wonderland

wonderland

annie leibovitz

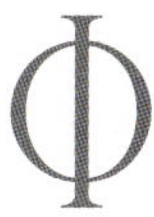

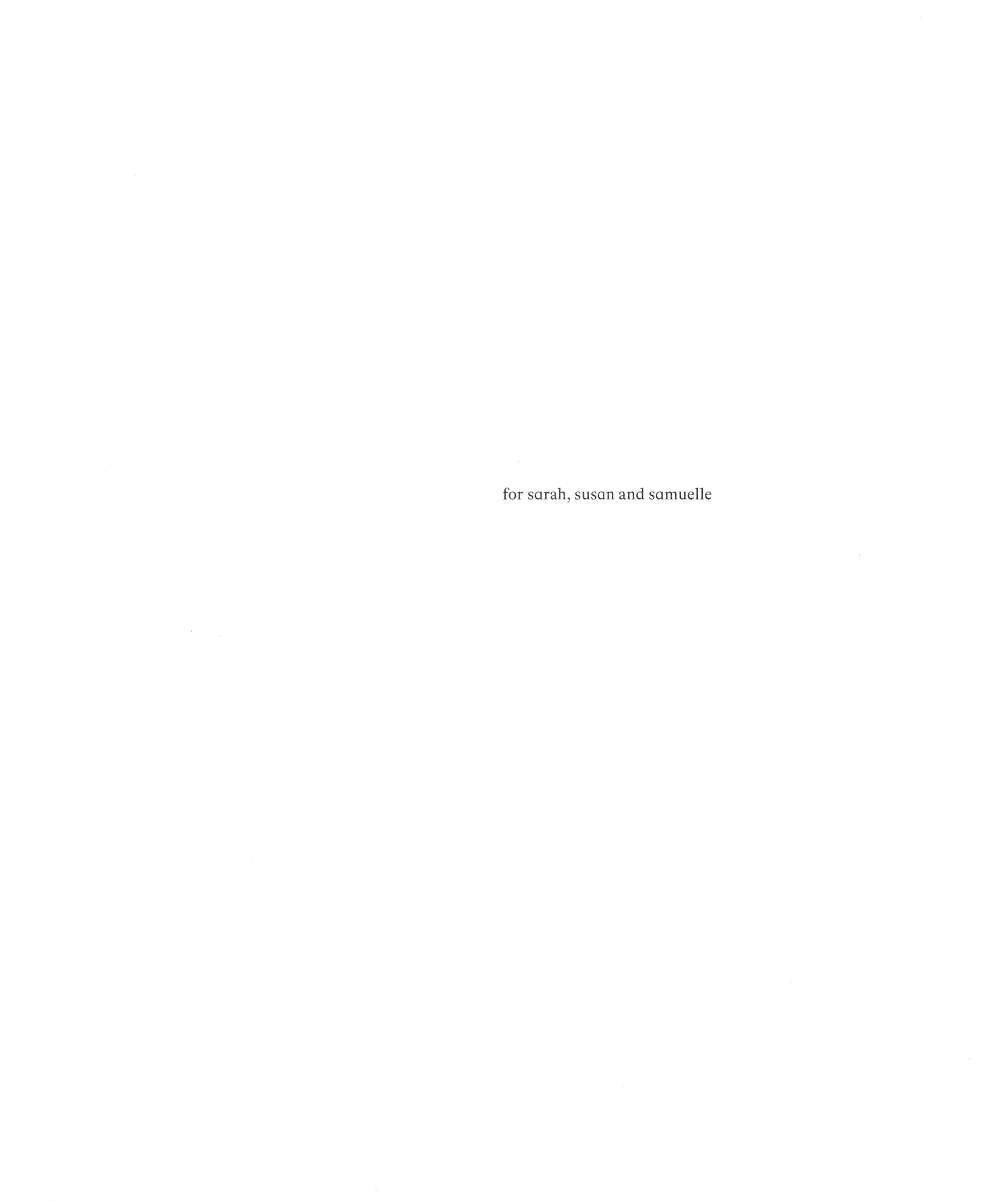

for sarah, susan and samuelle

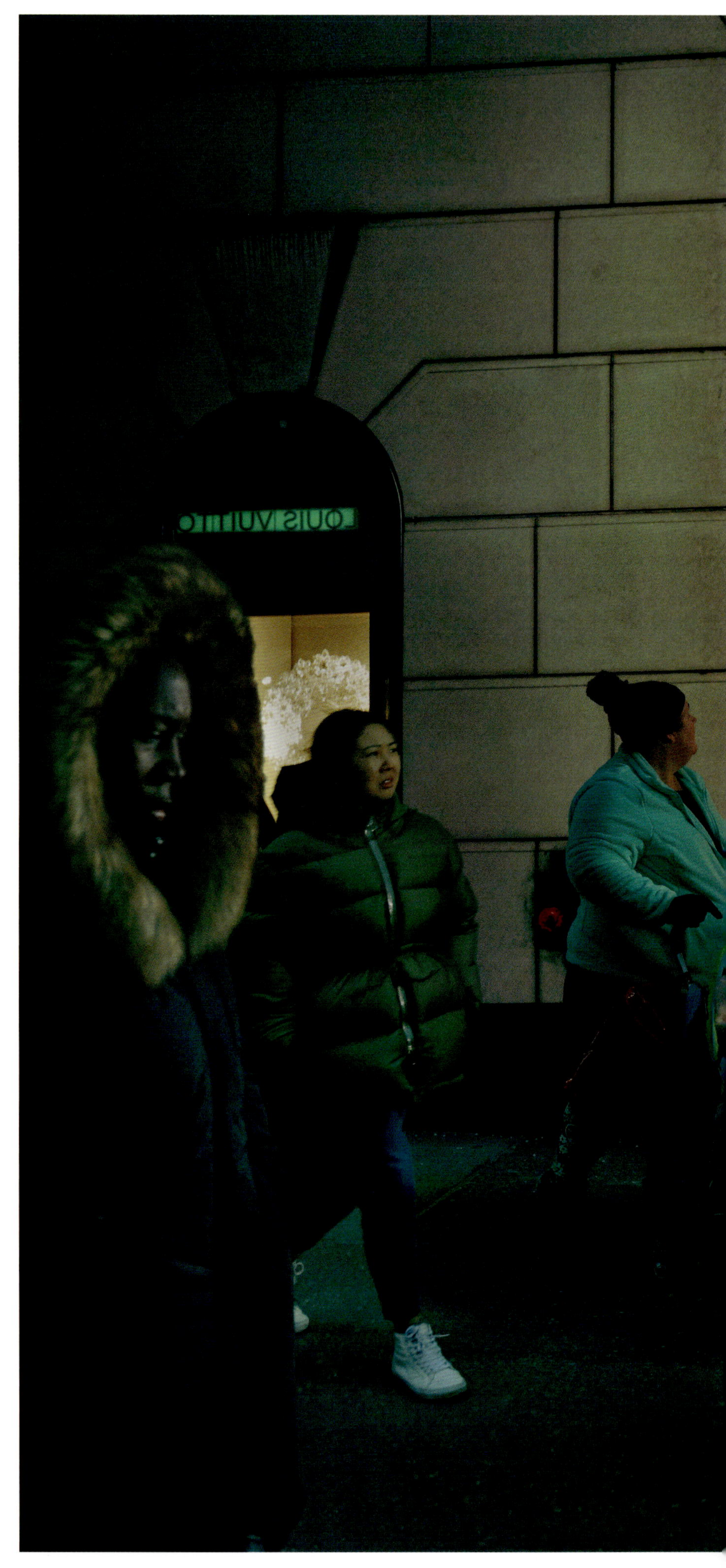

Lena Dunham,
Bergdorf Goodman,
New York City, 2013

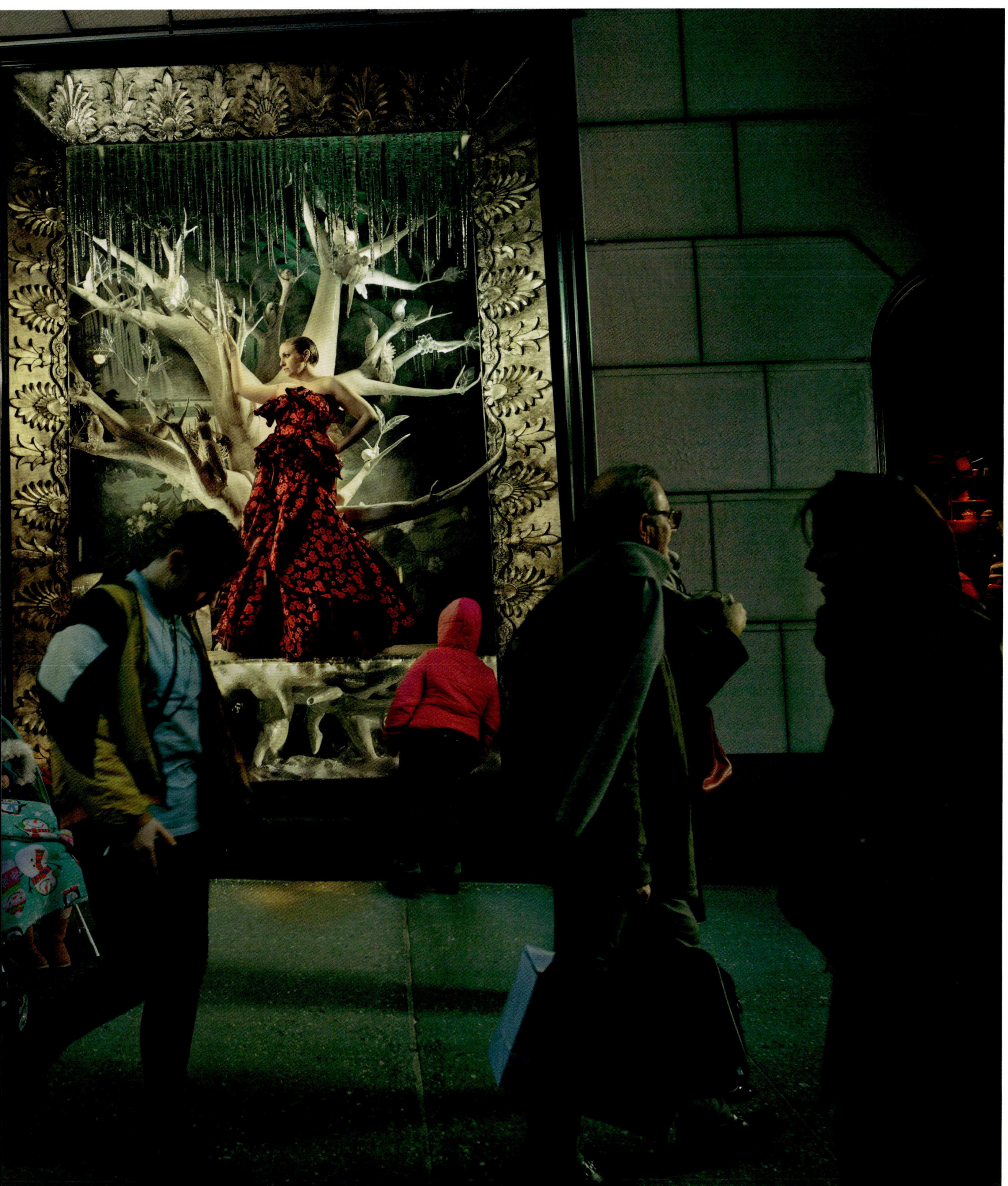

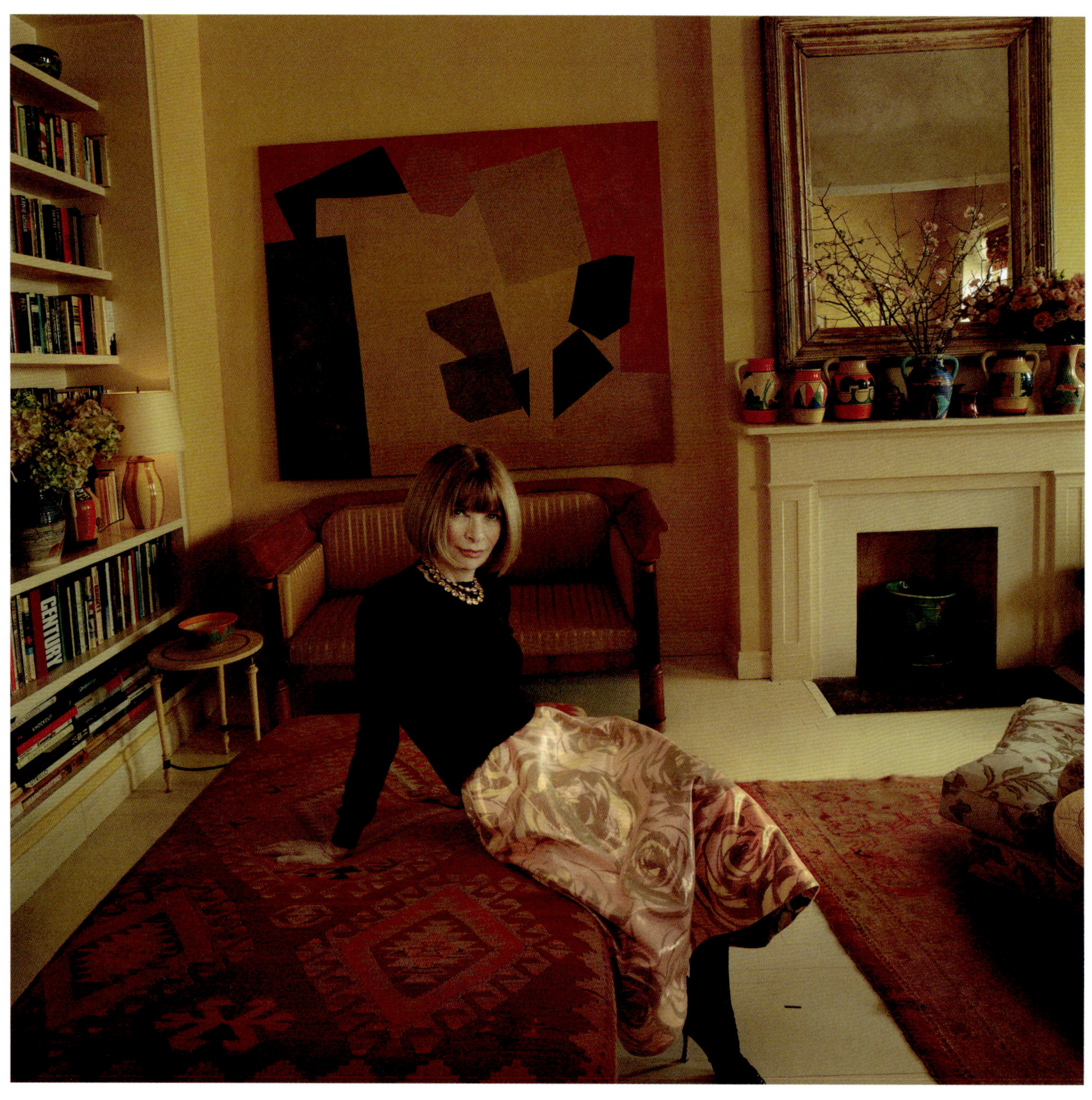

Anna Wintour,
New York City, 2015

One of the great pleasures of working as an editor is sending artists out into the world and being astonished by the work that they bring home. For the past three decades, I've found myself lucky to be able to send Annie Leibovitz to take photographs for *Vogue*, and for the same three decades, I have had the regular experience of being dazzled by treasure on her return. Nothing is unphotographable for Annie; no request is too outlandish, too bizarre, too hard. Over the years, her photographs have carried us into the lives of court barristers and tennis-court champions, bright-eyed teenage movie stars and stolid, cool-eyed queens. To render such a vivid range in portraiture is remarkable. To do it while making each picture one's own, as Annie has, approaches the miraculous.

The photographs in this collection offer a tour of Annie's varied talents and a record of one artist's progress through a changing world. The majority of them were commissioned for *Vogue*—a fact that I regard with more wonder than pride. Long before becoming the magazine's editor, in 1988, I admired Annie's photographs in publications such as *Rolling Stone* and *Vanity Fair*. But I never thought that we'd succeed in becoming a home for her, because I never thought that fashion, as an enterprise, would hold much interest in her eyes. Style, yes—one only had to glance at Annie's early work to appreciate her natural eye for combination, composition, color, form, and tone. But fashion photography involves close collaboration among photographers and fashion editors, and I assumed that Annie preferred to do her imaginative work herself.

I was wrong. Within a few years, Annie—in collaboration with such visionary editors as Grace Coddington, Tonne Goodman, Sara Moonves, Phyllis Posnick, Camilla Nickerson, and Alexandra Kotur—had not merely taken to fashion but produced many of the canonical portraits of our time. There's Hansel and Gretel, brought to life by Lily Cole, Lady Gaga, and Andrew Garfield in a magical series that bleeds into our own imaginations. There's Ben Stiller, in 2001, gadding about Paris with chic women—a straightforward enough assignment, but one that Annie imbued with genius. Note how each photograph in that series lives fully in its Parisian era and aesthetic, from the louche fin de siècle hunting lounge to the exotic Art Nouveau bath, the merry flapper frolic to the Technicolor poolside sprawl. Such portraits are rich in mood without being moody. They speak for themselves without revealing all their secrets.

Annie extends that wild imagination beyond fashion. In general, magazine photography claims its audience in at least one of three ways. It can offer news, in an image that captures a change in progress or a view of what was previously unseen. It can be, like a sumptuous couture dress, rich, beautiful, and well-made, a piece of art one *wants* to see spread on the page. Or it can show a keen human awareness, reaching out to touch the reader with especial authenticity.

All these virtues shimmer through the photographs that follow. We find Annie in the Democratic Caucus Room with Congresswoman Nancy Pelosi and close up beside the motorcade at President Barack Obama's first inauguration: portraits of the news as it is made. We see her laying sumptuous claim to the page in her impossibly gorgeous, nearly painterly portraits of Kirsten Dunst as Marie Antoinette and Keira Knightley as Dorothy Gale. And we can appreciate her sensitivity to human moments as Eddie Redmayne (playing an early twentieth-century trans woman) and Olivier Theyskens (kneeling in a mirrored room) meet the camera with their eyes. This book is filled with expressions so subtle and fleeting that one doesn't expect to find them caught on film. It is a testament to Annie's skill in putting her subjects at ease that she has caught them for posterity and the page.

What is most special about these photographs, though, is that they work on all three levels at once. Every "news" photograph is also a human portrait; every posed tableau contains a fresh vantage and thus a little bit of news. How else can we explain her masterly renderings of RuPaul in the garb of different eras—a study of femininity that also narrates one person's changing experience? How else can we explain our delight in the peculiar pastoral of Adam Driver in the Irish countryside with a ram on his shoulders? The images in this book are all portraits of people, which is to say that all have long stories behind them. Annie's gift—one of many—is to be able to elaborate a complete narrative in just one frame.

Remarkable images don't arrive without remarkable effort, as anybody who has worked with Annie knows. She spends hours preparing for a portrait session before the subjects even arrive. When the shooting begins, she's a bundle of nerves chased by the clock. An uninformed observer could be forgiven for taking her to be a young photographer plunged into her first big job; it's that denial of complacency, her way of treating every photograph as both her first and final effort, that brings such expanse to her range. Annie has many laurels, but she rests on none of them. She is always the first person to tell me that she thinks a spread—her own—just isn't good enough. (She's usually wrong.) Seeing her photographs collected here summons up memories of the work we've done together, of the passage through a sometimes thrilling, sometimes baffling, always changing world we've shared.

I have personal favorites among these portraits, especially those that seem to capture friends and artists dear to me: John Galliano in his perversely ornate bath, Karl Lagerfeld working at a desk piled high with paper, and of course Natalia Vodianova as Alice wandering a Wonderland of fine designers. Like Alice, Annie seems to travel through the world in the way of a wonderstruck stranger, meeting all the mad hatters and grinning cats, dreaming remarkable dreams, and alternating between being scarcely visible and standing strikingly tall. She is our guide on journeys that we wish we all could take. These photographs open up an entry into her extraordinary world and lead us out the other end, toward a future that, we hope, we can watch unfold through her lens.

—Anna Wintour

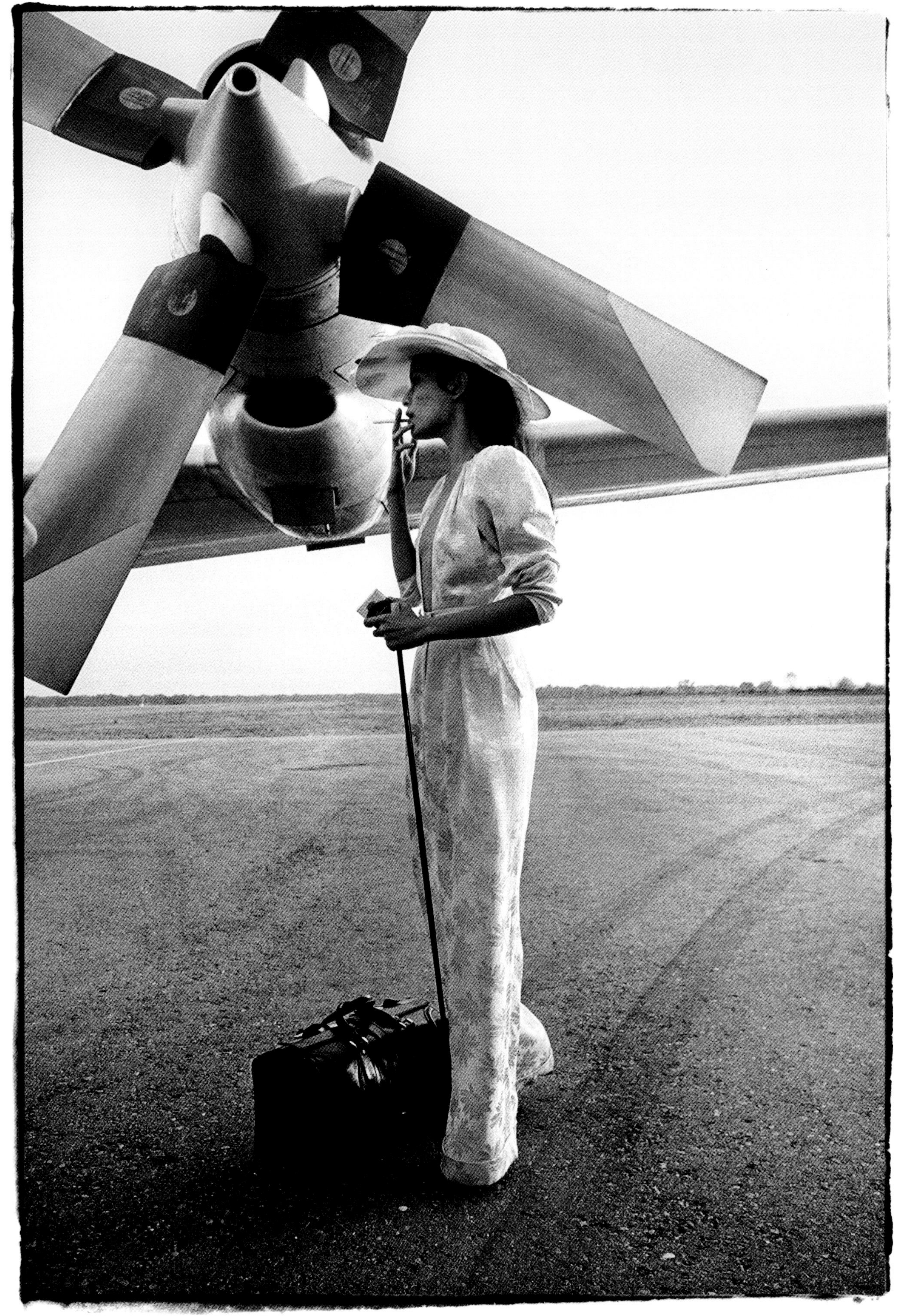

Bianca Jagger,
the Rolling Stones
American Tour 1972,
Kansas City, Missouri

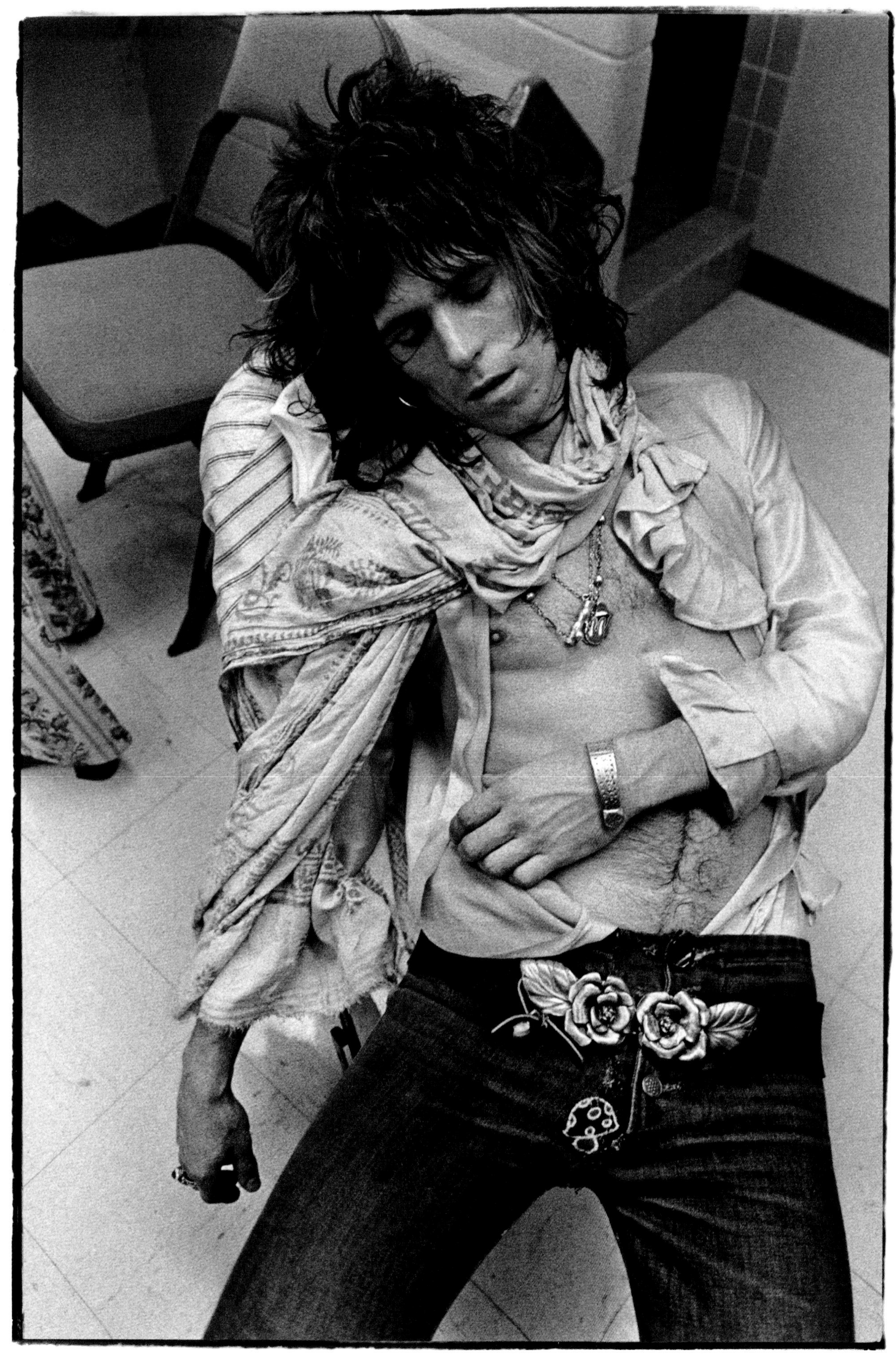

Keith Richards,
the Rolling Stones
American Tour 1972,
Fort Worth, Texas

I was going to school at the San Francisco Art Institute in the early 1970s, when I started working for *Rolling Stone*. We studied Henri Cartier-Bresson and Robert Frank—personal reportage. Cartier-Bresson and Robert Frank had the ability to pack the world into a 35 mm rectangle. What I learned from them was the model for my early work at the magazine.

I lived in San Francisco, but many of my assignments started coming out of Los Angeles, so I would throw my lights and cameras into the back of the car and drive down the coast. Those drives were great thinking sessions. In between shoots, I would find myself at the newsstand on Las Palmas, poring through magazines from Europe and New York. It was another world. Richard Avedon, Helmut Newton, Guy Bourdin, Irving Penn. I studied their lighting and composition. They were brilliant. The imagery was powerful—sexy, contemporary, bold, graphic. I was seeing color for the first time. I couldn't afford to buy the magazines, but I would stand there for hours and then go to Musso and Frank's, which was around the corner, to meet with Eve Babitz and eat sand dabs and talk.

When I met Bea Feitler in New York a few years later, it was as if a portal had opened to that world. The refrigerator in Bea's Central Park South apartment (which Horst had photographed, with its balcony and beautiful view) only had champagne in it. Bea was something. When she was still in her early twenties, she had been a revolutionary art director, along with Ruth Ansel, at *Harper's Bazaar*, where they gave Diane Arbus assignments, including fashion assignments.

Bea would talk about her adventures covering the couture in Paris with Richard Avedon and Bill King. They would see the shows and photograph the dresses in a few days. The magazines would have the clothes at night, and the buyers had them during the day. Photographers and editors stayed up working around the clock, and everyone got drunk and crazy and wild. I listened to Bea's stories with awe.

Bea was my mentor in photography, not just fashion photography. She was the first art director of *Ms.* magazine, where she created a distinctive look with uninhibited typography and layouts. I met her when she asked me to do a shoot for *Ms*. Then she came out to California to do some work for *Rolling Stone*, including a special issue of my photographs. Since I was working with journalists, I had been looking at the Depression-era documentarians and *Life* magazine photographers, most importantly Eugene Smith. His photo-essays had the most profound effect on me. Smith never put his camera down, day or night. And he had a point of view.

Bea encouraged me to take my first fashion assignment. In 1977, *New West*, which had just been launched by Clay Felker as a West Coast version of *New York*, asked me to do a shoot with Margaux Hemingway, the granddaughter of Ernest Hemingway. Margaux was a six-foot-tall supermodel with a million-dollar contract from Fabergé. She had been on the covers of *Time* and *Vogue*. She was friends with two of the most important hair and makeup people, Way Bandy and Maury Hopson, and she wouldn't go anywhere without them. When Bea advised me to take the job, she also gave me the best advice I ever got about fashion photography. "You can take the photograph any way you want," she said. "But you must always see the clothes. You must be true to the fashion."

That's how I found myself in the middle of nowhere with a high-end fashion team. I had decided to do the shoot in Plains, Georgia, a tiny town surrounded by peanut fields. Jimmy Carter had just become president and Plains was his home. I had spent a lot of time in Plains covering the election, and I guess I went there because I could. It seemed somehow relevant and the landscape was intriguing. Jimmy Carter's brother, Billy, had a run-down gas station in Plains, and he agreed to pose with Margaux, who was wearing skin-tight gold lamé jeans from Fiorucci. The glittery Fiorucci store on 59th Street in New York, the first concept store, had just opened. The concept was that it was a nightclub during the day. People were dancing in the windows. Andy Warhol and Cher and Jackie Onassis shopped at Fiorucci. The teenage Marc Jacobs hung out there and persuaded his grandmother to buy him a pair of Fiorucci jeans. Billy's gas station in Plains, on the other hand, as he explained to us, was pretty much a front for selling beer out of the back room.

I didn't know what I was doing with Margaux, but she was very sure of herself. It was a revelation to work with a subject who liked to be photographed and knew how to play and collaborate with the photographer. I was in over my head with Way and Maury though.

They were in their own world, and I was just trying to figure out how to take the pictures.

A few years later, in the early eighties, when Bea designed the prototype for the relaunch of *Vanity Fair*, she pulled me into the world of Condé Nast. It was a legendary world where photographers were recognized as artists. I left *Rolling Stone* and started working for *Vanity Fair*, and occasionally I would get an assignment for a portrait from *Vogue*. But I couldn't believe it when Anna Wintour asked me to shoot the couture in Paris with Kate Moss.

Vogue booked me into the Ritz. Coco Chanel had lived in the Ritz. She moved into a suite there in 1934 and stayed until her death in 1971. Her boutique was across the street. Scott and Zelda Fitzgerald and Cole Porter were regulars. Proust, on his deathbed, sent out for his favorite beer from the Ritz bar. Robert Capa and Ingrid Bergman started an affair there. Susan Sontag and I would stay at L'Hotel, on the Left Bank, where Oscar Wilde died. We always stayed on the Left Bank so that we could walk to the Café de Flore. But the Ritz is the most romantic hotel in Paris. Staying there was like some kind of dream.

Then Anna said that Sean Combs, or Puff Daddy, as he was then called, would be part of my shoot.

Puff Daddy booked himself into the Hyatt.

I began to understand what Anna was doing. Everything started coming together. It was brilliant and ahead of its time. The shoot was a cross-cultural straddling of two worlds: rap culture and high fashion. And of course they weren't all that different.

Grace Coddington was the editor on the shoot. She didn't have a problem with Puff Daddy, but I could tell that she was skeptical about me. I've worked with Grace many times since then, and every time is like starting from scratch. The best work I've done in fashion is most likely my work with Grace, but every single time we work together, Grace points out that I know absolutely nothing.

Grace and Anna let me go to all the fashion shows, even though I knew that they didn't expect me to. In the back of my mind were the great old fashion stories, particularly Avedon's shoot for *Harper's Bazaar* with Mike Nichols and Suzy Parker as movie stars who are having an affair in Paris: escaping paparazzi in Maxim's, flirting, fighting. We started at the Hyatt in Puff Daddy's room. Then we went all over Paris. We shot on the Pont Alexandre III and during a party that Puff Daddy threw for himself at a hip new restaurant.

Kate Moss made me feel like I was the greatest photographer who ever existed. She knows how to transform a dress. Puffy was with us for two days, and on the third day we worked with Kate alone, in an abandoned paint factory outside of Paris.

The haute couture scene that Bea had described to me when I first met her was long past, but I would see some great shows in Paris over the years, especially that first season in 1999—Galliano's Dior show in the Orangerie at Versailles, Alexander McQueen's show for Givenchy, Versace at the Ritz, Karl Lagerfeld's collection for Chanel in the Louvre. They were performance art.

Looking back at my work, I see that fashion has always been there. It is the driving force in a portrait—whether it is Jerry Garcia in a black T-shirt, or Patti Smith in the much-imitated style that has endured for decades, or the Rolling Stones. But it was the photographs of showgirls I did for Tina Brown's *New Yorker* around the time of the Puff Daddy / Kate Moss shoot in Paris that changed my view of photography forever. That and studying David Hockney's work on perspective. I realized that one picture was never going to tell the story. When the women in Las Vegas arrived for their portrait sessions, I didn't recognize them. Then they changed into their costumes and became showgirls. We ran two photographs of each woman: a "real" portrait and the costumed one.

Fashion plays a part in the scheme of everything, but photography always comes first for me. The photograph is the most important part. And photography is so big that it can encompass portraiture, reportage, family photographs, fashion. There are so many ways to use photography.

I've never thought of myself as a fashion photographer, but my work for *Vogue* fueled the fire for a kind of photography that I might not otherwise have explored. I am forever grateful to Anna Wintour for letting me enter this world. She continues to be a complex, intriguing mystery to me, and I would lay down my life for her any day. The opportunity Anna gave me coincided with the moment I bought an apartment in Paris and began spending time there and also started a family. Some of the early fashion stories I did for *Vogue* were based on fairy tales that I would read to my children.

I held on to my fashion photographs over the years because I wasn't sure where they belonged. I had a little chapter on fashion in *At Work*, and I published a few of the pictures in *Portraits: 2005–2016*, but I didn't do a "fashion" book. Then I came to understand that all the pictures belong together.

—Annie Leibovitz

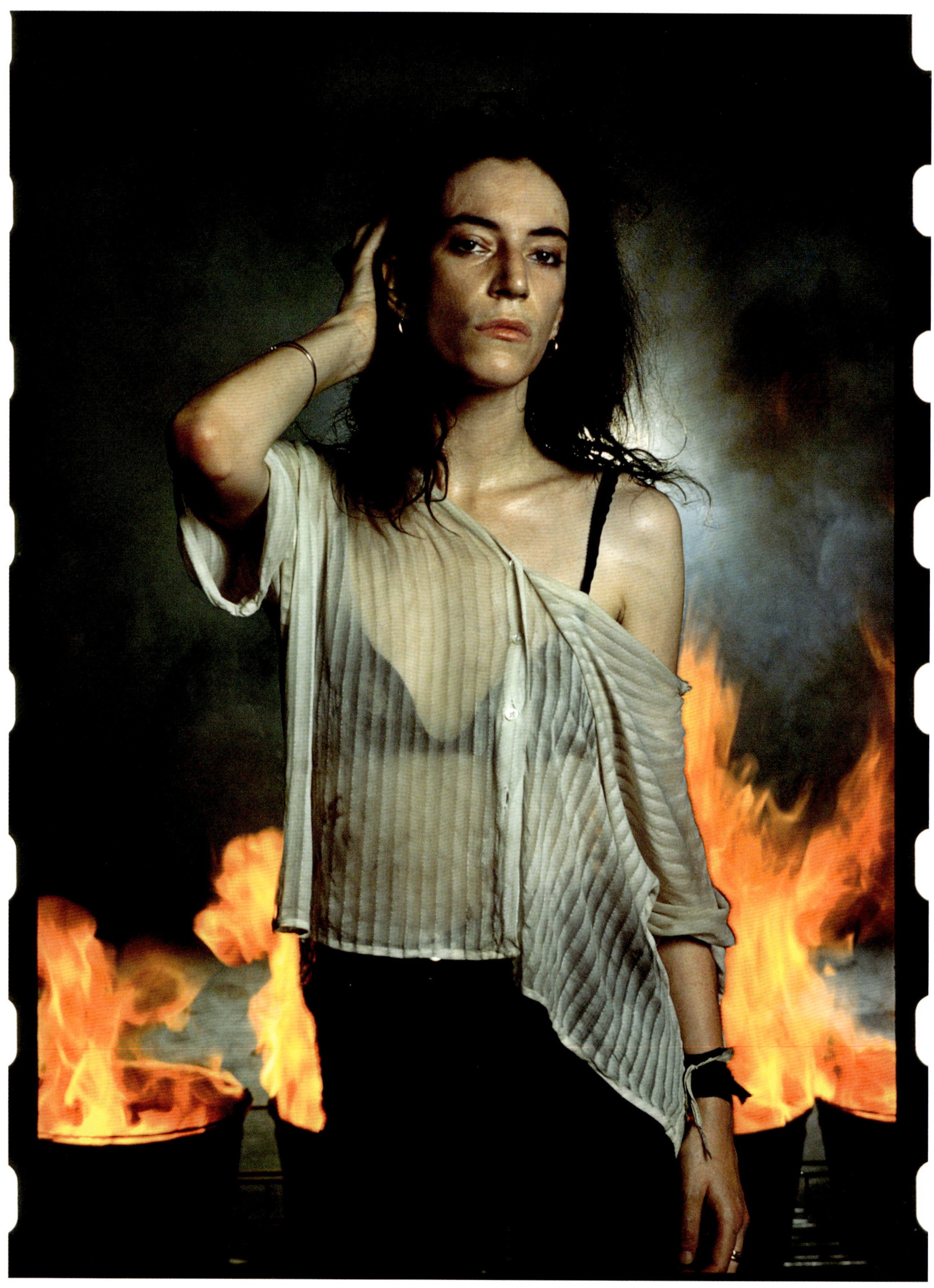

Patti Smith, New Orleans, 1978;
and New York City, 1996

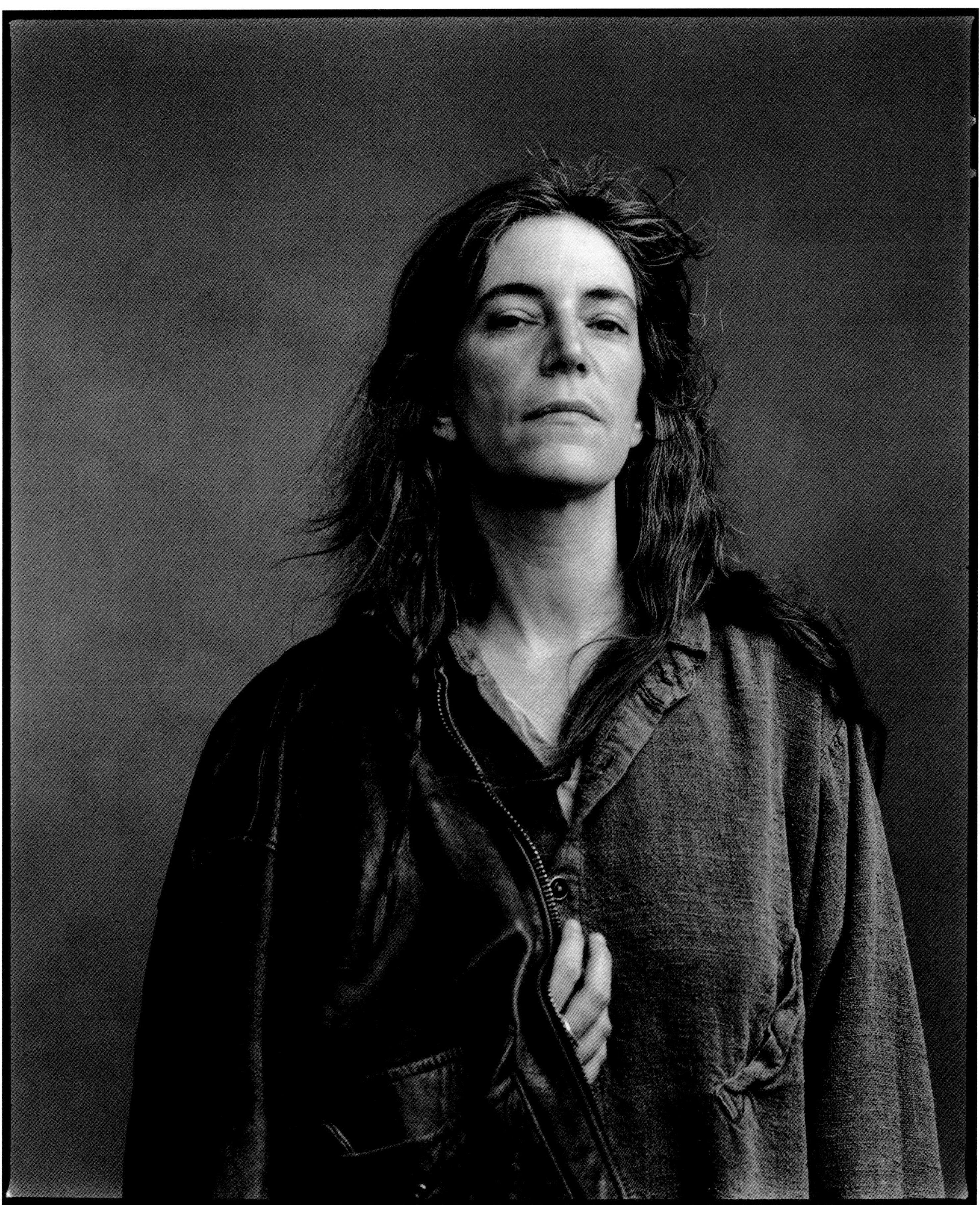

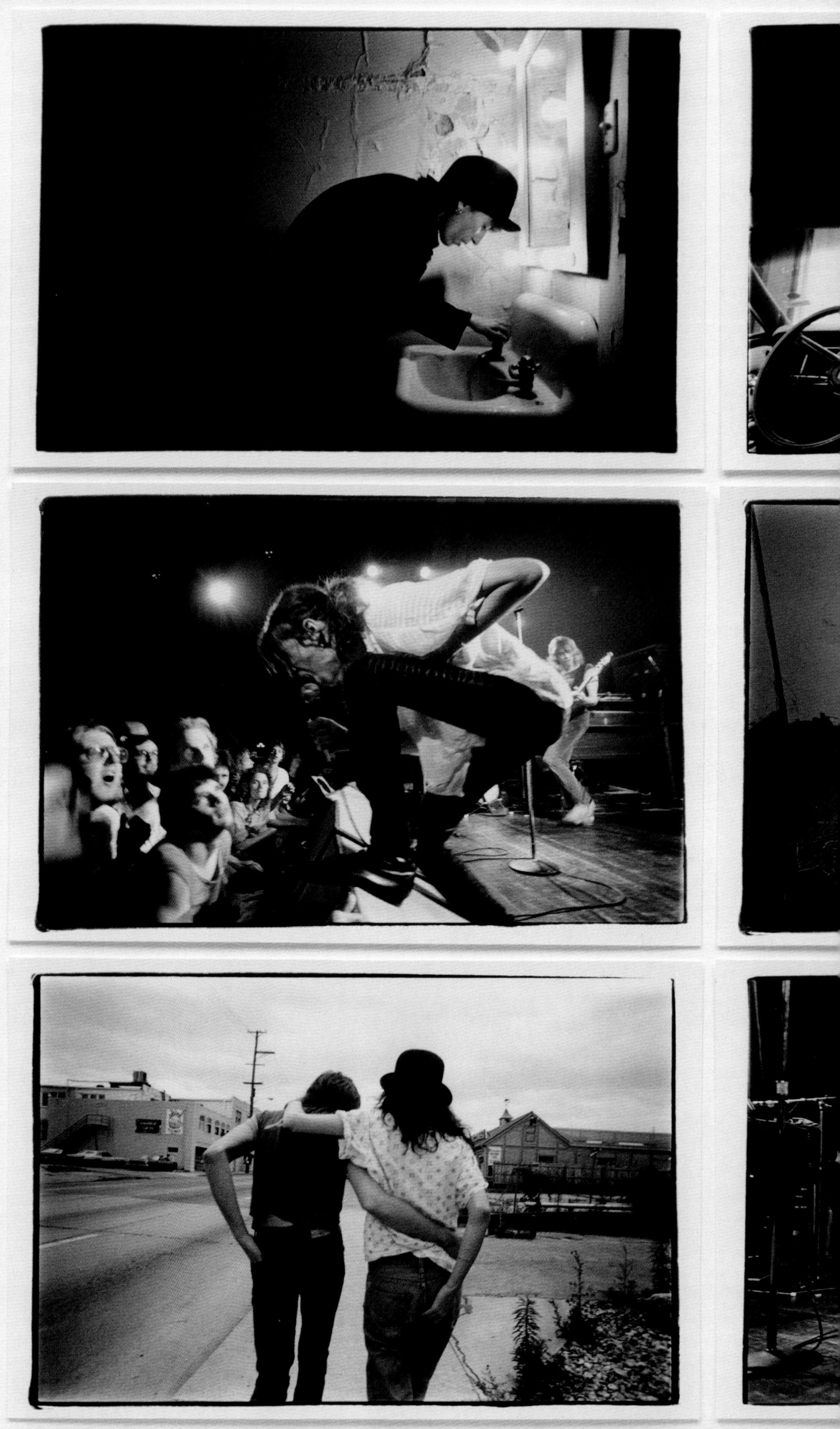

Patti Smith on tour
for *Easter*, 1978

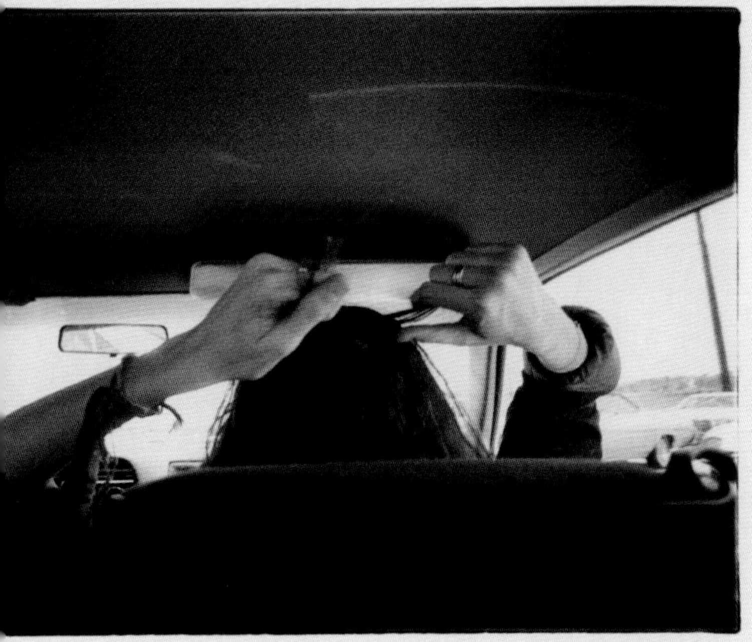
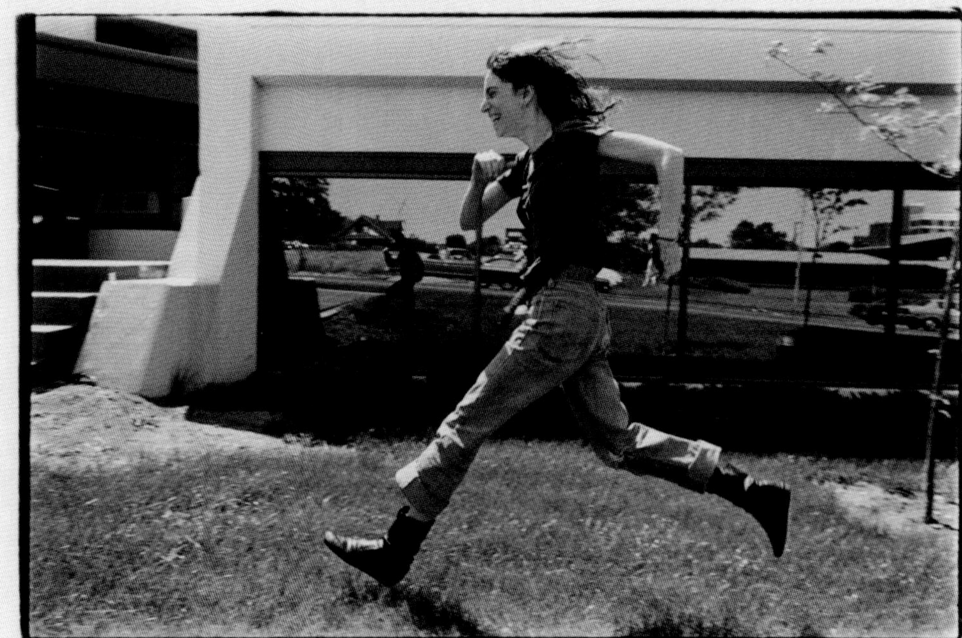
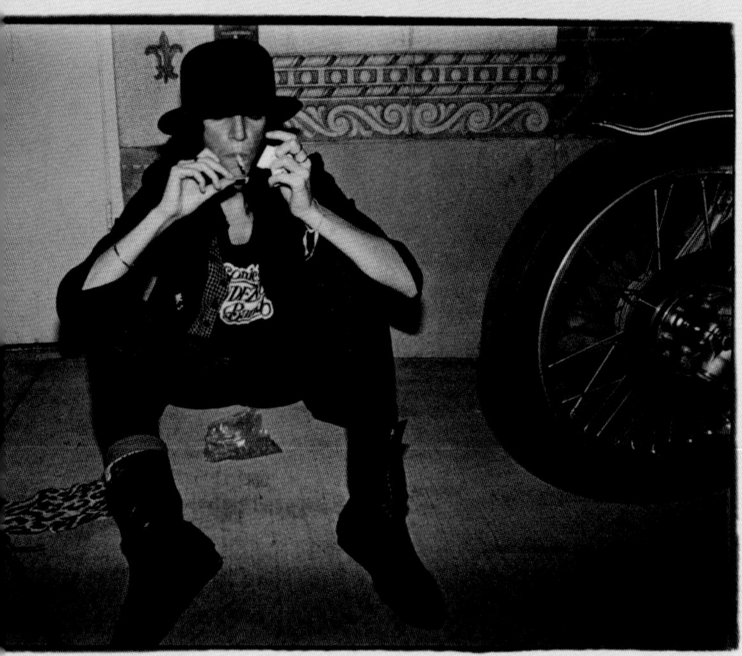
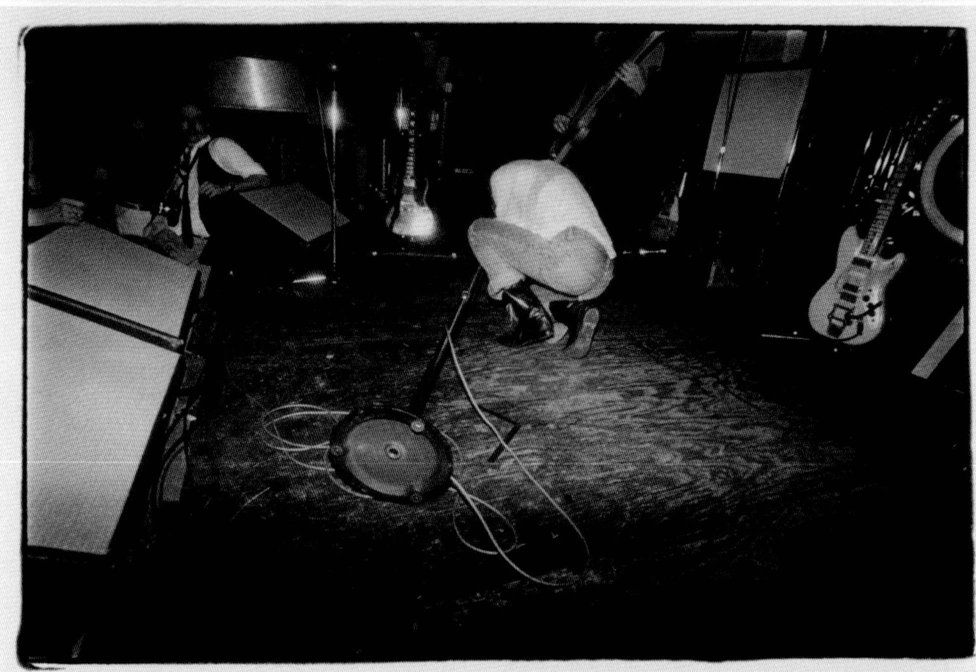
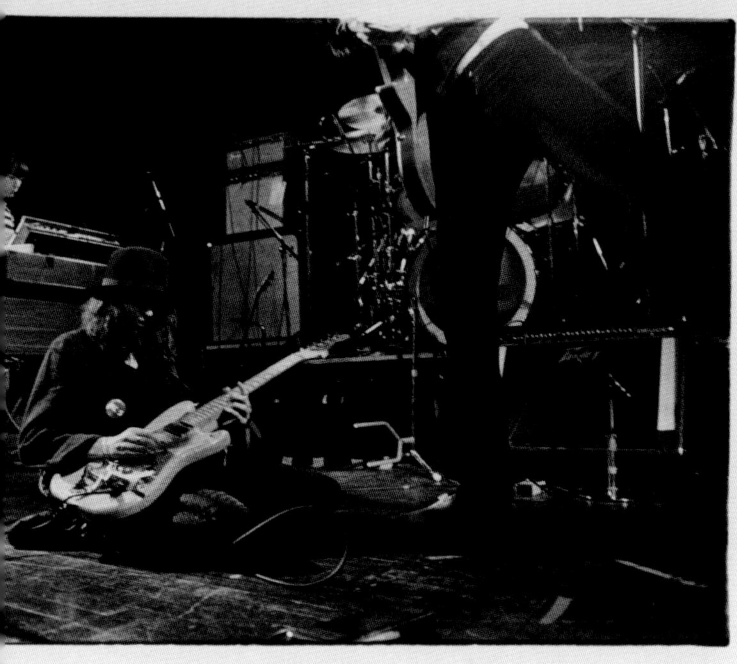
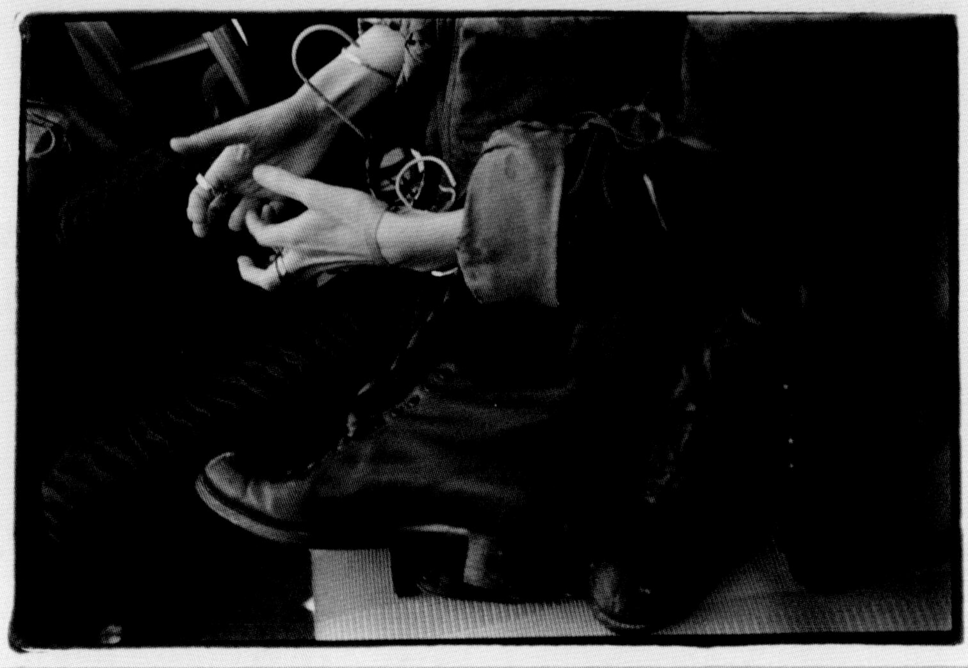

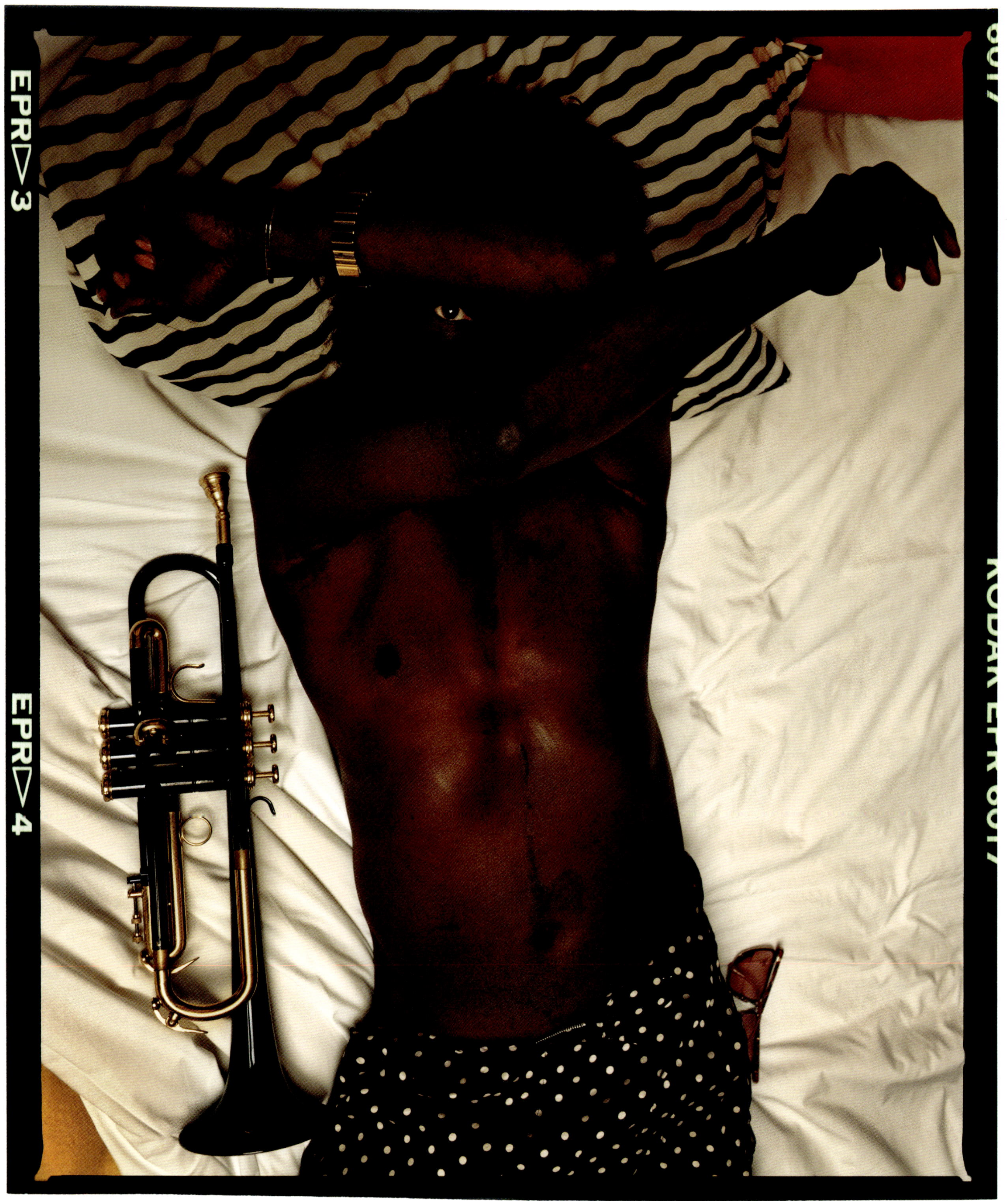

Miles Davis,
New York City, 1989

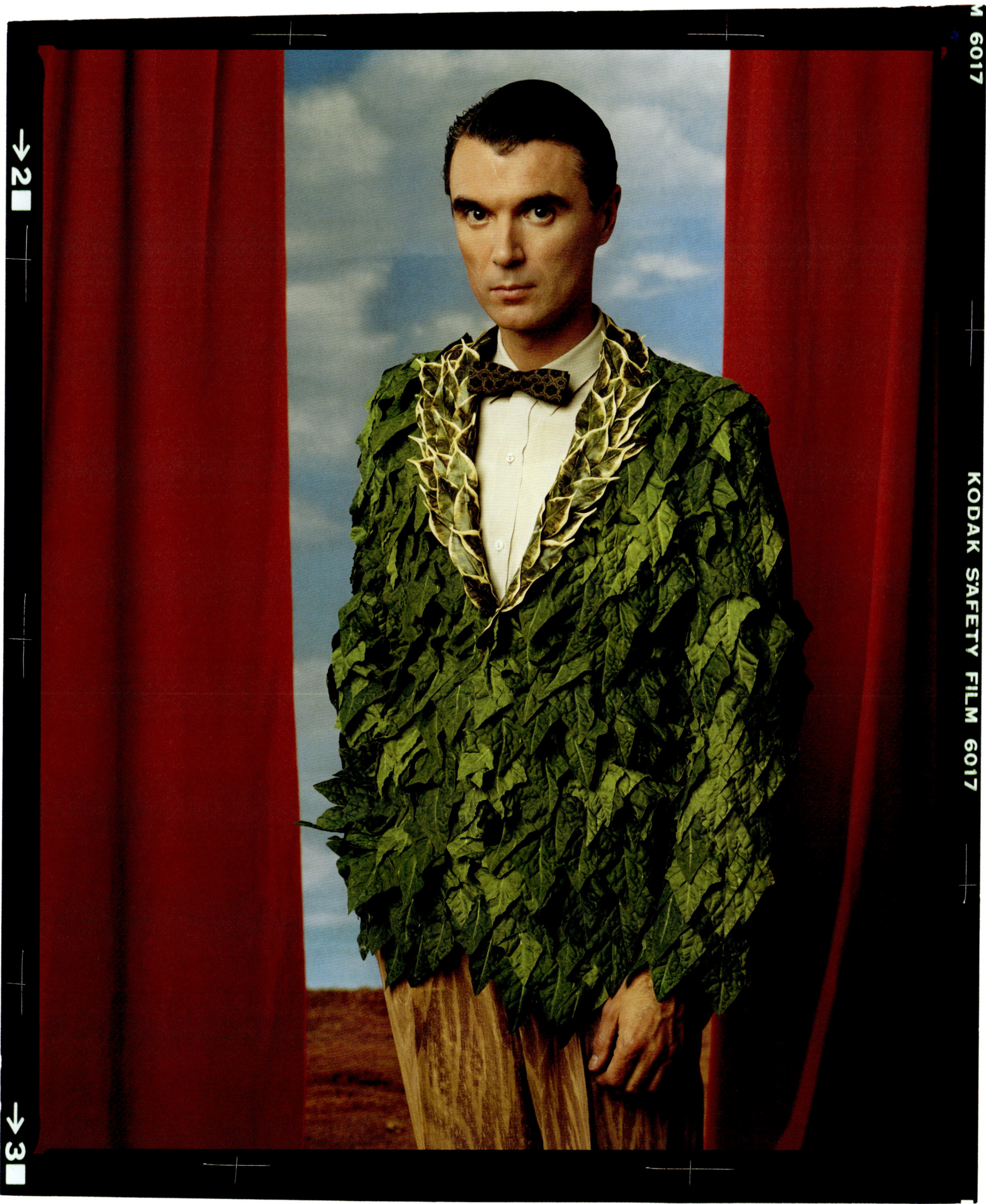

David Byrne,
Los Angeles, 1986

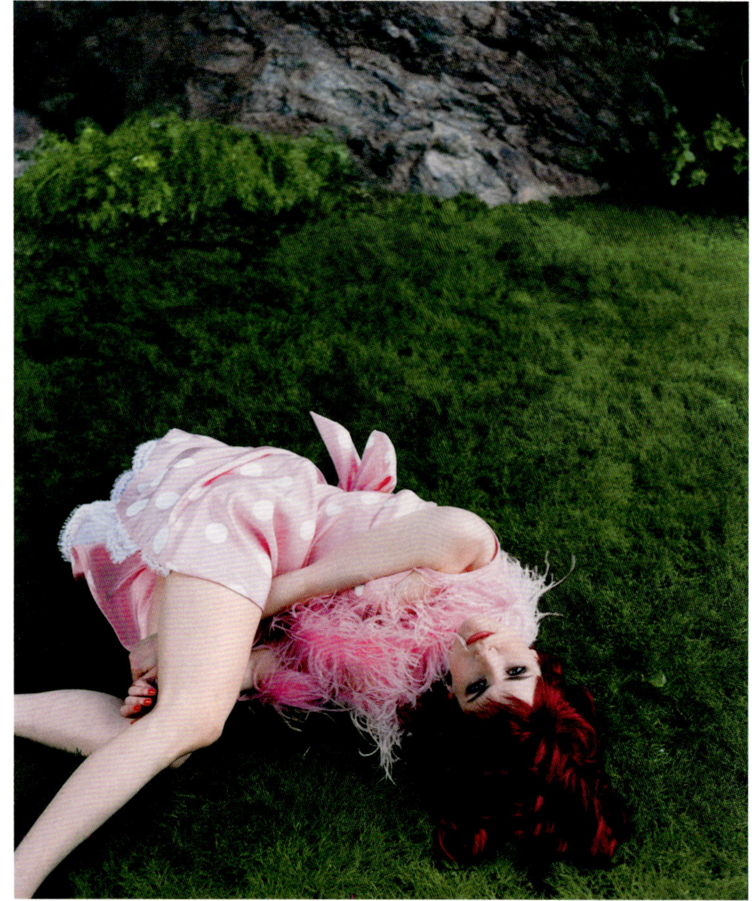

Jennifer Jason Leigh,
Palm Springs, California, 1994

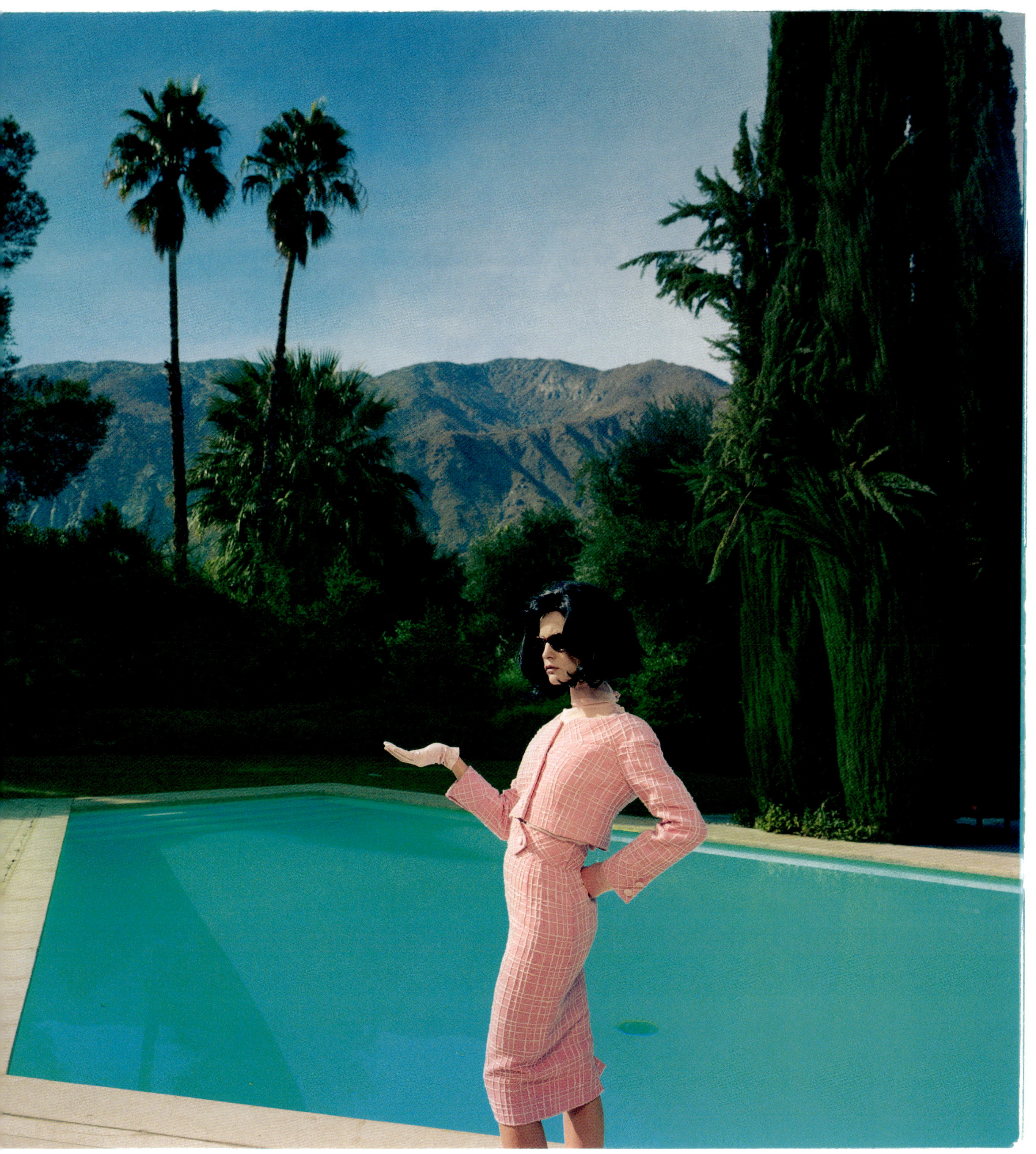

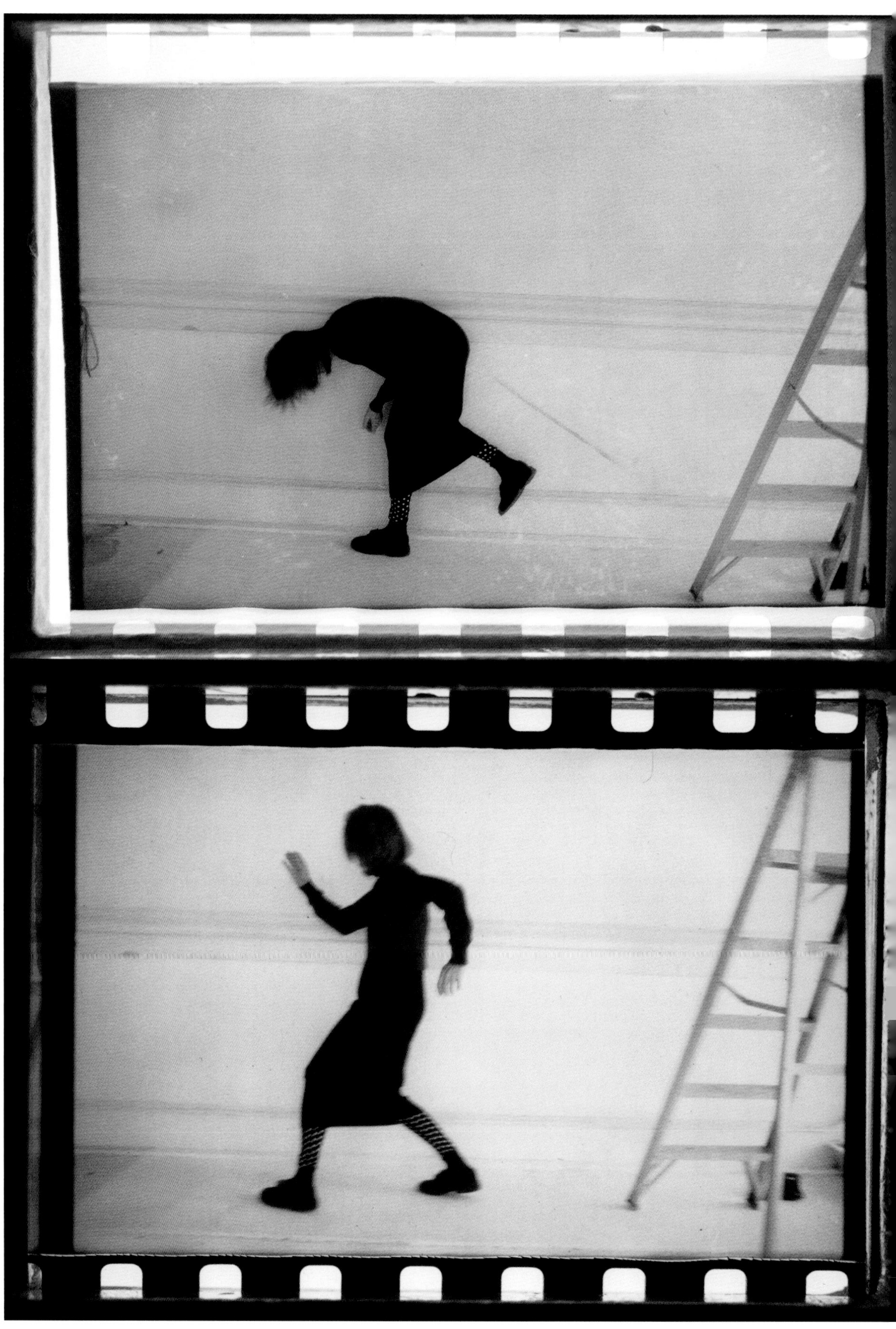

Diane Keaton,
Los Angeles, 1986

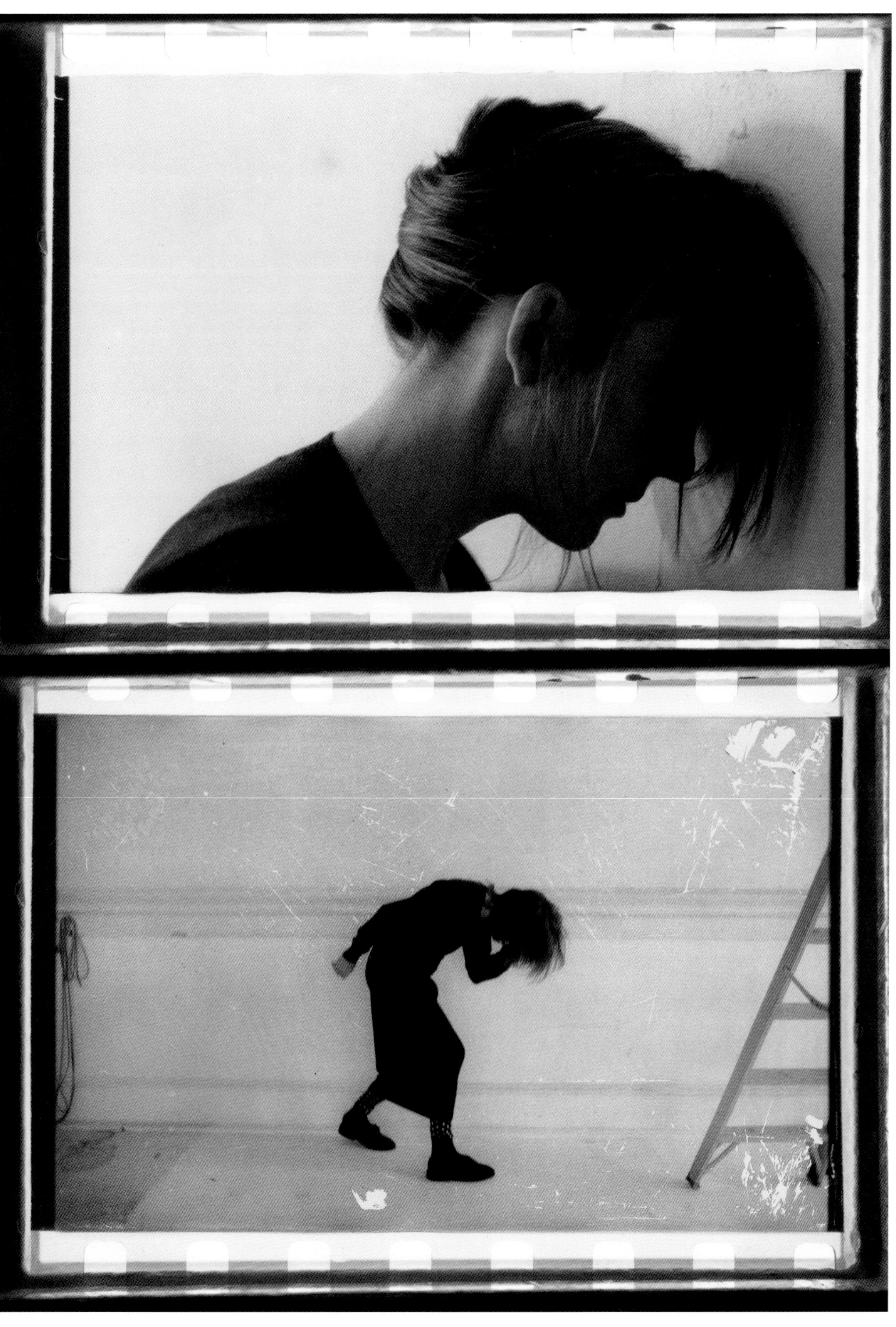

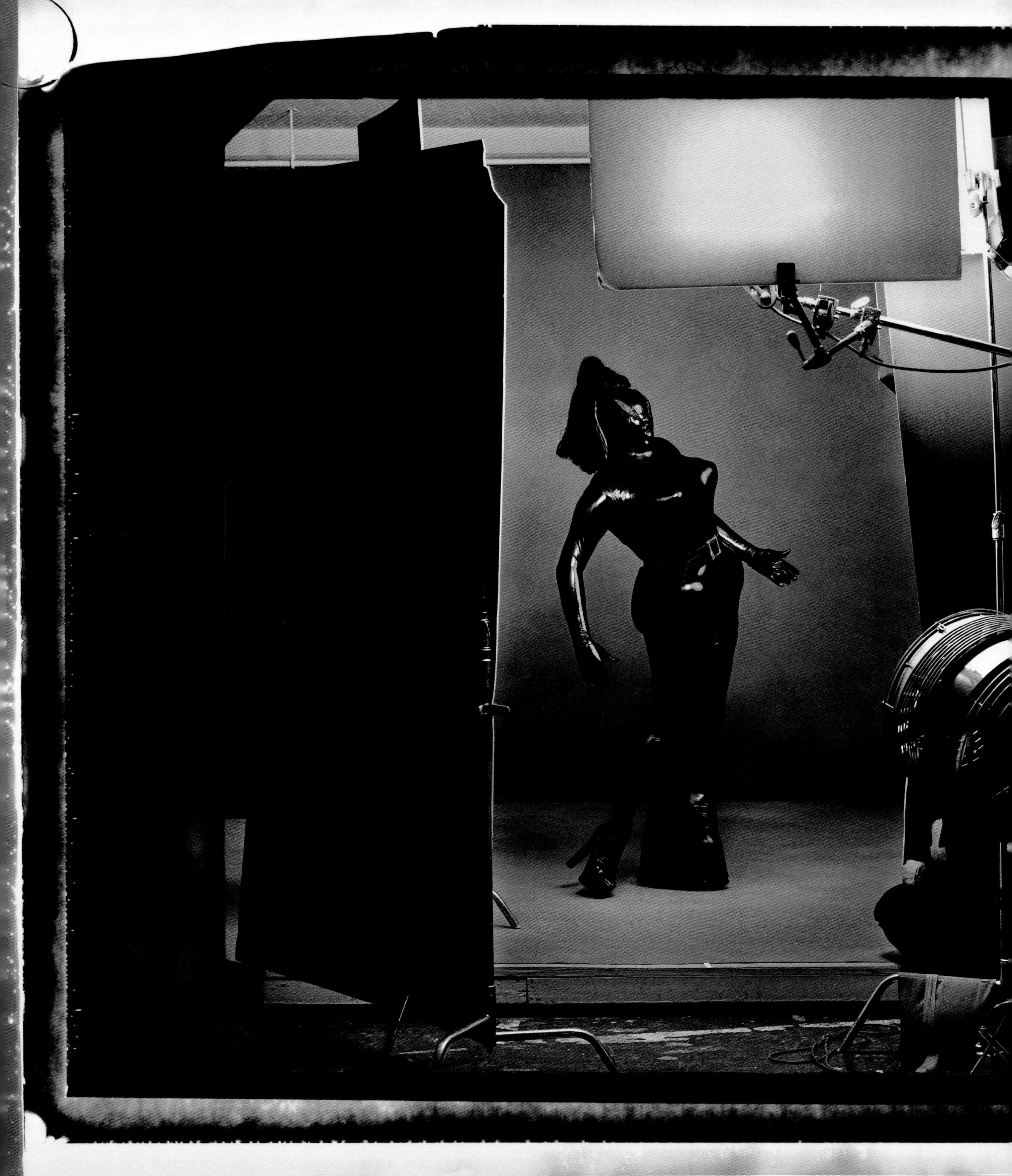

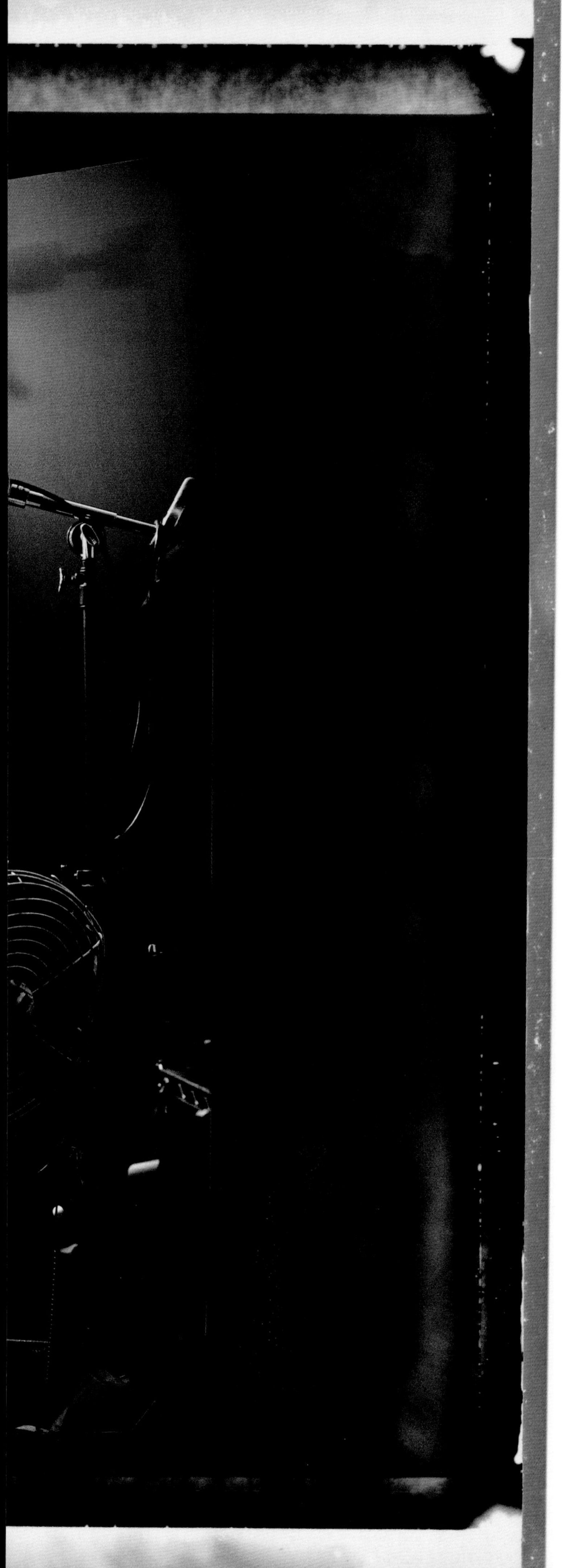

Leigh Bowery,
New York City, 1993

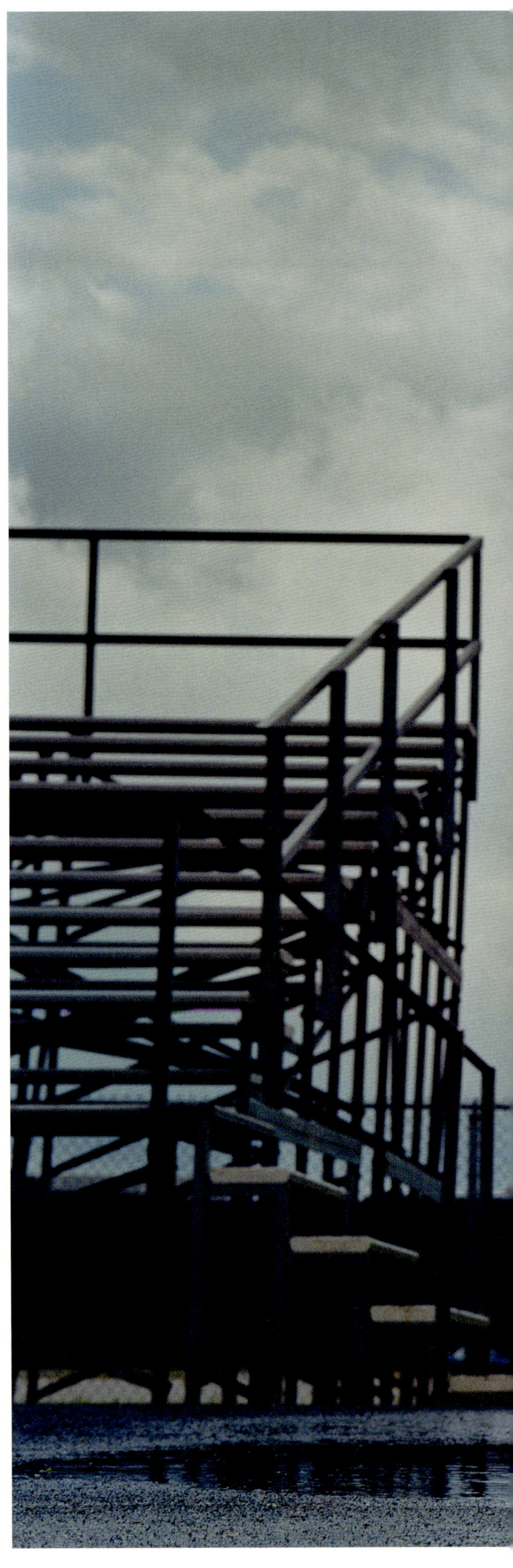

Carl Lewis,
Houston, Texas, 1994

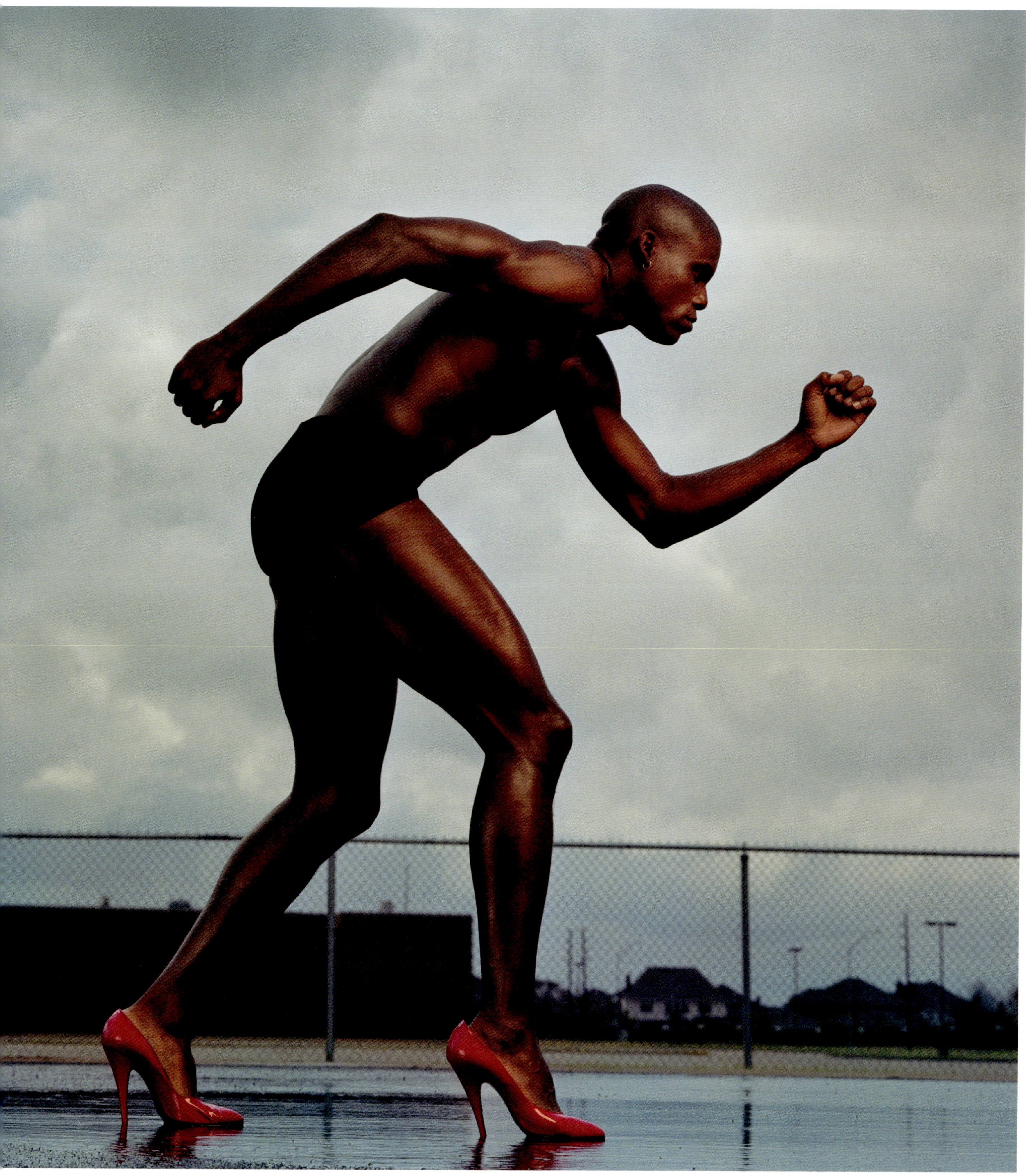

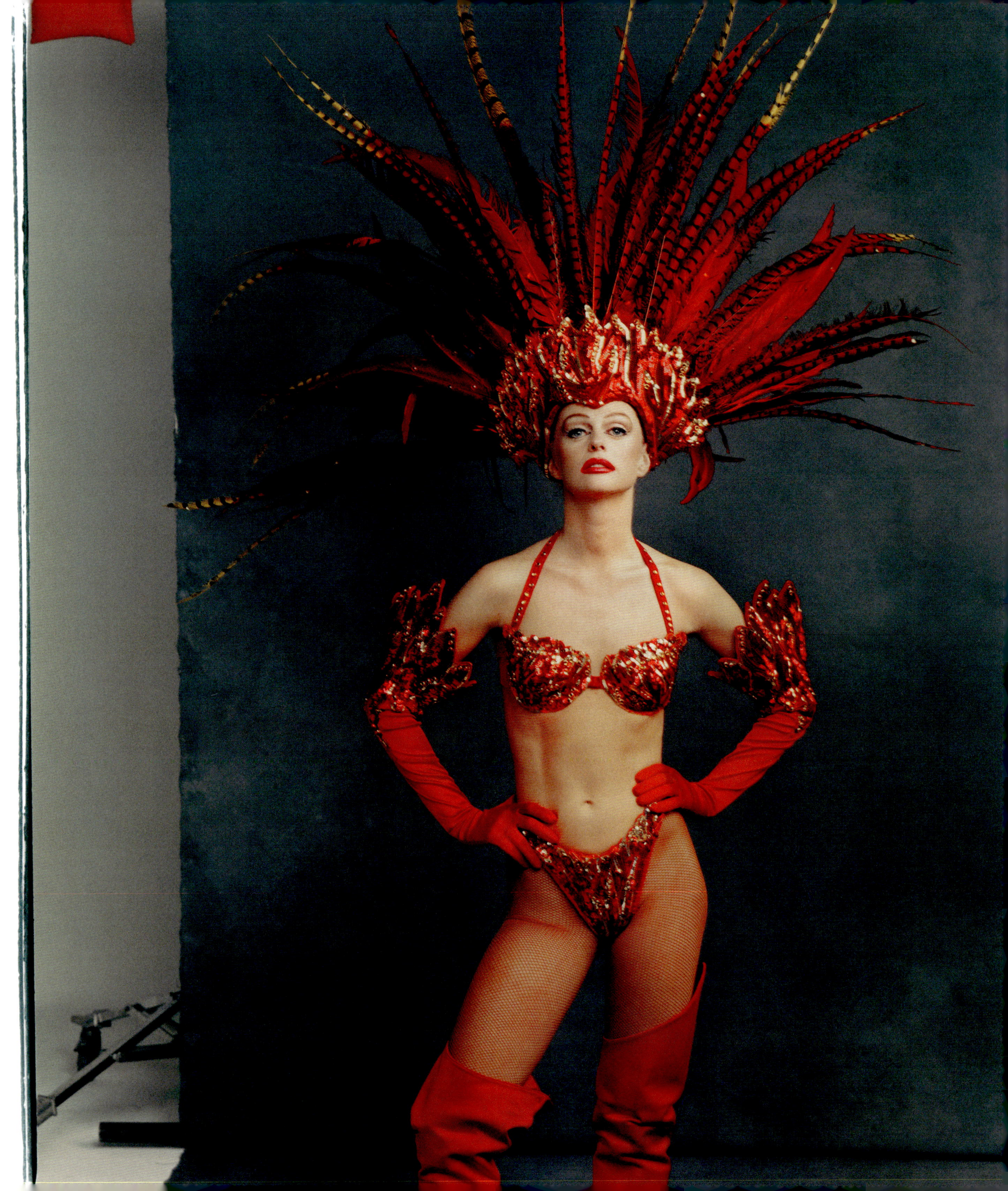

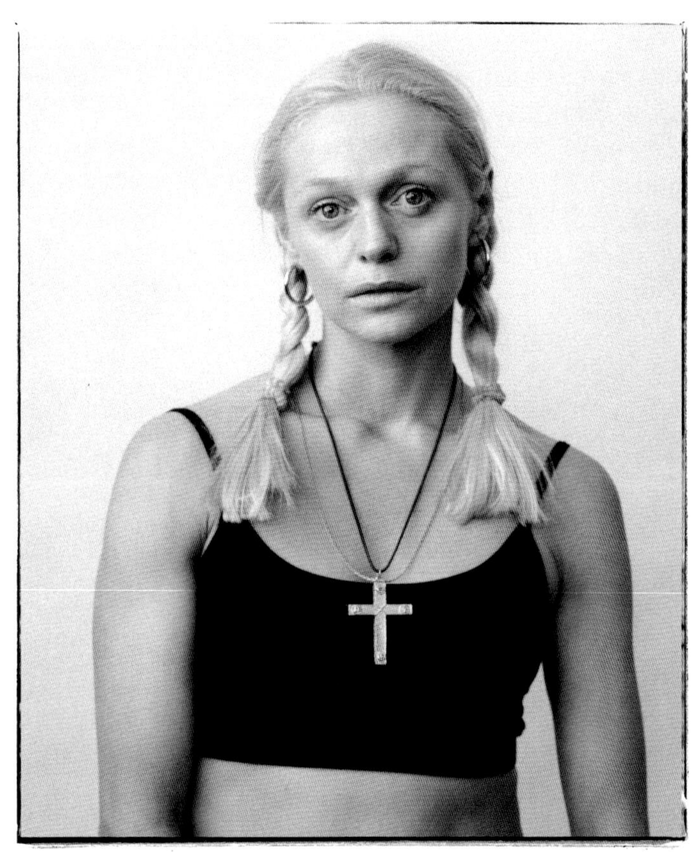

Akke Alma, Stardust Casino,
Las Vegas, Nevada, 1995

Akke Alma,
Las Vegas, Nevada, 1995

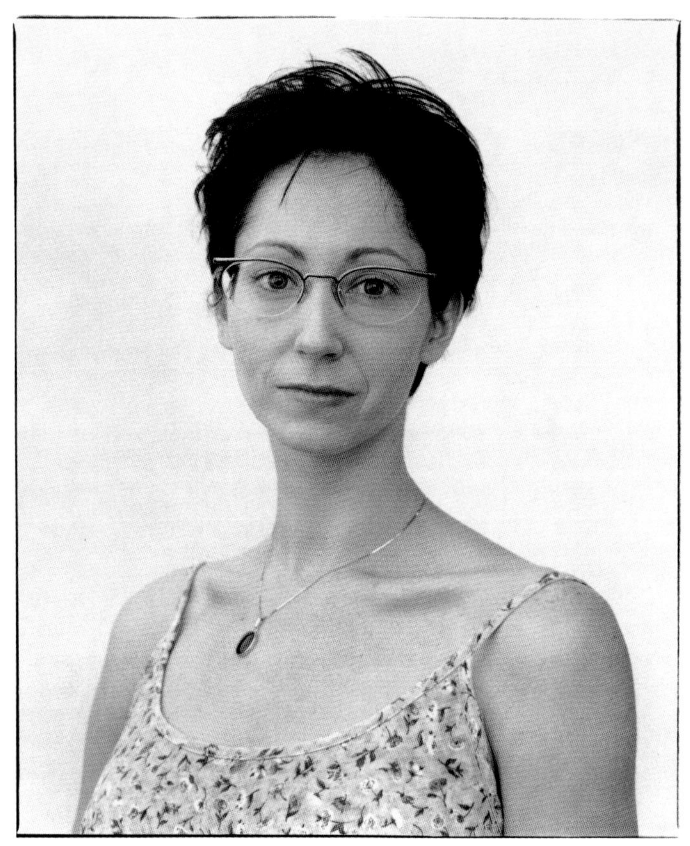

Susan McNamara,
Las Vegas, Nevada, 1995

Susan McNamara, Bally's Casino,
Las Vegas, Nevada, 1995

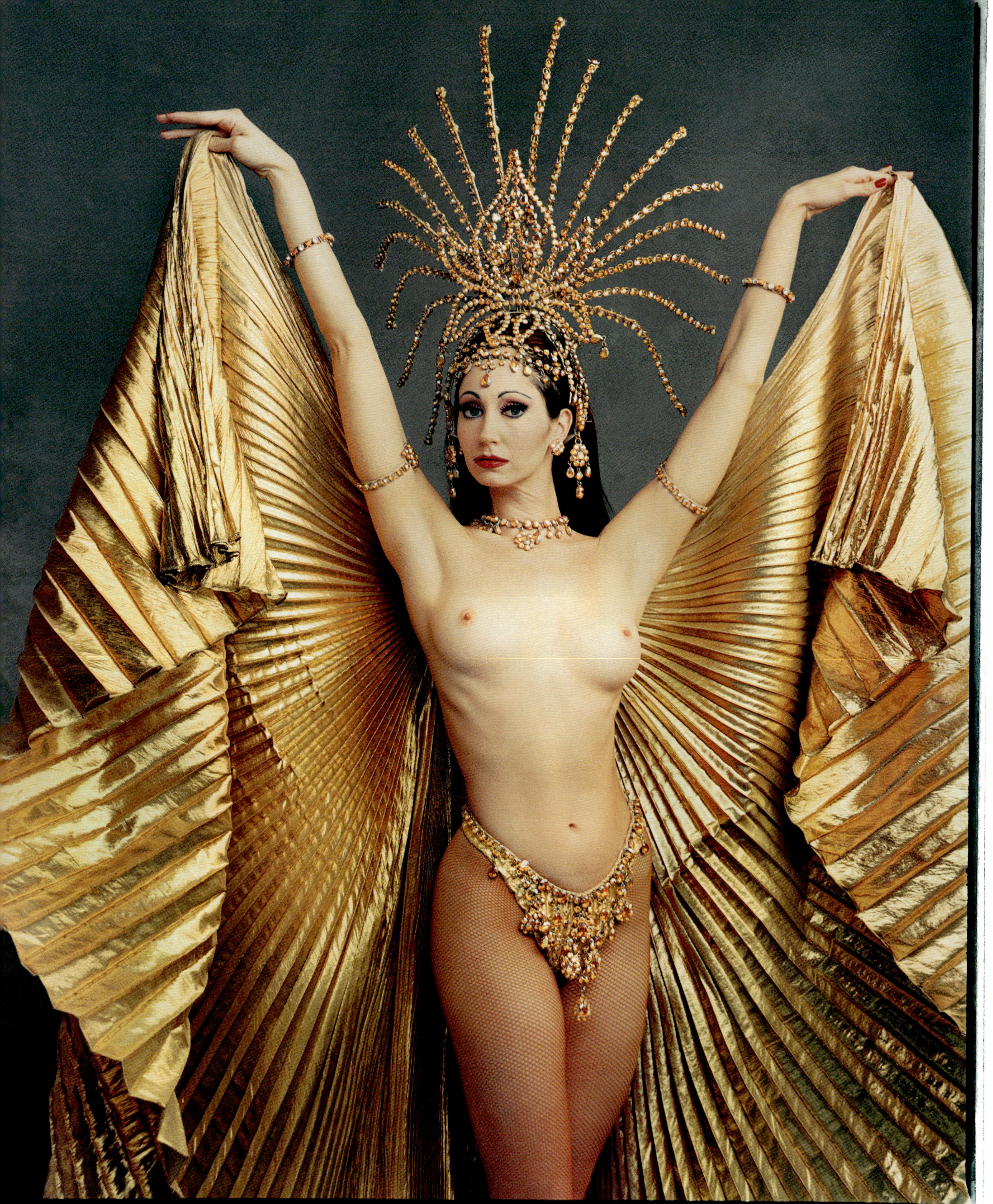

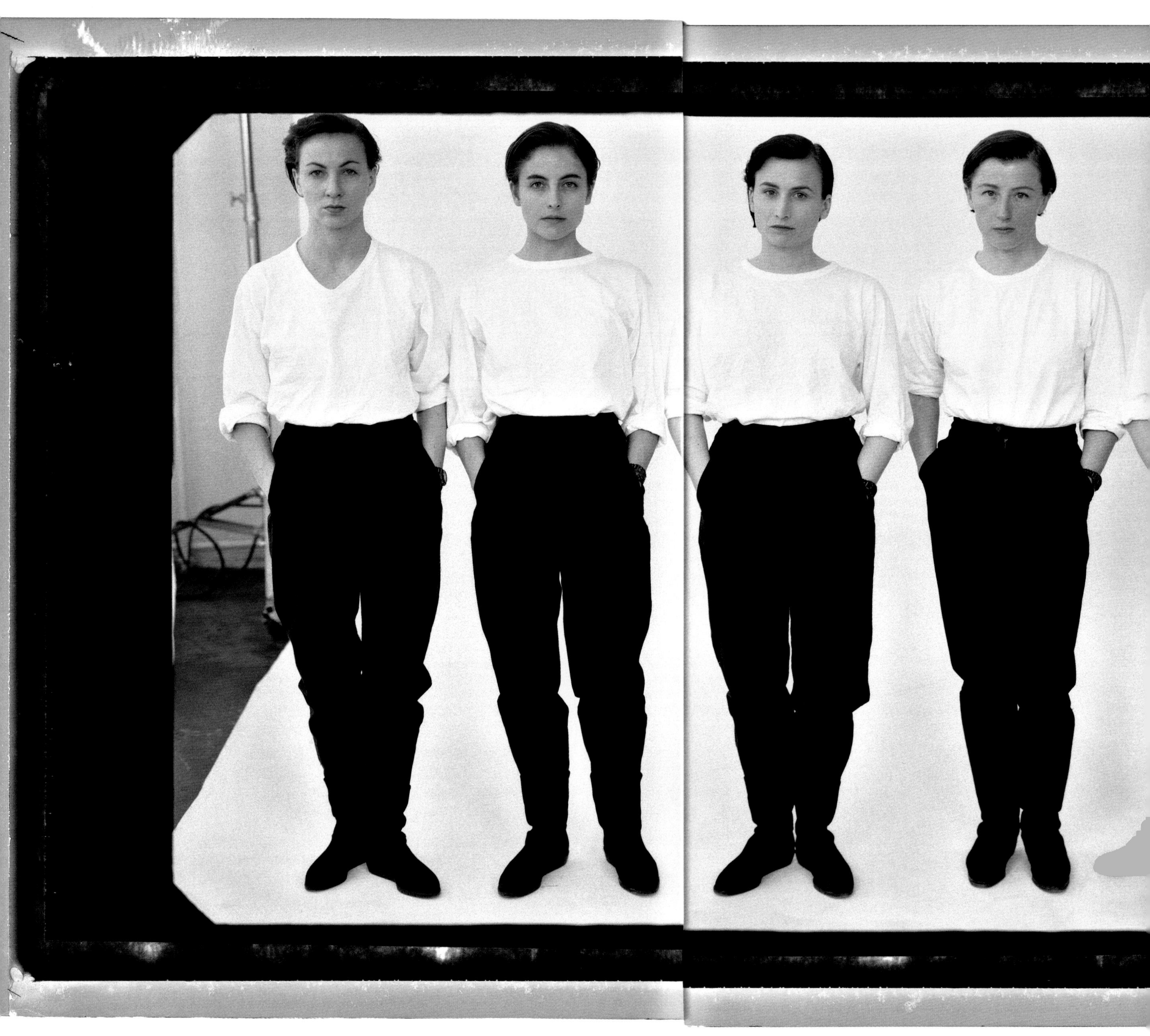

Cindy Sherman,
New York City, 1992

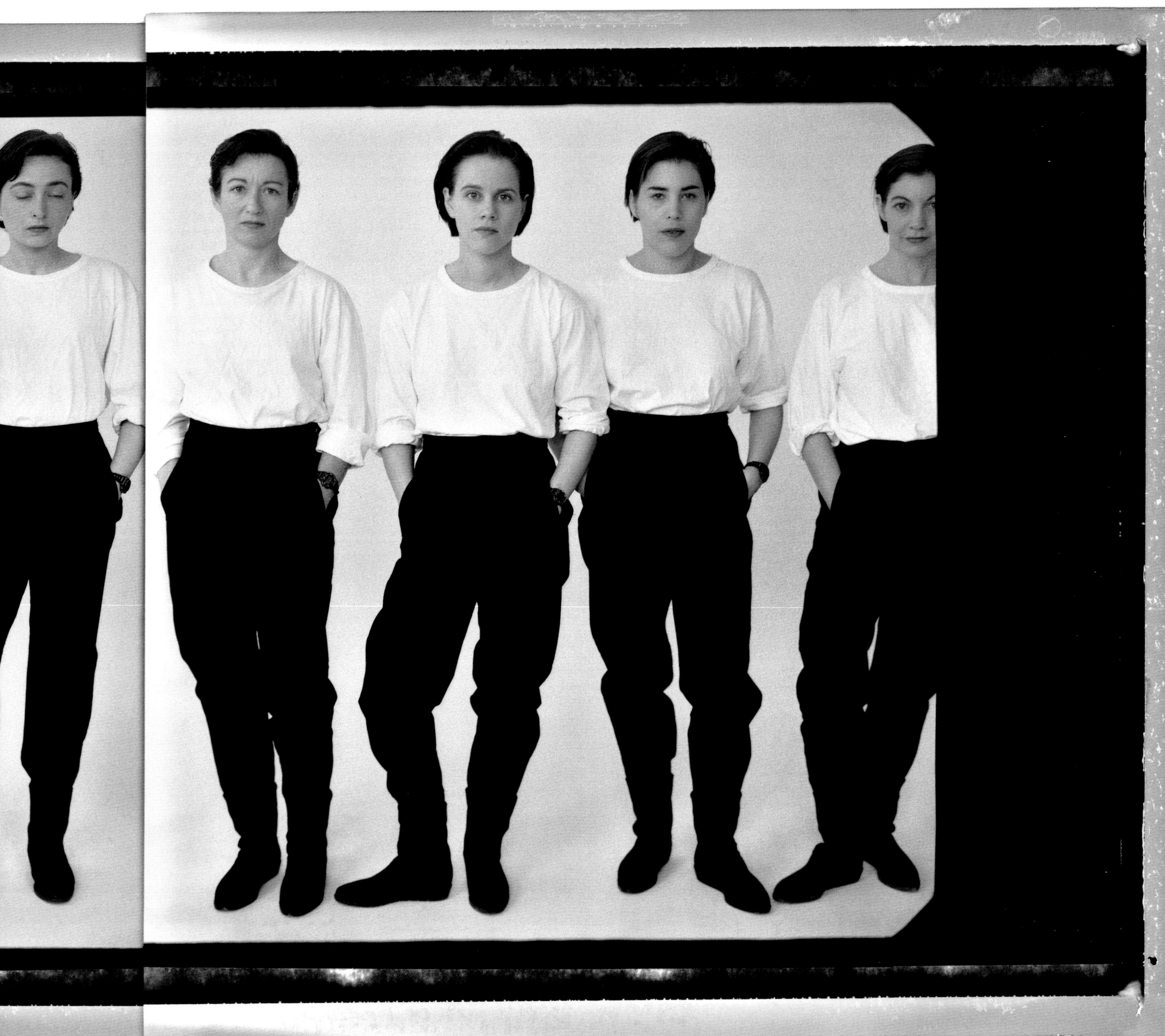

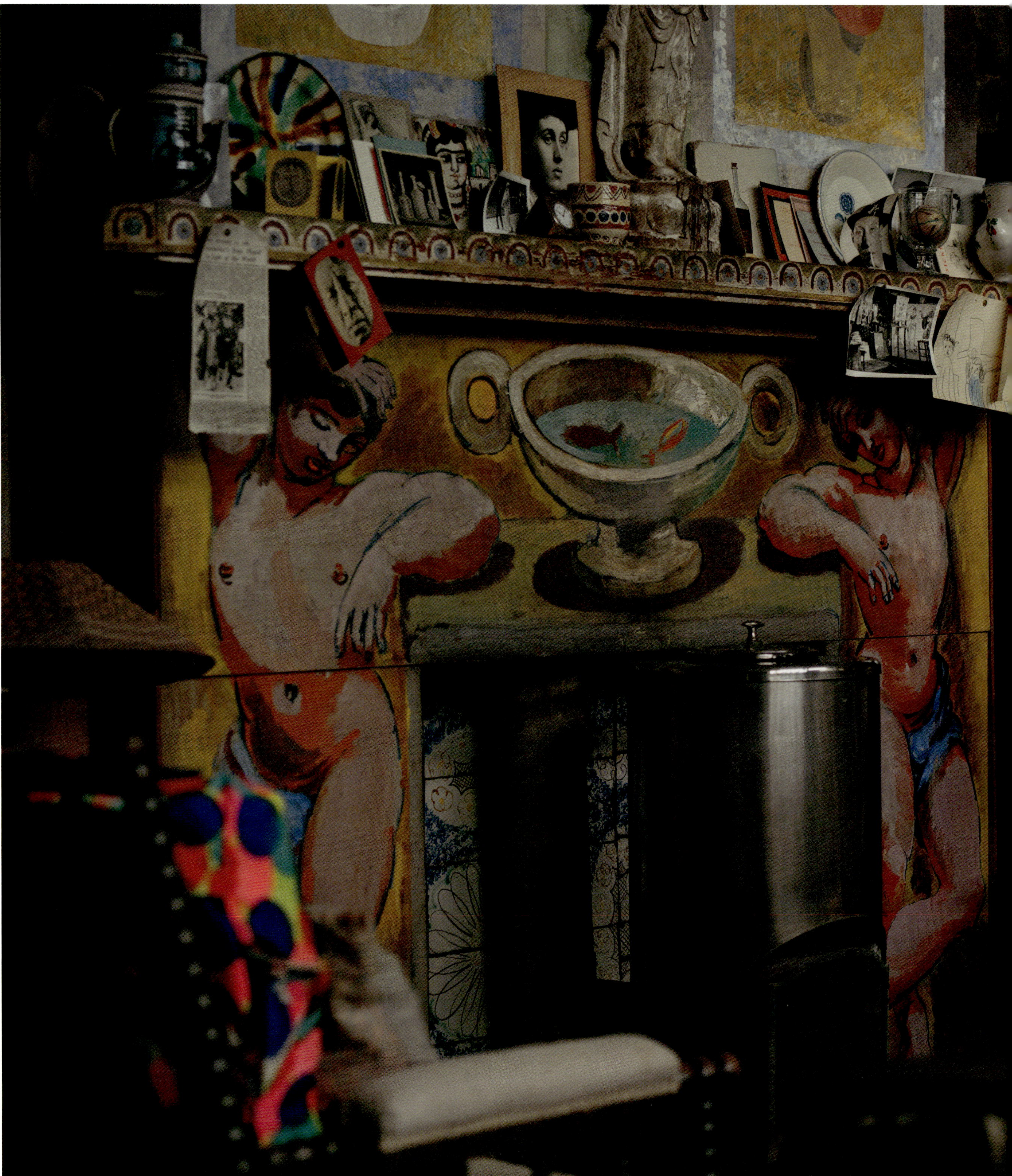

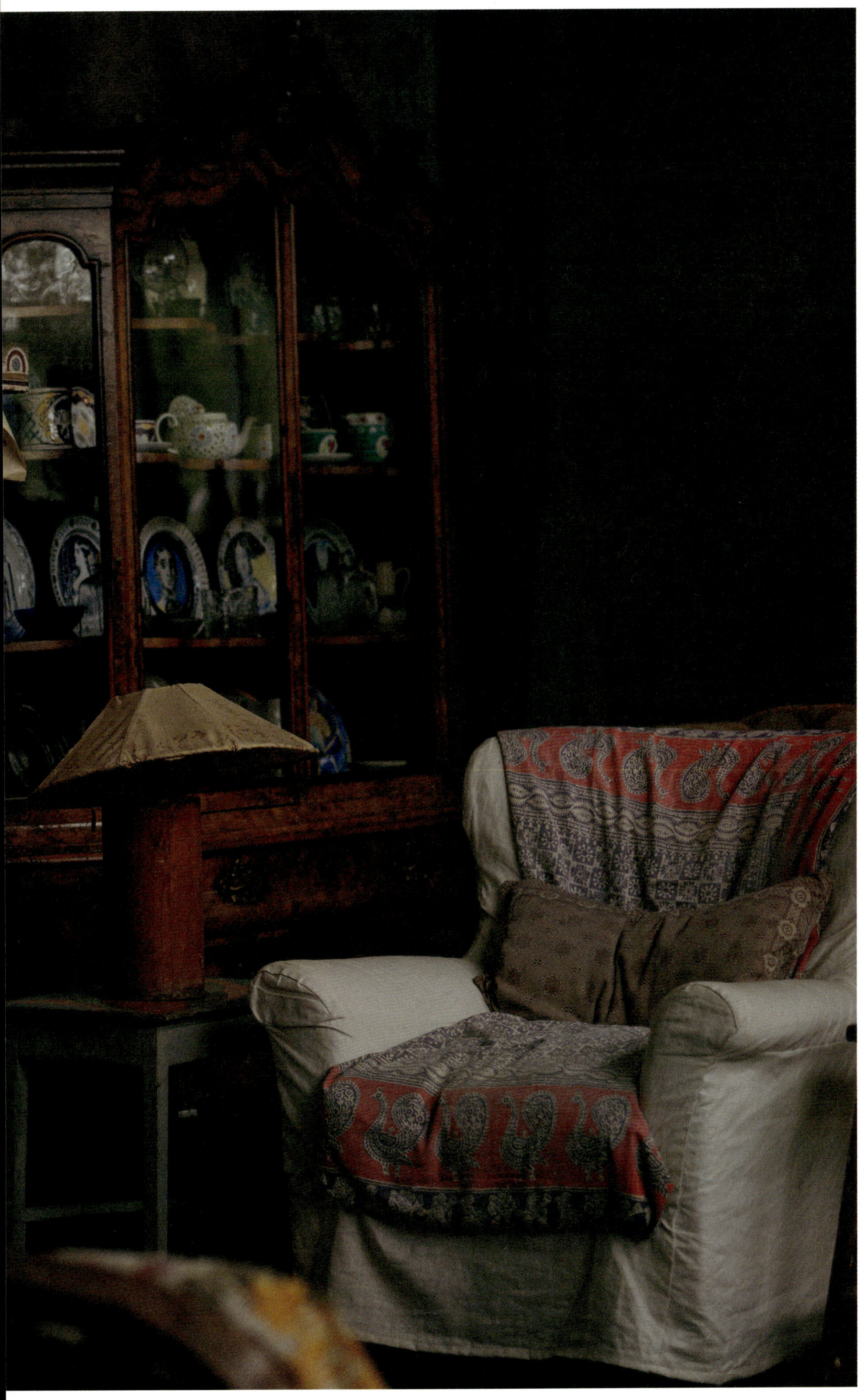

Charleston farmhouse,
East Sussex, England, 2010

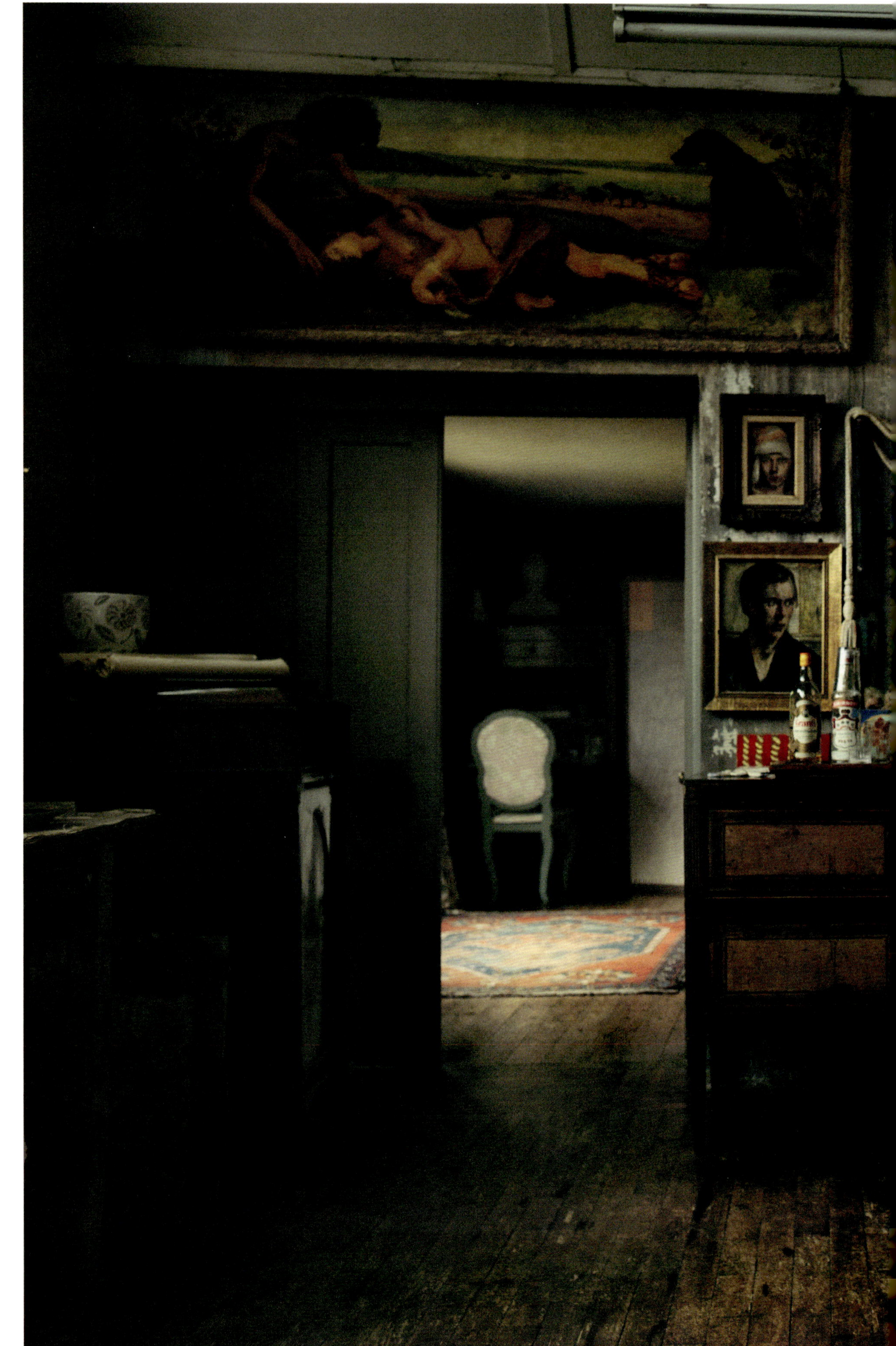

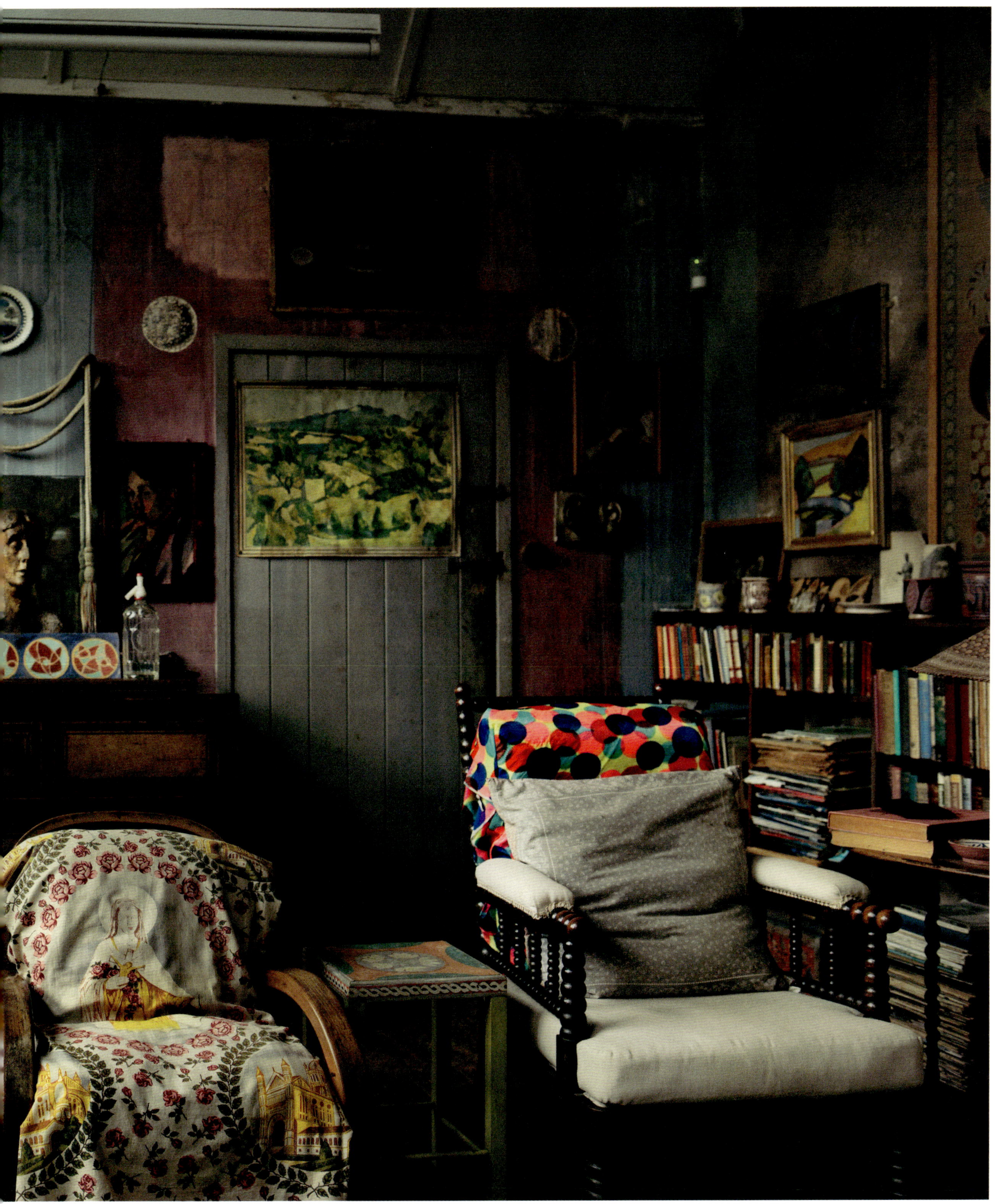

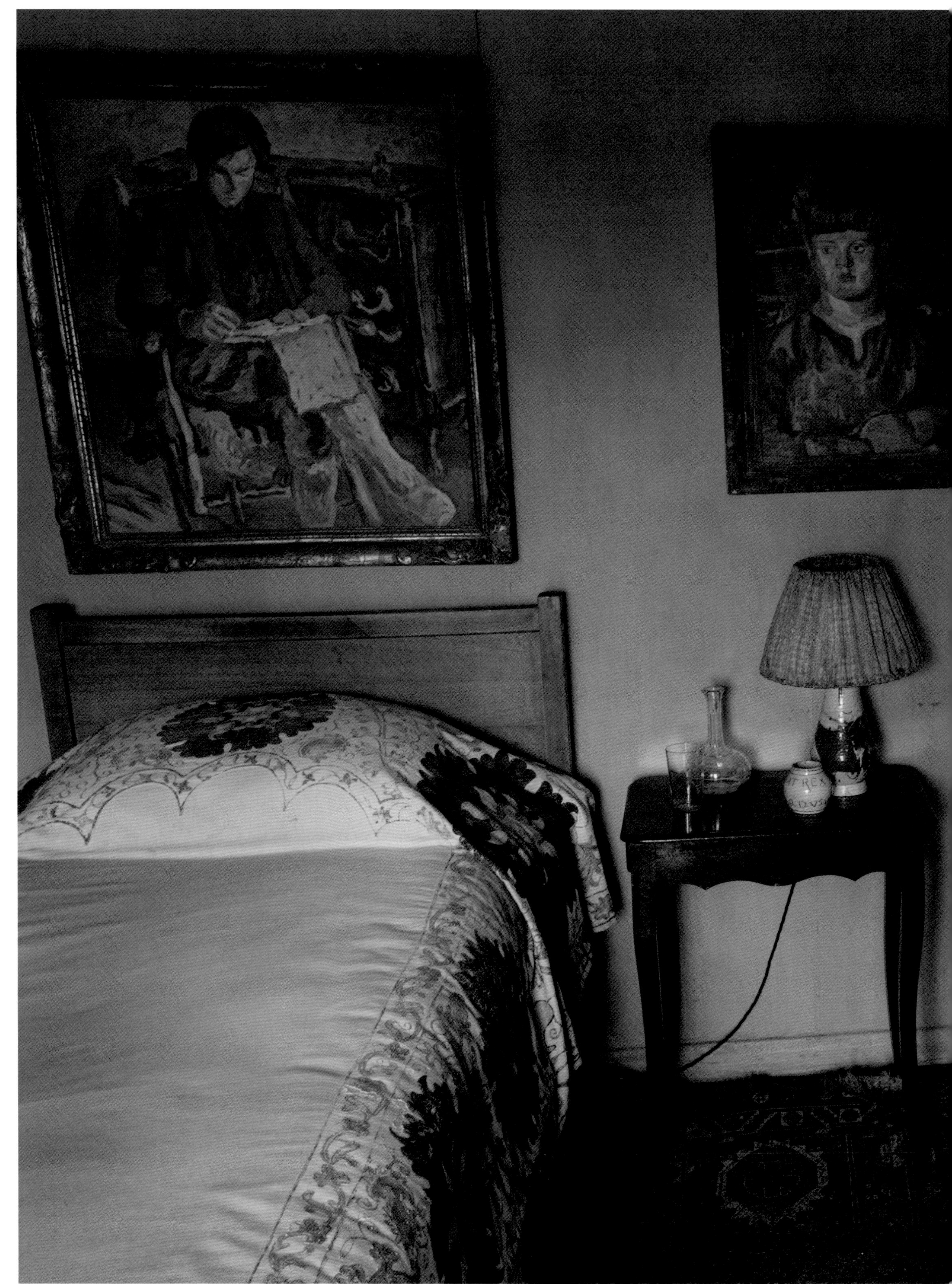

Vanessa Bell's bedroom,
Charleston farmhouse,
East Sussex, England, 2010

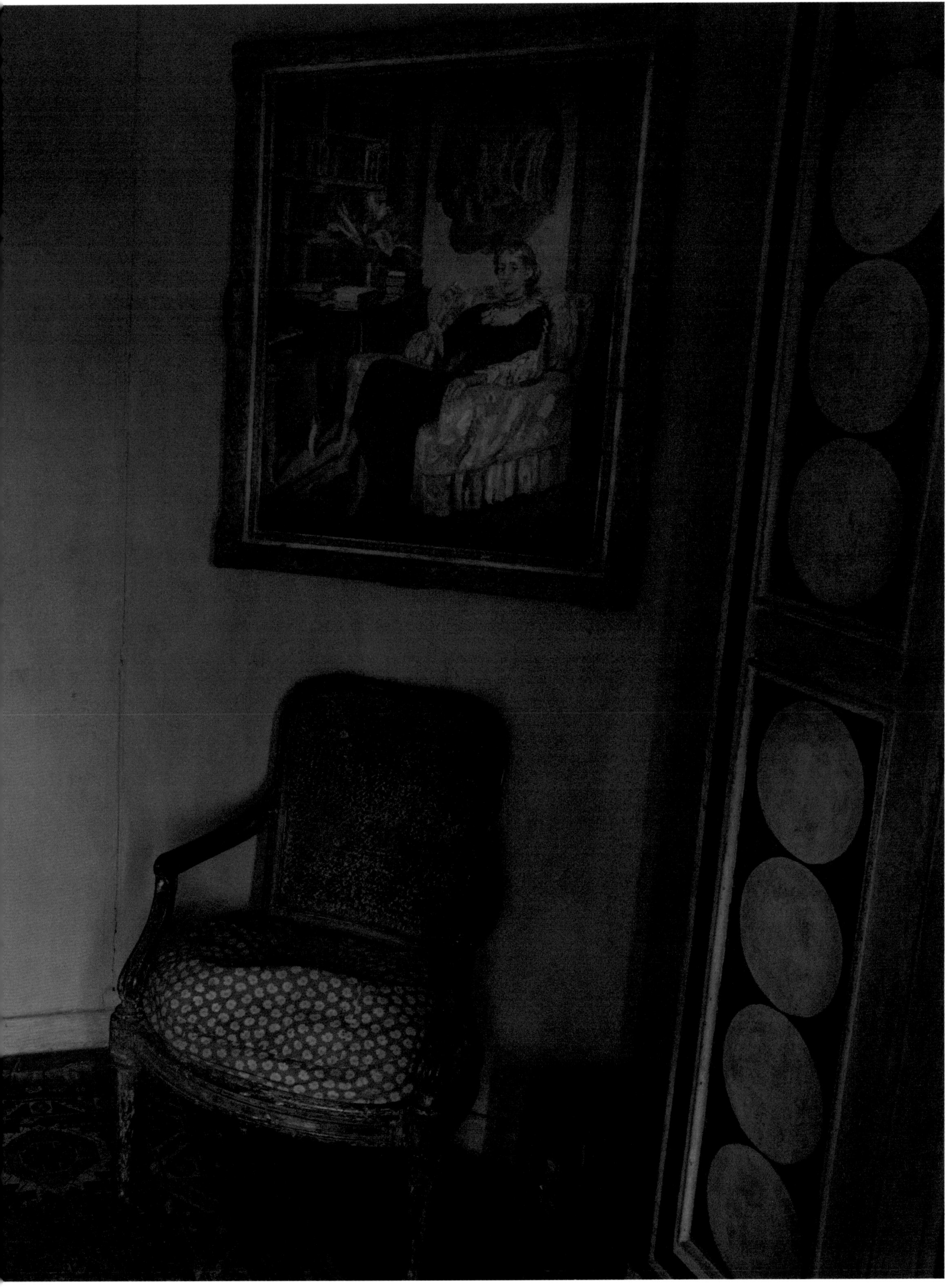

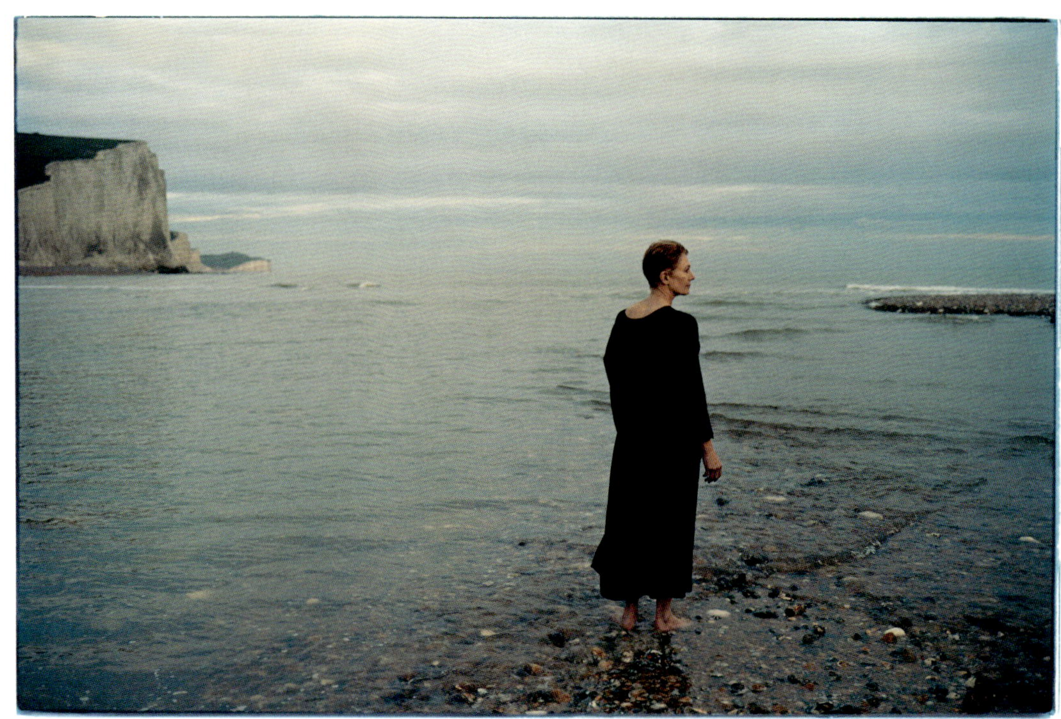

A crucial element of Annie's work is a sense of place. She is not by nature a studio photographer. The history of a place, its sounds and smells, influence a picture in ways that are impossible to achieve in a studio. She prefers her subjects to be in a location that is meaningful to them—it isn't just for background or decor. It has its own integrity, its own distinct characteristics.

In a body of work called *Pilgrimage*, there are no people in the pictures. Just places that are associated with people who mean something to her—Emily Dickinson's bedroom in Amherst, Massachusetts; Georgia O'Keeffe's houses in the New Mexico desert; a concert gown worn by Marian Anderson found in her rehearsal room in Connecticut; Eleanor Roosevelt's cottage in upstate New York; the chalk cliffs on the Isle of Wight where Julia Margaret Cameron took walks.

Charleston Farmhouse, in the Sussex Downs in England, is also part of that work. The Bloomsbury Group painters Vanessa Bell and Duncan Grant lived at Charleston in a romantically complicated household not far from the home of Bell's sister, Virginia Woolf. Several years earlier, Annie photographed Nicole Kidman at Charleston. Kidman was living in England with her then husband, Tom Cruise, while they made *Eyes Wide Shut*, Stanley Kubrick's final film, which was shot continuously for four hundred days. Kubrick had asked her to stay out of the sun for a year before they started filming. Her skin was pale, almost translucent.

Vanessa Redgrave, Seven Sisters cliffs, East Sussex, England, 1994

Nicole Kidman in the garden at Charleston farmhouse, East Sussex, England, 1997

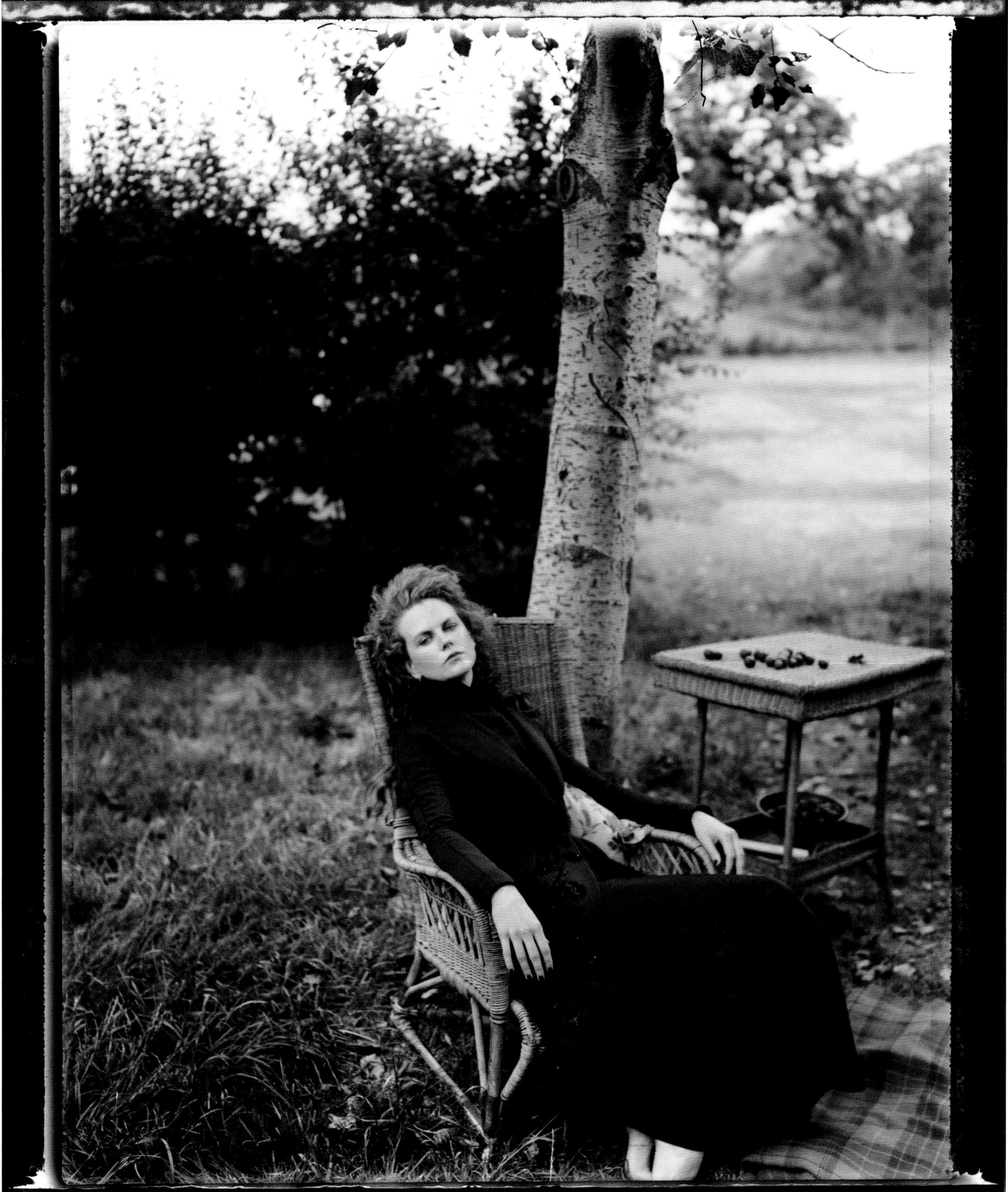

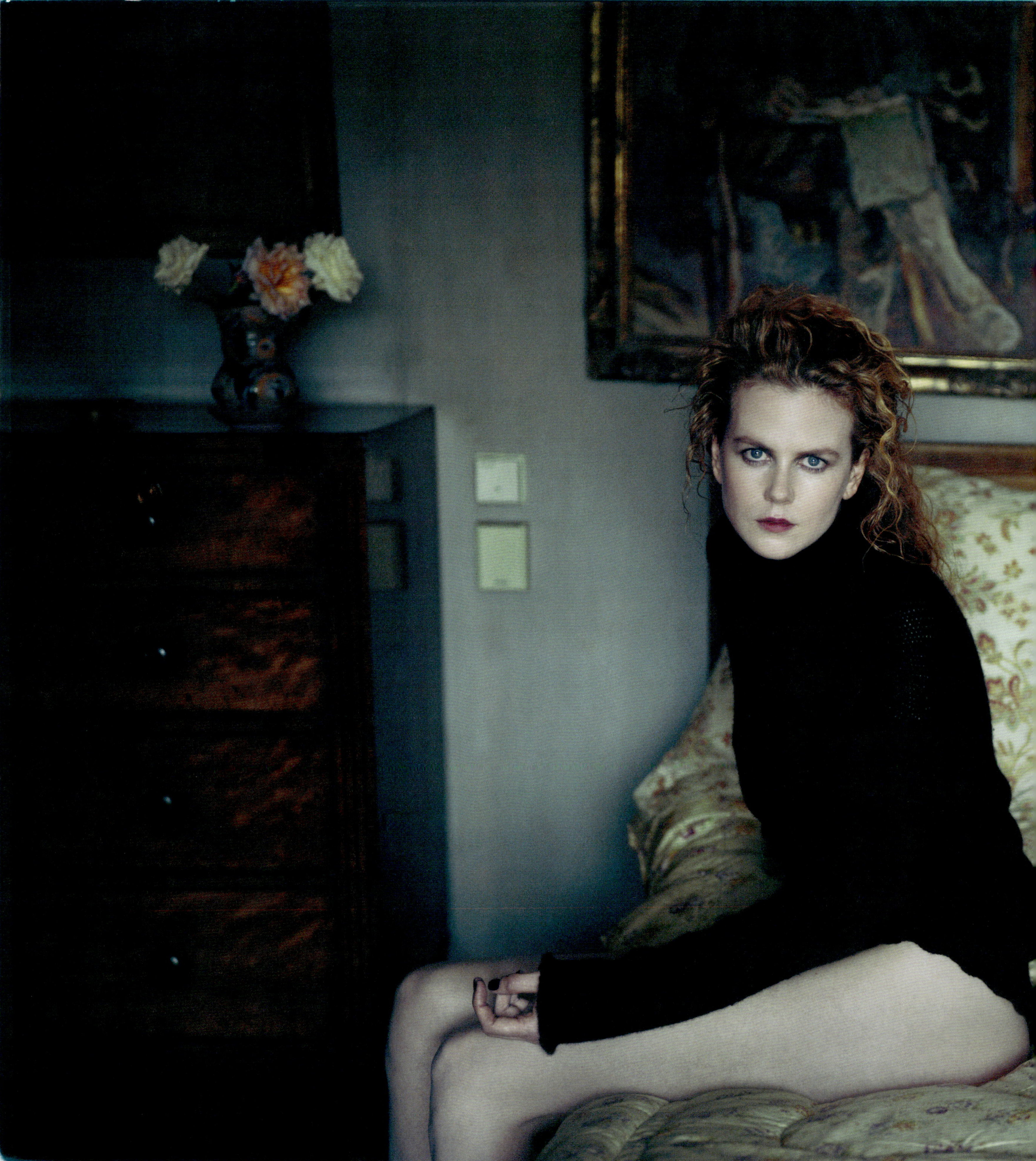

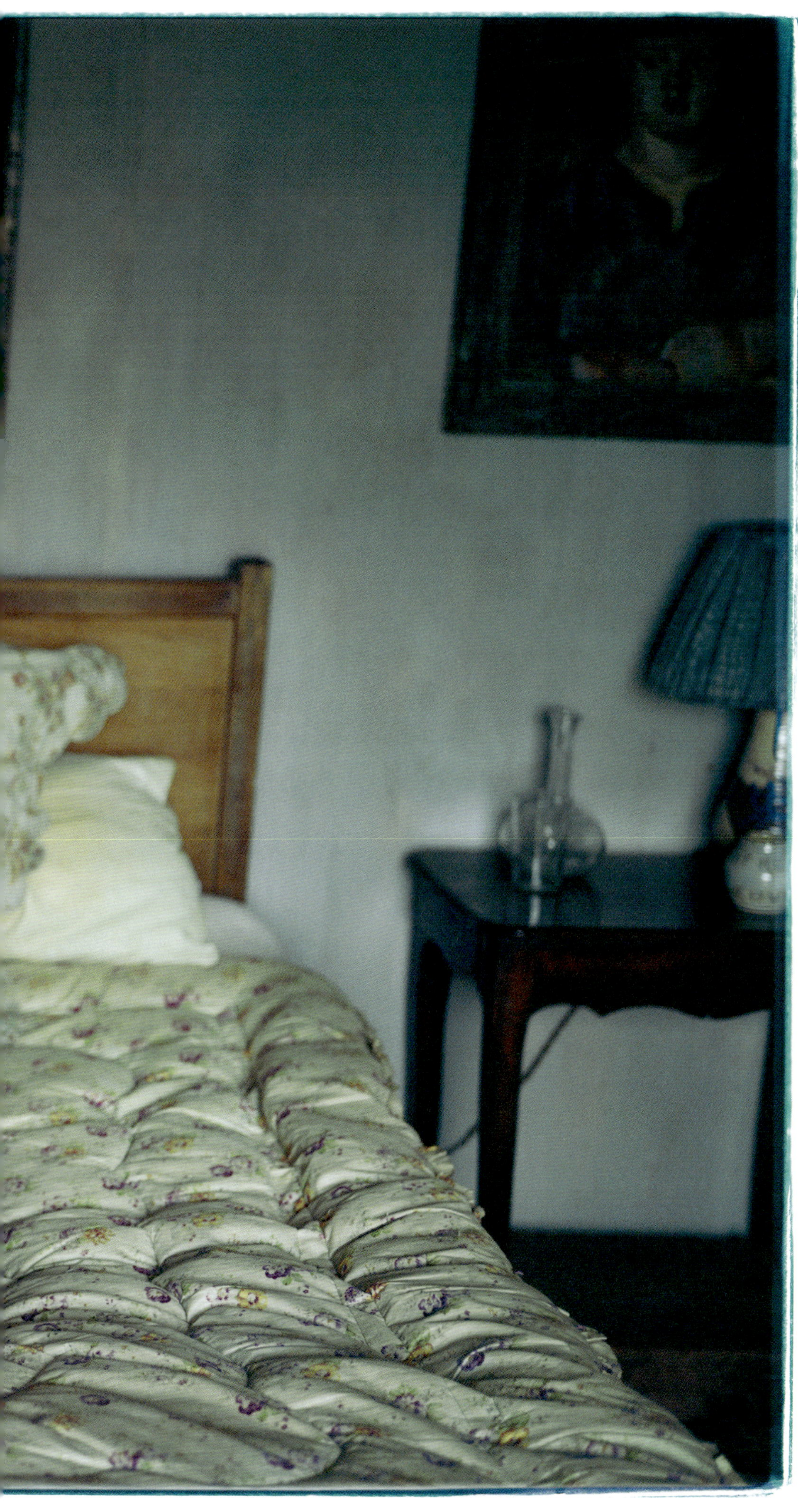

Nicole Kidman,
Charleston farmhouse,
East Sussex, England, 1997

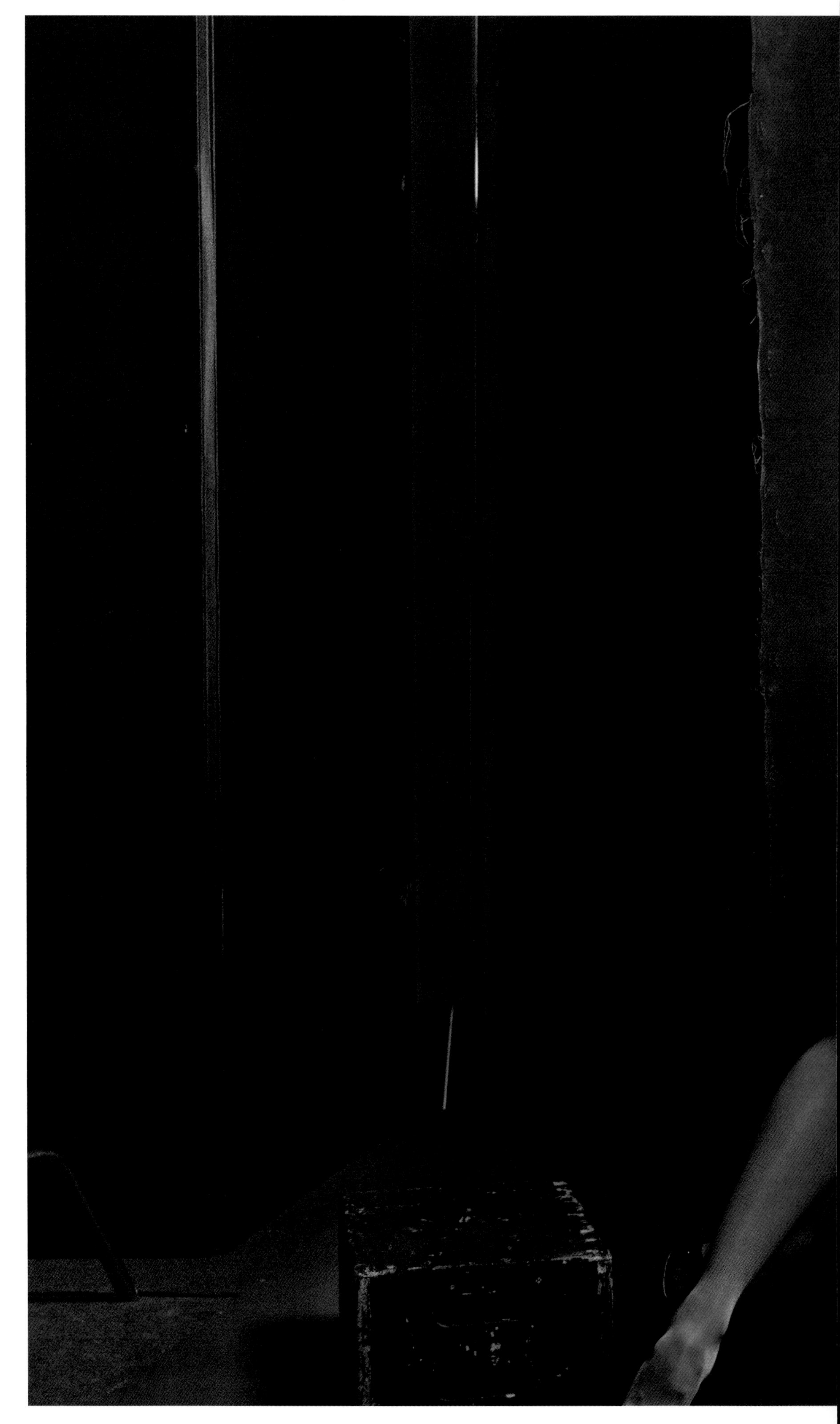

Nicole Kidman and Baz Luhrmann,
New York City, 2008

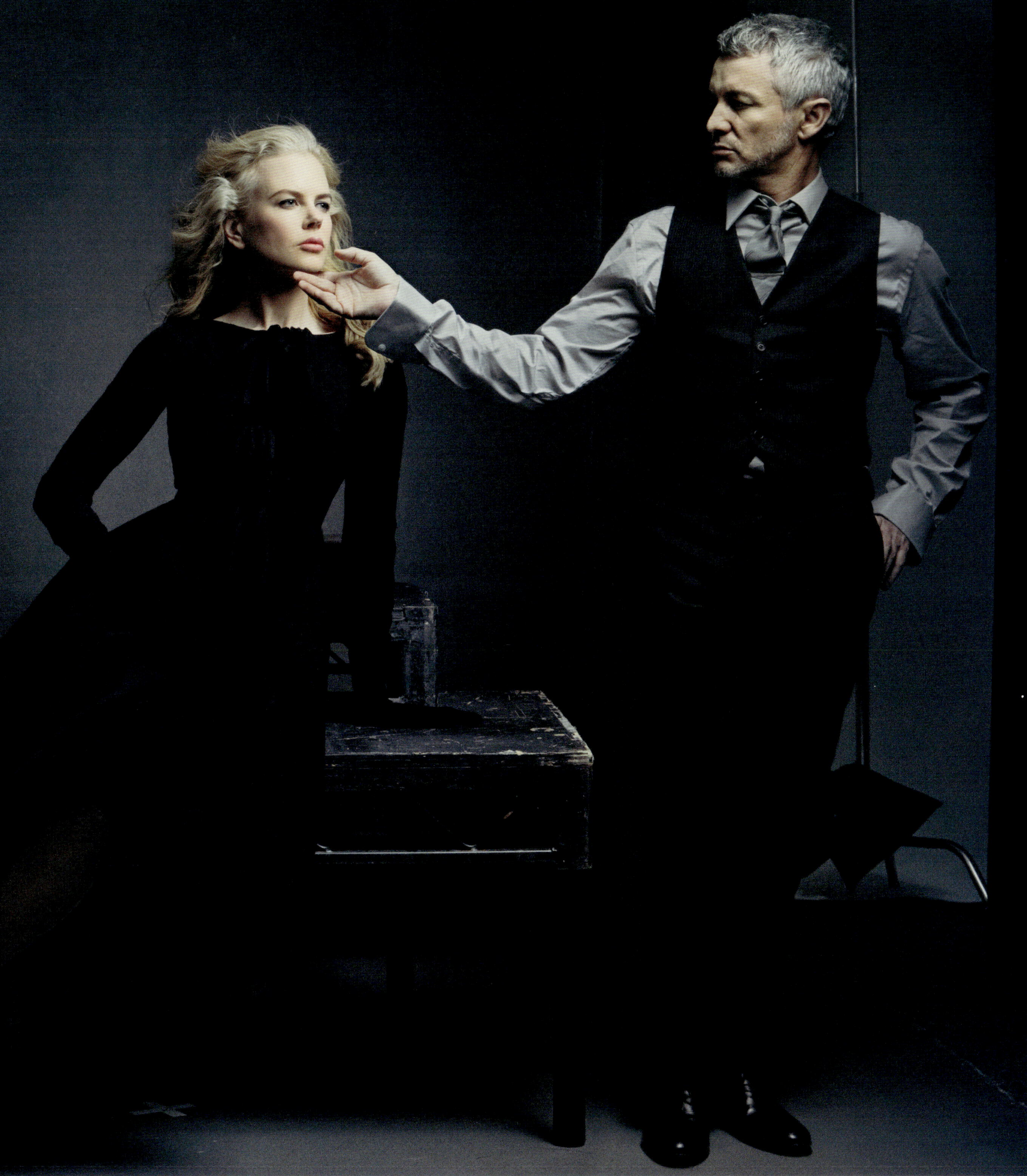

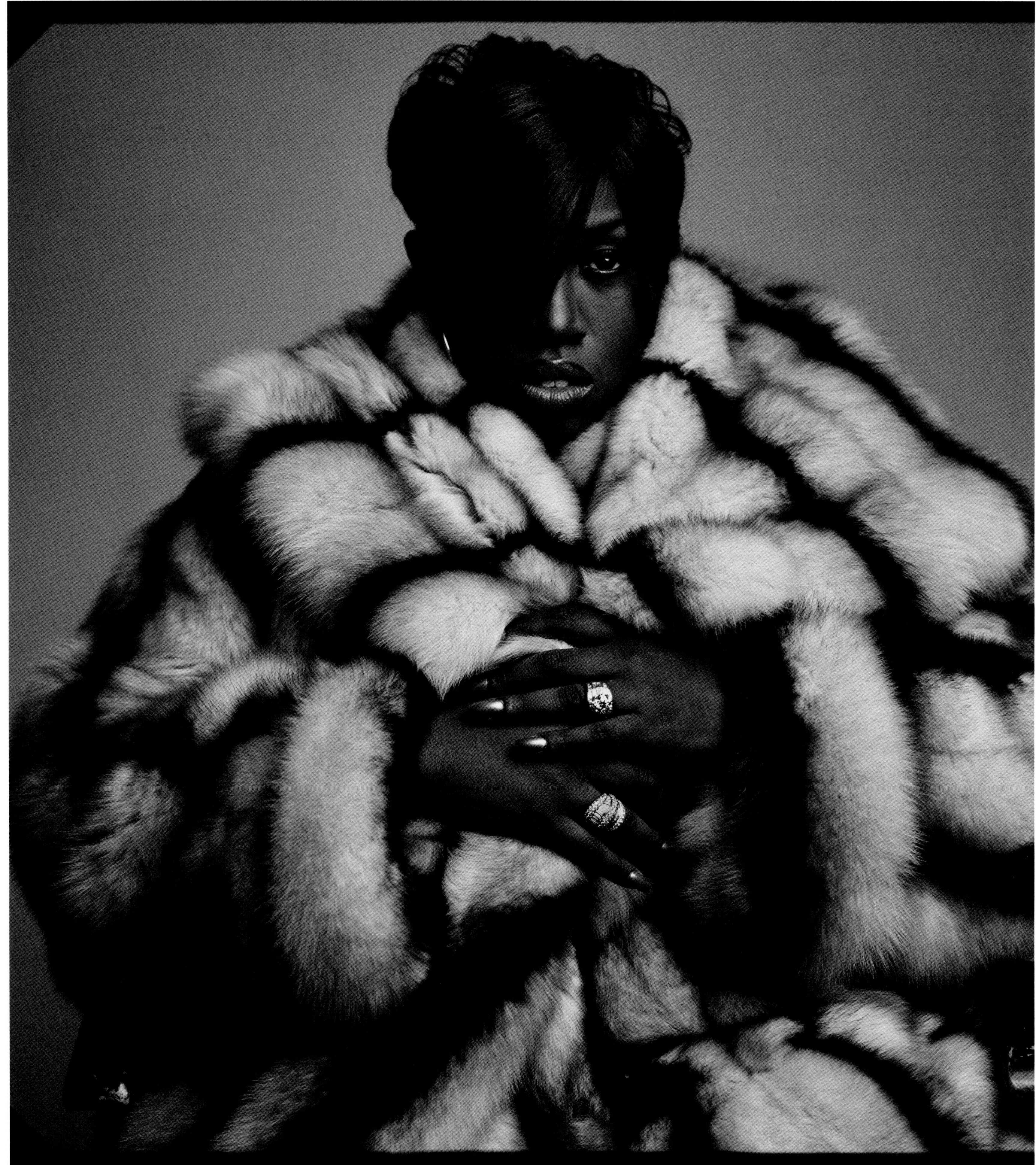

Missy Elliott,
New York City, 1999

Lil' Kim,
New York City, 1999

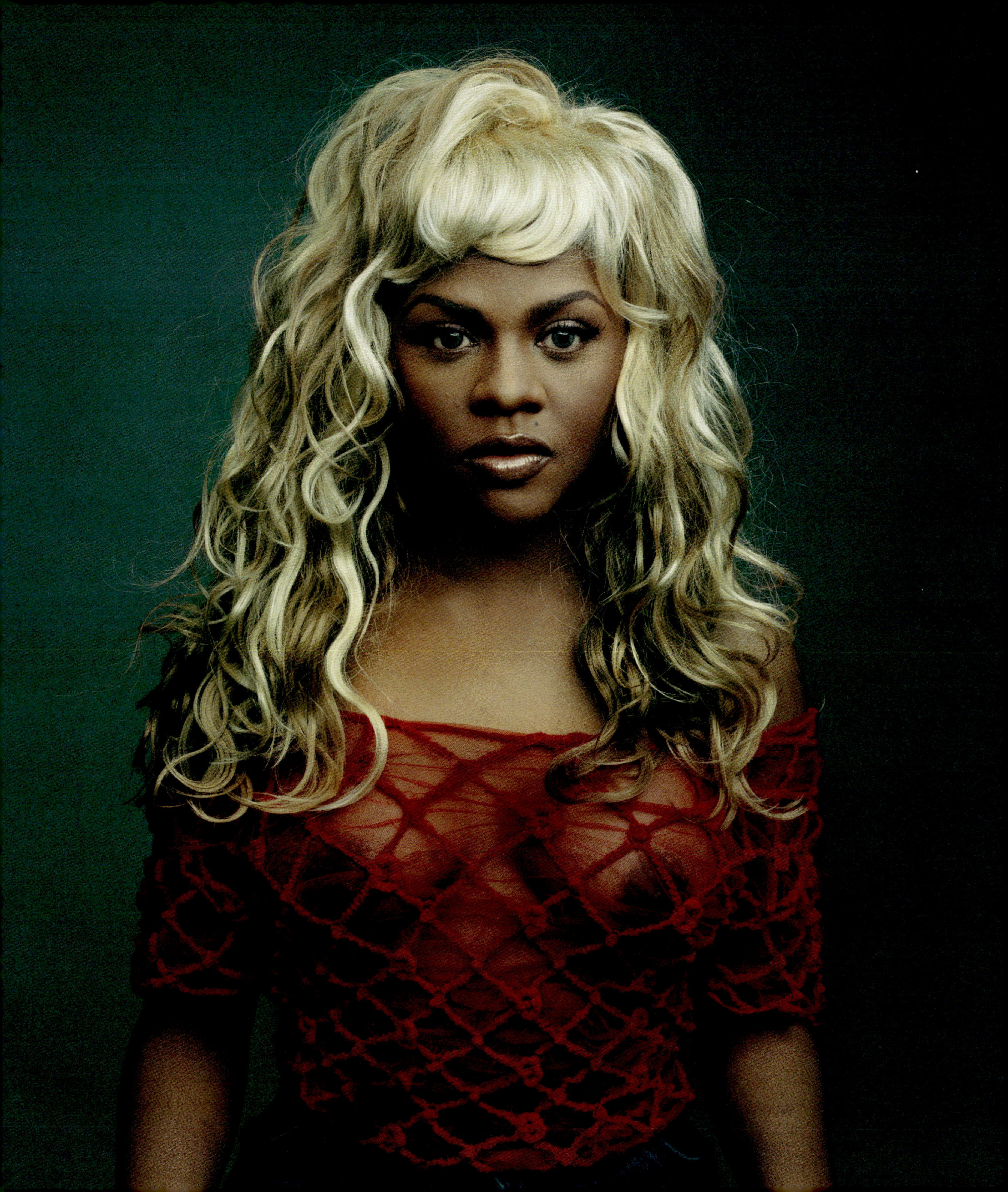

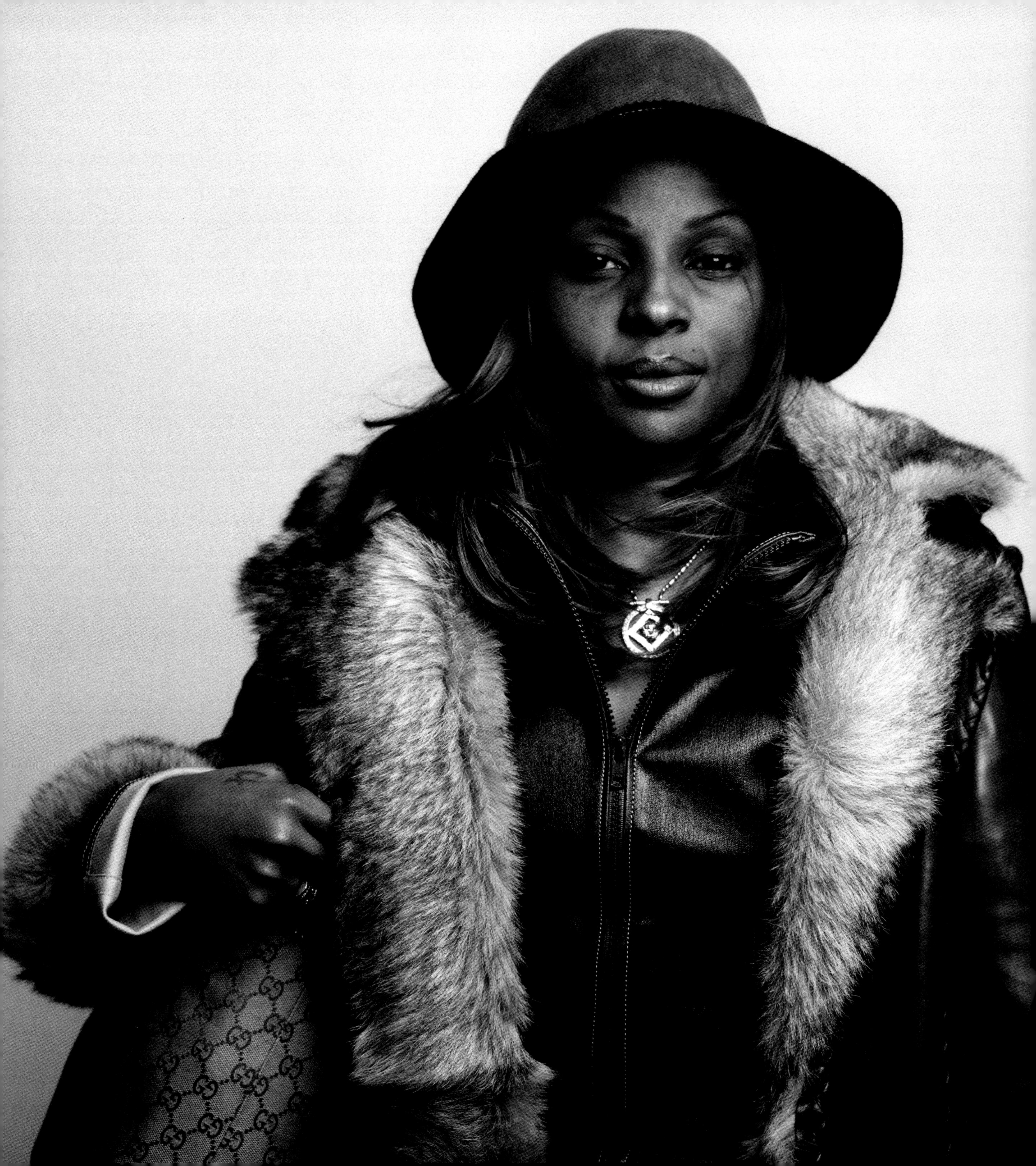

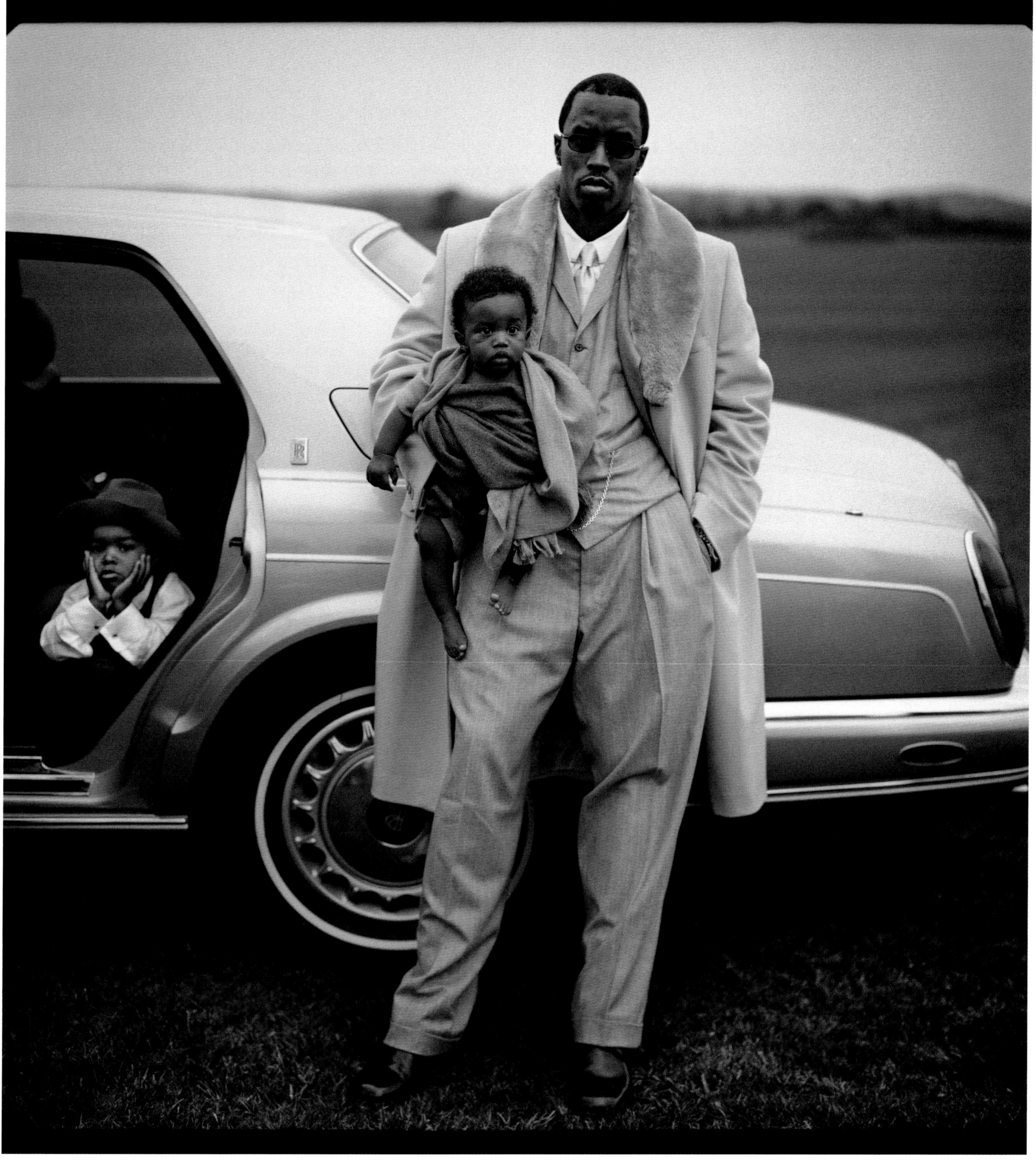

Mary J. Blige,
New York City, 1999

Sean Combs and his sons, Justin and Christian,
Bridgehampton, New York, 1998

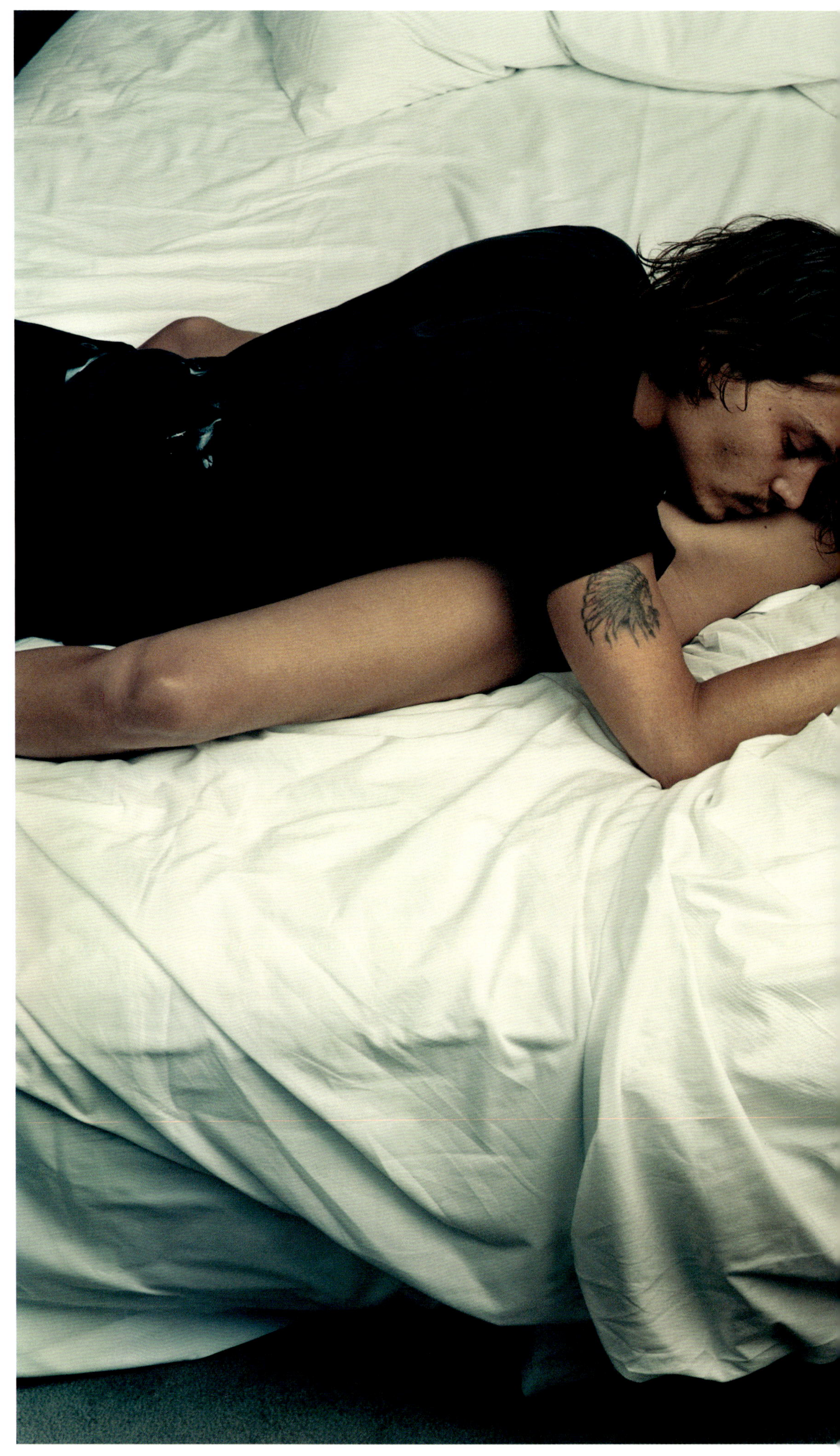

Johnny Depp and Kate Moss,
New York City, 1994

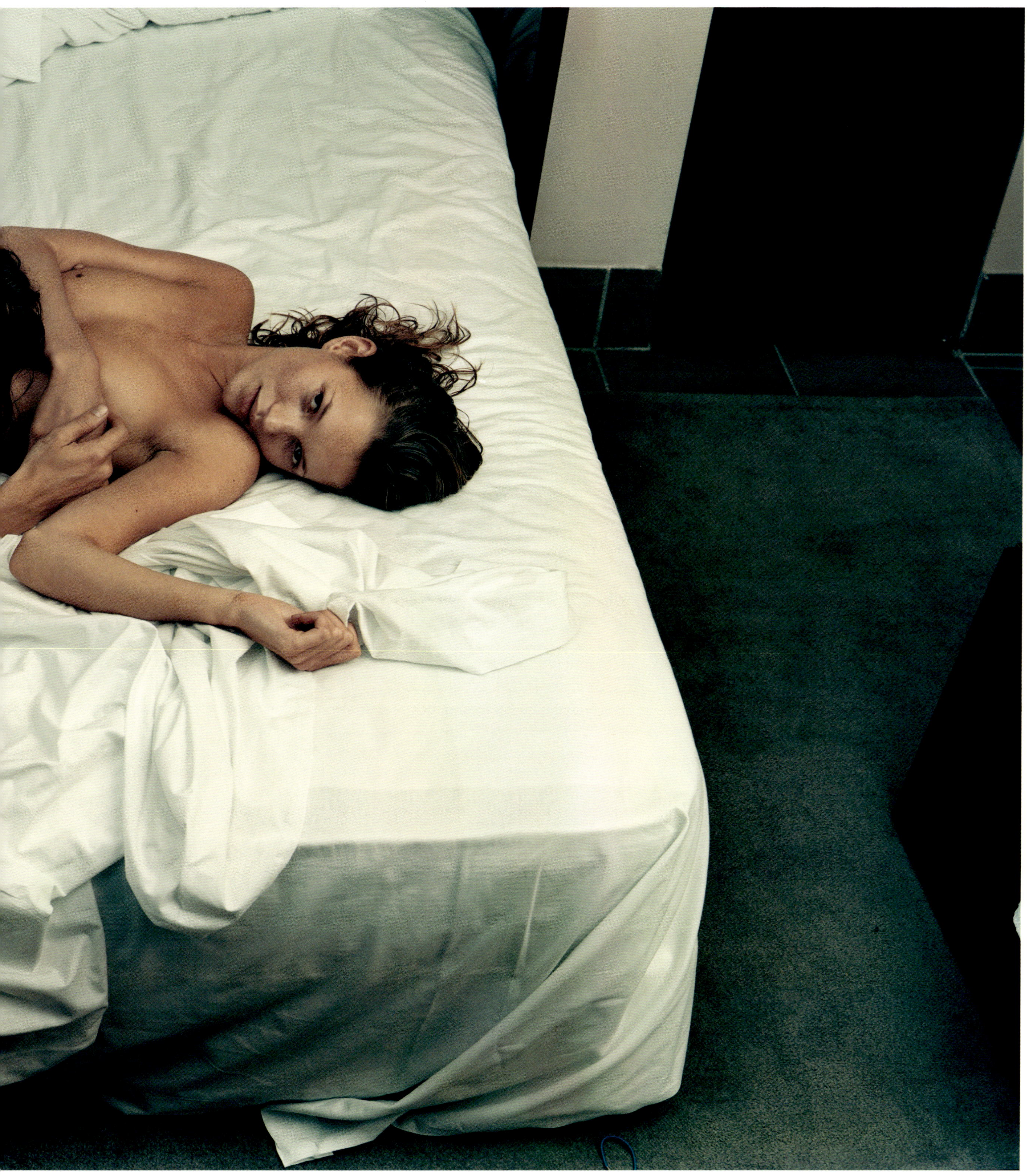

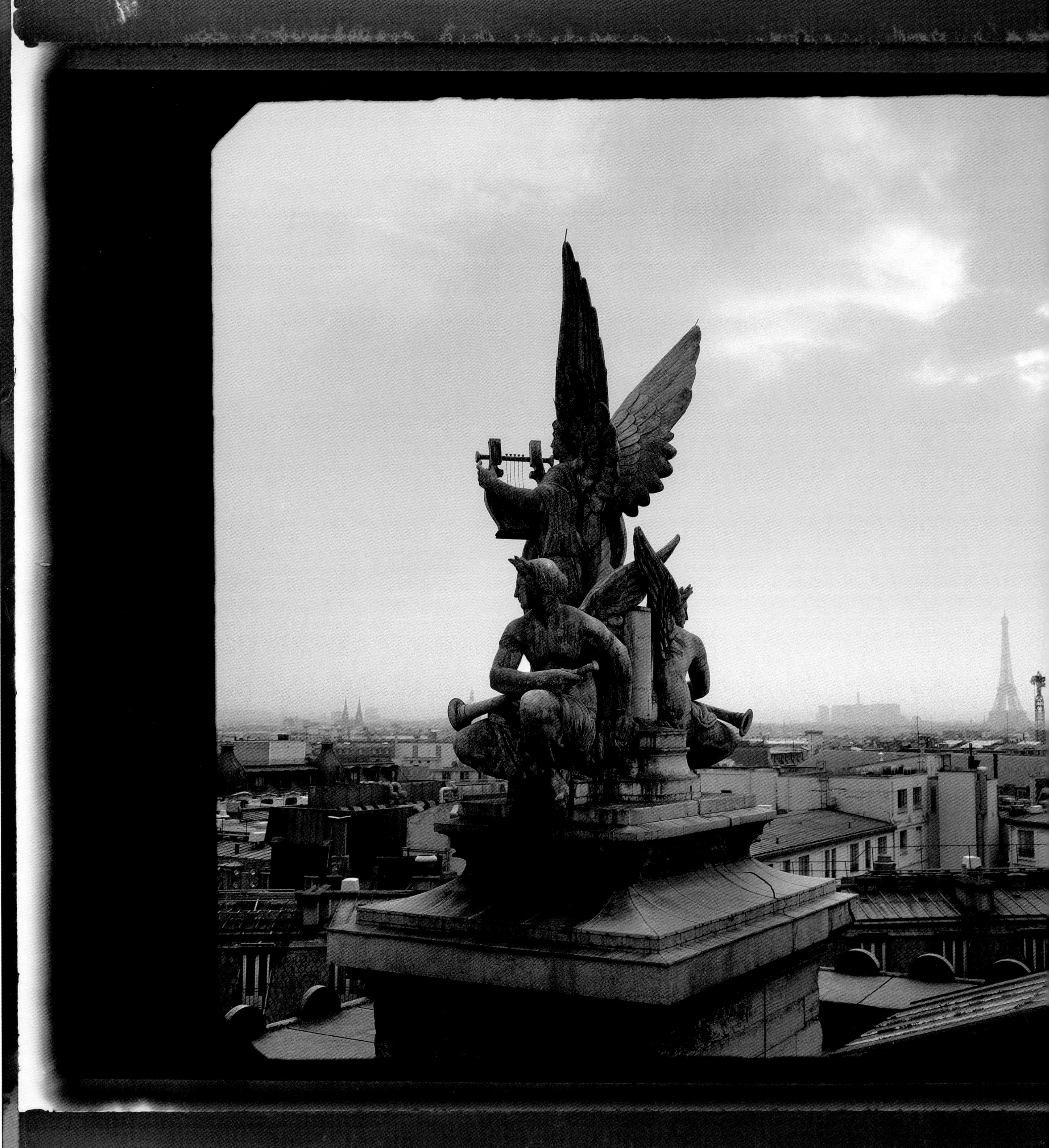

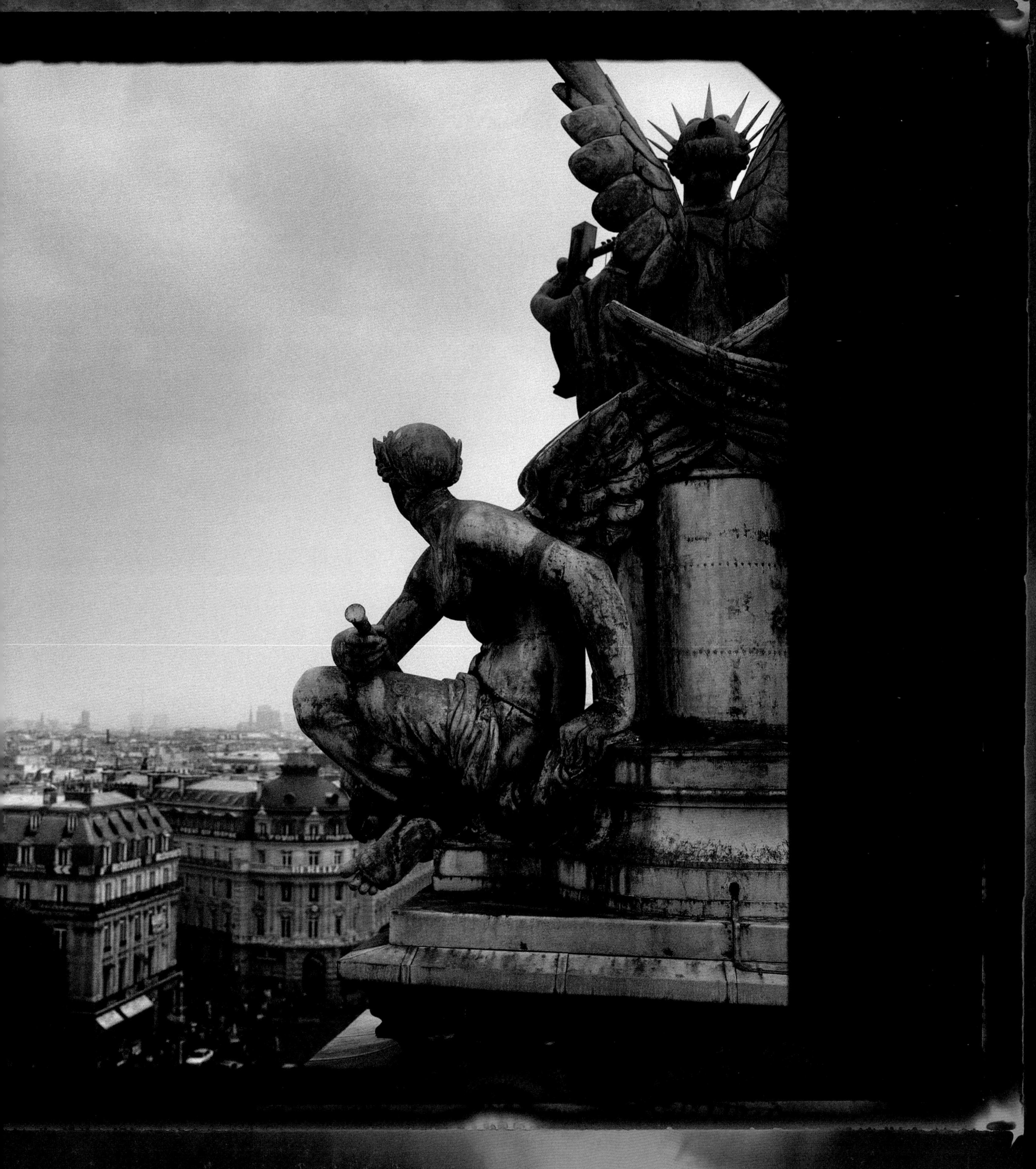

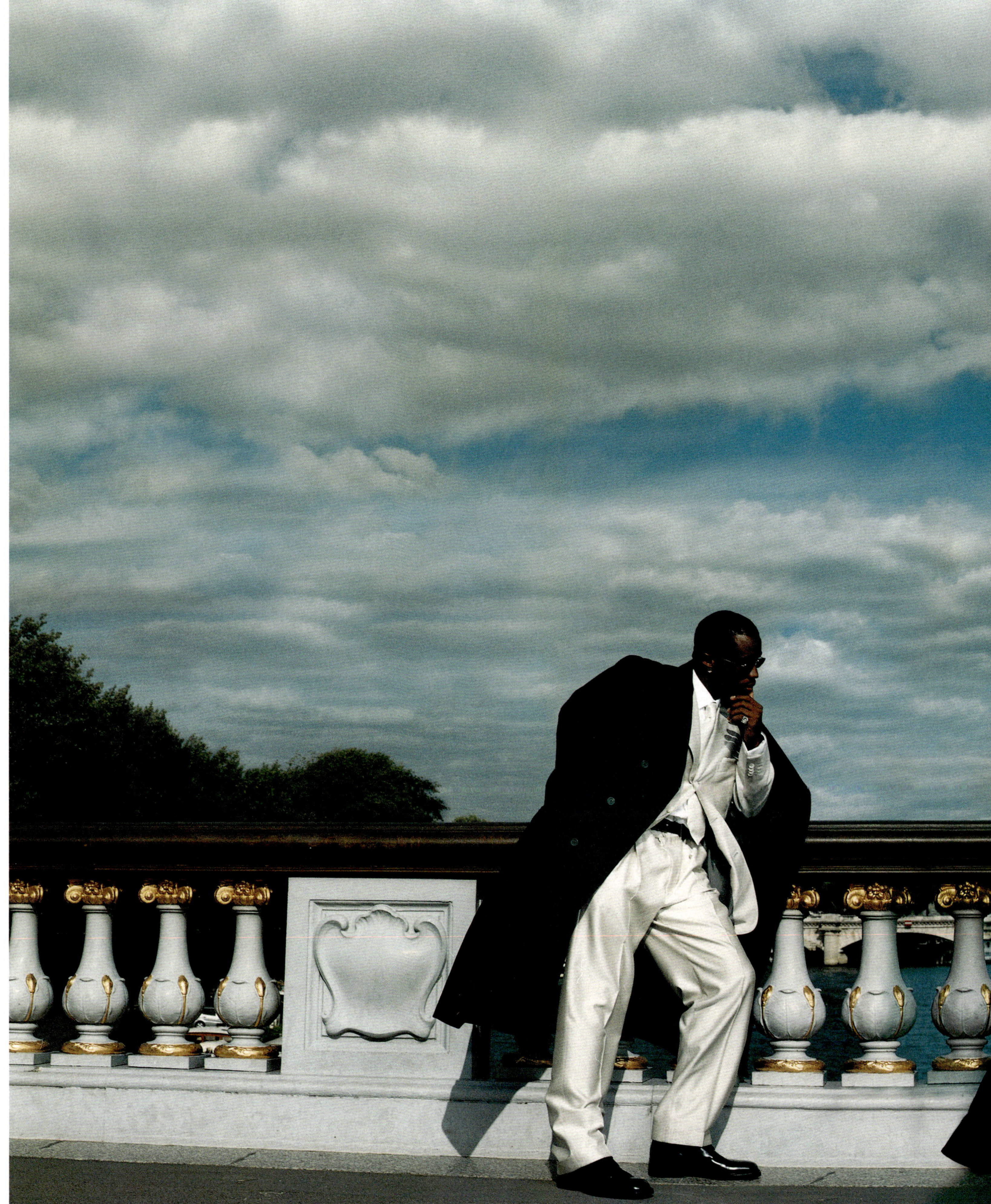

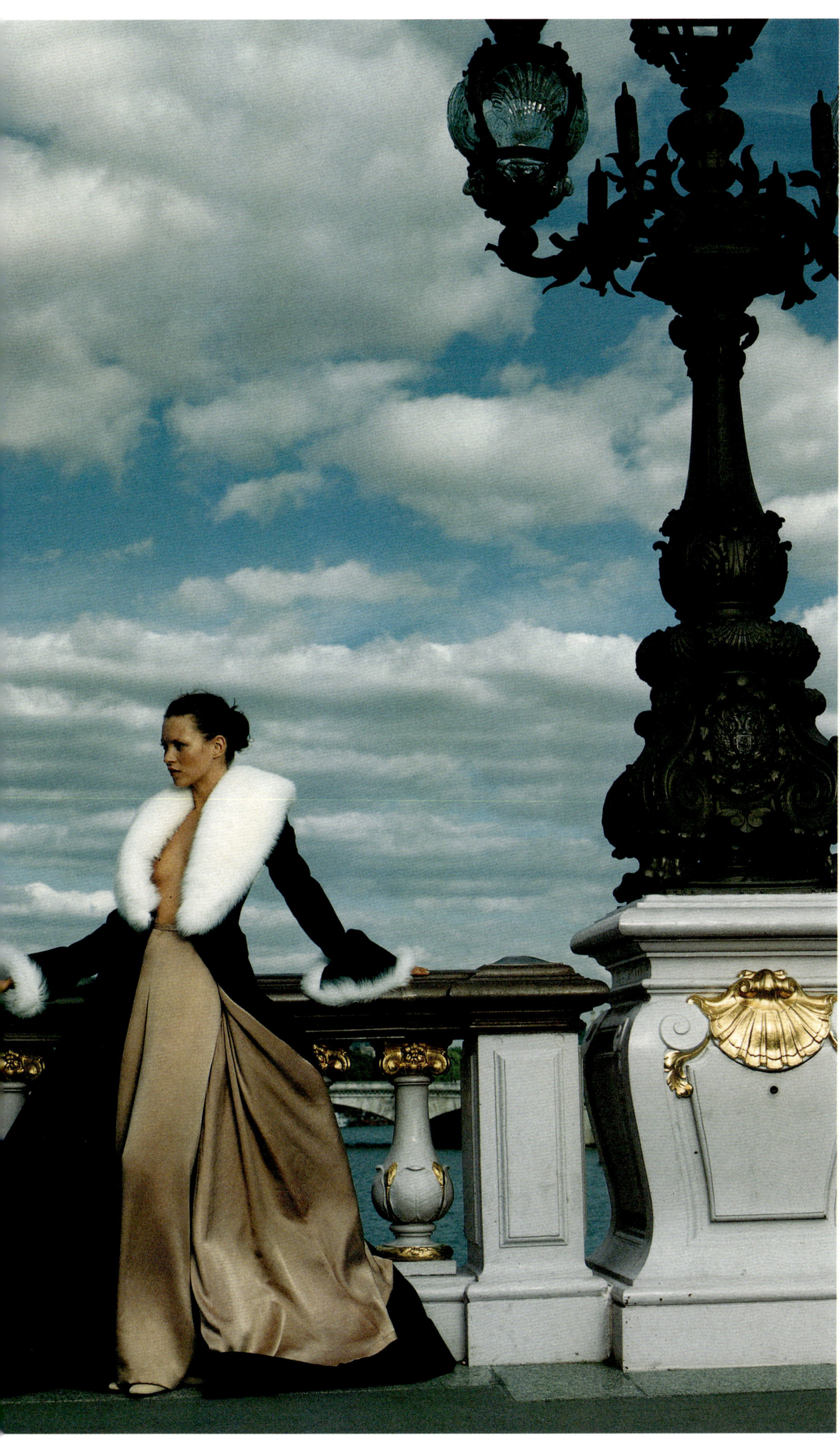

When *Vogue* sent Annie to Paris to cover the collections in 1999, she made her first foray into haute couture. She collaborated with Grace Coddington, who brought decades of cosmopolitan experience as a model and then a fashion editor. Annie brought enthusiasm and curiosity about a world she had only seen from afar. They created their first long narrative feature together on that trip.

Stories suited Annie's journalistic approach, and they were Grace's signature style since her days at British *Vogue*. Annie prepared by attending the designers' shows. Couture is an insulated world, and not many people have the opportunity to see what goes into it. It was in Paris that she came to understand what great artists the designers are.

Previous spread:
Palais Garnier, Paris, 1994

Sean Combs and Kate Moss,
Pont Alexandre III, Paris, 1999

Sean Combs spoke with Jonathan Van Meter about being asked to appear in *Vogue* for the first time: "I was designing my clothes and jewelry, and doing things that weren't being done in fashion. There wasn't a lot of Blackness in fashion or Black models on the runways. Back then, there was no one in the front rows. We weren't invited to anything. If you were Black and you were hip-hop, it was dangerous. I had grown up looking at *GQ* and *Vogue* and knowing who Anna Wintour was. When I got that call from her, I was blown away. She was bringing me into her world and letting me disrupt it."

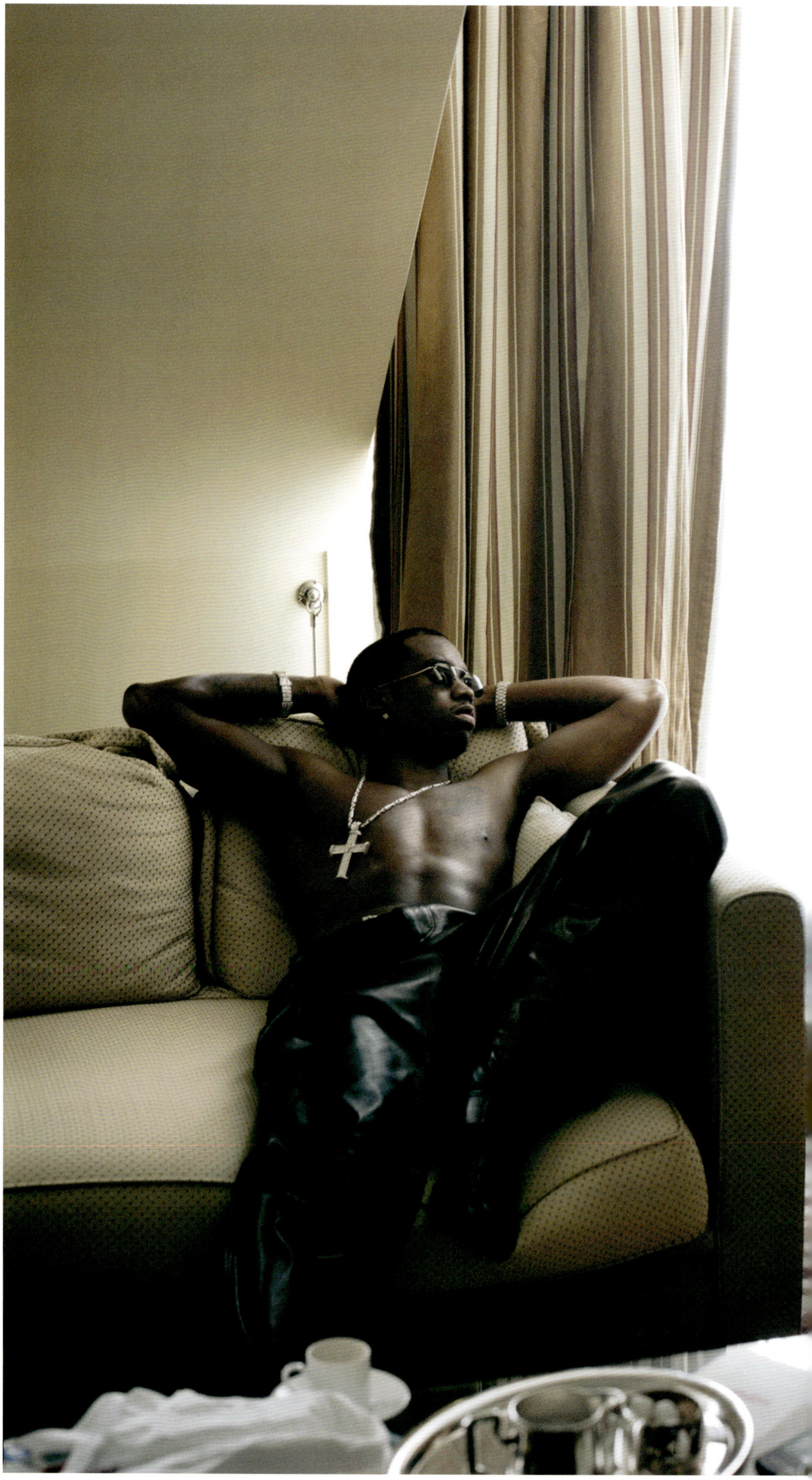

Hyatt Hotel, Paris, 1999

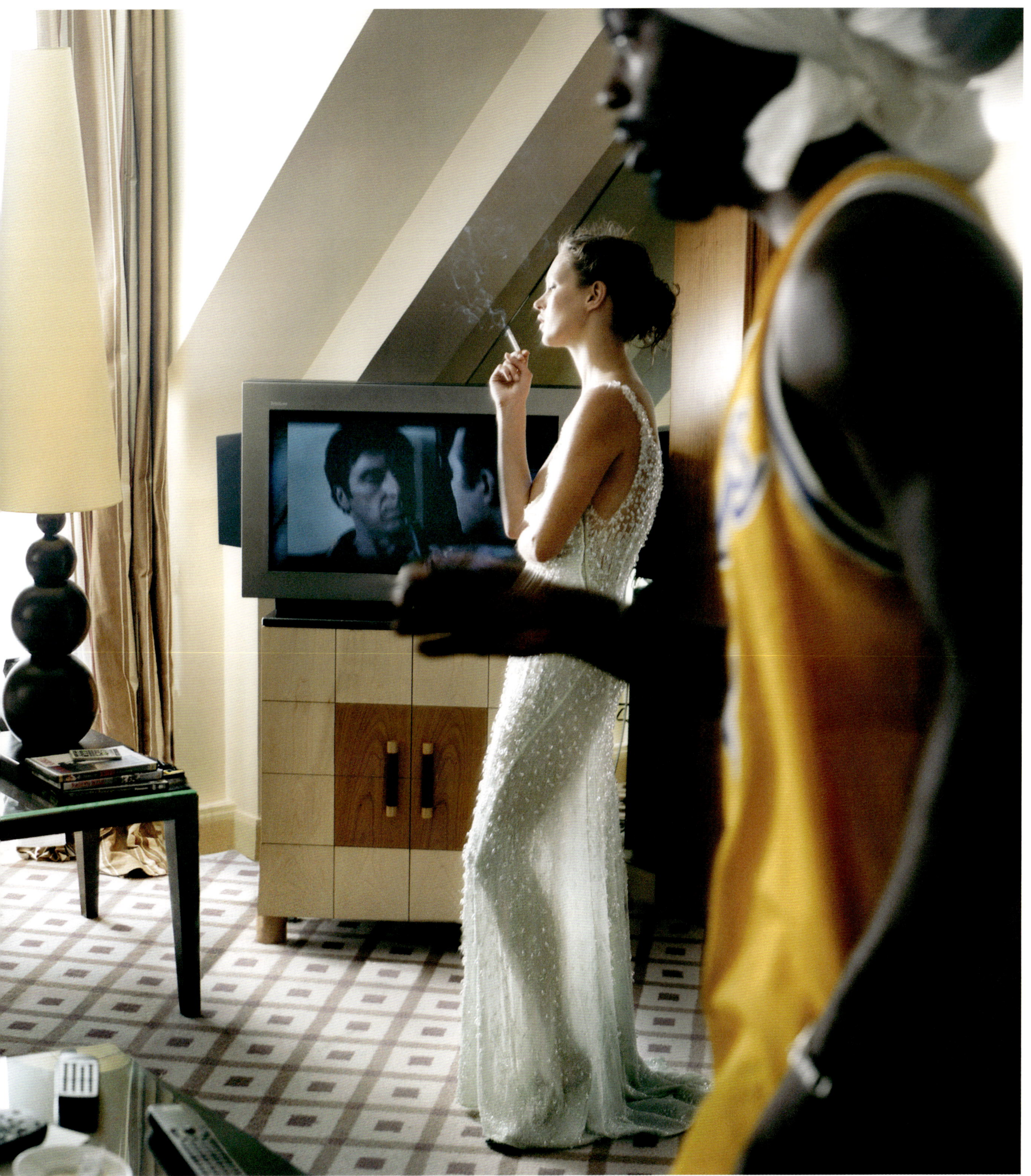

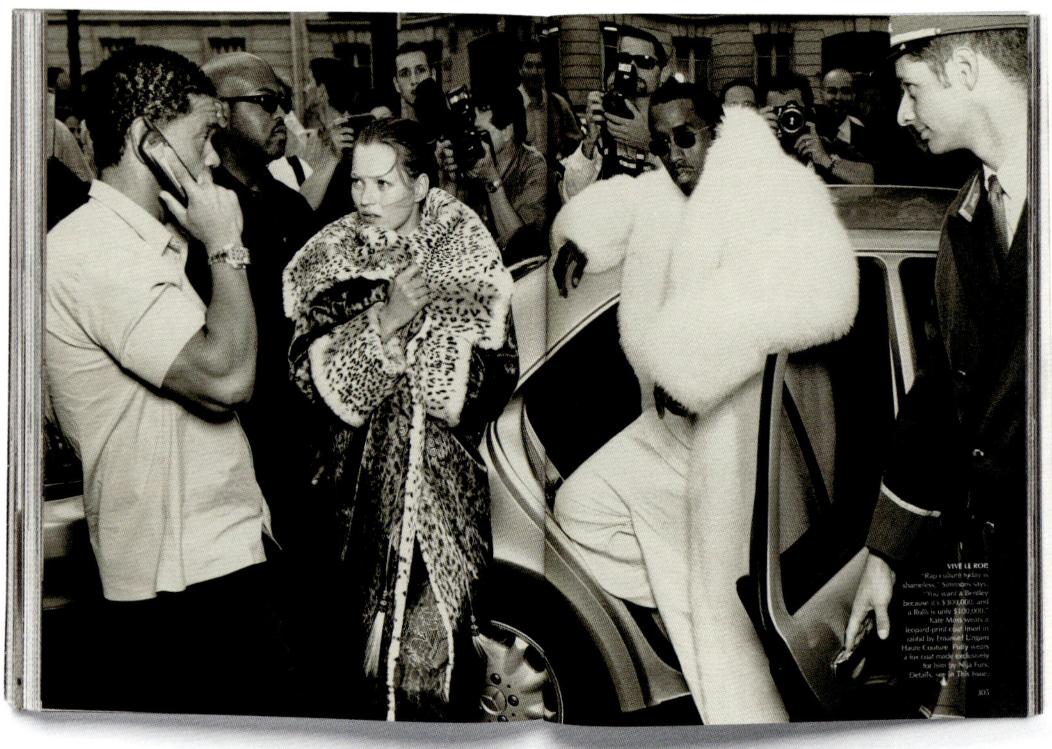

VIVE LE ROI!
"Rap culture today is shameless," Simmons says. "You want a Bentley because it's $300,000, and a Rolls is only $100,000." Kate Moss wears a leopard-print coat lined in rabbit by Emanuel Ungaro Haute Couture. Puffy wears a fox coat made exclusively for him by Nija Furs. Details, see In This Issue.

305

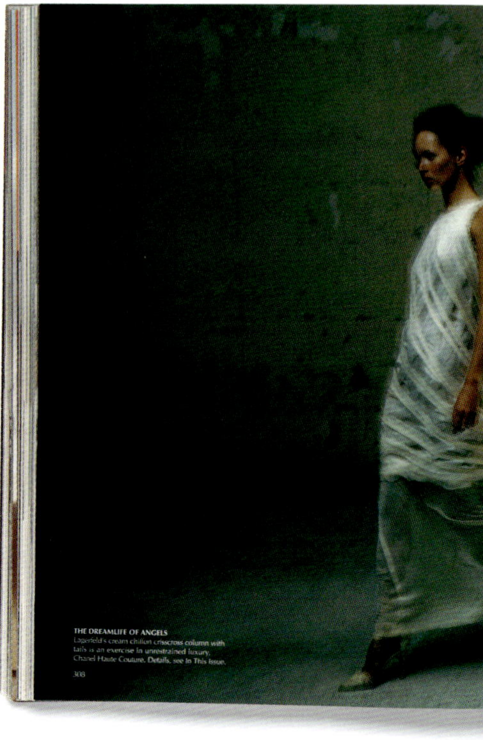

THE DREAMLIFE OF ANGELS
Lagerfeld's cream chiffon crisscross column with tails is an exercise in unrestrained luxury. Chanel Haute Couture. Details, see In This Issue.

308

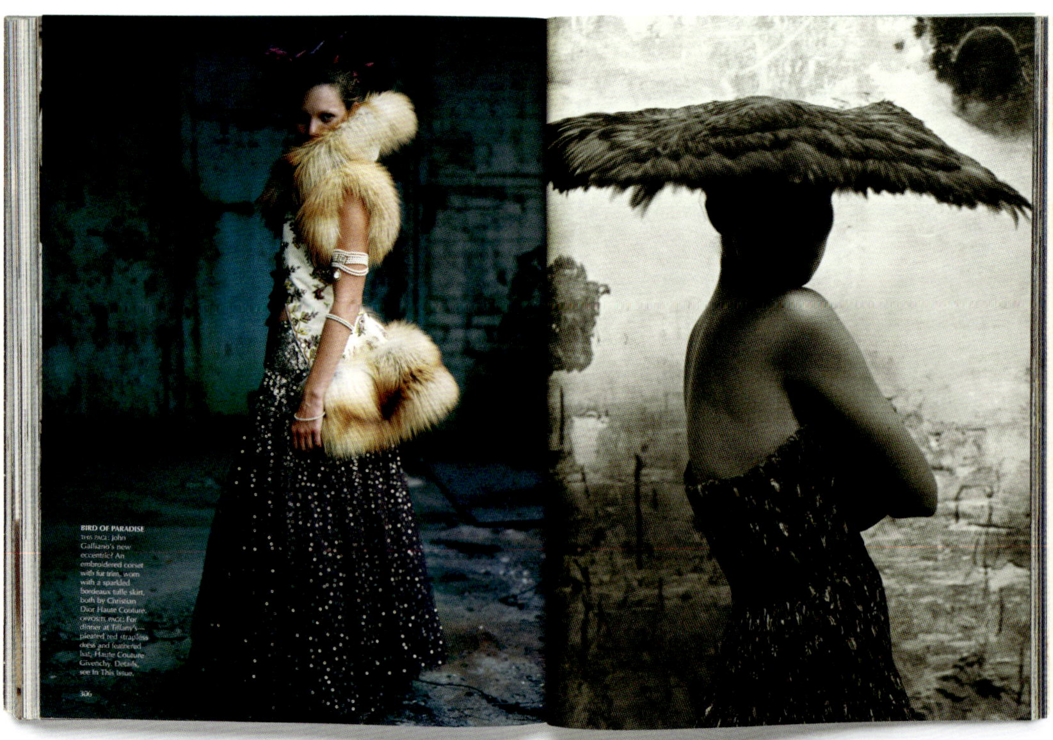

BIRD OF PARADISE
THIS PAGE: John Galliano's new eccentric! An embroidered corset with fur trim, worn with a sparkled bordeaux tulle skirt, both by Christian Dior Haute Couture. OPPOSITE PAGE: For dinner at Tiffany's—pleated red strapless dress and feathered hat, Haute Couture Givenchy. Details, see In This Issue.

306

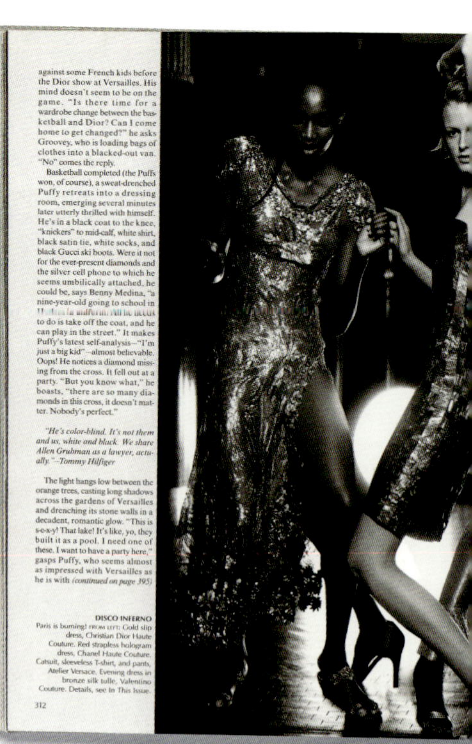

against some French kids before the Dior show at Versailles. His mind doesn't seem to be on the game. "Is there time for a wardrobe change between the basketball and Dior? Can I come home to get changed?" he asks Groovey, who is loading bags of clothes into a blacked-out van. "No" comes the reply.

Basketball completed (the Puffs won, of course), a sweat-drenched Puffy retreats into a dressing room, emerging several minutes later utterly thrilled with himself. He's in a black coat to the knee, "knickers" to mid-calf, white shirt, black satin tie, white socks, and black Gucci ski boots. Were it not for the ever-present diamonds and the silver cell phone to which he seems umbilically attached, he could be, says Benny Medina, "a nine-year-old going to school in [illegible] to do is take off the coat, and he can play in the street." It makes Puffy's latest self-analysis—"I'm just a big kid"—almost believable. Oops! He notices a diamond missing from the cross. It fell out at a party. "But you know what," he boasts, "there are so many diamonds in this cross, it doesn't matter. Nobody's perfect."

"He's color-blind. It's not them and us, white and black. We share Allen Grubman as a lawyer, actually."—Tommy Hilfiger

The light hangs low between the orange trees, casting long shadows across the gardens of Versailles and drenching its stone walls in a decadent, romantic glow. "This is s-e-x-y! That lake! It's like, yo, they built it as a pool. I need one of these. I want to have a party here," gasps Puffy, who seems almost as impressed with Versailles as he is with *(continued on page 395)*

DISCO INFERNO
Paris is burning! FROM LEFT: Gold slip dress, Christian Dior Haute Couture. Red strapless hologram dress, Chanel Haute Couture. Catsuit, sleeveless T-shirt, and pants, Atelier Versace. Evening dress in bronze silk tulle, Valentino Couture. Details, see In This Issue.

312

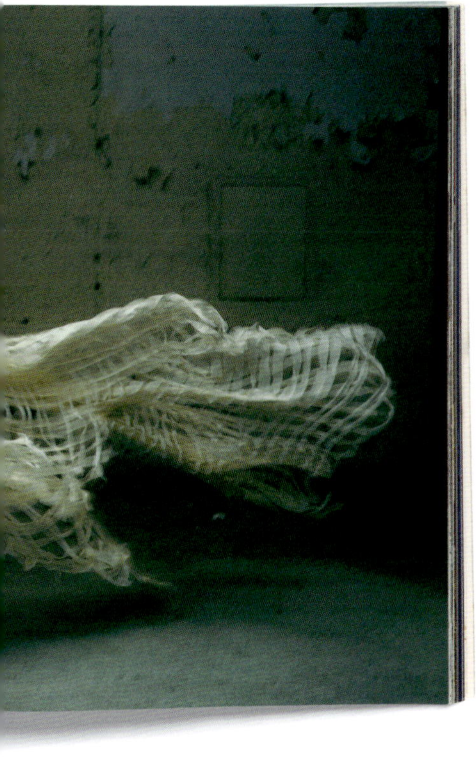

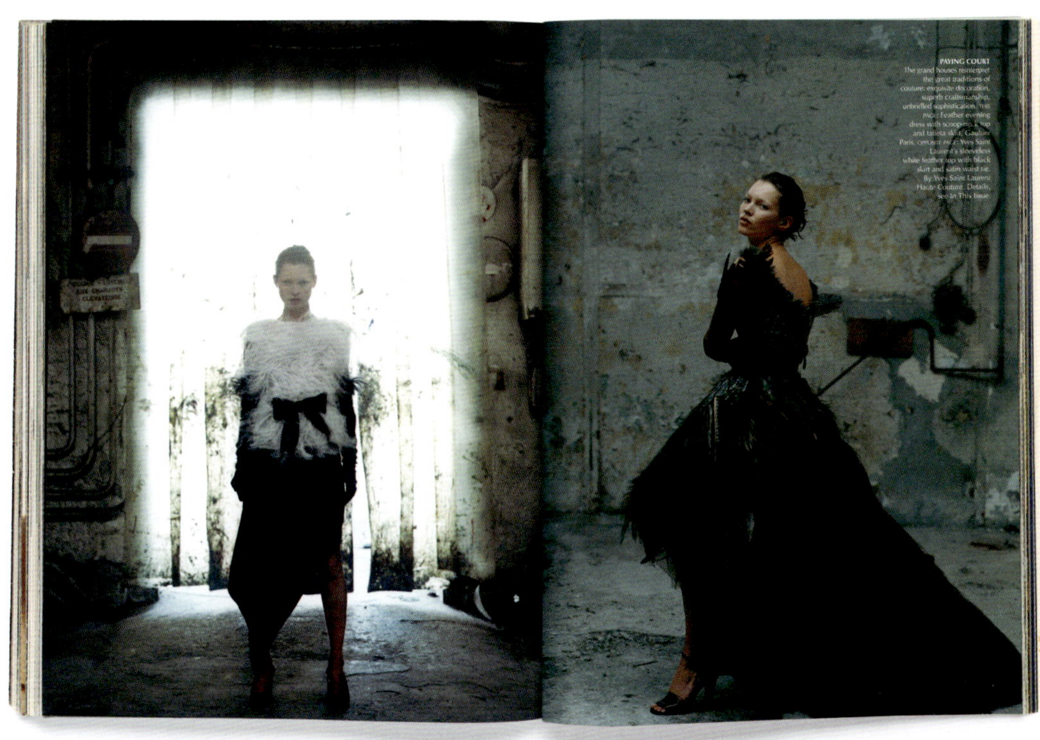
PAYING COURT
The grand houses reinterpret
the great traditions of
couture: exquisite decoration,
superb craftsmanship,
unbridled sophistication. THIS
PAGE: Feather evening
dress with scoop-neck top
and taffeta skirt, Gaultier
Paris. OPPOSITE PAGE: Yves Saint
Laurent's sleeveless
white feather top with black
skirt and satin waist tie.
By Yves Saint Laurent
Haute Couture. Details,
see In This Issue.

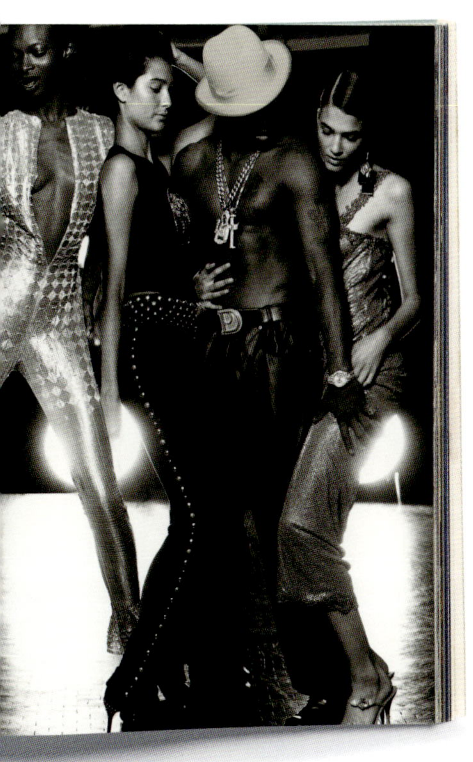

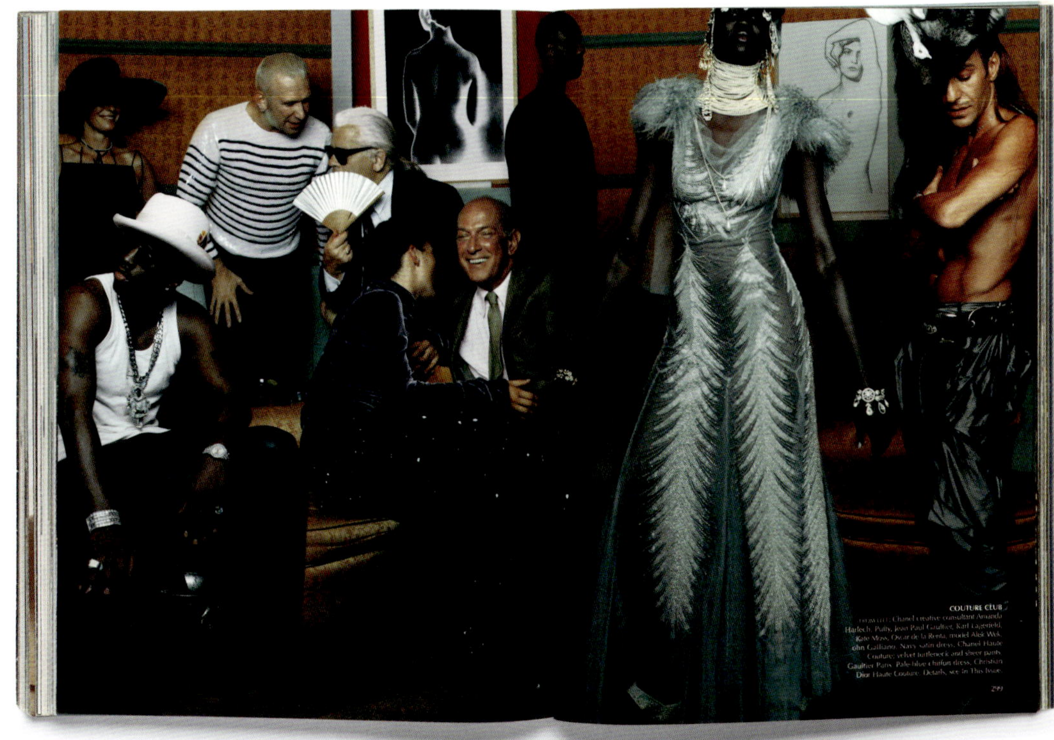
COUTURE CLUB
FROM LEFT: Chanel creative consultant Amanda
Harlech, Puffy, Jean Paul Gaultier, Karl Lagerfeld,
Kate Moss, Oscar de la Renta, model Alek Wek,
John Galliano. Navy satin dress, Chanel Haute
Couture; velvet turtleneck and sheer pants,
Gaultier Paris. Pale-blue chiffon dress, Christian
Dior Haute Couture. Details, see In This Issue.
299

Kate Moss, Paris, 1999

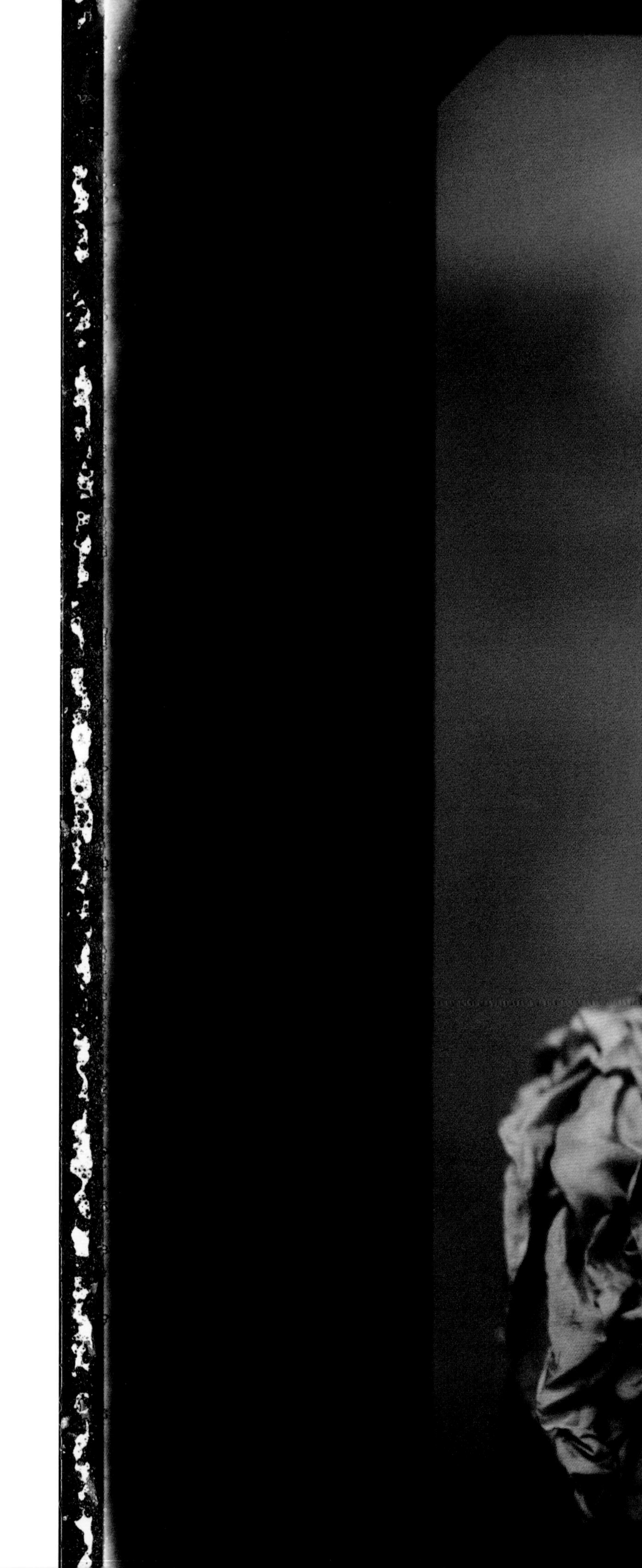

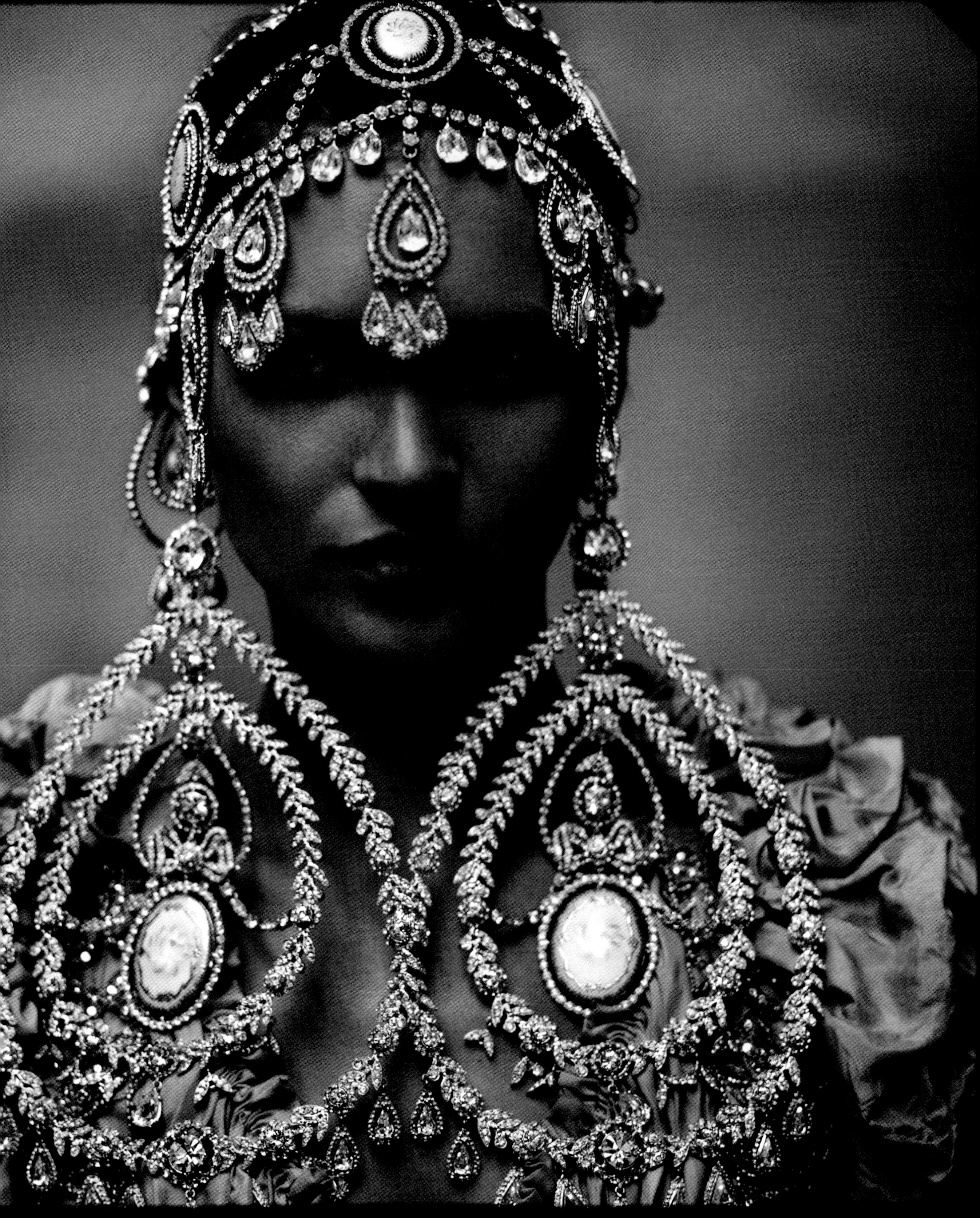

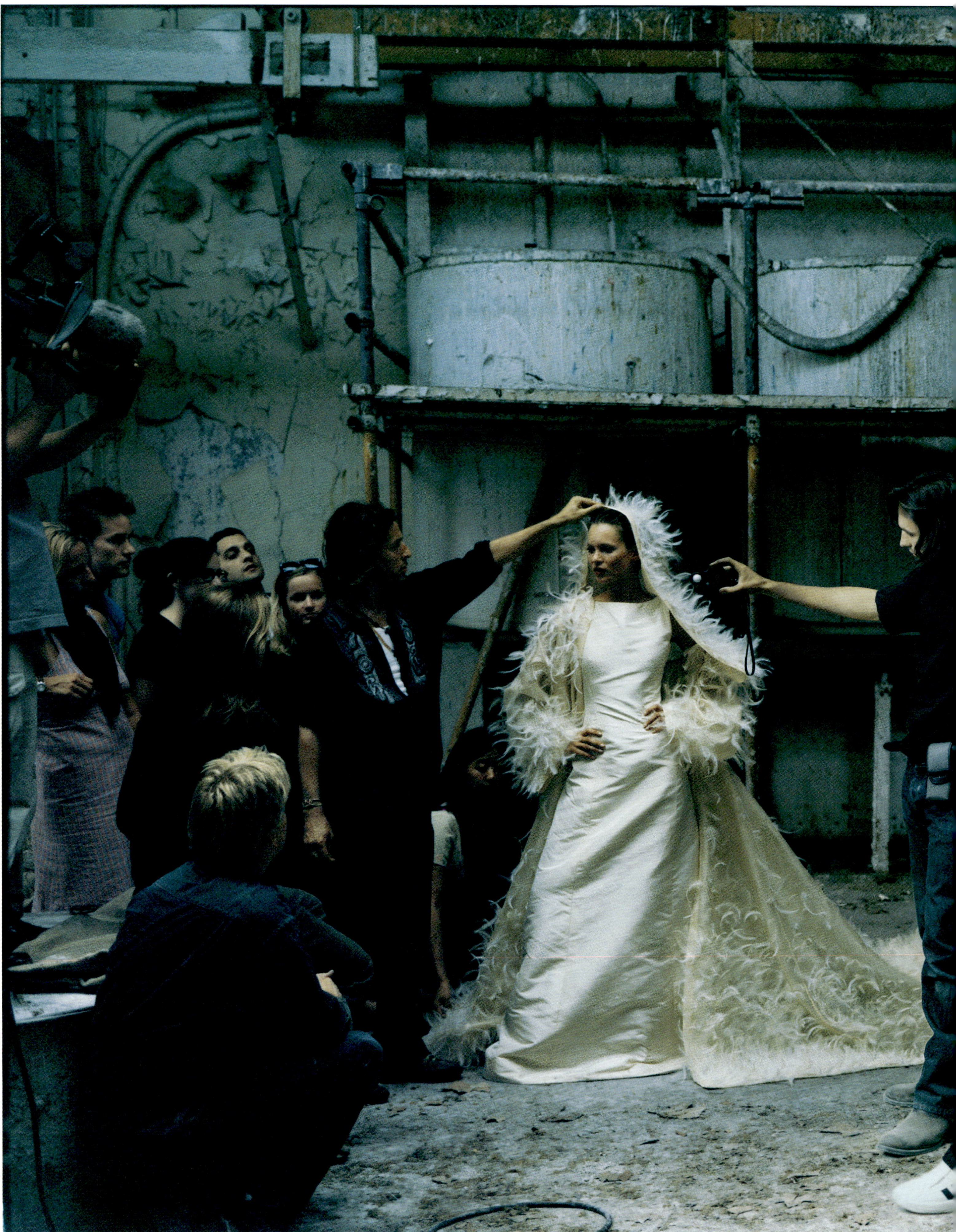

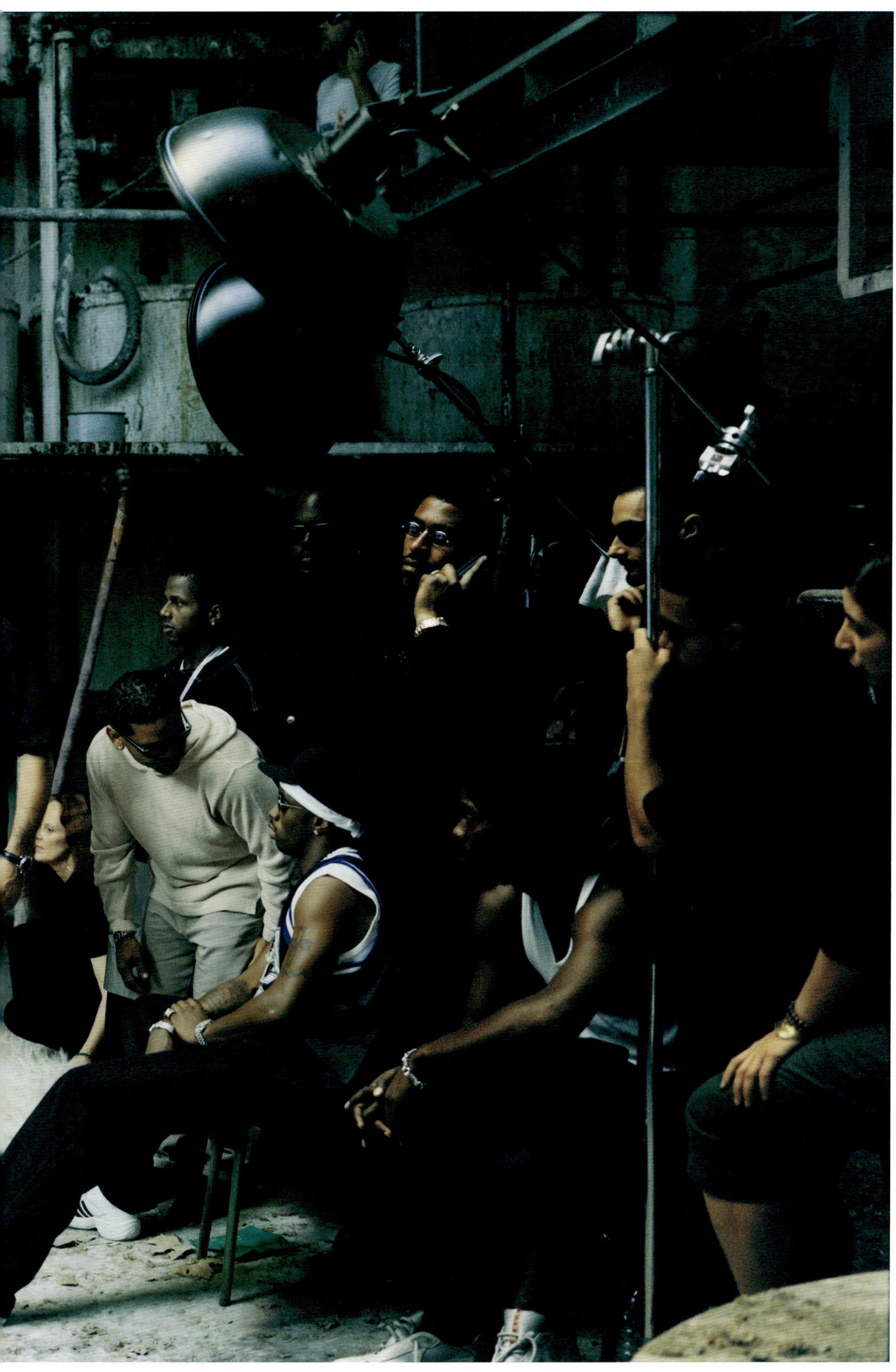

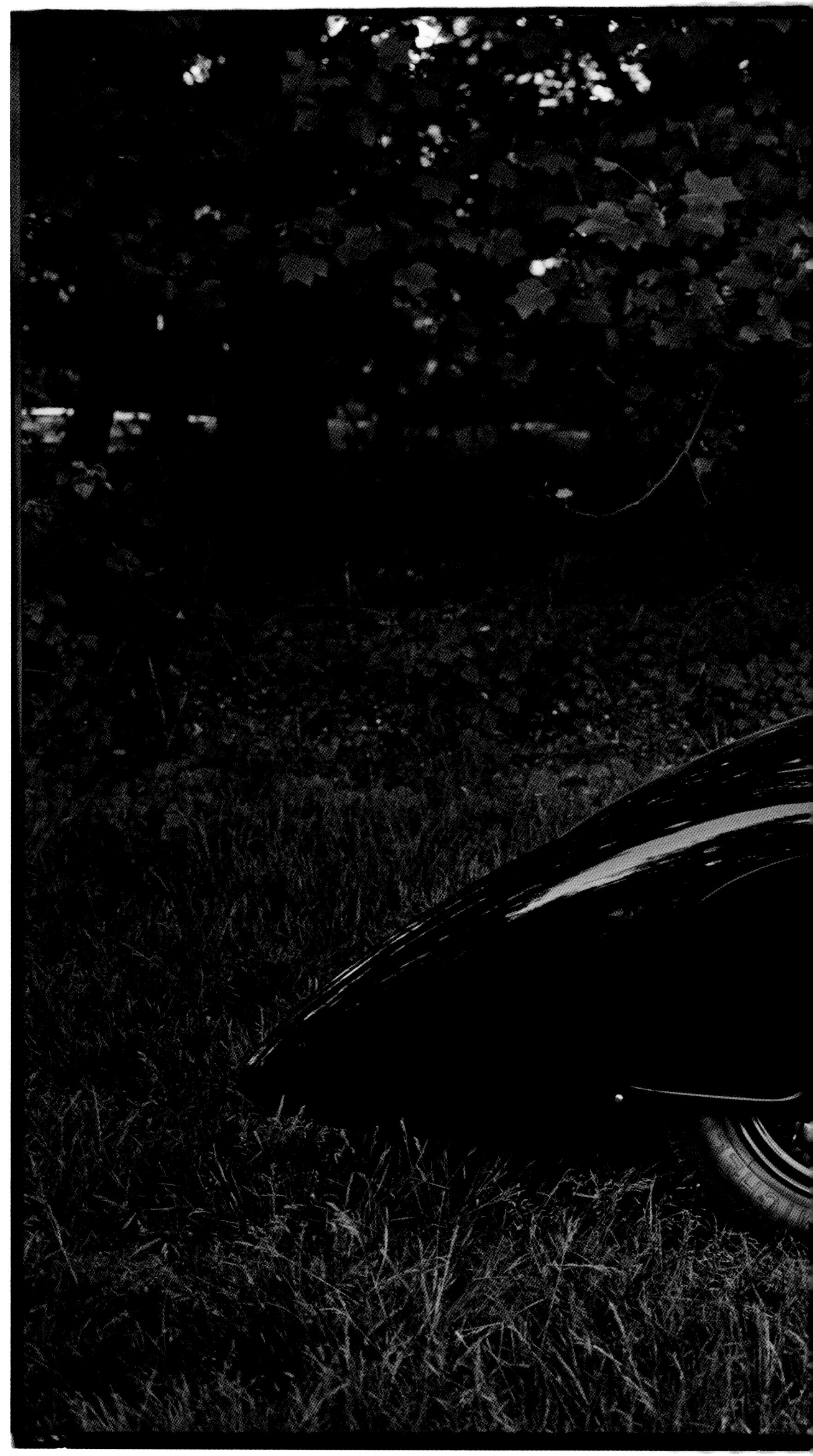

Ralph Lauren,
Bedford, New York, 1996

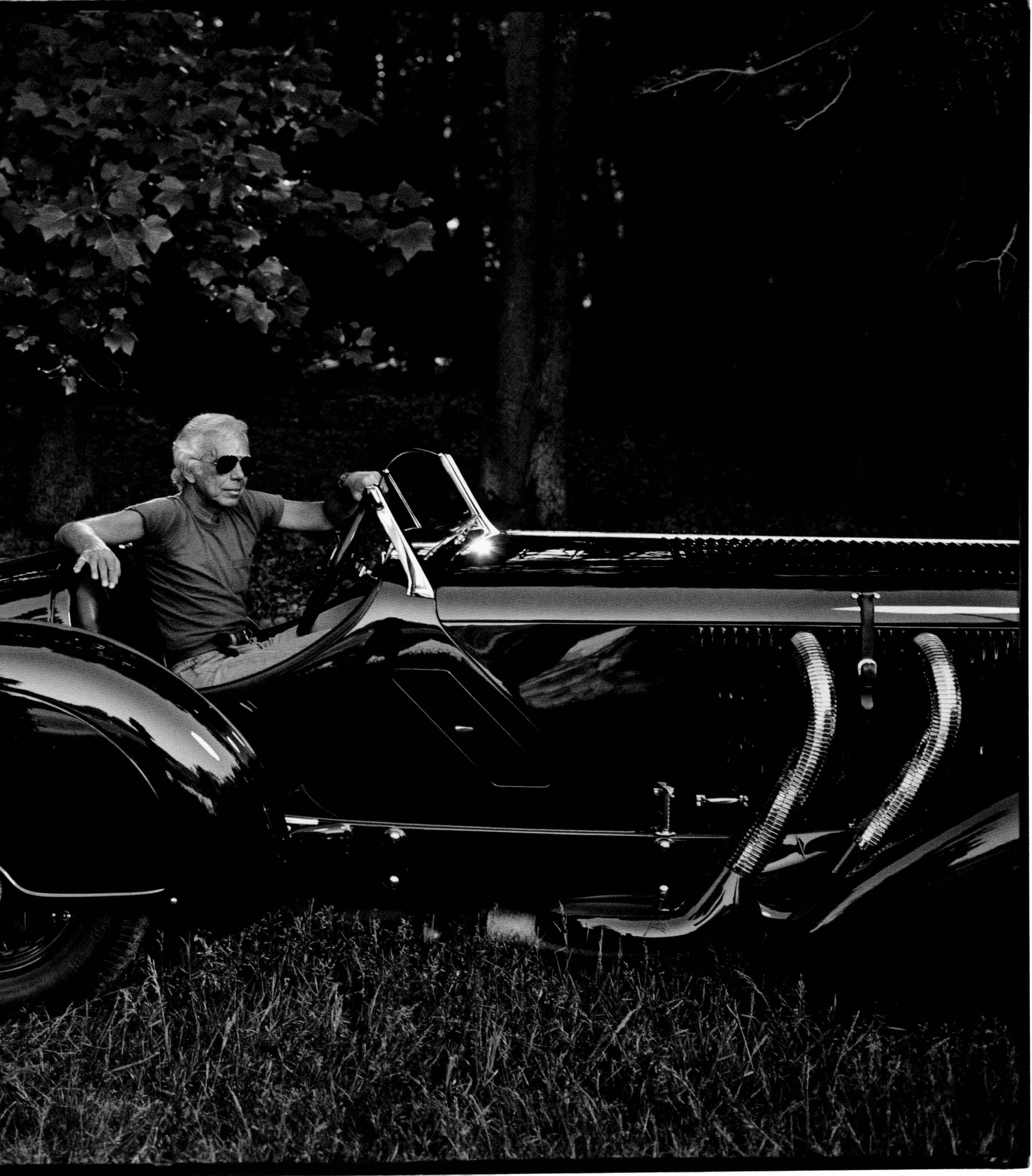

Calvin Klein and Carolyn Murphy,
New York City, 1999

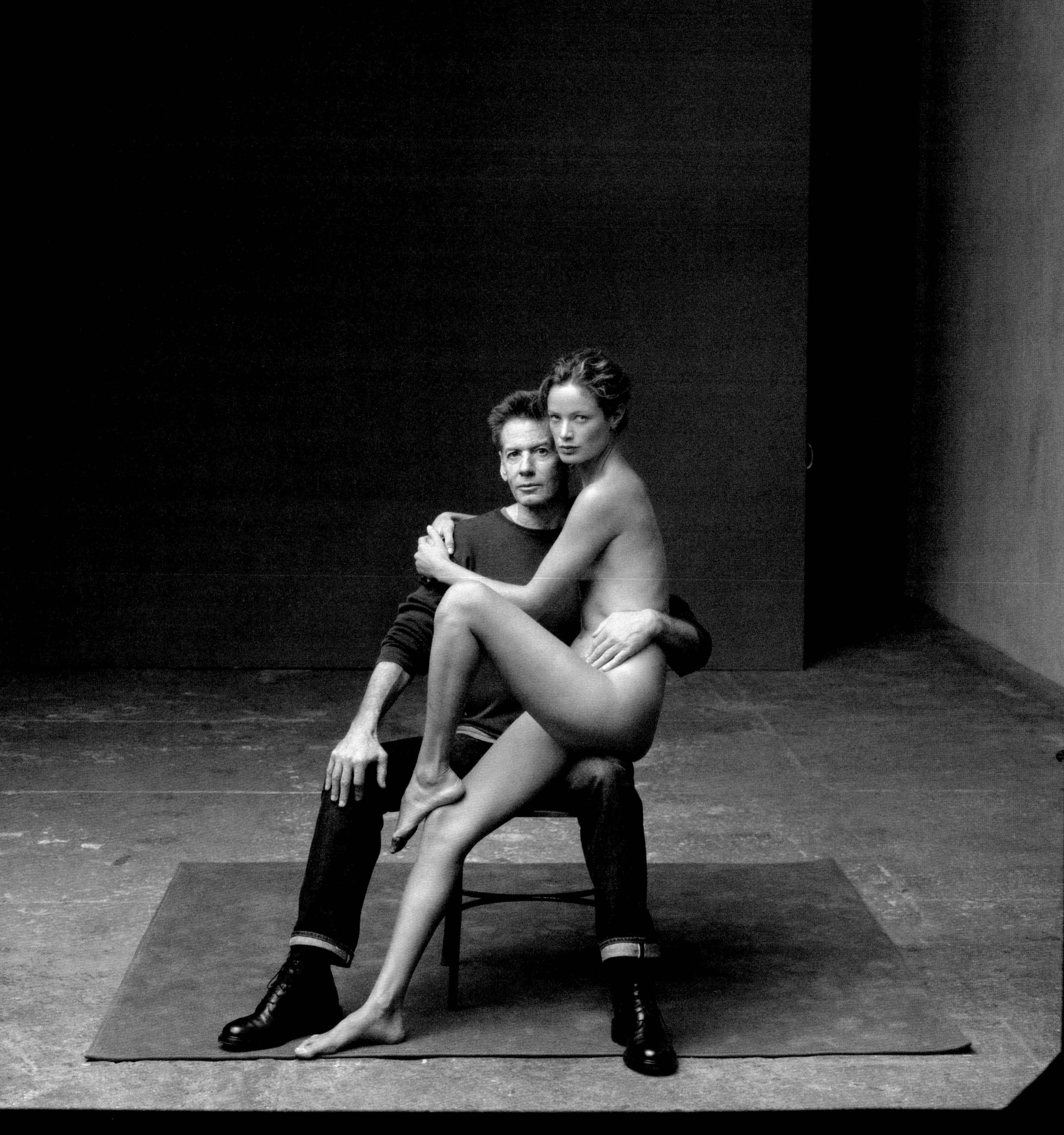

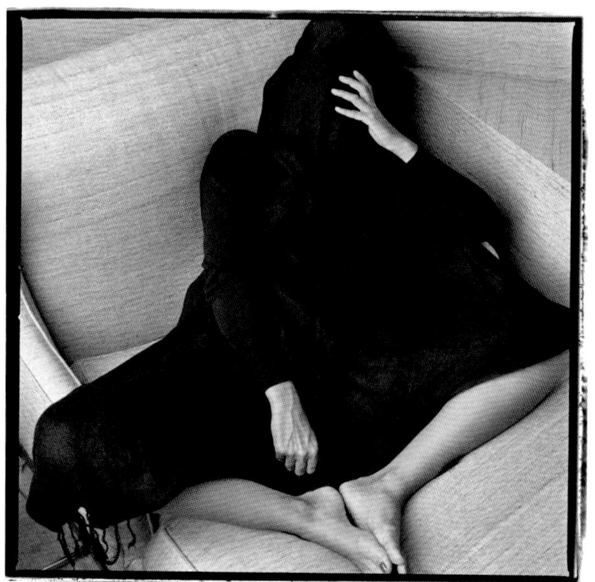

Donna Karan,
New York City, 1985

Donna Karan with her daughter,
Gabby, New York City, 1996

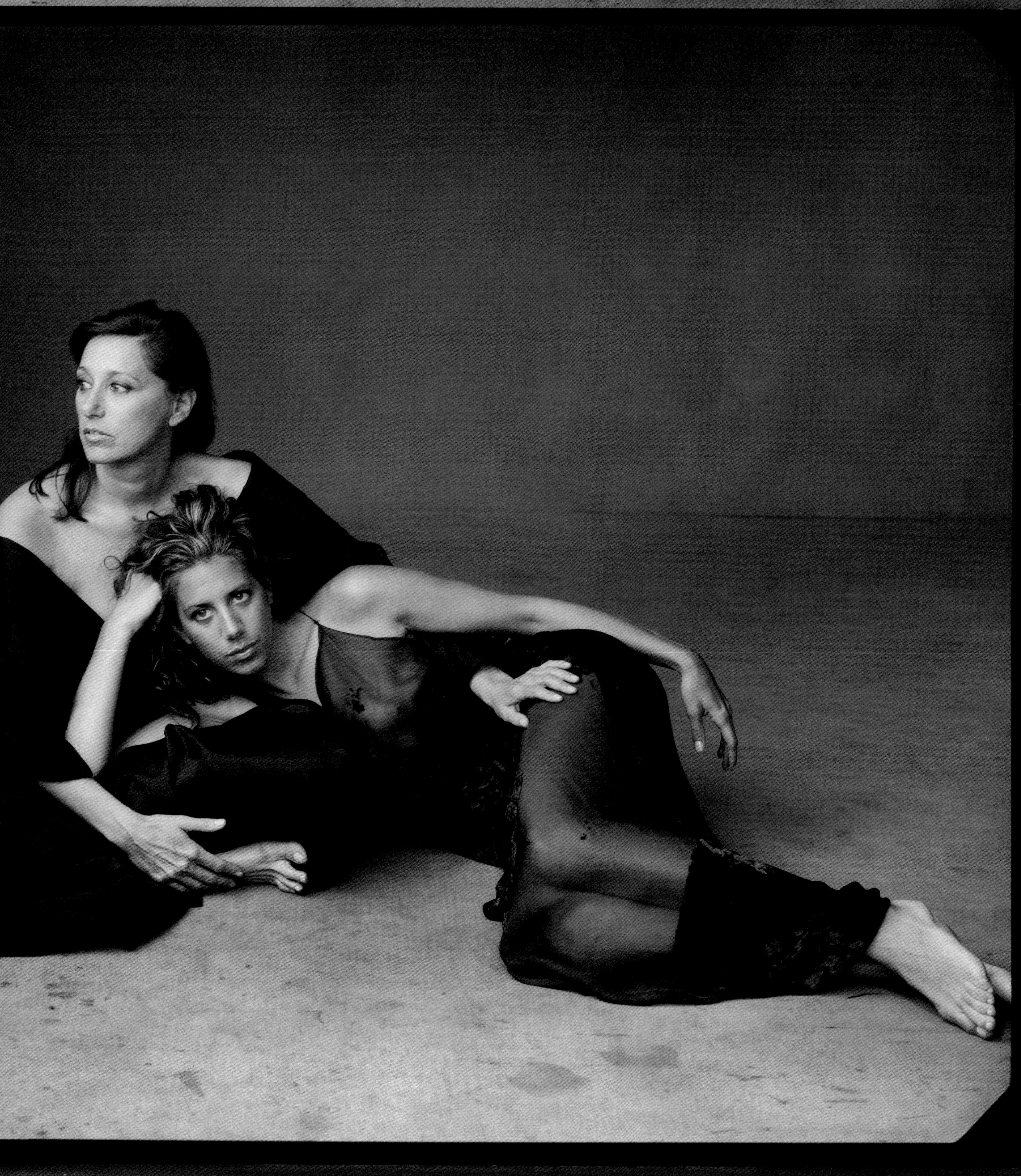

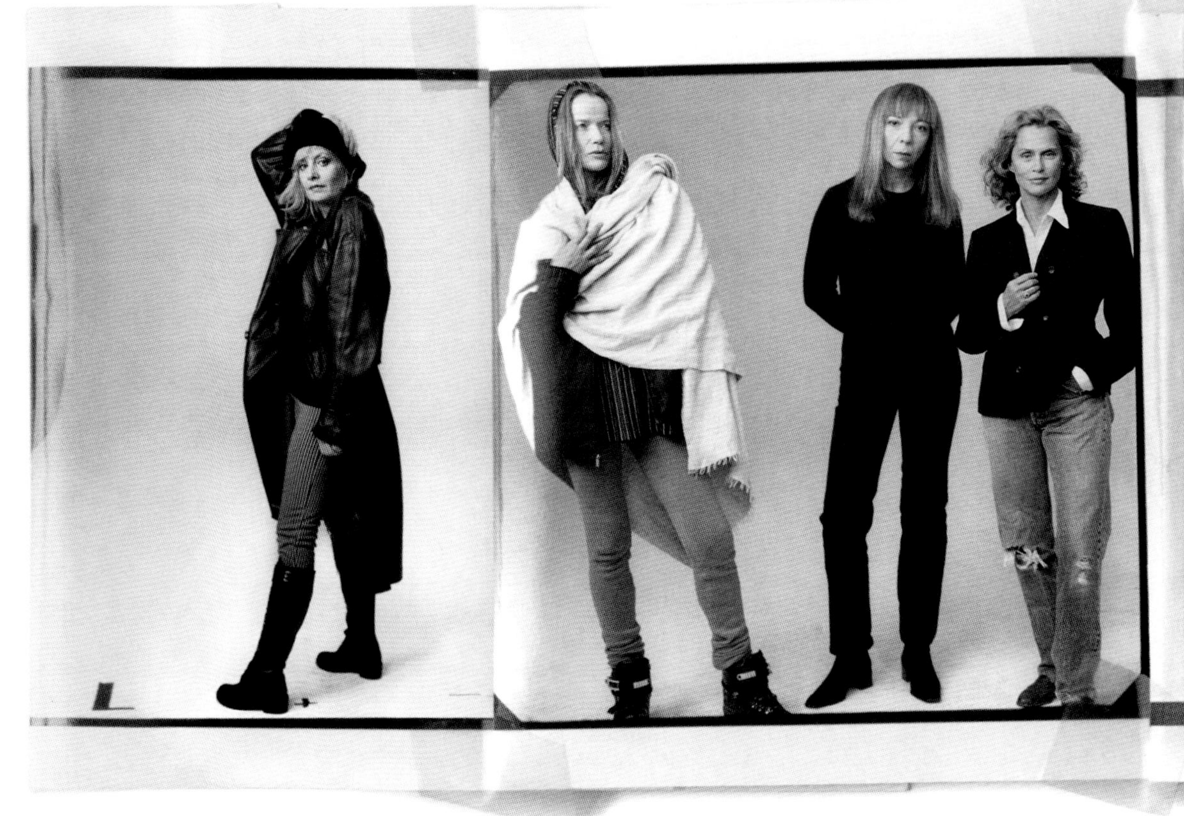

"When I was working on what would become the book *Women*, I began thinking about the women whose job it is to wear fashion. I decided that I wanted to photograph the important models of their time in the clothes they wear in real life. As they came into the studio, I asked them to walk directly over to where we were shooting. I worked with Polaroids. Christie Brinkley and Stella Tennant walked in with their babies. We didn't use the pictures in the book, but some of them were published in *Vogue* when the book came out."

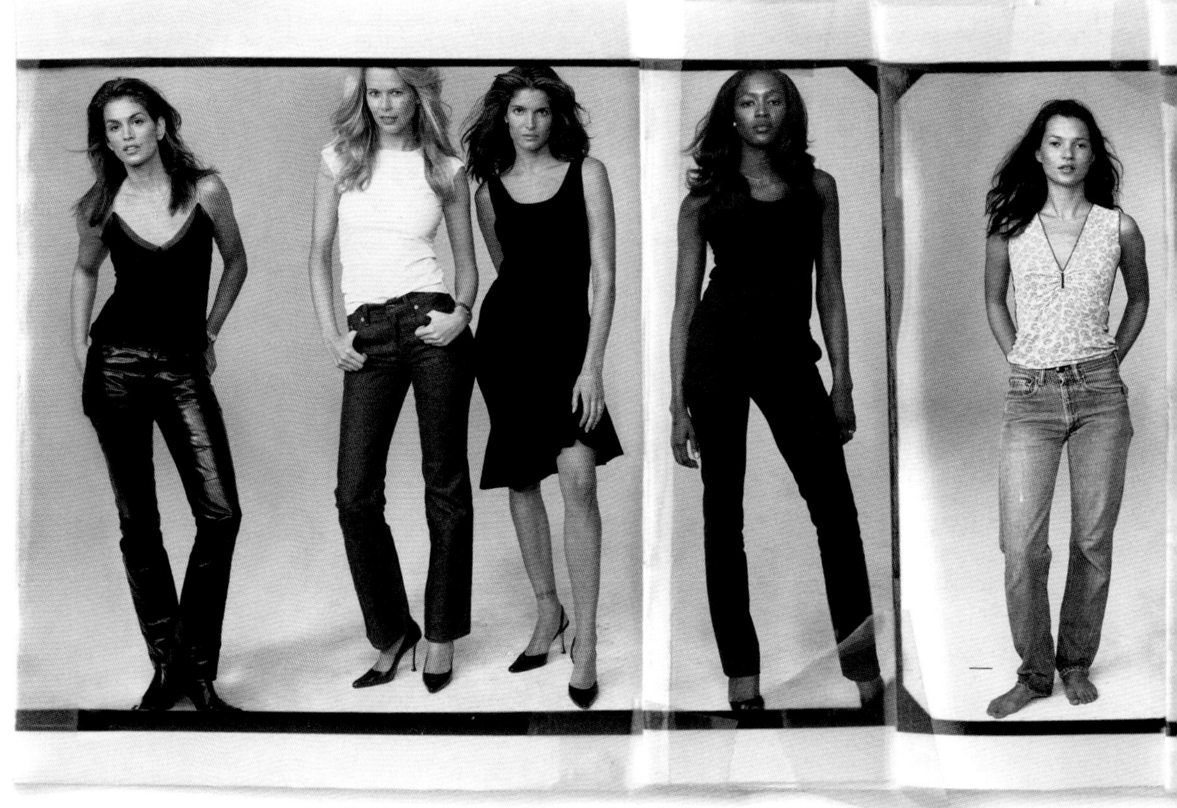

Twiggy, Veruschka, Penelope Tree, Lauren Hutton, Dayle Haddon, Marisa Berenson, Lisa Taylor, Rosie Vela, Patti Hansen, Isabella Rossellini, Christie Brinkley, Iman, Paulina Porizkova, Cindy Crawford, Claudia Schiffer, Stephanie Seymour, Naomi Campbell, Kate Moss, Stella Tennant, Amber Valletta, Shalom Harlow, Carolyn Murphy, Bridget Hall, Karen Elson, Alek Wek, Frankie Rayder, Audrey Marnay, Drive-In Studio, New York City, 1998

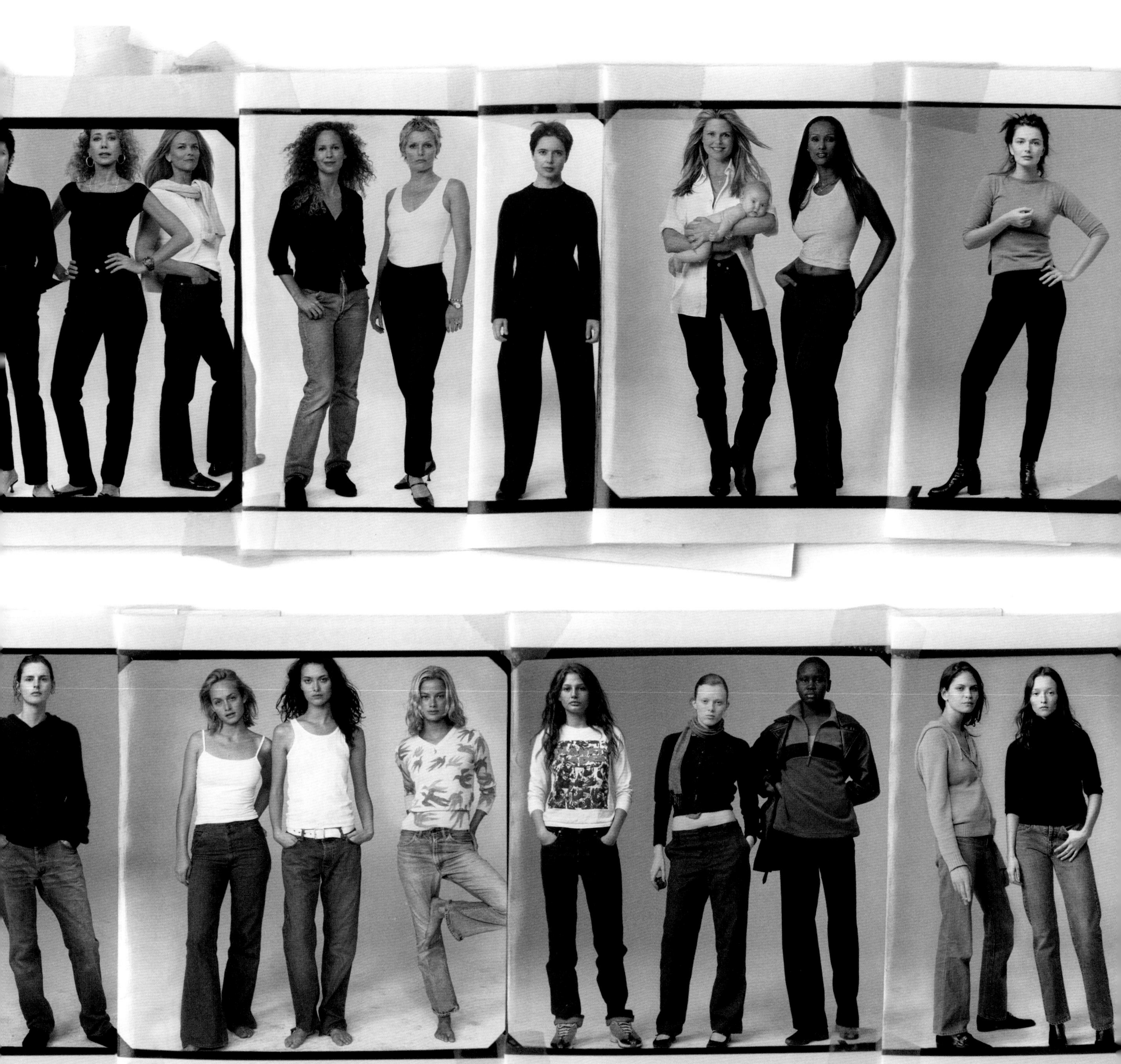

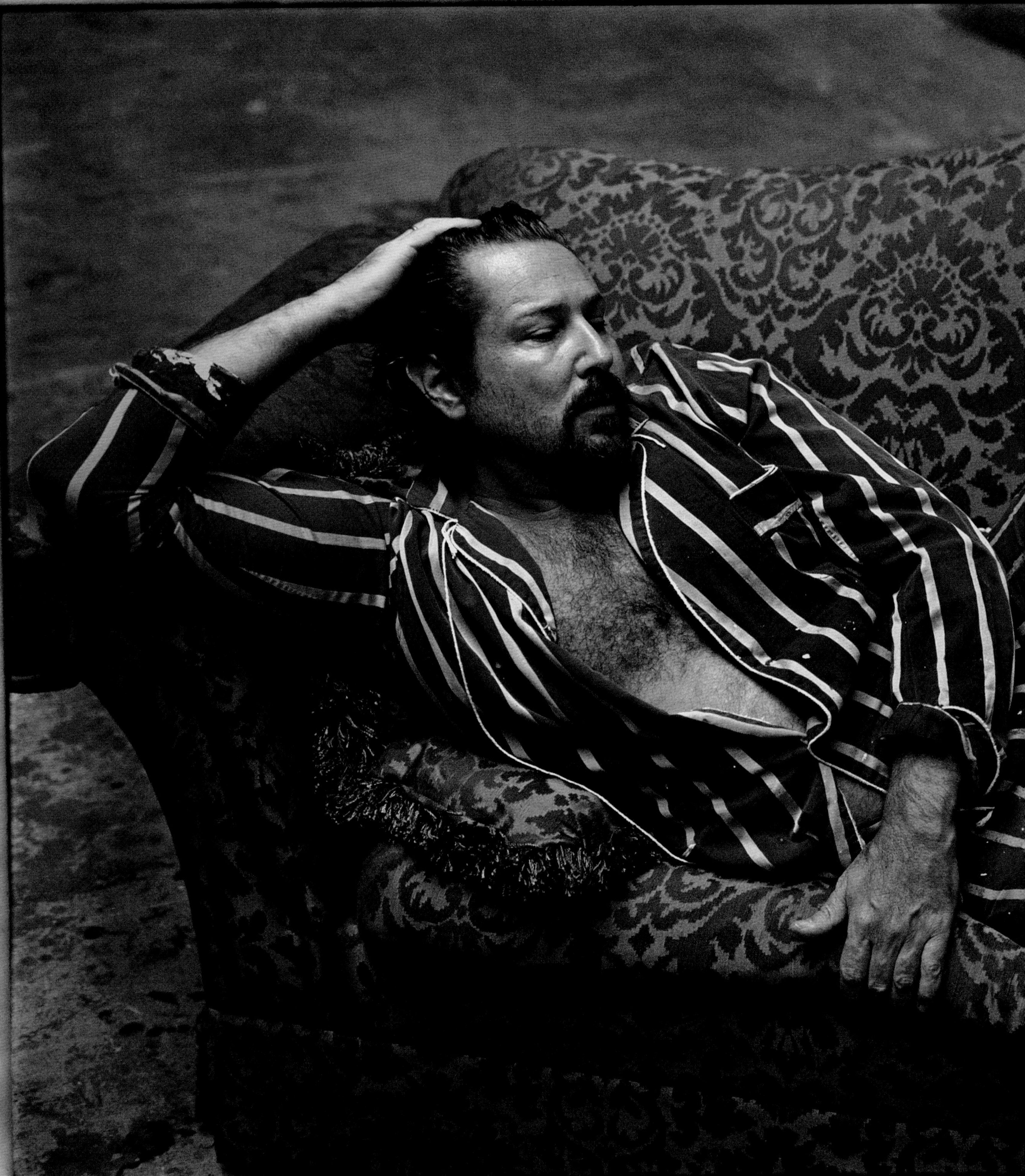

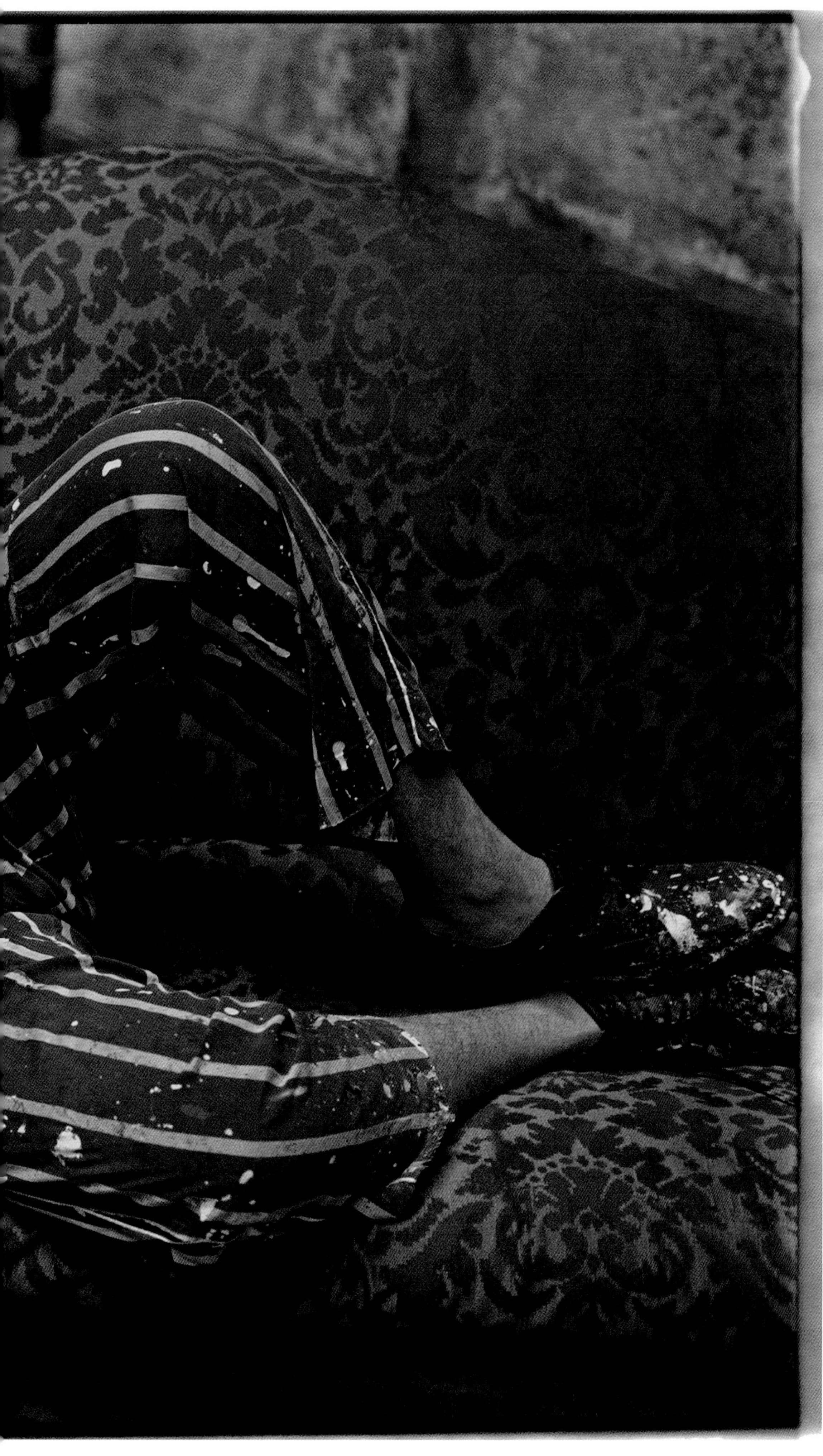

Julian Schnabel in his studio,
New York City, 1995

Matthew Barney,
Hotel New York,
Rotterdam, 1995

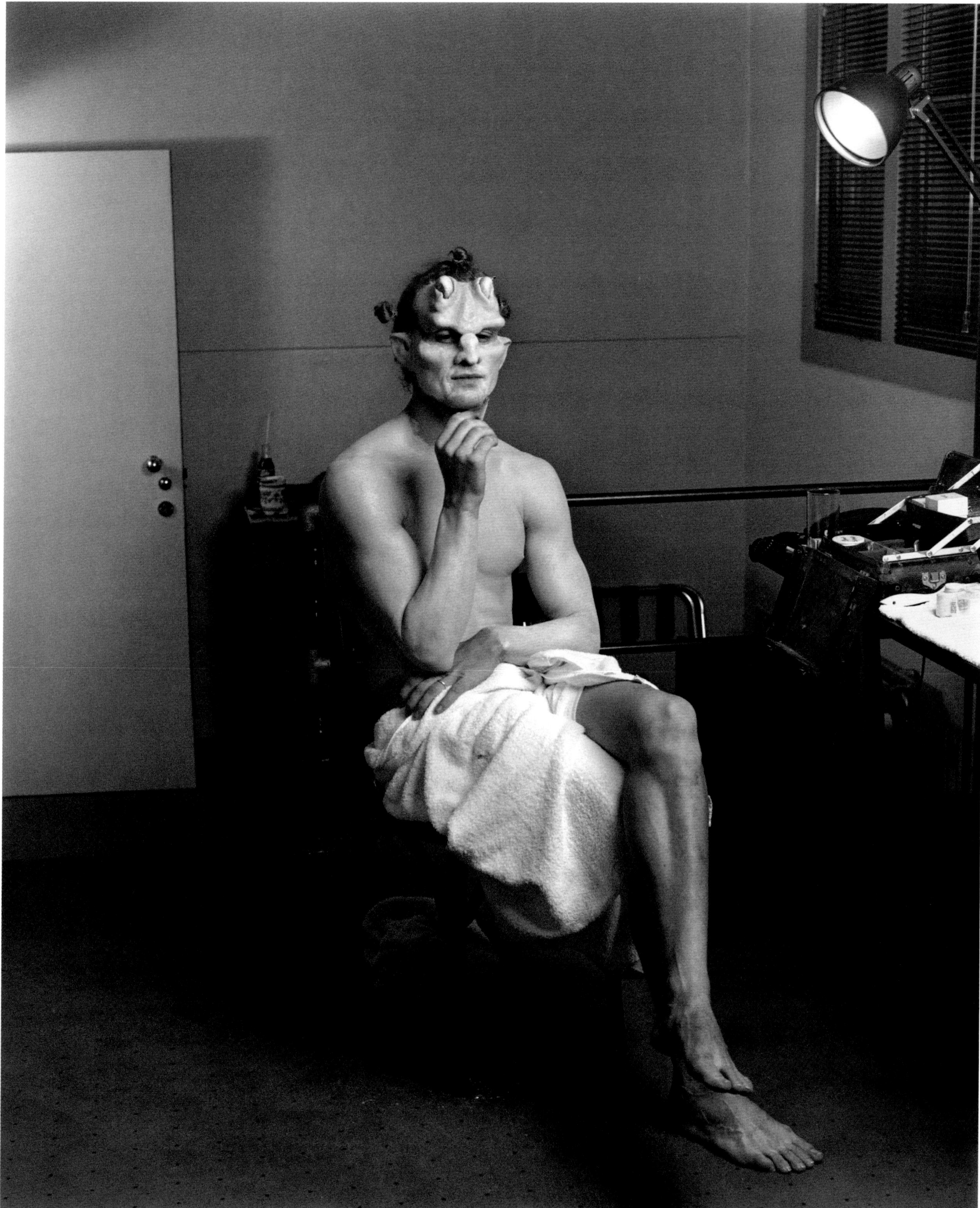

The second big couture shoot for *Vogue* that Annie and Grace Coddington collaborated on was an homage to fashion photography. It featured Stella Tennant and Ben Stiller, who had just made *Zoolander*, a parody of the world of male models. Annie had in mind Cecil Beaton, Helmut Newton, Richard Avedon, and Bruce Weber, among others.

The plastic bubble hanging surreally over the Seine was Melvin Sokolsky's invention for the Paris collections in *Harper's Bazaar* in 1963.

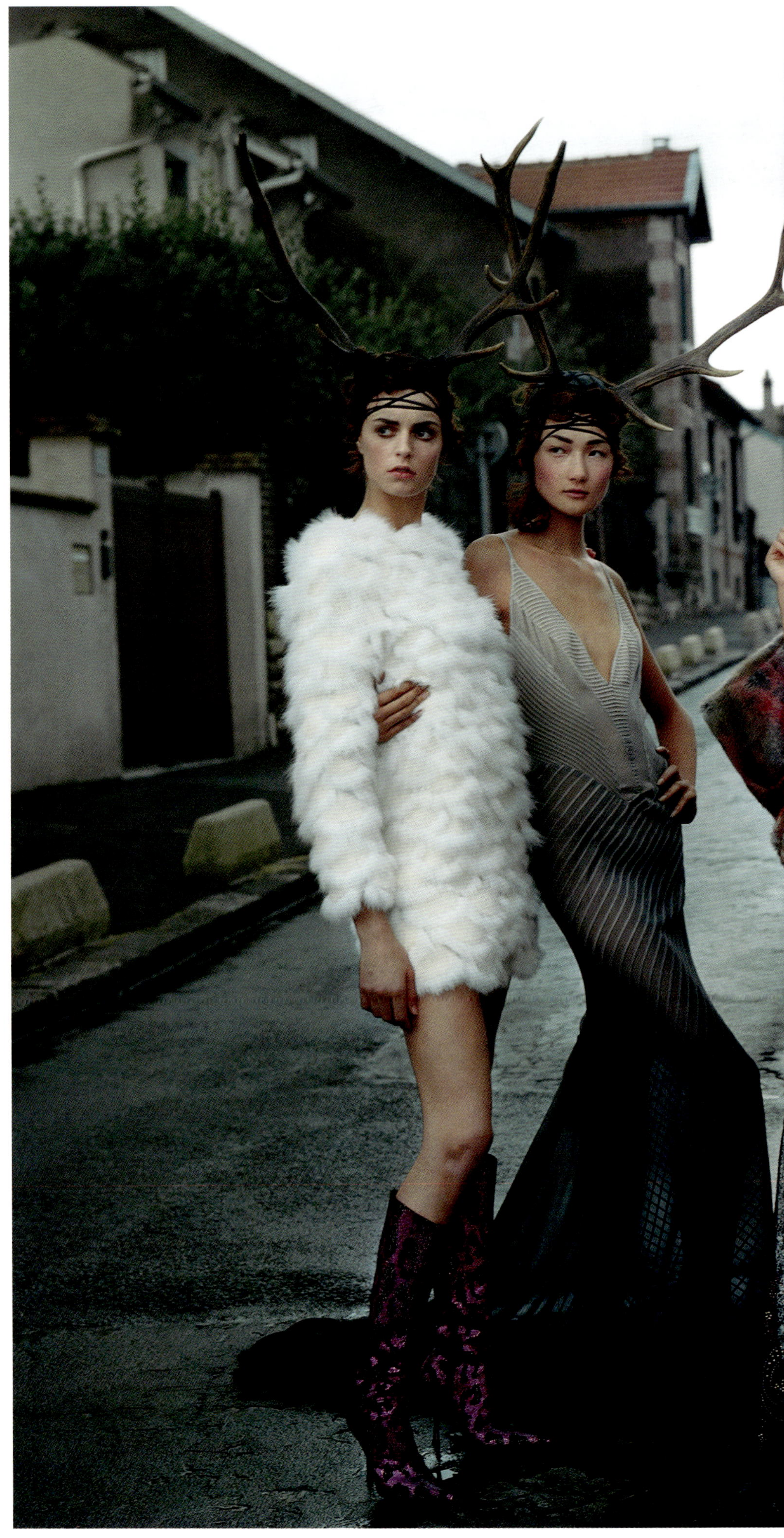

Ben Stiller with Jacquetta Wheeler, Ai Tominaga, Karolina Kurkova, Oluchi Onweagba, and Stella Tennant, Paris, 2001

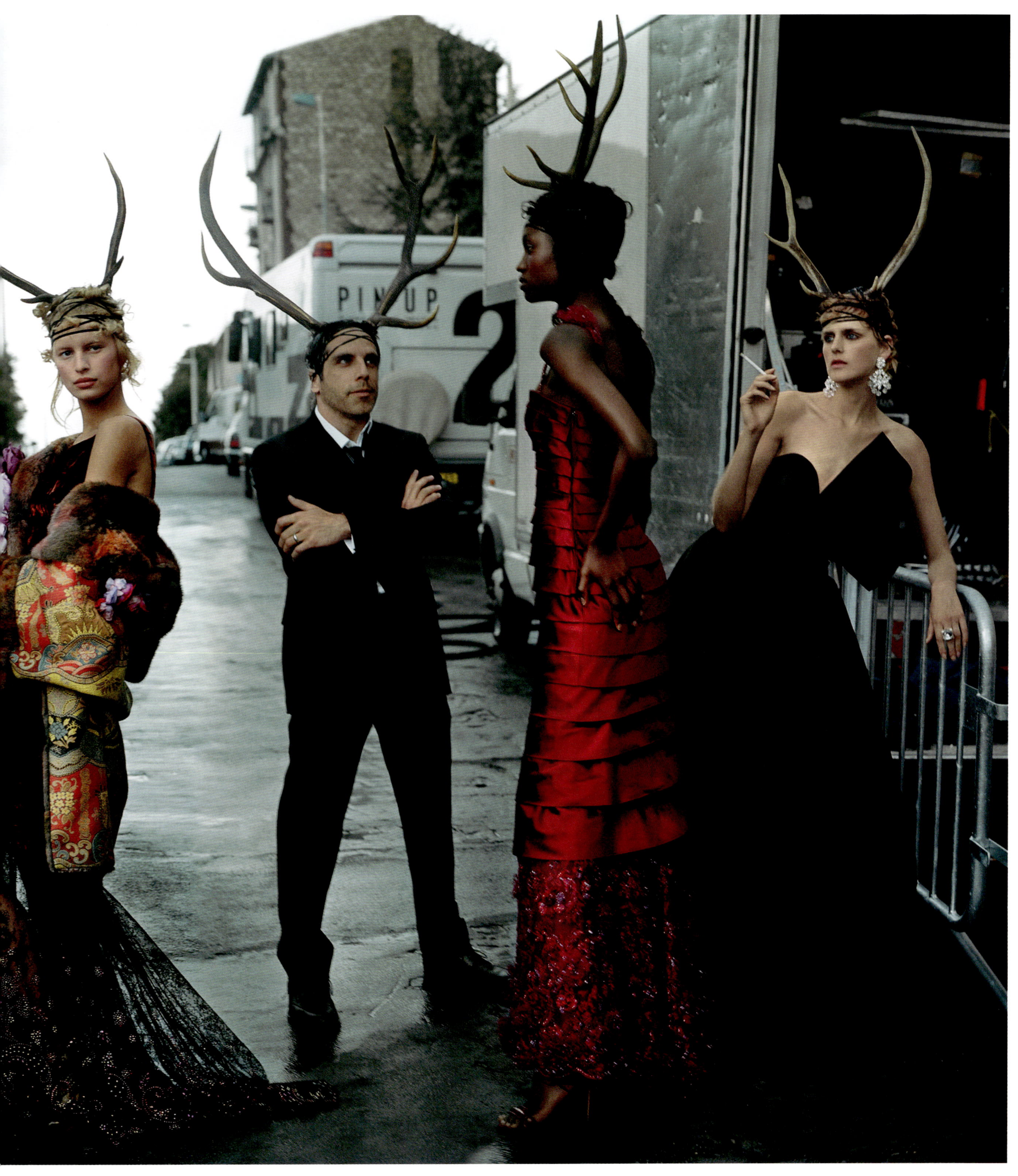
PIN UP

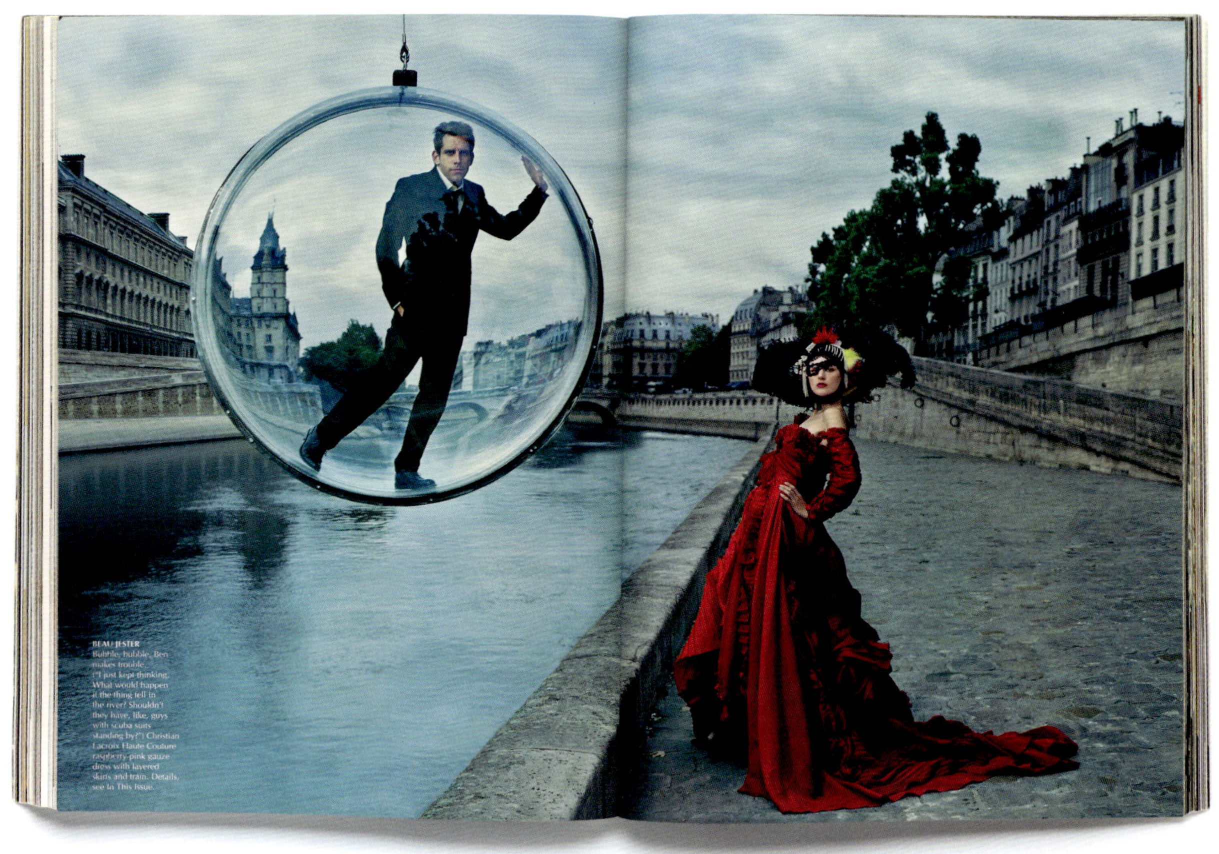
BEAU JESTER
Bubble, bubble, Ben makes trouble. ("I just kept thinking, What would happen if the thing fell in the river? Shouldn't they have, like, guys with scuba suits standing by?") Christian Lacroix Haute Couture raspberry-pink gauze dress with layered skirts and train. Details, see In This Issue.

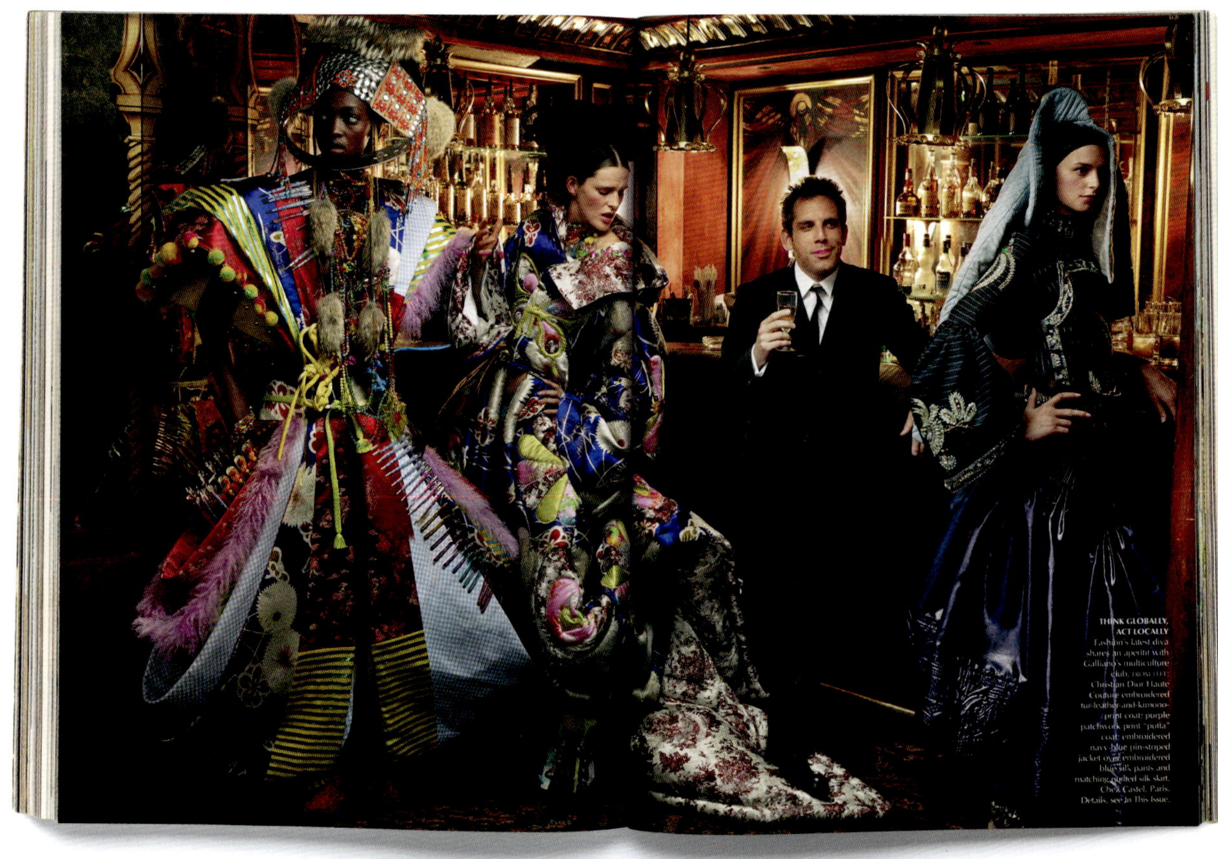
THINK GLOBALLY, ACT LOCALLY
Fashion's latest diva shares an aperitif with Galliano's multiculture club. FROM LEFT: Christian Dior Haute Couture embroidered fur-leather-and-kimono-print coat; purple patchwork print "puffa" coat; embroidered navy-blue pin-striped jacket over embroidered blue silk pants and matching quilted silk skirt. Chez Castel, Paris. Details, see In This Issue.

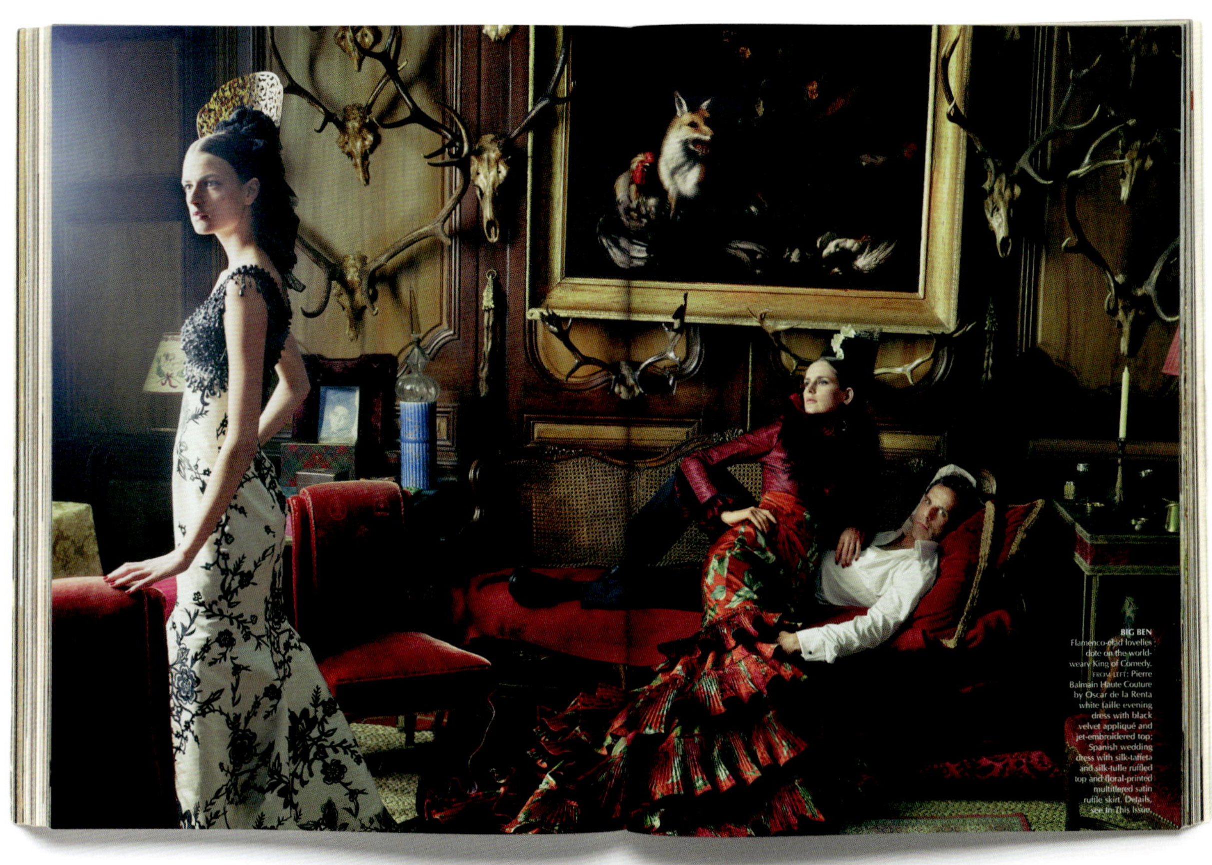
BIG BEN
Flamenco-clad lovelies dote on the world-weary King of Comedy. FROM LEFT: Pierre Balmain Haute Couture by Oscar de la Renta white faille evening dress with black velvet appliqué and jet-embroidered top; Spanish wedding dress with silk-taffeta and silk-tulle ruffled top and floral-printed multitiered satin ruffle skirt. Details, see In This Issue.

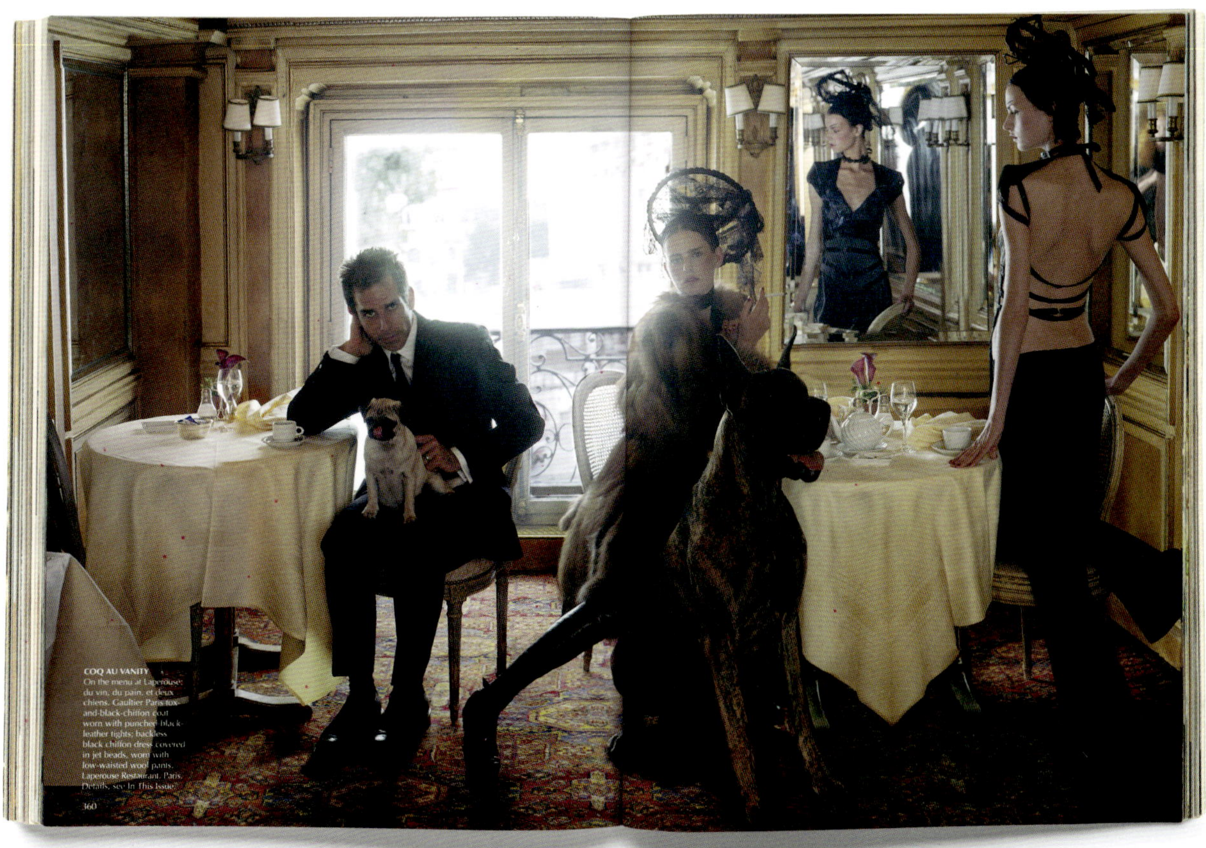
COQ AU VANITY
On the menu at Laperouse: du vin, du pain, et deux chiens. Gaultier Paris fox-and-black-chiffon coat worn with punched black-leather tights; backless black chiffon dress covered in jet beads, worn with low-waisted wool pants. Laperouse Restaurant, Paris. Details, see In This Issue.
360

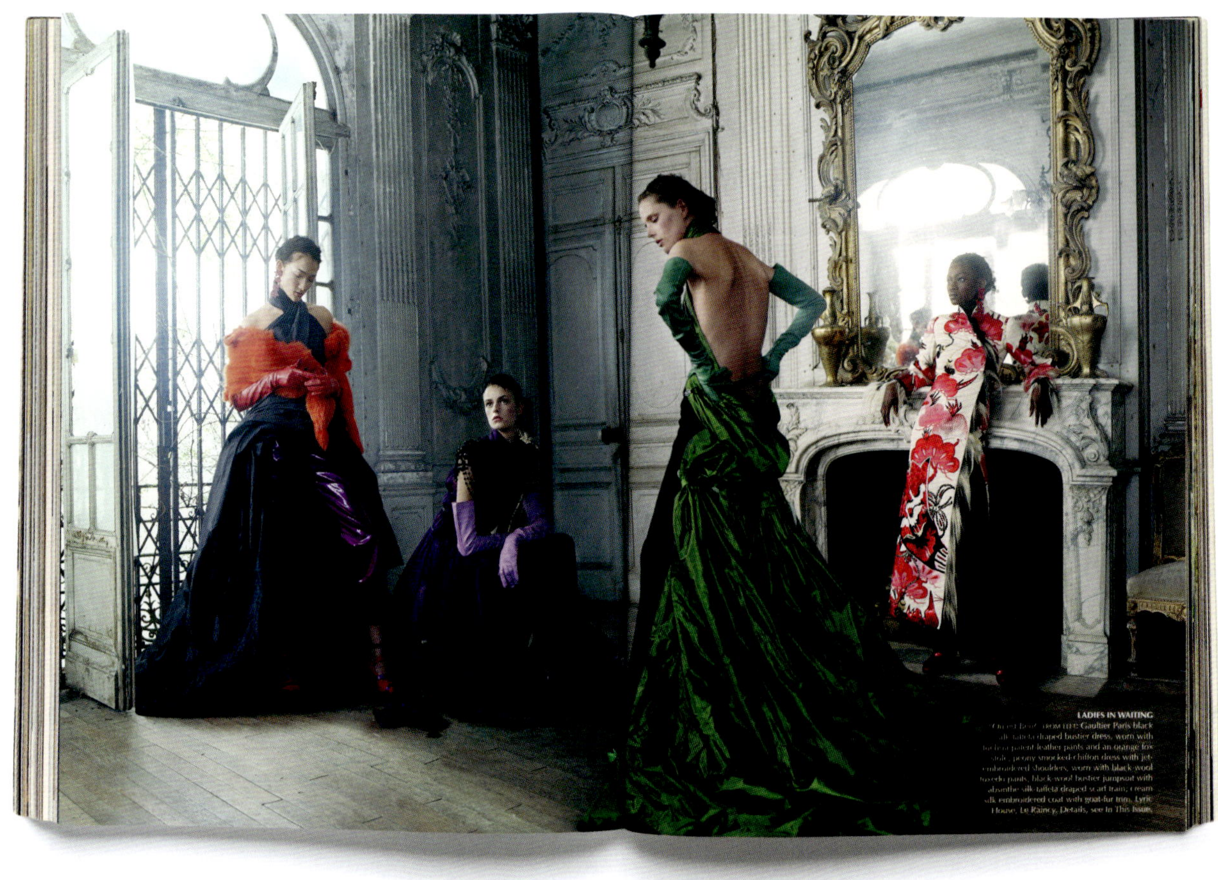
LADIES IN WAITING
House, Le Raincy. Details, see In This Issue.

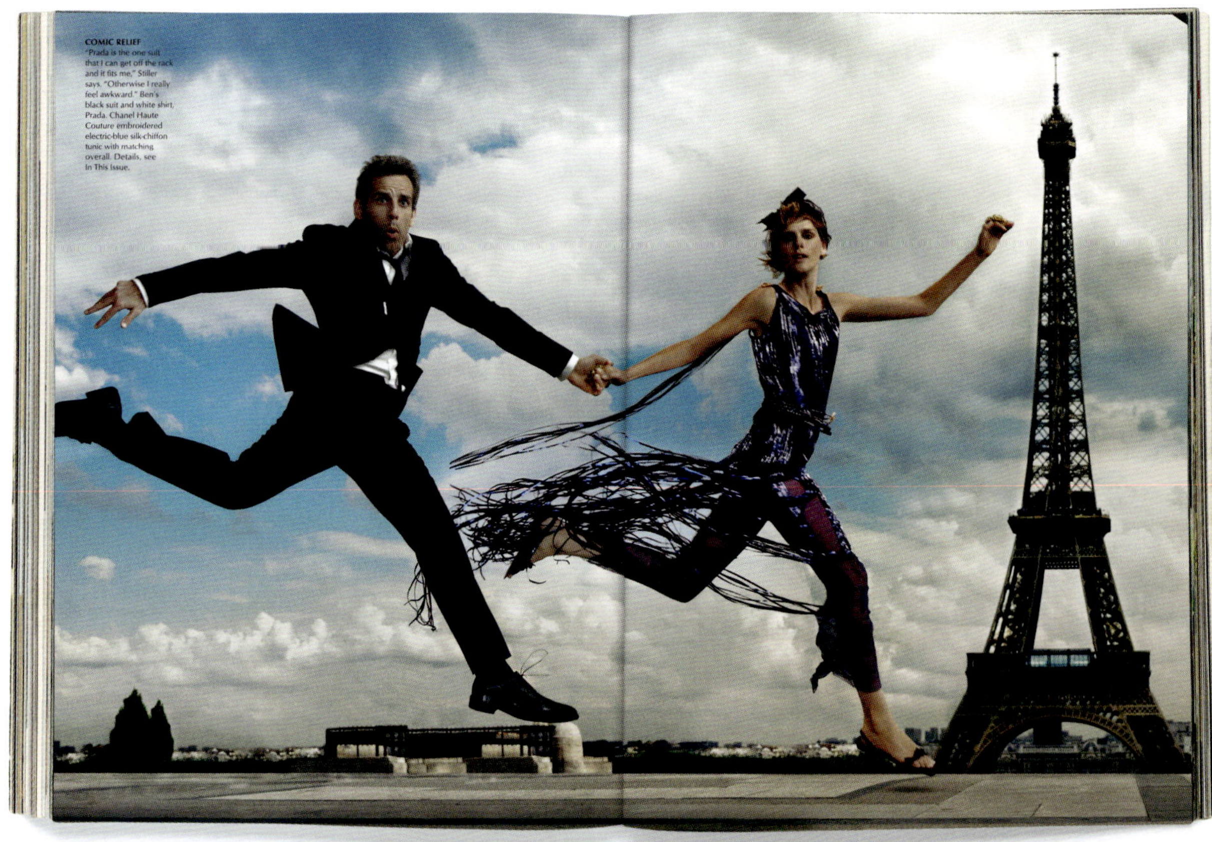
COMIC RELIEF
"Prada is the one suit that I can get off the rack and it fits me," Stiller says. "Otherwise I really feel awkward." Ben's black suit and white shirt, Prada. Chanel Haute Couture embroidered electric-blue silk-chiffon tunic with matching overall. Details, see In This Issue.

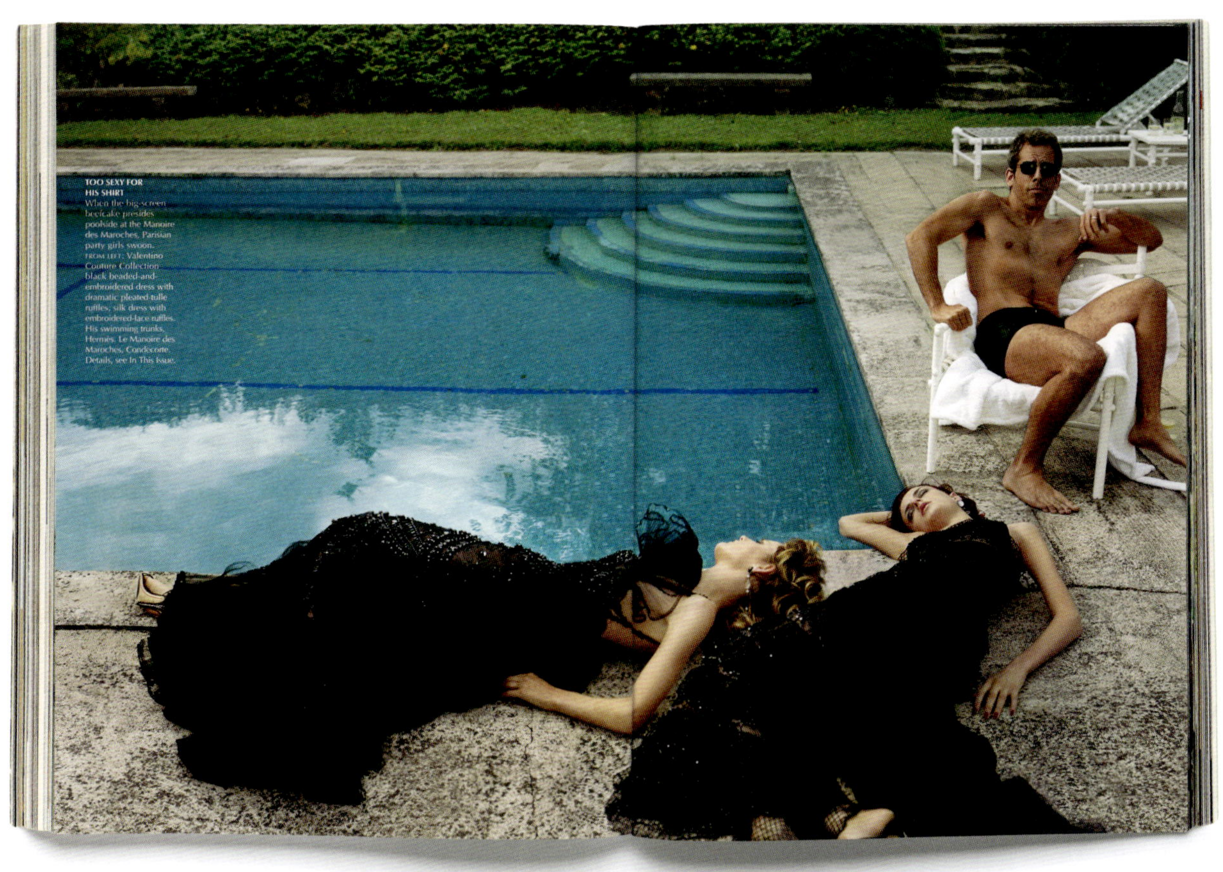
TOO SEXY FOR HIS SHIRT
When the big-screen beefcake presides poolside at the Manoire des Maroches, Parisian party girls swoon. FROM LEFT: Valentino Couture Collection black beaded-and-embroidered dress with dramatic pleated-tulle ruffles; silk dress with embroidered-lace ruffles. His swimming trunks, Hermès. Le Manoire des Maroches, Condecorte. Details, see In This Issue.

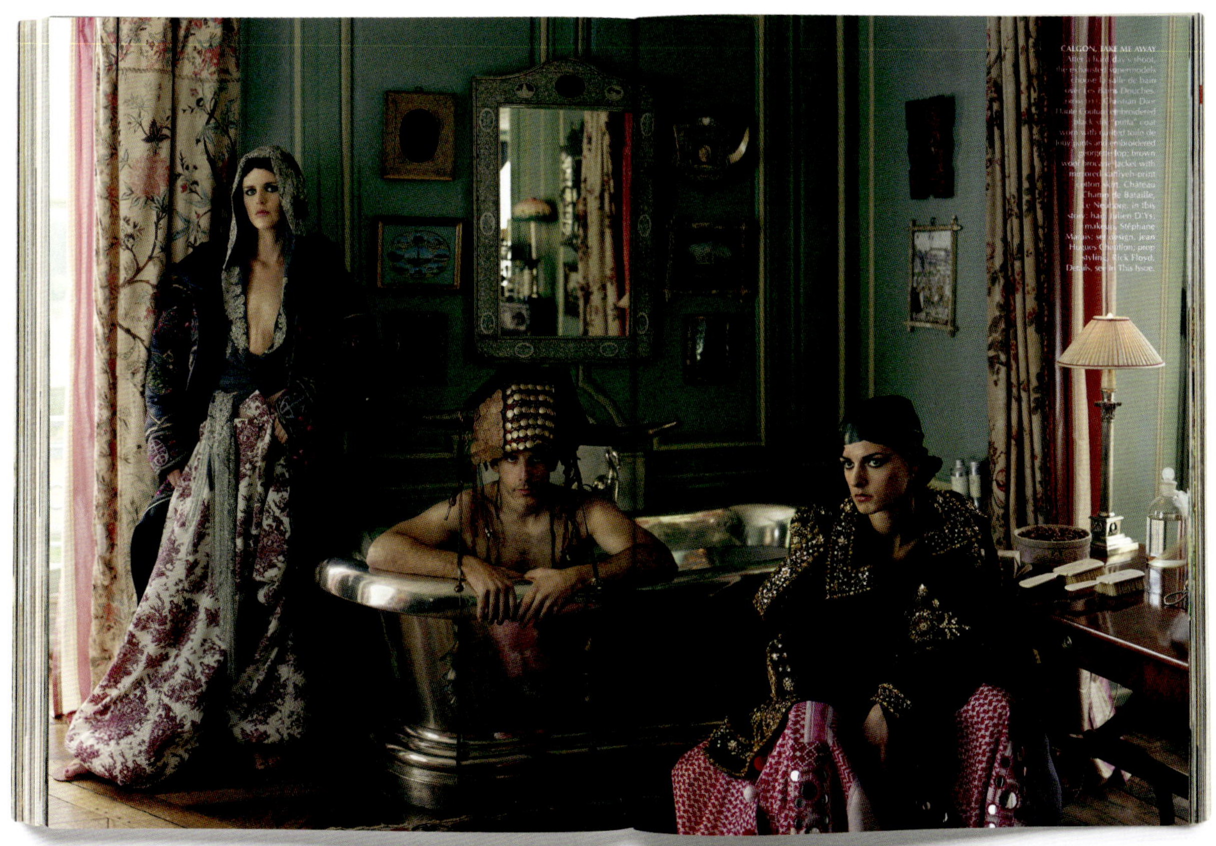
CALGON, TAKE ME AWAY
After a hard day's shoot, the exhausted supermodels choose la salle de bain over Les Bains Douches. FROM LEFT: Christian Dior Haute Couture embroidered black silk "punta" coat worn with quilted toile de Jouy pants and embroidered georgette top; brown wool brocade jacket with mirrored kaffiyeh-print cotton skirt. Château Champ de Bataille, Le Neubourg. In this story: hair, Julien D'Ys; makeup, Stéphane Marais; set design, Jean Hugues Chatillon; prop styling, Rick Floyd. Details, see In This Issue.

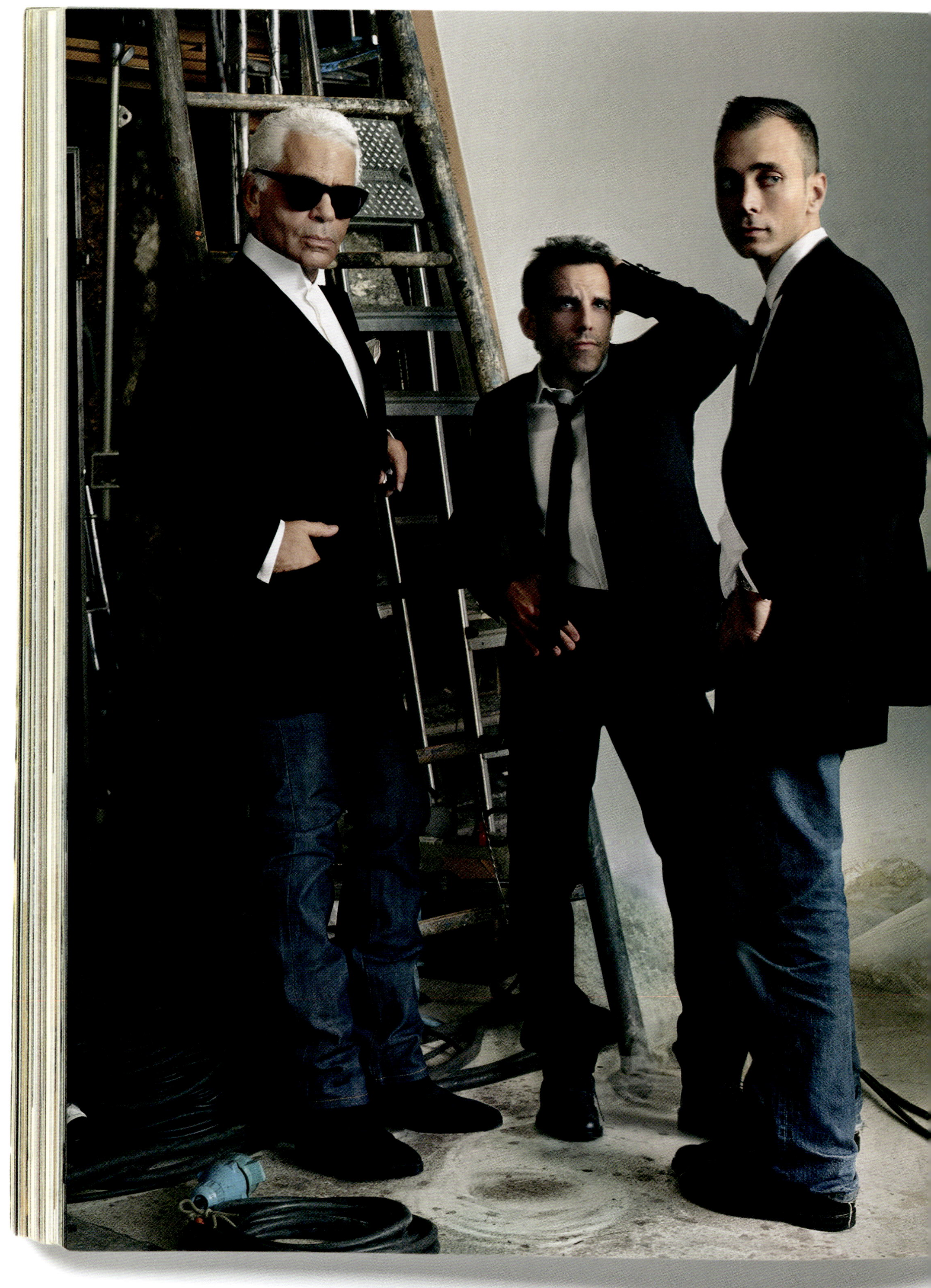

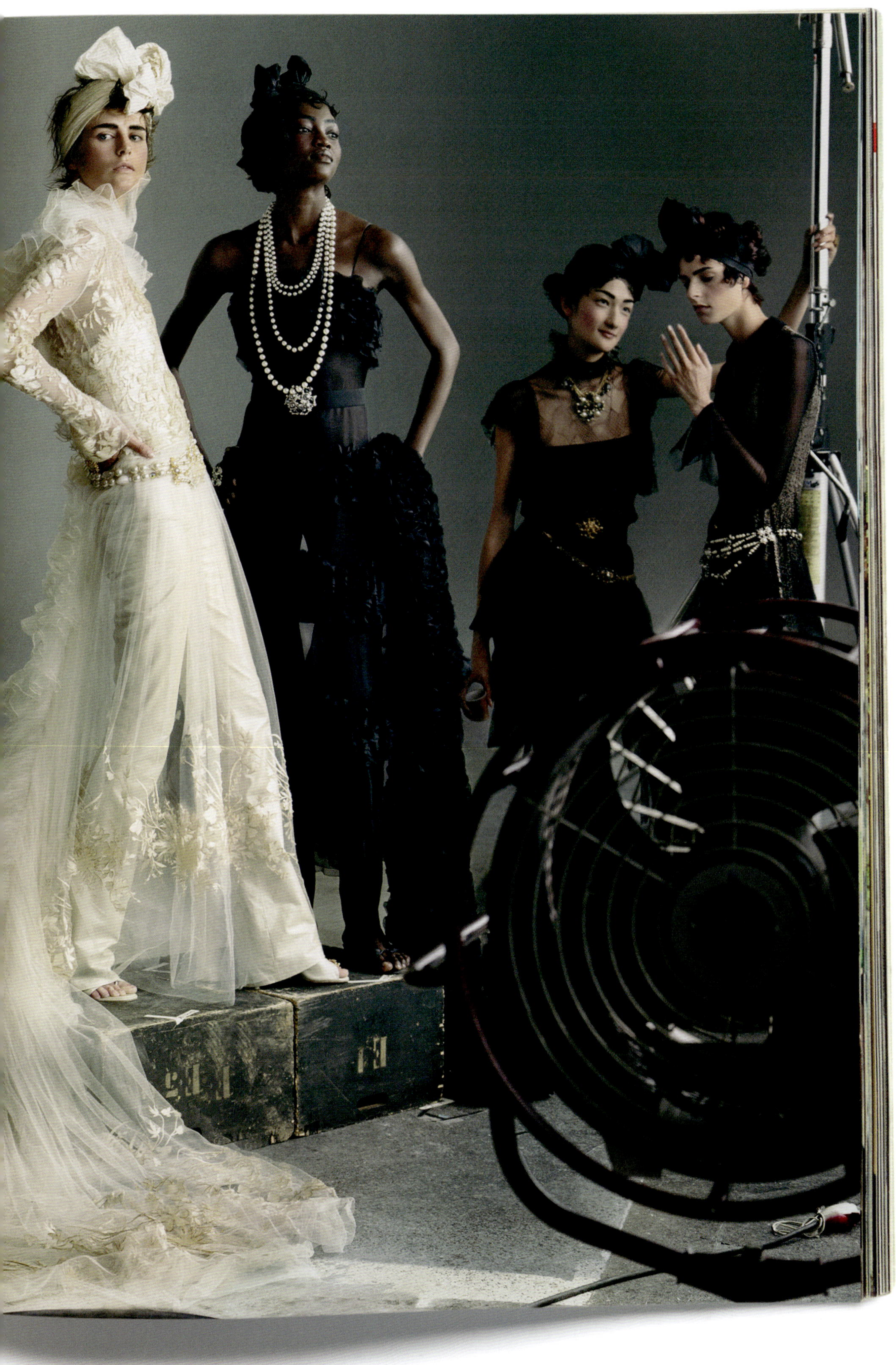

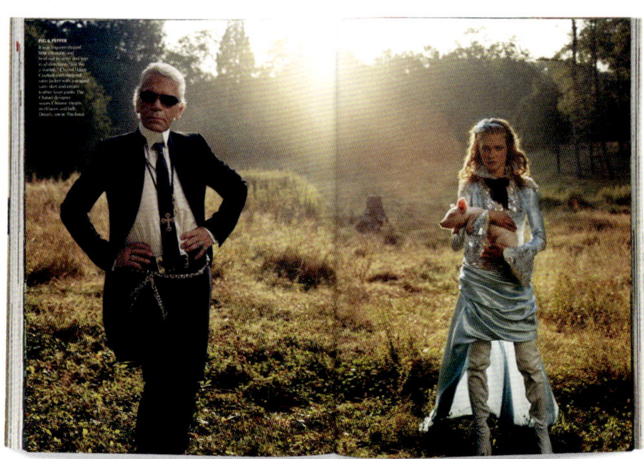

The *Alice in Wonderland* story was set in the Louis XVI folly garden of the château in Corbeil-Cerf in northern France. Grace Coddington asked designers to make blue dresses. Alice was portrayed by Natalia Vodianova. The designers themselves were cast in specific roles: Tom Ford as the White Rabbit, Marc Jacobs as the Caterpillar, Jean Paul Gaultier as the Cheshire Cat, Viktor and Rolf as Tweedledum and Tweedledee, Donatella Versace as the Gryphon and her friend Rupert Everett as the Mock Turtle, the milliner Stephen Jones as the Mad Hatter, Christian Lacroix as the March Hare, John Galliano as the Queen of Hearts, and Nicolas Ghesquière as Alice's black cat. Karl Lagerfeld said that he wanted to play himself or the White Rabbit. Since Tom Ford had already been promised the White Rabbit part, Lagerfeld was cast as the duchess whose baby turns into a pig. When he arrived on set he didn't want anything to do with the pig.

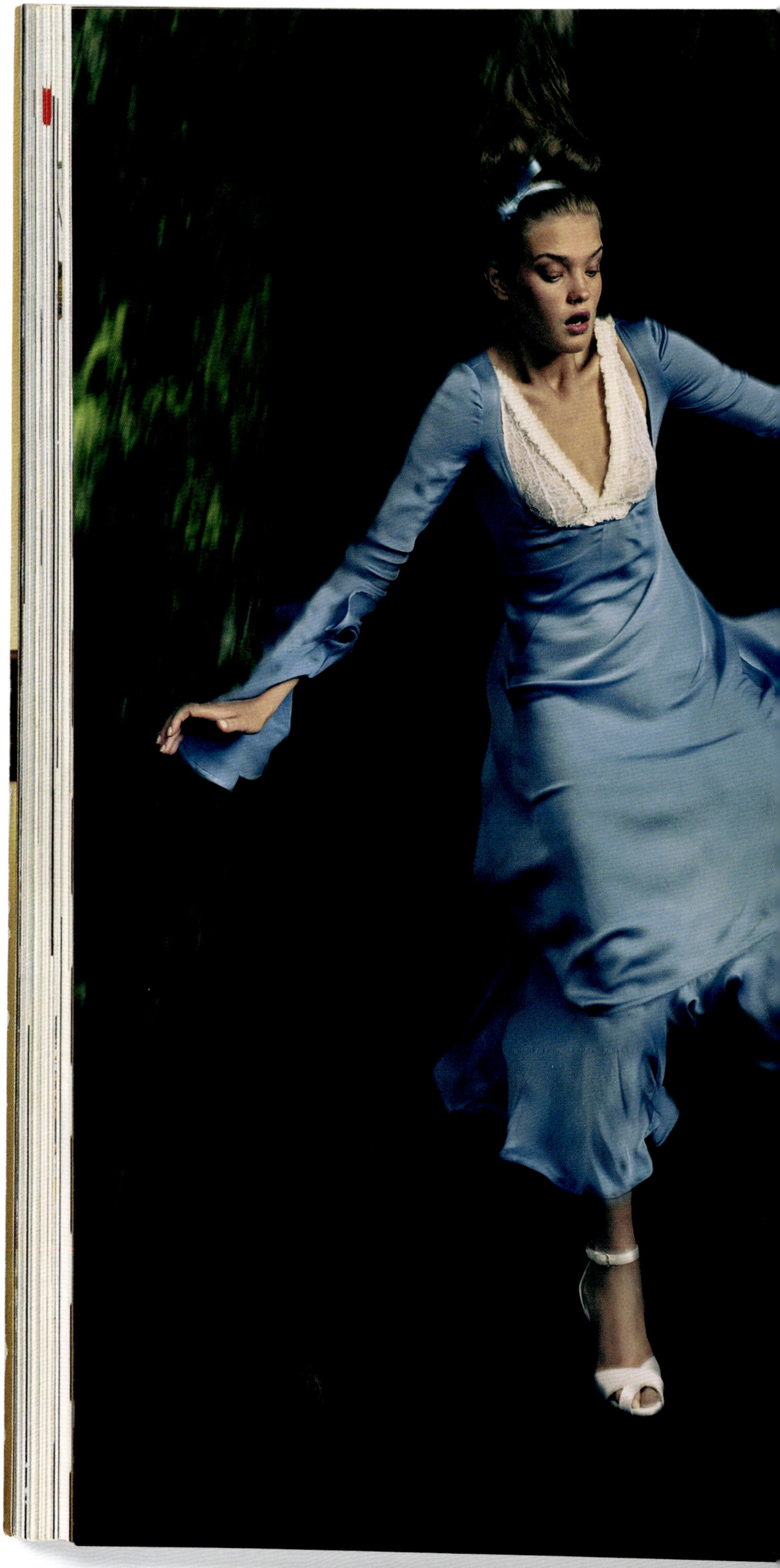

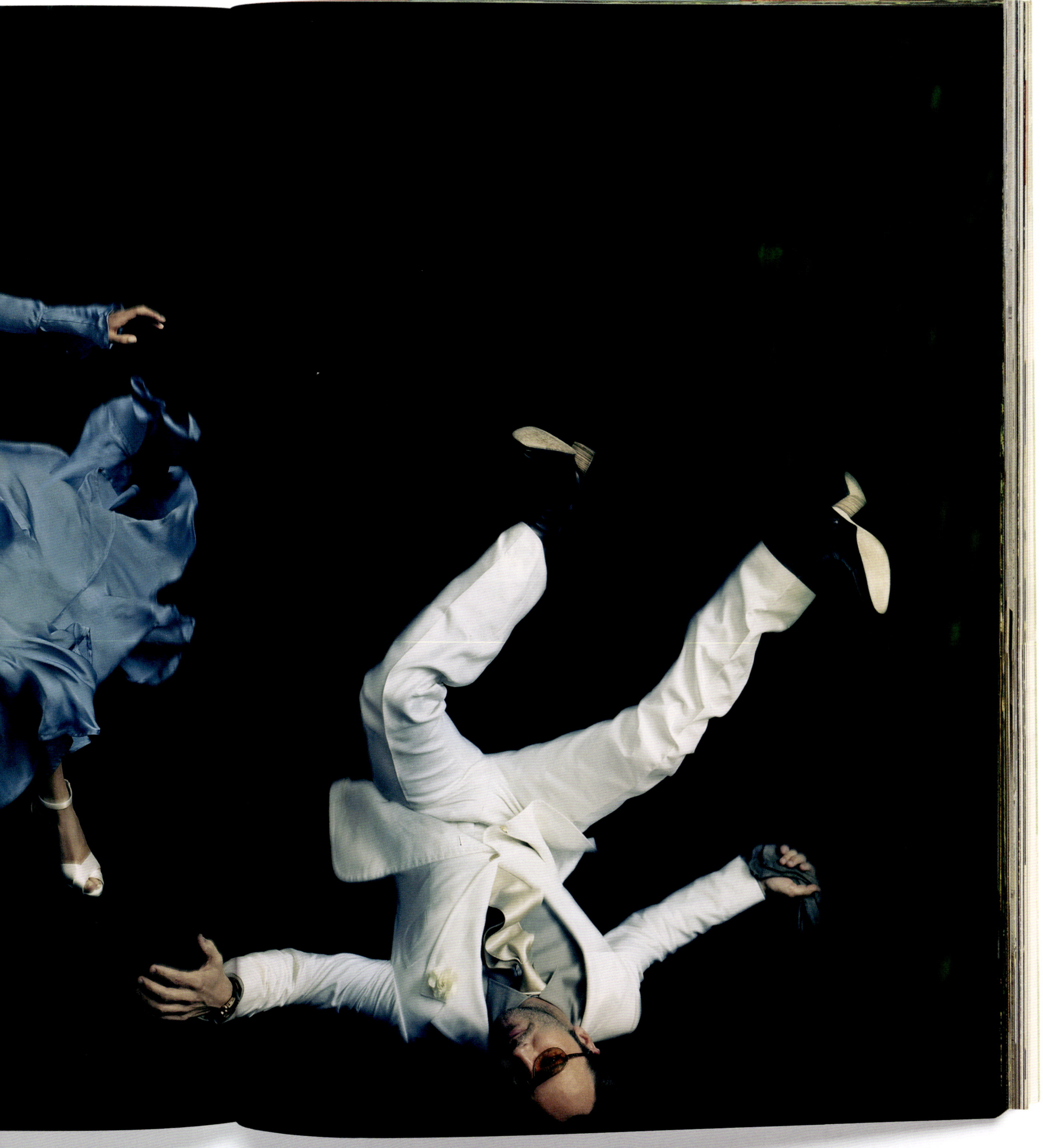

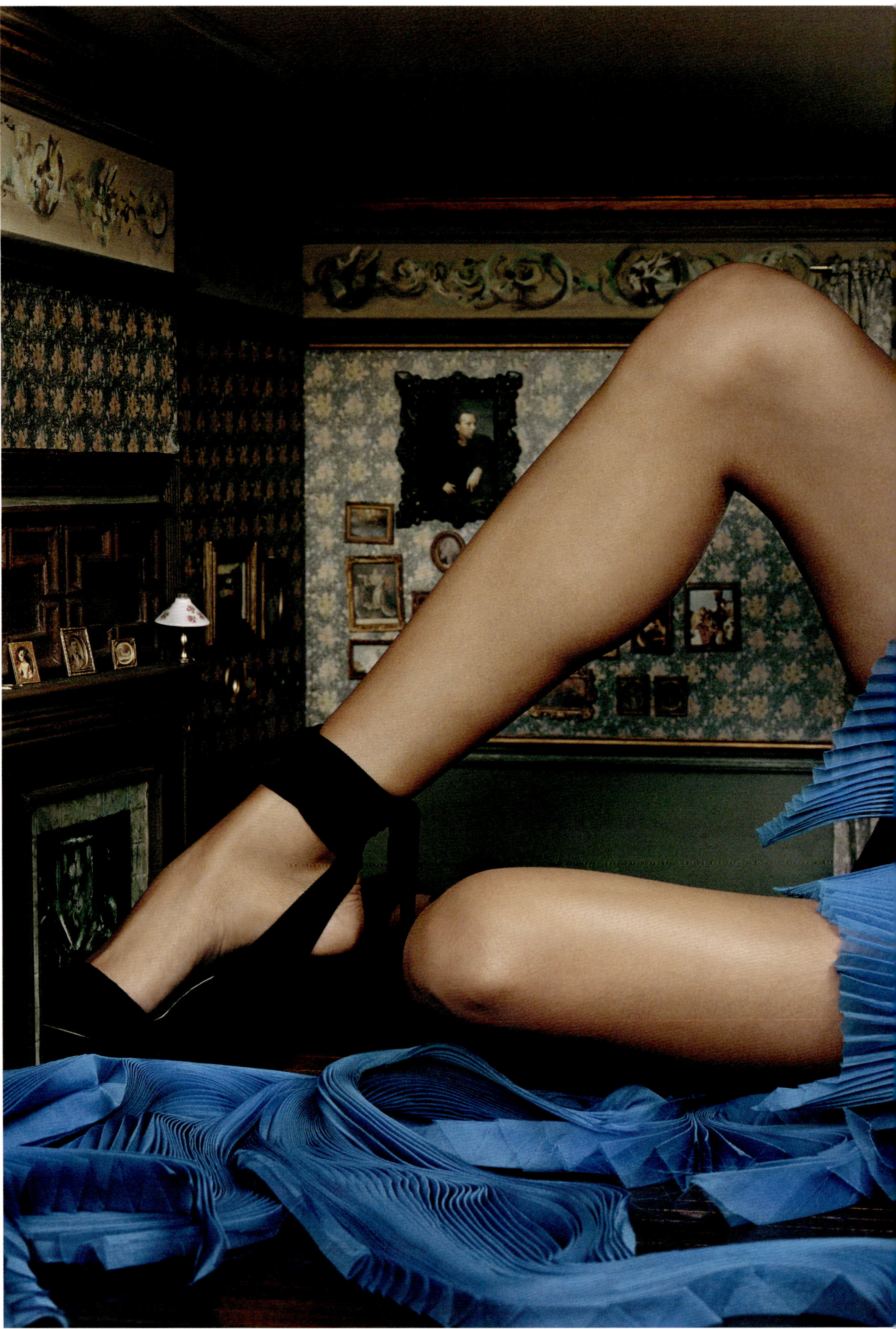

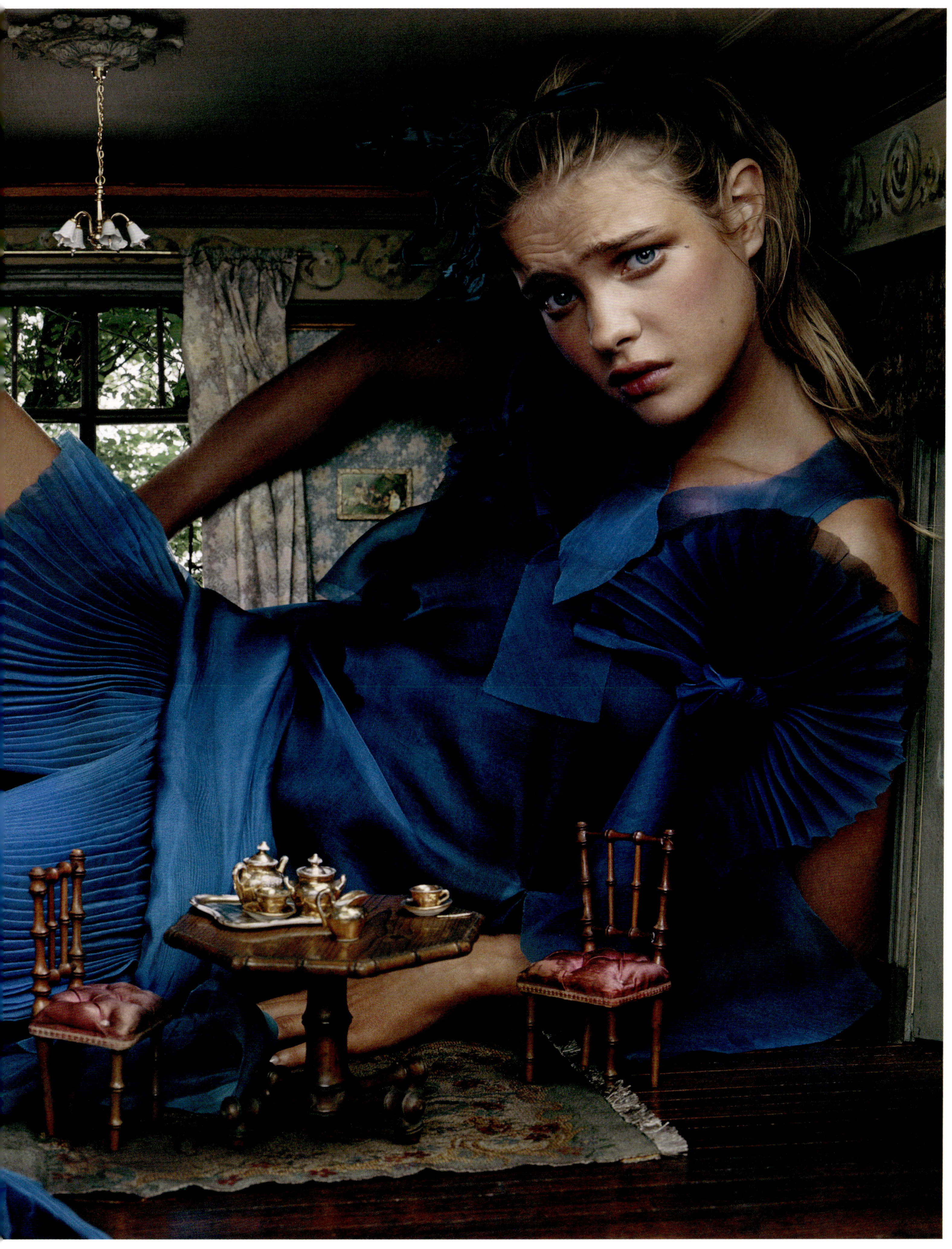

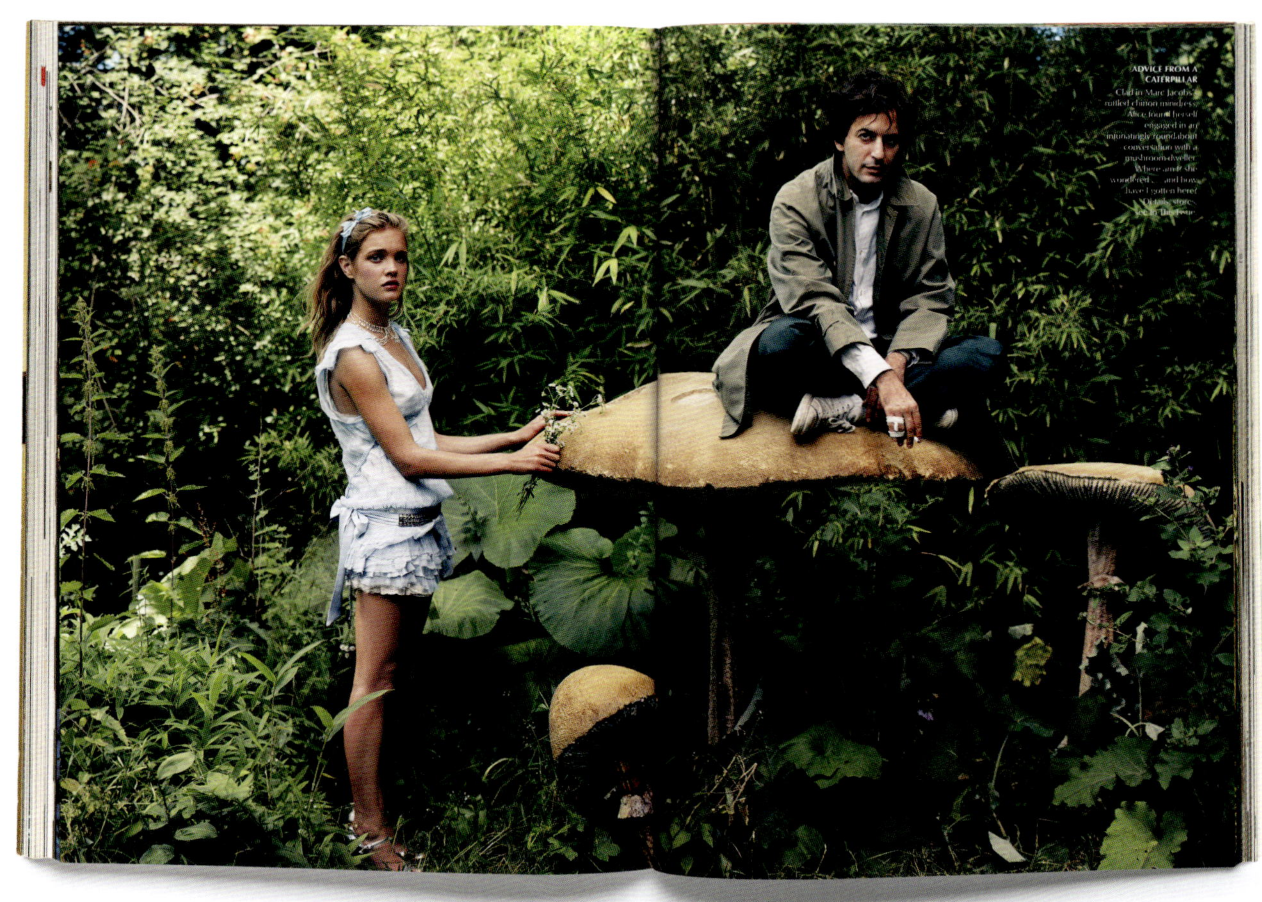
ADVICE FROM A CATERPILLAR
Clad in Marc Jacobs's ruffled chiffon minidress, Alice found herself engaged in an infuriatingly roundabout conversation with a mushroom-dweller. Where am I? she wondered . . . and how have I gotten here? Details, stores, see In This Issue.

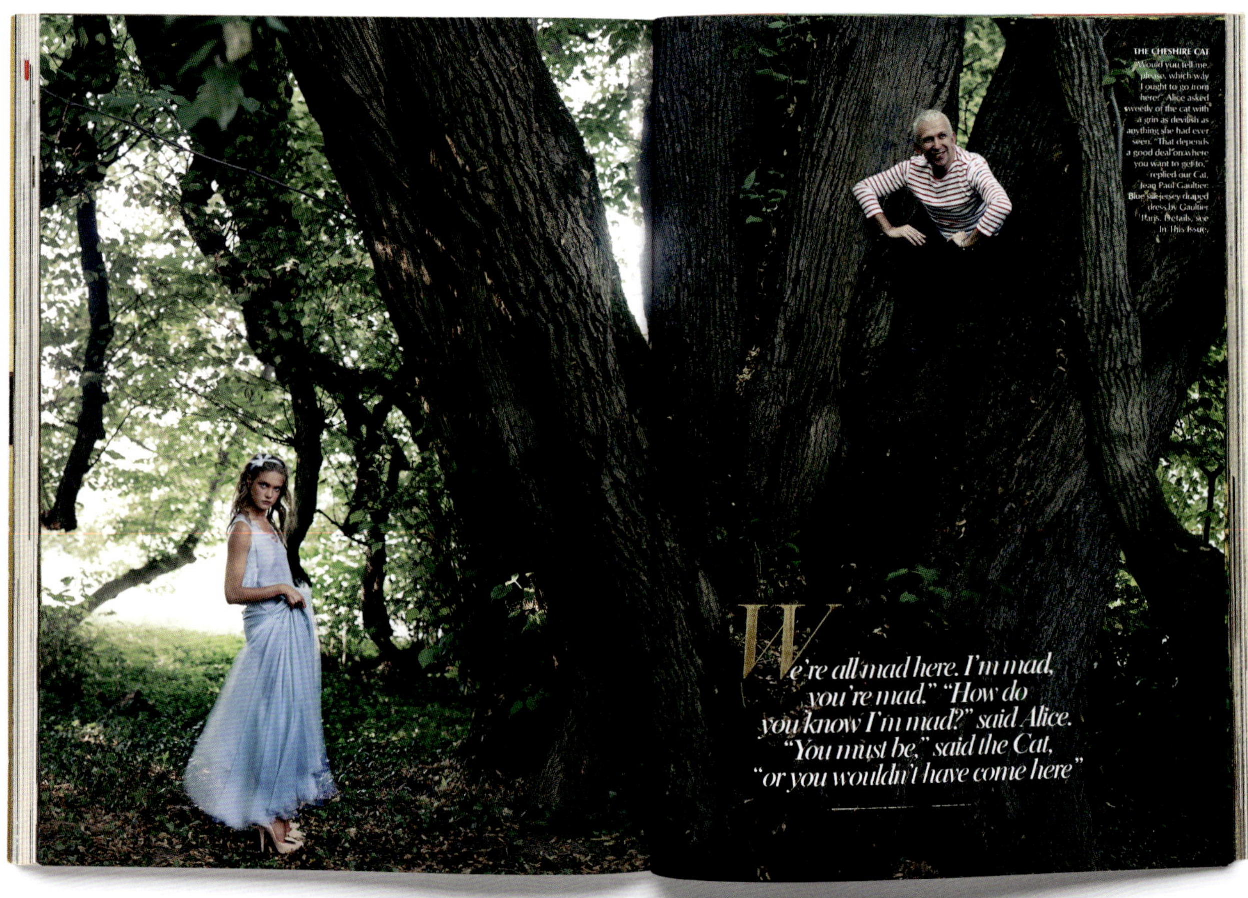
THE CHESHIRE CAT
"Would you tell me, please, which way I ought to go from here?" Alice asked sweetly of the cat with a grin as devilish as anything she had ever seen. "That depends a good deal on where you want to get to," replied our Cat, Jean Paul Gaultier. Blue silk-jersey draped dress by Gaultier Paris. Details, see In This Issue.
"We're all mad here. I'm mad, you're mad." "How do you know I'm mad?" said Alice. "You must be," said the Cat, "or you wouldn't have come here"

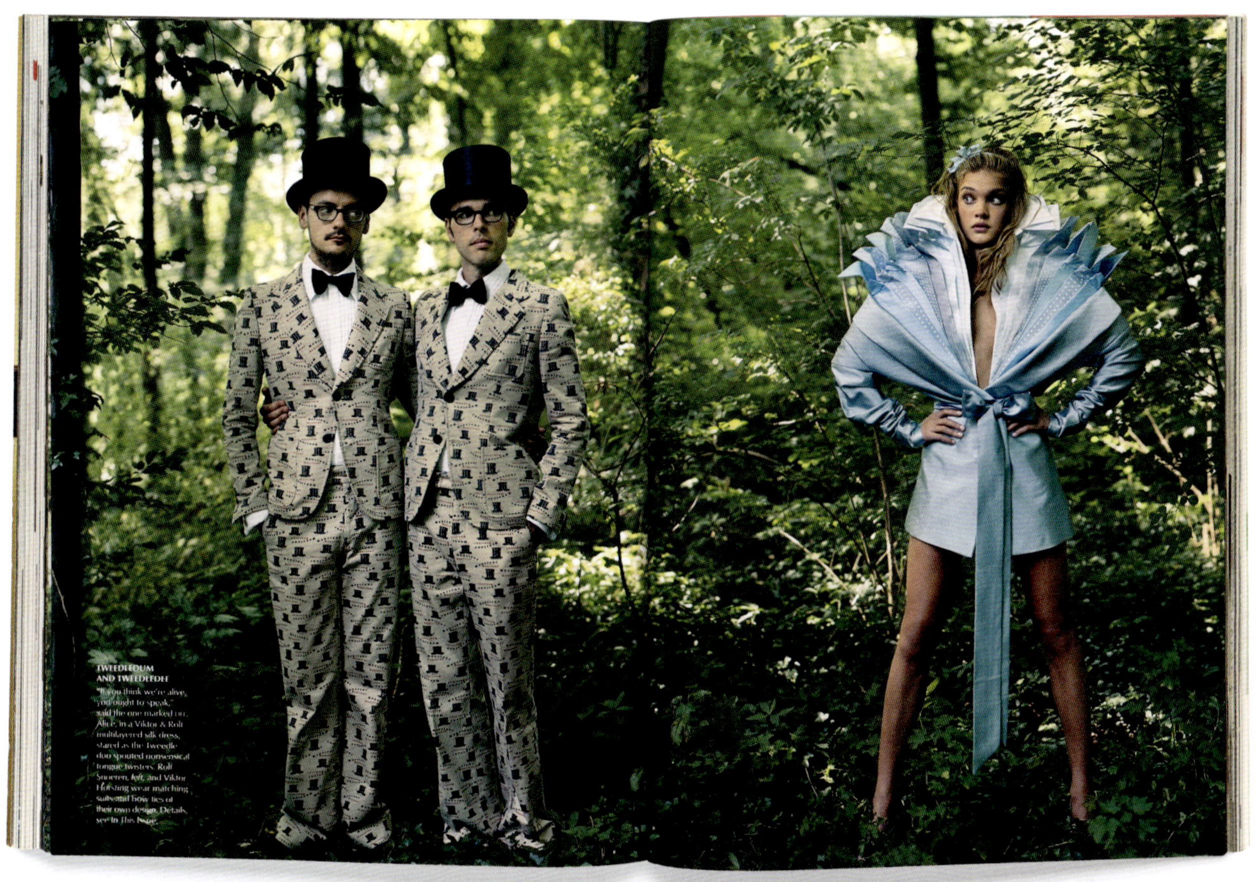

TWEEDLEDUM AND TWEEDLEDEE
"If you think we're alive, you ought to speak," said the one marked DUM. Alice, in a Viktor & Rolf multilayered silk dress, stared as the Tweedle duo spouted nonsensical tongue twisters. Rolf Snoeren, *left*, and Viktor Horsting wear matching suits and bow ties of their own design. Details, see In This Issue.

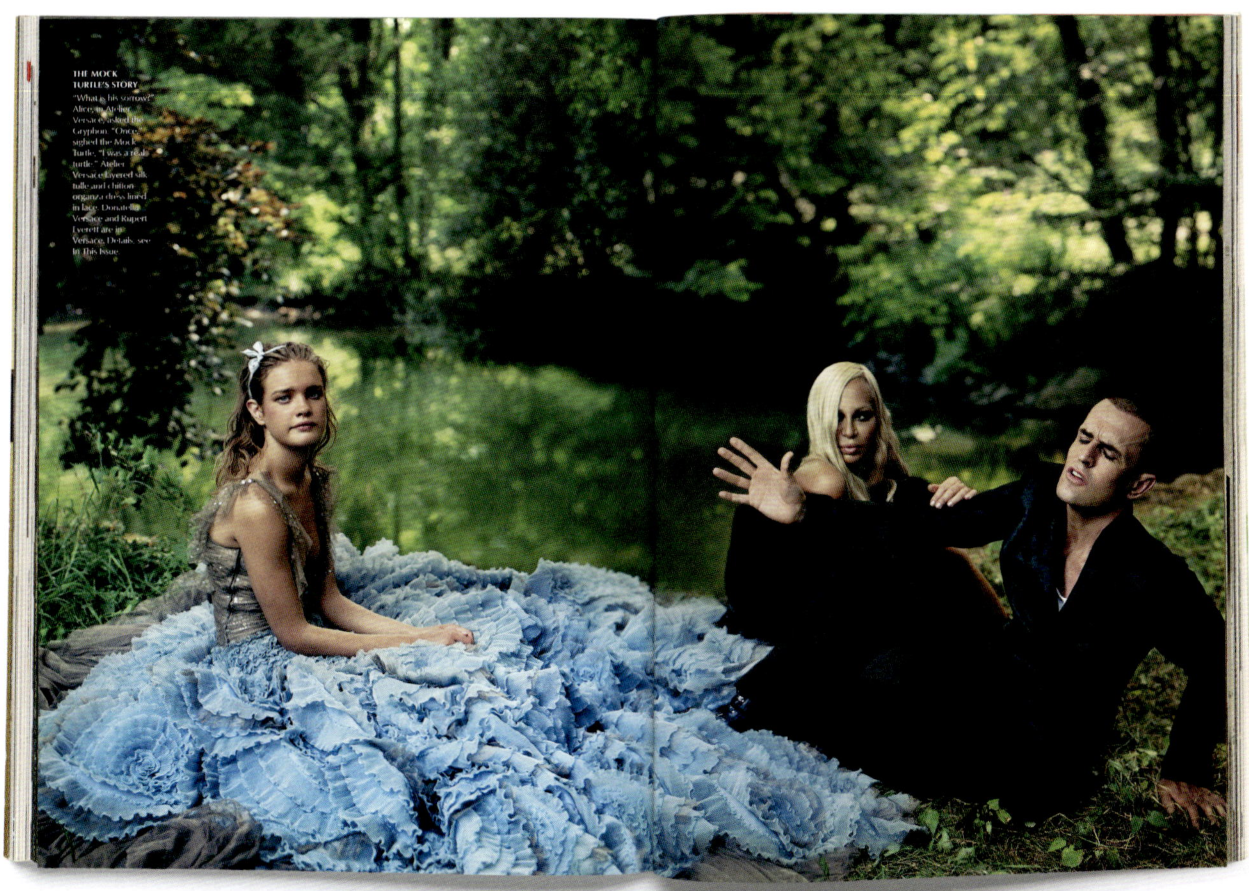

THE MOCK TURTLE'S STORY
"What is his sorrow?" Alice, in Atelier Versace, asked the Gryphon. "Once," sighed the Mock Turtle, "I was a real turtle." Atelier Versace layered silk tulle and chiffon organza dress lined in lace. Donatella Versace and Rupert Everett are in Versace. Details, see In This Issue.

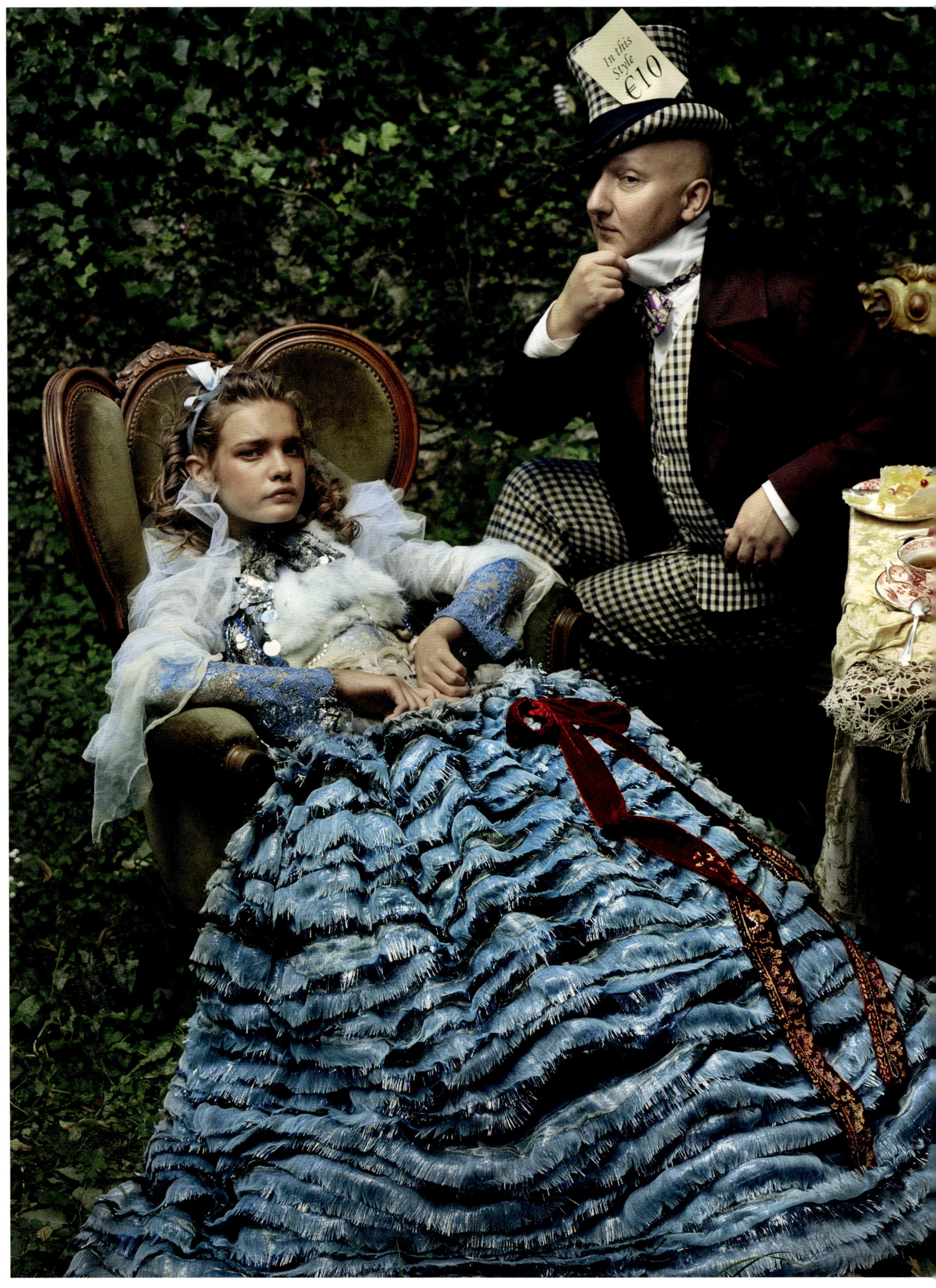
In this
Style
€10

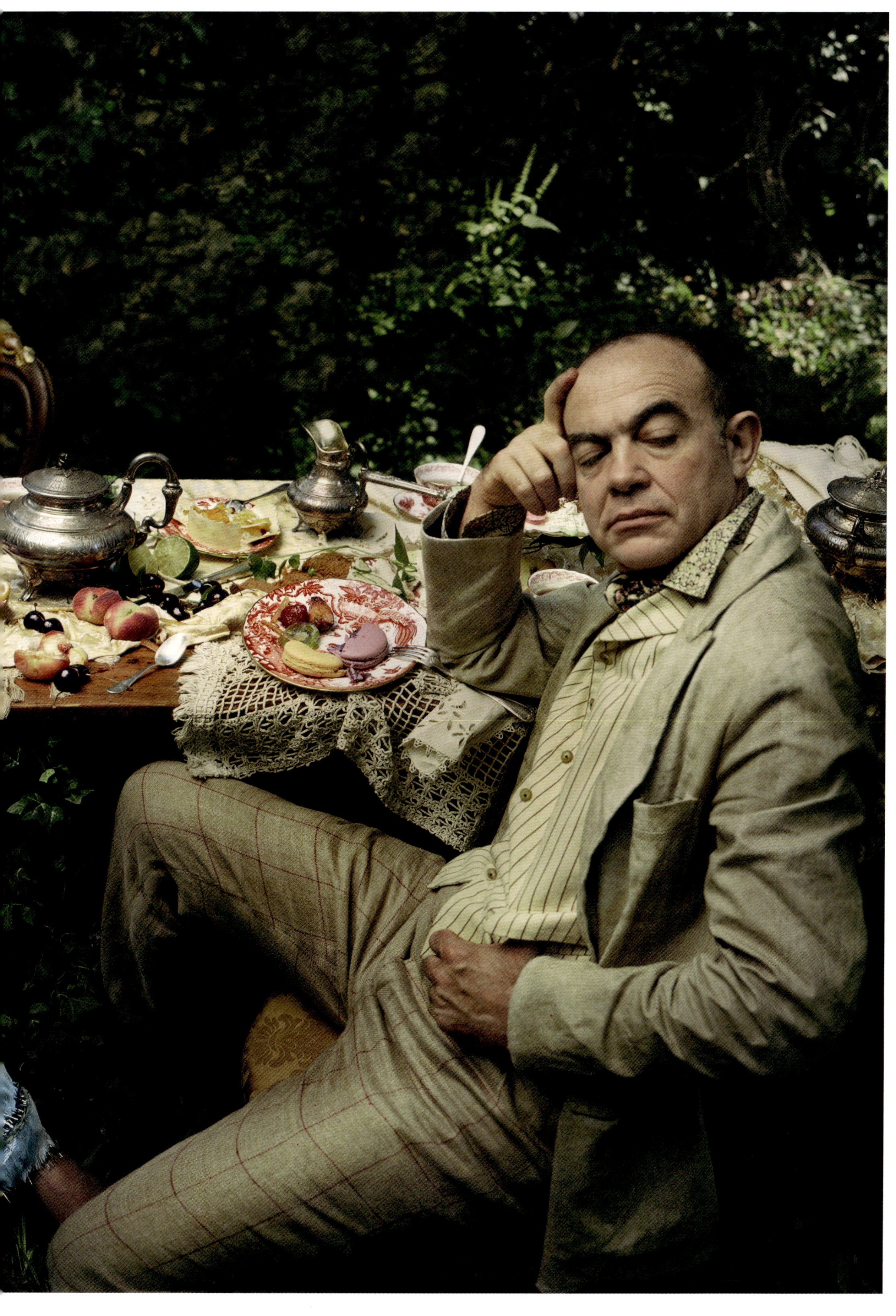

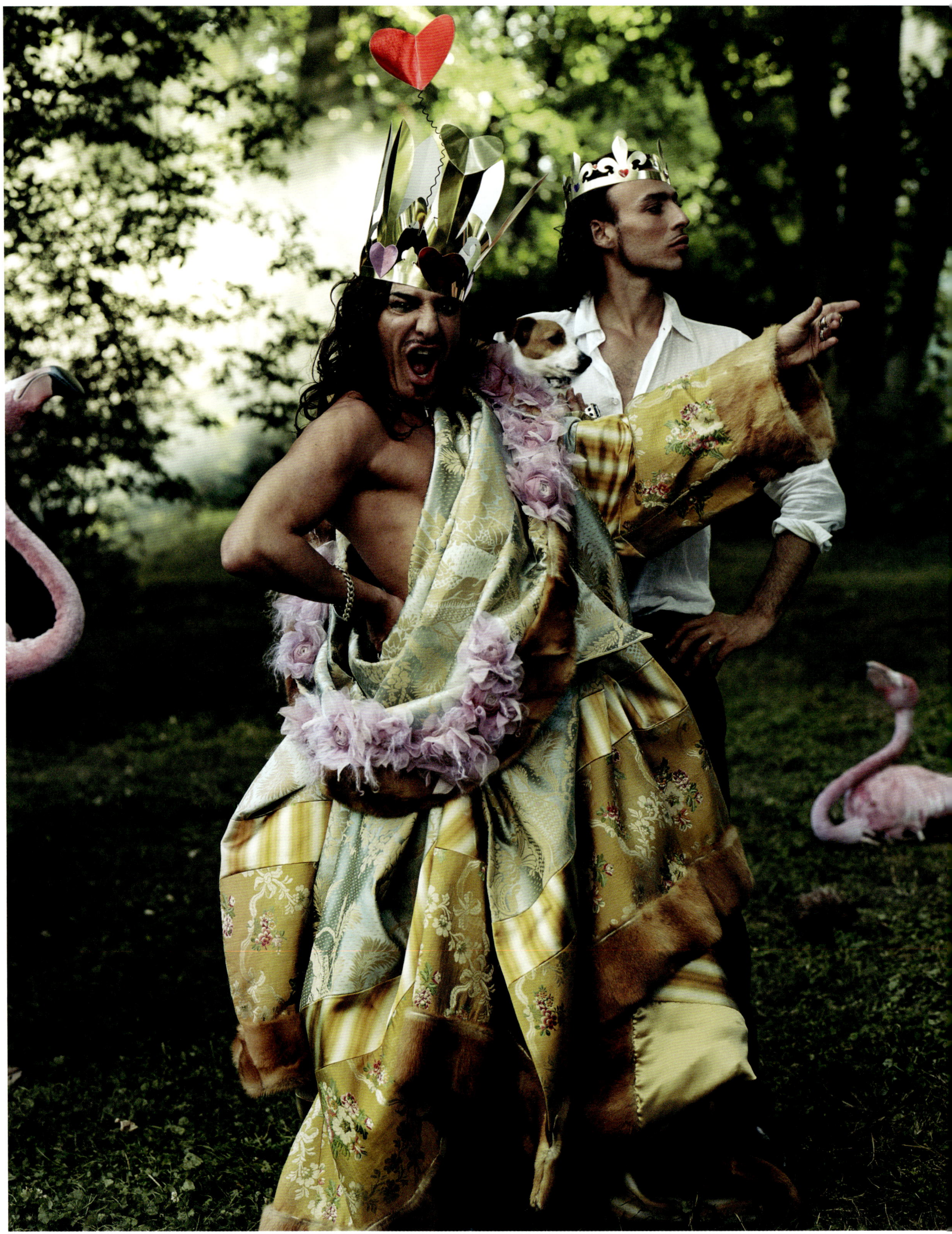

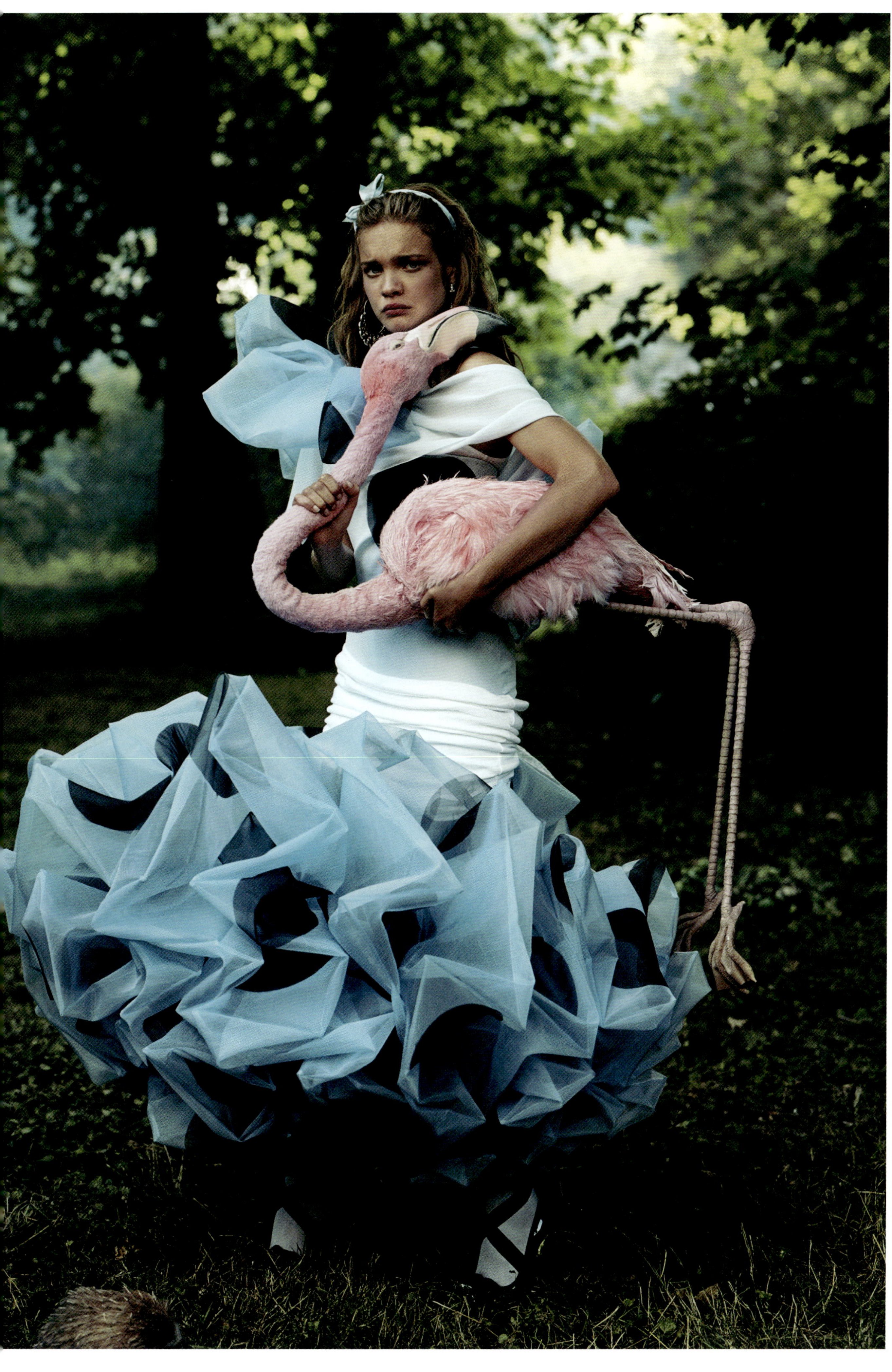

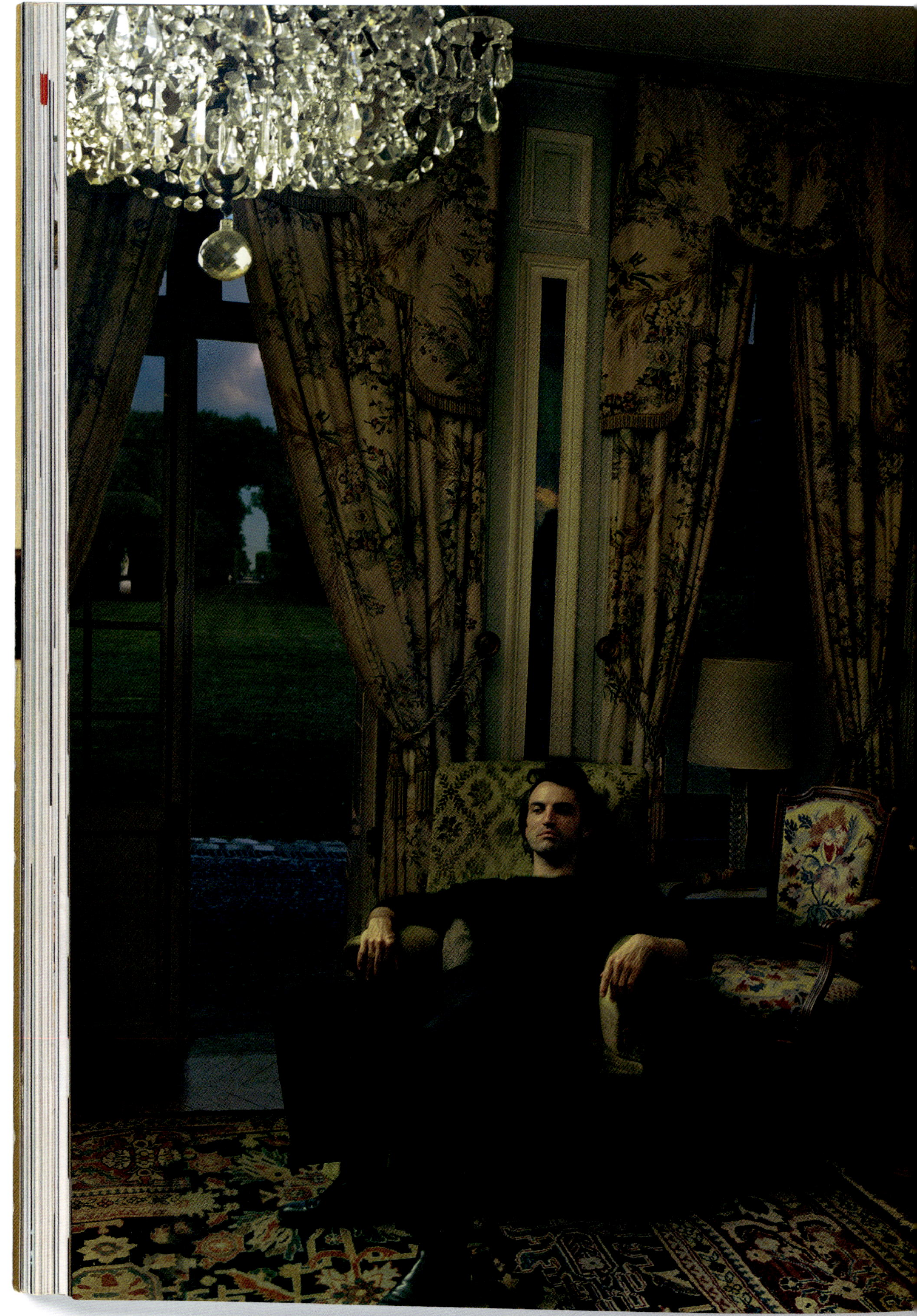

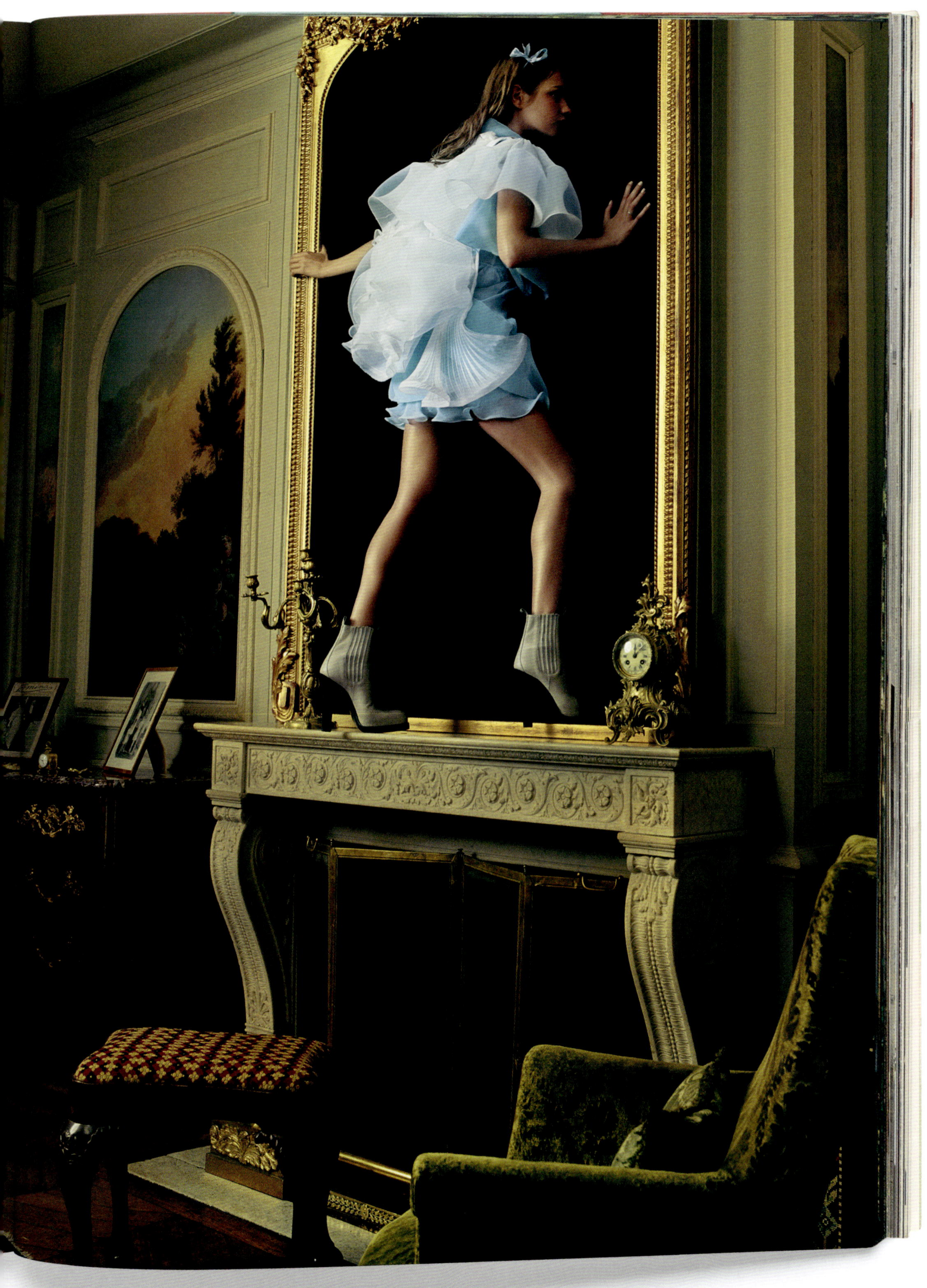

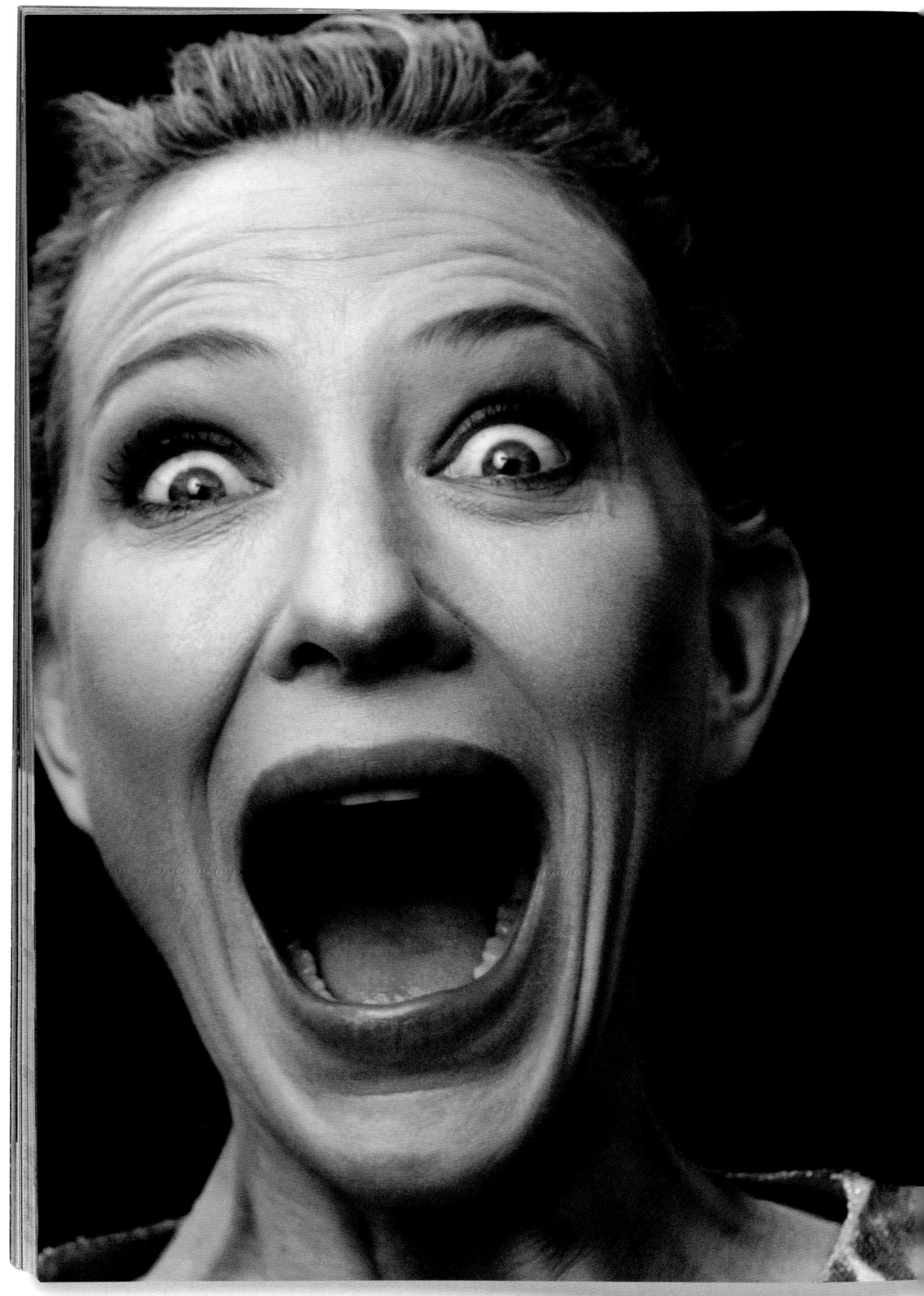

Cate Blanchett,
London, 2009

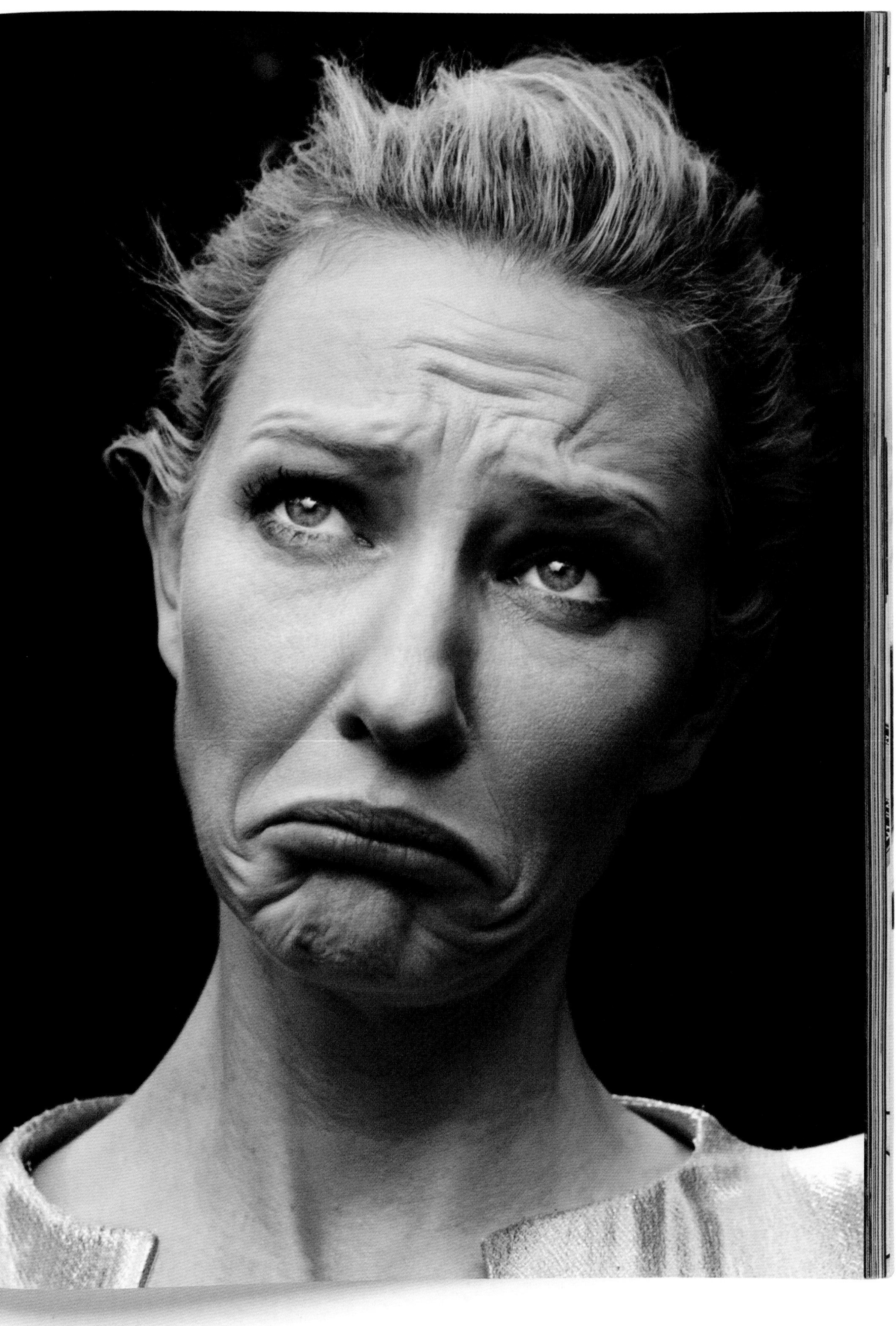

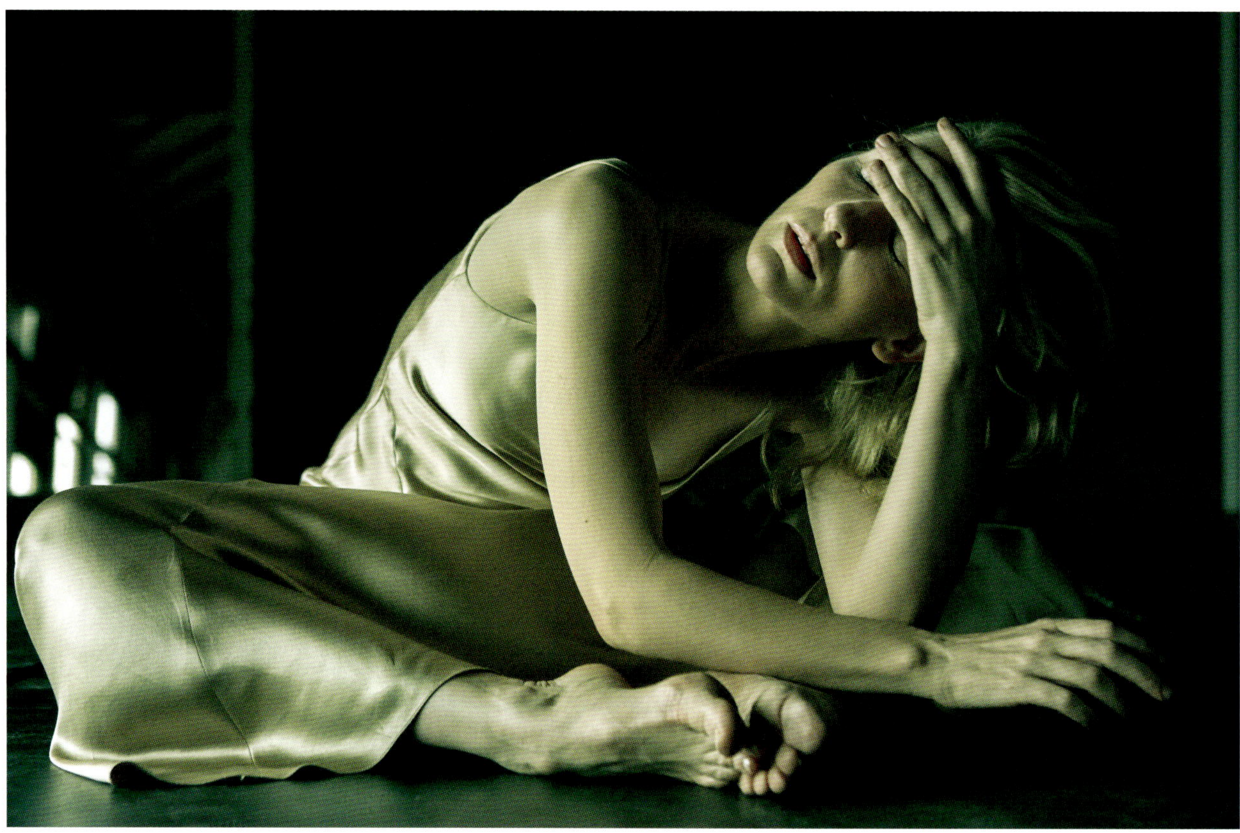

"When I look through the pictures from this shoot with Cate Blanchett, I see her working, dancing with all her heart, her passion. Cate is a creature of the theater. She doesn't resist the camera.

Very early on, I did a shoot with Cate in the Mojave Desert. We built a glass house in the middle of nowhere. It was blisteringly hot, miserable, a sort of Outward Bound experience gone wrong. And then it started to snow. Another time, we worked on a rooftop in London in the pouring rain. She never complained.

Cate once said to me, after we had worked on many shoots together over the years, 'You are never satisfied, are you?' That haunts me, because she is most likely right."

Cate Blanchett,
Sydney Theatre Company,
Sydney, Australia, 2008

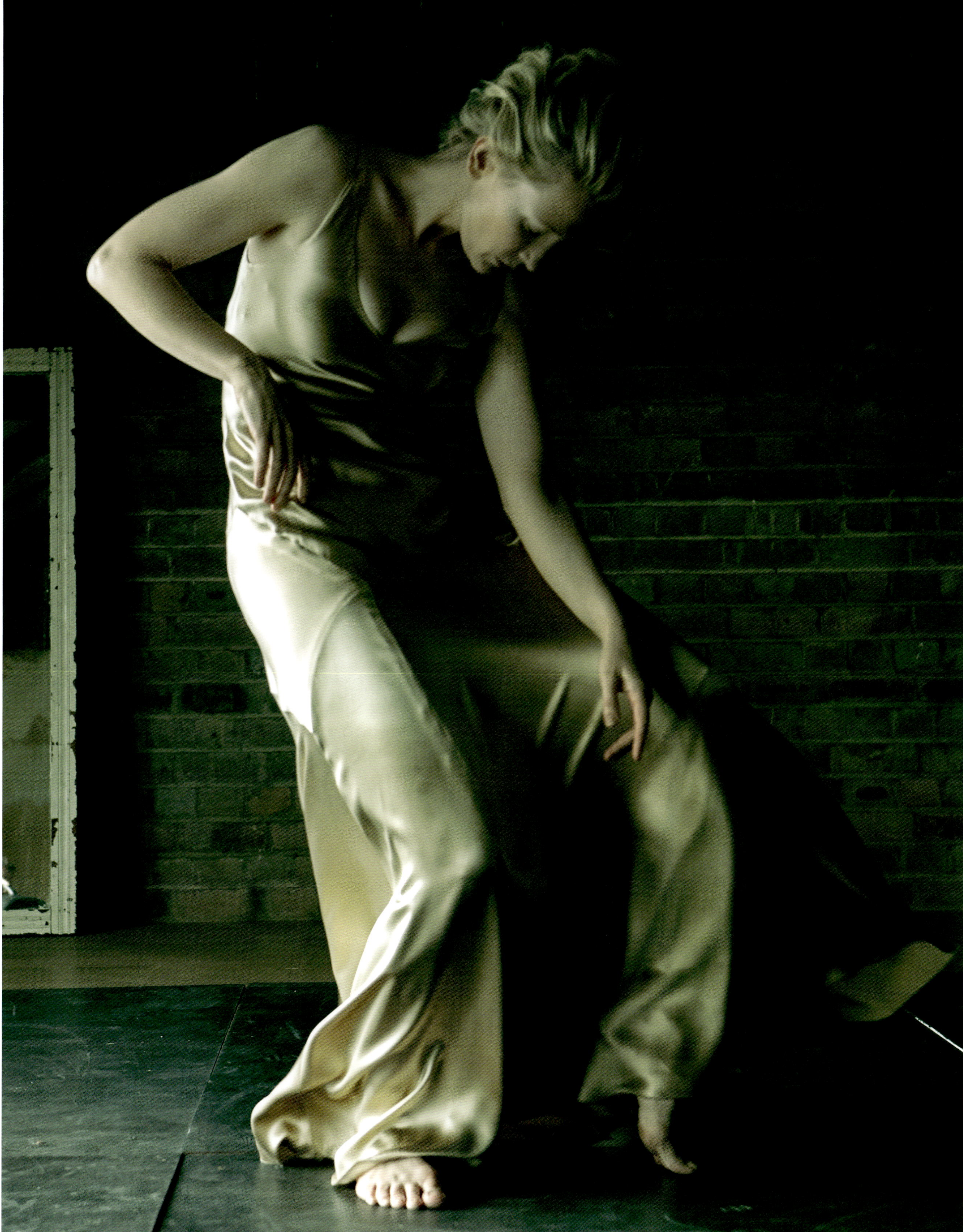

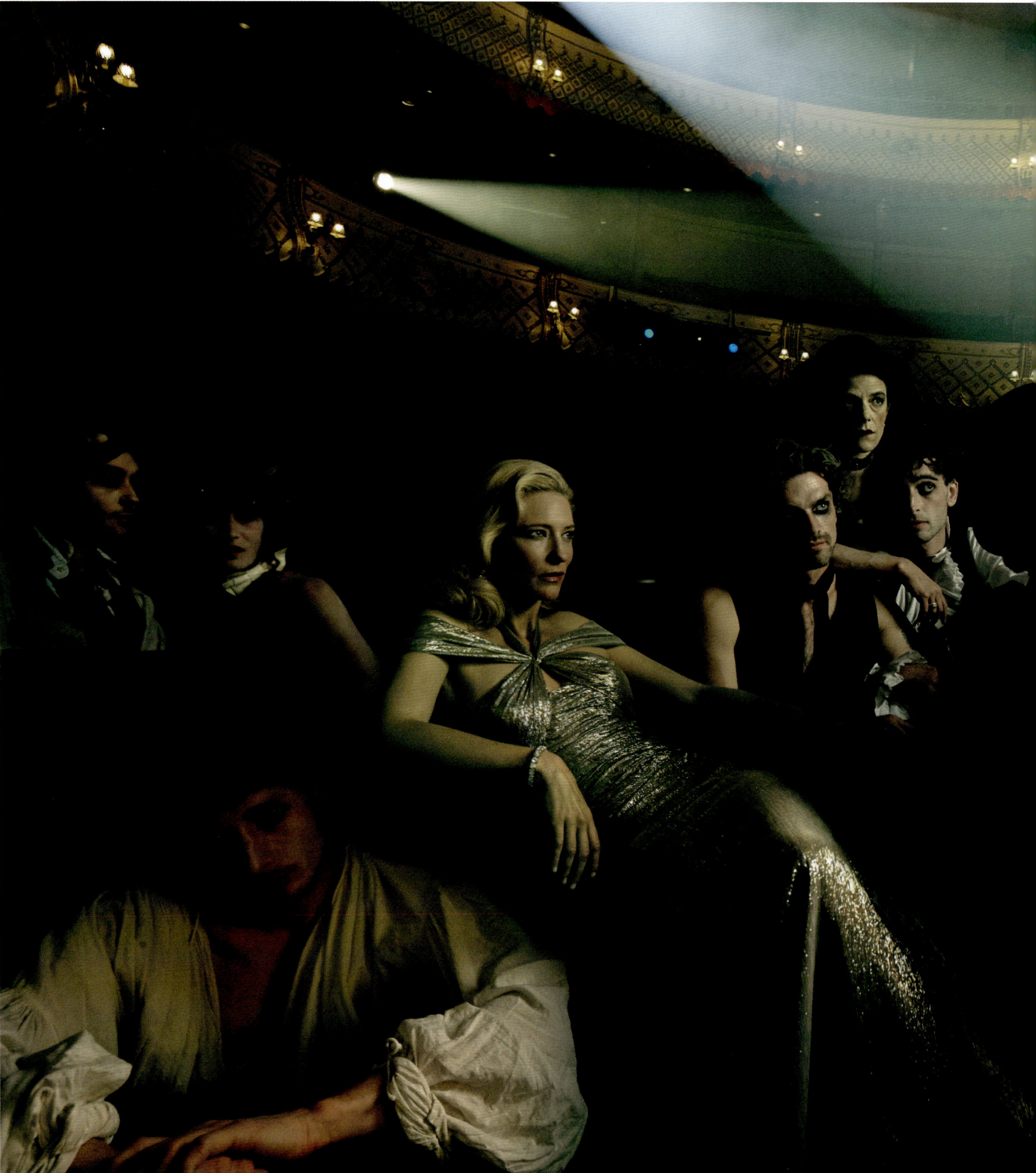

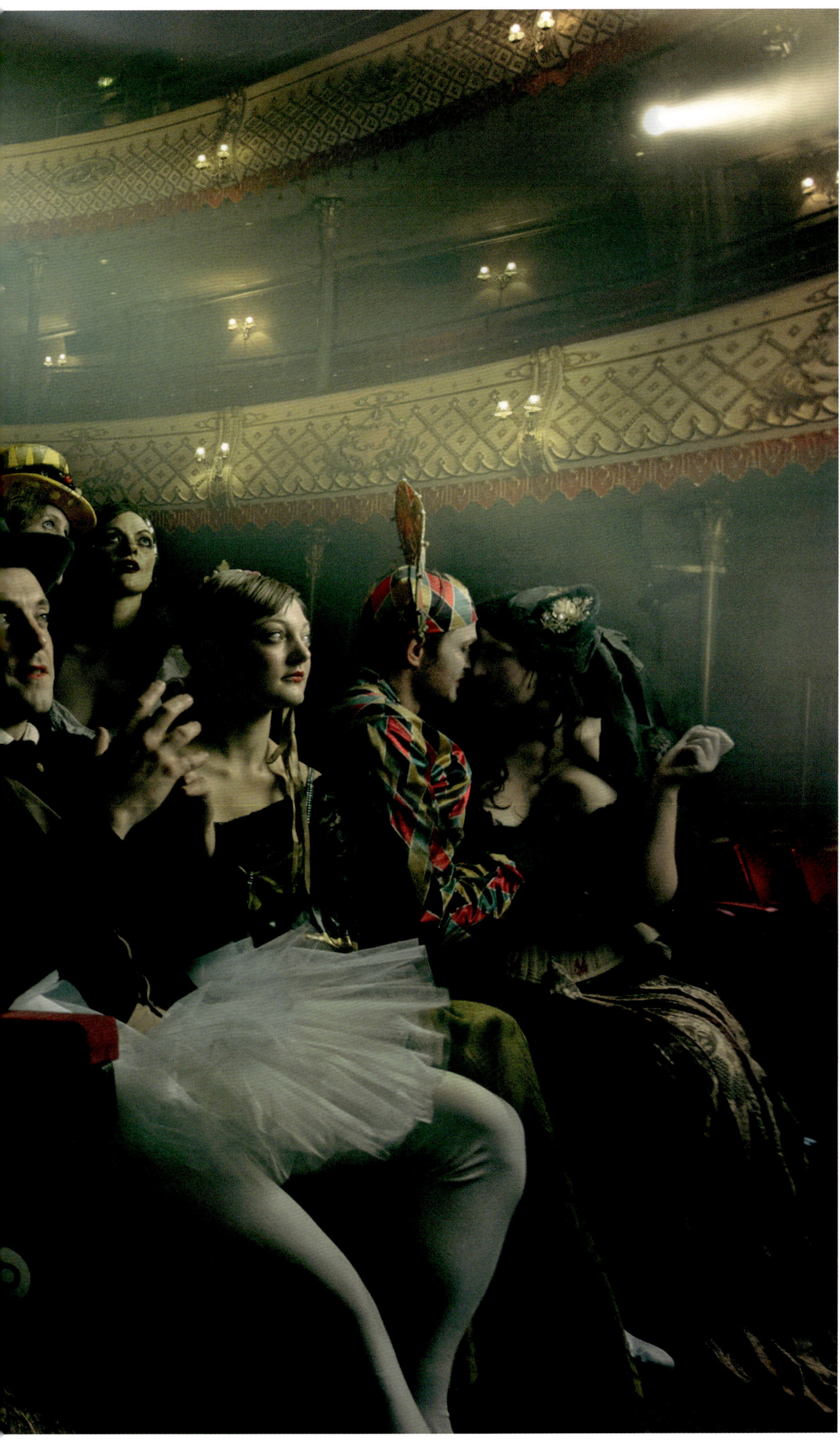

Cate Blanchett, the Old Vic,
London, 2009

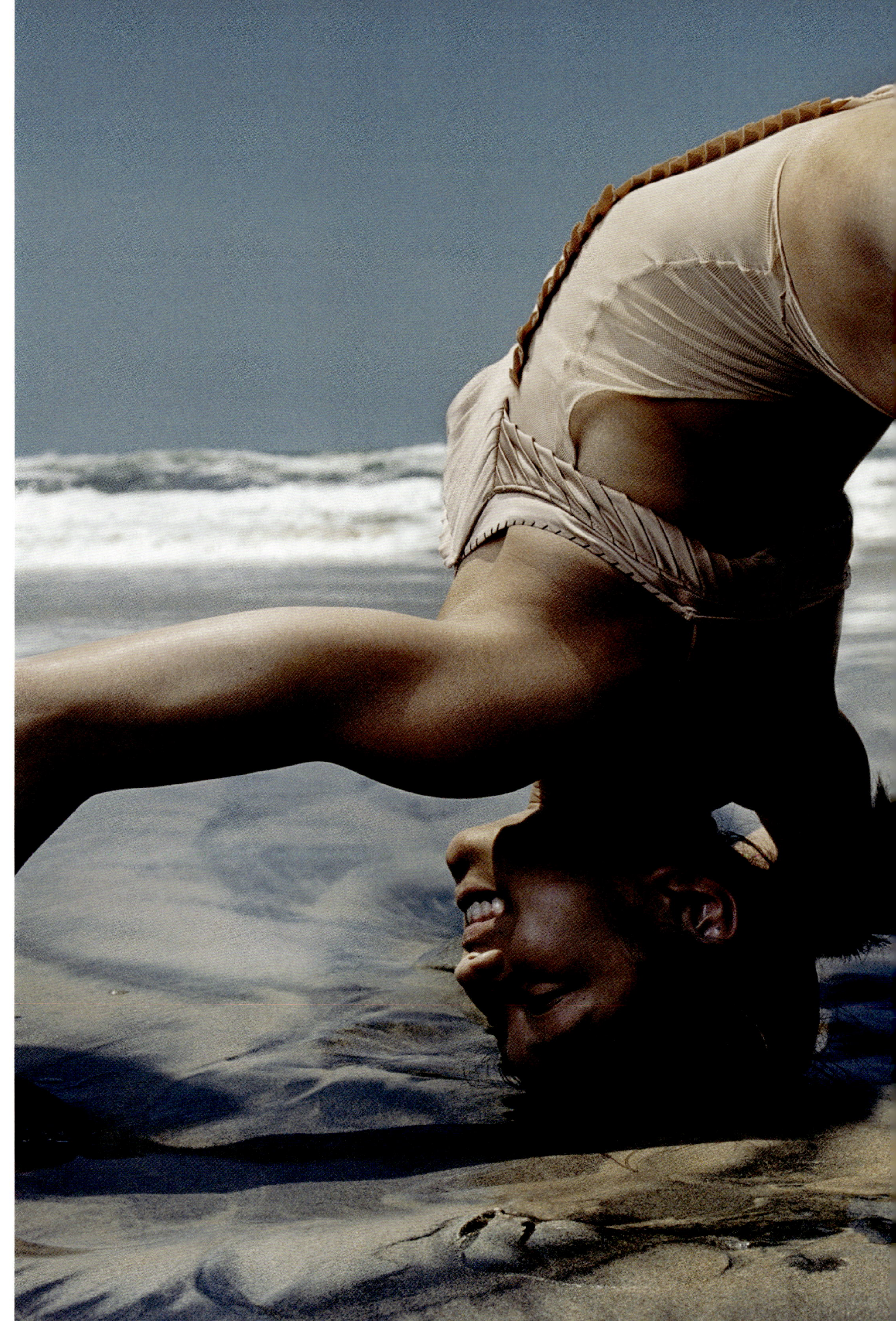

Allyse Ishino,
XXVIII Summer Olympics
US women's gymnastic team,
San Diego, California, 2004

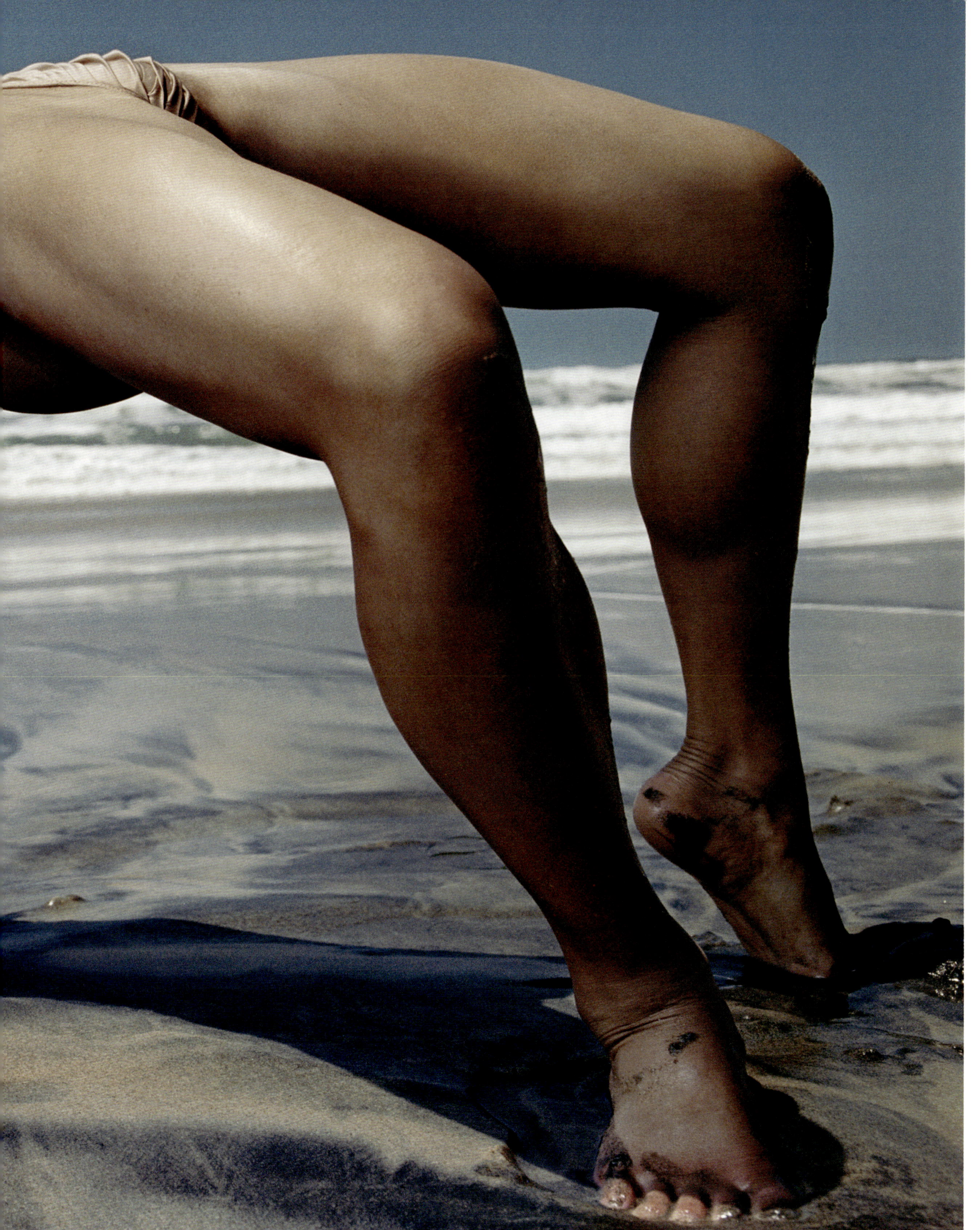

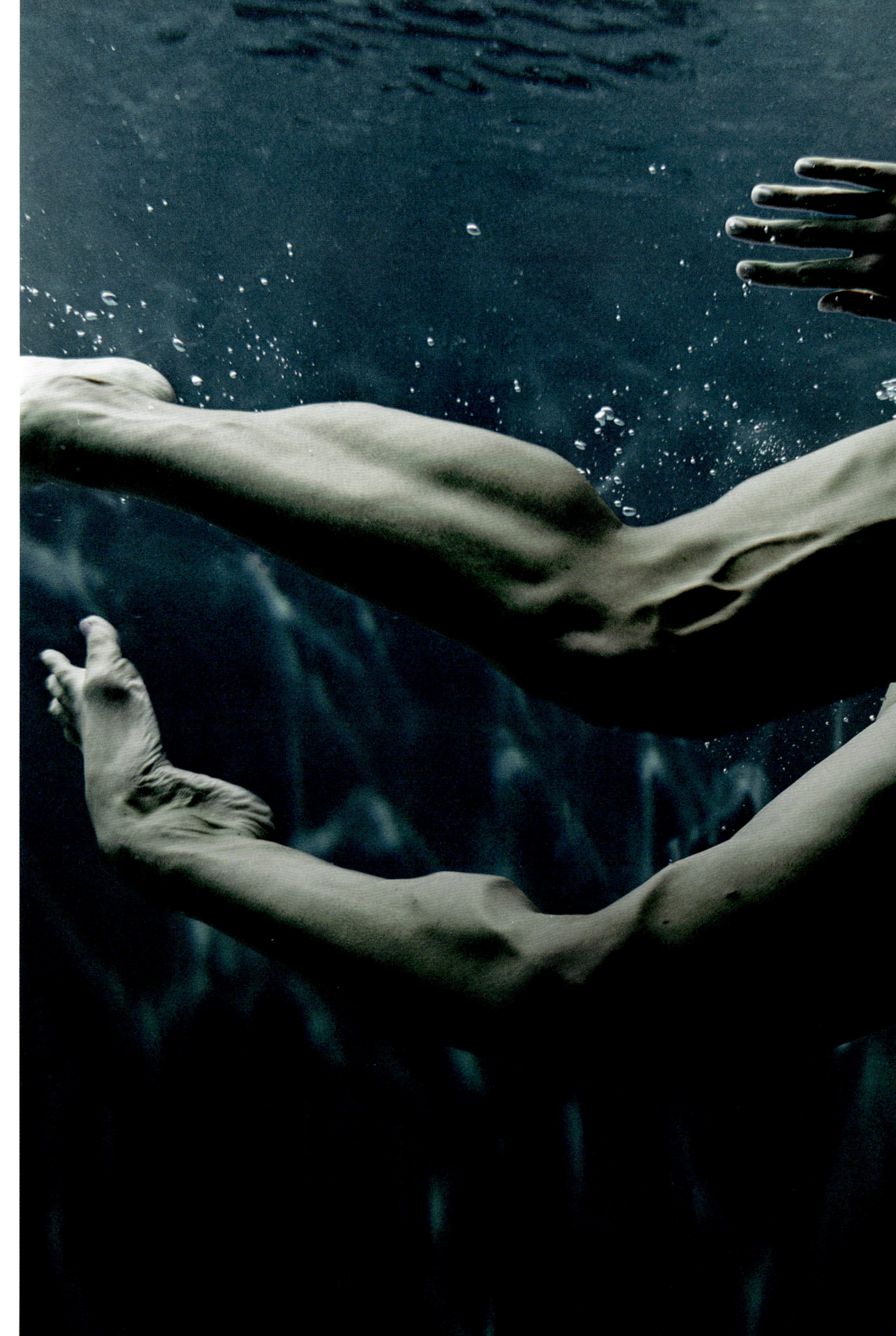

Natalie Coughlin,
XXVIII Summer Olympics
US women's swimming team
gold medalist, Los Angeles, 2004

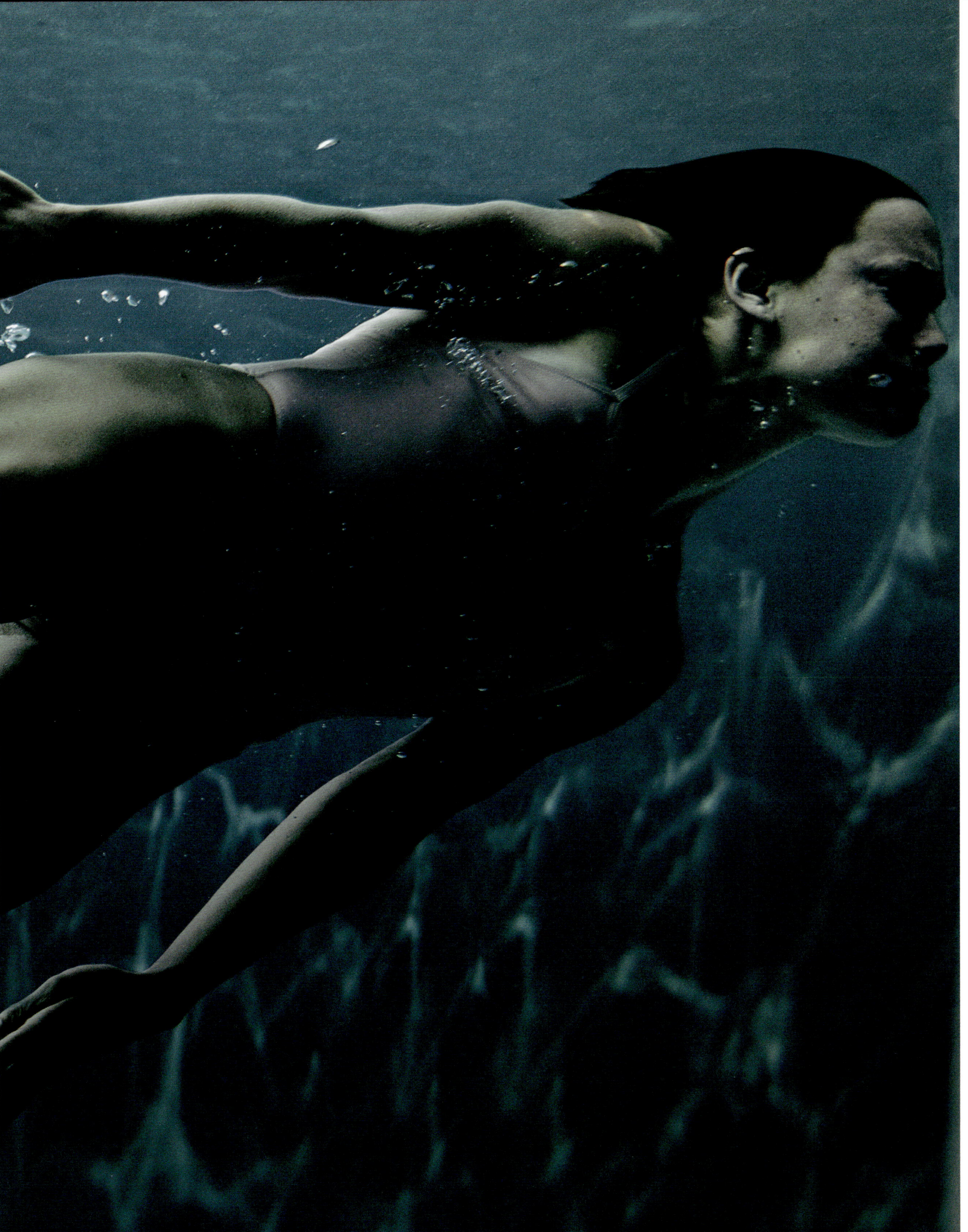

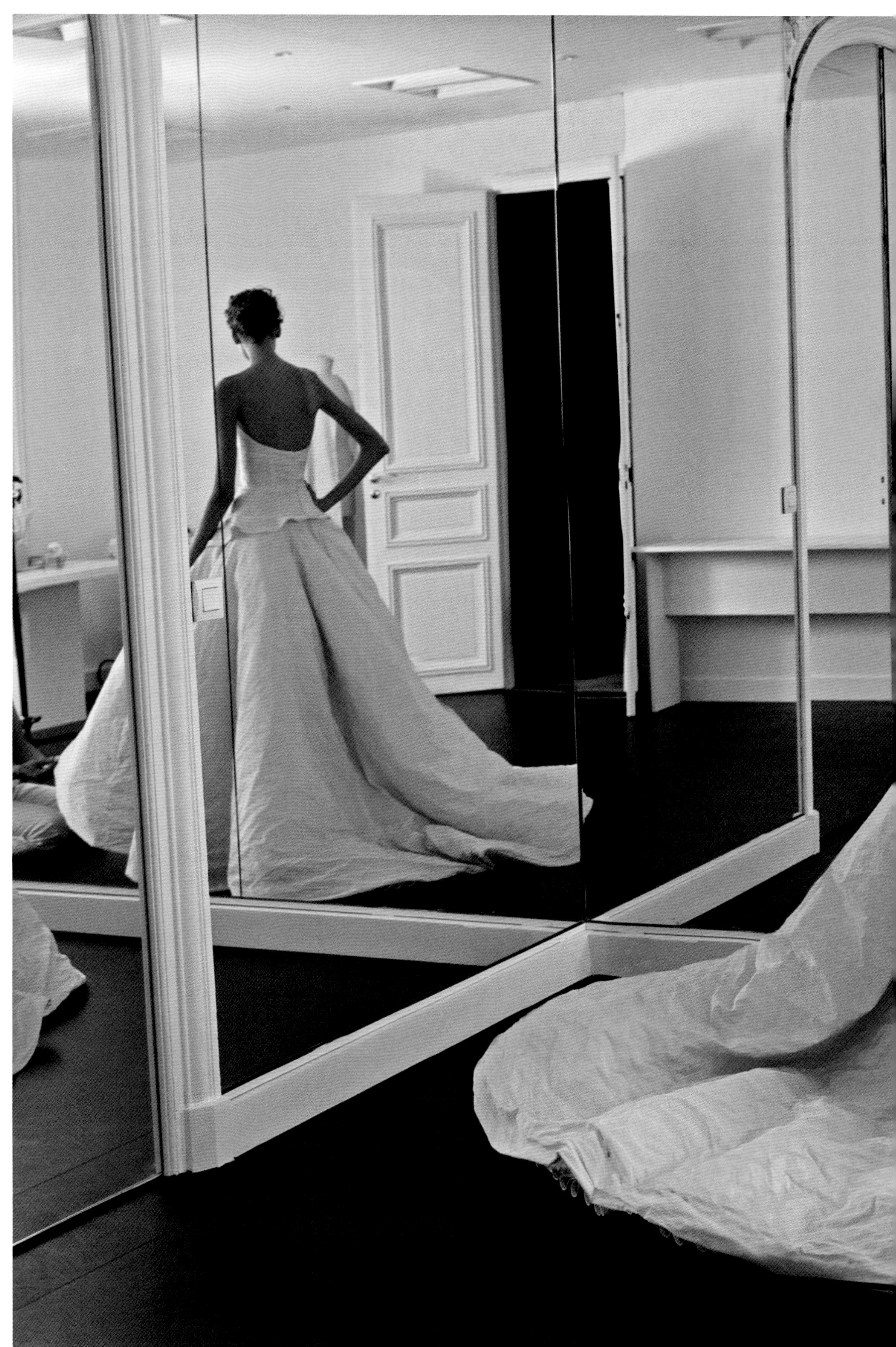

Olivier Theyskens, Paris, 2004

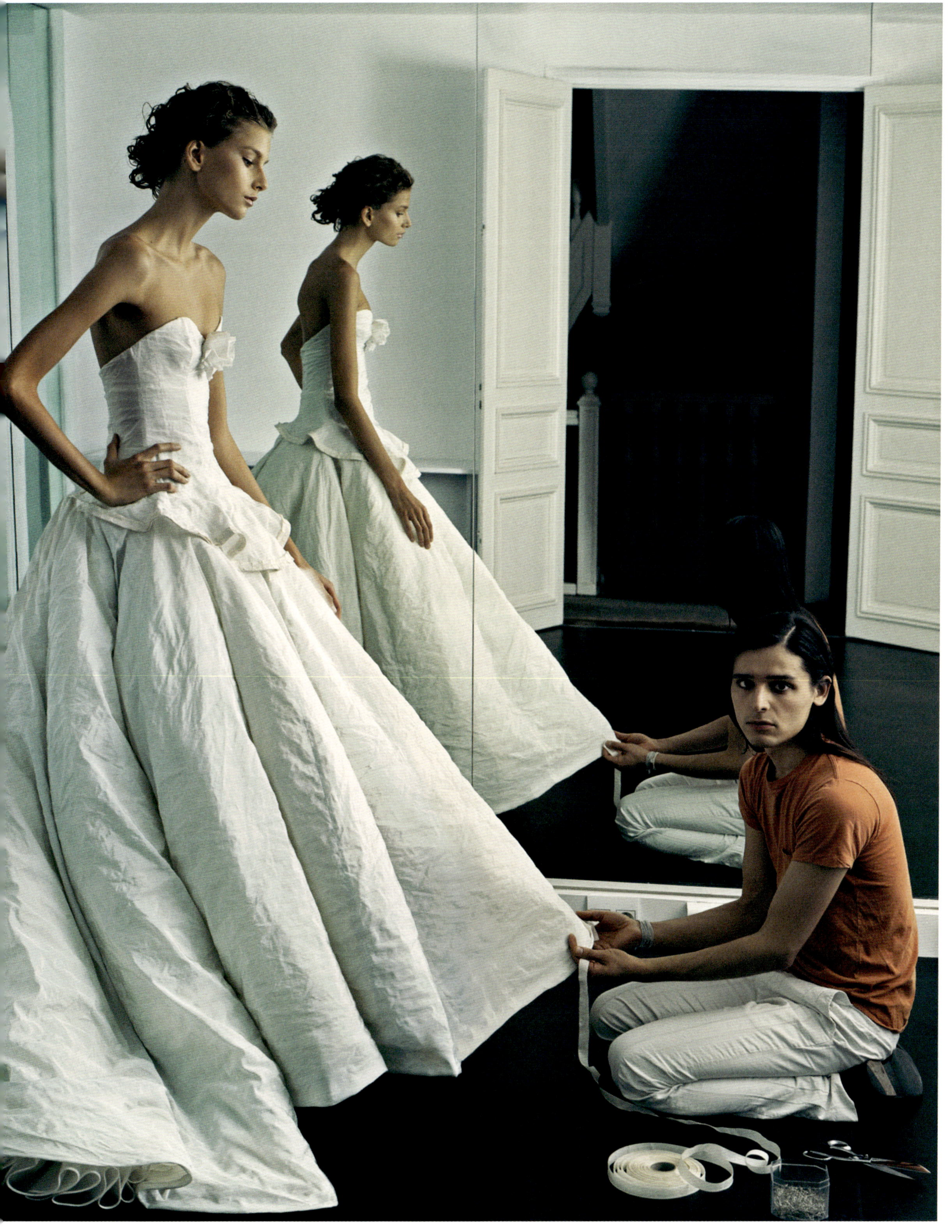

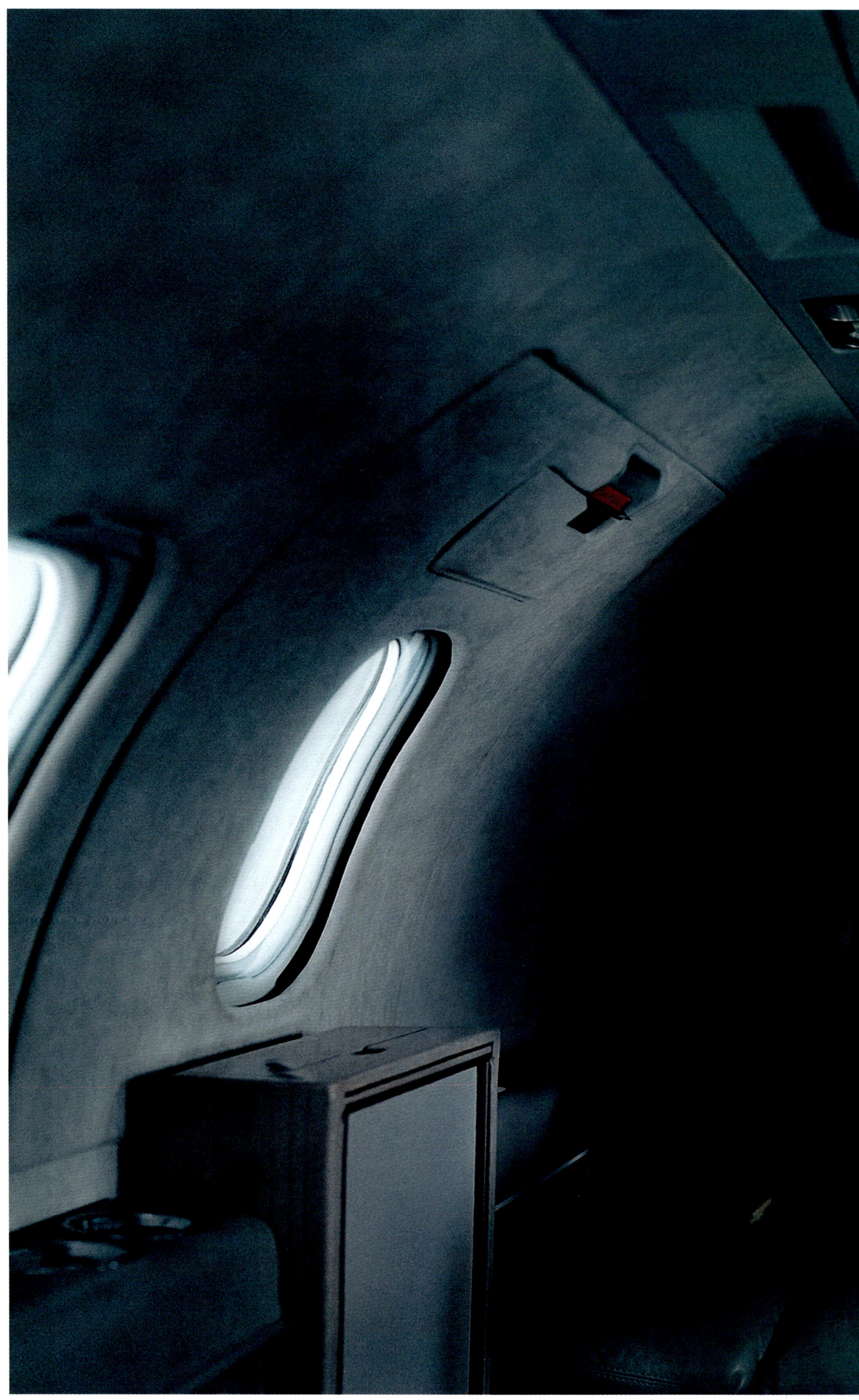

Jil Sander,
Teterboro Airport,
New Jersey, 1996

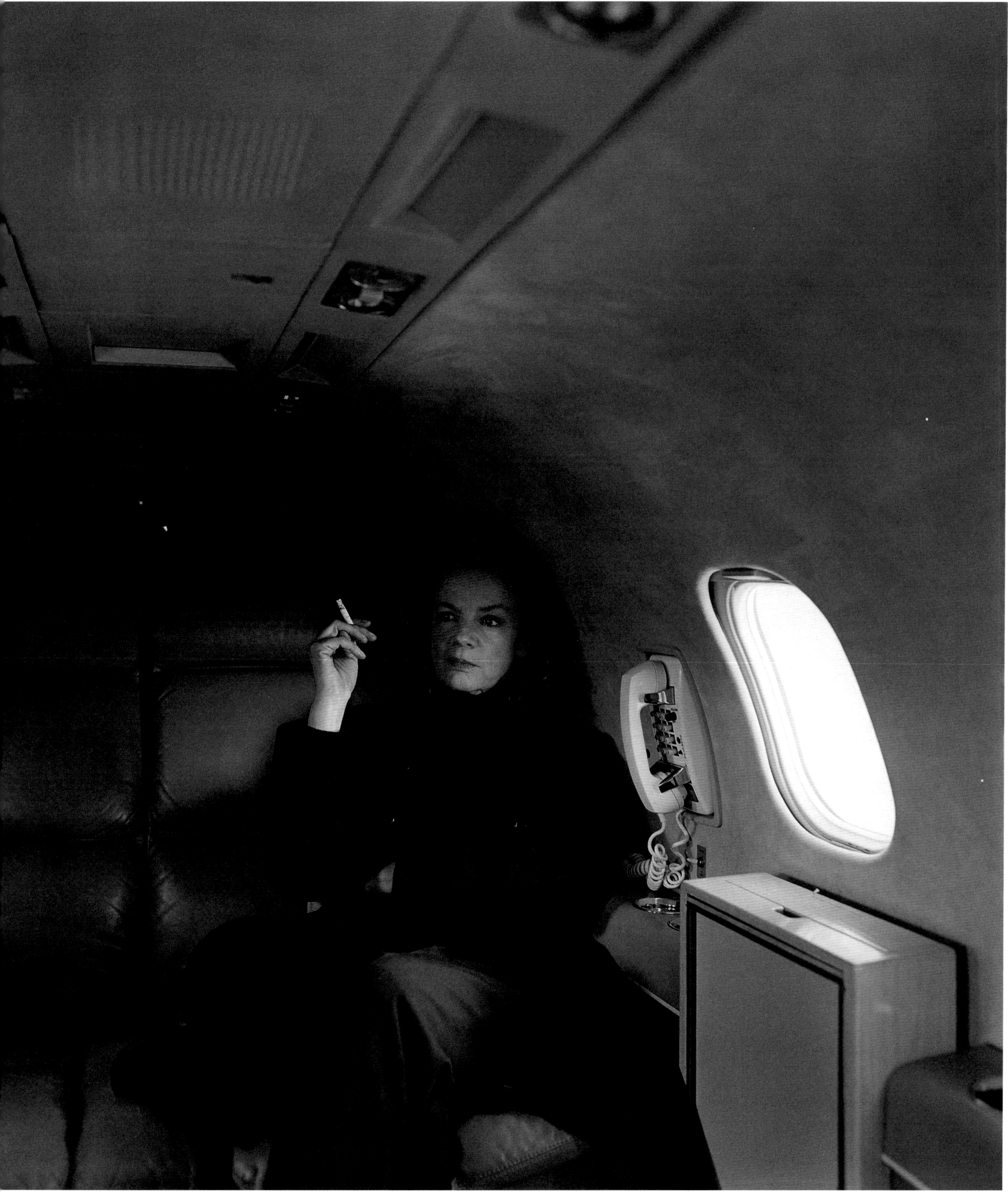

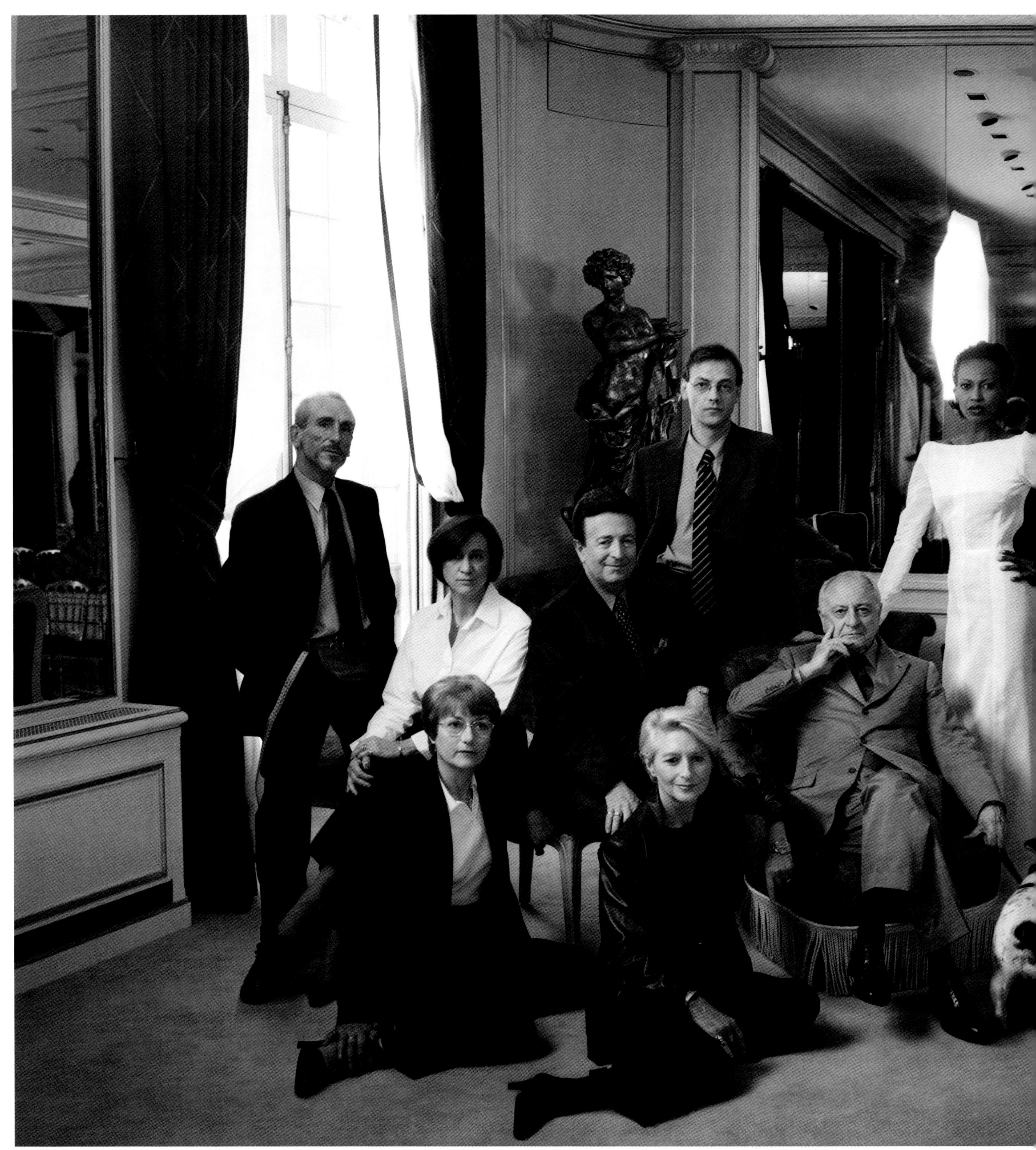

Yves Saint Laurent with M. Alain, Mme. Georgette, Mme. Colette, M. Jean-Pierre, M. Philippe, Mme. Fréderique, Pierre Bergé, Amalia, Catherine Deneuve, Loulou de la Falaise, Anne-Marie Muñoz, and Betty Catroux, Yves Saint Laurent Haute Couture House, Paris, 2000

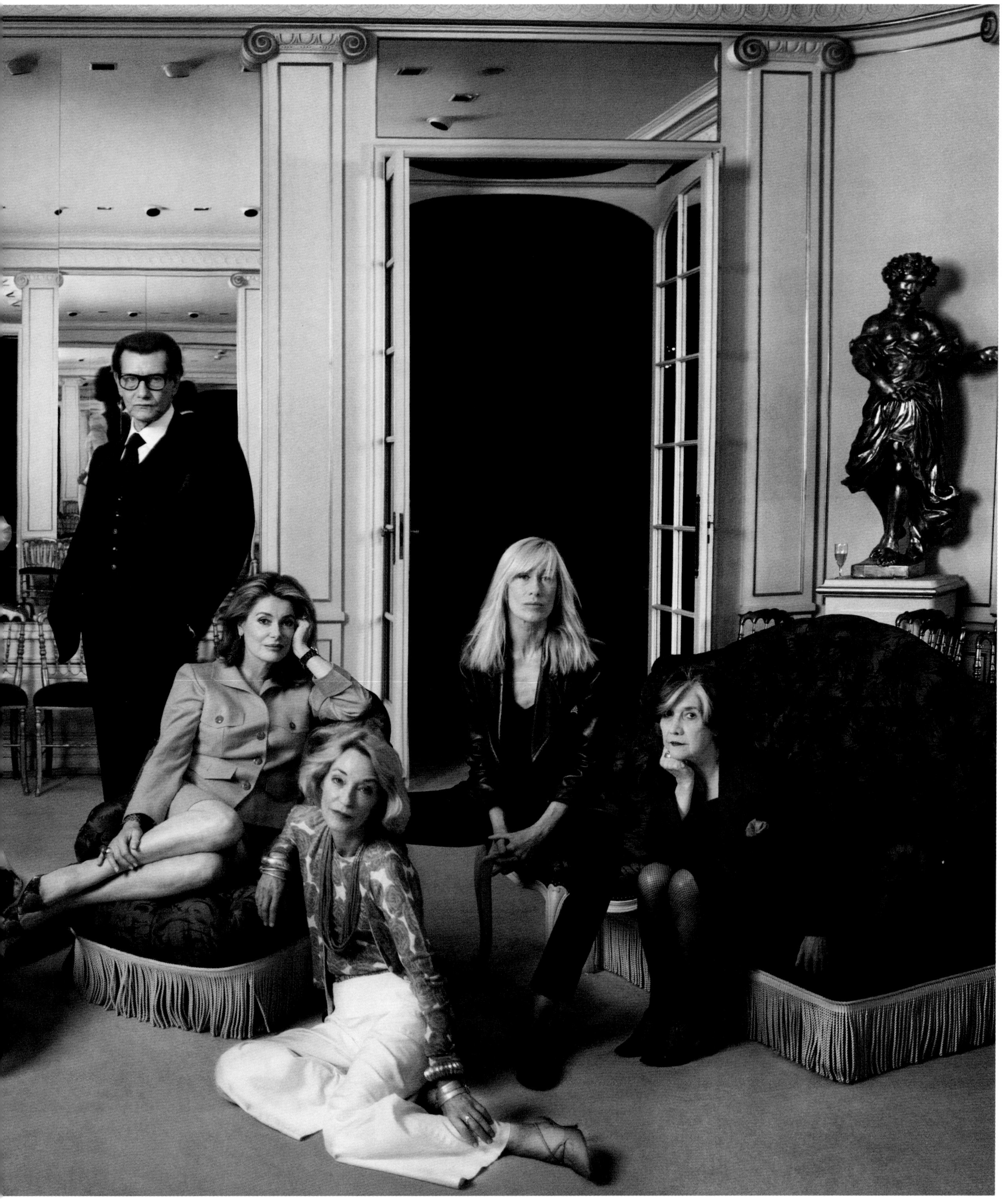

Seduction was the theme of *Dangerous Liaisons: Fashion and Furniture in the Eighteenth Century*, an exhibition curated by Harold Koda and Andrew Bolton for the Metropolitan Museum of Art's Costume Institute in the spring of 2004. Mannequins in opulent dresses were posed in tableaux based on famous paintings of the period. The sexually charged scenes, set in rooms filled with rococo and neoclassical furniture and art, evoked the decadence and excesses of the French court in the years before the Revolution.

The Met's concept for its show was melded with the spring couture collections for Annie's shoot. Gisele Bündchen, Karen Elson, Daria Werbowy, Gemma Ward, Lily Cole, Gérard Depardieu, Louis Garrel, and Hugh Dancy were photographed on locations an hour or so north of Paris—in Noailles and at the Château de Chaalis, which was a magnificent abbey in the fourteenth century and later became one of France's most imposing private homes. The château's largest room was packed with wigs and clothes and hair-and-makeup stations. The billiards room was set up for a scene in which the women would be playing pool and people would be flirting. The models were all wearing enormous Galliano dresses and had towering hairdos, and when they tried to come in, they couldn't fit through the door.

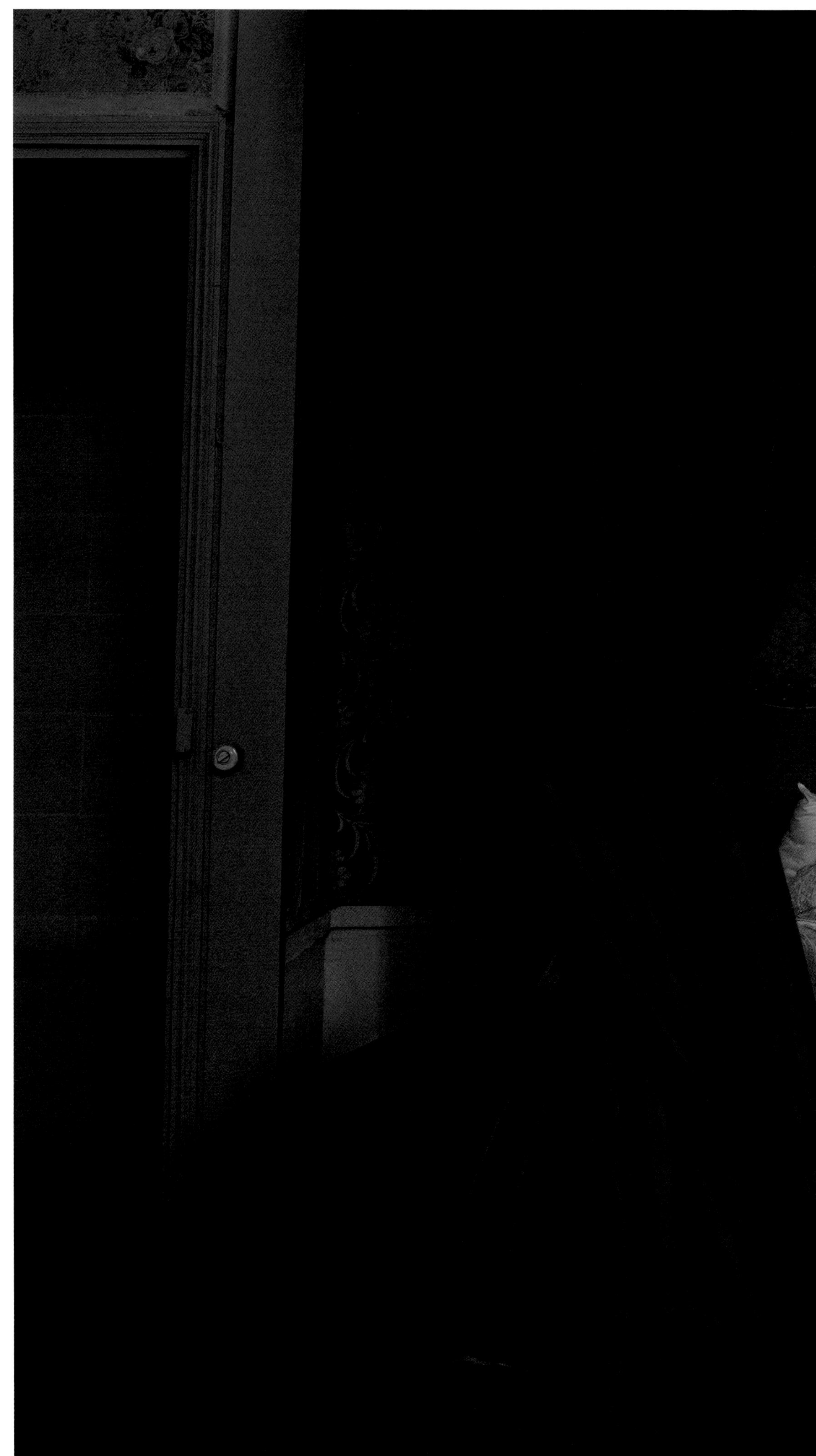

Gisele Bündchen and
Gérard Depardieu,
Noailles, France, 2004

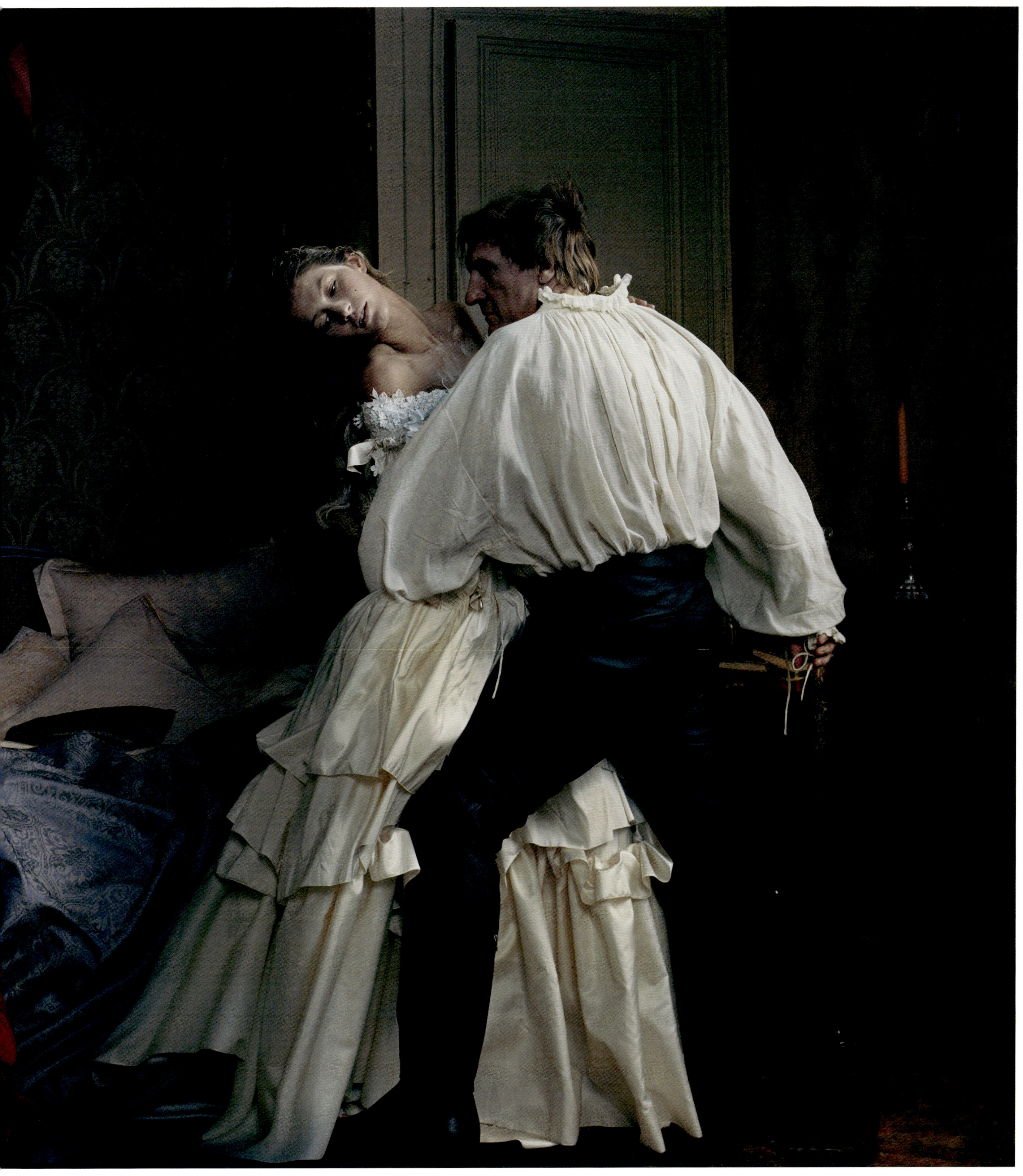

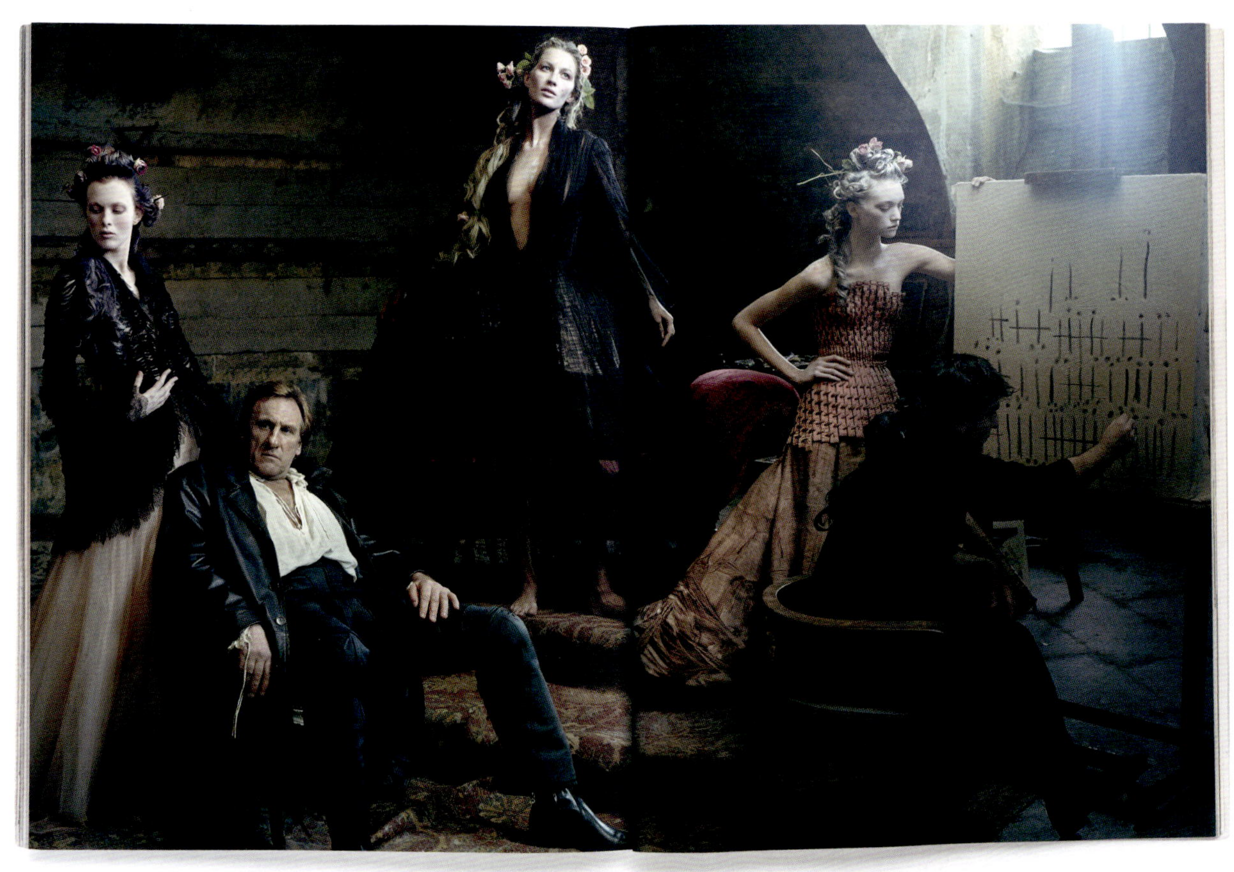

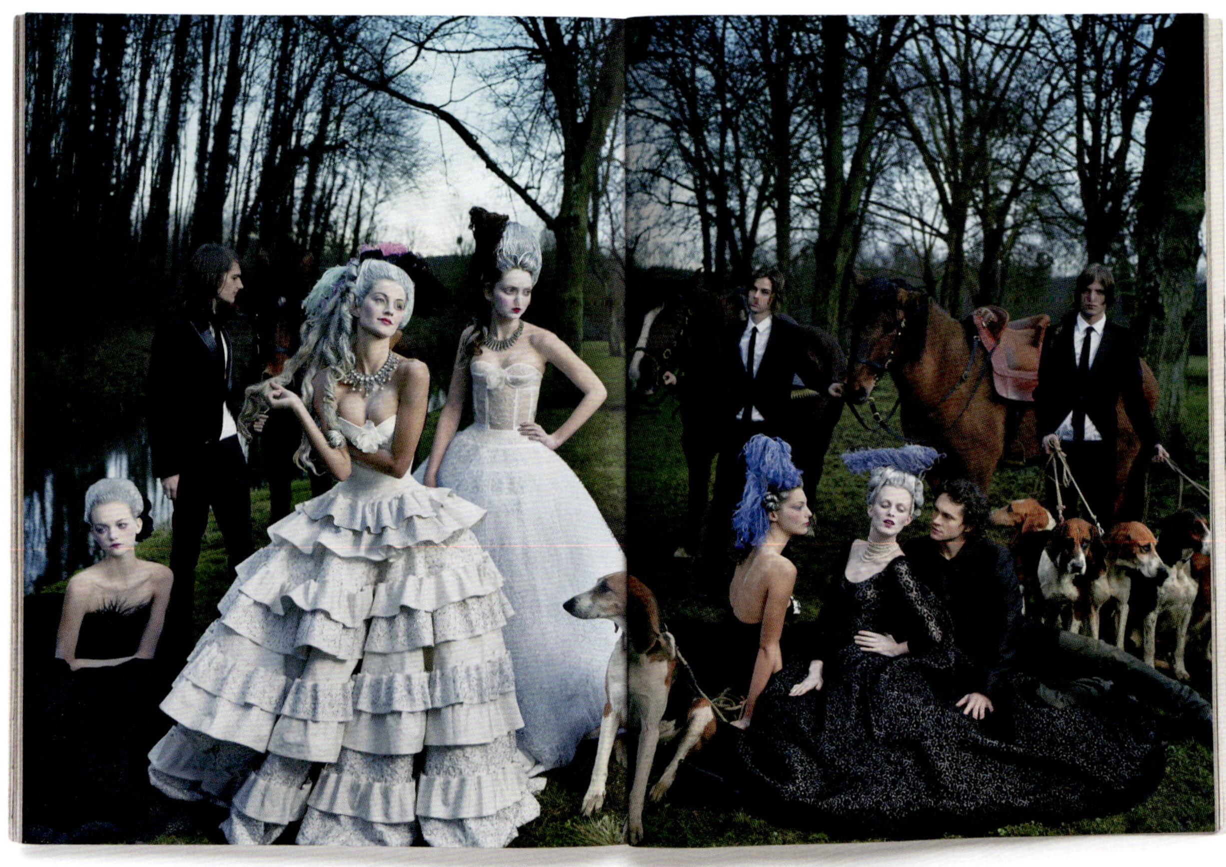

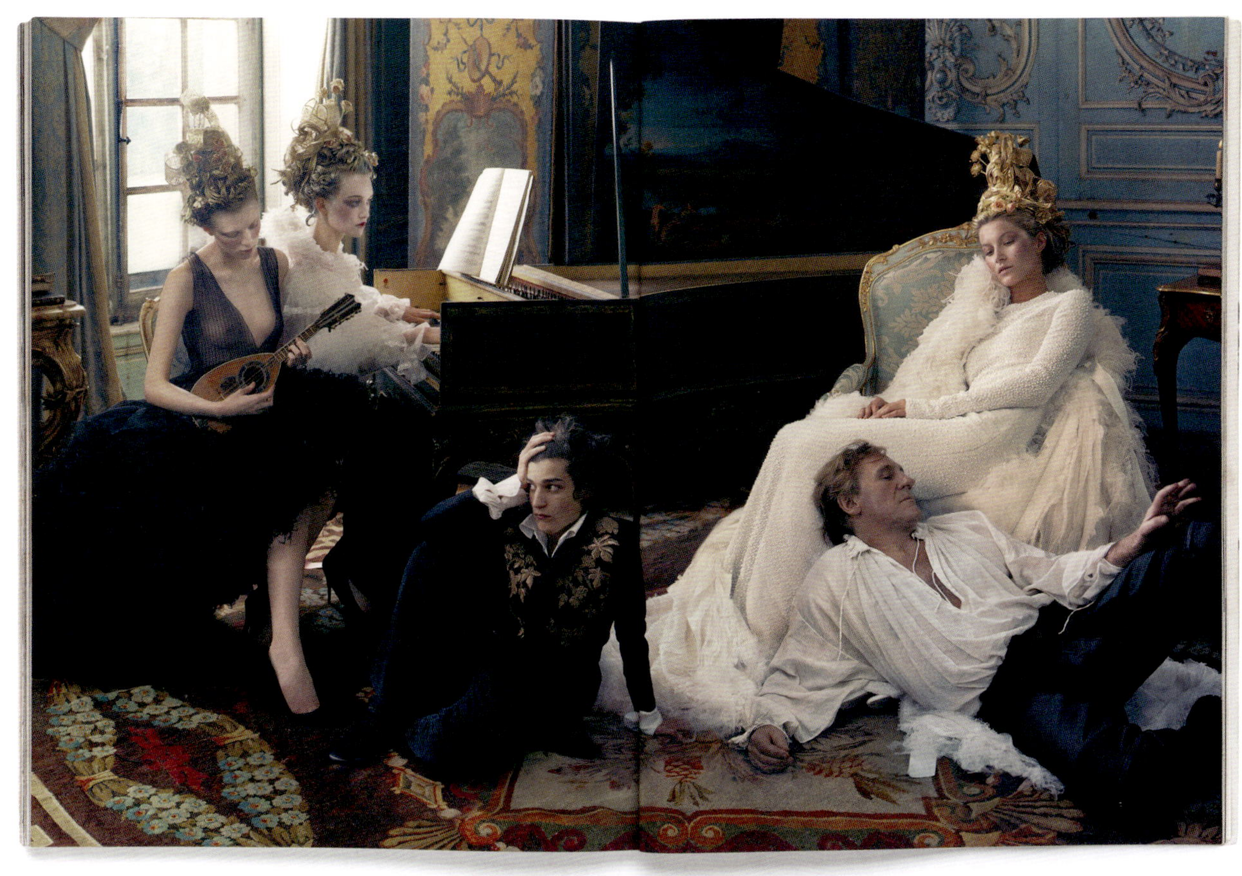

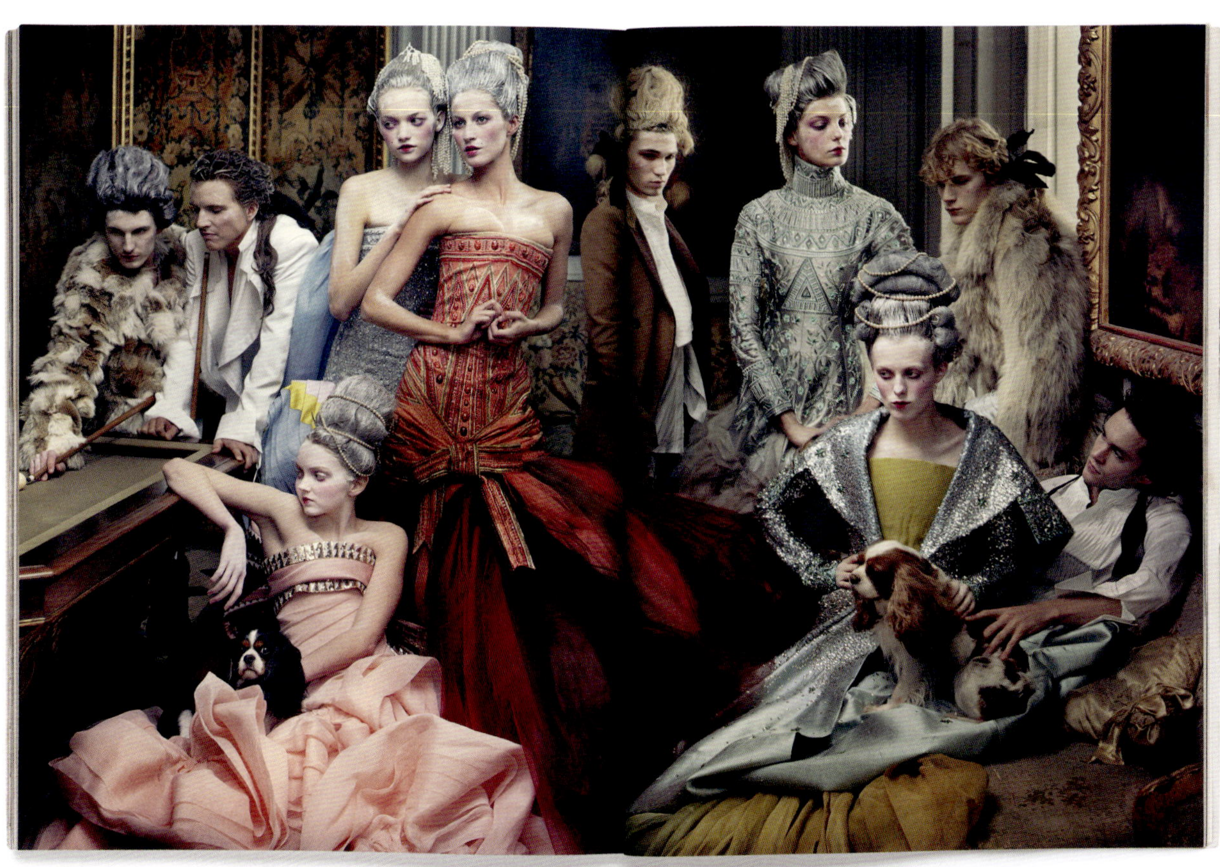

The *Wizard of Oz* story was made with a distinguished roster of artists. Alba and Francesco Clemente were Auntie Em and Uncle Henry. John Currin said that he wanted to be the Tin Man. Brice Marden was cast as the Scarecrow, Kara Walker was Glinda the Good Witch, Jasper Johns the Cowardly Lion, Chuck Close the Wizard, Kiki Smith the Wicked Witch. Keira Knightley was Dorothy. The Penn State Marching Band was enlisted to troop up and down the yellow brick road.

For Jeff Koons's performance as the Flying Monkey, he was covered in gold body makeup, harnessed to huge wings, and hoisted aloft by a crane.

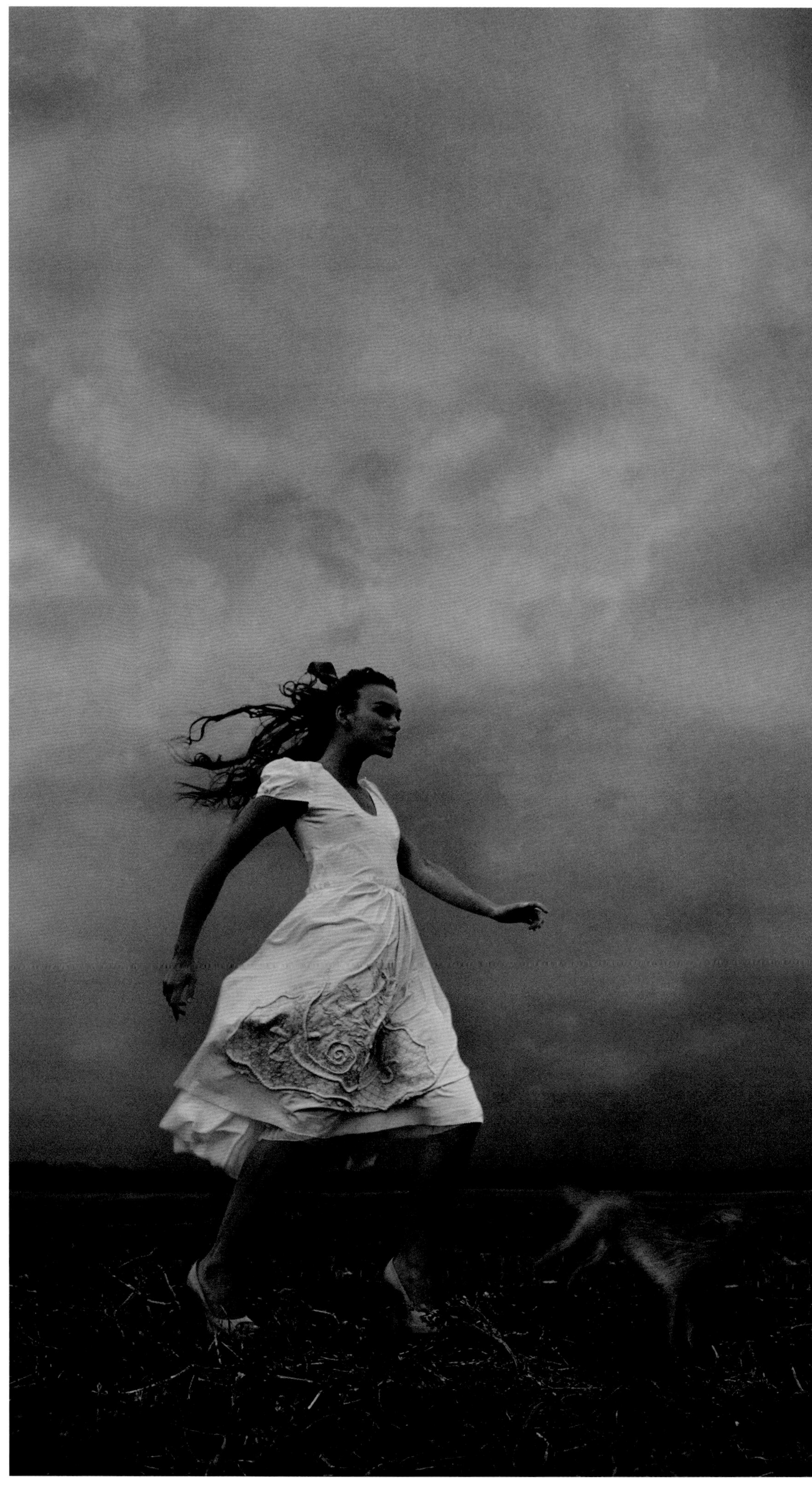

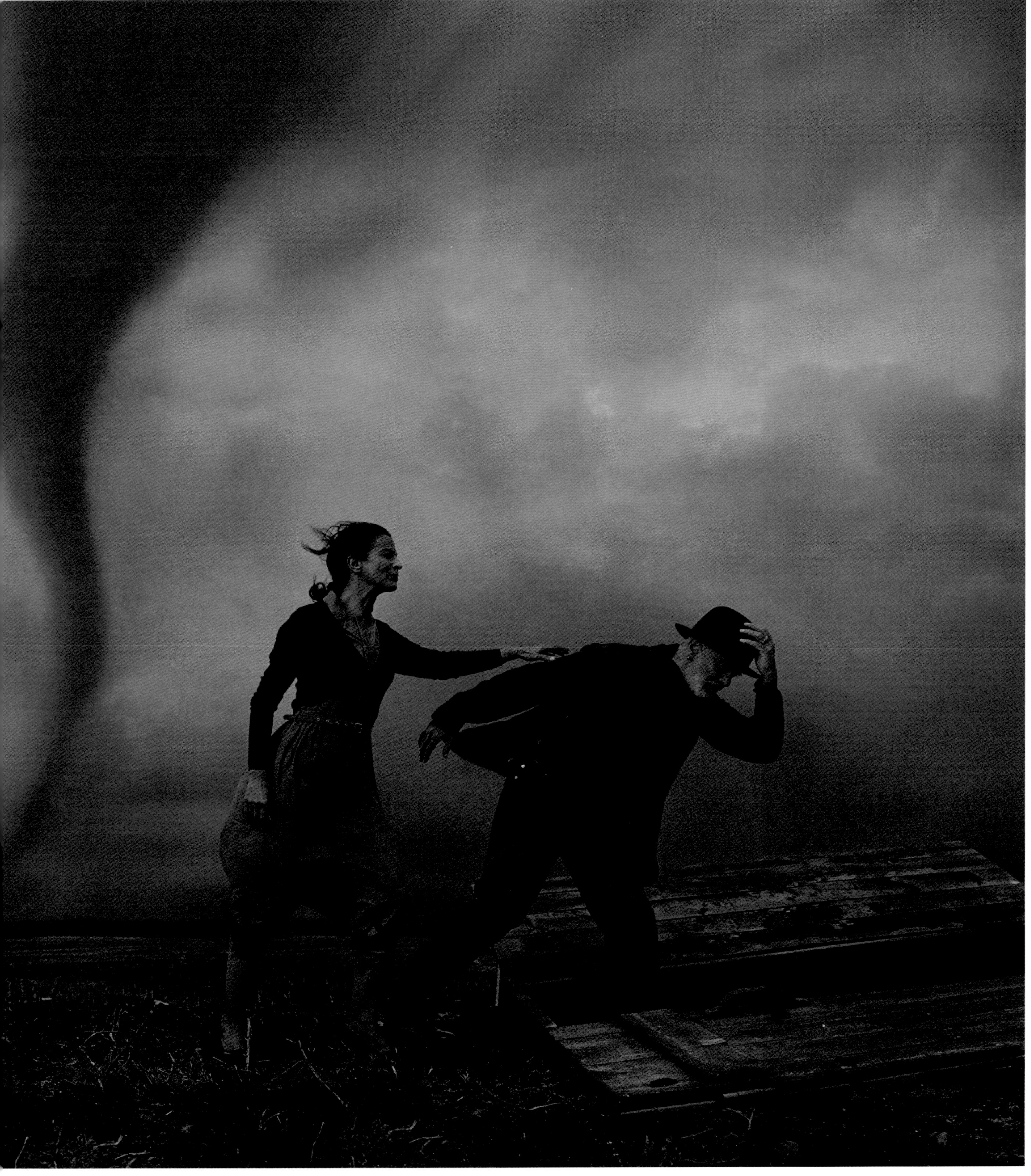

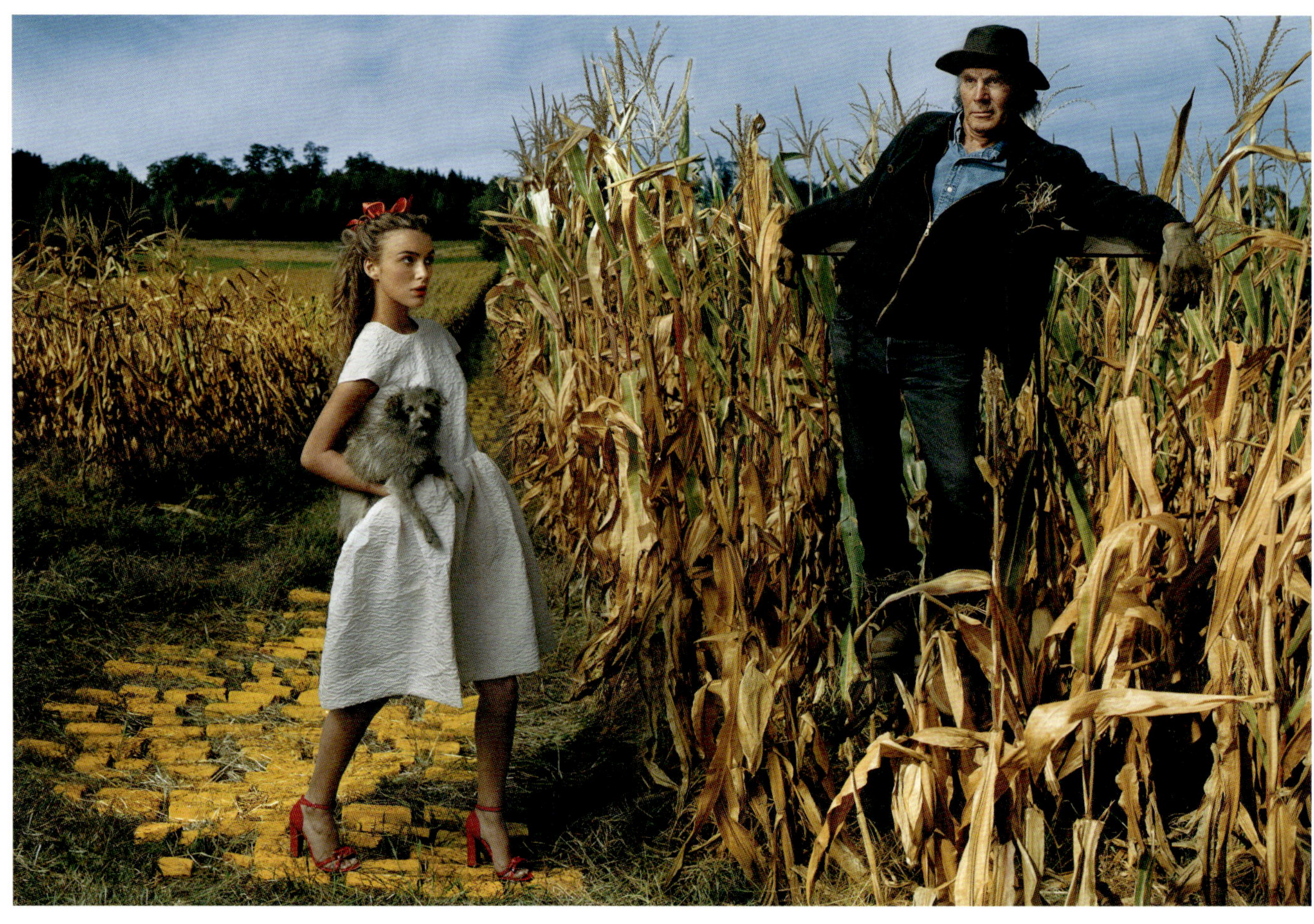

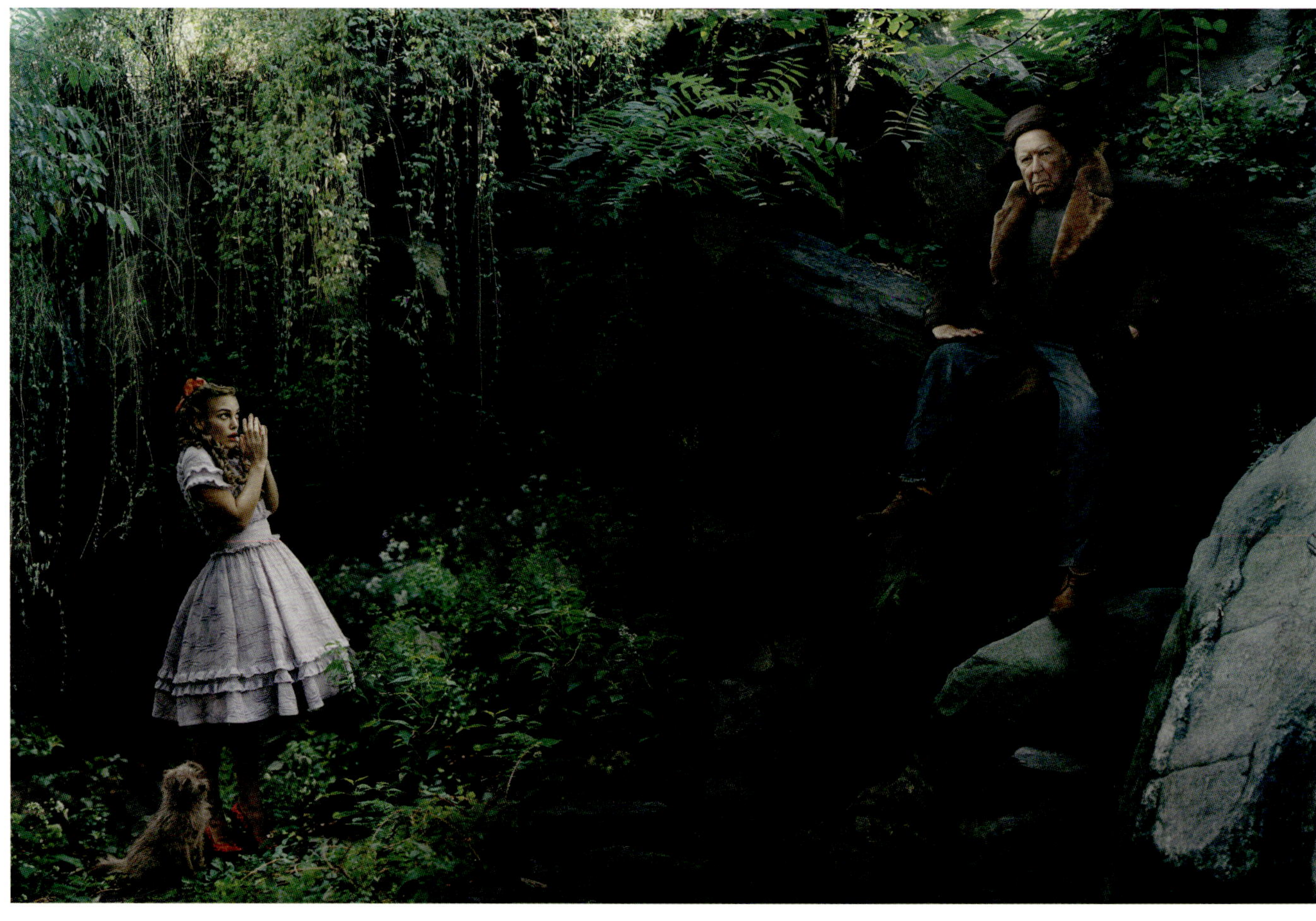

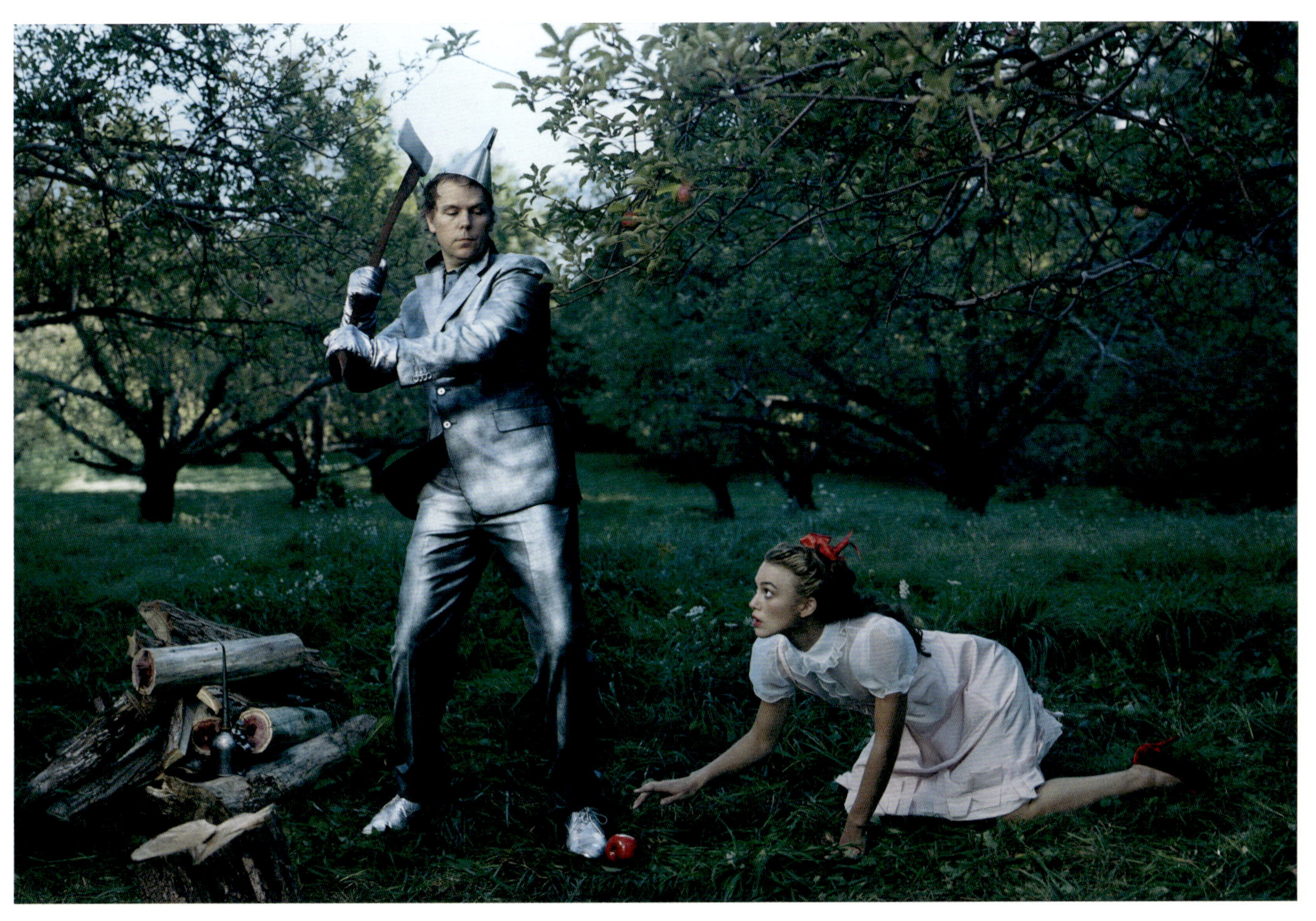

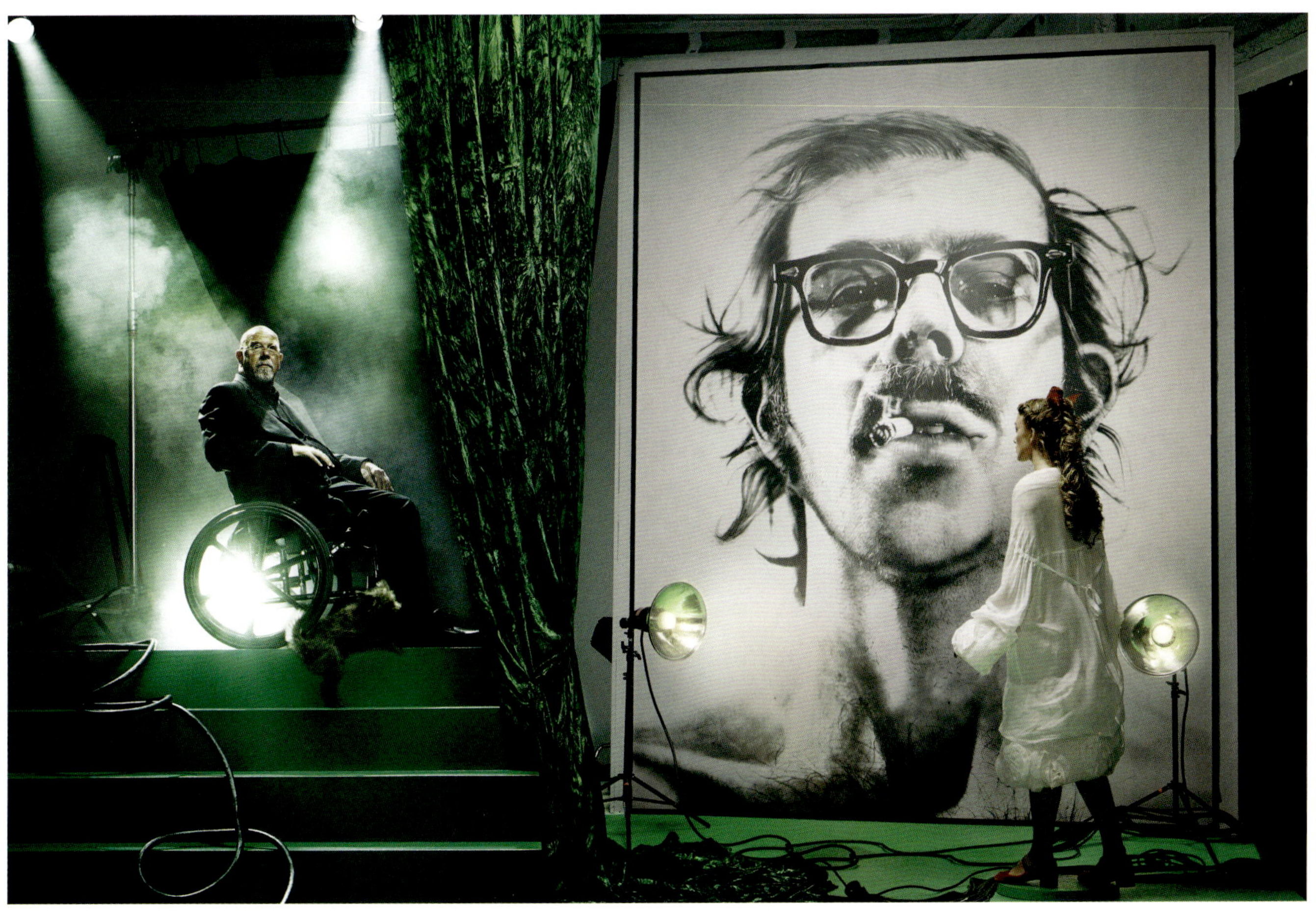

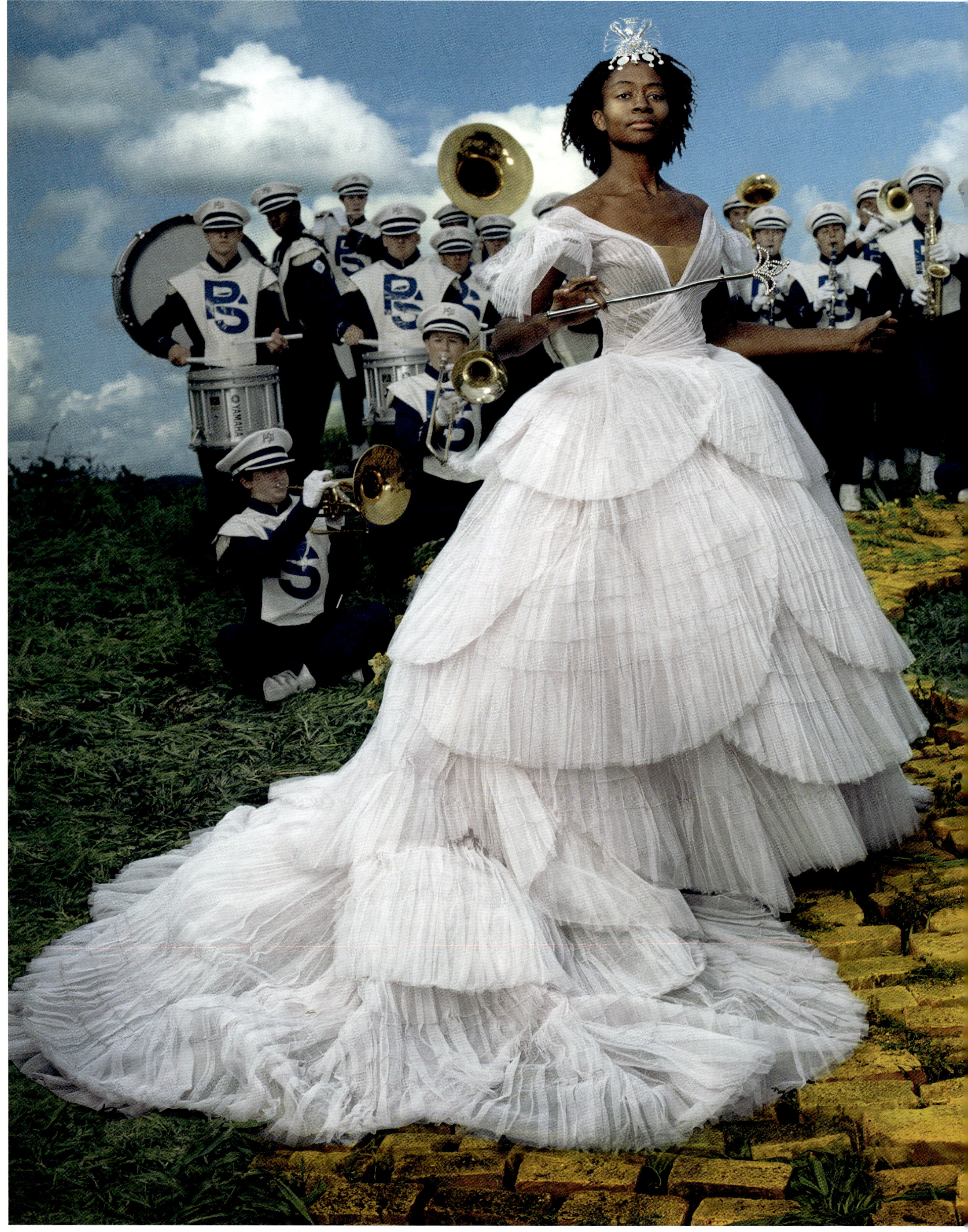
YAMAHA

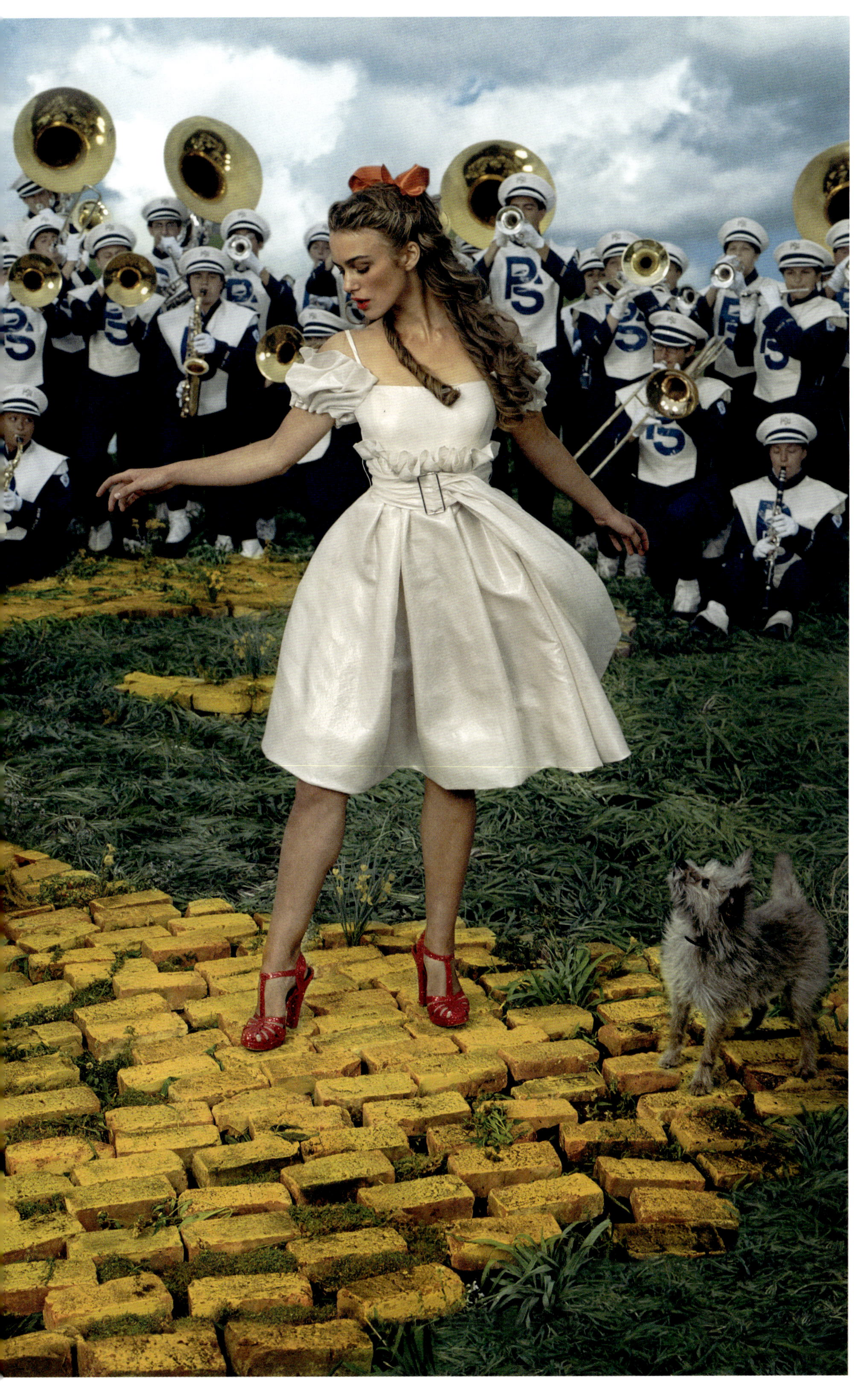

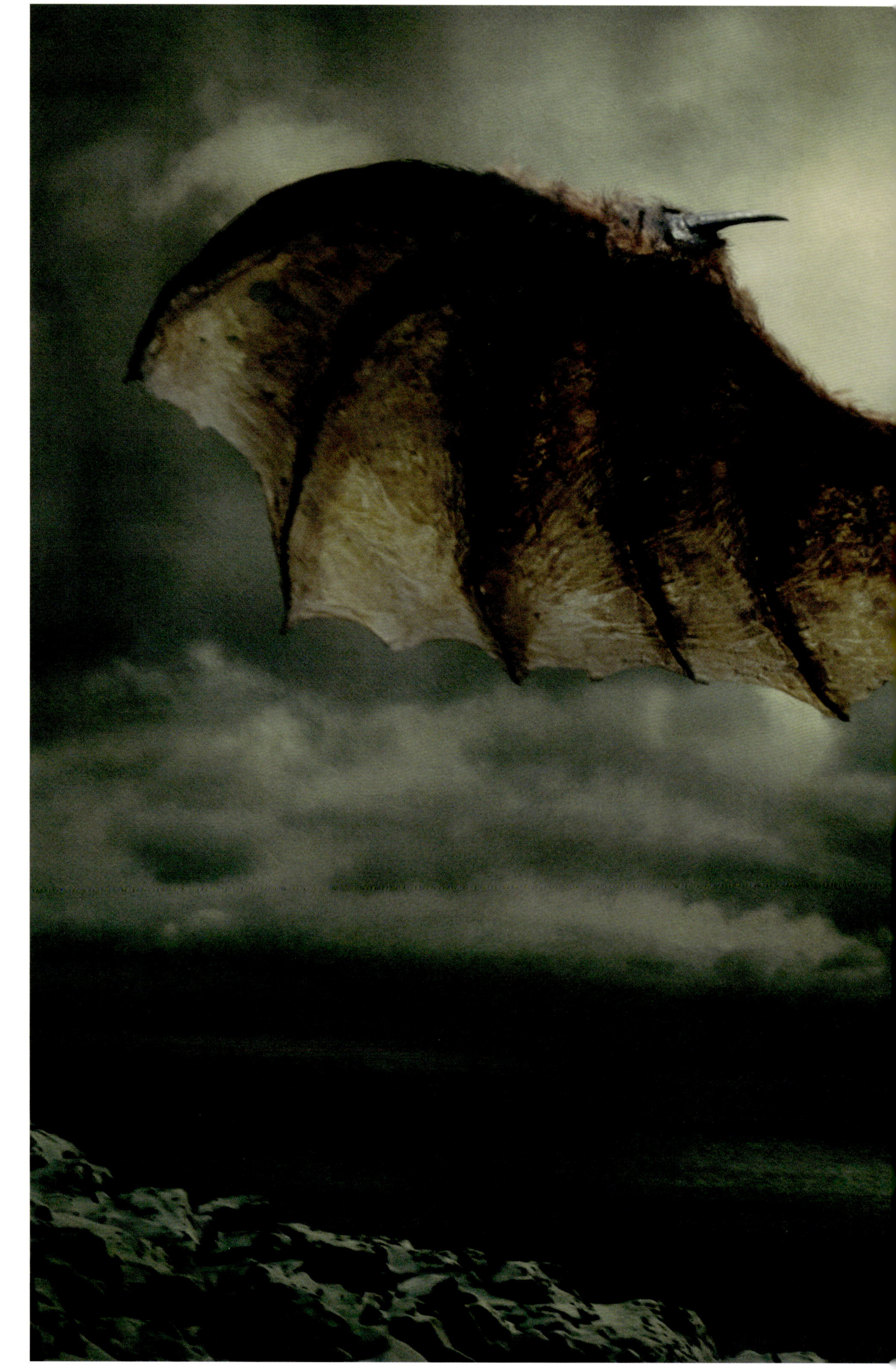

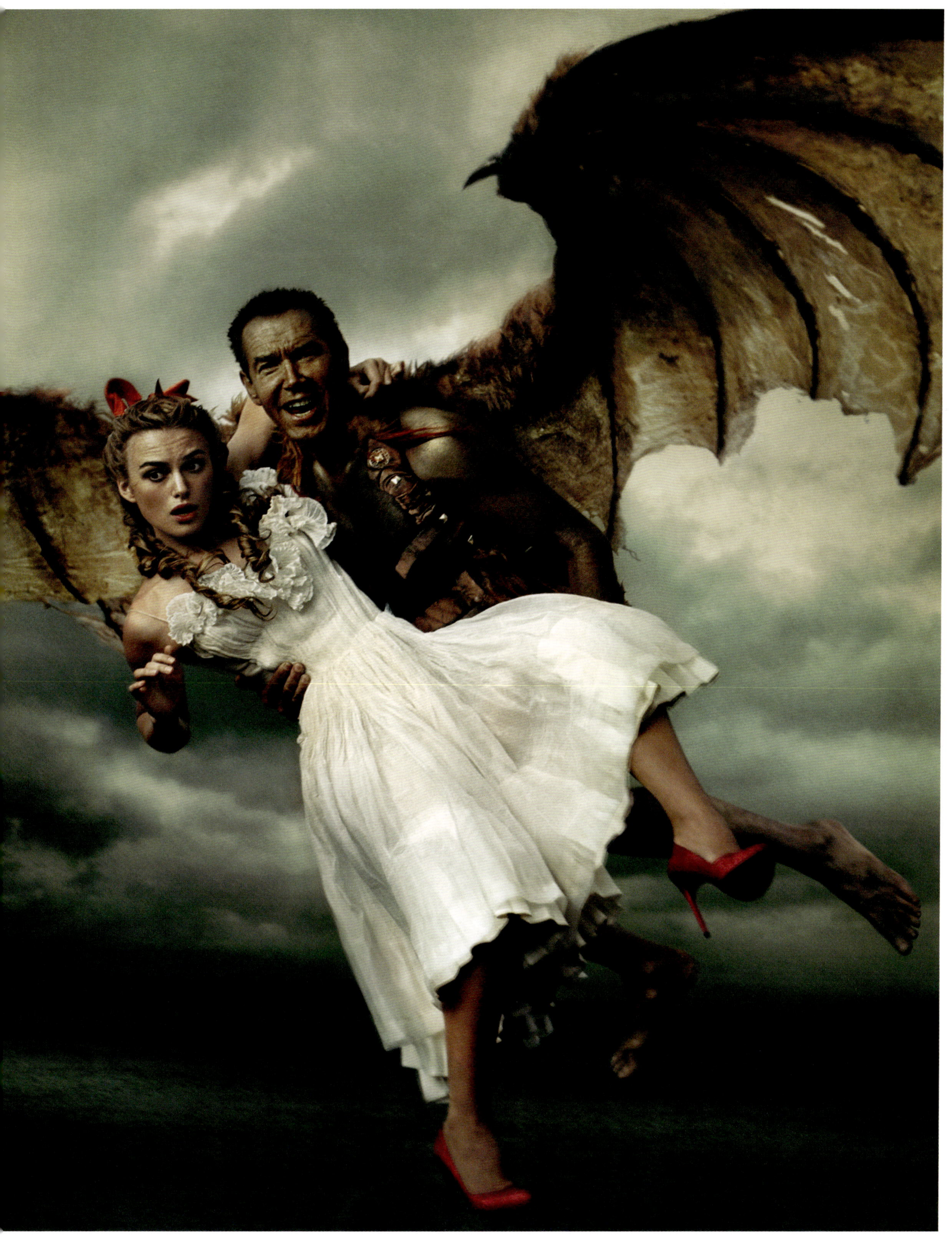

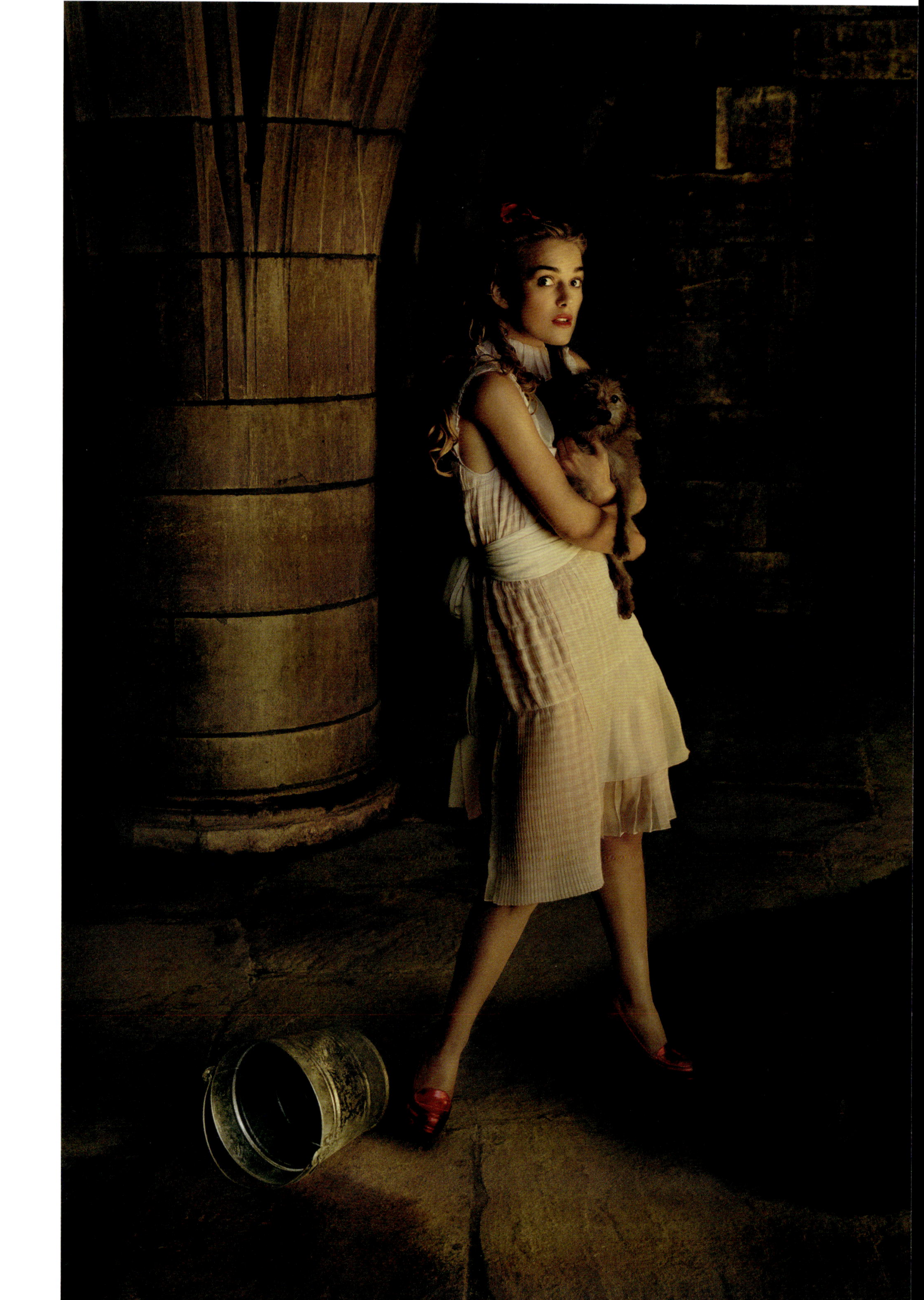

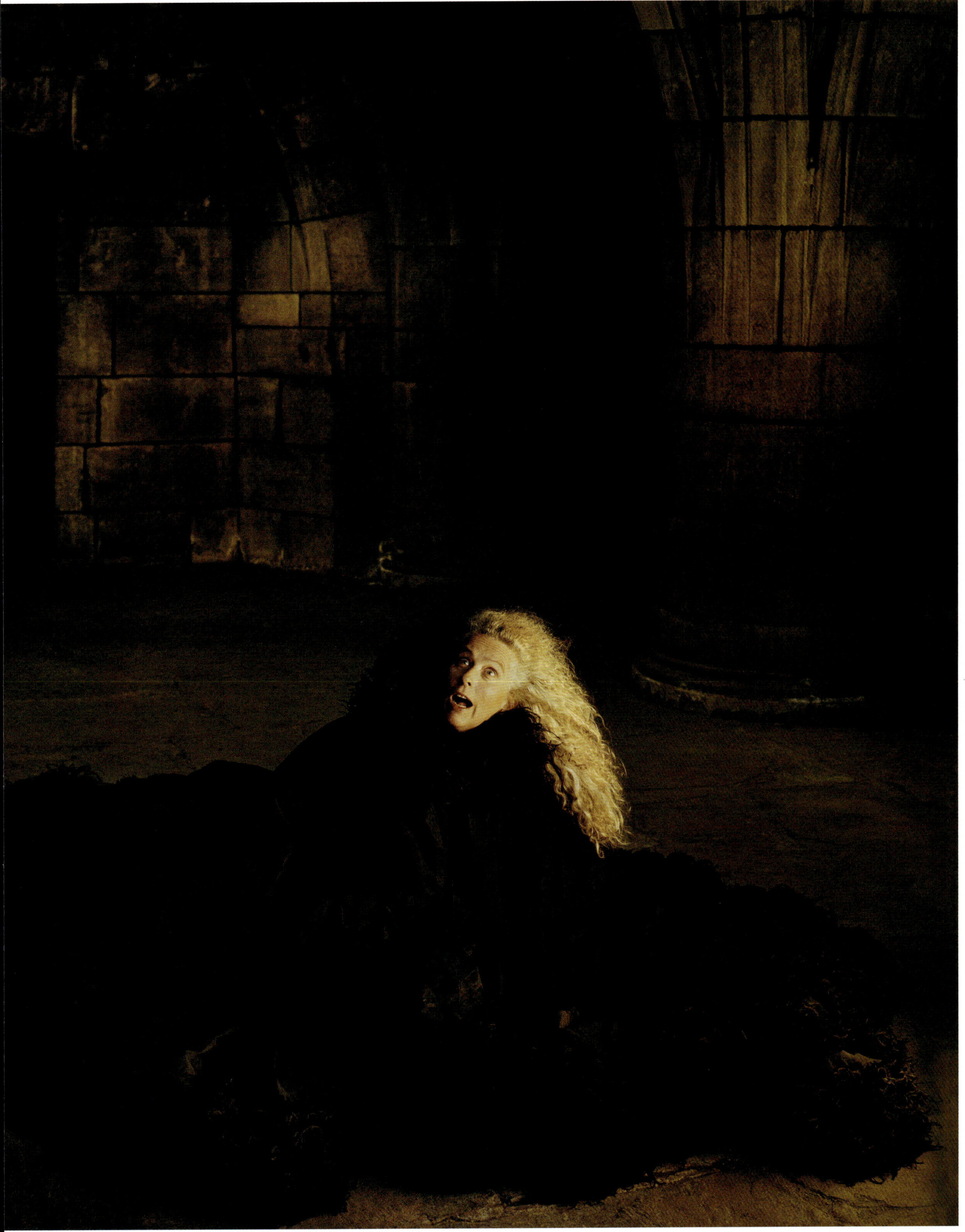

The music world was Annie's primary subject during her early years at *Rolling Stone*. She first photographed Dolly Parton in 1977. Nearly thirty years later, she asked Parton and Steve Earle to come by for a day and sit in on a shoot she did with Joaquin Phoenix and Reese Witherspoon. They had just played Johnny Cash and his wife, June Carter Cash, in the film *Walk the Line*.

The photographs were made at the sprawling wood-and-stone house on the edge of Old Hickory Lake, north of Nashville, where Johnny and June had spent their entire married life. It burned down two years later.

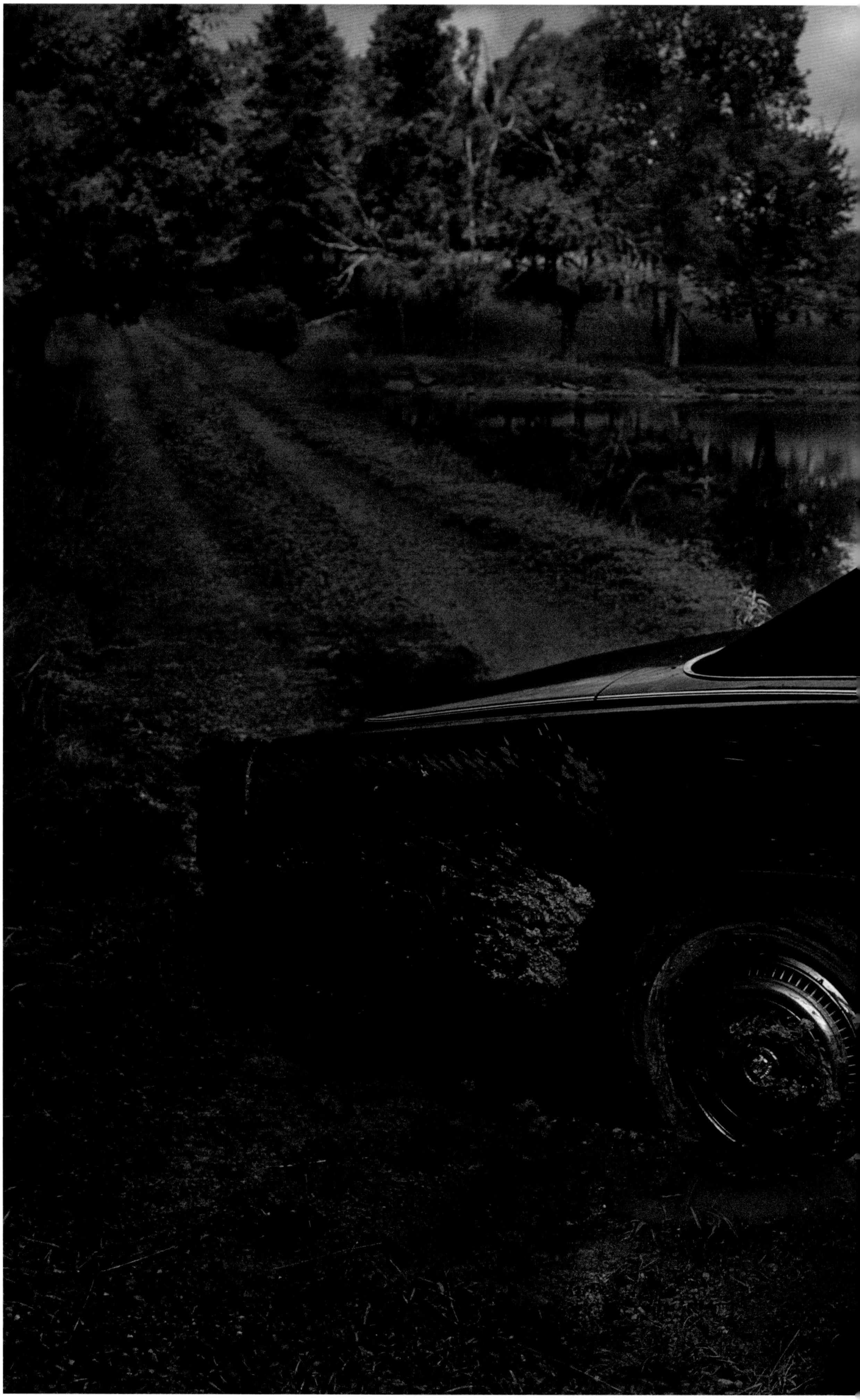

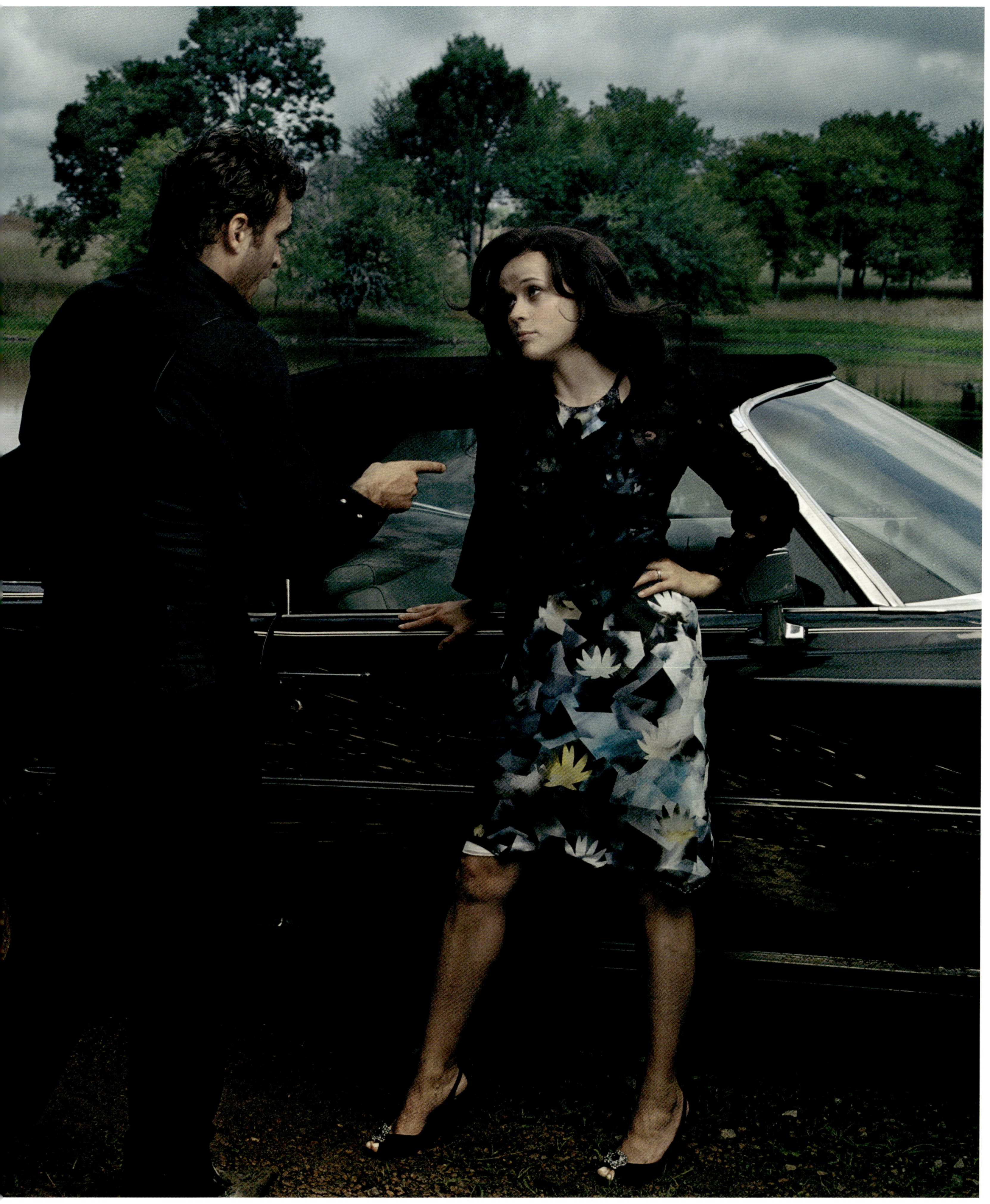

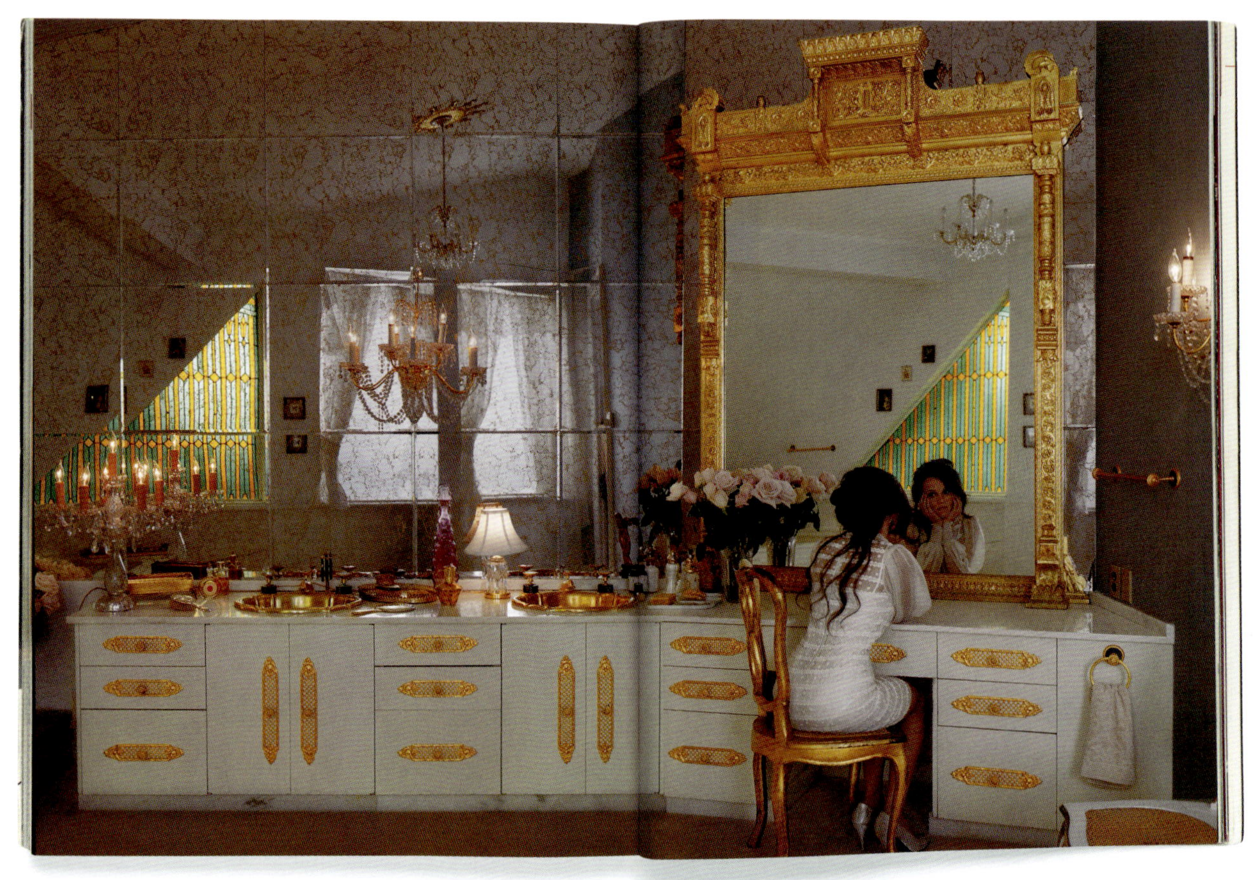

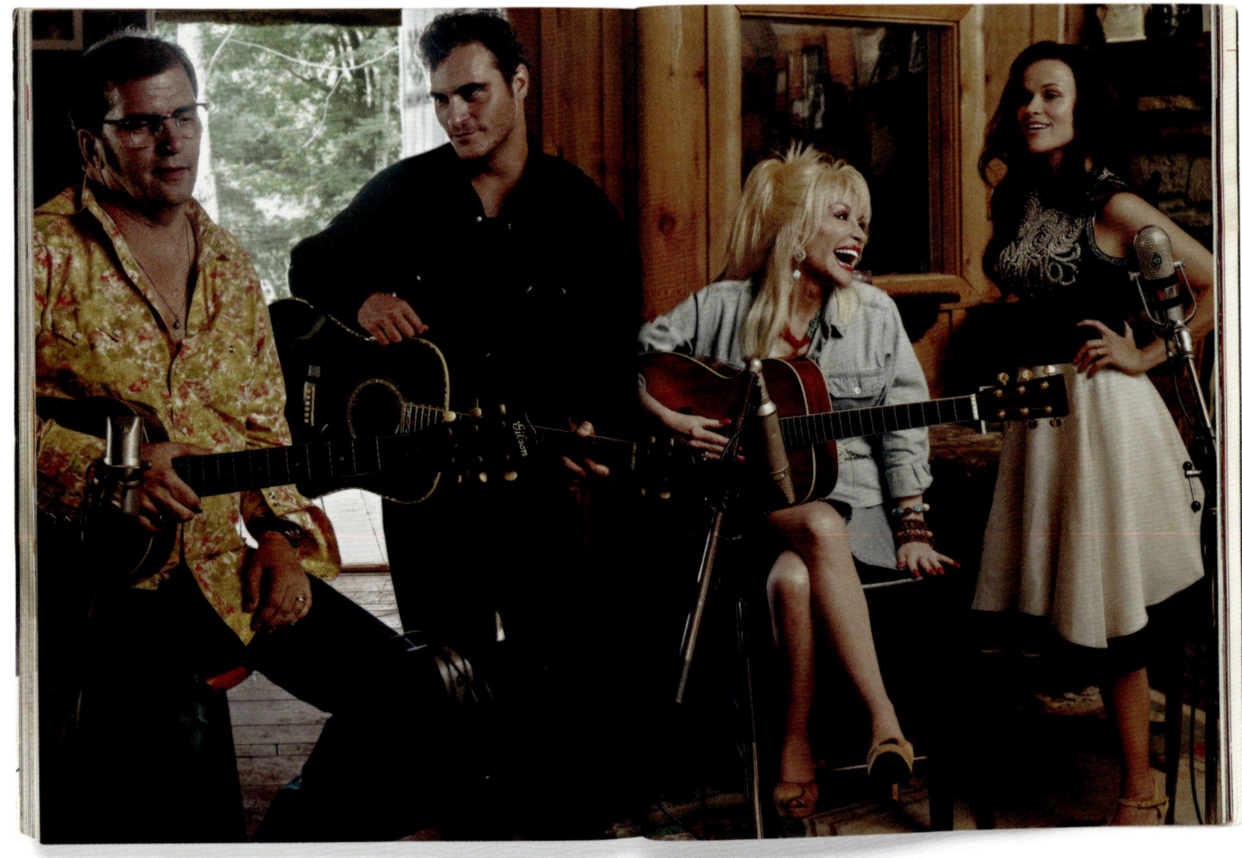

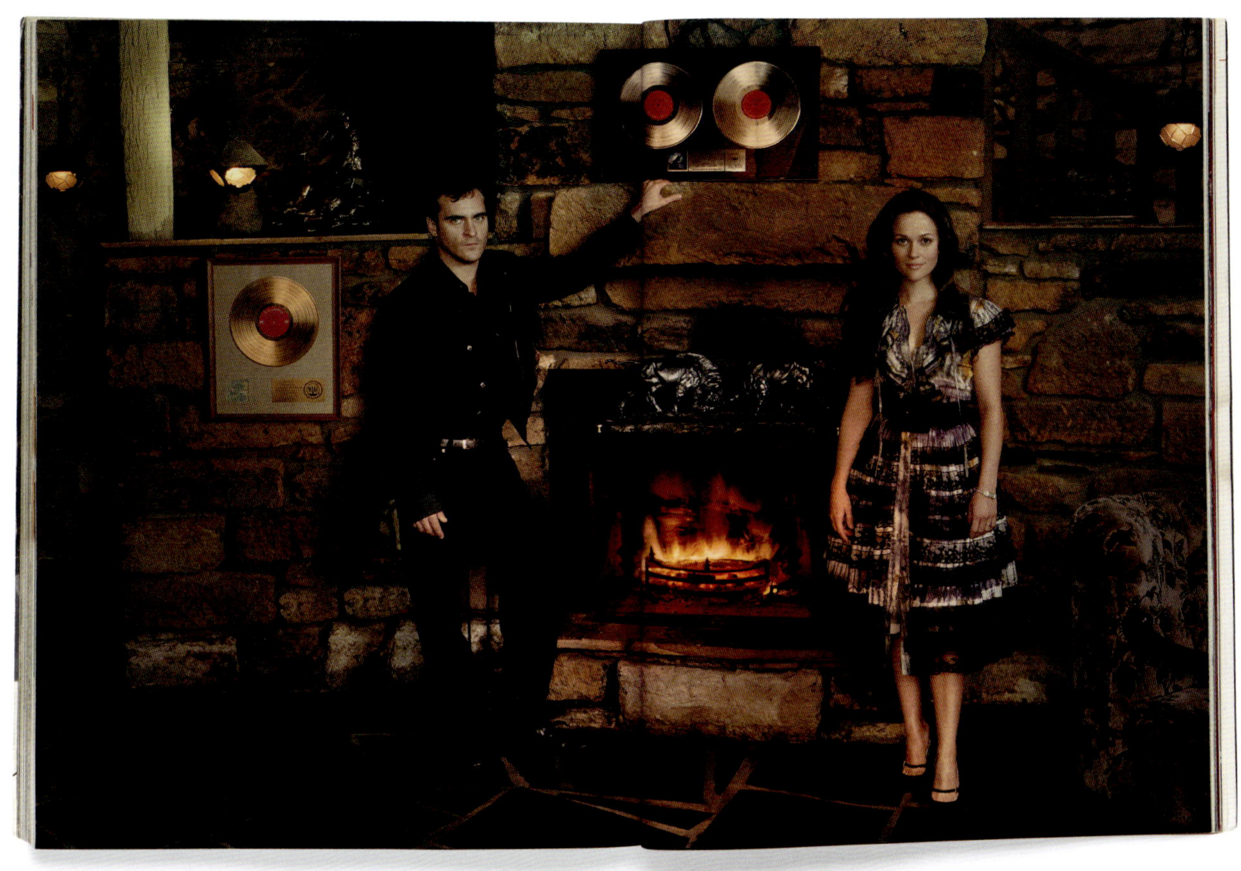

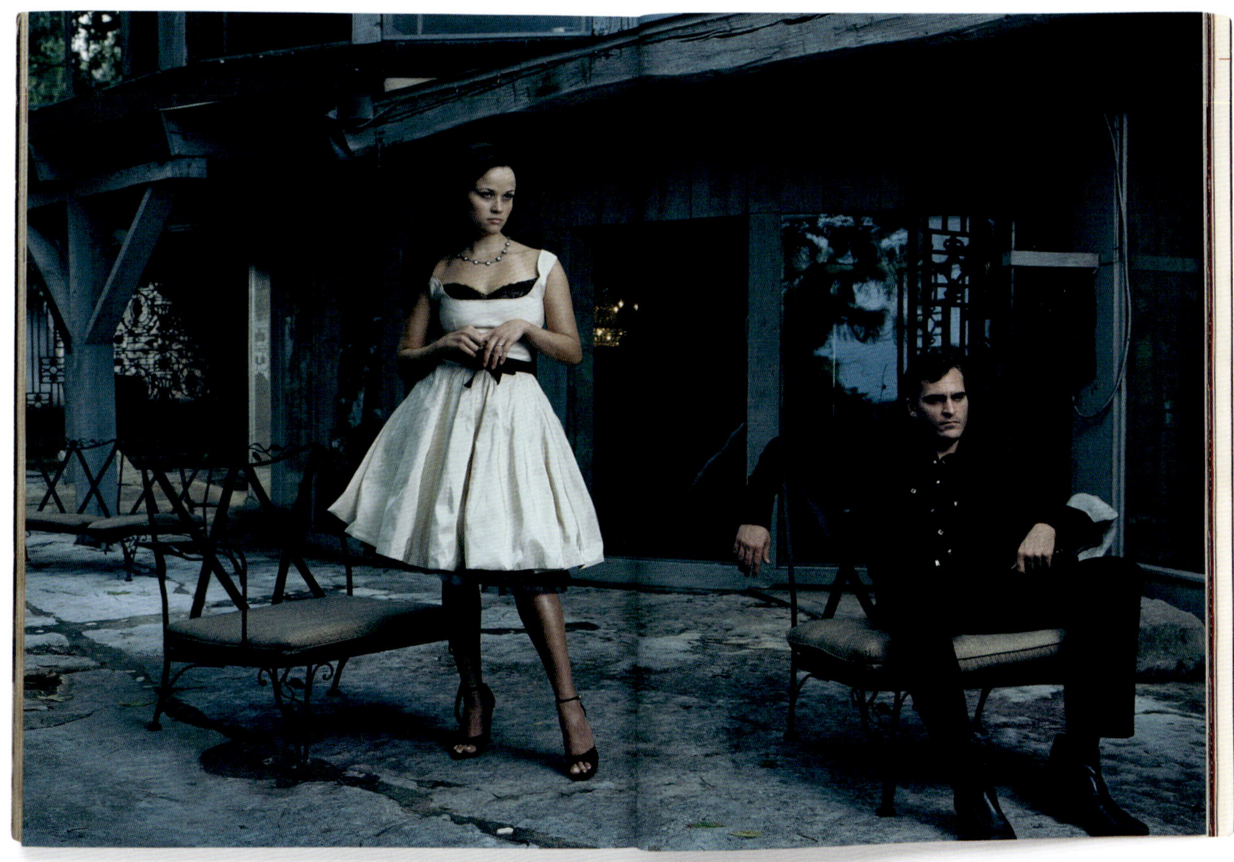

Angelina Jolie piloted her single-engine plane into a derelict airport halfway between LA and Las Vegas to meet Annie for a shoot in 2006. The army had used the airport during World War II, but now there were just dusty runways and some sheds and huge old hangars. Angelina and Brad Pitt parked their motorcycles there for occasional rides into the desert. Most of the shoot took place north of the airport in Death Valley sand dunes.

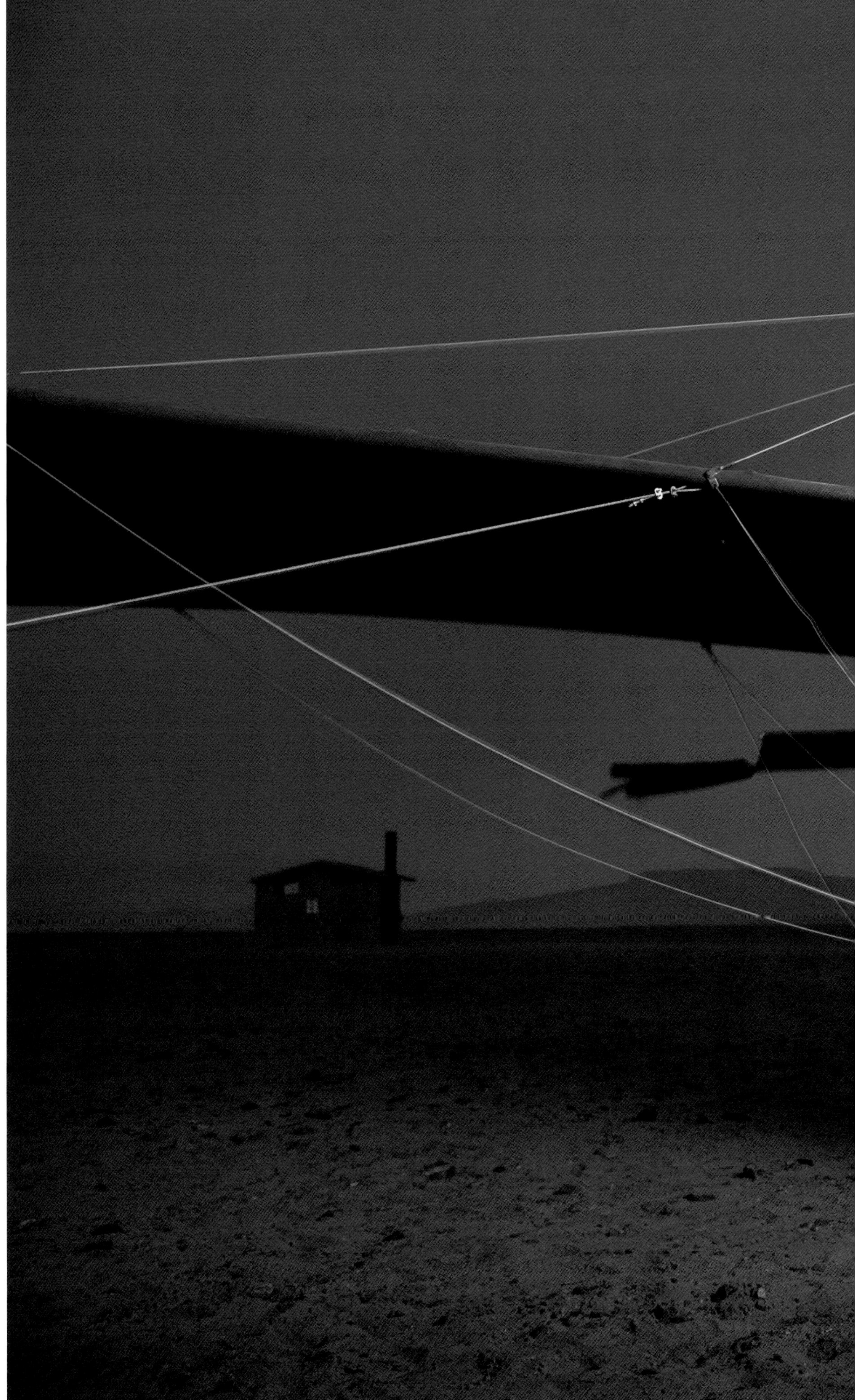

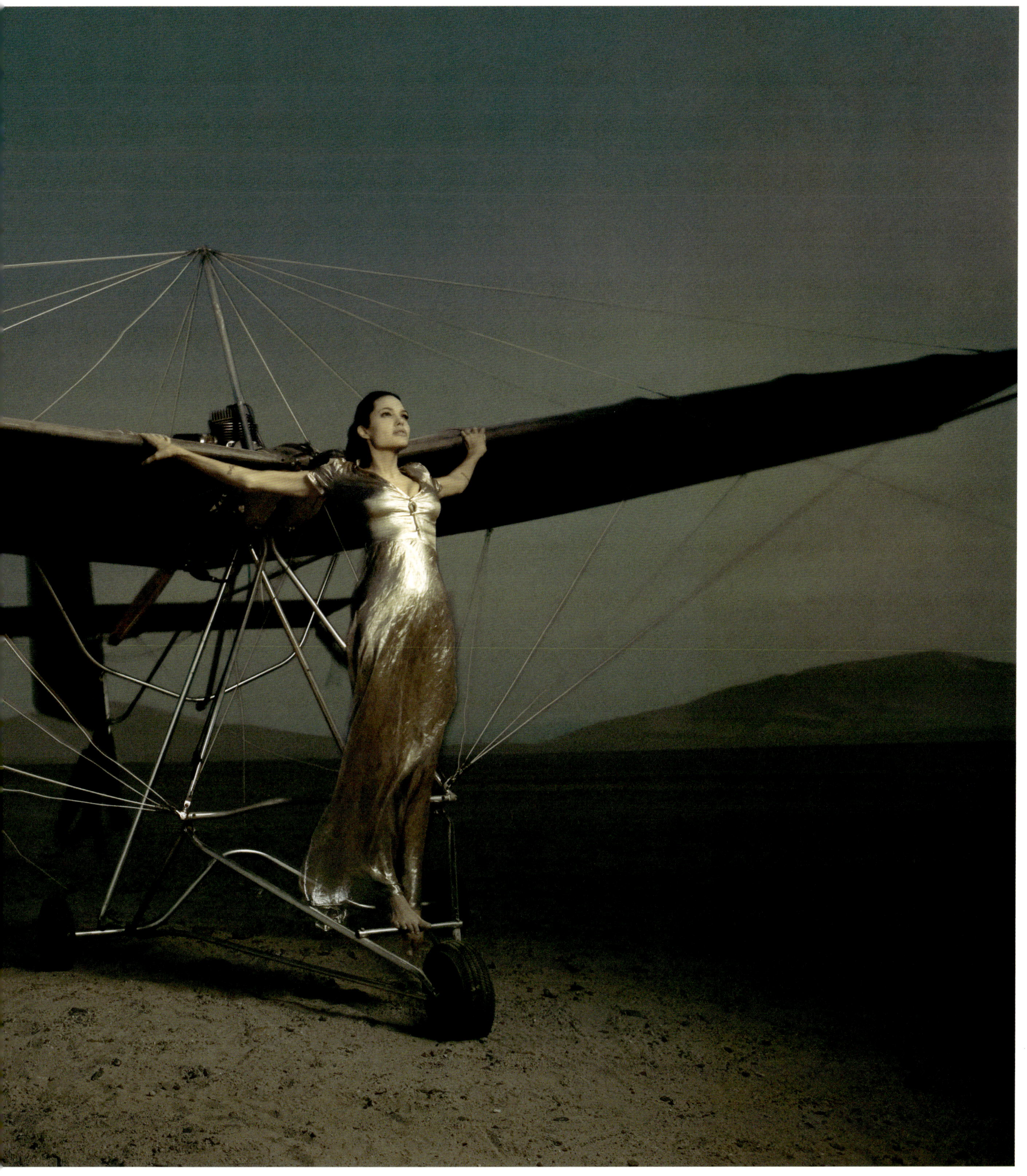

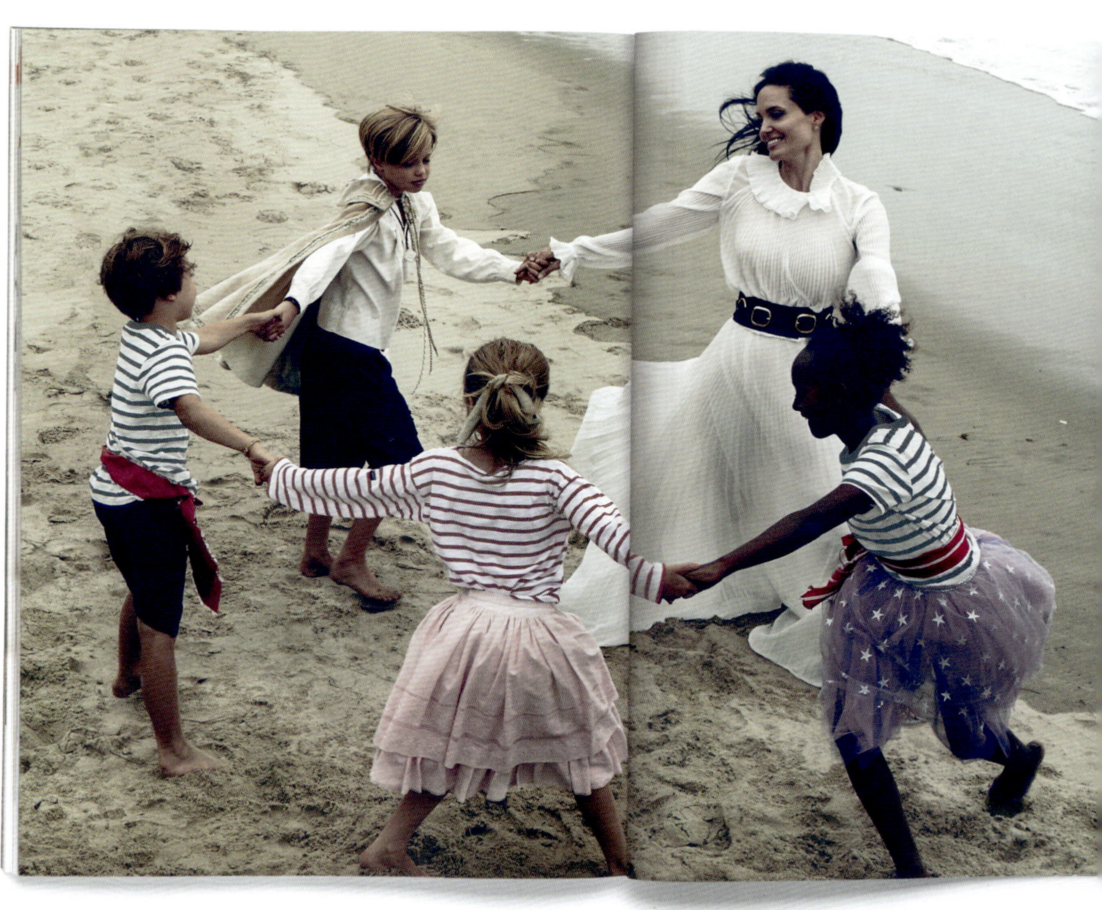

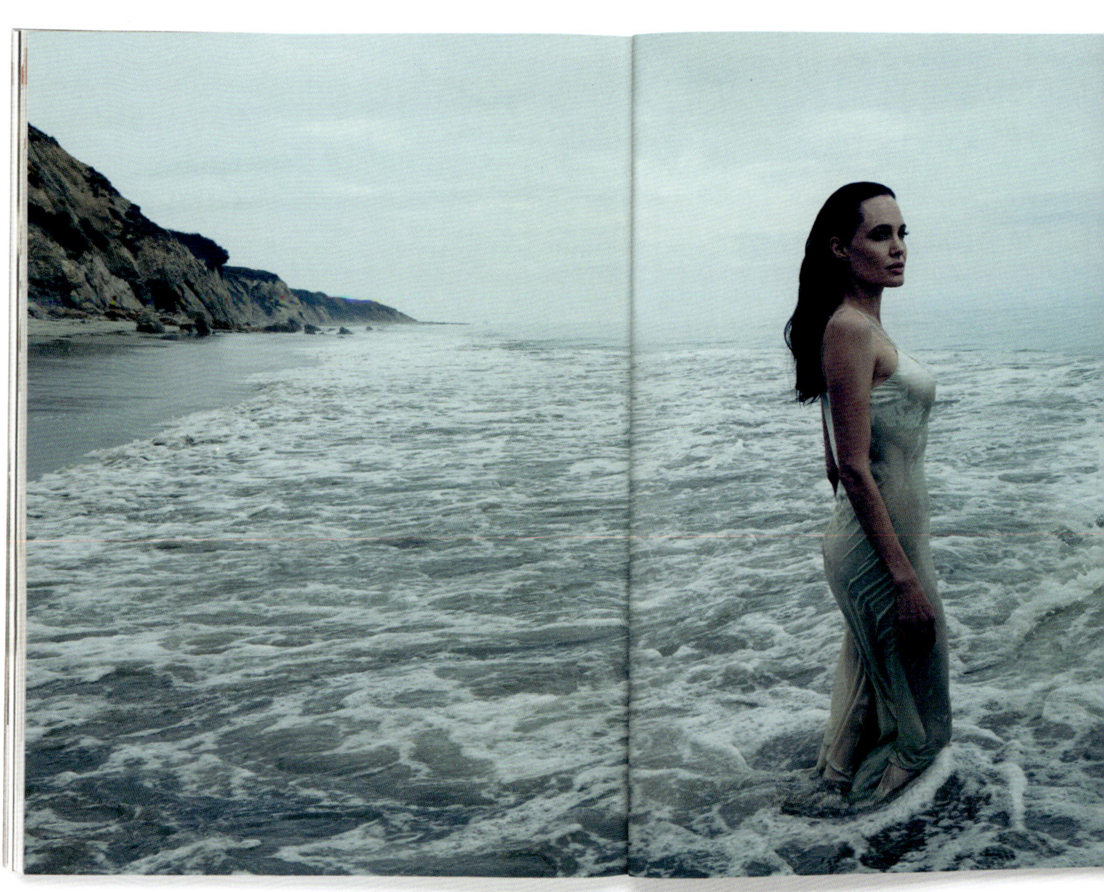

Angelina Jolie on the beach near her house on the coast of Southern California in 2015 with her six children—Maddox, Pax, Zahara, Shiloh, Knox, and Vivienne—and Brad Pitt.

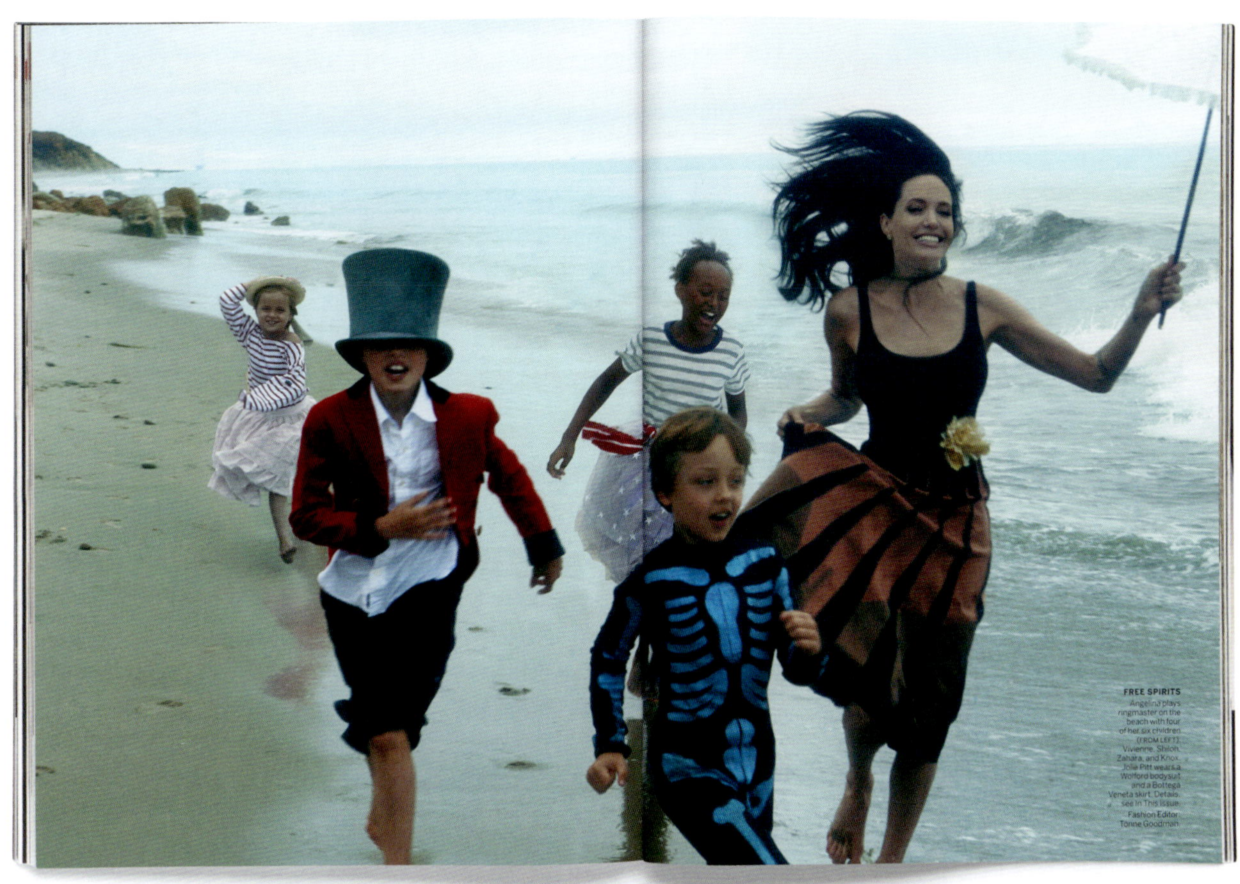
FREE SPIRITS
Angelina plays ringmaster on the beach with four of her six children (FROM LEFT): Vivienne, Shiloh, Zahara, and Knox. Jolie Pitt wears a Wolford bodysuit and a Bottega Veneta skirt. Details, see In This Issue.
Fashion Editor: Tonne Goodman

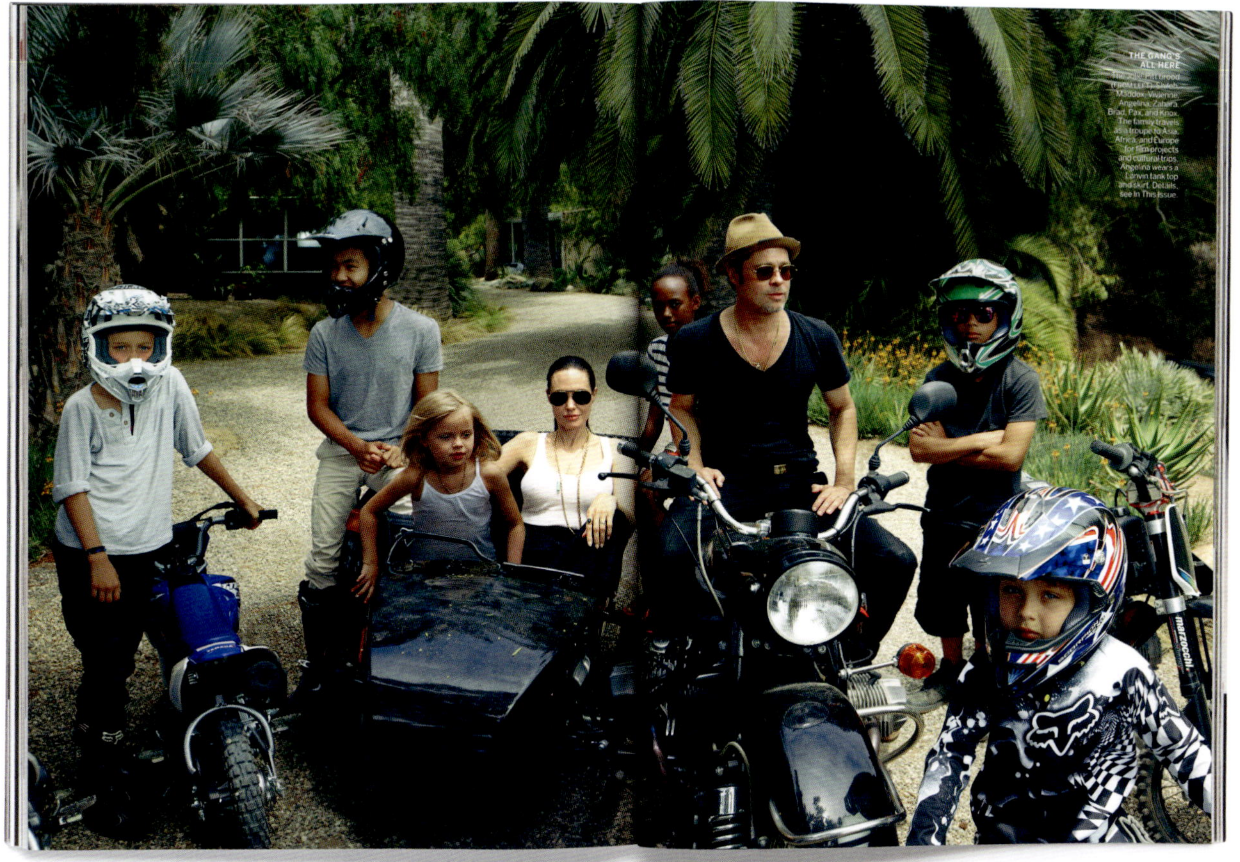
THE GANG'S ALL HERE
The Jolie-Pitt brood (FROM LEFT): Shiloh, Maddox, Vivienne, Angelina, Zahara, Brad, Pax, and Knox. The family travels as a troupe to Asia, Africa, and Europe for film projects and cultural trips. Angelina wears a Lanvin tank top and skirt. Details, see In This Issue.

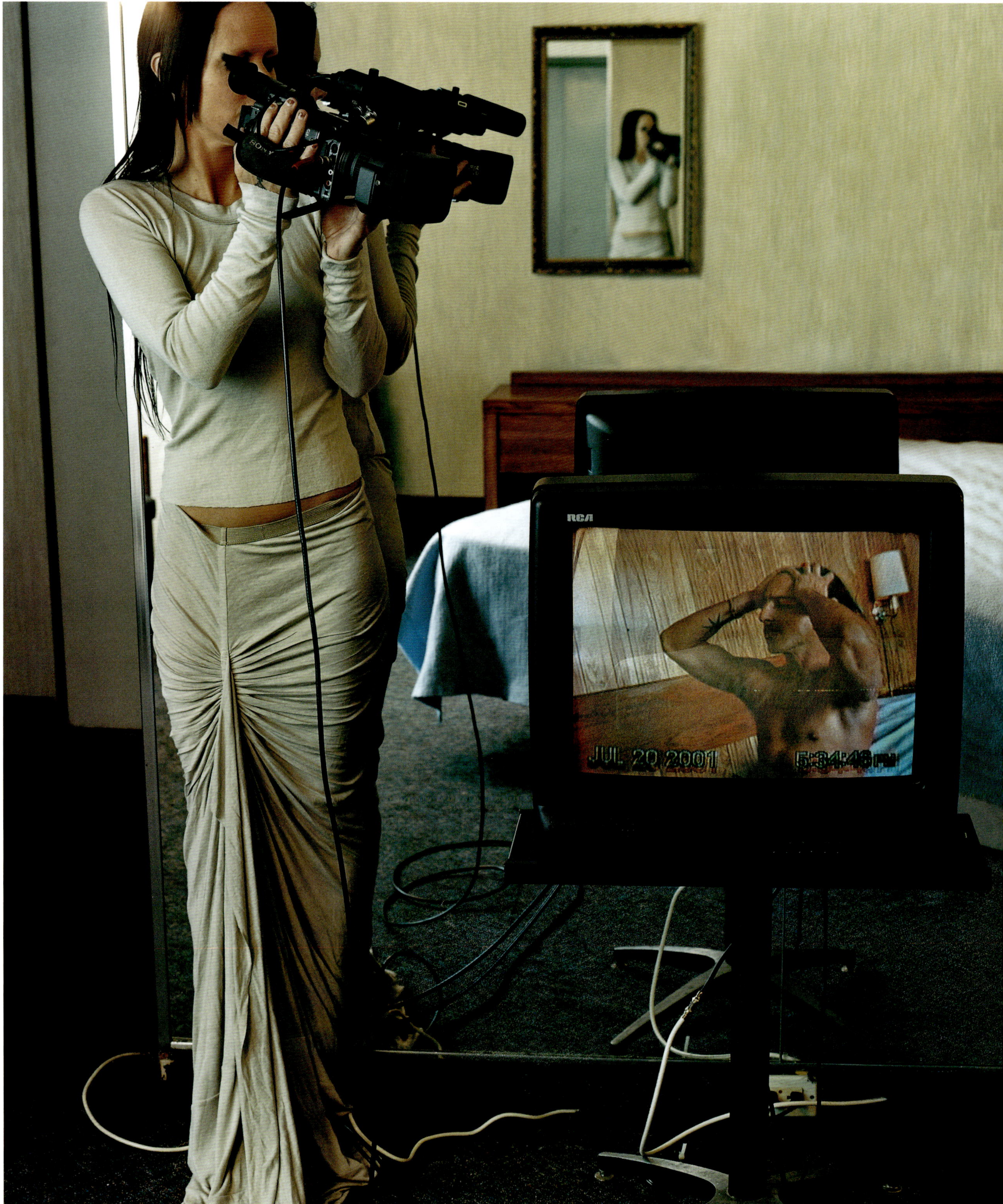
SONY
RCA
JUL 20 2001

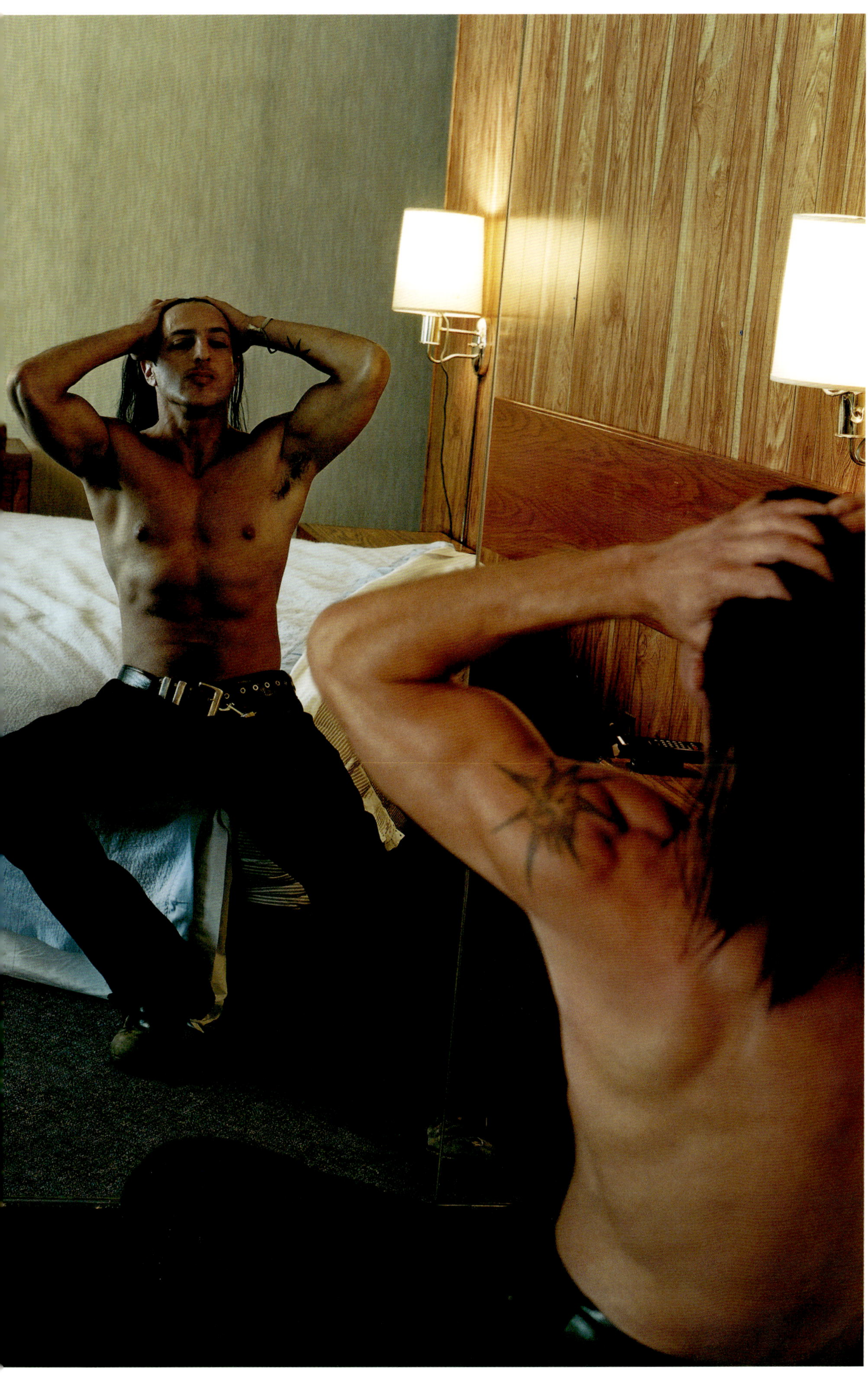

Rick Owens with Kembra Pfahler,
Secaucus, New Jersey, 2001

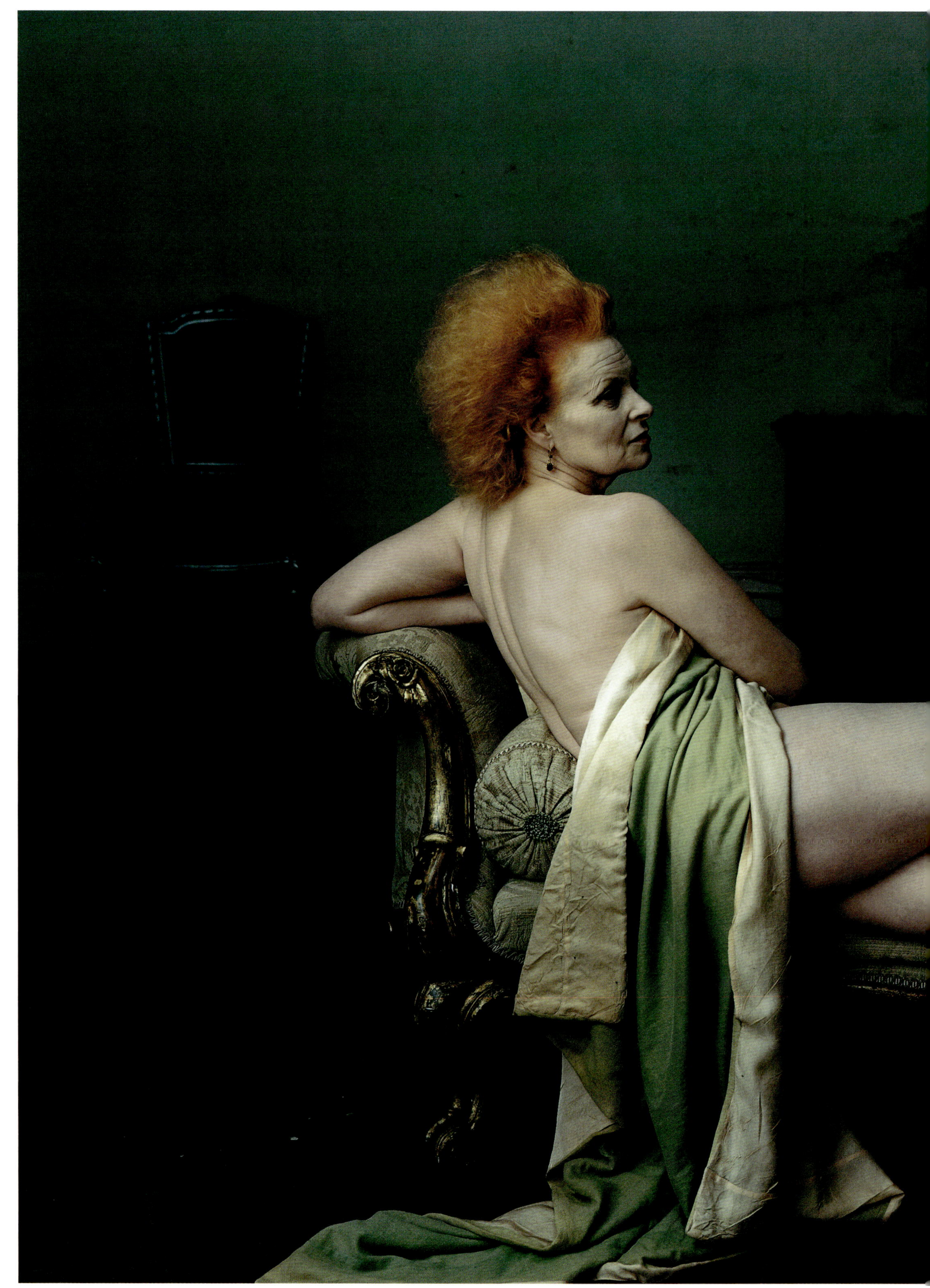

Vivienne Westwood and her husband, Andreas Kronthaler, London, 2001

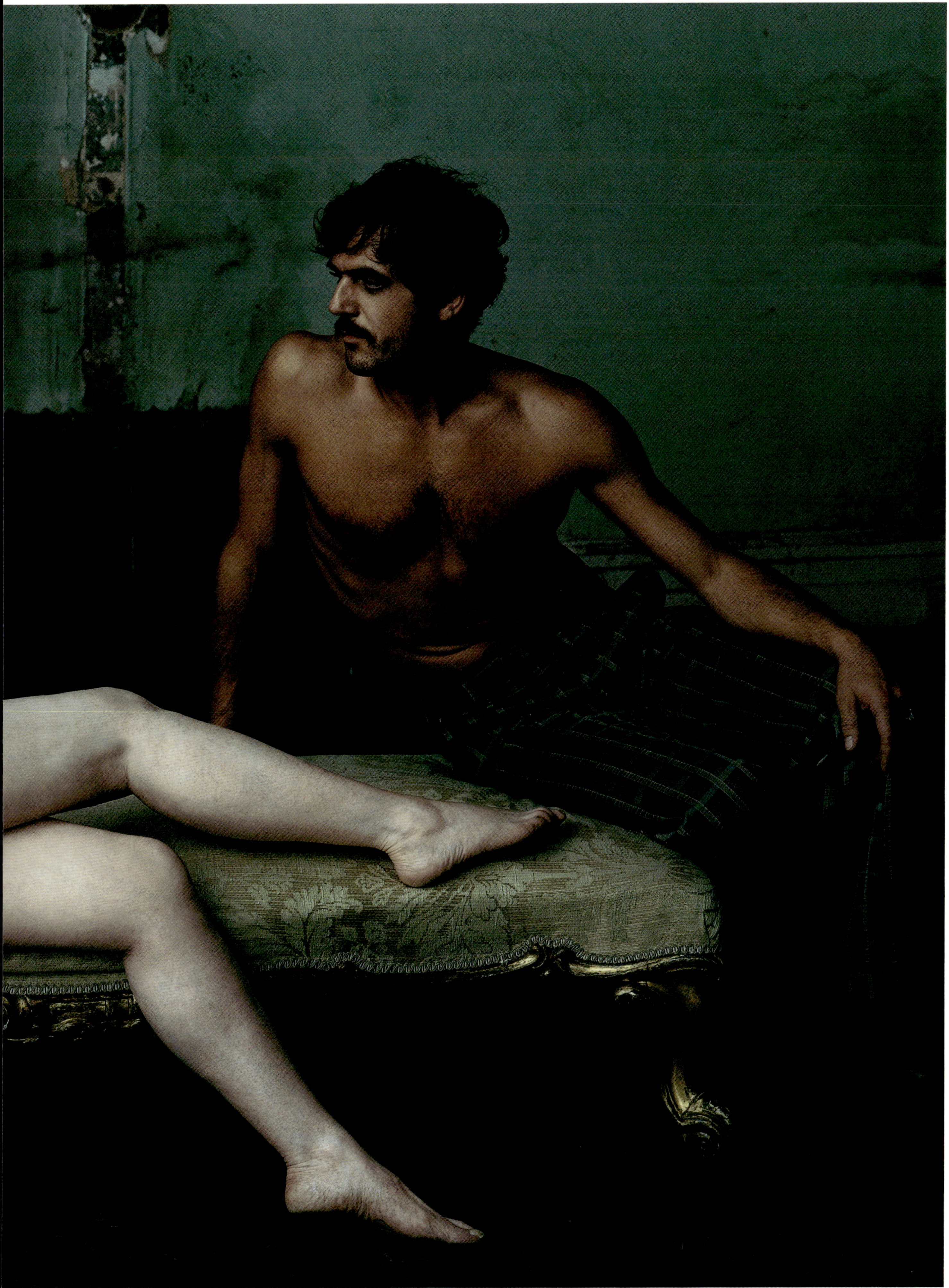

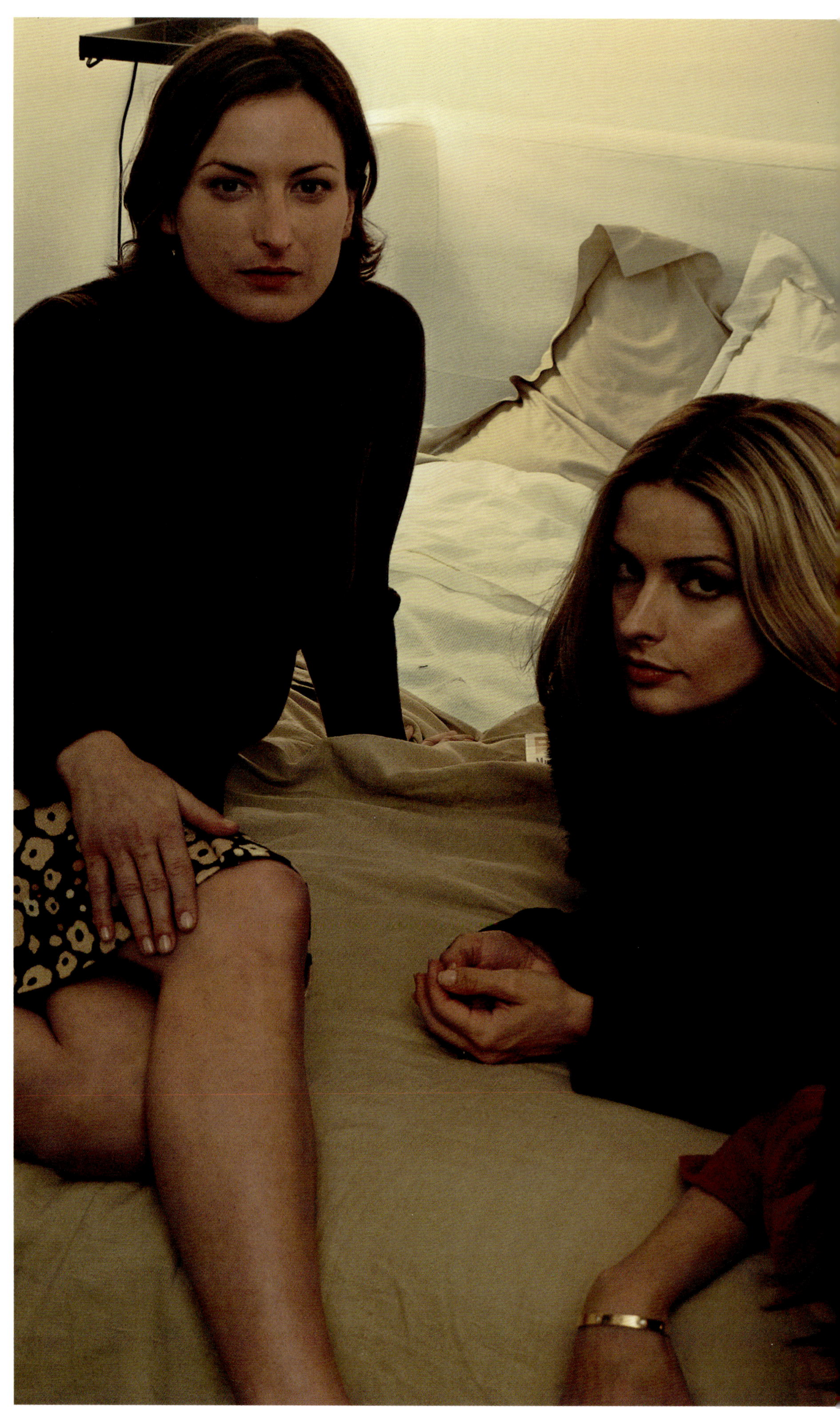

Marc Jacobs with Zoe Cassavetes, Lisa Marie, Sofia Coppola, Venetia Scott, and Robert Duffy, Mercer Hotel, New York City, 2000

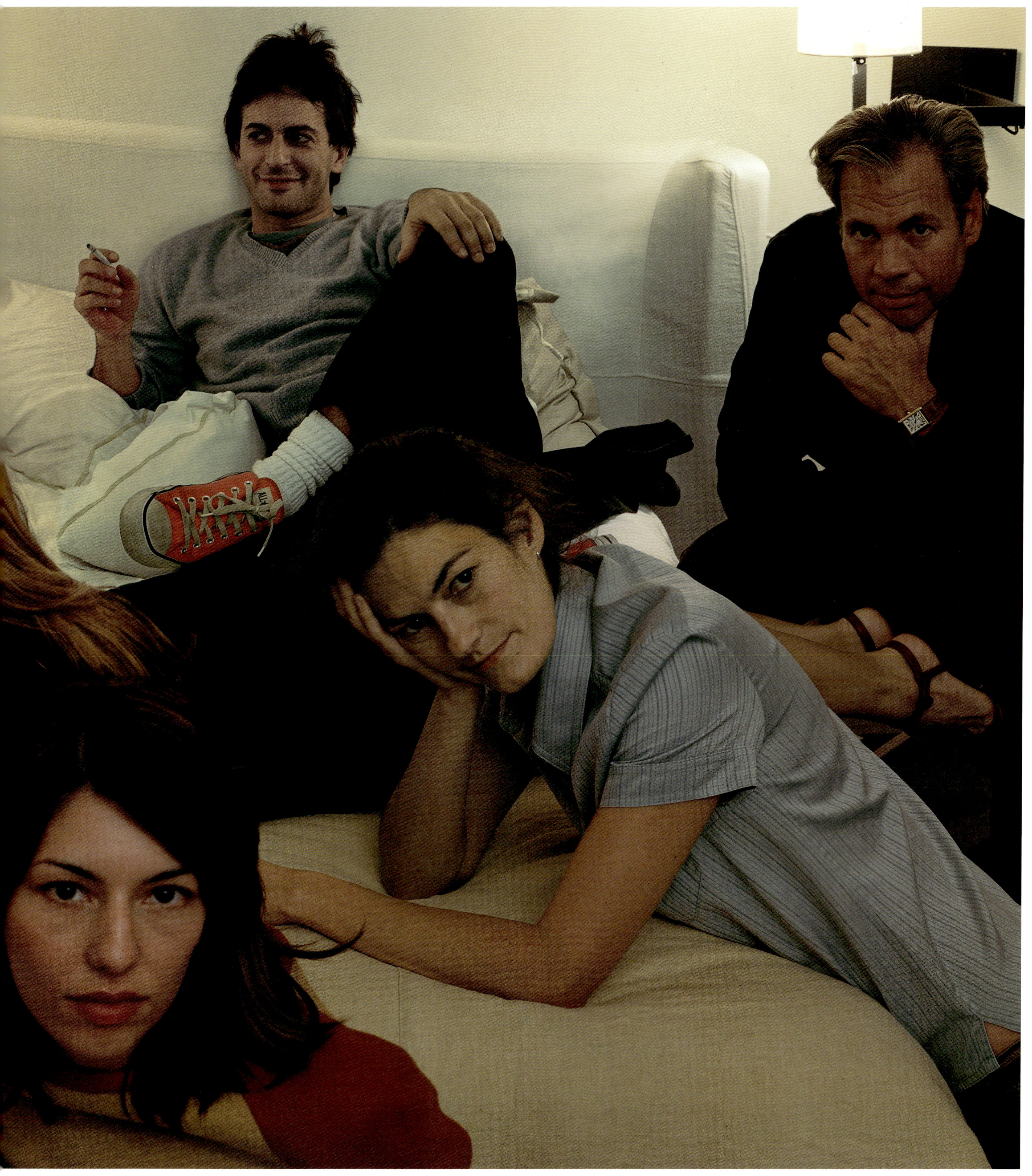

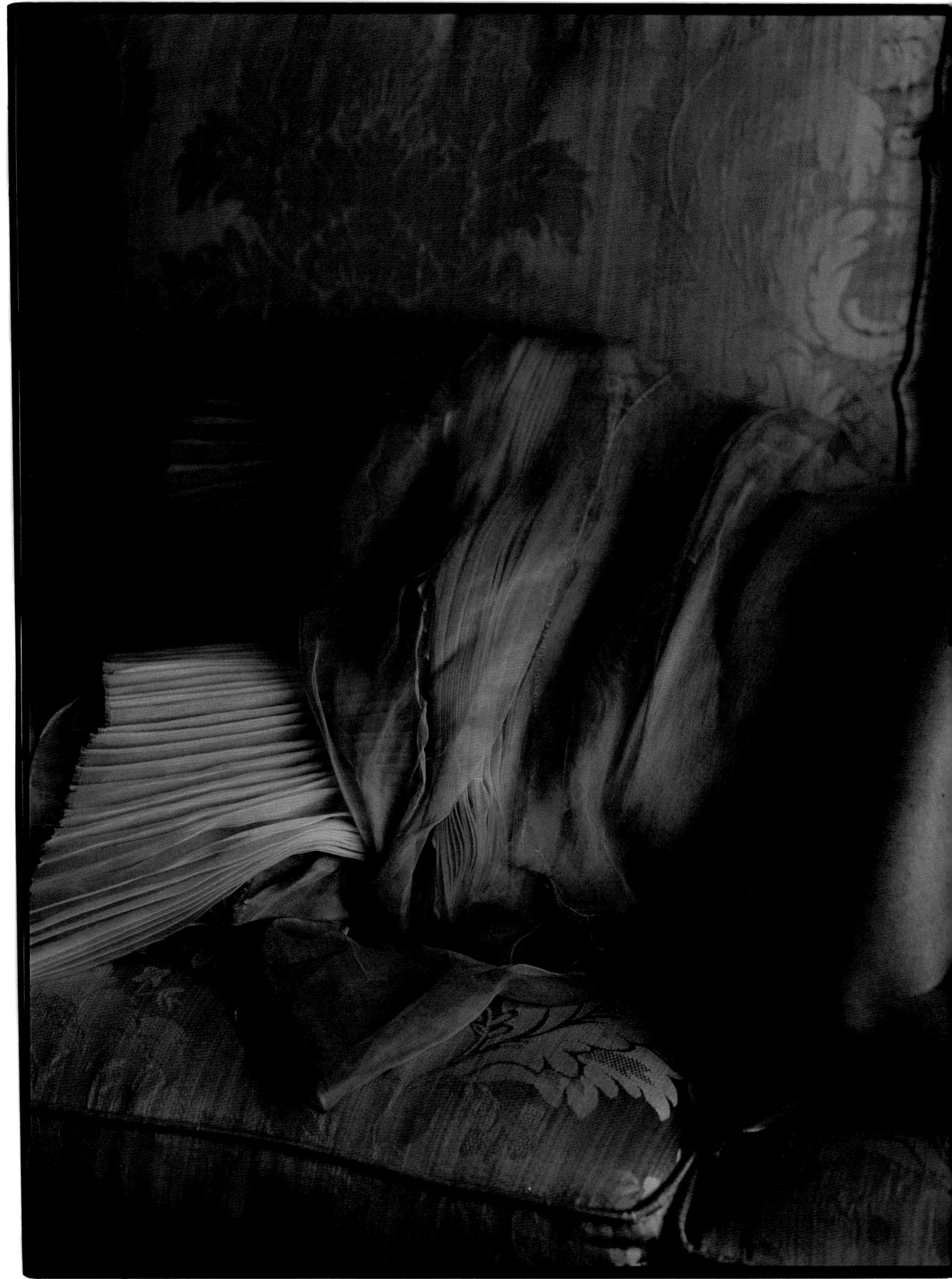

Sofia Coppola,
New York City, 2003

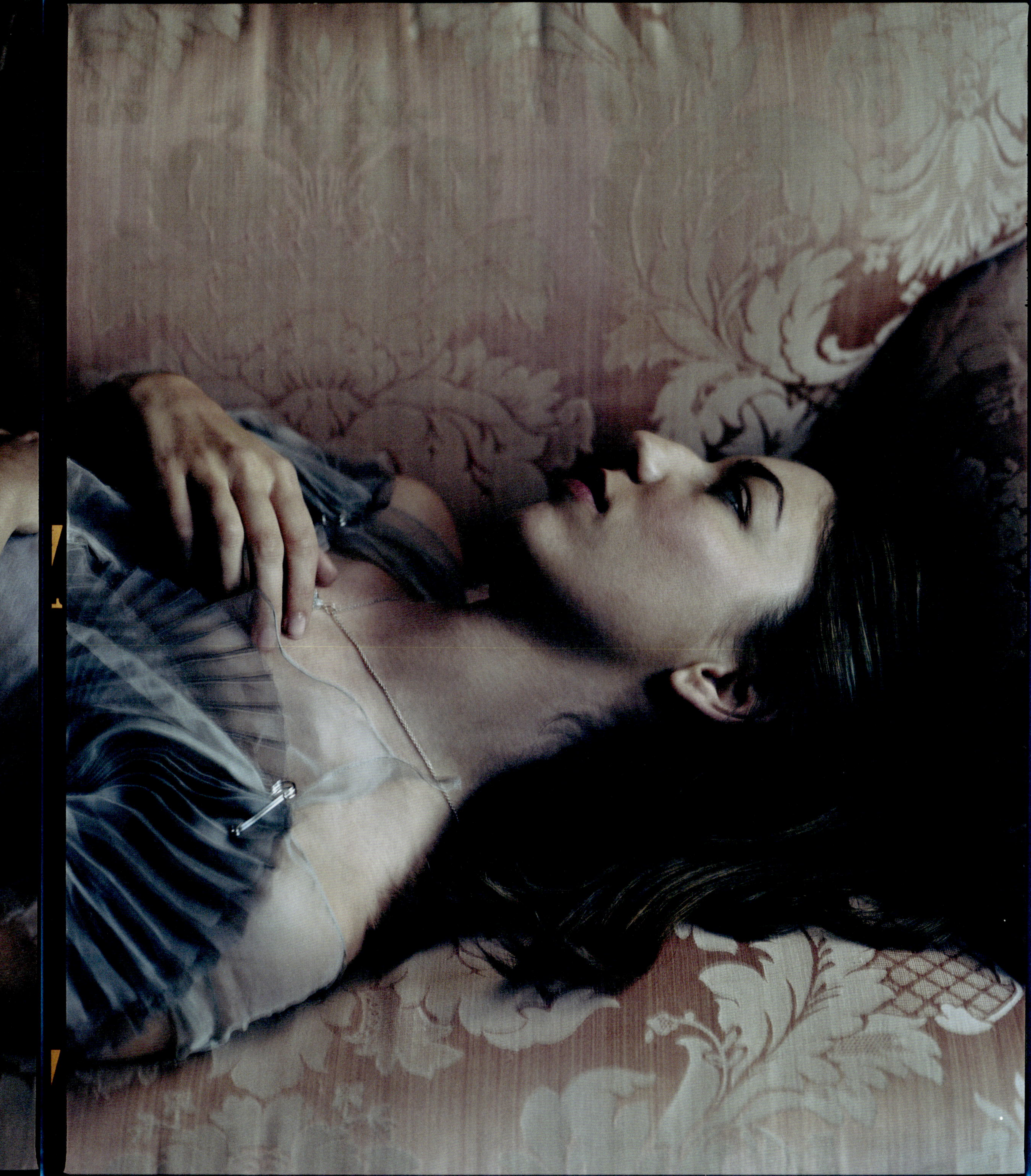

"Working in Versailles was like a dream. Sofia Coppola had just made *Marie Antoinette* there with Kirsten Dunst, and the grand rooms and gardens of the château were opened up for a fashion shoot for the first time in twenty-five years.

I was planning to set a scene in the Conciergerie in Paris, where Marie Antoinette was imprisoned before she was guillotined, but that was not the story Anna Wintour had in mind. She called from New York with instructions: 'Don't make it depressing. Don't make it dark and don't make it depressing.'"

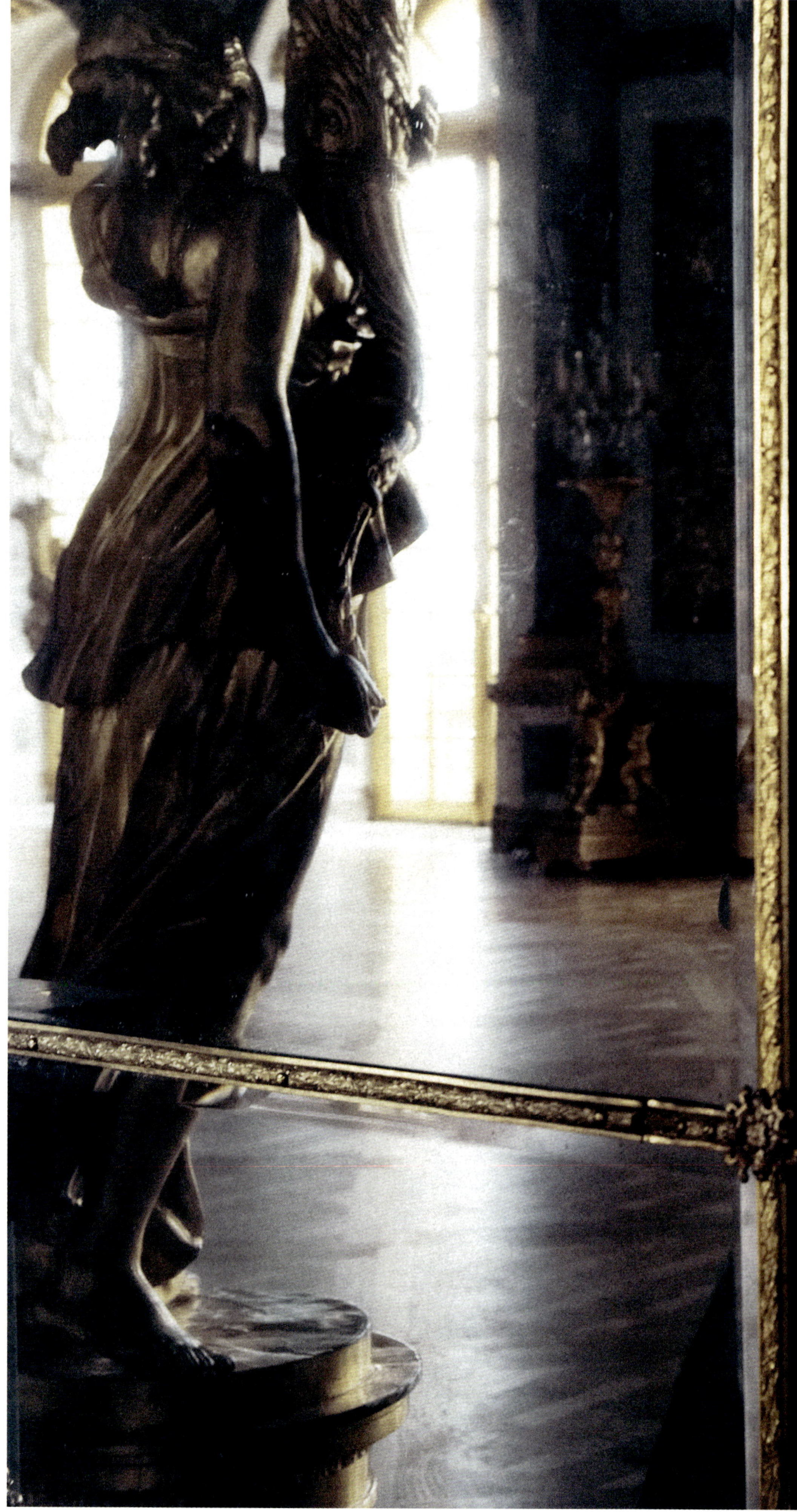

Kirsten Dunst and Jason Schwartzman,
Hall of Mirrors, Versailles, France, 2006

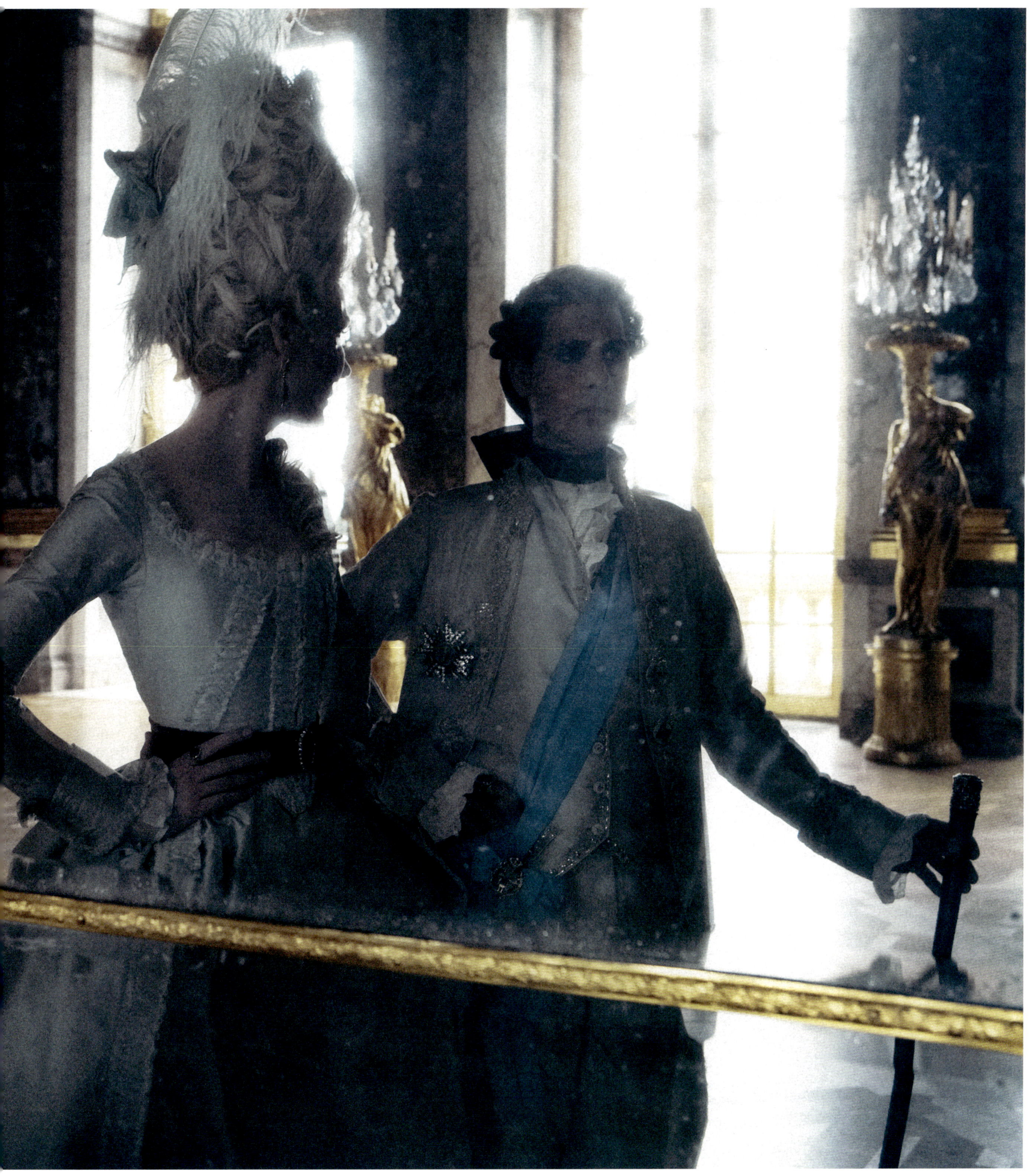

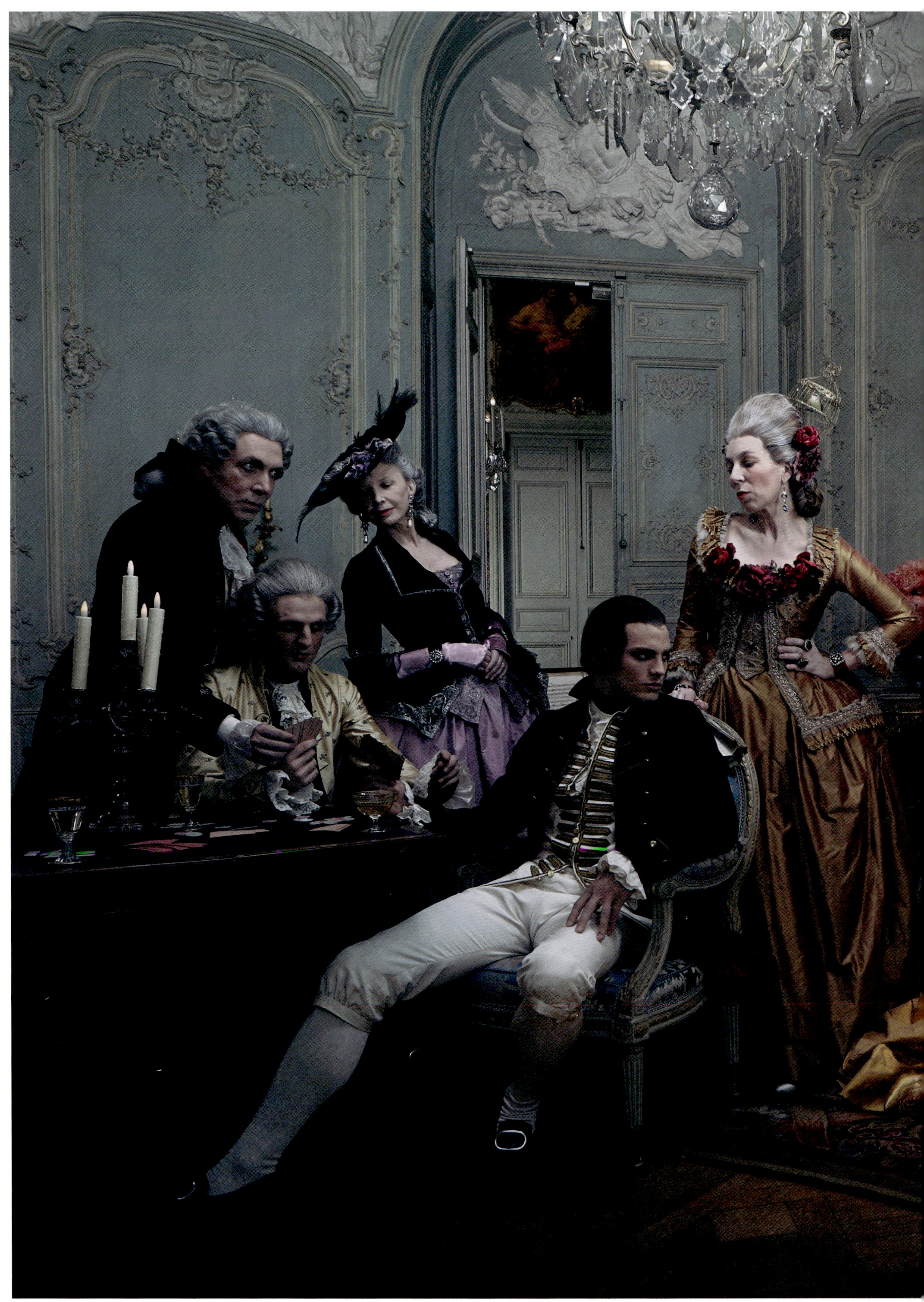

The Hôtel de Soubise,
now the National Archives,
Paris, 2006

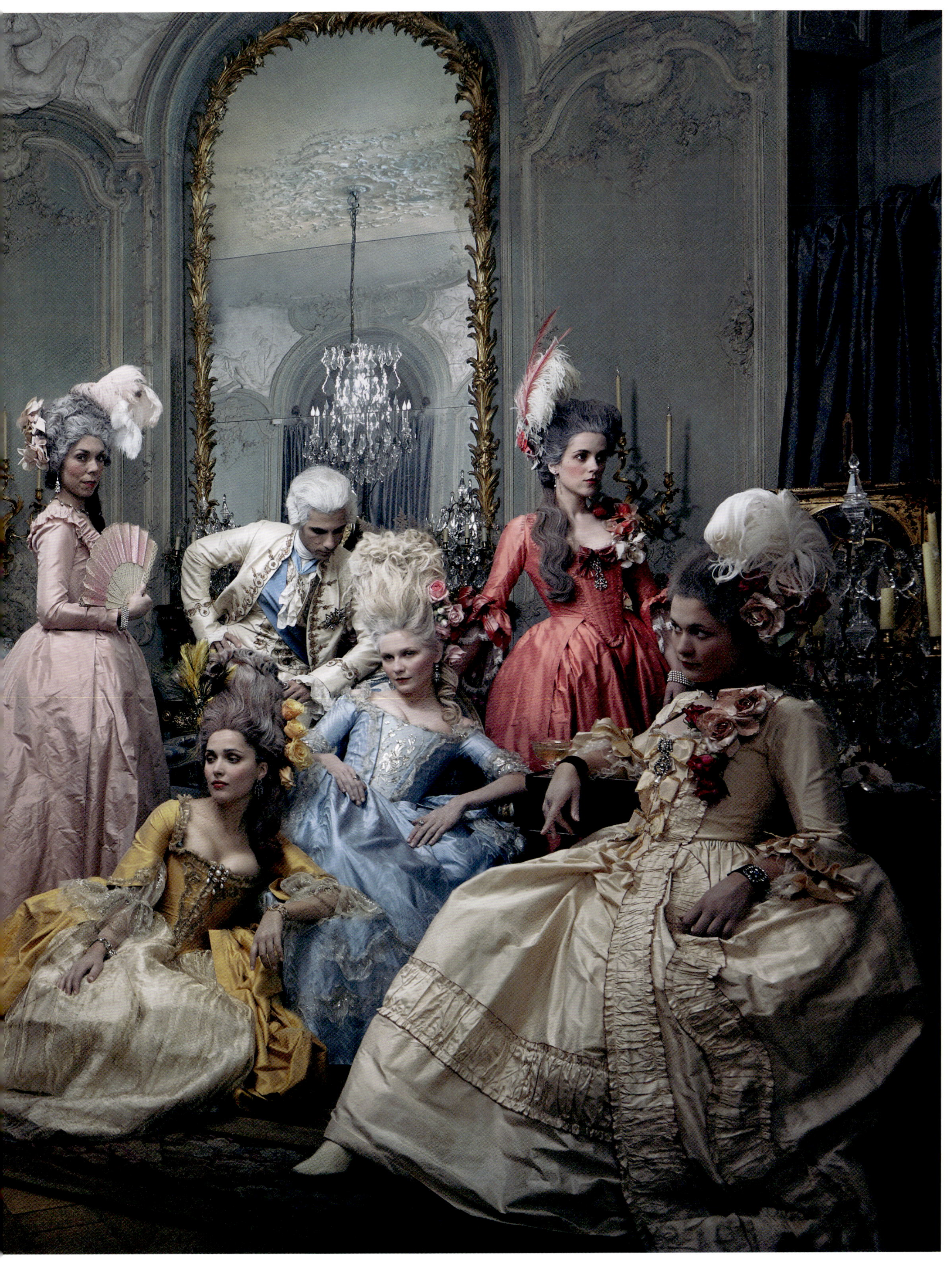

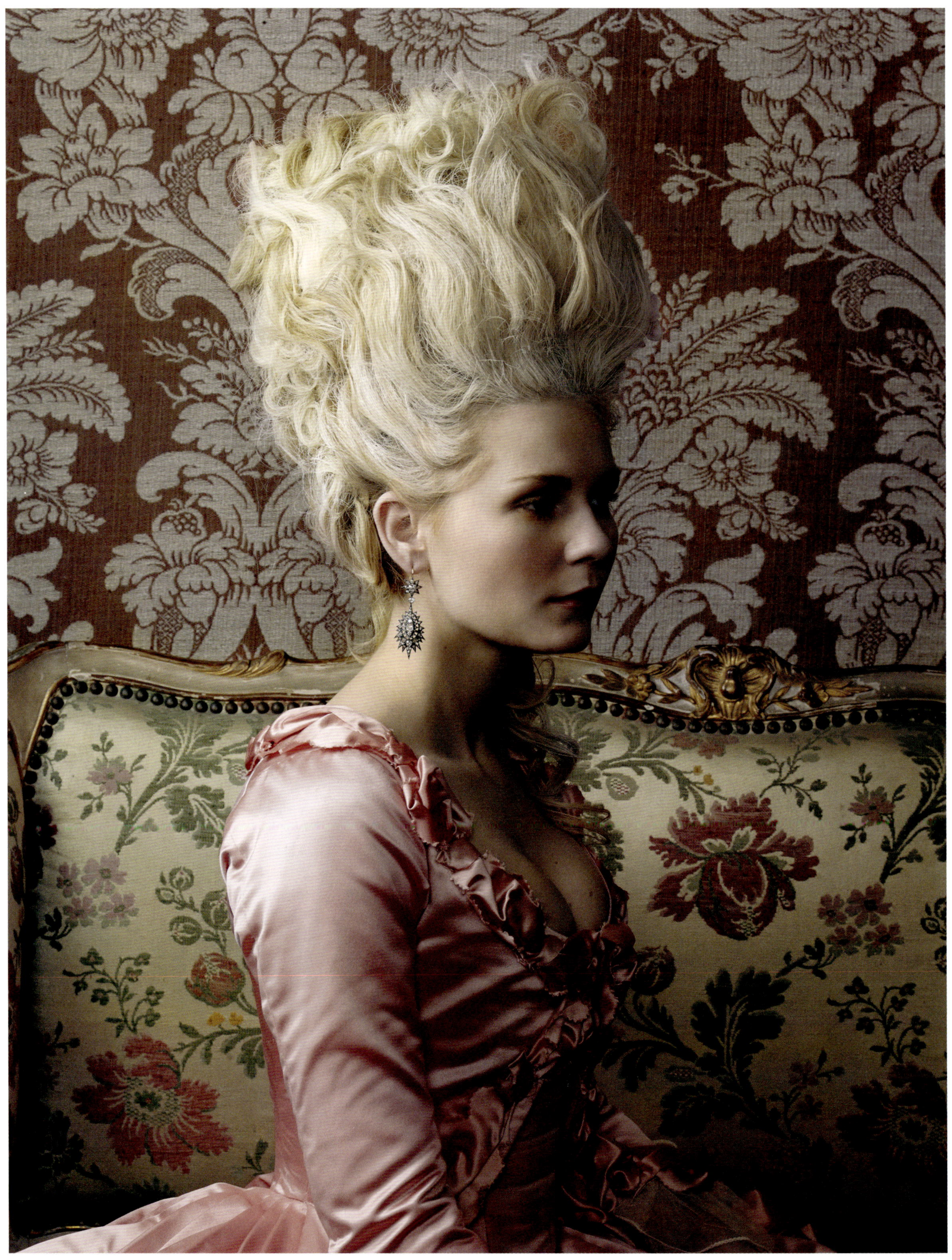

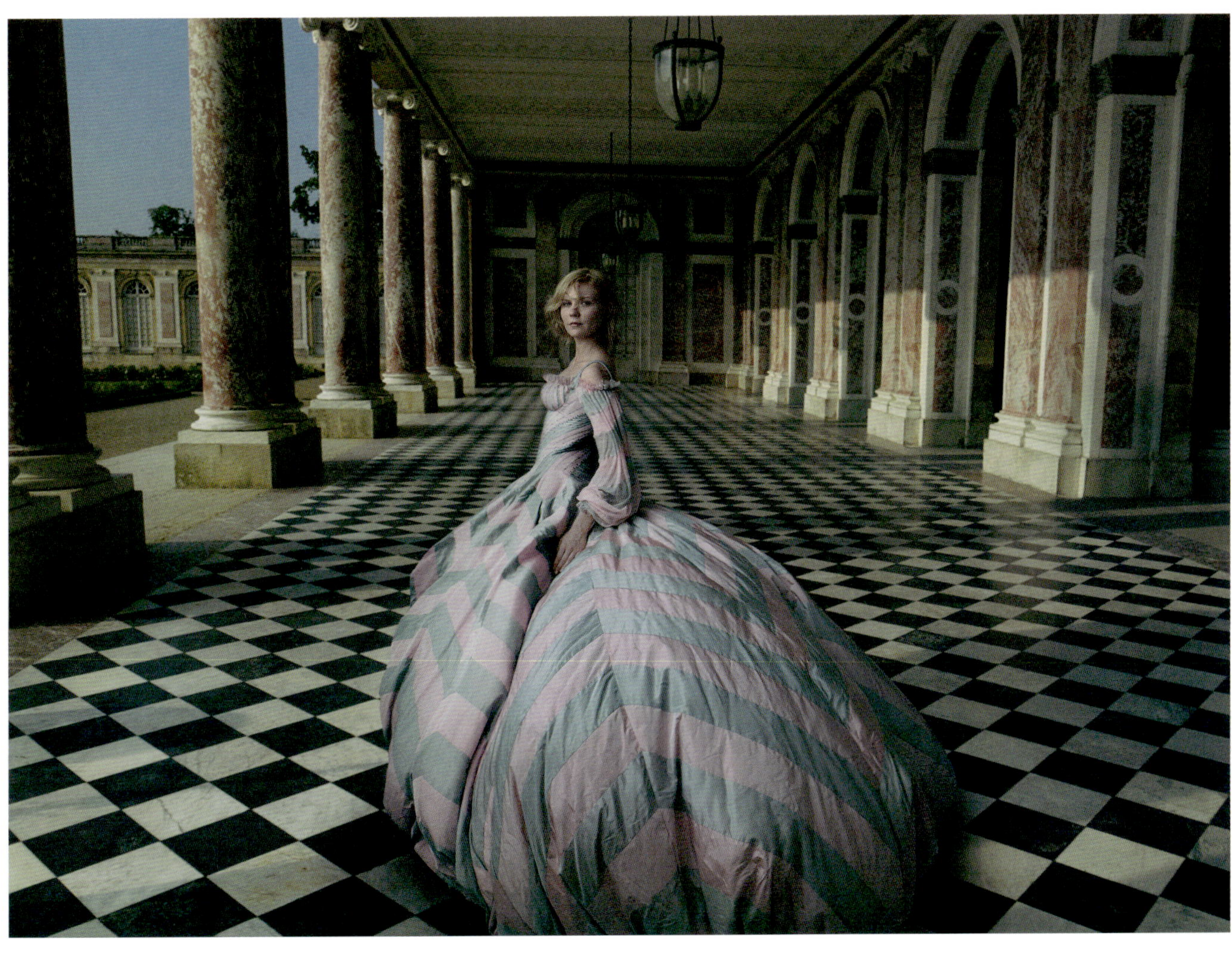

Le Petit Trianon

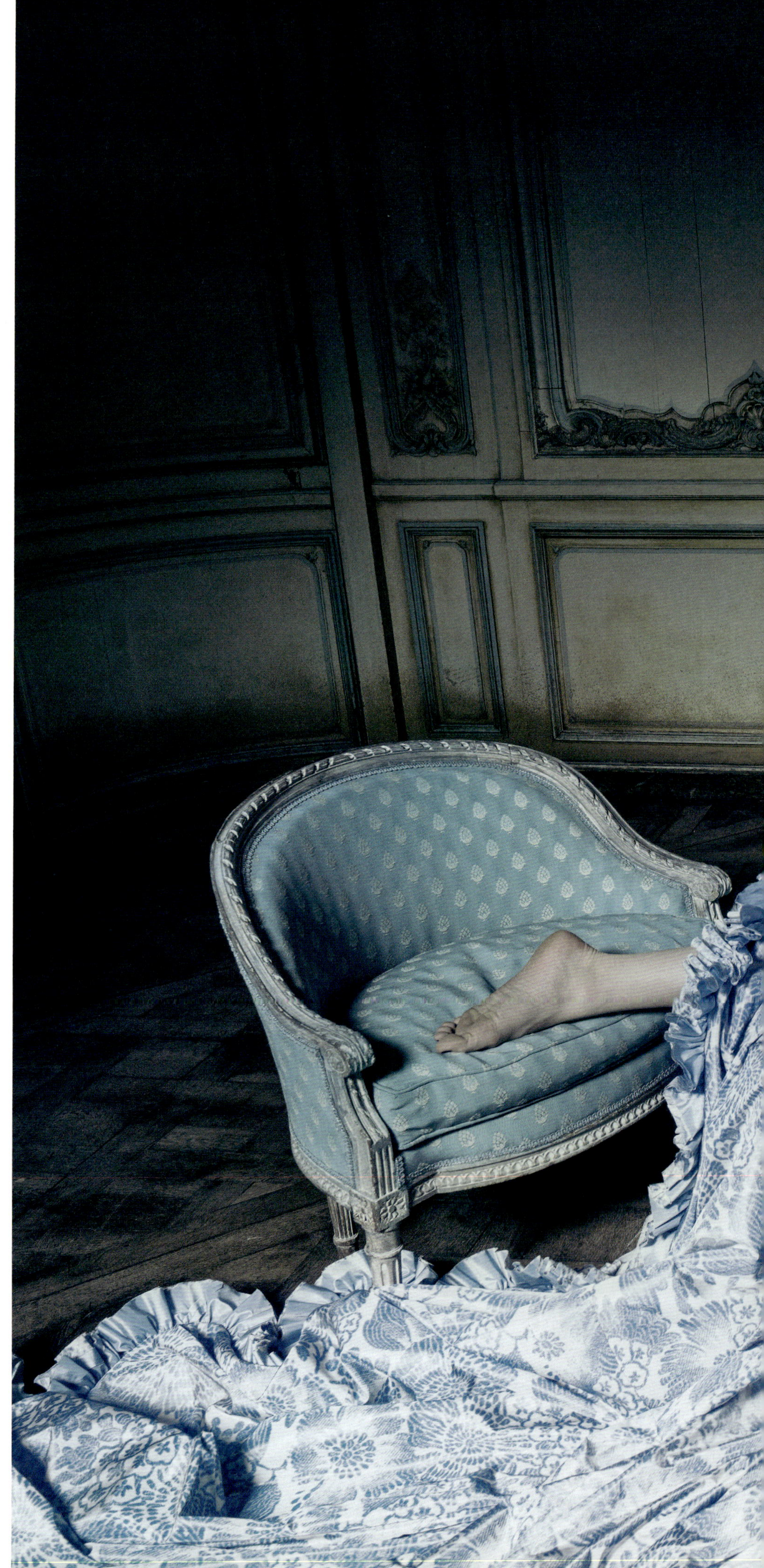

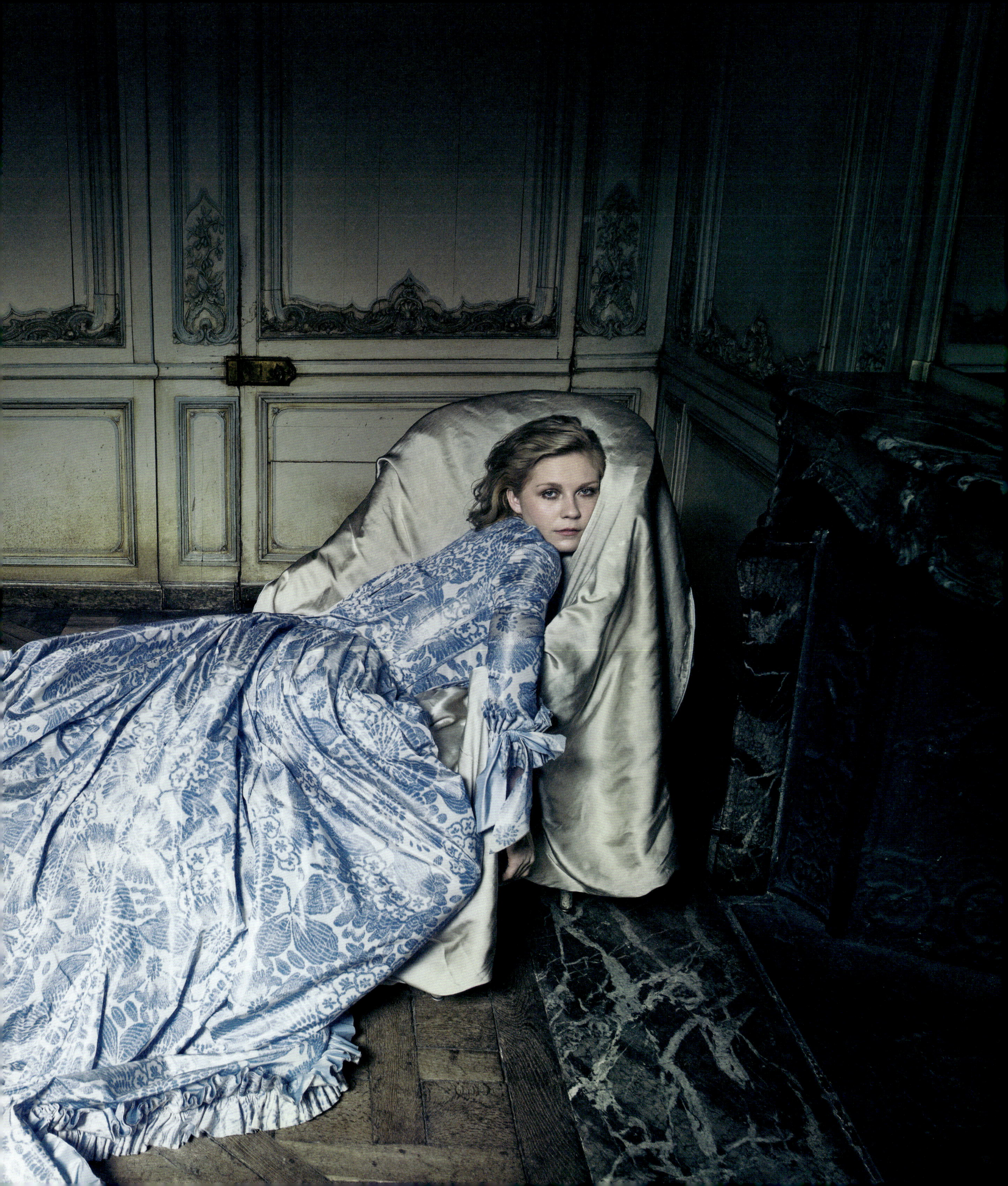

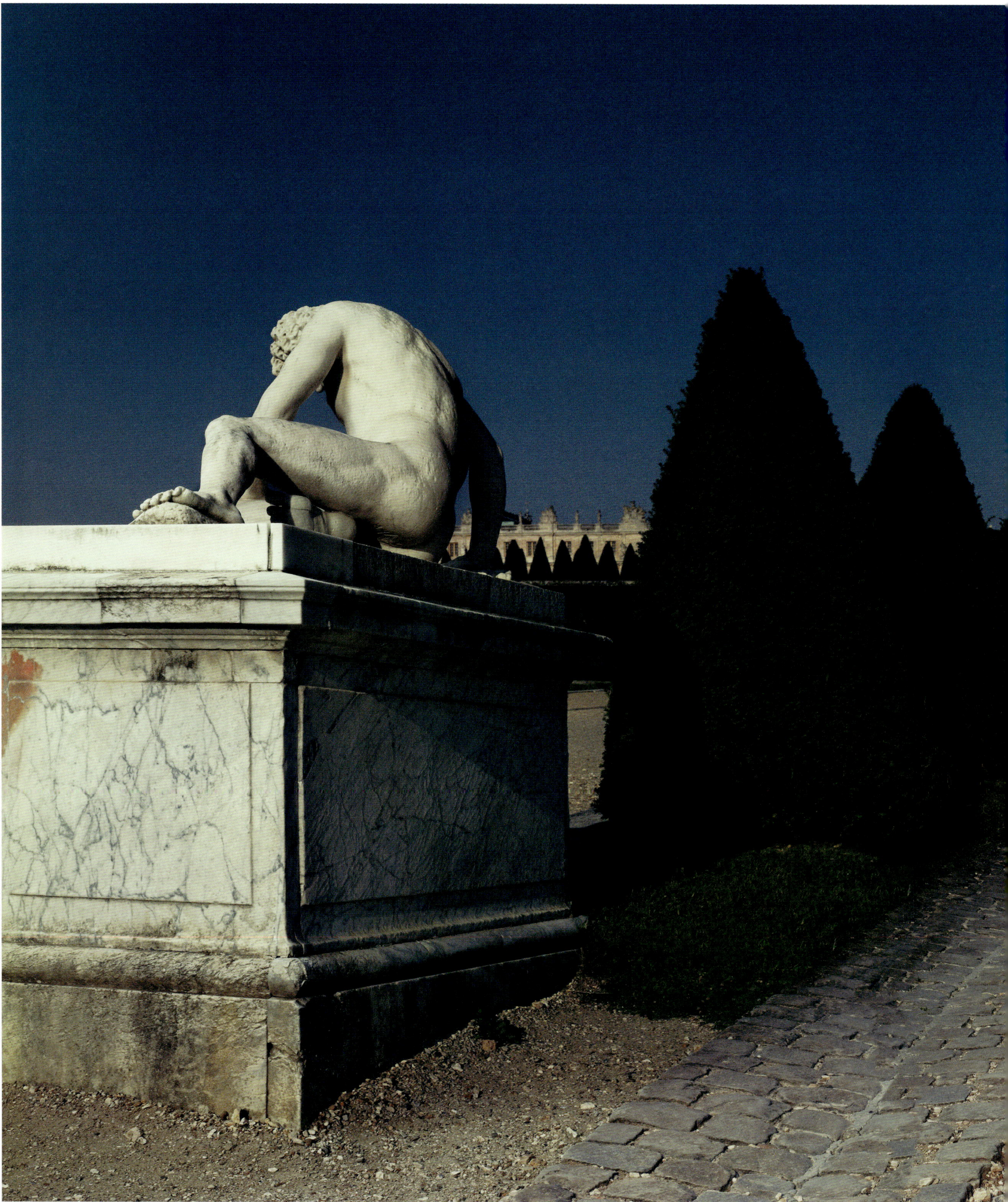

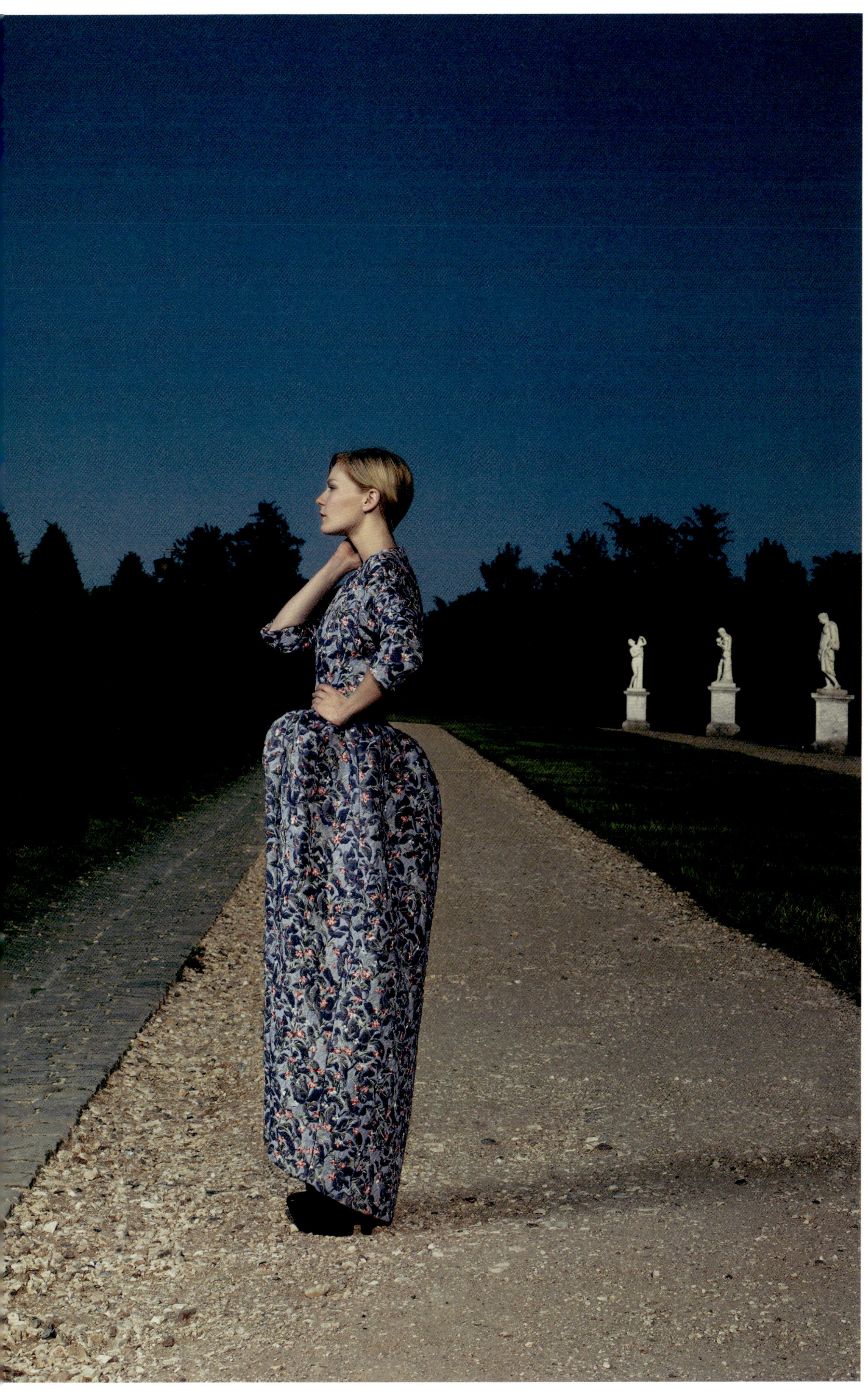

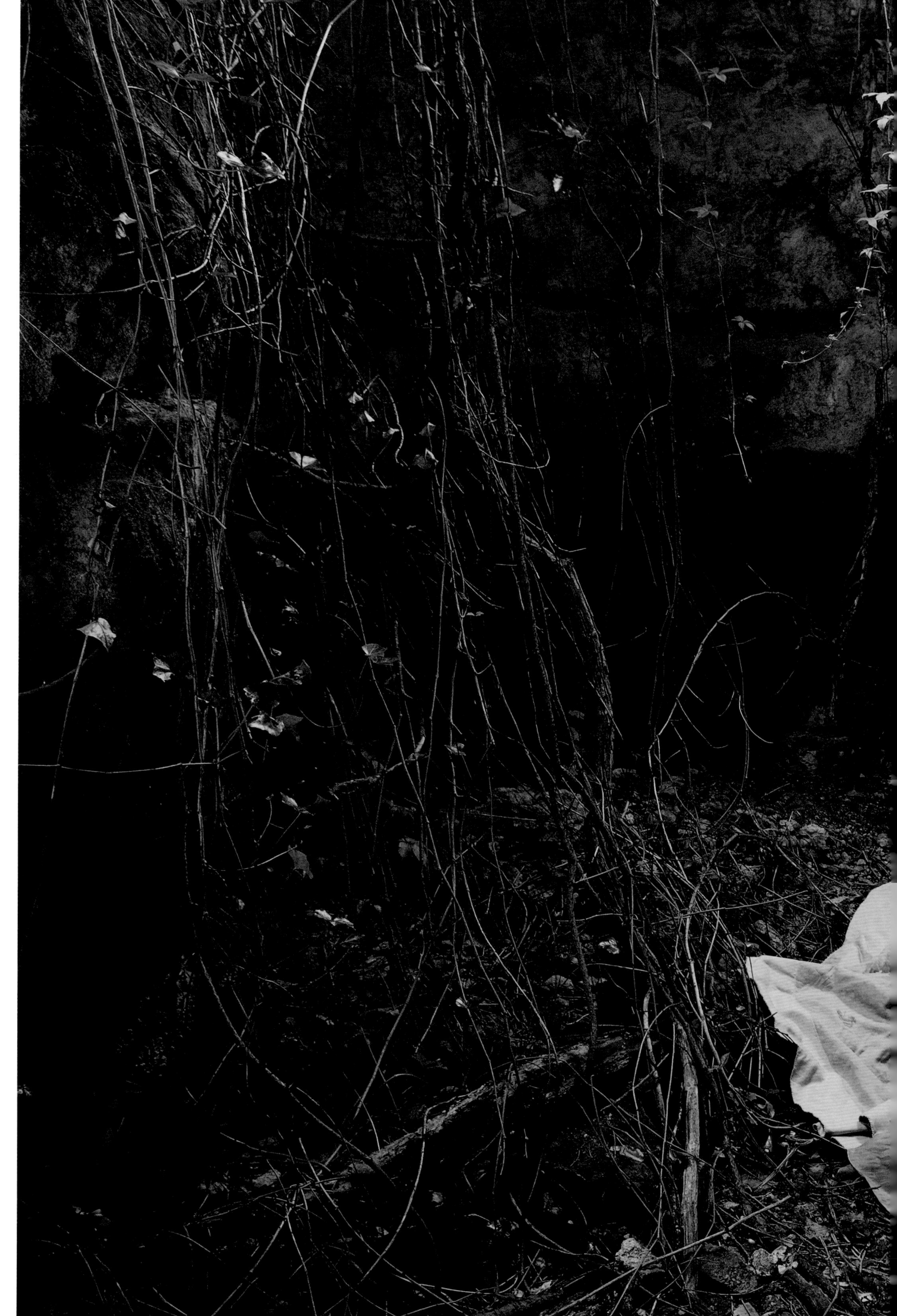

One scene in the Marie Antoinette story took place at the bottom of a cave on the grounds of the Château de Stors, north of Paris. In the eighteenth century, the owner kept two bears there.

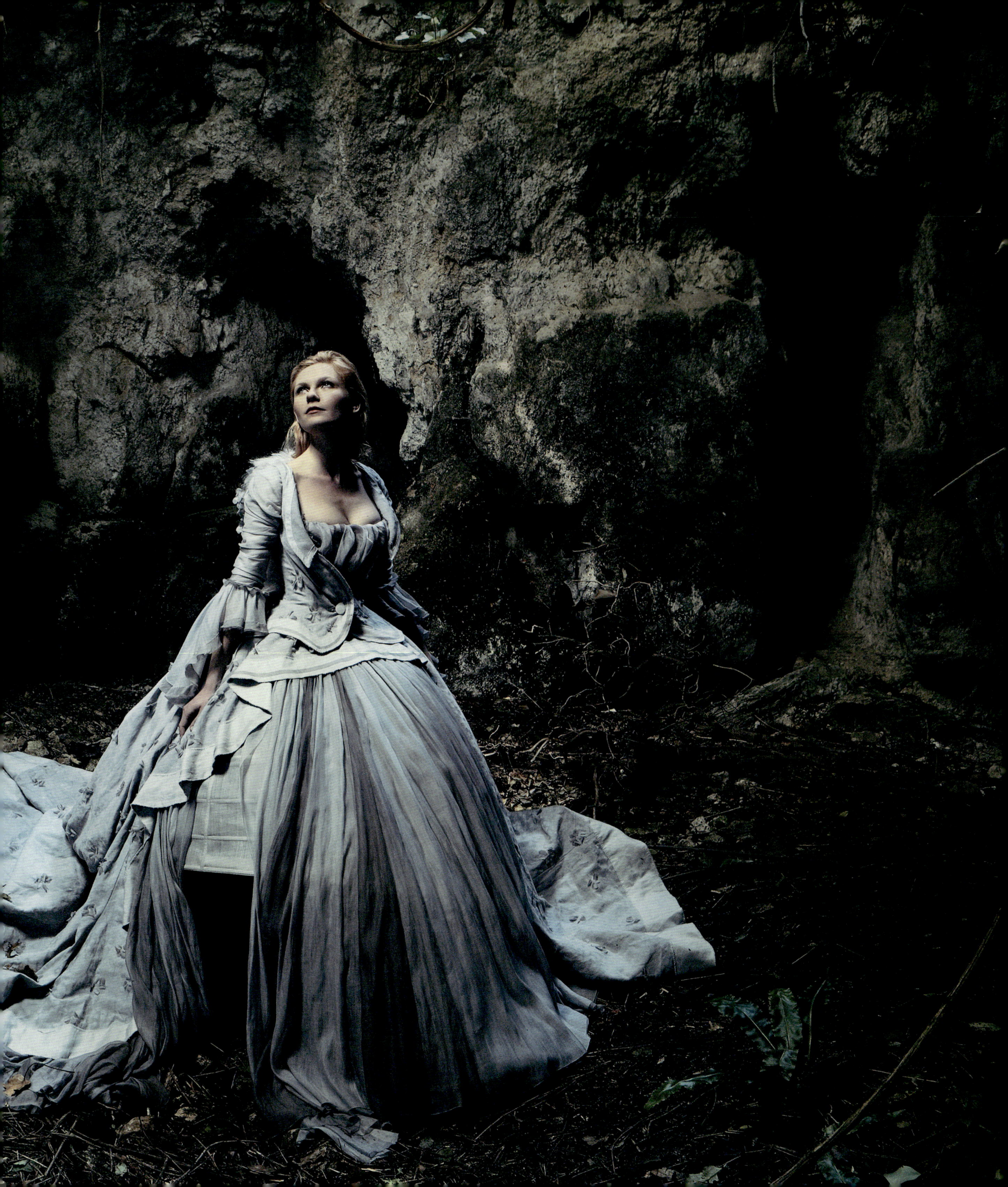

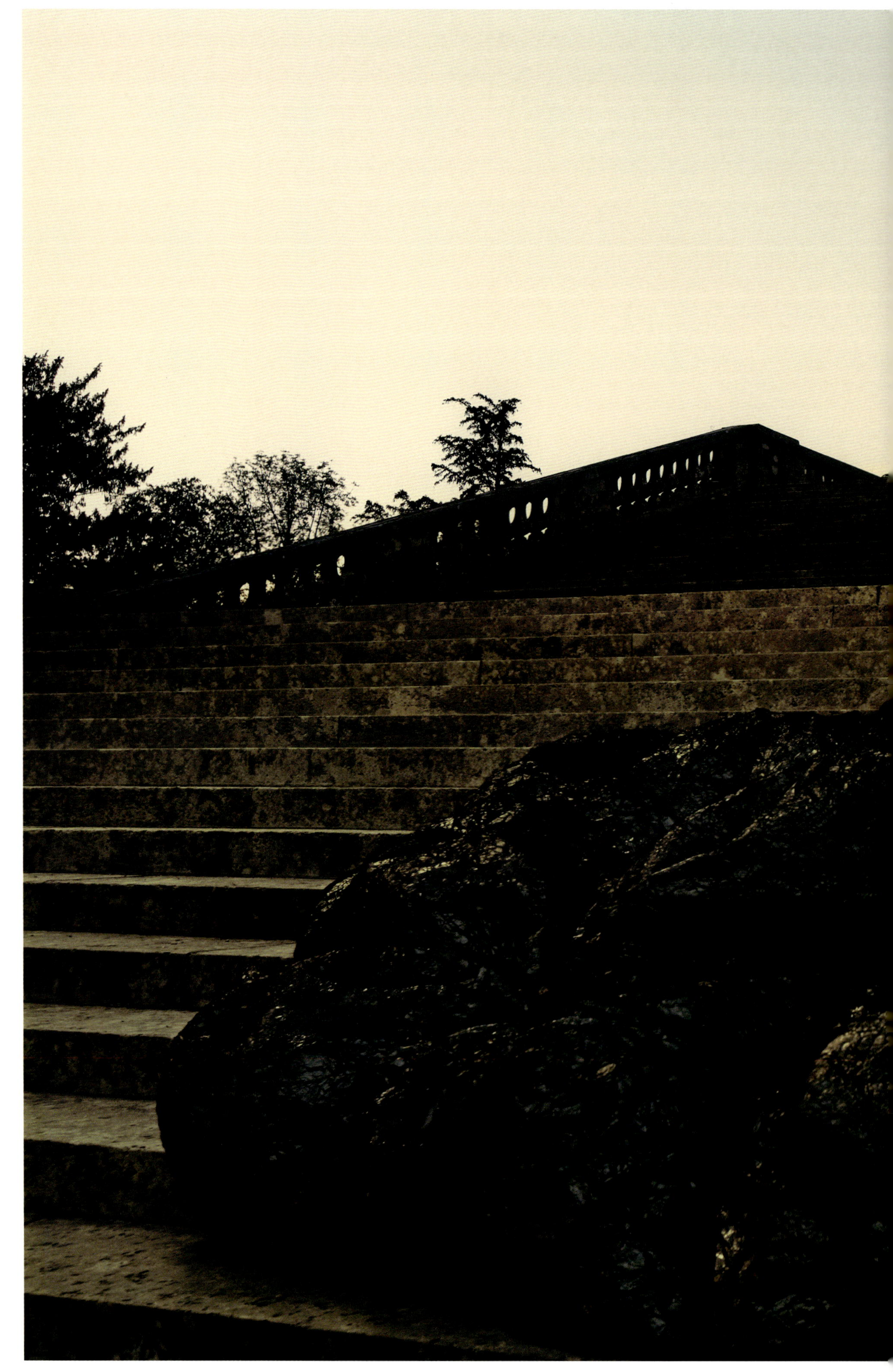

The Hundred Steps
leading to the Orangerie,
Versailles, France, 2006

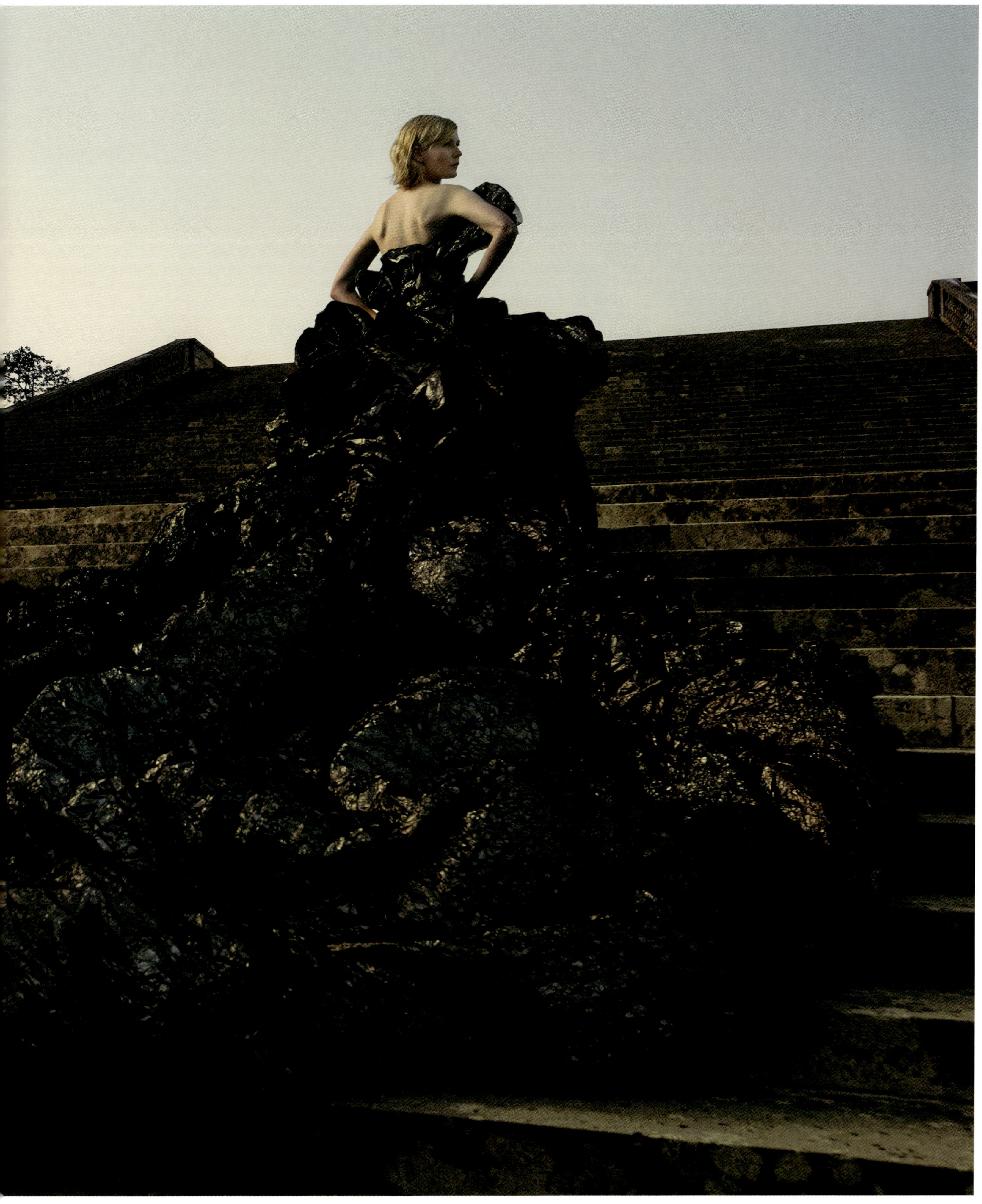

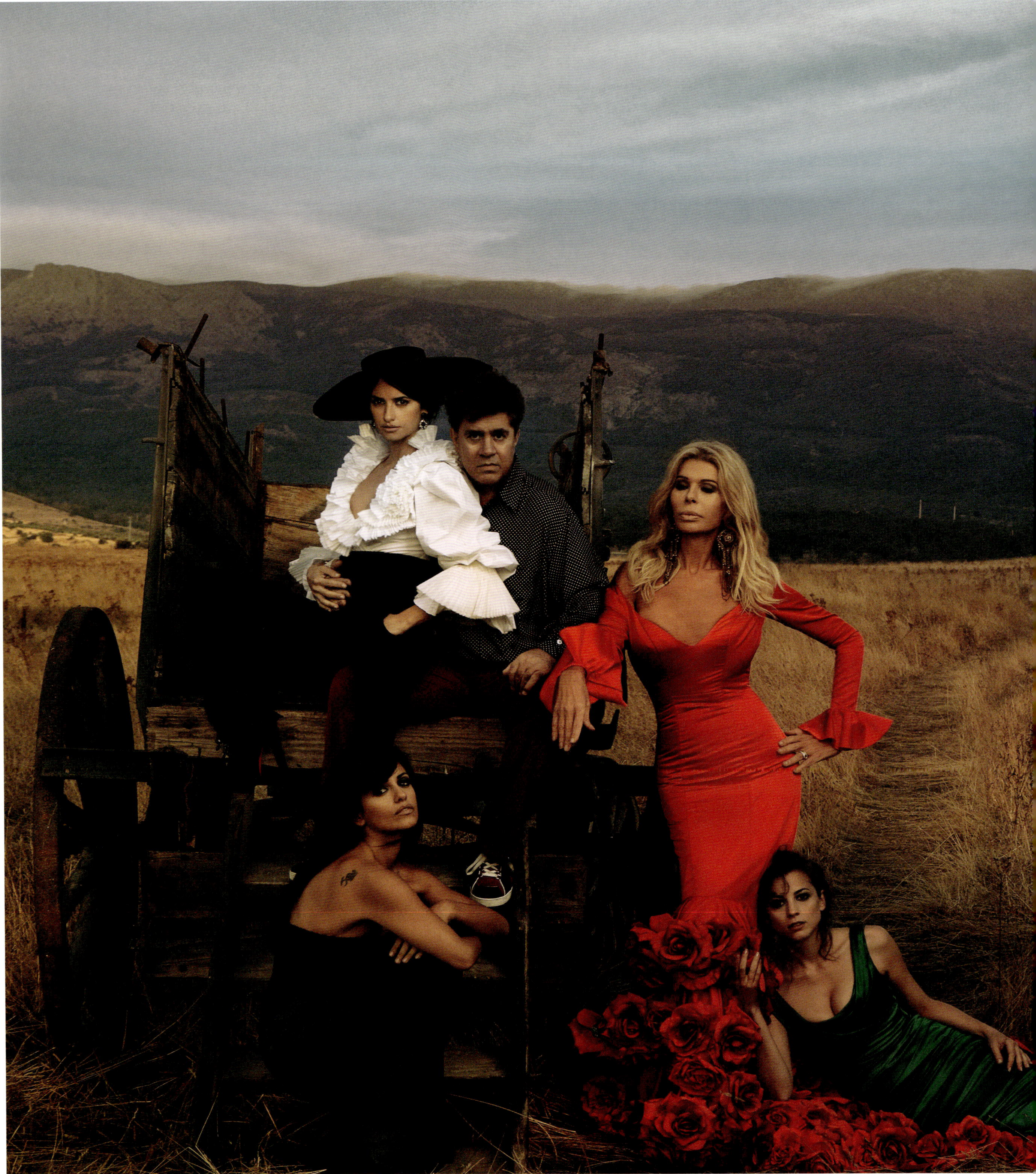

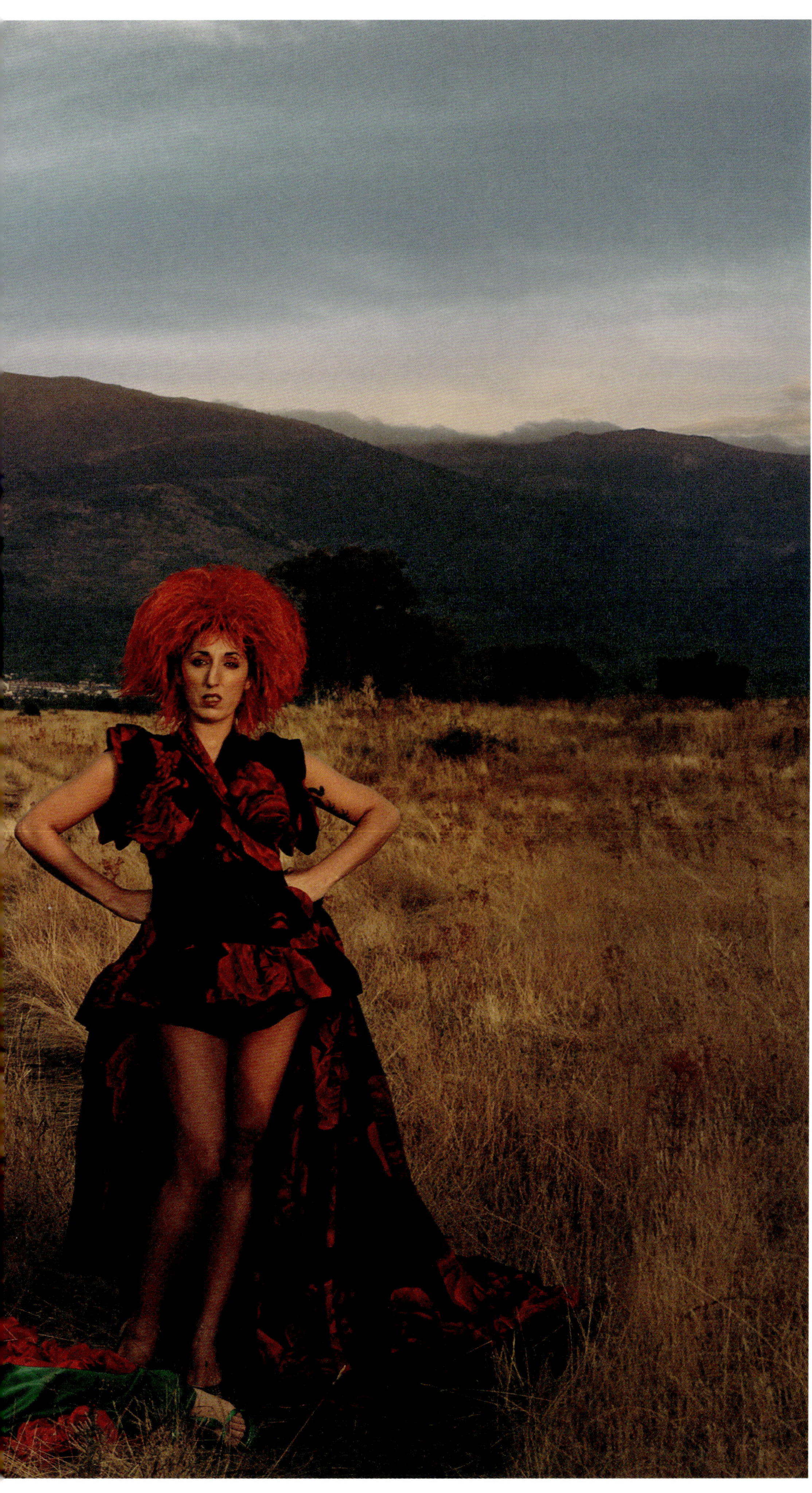

“I had photographed Penélope Cruz several times before, but the shoot in Spain was different. Penélope was so relaxed and confident. She was proud to be at home. Pedro Almodóvar, who calls her his muse, was part of the shoot.”

Penélope Cruz, Pedro Almodóvar, Bibiana Fernández, Rossy de Palma, Leonor Watling, and Penélope’s sister, Mónica, outside of Madrid, 2007

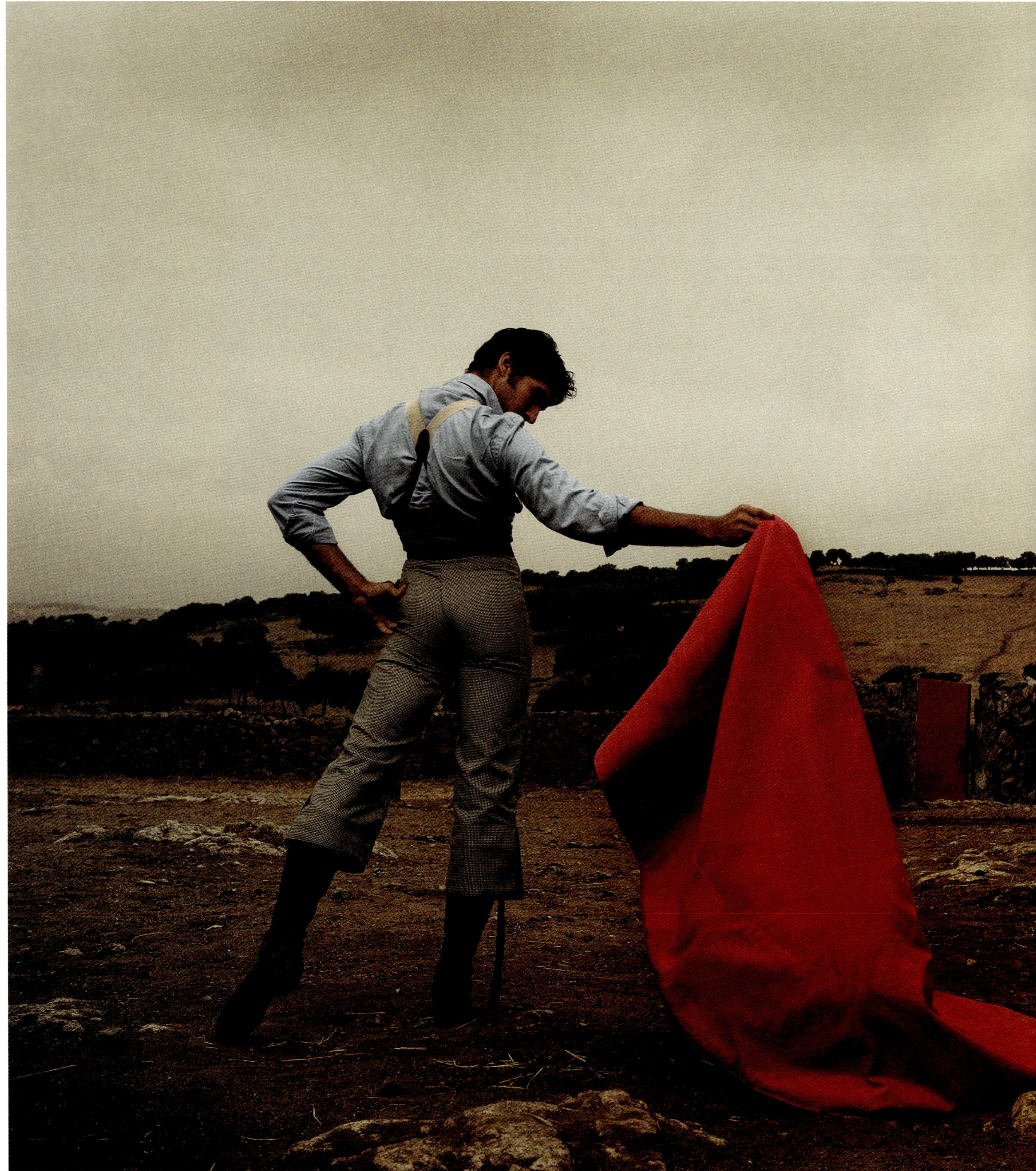

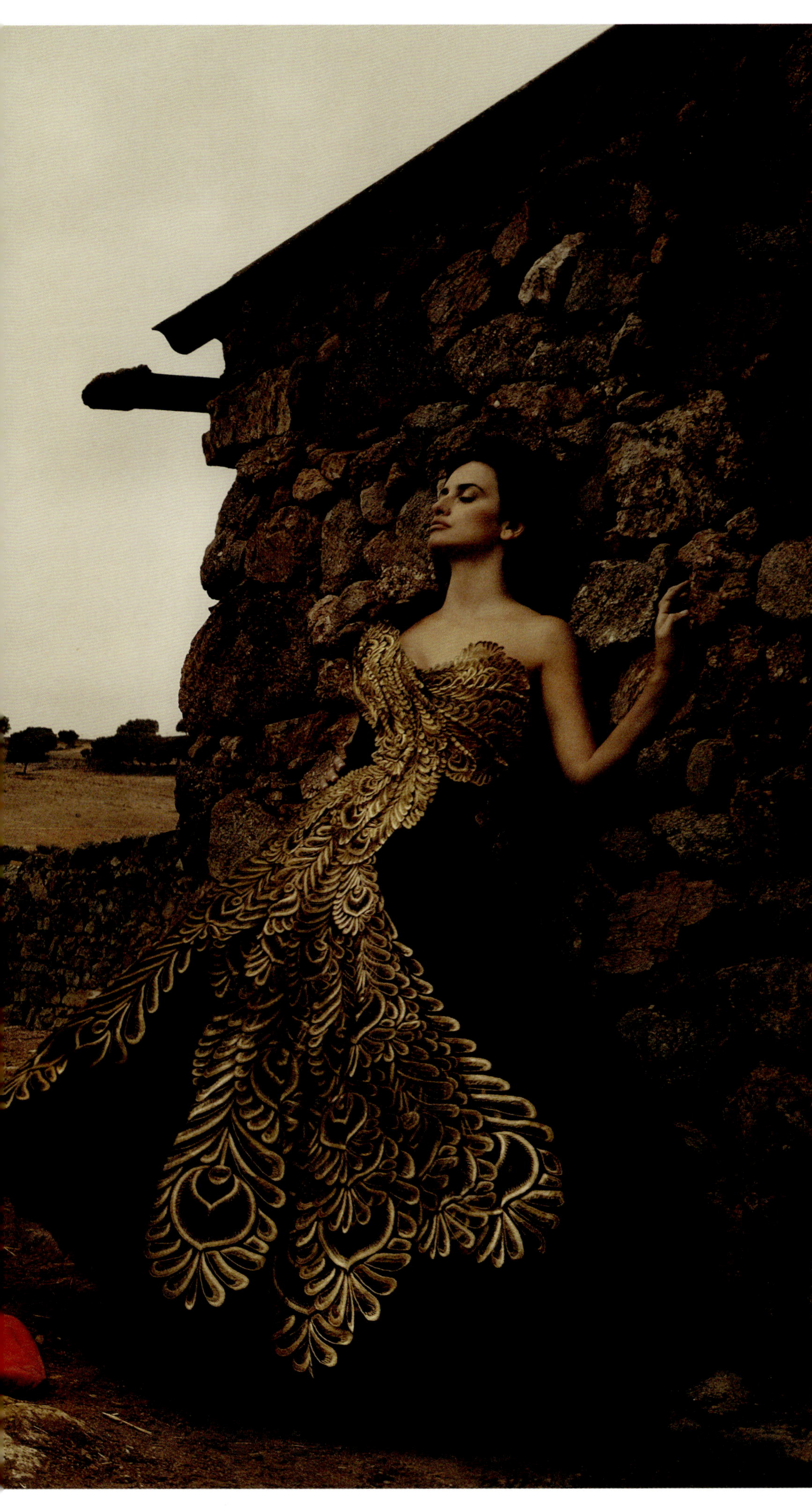

"Cayetano Rivera Ordóñez is from a famous bullfighting family. His great-grandfather was the model for the matador in Ernest Hemingway's *The Sun Also Rises*.

The day before the shoot, he had been gored in the thigh. While we were working, blood began seeping through his pants."

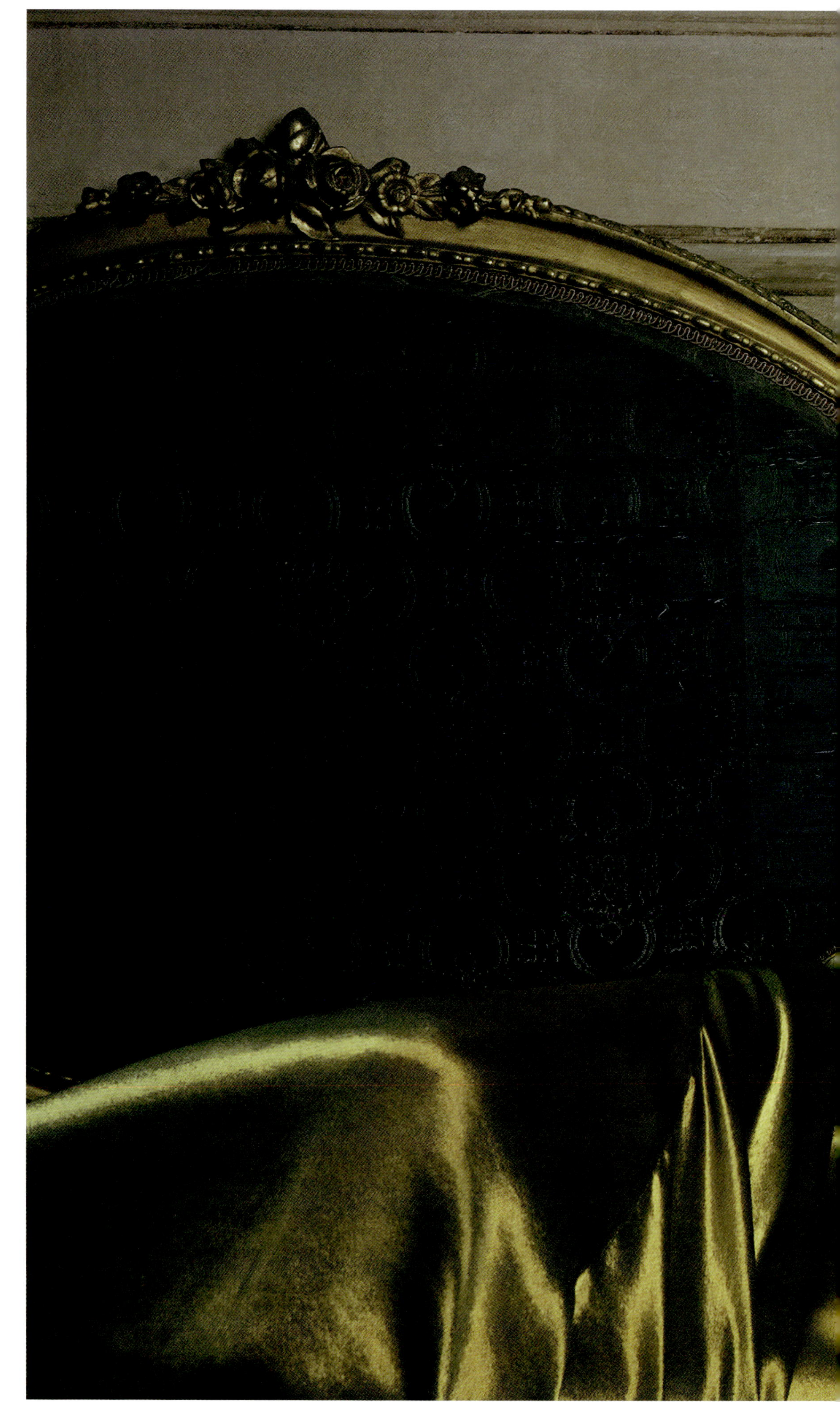

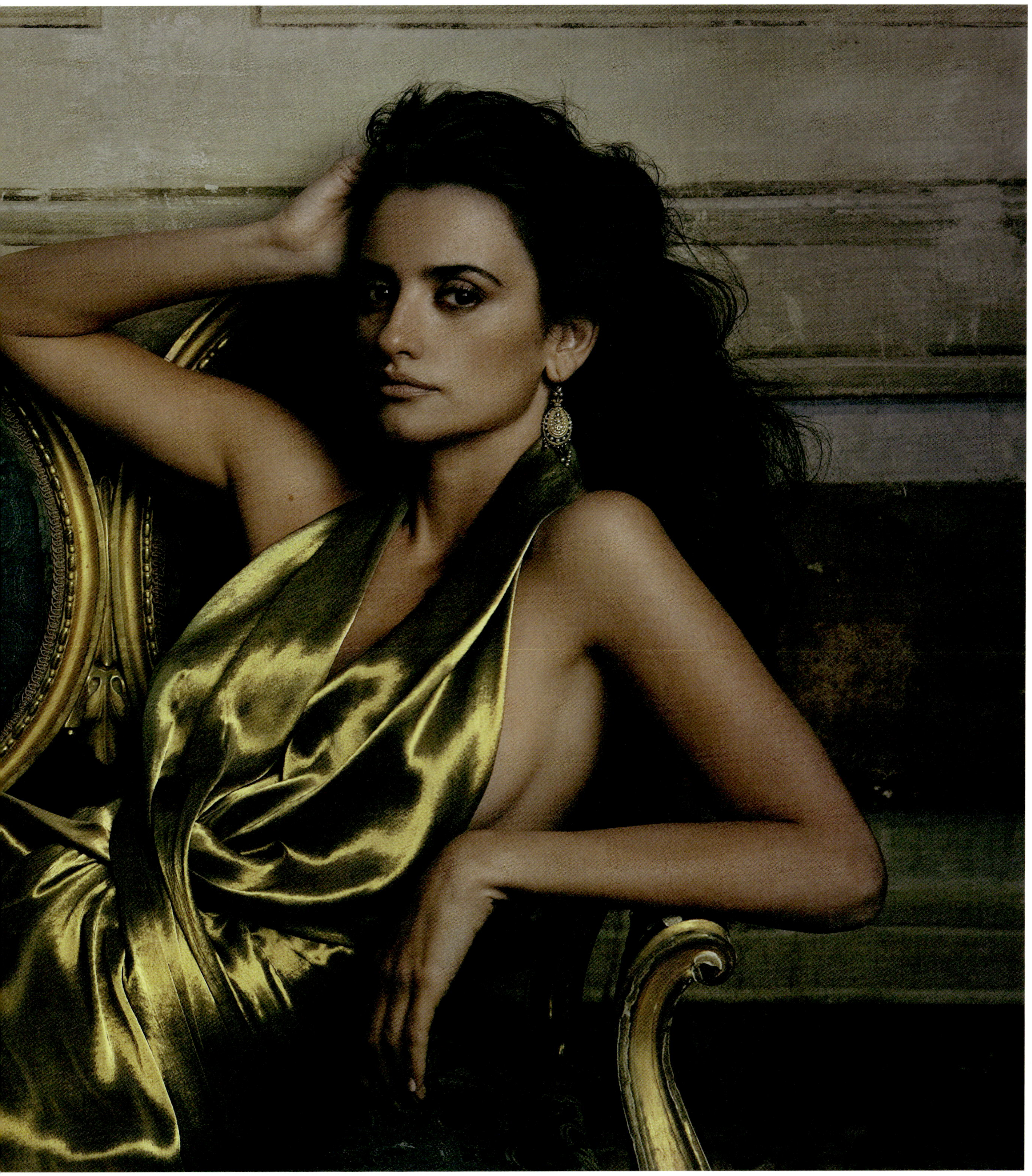

Cruz is in full air-drum mode, shaking her head and furiously swatting the space between her legs, transformed into a wild, carefree teenager before my eyes. I don't know what kind of unintentional look I must be giving her, but she clearly knows how funny this is because she suddenly glances across at me, squeezes my knee, and bursts out laughing.

"Penélope is such a goofball," Scarlett Johansson tells me later. "It's hilarious because here's this beautiful creature who is so serious about her acting and about her humanitarian work. And then she plays air drums, and you're like, Oh, my God, you're just like that nerd at summer camp!"

By about eight in the evening, I'm ready to get some rest. But Penélope's energy is entirely undimmed. She looks out the window, and an idea pops into her head: "Since we're passing, do you want to dash into Prada for ten minutes?" Her ten-minute dash is admirably efficient: It yields a black wool fall jacket, a Kim Novak–esque gray suit, a bottle-green cardigan, and a sublime black forties-inspired dress. "Remember that line I have in *All About My Mother?*" she smiles, recalling her role as the HIV-positive Sister Rosa: "'Prada seems to me ideal for nuns.'"

A few days later, when I meet Almodóvar in London between rehearsals for the stage version of that movie, he tells me about the plans he has for his muse. "If I were to make a period movie, I would cast her as a nineteenth-century European," he says. "I can see Penélope perfectly as the Claudia Cardinale character in *The Leopard.* Then there's another side to her that has not really been developed, which is comedy. I see her as ideally suited to a screwball comedy—she could be Holly Golightly or another Audrey Hepburn character, the one in *Two for the Road.* And the third kind of role I have in mind is a darker character, a film noir heroine along the lines of Gene Tierney: a mysterious woman—tough, romantic, disillusioned."

The list is extraordinary: partly because of the detail with which Almodóvar has already imagined these hoped-for creations, down to the makeup and hairstyles, and partly because he knows Penélope can be all of those things. I say she clearly inspires him to an incredible extent, and Almodóvar smiles: "There are so many things I'd like to do with her that I hope we can go on working together for the rest of our lives." □

346

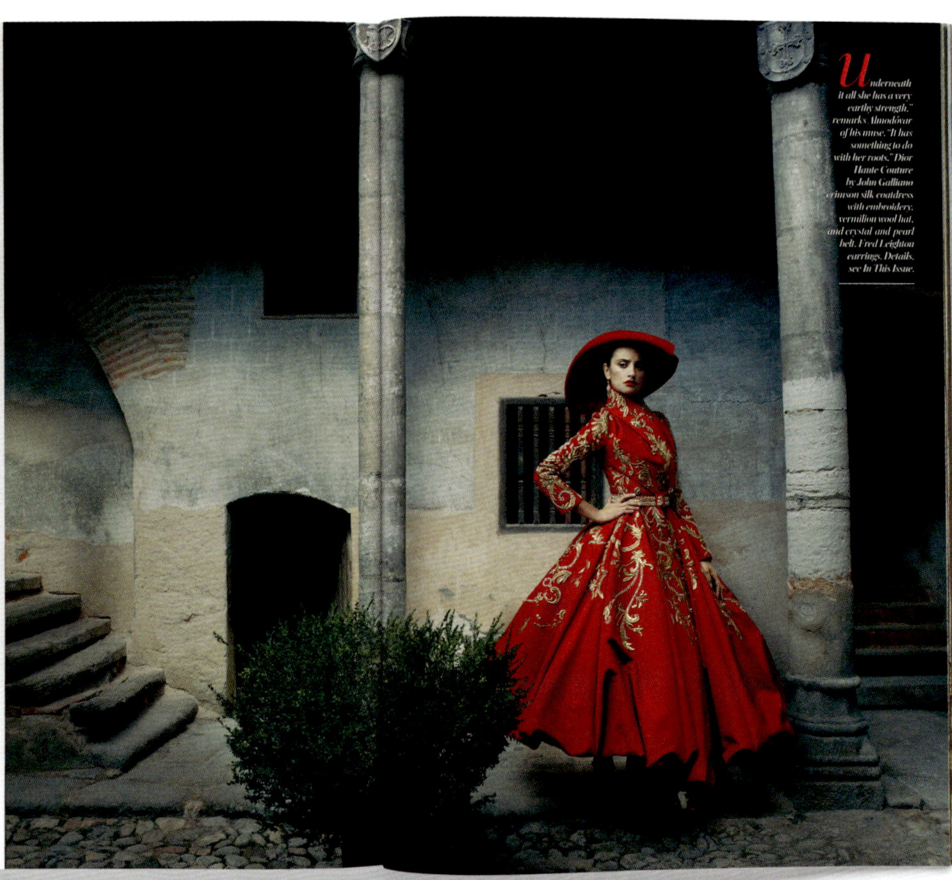

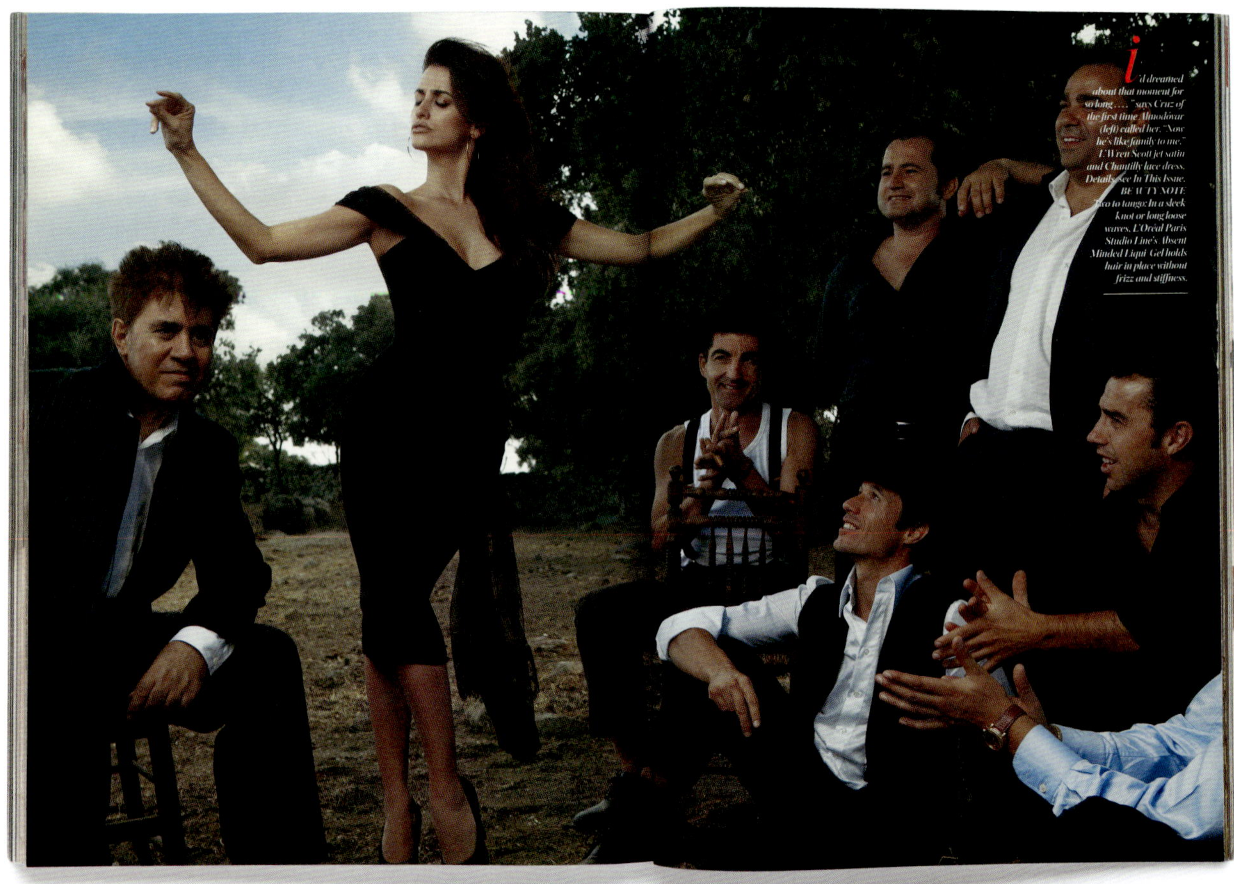

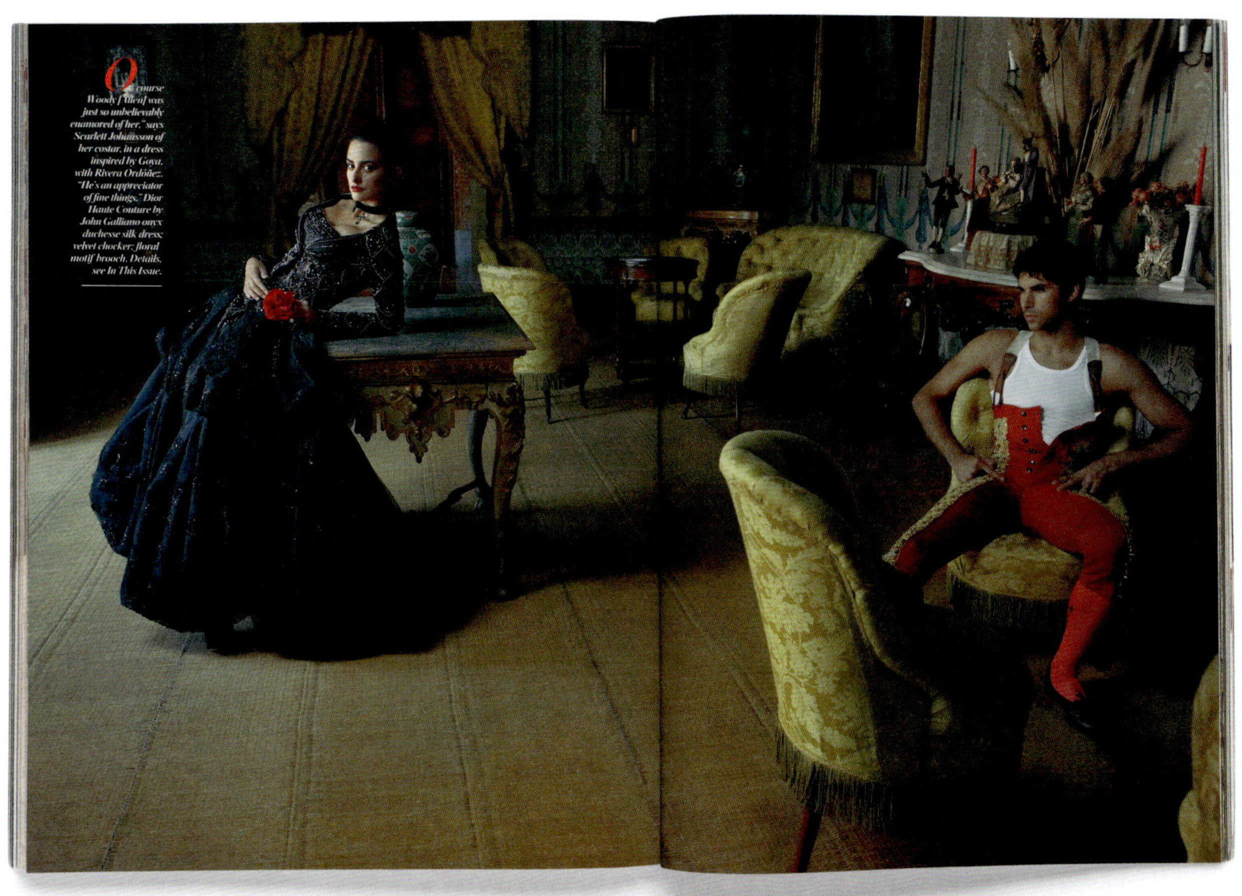

Of course Woody [Allen] was just so unbelievably enamored of her," says Scarlett Johansson of her costar, in a dress inspired by Goya, with Rivera Ordóñez. "He's an appreciator of fine things." Dior Haute Couture by John Galliano onyx duchesse silk dress; velvet chocker; floral motif brooch. Details, see In This Issue.

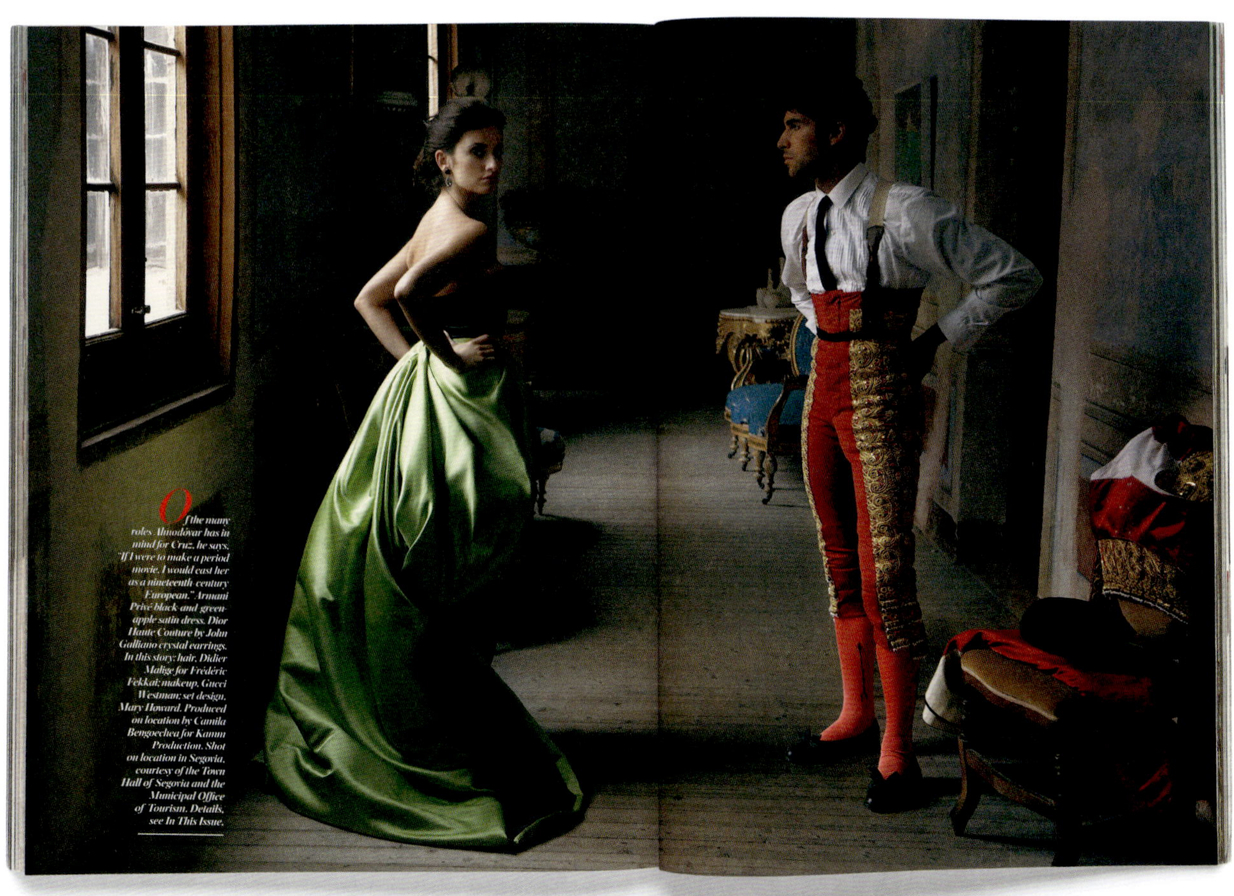

Of the many roles Almodóvar has in mind for Cruz, he says, "If I were to make a period movie, I would cast her as a nineteenth-century European." Armani Privé black-and green-apple satin dress. Dior Haute Couture by John Galliano crystal earrings. In this story: hair, Didier Malige for Frédéric Fekkai; makeup, Gucci Westman; set design, Mary Howard. Produced on location by Camila Bengoechea for Kamm Production. Shot on location in Segovia, courtesy of the Town Hall of Segovia and the Municipal Office of Tourism. Details, see In This Issue.

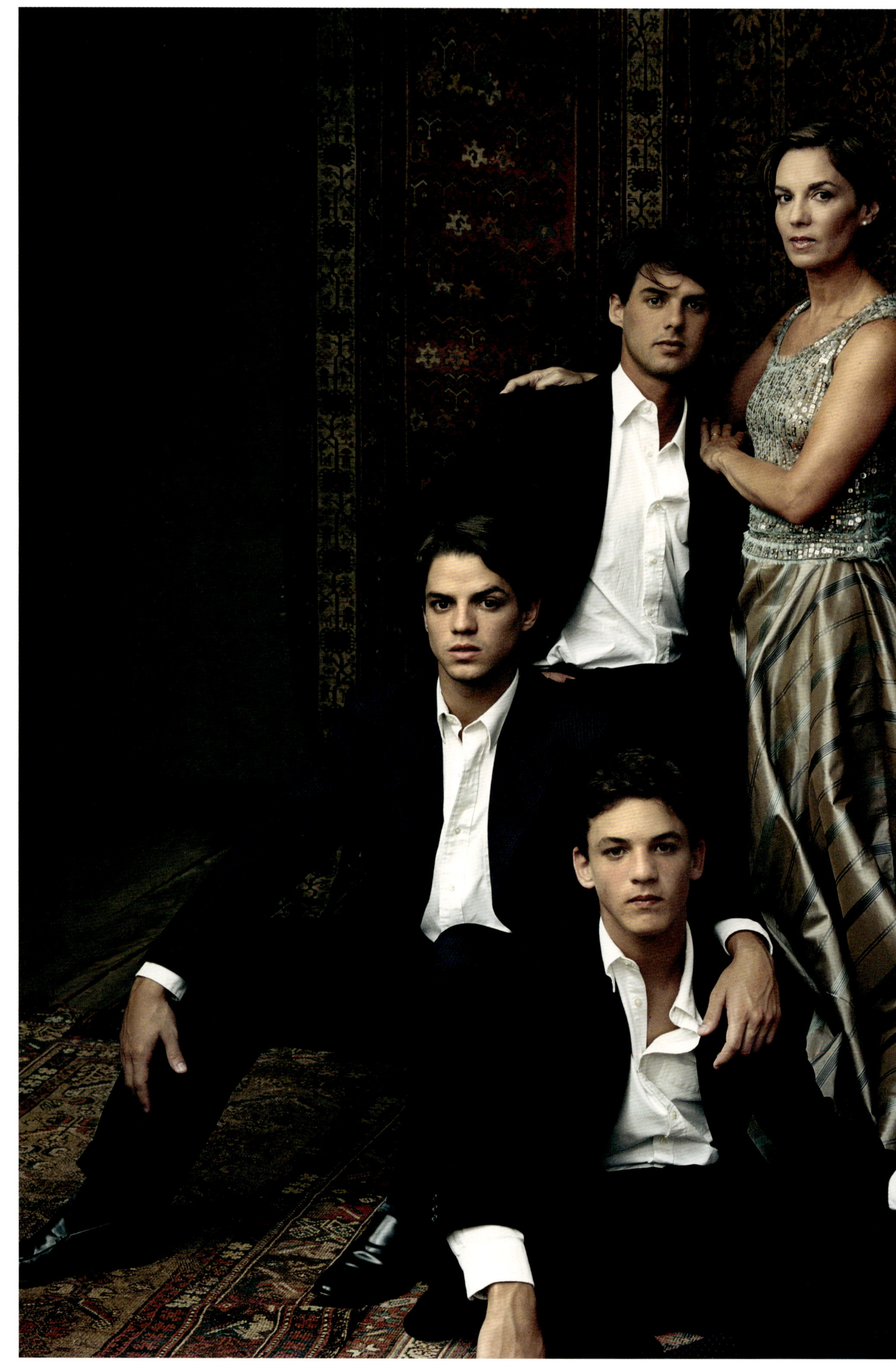

Carolina Herrera with her four daughters and their children, New York City, 2004: Mercedes Mendoza and her sons, Roberto, Federico, and Rodrigo; Ana Luisa Calicchio with Axel; Carolina Jr. with Oriana; Carolina Herrera with baby Carolina Lansing; Patricia Lansing

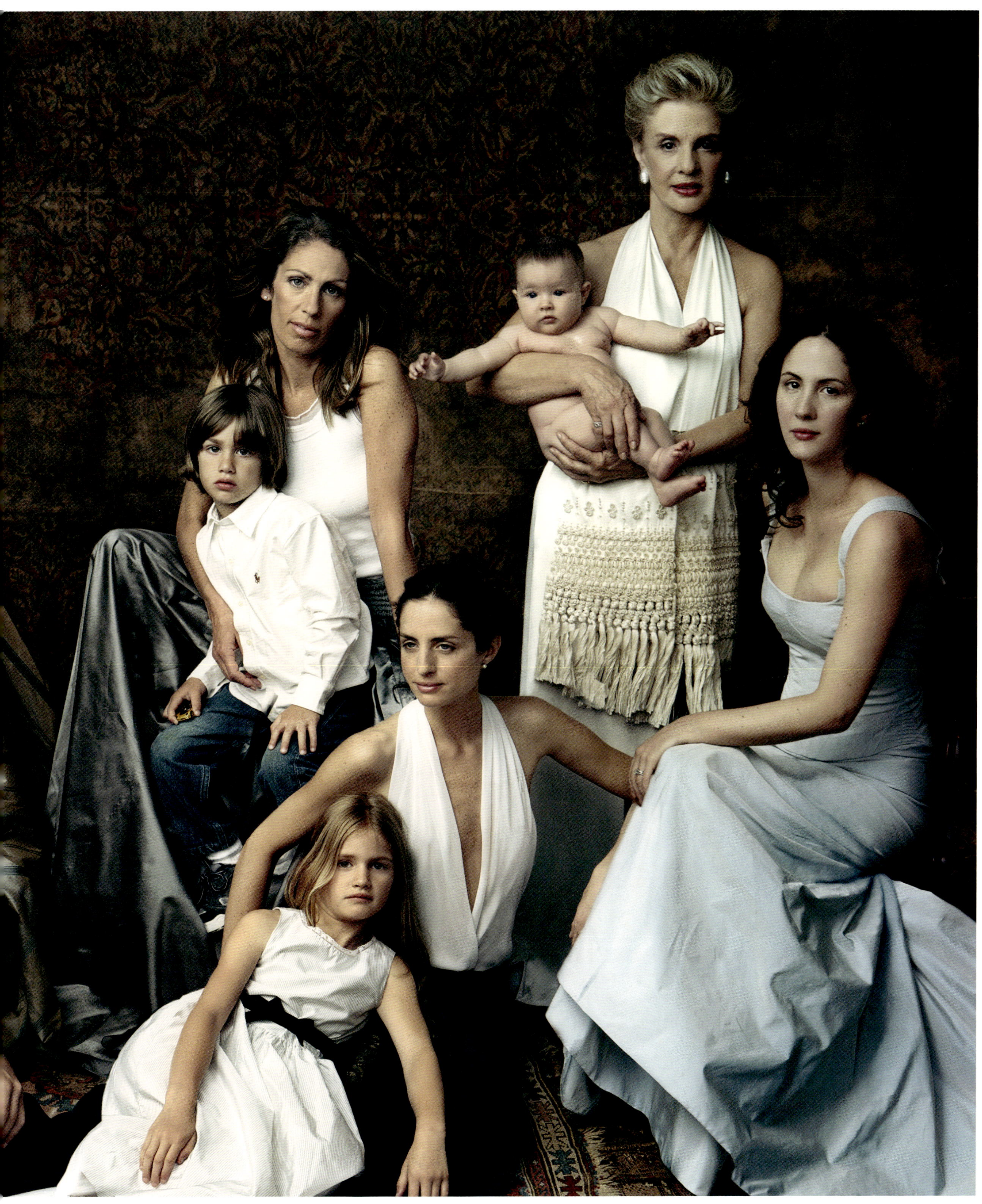

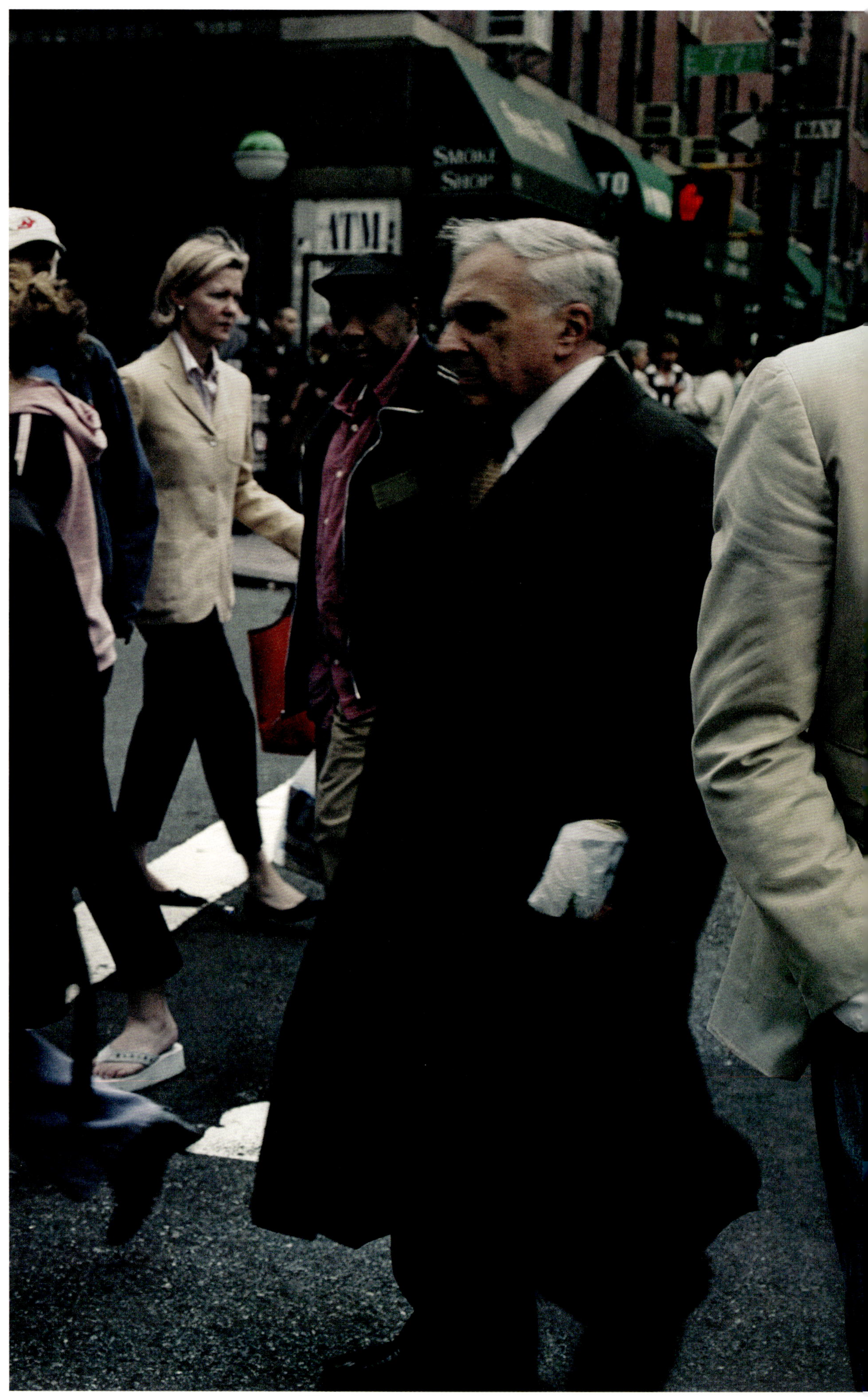

Andy and Kate Spade,
New York City, 2004

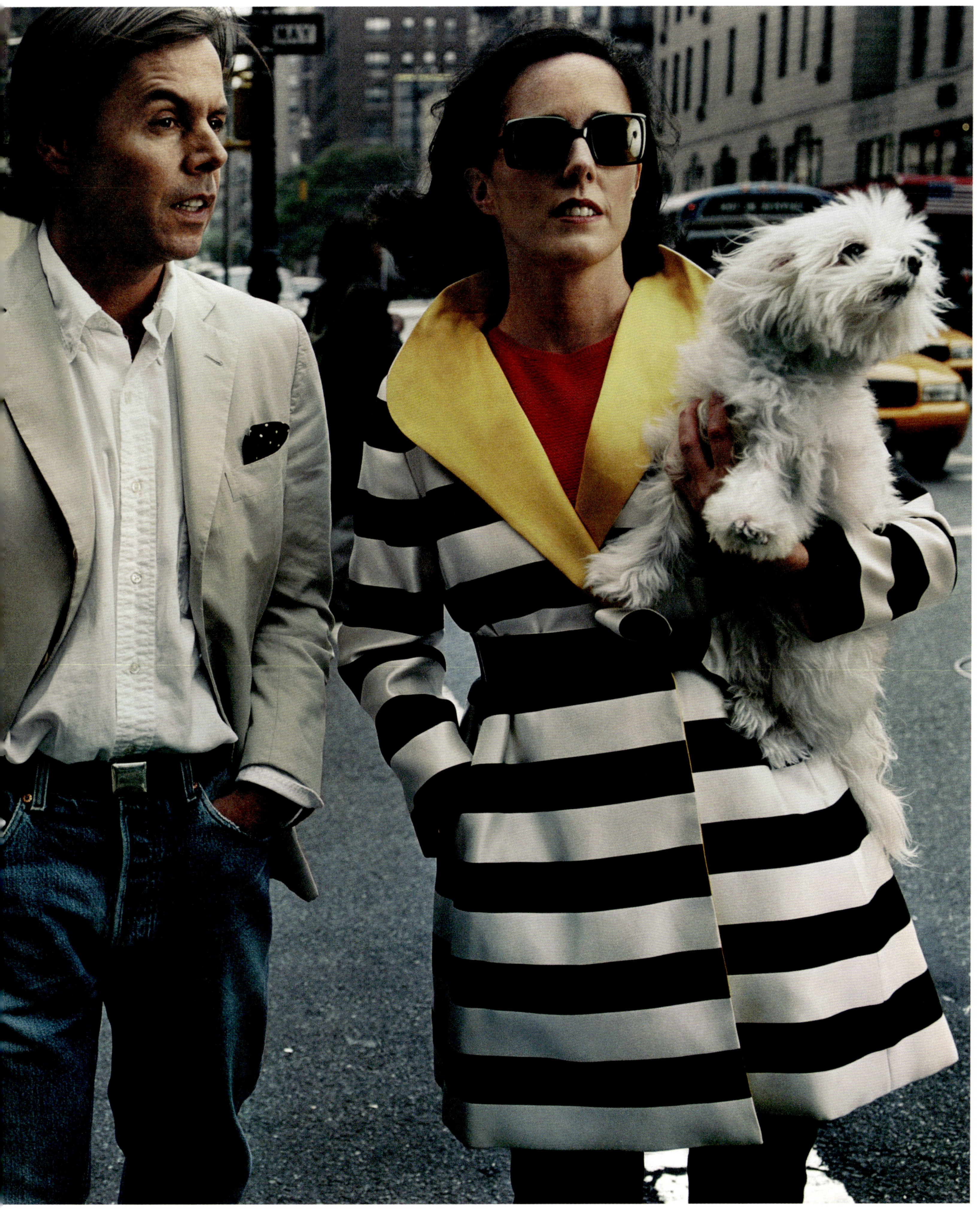

In 2005 the Plaza Hotel in New York was shut down, and the interiors were dismantled for a liquidation sale. New owners were turning much of the building into multimillion-dollar condominiums that would serve as pieds-à-terre for wealthy foreigners. It was the end of something.

The opulent hotel had flourished at the corner of Central Park South and Fifth Avenue for nearly a hundred years. Truman Capote threw his Black and White Ball in the Grand Ballroom of the Plaza for five hundred guests, who ate chicken hash and spaghetti at midnight. Cary Grant drank a cosmopolitan under the murals of the Oak Bar before kidnappers dragged him away in *North by Northwest*. Eloise, the resident six-year-old enfant terrible created by Kay Thompson for her nightclub act in the hotel's Persian Room, skipped along the halls, banging on doors before pouring water down the mail chute.

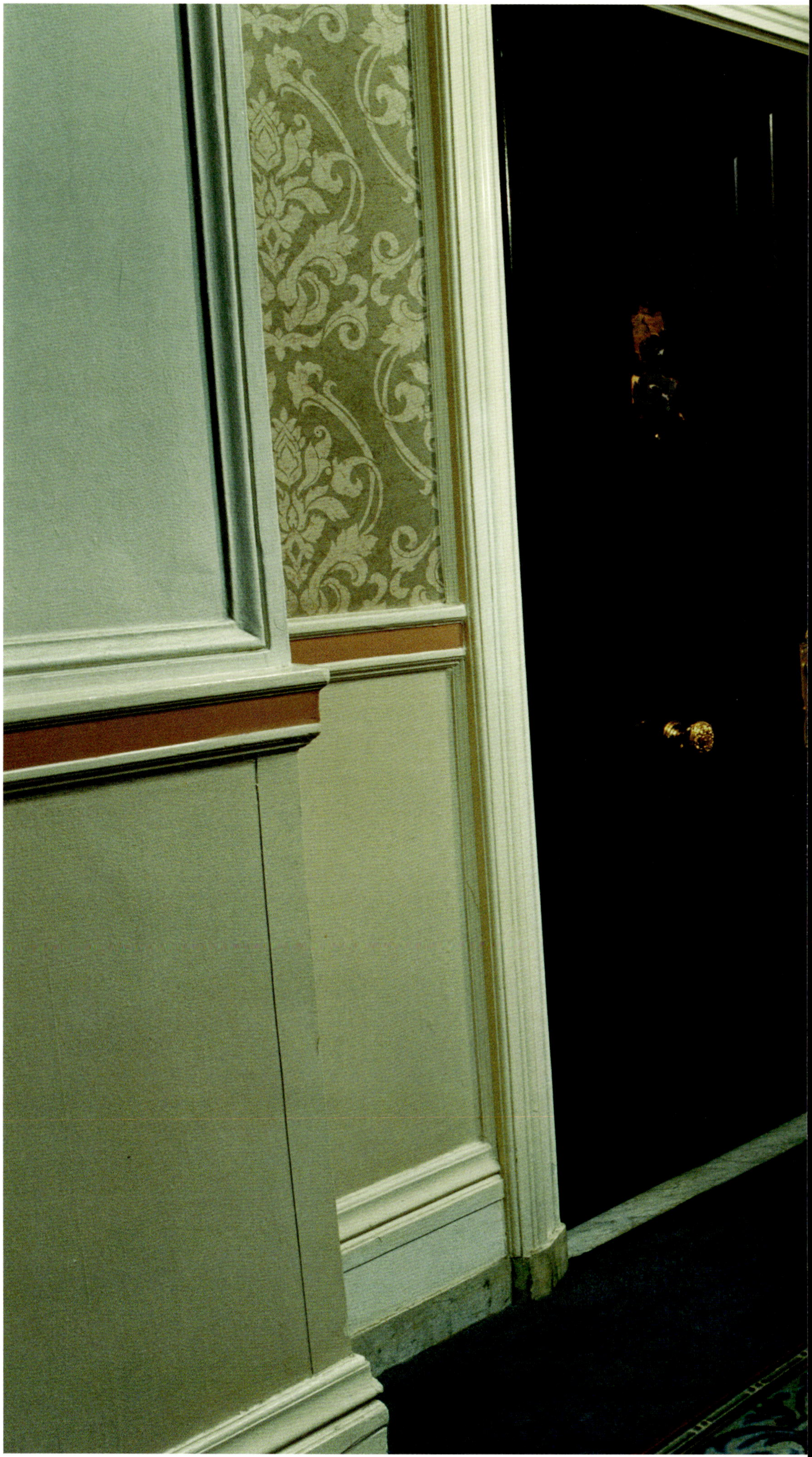

Sarah Jessica Parker,
the Plaza Hotel,
New York City, 2005

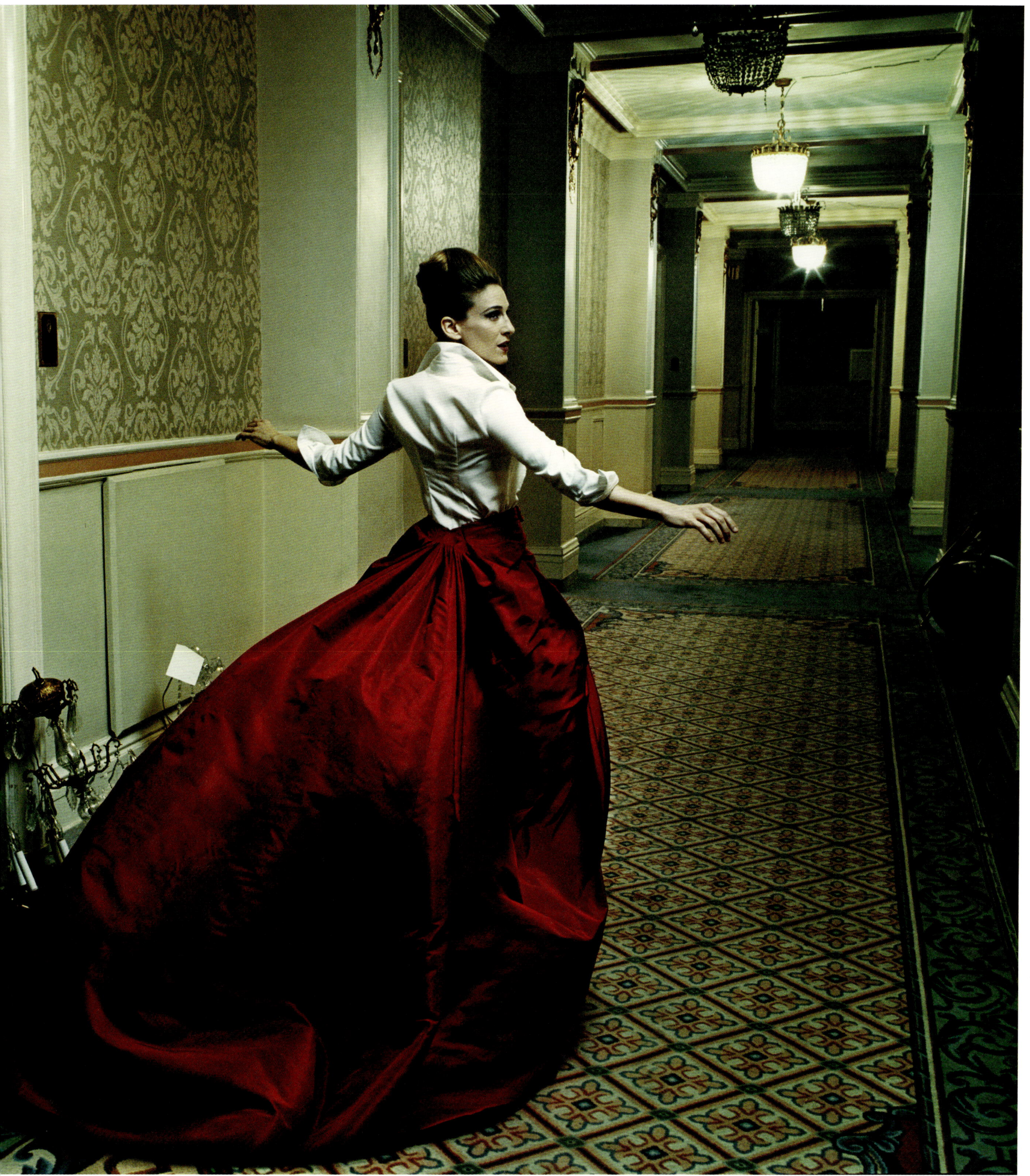

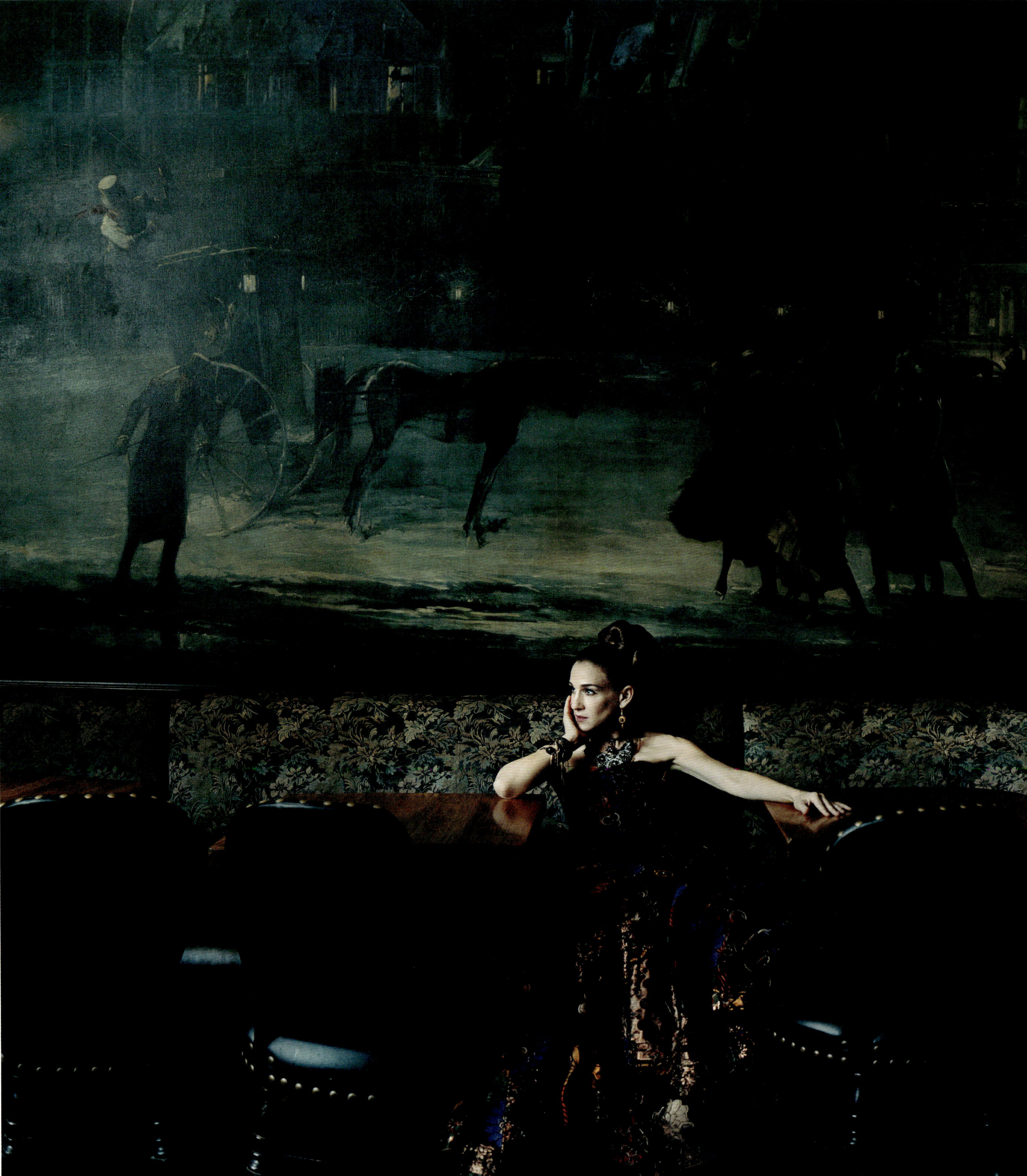

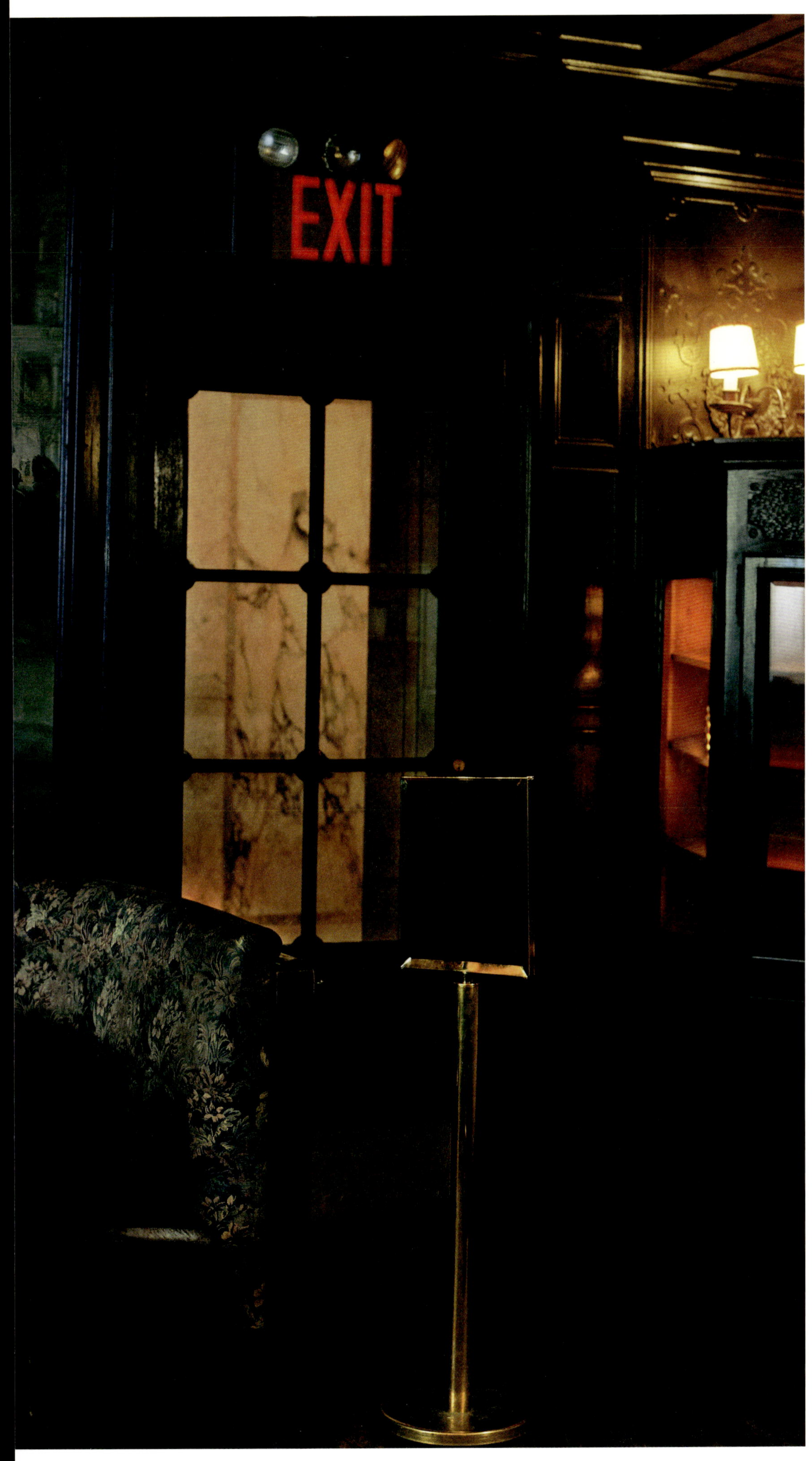

The Oak Room at the Plaza

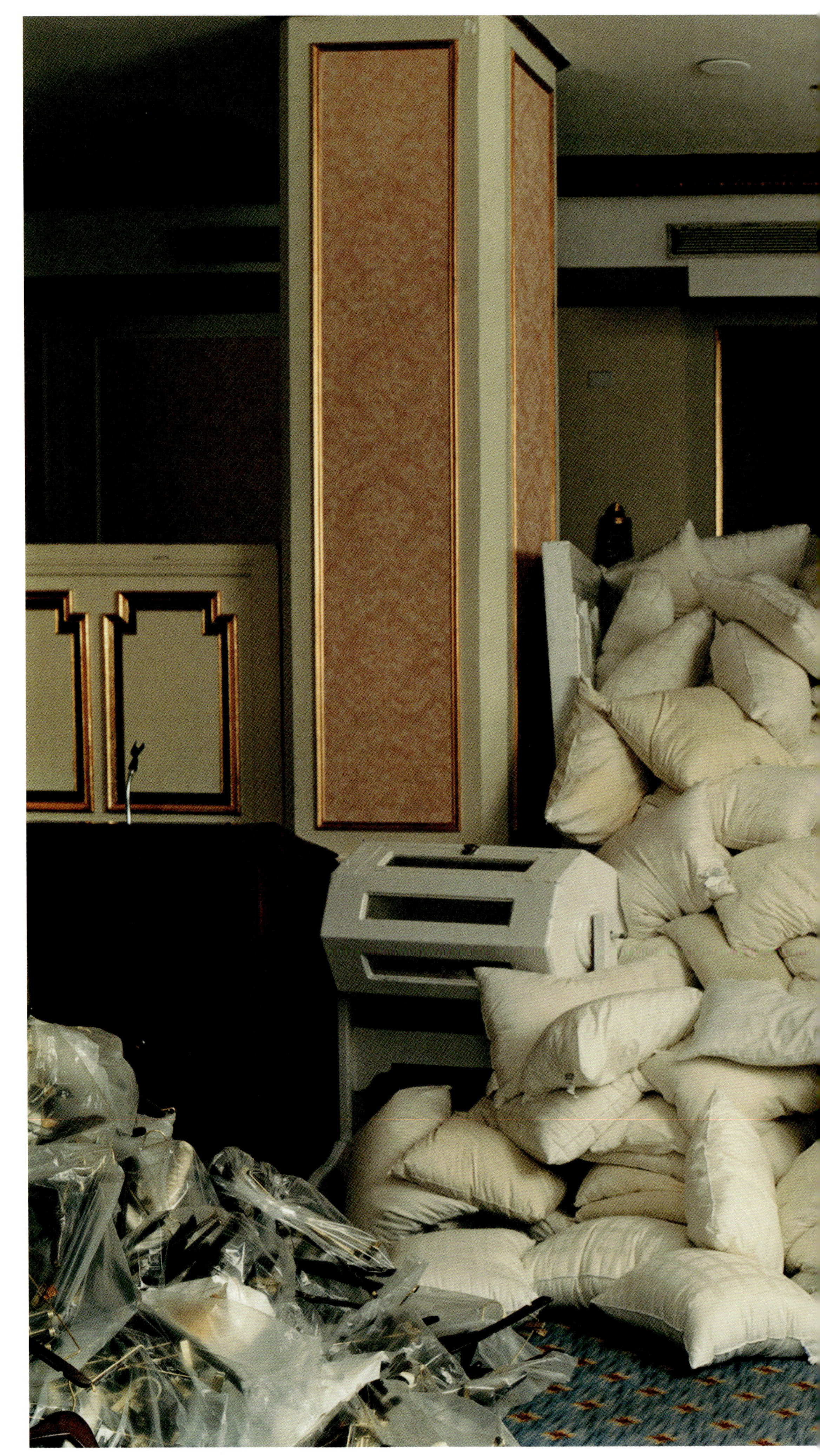

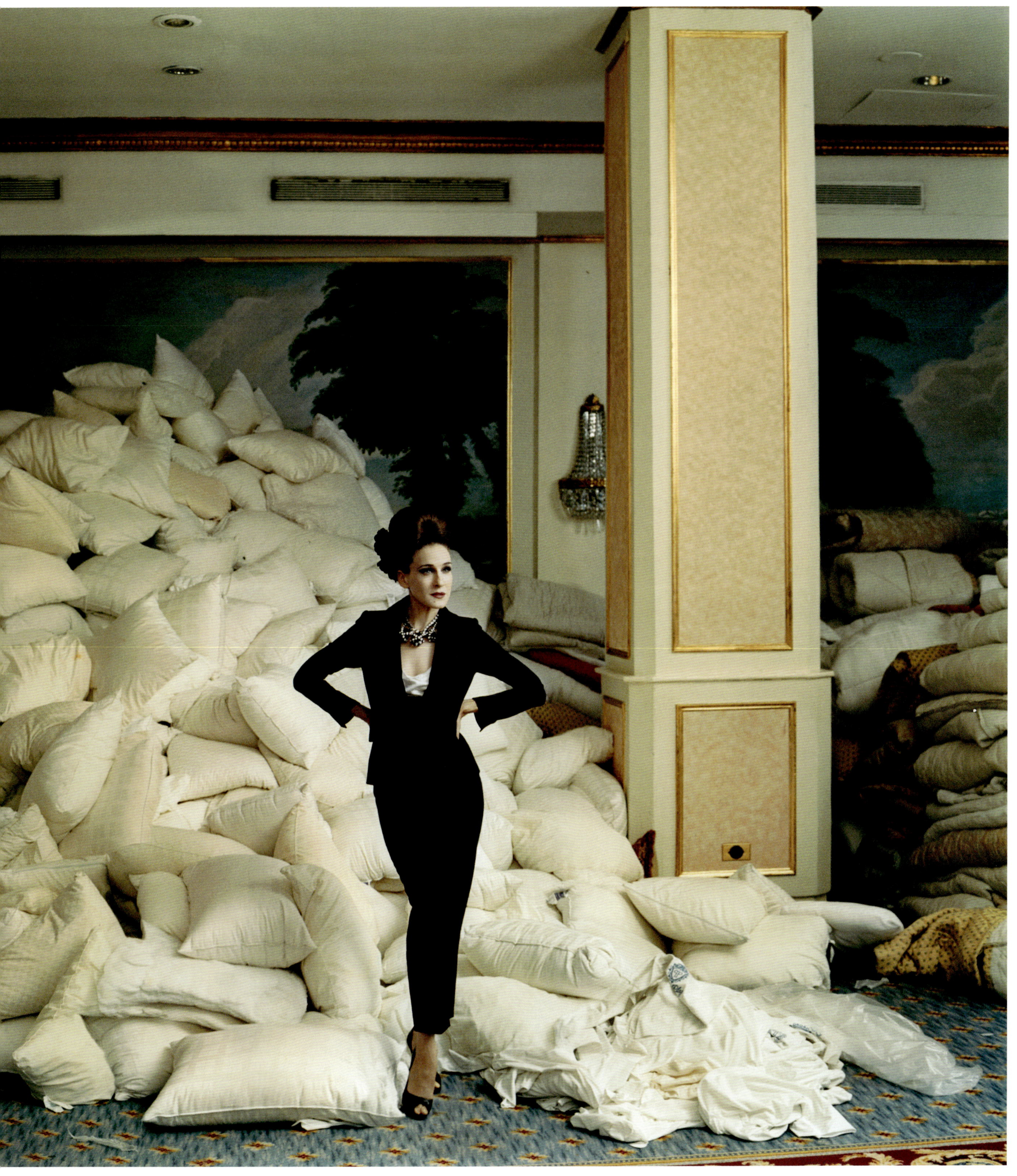

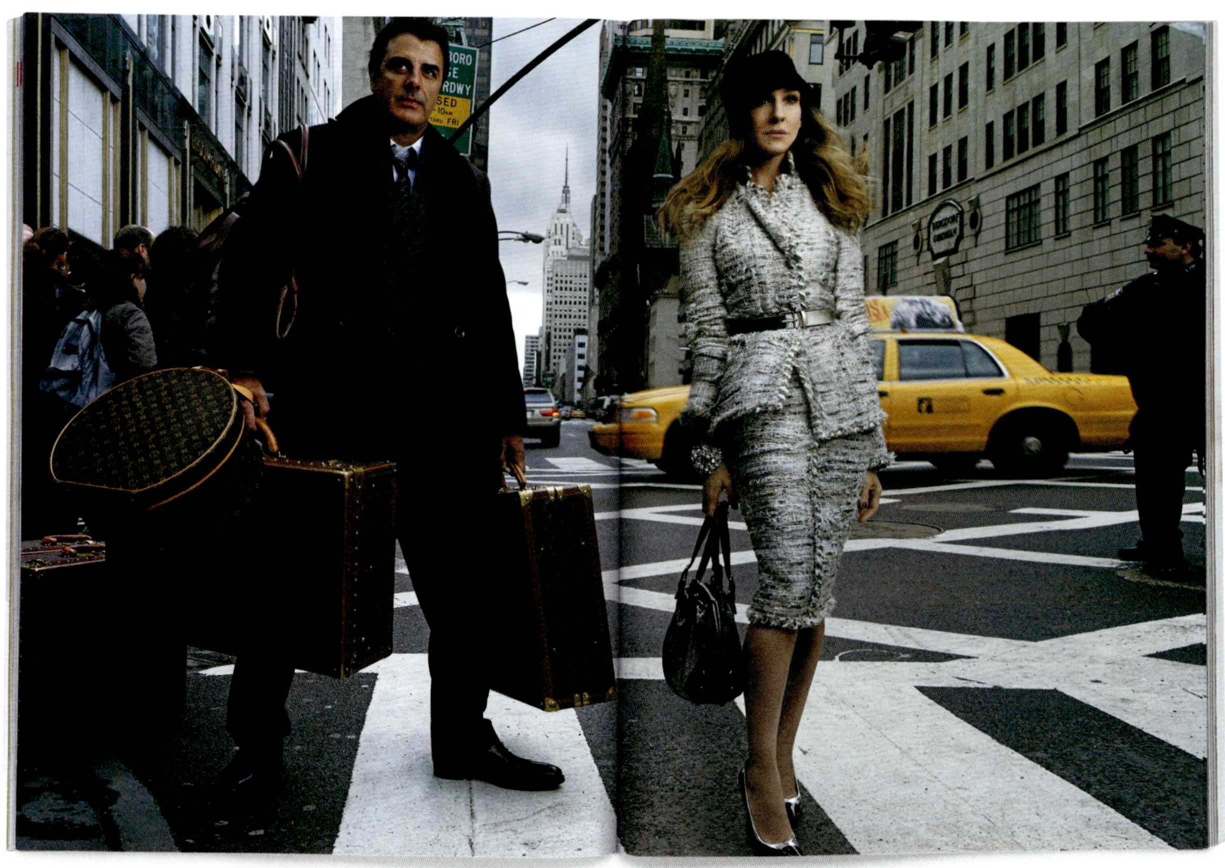

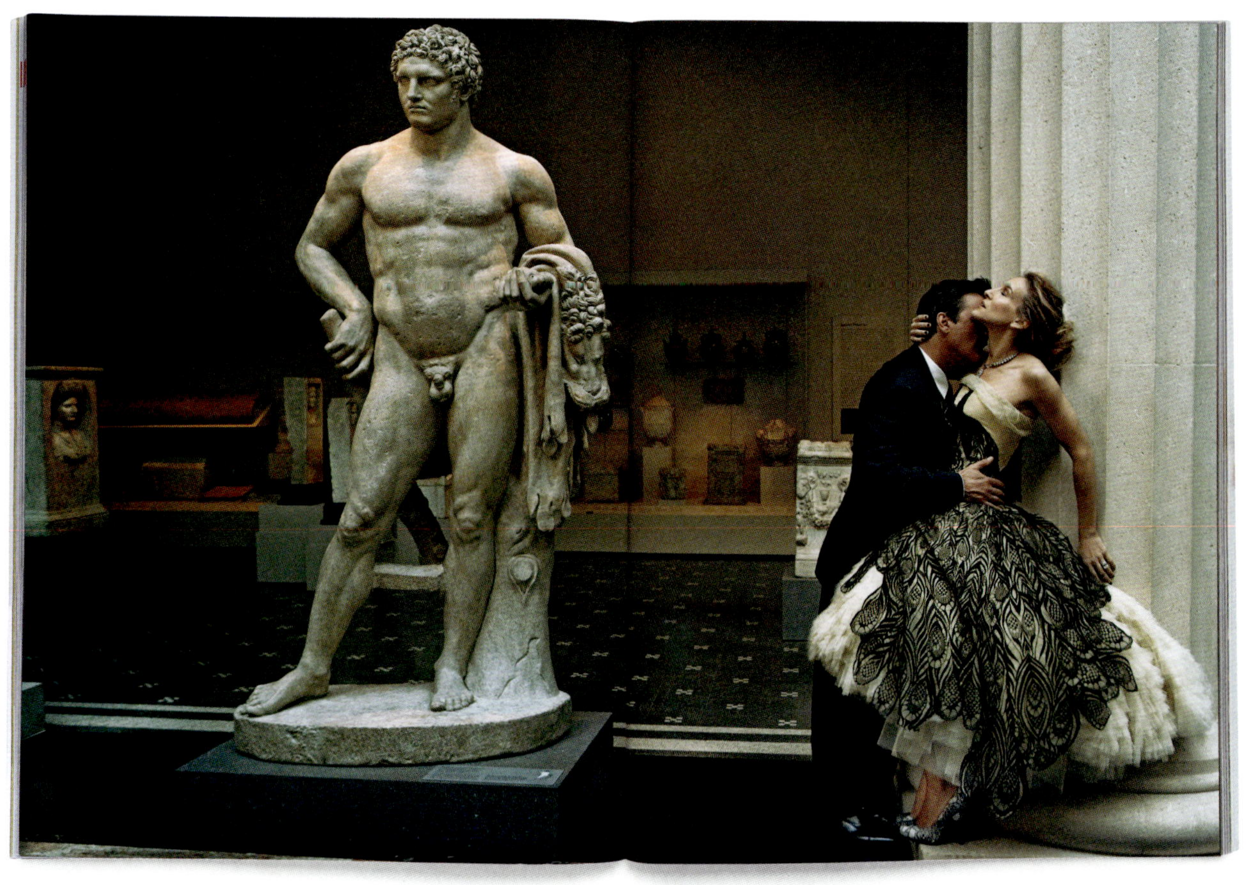

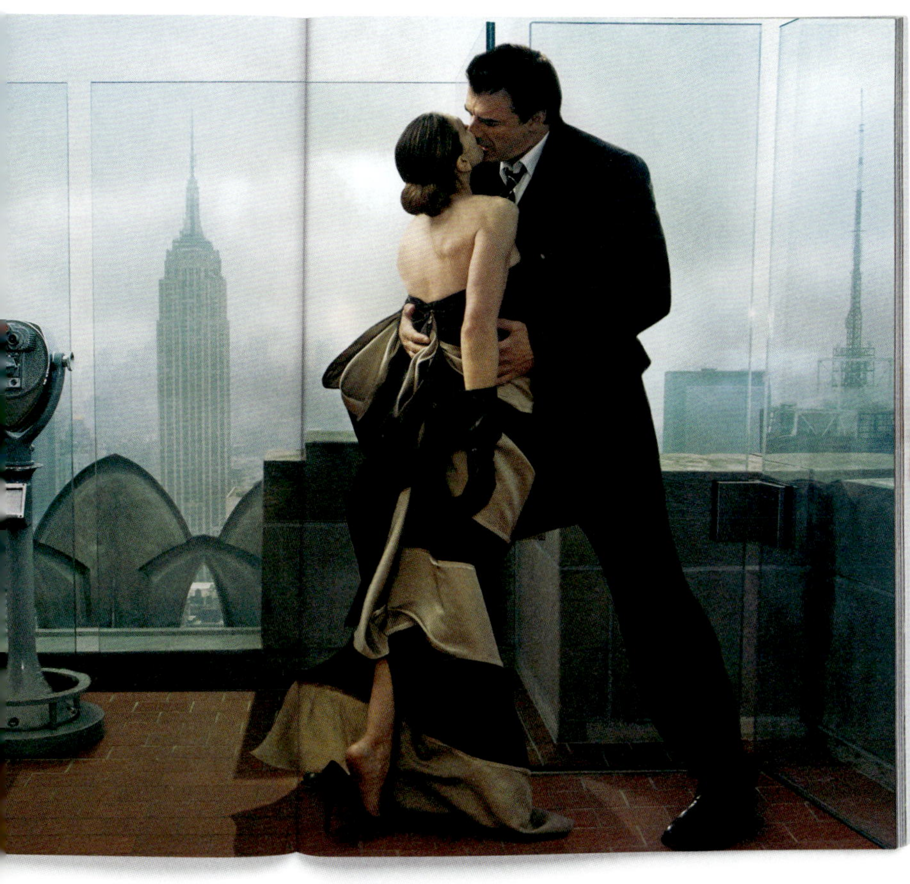

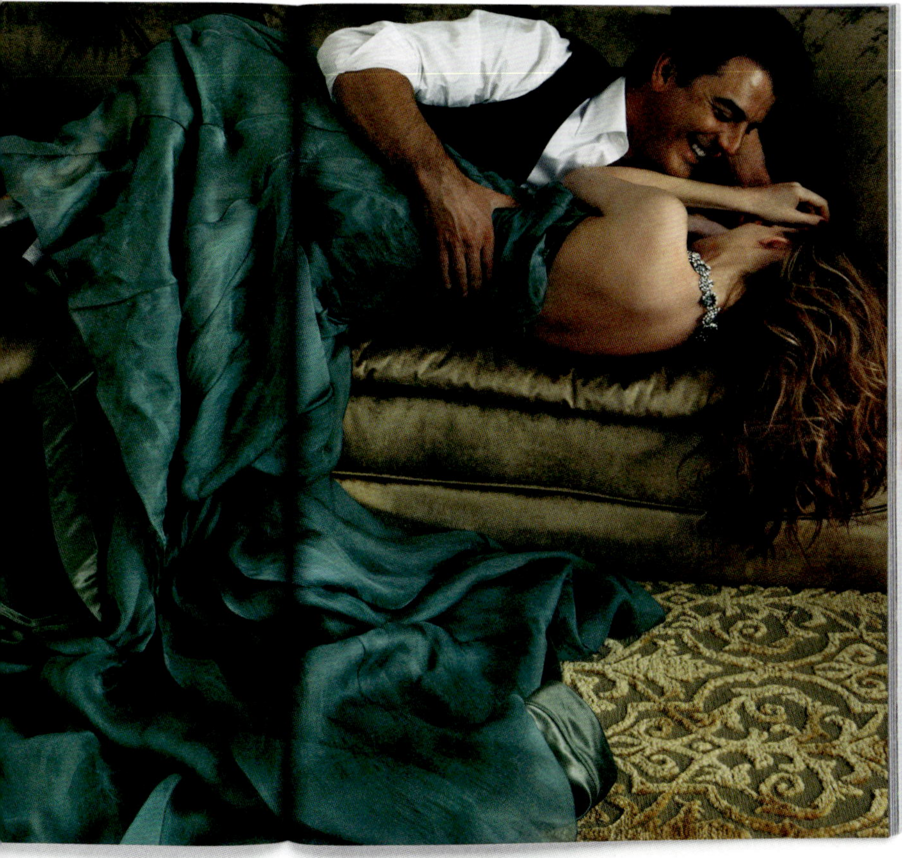

"We went all over New York for the shoot with Sarah Jessica Parker and Chris Noth: back to the Plaza, to the Greek and Roman galleries at the Metropolitan Museum of Art, and to the Top of the Rock, the observation deck at 30 Rockefeller Plaza."

New York City, 2008

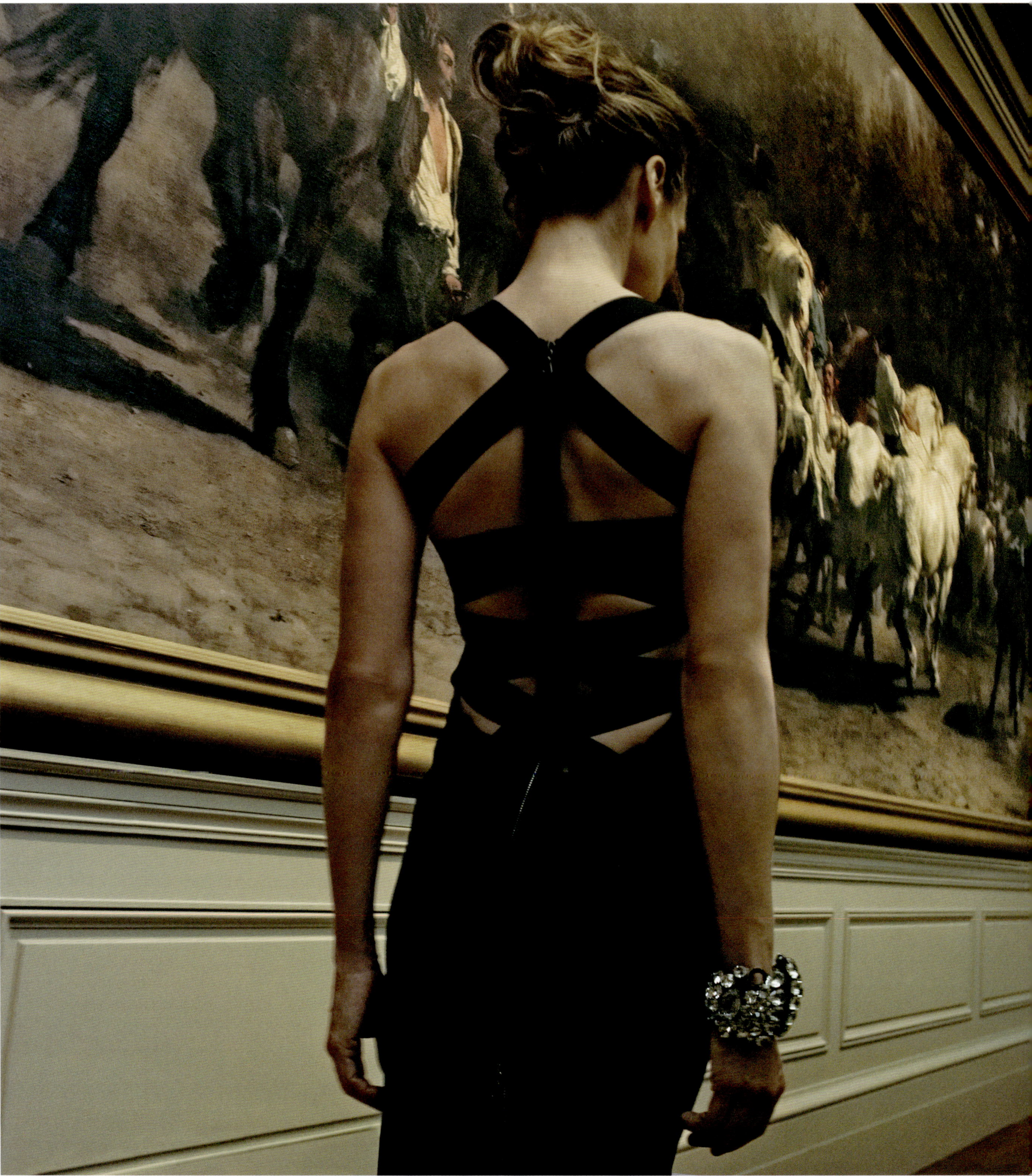

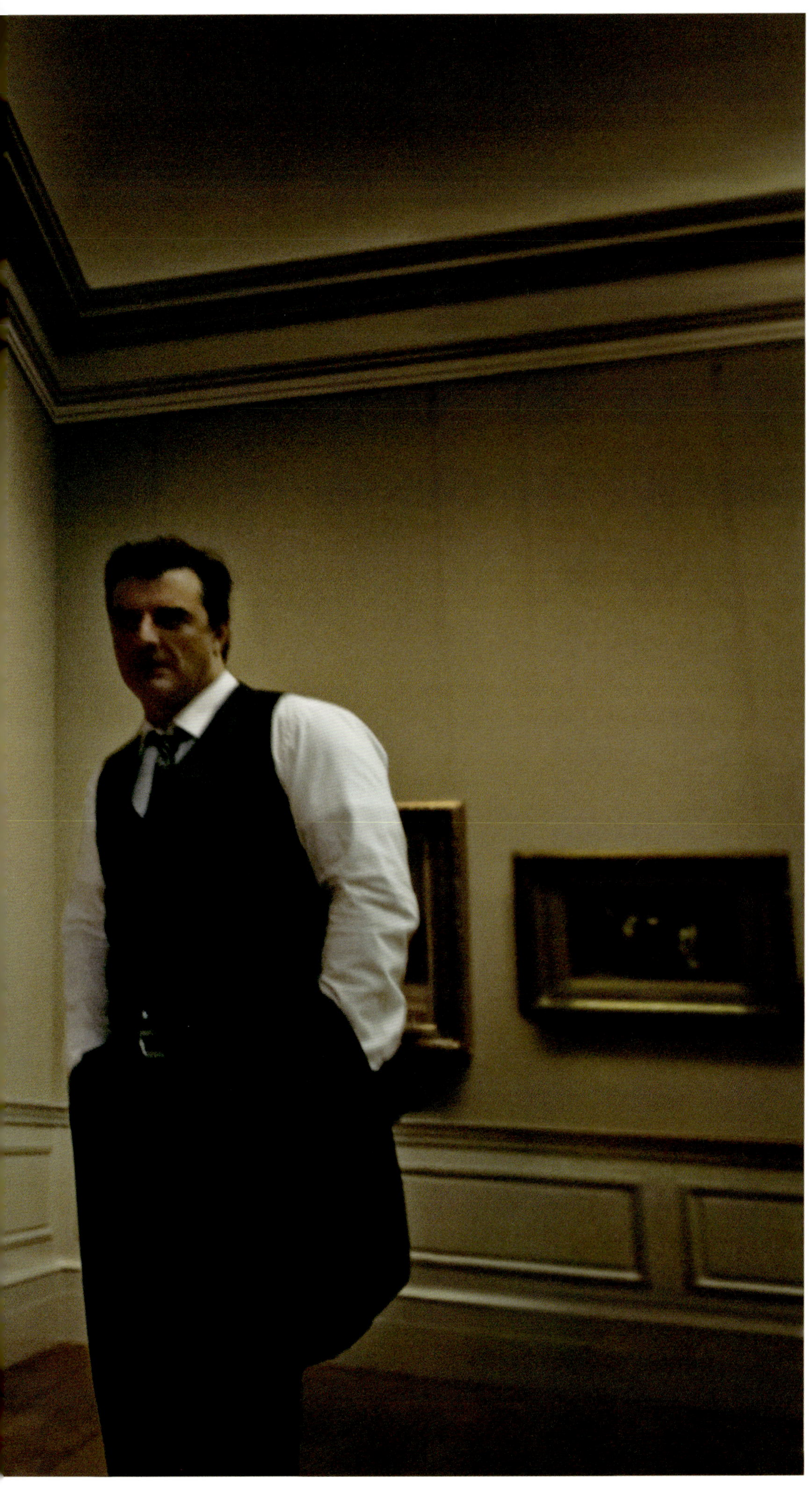

In the nineteenth- and early twentieth-century European galleries at the Metropolitan Museum of Art, New York City, 2008

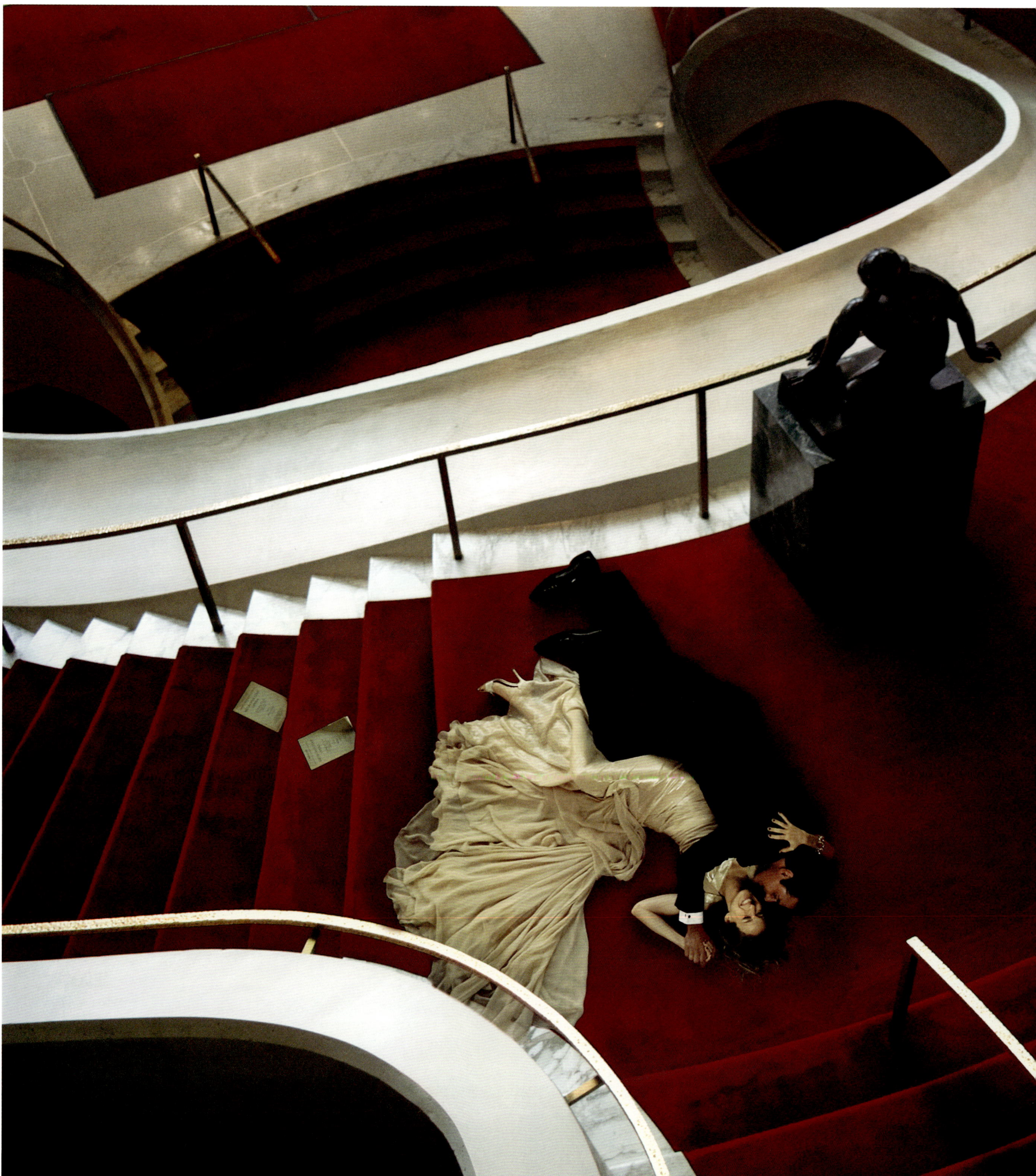

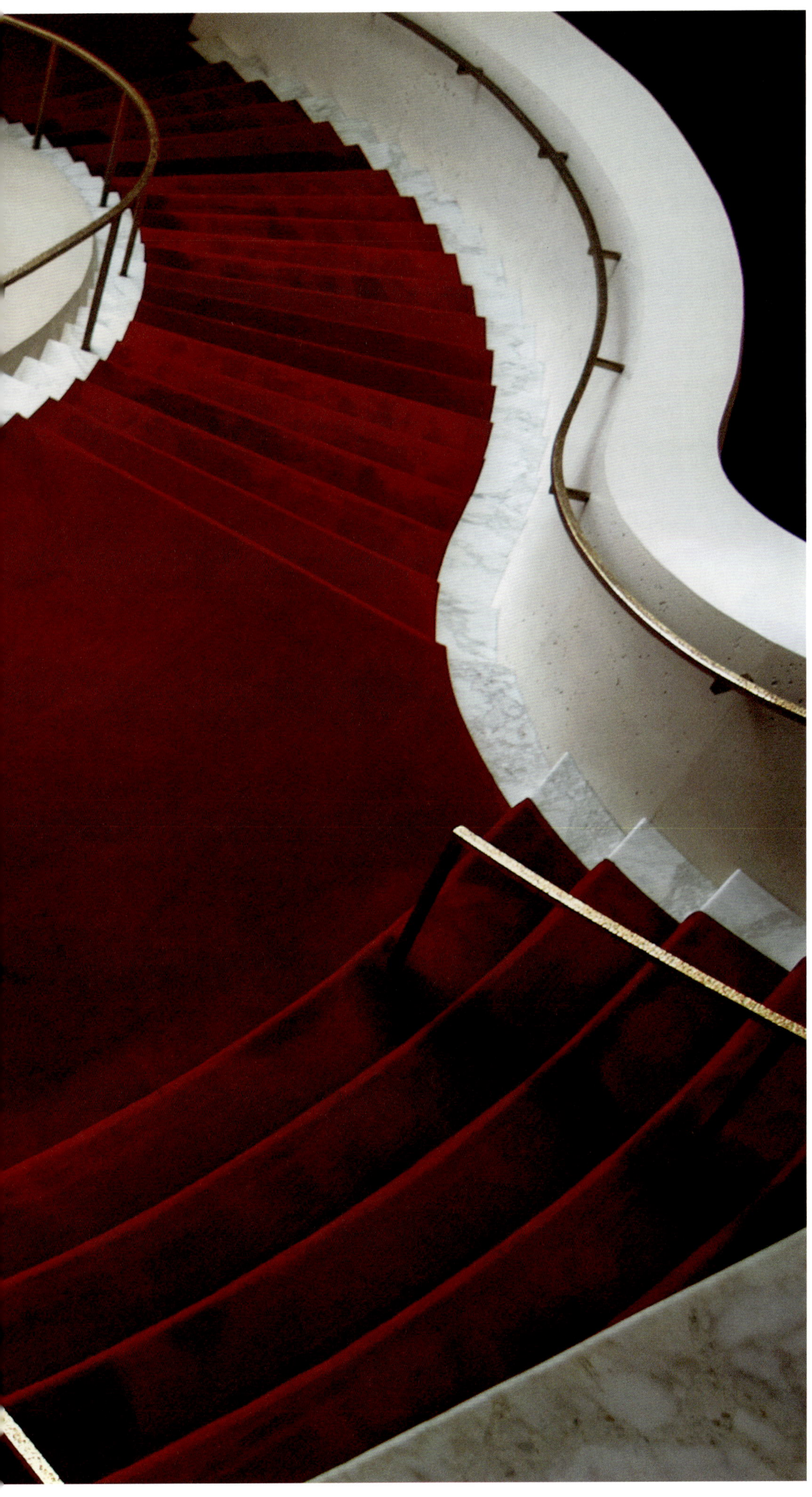

The grand staircase at the
Metropolitan Opera

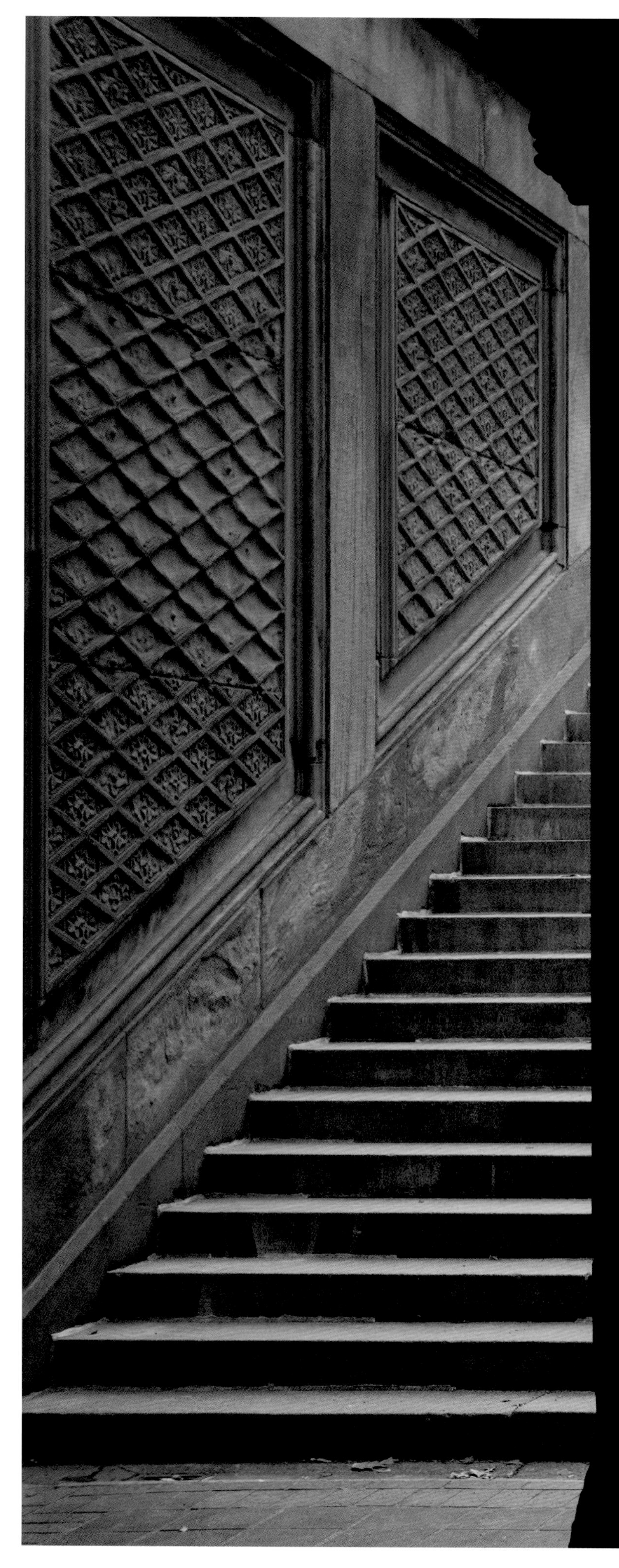

Bethesda Terrace in Central Park

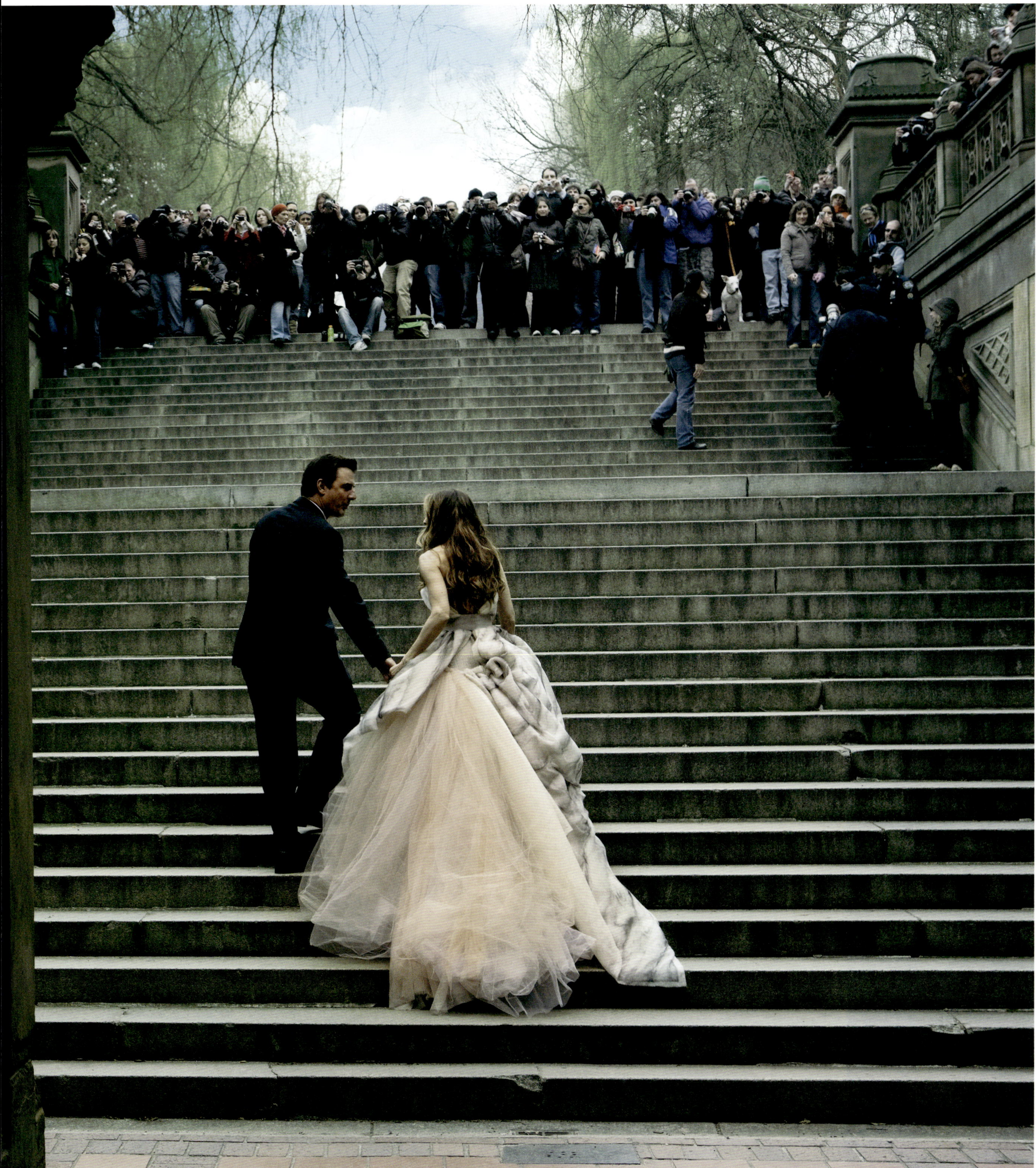

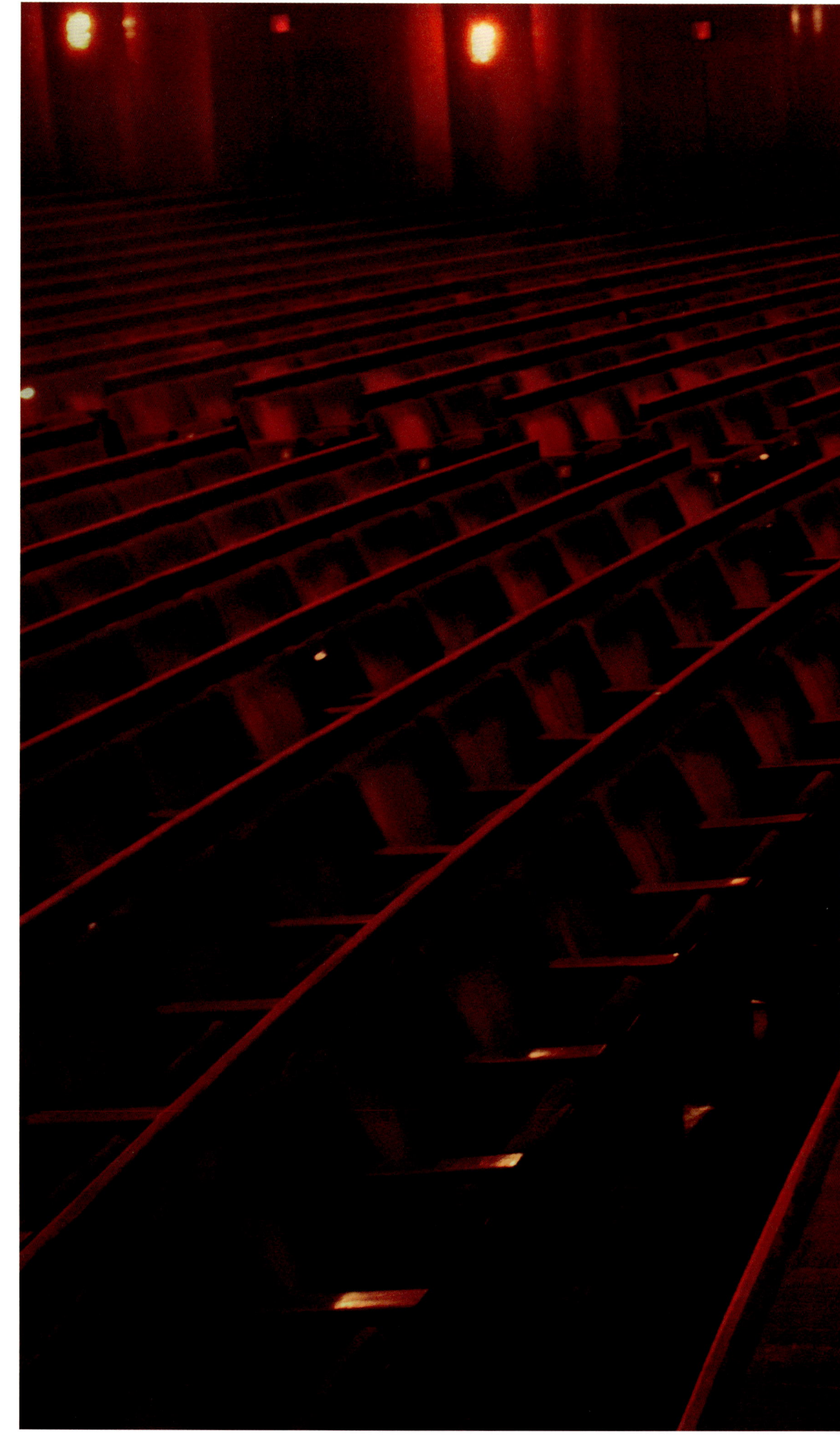

Renée Fleming,
Metropolitan Opera,
New York City, 2008

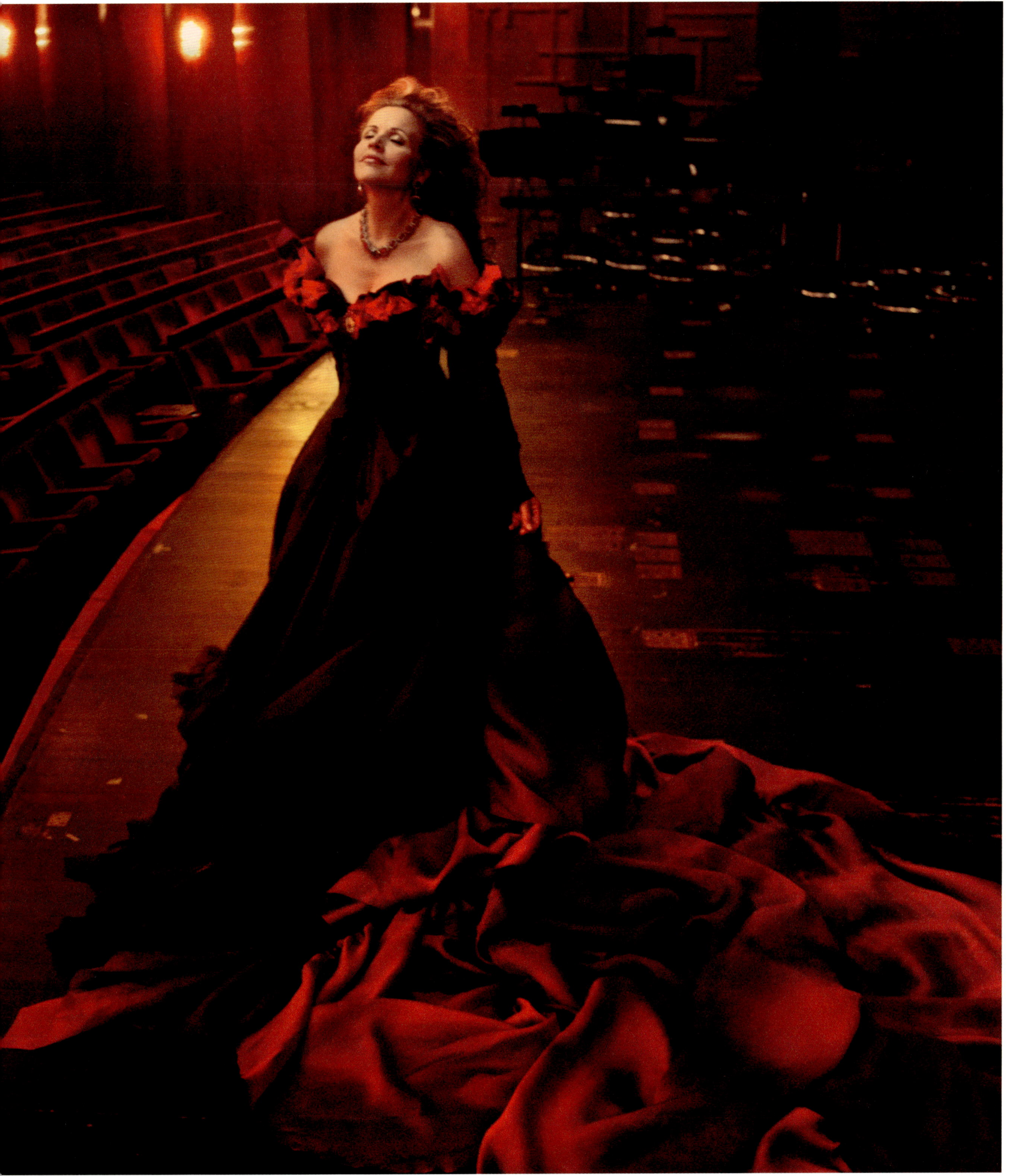

Annie has a long history of working with dancers. In 1990 she spent weeks with Mikhail Baryshnikov and Mark Morris documenting the creation of their White Oak Dance Project. Her mother studied with Martha Graham. She has written about the special sort of grace that dancers have, the sense of movement that their bodies retain.

For the *Romeo and Juliet* shoot, Annie worked with Roberto Bolle, an Italian ballet star who had appeared in productions of *Romeo and Juliet* many times in many places. Men from the chorus of the Broadway revival of *South Pacific* were the warring Montagues and Capulets. Juliet was played by the model Coco Rocha.

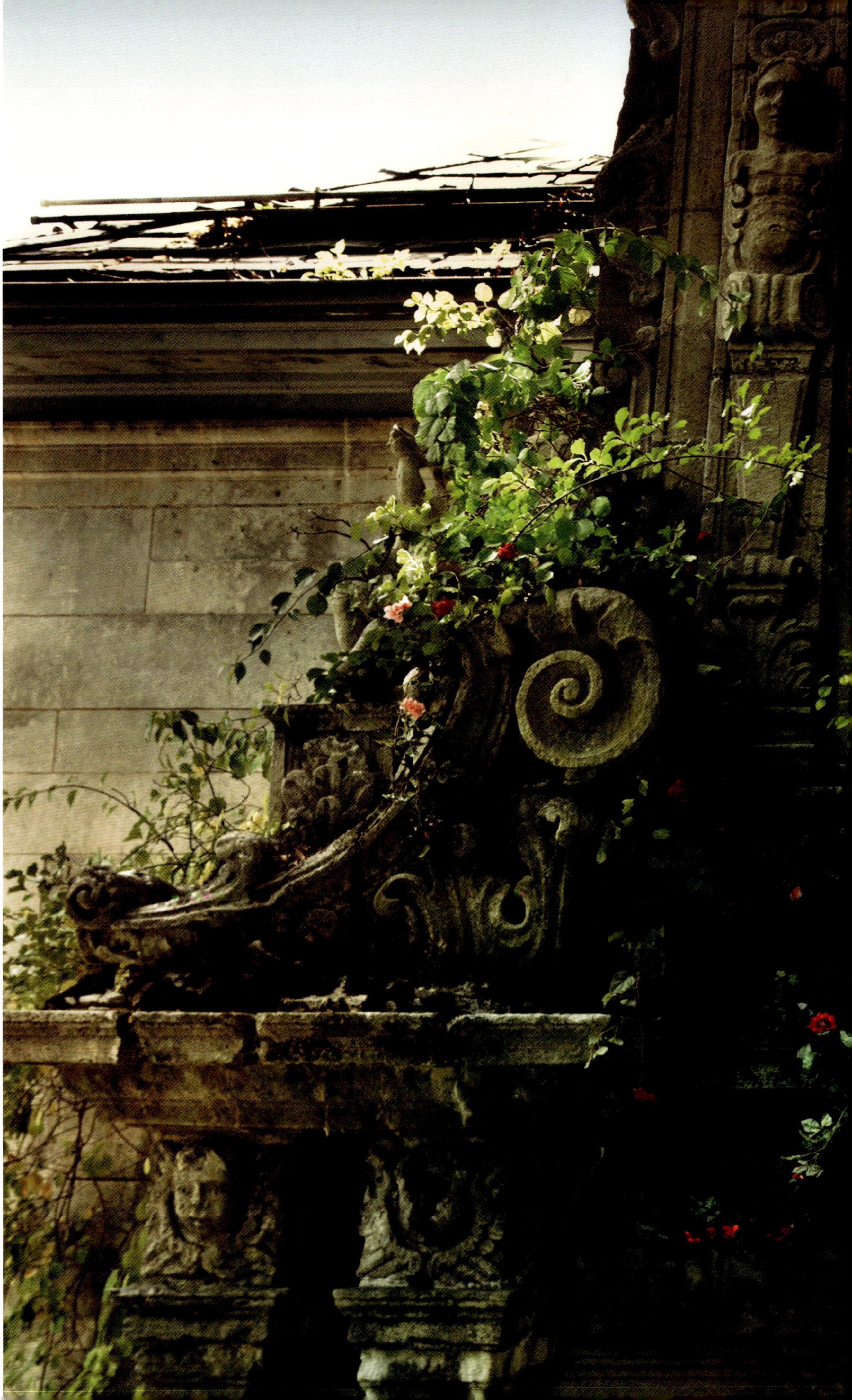

Roberto Bolle and Coco Rocha,
New York City, 2008

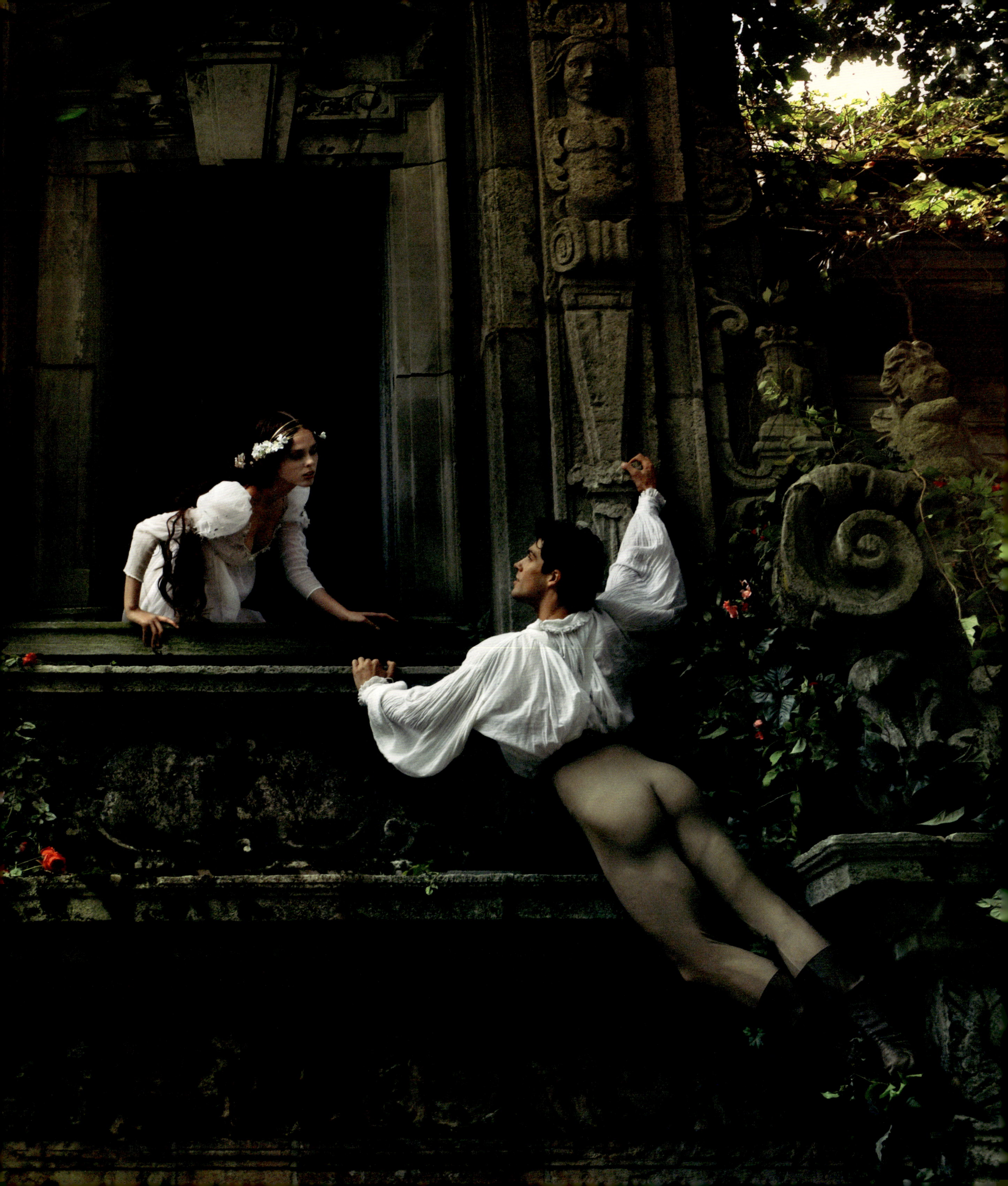

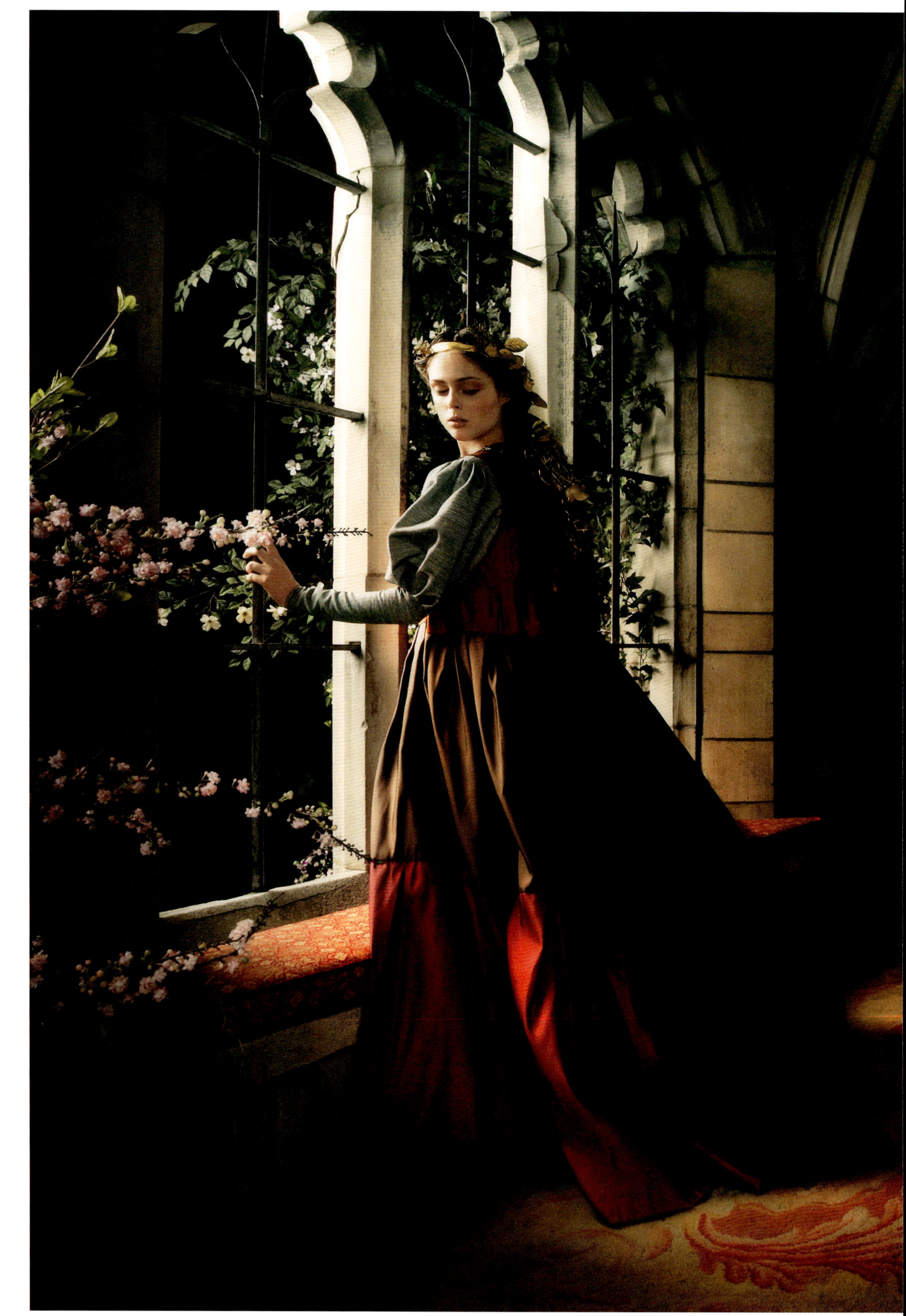

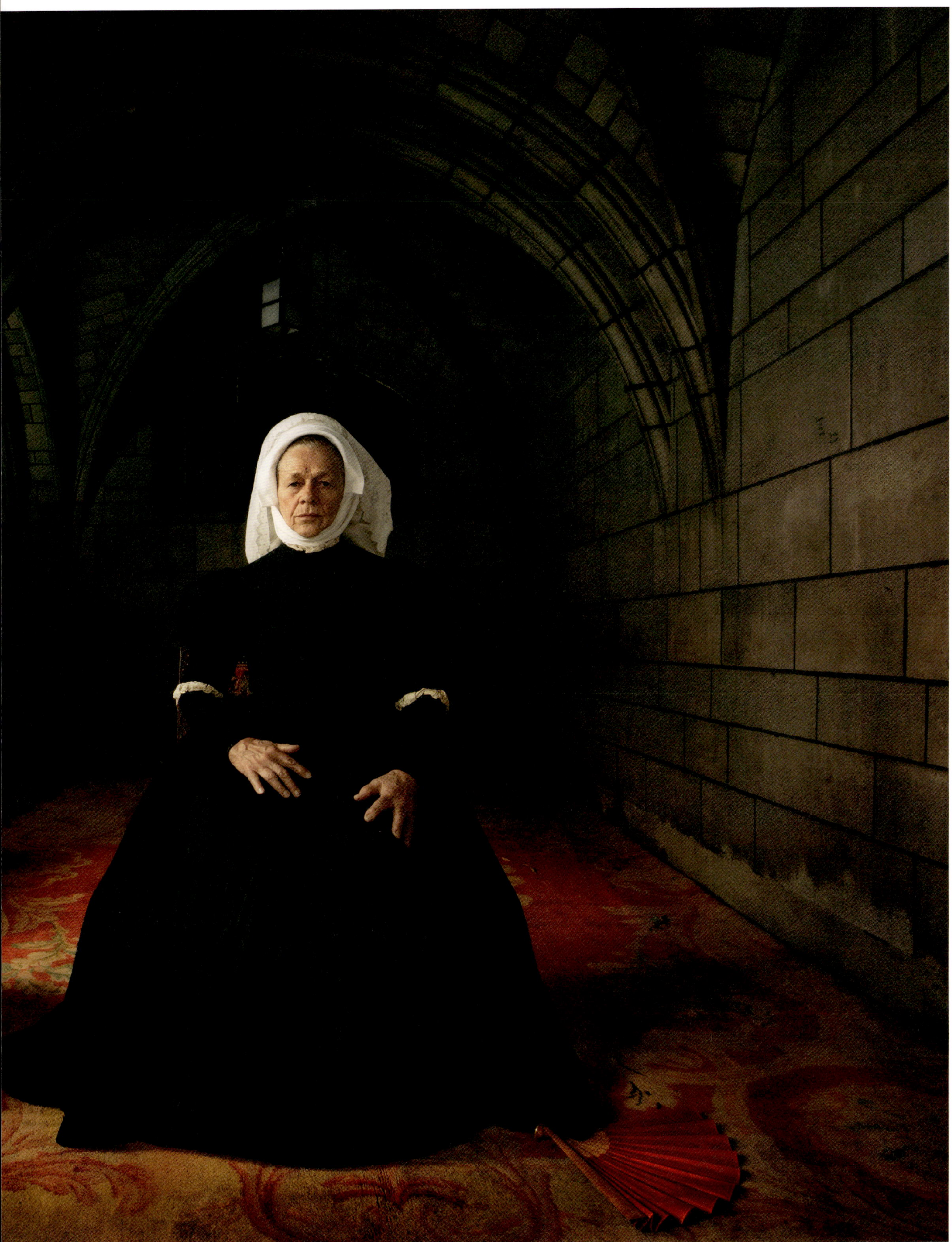

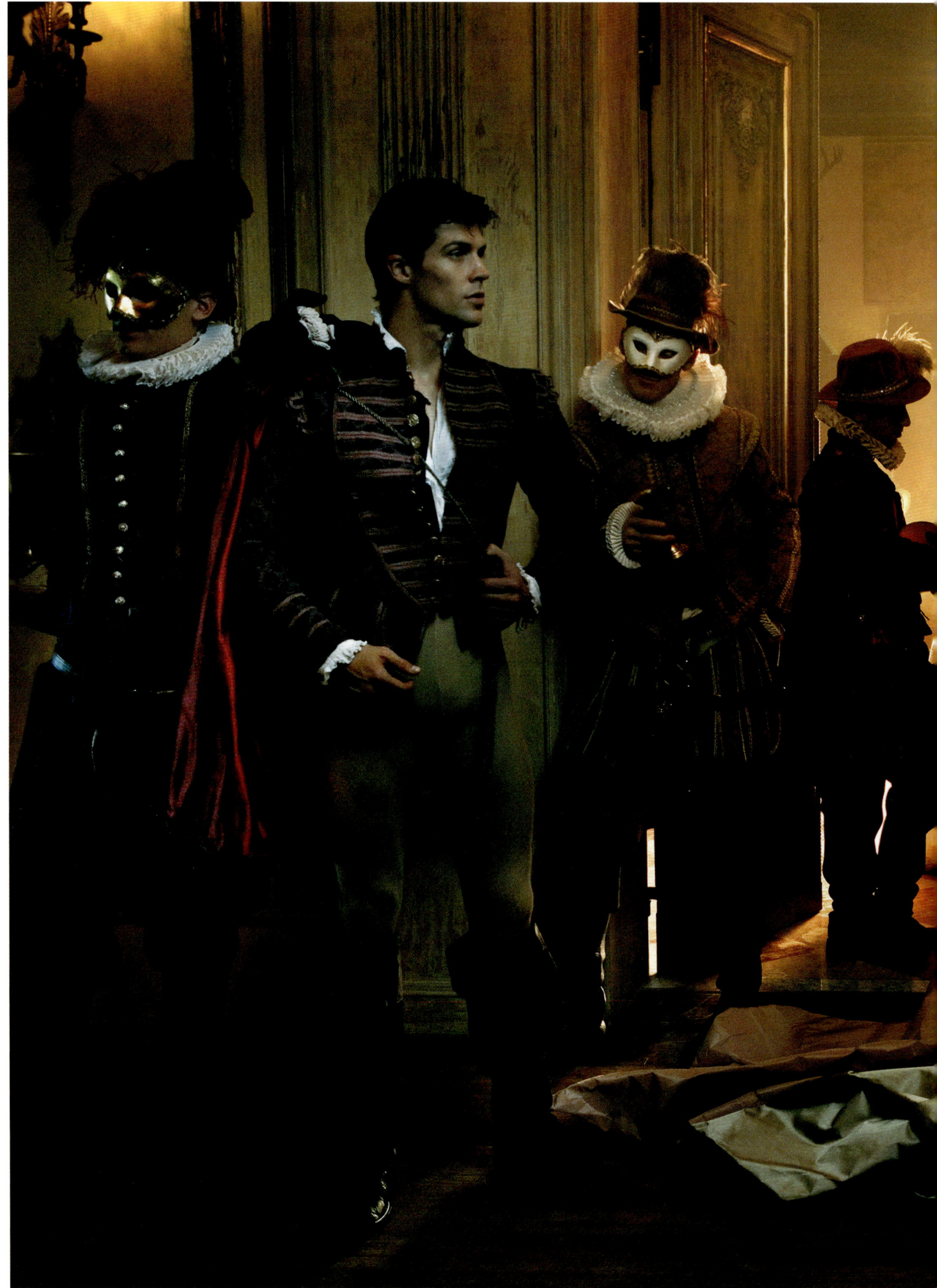

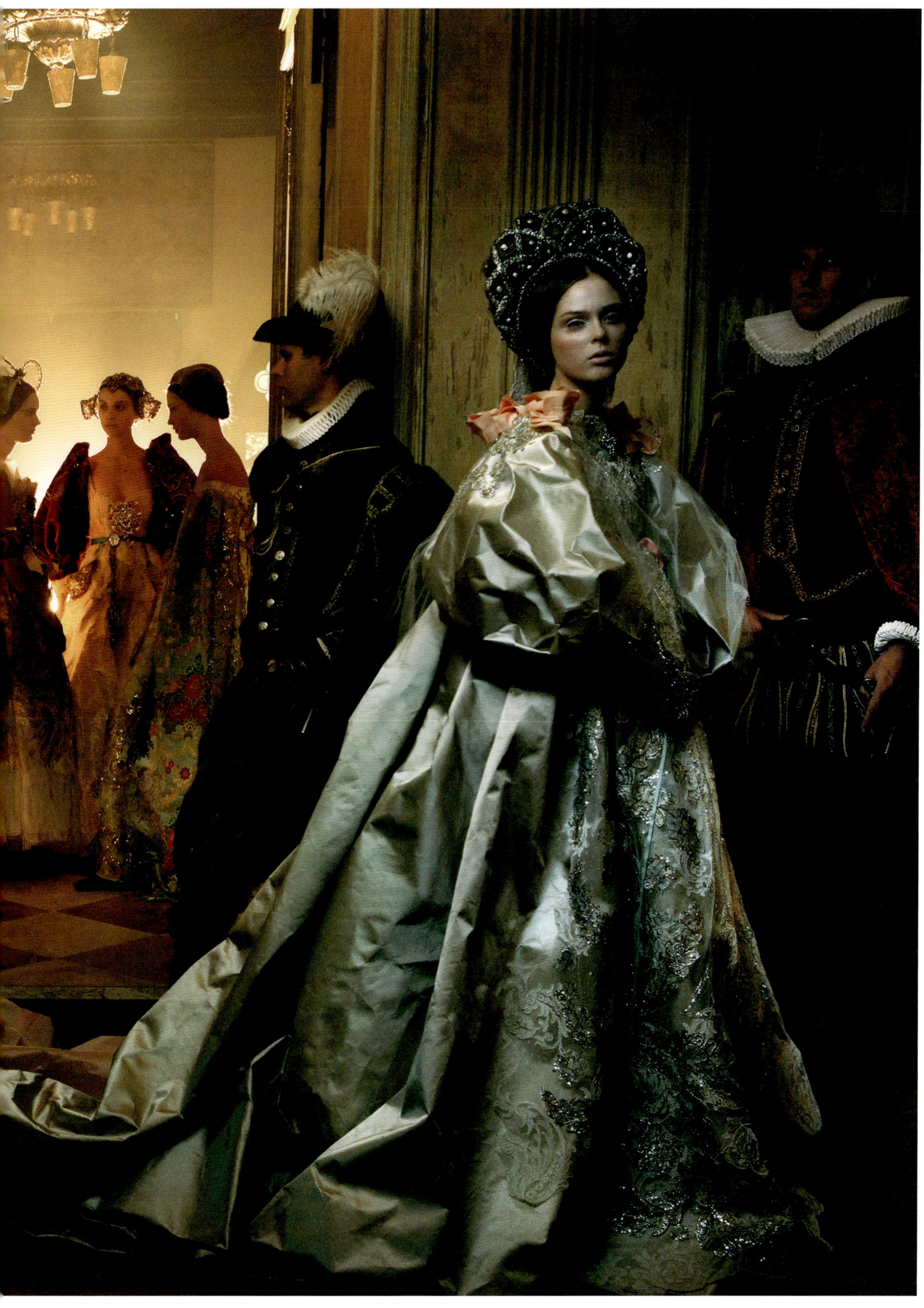

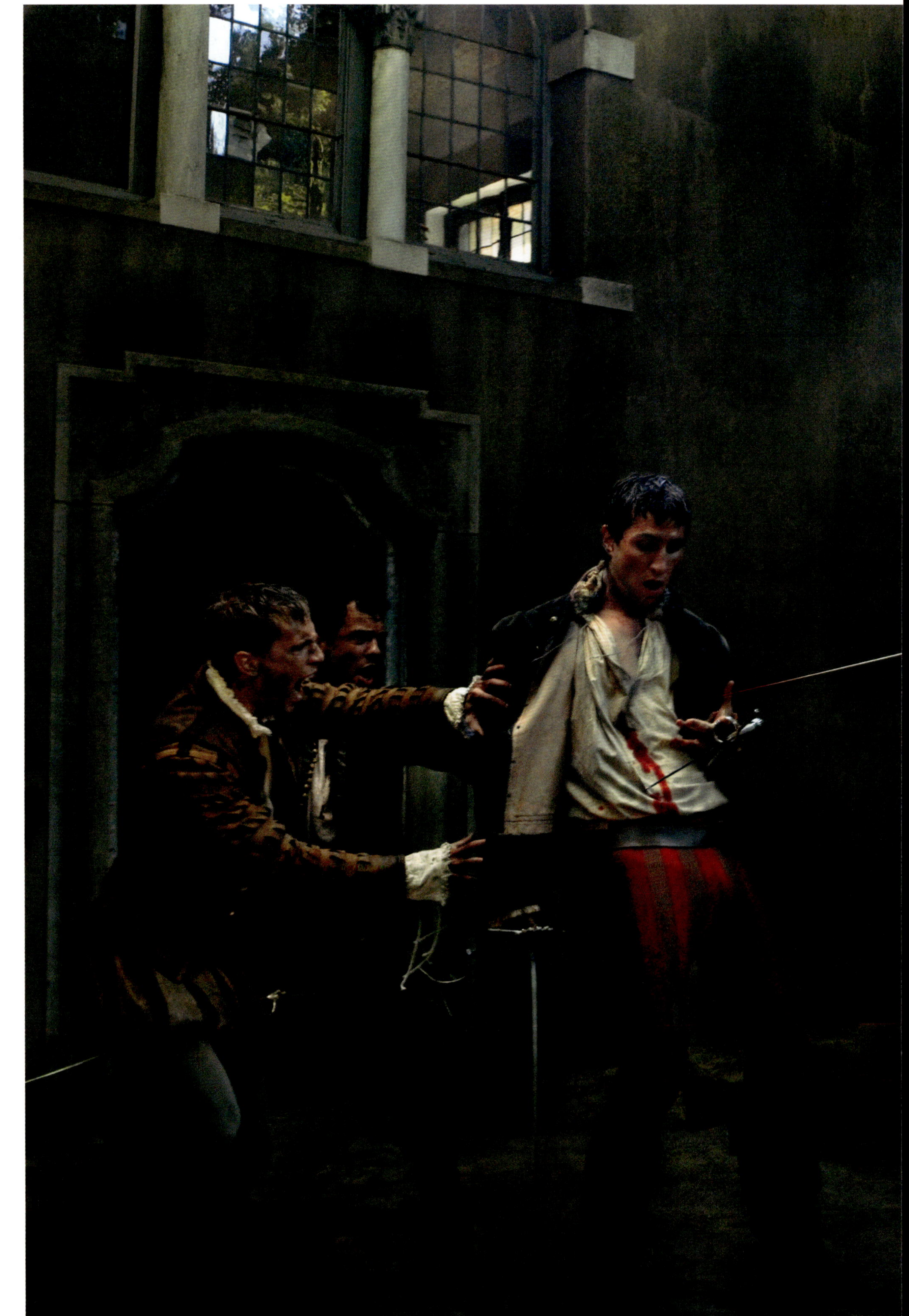

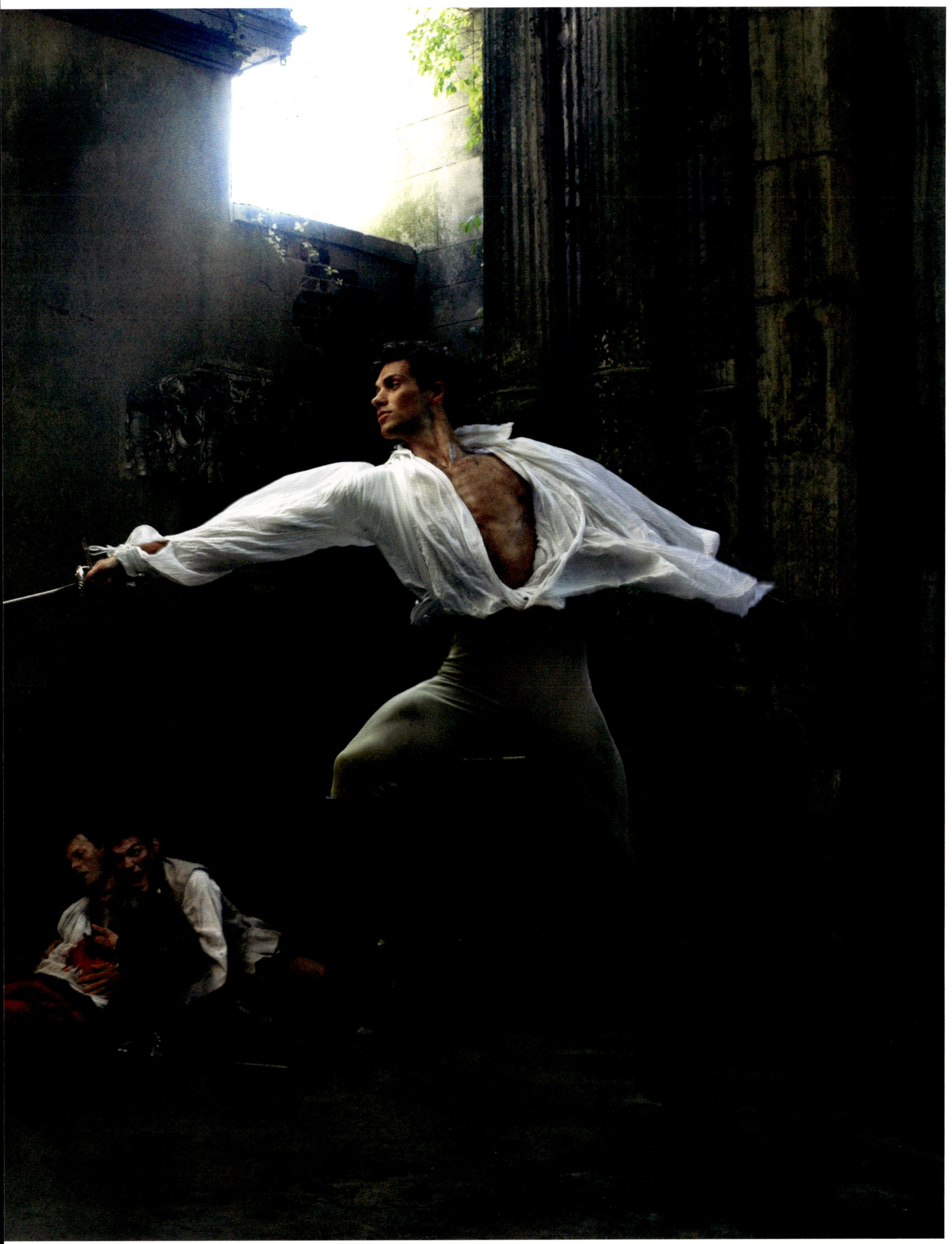

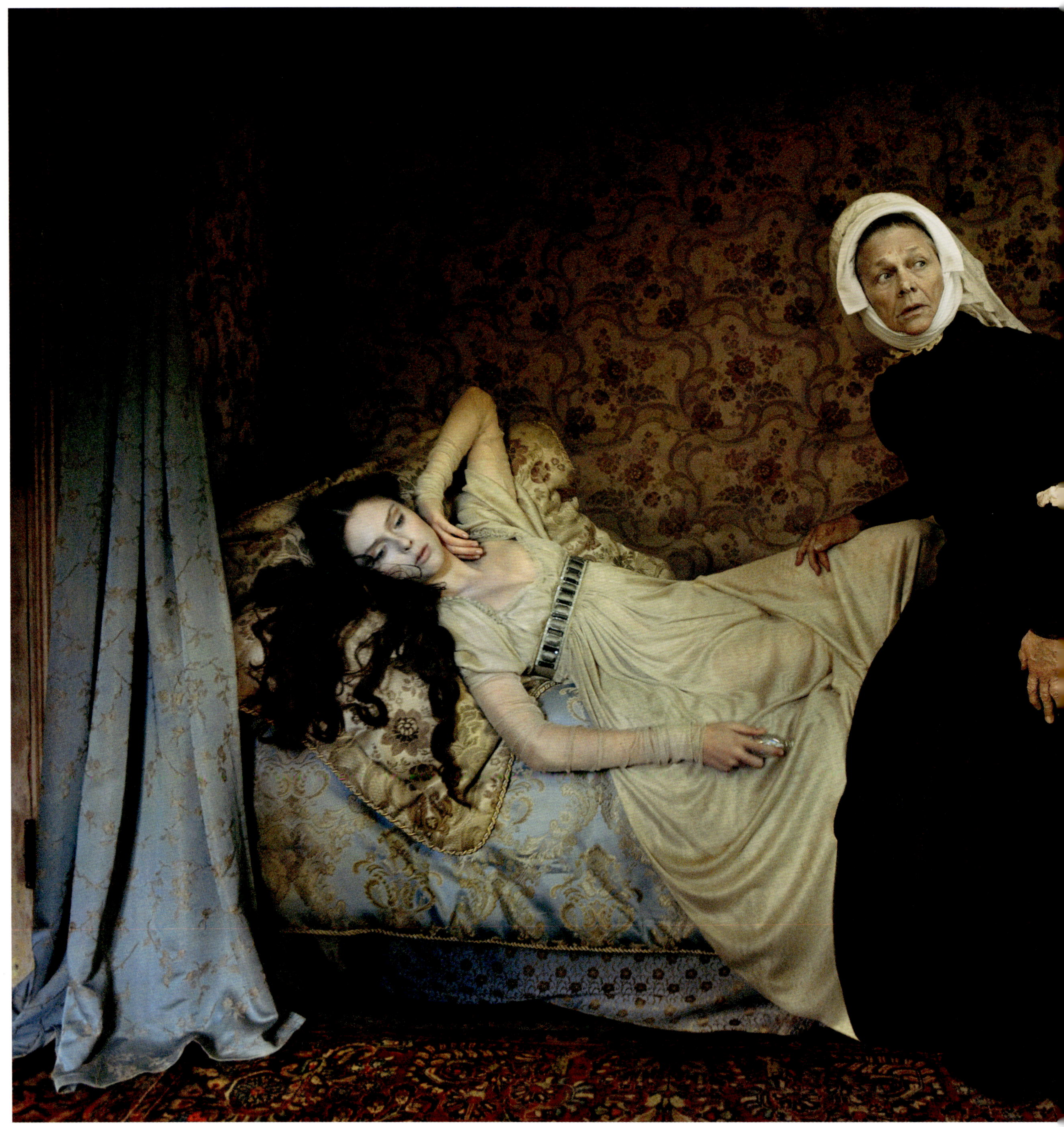

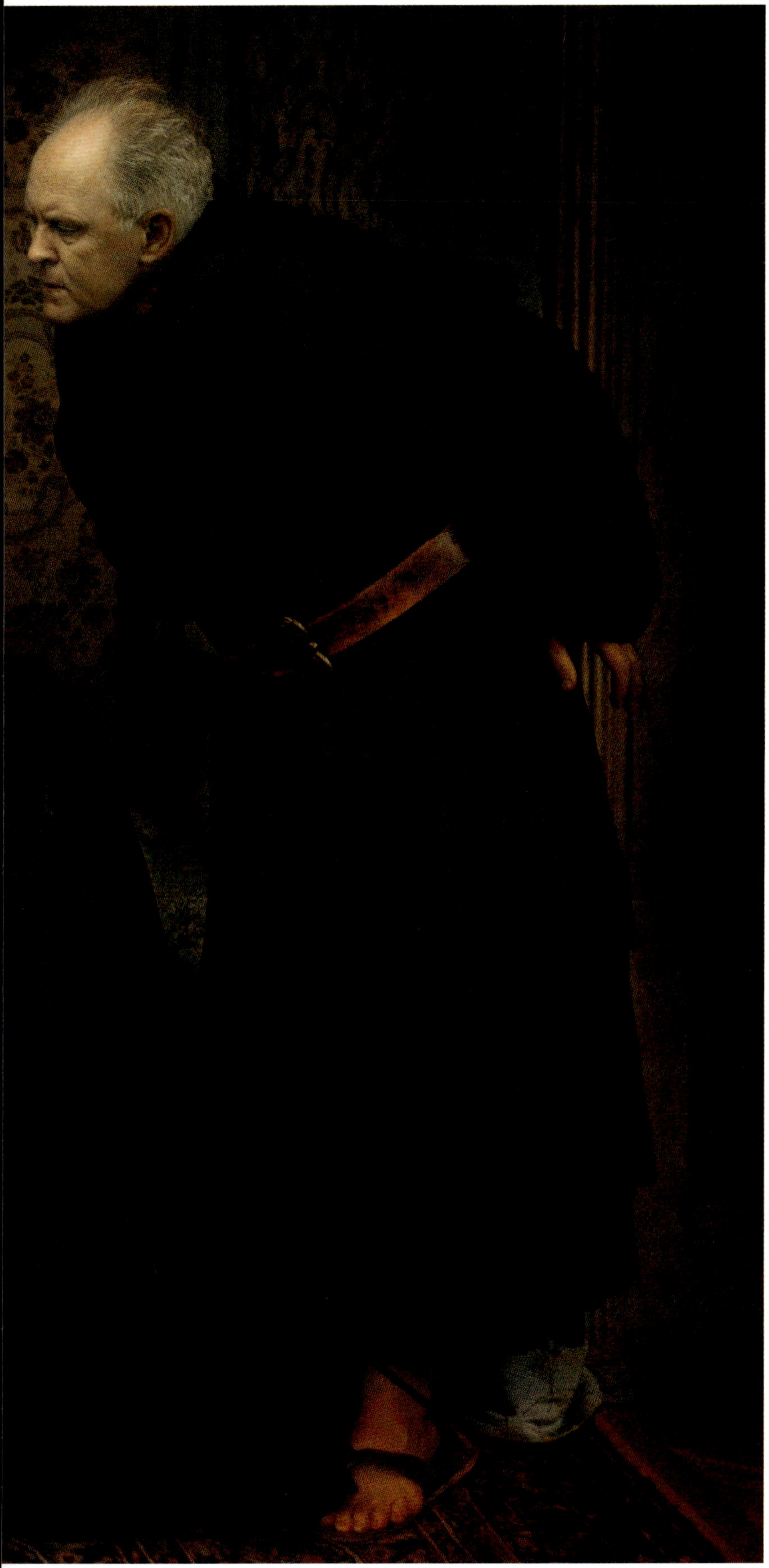

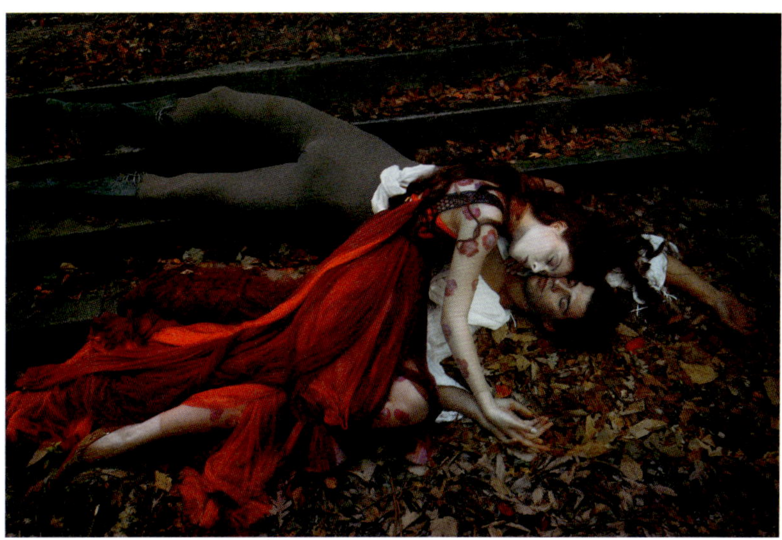

The supporting cast for the *Romeo and Juliet* story included John Lithgow as Friar Laurence and Estelle Parsons as the Nurse.

"Karen Elson is a musician and an actor. She understands performance, and she is a modern woman."

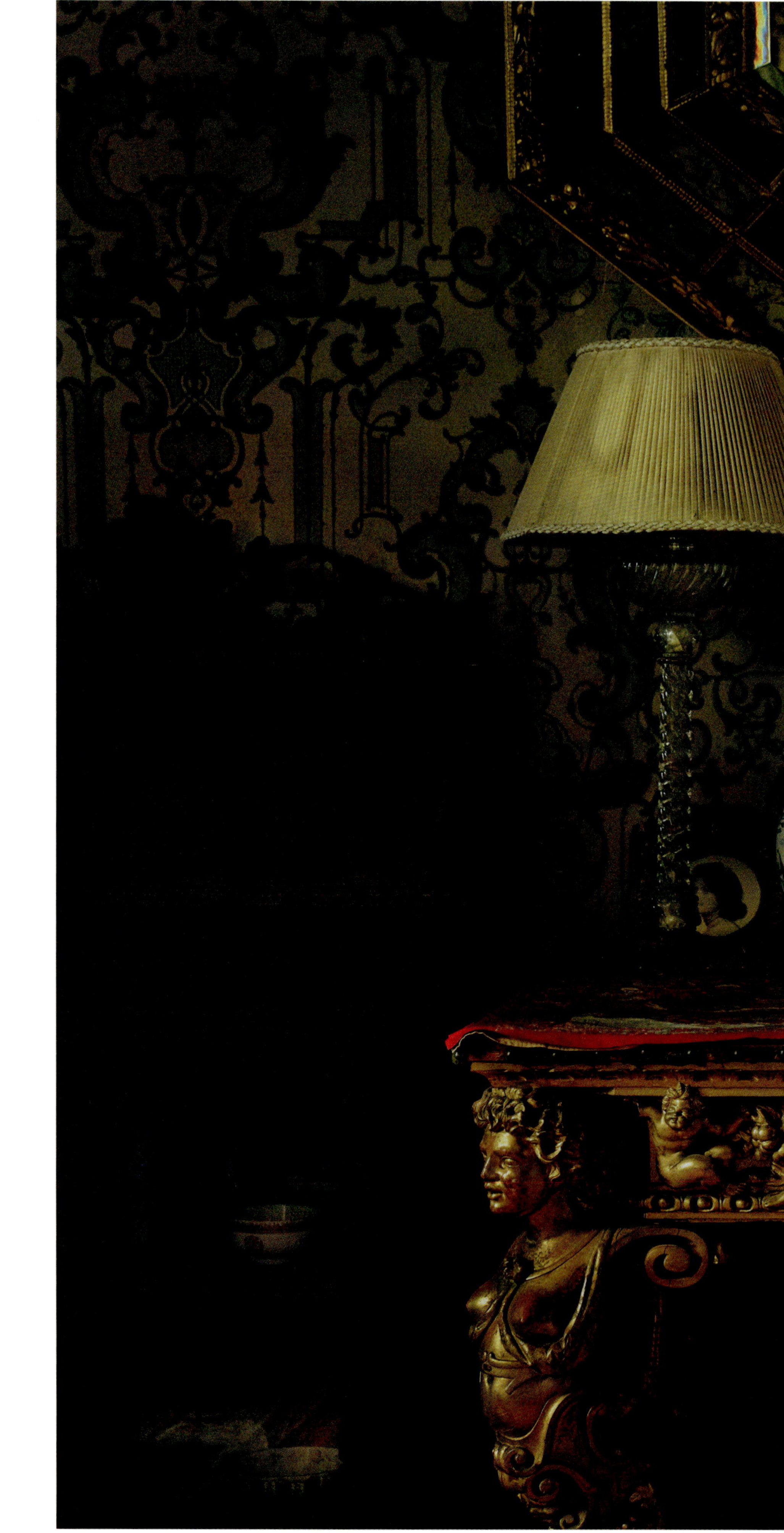

Rokeby, an old estate on the Hudson River in upstate New York, 2013

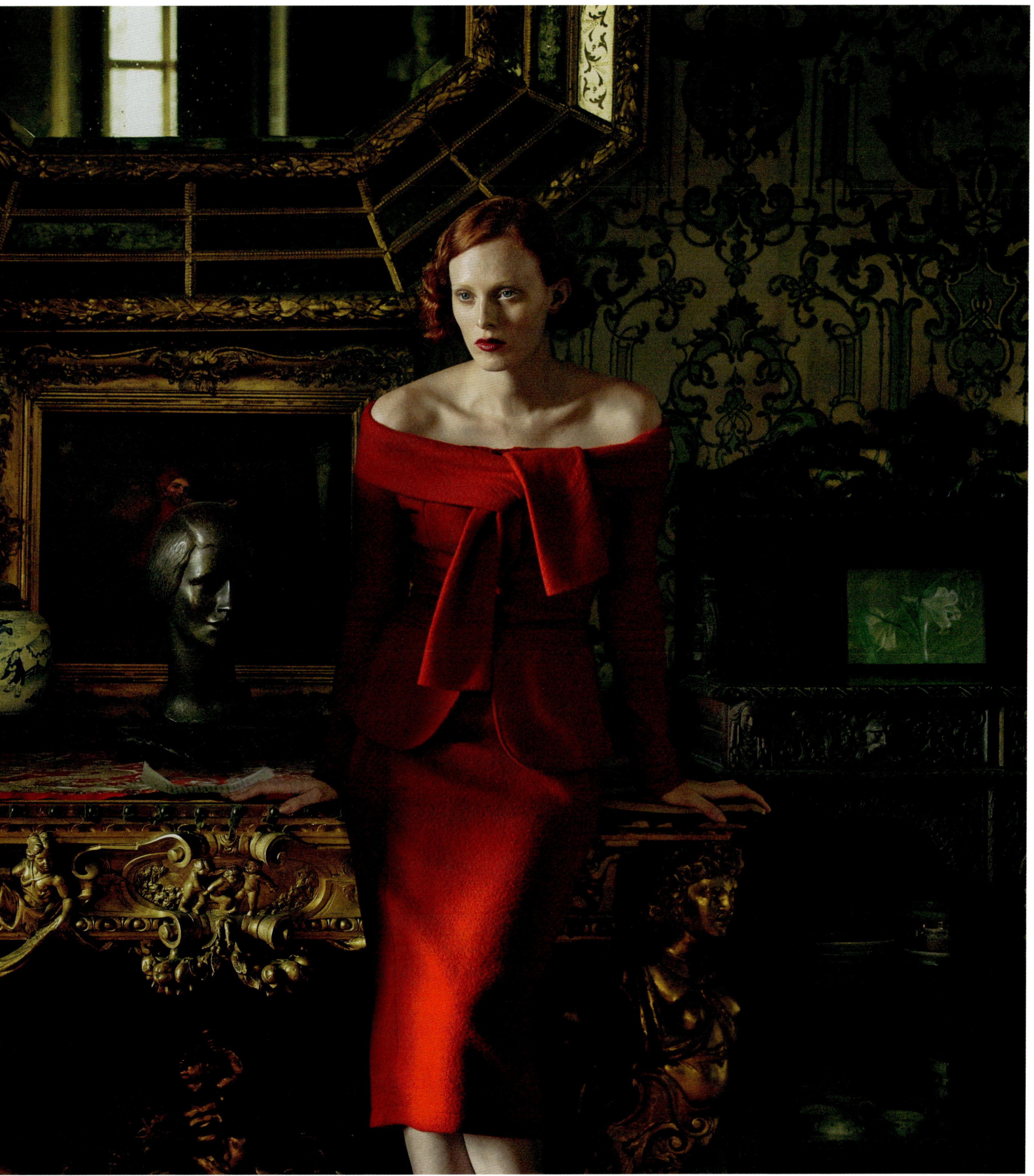

In 2013, when Harold Pinter's play *Betrayal* was revived in New York, Karen Elson was cast in Annie and Grace Coddington's interpretation of the story, along with the actors Hugh Dancy and Michael Shannon. *Betrayal* is a Proustian web of lies, half-truths, and uncertain motives, based on a real extramarital affair that Pinter carried on for years.

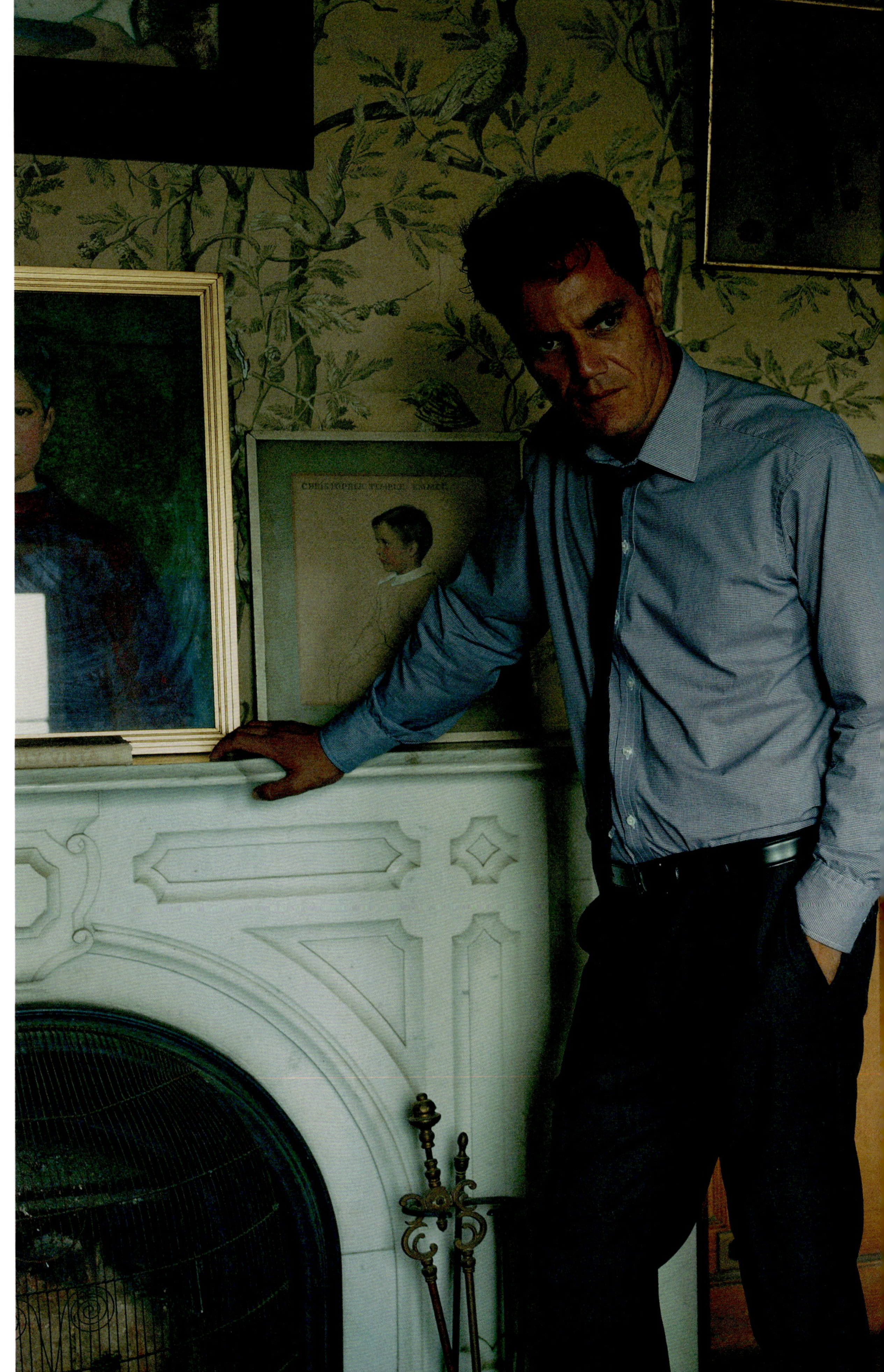

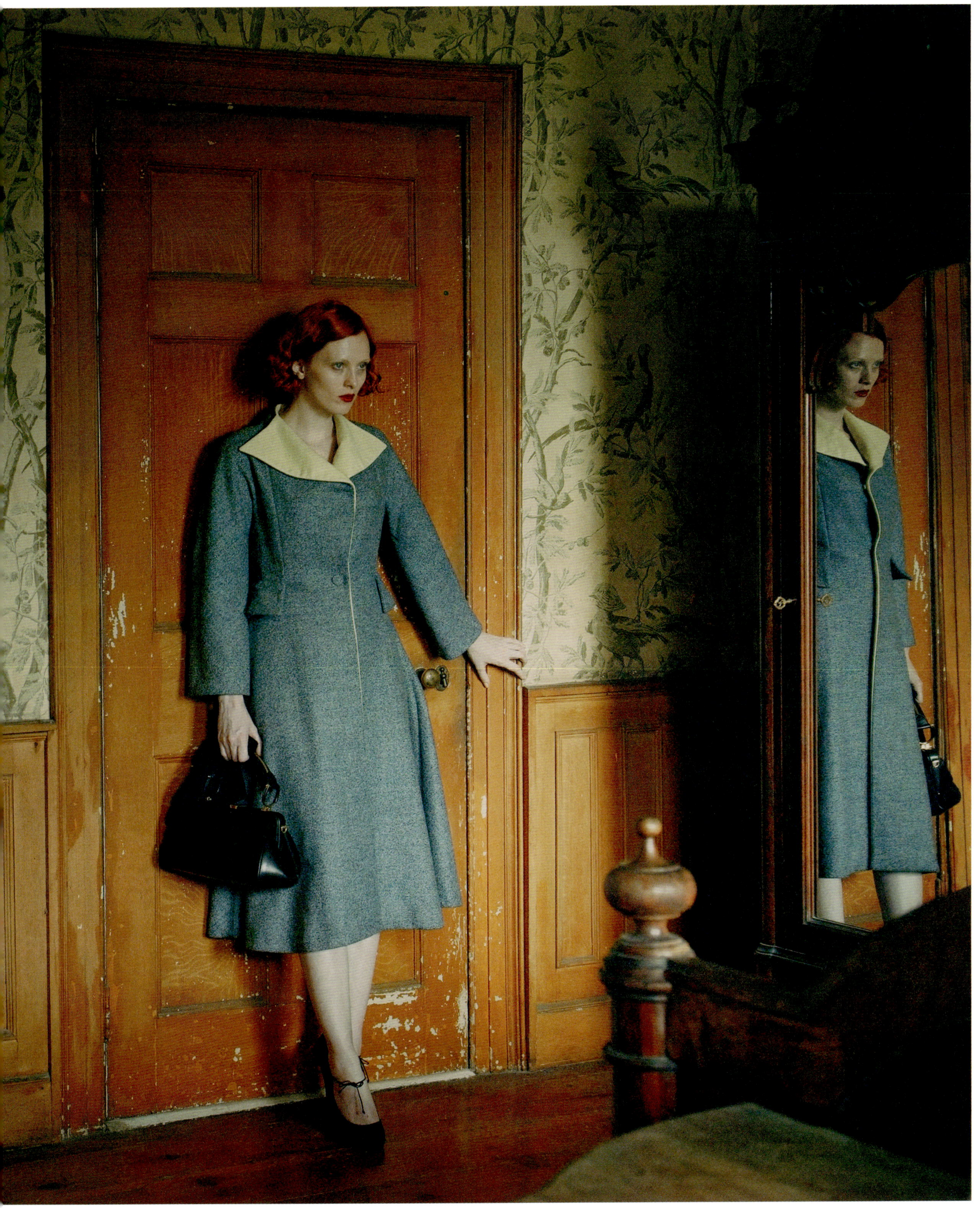

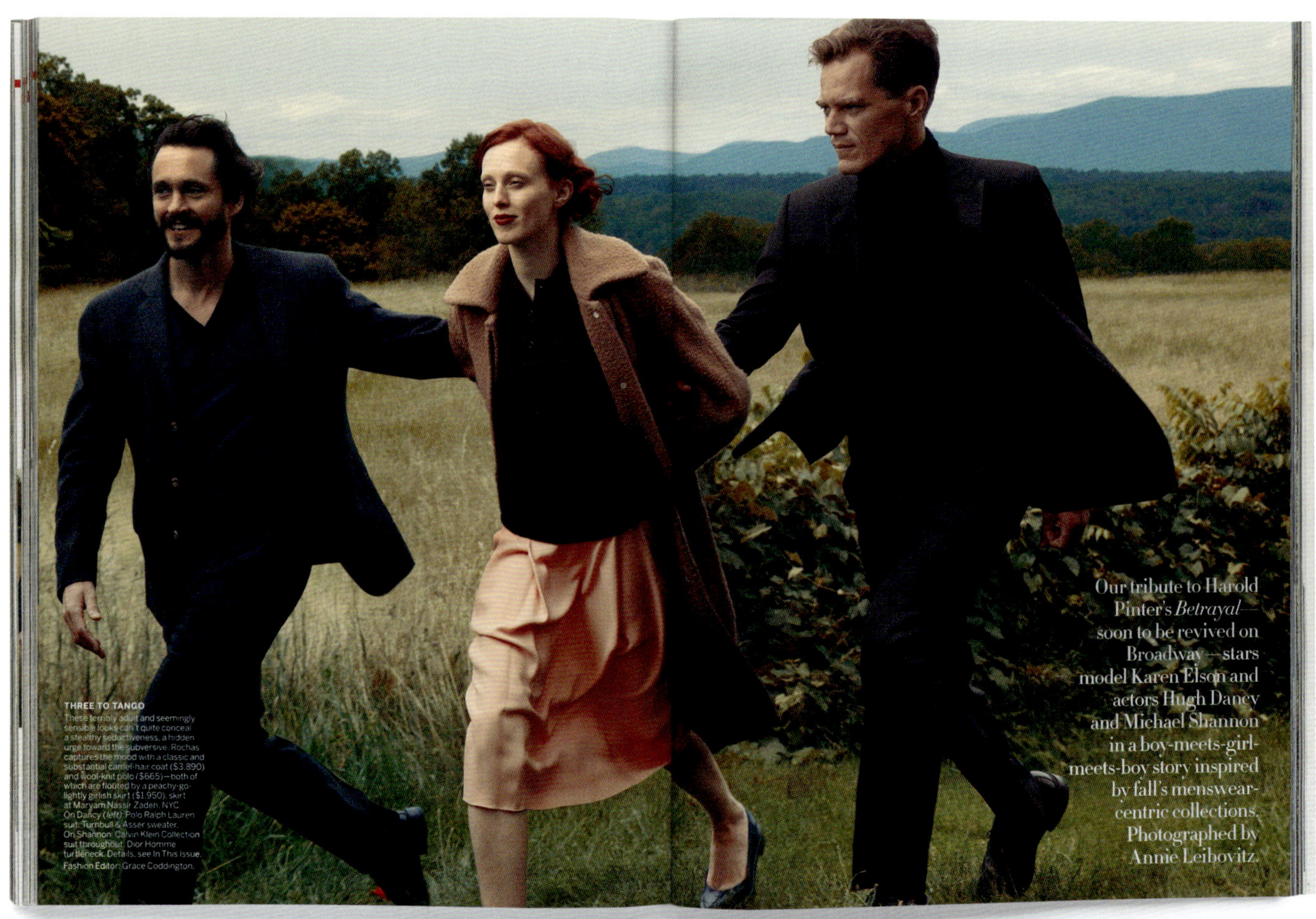

THREE TO TANGO
These terribly adult and seemingly sensible looks can't quite conceal a stealthy seductiveness, a hidden urge toward the subversive. Rochas captures the mood with a classic and substantial camel-hair coat ($3,890) and wool-knit polo ($665)—both of which are flouted by a peachy-go-lightly girlish skirt ($1,950); skirt at Maryam Nassir Zadeh, NYC. On Dancy (*left*): Polo Ralph Lauren suit; Turnbull & Asser sweater. On Shannon: Calvin Klein Collection suit throughout; Dior Homme turtleneck. Details, see In This Issue. Fashion Editor: Grace Coddington.

Our tribute to Harold Pinter's *Betrayal*—soon to be revived on Broadway—stars model Karen Elson and actors Hugh Dancy and Michael Shannon in a boy-meets-girl-meets-boy story inspired by fall's menswear-centric collections. Photographed by Annie Leibovitz.

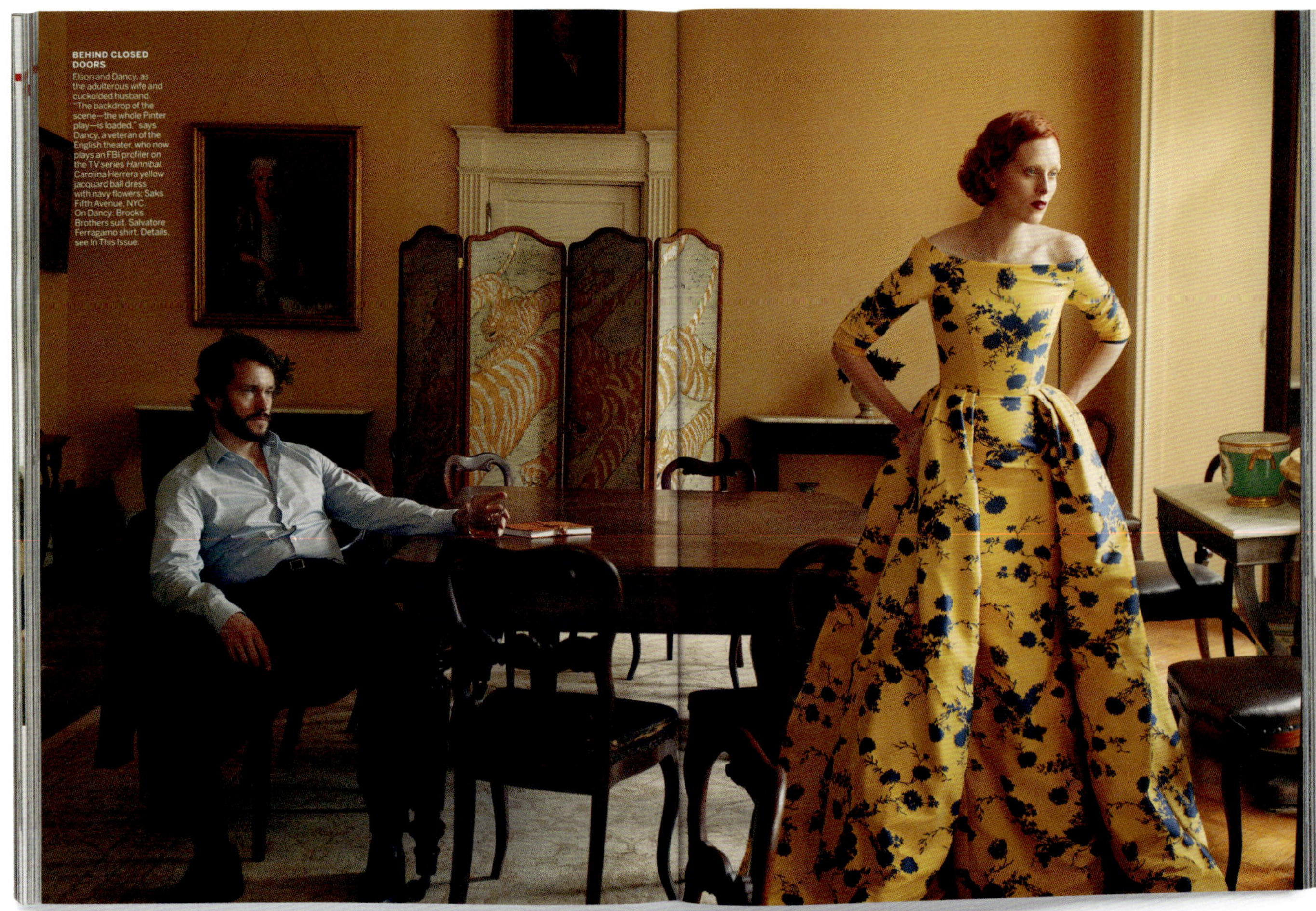

BEHIND CLOSED DOORS
Elson and Dancy, as the adulterous wife and cuckolded husband. "The backdrop of the scene—the whole Pinter play—is loaded," says Dancy, a veteran of the English theater, who now plays an FBI profiler on the TV series *Hannibal*. Carolina Herrera yellow jacquard ball dress with navy flowers; Saks Fifth Avenue, NYC. On Dancy: Brooks Brothers suit; Salvatore Ferragamo shirt. Details, see In This Issue.

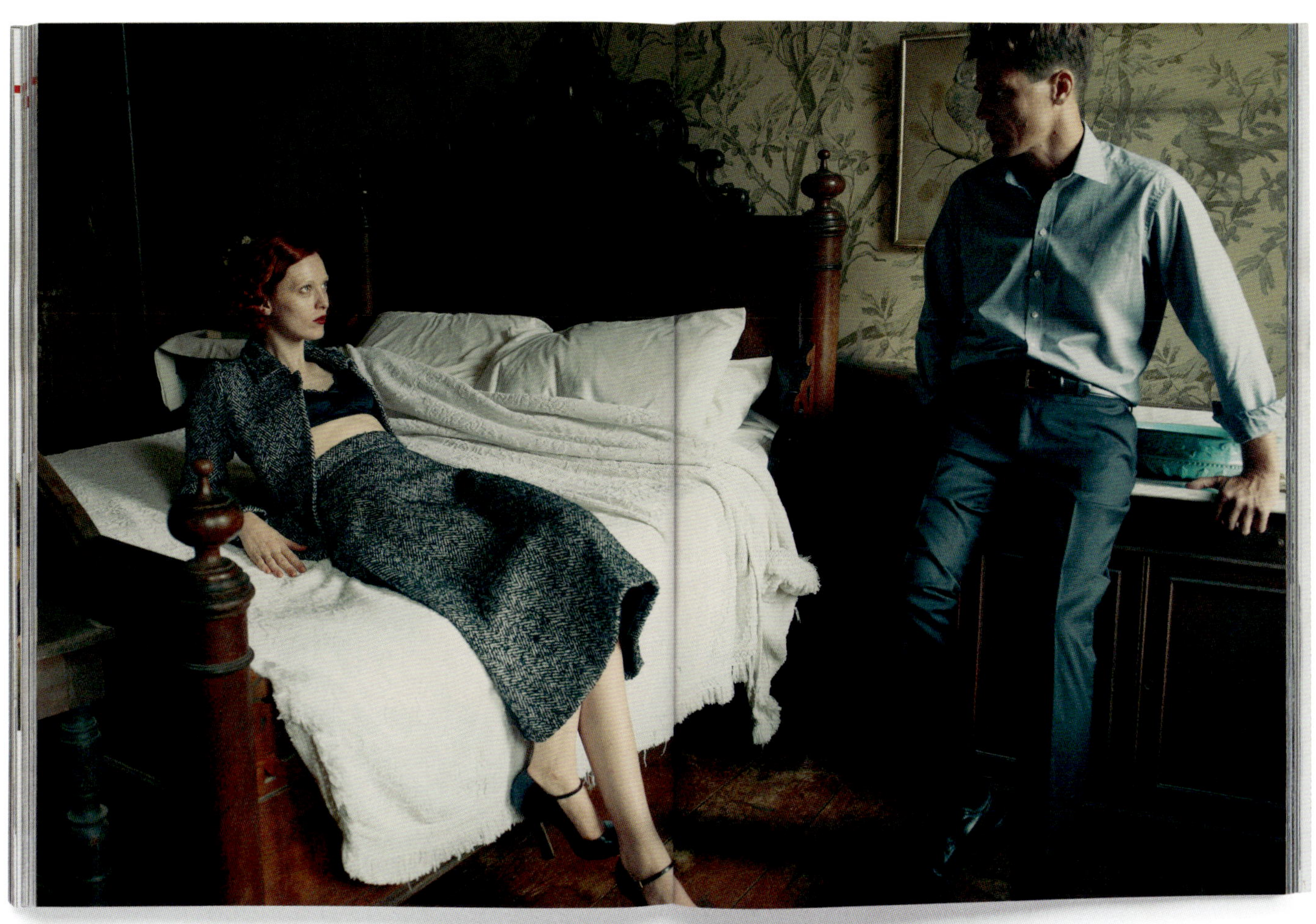

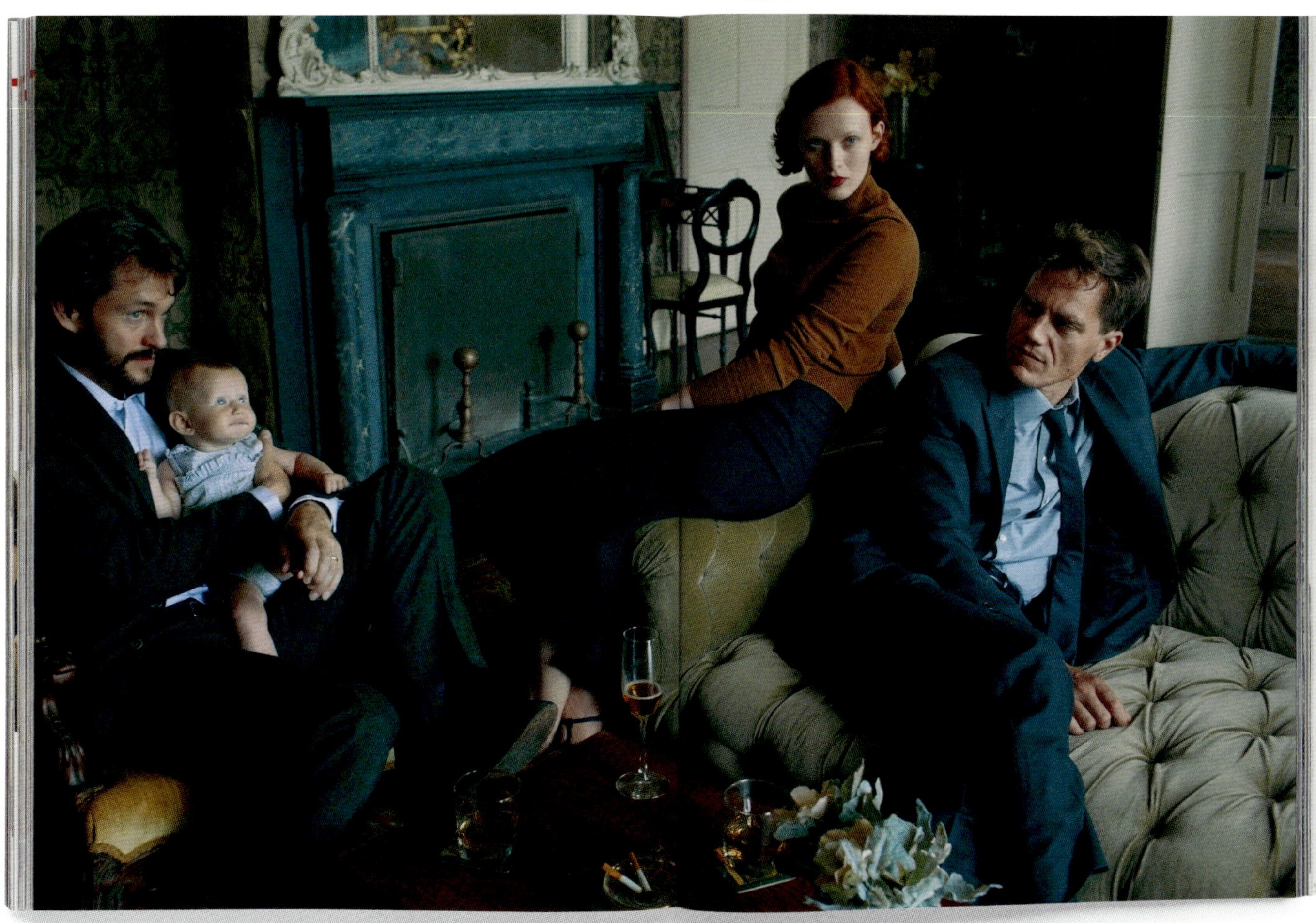

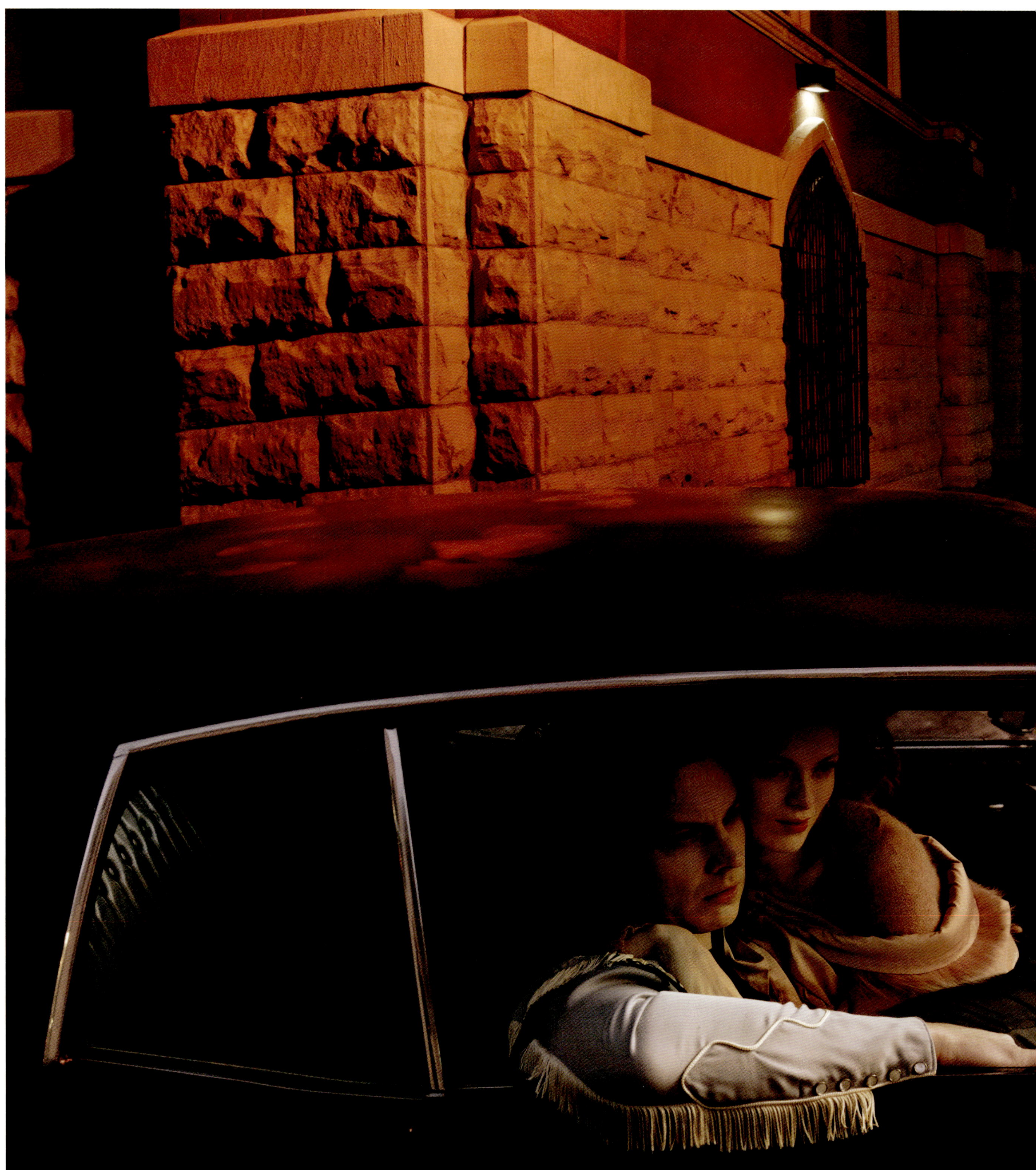

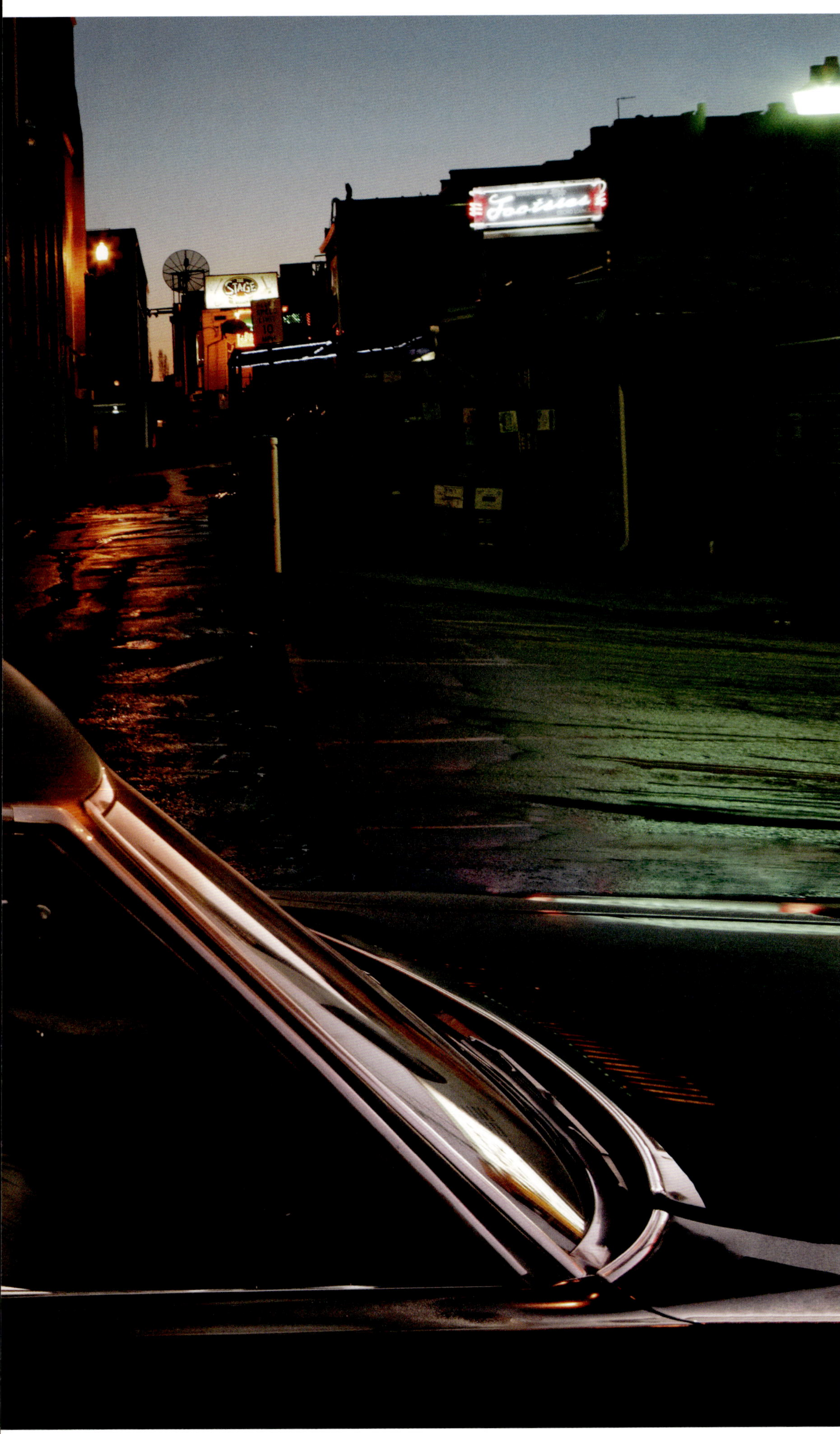

Karen Elson met Jack White in 2005 when she performed in a music video for a song by the White Stripes. They were married shortly thereafter, moved to Nashville, and had two children. He worked with Karen on her first album as a singer/songwriter, which they recorded in a studio in their garden.

Ryman Auditorium,
Nashville, 2010

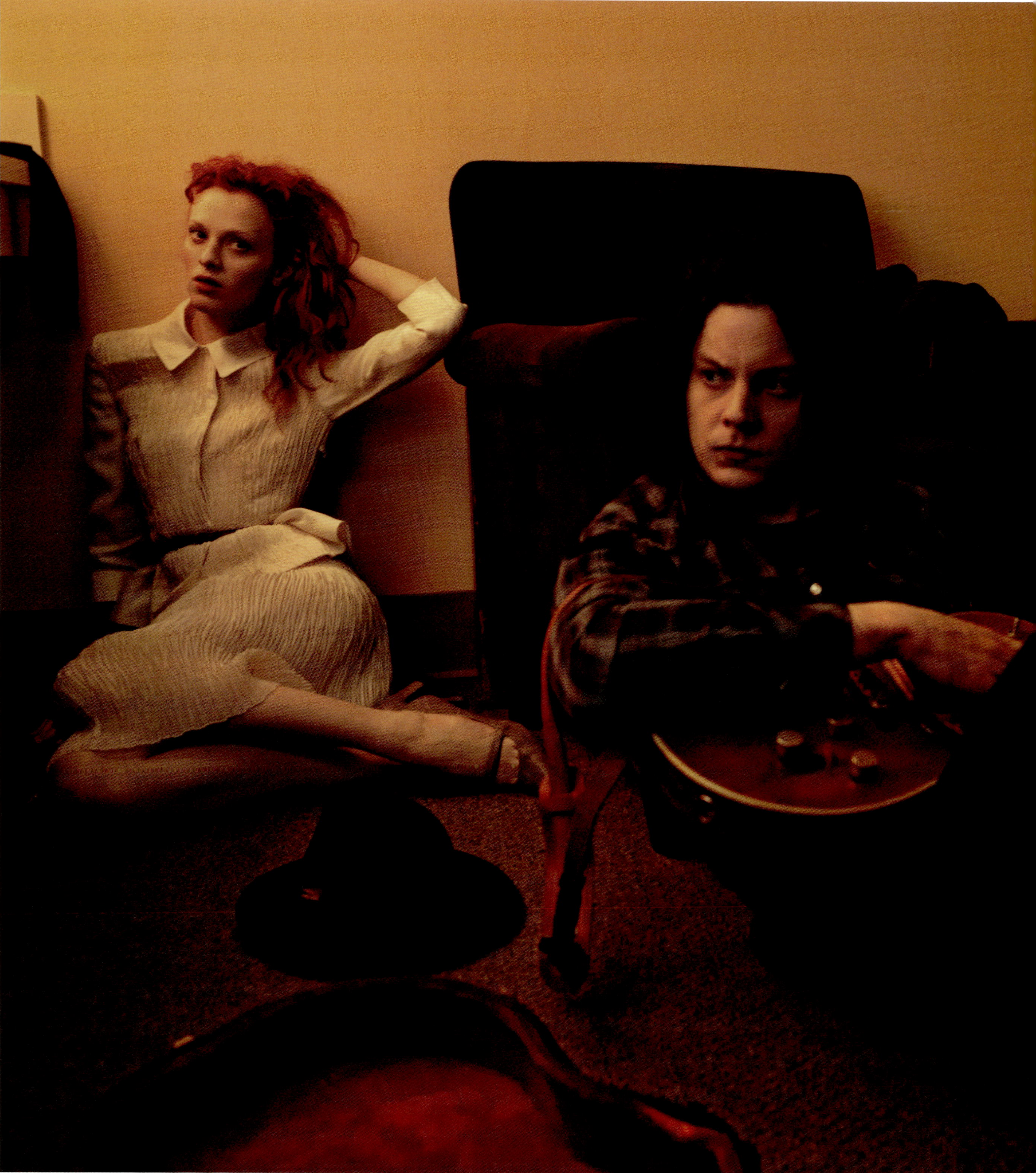

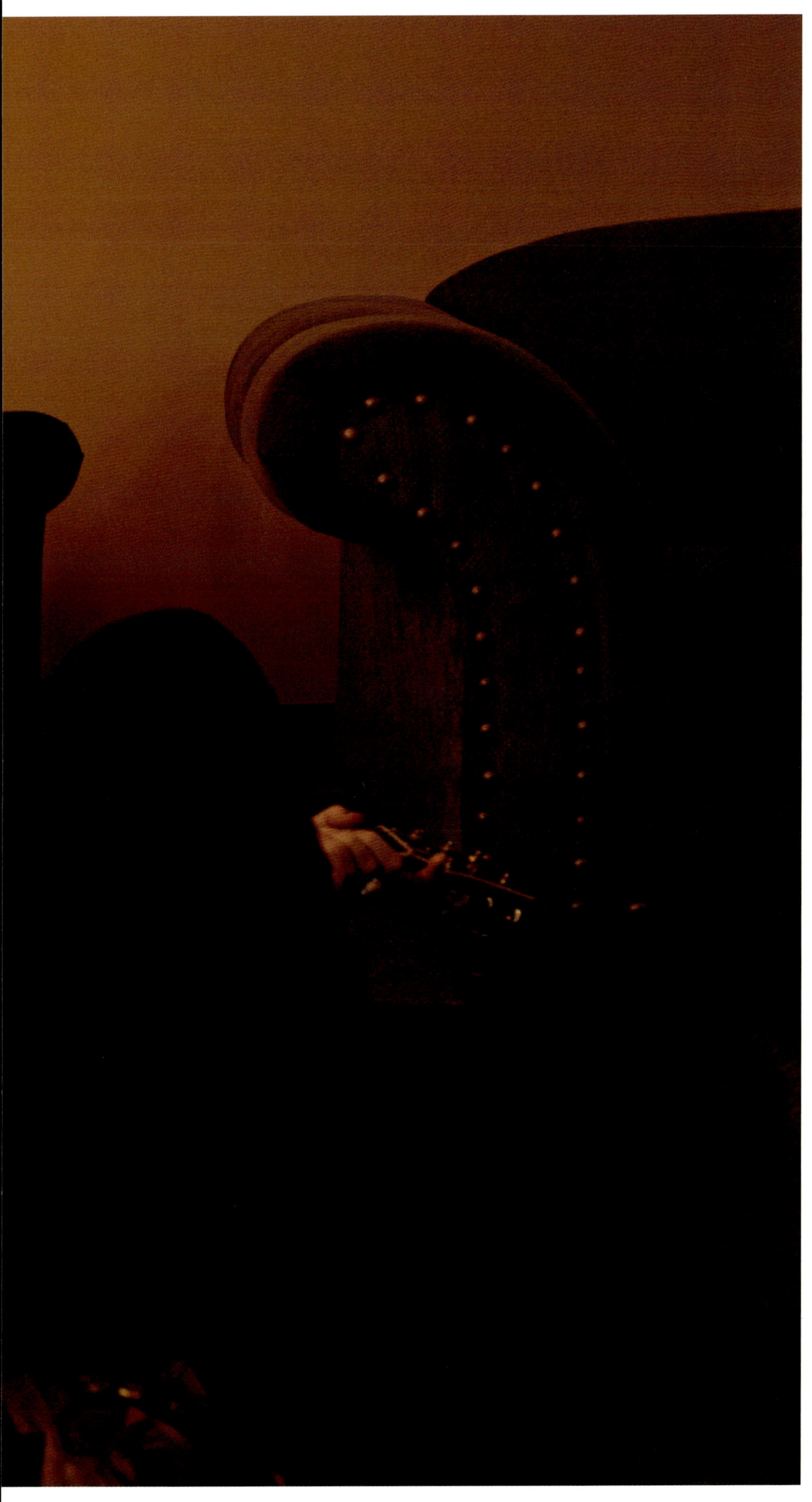

Dressing room at the Ryman
Auditorium, Nashville

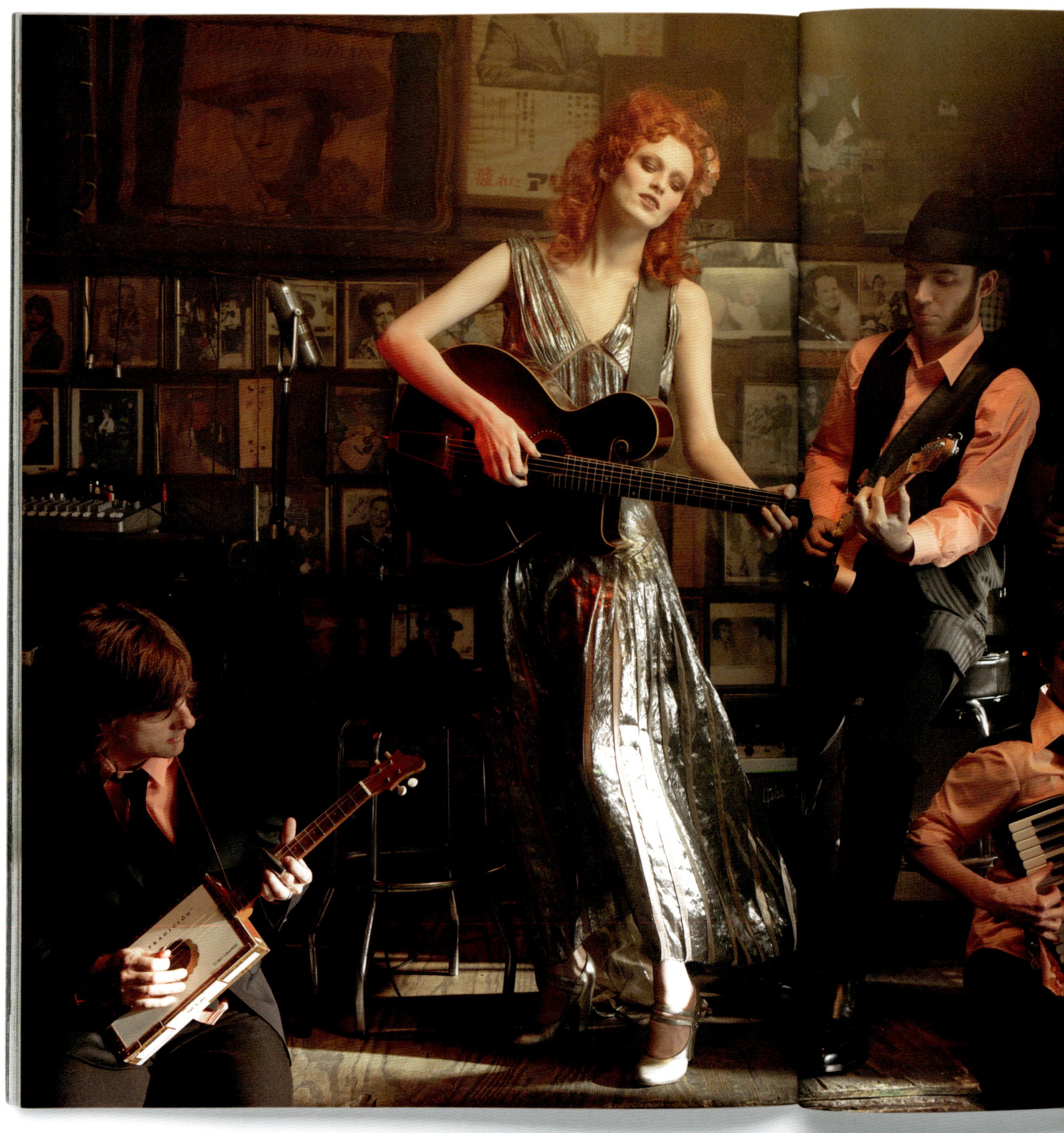
TRADICIÓN
TORO GRANDE

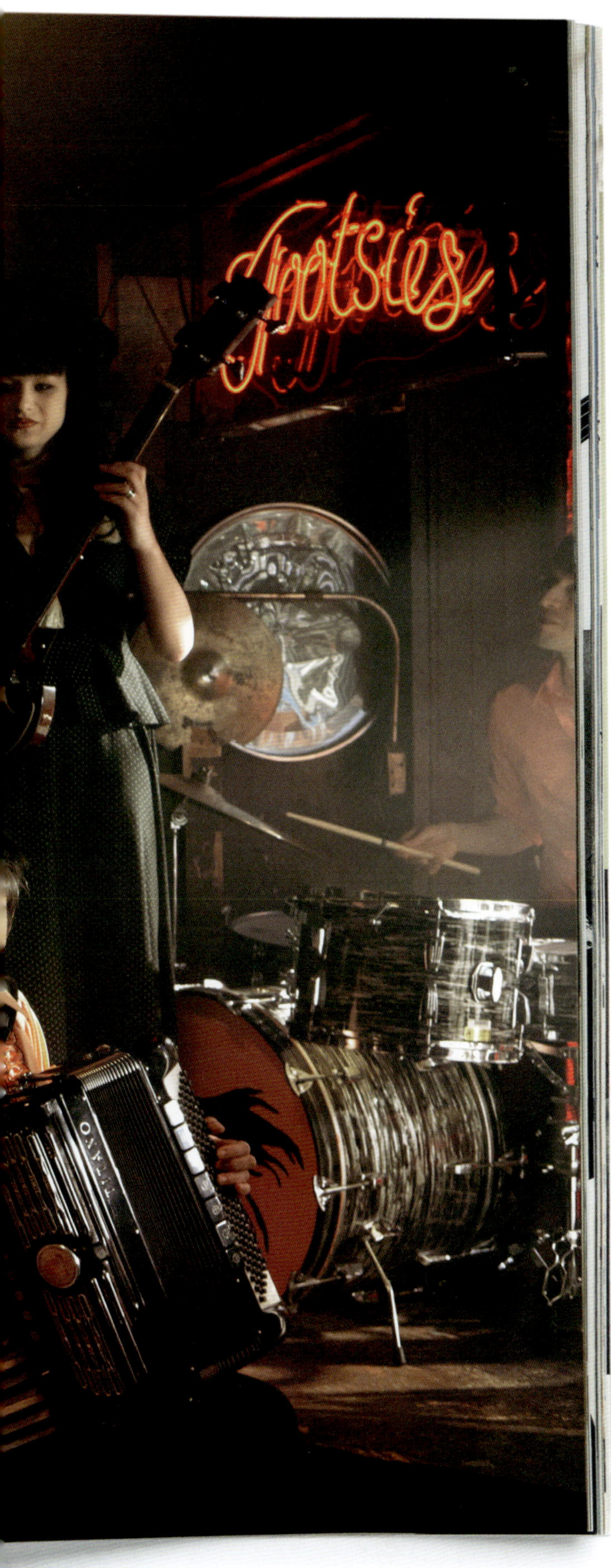

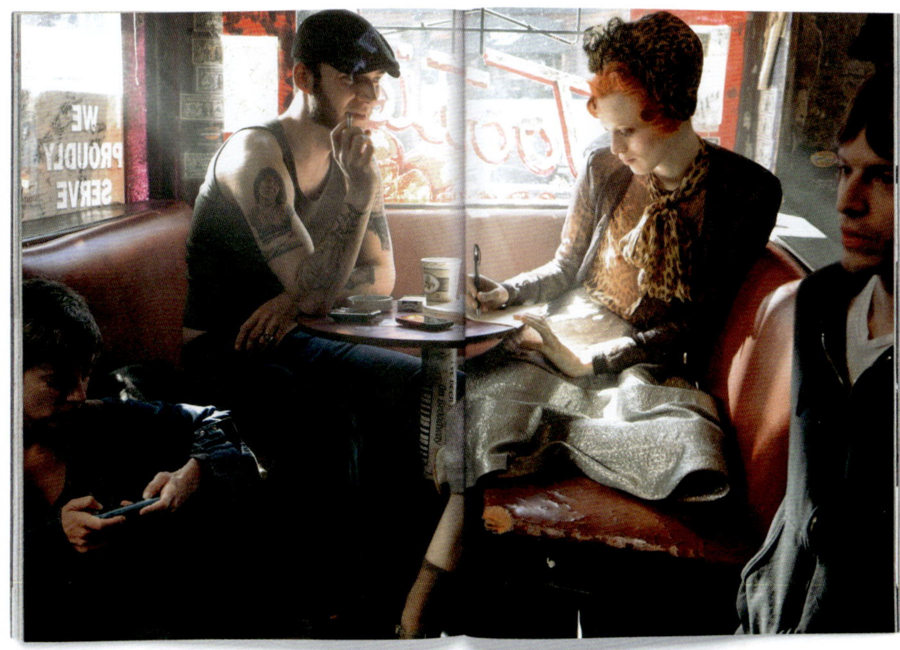

Karen Elson and her band at Tootsie's Orchid Lounge, Nashville

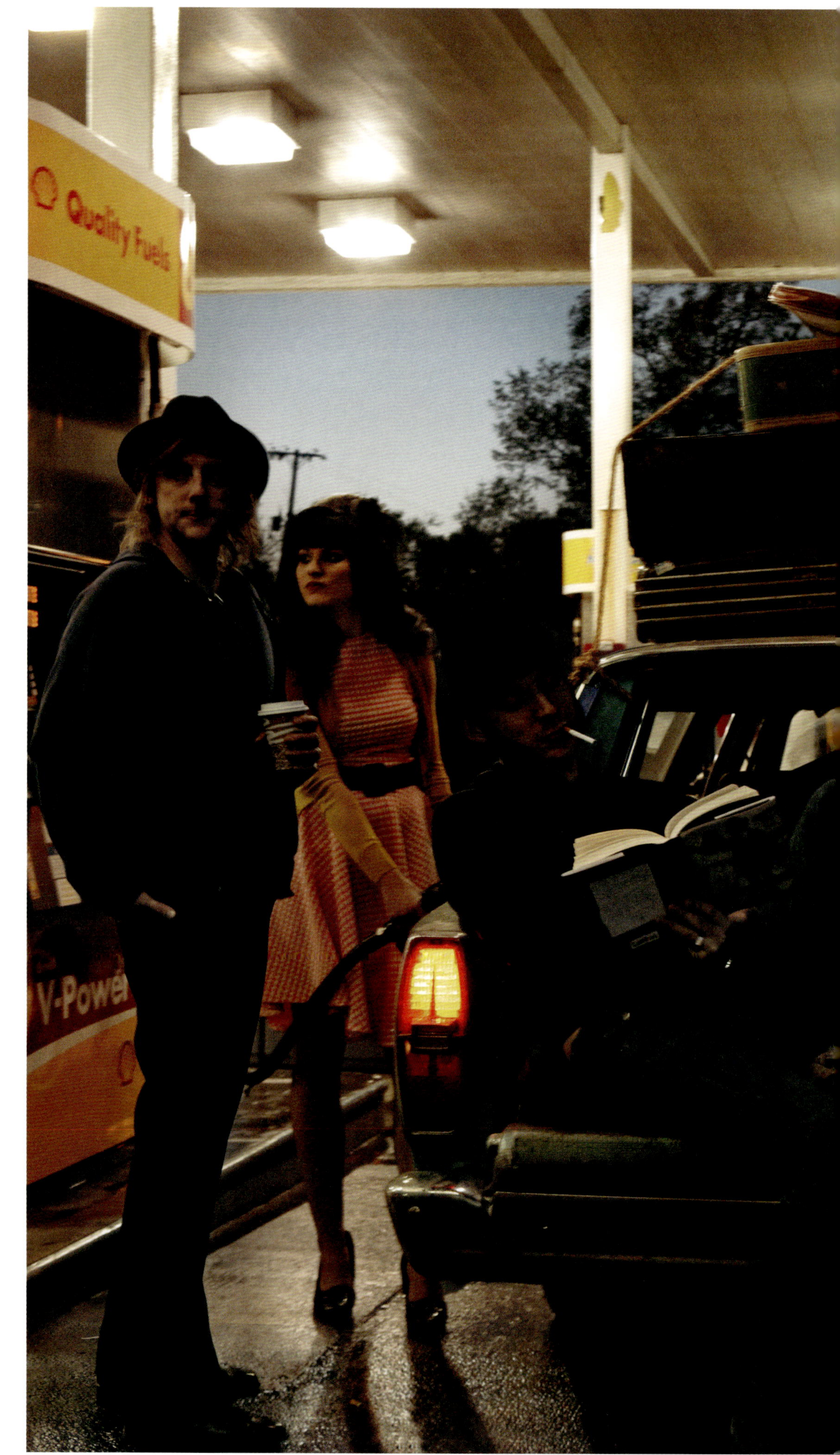
Quality Fuels
V-Power

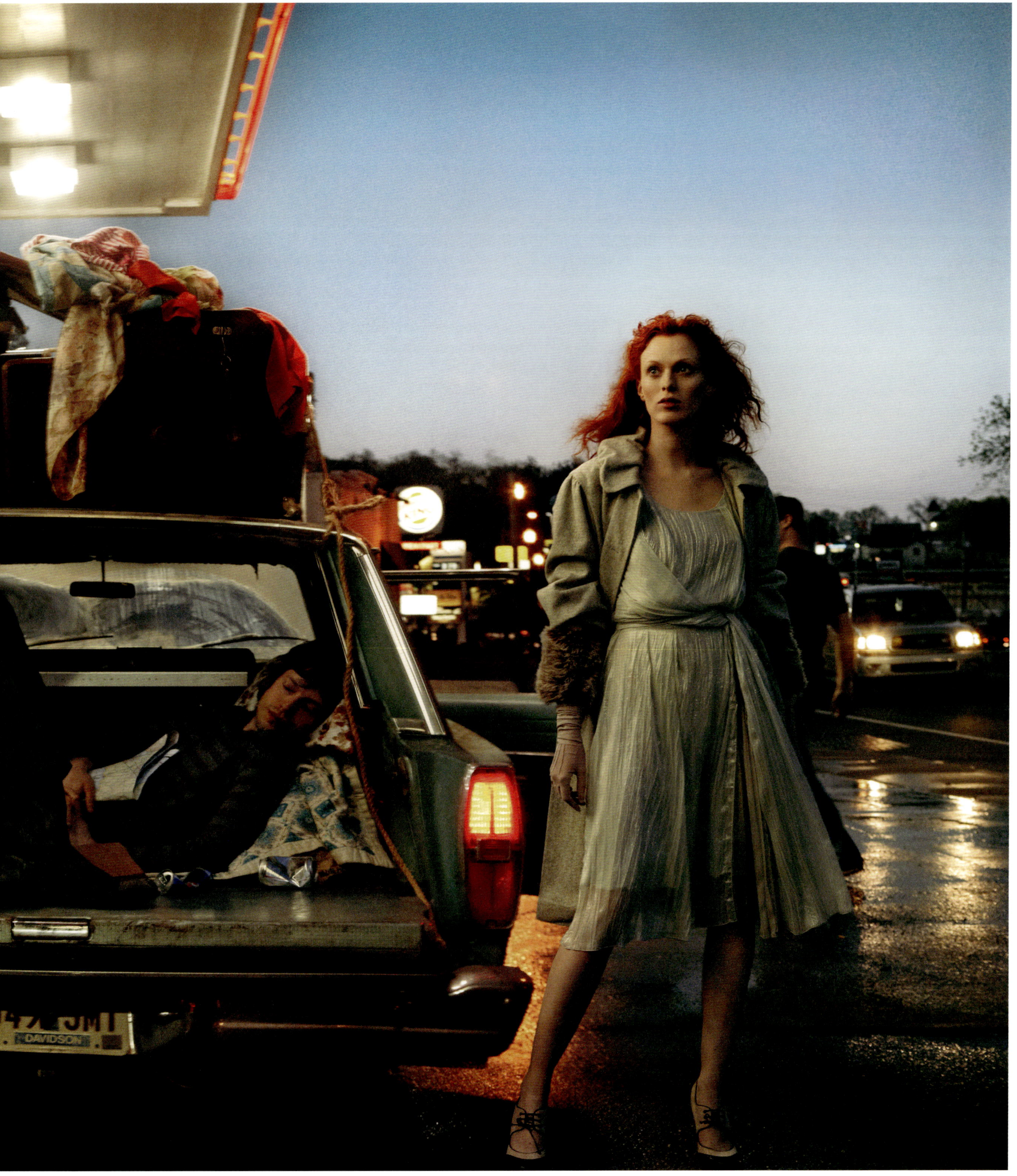
DAVIDSON

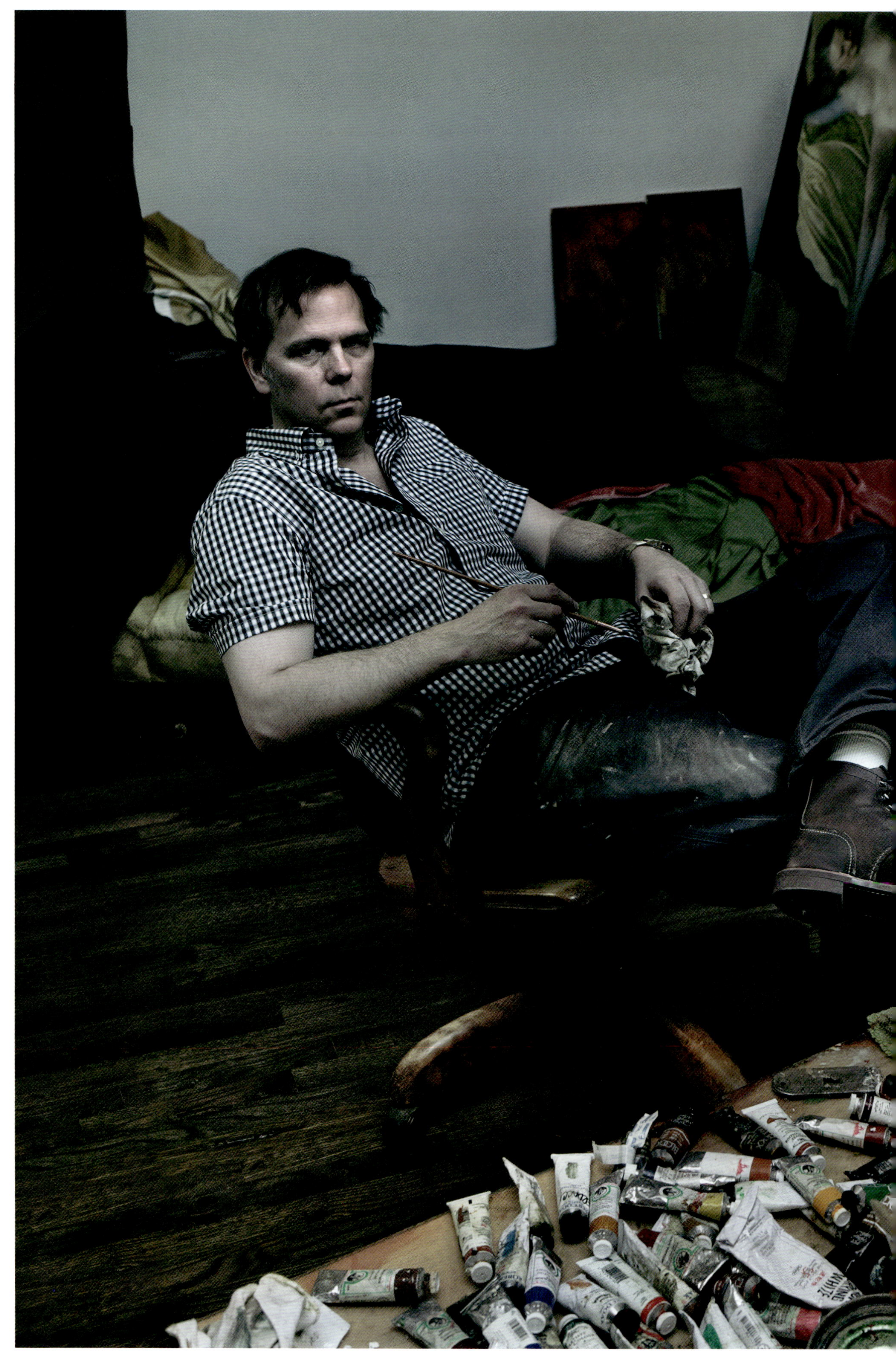

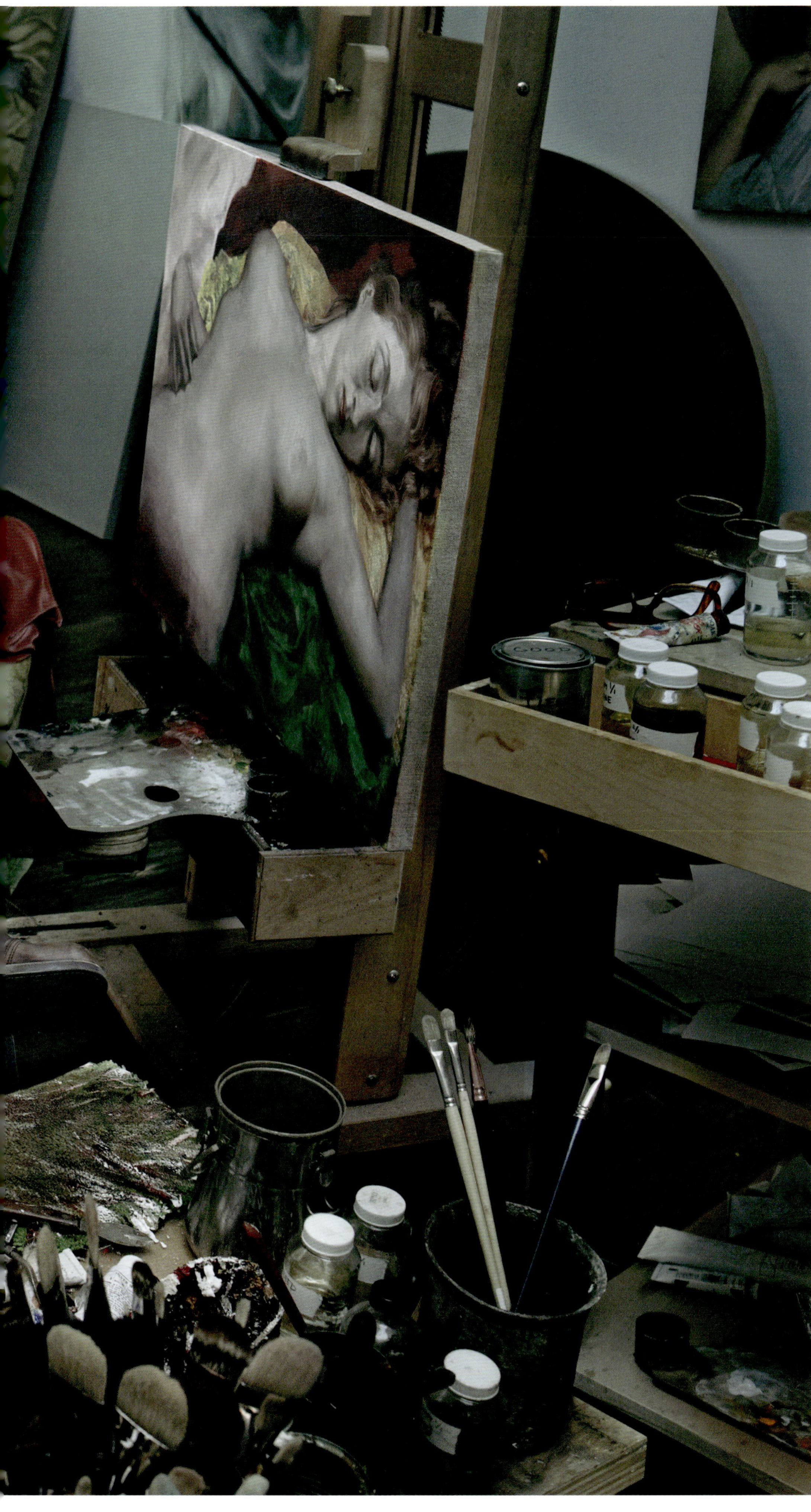

John Currin, New York City, 2011

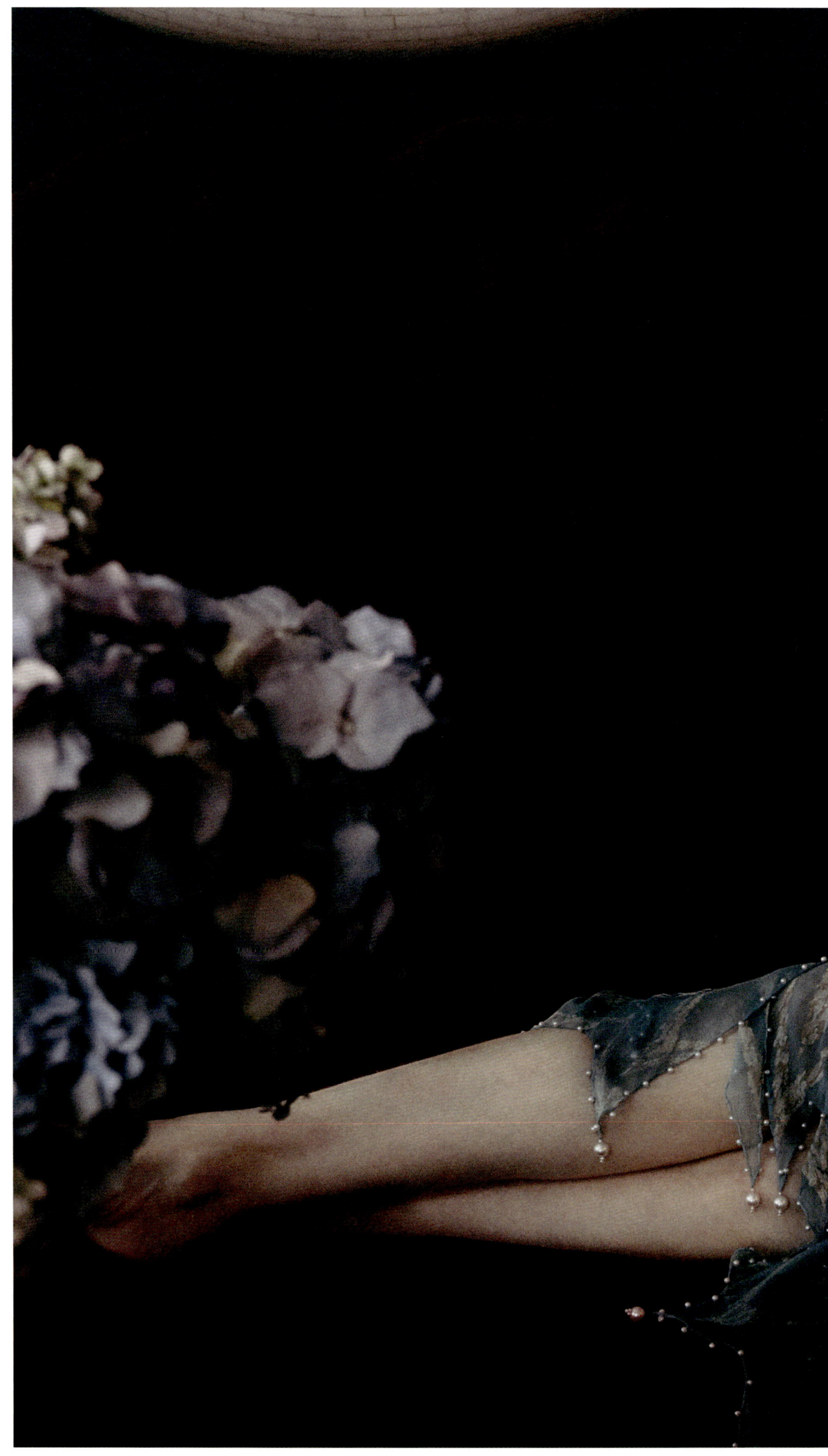

Rachel Feinstein with
her daughter, Flora Currin,
New York City, 2010

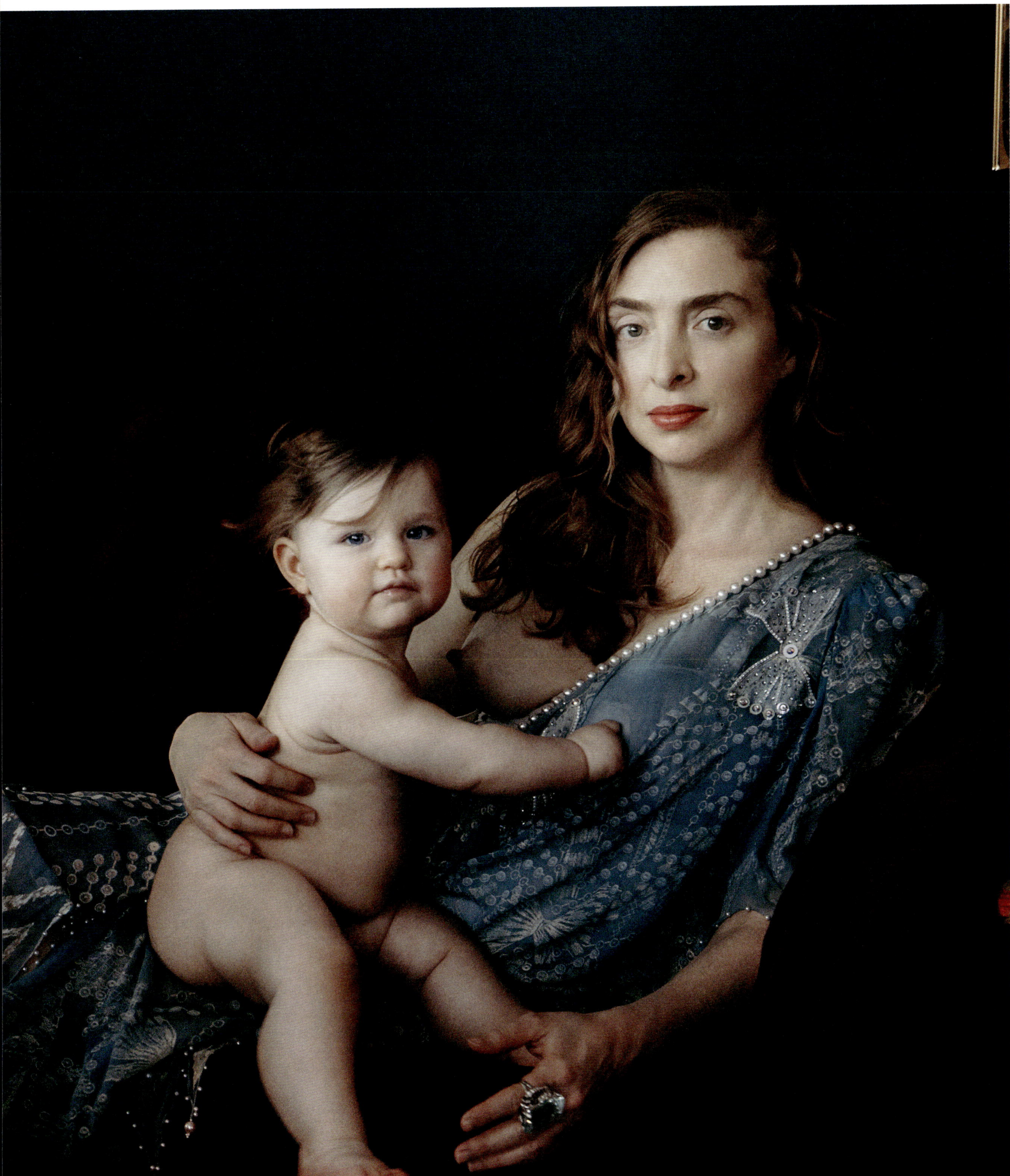

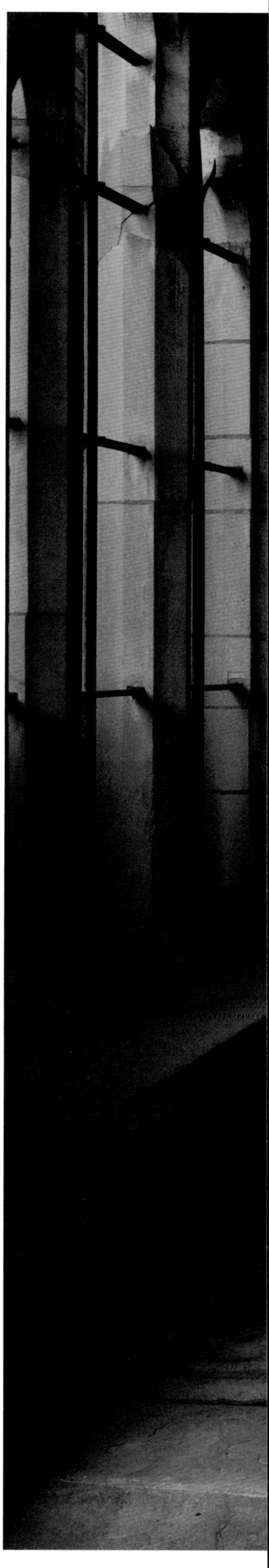

Francesco Vezzoli with his mother,
Titti Guizzi-Vezzoli, New York City, 2010

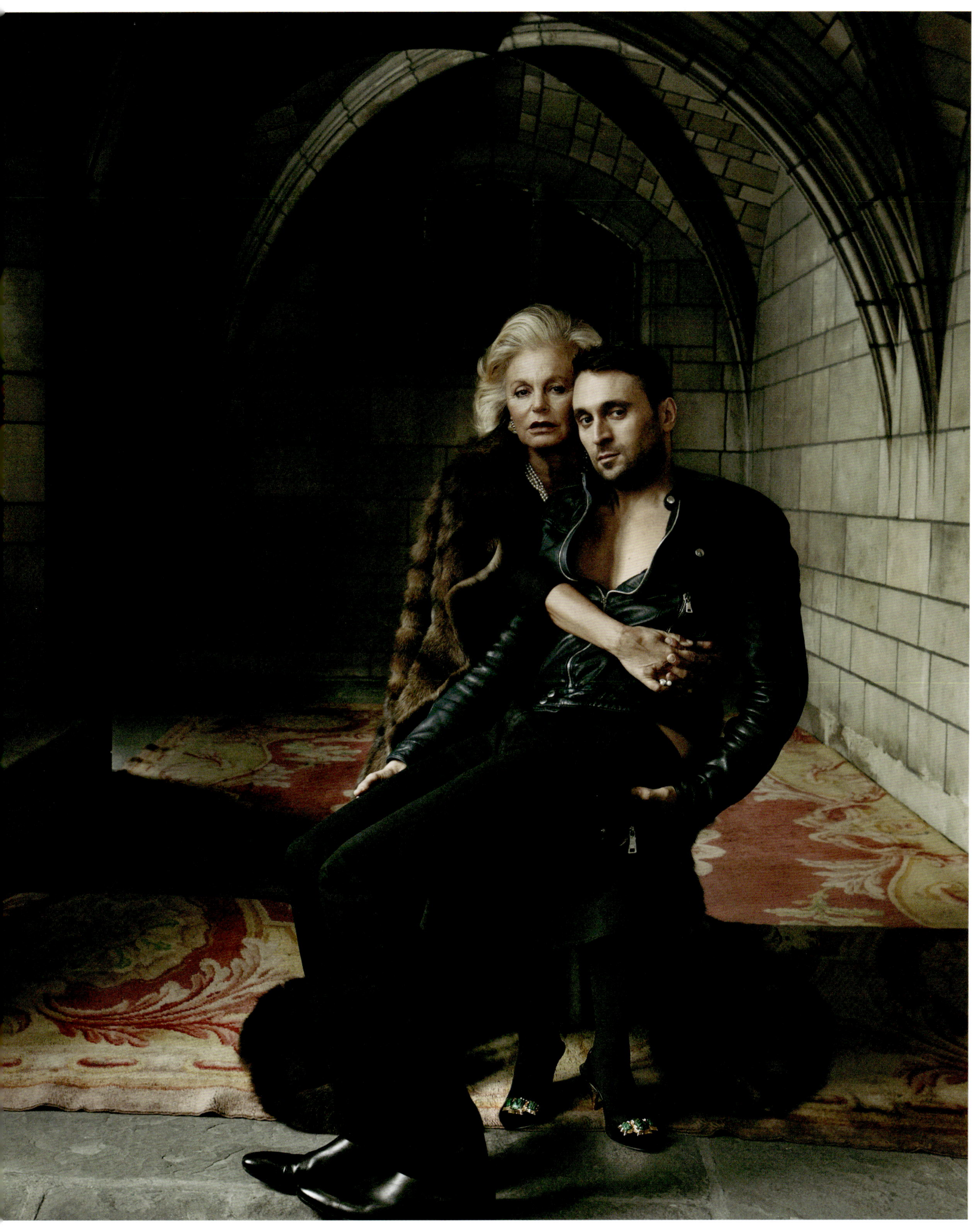

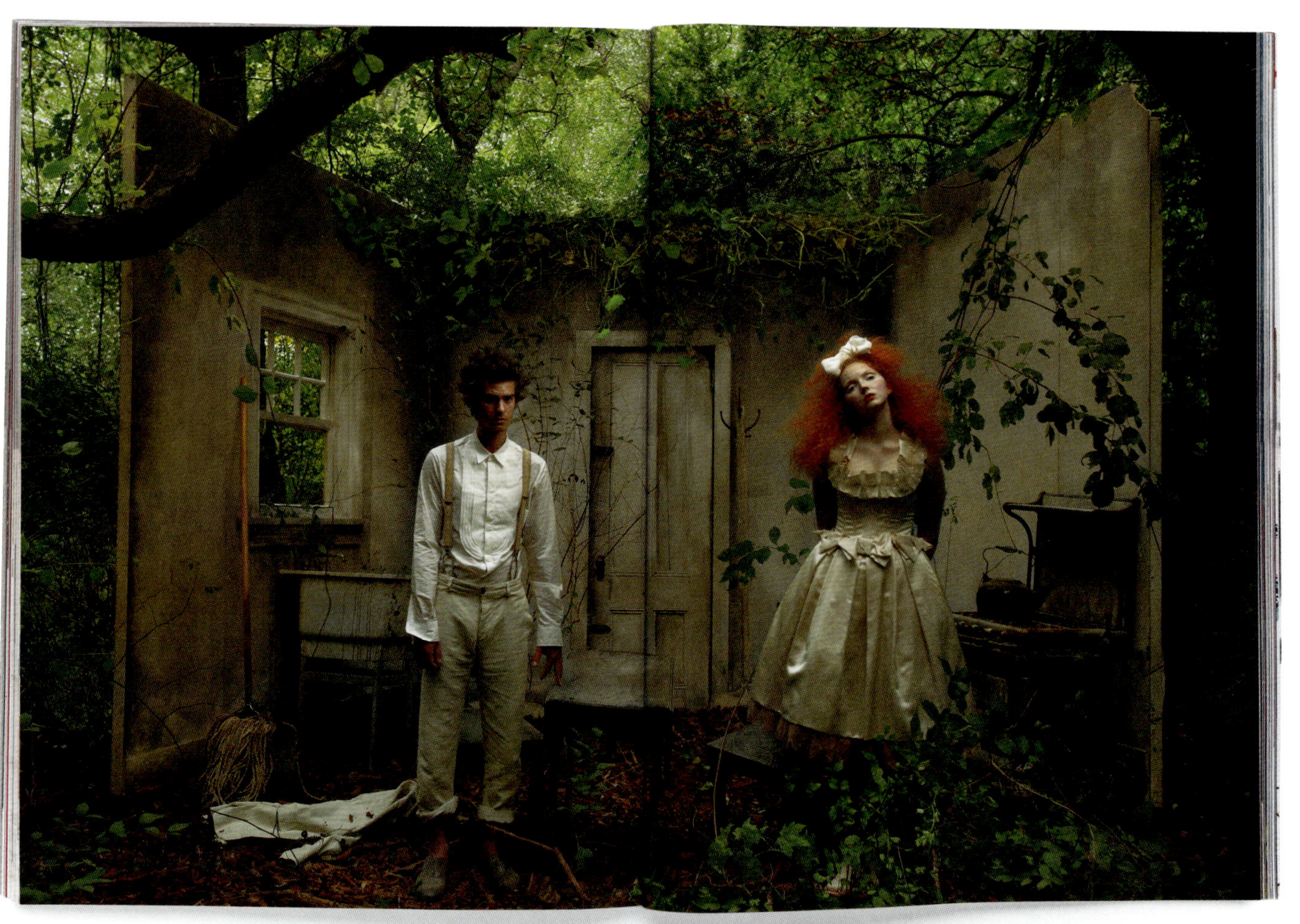

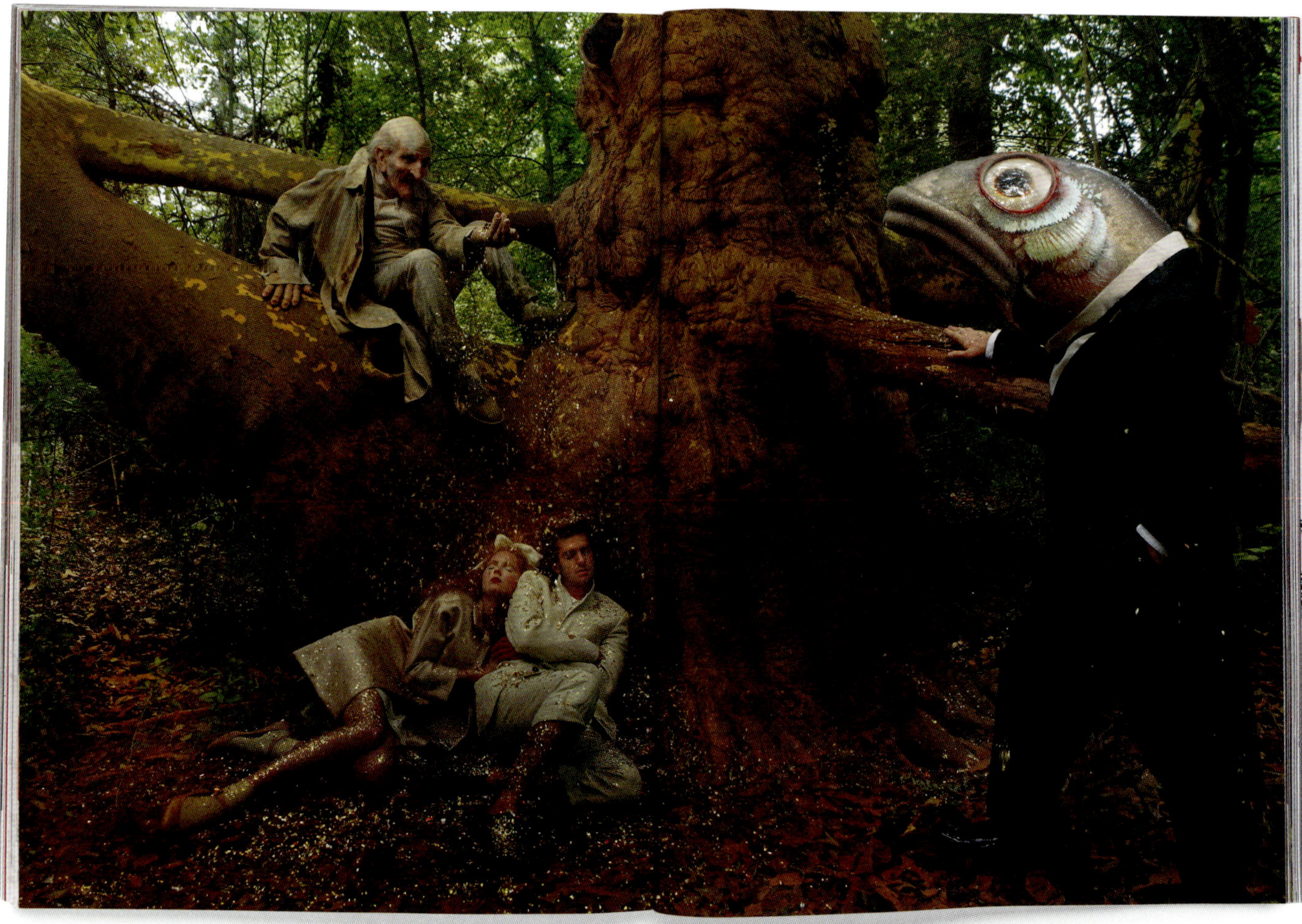

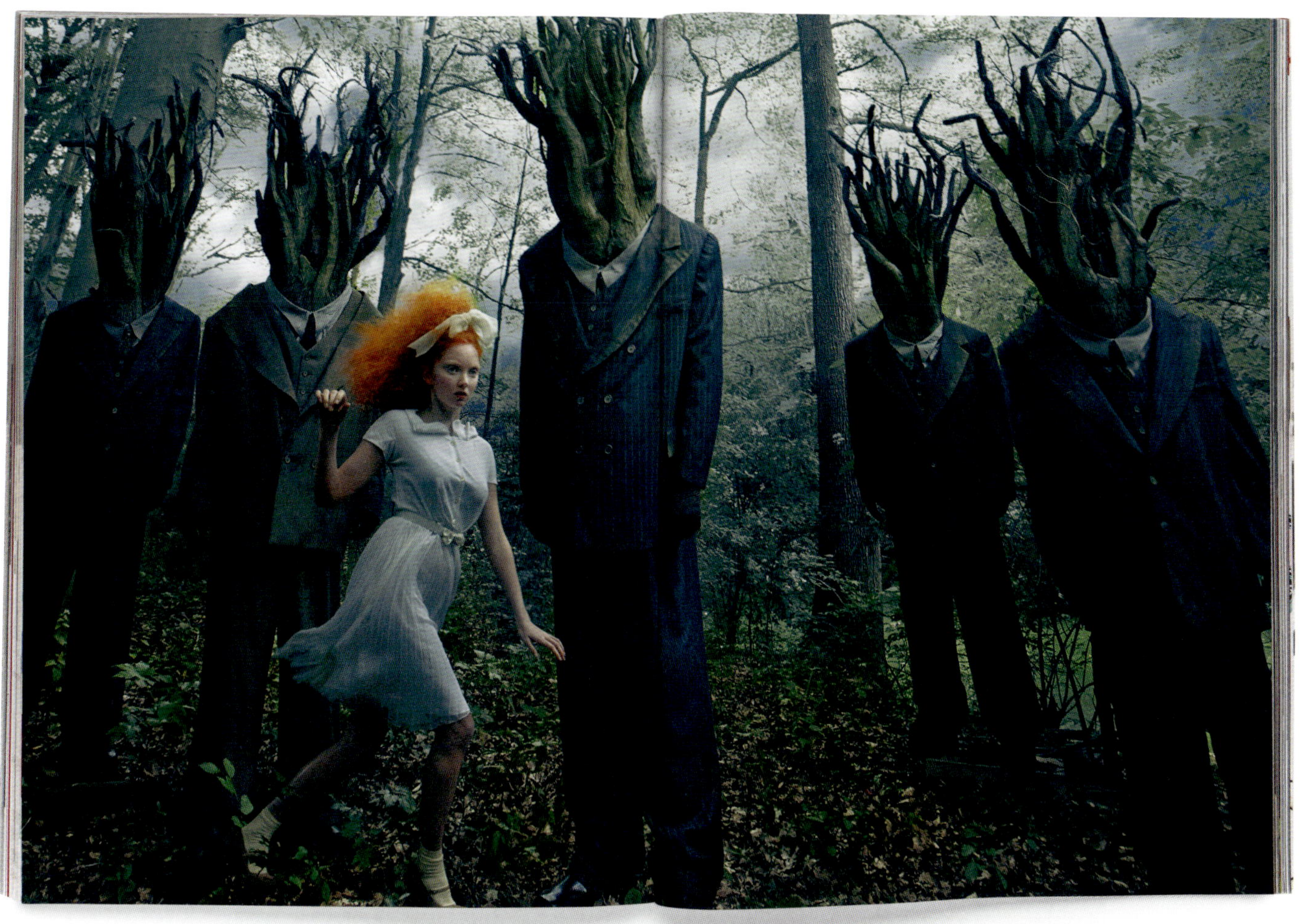

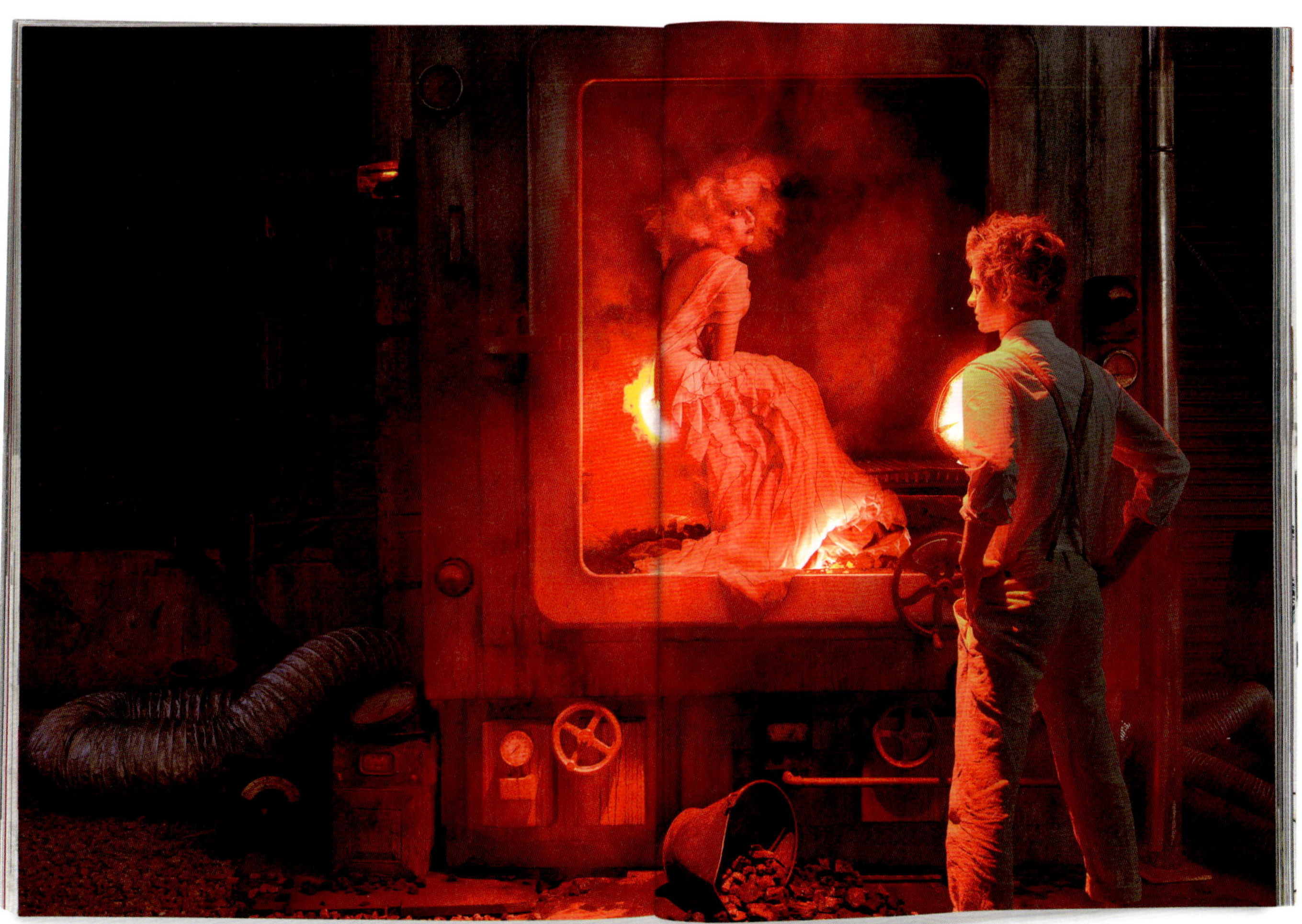

"When the Metropolitan Opera was mounting a production of Engelbert Humperdinck's version of the *Hansel and Gretel* story in 2009, Grace Coddington and I borrowed the Met's fantastic costumes for the Tree-men, the Sandman, and a Fish Maître d'. Grace dressed Lily Cole and the actor Andrew Garfield in white. Anna Wintour cast Lady Gaga as the Witch. She was just coming off her first global multimedia tour.

None of us knew what to expect when Lady Gaga arrived on set. She was wearing a long rubber raincoat. Her hair was slicked back and she wasn't wearing any makeup. She was a striking presence. 'She has absolutely nothing on under that coat,' Grace whispered to me."

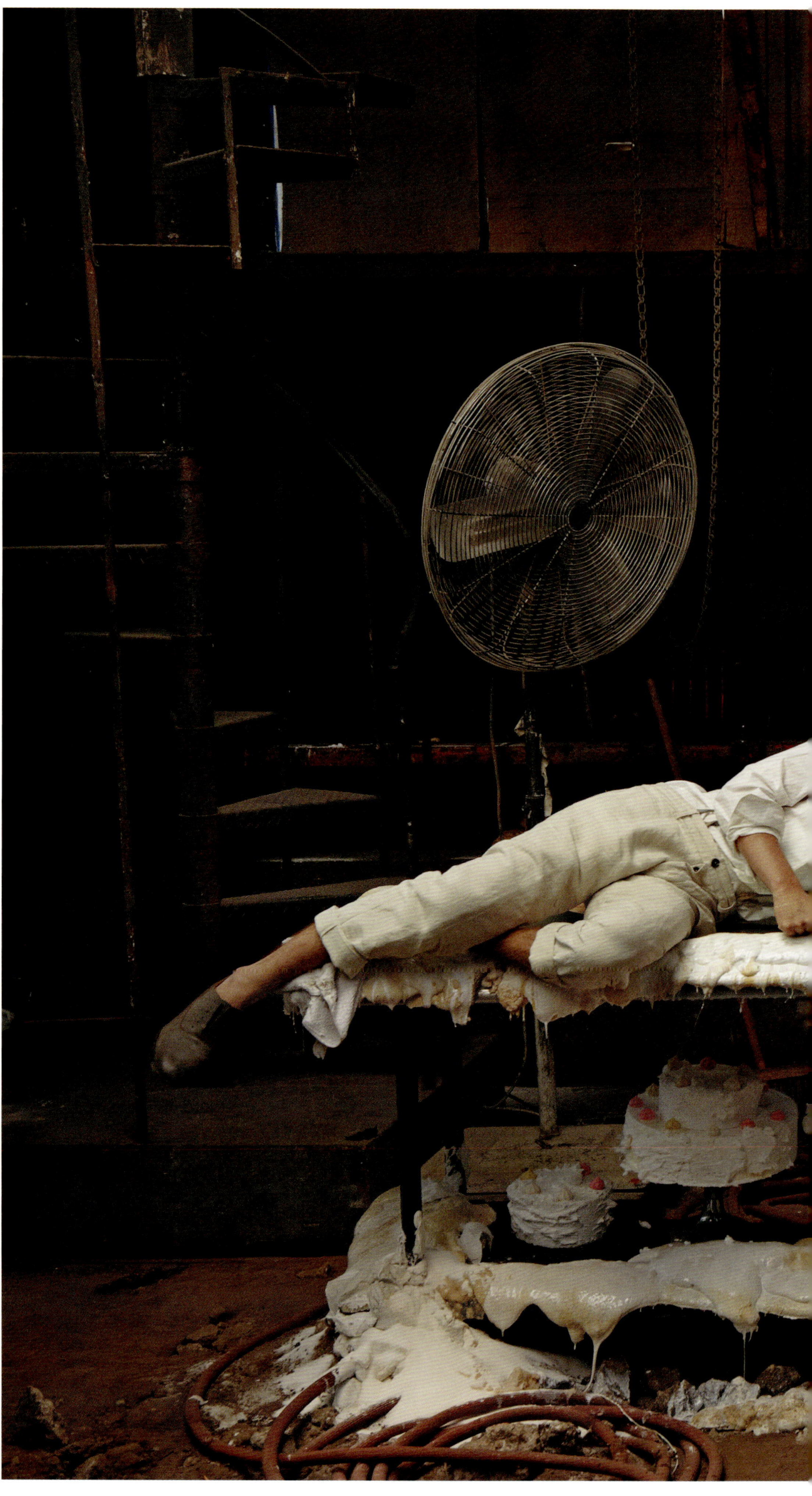

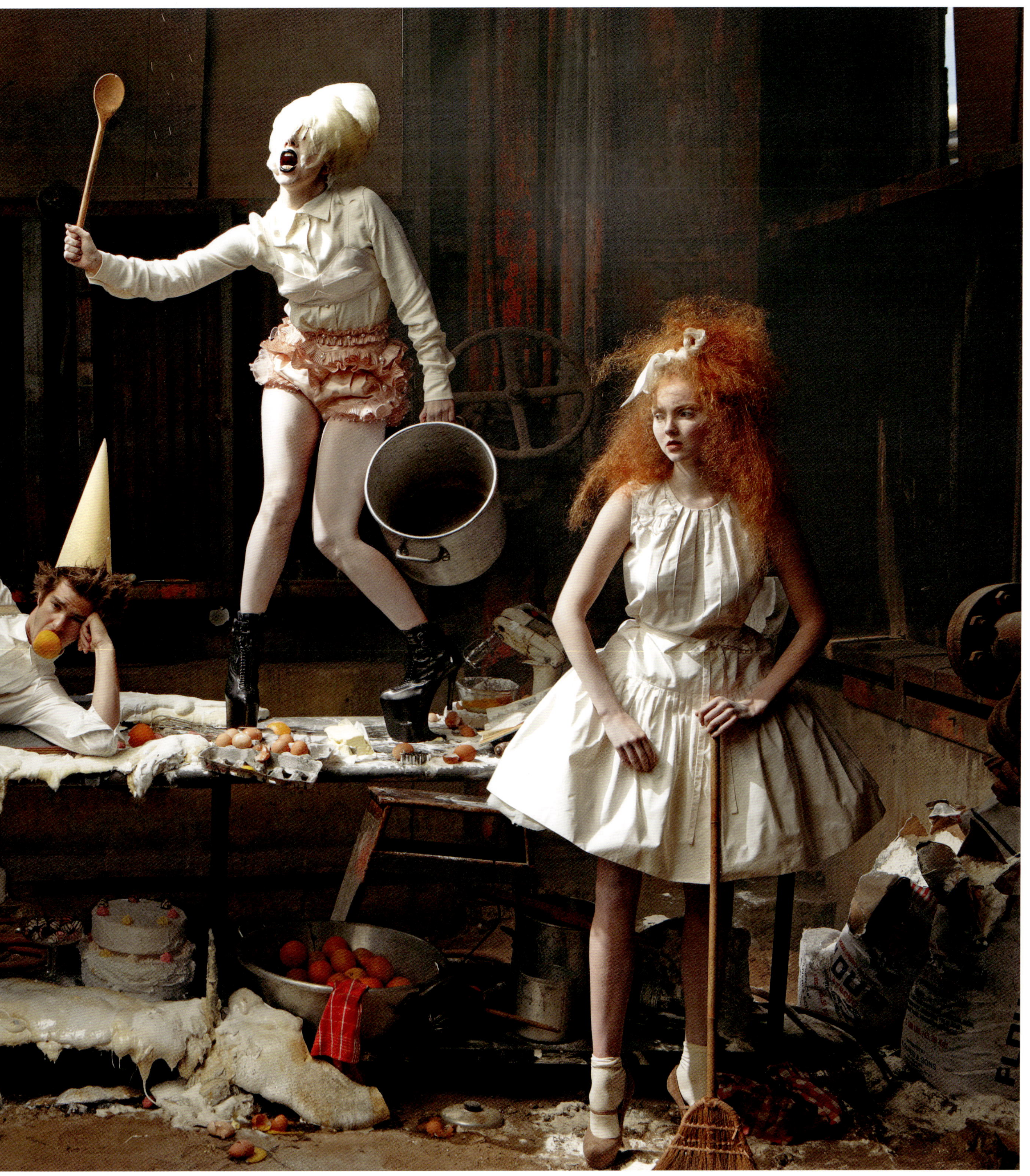

Julien d'Ys took his name from the mythical city of Ys, which was said to have been built below sea level off the coast of Brittany (where he was born) in the fourth century and then submerged in an act of pique by a beautiful and wicked woman. Julien was almost always the hair stylist on Annie's shoots with Grace Coddington; he was her comrade. Dates of shoots would be moved to accommodate his schedule. Sometimes he could be seen walking around the location, collecting twigs or leaves that would make their way into his creations.

Julien d'Ys with Raquel Zimmermann,
New York City, 2008

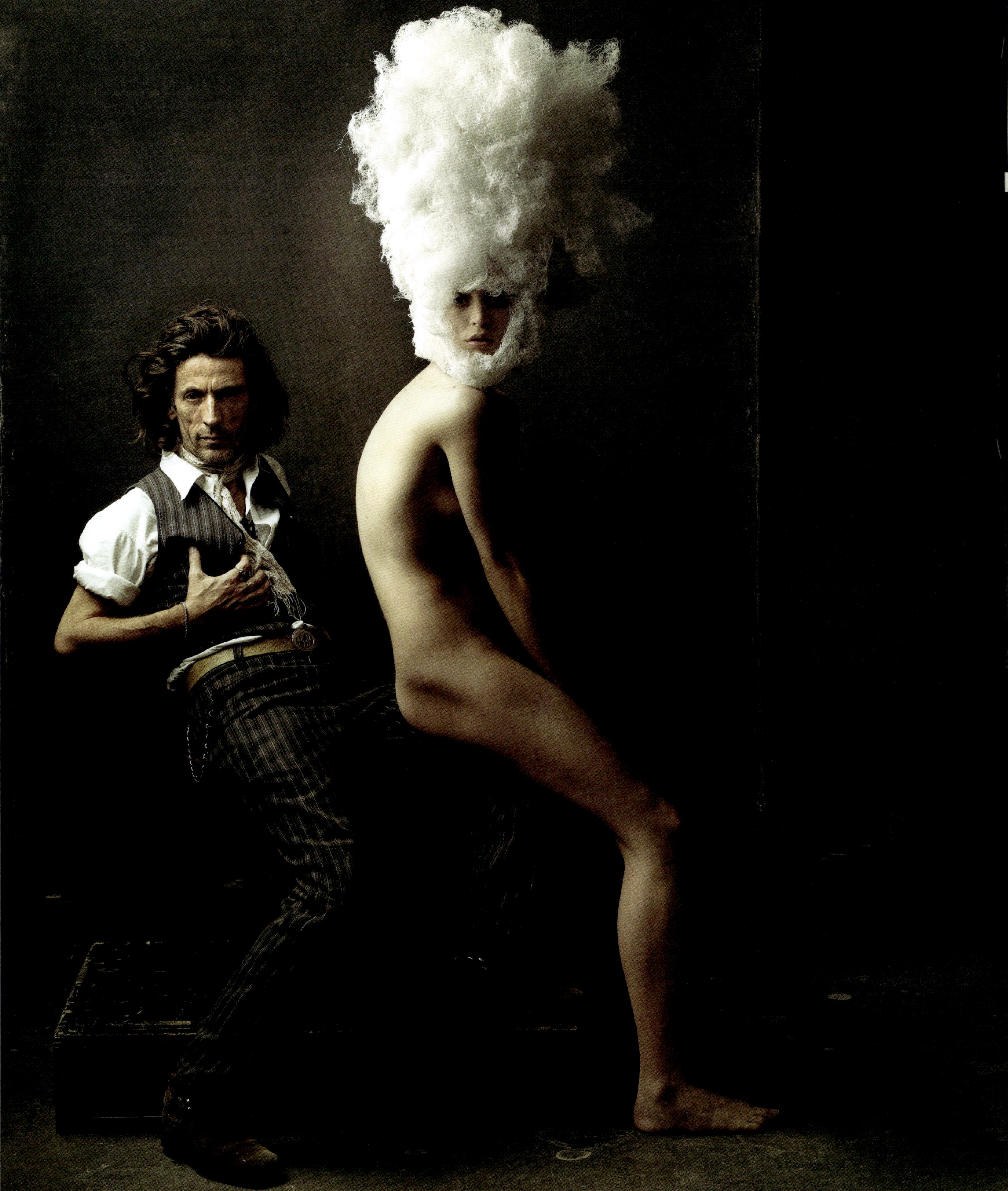

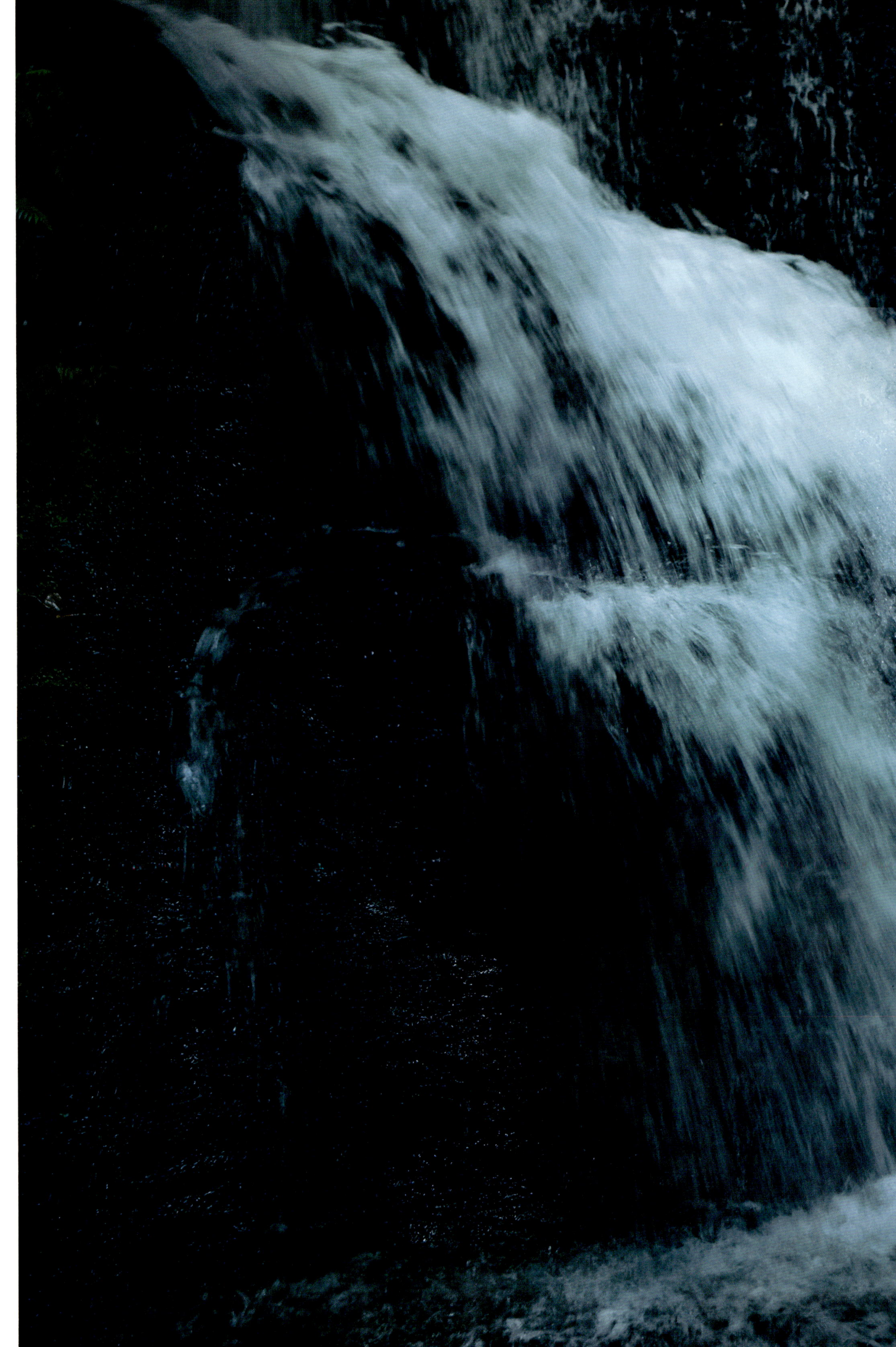

Charlize Theron, Bushkill
Falls, Pennsylvania, 2011

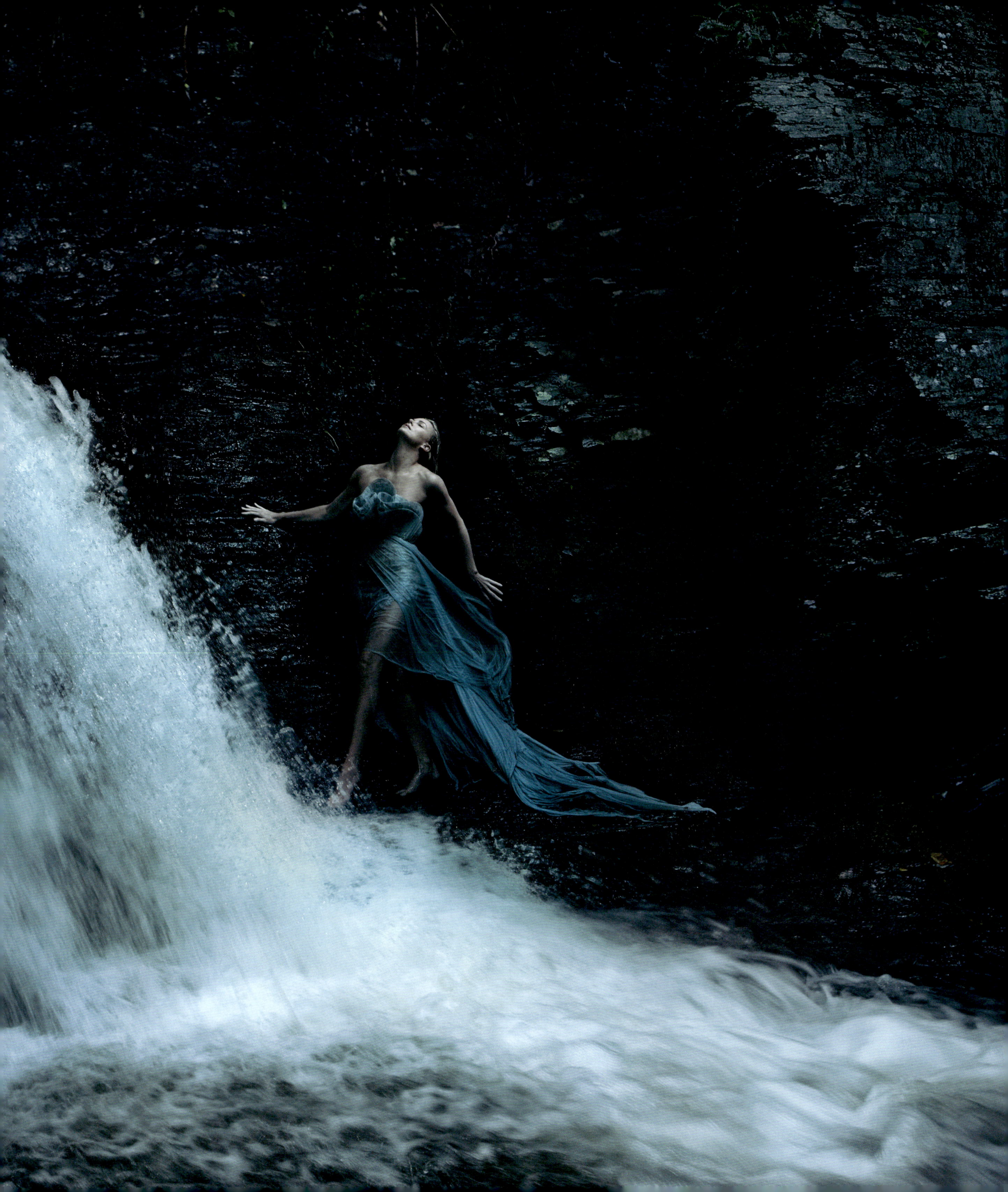

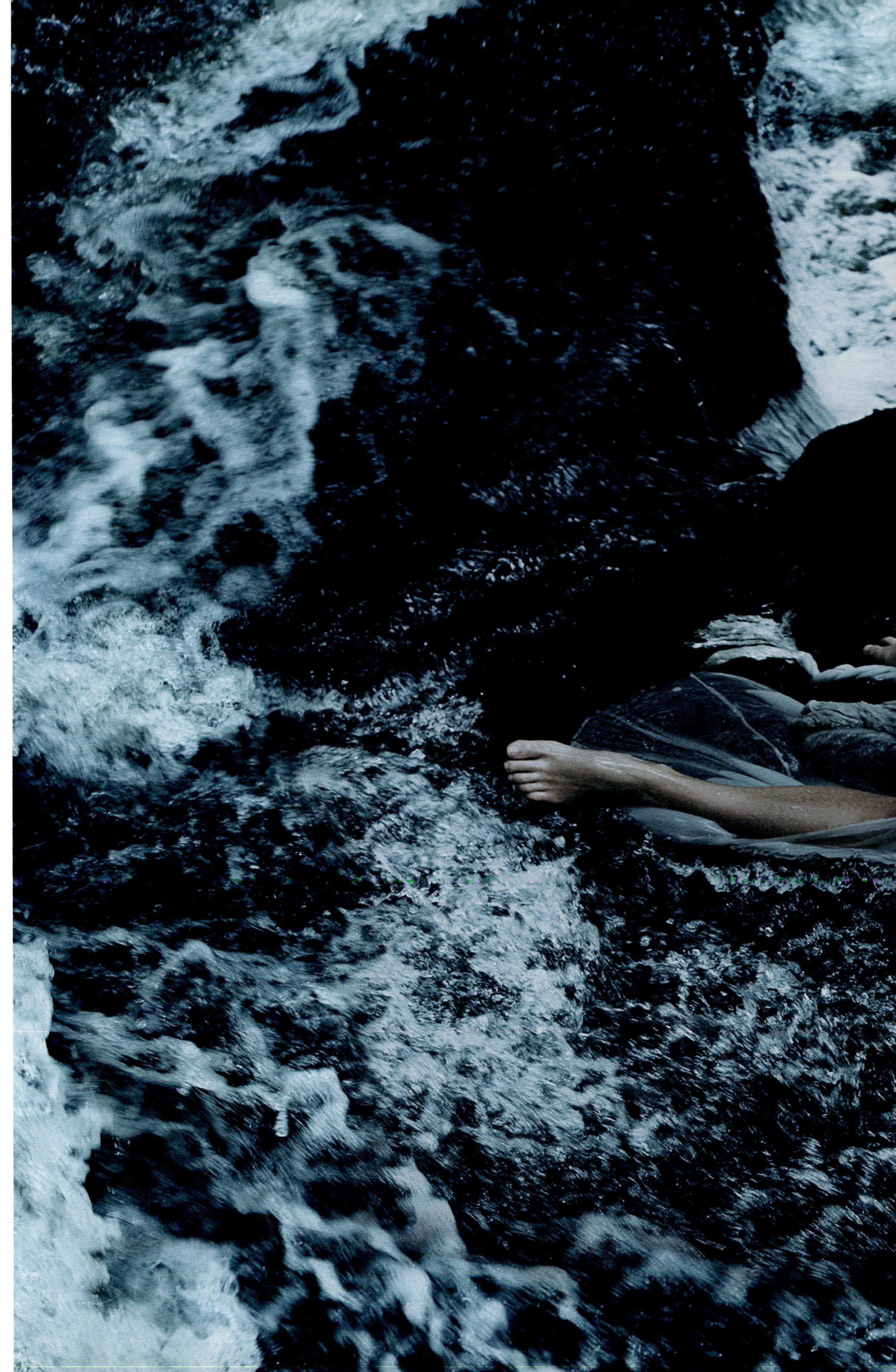

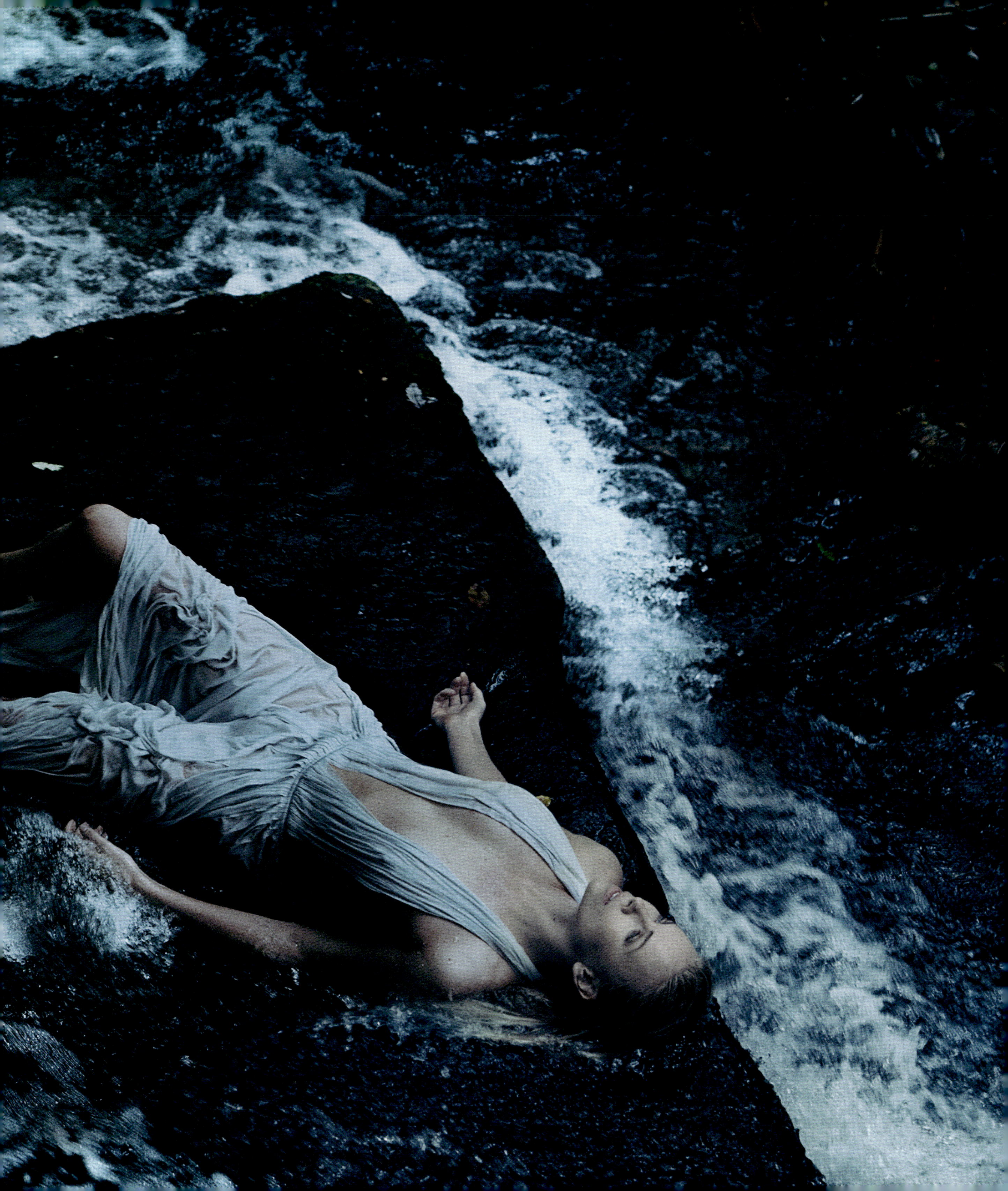

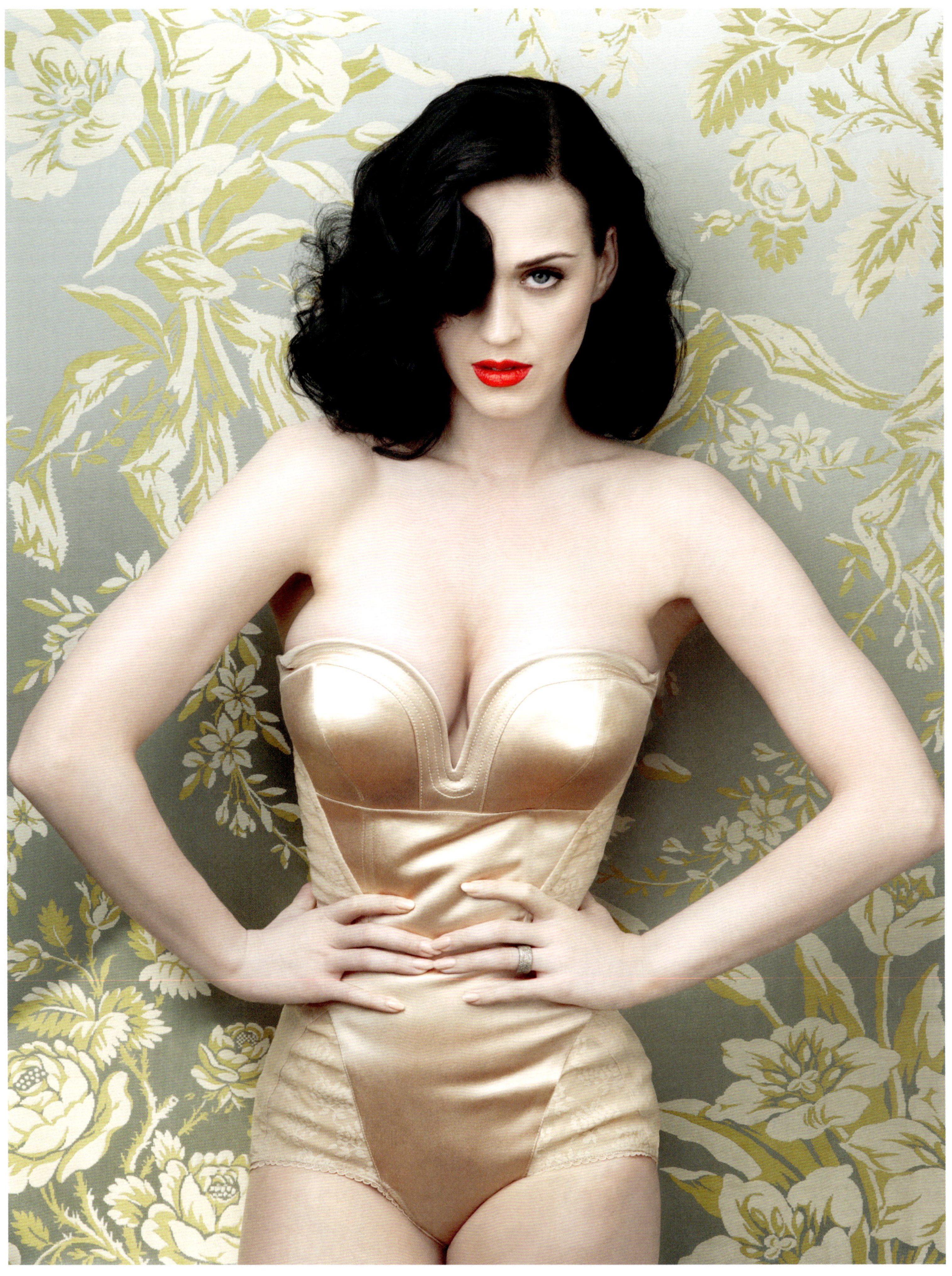

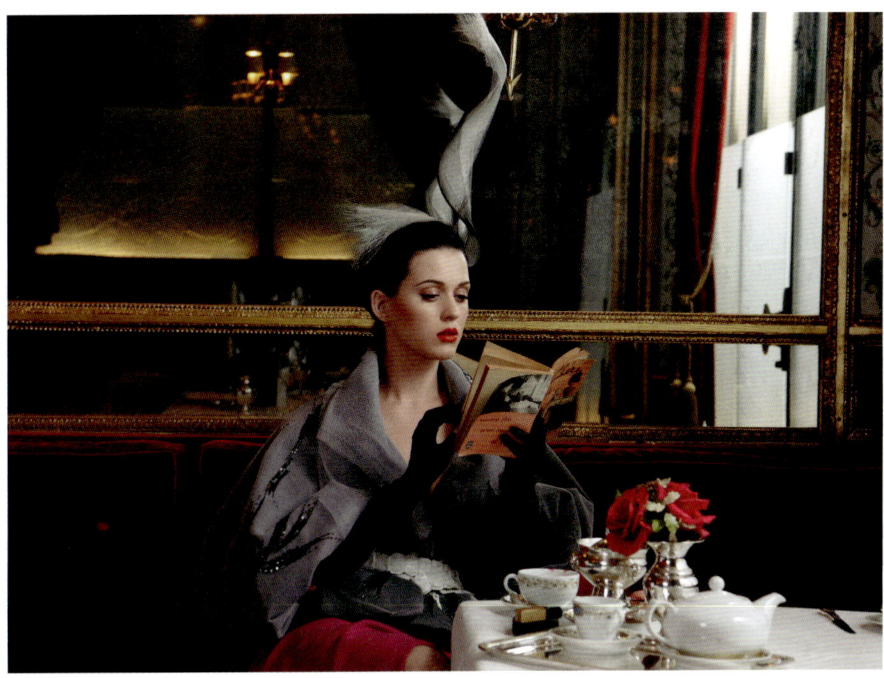

"Katy Perry was just starting out on a long international concert tour and was playing two nights in an arena on the outskirts of Paris. We did a shoot with her on her day off.

I had been working in Paris regularly for over a decade by then, and I knew the city well. That shoot became a kind of love letter to Paris. The scene on the merry-go-round came about because my children more or less lived on them when we were there. You don't realize that it is a city of merry-go-rounds until you have children.

This was a cover story for *Vanity Fair*, and the magazine wanted it to be a fashion story. I had resisted doing fashion for them, but all the portraits were turning into fashion shoots to some extent, and I succumbed. I had resisted because unless you're doing stories where you want some kind of role-playing, it seems more interesting to let the subjects remain themselves, with their own style. Katy has a very theatrical personality, so what we did wasn't a stretch."

Katy Perry reading Colette's *Chéri* at Le Grand Véfour in Paris, 2011

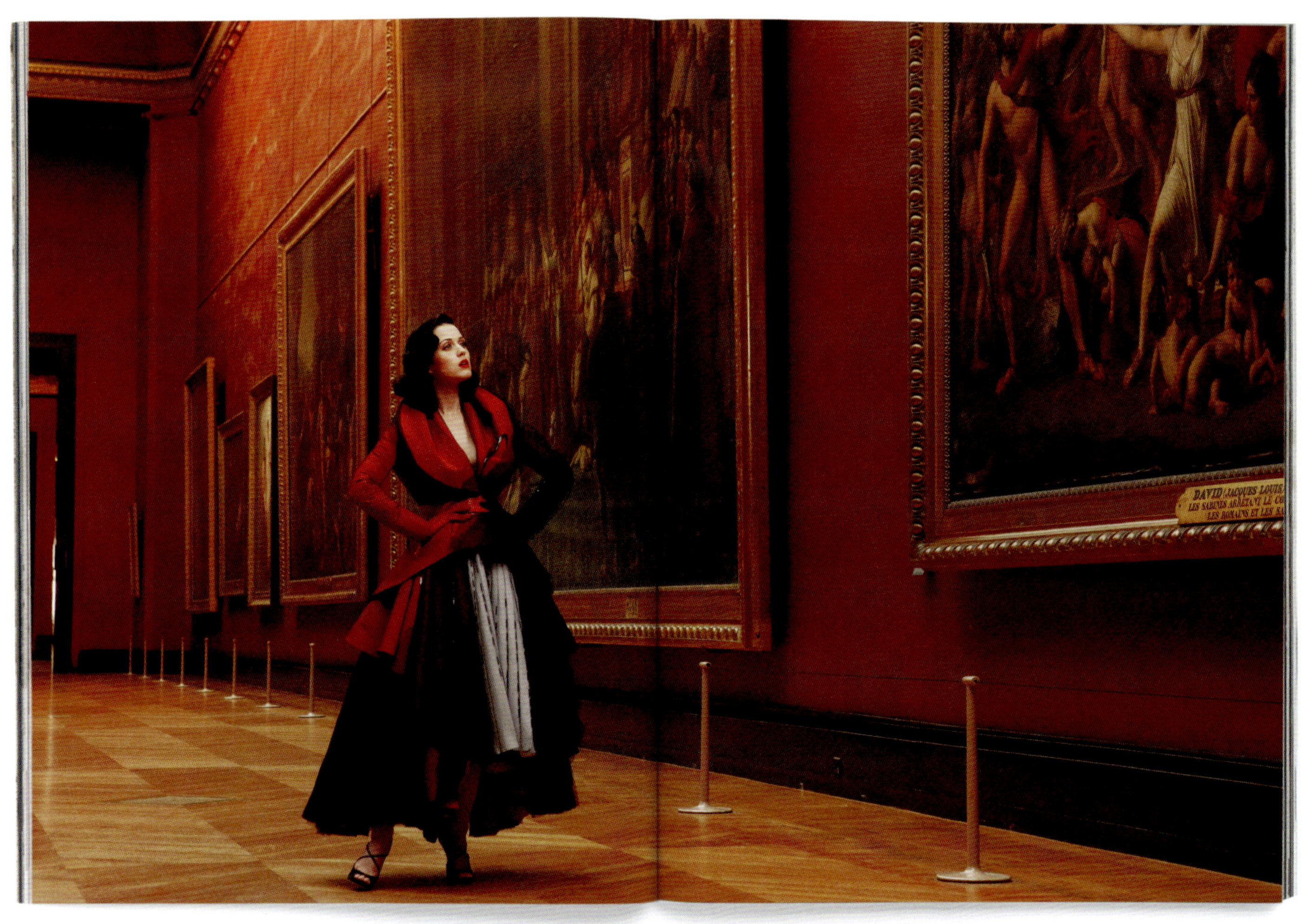
DAVID (JACQUES LOUIS
LES SABINES ARRÊTANT LE
LES ROMAINS ET LES

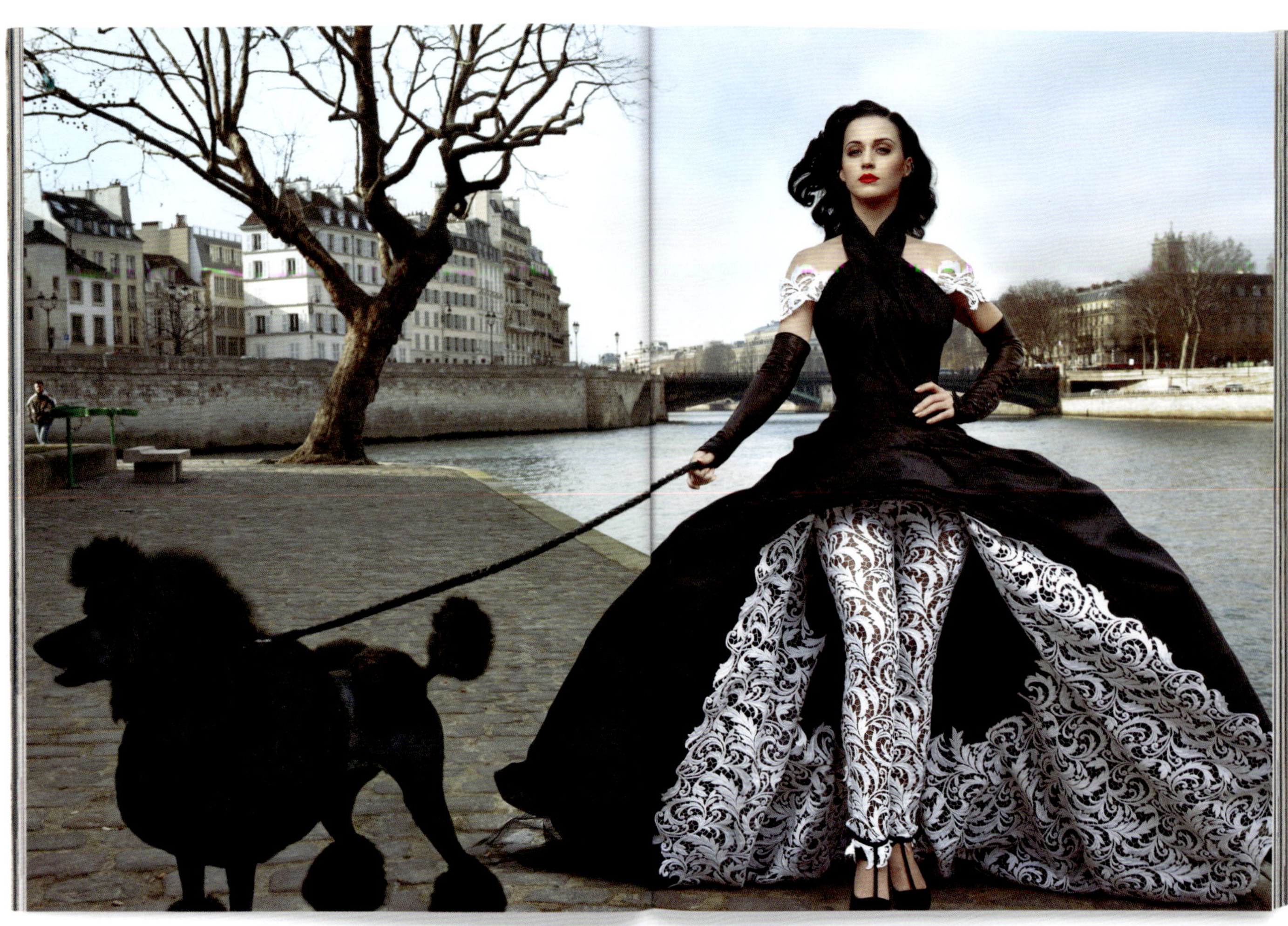

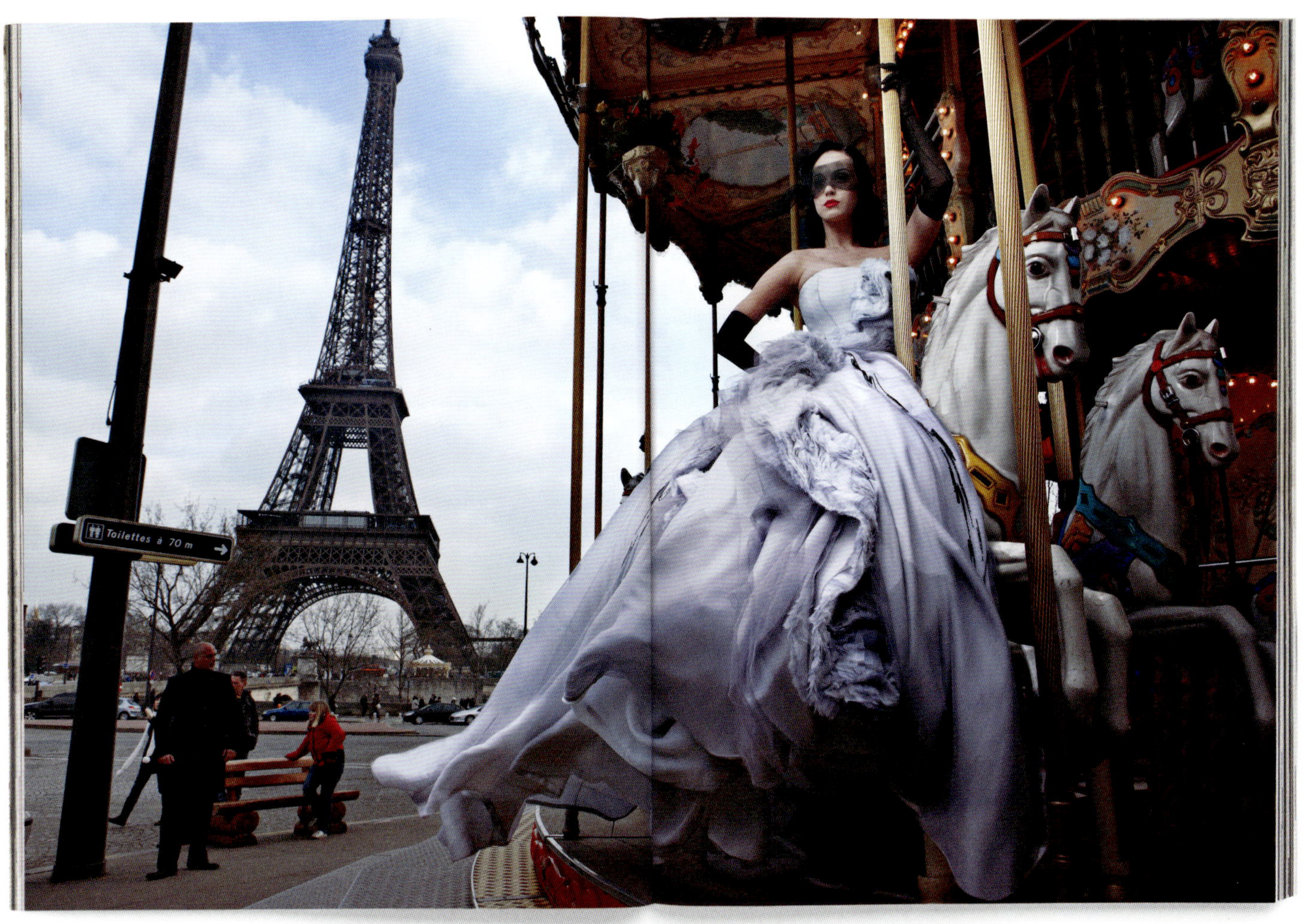
Toilettes à 70 m

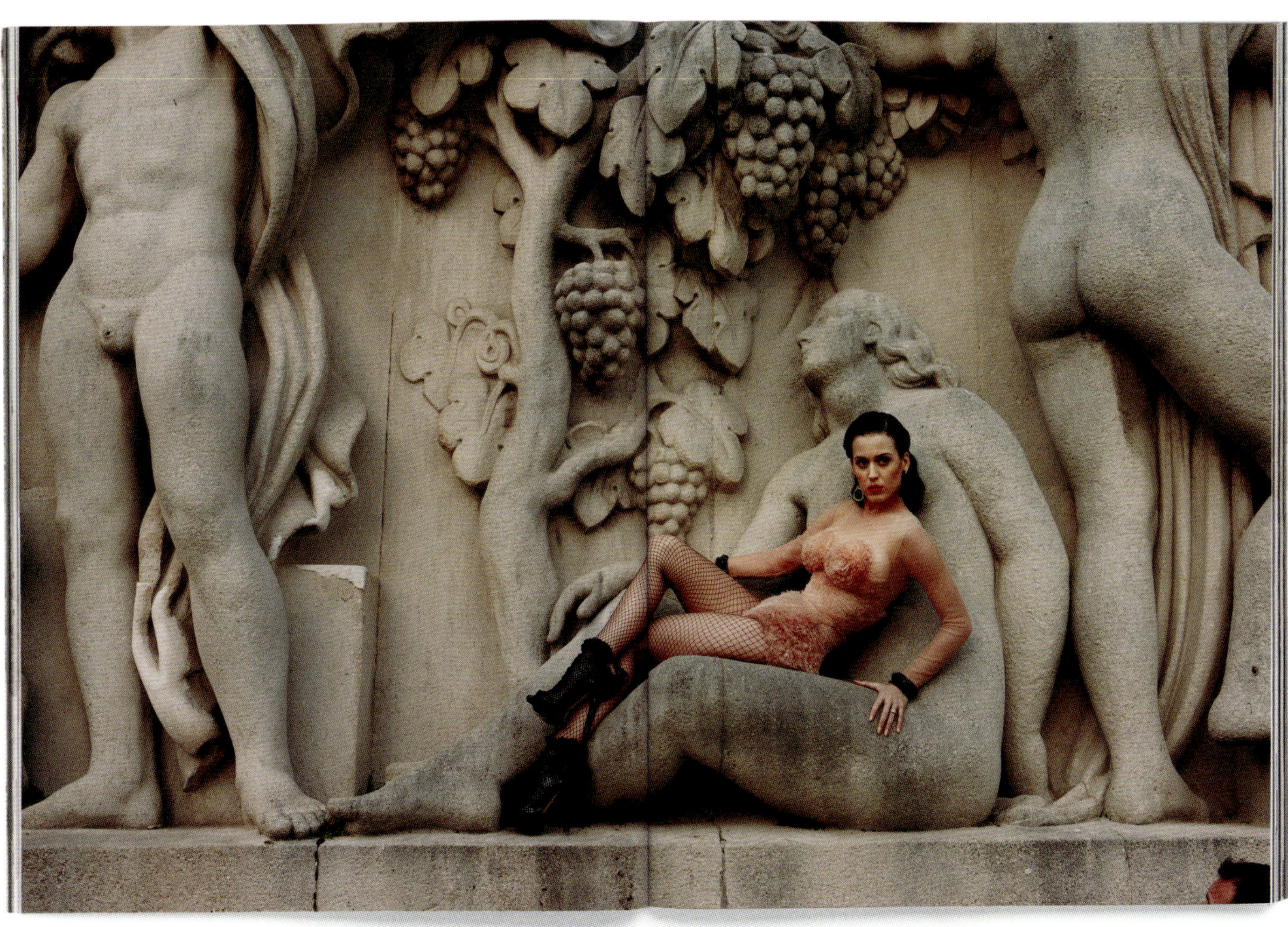

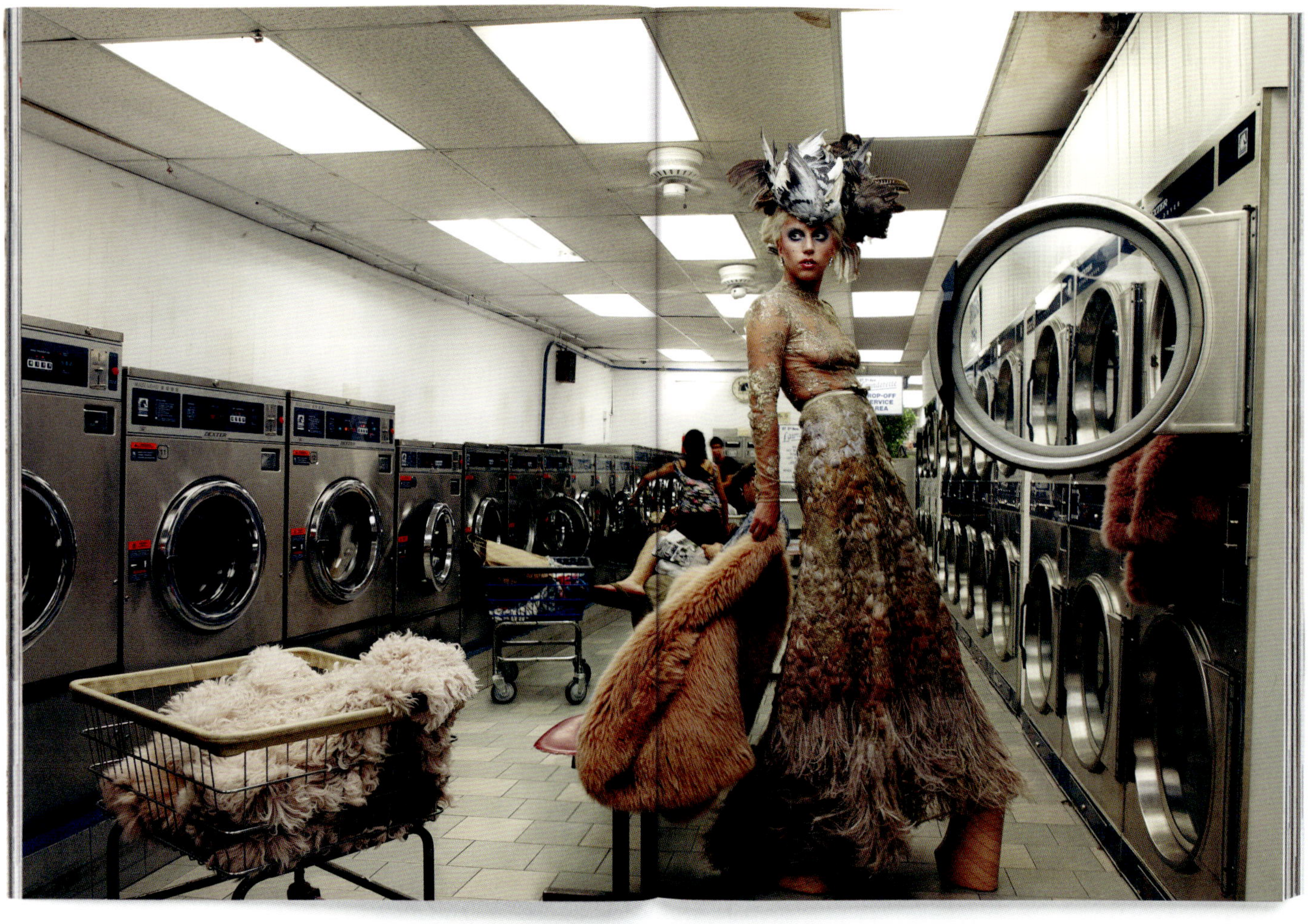

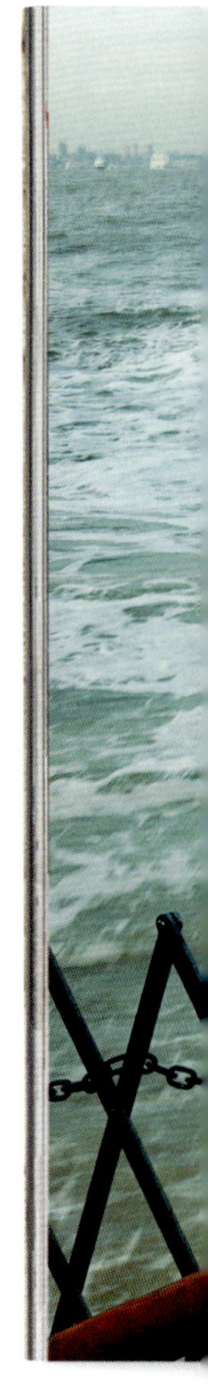

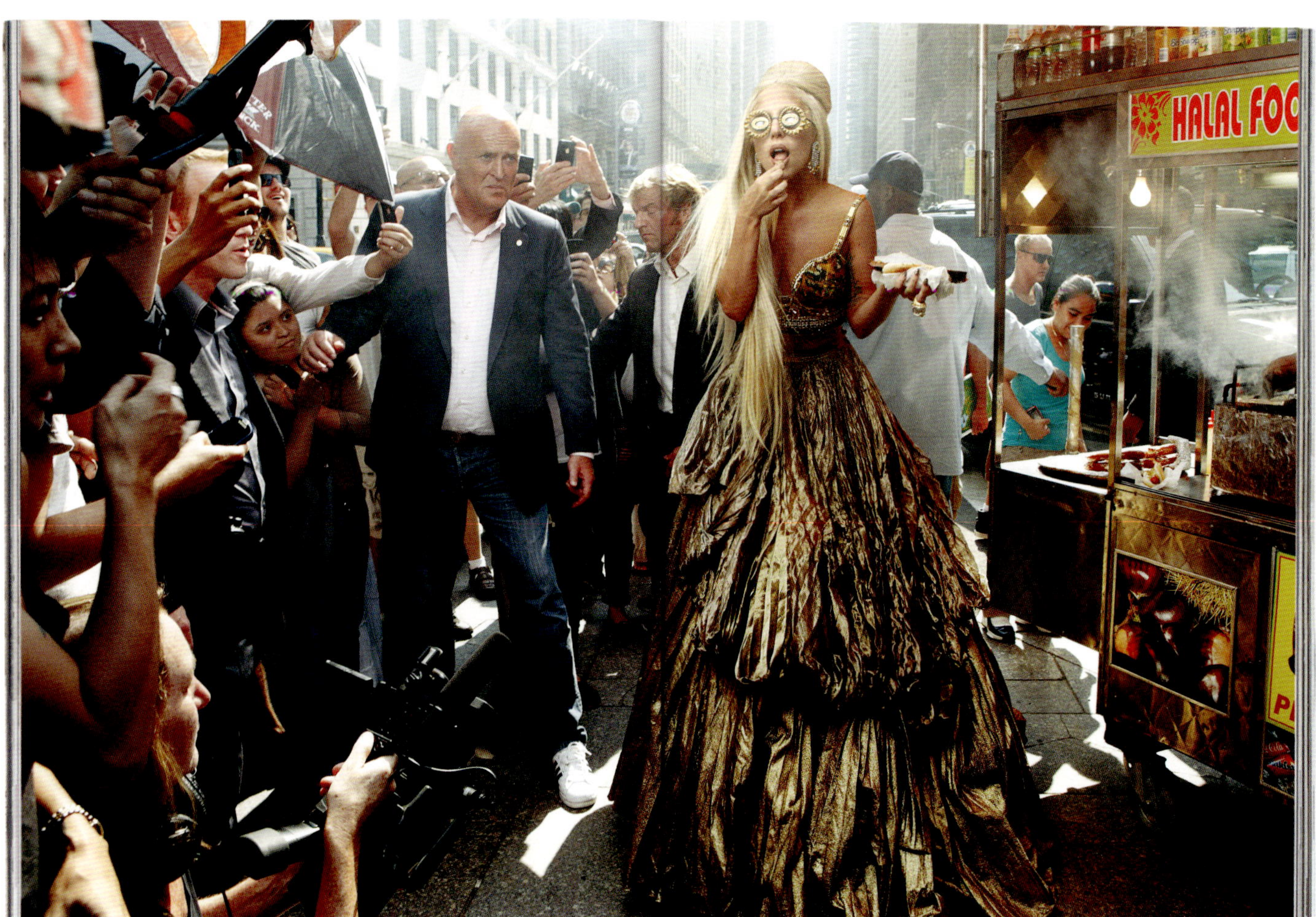

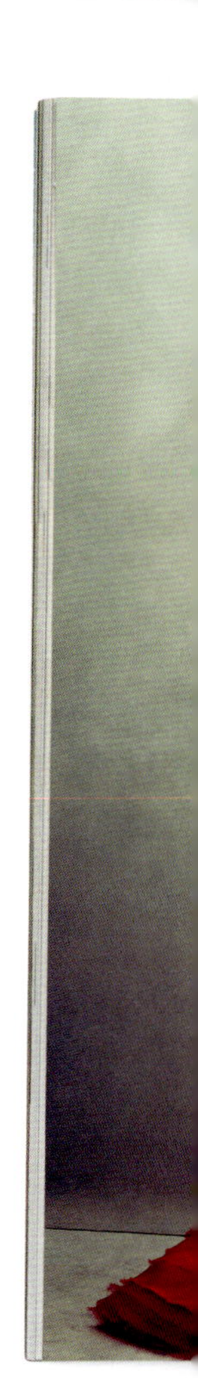

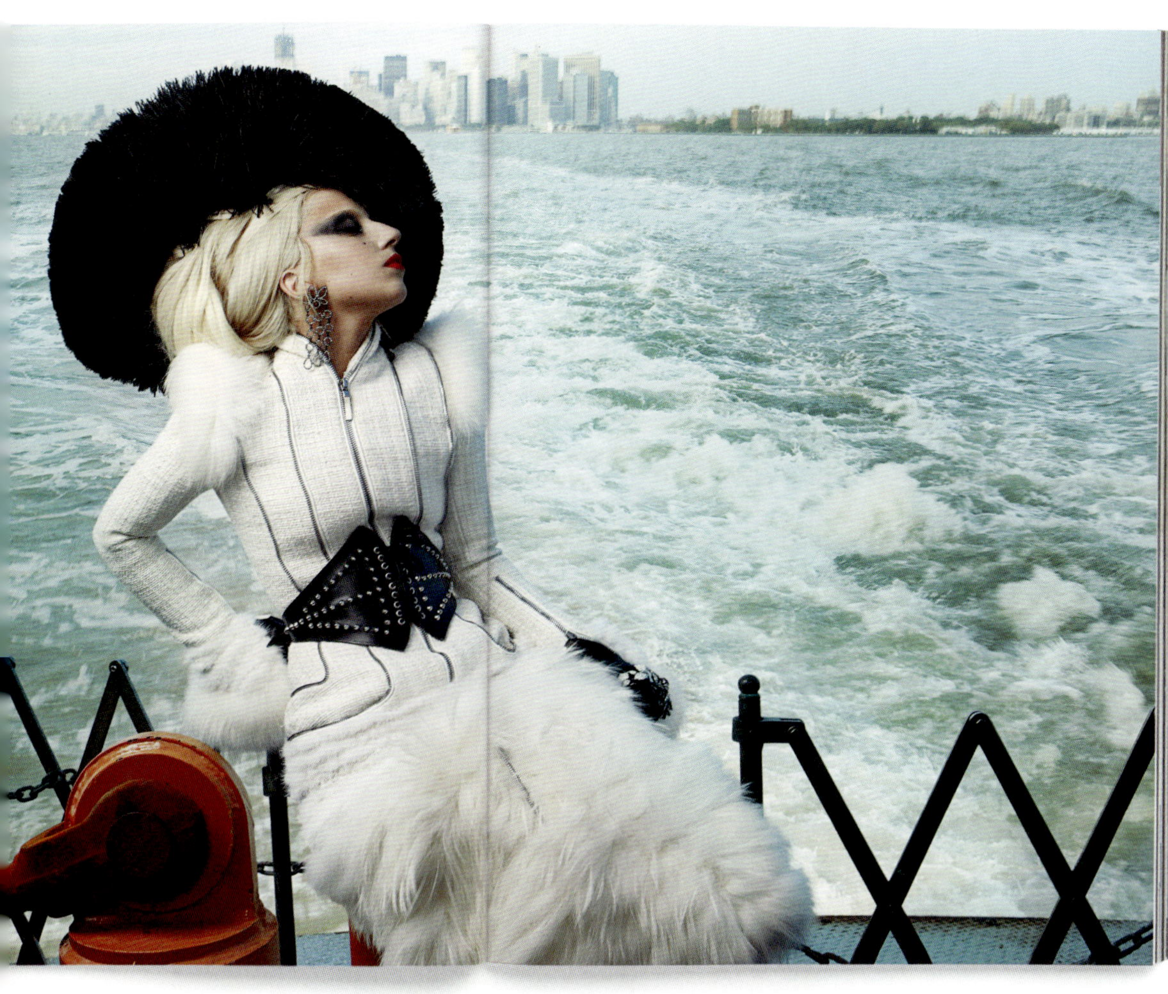

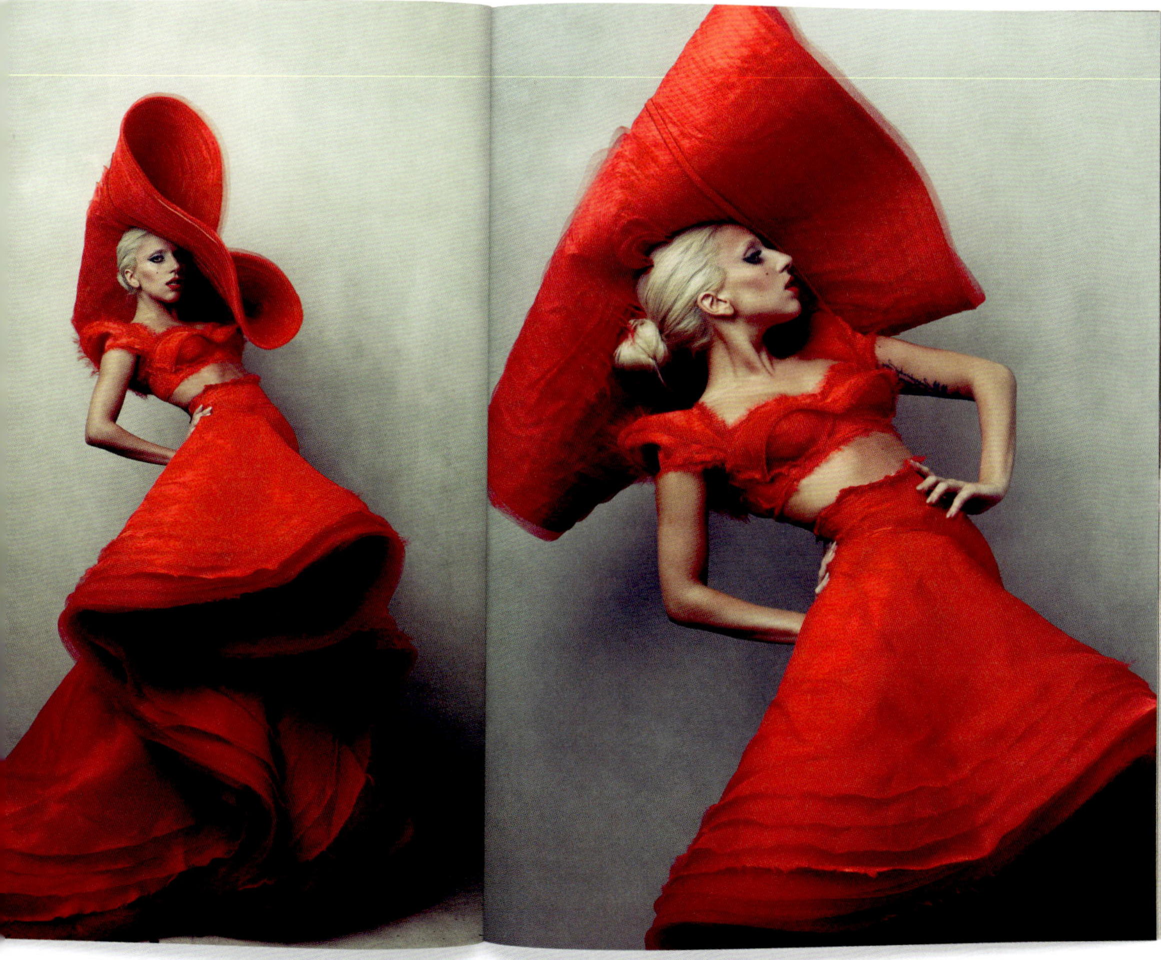

"Lady Gaga is a New Yorker through and through. We set our shoot with her on the Staten Island Ferry, at a hot-dog stand in Midtown Manhattan, and in a laundromat in the East Village near where she once had a place. She had recorded 'The Lady Is a Tramp' with Tony Bennett for his new album and he was making a portrait of her, so we ended up in his painting studio overlooking Central Park.

In retrospect, I think I missed the real story. Lady Gaga knew that she was going to be besieged by the paparazzi, and she had brought several changes of her own clothes with her. She wanted to be wearing something different when we moved locations. They were elaborate ensembles and it took a while to put them on. The shoes themselves were extraordinary—sculptured platforms a foot high. She couldn't walk in them without the help of two assistants, one on each arm."

New York City, 2011

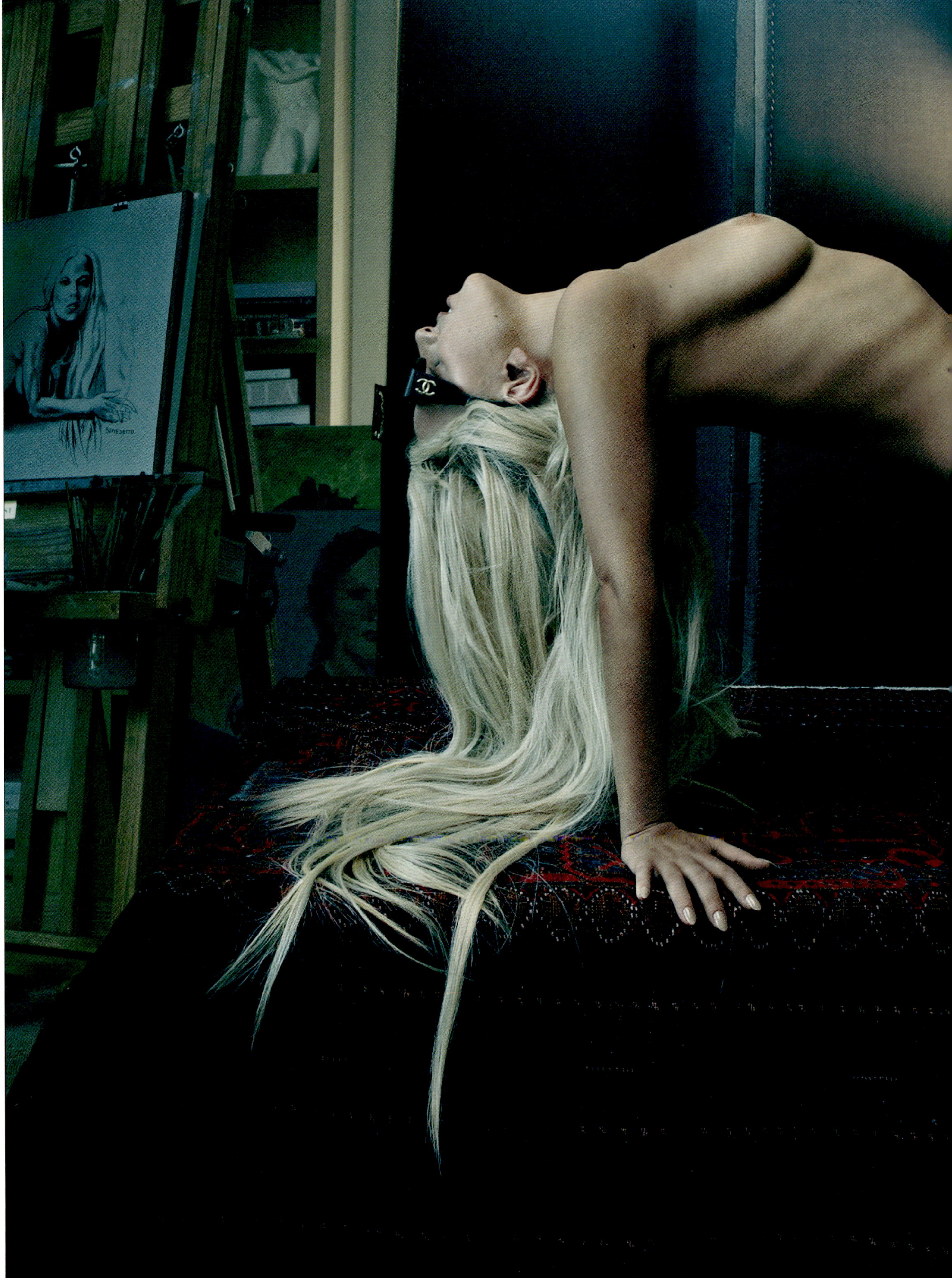
BENEDETTO

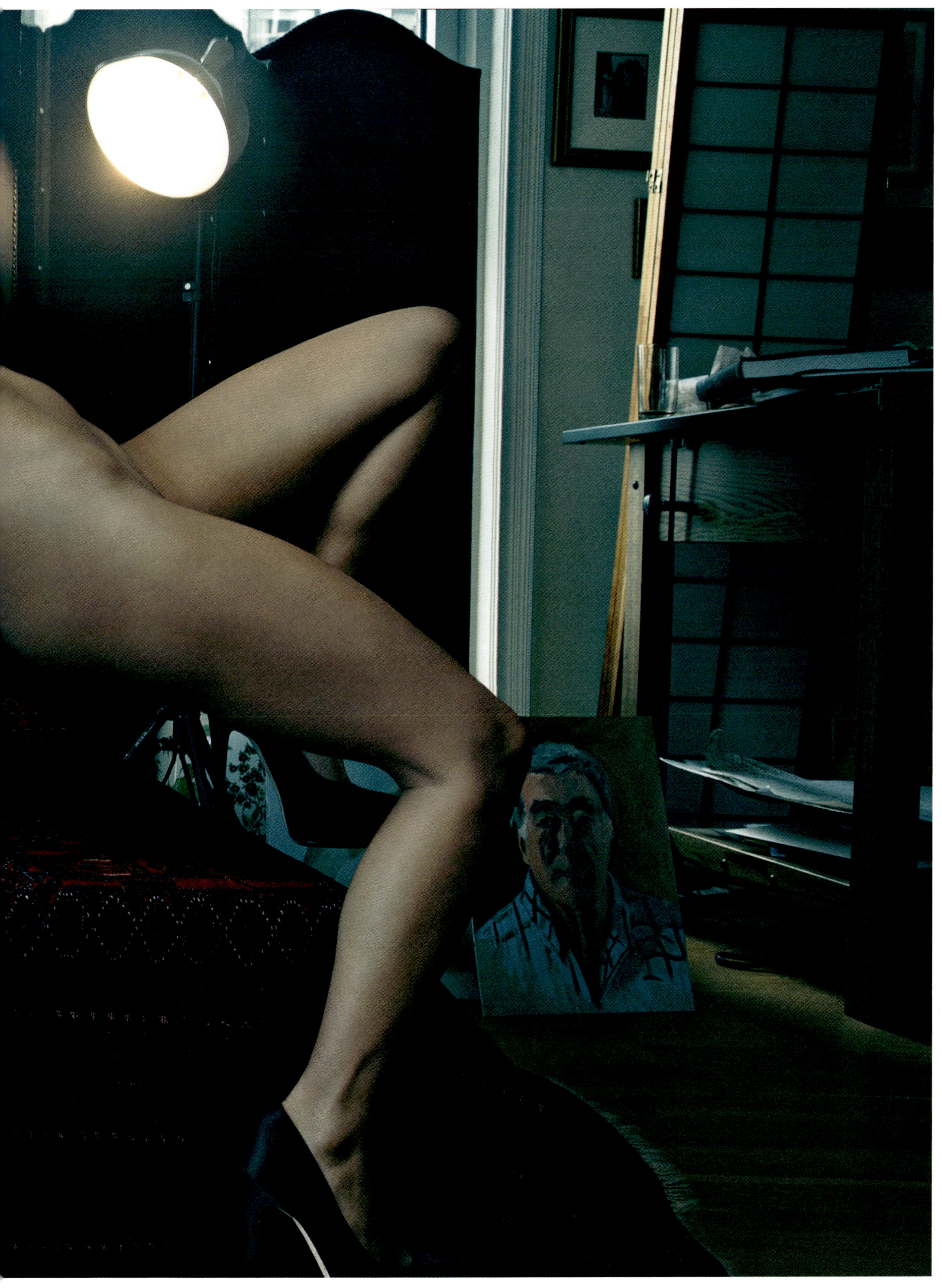

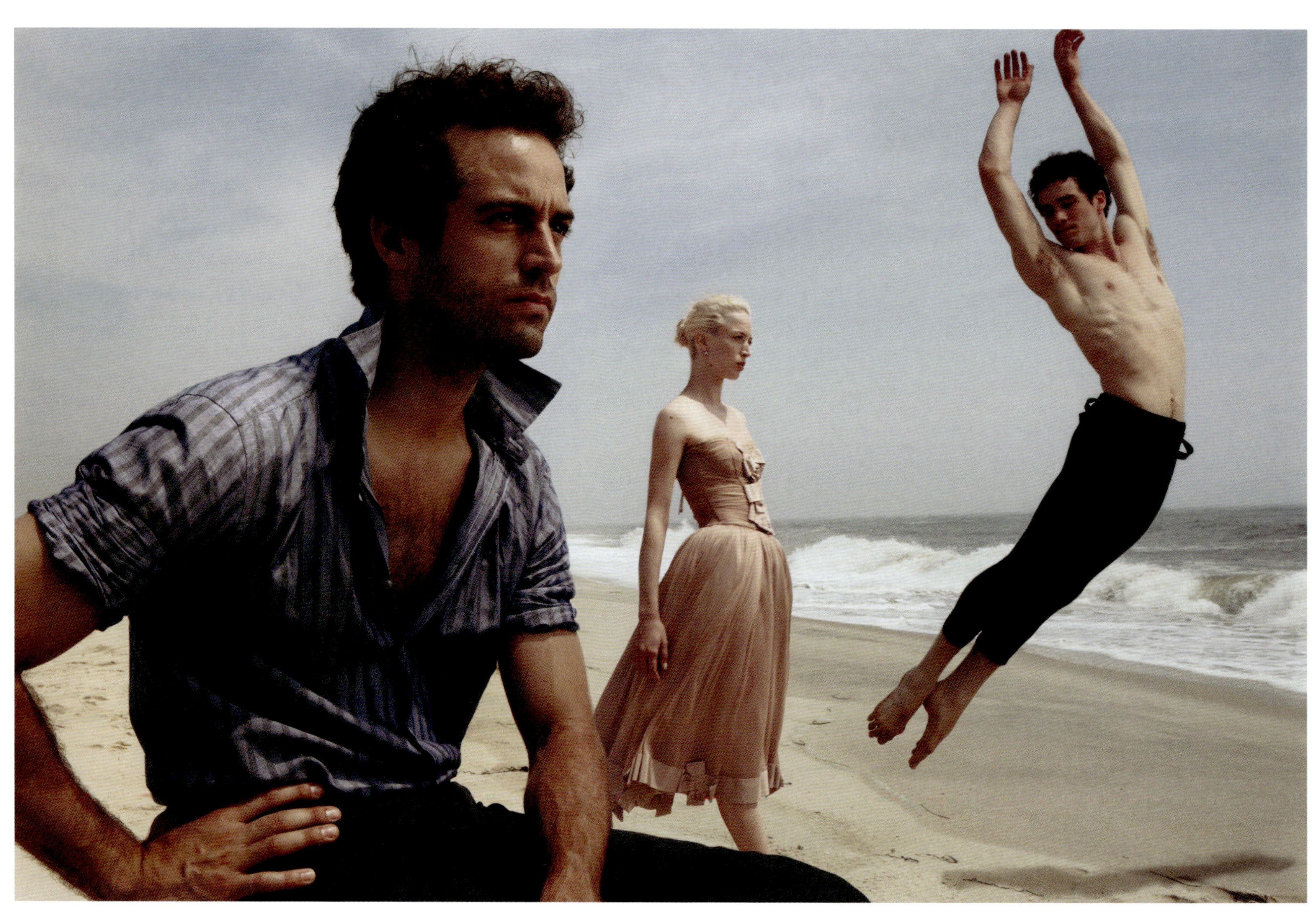

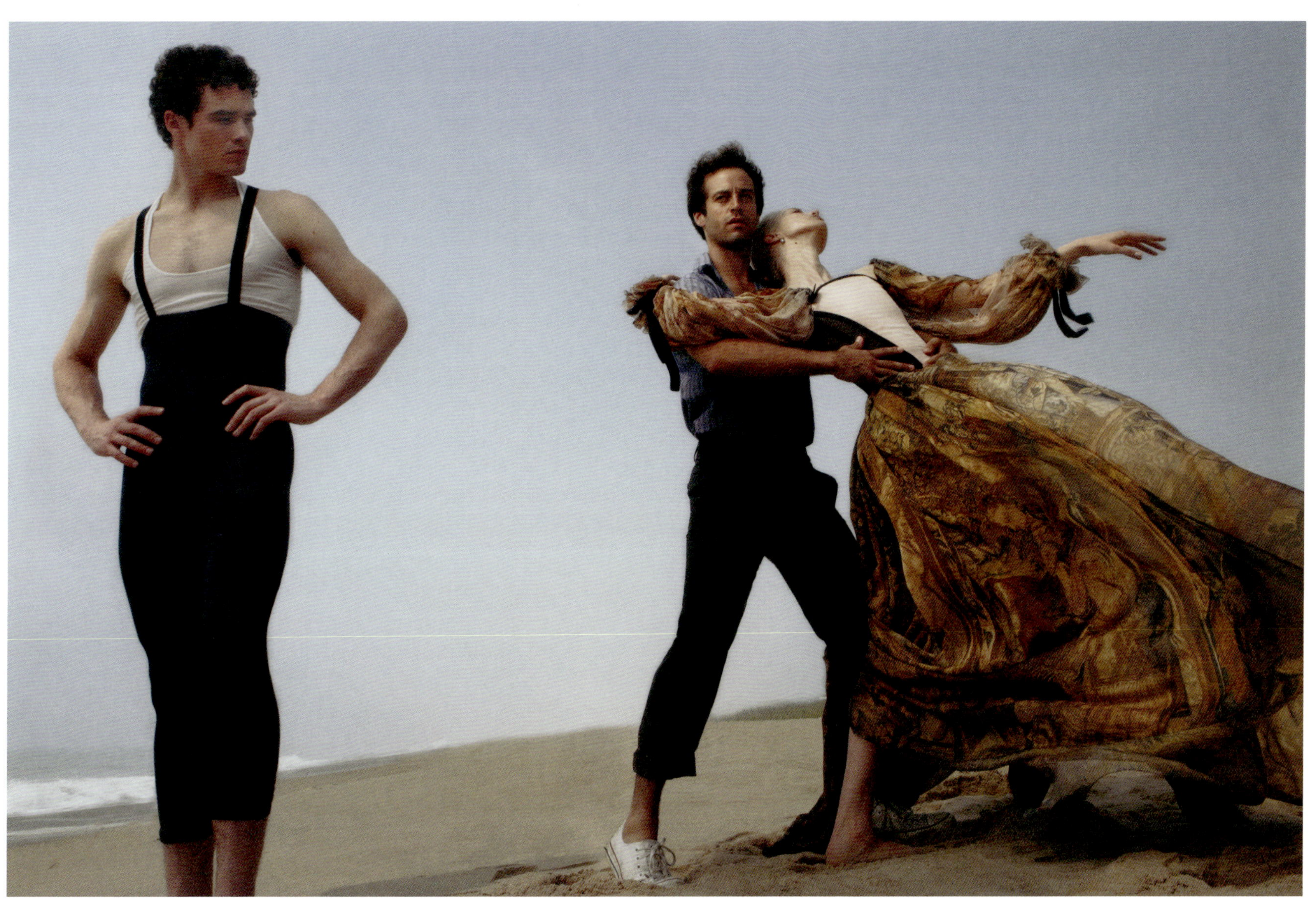

Benjamin Millepied, Cory Stearns, and Raquel Zimmermann, Watermill, New York, 2009

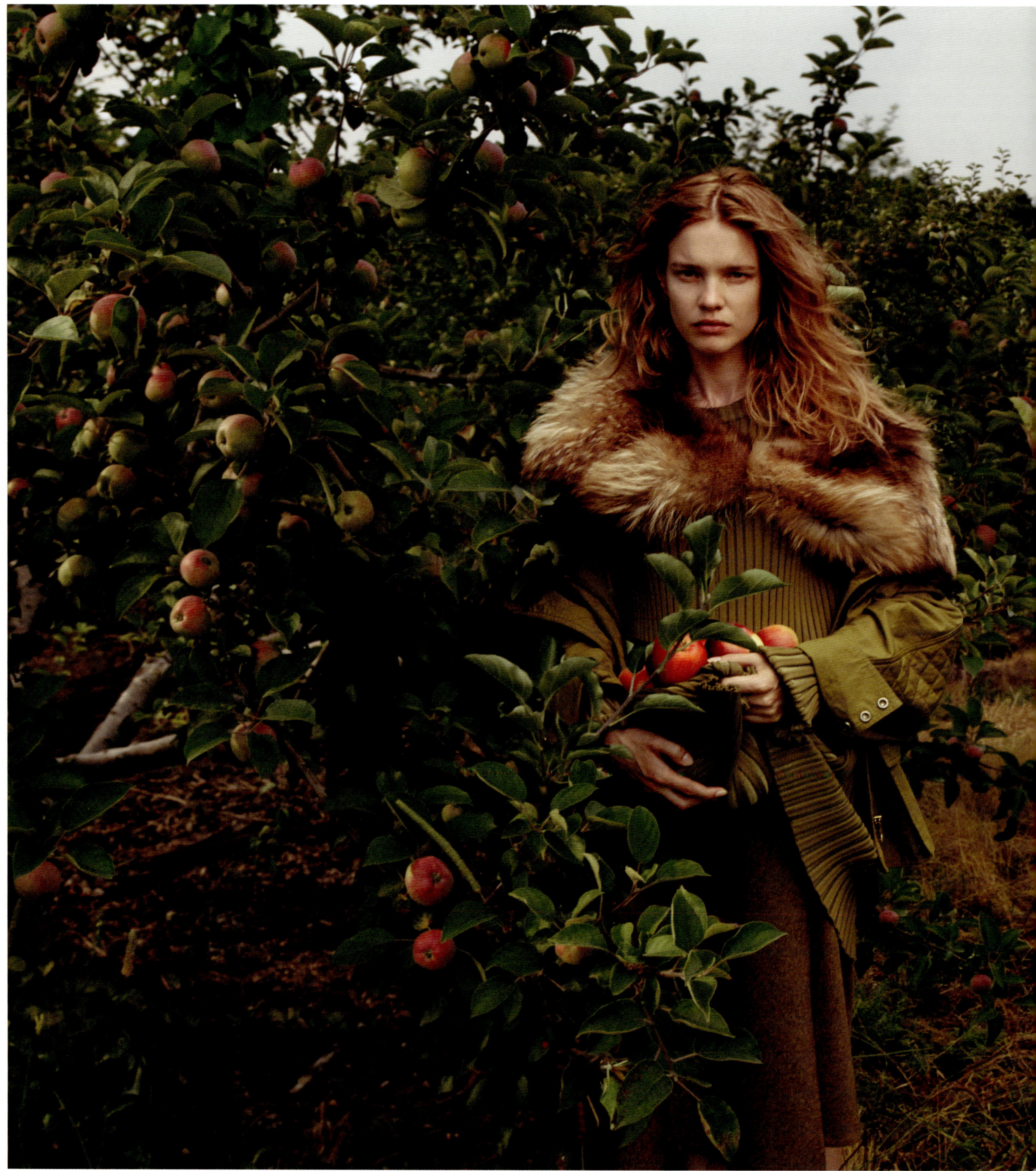

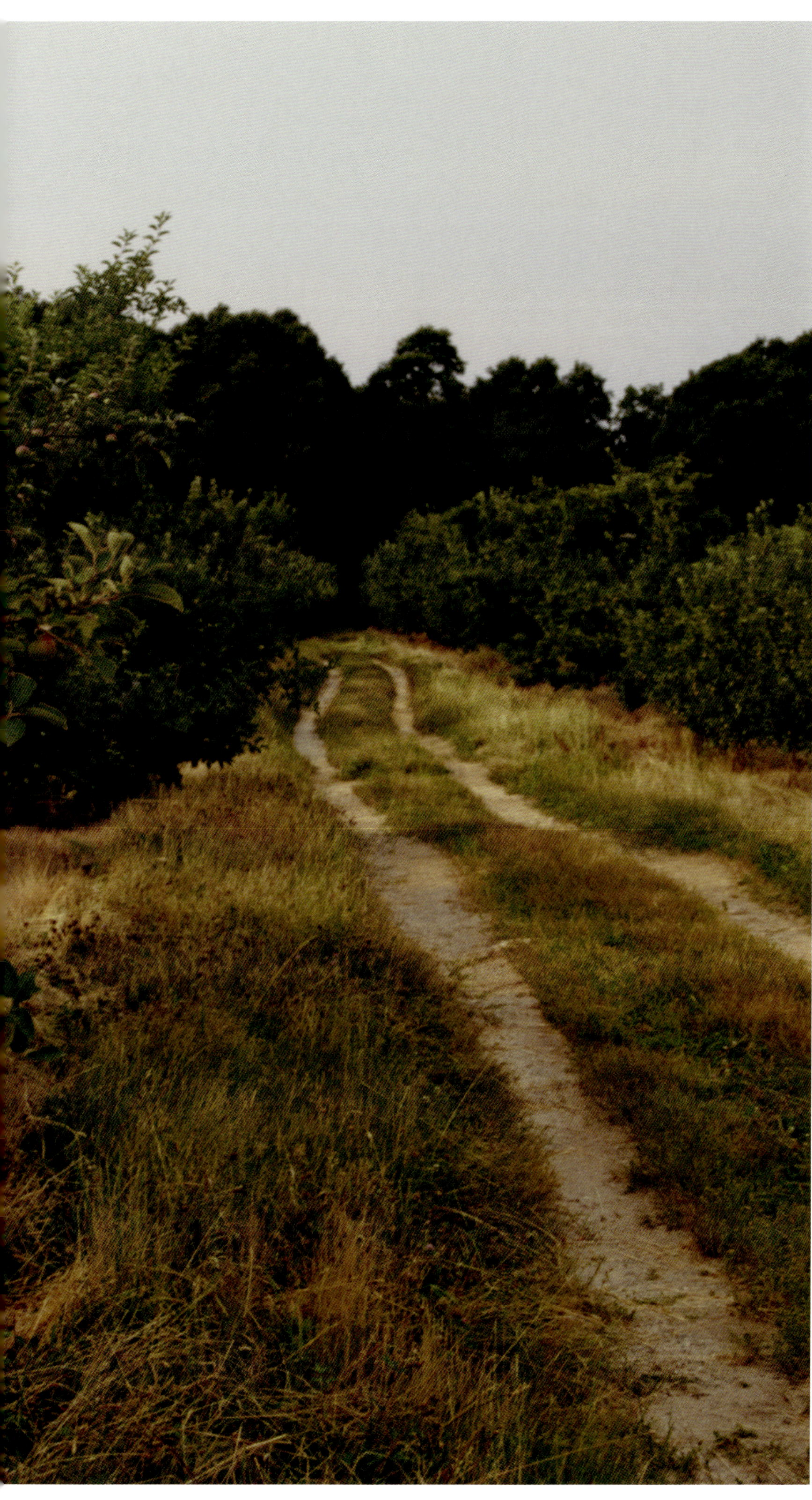

"When I first photographed Natalia Vodianova, it was for the *Alice in Wonderland* story, and she carried me through the shoot. She was charming and smart and talented and funny. And she was also a good actress. She was very aware of both sides of the camera. But one had the sense that there was something vulnerable lurking behind the gracious beauty. Years later, I photographed her in an apple orchard in upstate New York. When she was a girl in Russia, she sold apples with her mom in the streets. Her life was transformed when she was brought to Paris and became a model."

Montgomery Place,
Annandale-on-Hudson,
New York, 2014

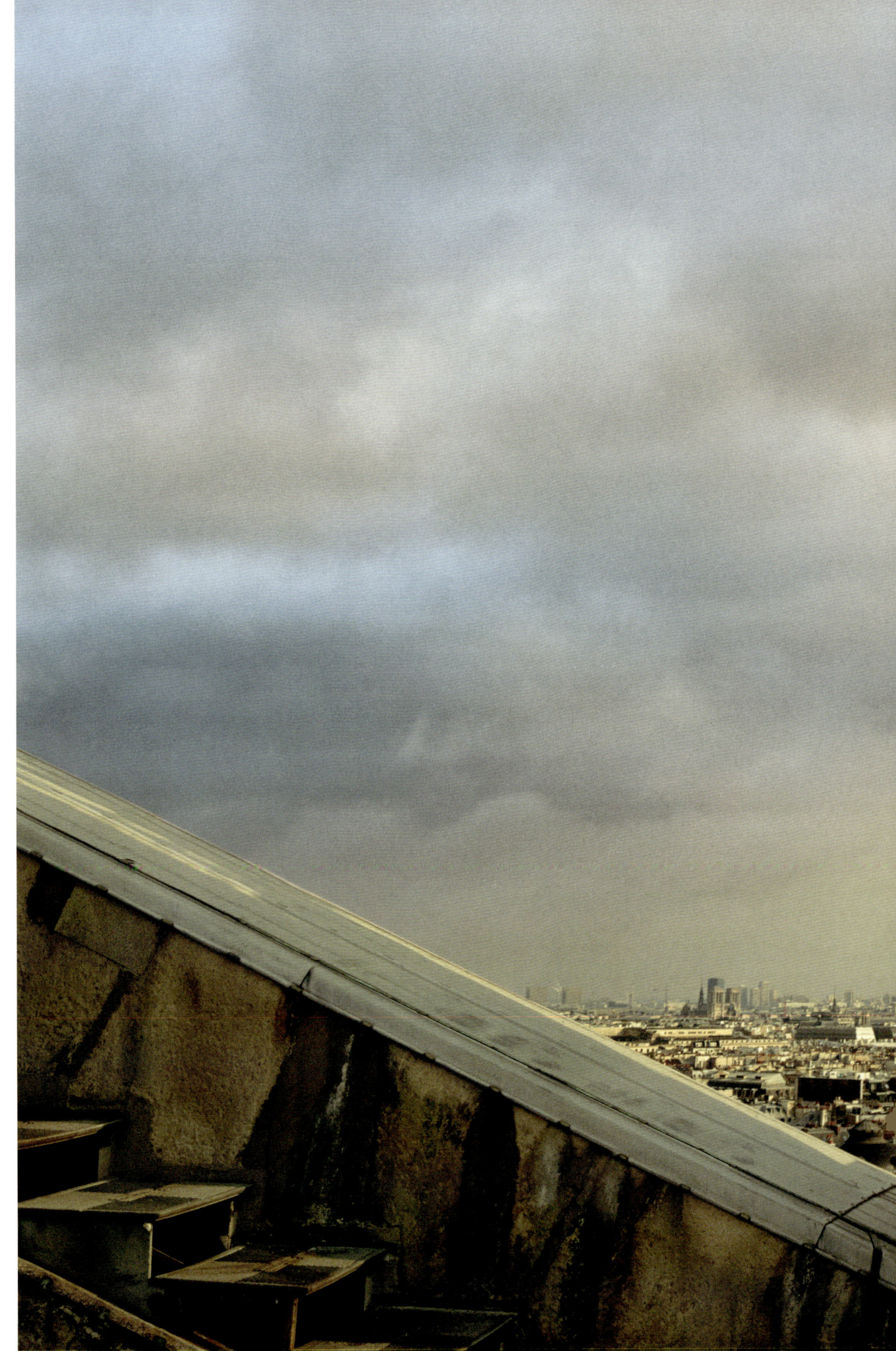

Natalia Vodianova,
Palais Garnier, Paris, 2014

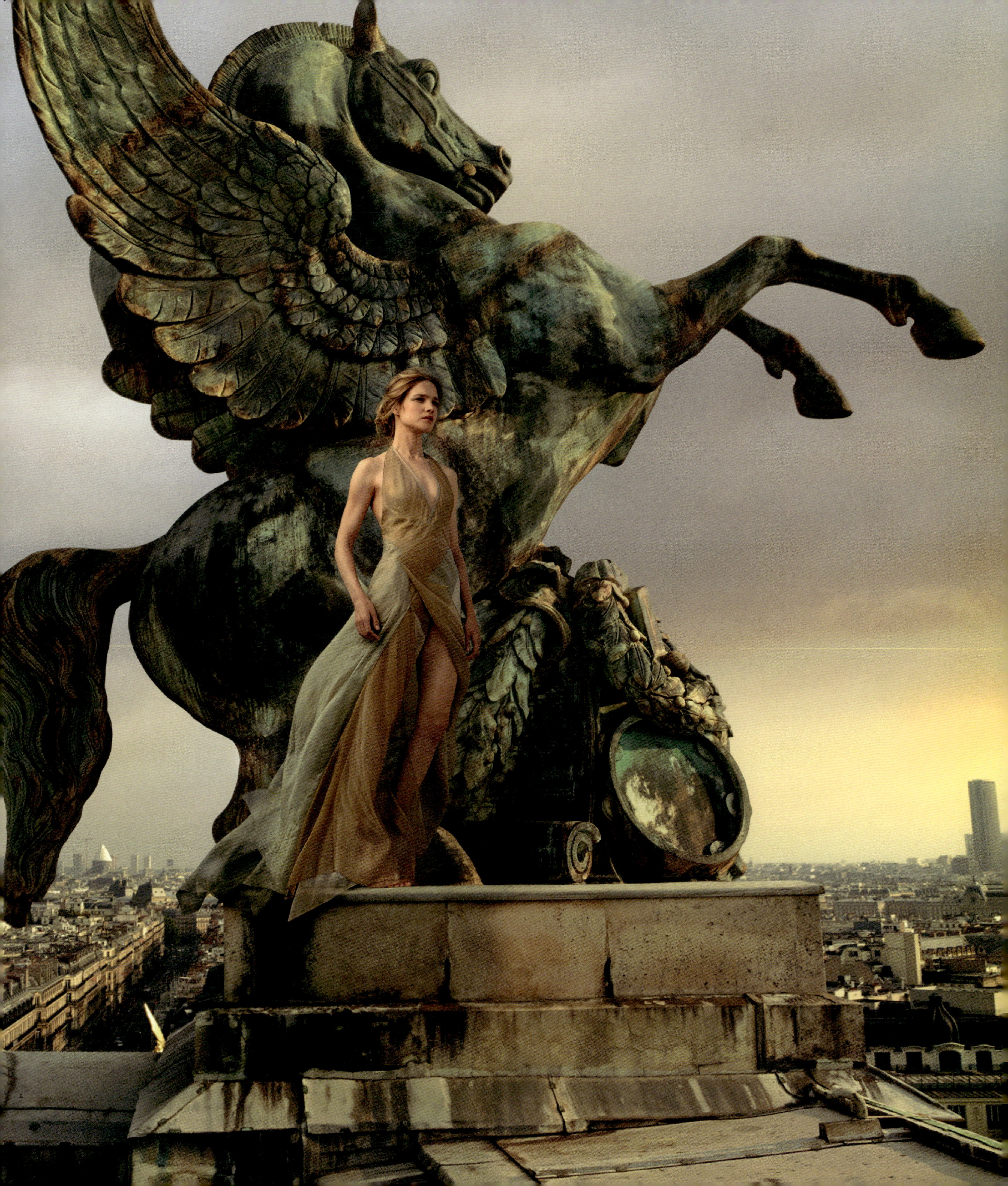

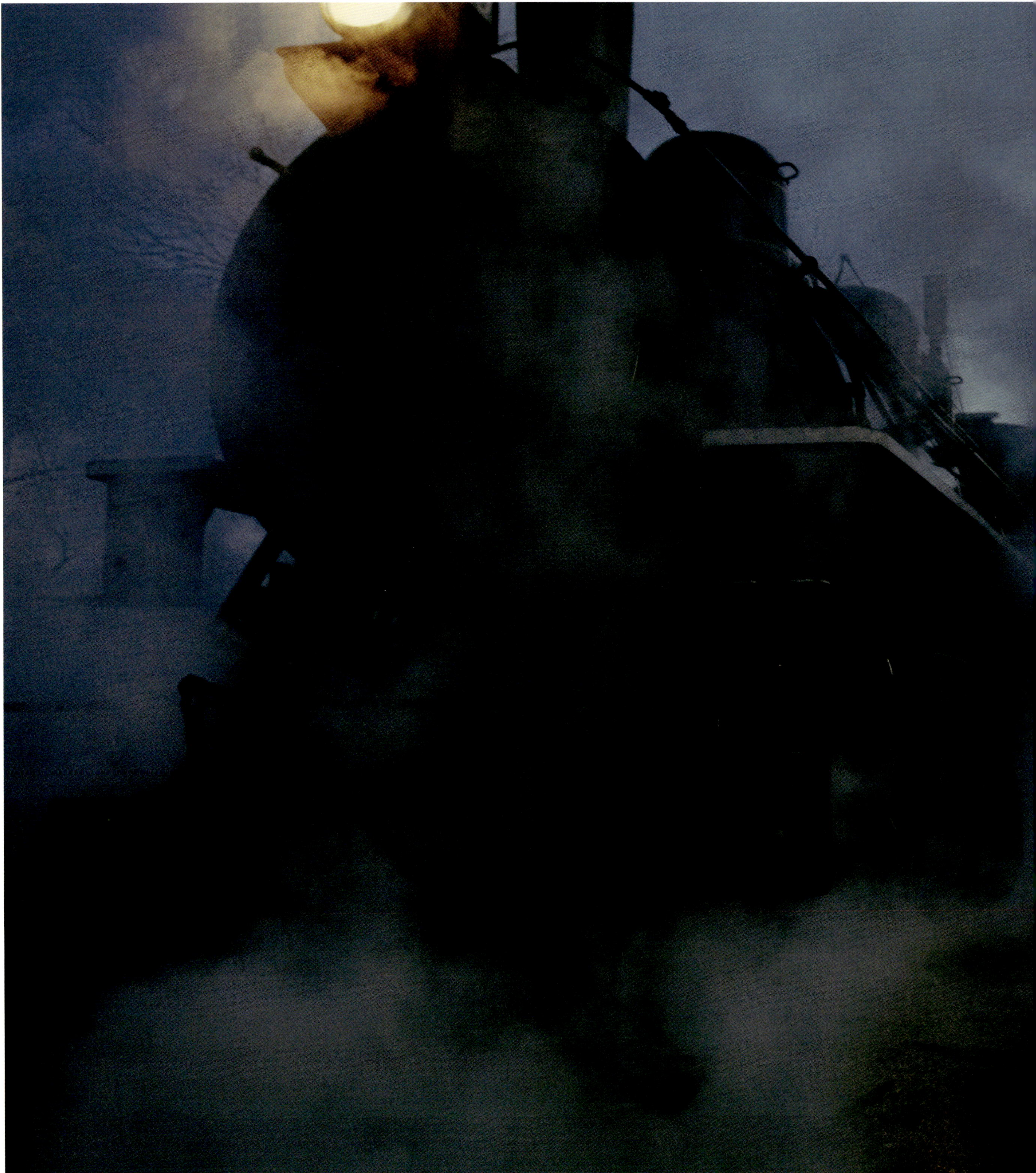

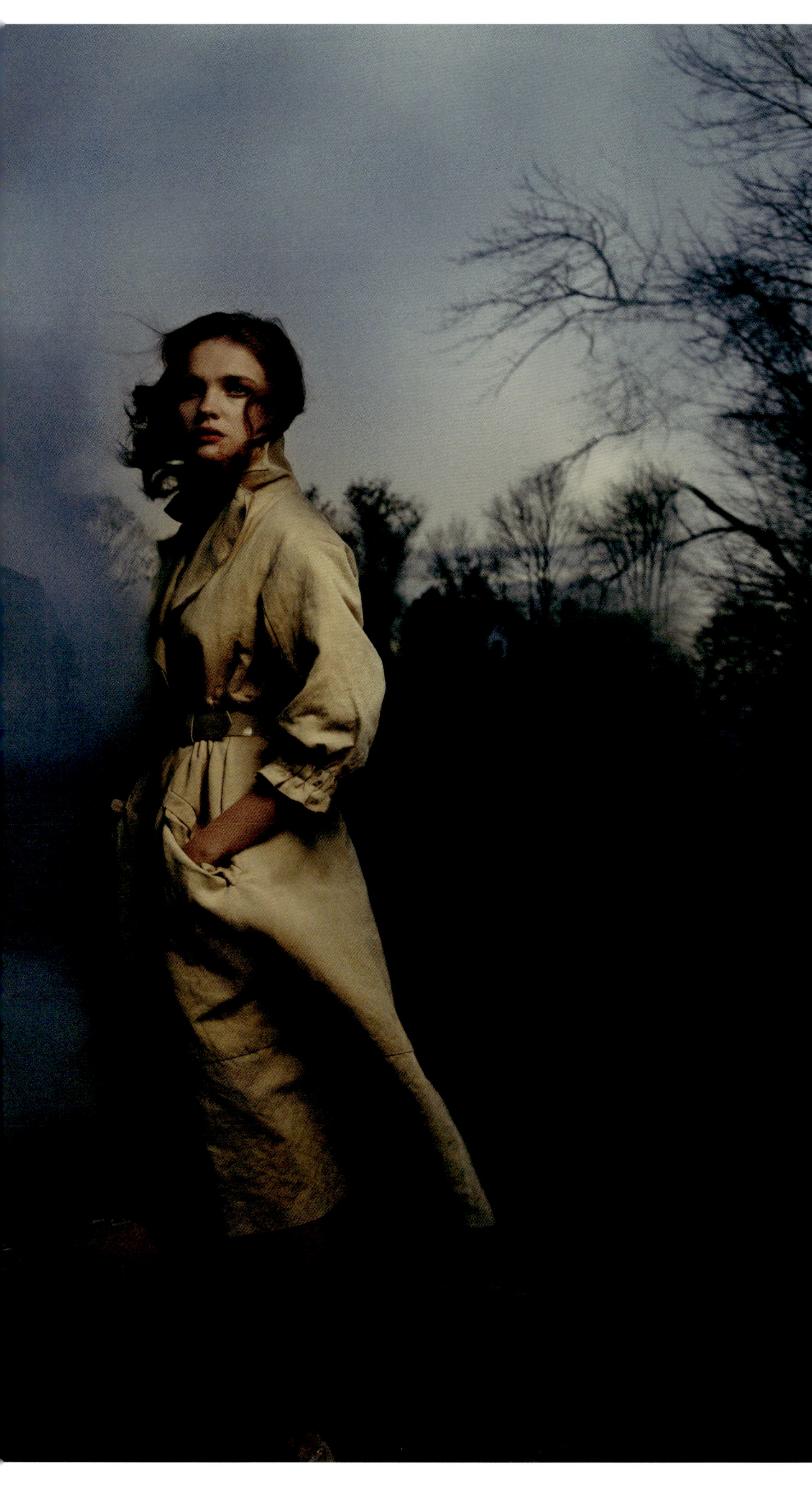

Trains are at the heart of the story of a doomed romance between two characters played by Natalia Vodianova and Sean Combs. The story was inspired by Combs's album *Last Train to Paris,* which is based on a real romance he had as a young man.

Natalia Vodianova, Valley Railroad, Essex, Connecticut, 2009

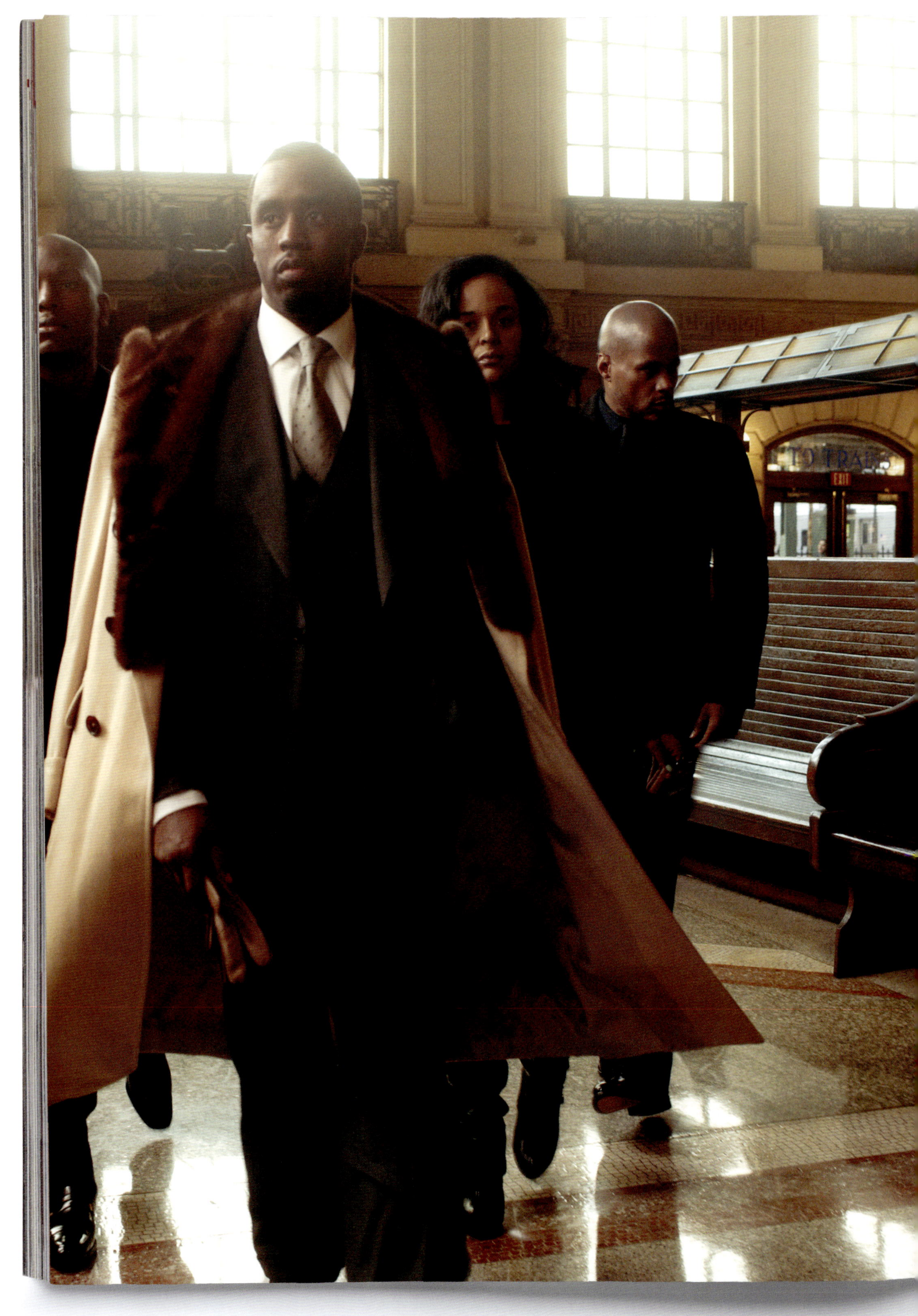

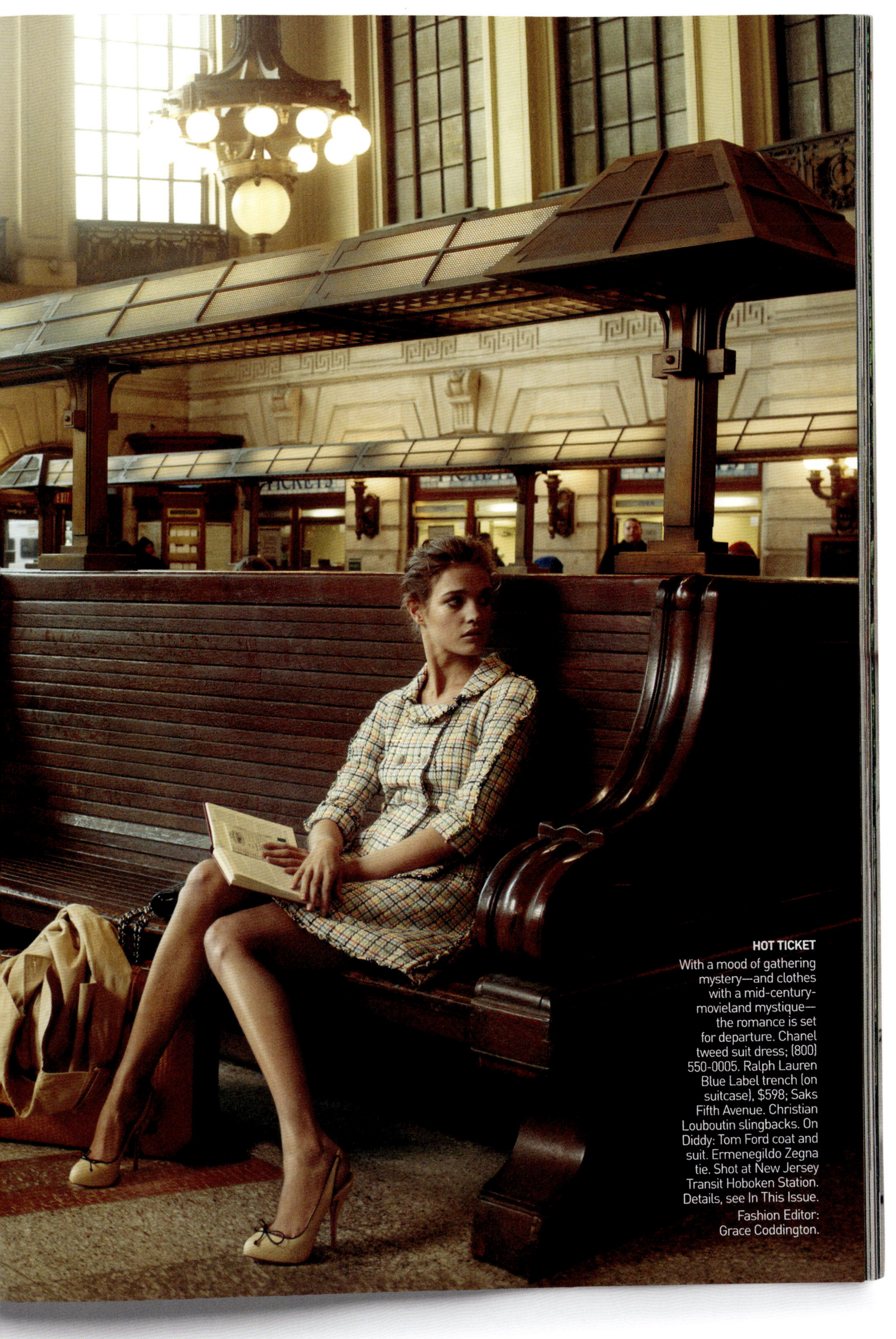

HOT TICKET

With a mood of gathering mystery—and clothes with a mid-century-movieland mystique—the romance is set for departure. Chanel tweed suit dress; (800) 550-0005. Ralph Lauren Blue Label trench (on suitcase), $598; Saks Fifth Avenue. Christian Louboutin slingbacks. On Diddy: Tom Ford coat and suit. Ermenegildo Zegna tie. Shot at New Jersey Transit Hoboken Station. Details, see In This Issue.

Fashion Editor: Grace Coddington.

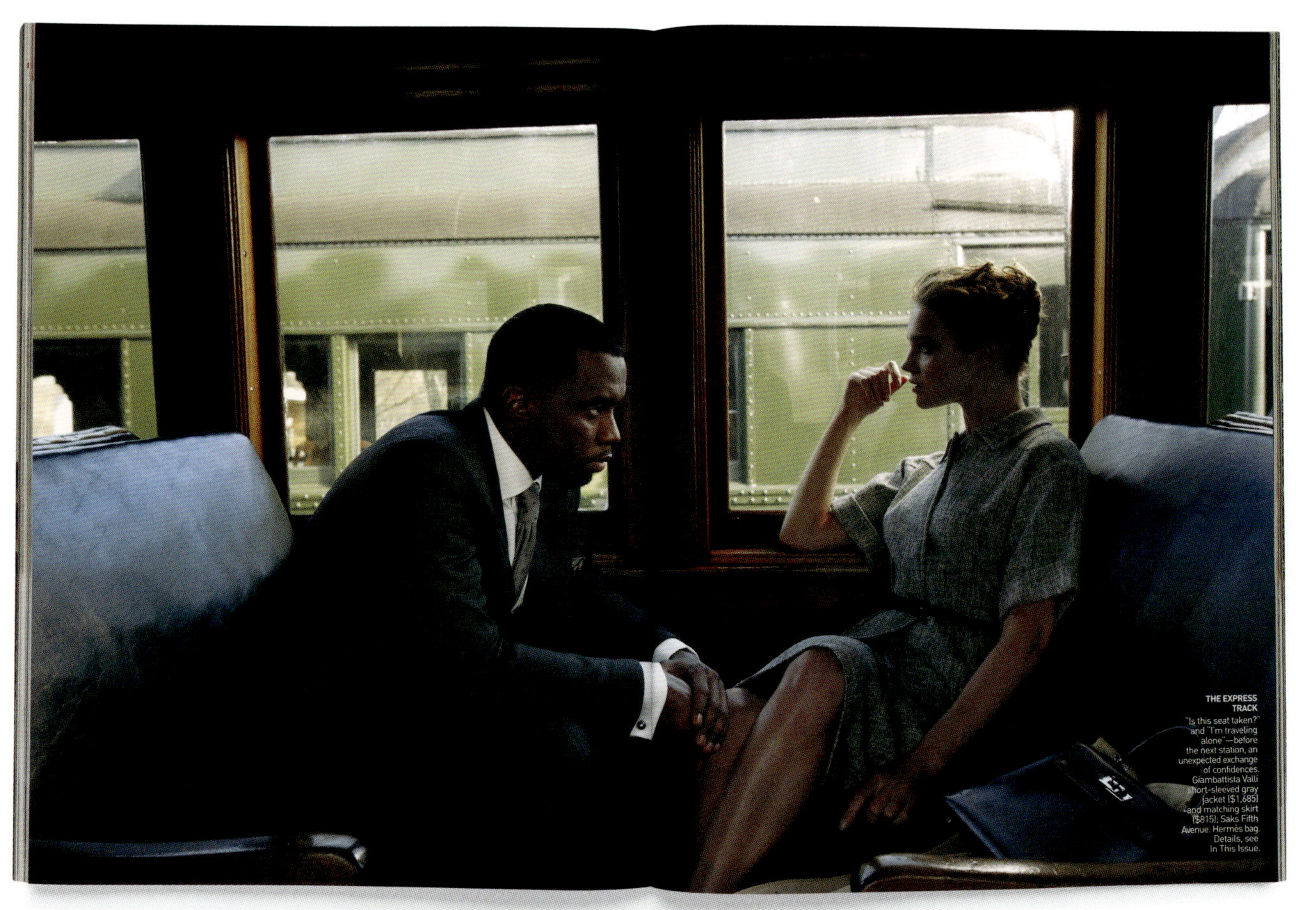
THE EXPRESS TRACK
"Is this seat taken?" and "I'm traveling alone"—before the next station, an unexpected exchange of confidences. Giambattista Valli short-sleeved gray jacket ($1,685) and matching skirt ($815); Saks Fifth Avenue. Hermès bag. Details, see In This Issue.

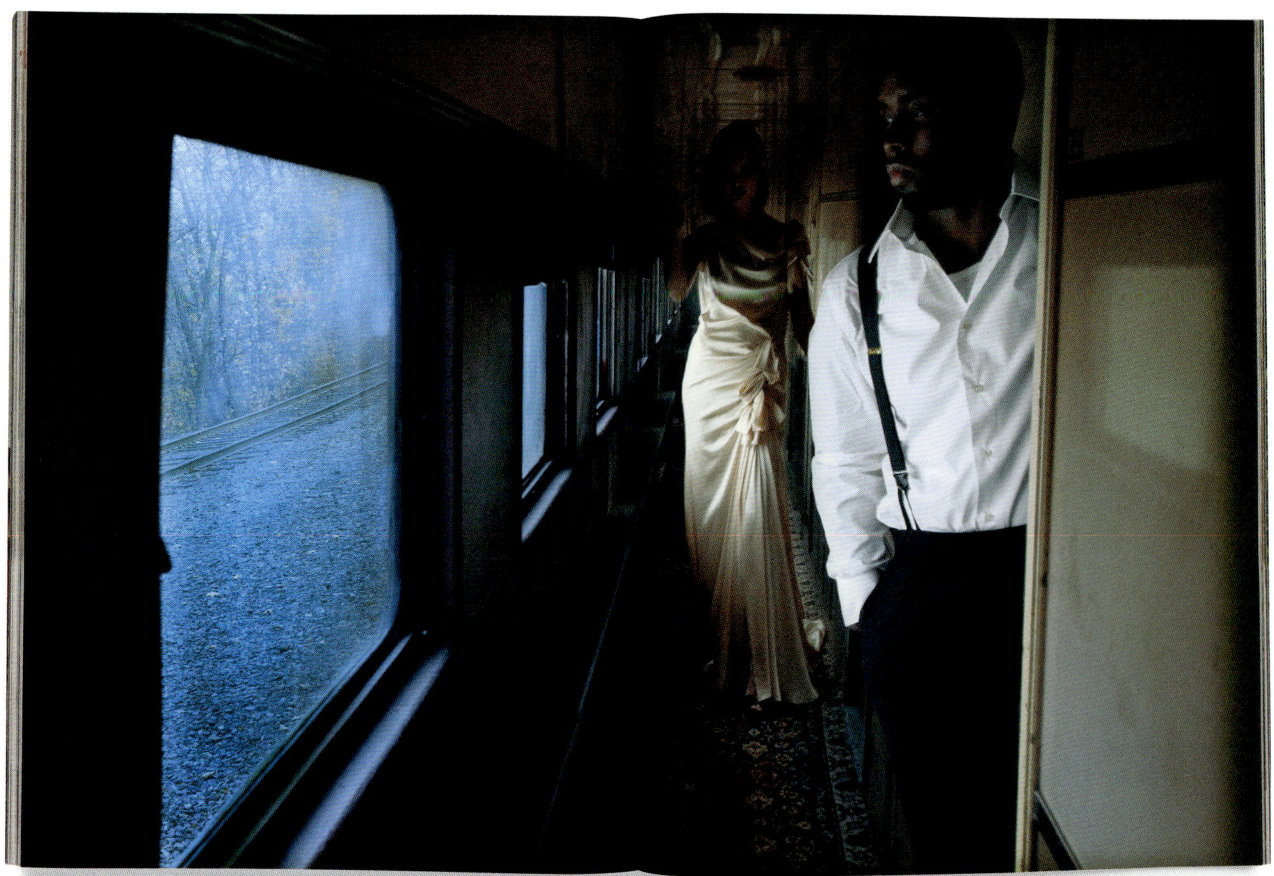

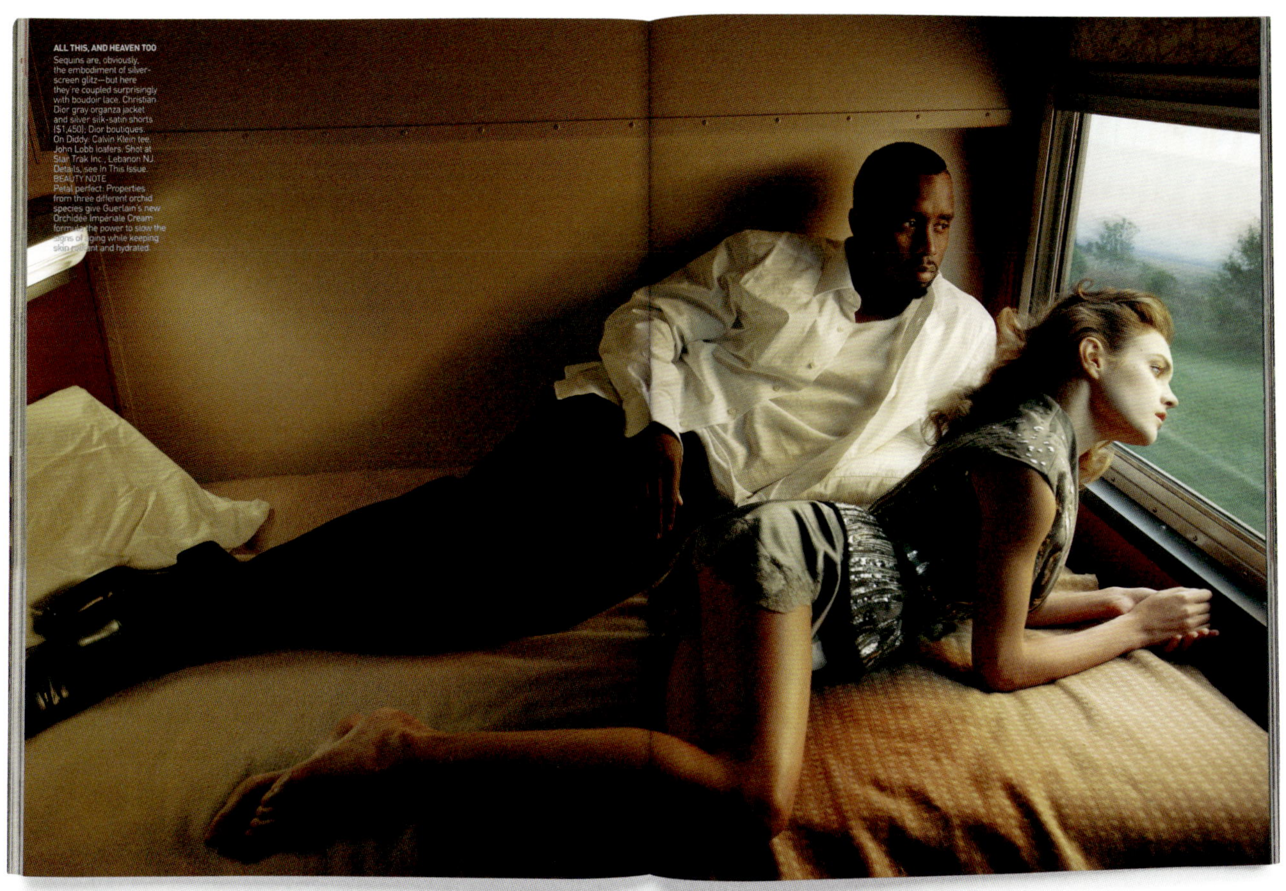
ALL THIS, AND HEAVEN TOO
Sequins are, obviously, the embodiment of silver-screen glitz—but here they're coupled surprisingly with boudoir lace. Christian Dior gray organza jacket and silver silk-satin shorts ($1,450); Dior boutiques. On Diddy: Calvin Klein tee. John Lobb loafers. Shot at Star Trak Inc., Lebanon NJ. Details, see In This Issue.
BEAUTY NOTE
Petal perfect: Properties from three different orchid species give Guerlain's new Orchidée Impériale Cream formula the power to slow the signs of aging while keeping skin radiant and hydrated.

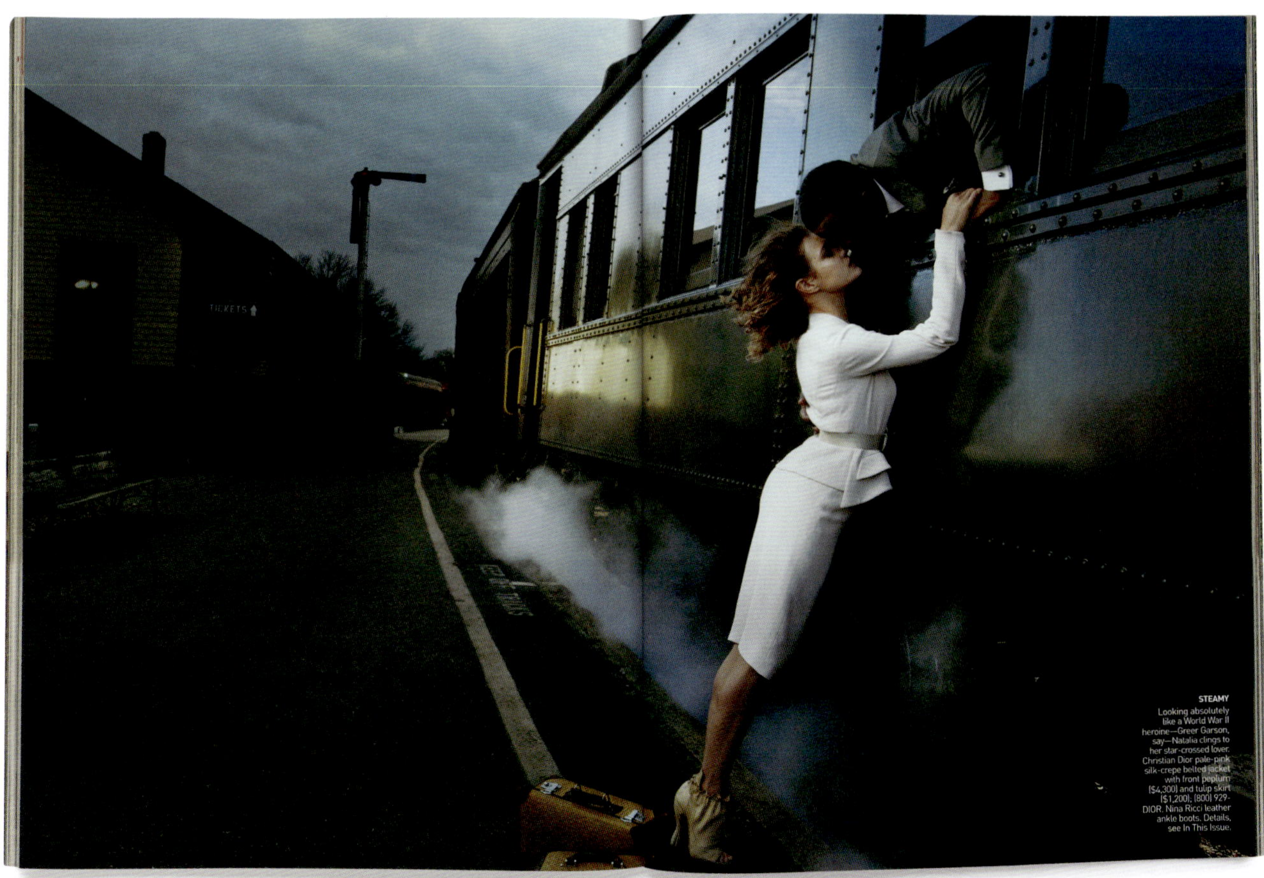
TICKETS
STEAMY
Looking absolutely like a World War II heroine—Greer Garson, say—Natalia clings to her star-crossed lover. Christian Dior pale-pink silk-crepe belted jacket with front peplum ($4,300) and tulip skirt ($1,200); (800) 929-DIOR. Nina Ricci leather ankle boots. Details, see In This Issue.

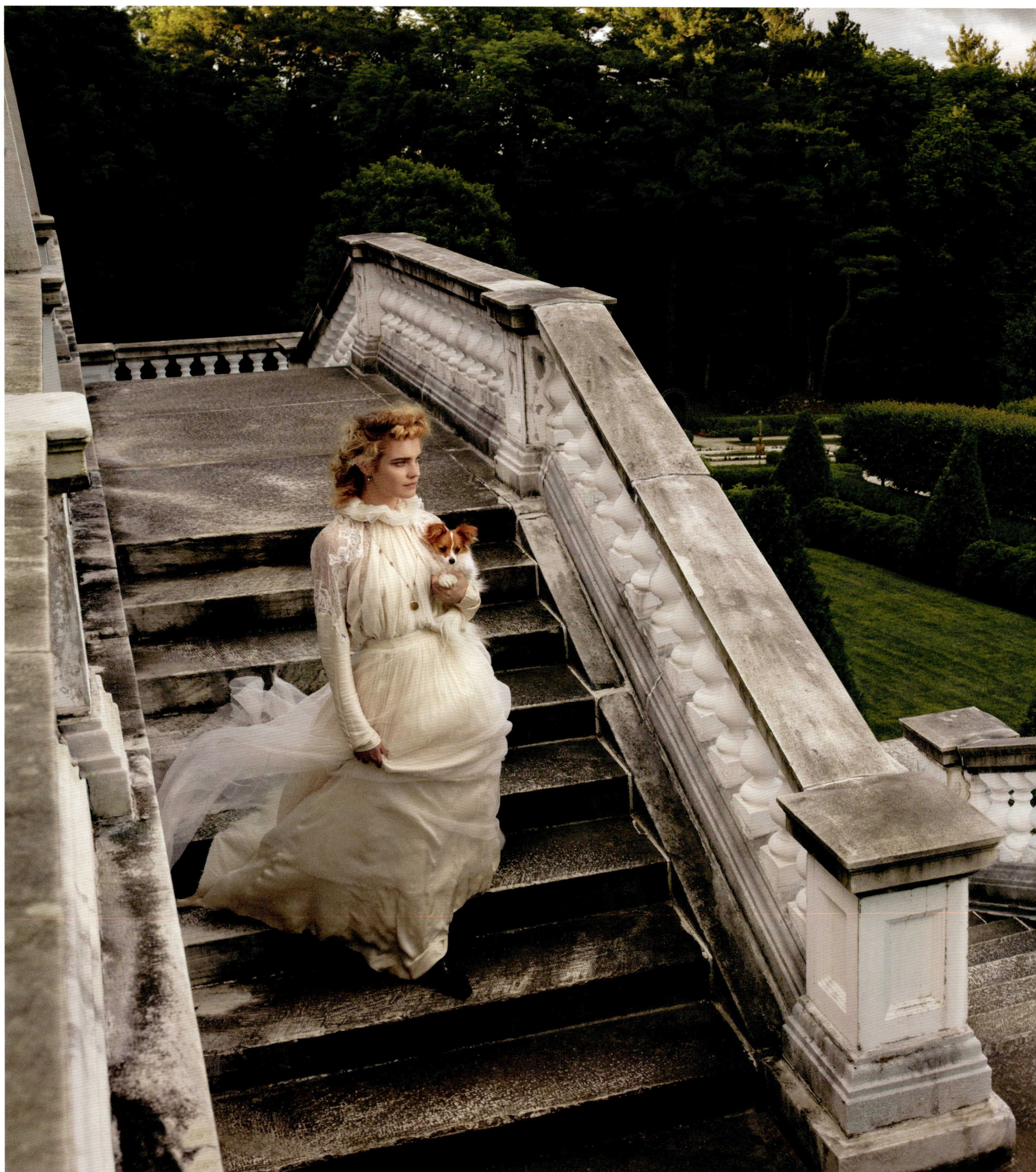

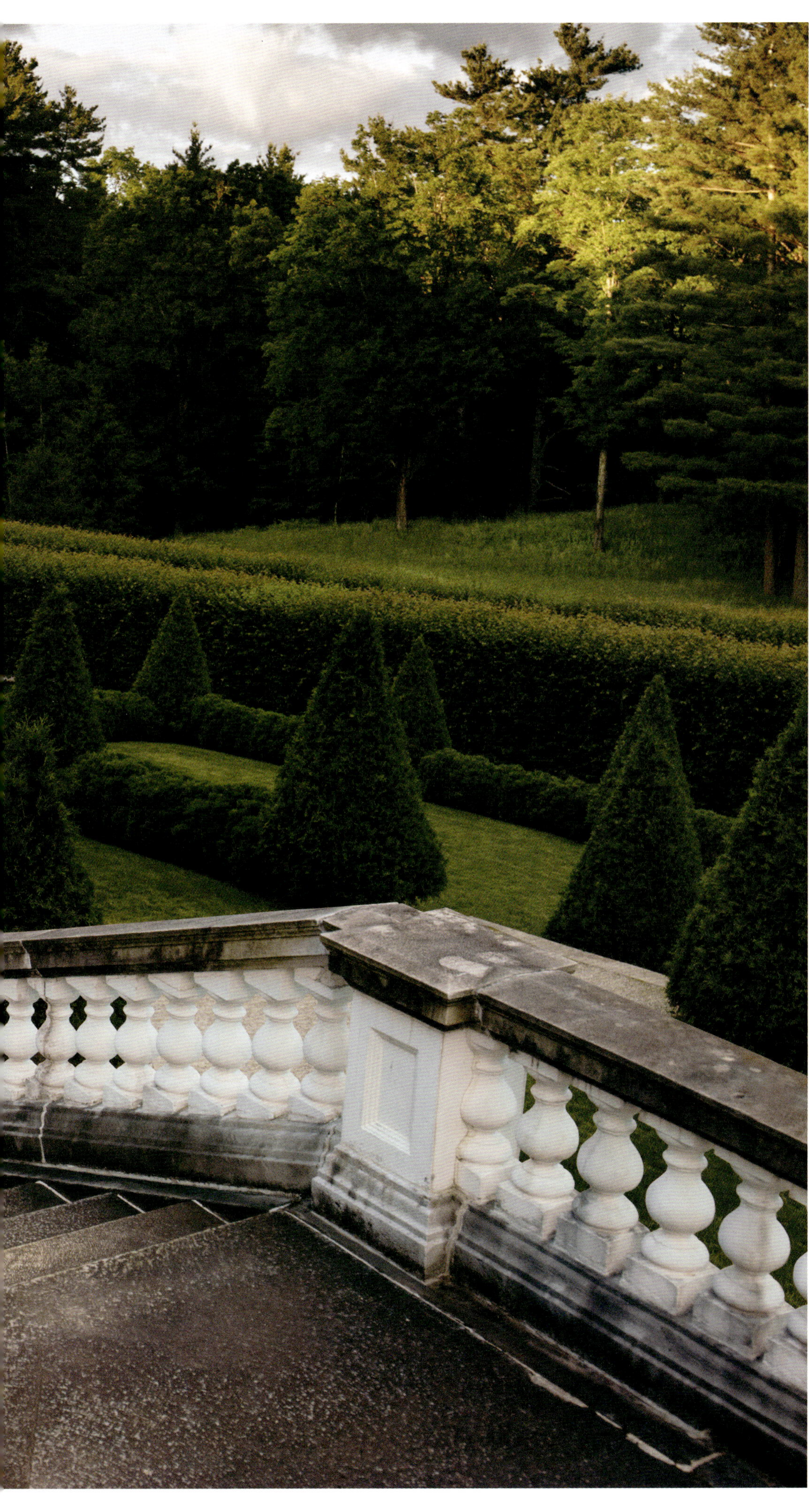

In upstate New York, there are ruins of a house overlooking the Hudson River that Edith Wharton visited as a child. It was her aunt's house, and she later used it as a model for grand Hudson River Valley estates in her novels. It was huge, with a four-story tower and terracotta chimneys and ornate balconies. At one time, it had the most extraordinary view of the river.

Wharton disliked the place. In her memoirs she described it as "Hudson River Gothic." In 1902, when she built her own house, The Mount, in the Berkshire Mountains of Massachusetts, she strove for simplicity. The Mount is elegant, expansive, symmetrical, with vast classical gardens. Wharton had written about interior decoration and also an important book on garden design. She wrote several novels and stories at The Mount before moving to Europe, where she died in 1937, at her house outside of Paris.

After Wharton sold The Mount, it went through hard times. It was a residence for a girls' school for many years. There was a chemistry lab in the kitchen. Then it was boarded up for a while. Then a troupe of actors lived there and performed Shakespeare plays in the overgrown gardens. By the early eighties there was an official restoration process in place, and in 2002, a hundred years after Wharton moved in, The Mount was opened to the public as a historic house.

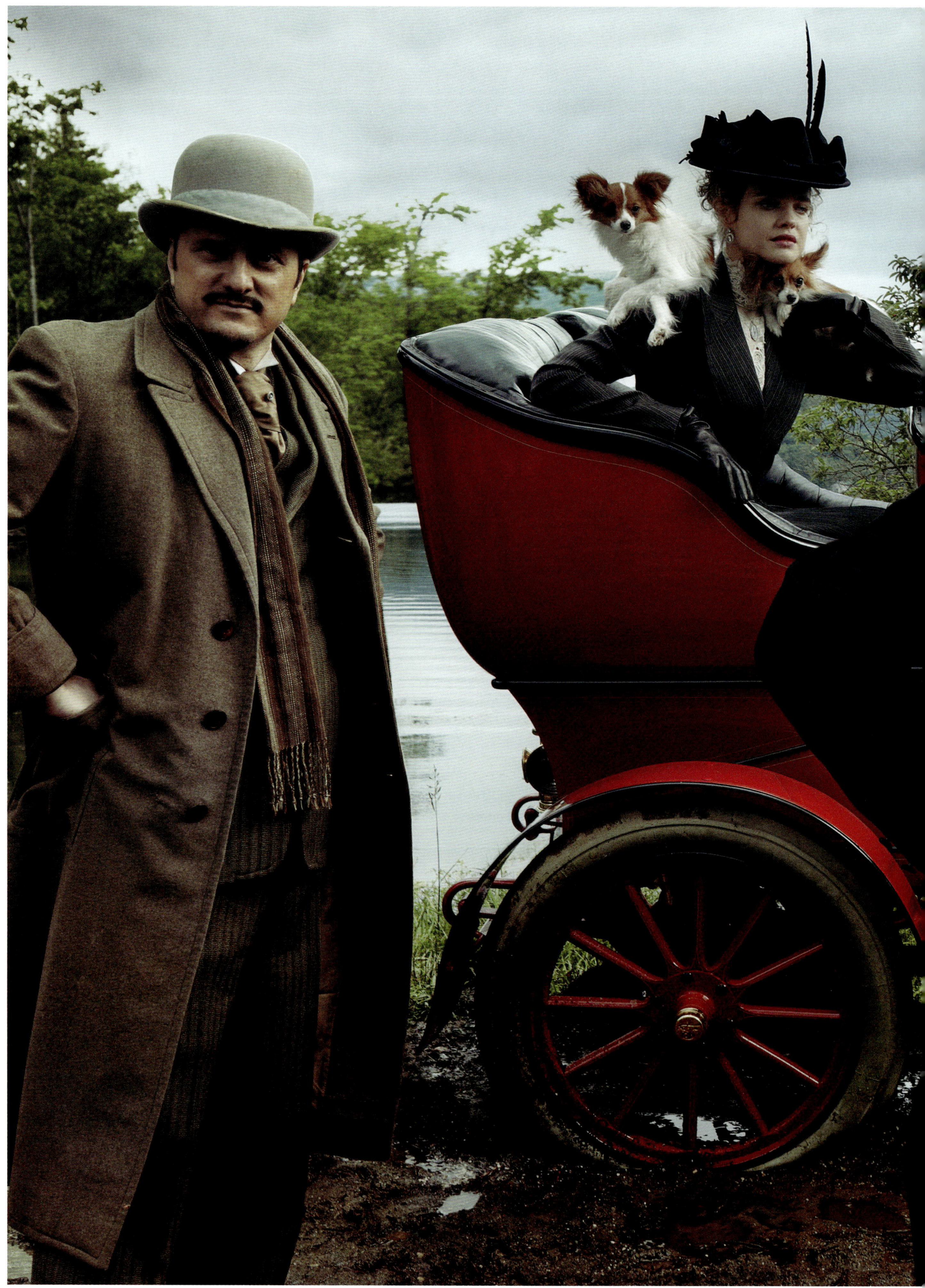

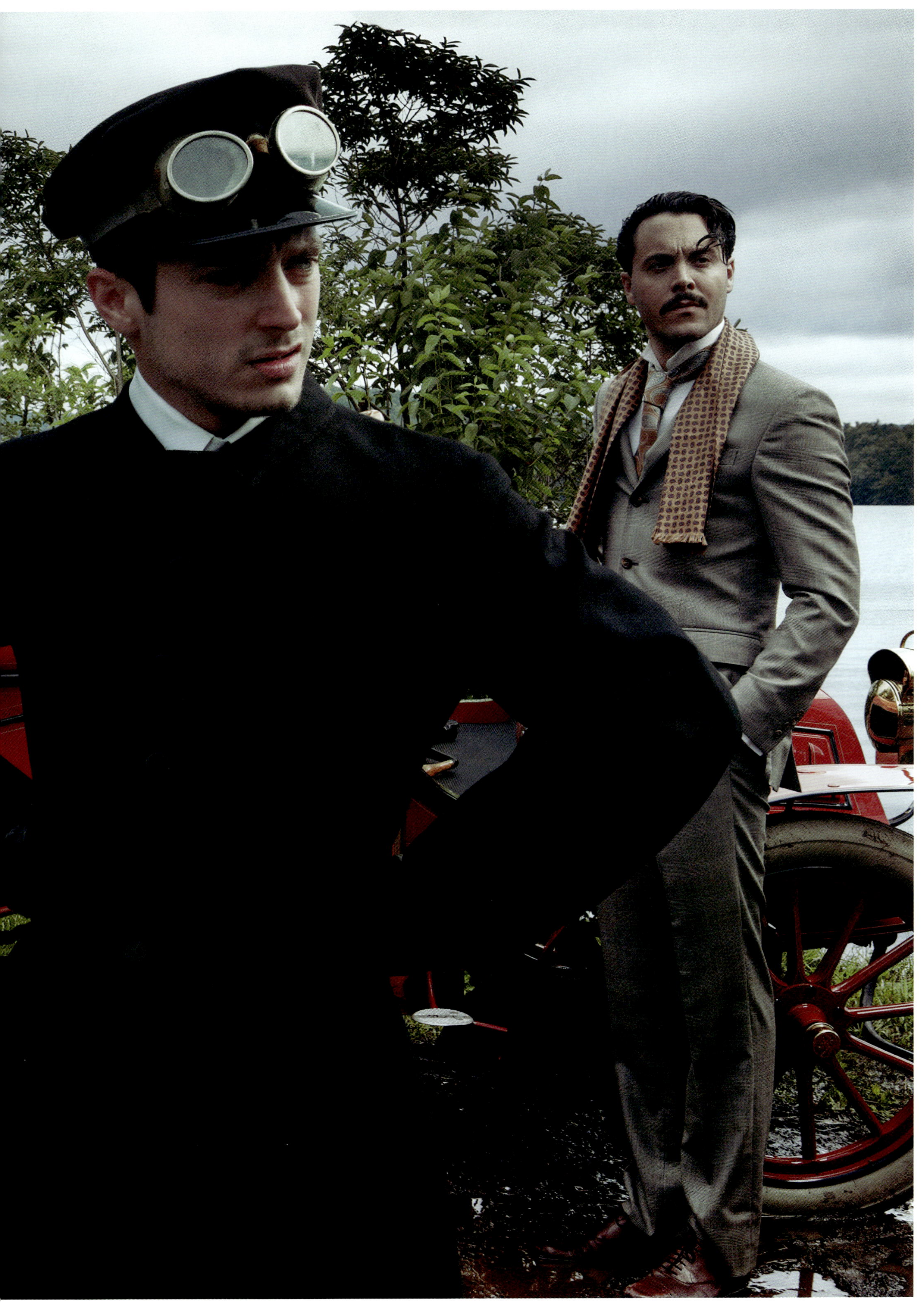

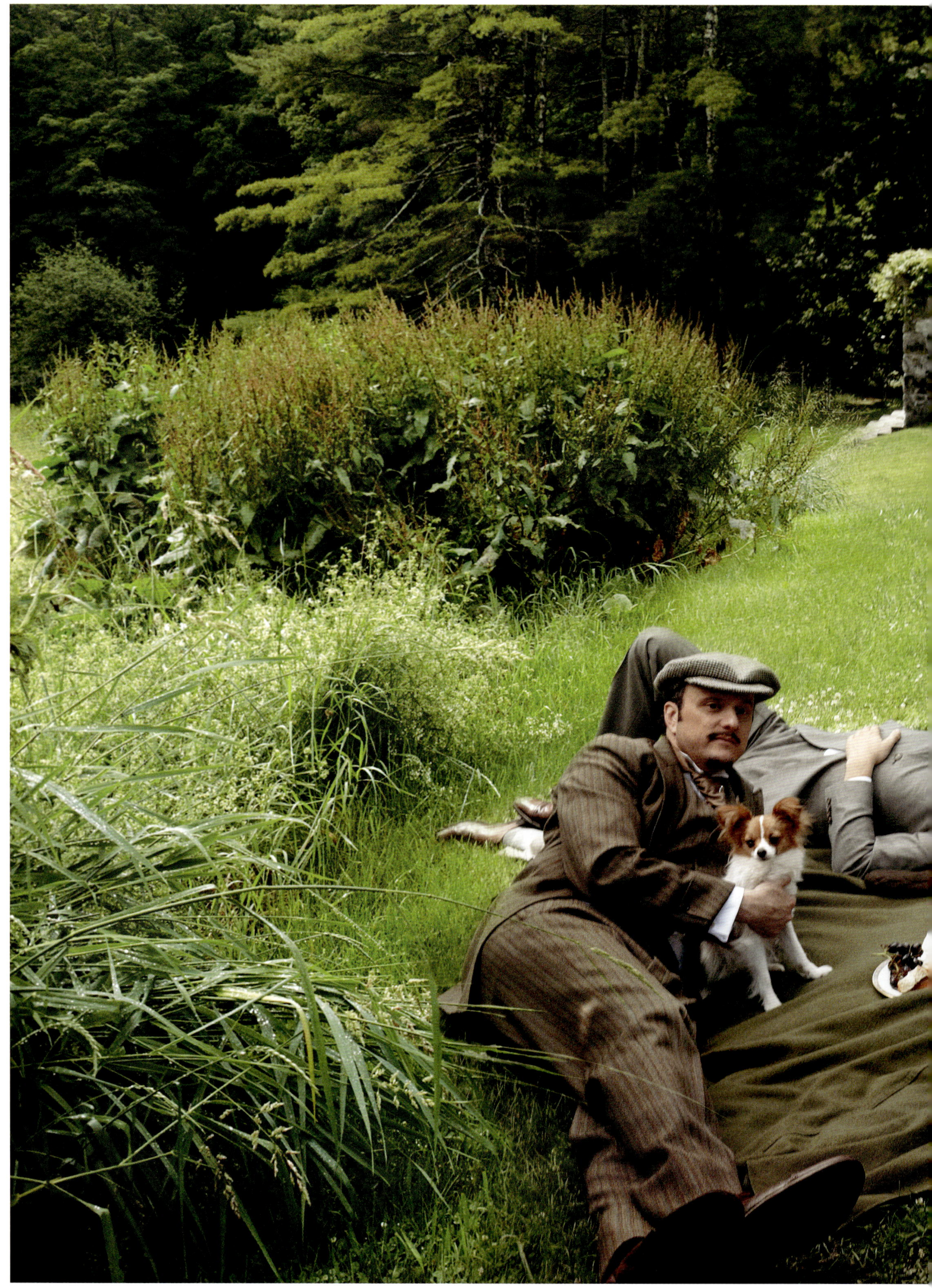

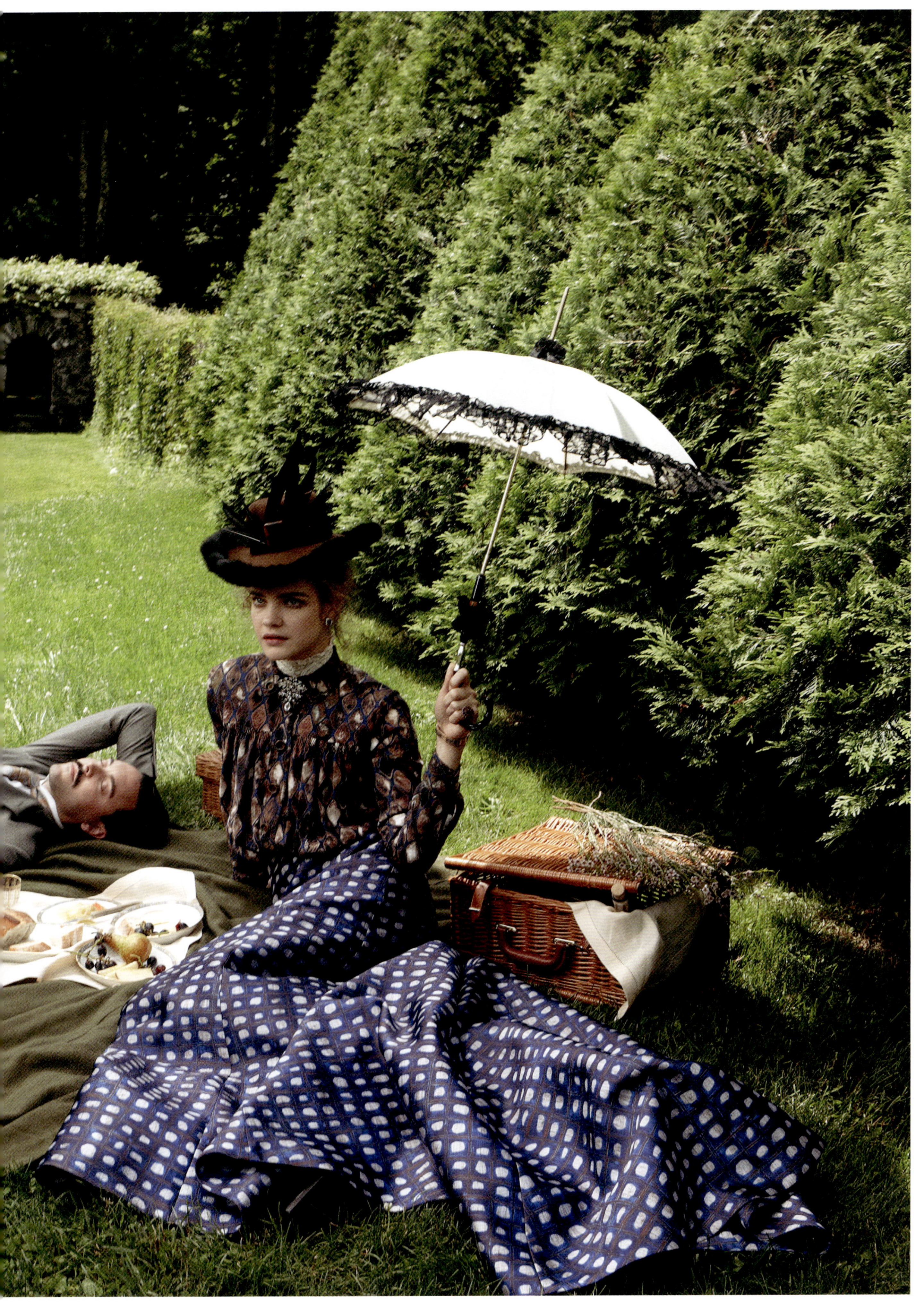

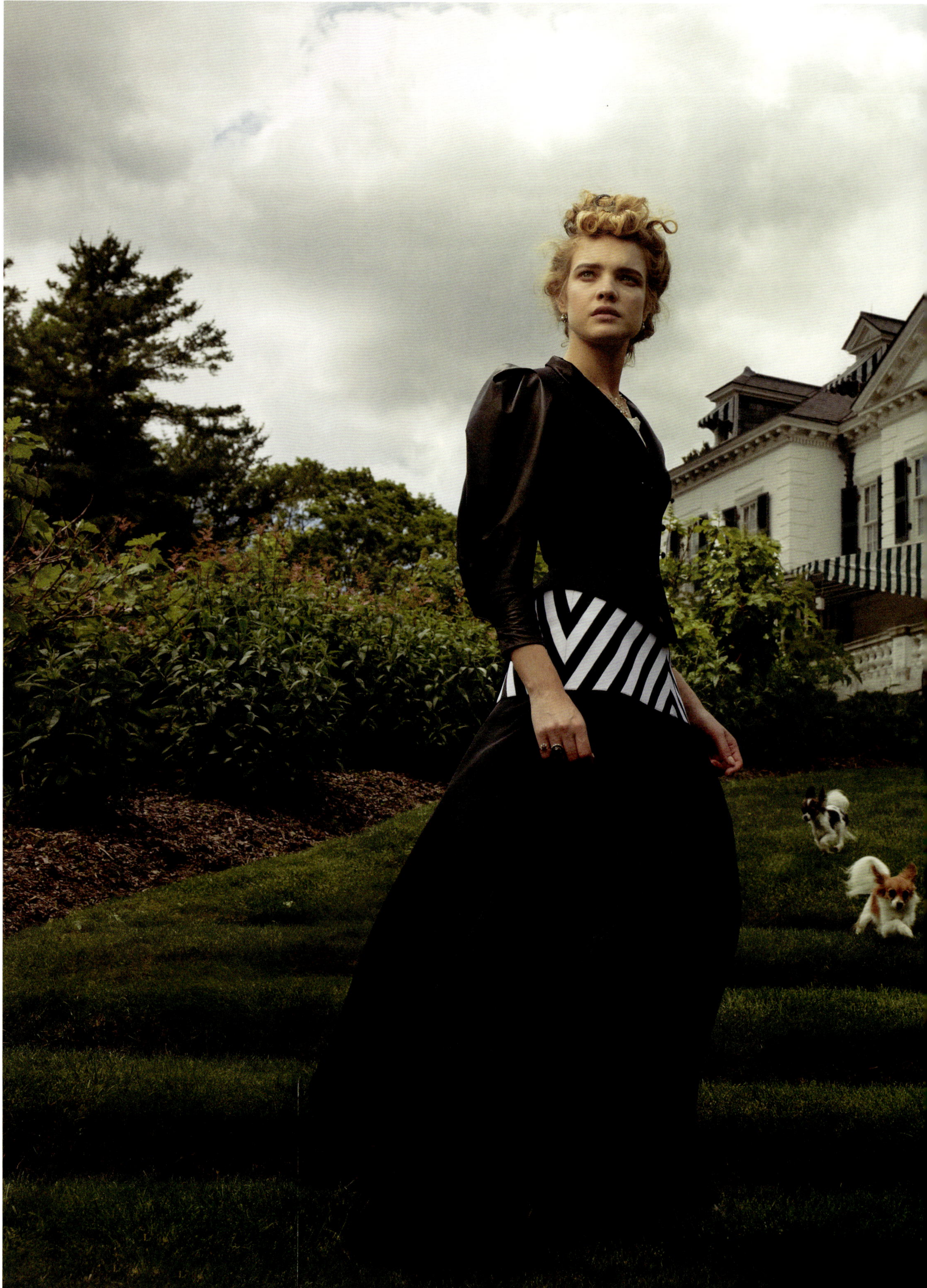

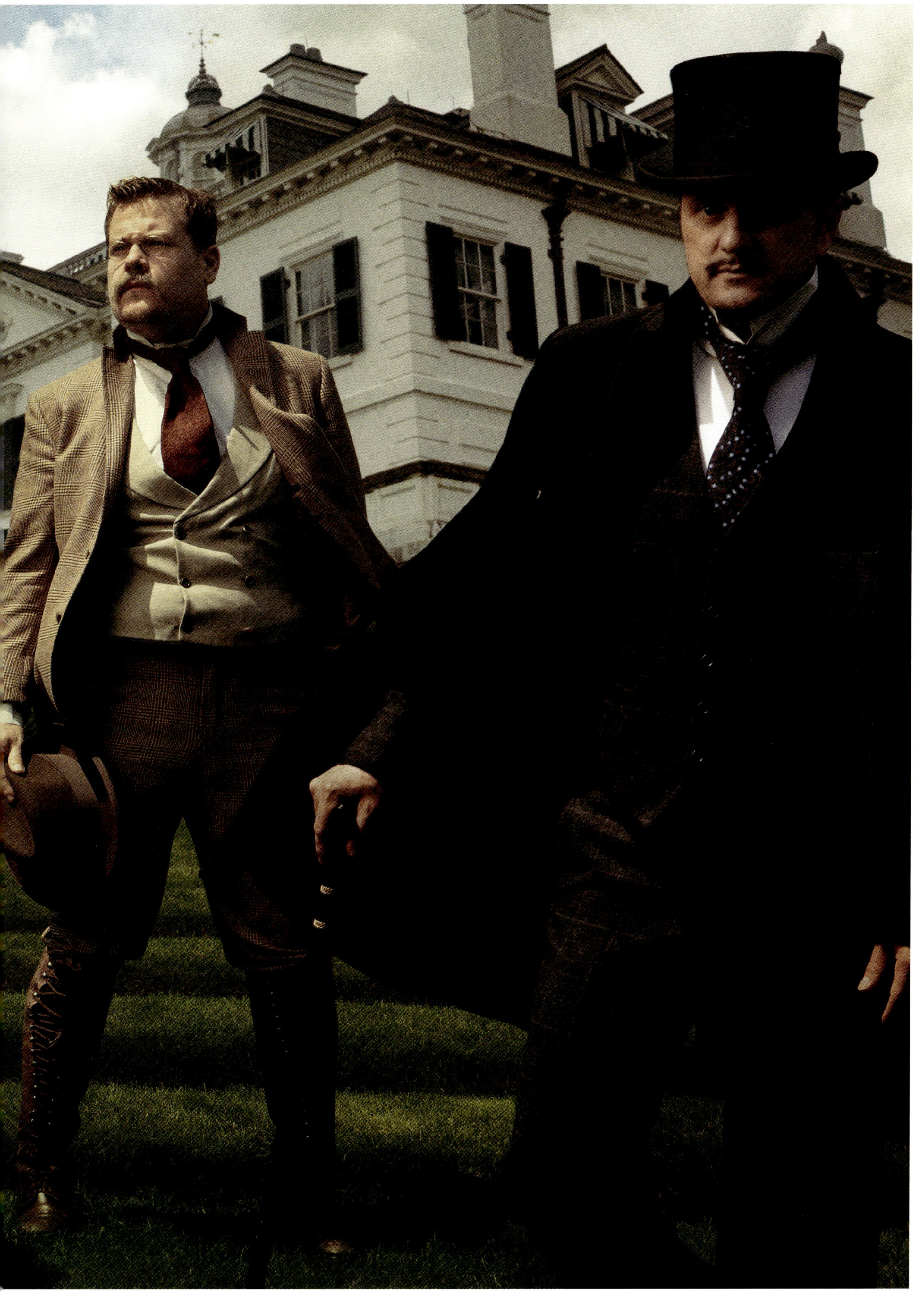

"When Anna asked me if I wanted to shoot at The Mount, I said yes immediately. It took four days and we never had to leave the grounds. We stayed in little guest-houses and ate all our meals there. At the last minute, Anna called and said that her friend James Corden was coming to play a part. Although he was appearing on Broadway, he could drive up during the day, we could photograph him, and he could make it back to New York in time for his performance. We scrambled to think of a role for him and decided that he could be Theodore Roosevelt, who was president when Wharton lived at The Mount. They were good friends.

The other characters were frequent guests. The novelist Jeffrey Eugenides played Henry James, the actor Jack Huston was Morton Fullerton, James's friend and Wharton's lover. The artist Nate Lowman played Daniel Chester French, Wharton's neighbor. The writer Jonathan Safran Foer played the original architect of The Mount, Ogden Codman. Max Minghella was the painter Maxfield Parrish; Juno Temple played Anna Bahlmann, Wharton's secretary and confidante; Elijah Wood was her chauffeur, Charles Cook; the writer Junot Díaz was the erudite diplomat Walter Berry. Mamie Gummer was Wharton's niece, Beatrix Farrand, and Natalia Vodianova was Wharton.

Grace brought eight sets of clothes for Natalia and put them on a rack. I asked her if that was all she had, and she said yes. She was very confident. And in fact, they were perfect. Exquisite. I used everything Grace brought and made eight pictures."

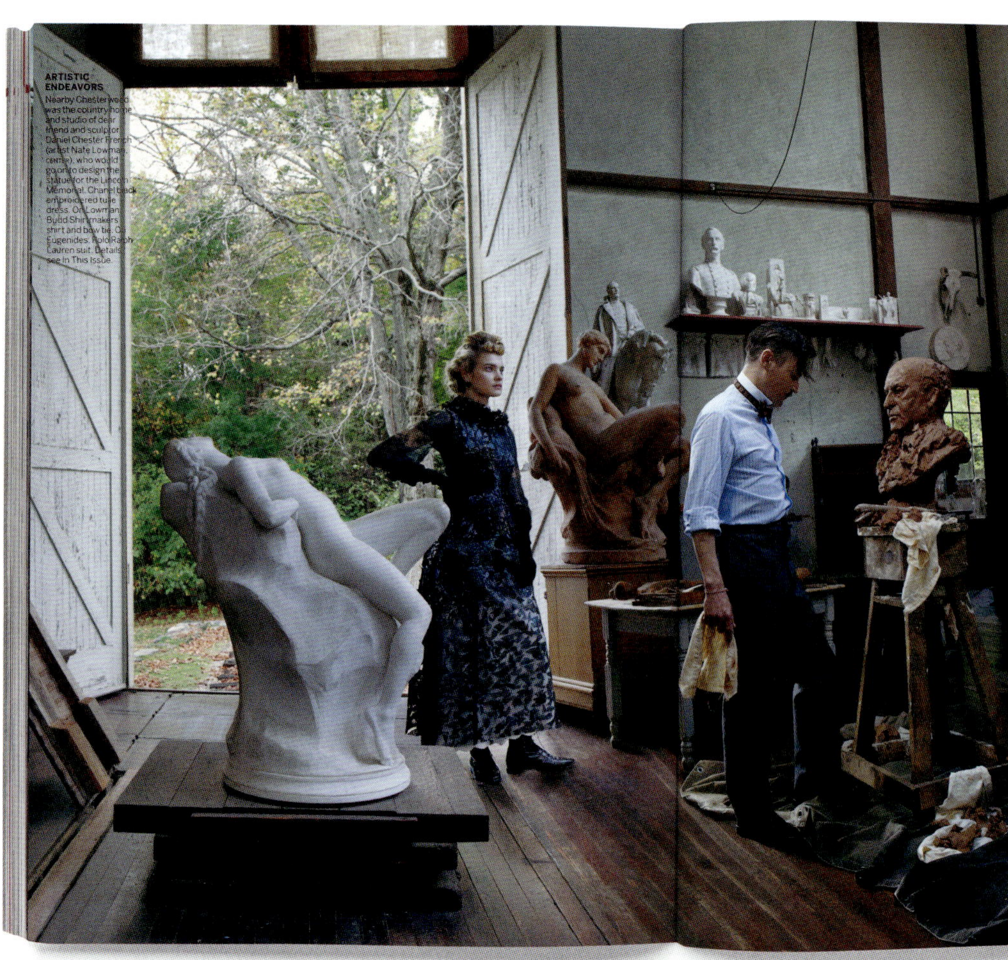

A WOMAN OF LETTERS
Anna Bahlmann (actress Juno Temple, NEAR LEFT) was Wharton's faithful secretary and lifelong confidante. On Vodianova: Alberta Ferretti chiffon dress with crystal collar. On Temple: Ralph Lauren Collection jacket and skirt, made for *Vogue*. Vintage Ralph Lauren Collection lace blouse. Details, see In This Issue.

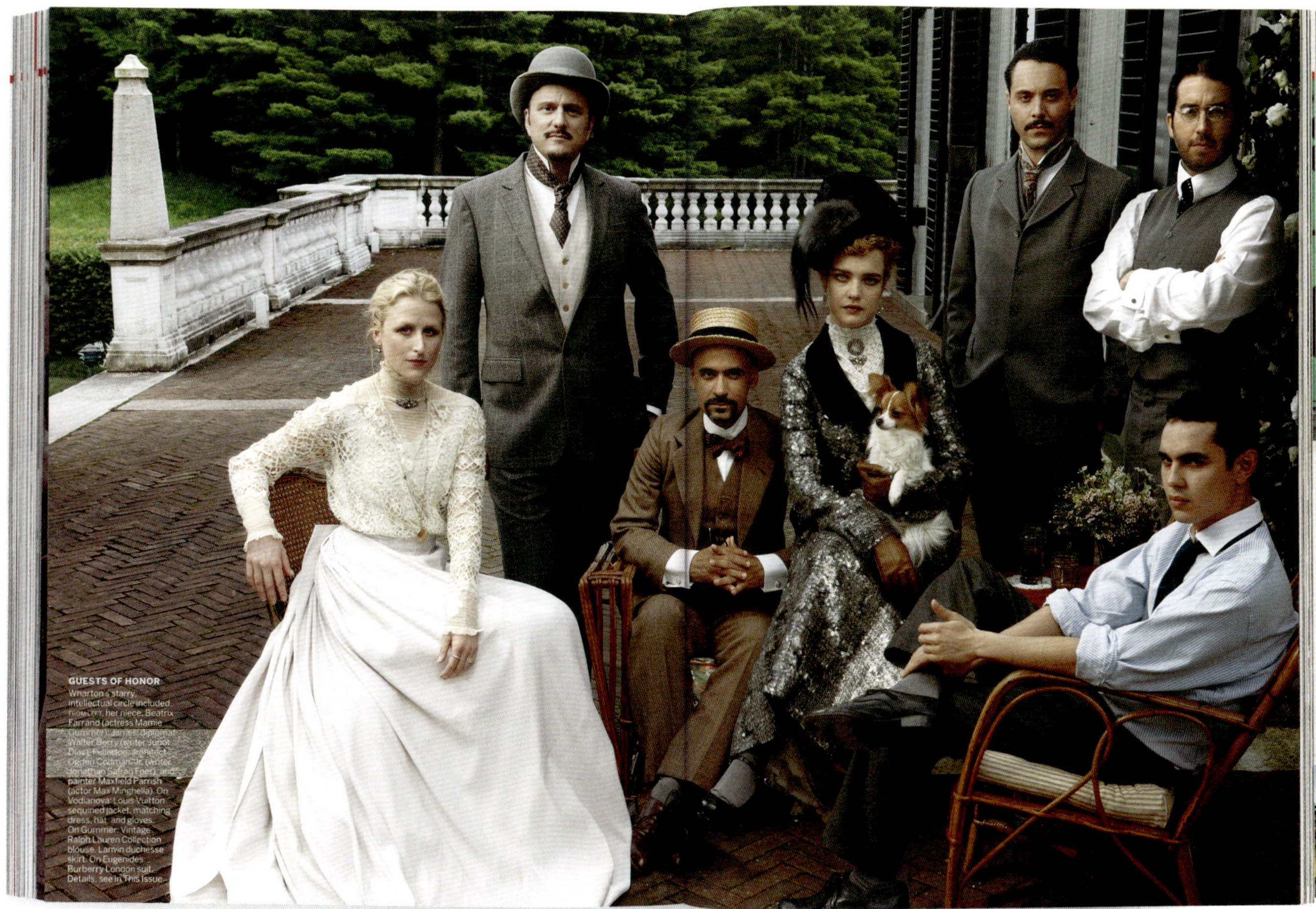
GUESTS OF HONOR
Wharton's starry, intellectual circle included, her niece, Beatrix Farrand (actress Mamie
Walter Berry (writer Junot
Ogden Codman Jr. (writer
painter Maxfield Parrish (actor Max Minghella). On Vodianova: Louis Vuitton sequined jacket, matching dress, hat, and gloves. On Gummer: Vintage Ralph Lauren Collection blouse. Lanvin duchesse skirt. On Eugenides: Burberry London suit. Details, see In This Issue.

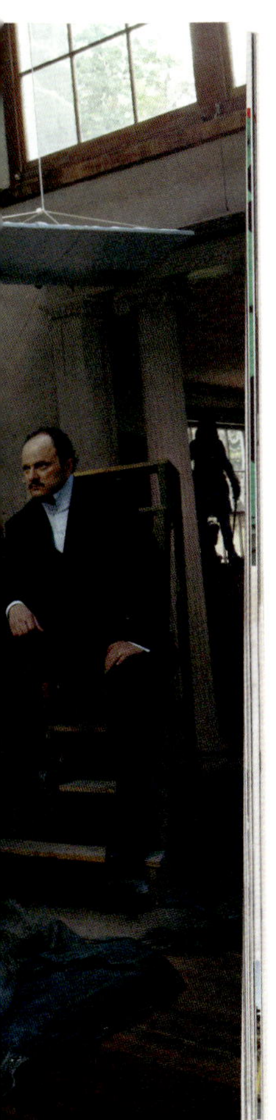

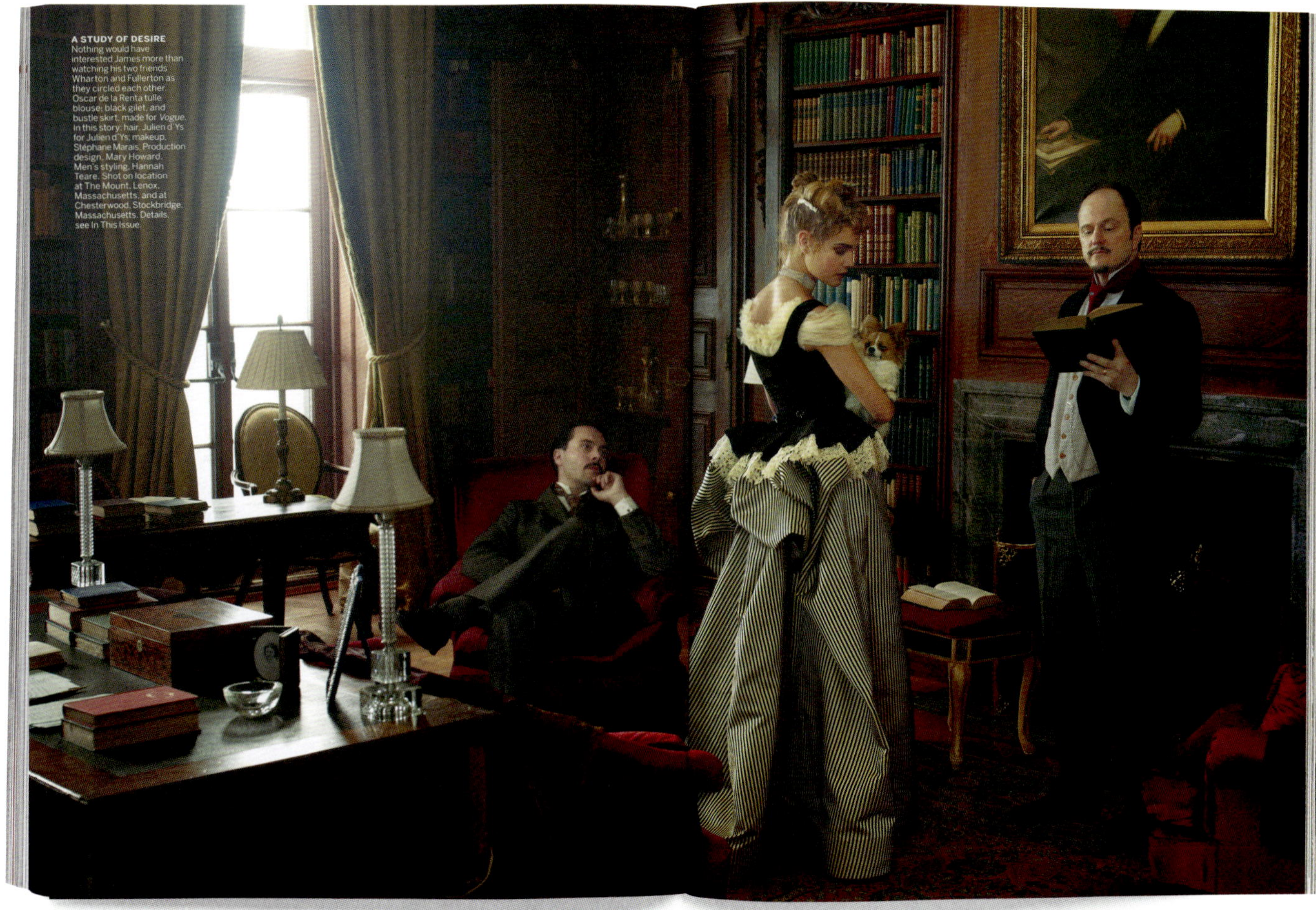
A STUDY OF DESIRE
Nothing would have interested James more than watching his two friends Wharton and Fullerton as they circled each other. Oscar de la Renta tulle blouse, black gilet, and bustle skirt, made for *Vogue*. In this story: hair, Julien d'Ys for Julien d'Ys; makeup, Stéphane Marais. Production design, Mary Howard. Men's styling, Hannah Teare. Shot on location at The Mount, Lenox, Massachusetts, and at Chesterwood, Stockbridge, Massachusetts. Details, see In This Issue.

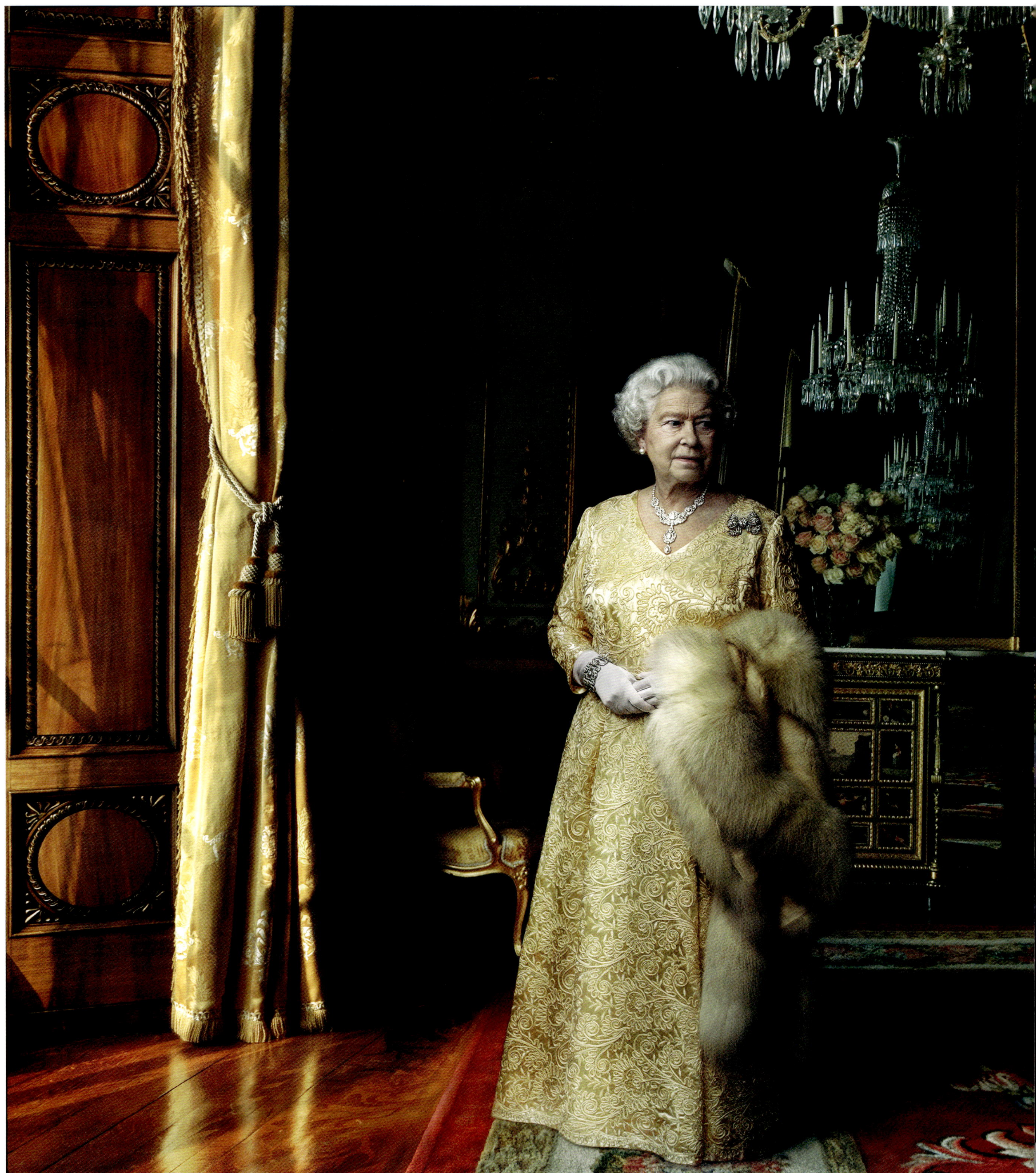

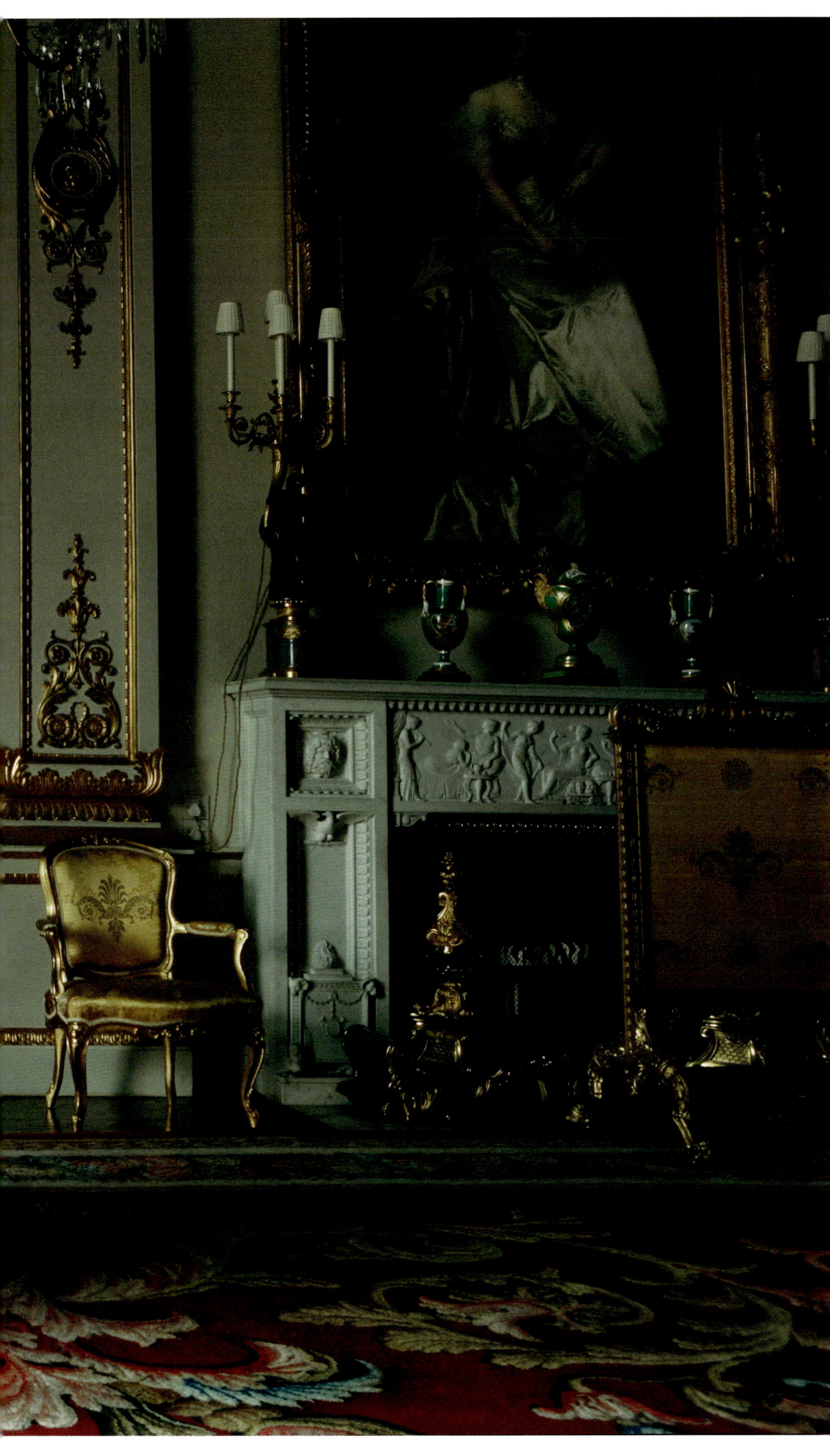

The first time Annie was asked to photograph Queen Elizabeth, on the occasion of the Queen's visit to Jamestown, Virginia, for the four hundredth anniversary of the founding of the British colony there, Annie said that she would like to make a portrait of the Queen on a horse on the grounds of Windsor Castle, her country home. That was not possible, she was told. No horse. No Windsor Castle. The Queen would be in London, at Buckingham Palace. Except for the horse and the location, Annie was given artistic leeway, and she decided that a formal portrait in the grand rooms of the palace was in order. She was asked what clothes and jewelry the Queen should wear and was given catalogs of robes and tiaras and brooches to make her choices.

Queen Elizabeth II, the White Drawing Room, Buckingham Palace, London, 2007

The second portrait session Annie had with the Queen was very different from the first one. Annie had asked to photograph her at Balmoral Castle, in Scotland, which has thousands of acres of forests and moors. She imagined the Queen driving a Range Rover and wearing rubber boots. But there would be no Balmoral. The portrait was made at Windsor, and the Queen had her own ideas about what the pictures should be. The occasion was her ninetieth birthday, and she wanted portraits with her grandchildren and great-grandchildren, her daughter, and her dogs.

Queen Elizabeth II with her grandchildren (James, Viscount Severn, and Lady Louise) and her great-grandchildren (Mia Tindall, Princess Charlotte, Savannah Phillips, Prince George, and Isla Phillips), in the Green Drawing room at Windsor Castle, Berkshire, England, 2016

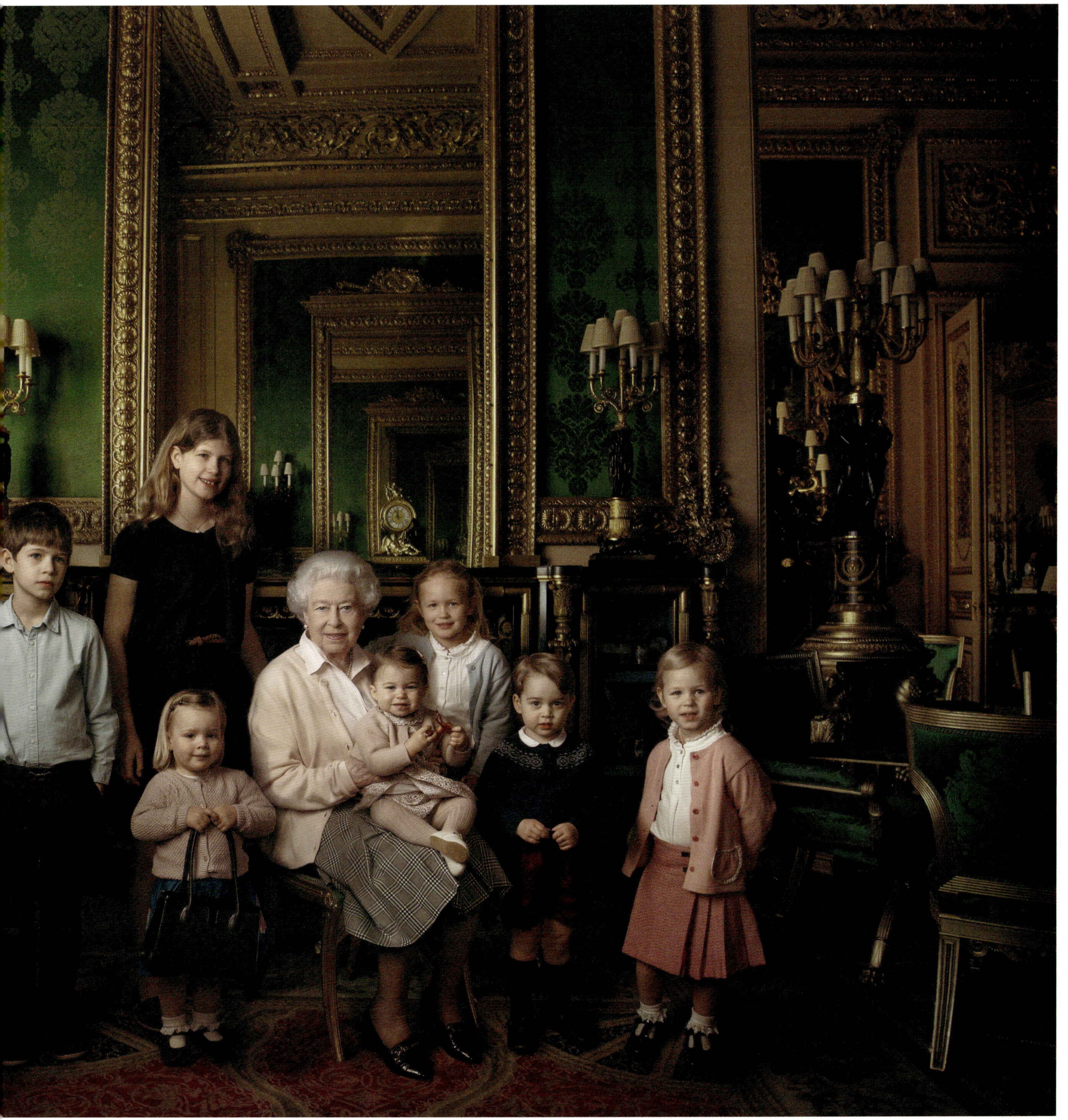

The Queen went out walking with her dogs every day. She did drive her Range Rover over to the shoot on the stairs. The dogs were in the car with her.

The Queen grew up with corgis, fearless little dogs bred for herding cattle. Her father brought a corgi home when she was seven, and she was not without one—and usually several—for decades afterward. She personally oversaw the royal corgi-breeding program. Dorgis came on the scene when one of the corgis mated with Princess Margaret's dachshund. Willow and Holly were the last corgis bred by the Queen.

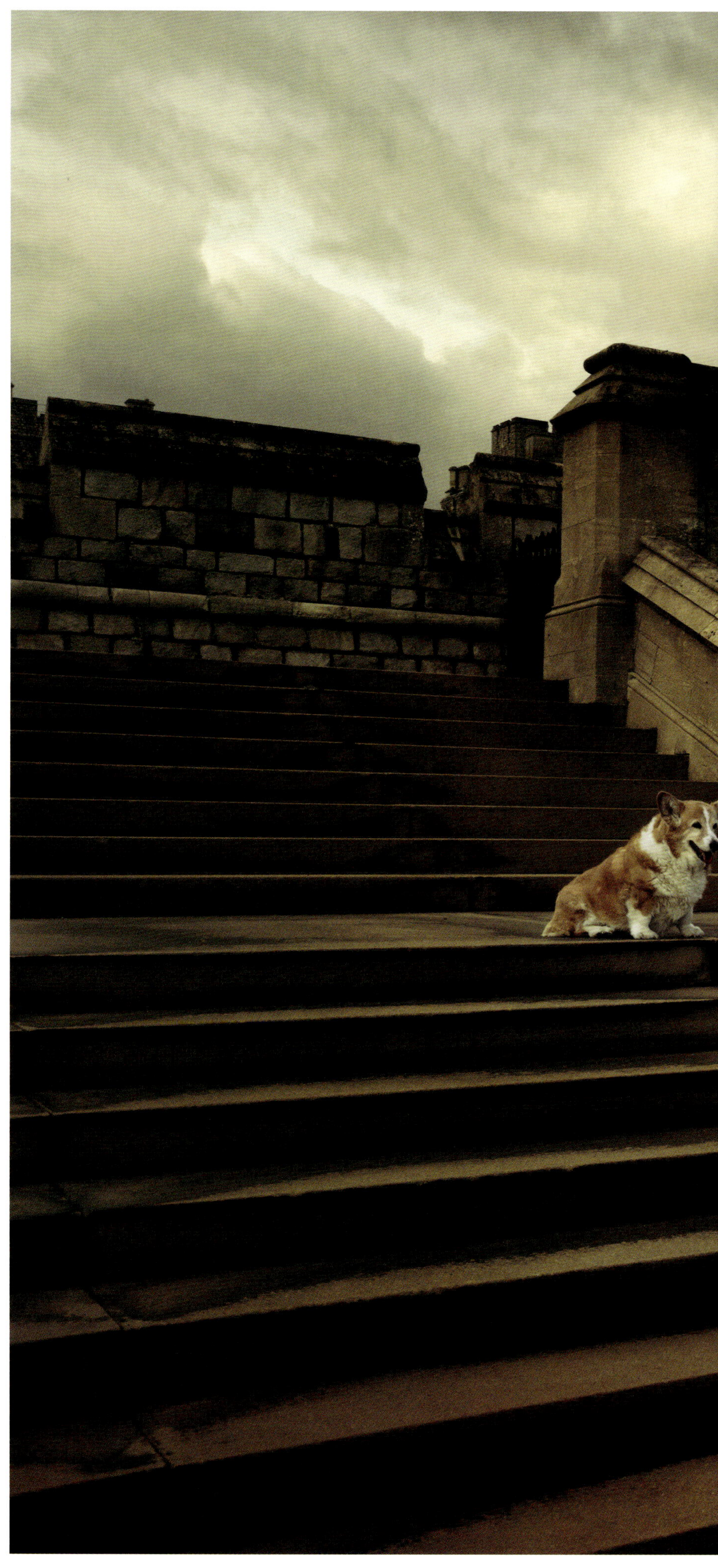

Queen Elizabeth II with corgi Willow, dorgi Vulcan, corgi Holly, and dorgi Candy, Windsor Castle, Berkshire, England, 2016

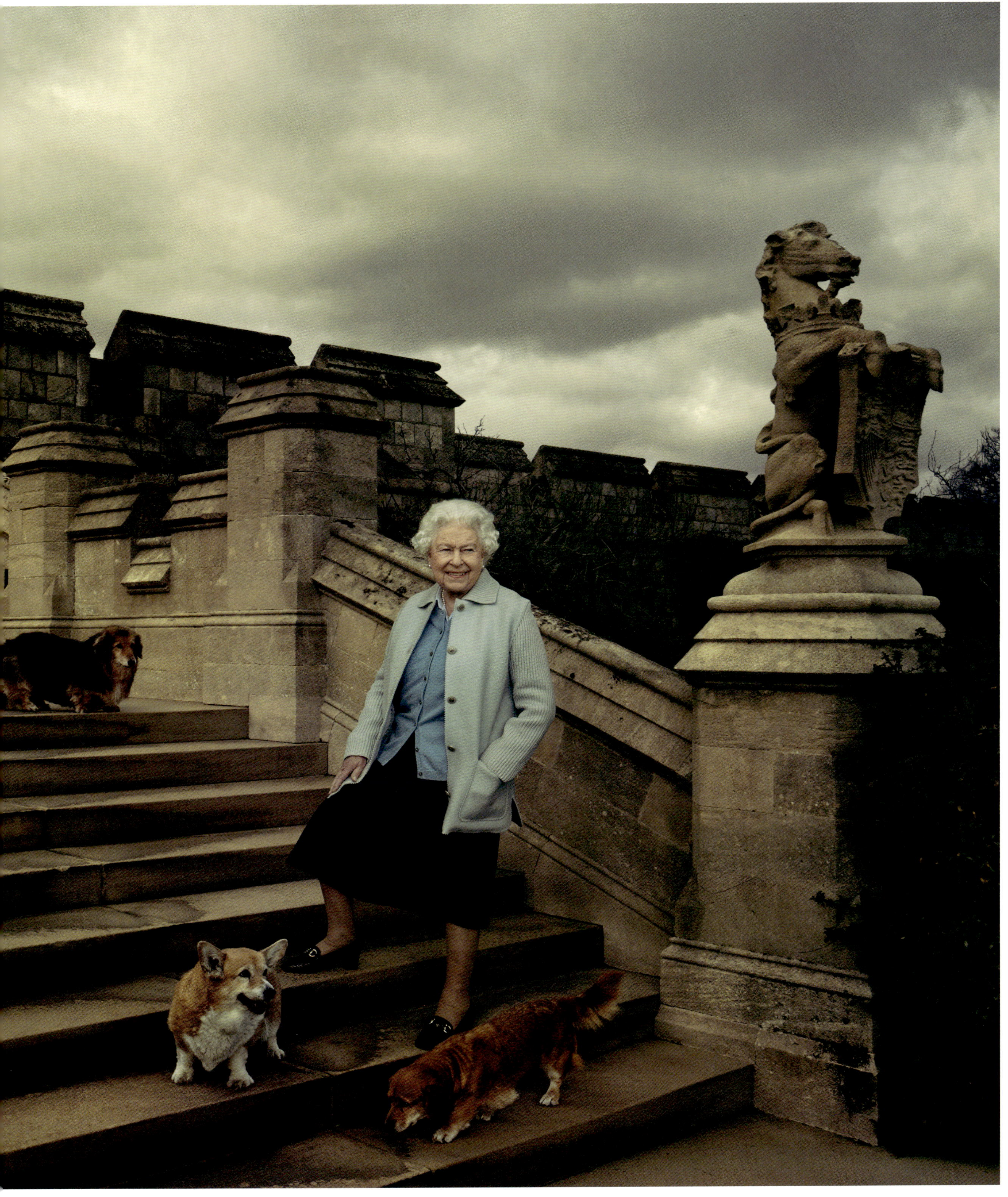

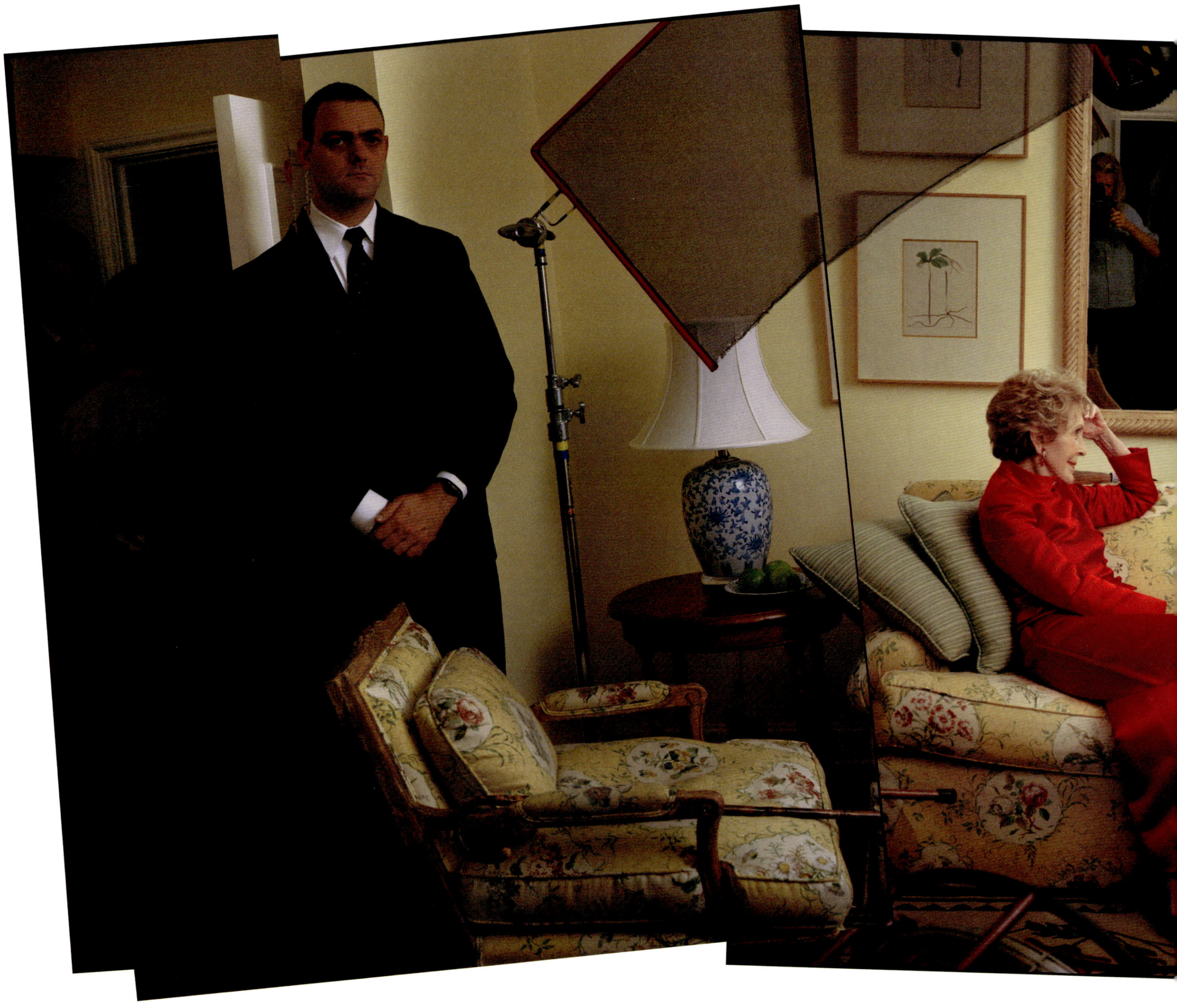

Nancy Reagan and Bobby Short,
Hotel Bel-Air, Los Angeles, 2002

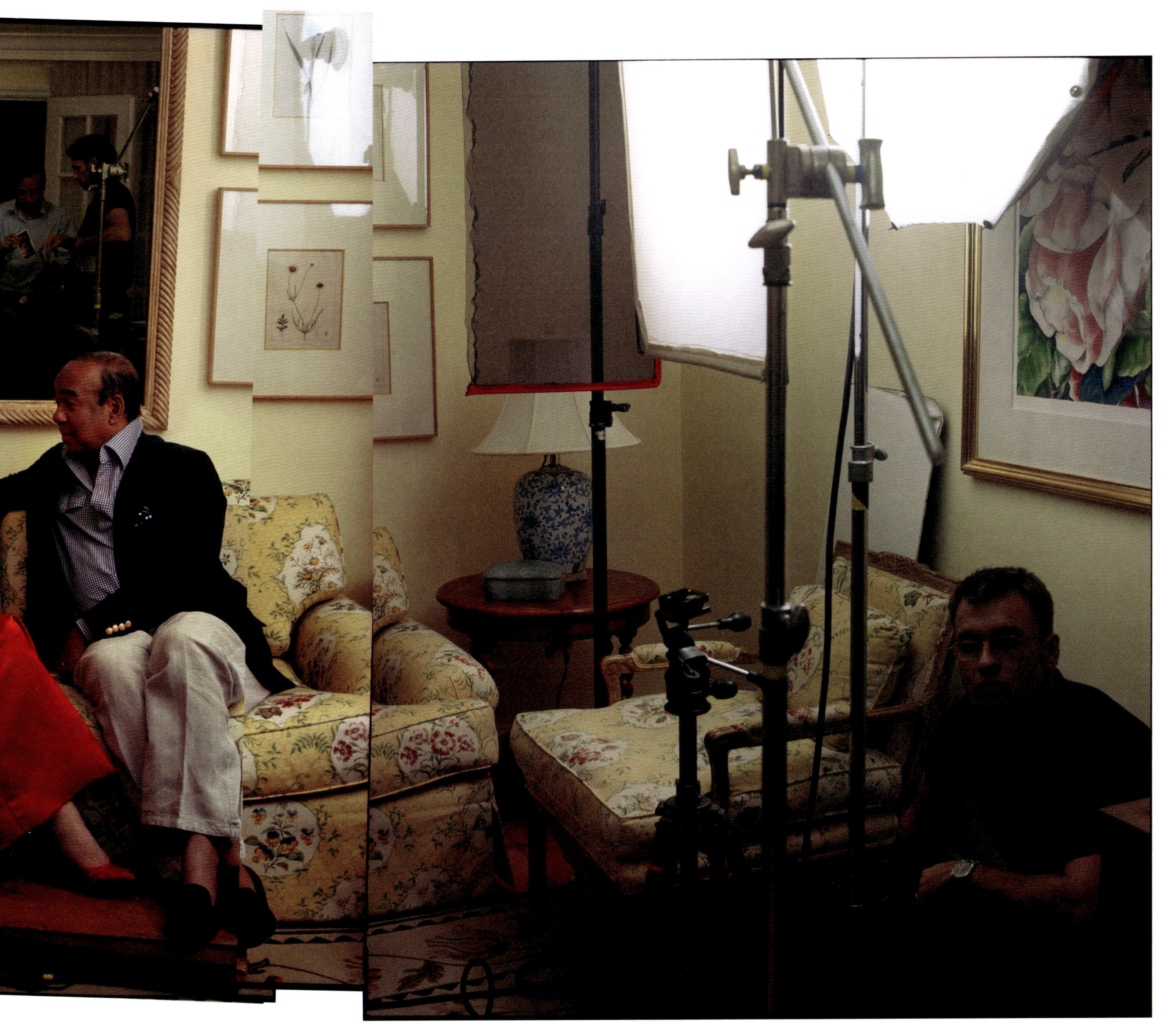

The portrait of the wife of the US president has been a tradition at *Vogue* since 1929, when Lou Hoover sat for Edward Steichen. It became even more important when Anna Wintour became *Vogue*'s editor. Anna is passionately interested in politics and especially in women who are in politics.

The first formal portrait of a First Lady Annie made for *Vogue* was during a sitting with Hillary Clinton in 1993, the first year of her husband's presidency, when her poll numbers were better than his and just before she presented her health plan to Congress. In 2001 Annie photographed Laura Bush in the Vermeil Room, the foyer for the ladies' powder room on the ground floor. Official portraits of First Ladies are hung in the Vermeil Room. The first time Annie made a formal portrait of Michelle Obama, George W. Bush was still president.

The role of a First Lady was altered most profoundly by Hillary Clinton. After the Clintons left the White House, she was the senator from New York, the US Secretary of State, and almost, by a thread, president herself. Those photographs belong with the many portraits Annie has made of women who hold positions of power in their own right, including Ruth Bader Ginsburg and Sandra Day O'Connor, the first two women to serve as US Supreme Court justices, and Nancy Pelosi, the first woman to hold the office of Speaker of the US House of Representatives, which made her second in the line of presidential successors.

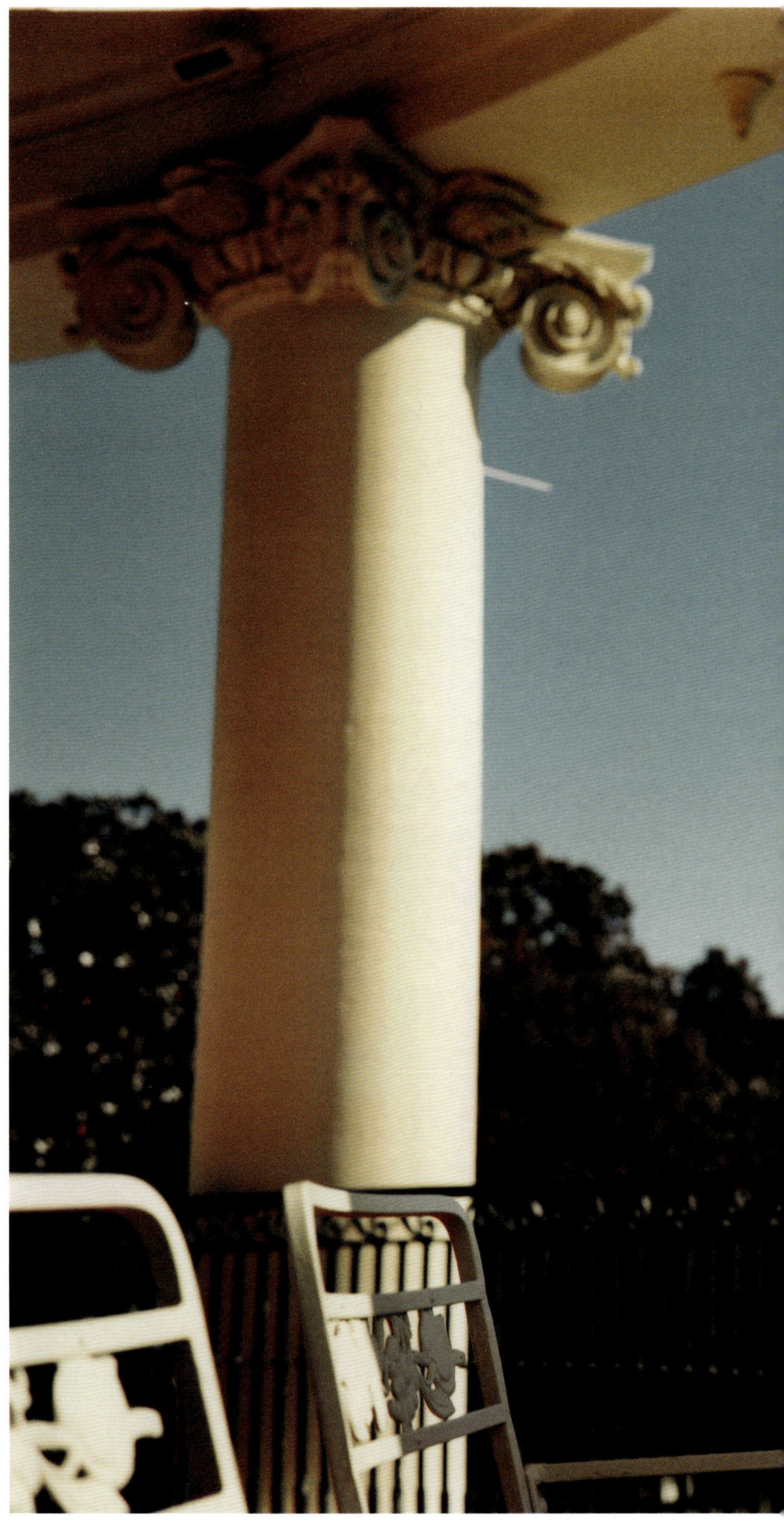

Hillary Clinton on the Truman Balcony of the White House, Washington, DC, 1998

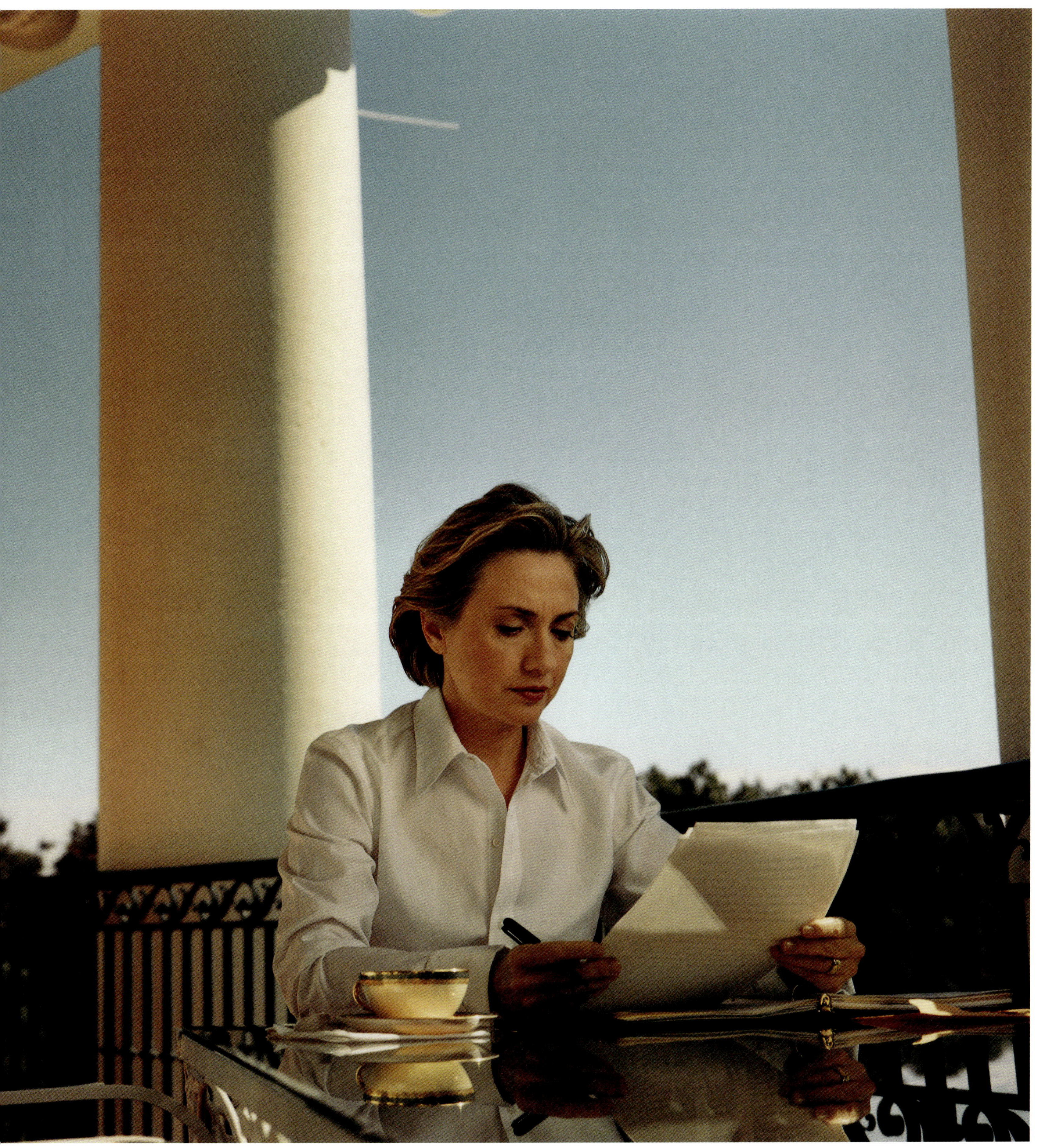

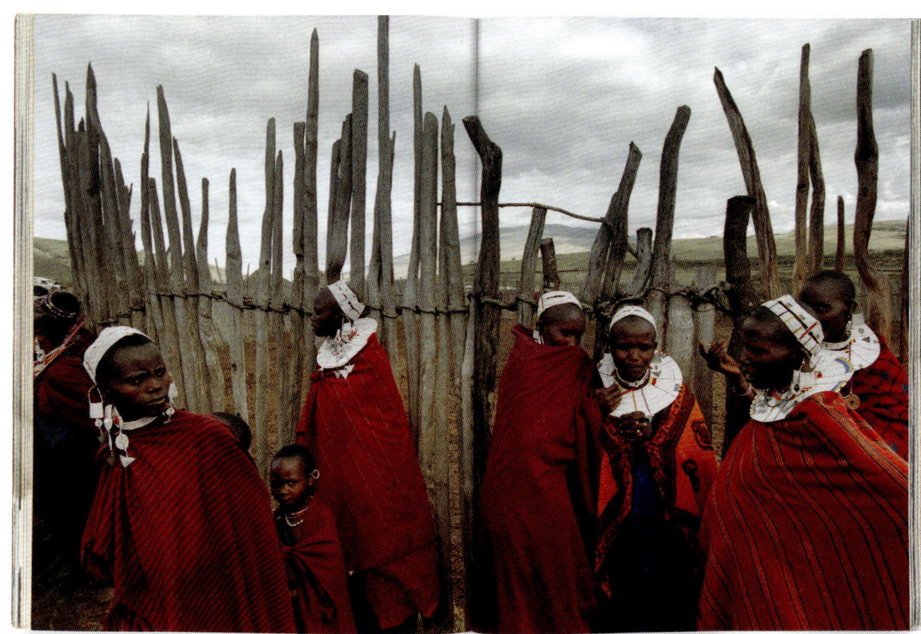
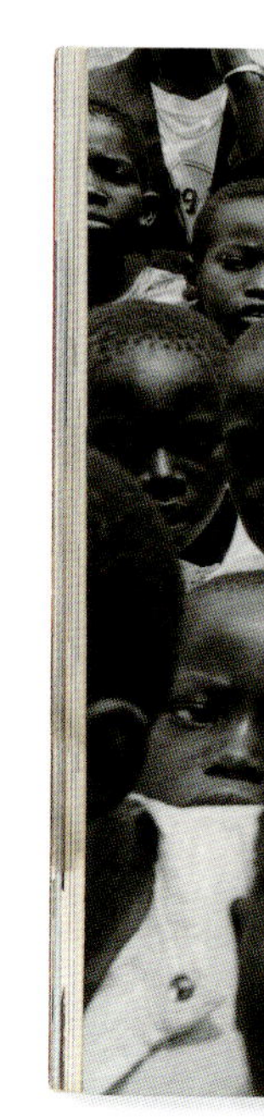

"Hillary and Chelsea Clinton made a twelve-day trip to Africa in 1997, and I went along to document it for *Vogue*. I was a little rusty doing that kind of work, and I was in a pool of the best photojournalists in the world, which sometimes seemed a little embarrassing. But just being in Africa was so moving that it didn't matter if I was dropping rolls of films all the time.

Watching Hillary at work was a revelation. The purpose of the trip was to support the rights of women and girls. She would go into a village and meet with the elders and the women and really listen to what they had to say—sitting at folding tables arranged in a circle so that no one had a more important seat than anyone else. When everyone had had a turn at speaking, Hillary would comment in a way that made it clear that what they had said was important and mattered."

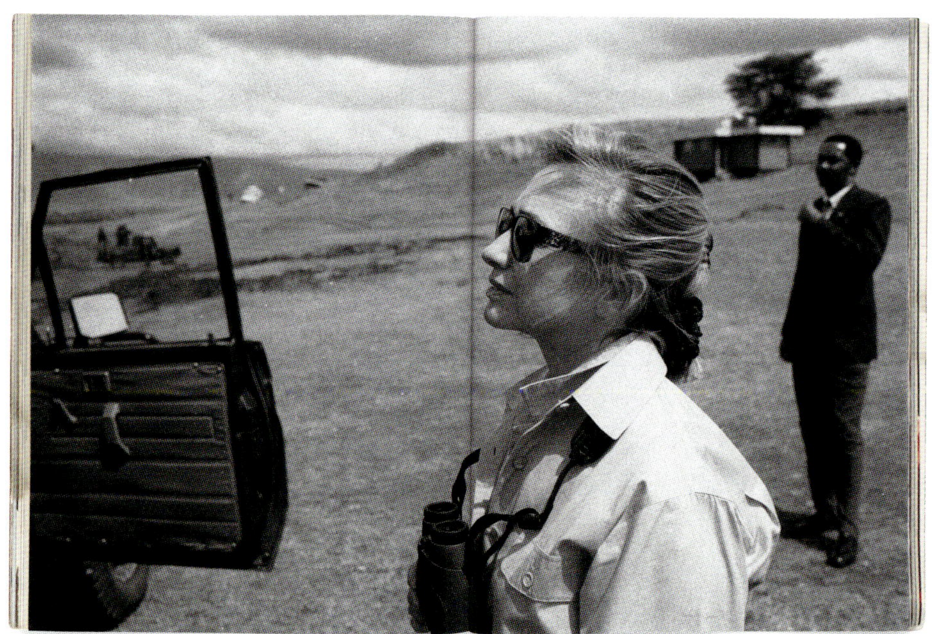

Top row: Masai villagers in Ngorongoro Conservation Area, Tanzania; a Masai village, Arusha, Tanzania; the women of the Victoria Mxenge Housing Project Initiative in Cape Town, South Africa, put the finishing touches on a renovated home. Bottom row: Ngorongoro Conservation Area; men in traditional costume, Victoria Falls; Ngorongoro Conservation Area.

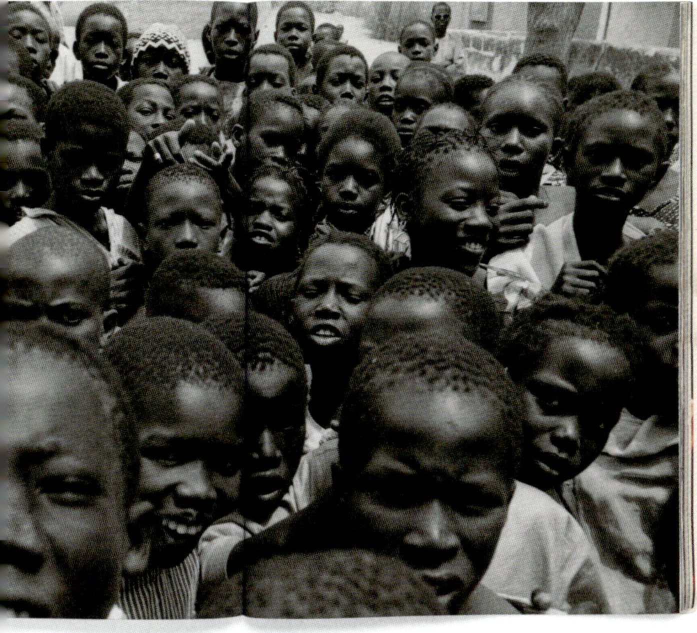

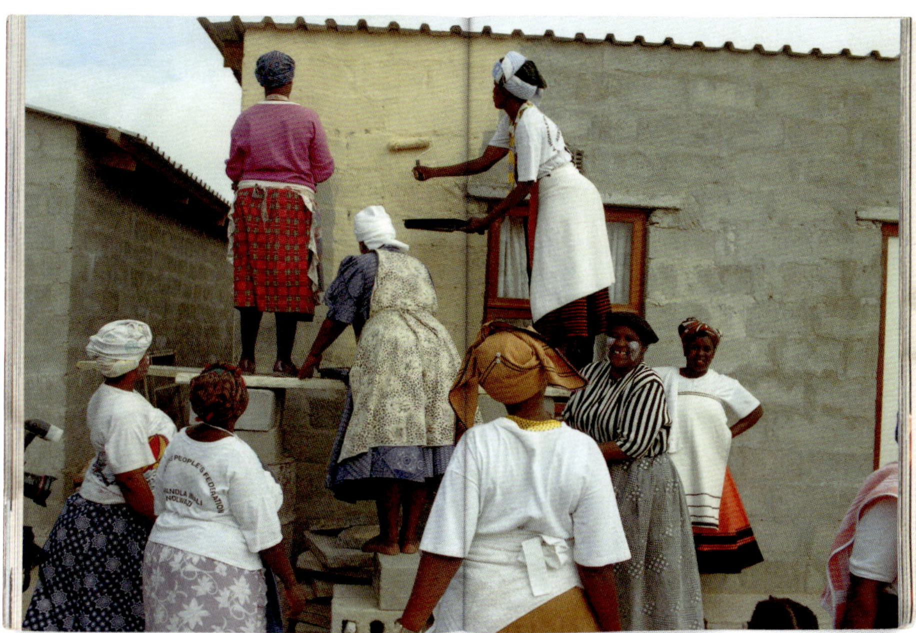

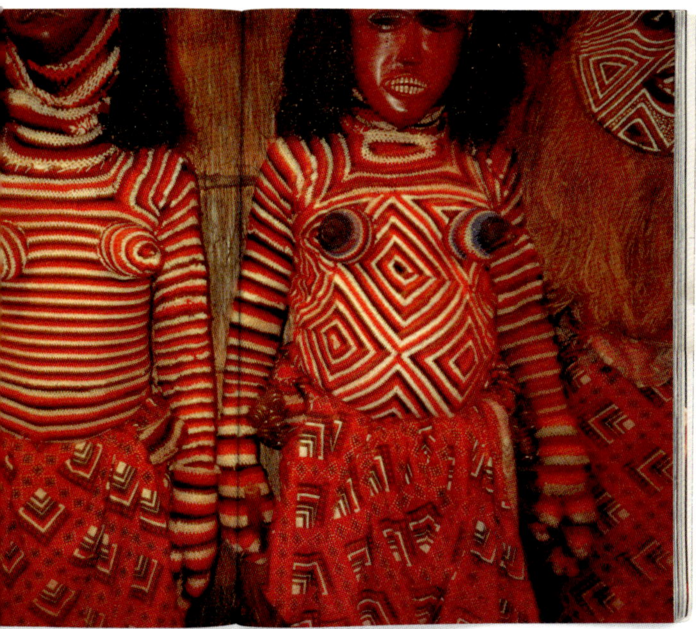

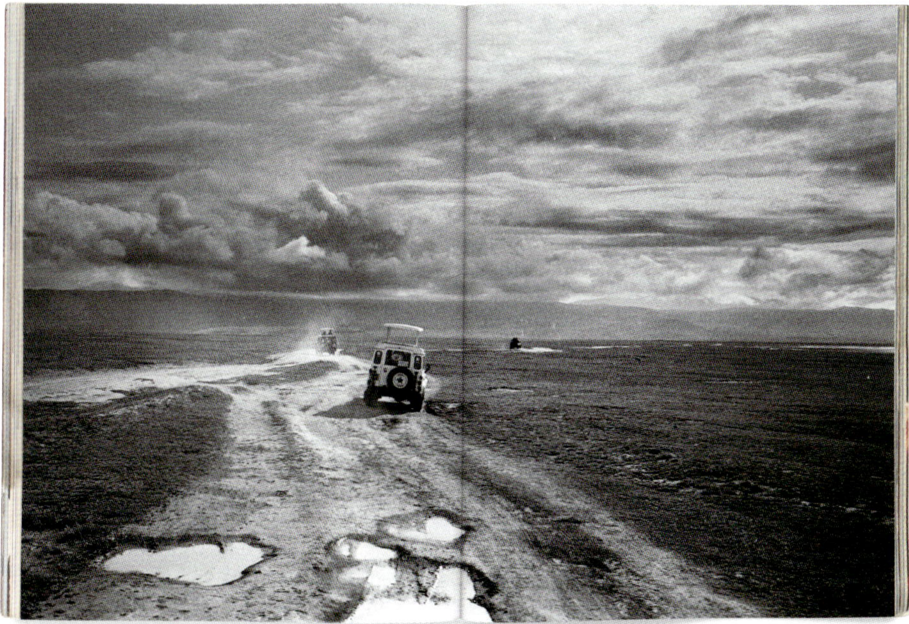

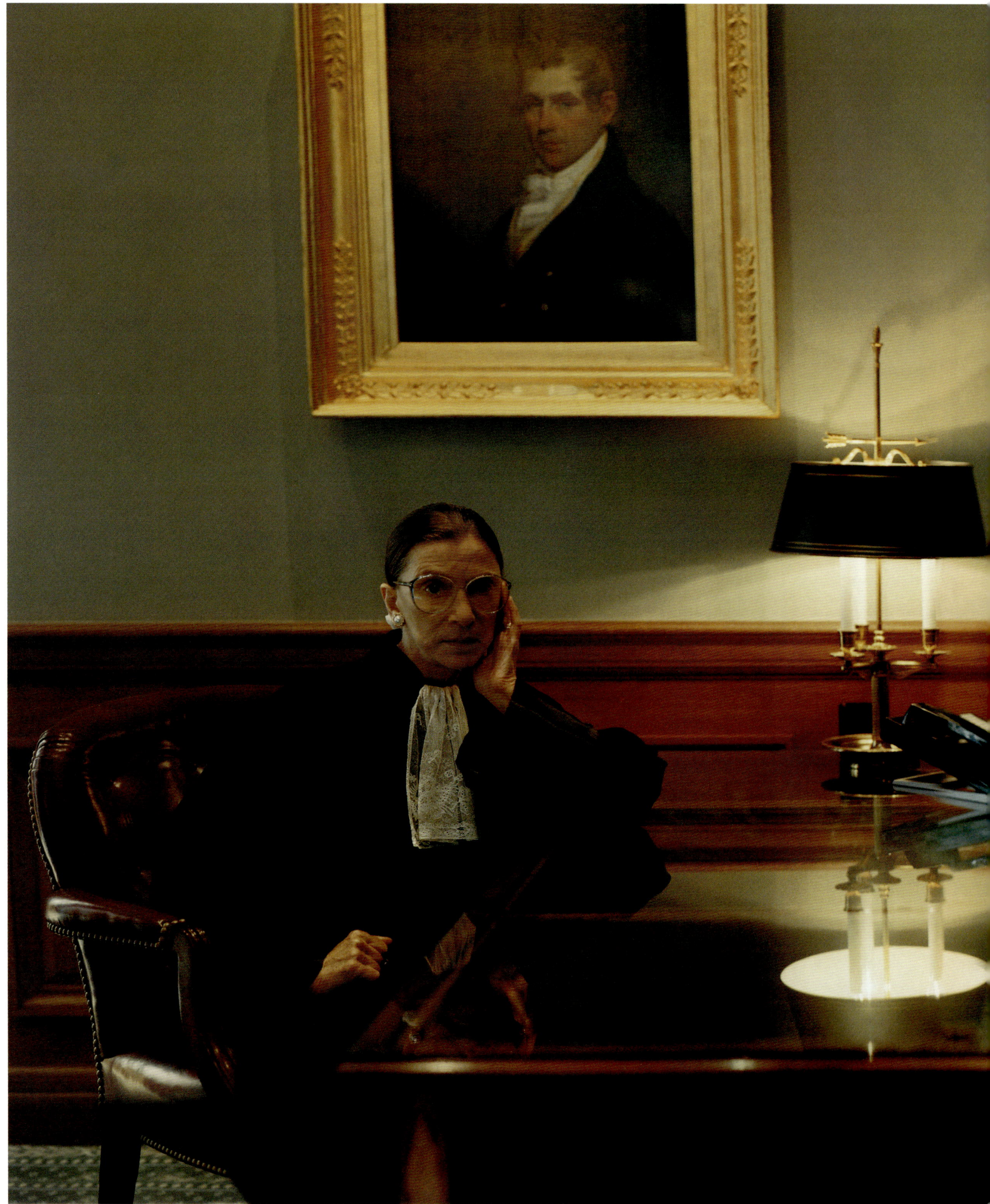

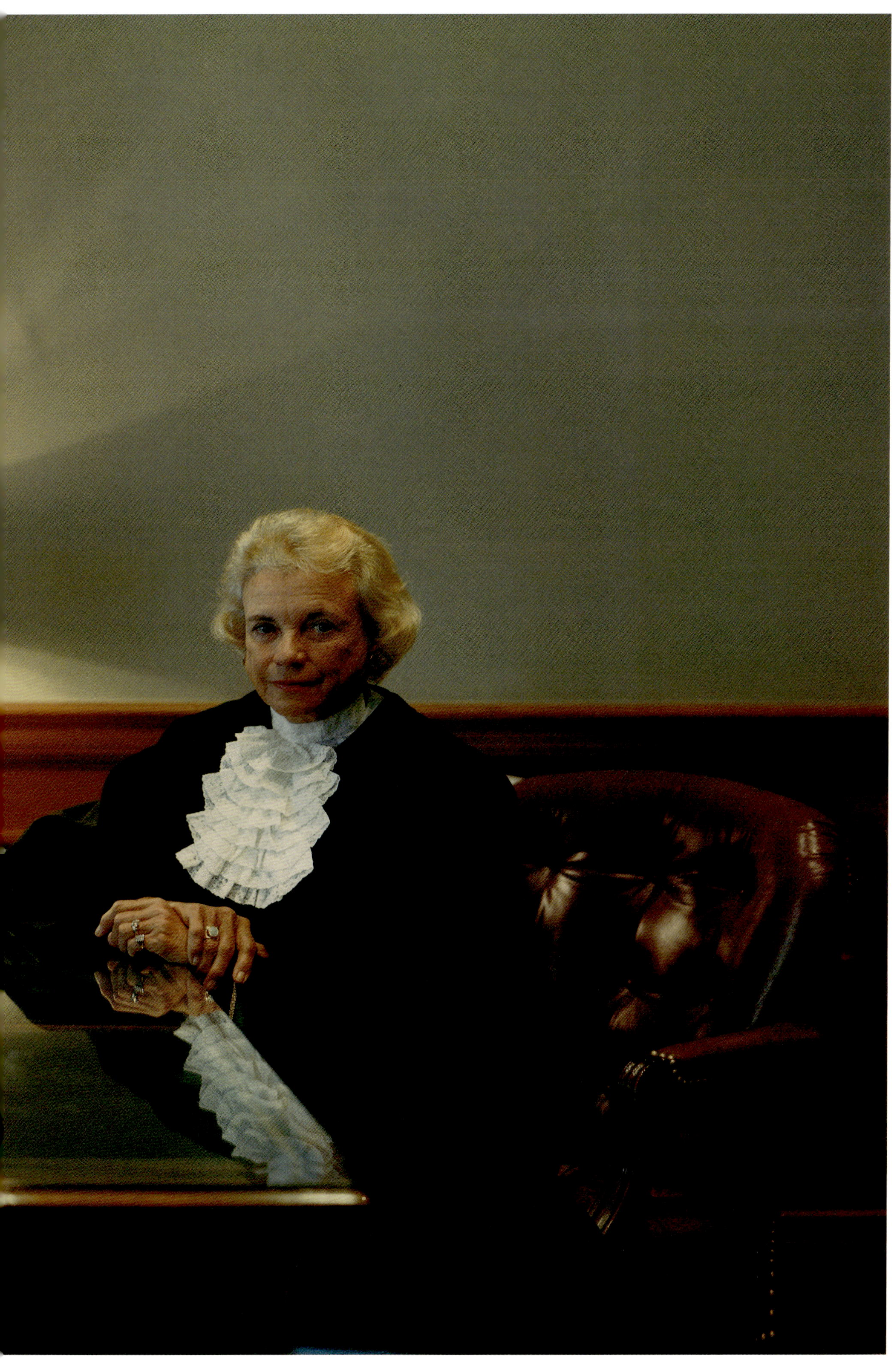

Justices Ruth Bader Ginsburg and
Sandra Day O'Connor, Supreme Court,
Washington, DC, 1997

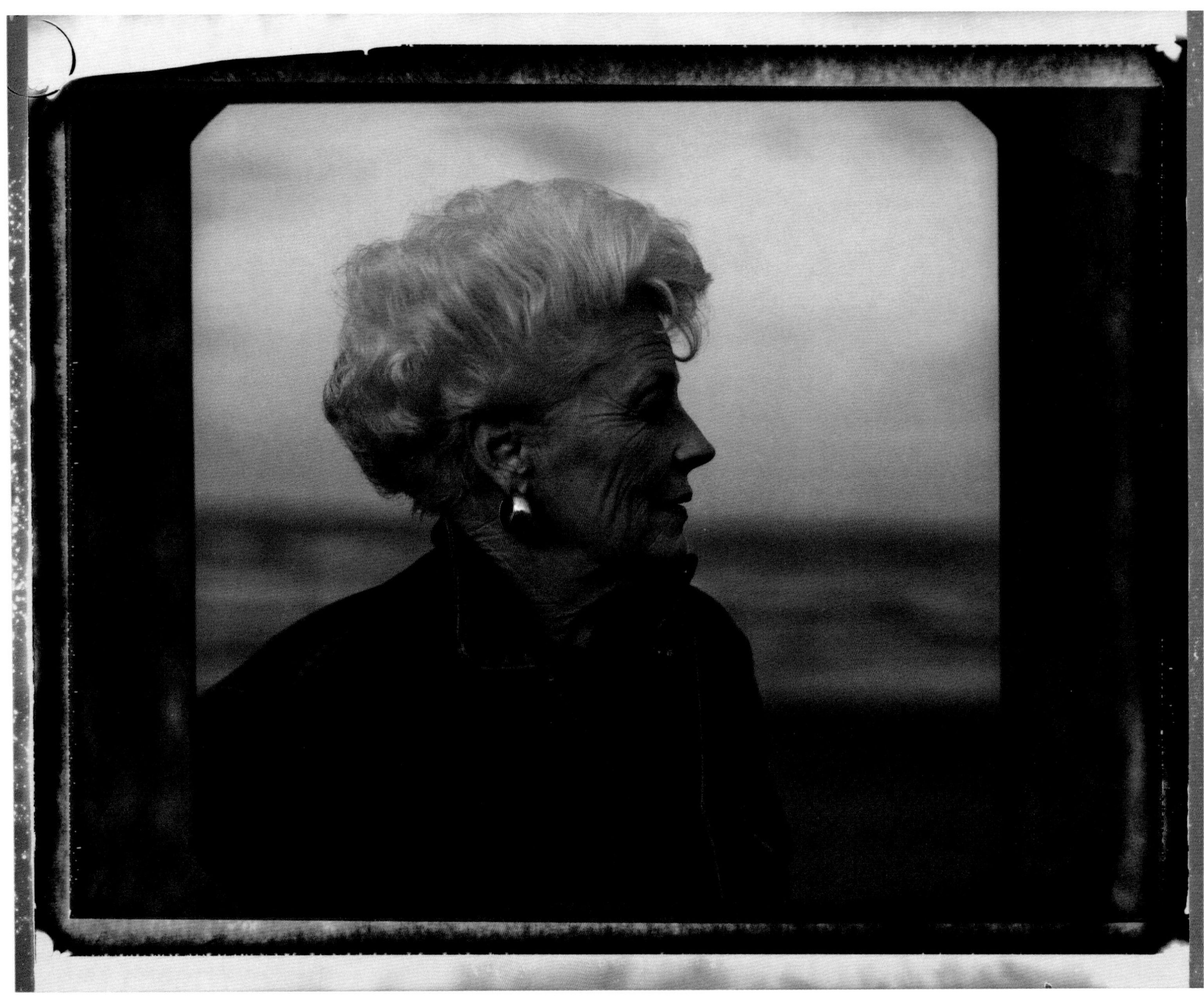

Barbara Jordan's voice, as many of her admirers noted, was like the voice of God. Deep, resonant, mellifluous, authoritative. The daughter of a poor Baptist minister, she was a gifted orator, melding the cadences of a down-home preacher with the elegant articulation and witty arguments of a lawyer trained at Boston University's School of Law. She was the first African American woman elected to Congress from a Southern state. That state was Texas, where she had shaped a political career in the wake of the 1965 Voting Rights Act. Her voice was first heard on a national level when she made an impassioned defense of the Constitution during the House Judiciary Committee's hearings on the impeachment of Richard Nixon. The arc of her career was directed toward fulfilling the promise of the civil rights movement. She retired from Congress in 1979 but continued to teach ethics at the University of Texas in spite of being wheelchair-bound with multiple sclerosis. "She forever redefined what it meant to be a Texan in the eyes of this nation," Ann Richards said in a eulogy at Jordan's funeral in 1996. The two women had been close friends for years. Richards was the flamboyant, irreverent, progressive governor of Texas from 1991 to 1995.

Ann Richards,
Honey Grove,
Texas, 1992

Barbara Jordan,
Austin, Texas, 1989

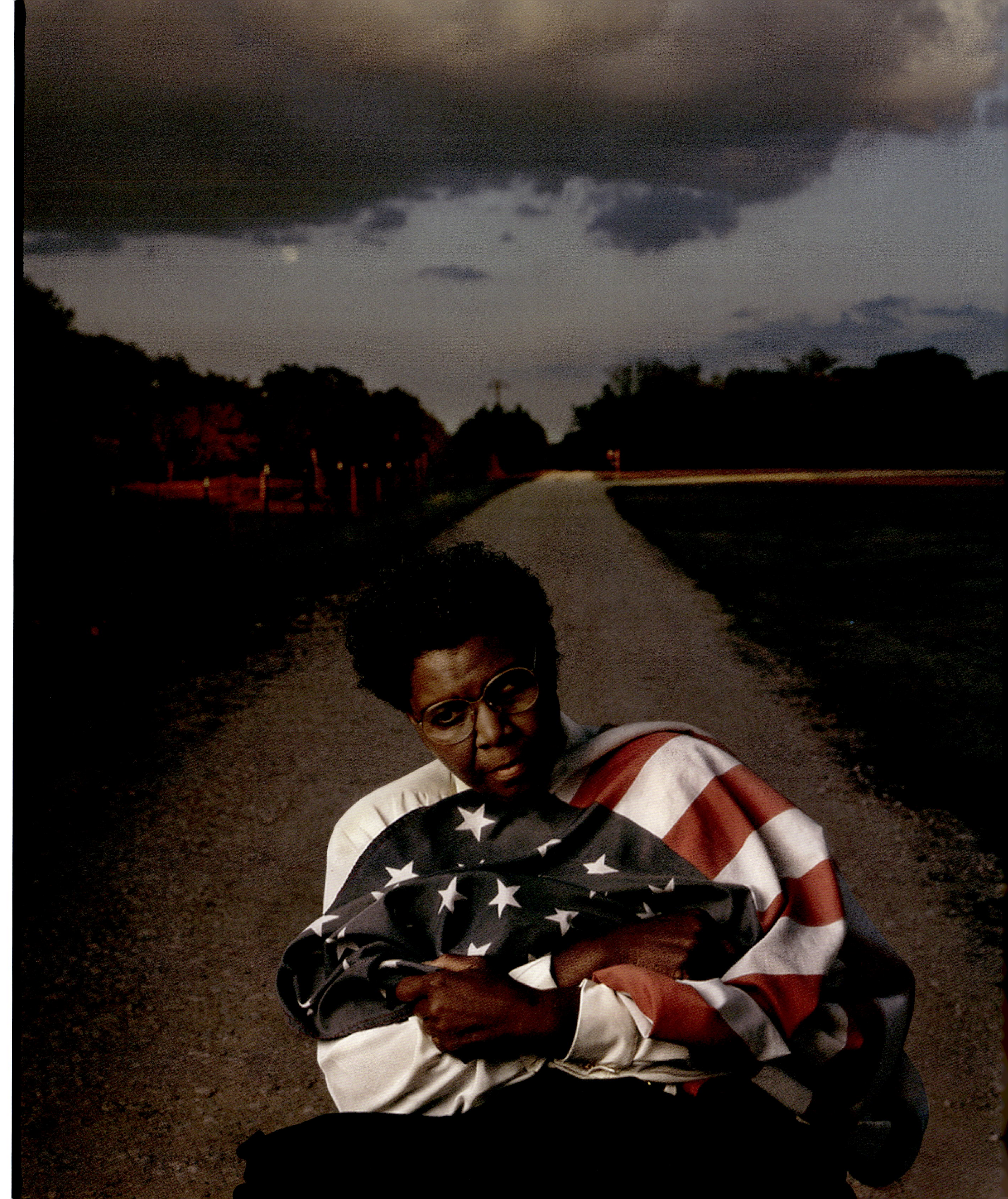

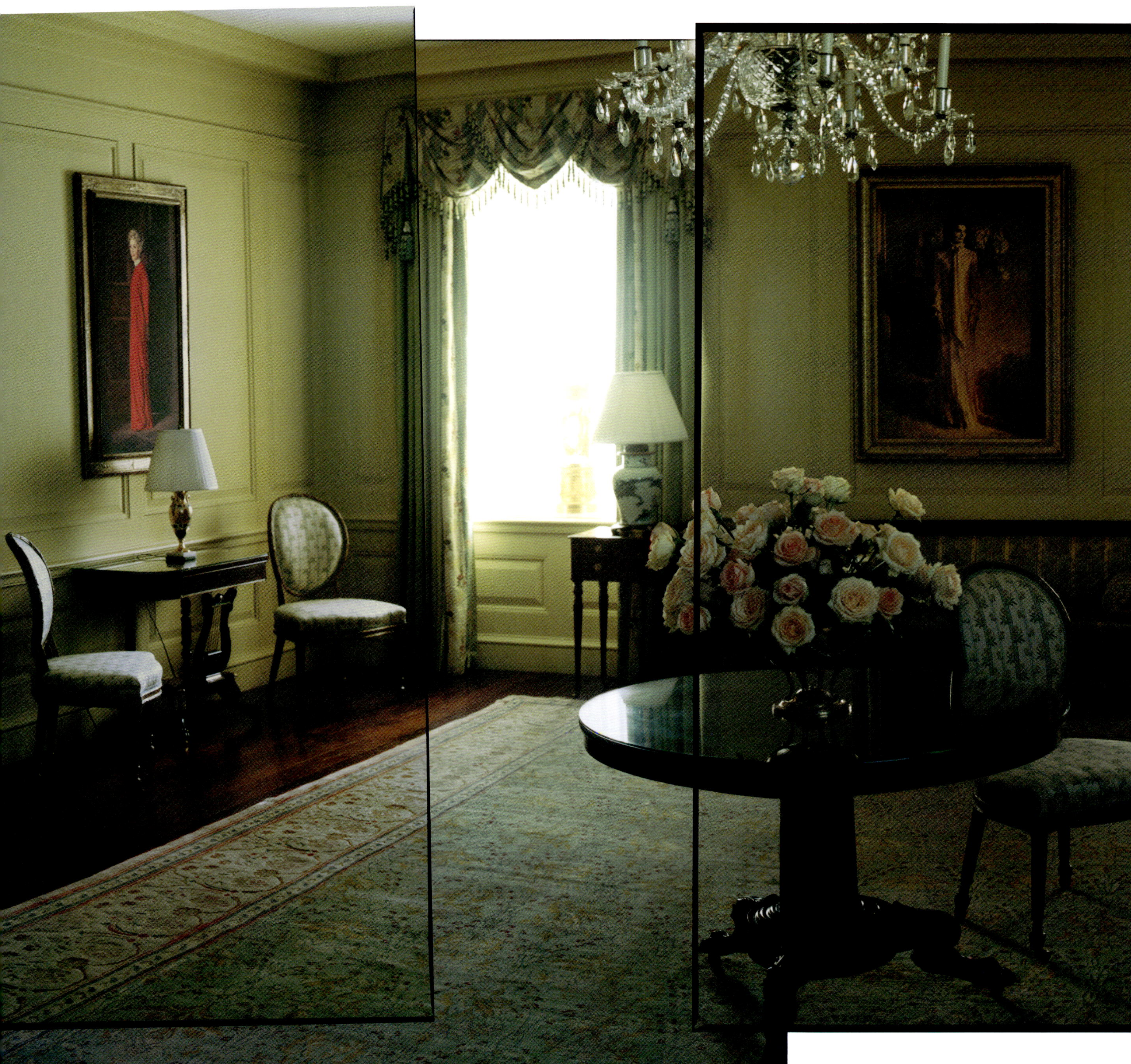

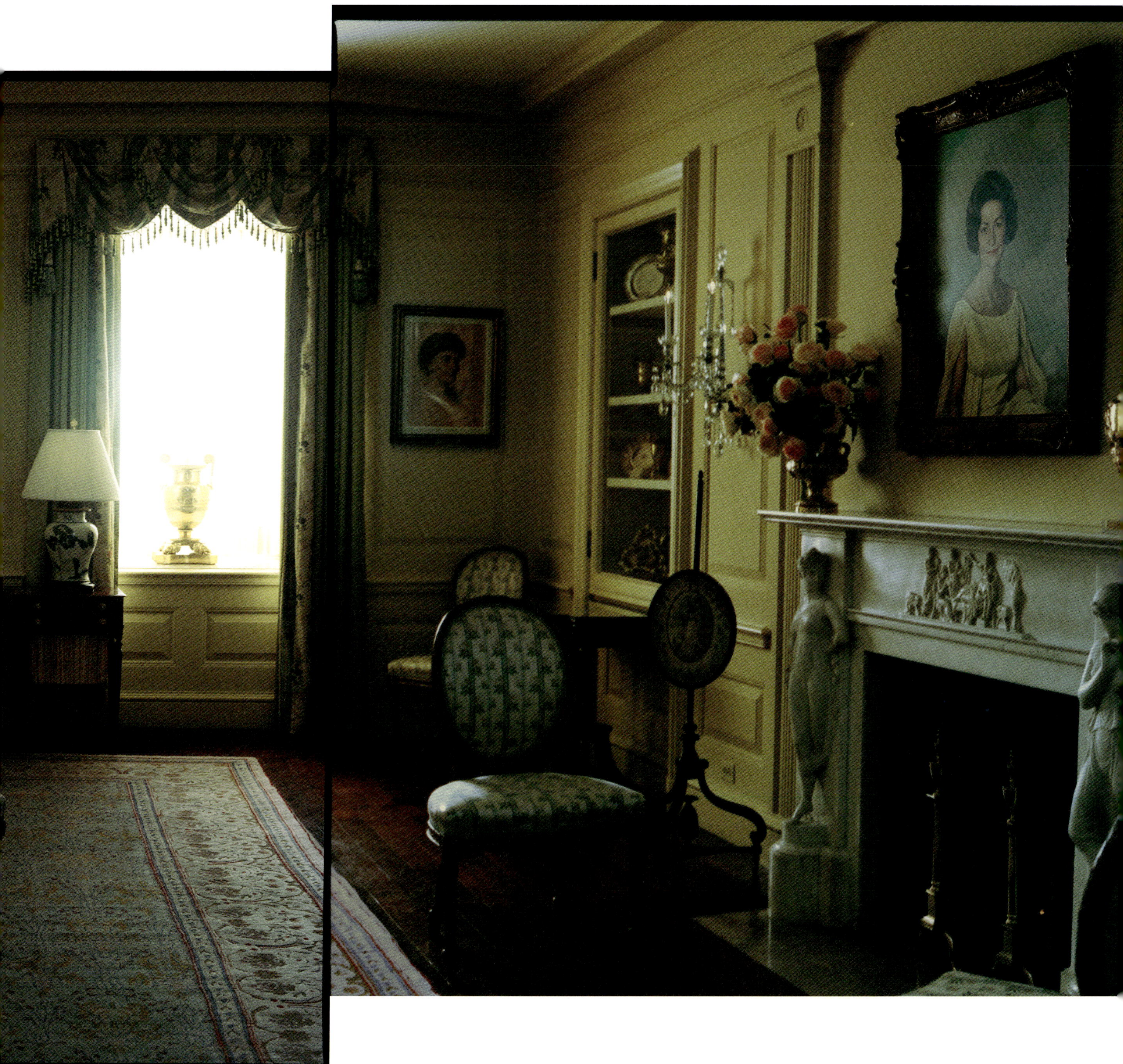

The Vermeil Room, with portraits of Nancy Reagan, Jacqueline Kennedy, Ellen Wilson, and Lady Bird Johnson, the White House, Washington, DC, 2001

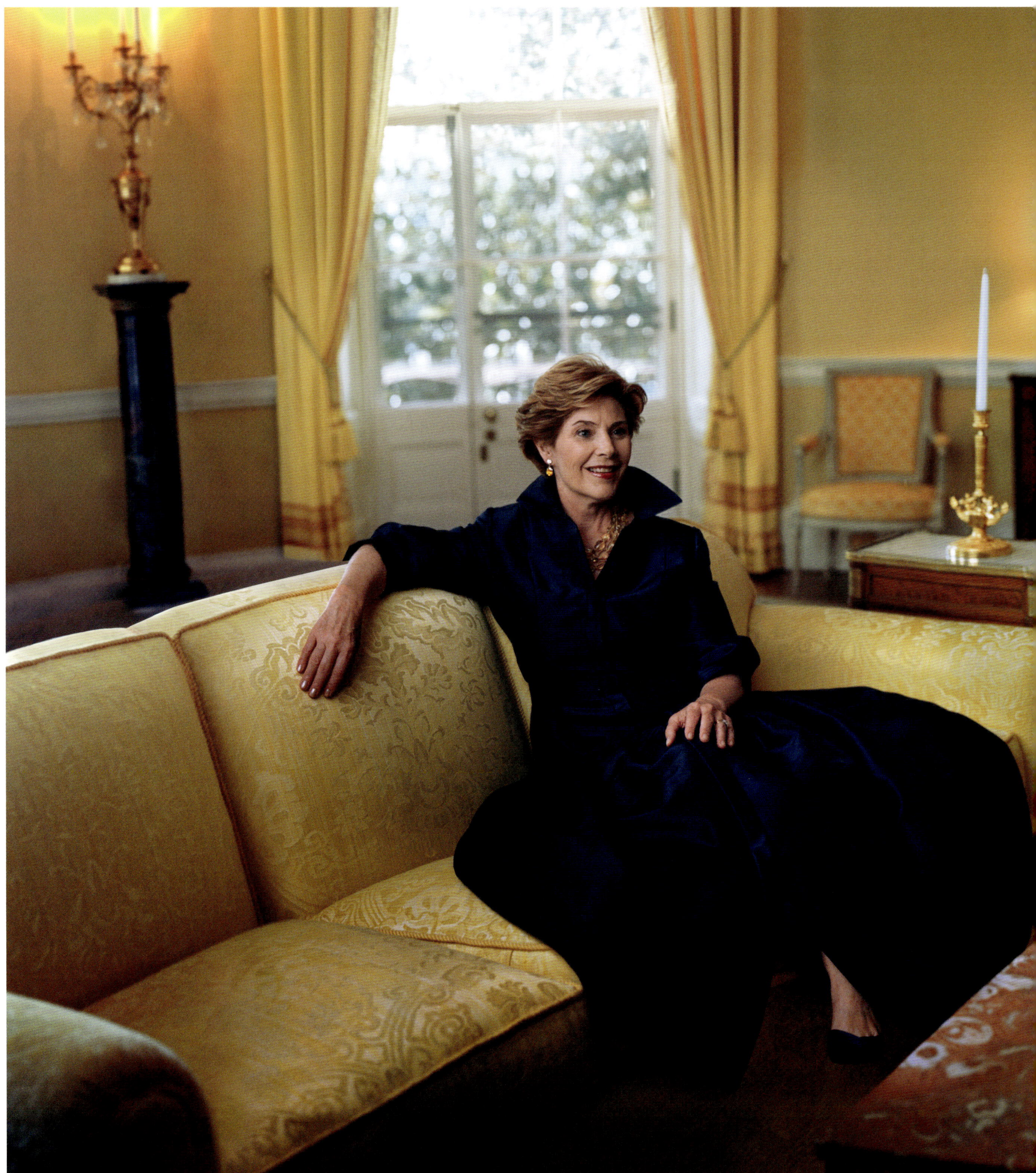

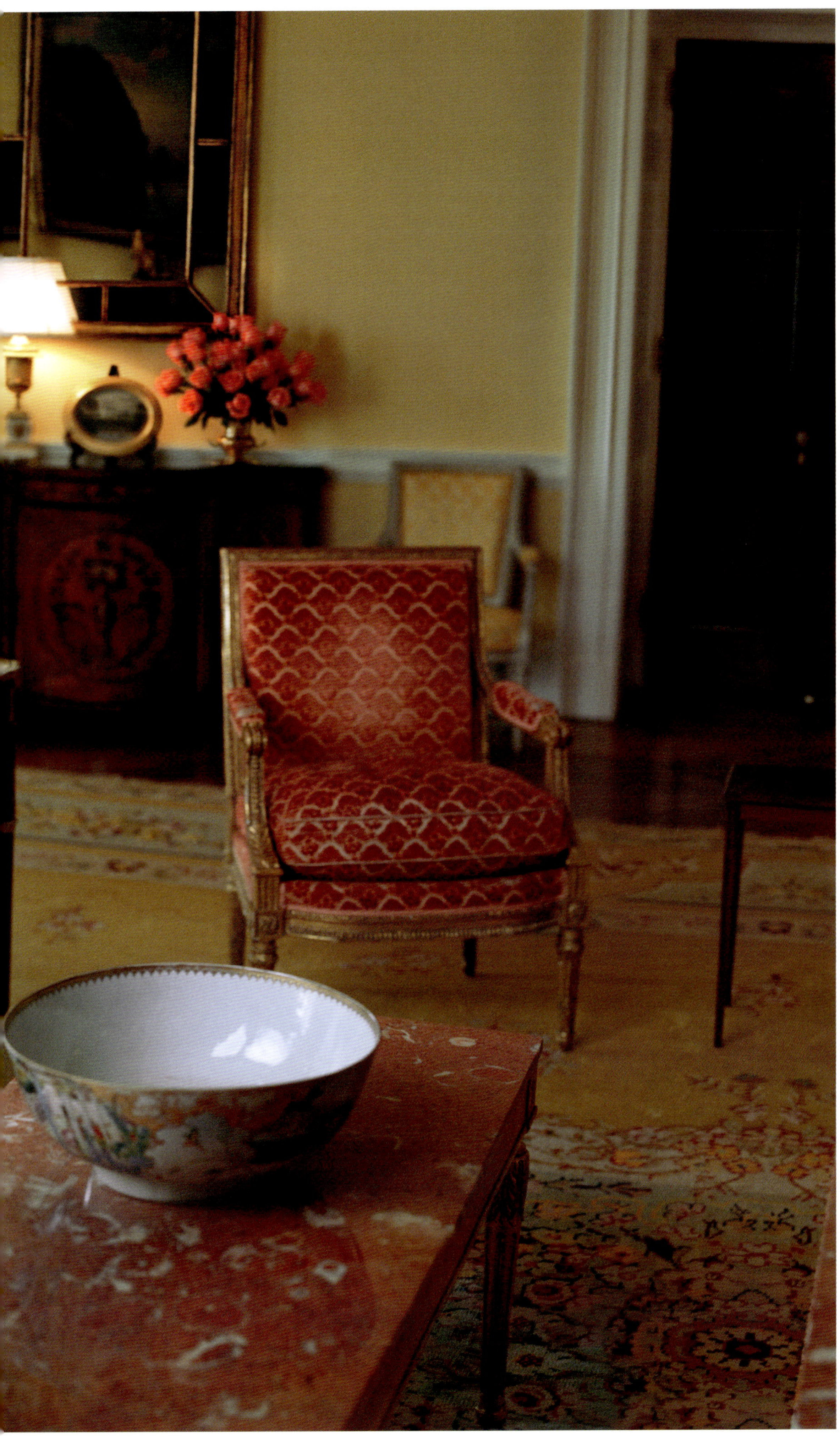

Laura Bush in the private quarters of the White House, Washington, DC, 2004

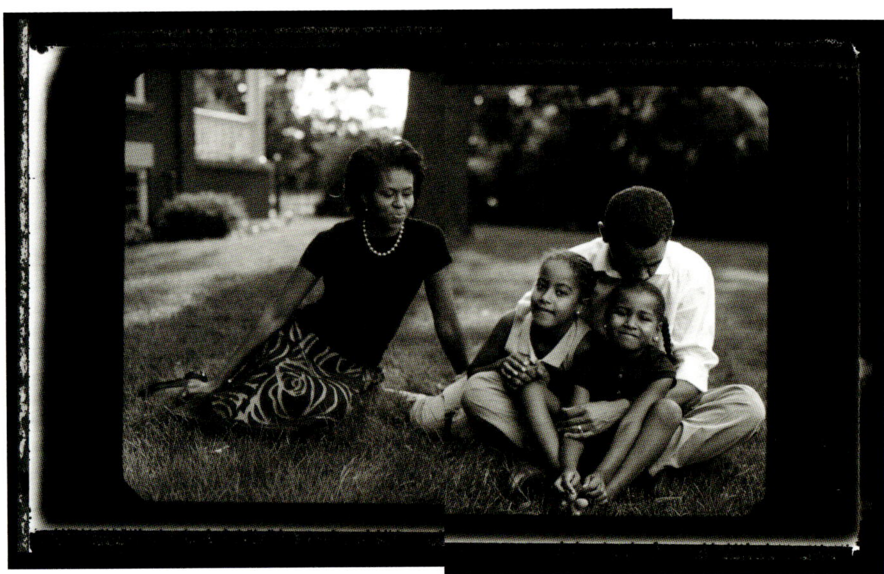

"I first photographed Michelle Obama in 2004, when her husband was running for the Senate. I met her and her children at his campaign headquarters. Three years later, when I made a formal portrait, he was about to be elected president. We couldn't imagine then what a significant place she would make for herself in the national psyche. She was a working woman who would become a very modern First Lady—stylish, pragmatic, engaged."

Michelle and Barack Obama with their daughters, Malia and Sasha, in the backyard of their house in Hyde Park, Chicago, 2006

Michelle Obama, Chicago, 2007

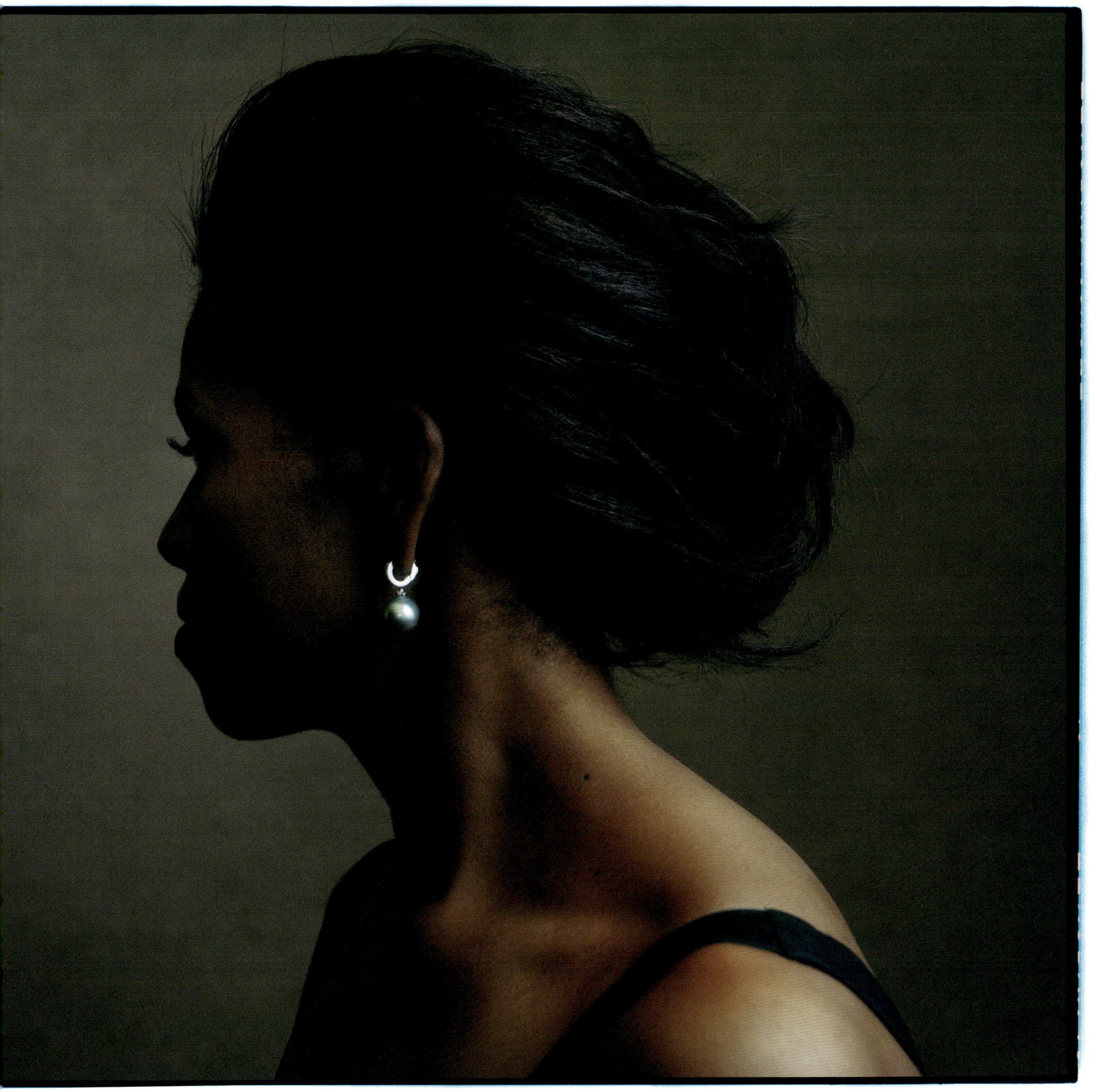

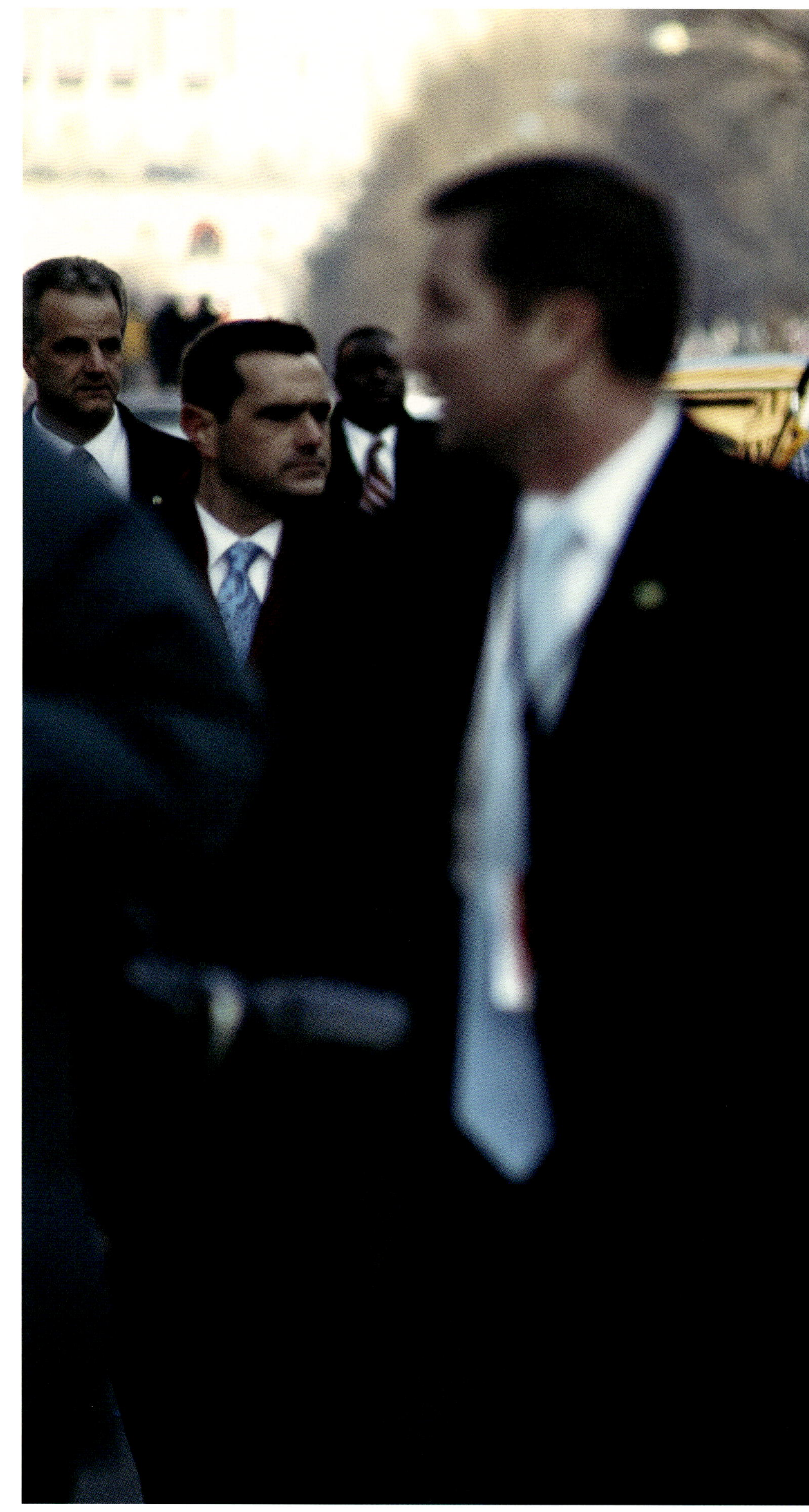

Barack and Michelle Obama, Inauguration Day, Washington, DC, January 20, 2009

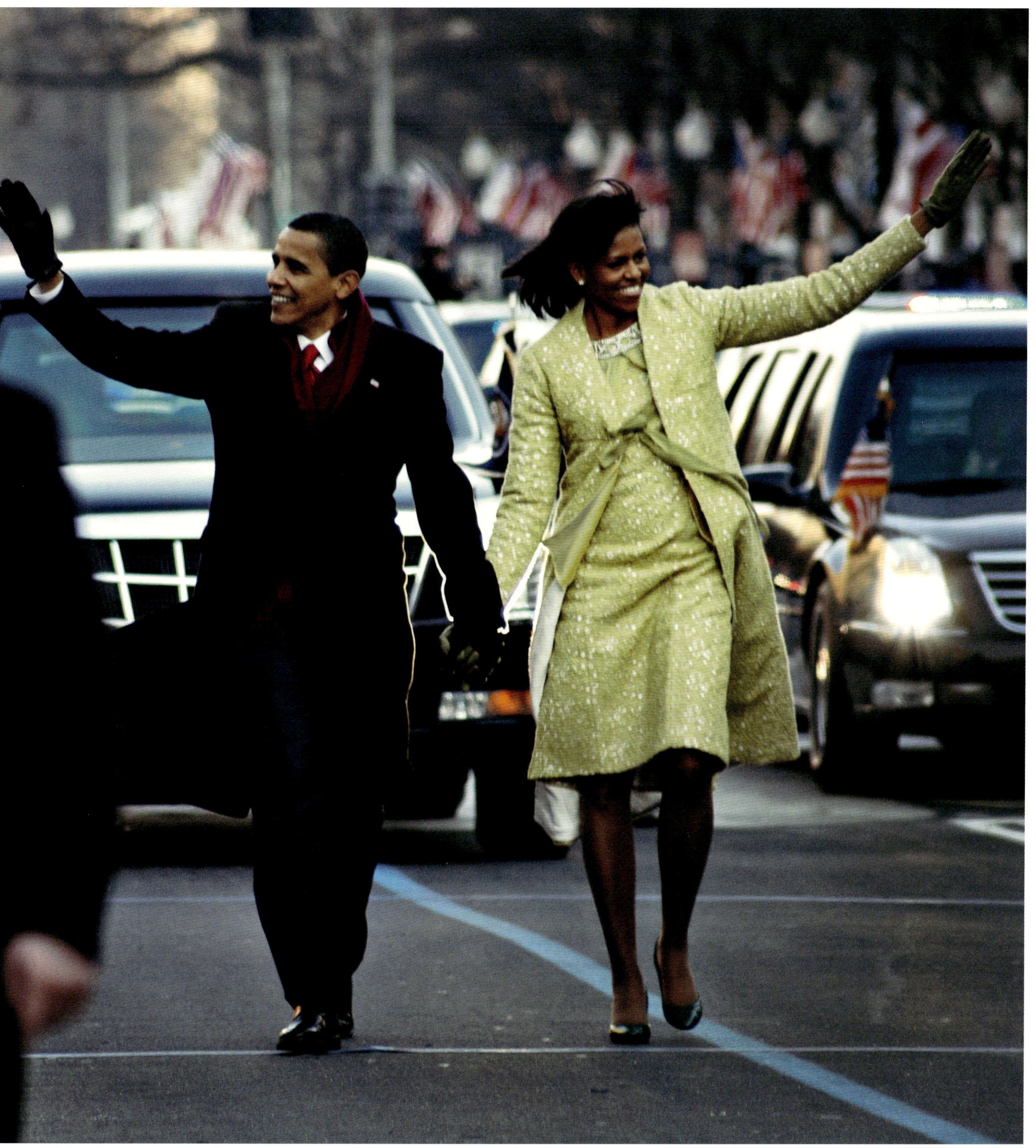

"The Obamas stayed at the Hay-Adams Hotel in the days leading up to the inauguration in January 2009. You could see the White House out the window. We did a cover shoot for *Vogue* there. The second *Vogue* cover portrait I made of Michele Obama appeared at the beginning of her husband's second term. The third cover was at the end, when they were leaving."

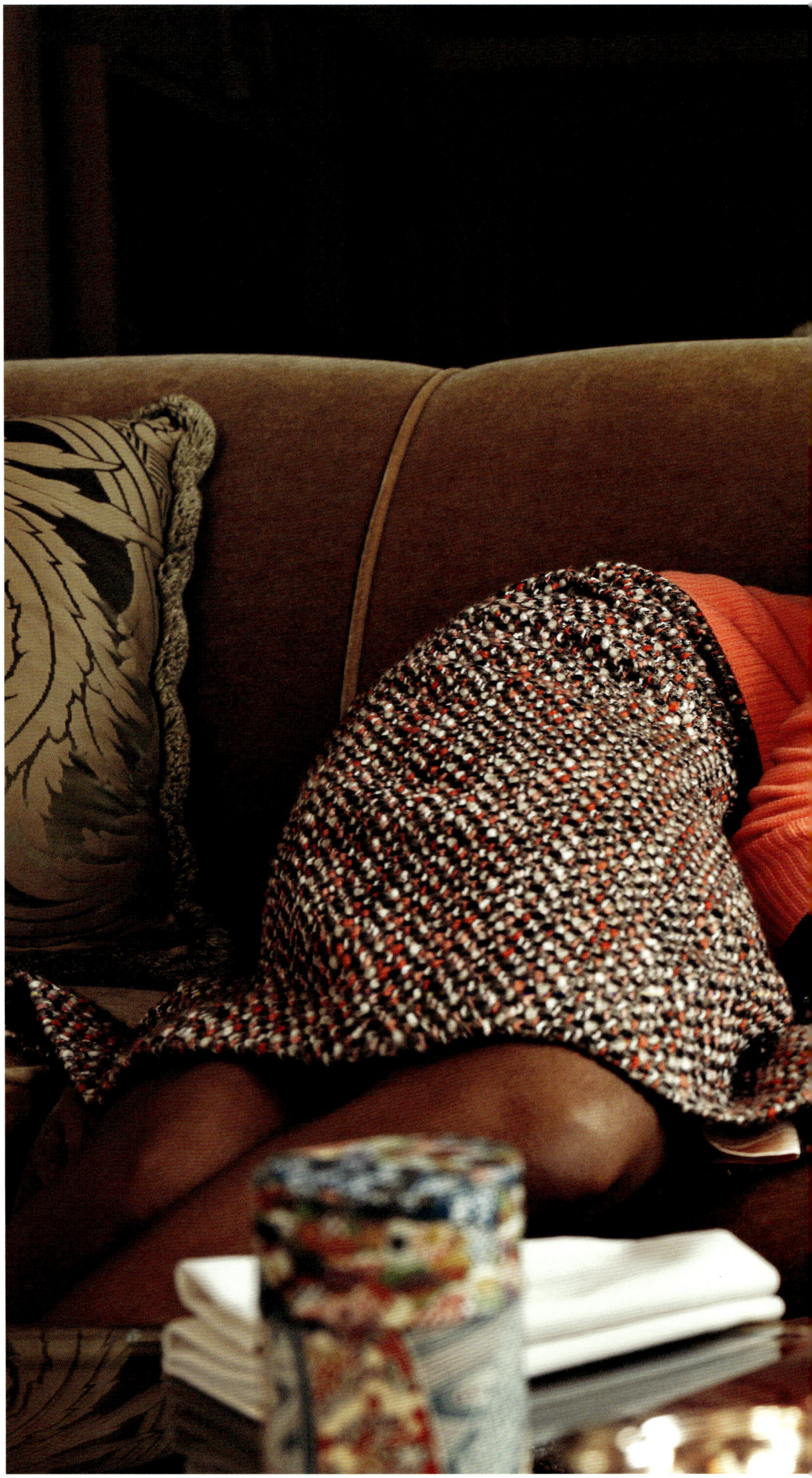

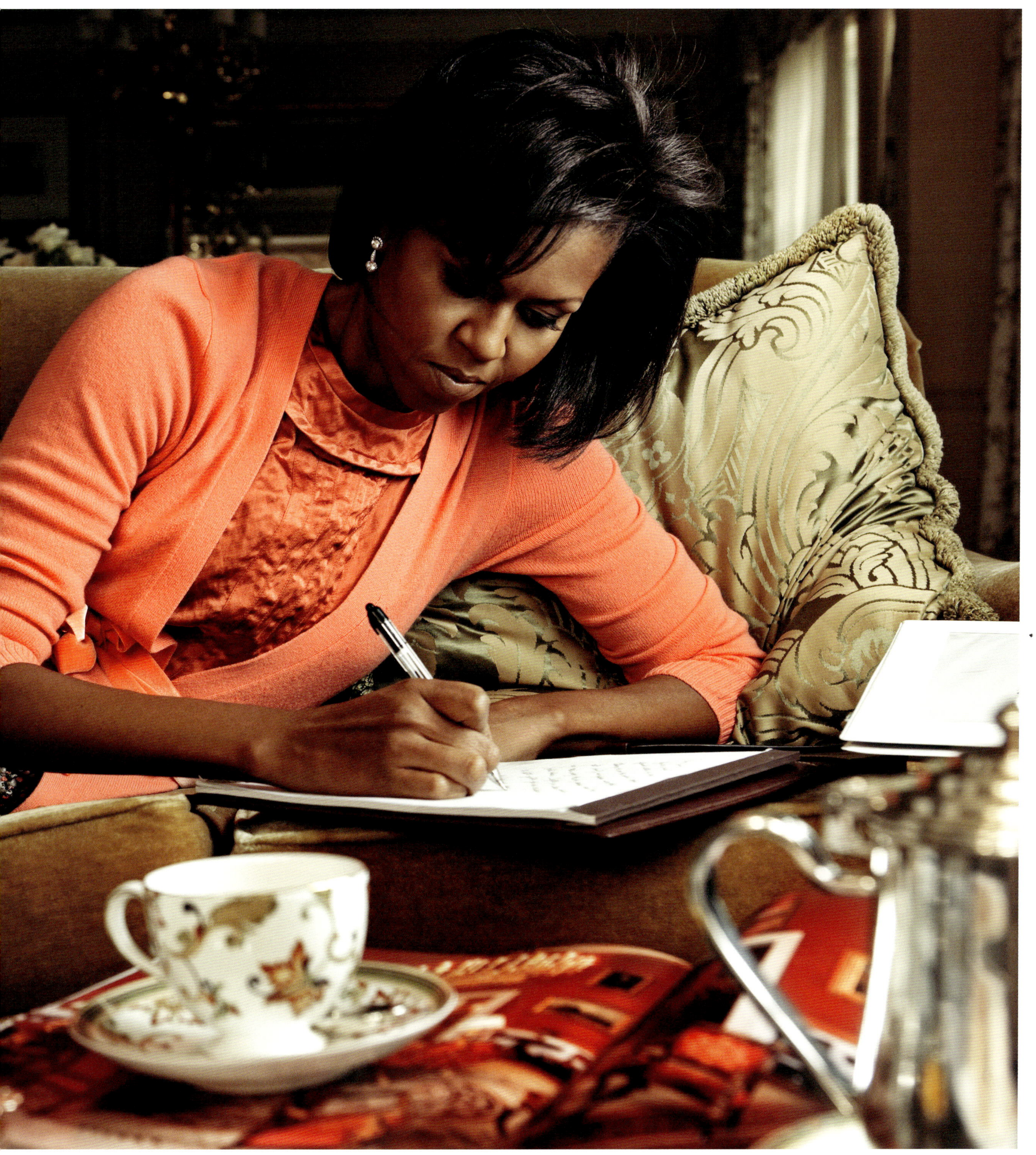

"I was ambivalent about including this portrait of Michelle Obama in the Red Room of the White House in this book. She is the epitome of accessibility and the portrait is formal. On the other hand, she is the first African American First Lady. She took on a historical role that the portrait refers to implicitly. She did it graciously and with elegance."

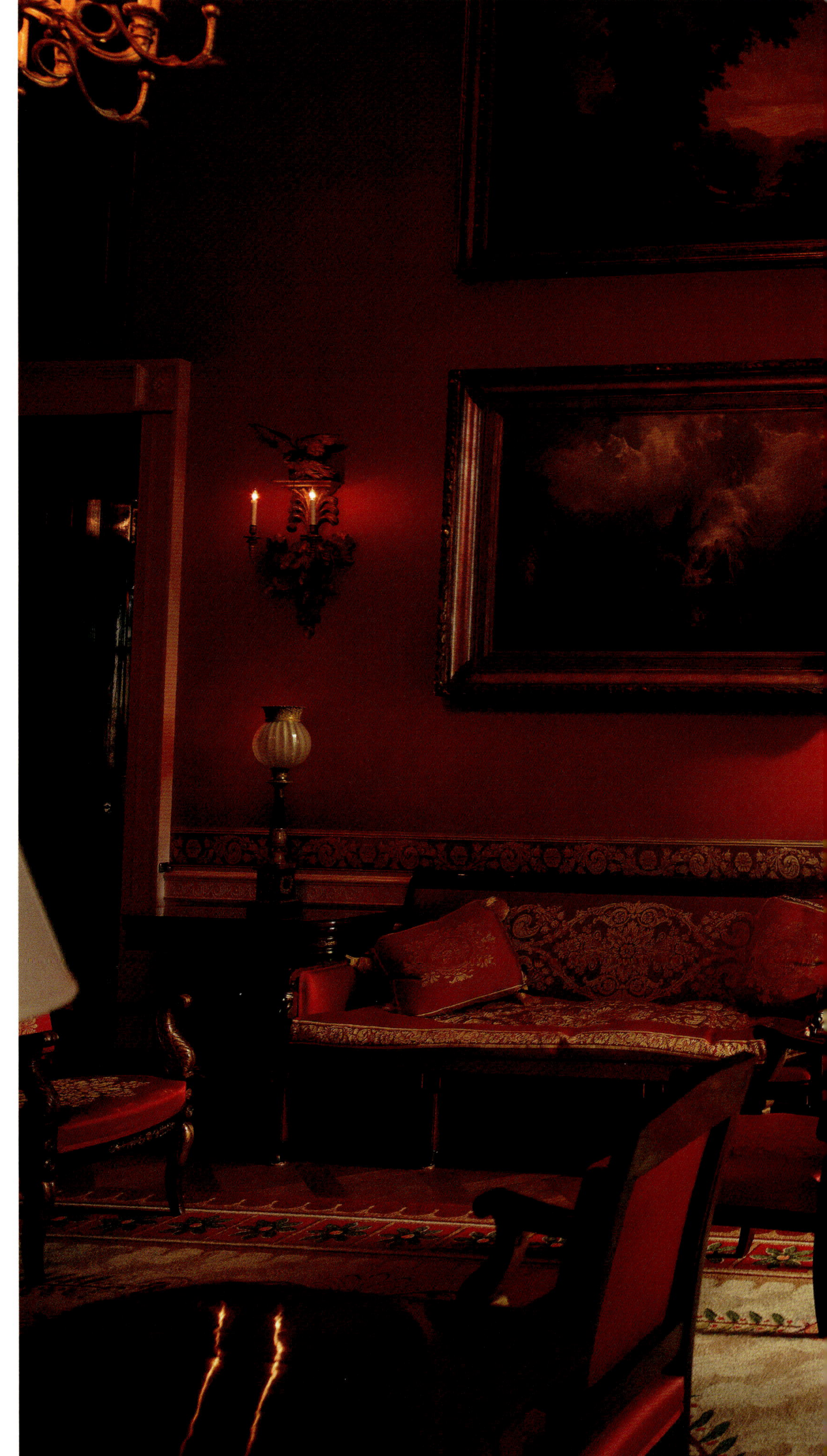

Michelle Obama, the Red Room of the White House, 2013

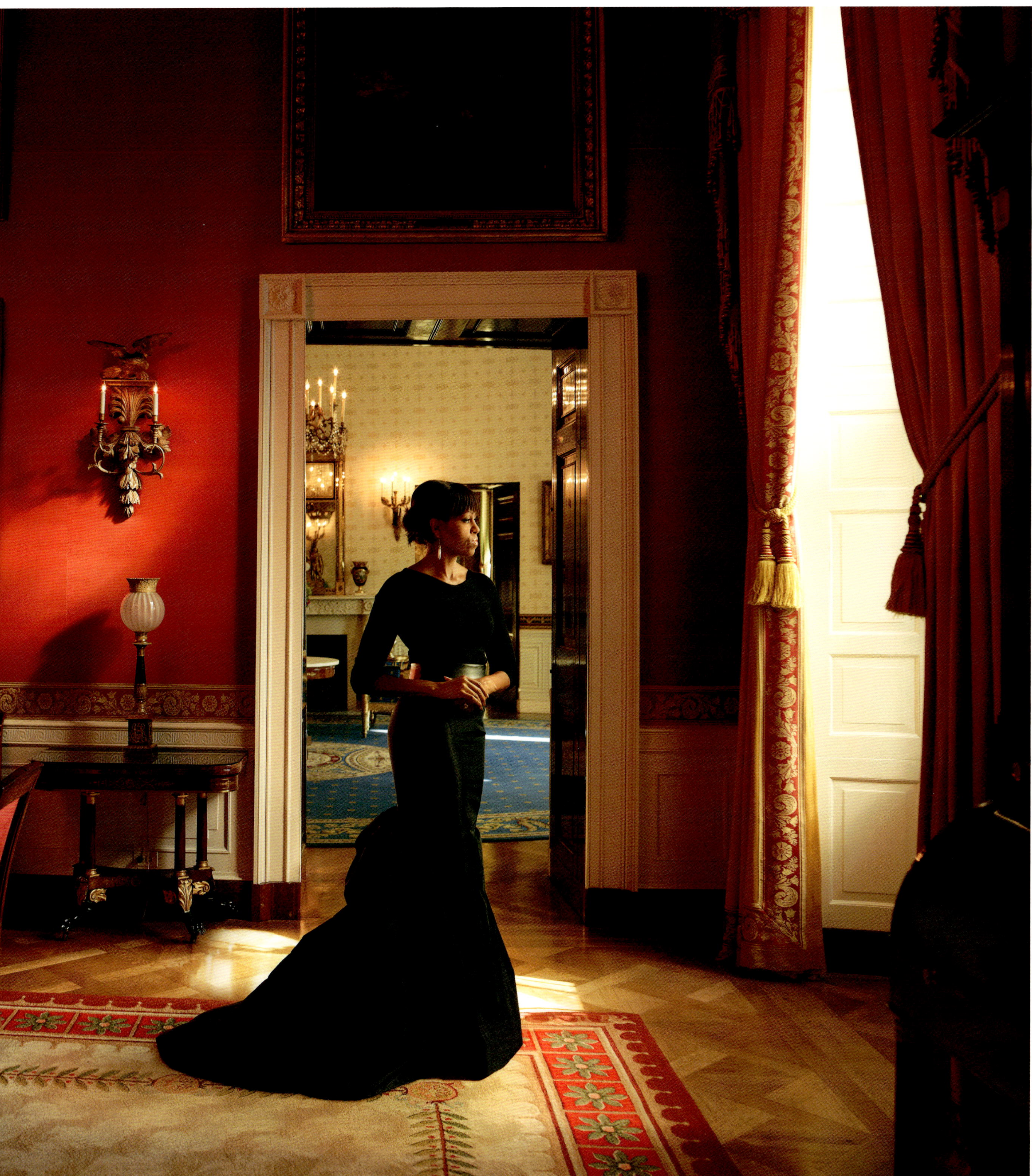

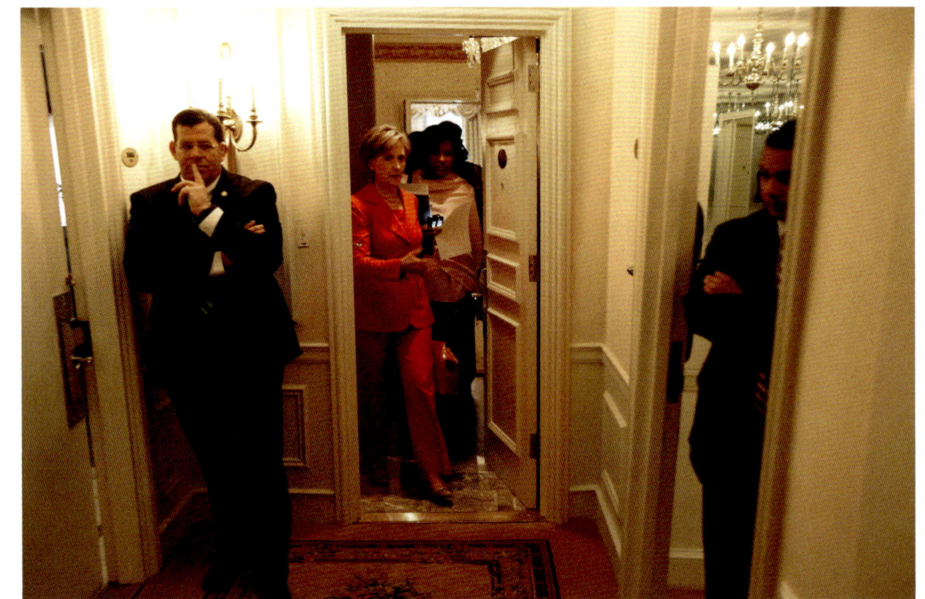
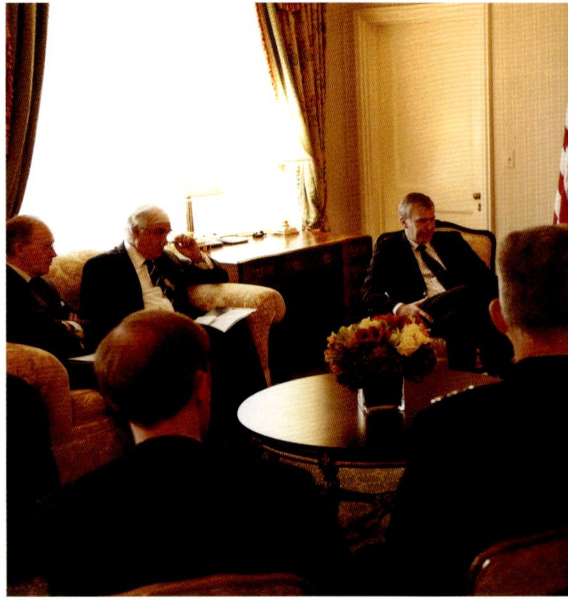
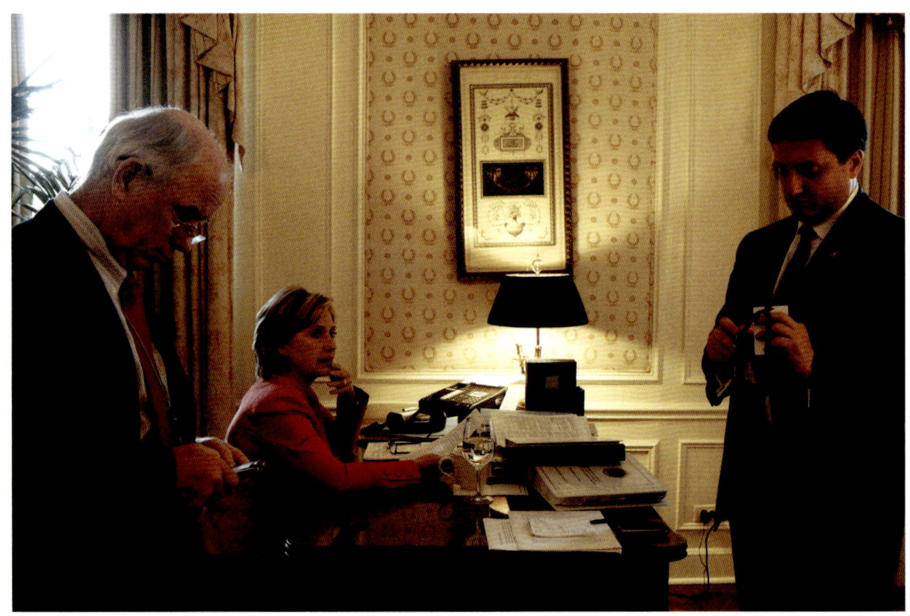
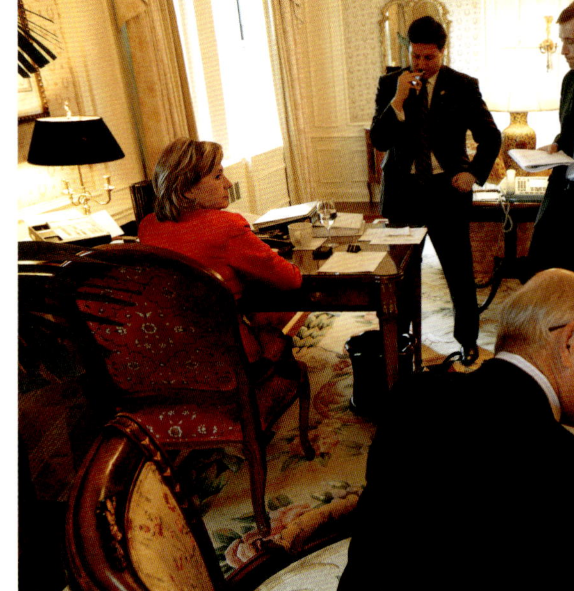
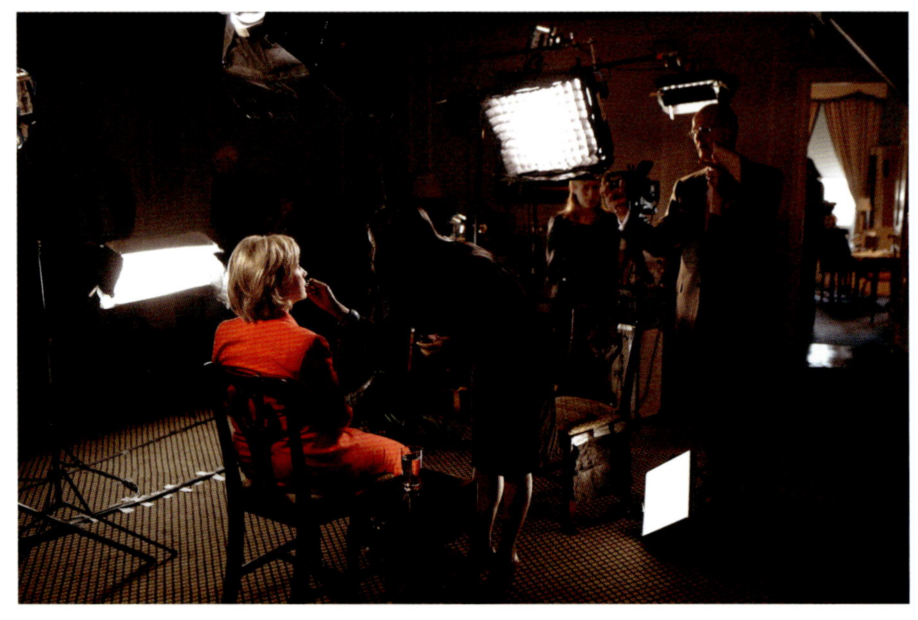
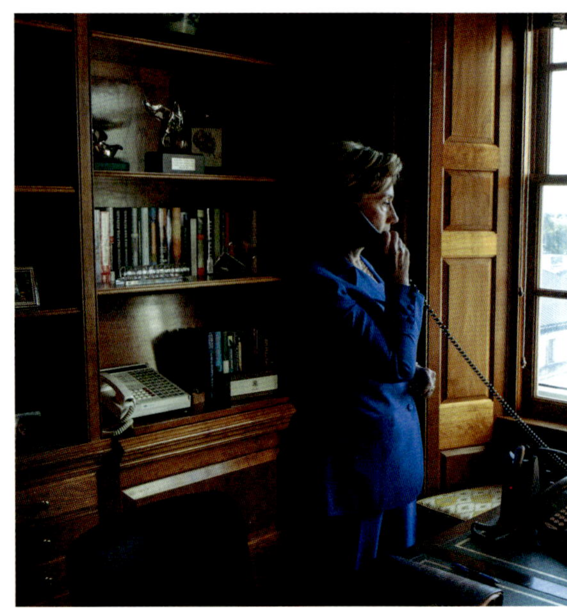

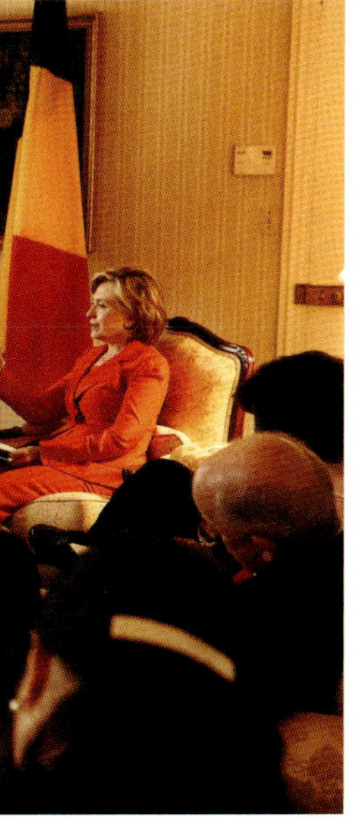

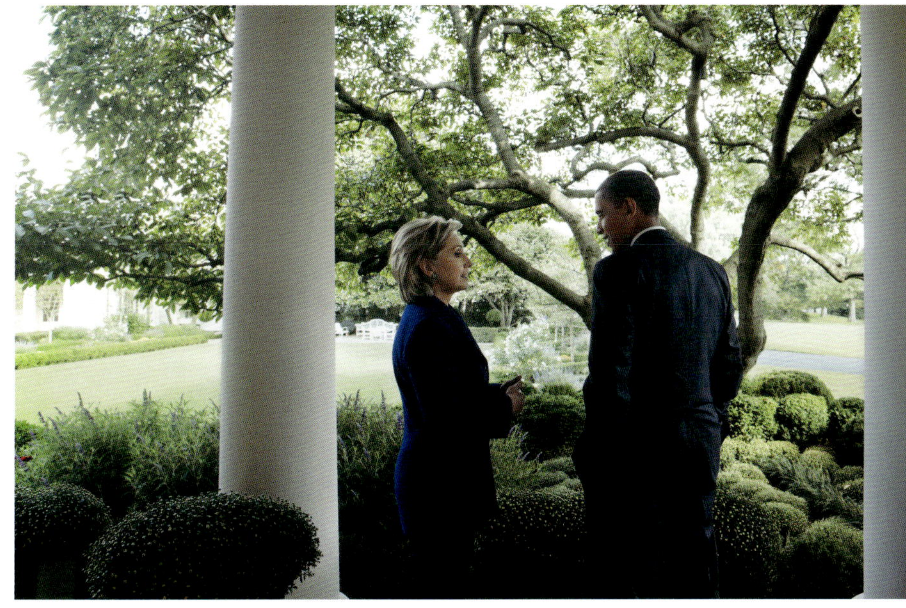

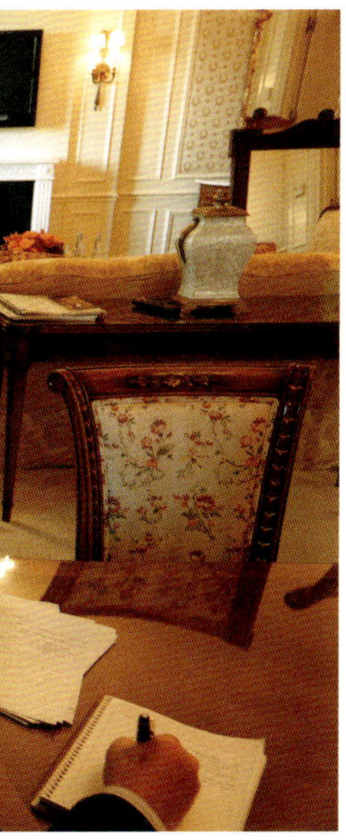

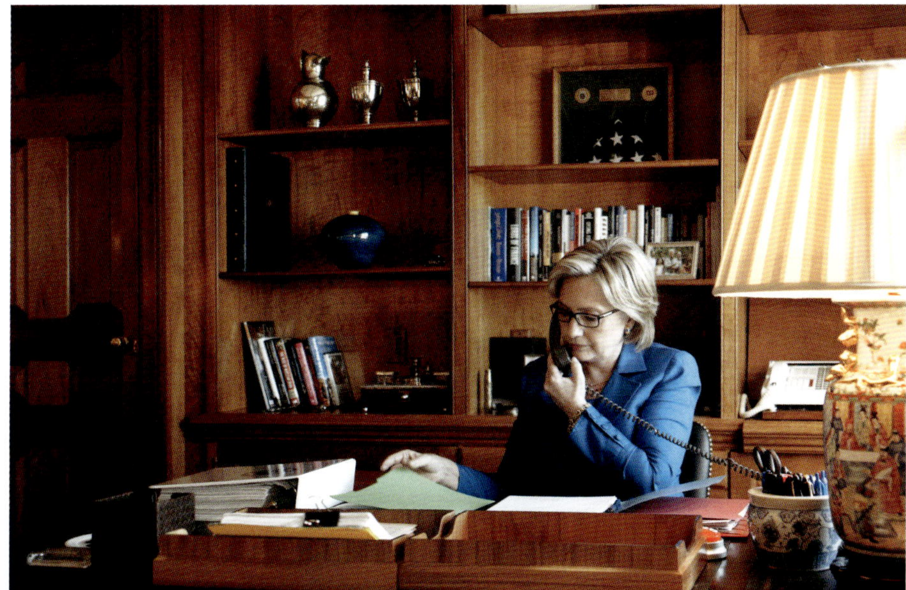

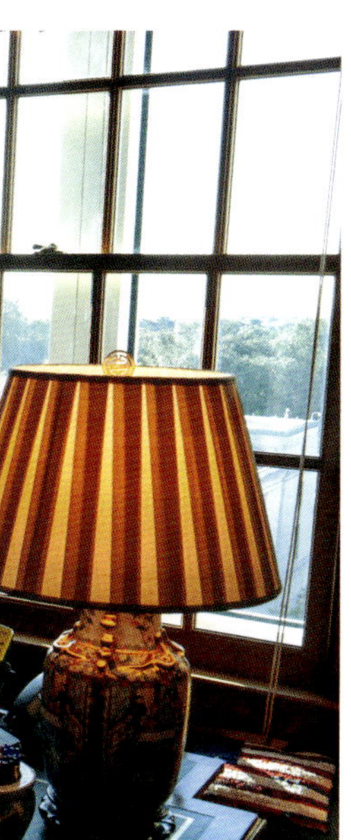

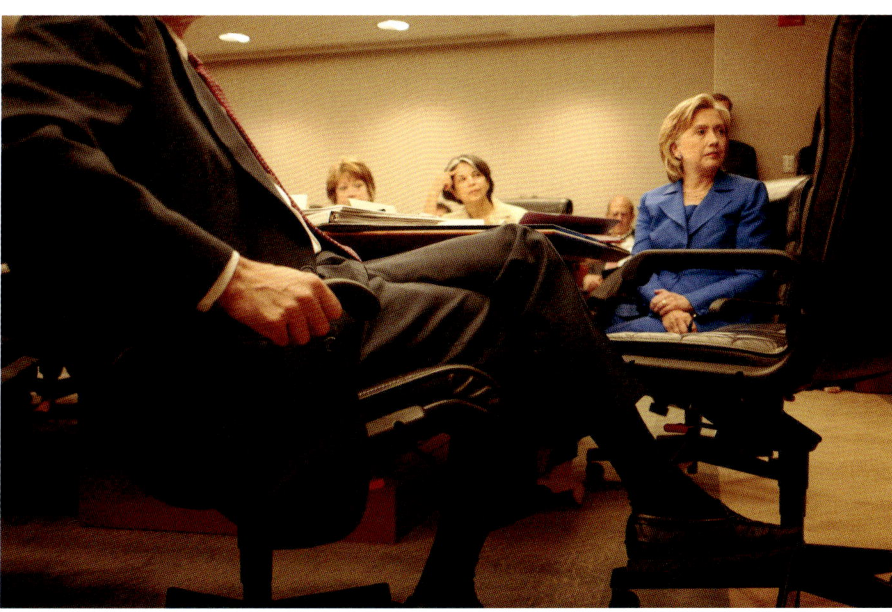

Hillary Clinton was helping to get her husband elected president in 1992, when Annie first photographed her. Annie was also with her in Africa when she was First Lady and again on the night she was elected a US senator from New York.

In 2009, after Barack Obama persuaded Hillary to be his Secretary of State, Annie followed her as she attended meetings in Washington, DC and in New York during the annual session of the United Nations General Assembly, much of which unfolded in the suites and ballrooms of the Waldorf-Astoria hotel on Park Avenue.

Hillary was the first former First Lady to be a member of the cabinet. She traveled to more countries than any other Secretary of State, covering almost a million air miles. Her philosophy was that face-to-face meetings between people was the best way to make connections. Being there was crucial.

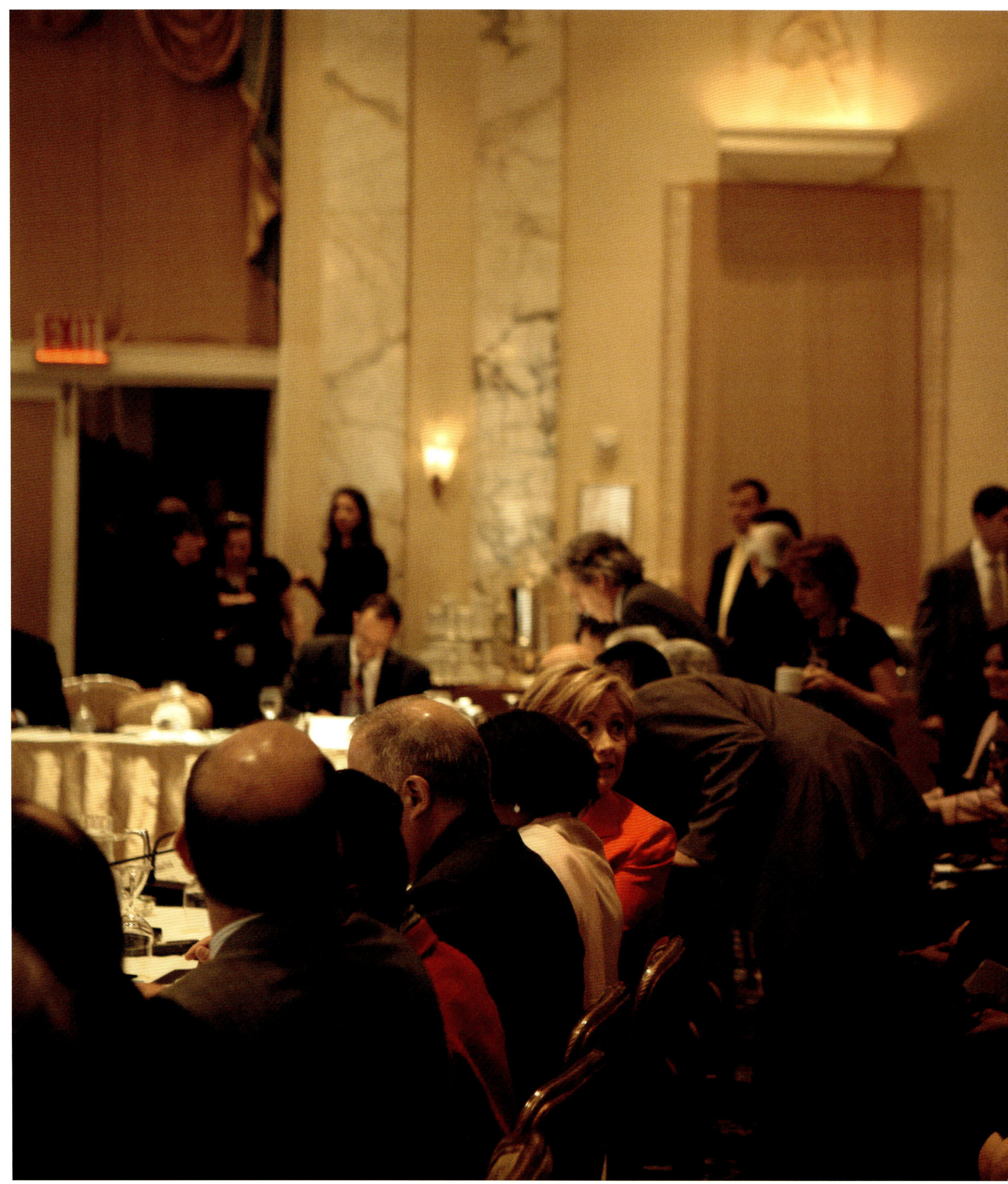
EXIT

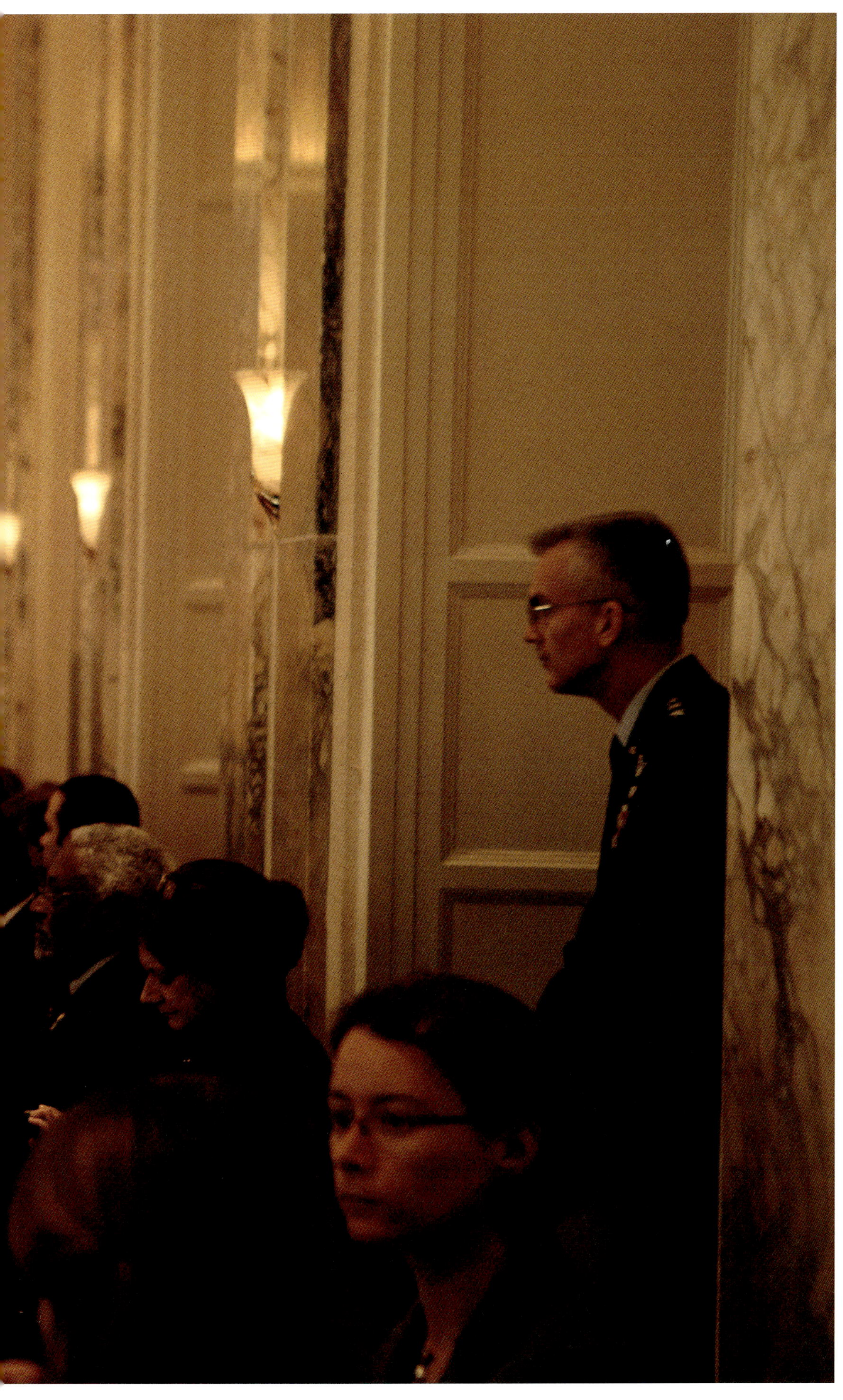

Hillary Clinton at the sixty-fourth session of the United Nations General Assembly, Waldorf Astoria hotel, New York City, 2009

“Sometimes you just can’t make it up. I photographed Donald Trump several times over the years. Phyllis Posnick was the editor on the sitting with Melania. Phyllis had worked a lot with Helmut Newton and Irving Penn, and she was always ready for things to go in unanticipated directions. Of all the fashion editors I’ve worked with, she has the best understanding of what goes into a photograph—what a good photograph is. The Trump plane and his Mercedes-Benz gullwing were already at the airport when we got there. We hadn’t planned on him being in the picture, but then he showed up because they were taking the plane back to New York when we finished.”

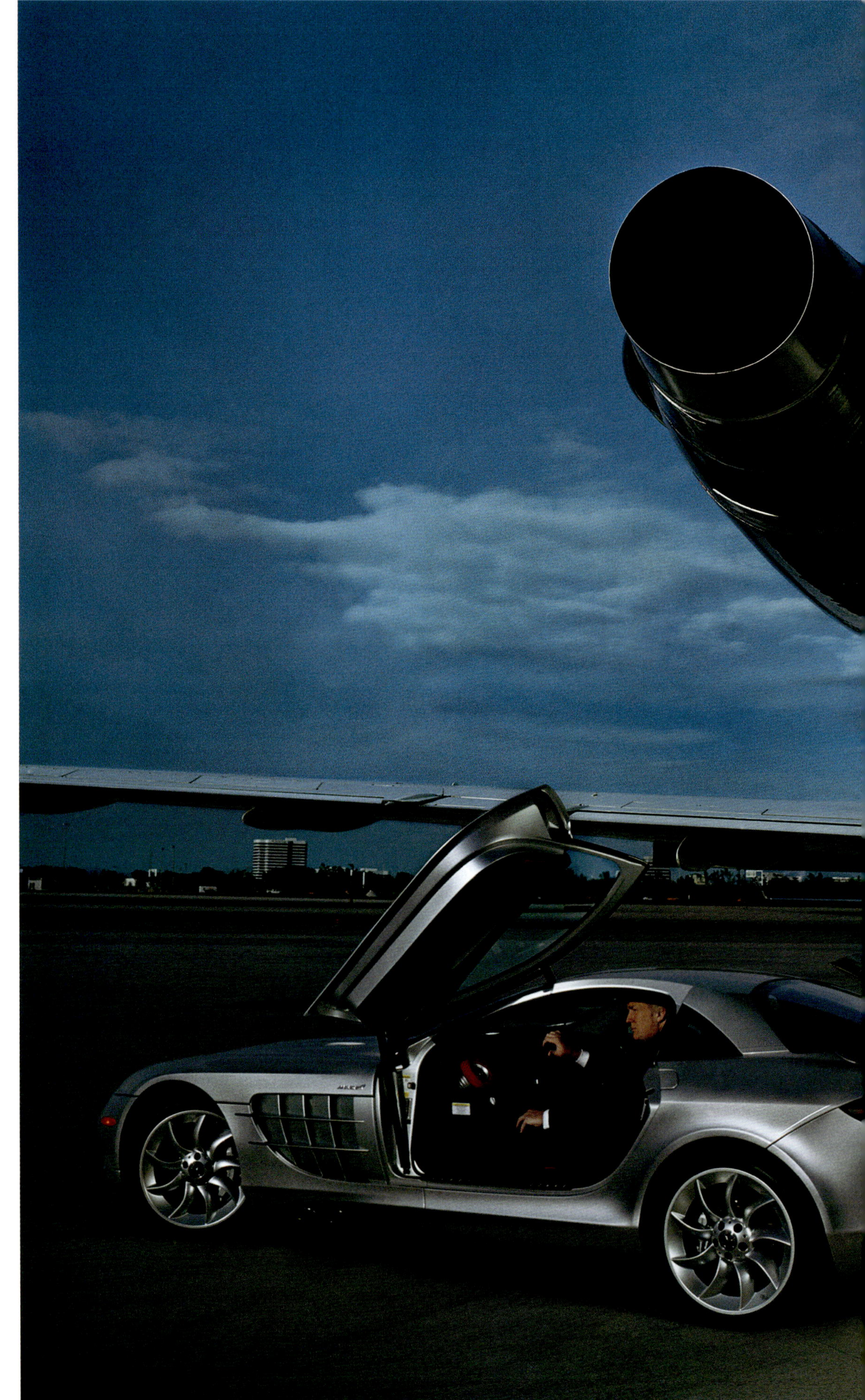

Donald and Melania Trump,
Palm Beach Airport, Florida, 2006

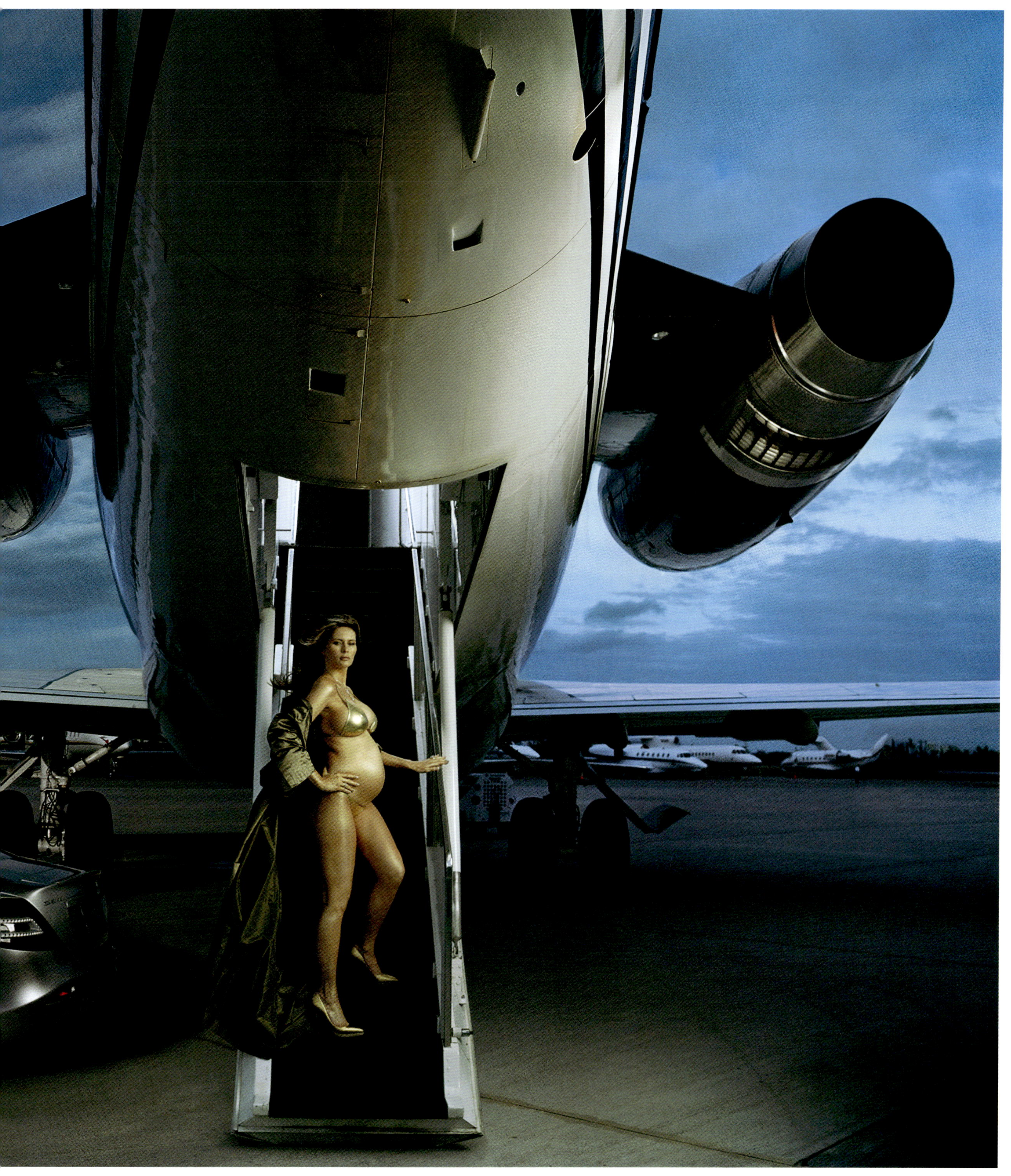

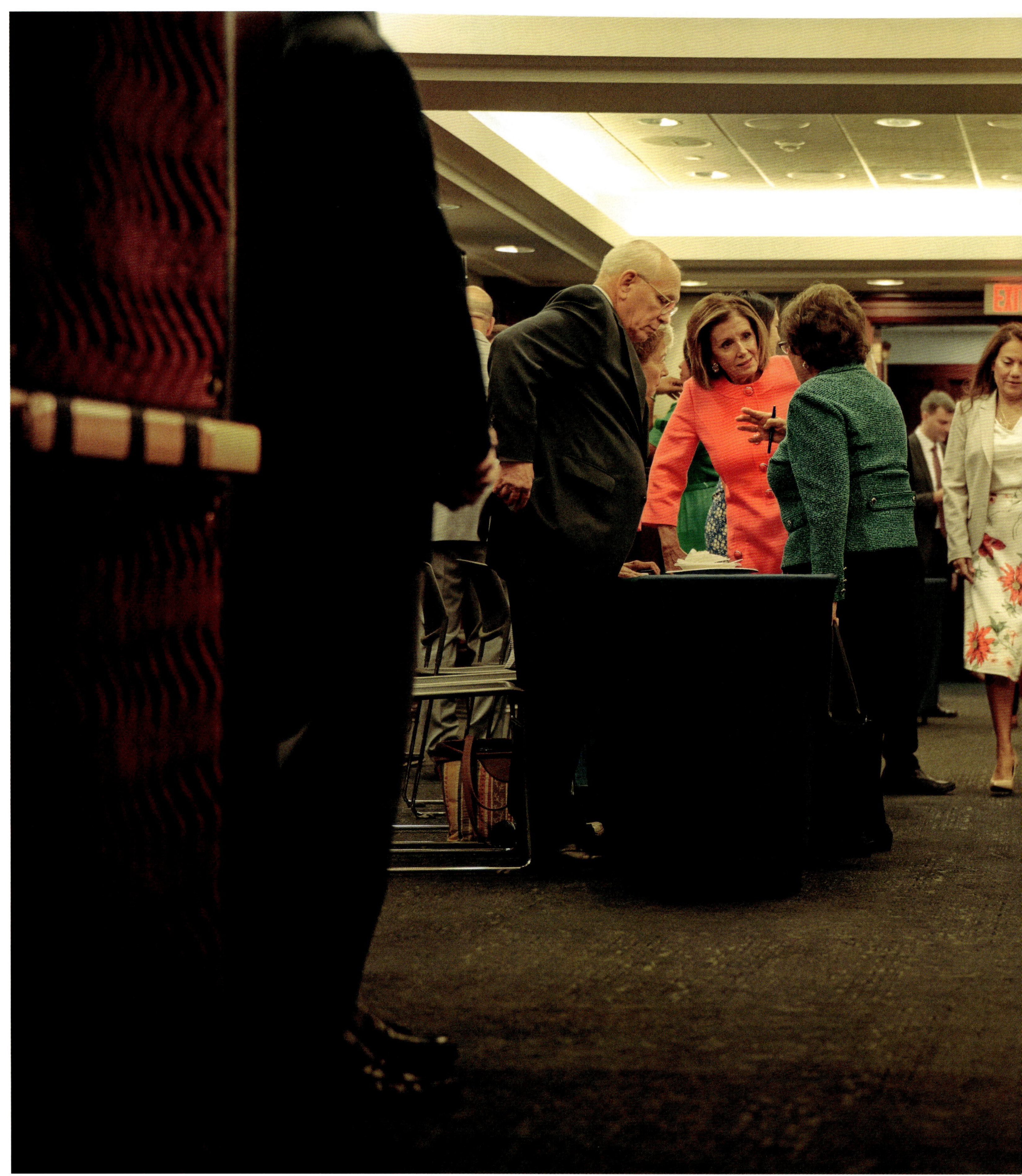
EXIT

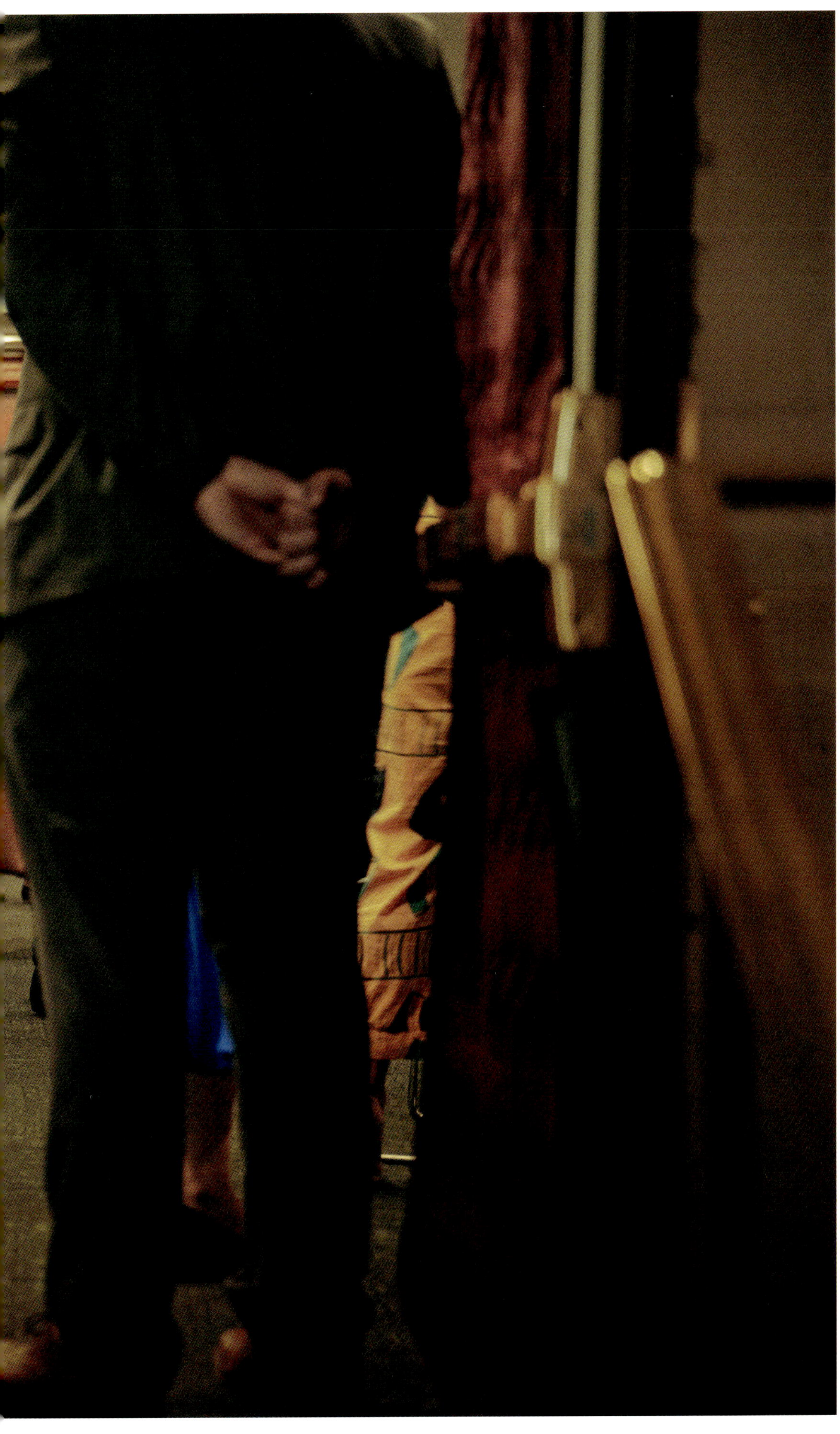

Nancy Pelosi in a morning meeting of Democratic floor leaders, US House of Representatives, Washington, DC, July 2019

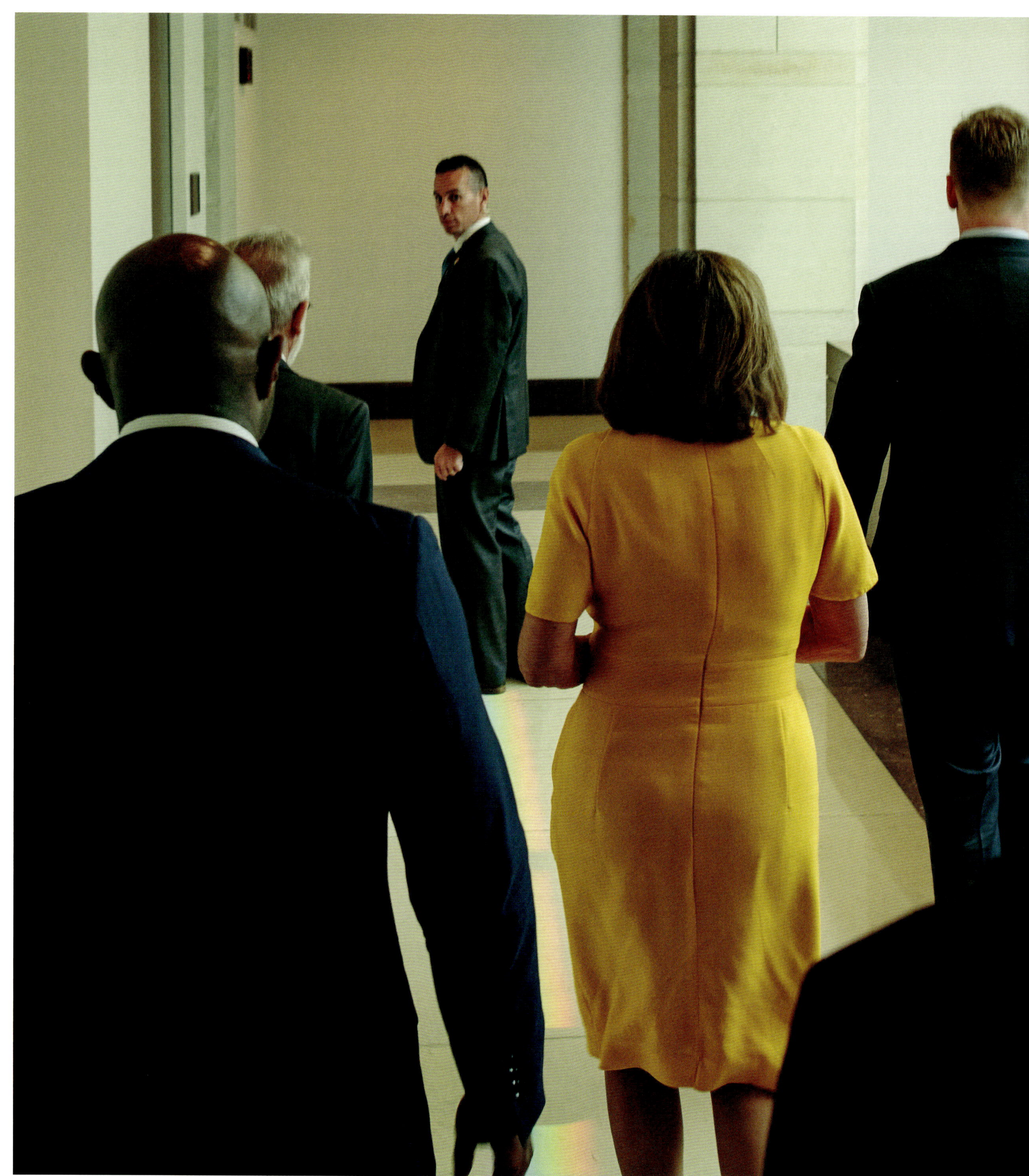

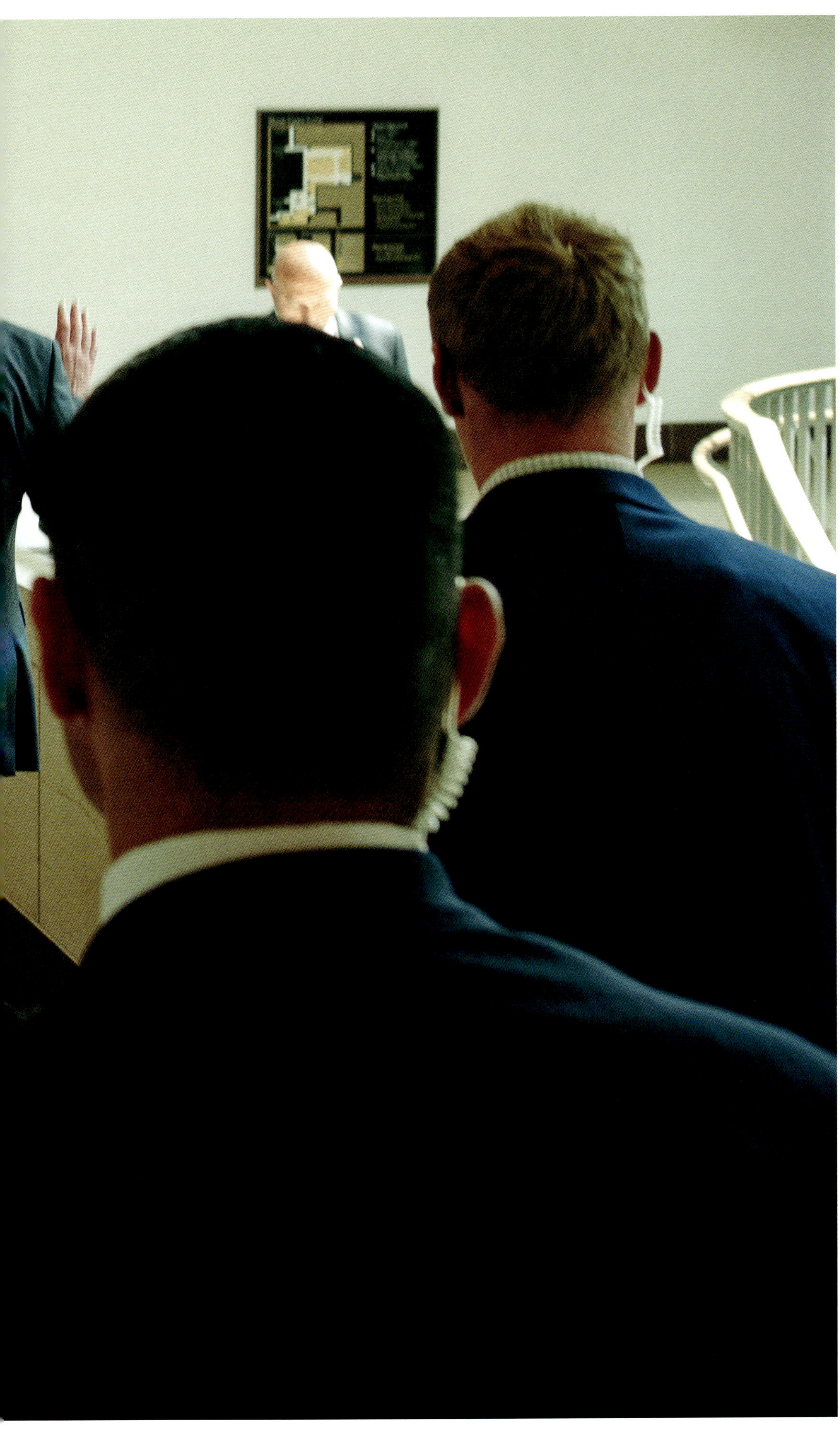

Nancy Pelosi with her
aides and security detail,
US House of Representatives,
Washington, DC, July 2019

When Nancy Pelosi met with Donald Trump in his office a few weeks after she became Speaker of the House late in 2018, the encounter was electric. They were discussing a potential shutdown of government, which Trump was threatening, and funding for a wall on the border with Mexico, which he had promised his base. Trump was patronizing. He called her "Nancy." He wagged his finger at her. She was calm. When he interrupted her, she interrupted him. She challenged him in a way that was then rare.

Photographs of Pelosi walking out of the White House in dark sunglasses and a red coat were quickly picked up as evidence that she was someone to contend with. "Along with her dark glasses, sharp heels and smile of post-combat exhilaration, the coat whispered 'burn' with a wink and a swish," Vanessa Friedman wrote the next day in the *New York Times*.

The *Times*'s comments about what Pelosi was wearing at the meeting with Trump and then again at her swearing in were criticized. Would what a man wore get that kind of attention? Friedman responded that it would be irresponsible not to cover the Speaker's style choices. "I don't think there's any question Ms. Pelosi picked a hot pink dress for her swearing in both because she knew it would make her stand out in what was still a room full of dark suits, and because of the symbolic nature of the occasion: a color traditionally associated with delicate femininity had become a color associated with a seat of power. That's a strategic and savvy choice."

A few months later, Annie spent two days following Pelosi around the Capitol. Meetings were scheduled every fifteen or twenty minutes, from seven in the morning until seven at night. It was hard to keep up with her. Pelosi walked everywhere and Annie couldn't get ahead of her. She was getting a glimpse of the perseverance and determination that would be so dramatically in evidence in the coming months and then, more spectacularly, in 2021.

Nancy Pelosi on the balcony of the Speaker's chamber, US House of Representatives, Washington, DC, July 2019

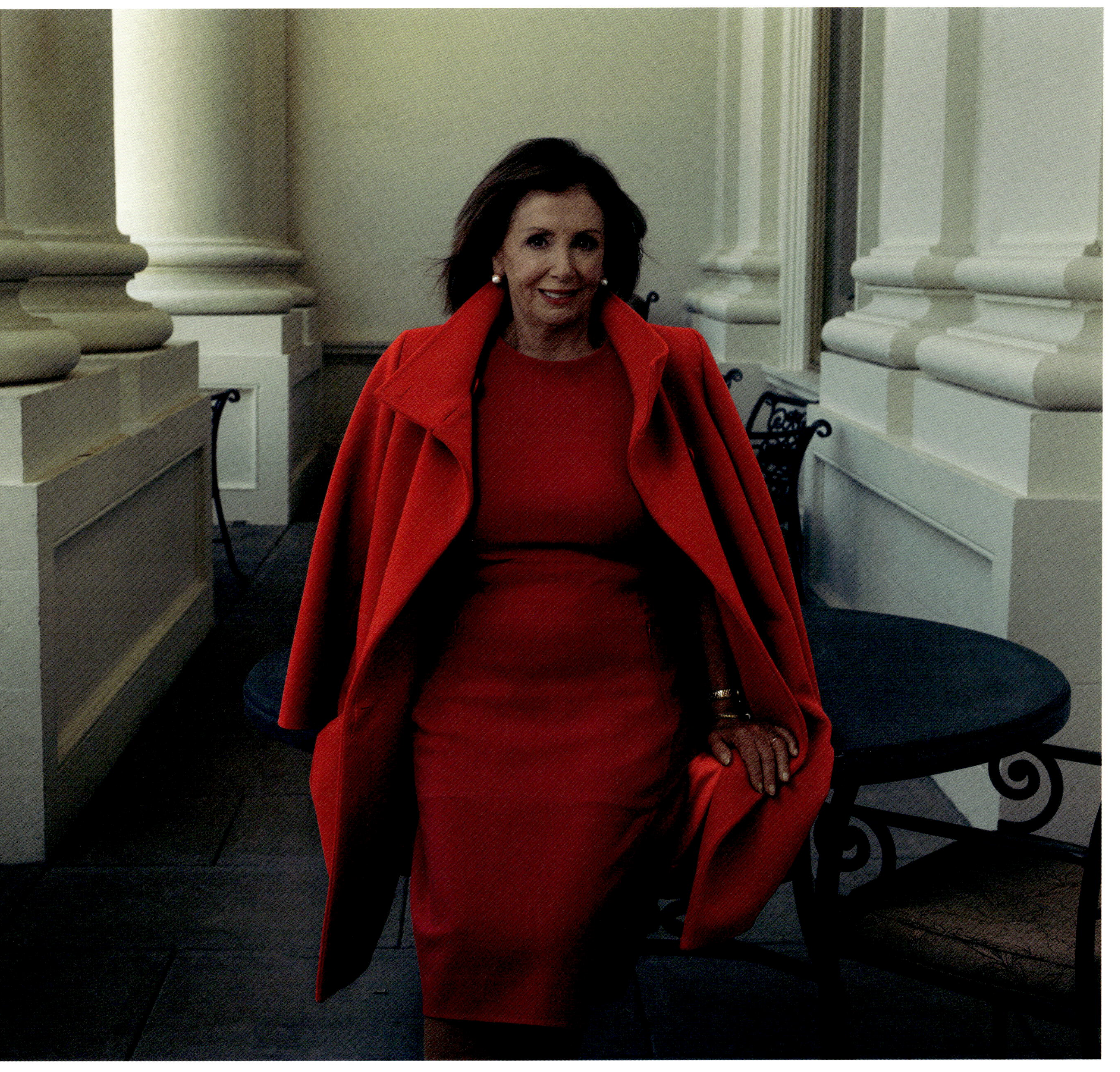

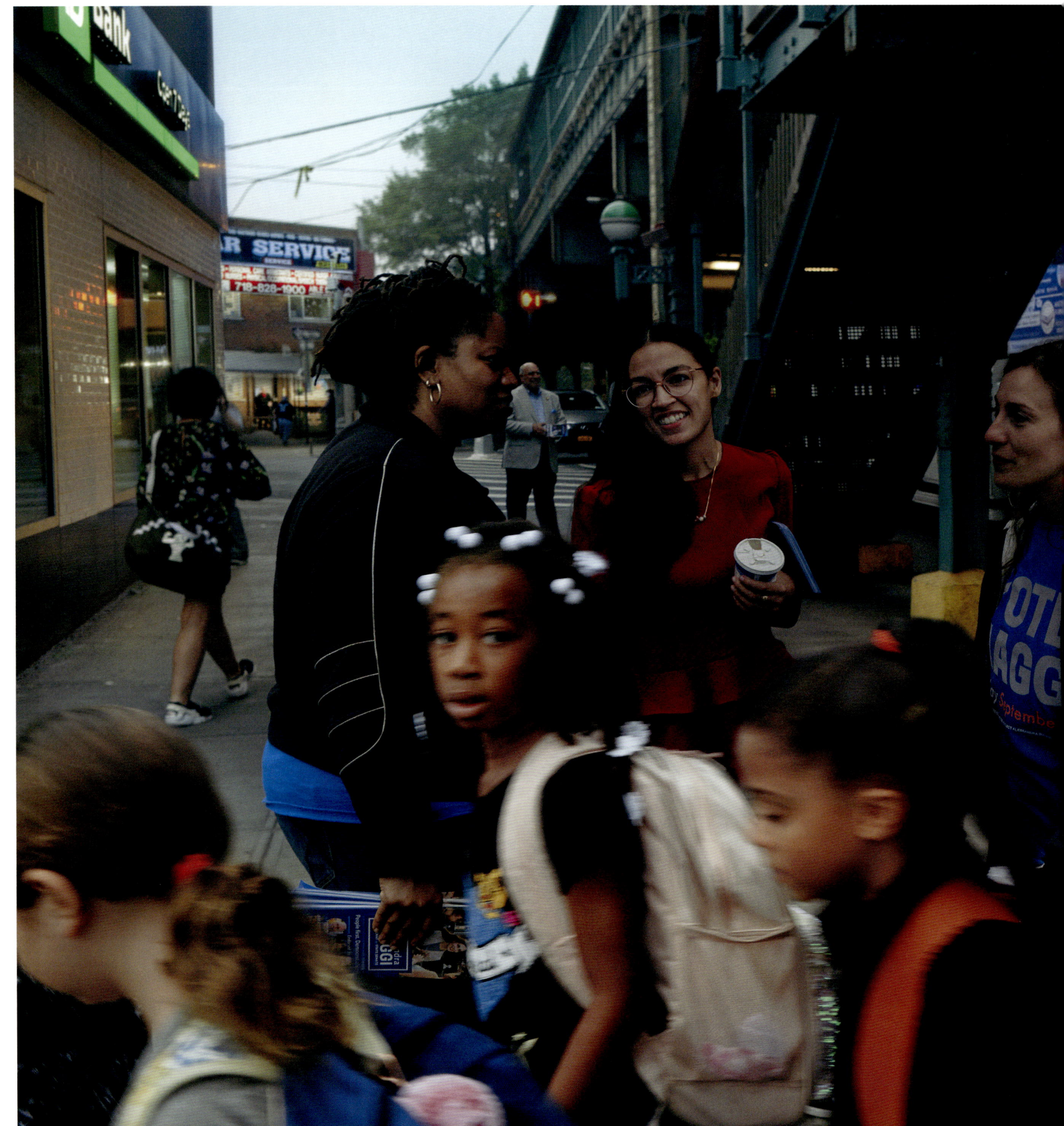
Bank
SERVICE
718-828-1900

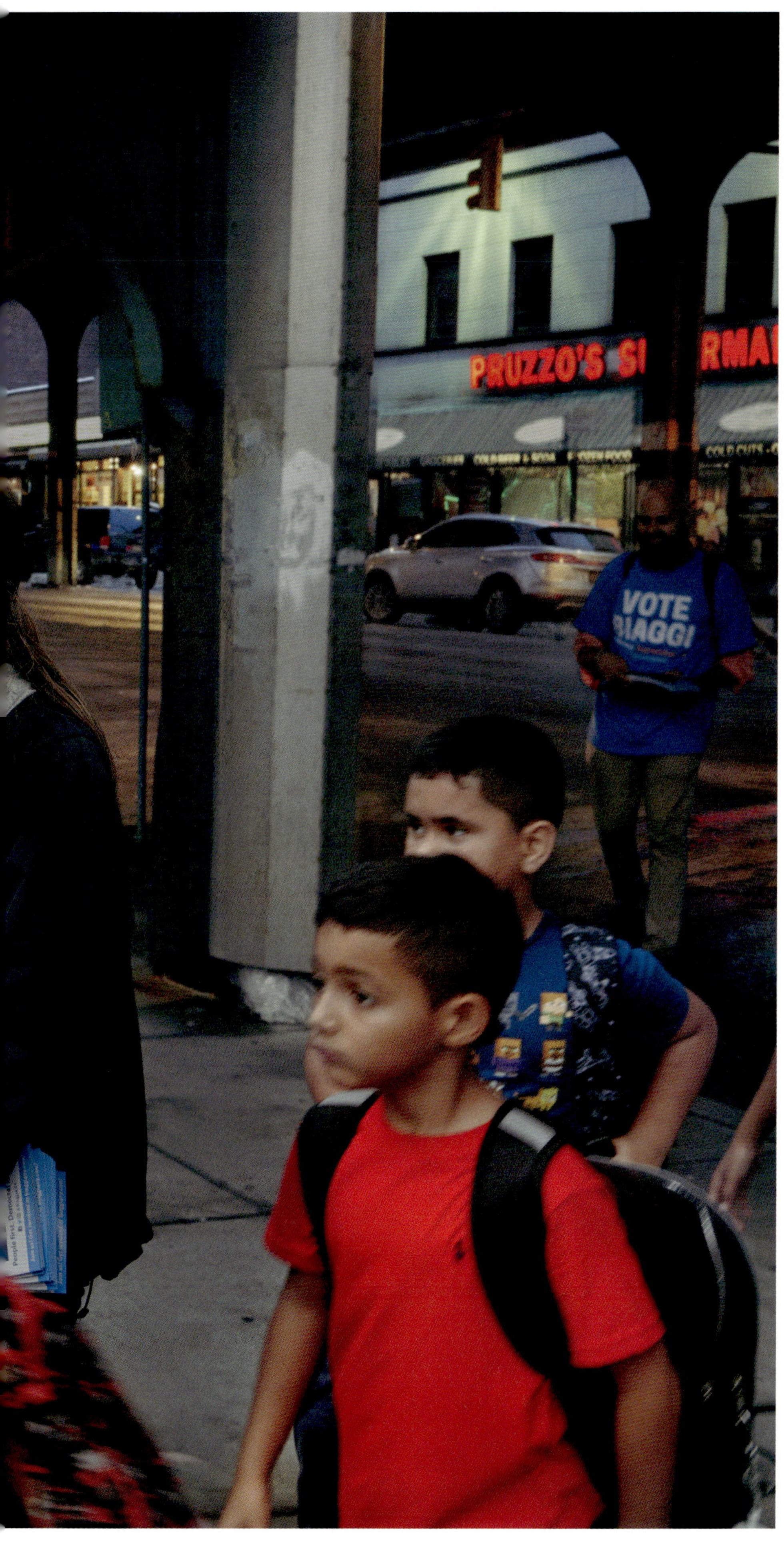

Alexandria Ocasio-Cortez campaigning for election to the House of Representatives, the Bronx, New York, 2018

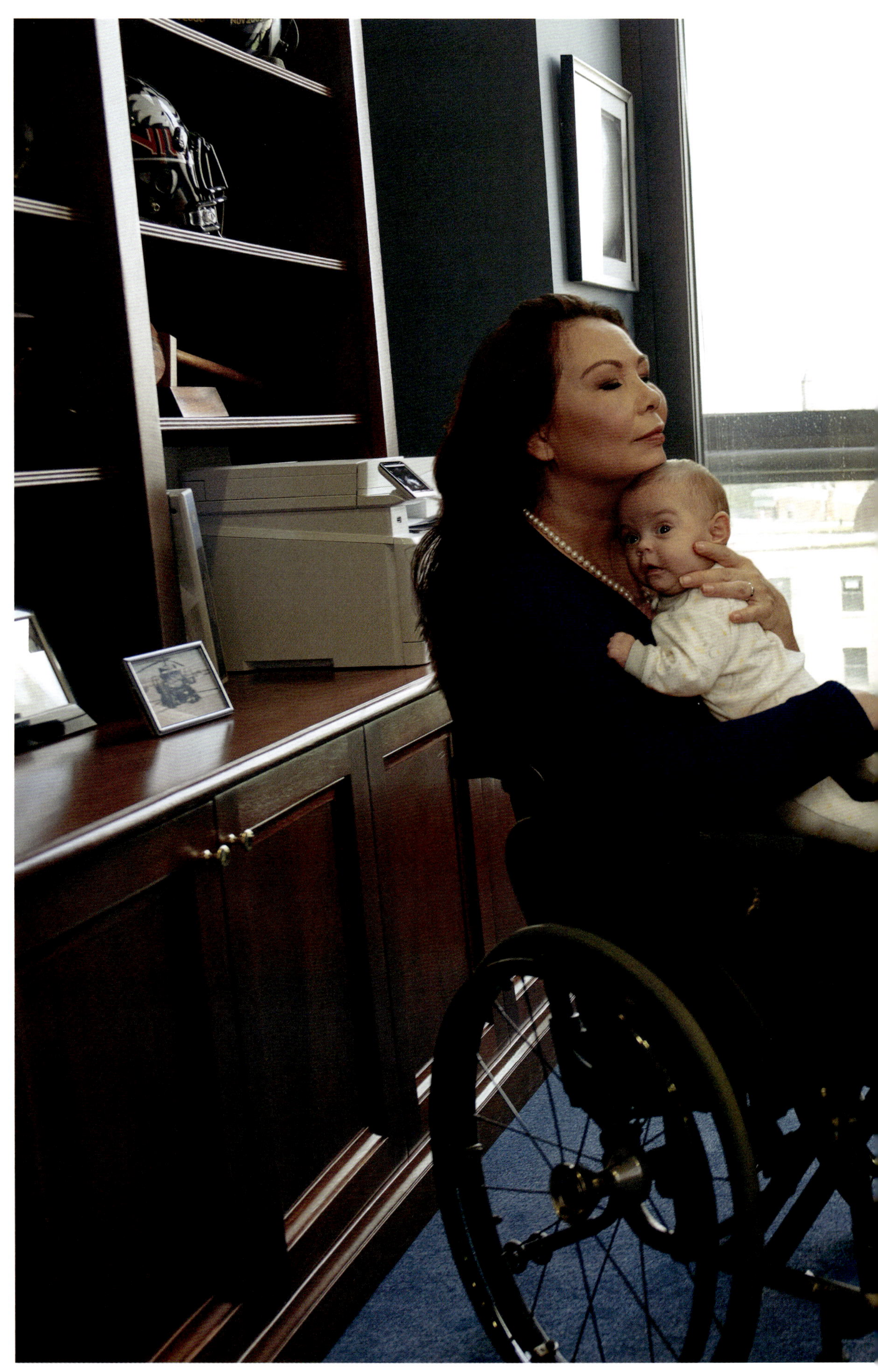

Senator Tammy Duckworth and her children, Abigail and Maile, Hart Senate Office Building, Washington, DC, 2018

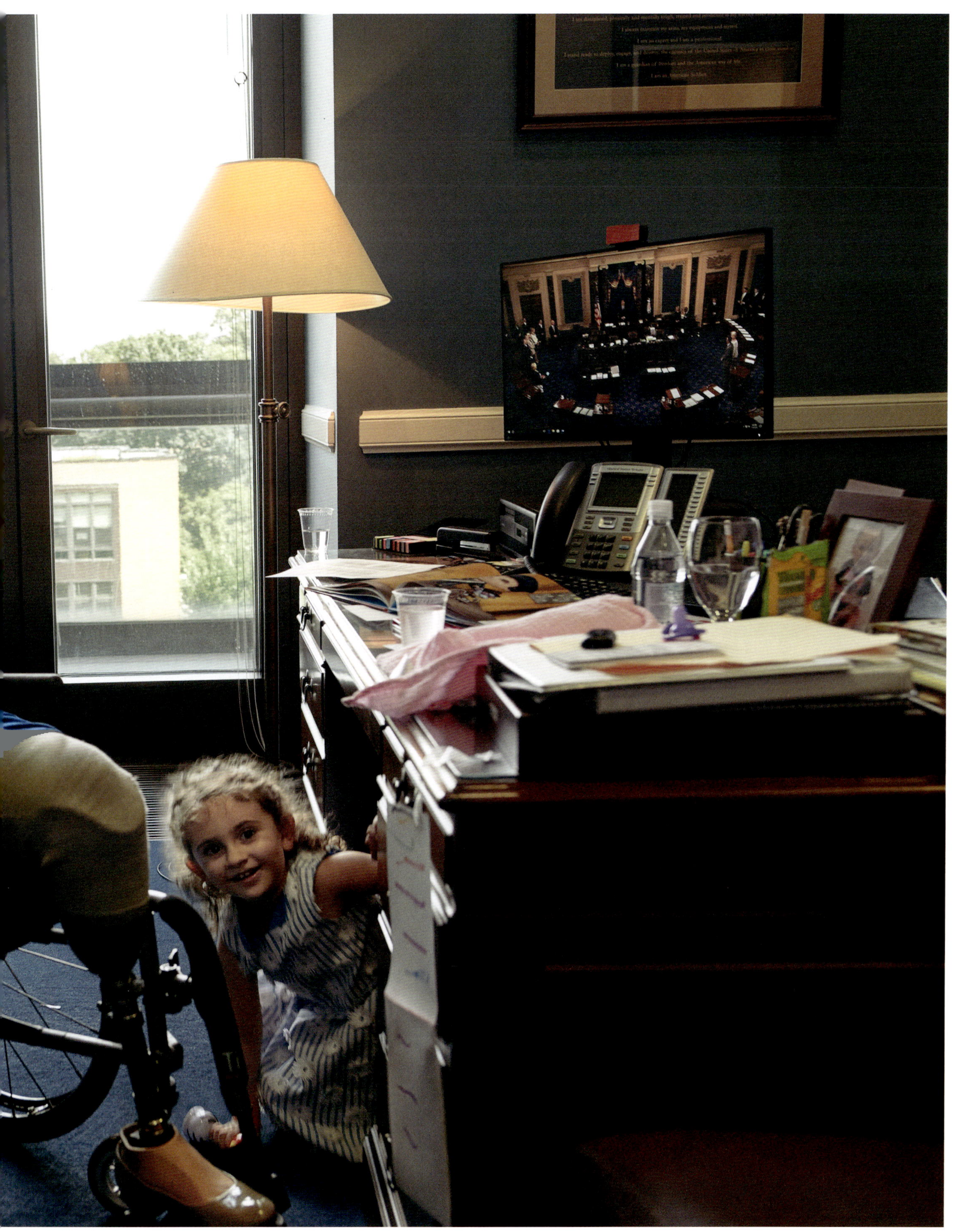

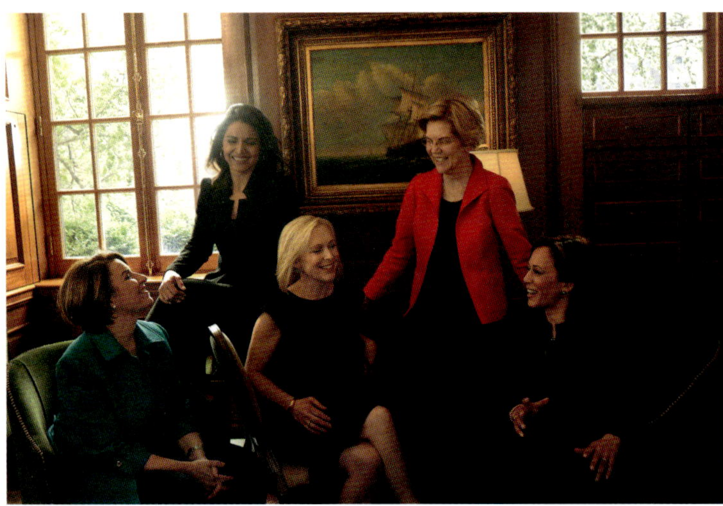

"The women who were campaigning for the Democratic nomination for president were pulled together for a shoot in Washington in the fall of 2019. I assumed that there would be a certain amount of tension in the room, but it was quite the opposite. They were happy to see one another and have a chance to catch up. And they all had a sense of humor. There was a vote in the Senate that morning, and they kept running in and out. In the end I think we had about twelve minutes to work. I had turned away from the group after I had what I thought was the last picture, and then I realized that something was going on behind me. It happened so fast that I didn't have time to bring my camera to my eye."

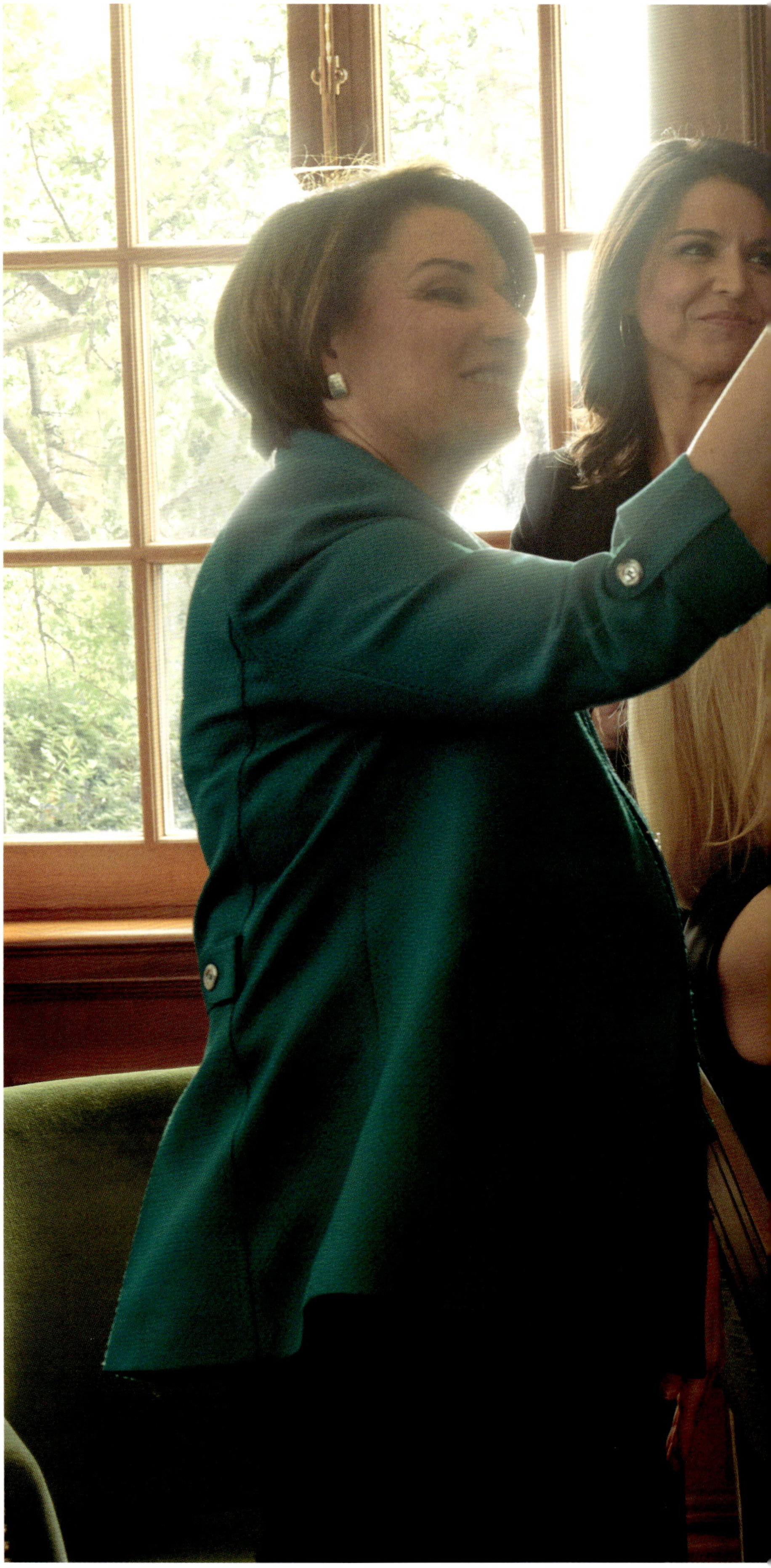

Senator Amy Klobuchar, Representative Tulsi Gabbard, Senator Kirsten Gillibrand, Senator Elizabeth Warren, and Senator Kamala Harris, the Jefferson Hotel, Washington, DC, 2019

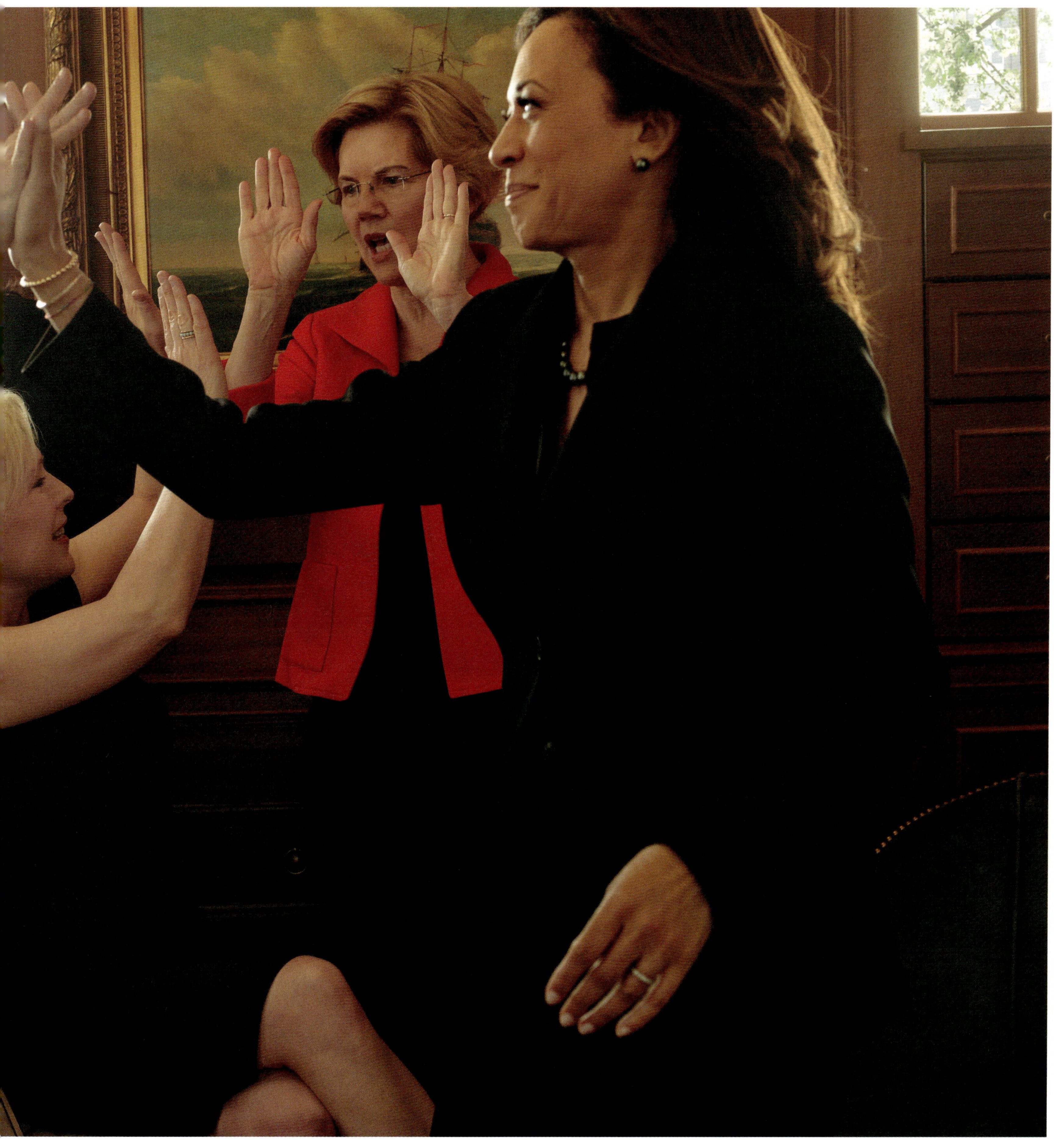

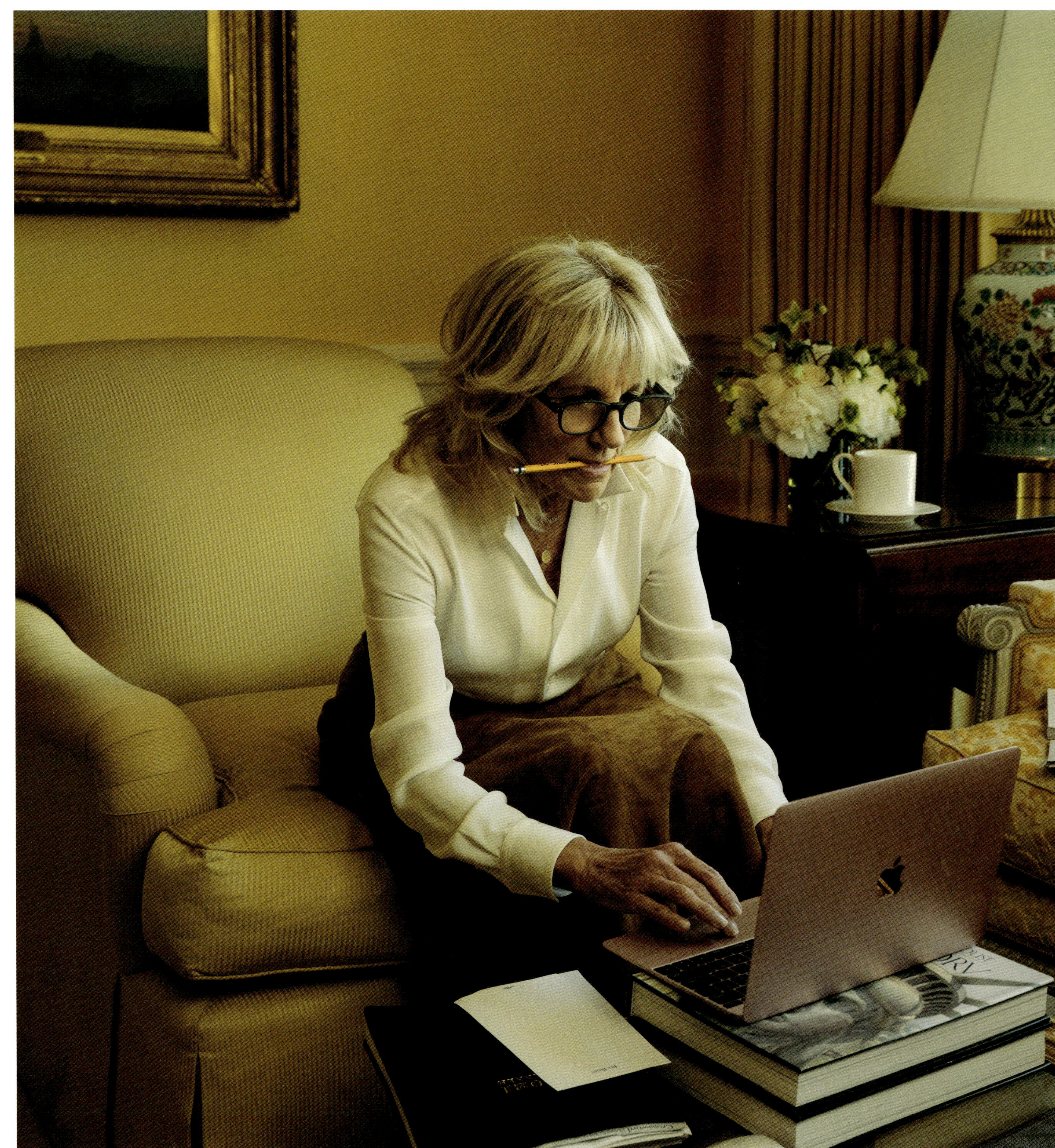

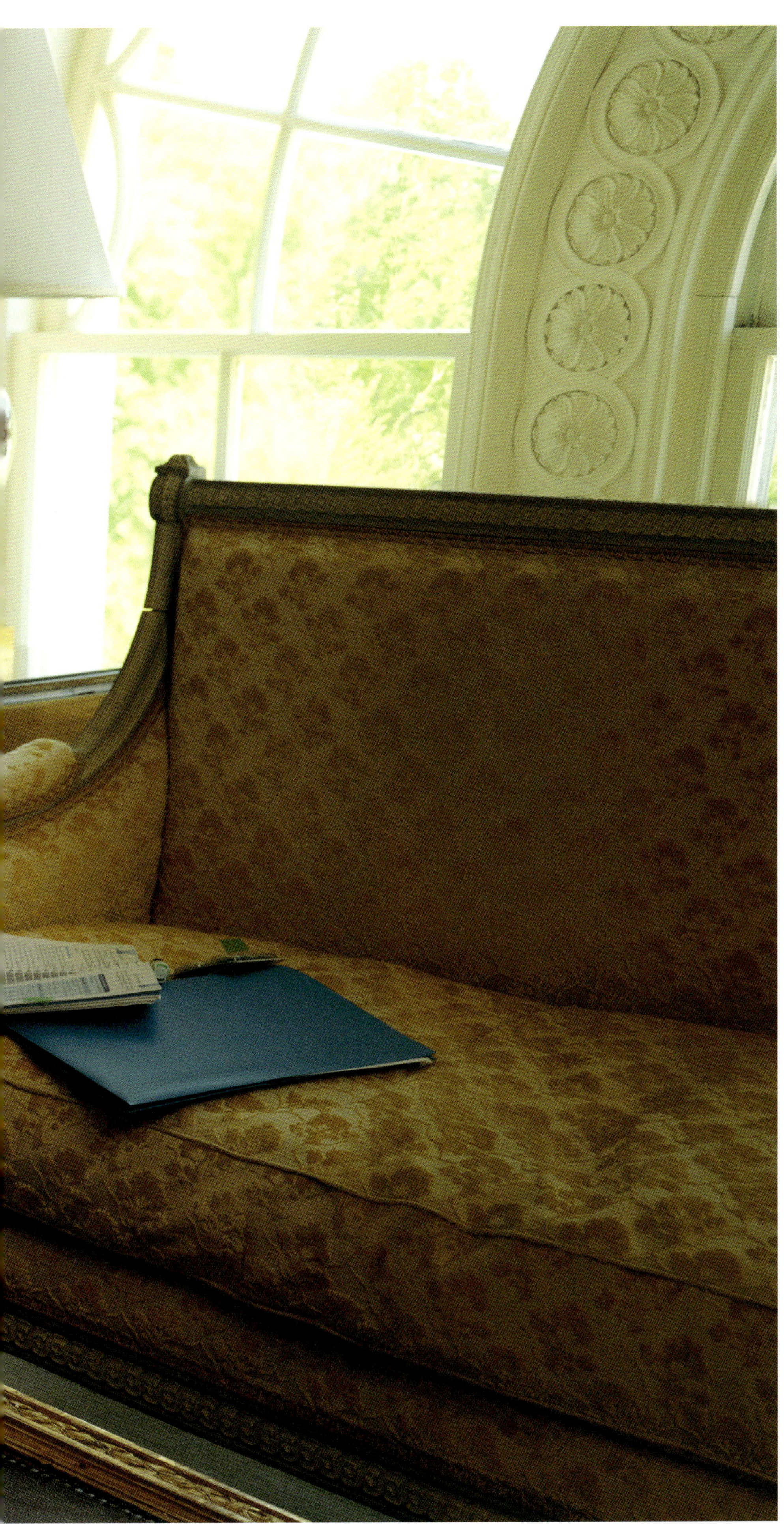

"During Joe Biden's first one hundred days as president, the White House was a workplace more than a residence or a museum. The Bidens went home to Delaware on the weekends when they could. When I met Dr. Biden for a fitting and a location scout, the furniture in the historic first-floor rooms had been placed to the side to make space for a virtual summit of world leaders on climate. It was a high-tech event, with video monitors everywhere. Due to COVID, there were no visitors and the White House was practically empty. Dr. Biden had an office in the East Wing, and she sometimes worked on the second floor, in the family's private residence. On the day of the shoot, the ninety-sixth day, she was grading papers for her writing classes at Northern Virginia Community College. 'I know it is the first one hundred days,' she said to me, 'but it feels like ten years.'"

Dr. Jill Biden, East Sitting Hall,
the White House, April 26, 2021

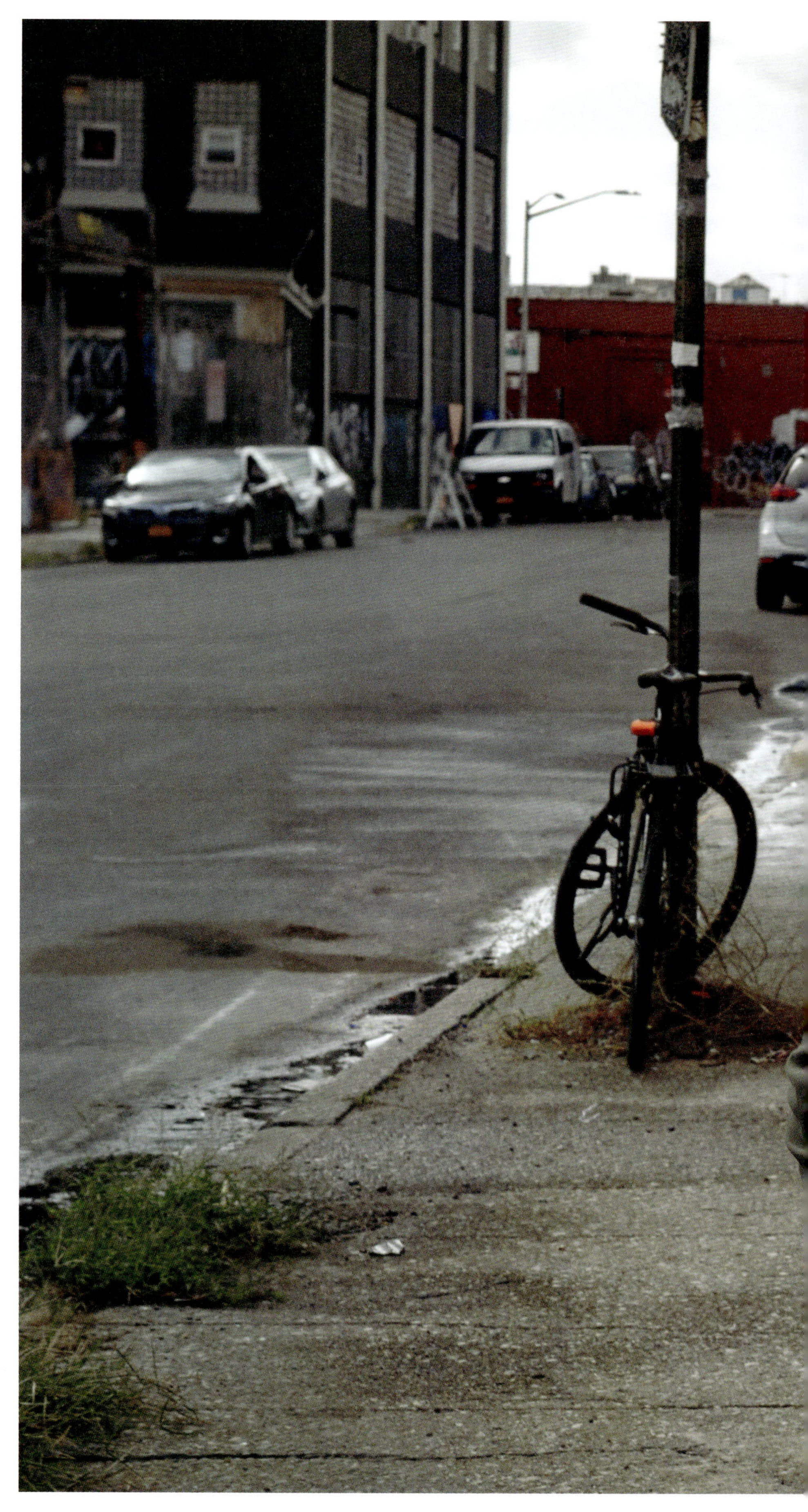

Gloria Steinem with Naomi Wadler, the twelve-year-old spokesperson for victims of gun violence, Brooklyn, New York, 2018

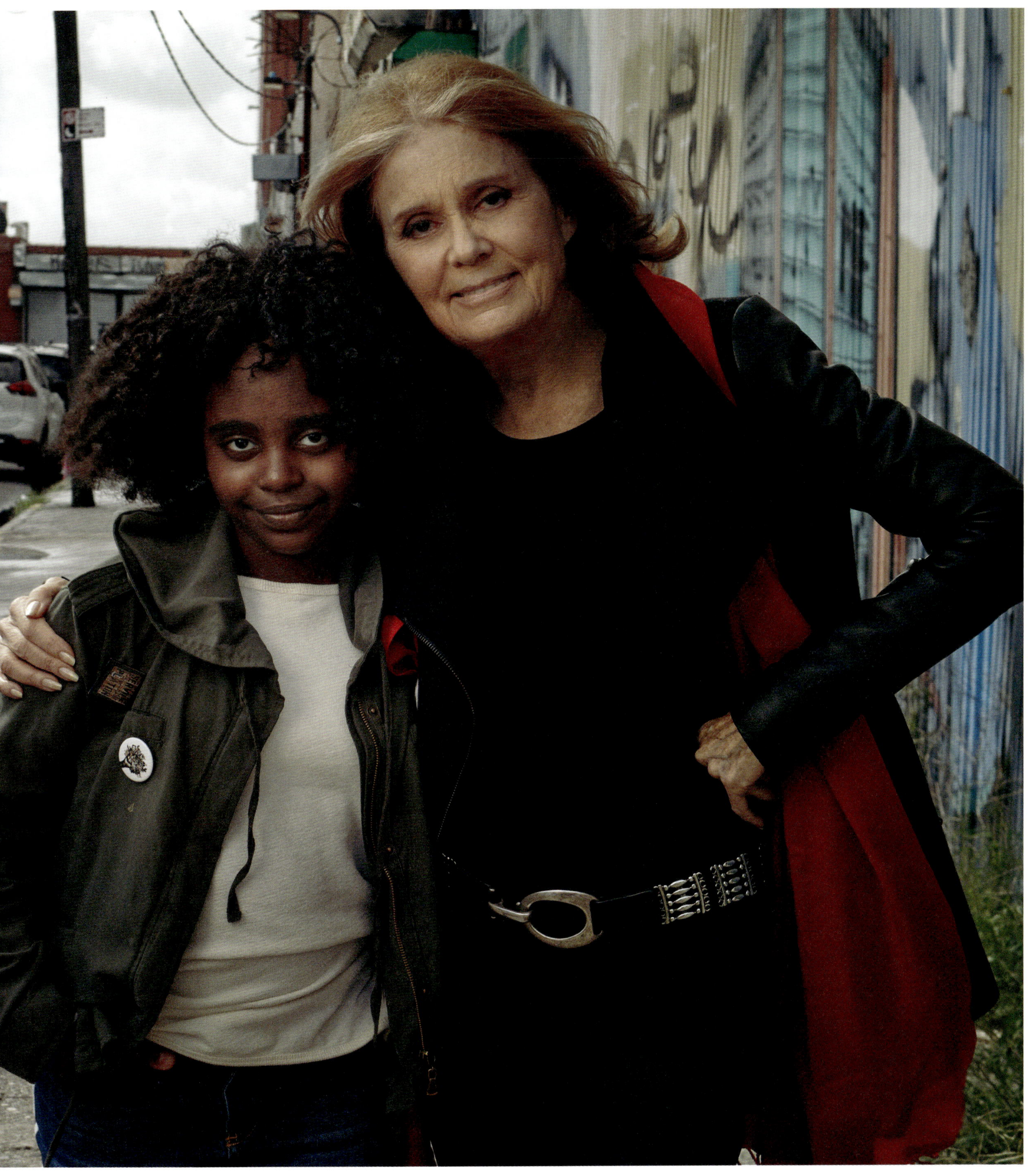

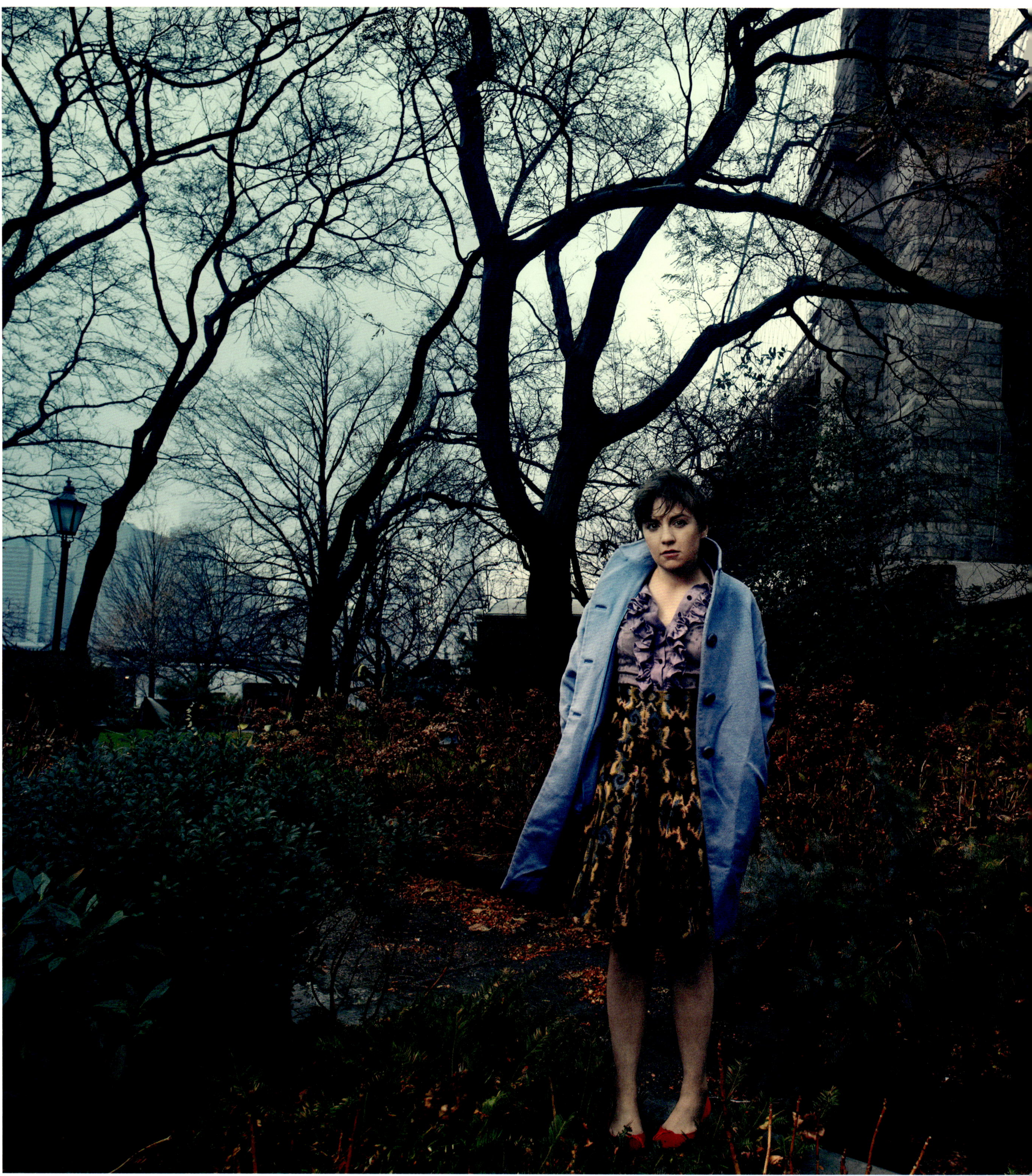

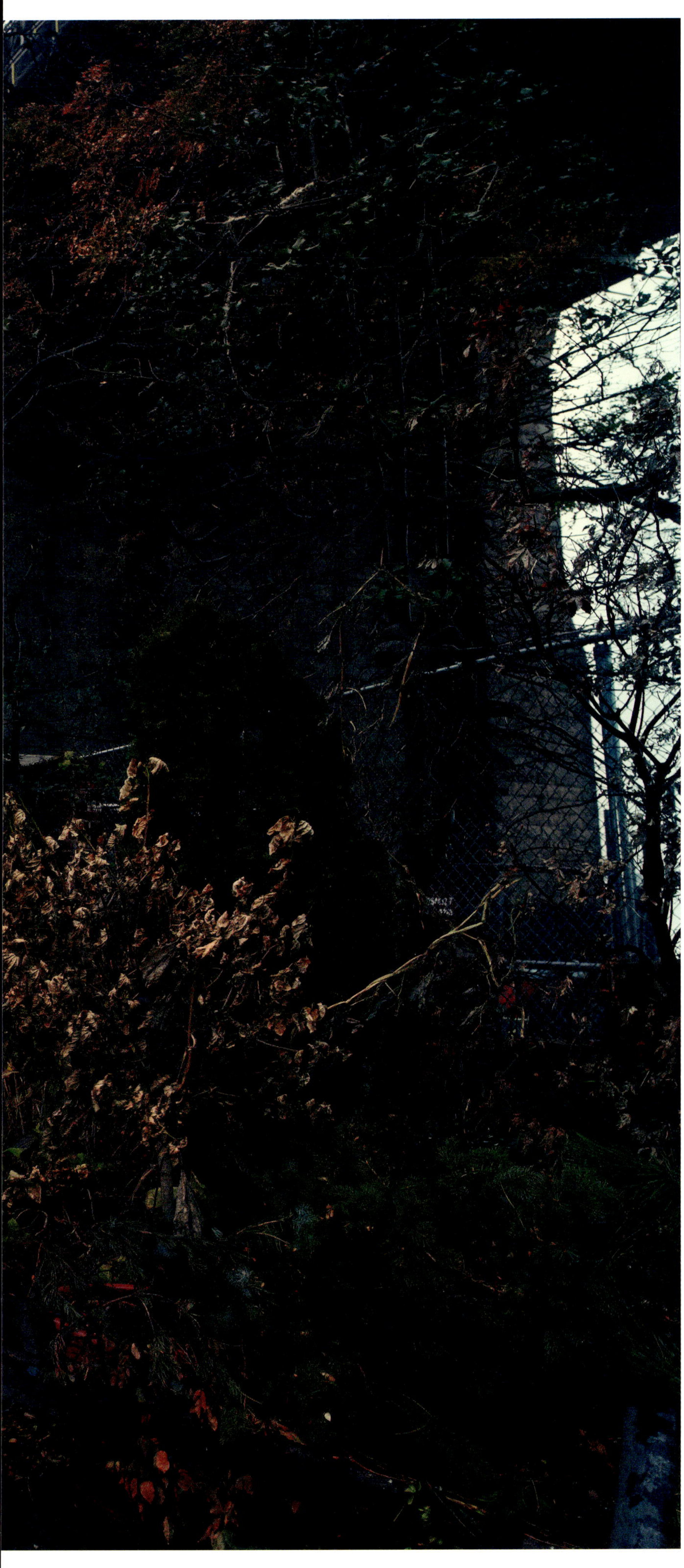

Lena Dunham grew up in Manhattan, in her parents' downtown artists' loft, but she went to school in Brooklyn. She was a student at St. Ann's, the progressive private school in Brooklyn Heights where other children of artists were sent. That life provided the material for her early work and established the emotional territory that evolved into *Girls*. Zac Posen was another St. Ann's student. He was six years older than Lena and was for a time her babysitter. He would pick her up in Tribeca and escort her to school on the subway. Posen designed costumes for school plays and created outfits for other students. By the time Lena was ready to graduate from St. Ann's, he had his own fashion label. He made her graduation dress, which is what she chose to wear in the first portrait Annie made of her, under the Brooklyn Bridge.

Lena Dunham, Brooklyn Bridge,
New York, 2012

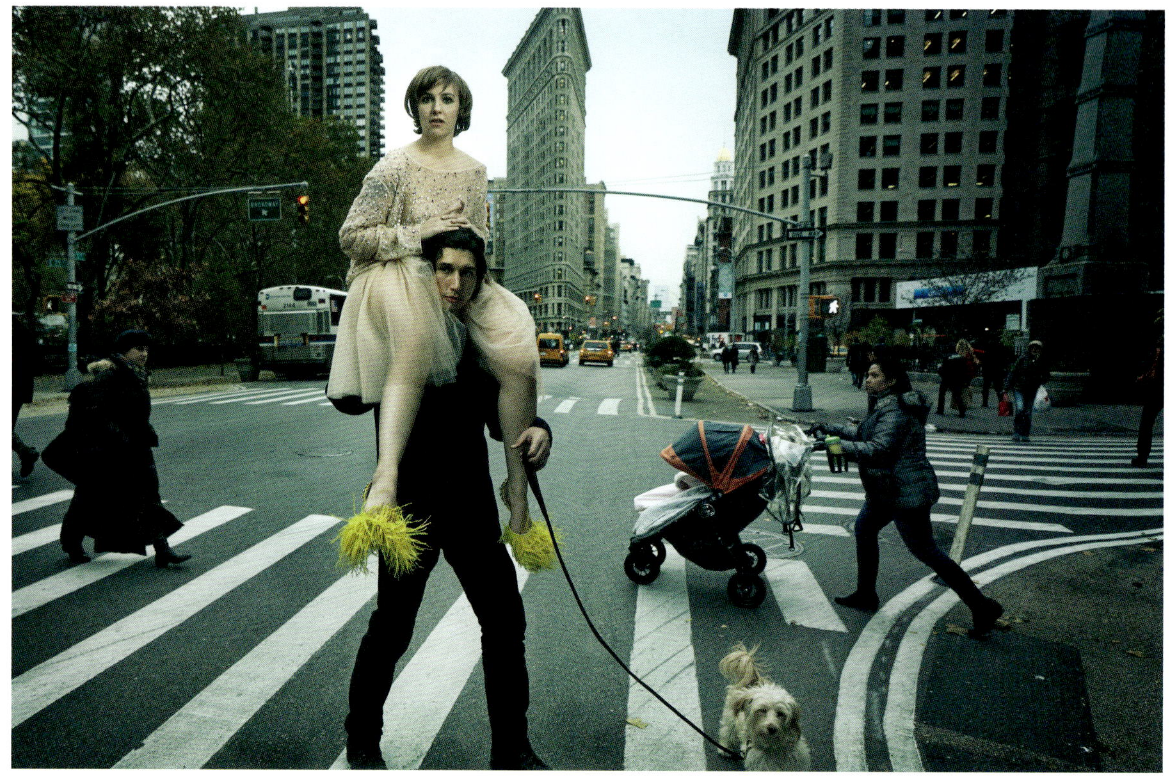

Lena Dunham first appeared in *Vogue* in 1998, when she was eleven, in an article about cool girls—the "girl who looks fabulous and seems to be everywhere that's worth going," as Plum Sykes, the author of the *Vogue* piece, put it. The young Lena showed Sykes a Helmut Lang–inspired dress she had made and explained that she would prefer to have something by Jil Sander. That was unfortunately out of reach because of her allowance, which was then five dollars a week.

Lena Dunham and Adam Driver,
New York City, 2013

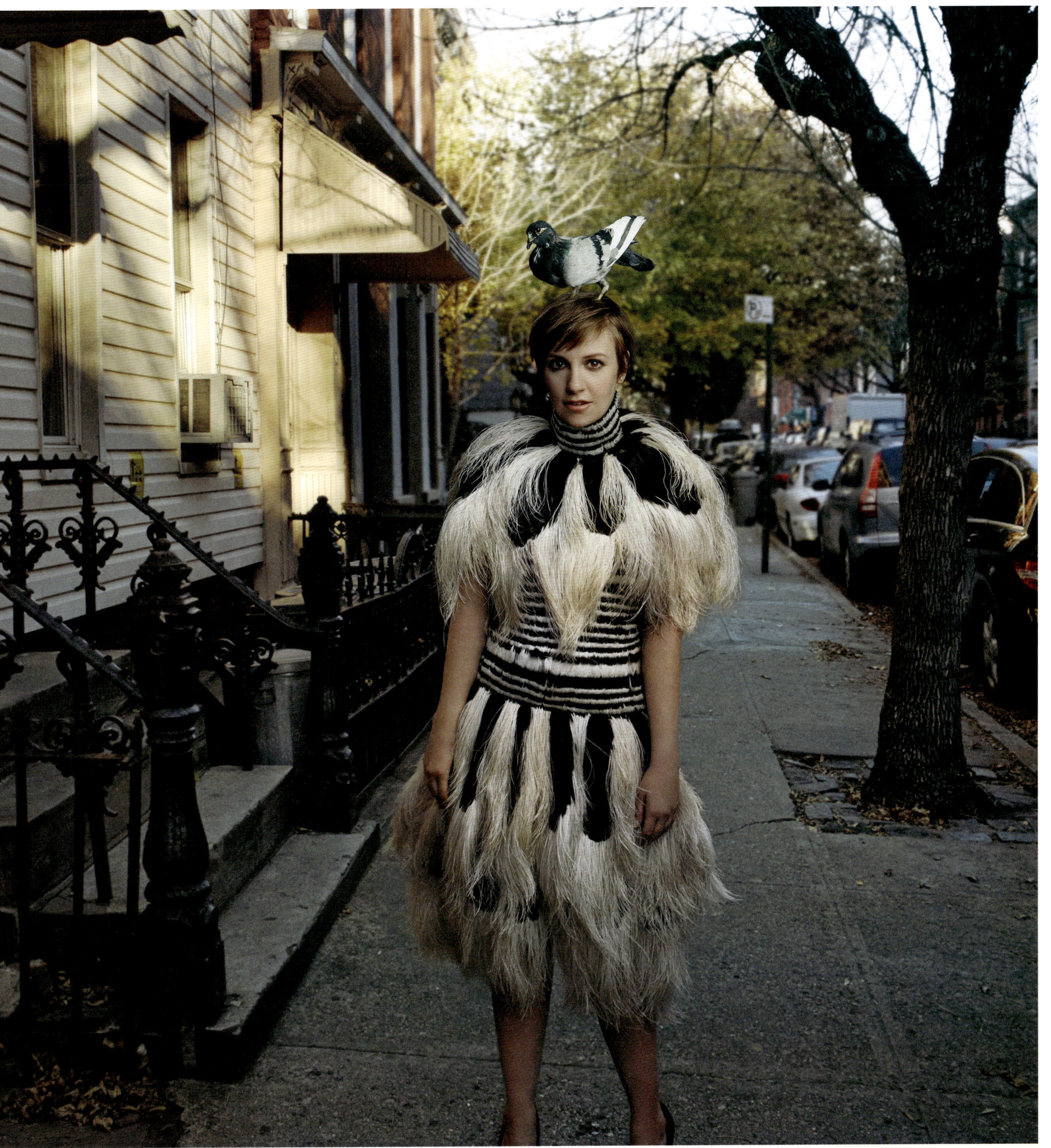

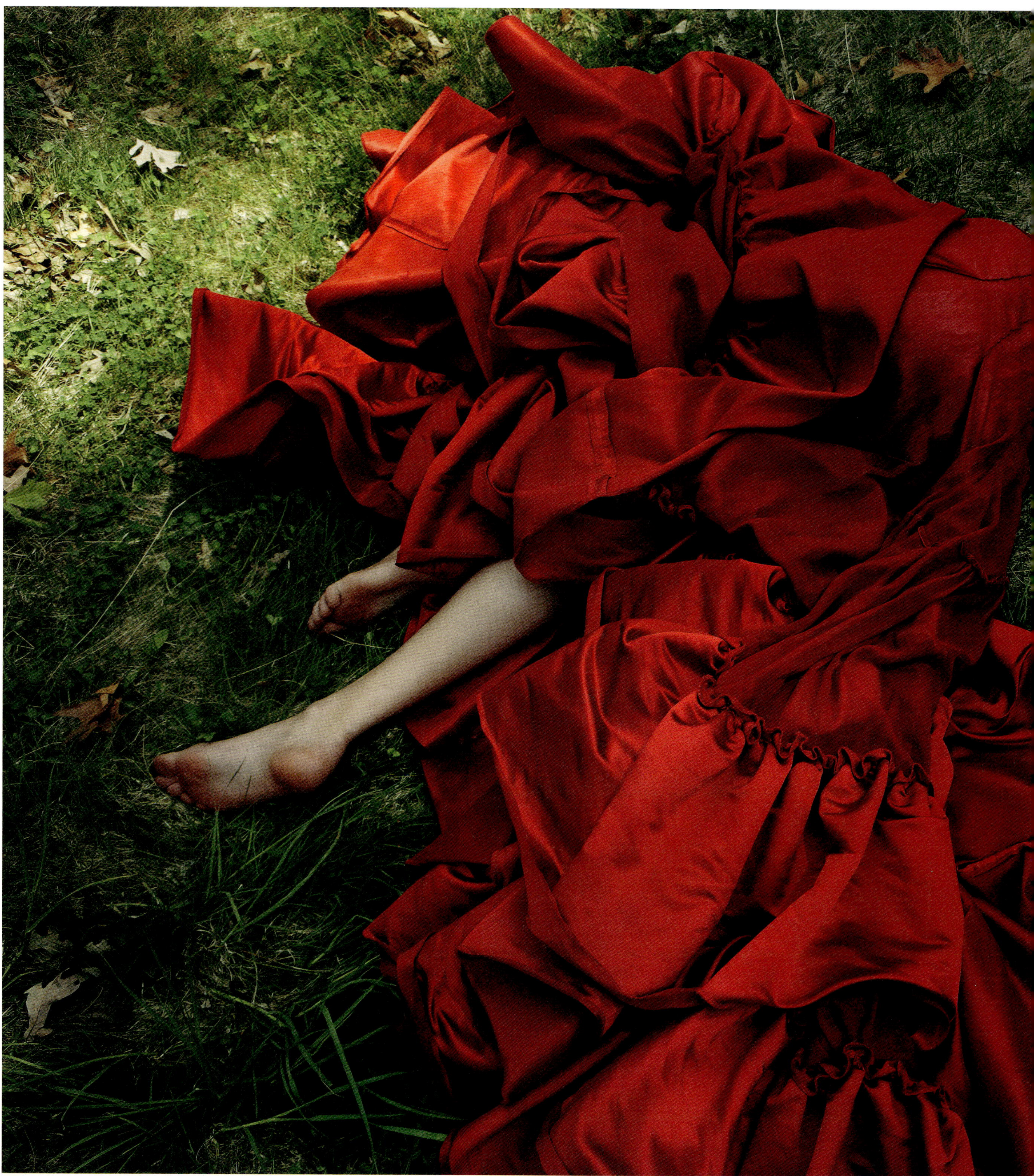

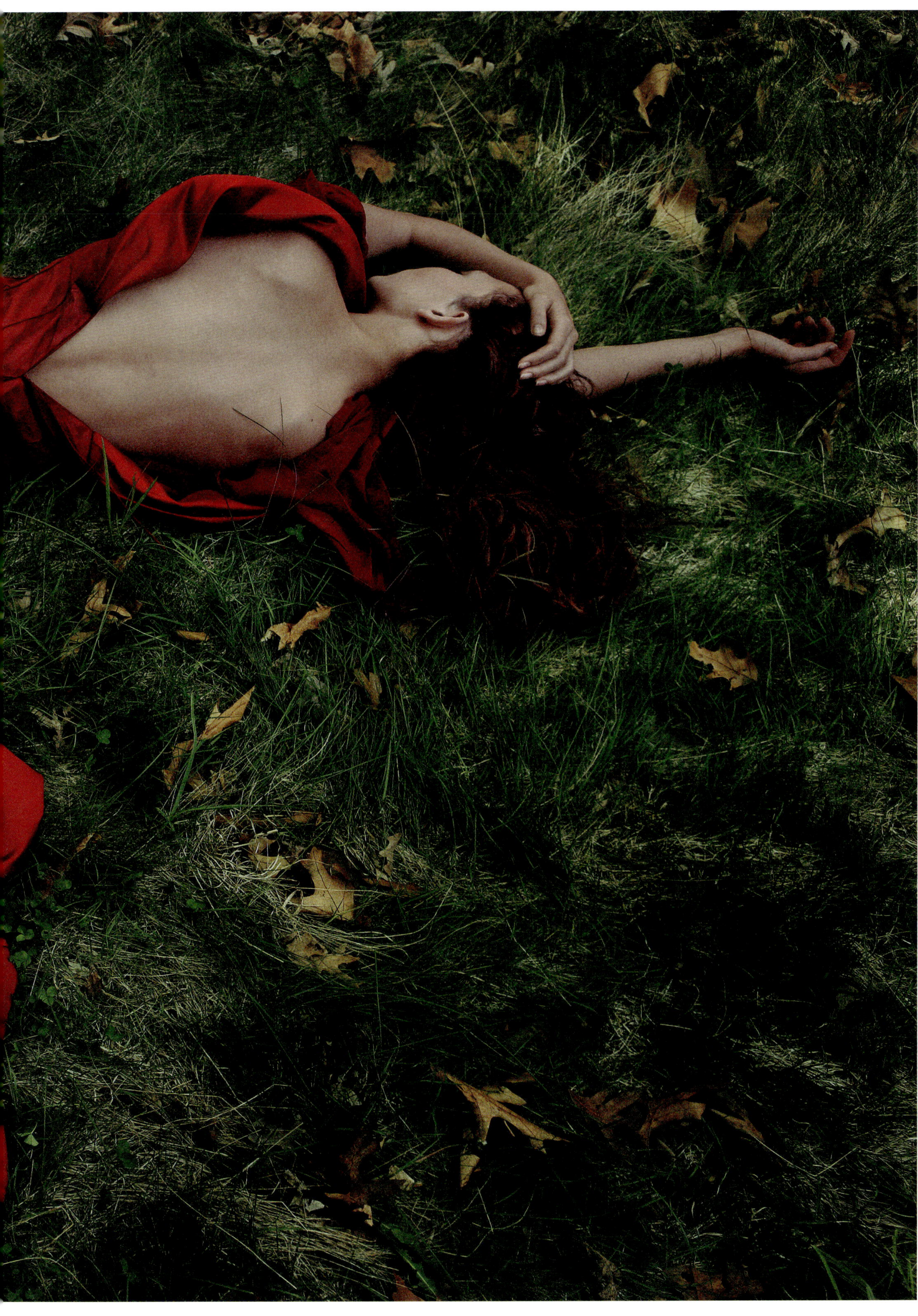

Karlie Kloss, Oak Terrace,
Tivoli, New York, 2009

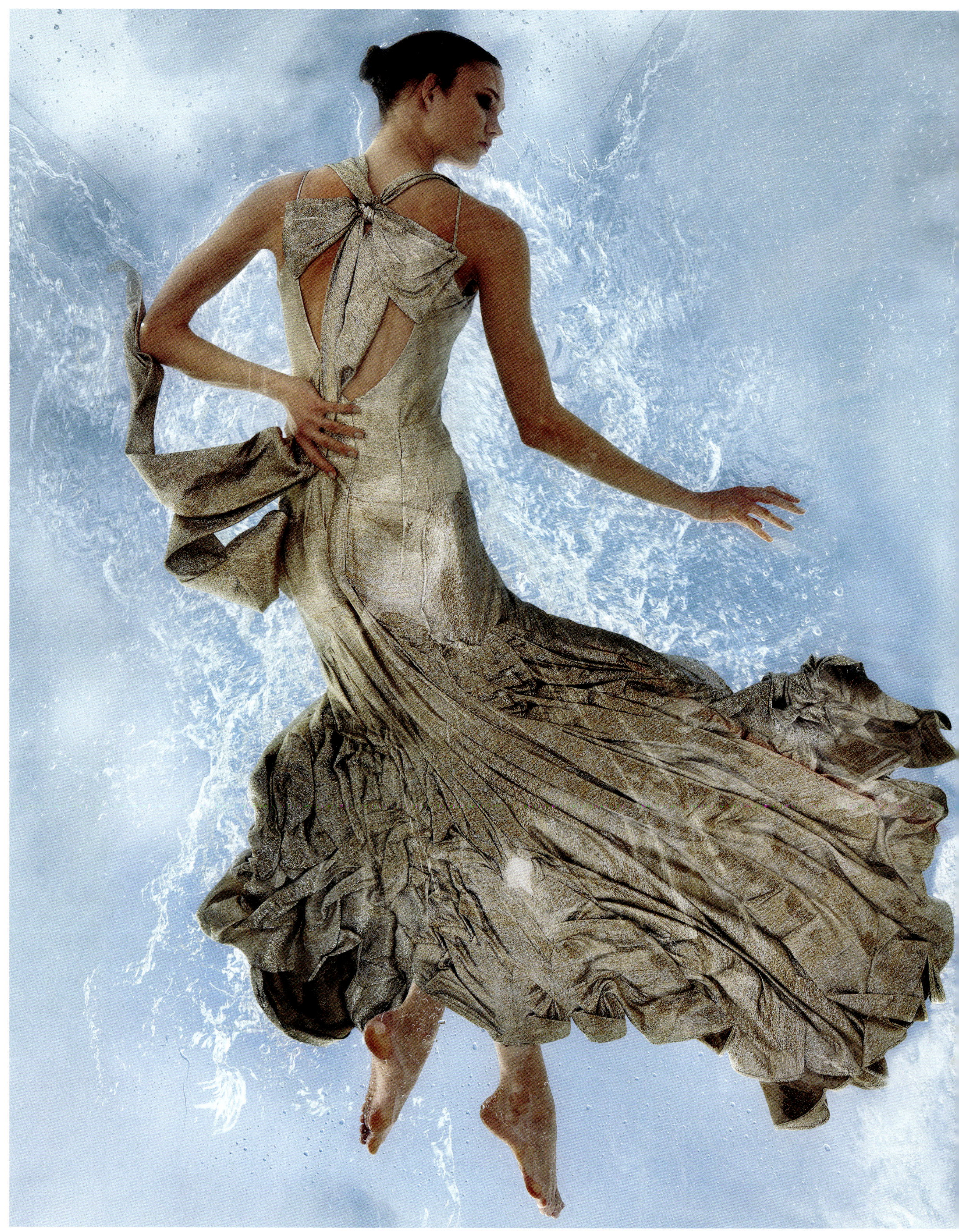

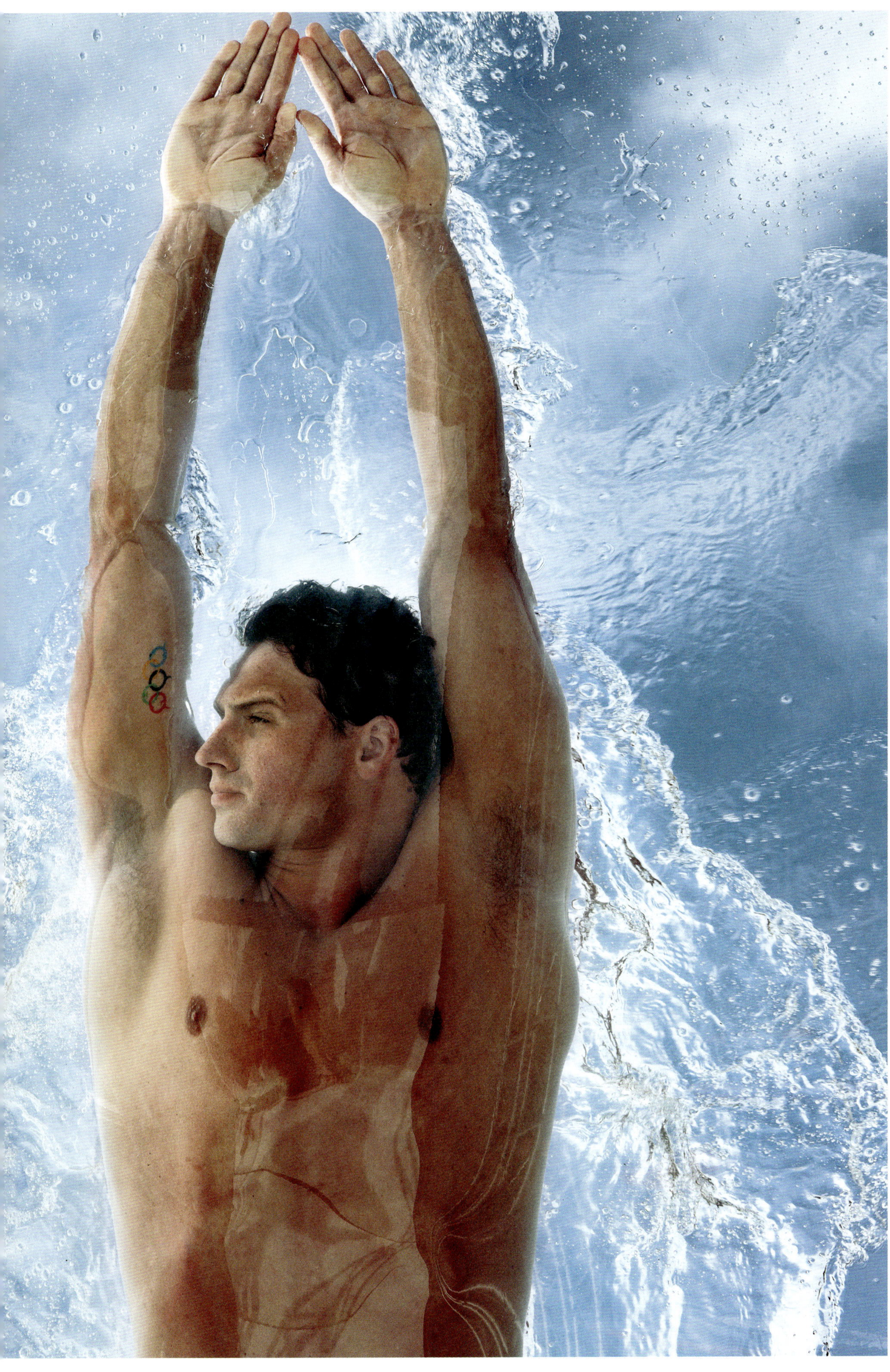

Karlie Kloss and Ryan Lochte,
Miami, 2012

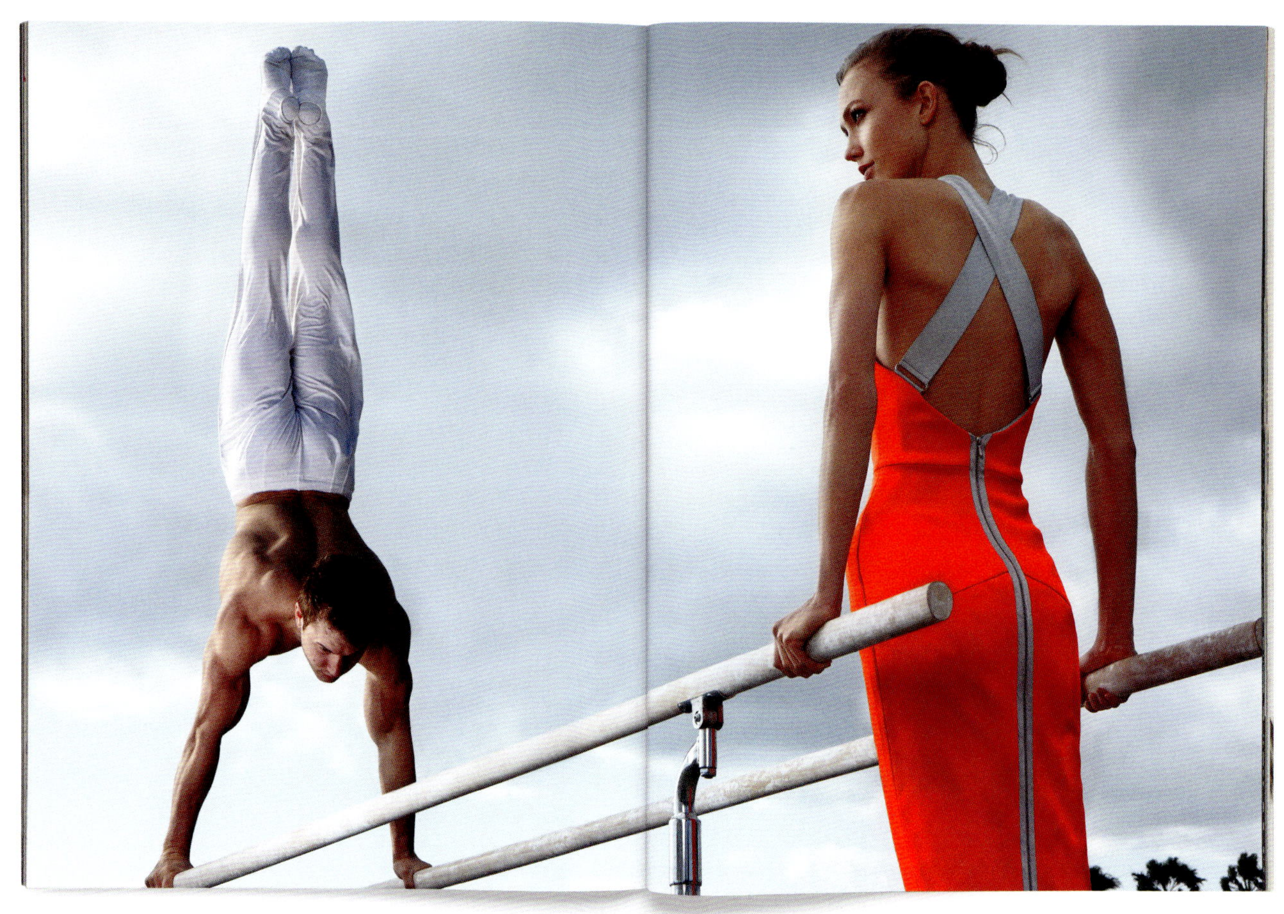

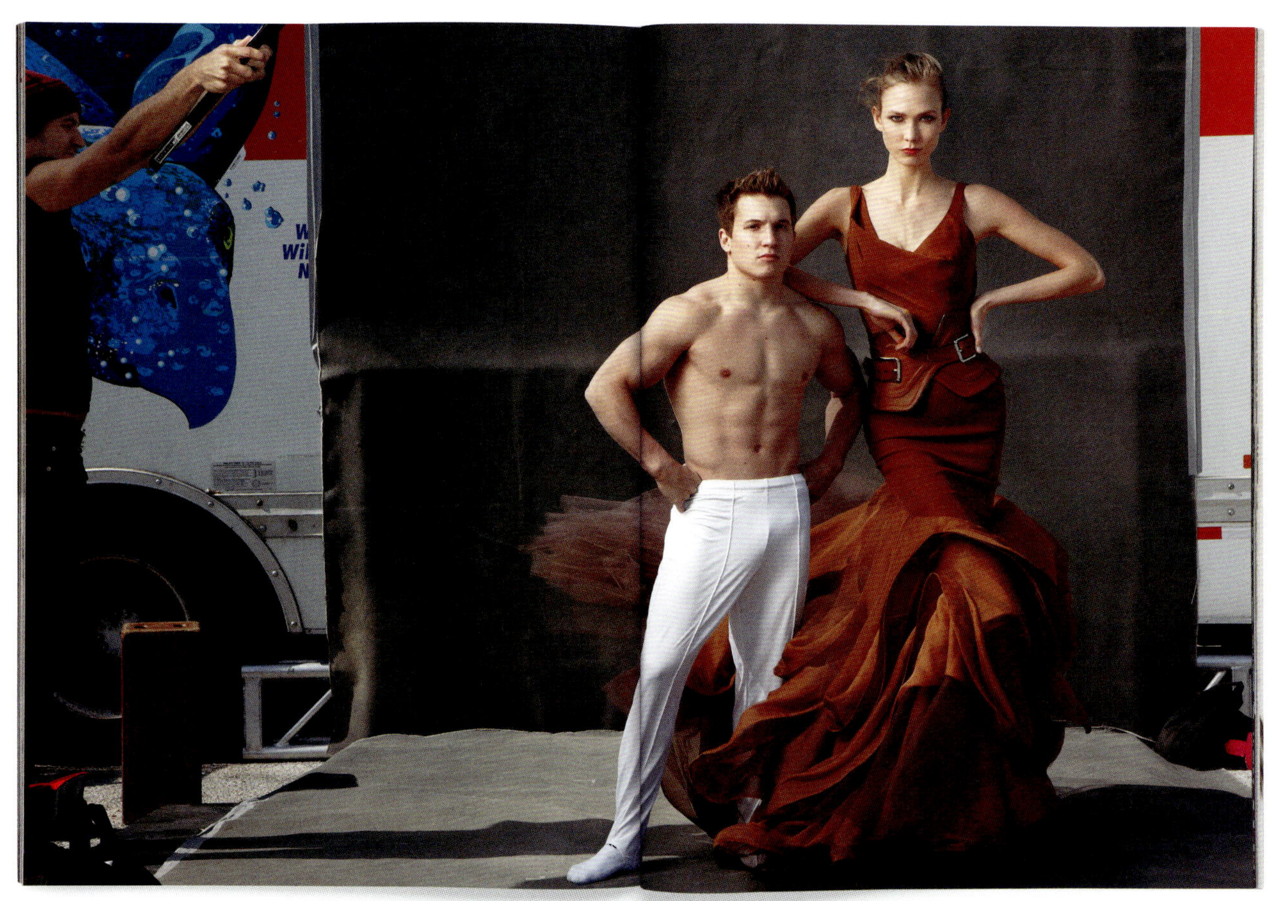

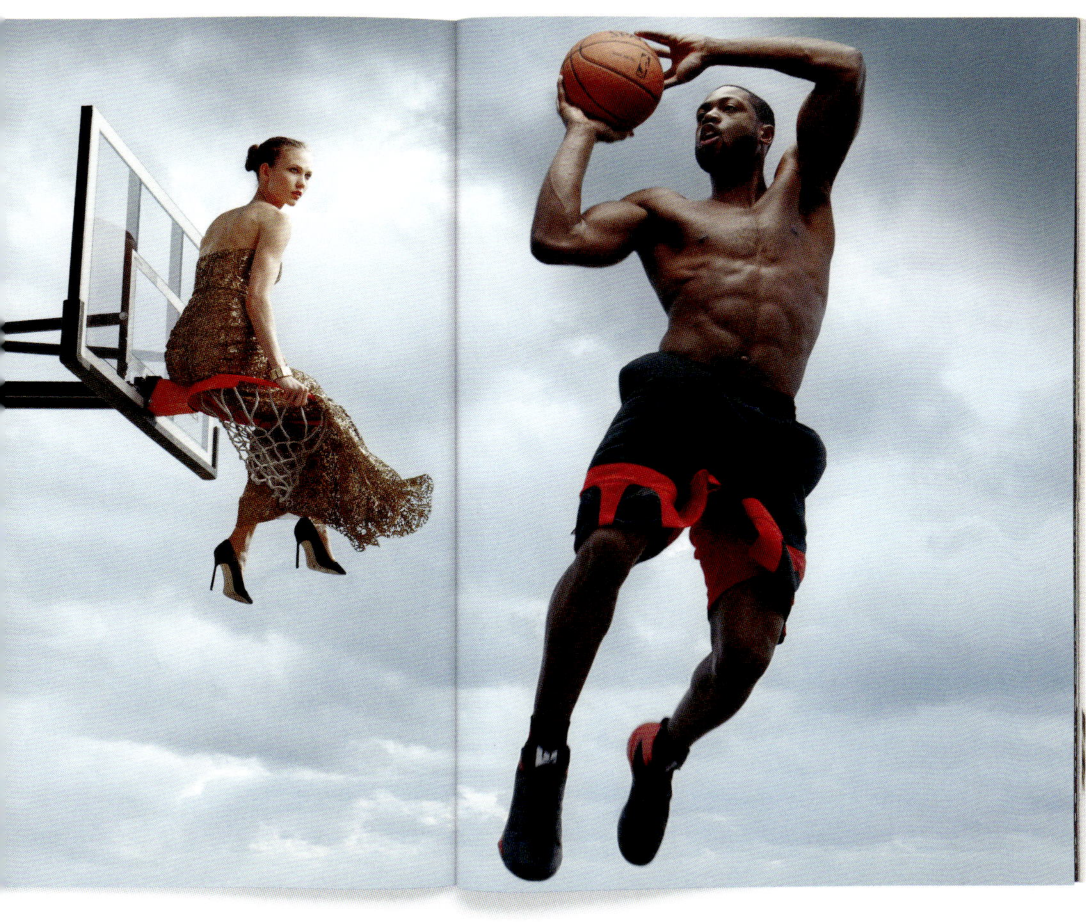

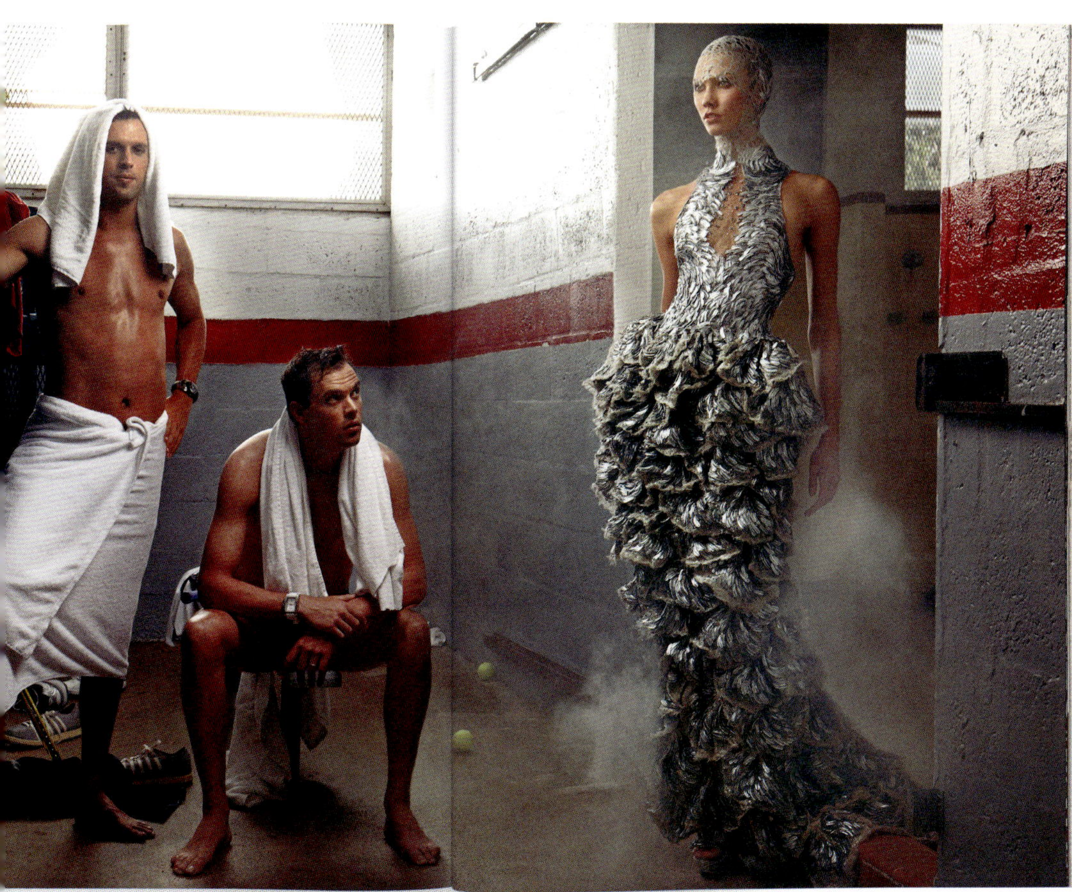

Karlie Kloss with athletes preparing for the 2012 Summer Olympics in London: gymnast Jonathan Horton, basketball player Dwyane Wade, and tennis doubles partners—and twin brothers—Bob and Mike Bryan

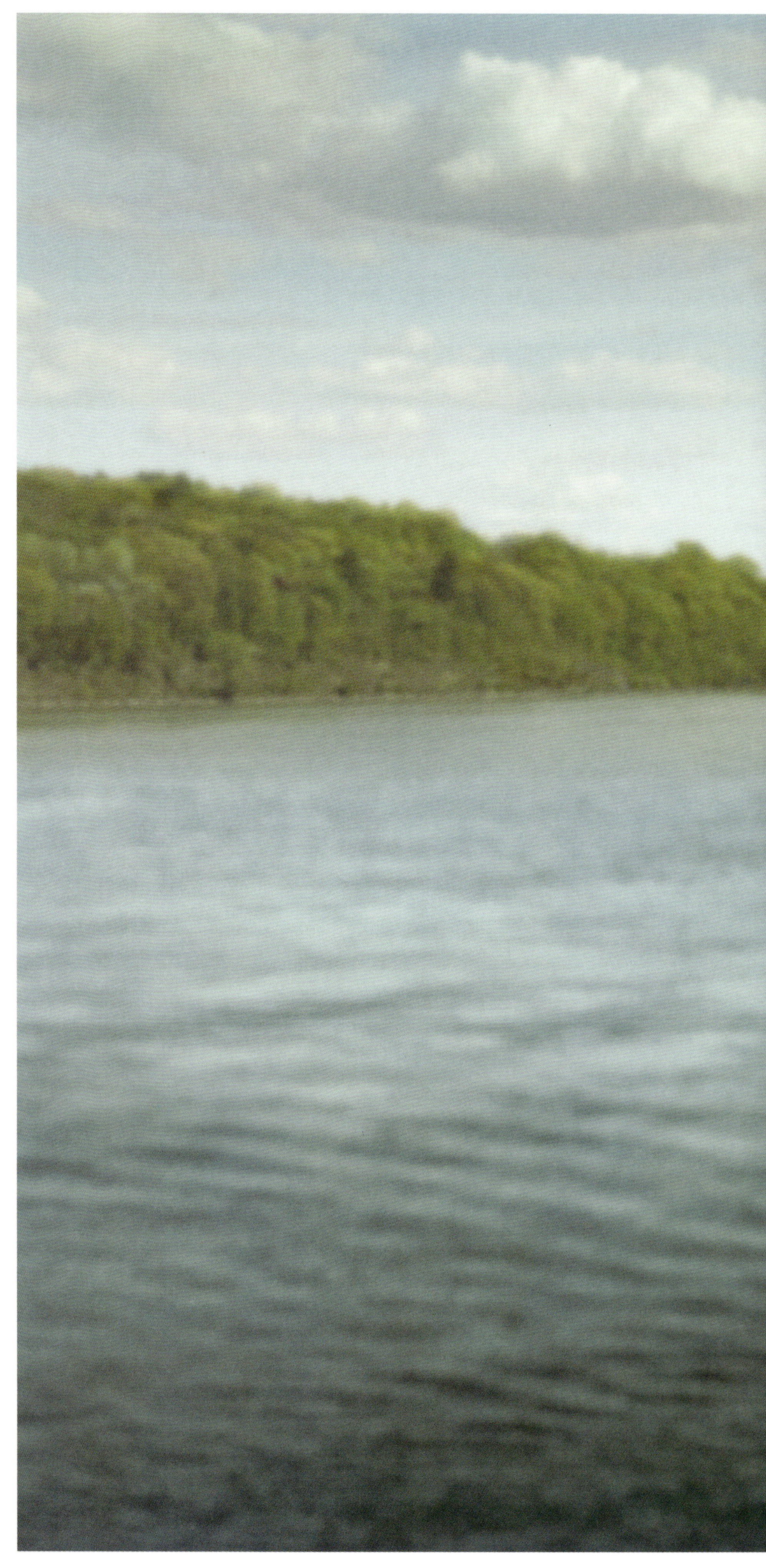

John Galliano, Saugerties,
New York, 2013

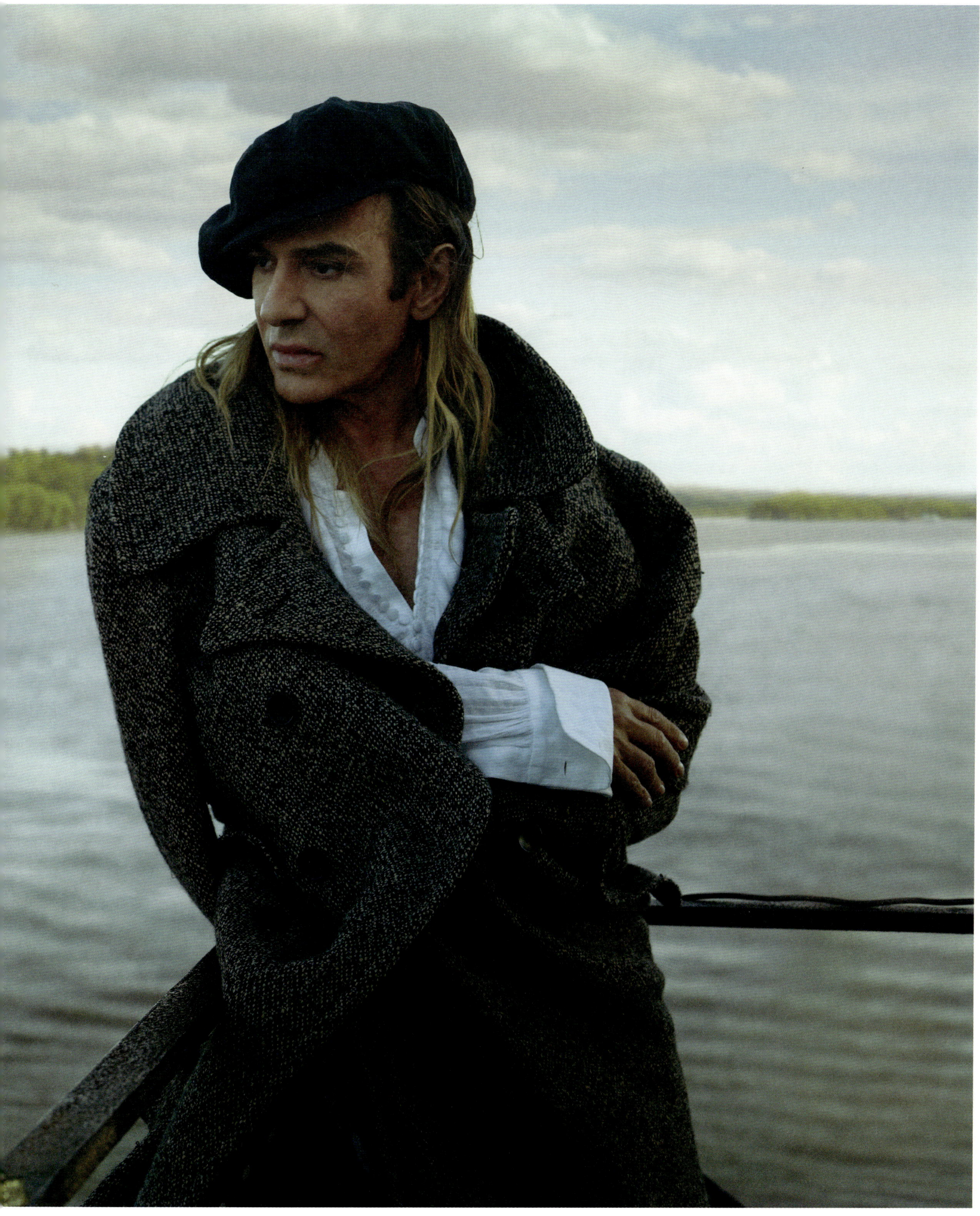

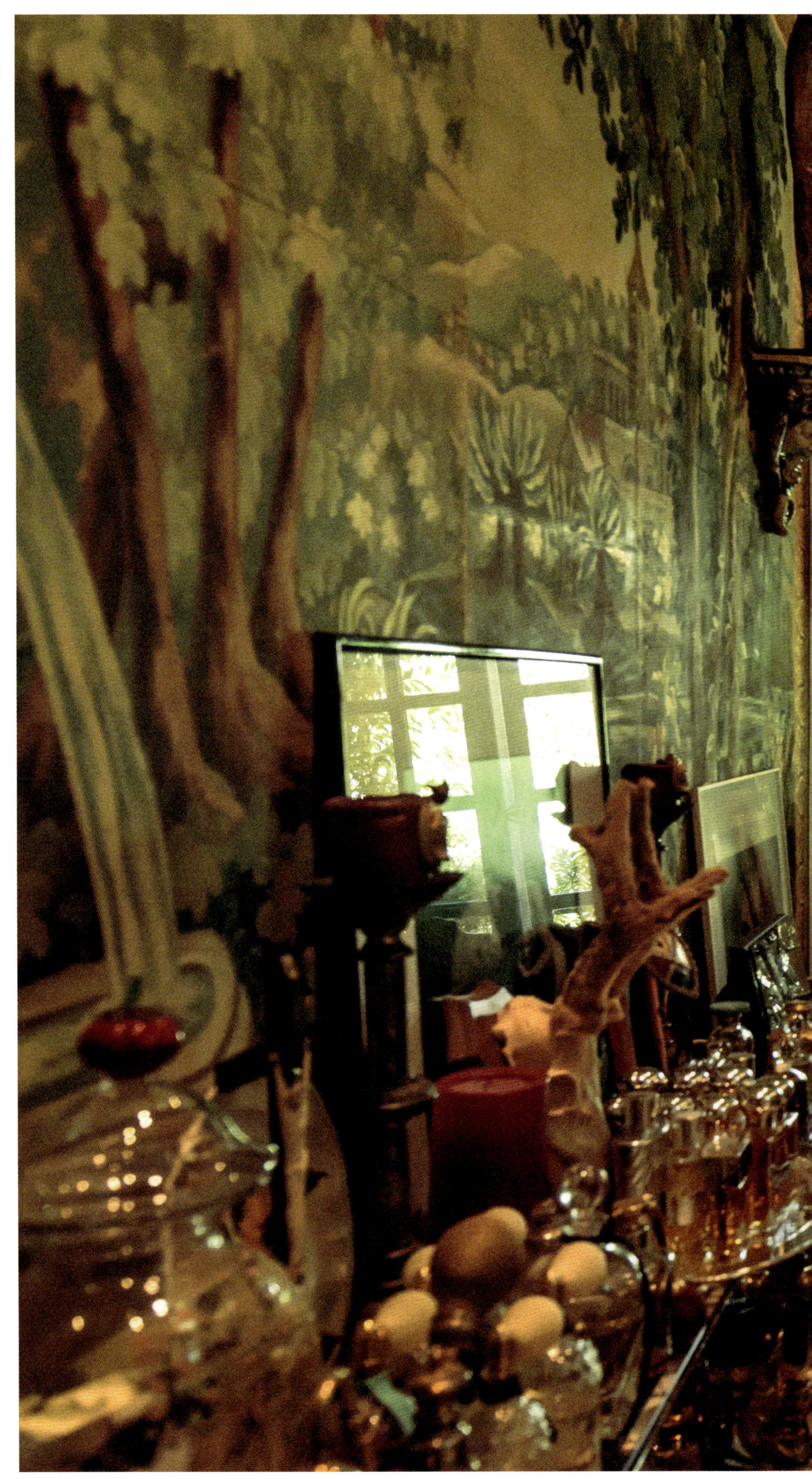

John Galliano, Paris, 2018

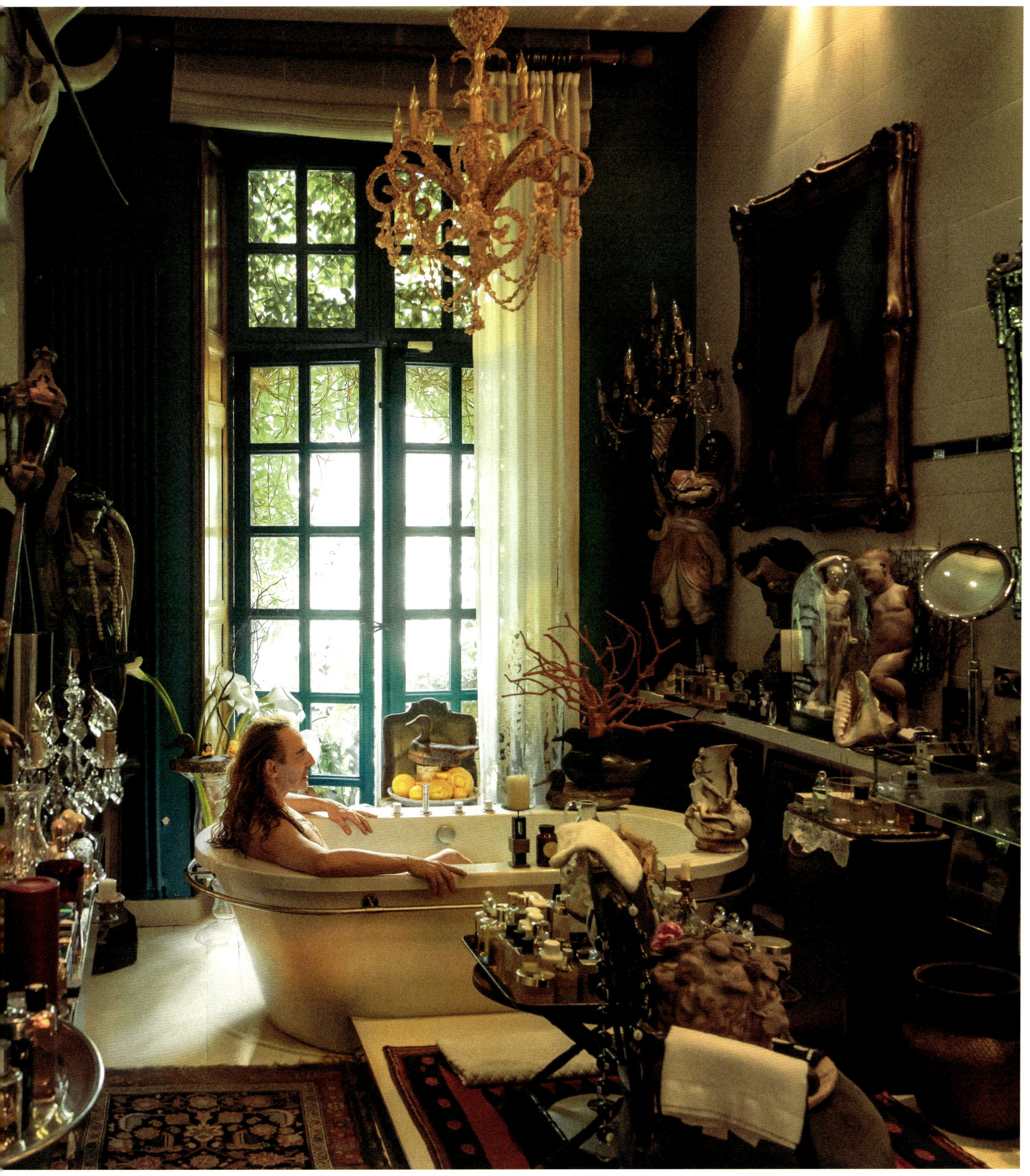

"By this time Daria Werbowy had pretty much retired in rural Ireland. She rarely agreed to be photographed and was talked into it only when she was assured that our story would be a romantic travel adventure through County Kerry with Adam Driver.

Julien D'Ys was the hair stylist. Soon after he arrived he put his hands in a creek and then got some dirt on them and rubbed it into Daria's hair. He said, 'Don't touch it.' There were just a few of us in a couple of cars driving around. She changed clothes in the back of a van."

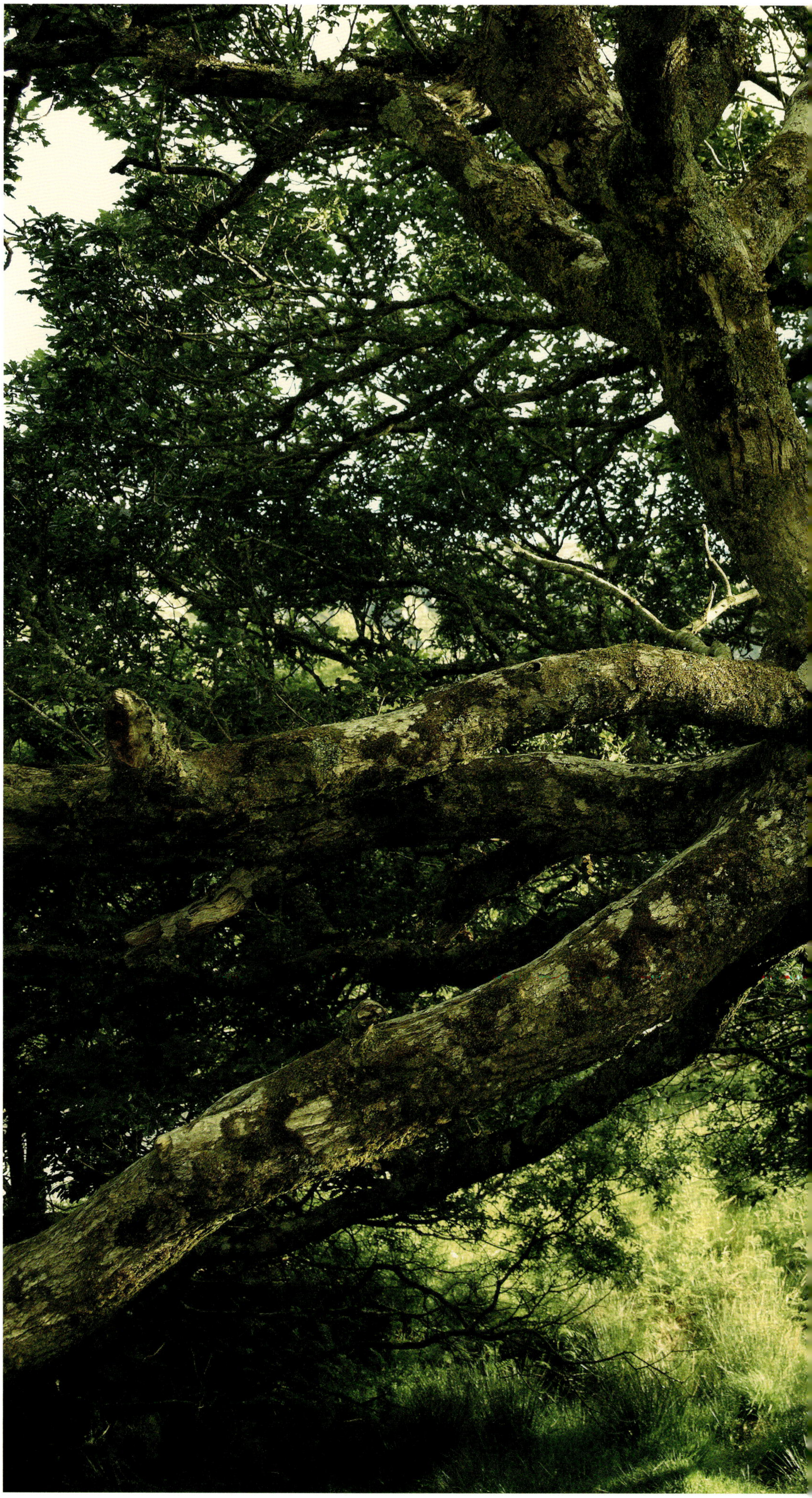

Daria Werbowy and Adam Driver,
County Kerry, Ireland, 2013

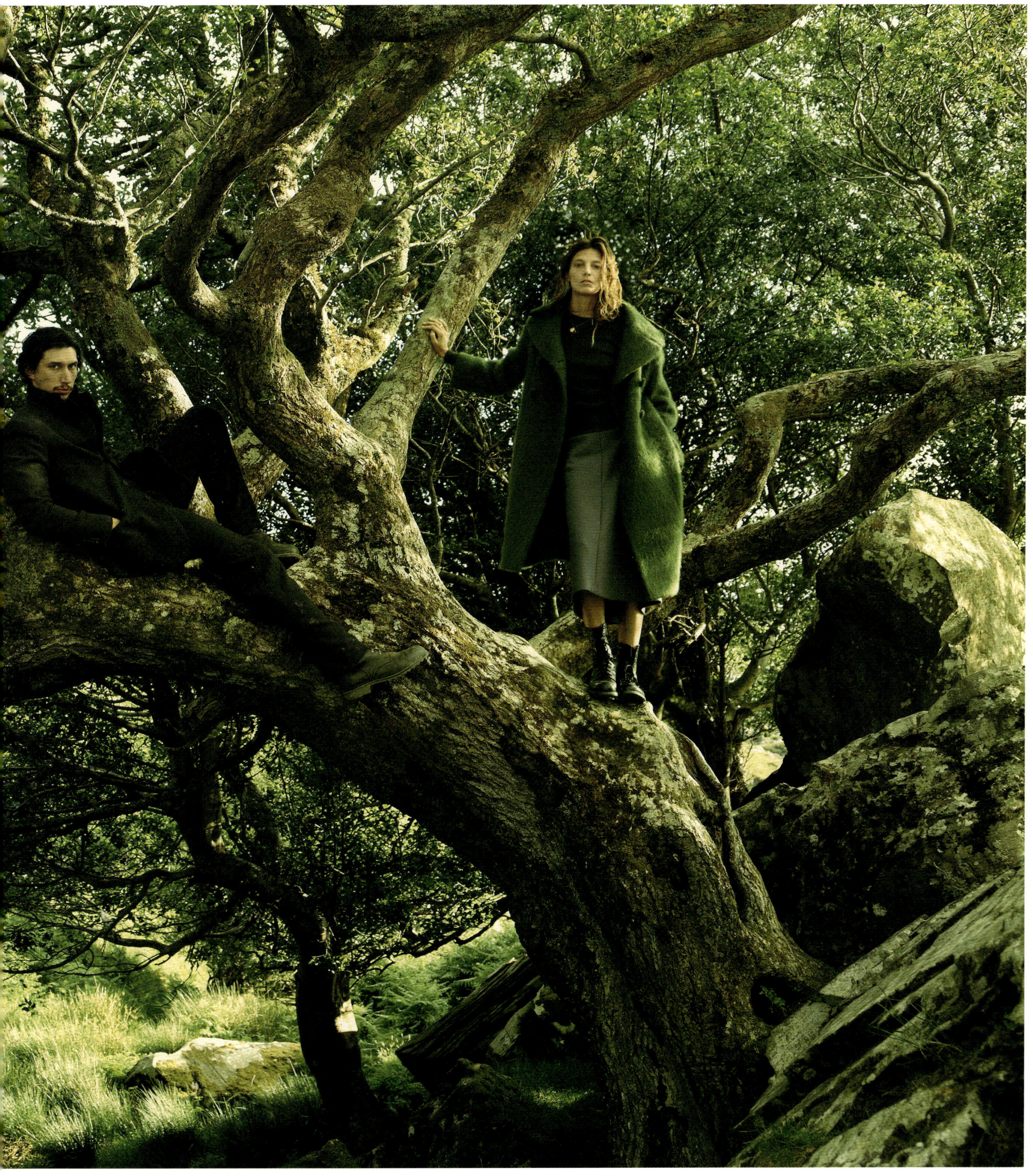

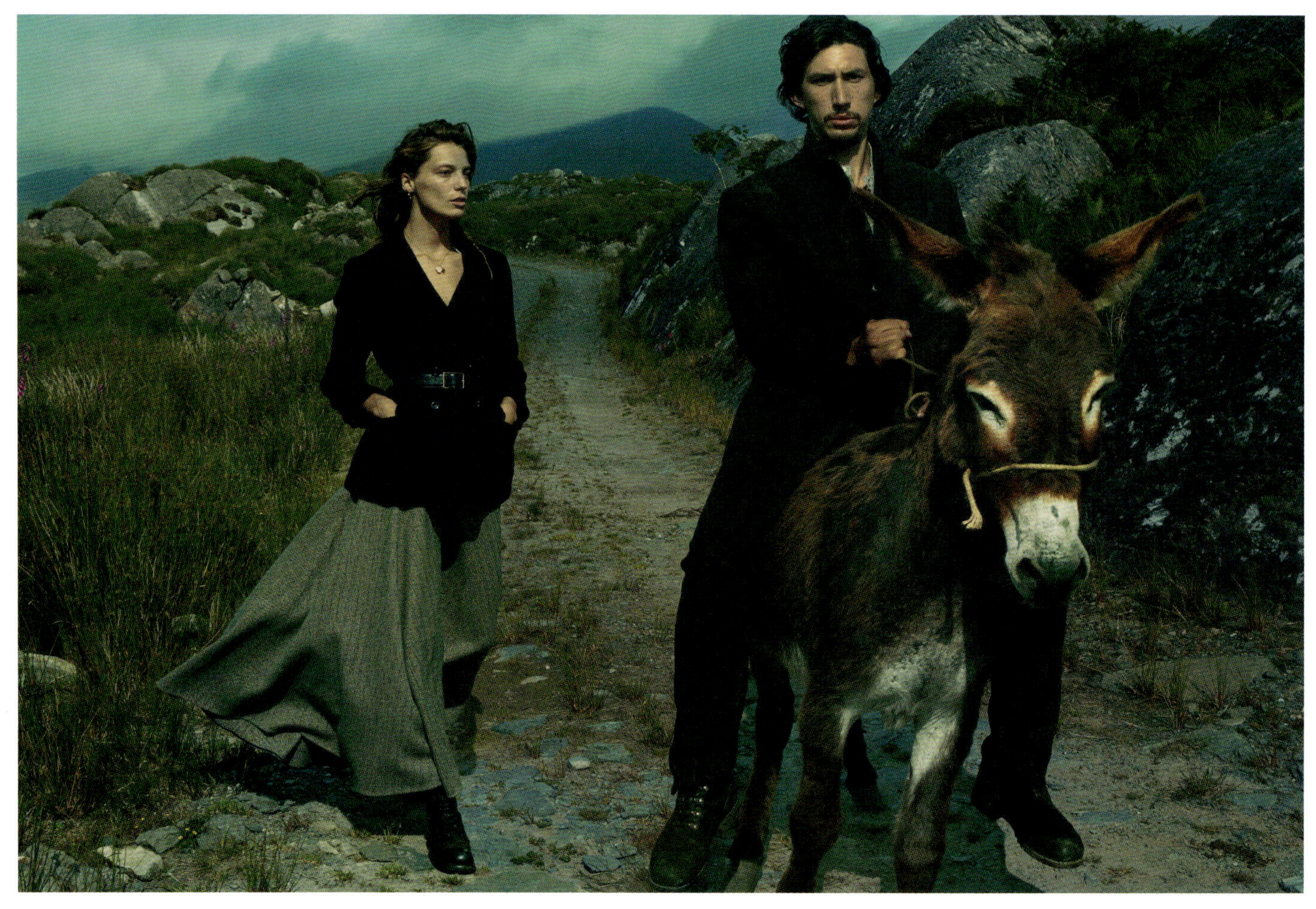

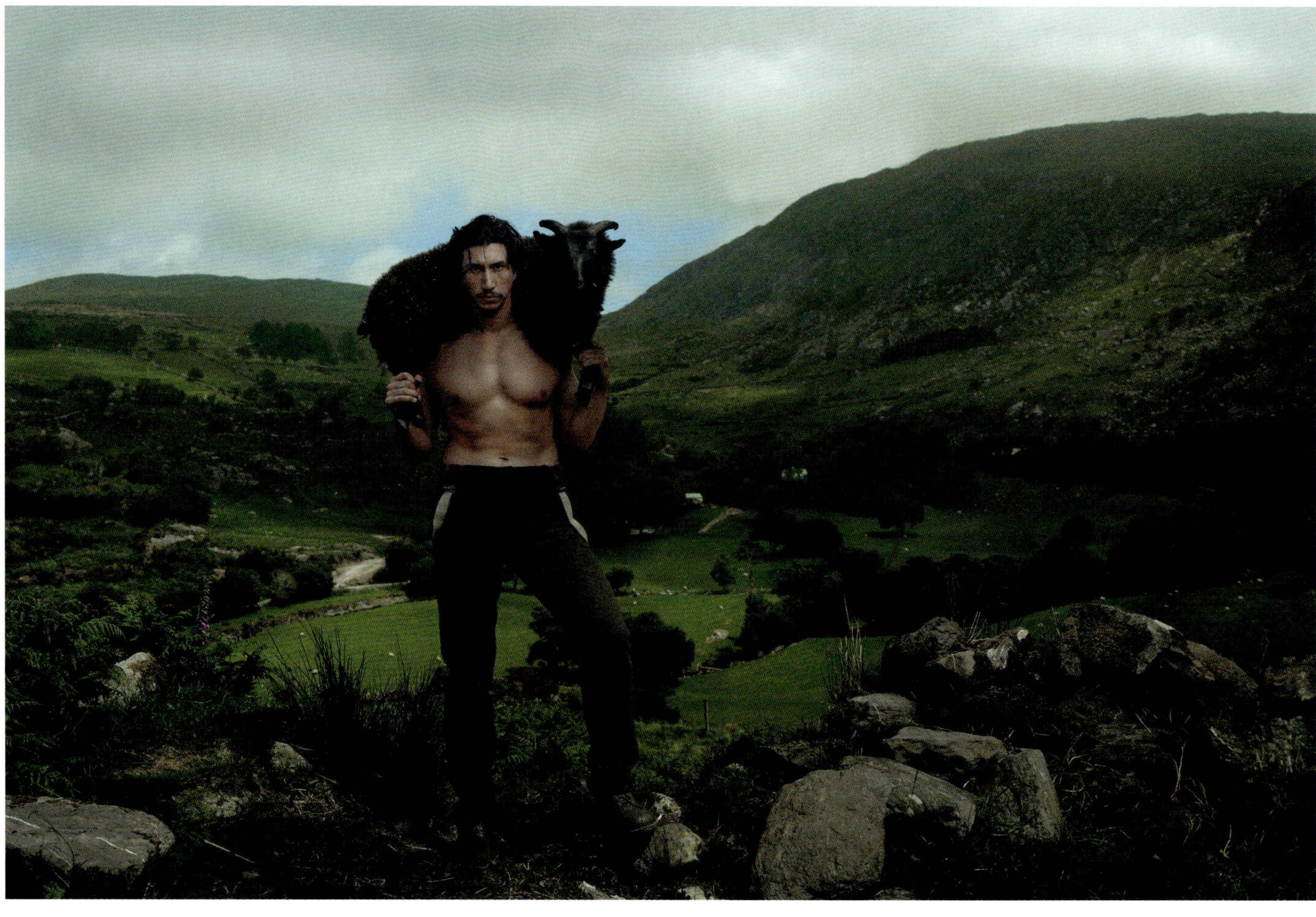

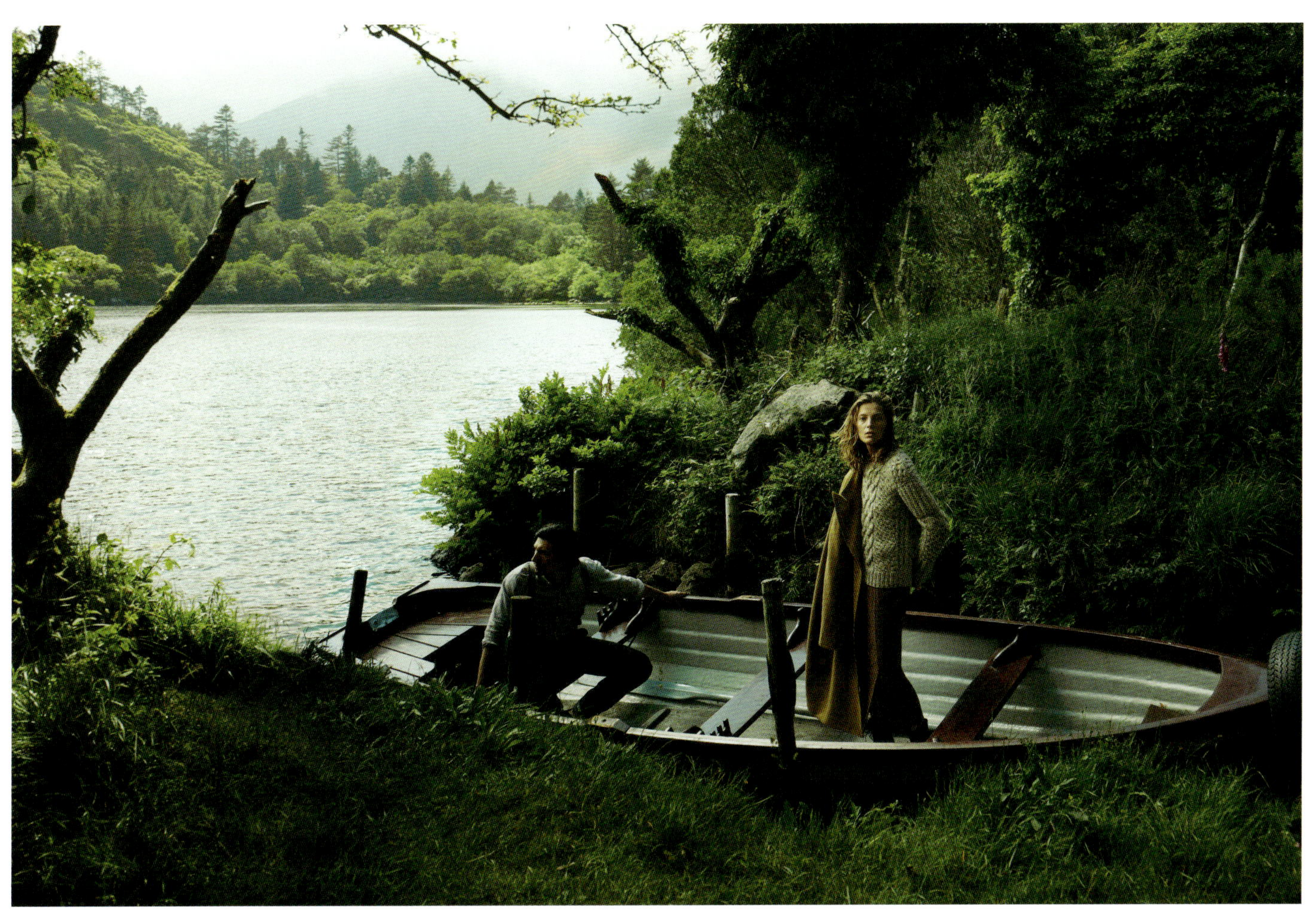

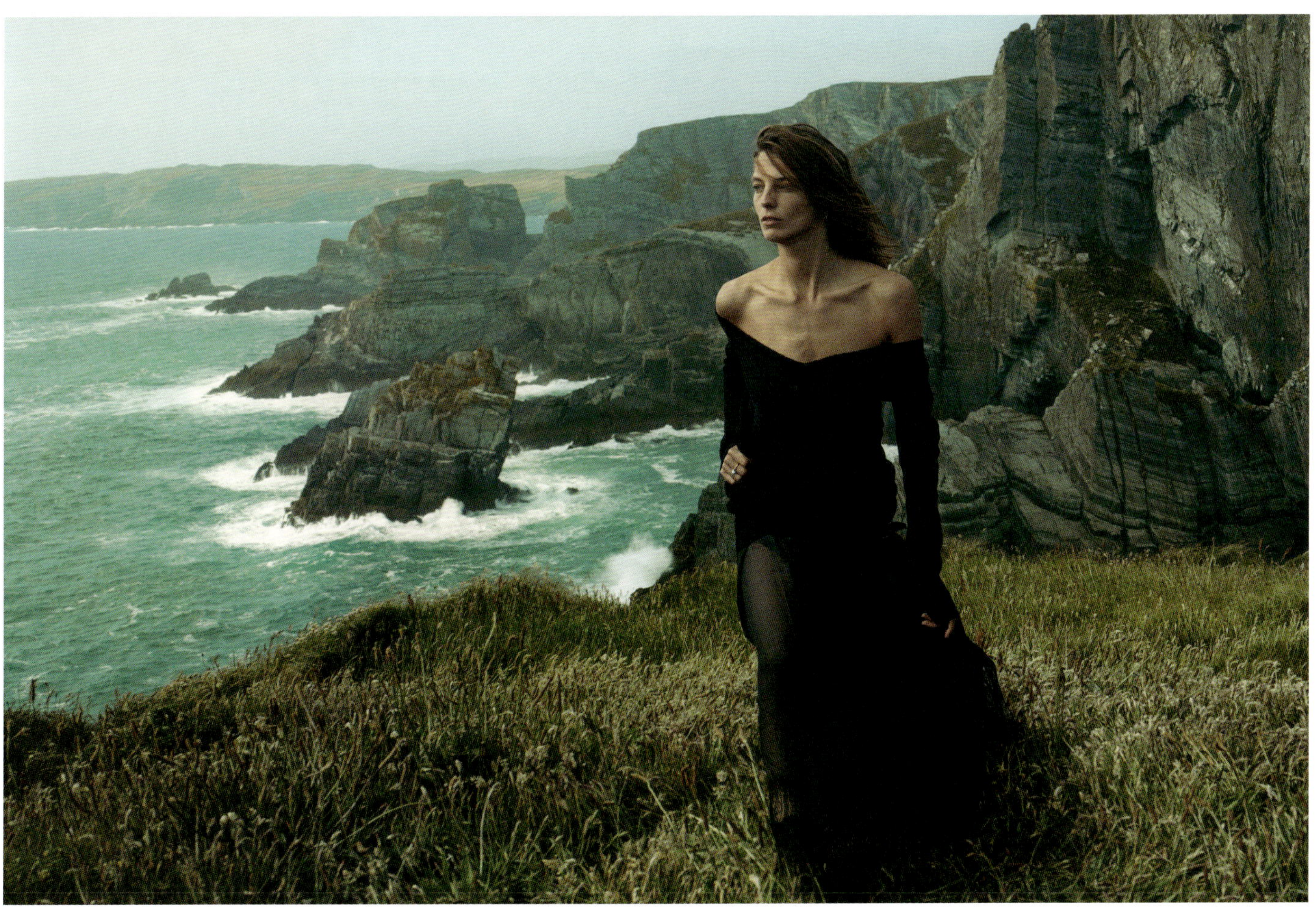

"When I was asked to make a *Vogue* cover for the magazine's 125th anniversary, I knew what I wanted as the setting. There was a global refugee crisis. In the United States, Donald Trump was trying to close the doors to the country. My grandparents were immigrants from Russia and Romania and had come through Ellis Island. Those early photographs by anonymous photographers of immigrants entering New York Harbor and seeing the Statue of Liberty for the first time are so moving."

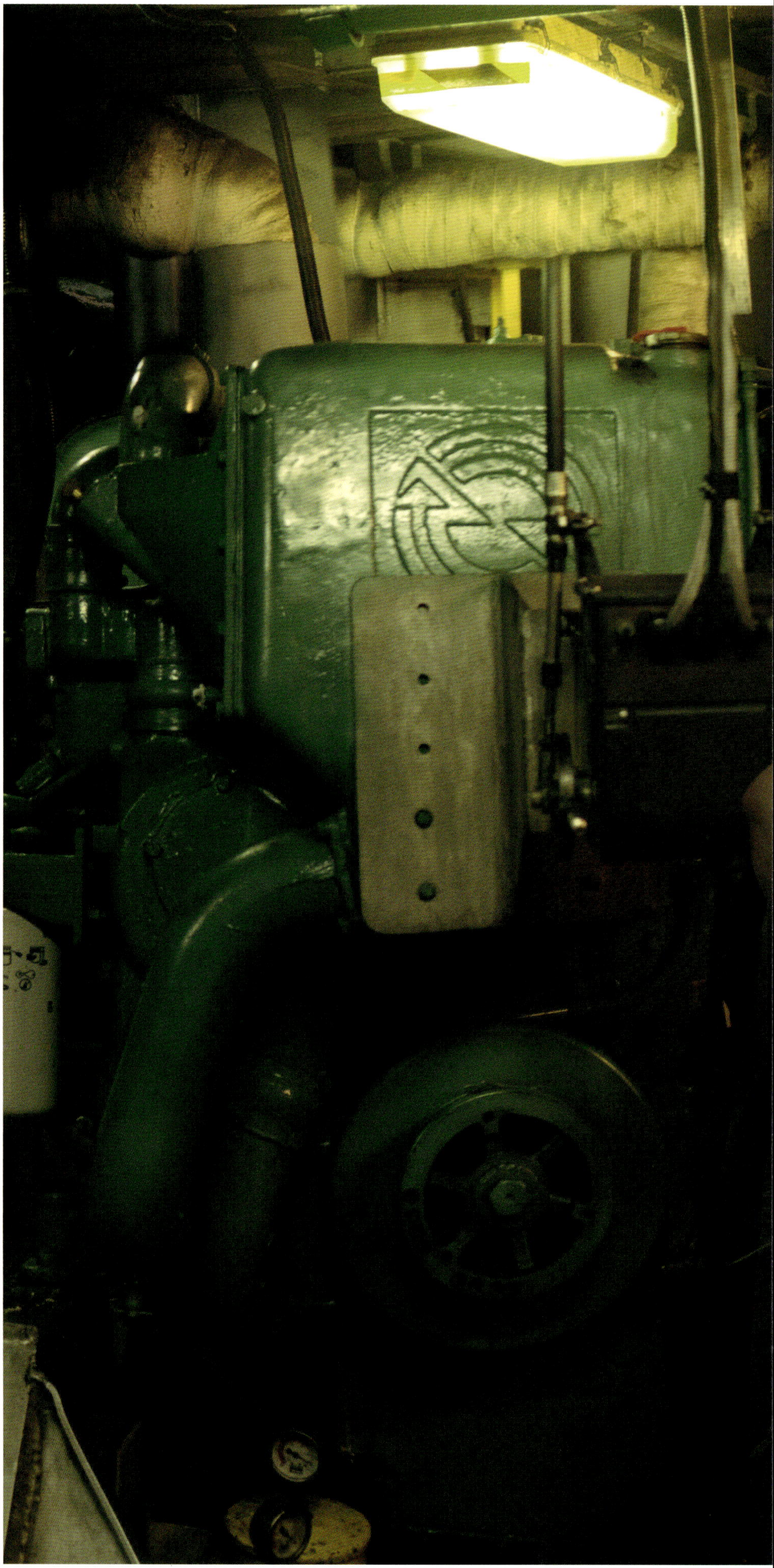

Jennifer Lawrence in the boiler room of the *Marjorie B. McAllister*, New York Harbor, 2017

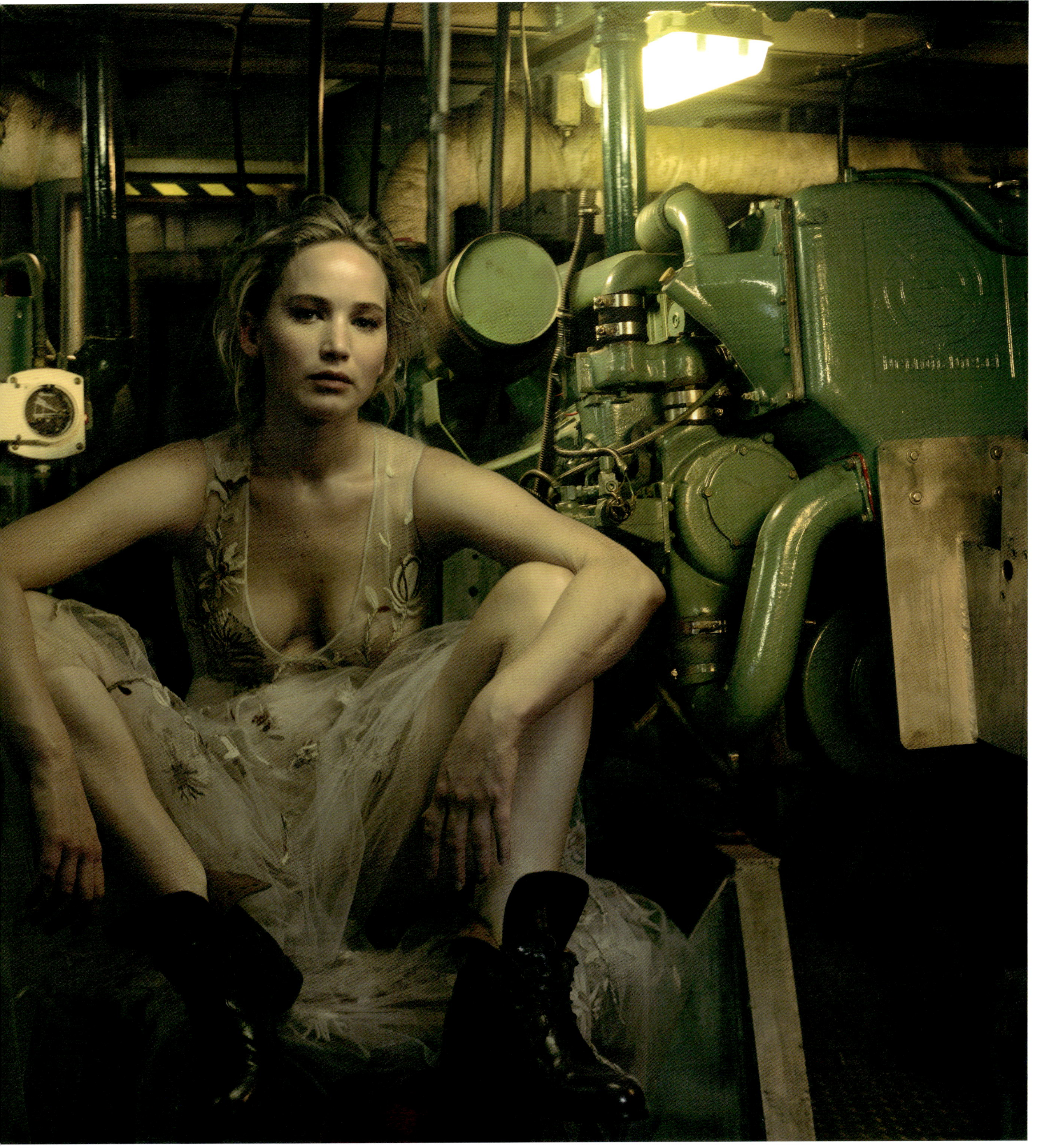

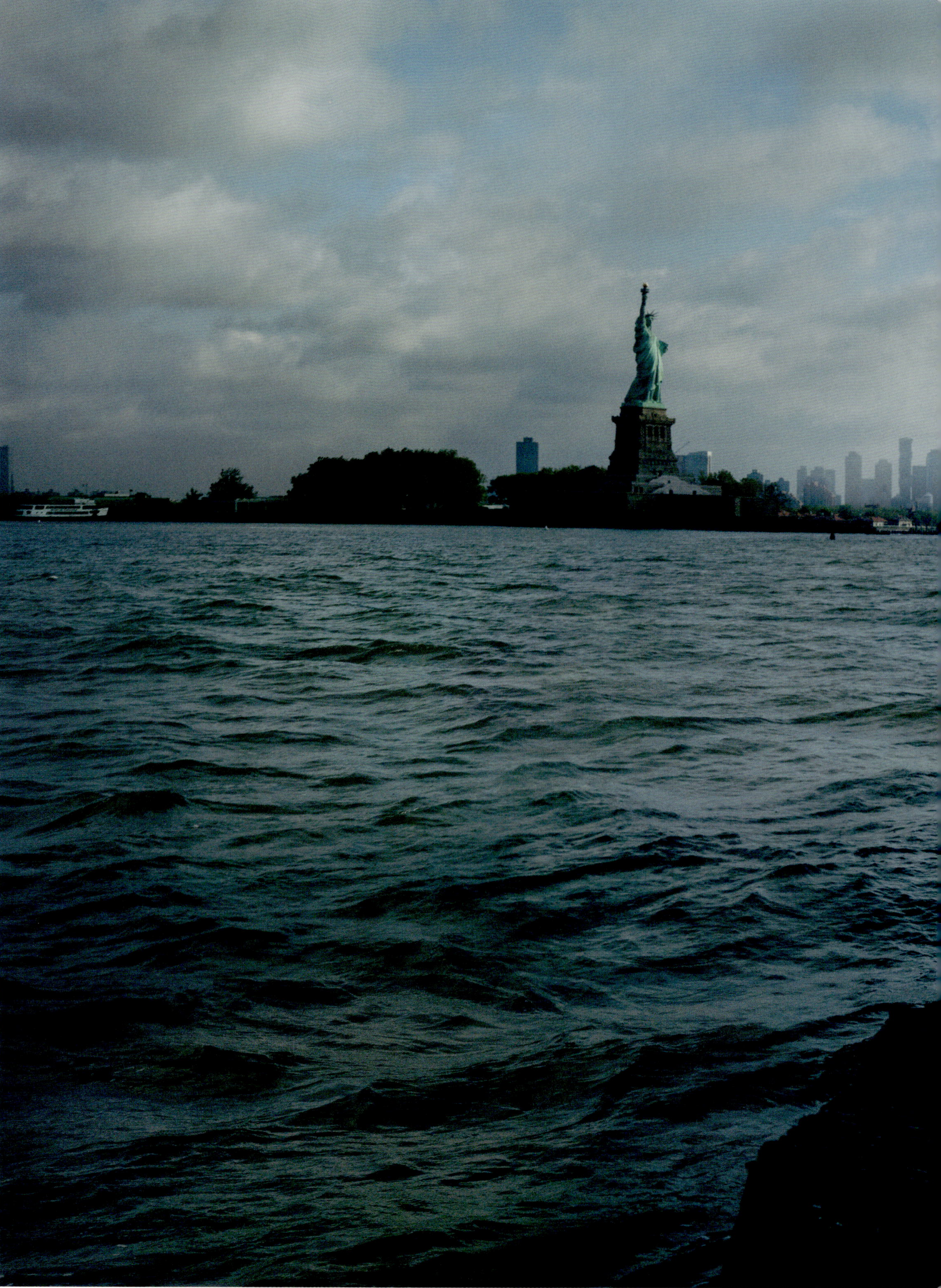

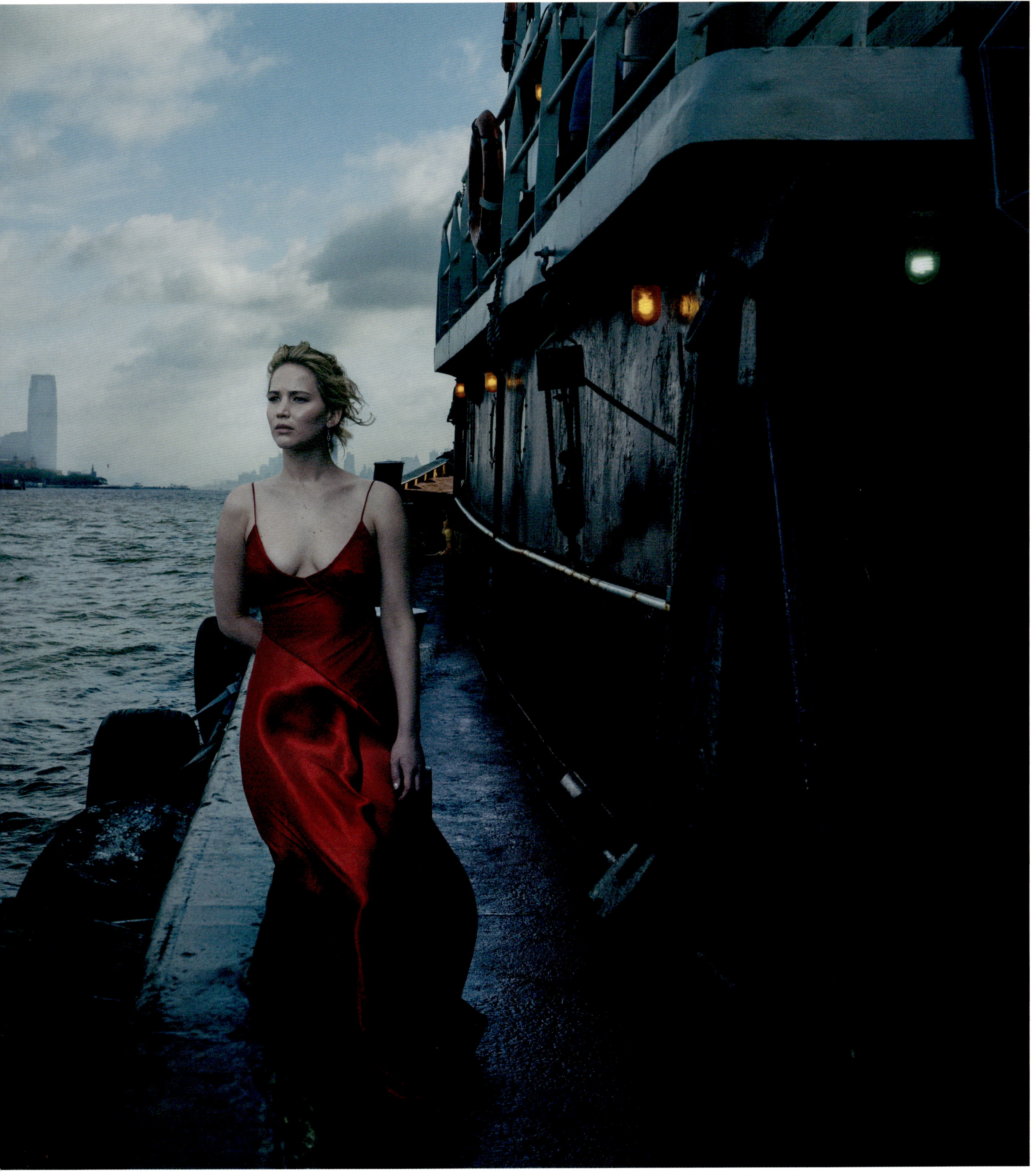

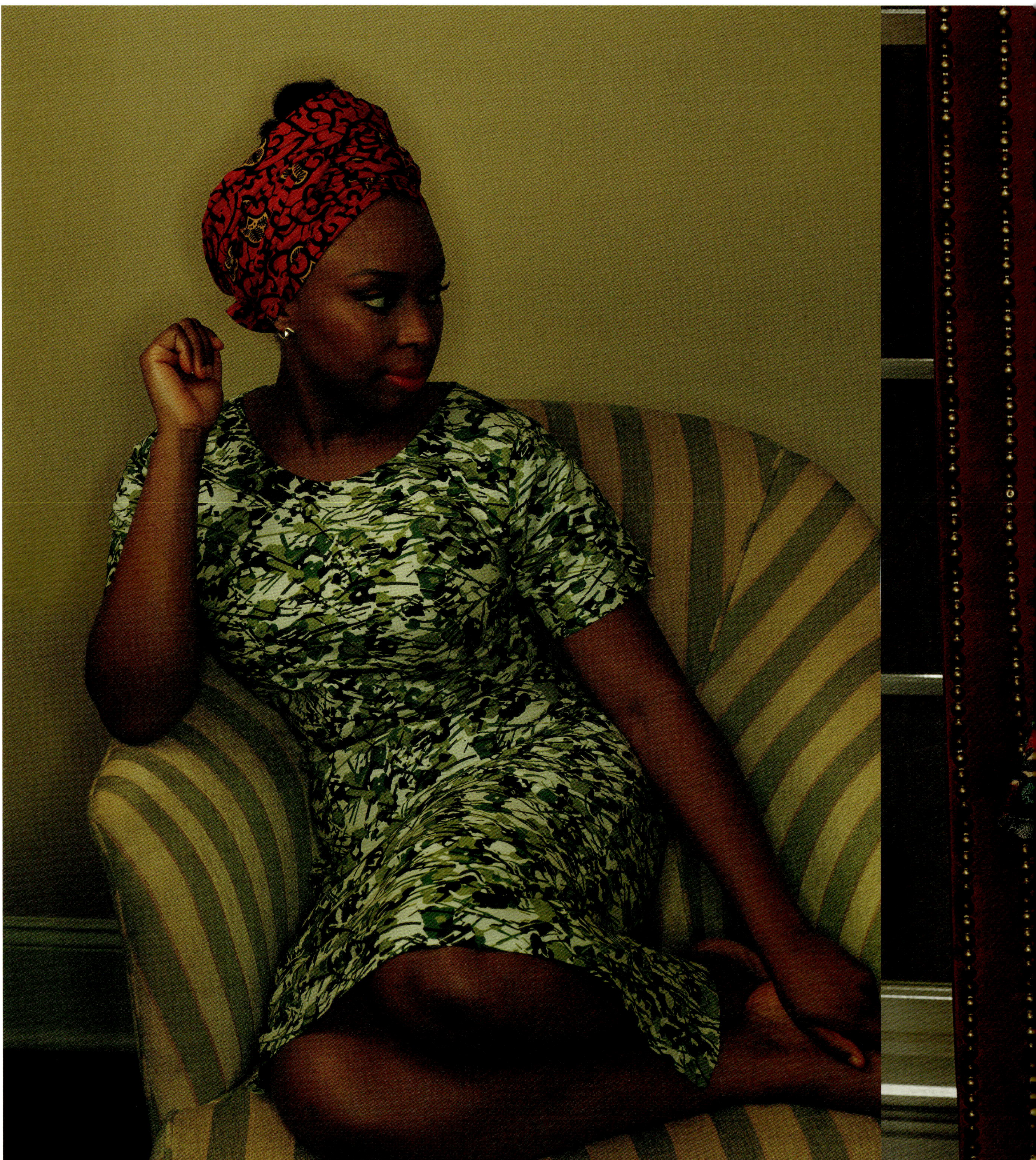

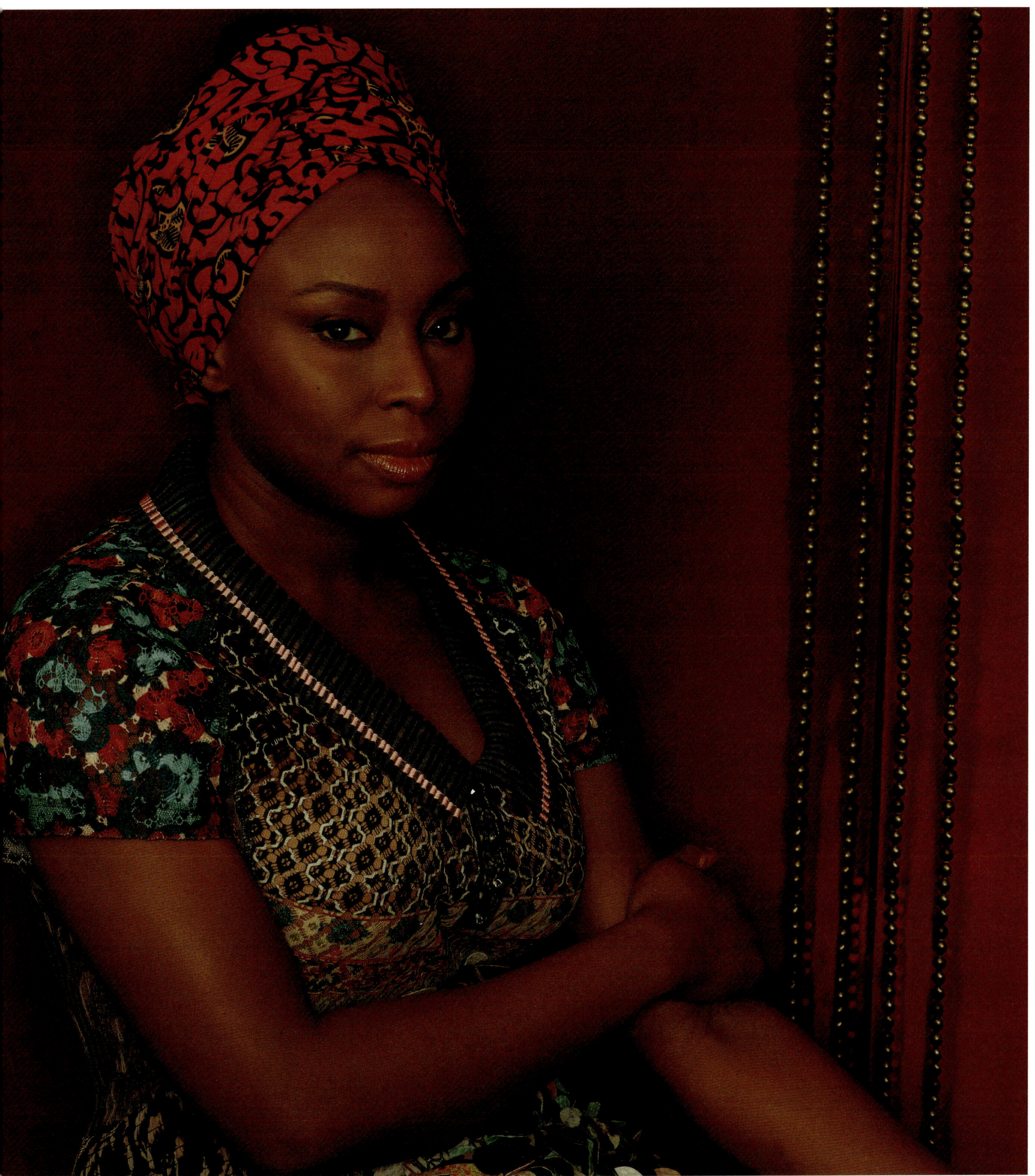

Previous pages: Chimamanda Ngozi Adichie,
Ellicott City, Maryland, 2016

Maya Angelou, New York City, 1999

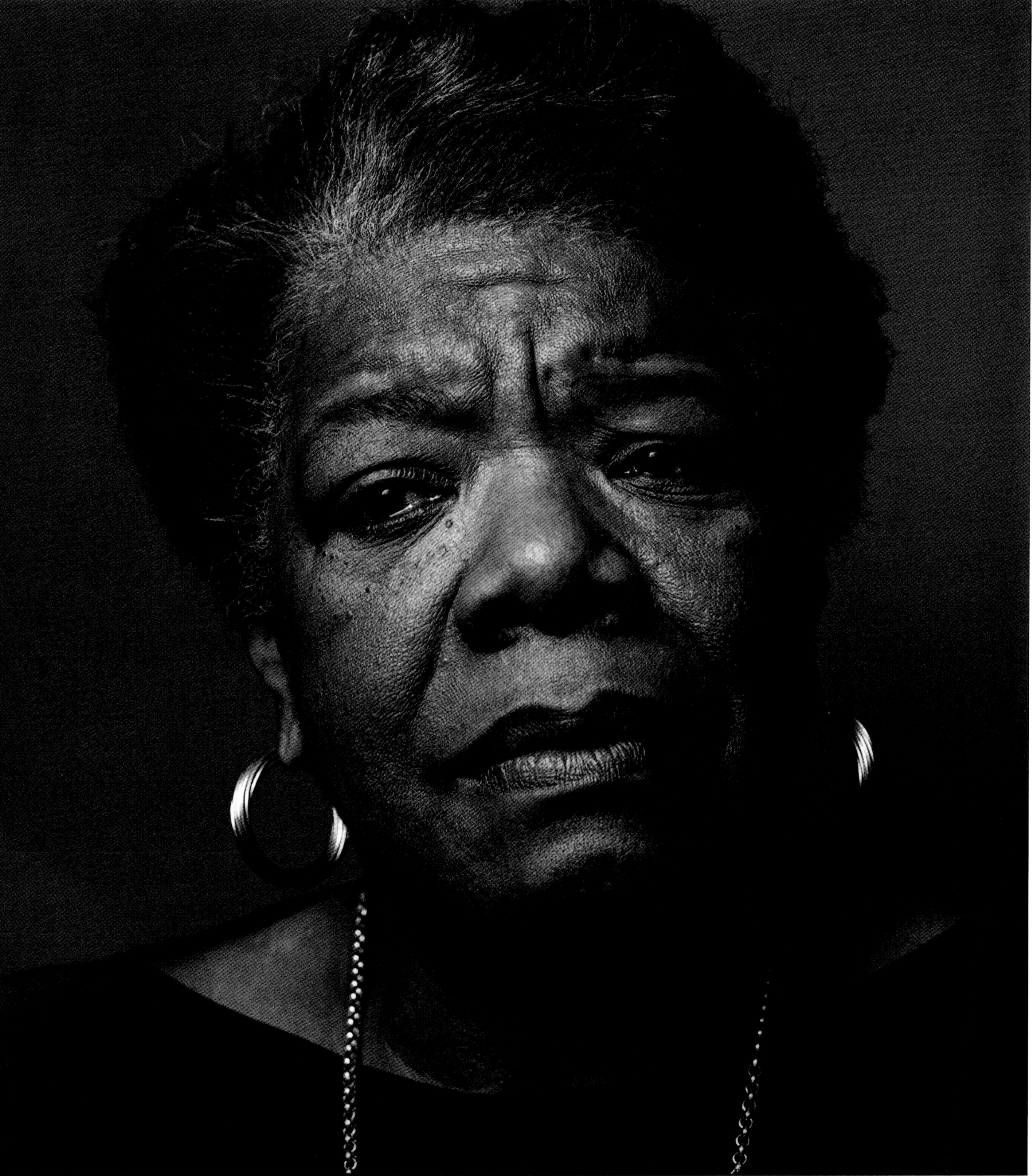

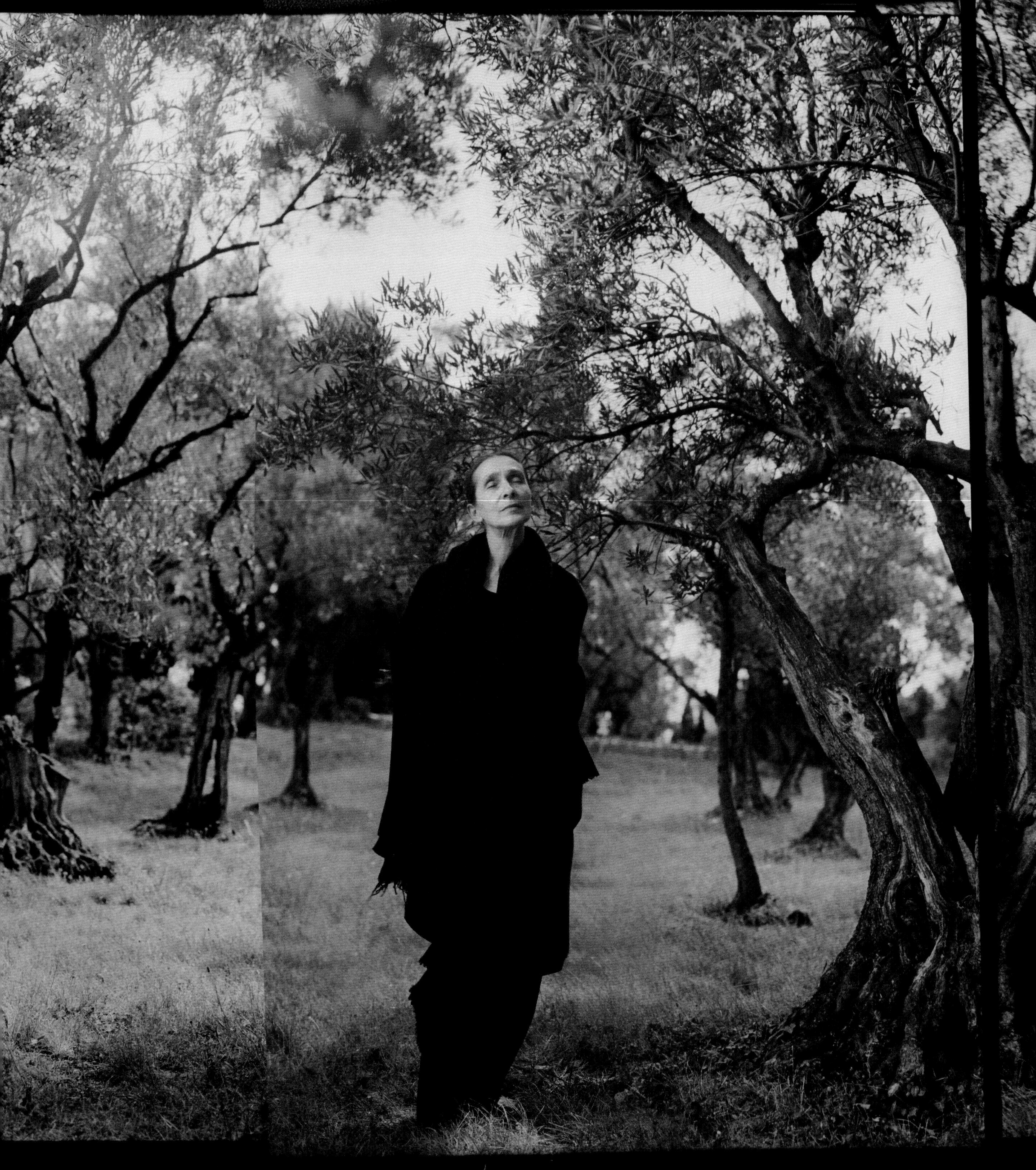

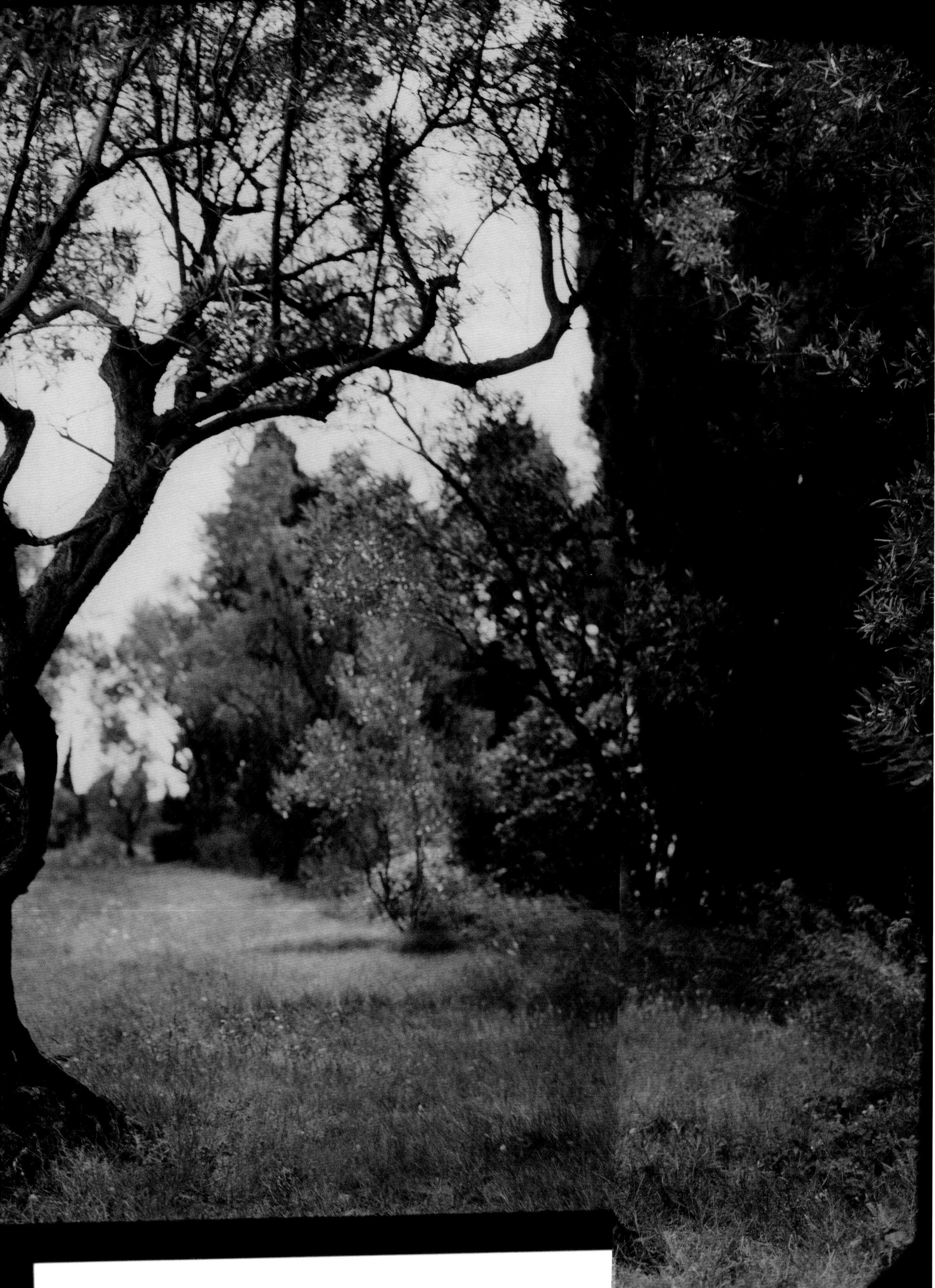

Pina Bausch,
Avignon,
France, 2000

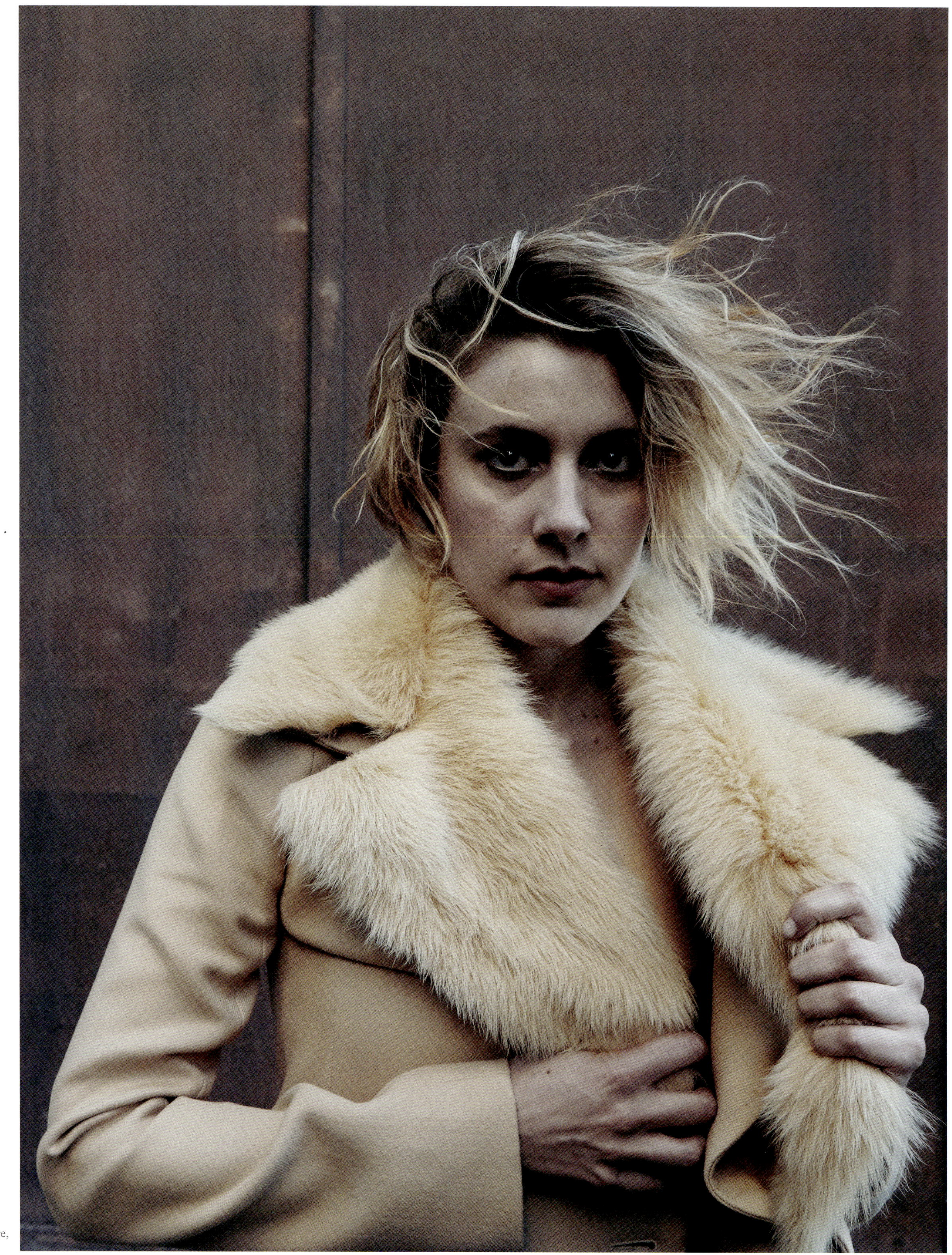

Greta Gerwig,
Paramount Sound Stage,
Los Angeles, 2016

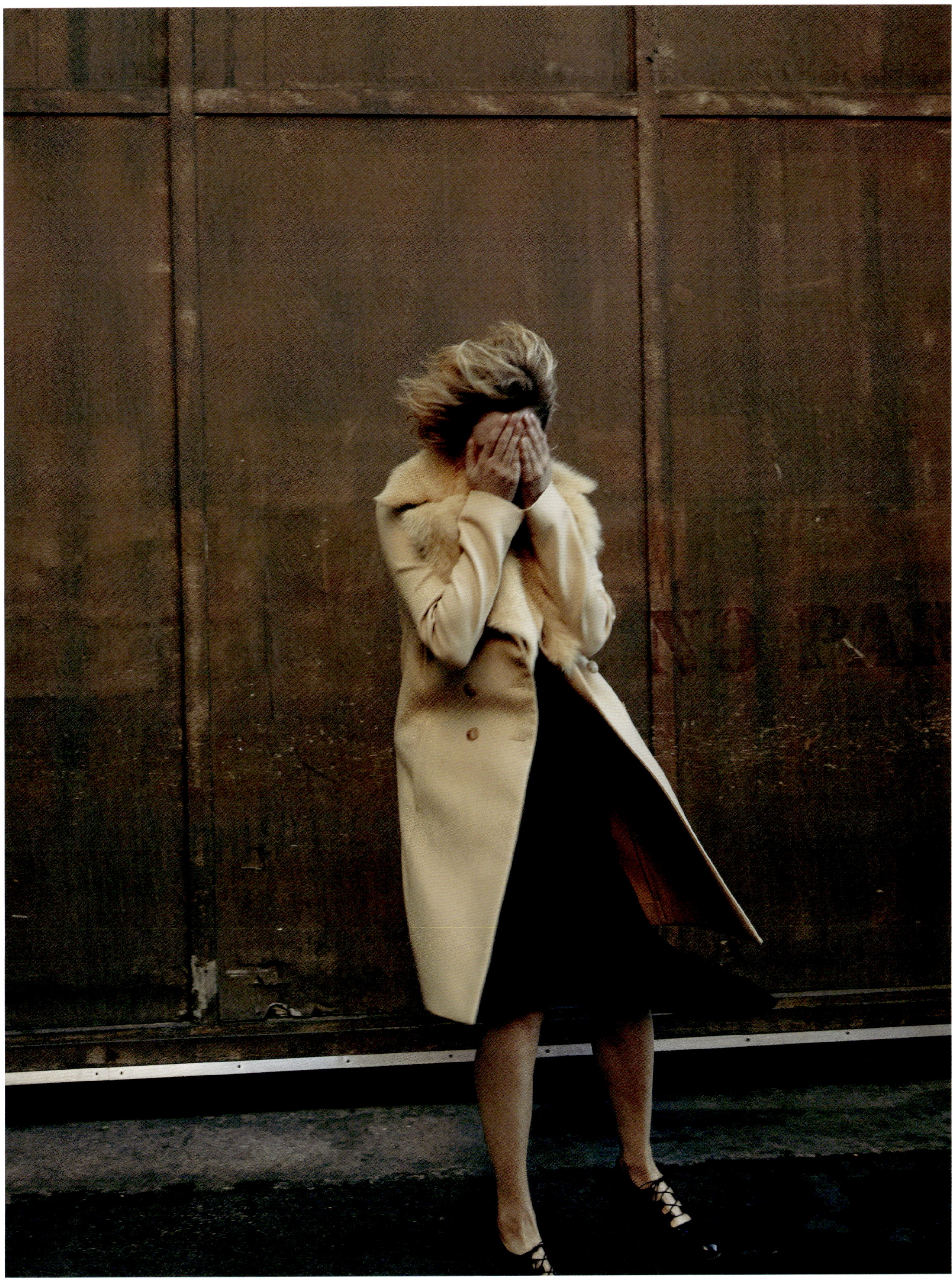

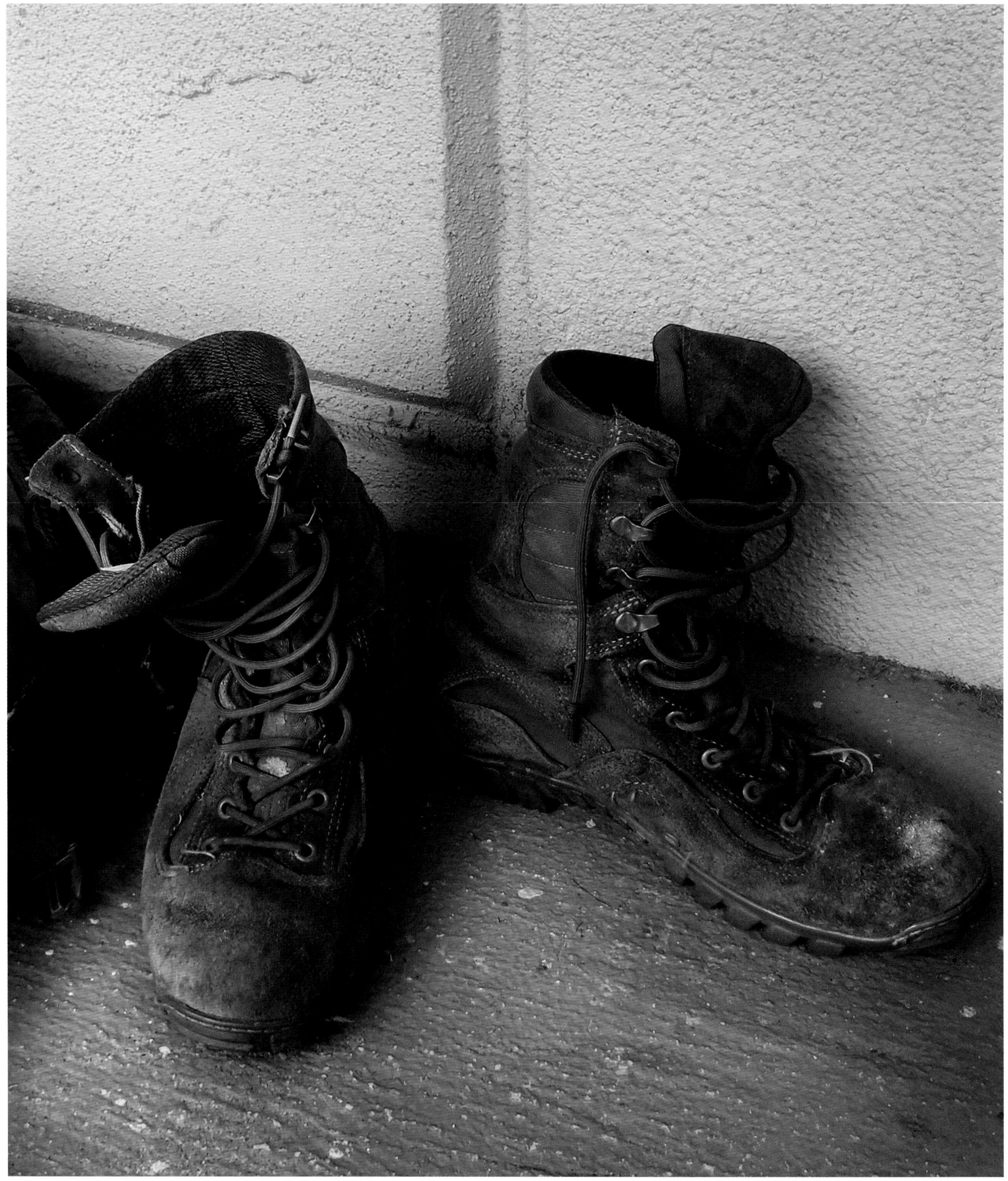

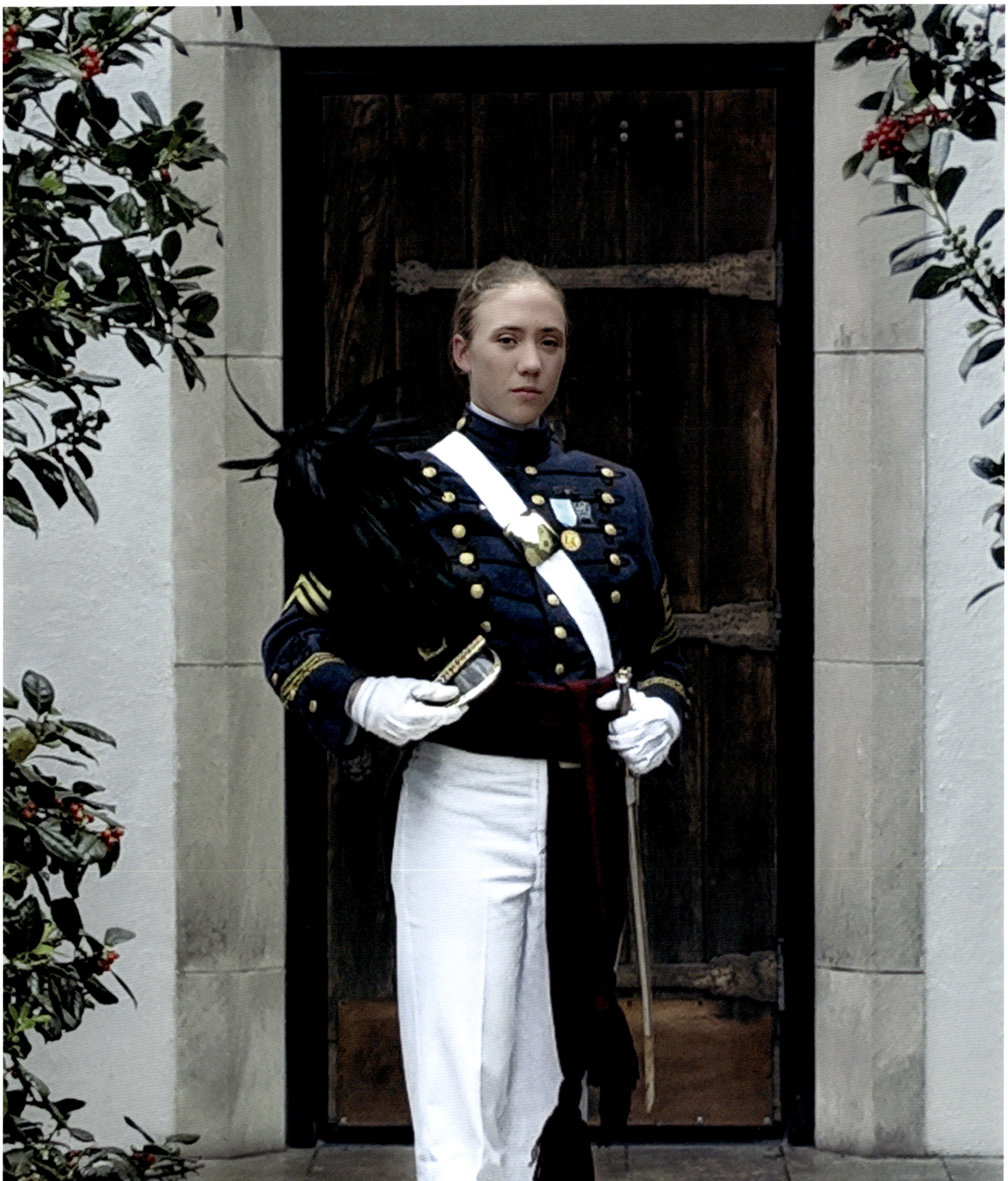

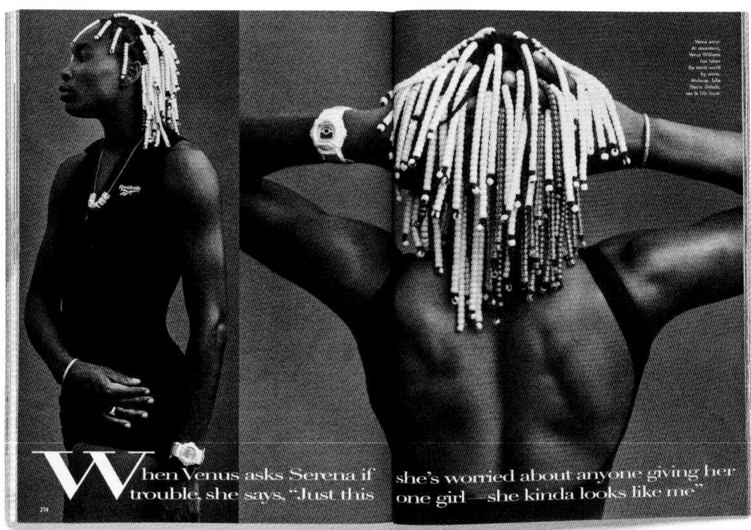
When Venus asks Serena if she's worried about anyone giving her trouble, she says, "Just this one girl—she kinda looks like me"

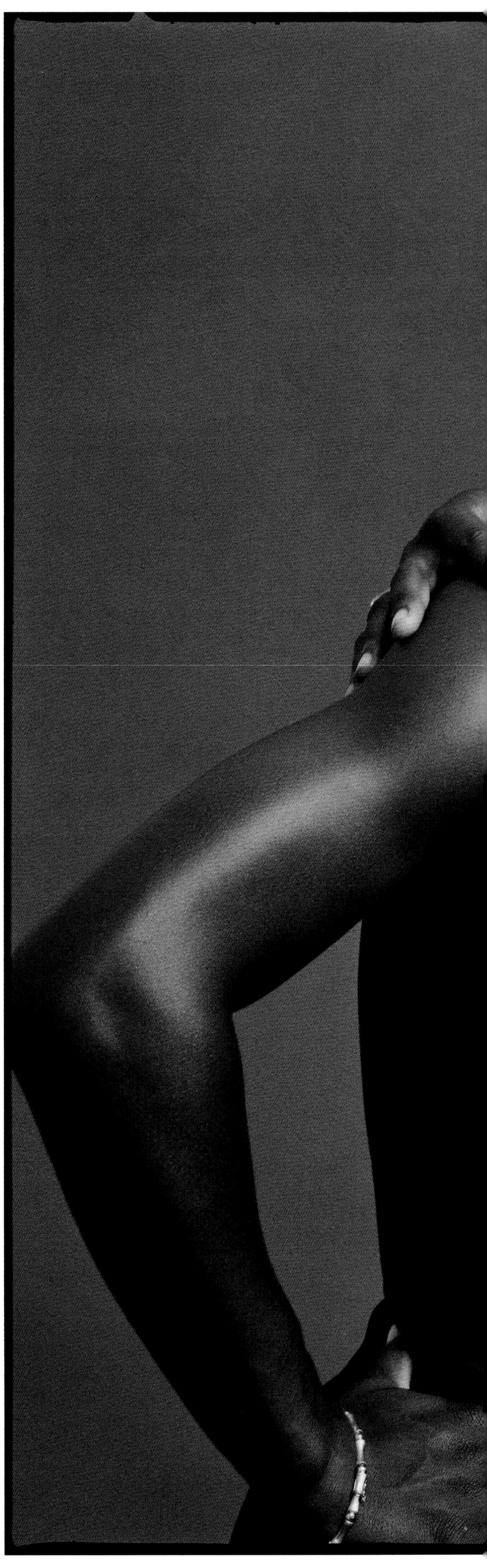

Venus Williams was seventeen and her sister Serena was sixteen when Annie first photographed them. They were newcomers to professional tennis, young Black women in a largely white sport. Four years later, Venus was the number-one women's player in the world. It was a spot she held only briefly that time, because a few months later, Serena was number one.

The Williams sisters transformed women's tennis. Their serves were aggressive, their on-court strategies tenacious and unyielding. Annie has photographed the Williams sisters many times over the years. That first sitting came with a *Vogue* fashion editor—Camilla Nickerson—and Carolina Herrera dresses. Annie was interested in the girls' physical power. But, of course—understandably—they were excited about the clothes.

Previous spread: Sarah Zorn was the first female regimental commander—the top cadet—in the history of the Citadel, the Military College of South Carolina, in Charleston. She graduated in 2019 and was commissioned as an officer in the army.

Venus Williams, Palm Beach Gardens, Florida, 1998

Serena and Venus Williams, Palm Beach Gardens, Florida, 1998

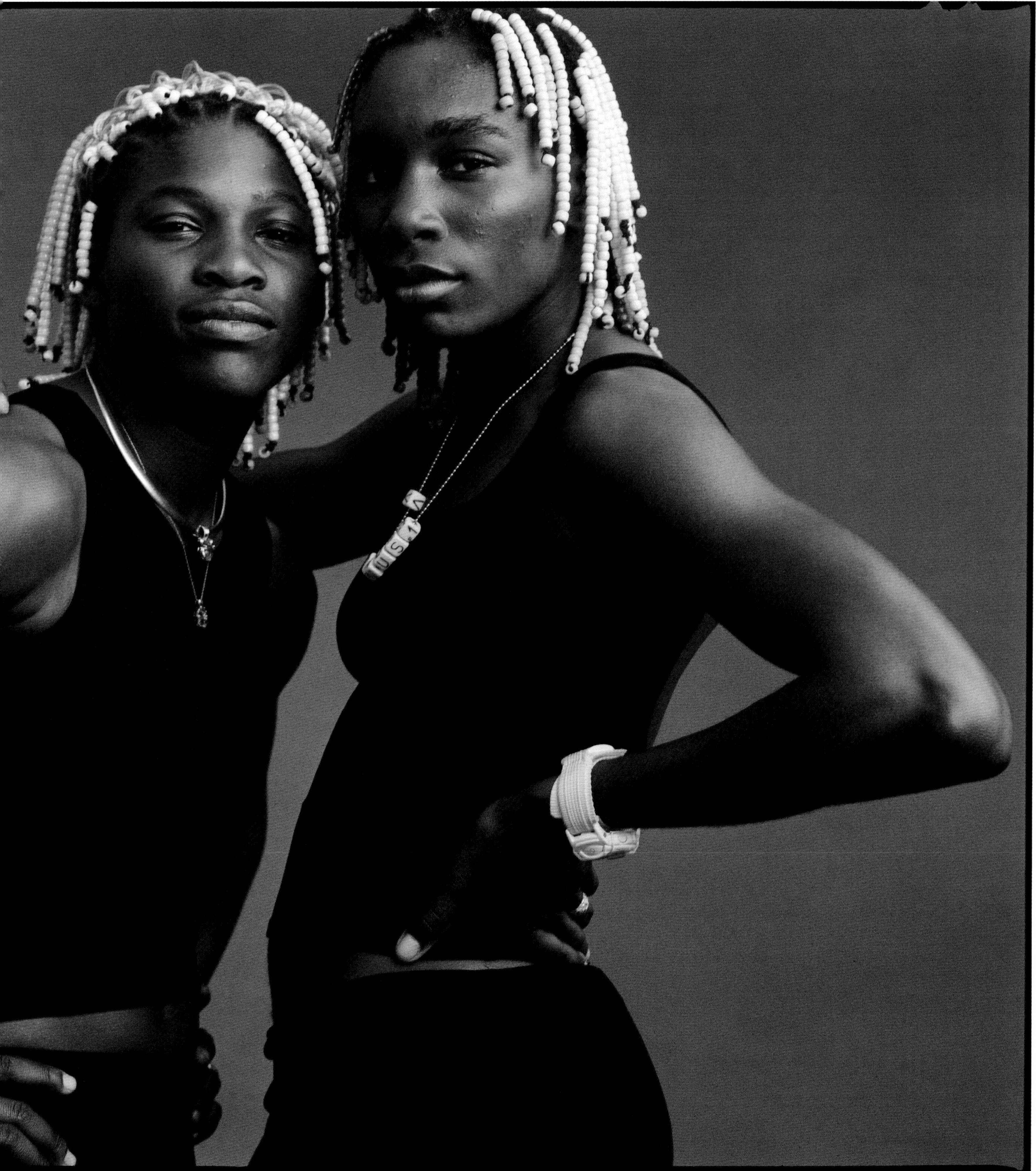

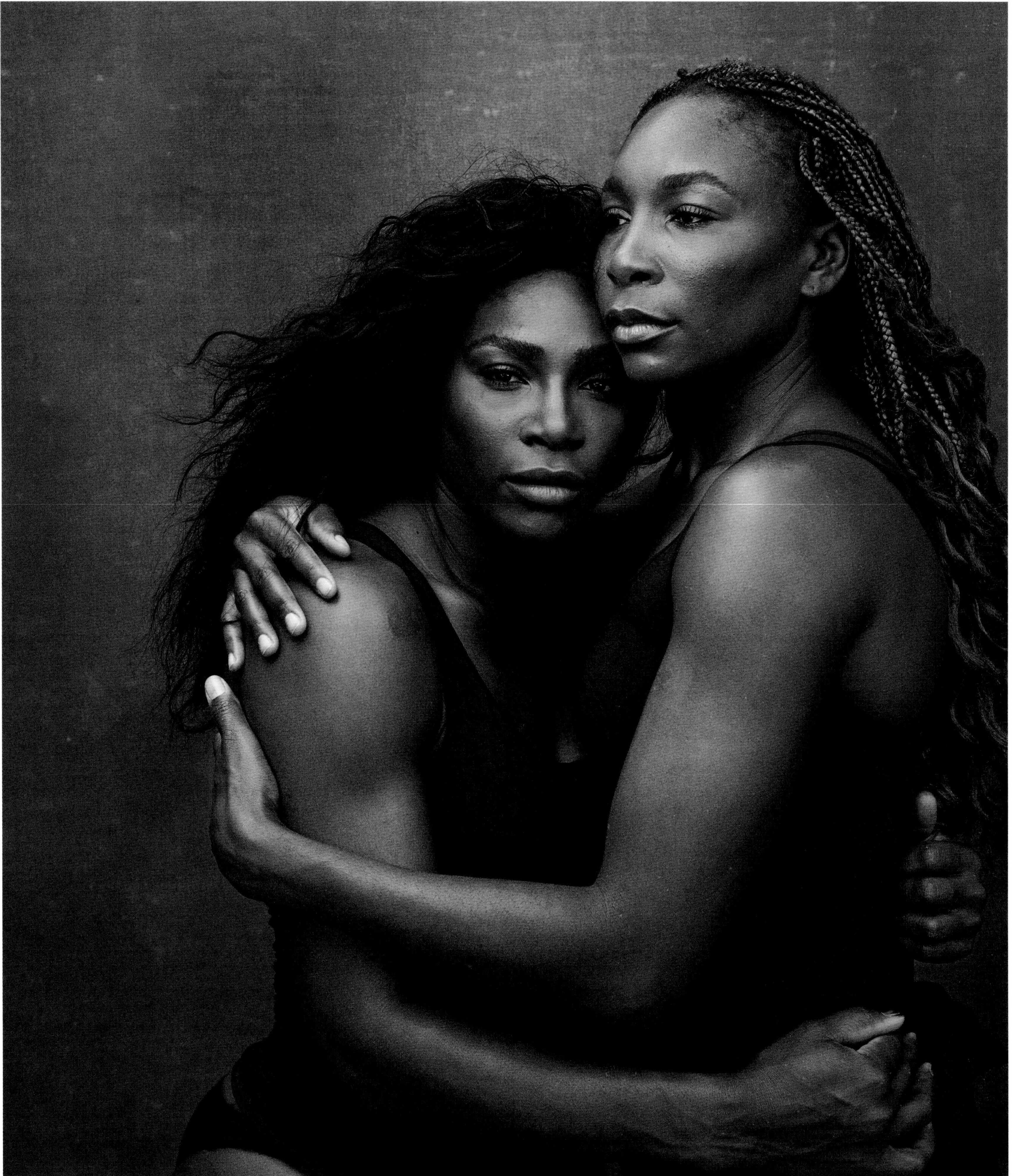

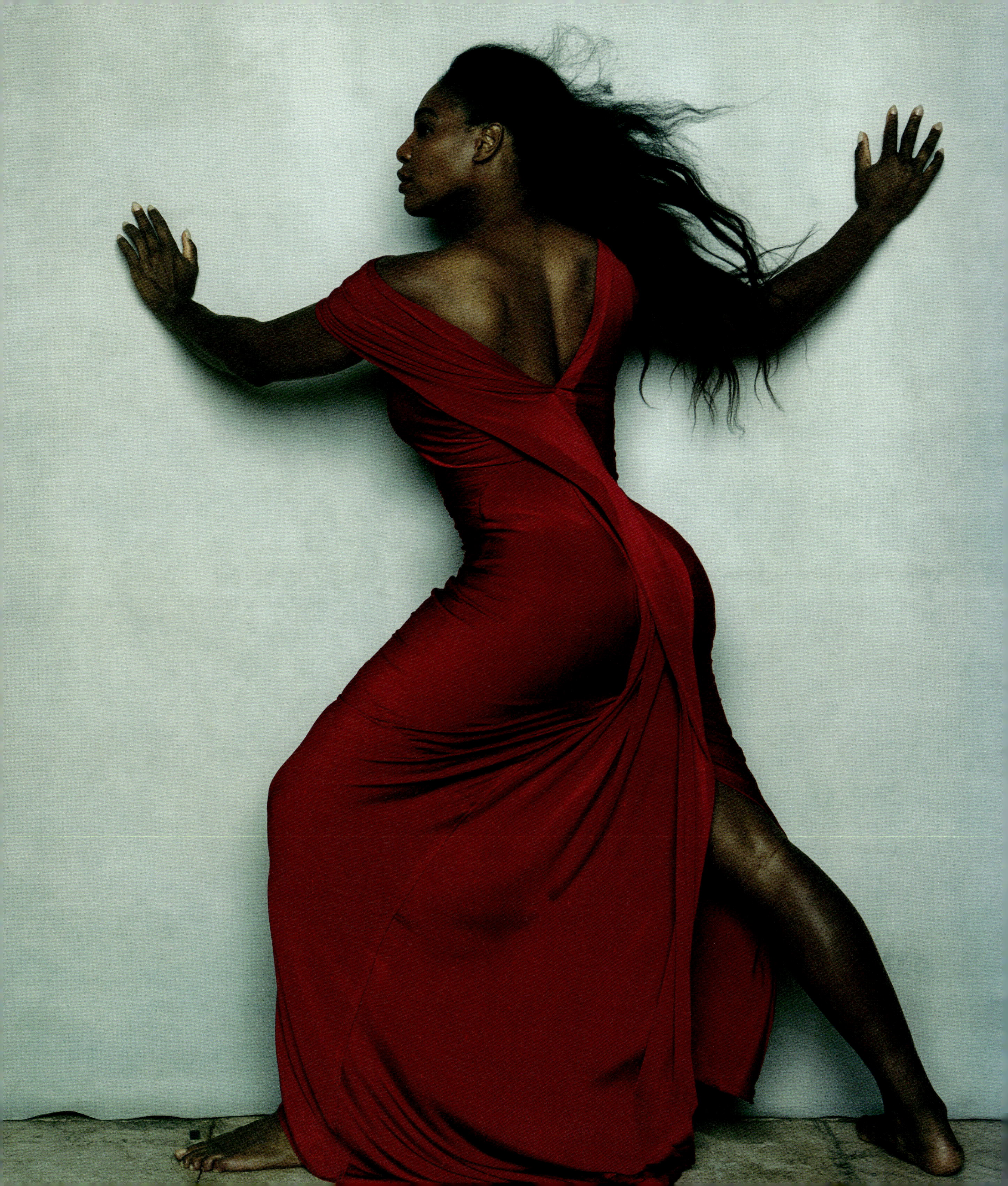

Serena Williams was pregnant when Annie photographed her for a *Vanity Fair* cover. She was the oldest woman in the game to hold the number-one title (she was thirty-five) and was unarguably the best women's tennis player in history. Maybe the greatest female athlete ever.

Previous pages: Serena and Venus Williams, Palm Beach, Florida, 2016. Serena Williams, Palm Beach, Florida, 2014

Serena Williams, Palm Beach, Florida, 2017

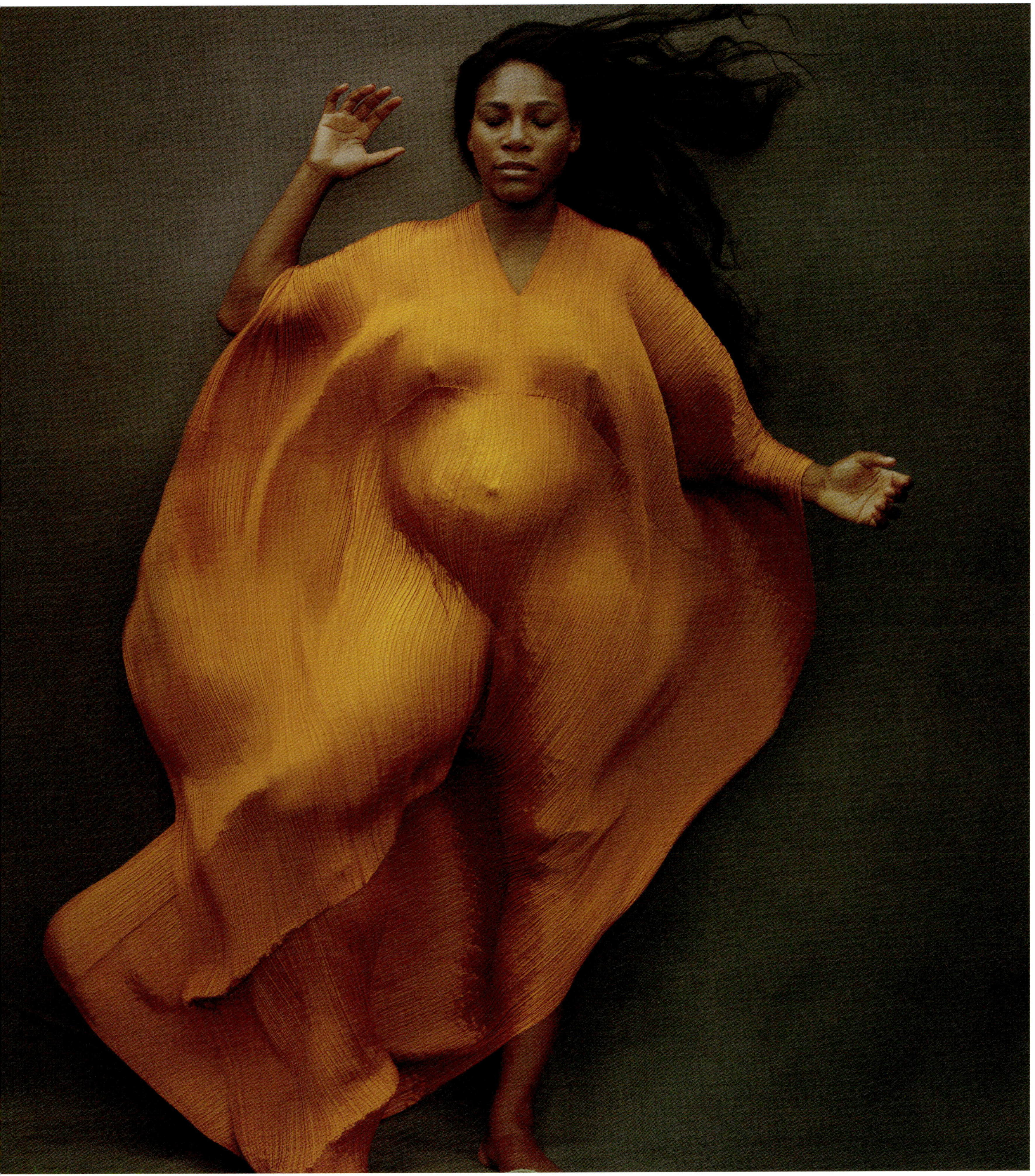

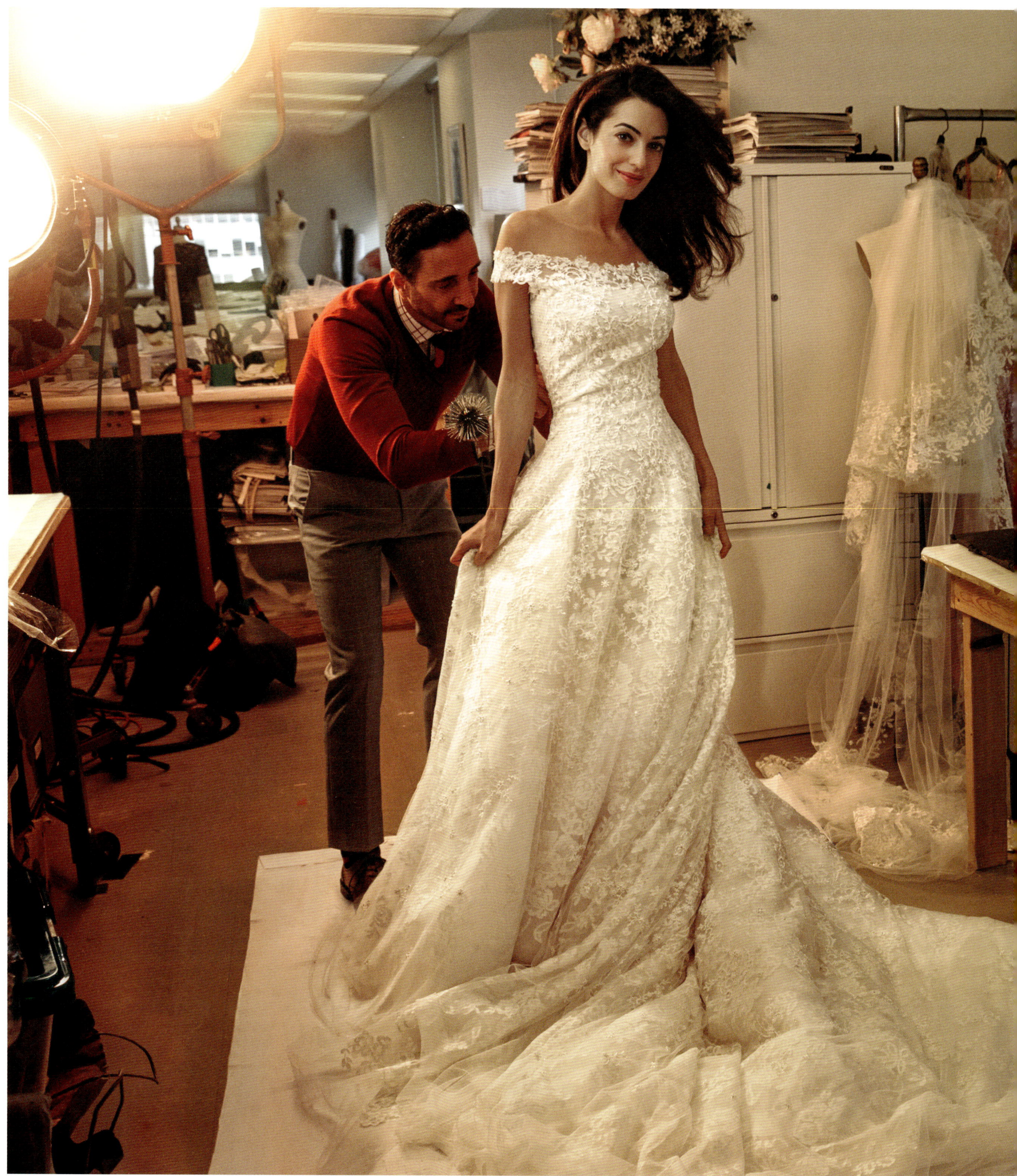

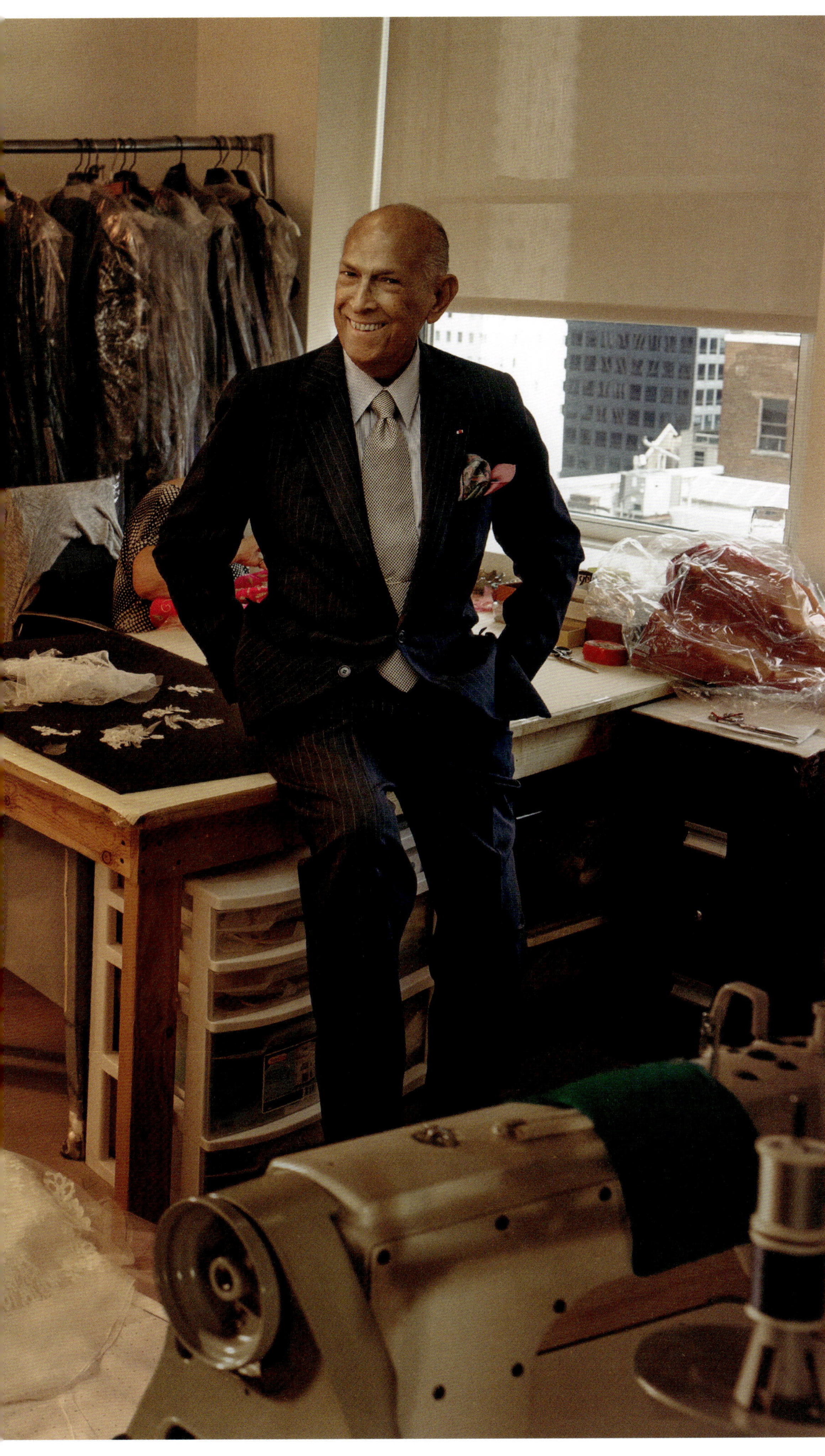

Amal Clooney's wedding dress was one of the last things that Oscar de la Renta designed. Amal and George Clooney were married in Venice on September 27, 2014.

Amal Clooney with Raffaele Ilardo and Oscar de la Renta in the de la Renta studio, New York City, 2014

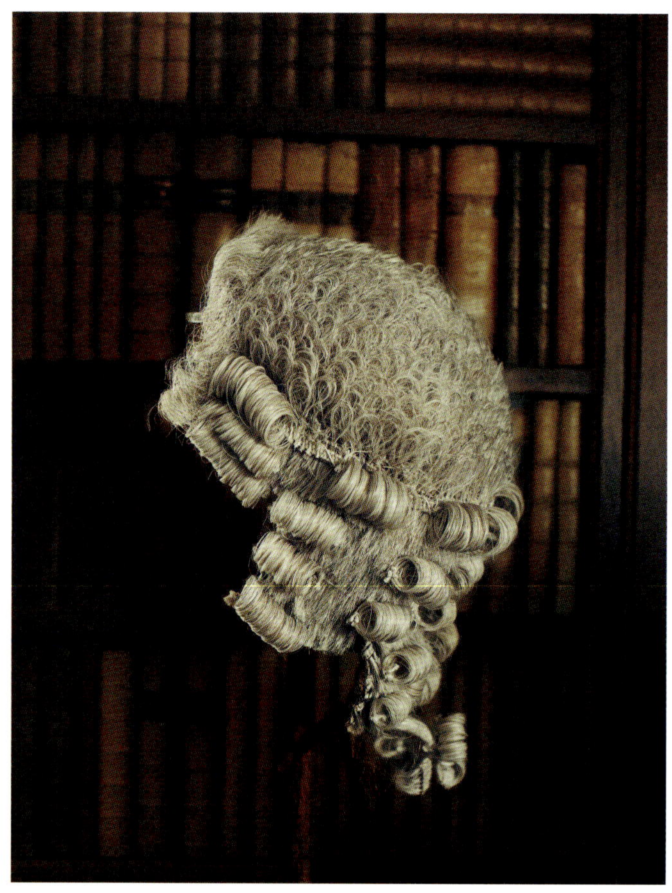

Amal Clooney was born in Lebanon and grew up in England. An international human rights lawyer with degrees from Oxford and the New York University Law School, she has pleaded the cases of vulnerable and exploited groups in international courts and on the floor of the United Nations. At the UN, she represented Nadia Murad, a Nobel Peace Prize laureate, arguing that Isis should be held accountable for genocide, war crimes, and crimes against humanity.

The horsehair wig and robe that Amal Clooney wears in court as a barrister are kept in her office at her home in southern England.

Berkshire, England, 2018

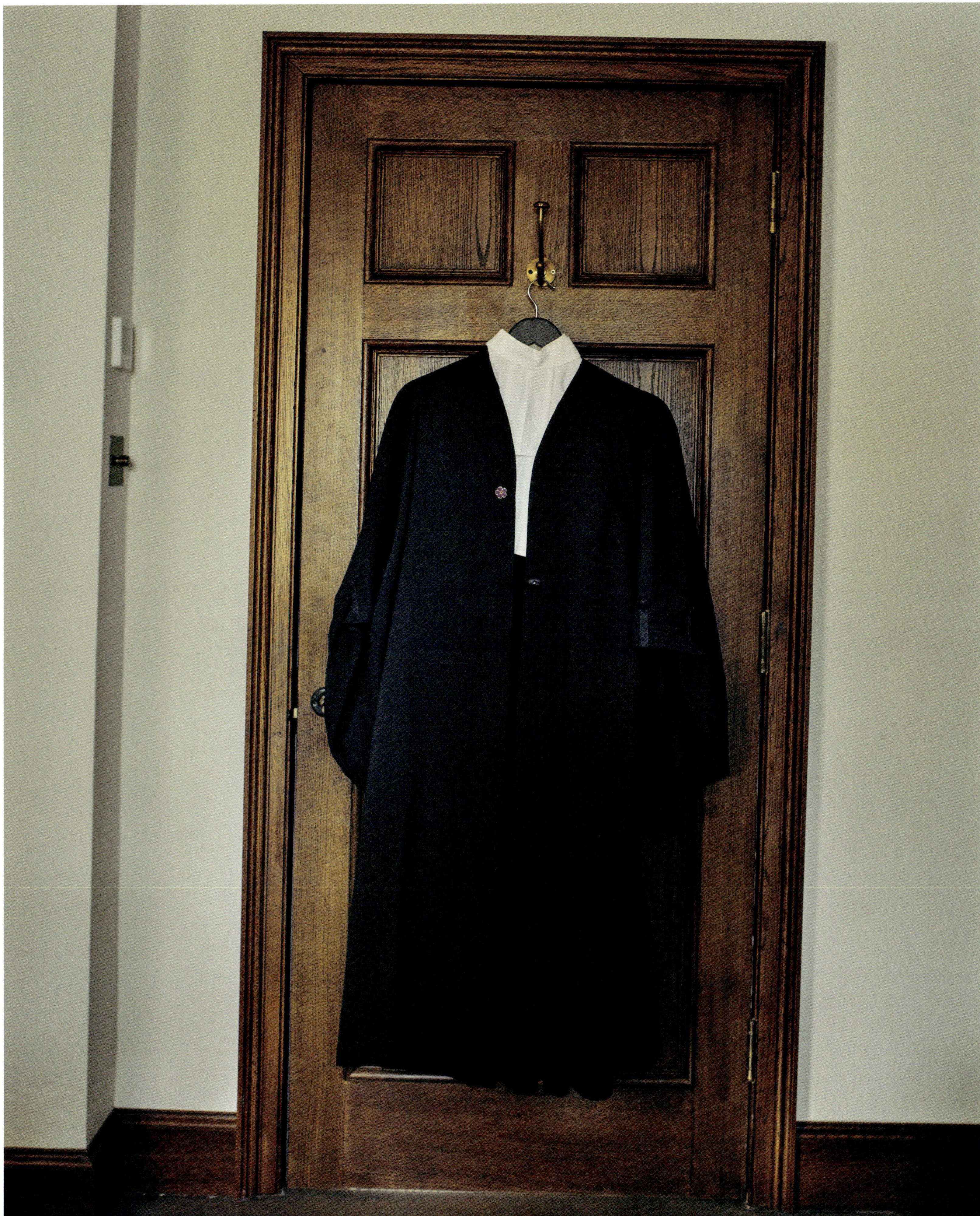

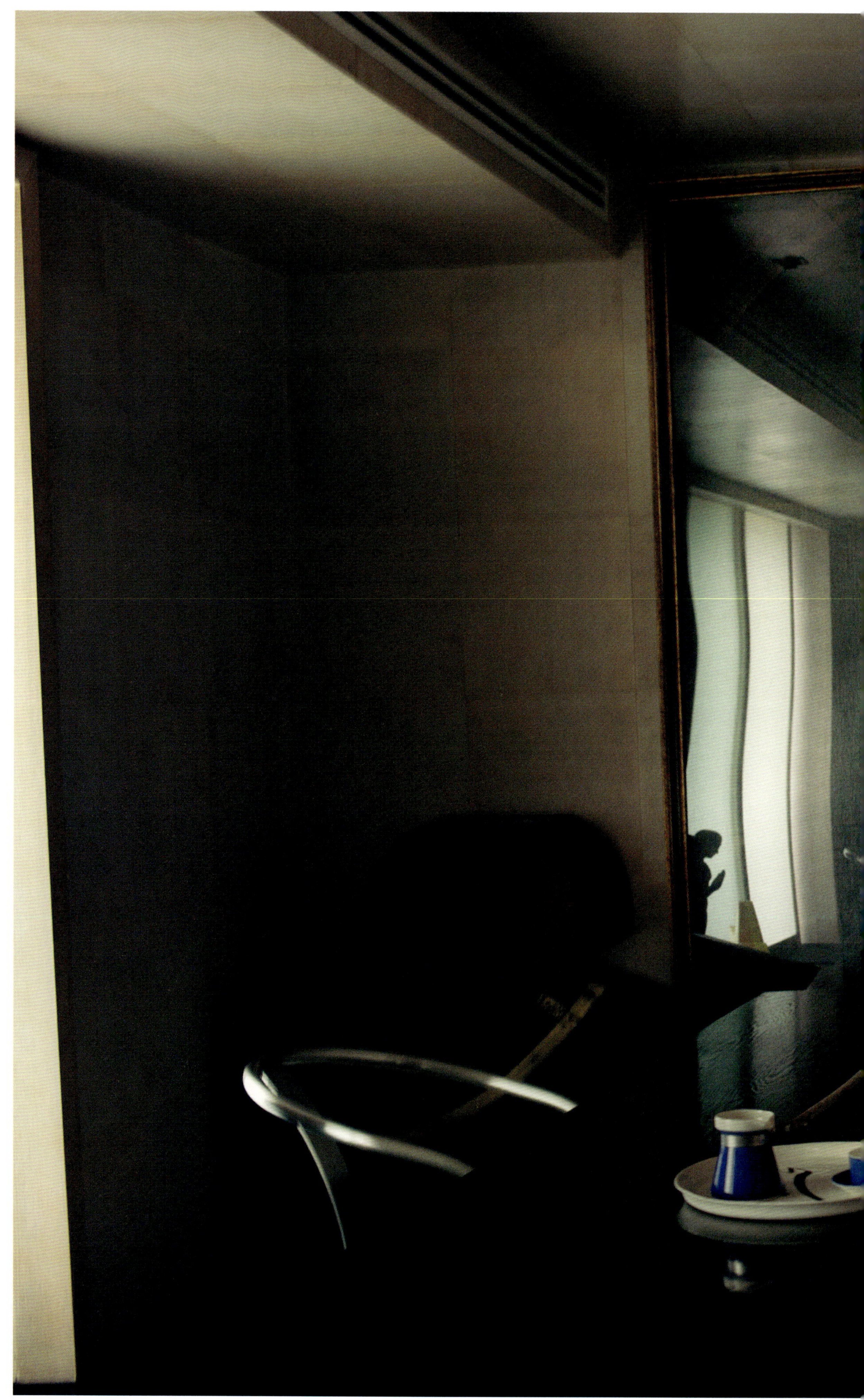

Giorgio Armani, Milan, 2012

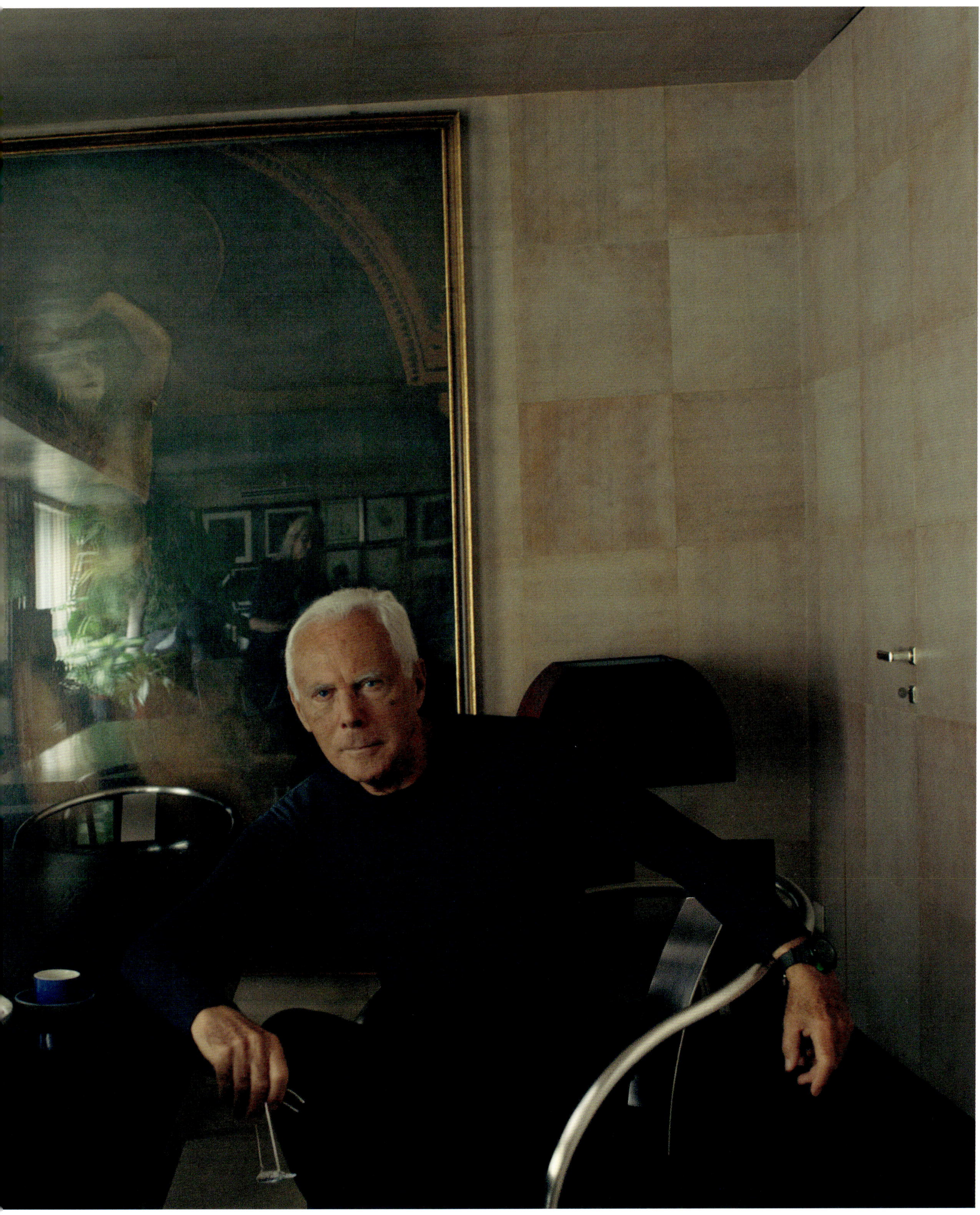

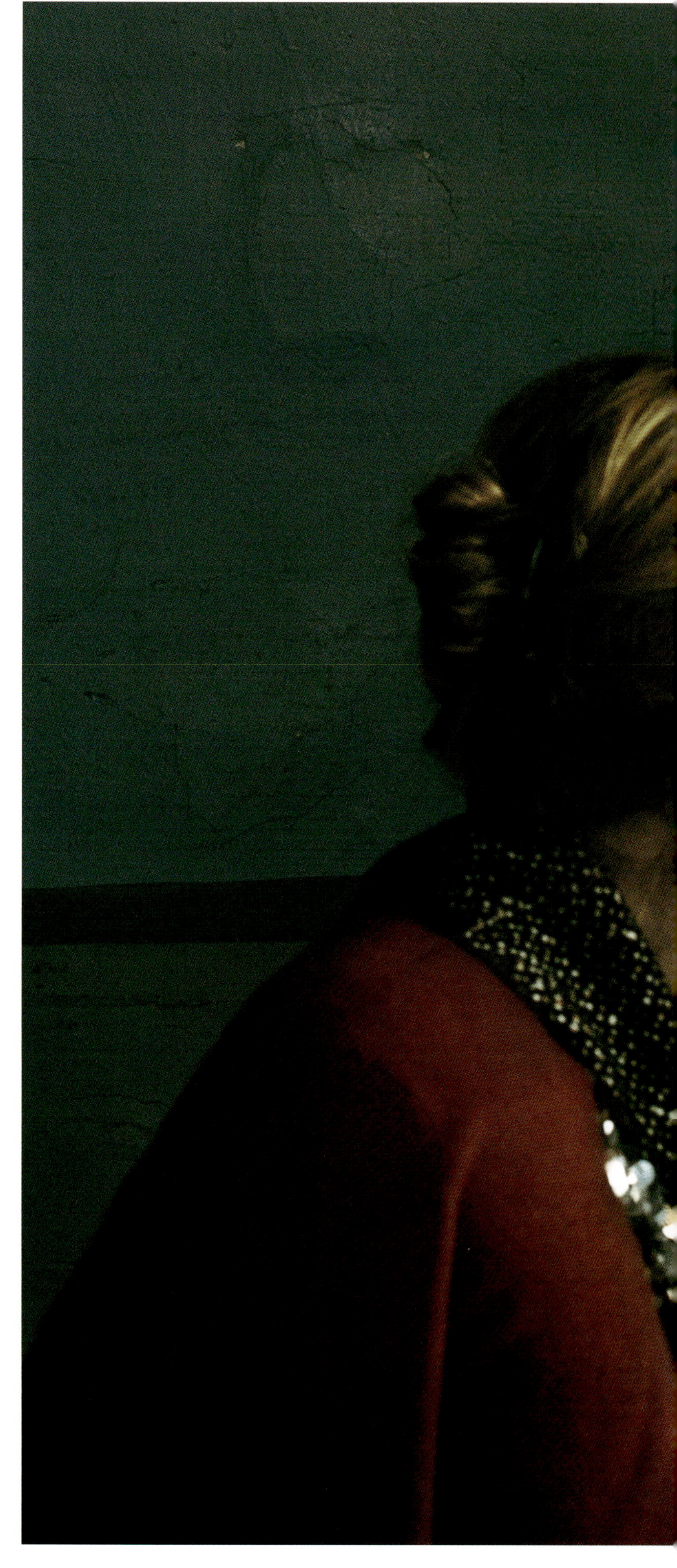

Miuccia Prada, Paris, 2000

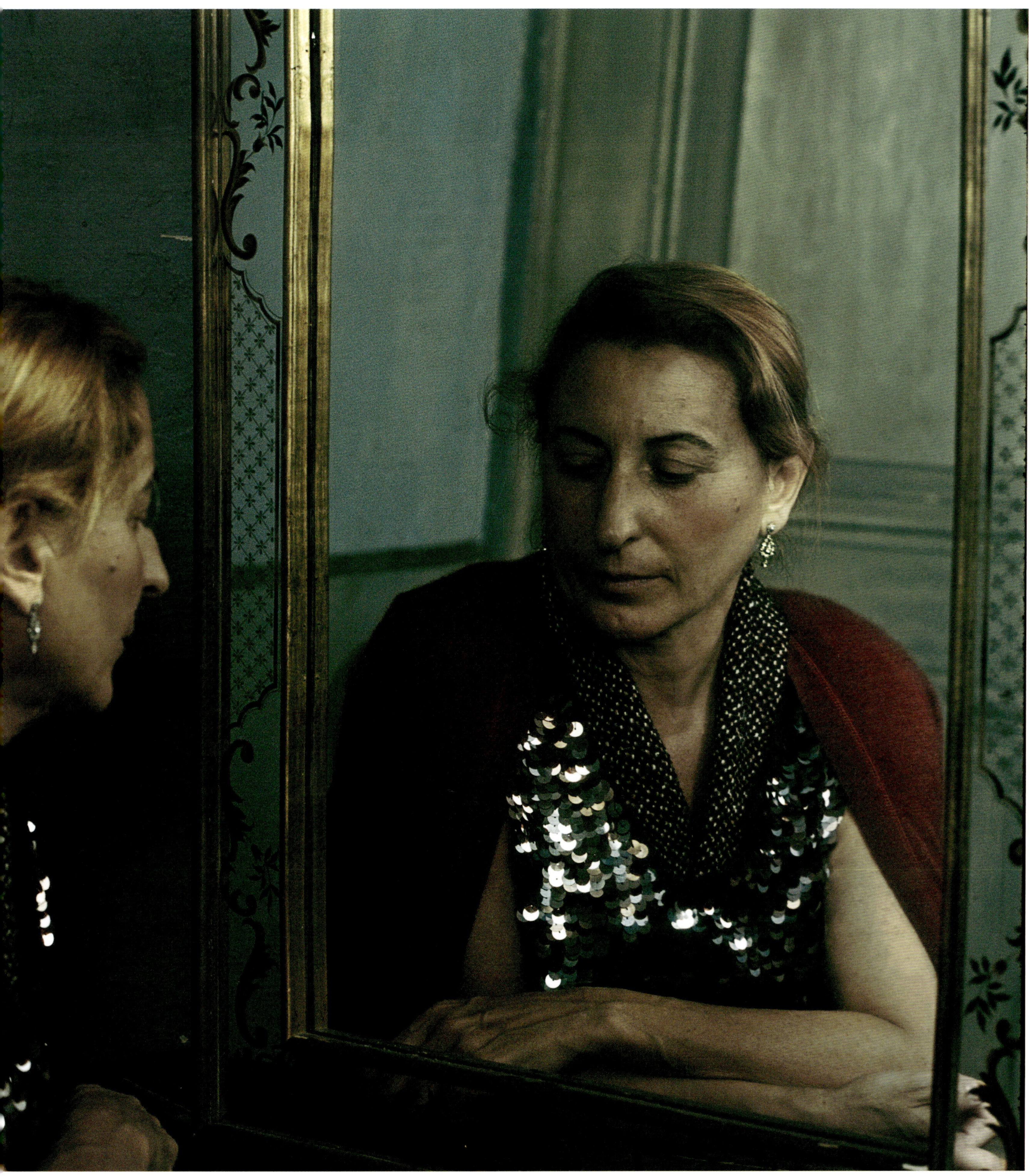

Andrew Bolton, head curator of the Costume Institute at the Metropolitan Museum of Art in New York, was instrumental in bringing fashion out of the basement, where Diana Vreeland valiantly toiled, and into the main galleries. His shows were at once scholarly and theatrical. *Alexander McQueen: Savage Beauty,* conceived and curated by Bolton in 2011, was meant to be experienced the way a McQueen runway show was experienced—that is, as Bolton wrote in the show's catalog, as "avant-garde installation and performance art."

In 2015 *China: Through the Looking Glass* brought curators from the museum's Department of Asian Art together with the Chinese film director Wong Kar-Wai. Bolton's 2018 show, *Heavenly Bodies: Fashion and the Catholic Imagination*, explored the impact of Catholicism on couture and became the museum's most-visited exhibition ever.

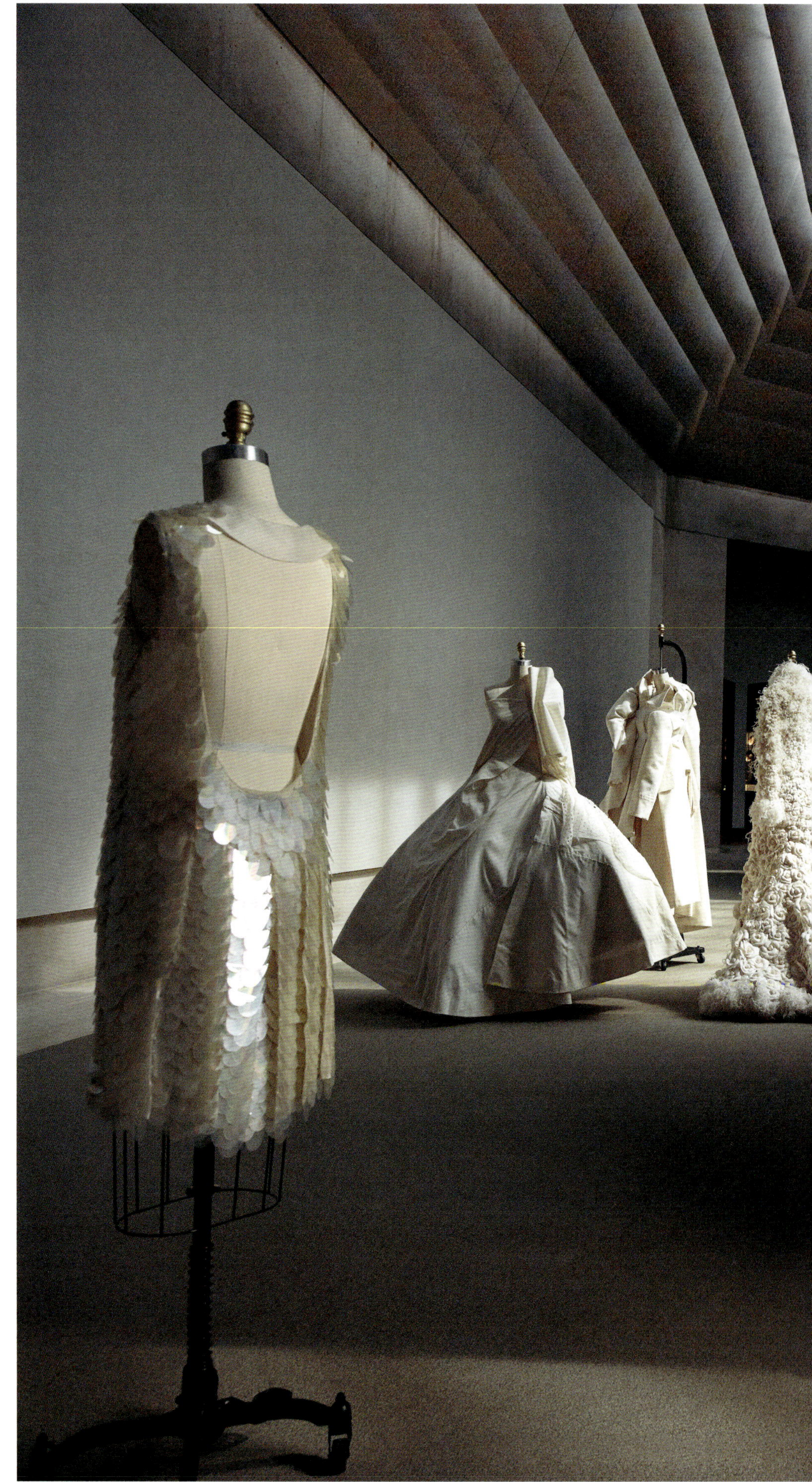

Andrew Bolton at the Metropolitan Museum of Art, New York City, 2016

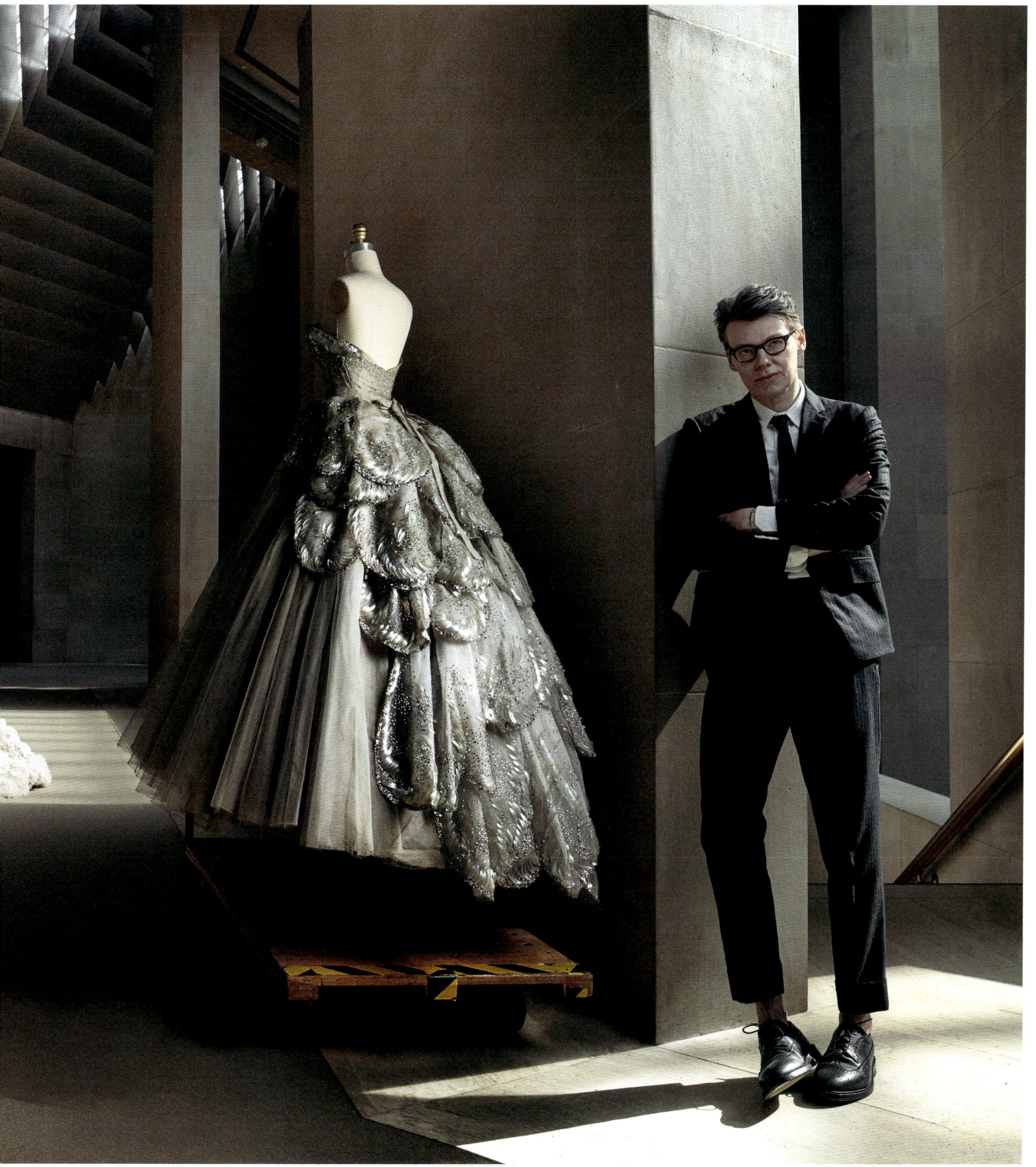

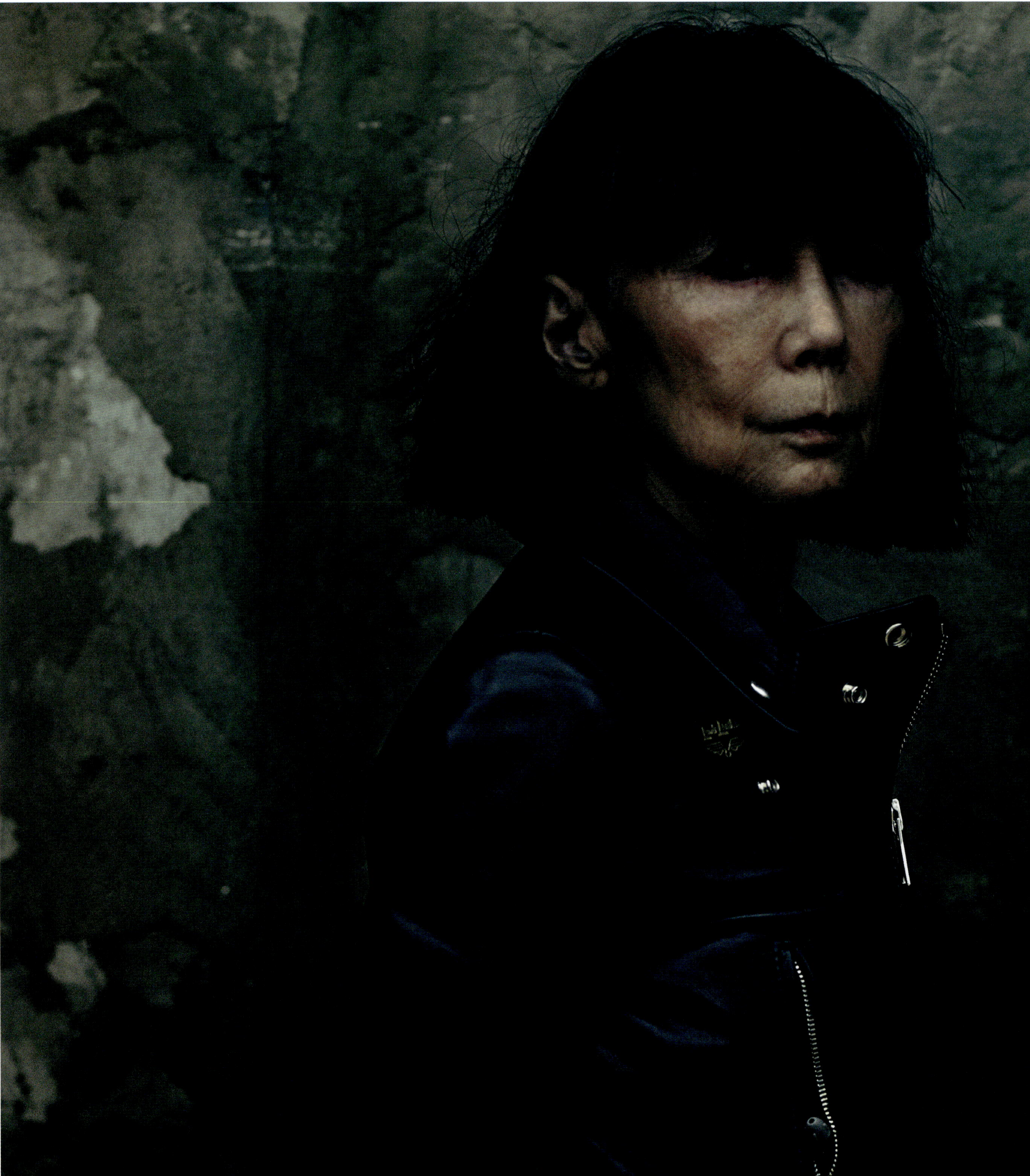

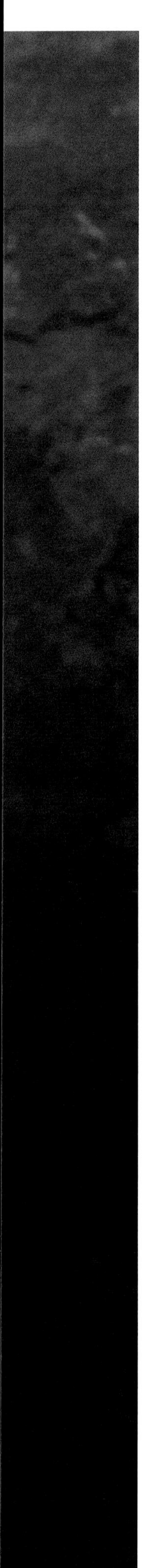

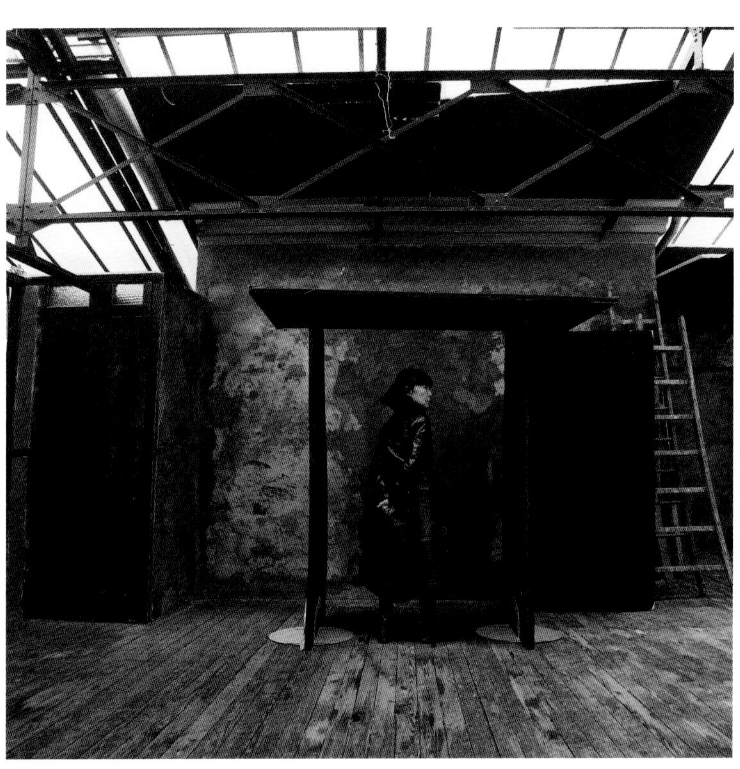

Rei Kawakubo, Paris, 2017

Claire Danes was photographed by Annie for the first time in 1992, as Danes reminded her when they were working on a *Vanity Fair* cover shoot some years later. Danes had been part of the portrait of Cindy Sherman in a lineup of stand-ins and actresses. Sherman had said that she wanted to disappear in the picture. There were multiple Sherman lookalikes in the white shirt and black pants she had been wearing when Annie met with her to discuss the shoot. Danes was on the end of the lineup, but she was cut out of the final picture.

Danes had been acting since she was a preteen. Twenty years after the Cindy Sherman shoot, she was the star of *Homeland*, coping with terrorism, official and clandestine surveillance, torture, personal betrayal, and espionage. She appeared on the cover of *Vogue* just as the third season started. *Homeland* was a very ambitious show and unusual, for the time, in having a woman at the center of what was essentially a contemporary political thriller.

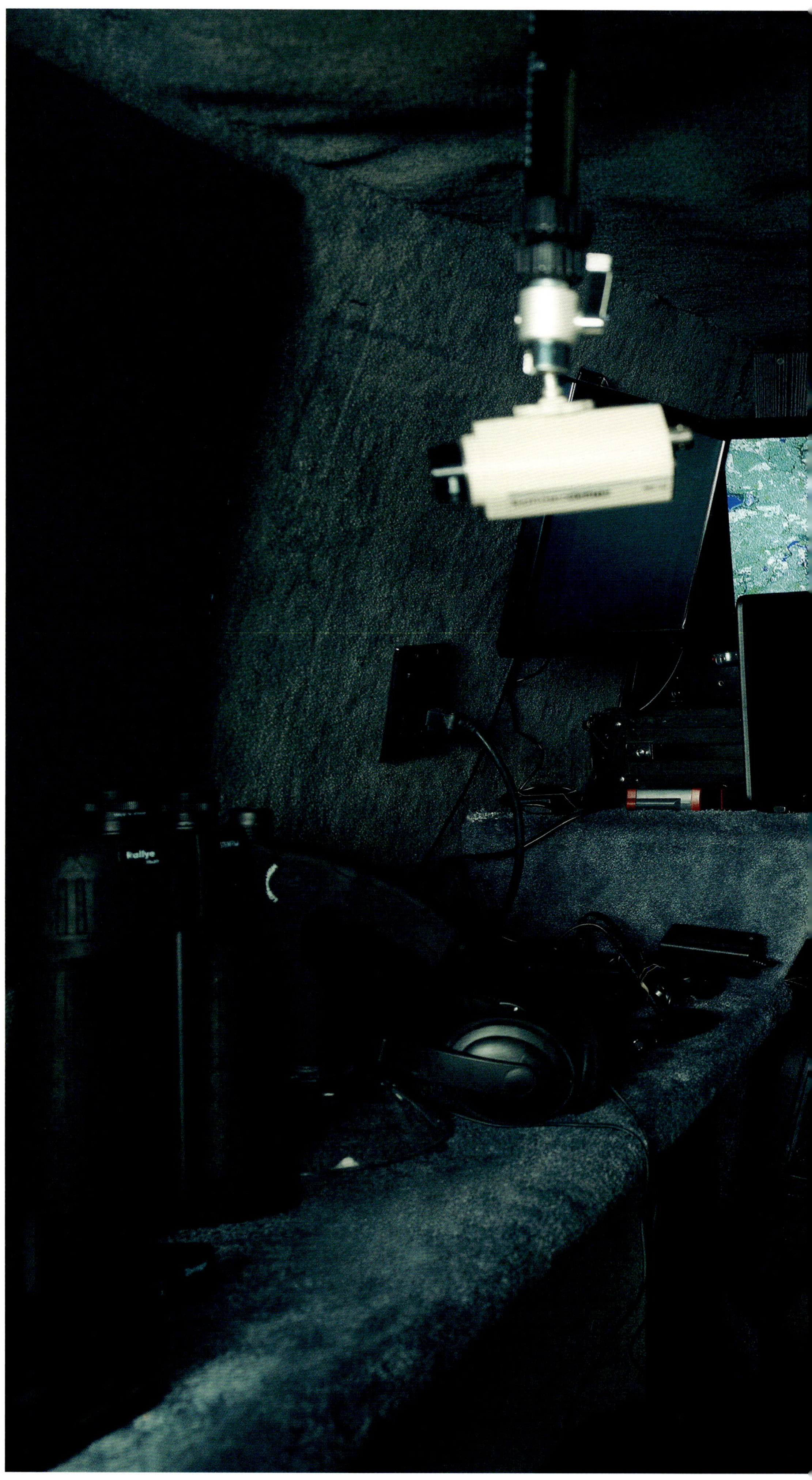

Claire Danes, New York City, 2013

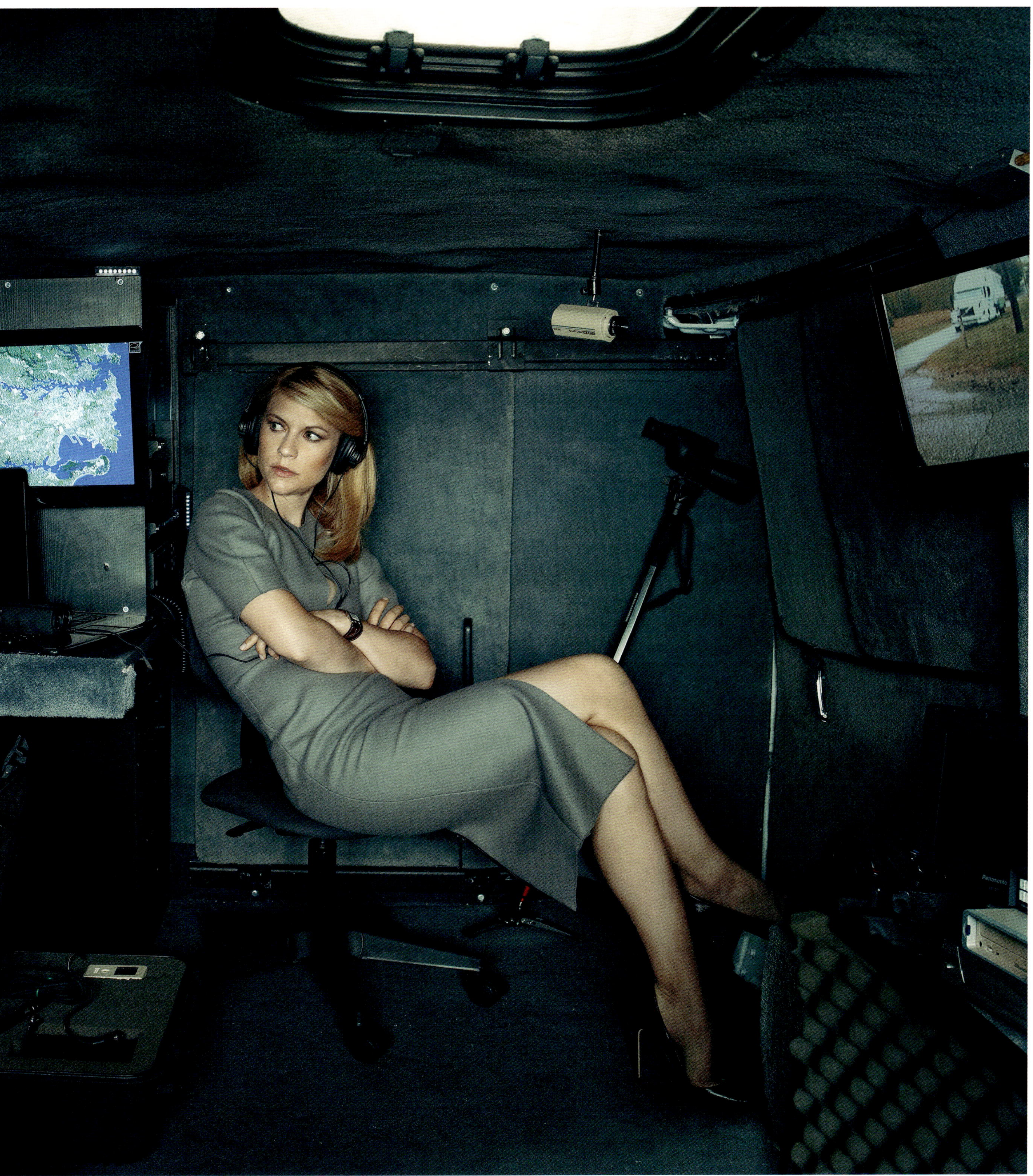

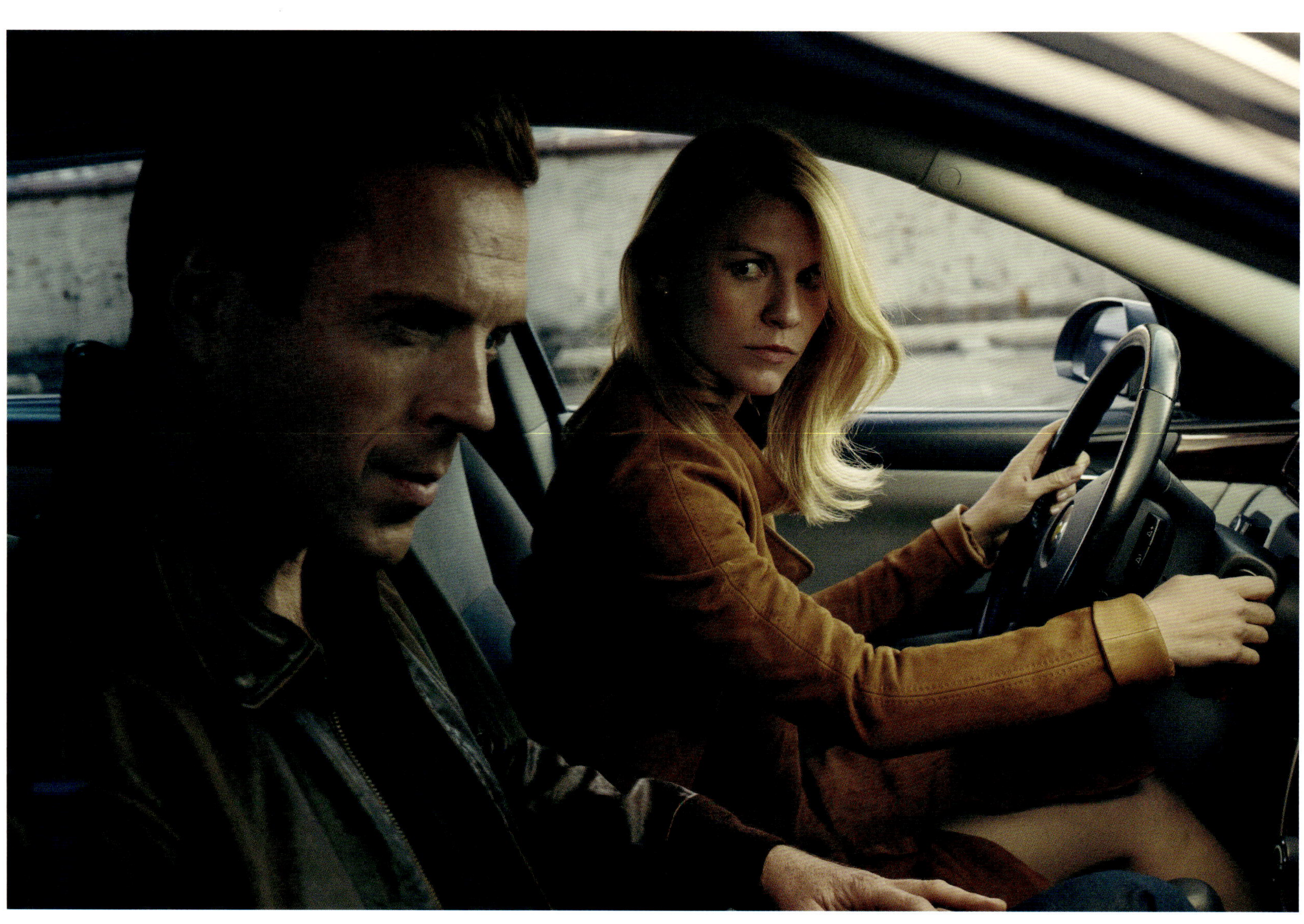

Claire Danes with Damian Lewis,
New York City, 2013

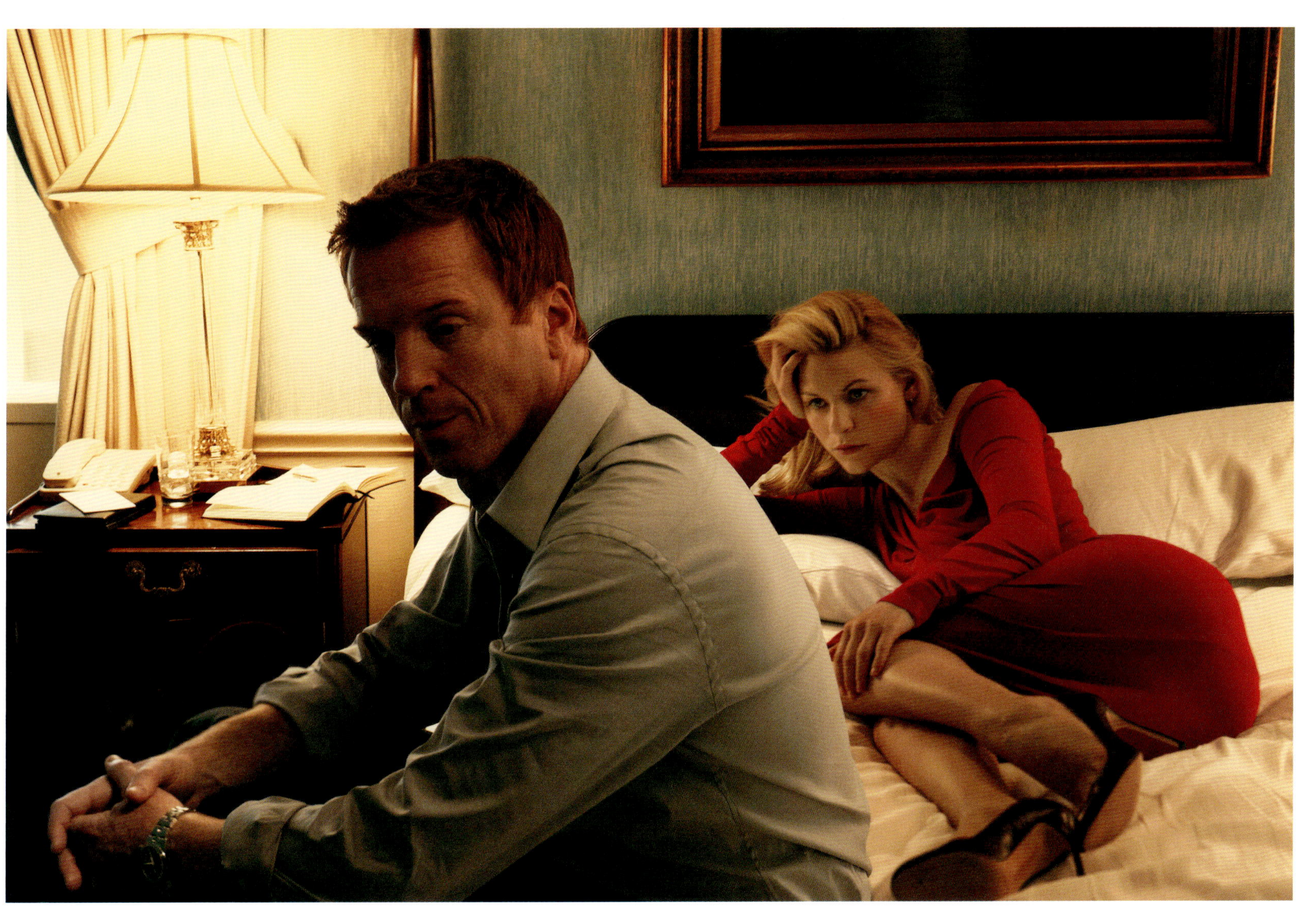

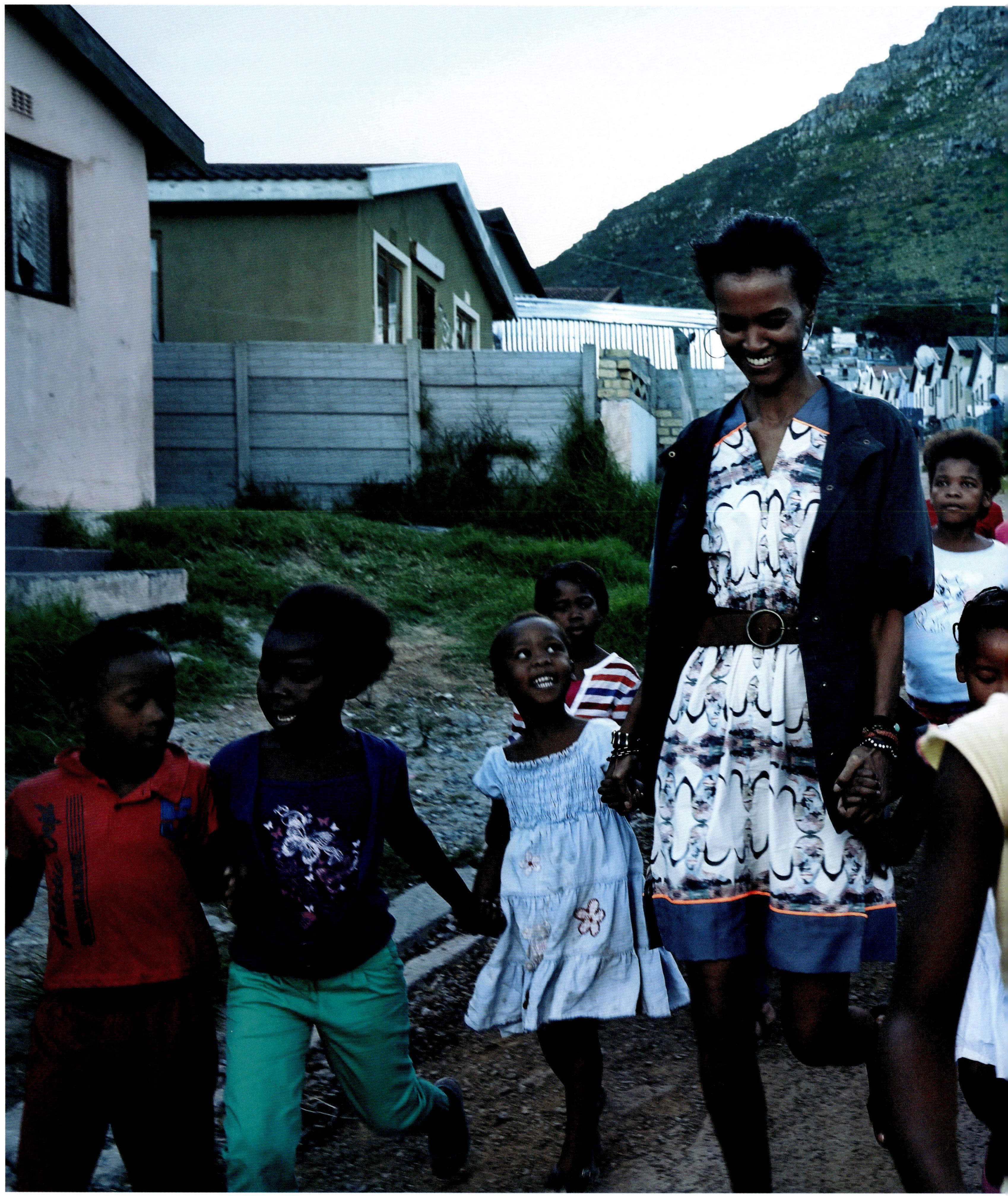

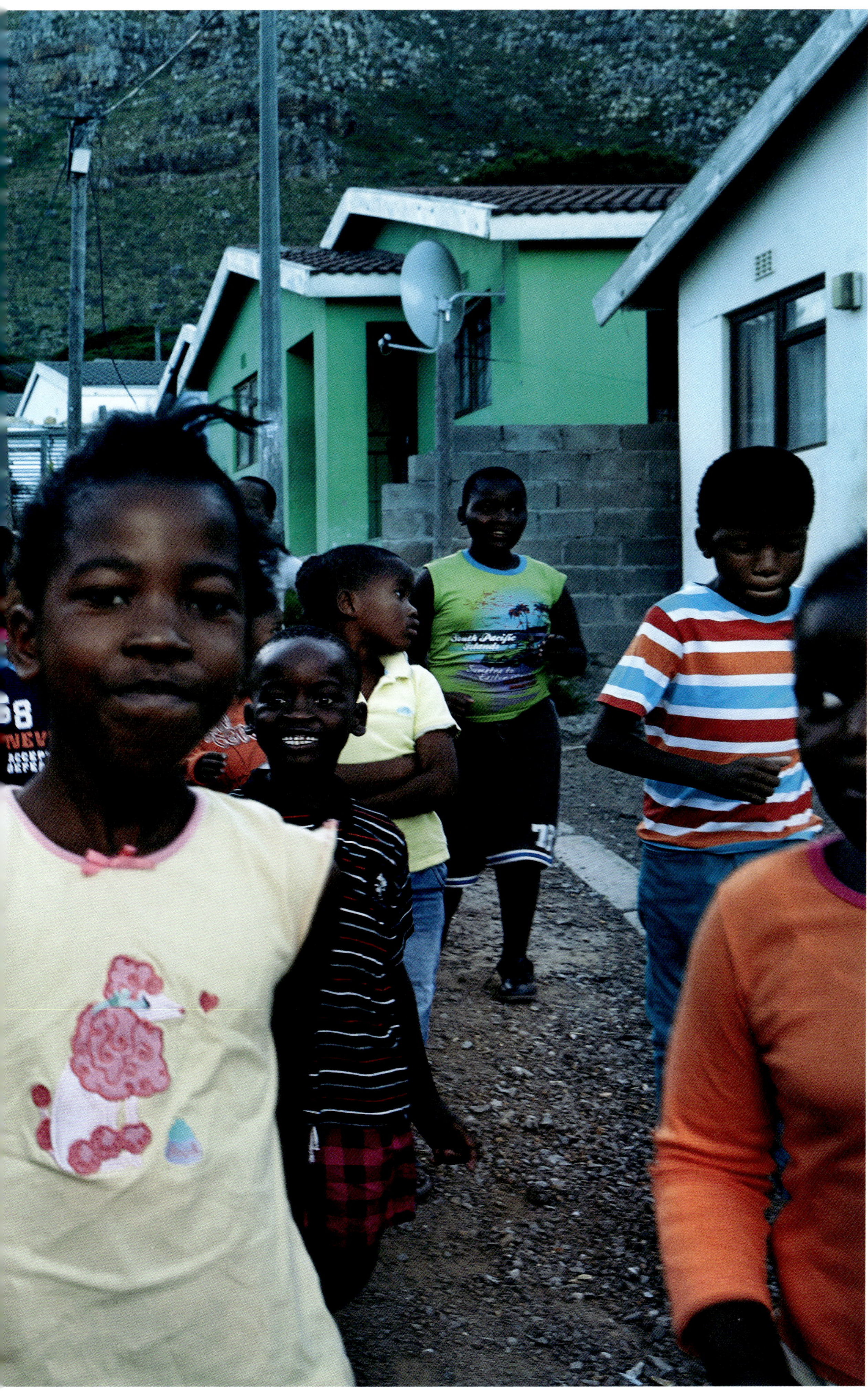

Liya Kebede has a foundation dedicated to maternal health in Ethiopia, her native country. It is the philanthropic arm of the design house she started to support traditional artisan weavers there. The foundation collaborates with nonprofit organizations across Africa. In 2014 Kebede and Victoria Beckham went to South Africa as representatives of the group of women fashion designers who were making the Born Free Collection, a limited-edition clothing line created to benefit organizations working to eliminate mother-to-child HIV transmission in Africa.

Imizamo Yethu, a settlement on the outskirts of Cape Town, 2014

Much of the work of preventing mother-to-child transmission of HIV is simply convincing women that their unborn children can be protected if a single pill is taken daily. Mothers2mothers, a grassroots, Africa-based organization, put Denise Manong, who was pregnant and HIV positive, on a drug-treatment program that kept her and her baby healthy. After the birth of her daughter, Denise herself became one of over a thousand mentor mothers in sub-Saharan Africa who have helped to virtually eliminate HIV in babies born in the mothers2mothers program.

Denise Manong and her daughter Linamandla, Khayelitsha township, Western Cape, South Africa, 2014

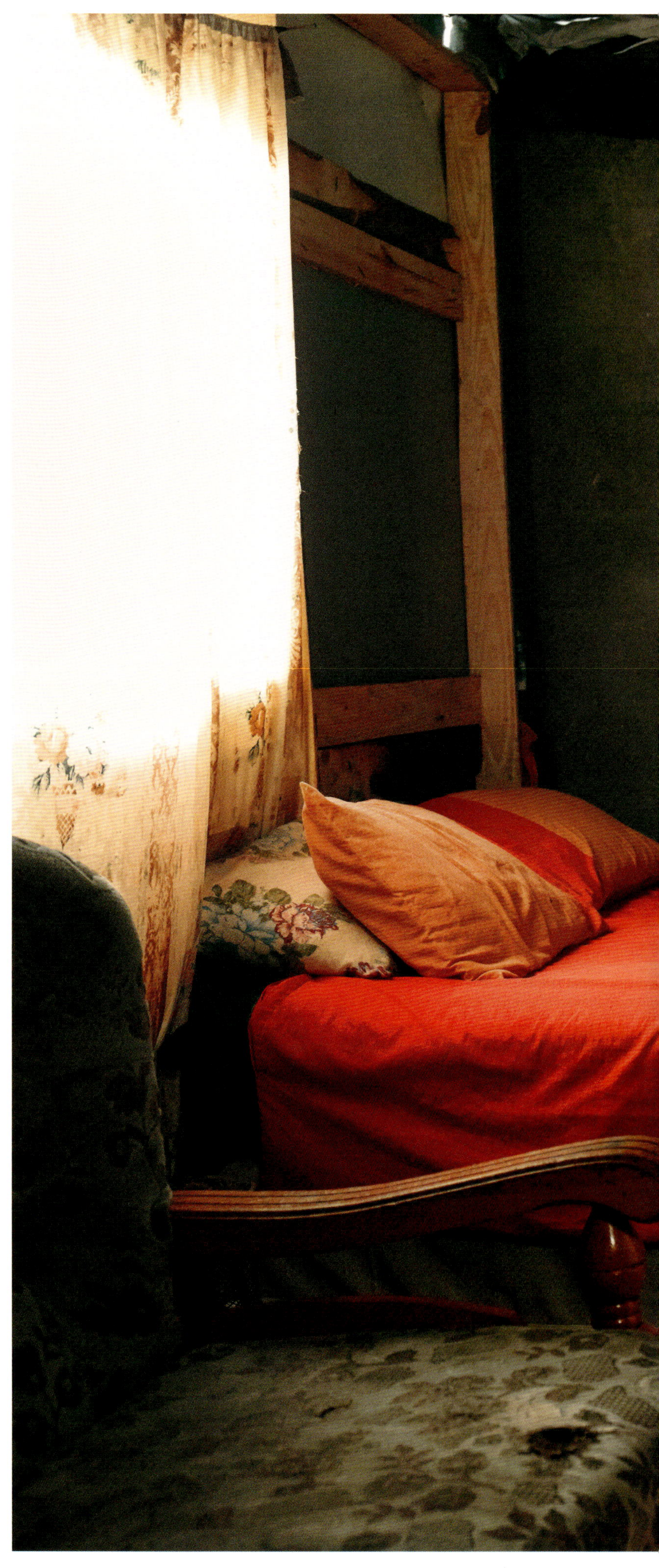

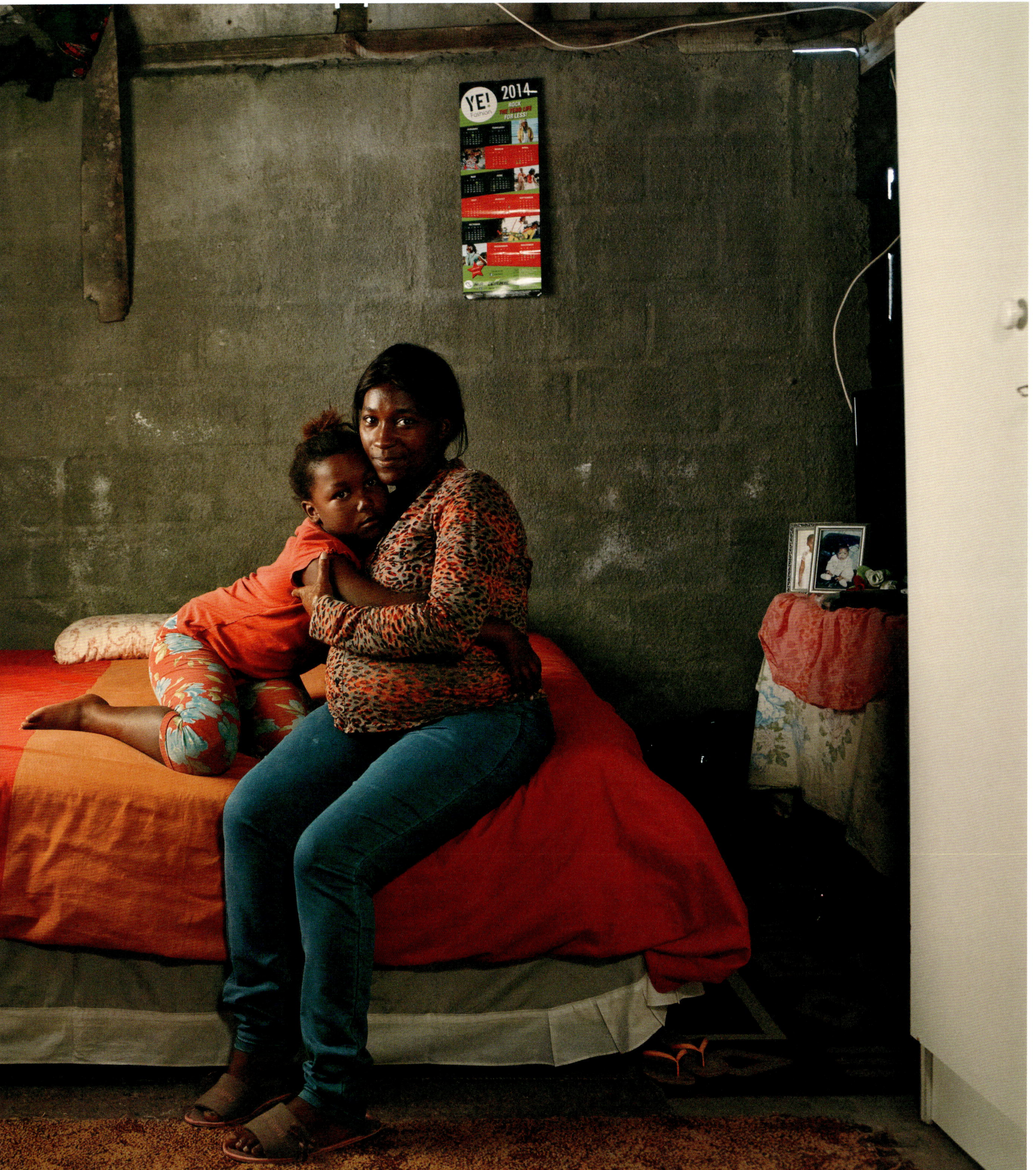
YE!
Fashion
2014
ROCK
FOR LESS!

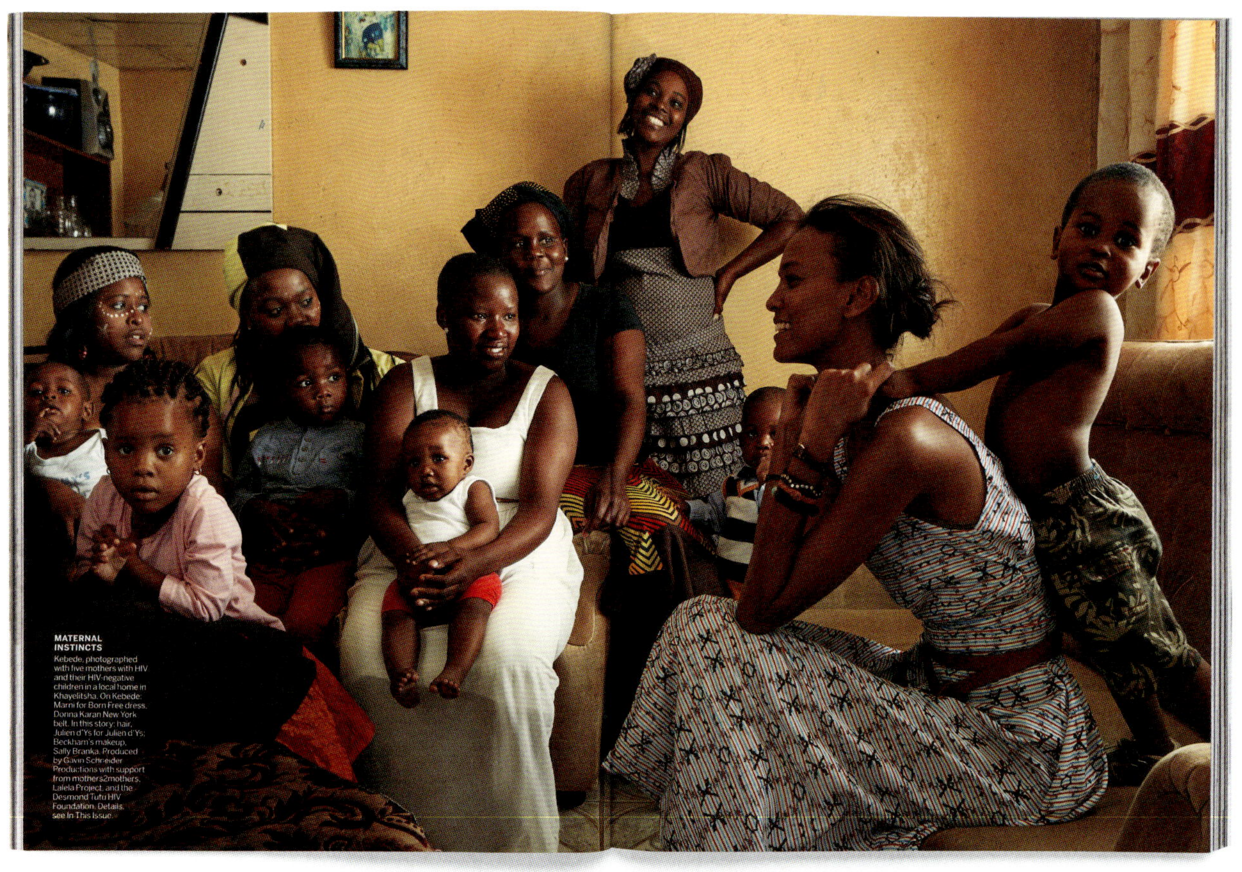

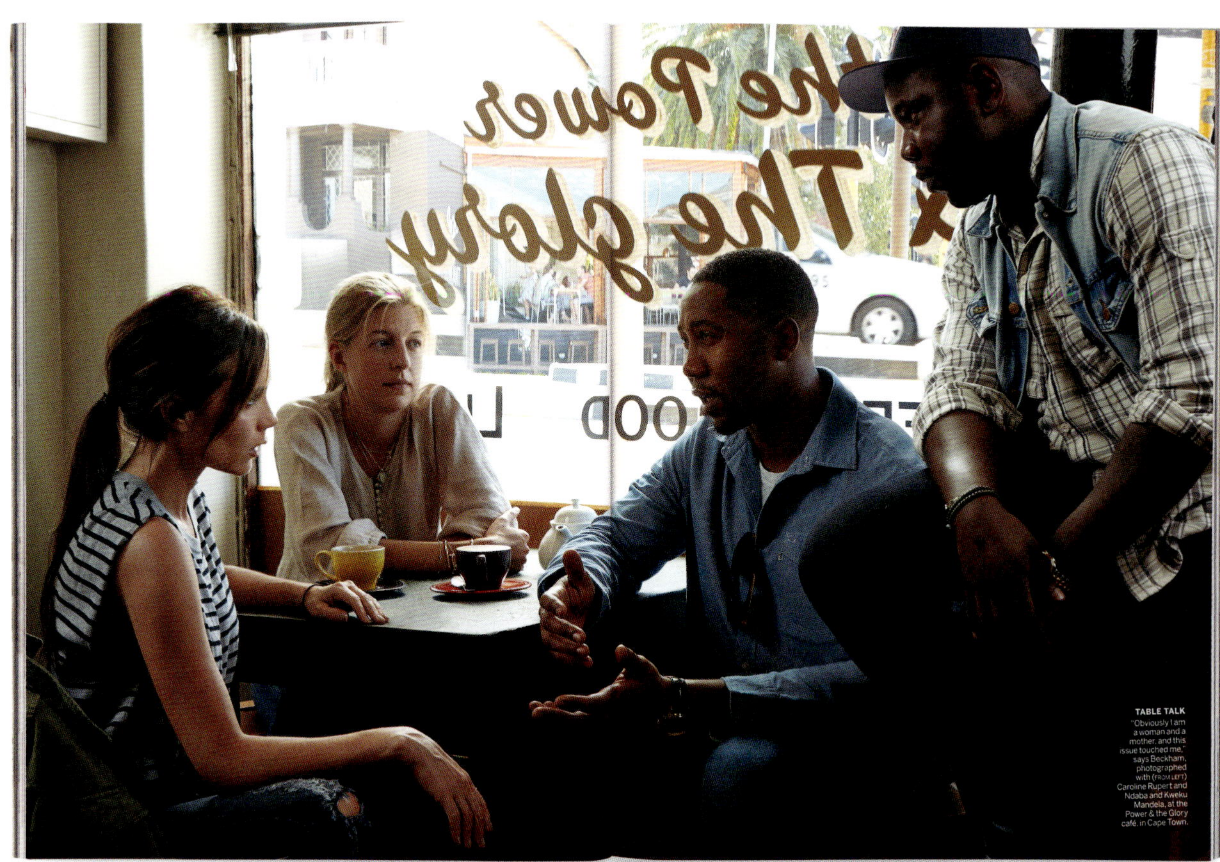

Liya Kebede with mothers and children in Khayelitsha township

Victoria Beckham with Caroline Rupert and Ndaba and Kweku Mandela, Nelson Mandela's grandsons, at the Power and the Glory café, Cape Town

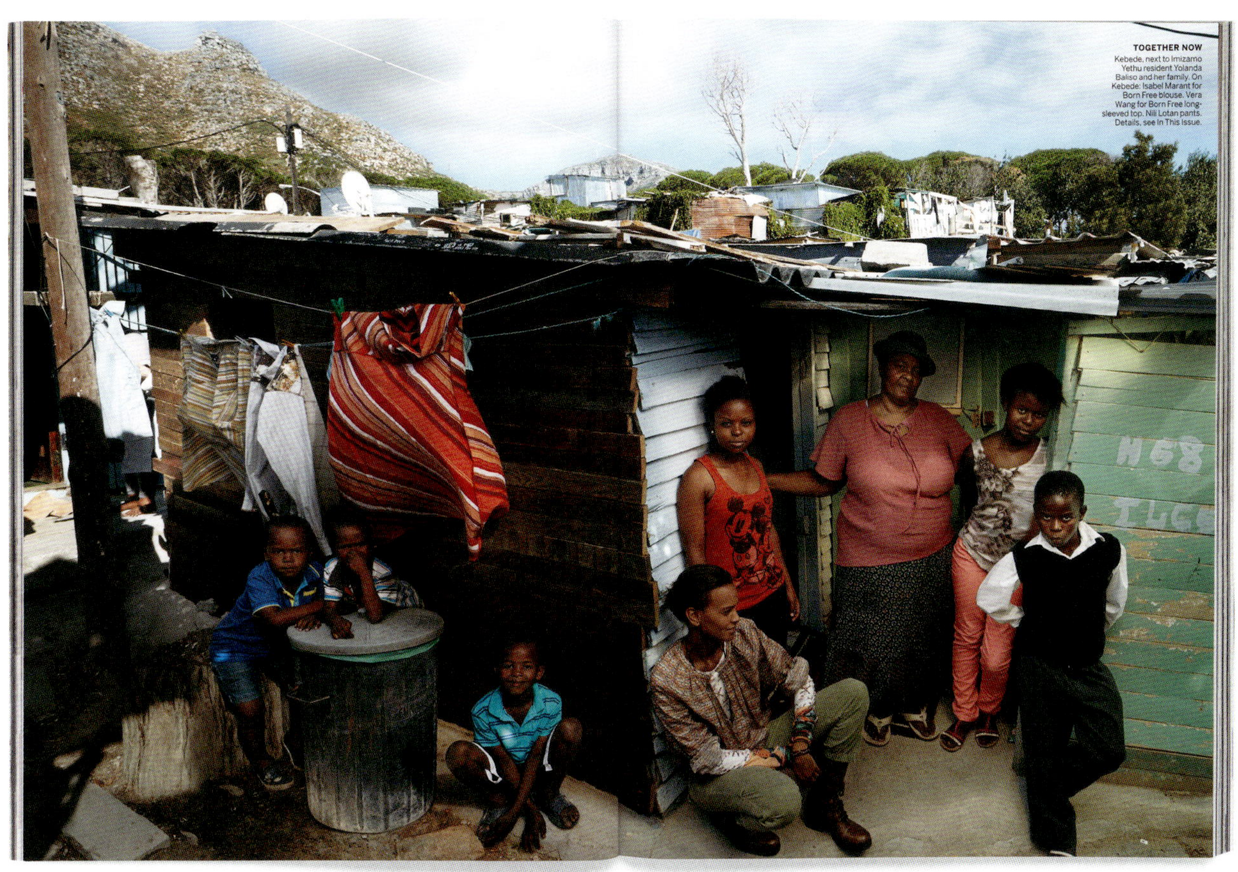

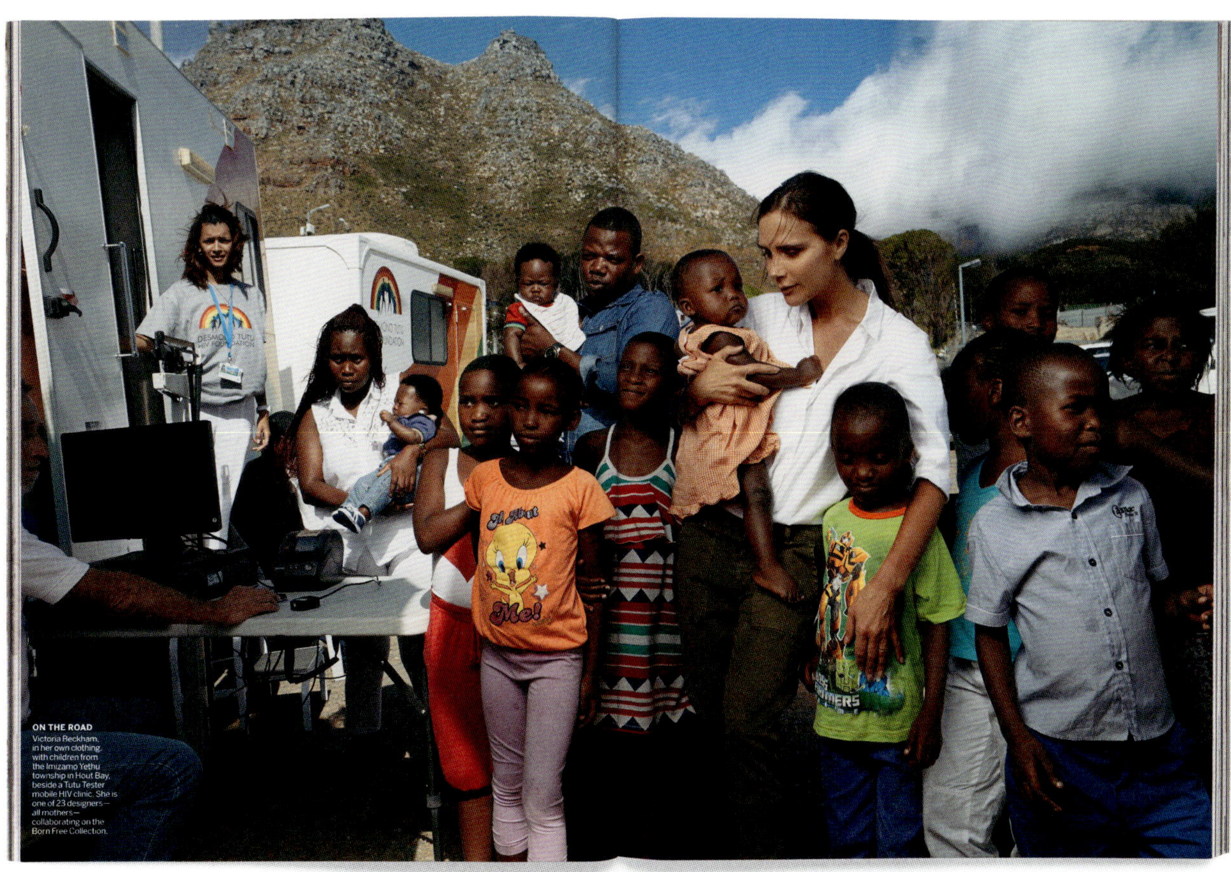

Liya Kebede with Yolanda Baliso and her family in the Imizamo Yethu settlement

Victoria Beckham at a mobile HIV clinic in Imizamo Yethu

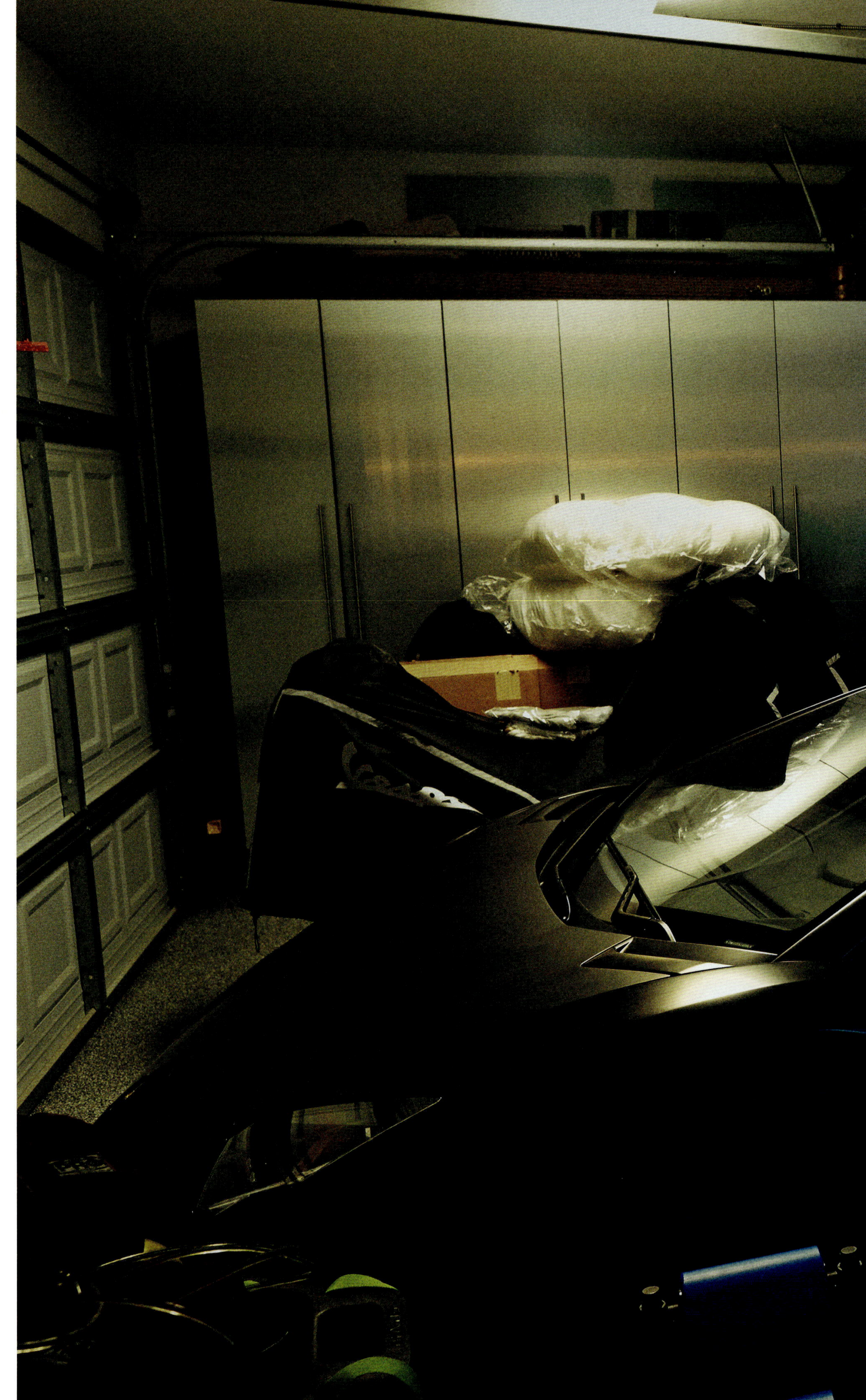

Kim Kardashian
and Kanye West,
Los Angeles, 2014

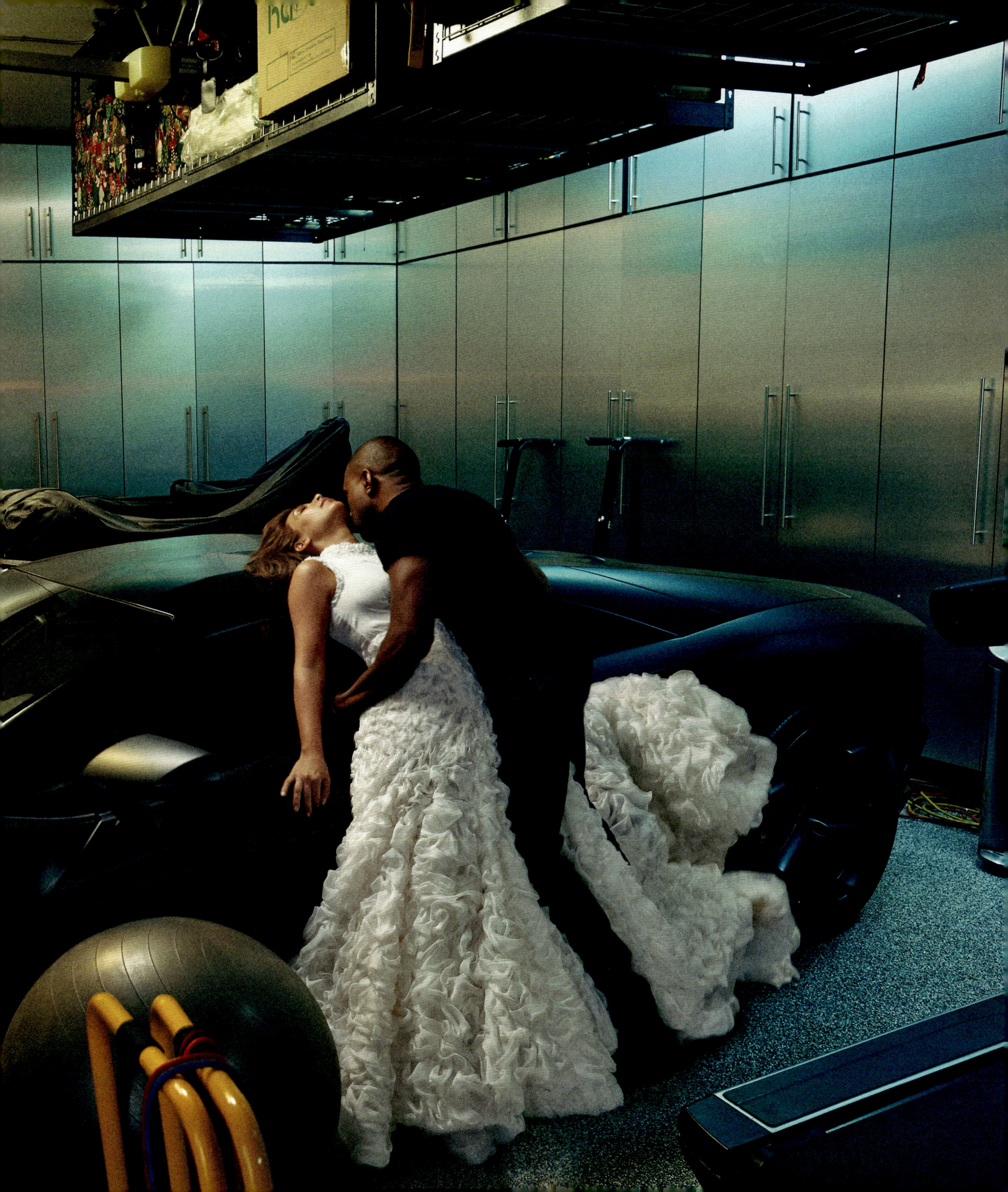

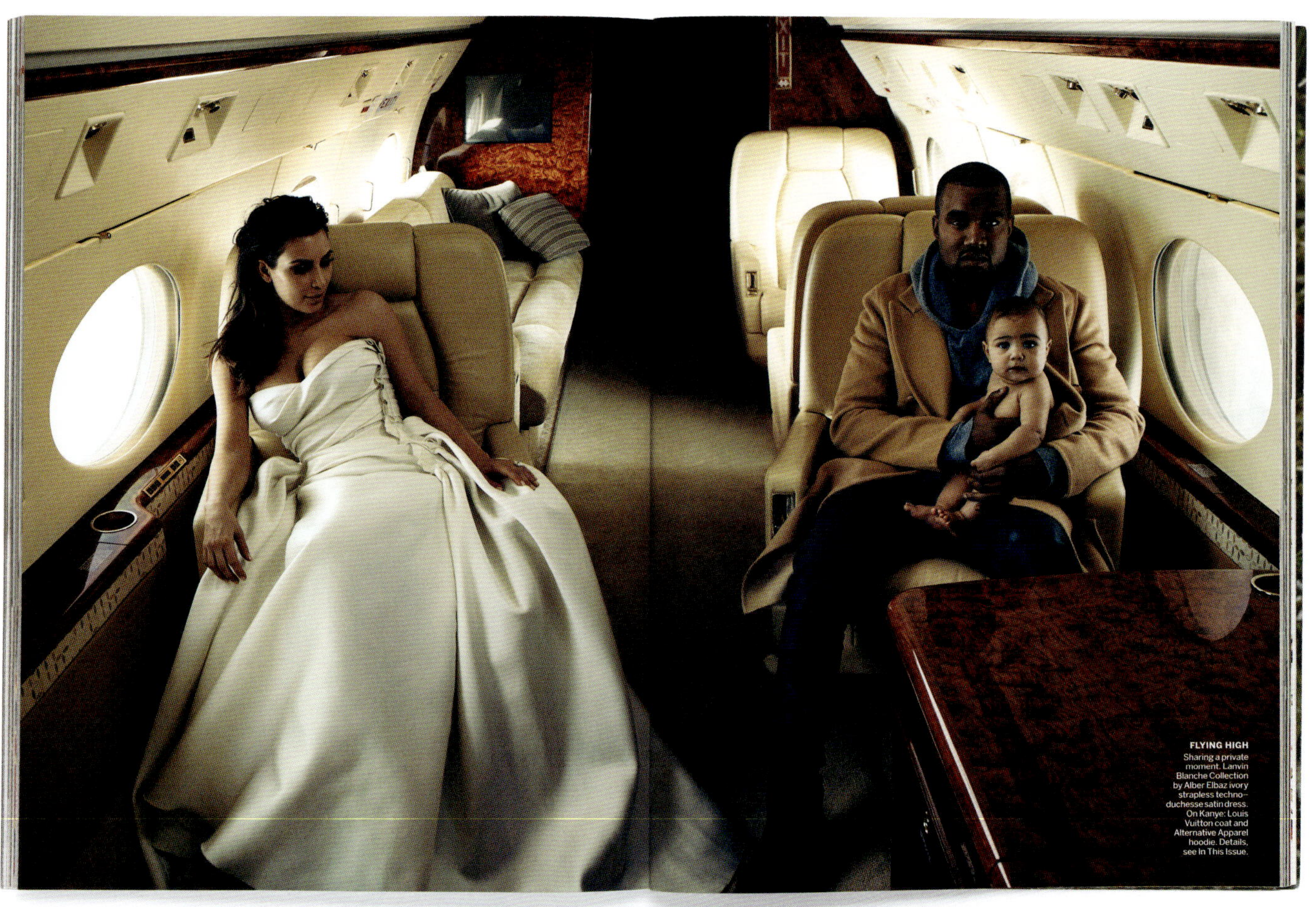
FLYING HIGH
Sharing a private moment. Lanvin Blanche Collection by Alber Elbaz ivory strapless techno–duchesse satin dress. On Kanye: Louis Vuitton coat and Alternative Apparel hoodie. Details, see In This Issue.

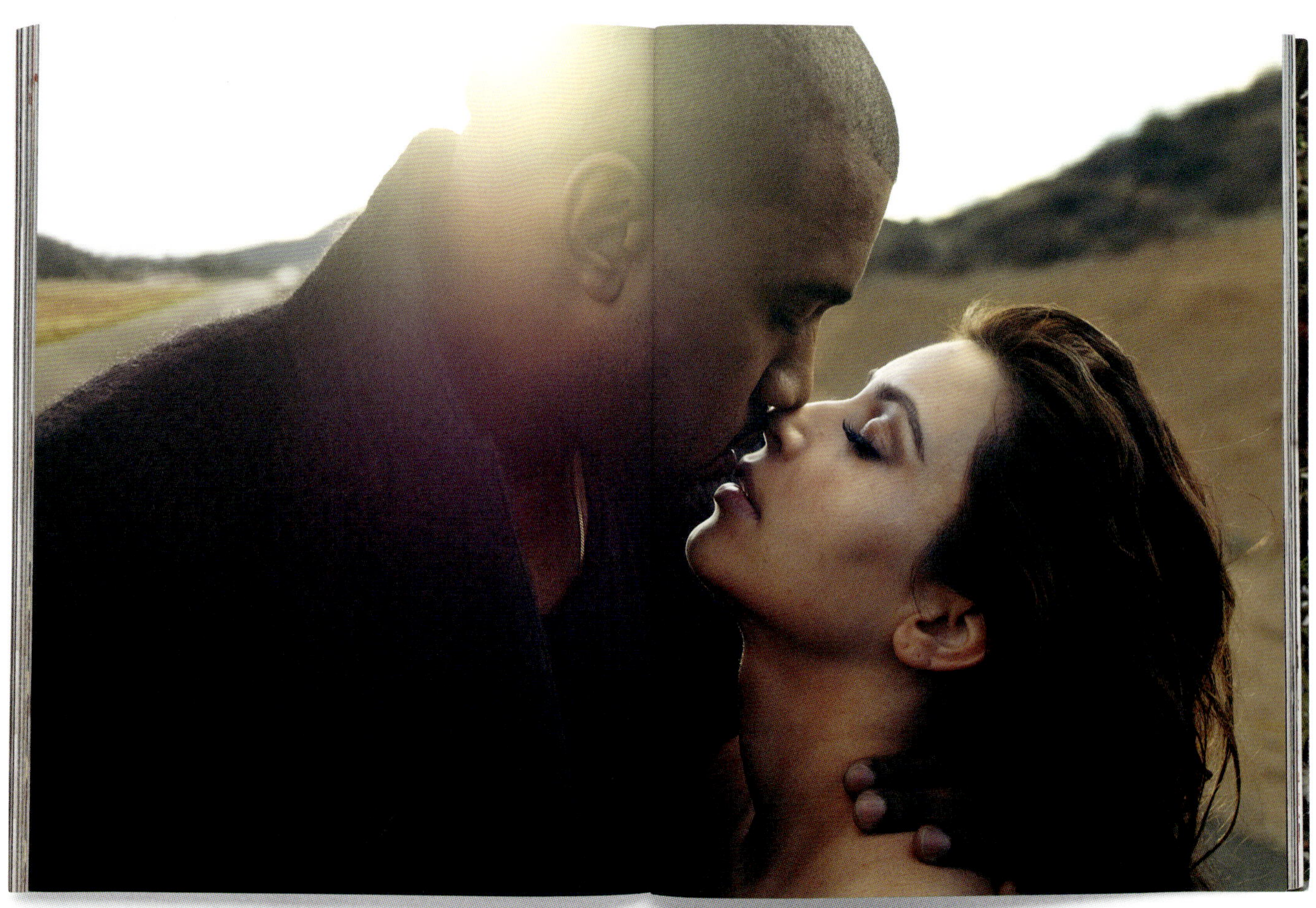

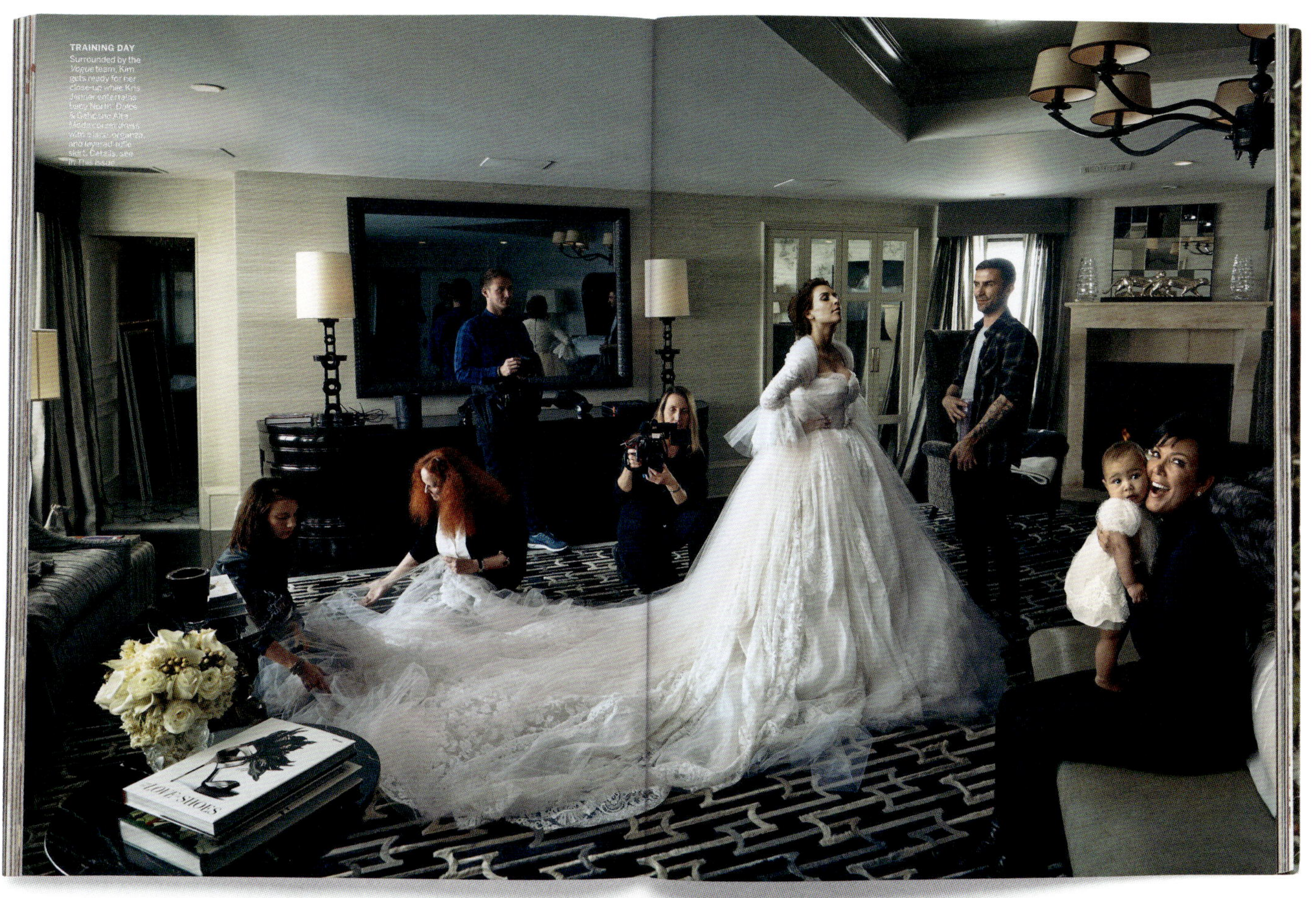
TRAINING DAY
Surrounded by the
Vogue team, Kim
gets ready for her
close-up while Kris
and layered tulle
skirt. Details, see
In This Issue.
LOVE SHOES

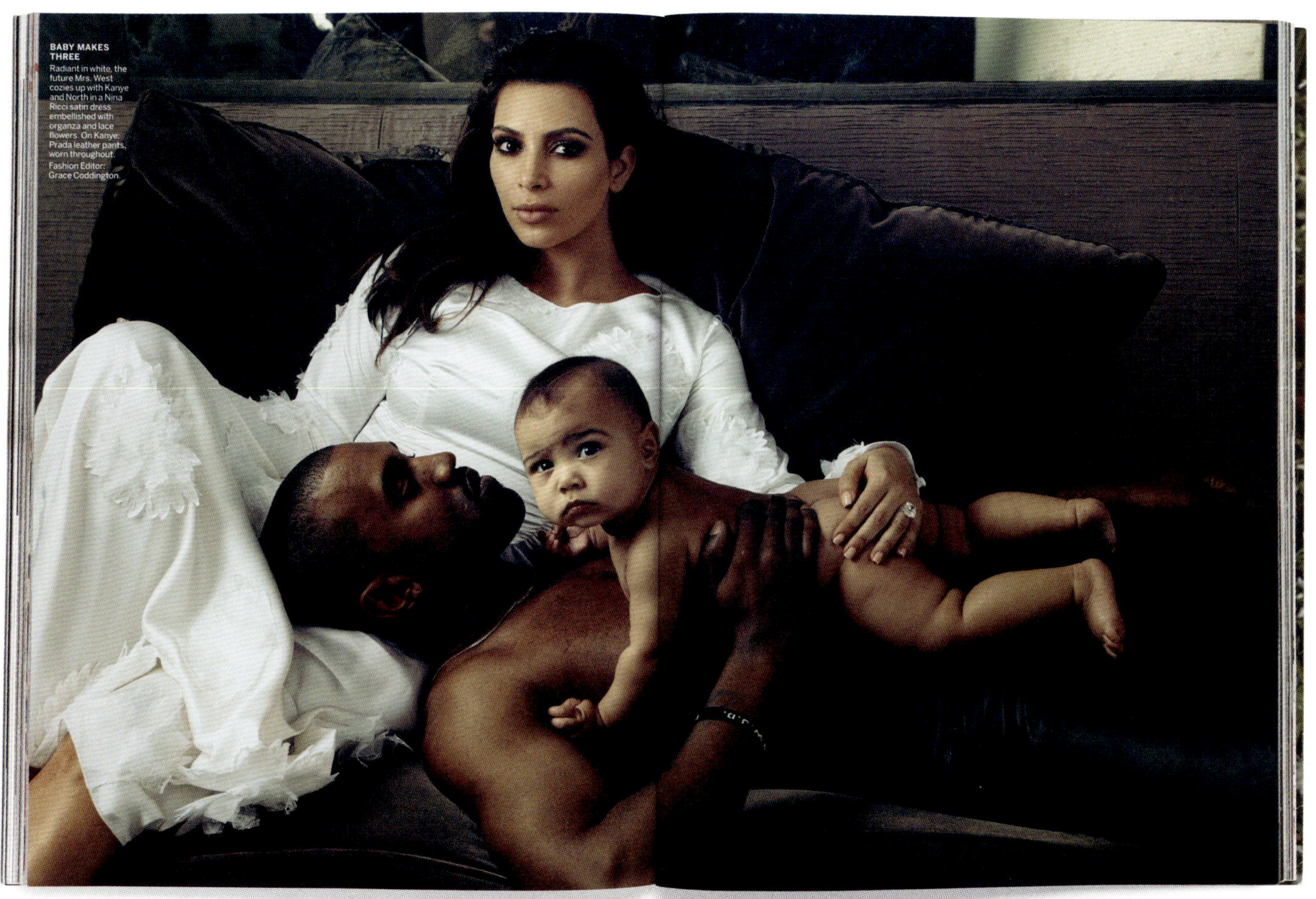
BABY MAKES THREE
Radiant in white, the future Mrs. West cozies up with Kanye and North in a Nina Ricci satin dress embellished with organza and lace flowers. On Kanye: Prada leather pants, worn throughout.
Fashion Editor: Grace Coddington.

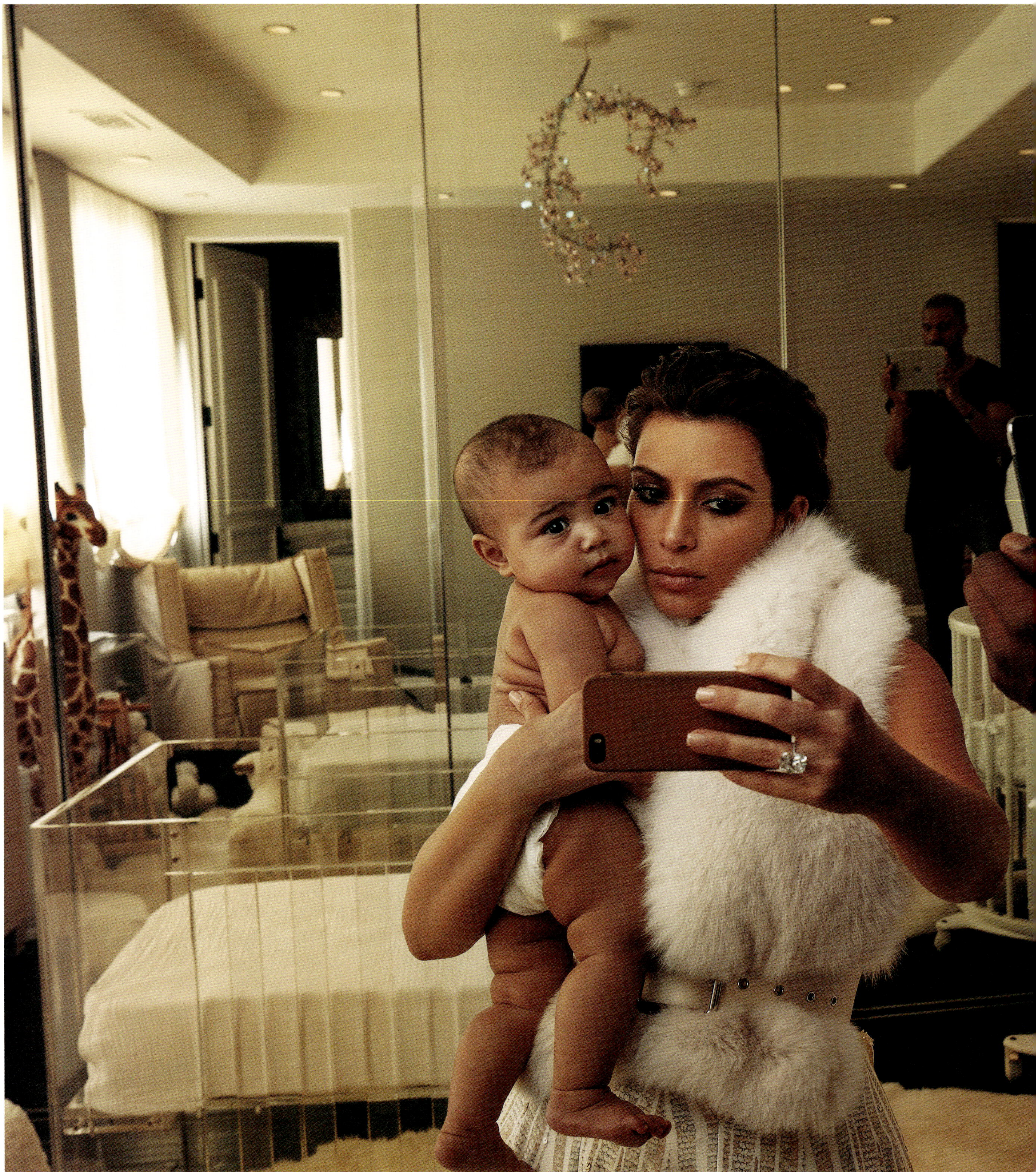

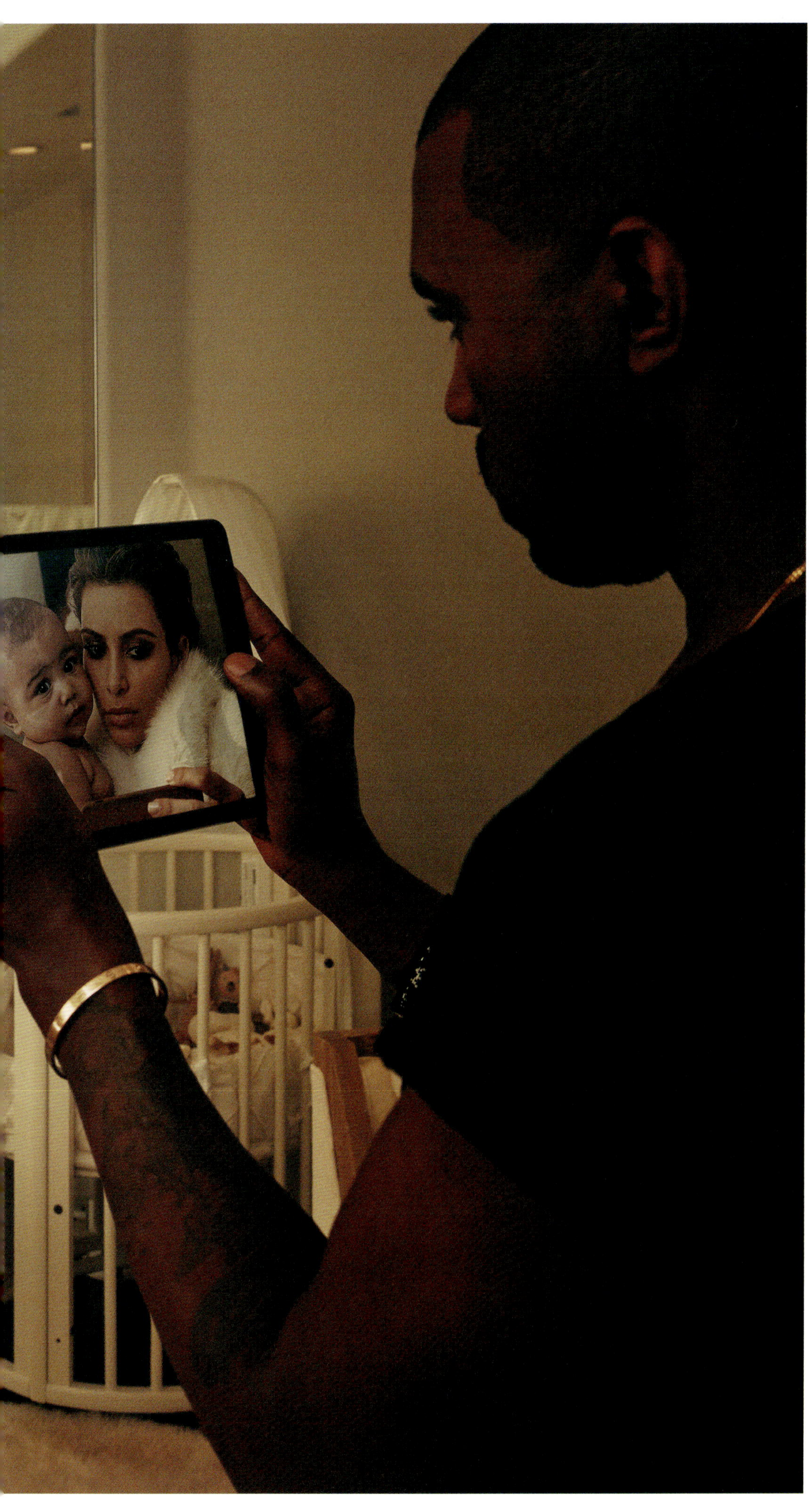

"Kim Kardashian and Kanye West were living at her mother's house when we did their prewedding shoot, because their new house wasn't ready. The concept was that we would do the whole shoot in her house, which was where *Keeping Up With the Kardashians* was set. The problem was that Kanye didn't want to be seen in his mother-in-law's house. 'There's not a room in the house that's me,' he said. 'Except the baby's room.' He kept talking about wanting to go to Paris."

Kim Kardashian, North West, and Kanye West, Los Angeles, 2014

"Caitlyn Jenner emerged over the course of the two days we photographed her in her house in Malibu. The house was in the mountains and it felt very isolated, but we were surrounded by paparazzi. They were in the adjacent hills with their telephoto lenses. The house had floor-to-ceiling windows, and we had to put scrims all around it.

I wasn't going to include the picture in the gold Halston dress in the story. Caitlyn put it on late on the last day of the shoot. When she came out of the dressing room, I thought that maybe everyone had started drinking, which they had. Oribe, who was doing her hair, and Mark Carrasquillo, who was in charge of makeup, were having champagne with her and they had gone too far . . . too much hair, too much makeup."

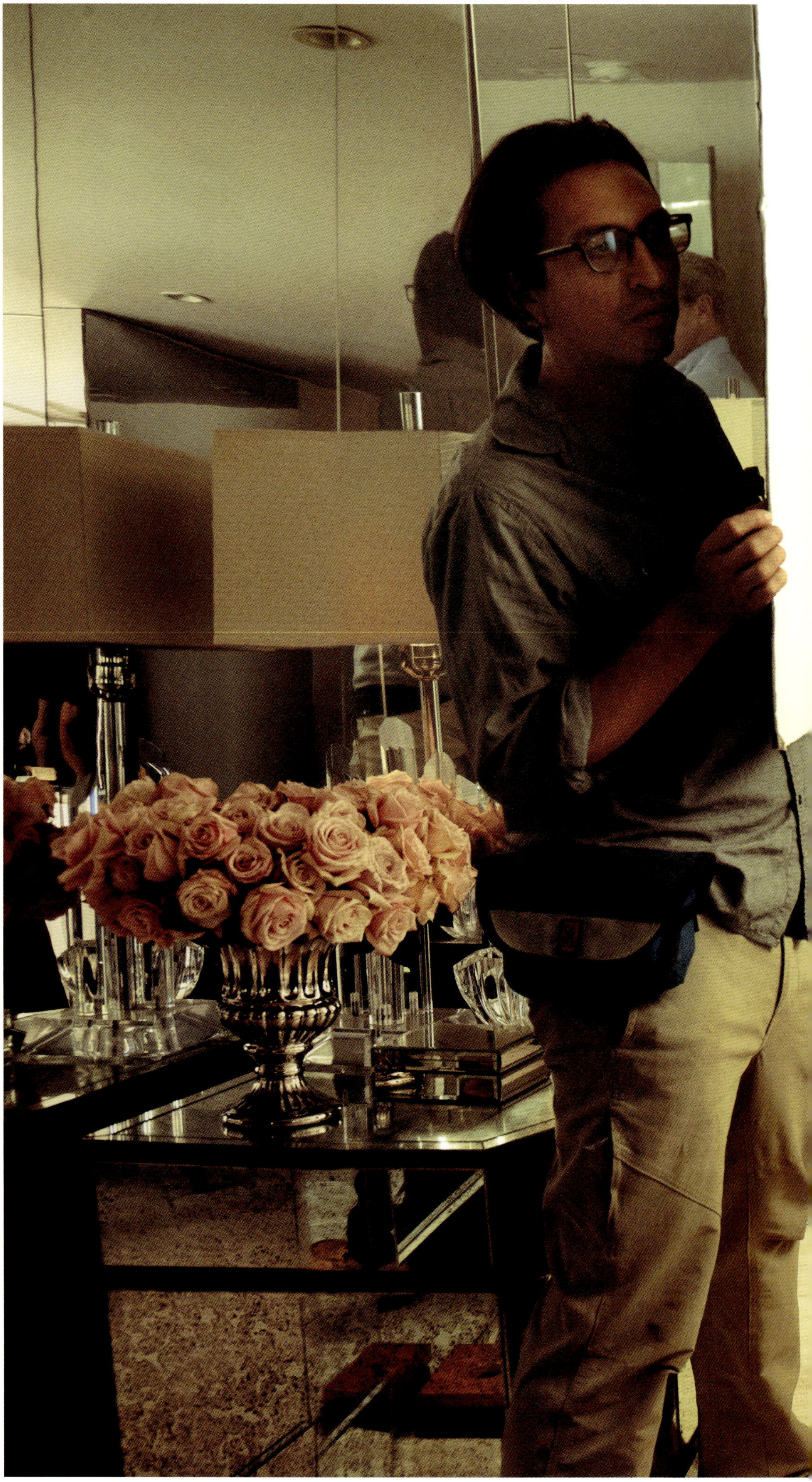

Malibu, California, 2015

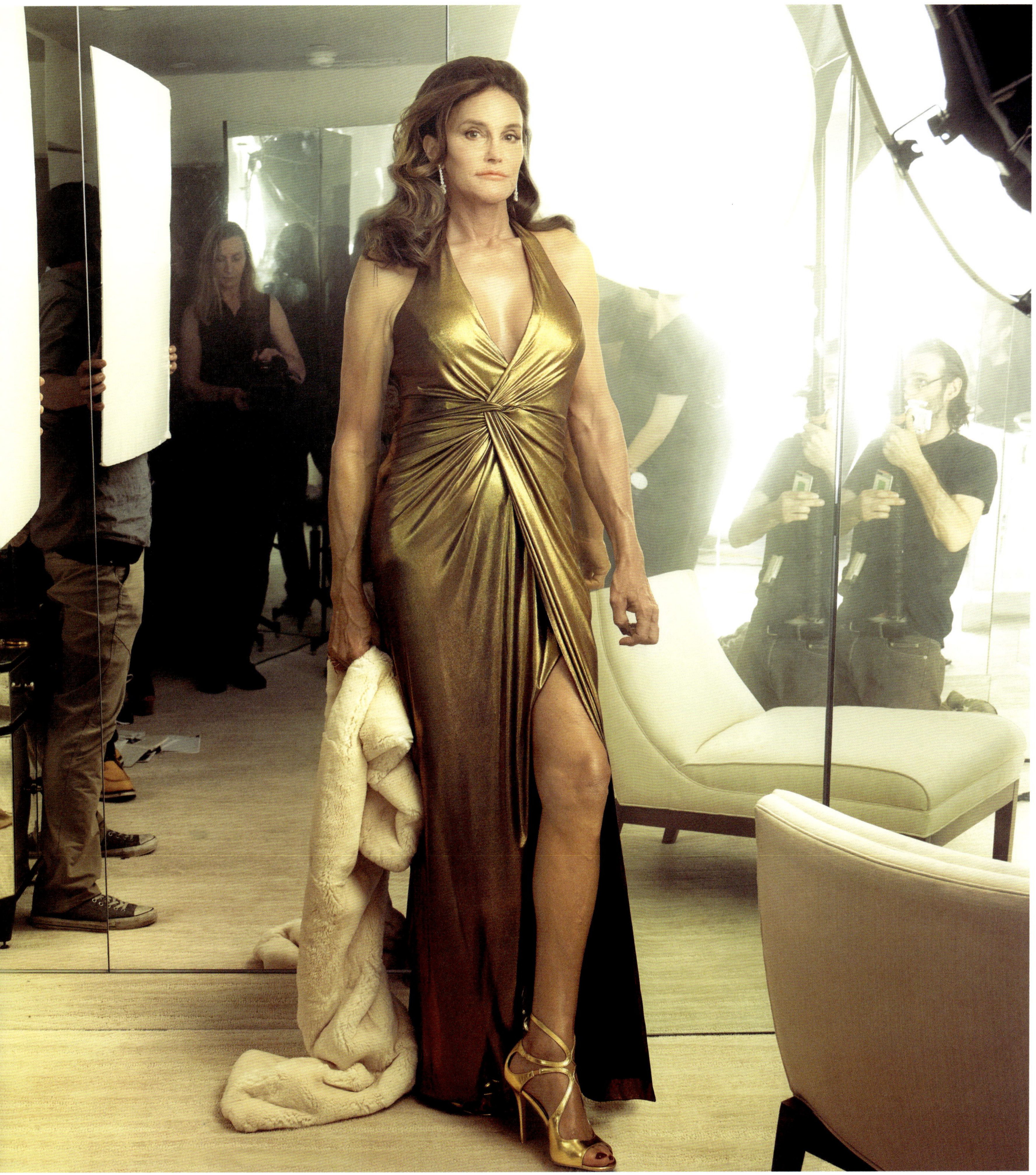

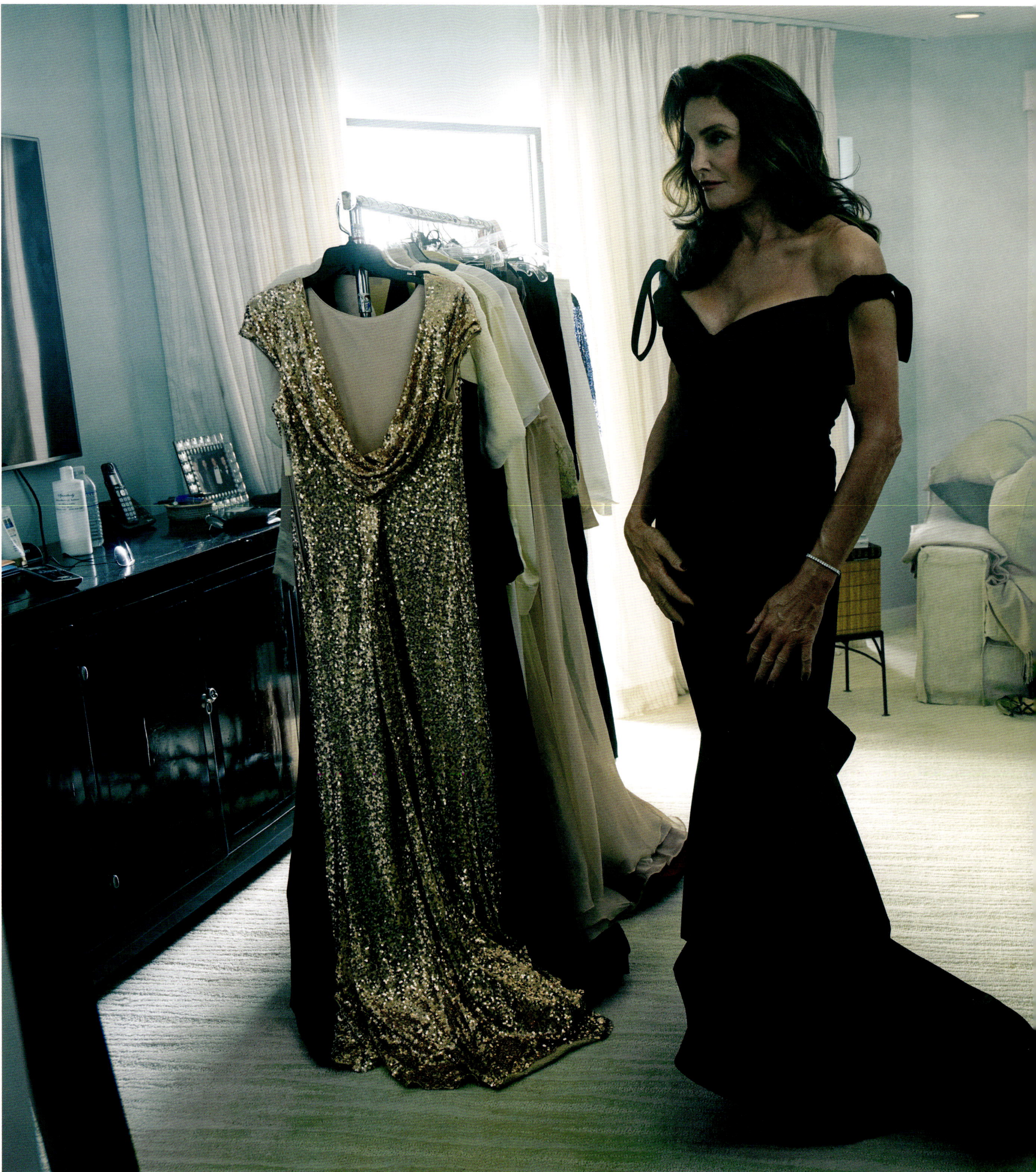

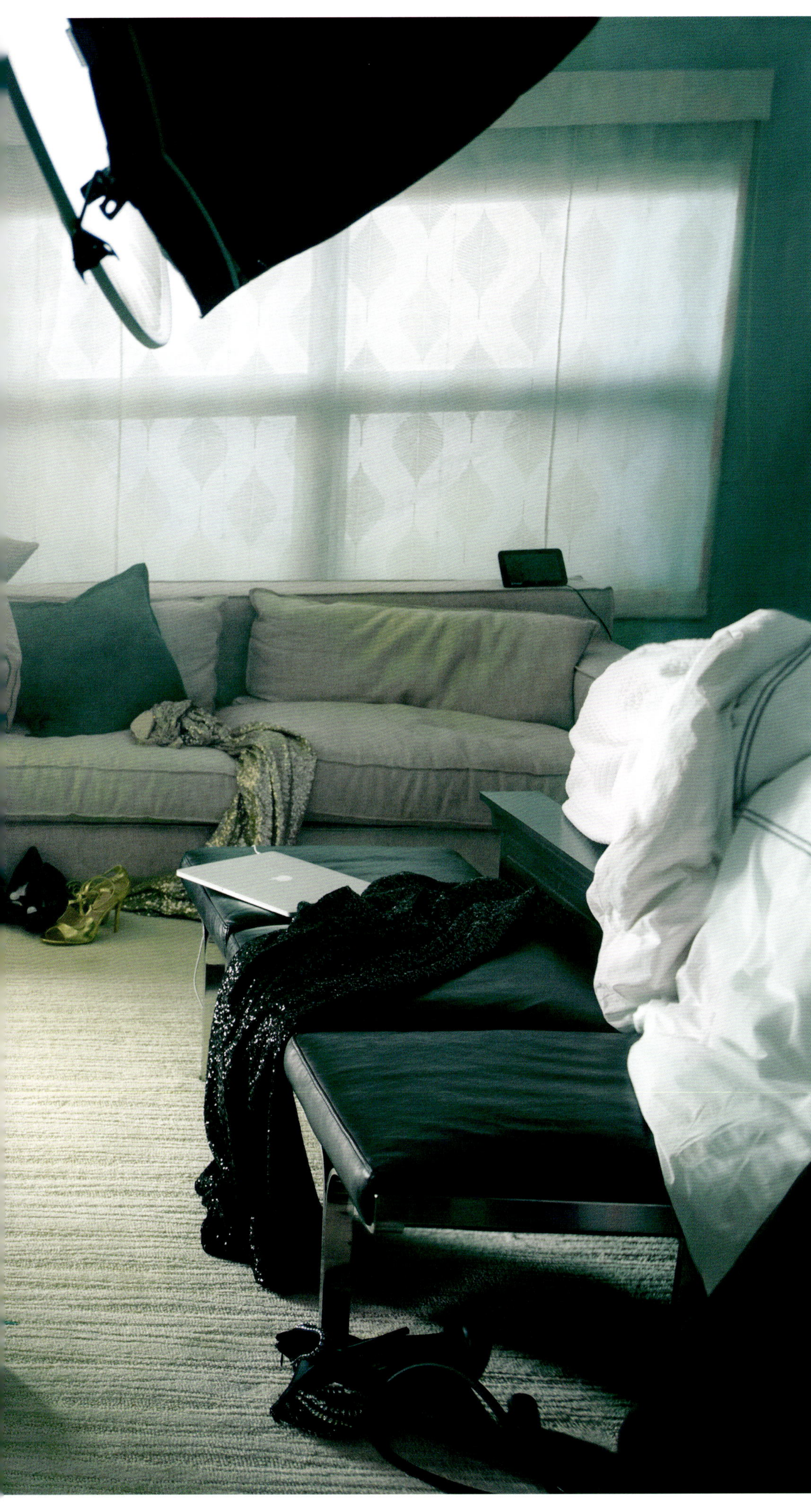

“I had started out thinking we would be conservative. We had a tremendous amount of reference material—classic photographs of women like Katharine Hepburn and Lauren Bacall. But Caitlyn just took over. She was very quiet on the first day and then she gained confidence.”

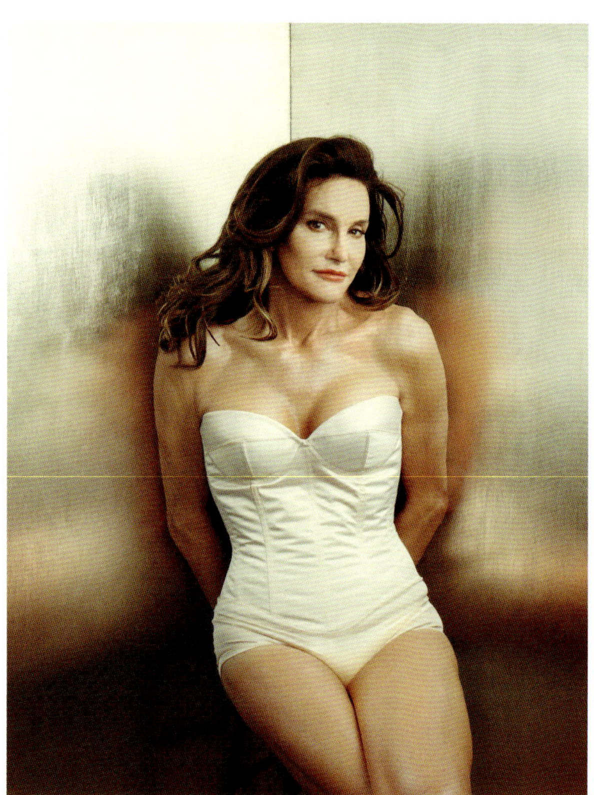

"What we were developing was an acquired look. A construction. This was not journalism. We weren't thinking about *Vanity Fair* or the cover. We just wanted to support Caitlyn as she became a woman. Our whole team wanted the process to be a success for her. The July 2015 cover revealed her name and image for the first time."

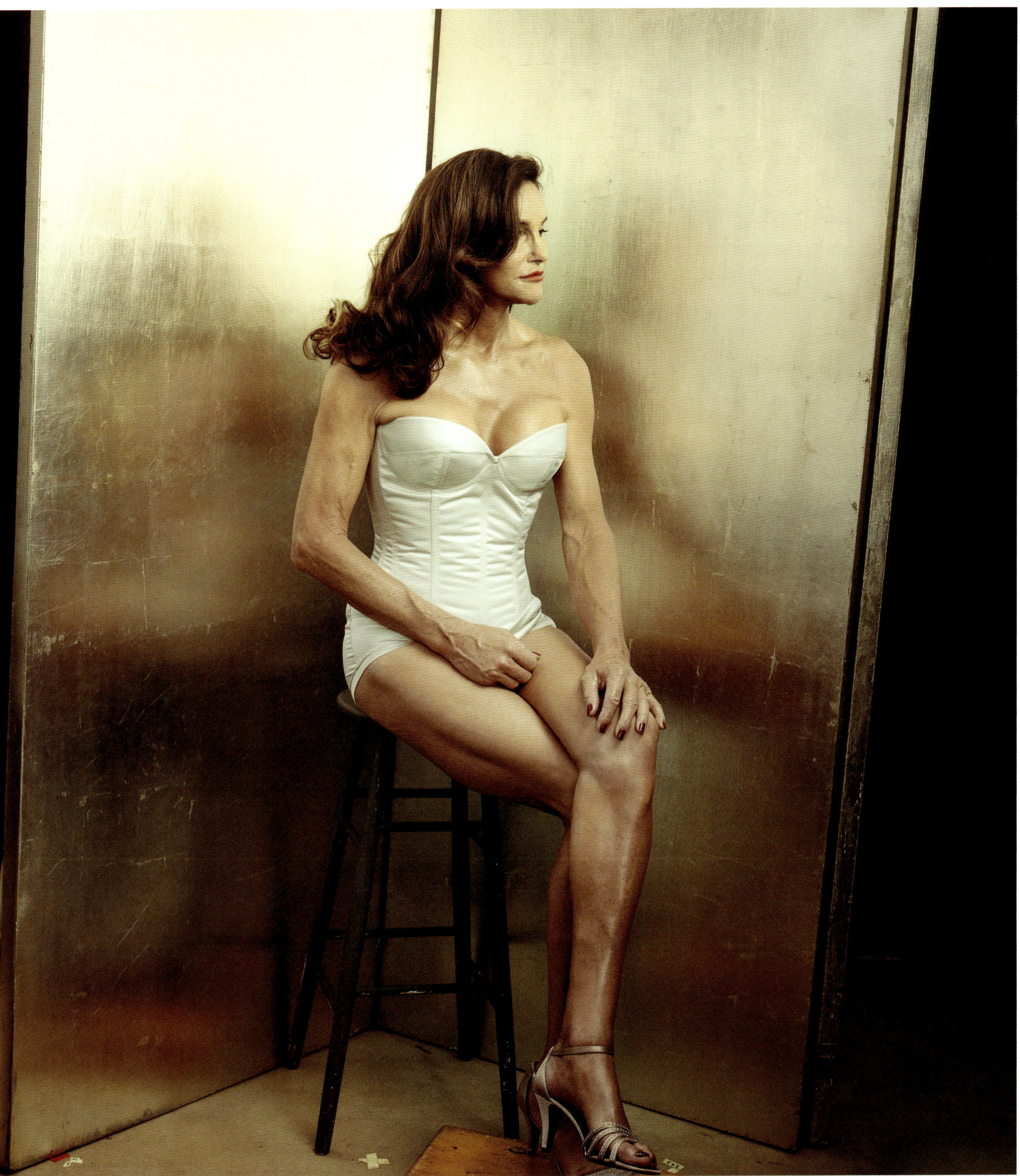

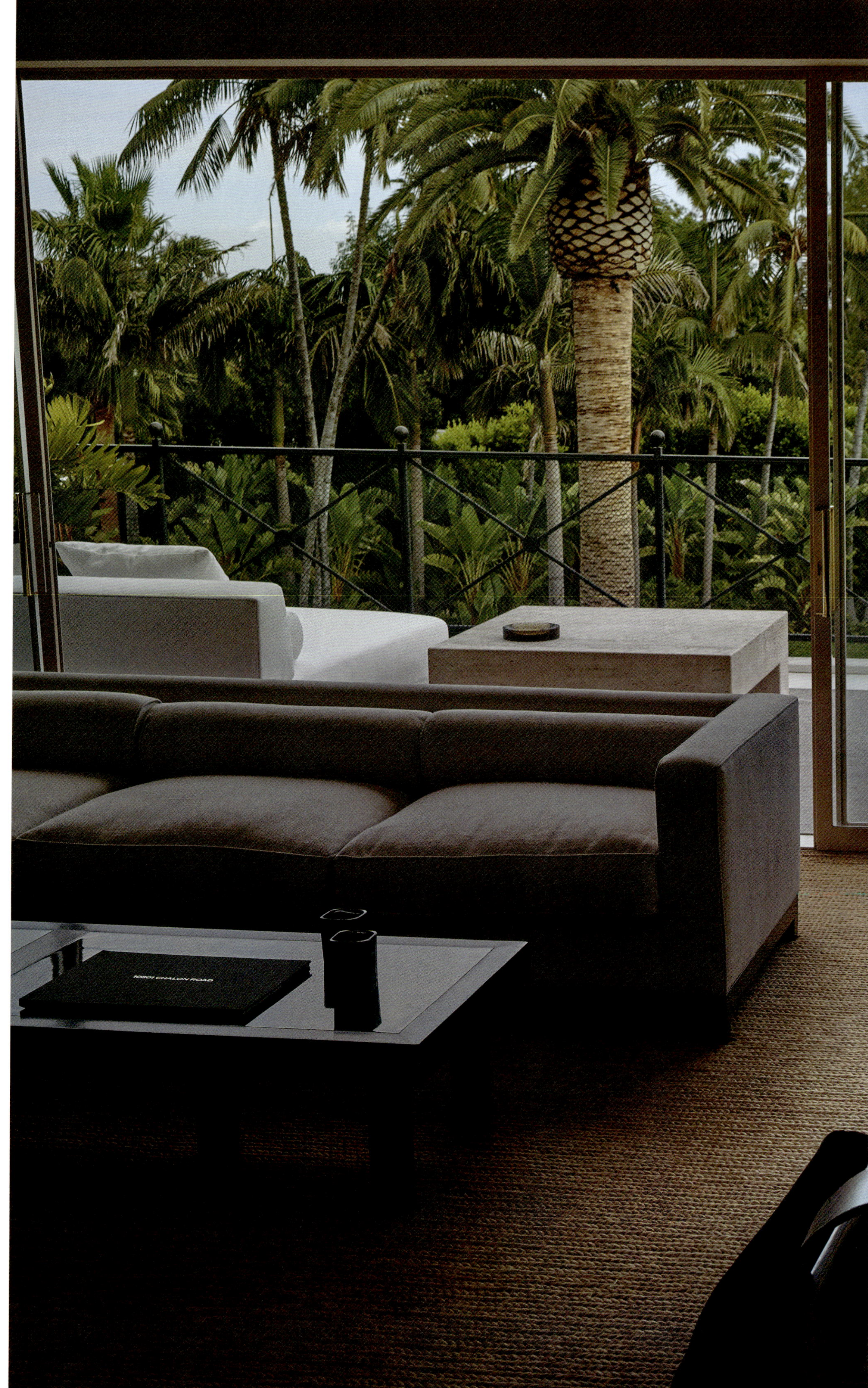

Tom Ford, Los Angeles, 2019

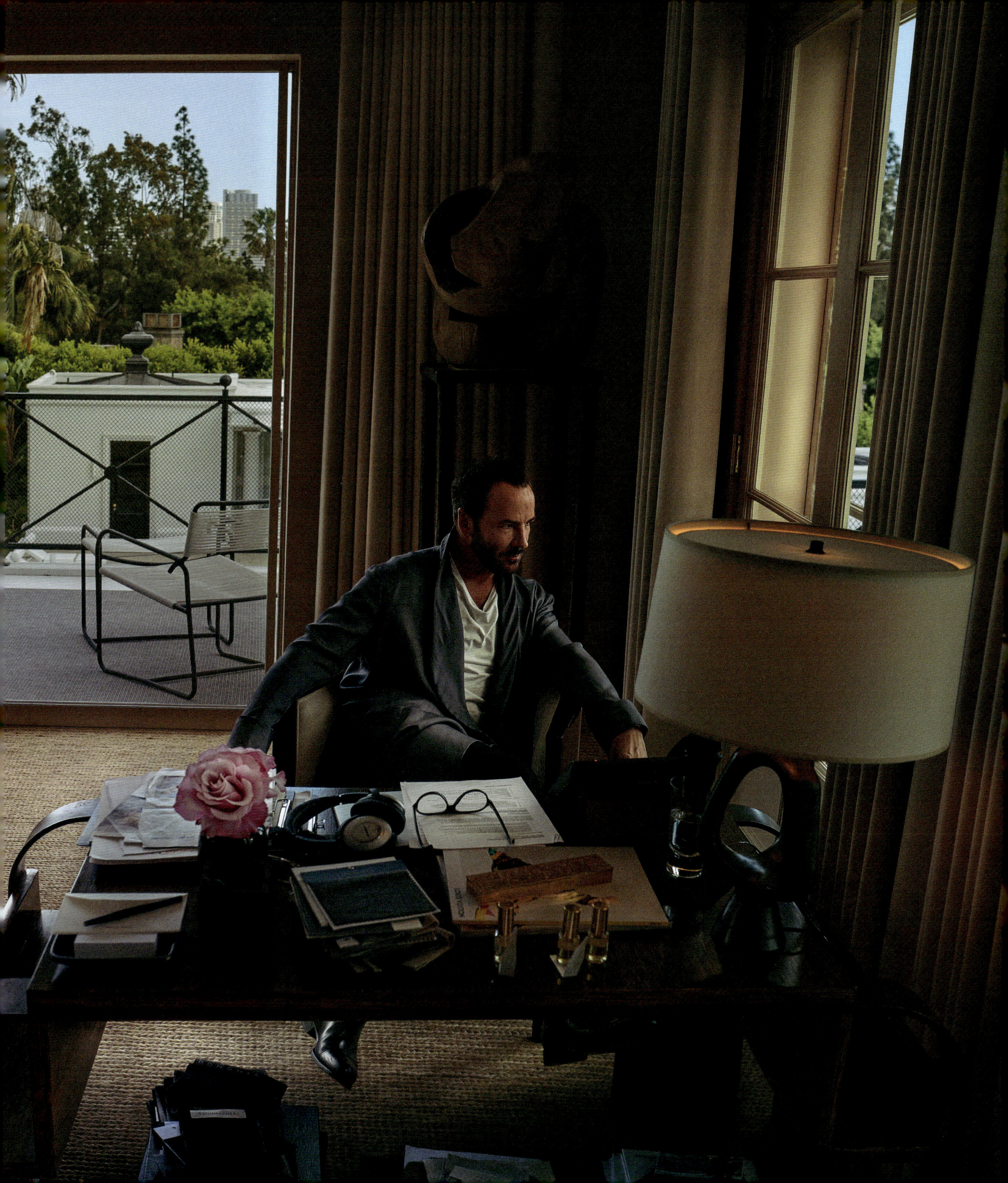

“A shoot can become so charged and intense that you enter a kind of zone. You are taken in. The rest of the world just disappears. Rihanna has a mesmerizing aura. Her confidence in her allure is conveyed in some intangible, mysterious way. I had seen a photograph of her dancing in the street in Barbados, where she grew up, during Mardi Gras, and I had tried for years to set up a trip with her there. Then when we were planning a cover shoot with her for *Vanity Fair*, we began hearing rumors that restrictions on travel to Cuba were going to be lifted. Why not do the Rihanna shoot in Havana? Before the old city was changed forever. It turned out that Rihanna wanted to go to Cuba too. She was interested in Cuban music and the legendary recording studios that were there before the revolution.”

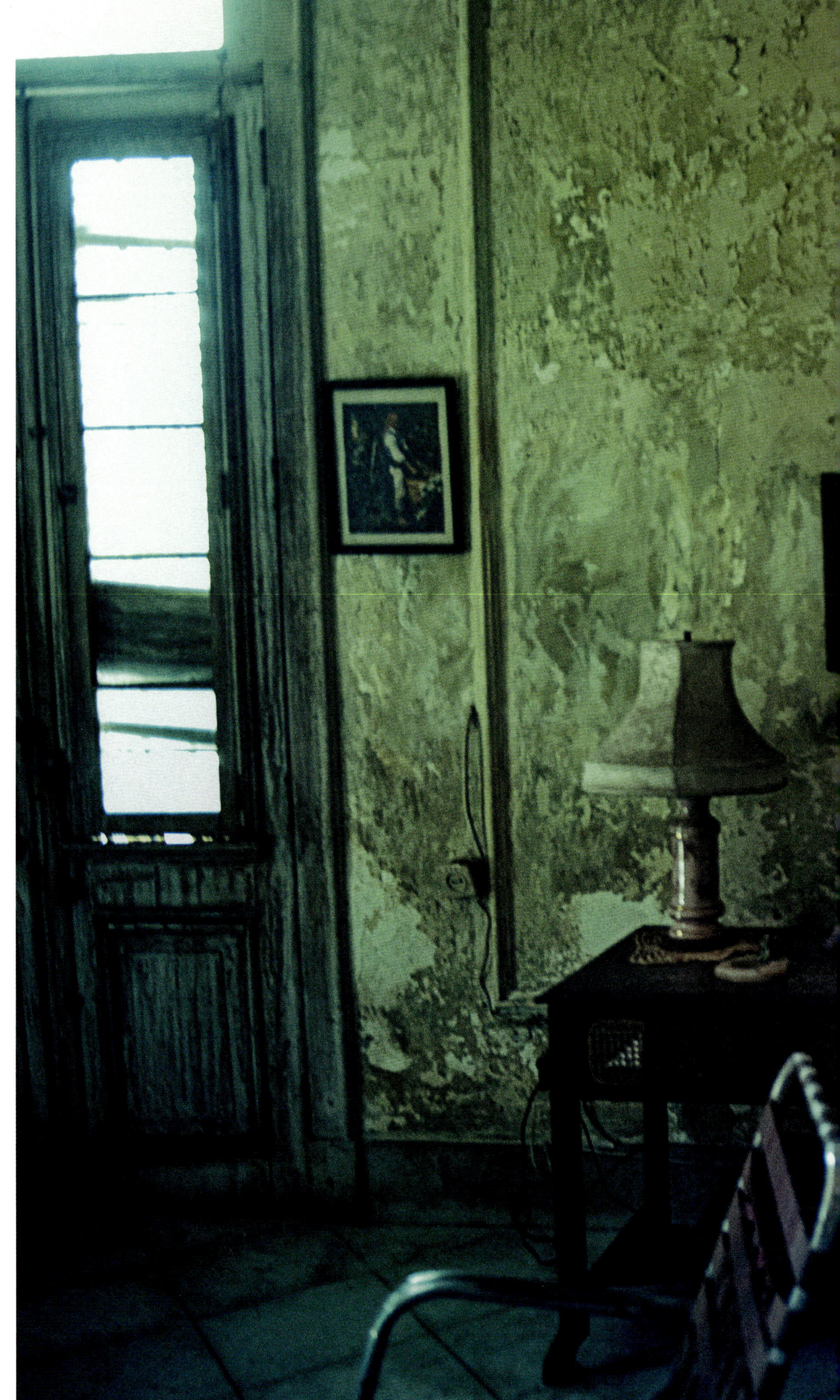

Havana, 2015

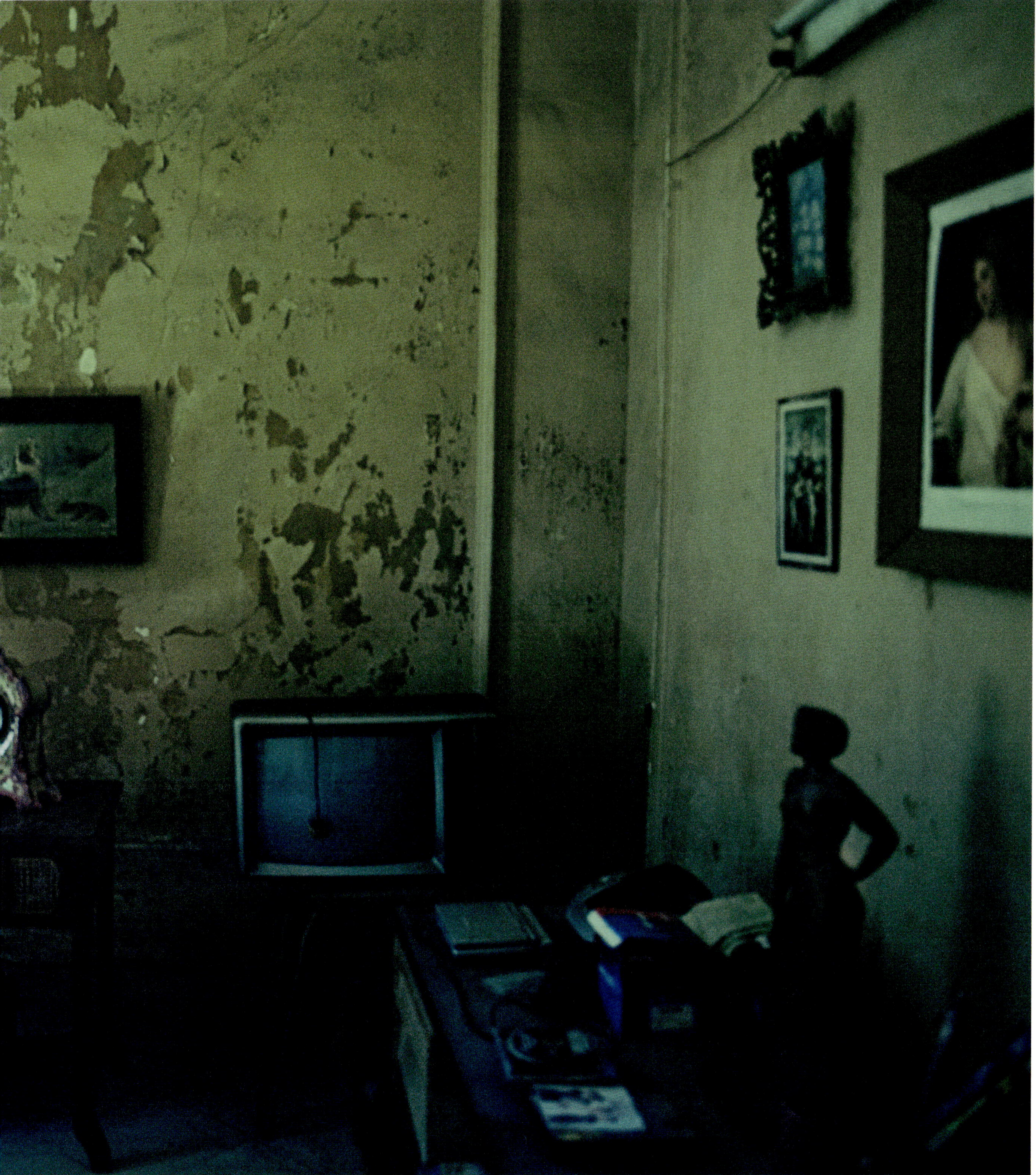

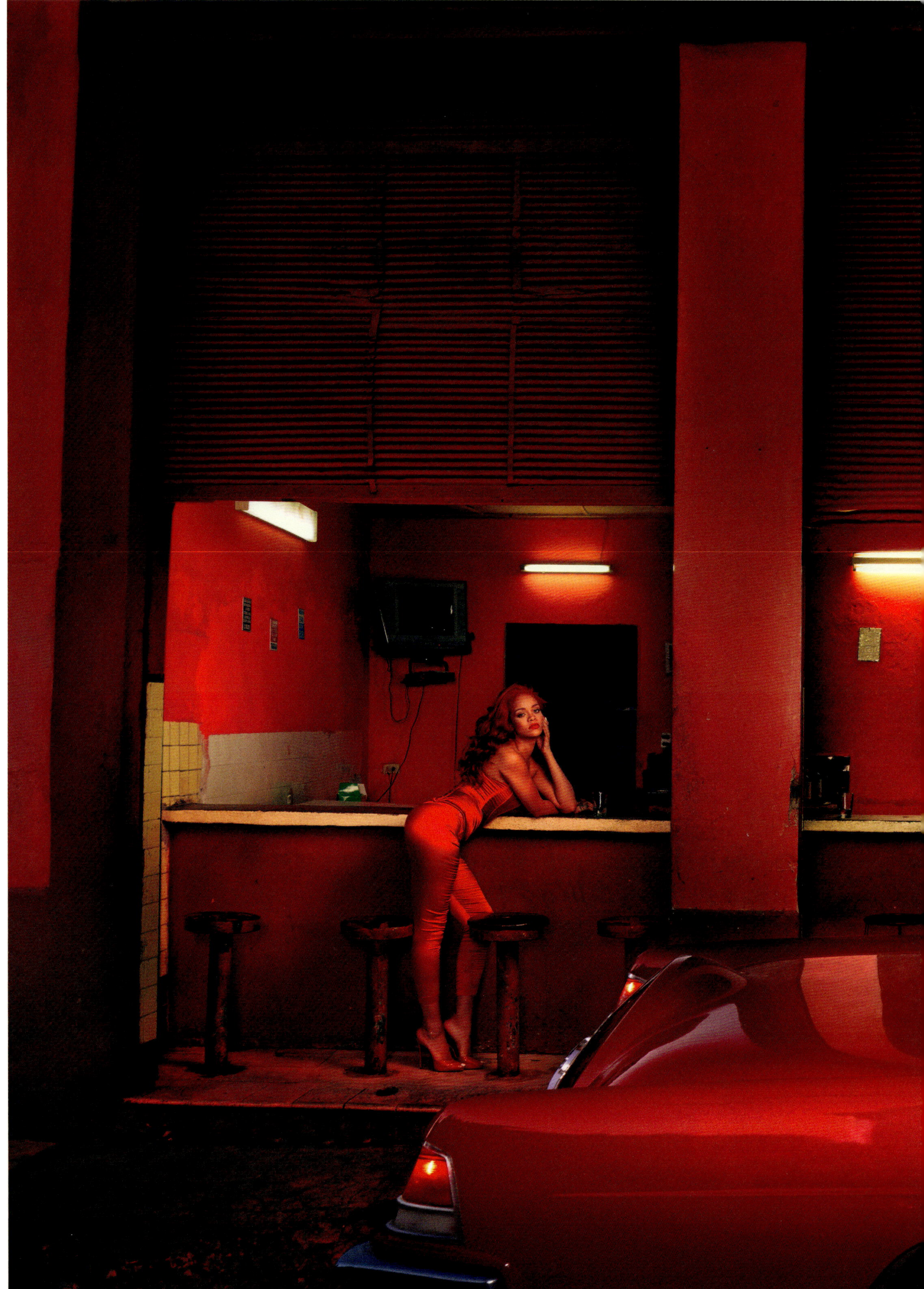

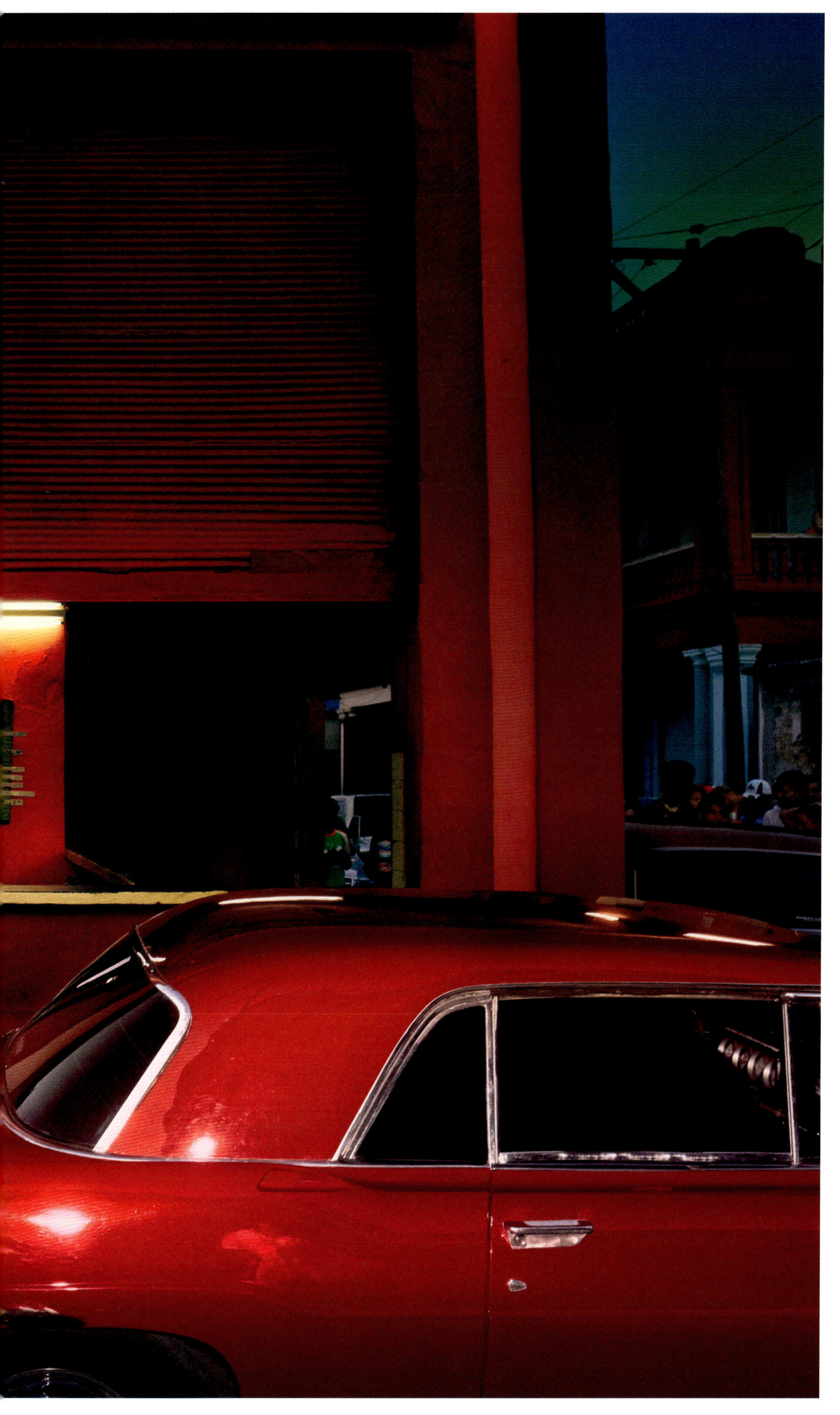

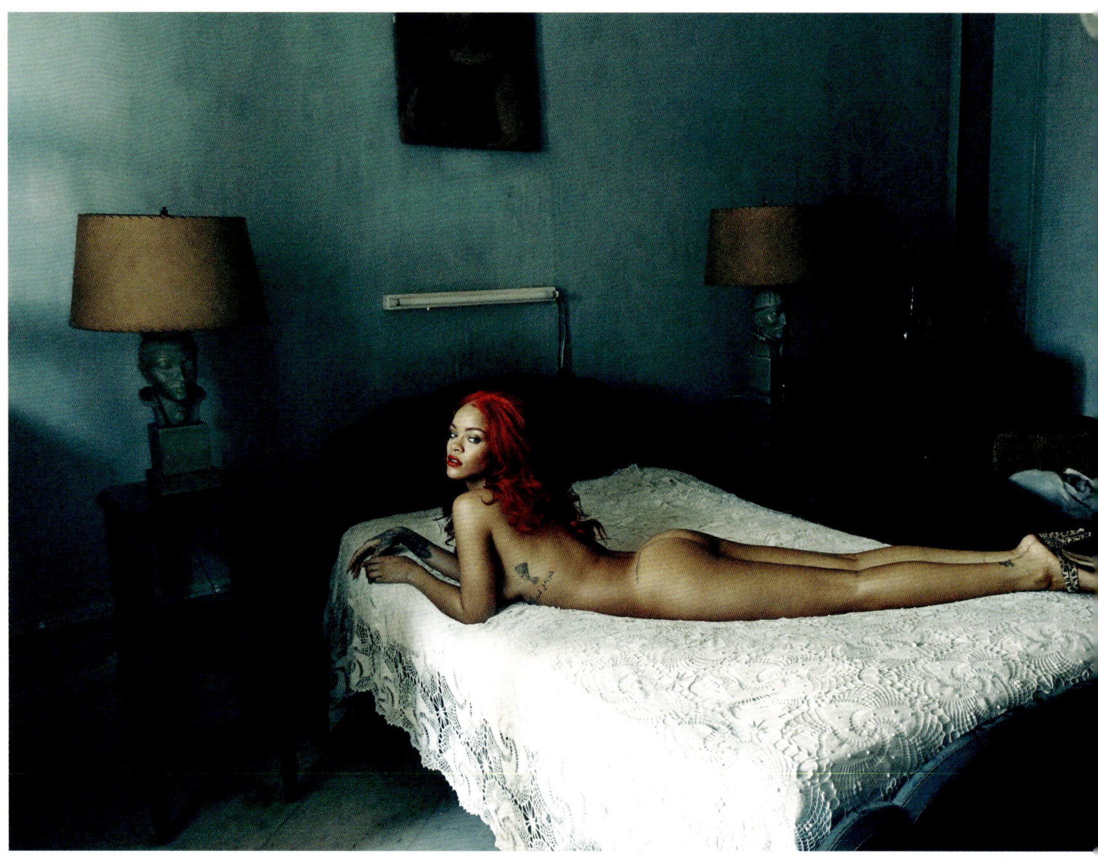

“Havana was hot and vivid and sexy. There were little bars on side streets and deteriorating 1930s villas and classic American cars. We used a 1956 Lincoln Continental Mark II that had been owned by the wife of Fulgencio Batista, Cuba’s last military dictator. Hundreds of people—fans—gathered around wherever we went. Rihanna would get into arguments with her bodyguards, who were trying to control the situation, but that was pretty much impossible. One afternoon I followed her into a particularly large crowd, trying to take her picture, and she took my arm and pulled me in deeper.”

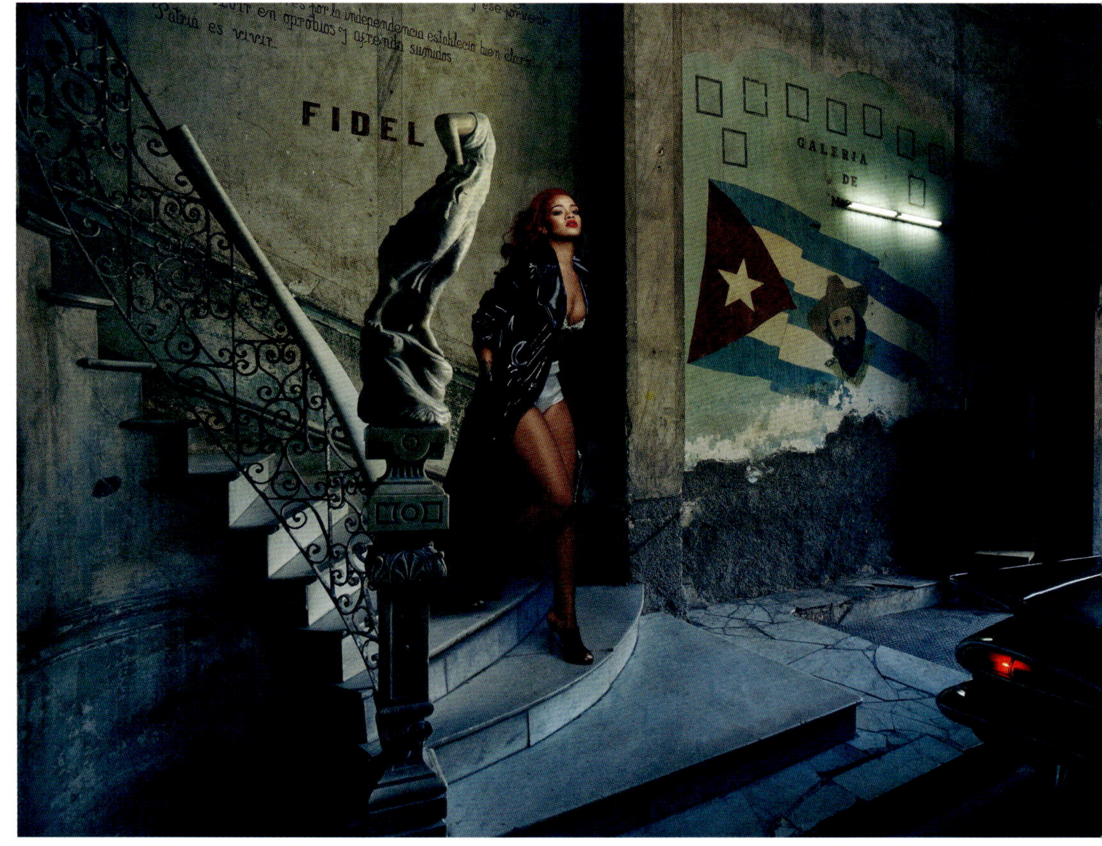

Rihanna, Havana, 2015

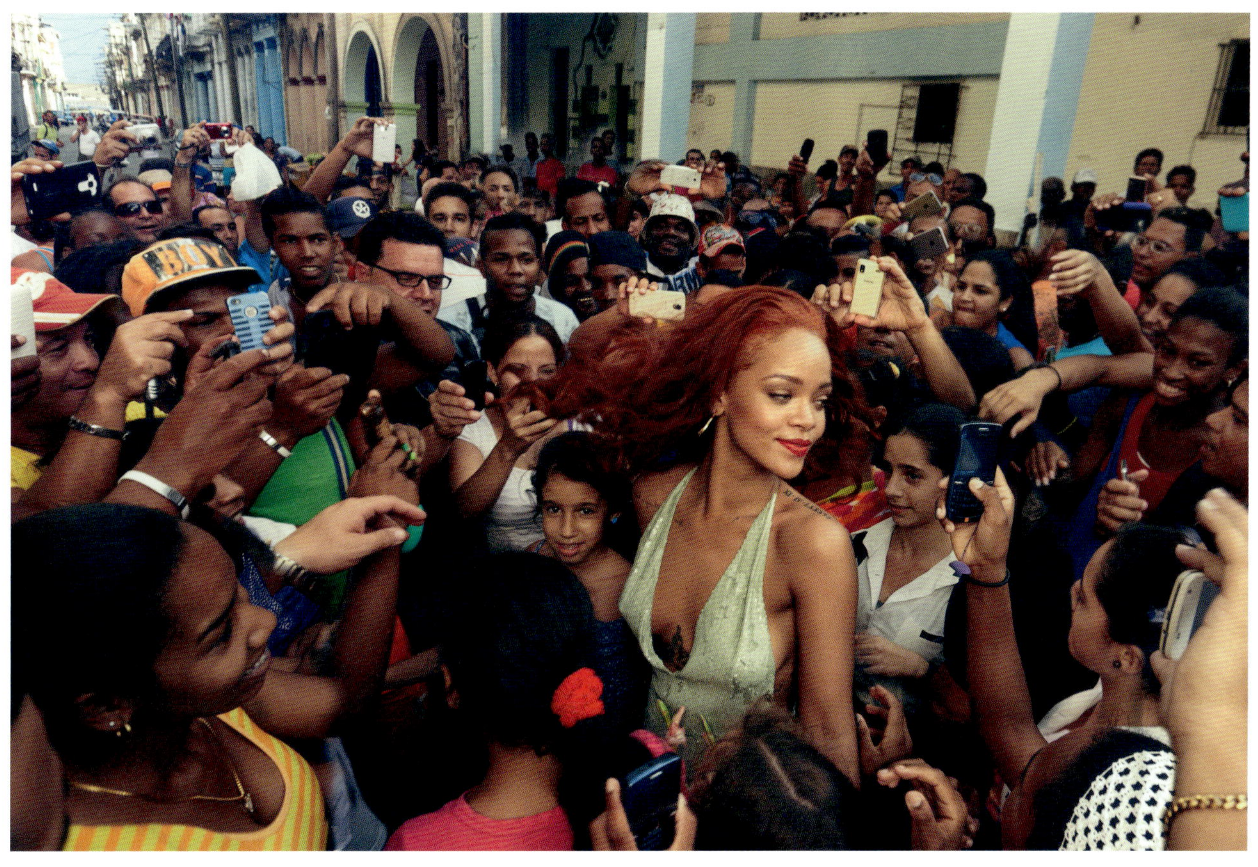

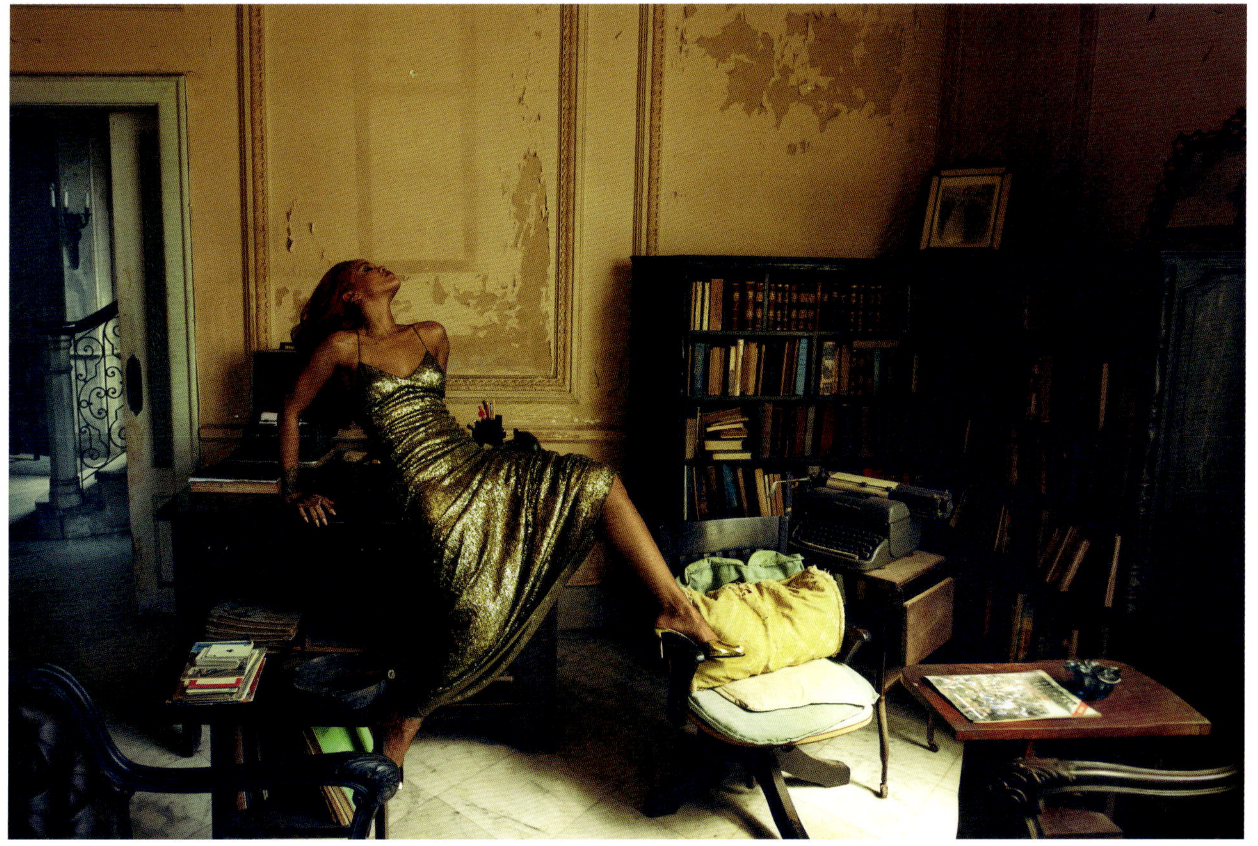

Annie's first shoot with Rihanna was for *Vogue* a few years before they went to Cuba, Rihanna has been on many *Vogue* covers since then, but that was the first time for her. Fashion editors were still learning to cope with bodies that weren't model sizes. Annie remembers that Tonne Goodman was having a hard time on that first Rihanna shoot. None of the clothes fit her. They ended up turning a Chanel dress around and Rihanna wore it backwards.

The move away from models on covers had been relatively sudden. Supermodels dominated magazines in the sixties, seventies, and eighties, but in the nineties that began to change. In 1999 four of *Vogue*'s twelve cover subjects were not models. By 2003 all twelve covers featured celebrities—actors, athletes, musicians. Many of them were women who had very clear ideas about what they would and would not wear. They were custodians of their own images.

Following spread: Eddie Redmayne as Lili Elbe in *The Danish Girl*, Hertfordshire, England, 2015

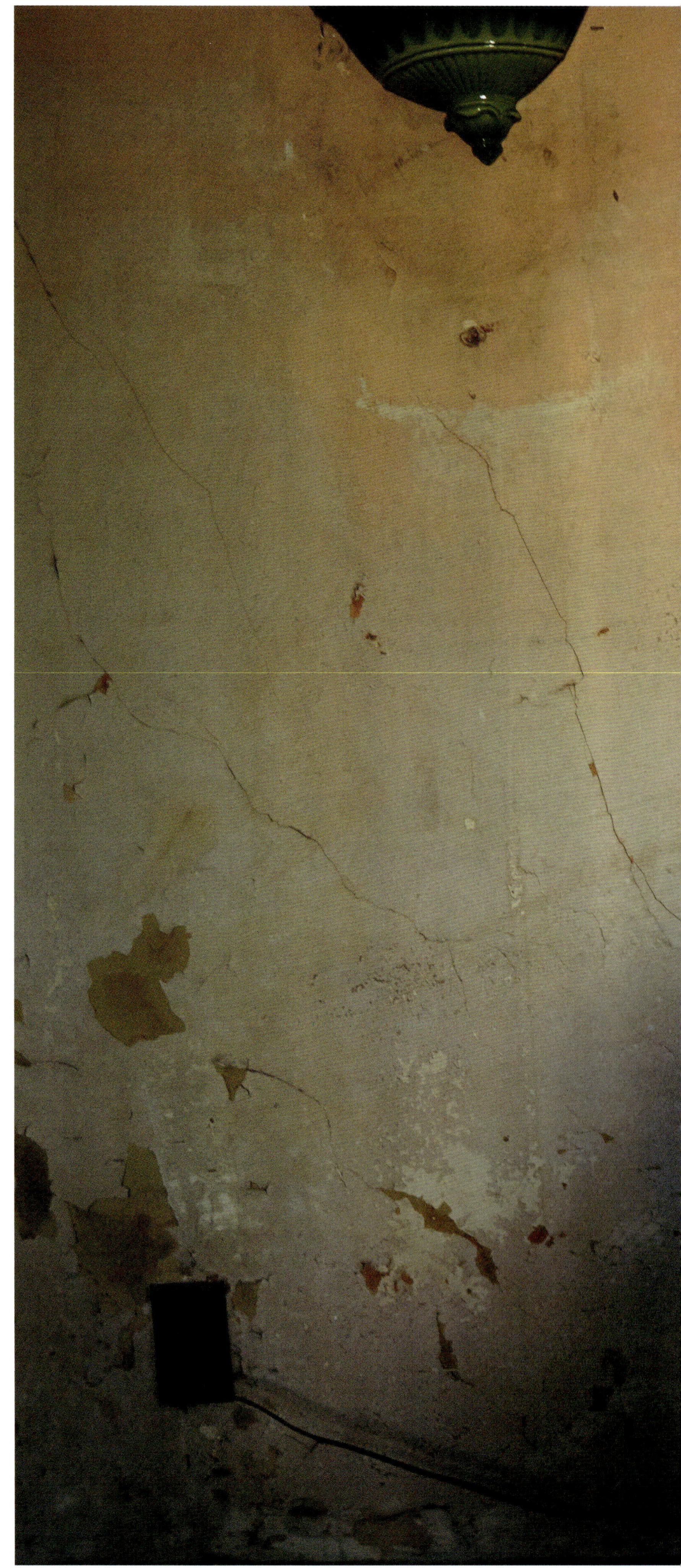

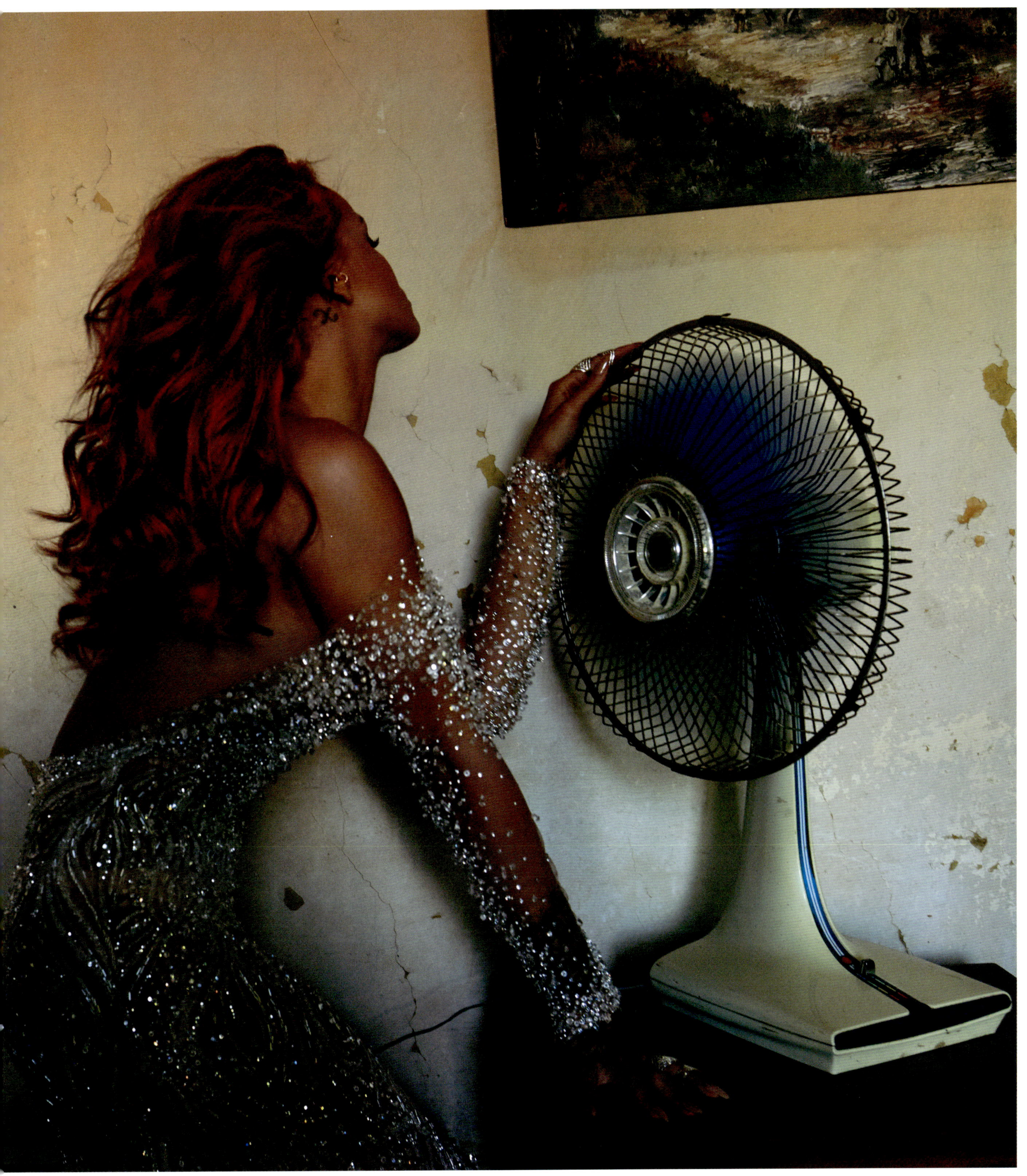

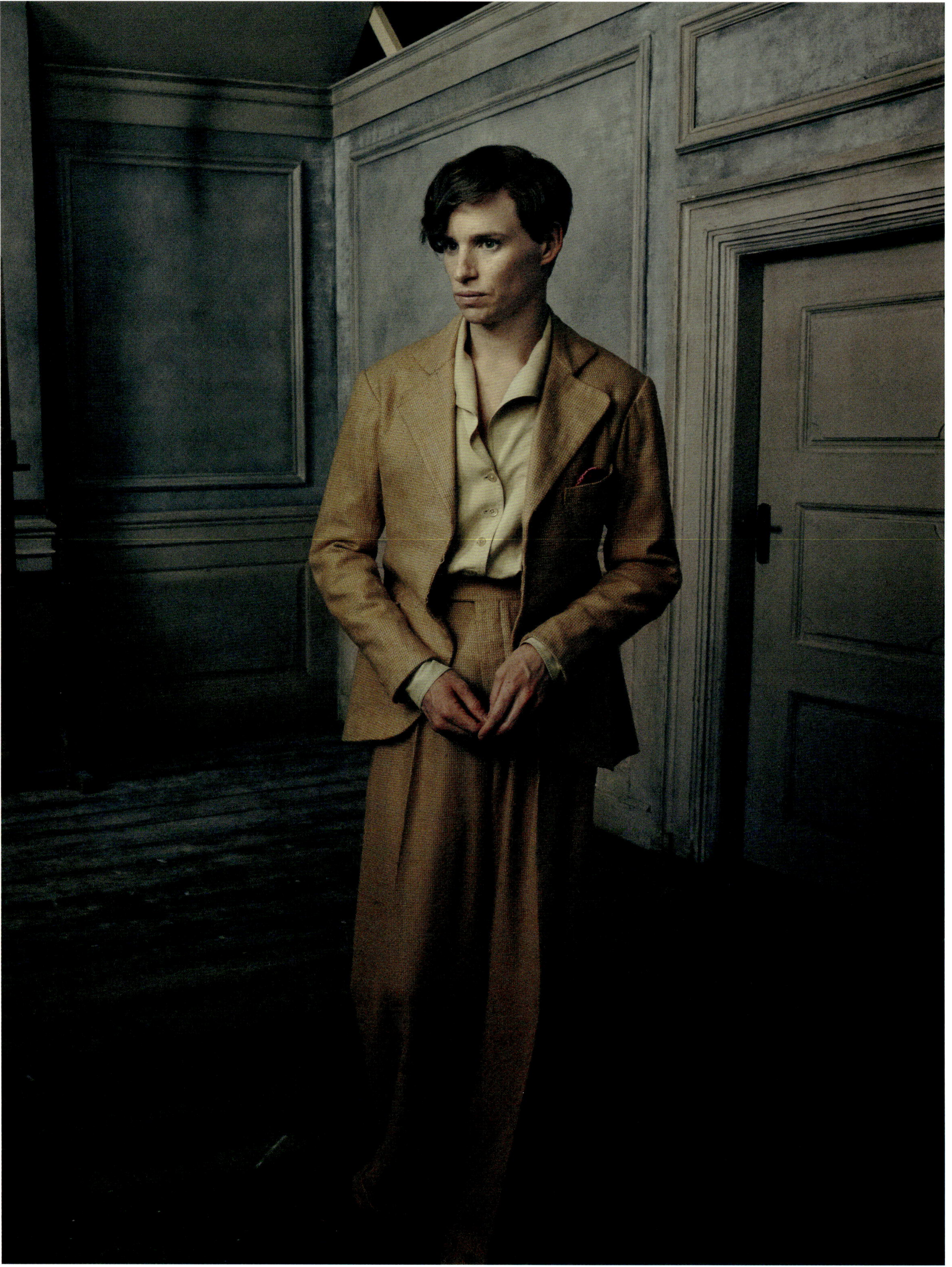

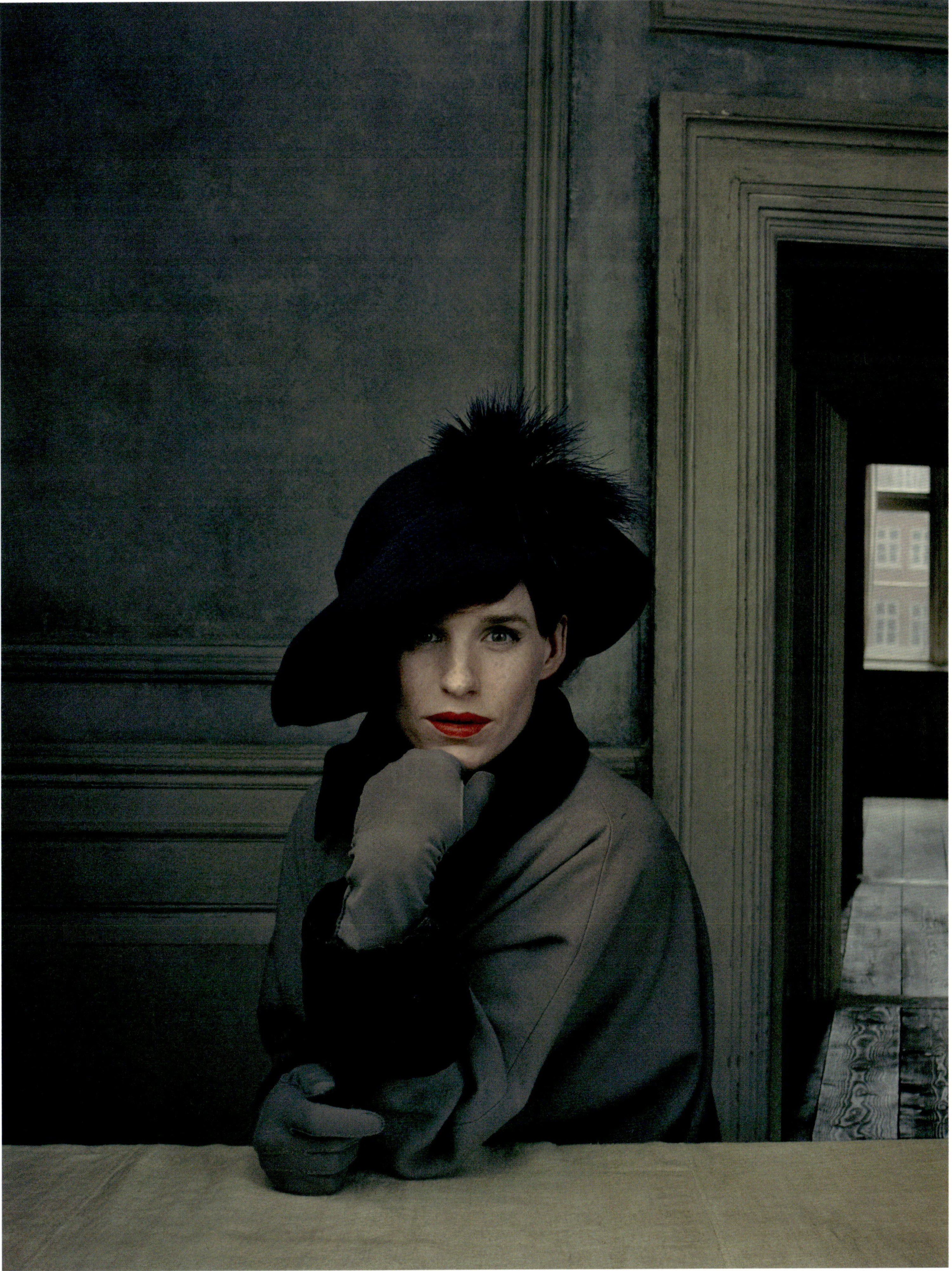

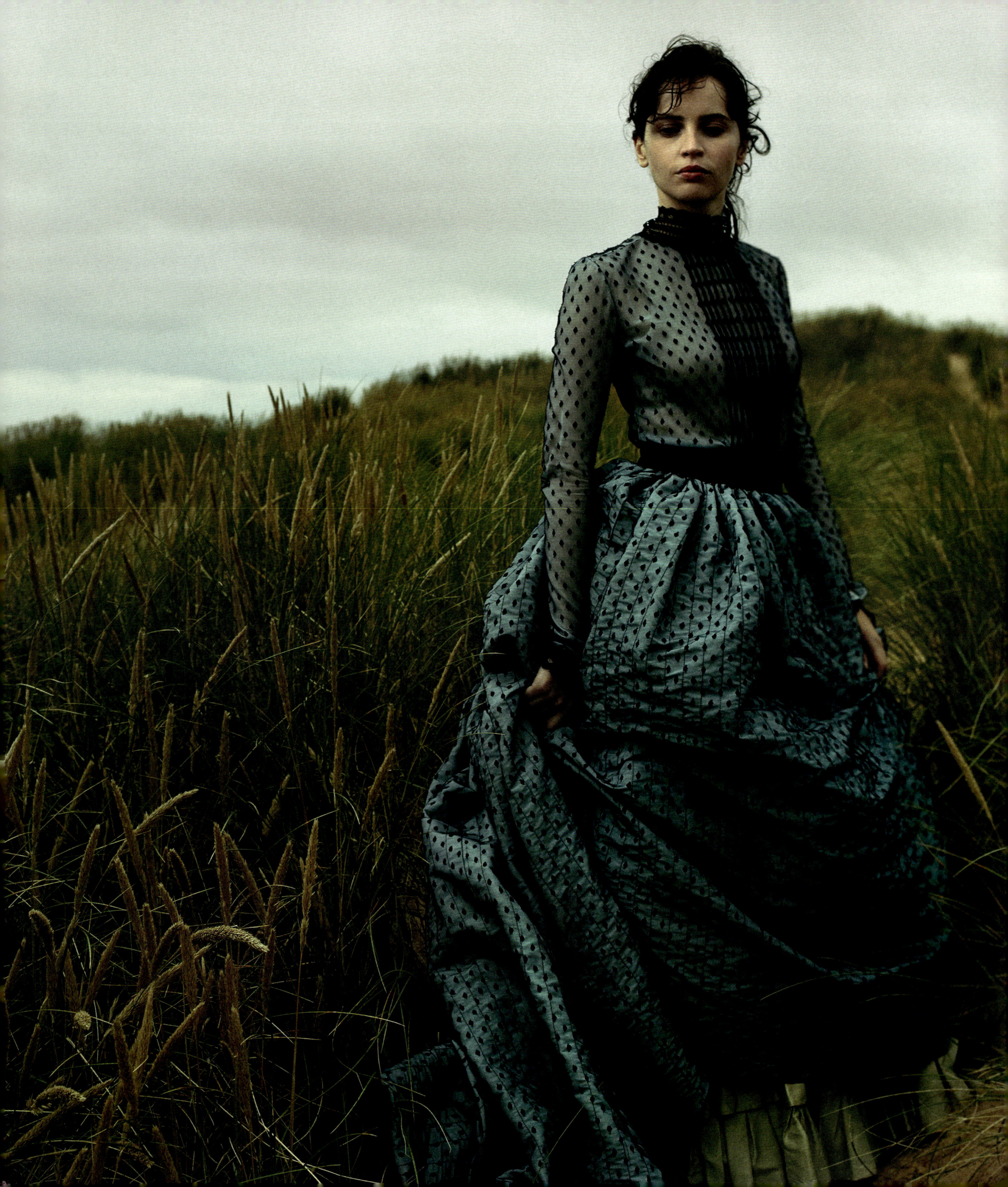

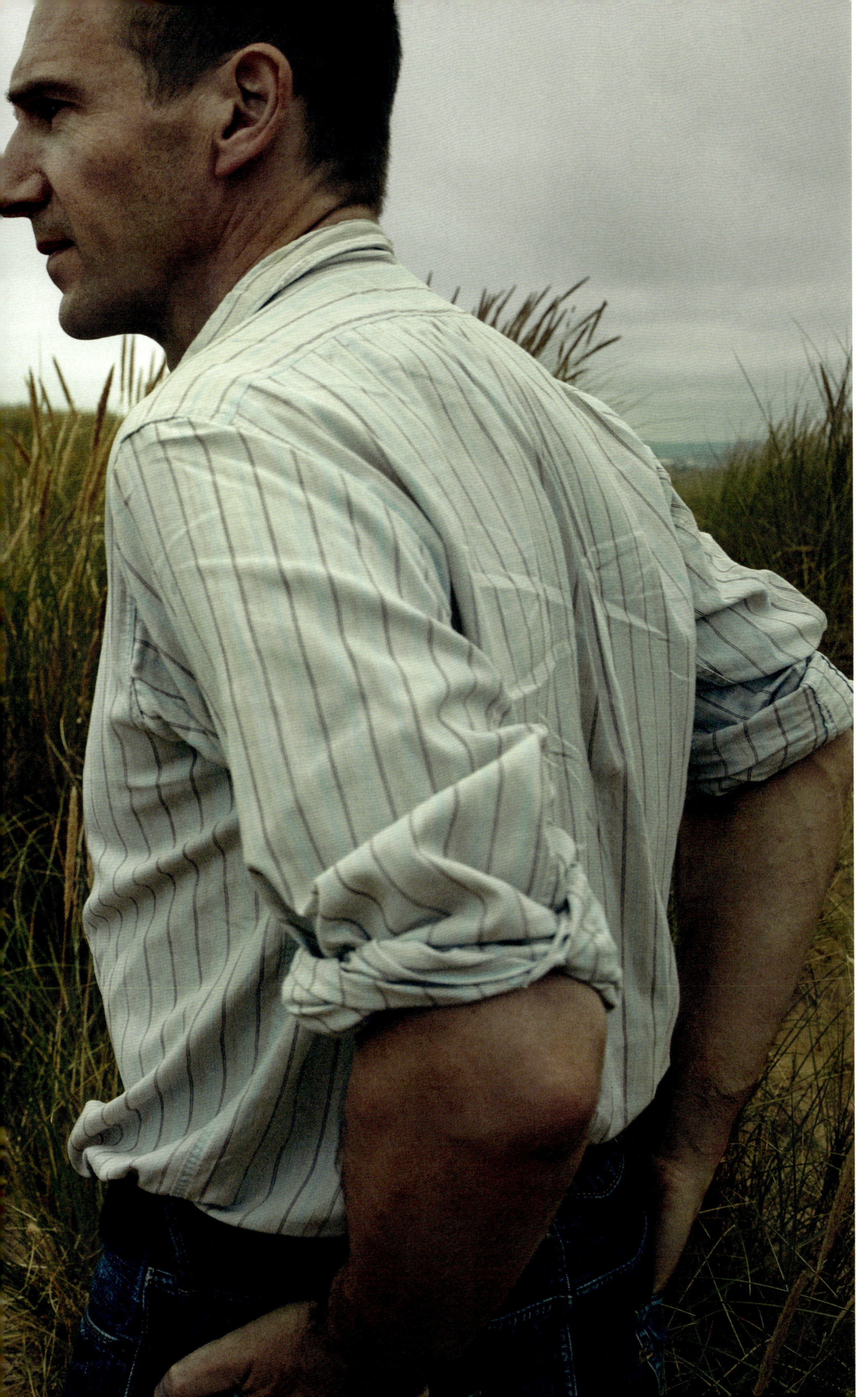

Ralph Fiennes directed and starred in *The Invisible Woman* (2013). He played Charles Dickens. Felicity Jones was Nelly Ternan, Dickens's young mistress in the last years of his life.

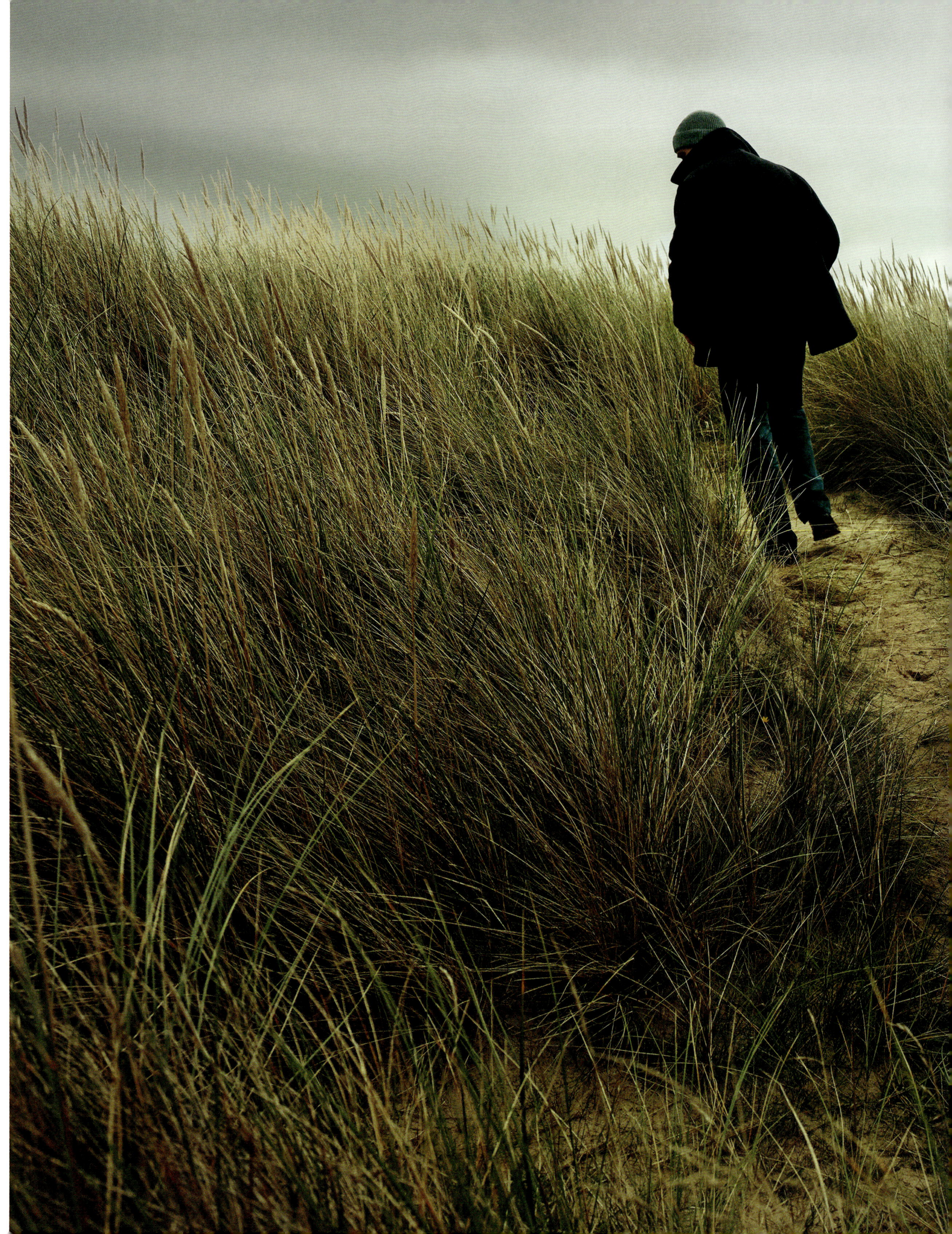

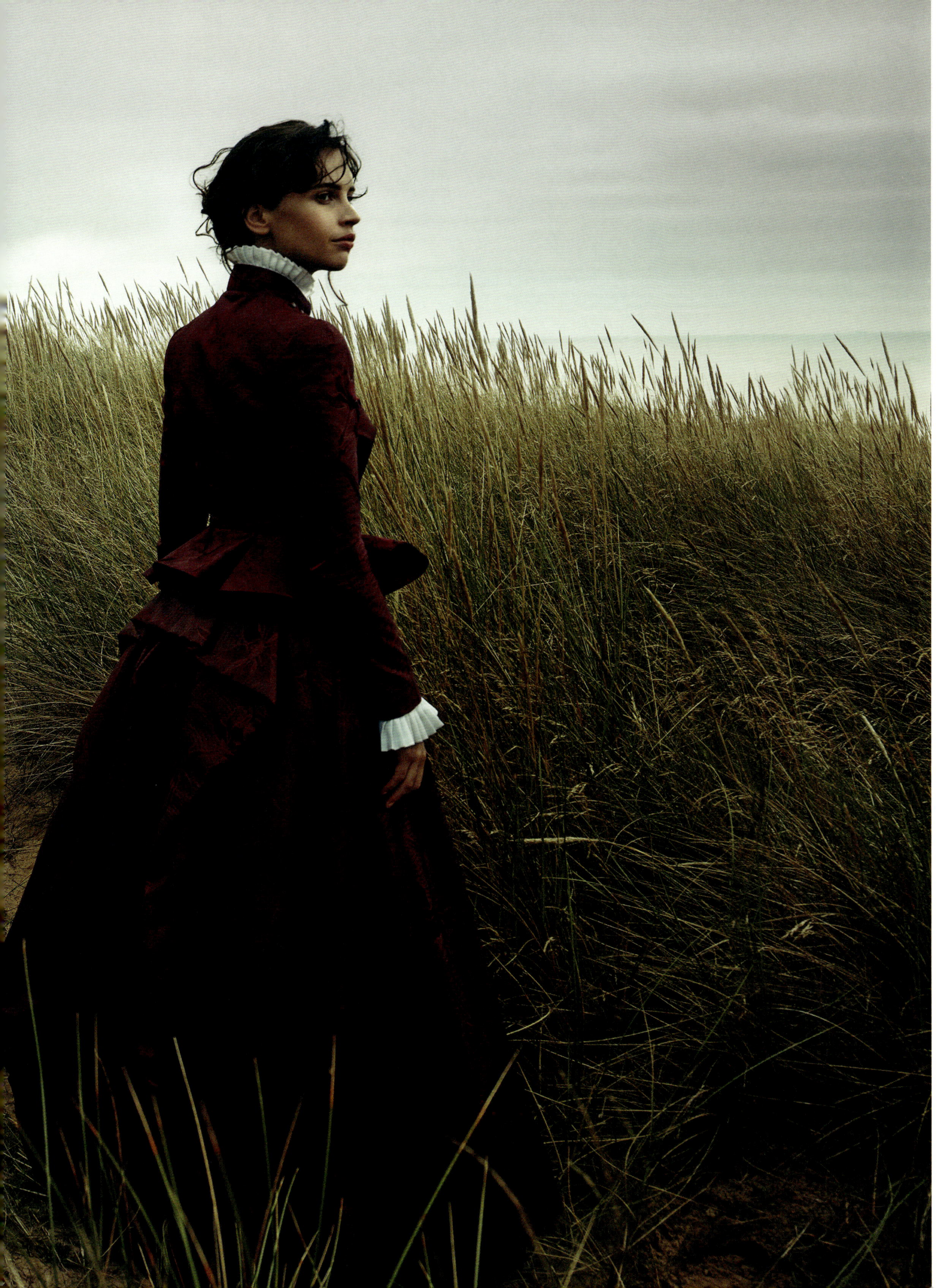

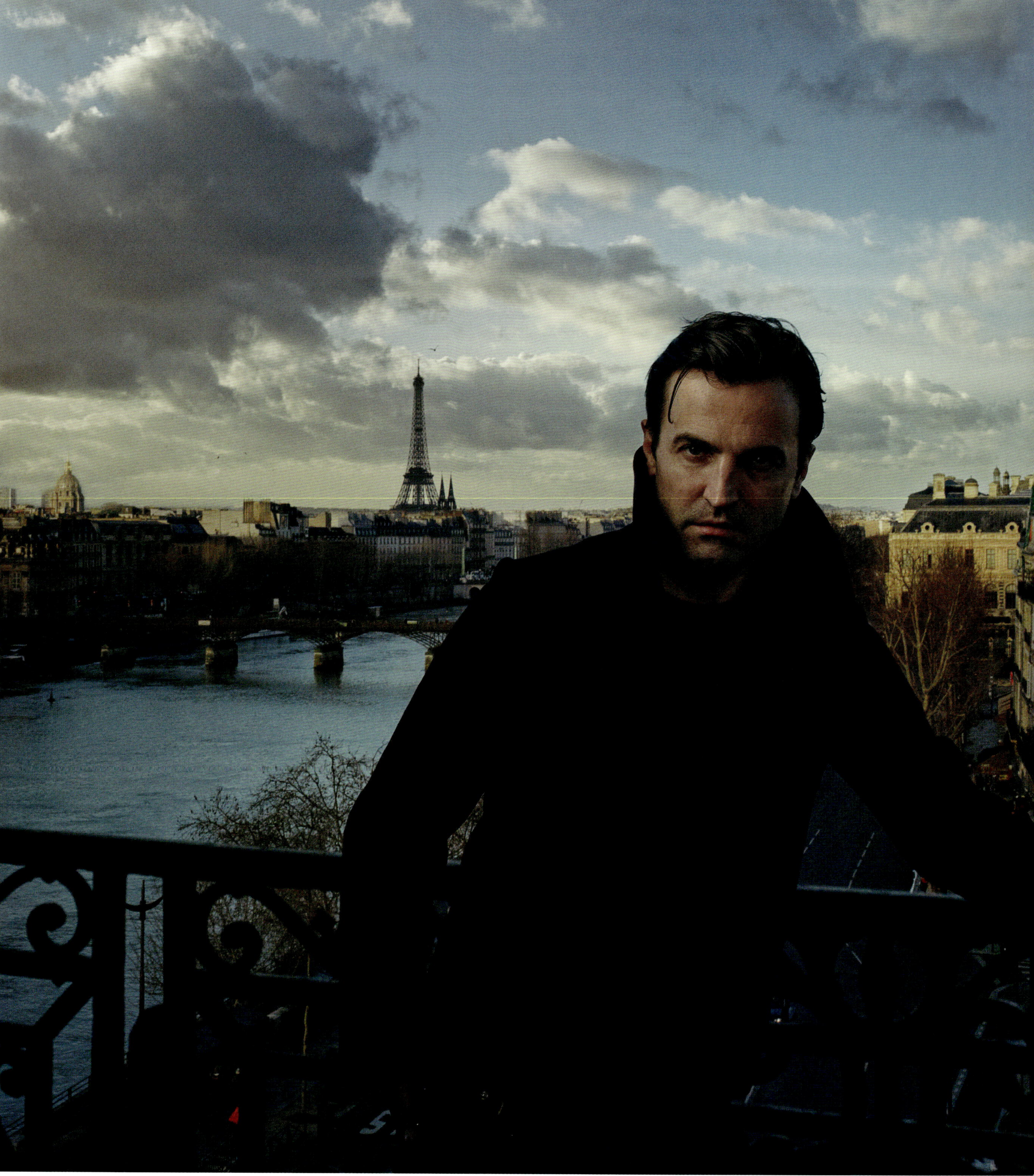

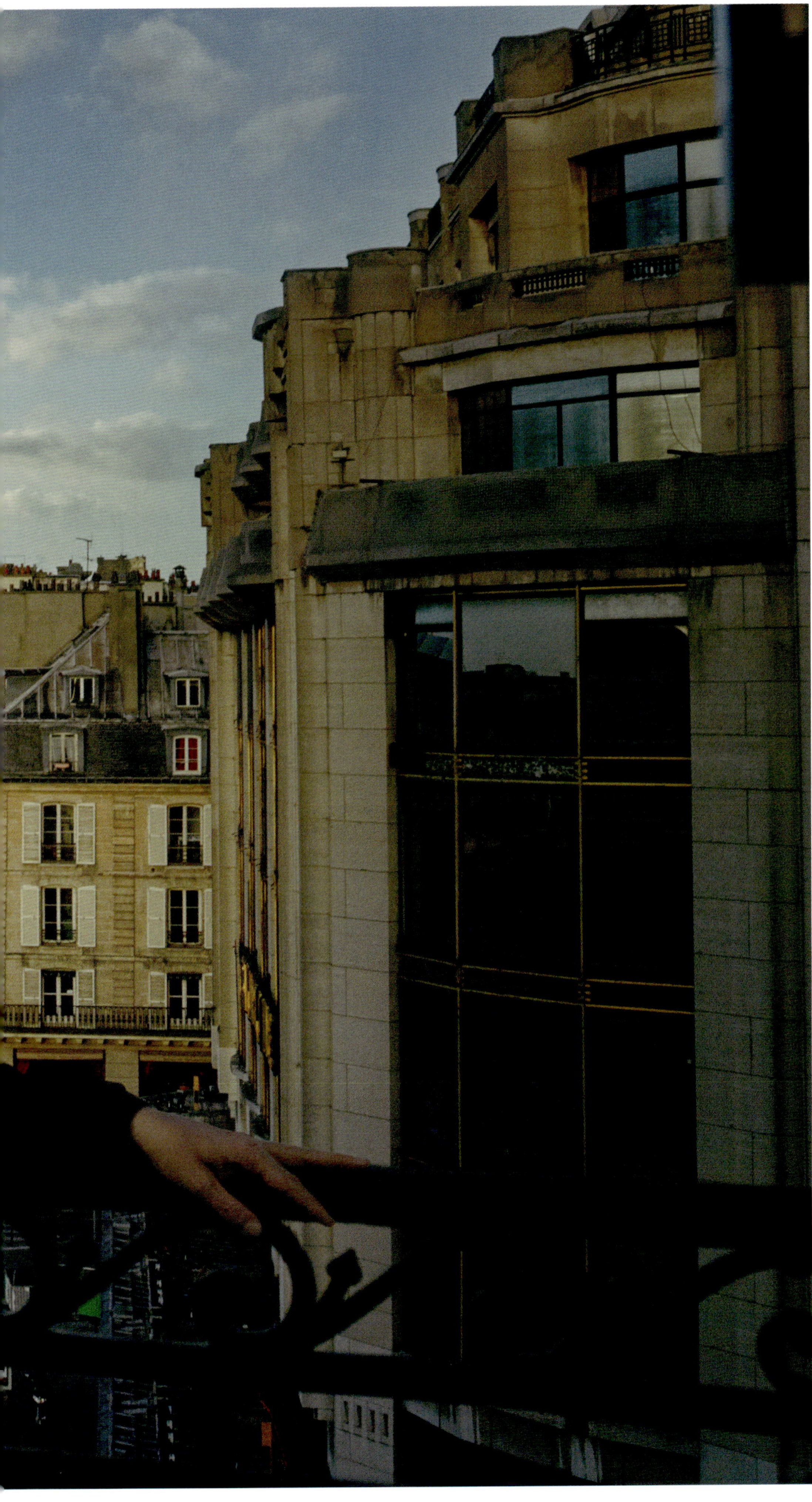

Nicolas Ghesquière,
Paris, 2014

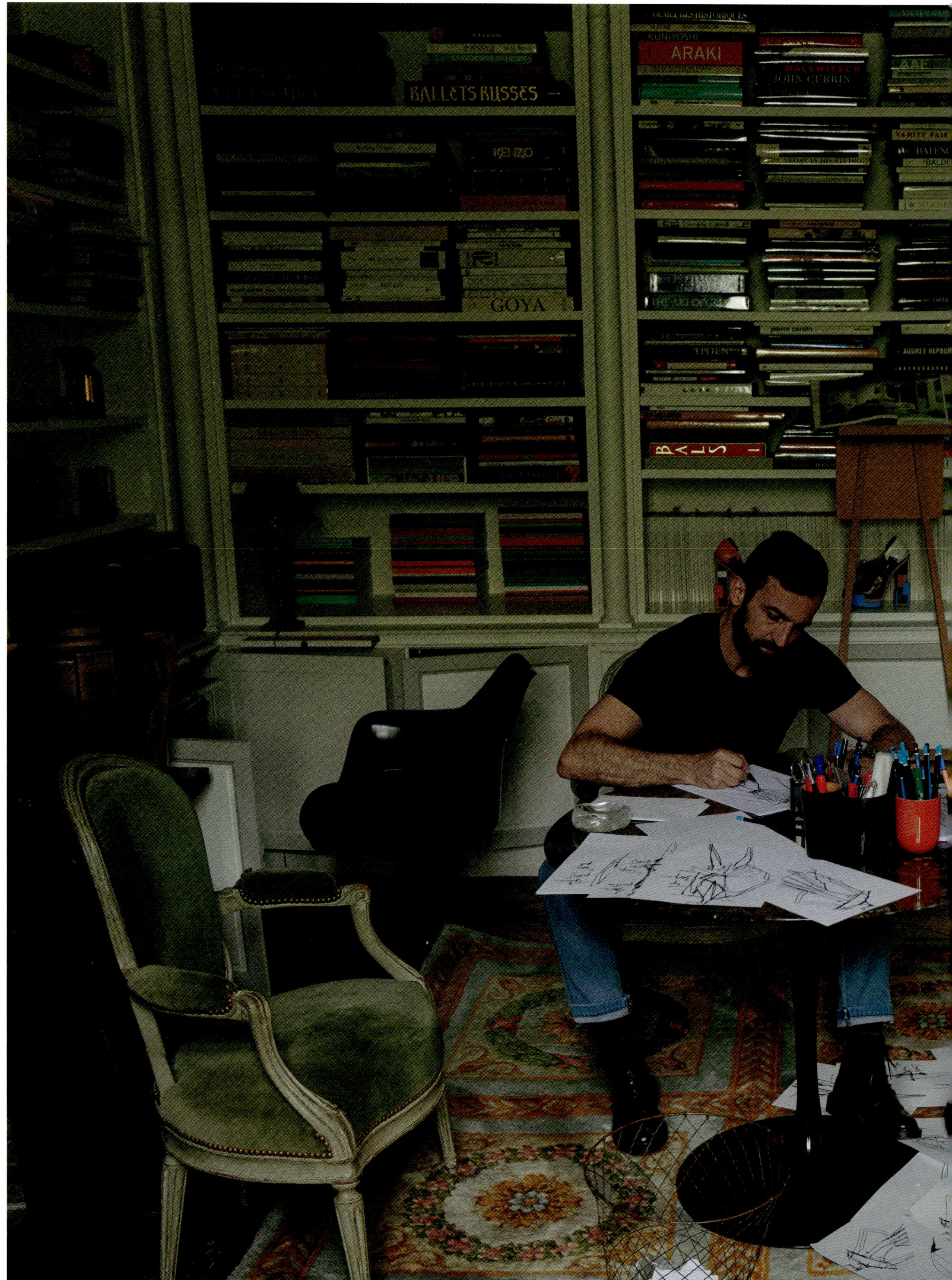
BALLETS RUSSES
KUNIYOSHI
ARAKI
MALEWITSCH
JOHN CURRIN
KENZO
VANITY FAIR
GOYA
DRESSED
pierre cardin
ALISON JACKSON
AUDREY HEPBURN

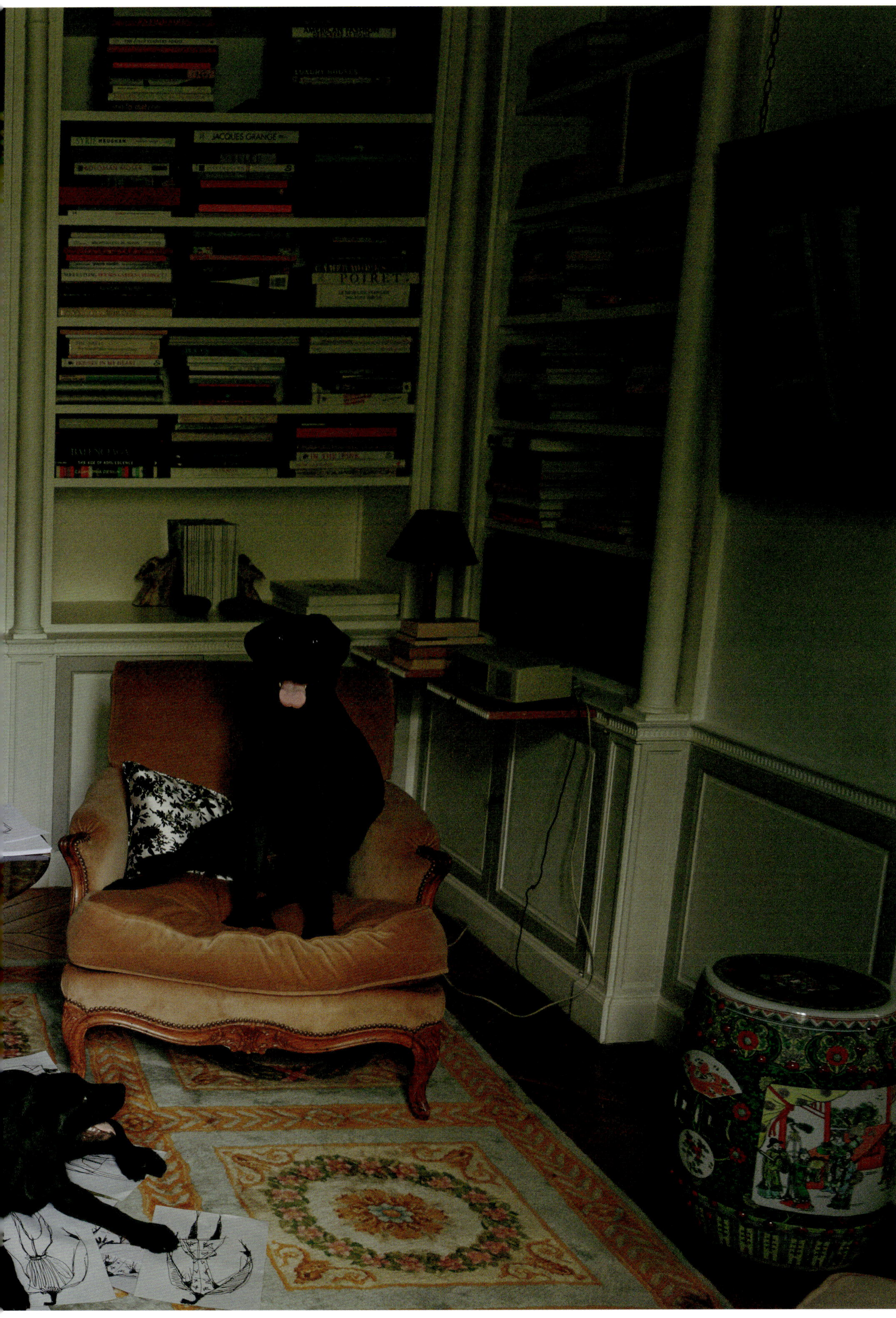

Nicolas Ghesquière, Montfort-l'Amaury, France, 2018

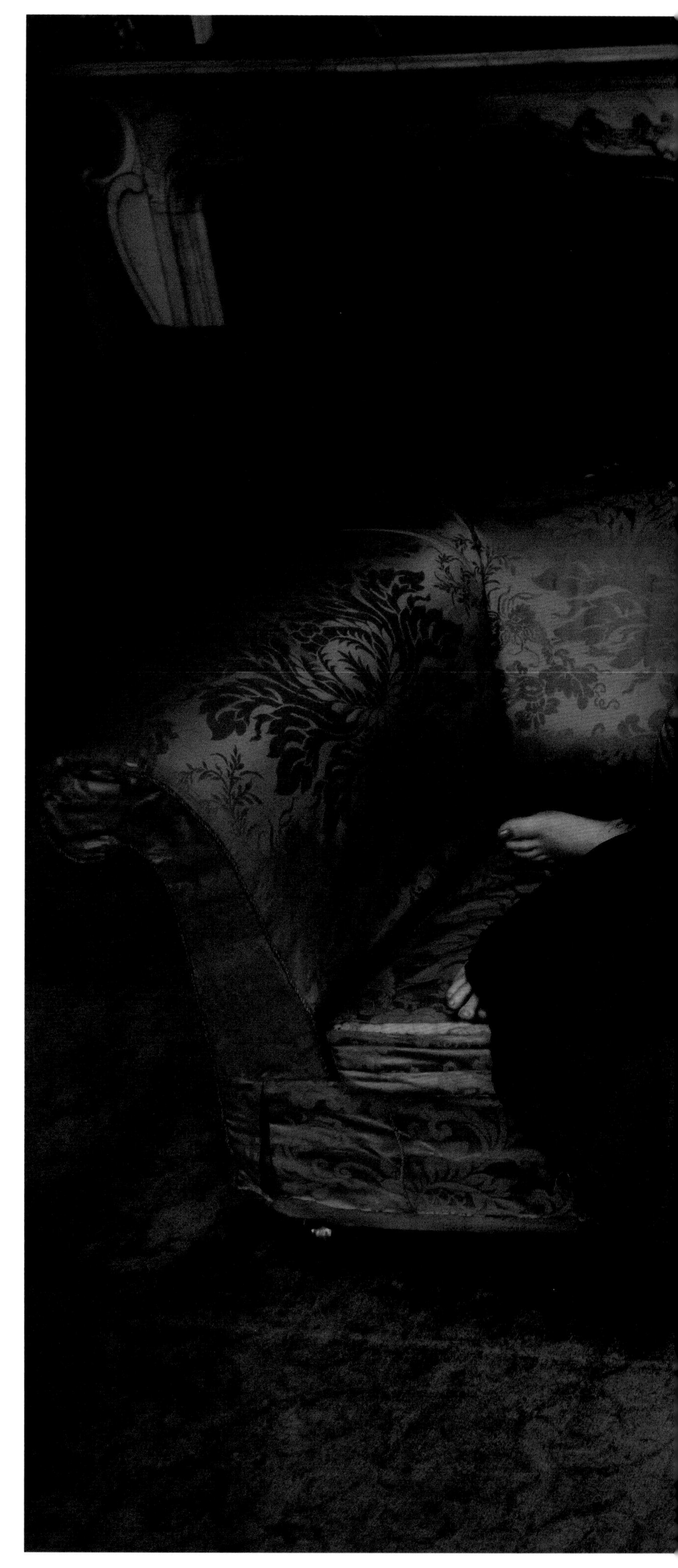

Adele, Watlington,
Oxfordshire, England, 2015

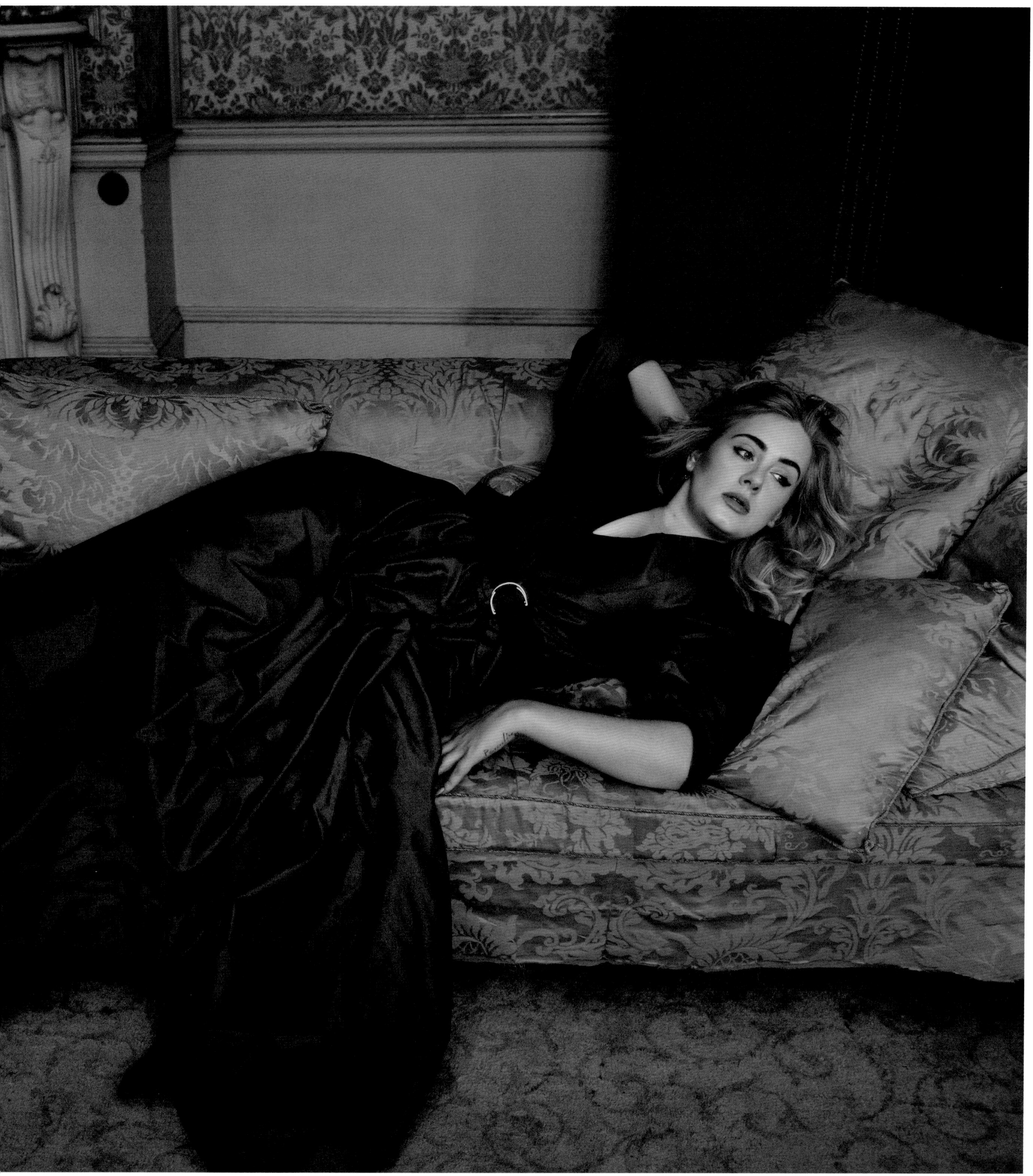

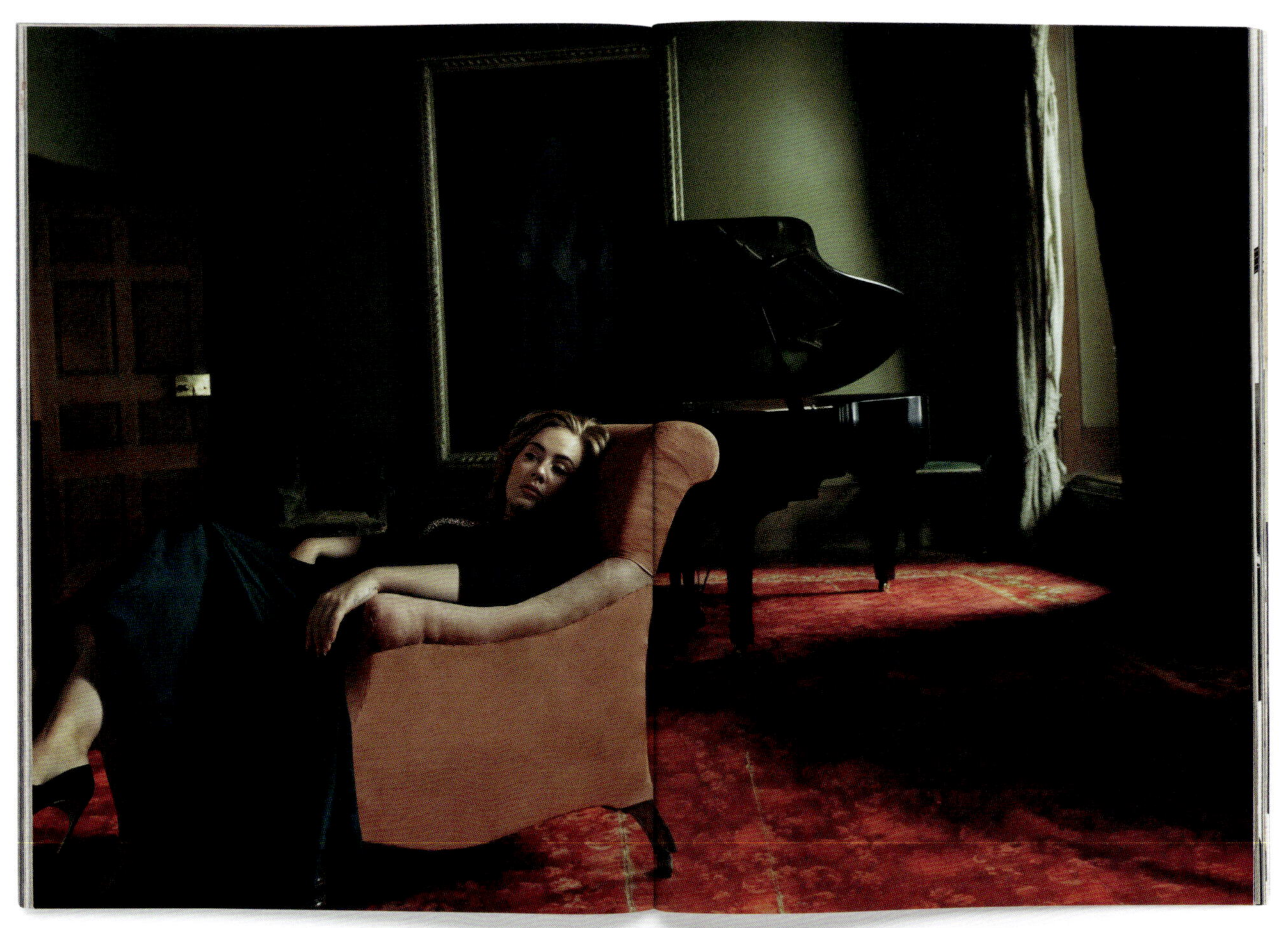

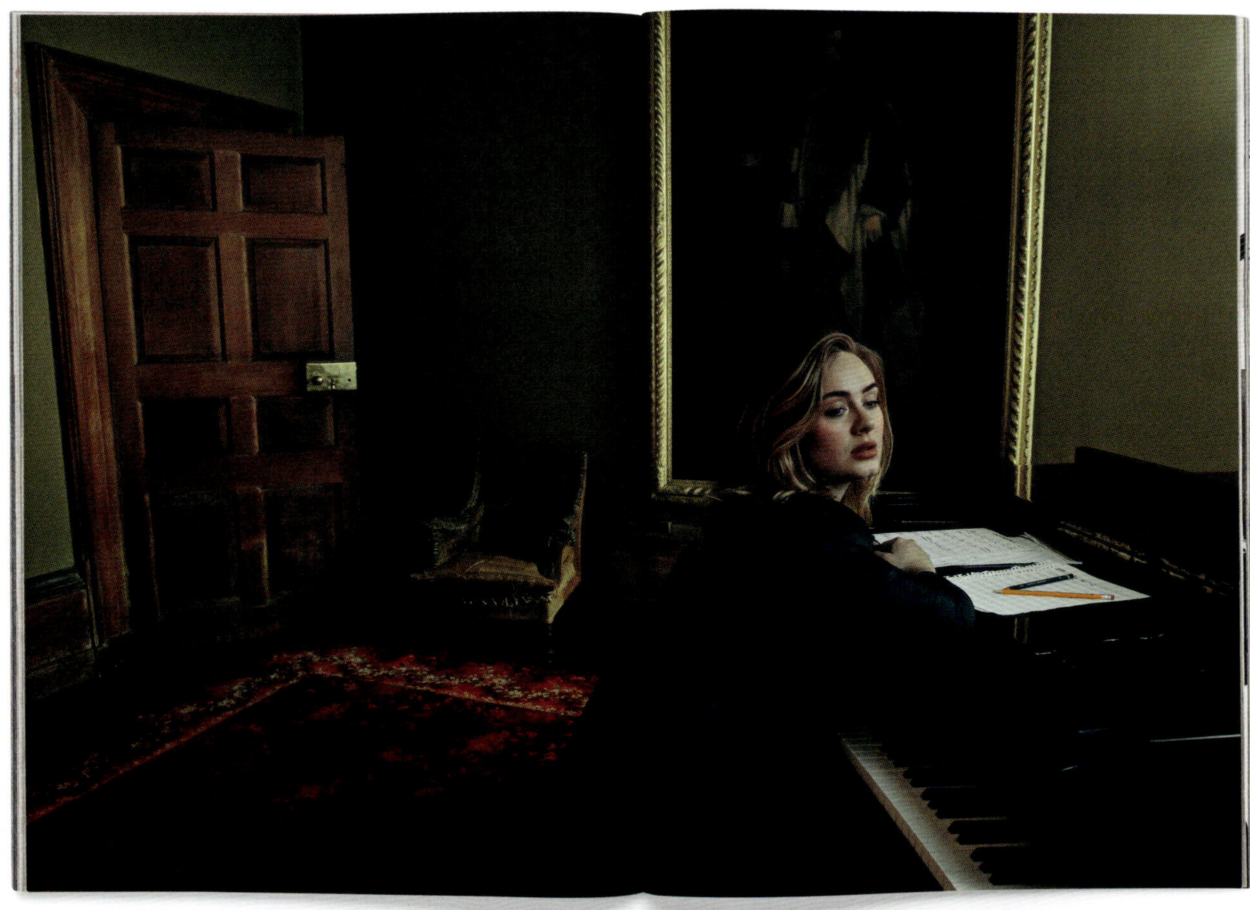

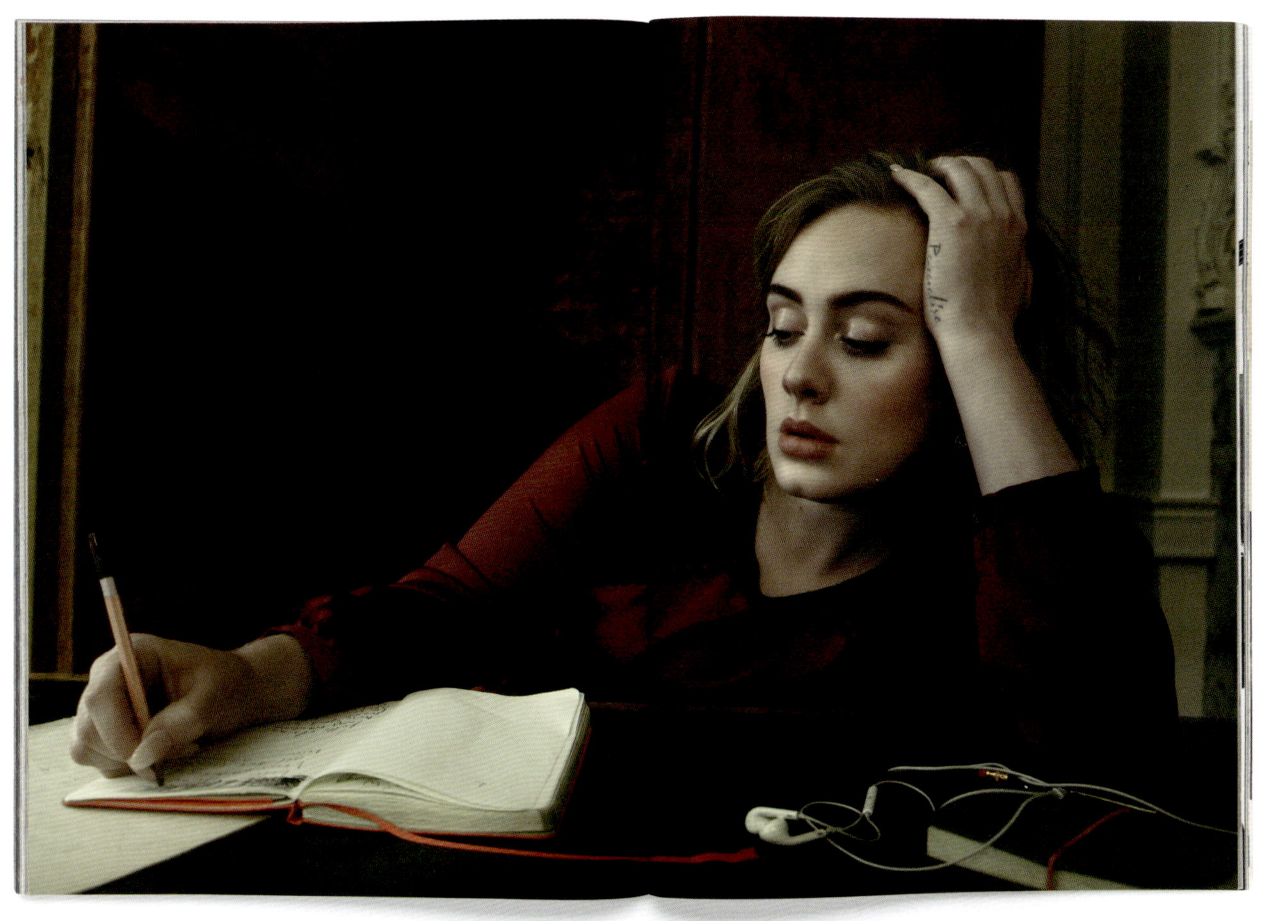

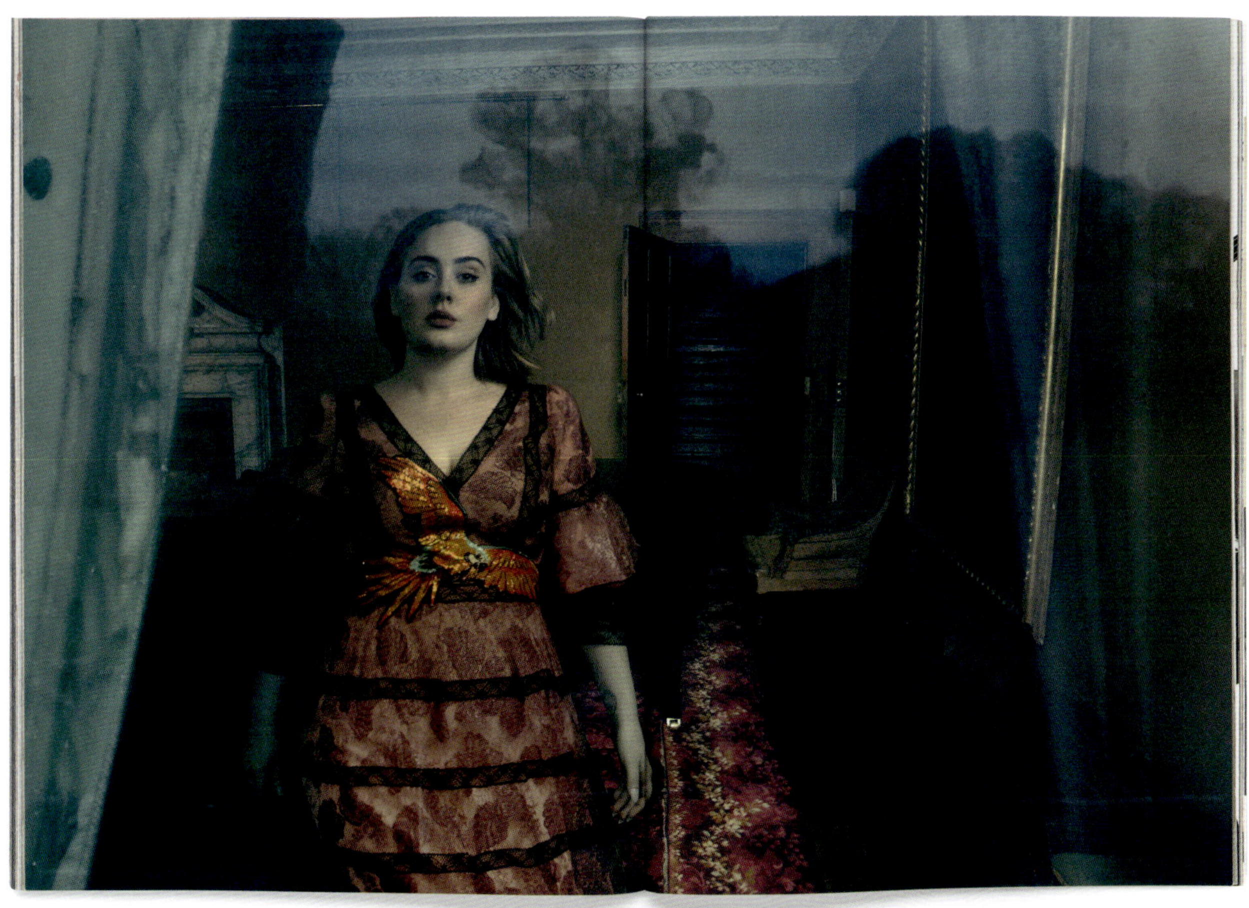

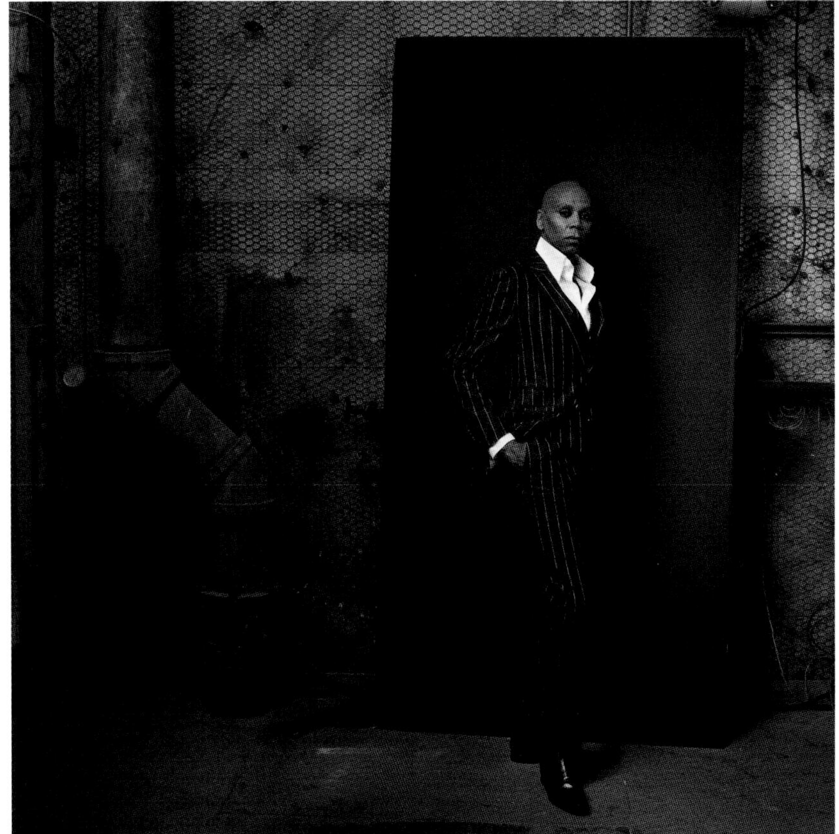

RuPaul honed his campy, knowing performance style in the downtown New York club scene of the late 1980s and early 1990s. It wasn't always drag. Sometimes he would show up at the Roxy, the cavernous gay club and roller disco, in a chicken suit. Then he had a hit dance record and launched his music career, followed by his acting career, and—all of this going on simultaneously—his career as a television personality and producer. Naturally elegant, witty, and charismatic, he led the integration of drag into the larger culture.

RuPaul, Warner Brothers Studio,
Burbank, California, 2019

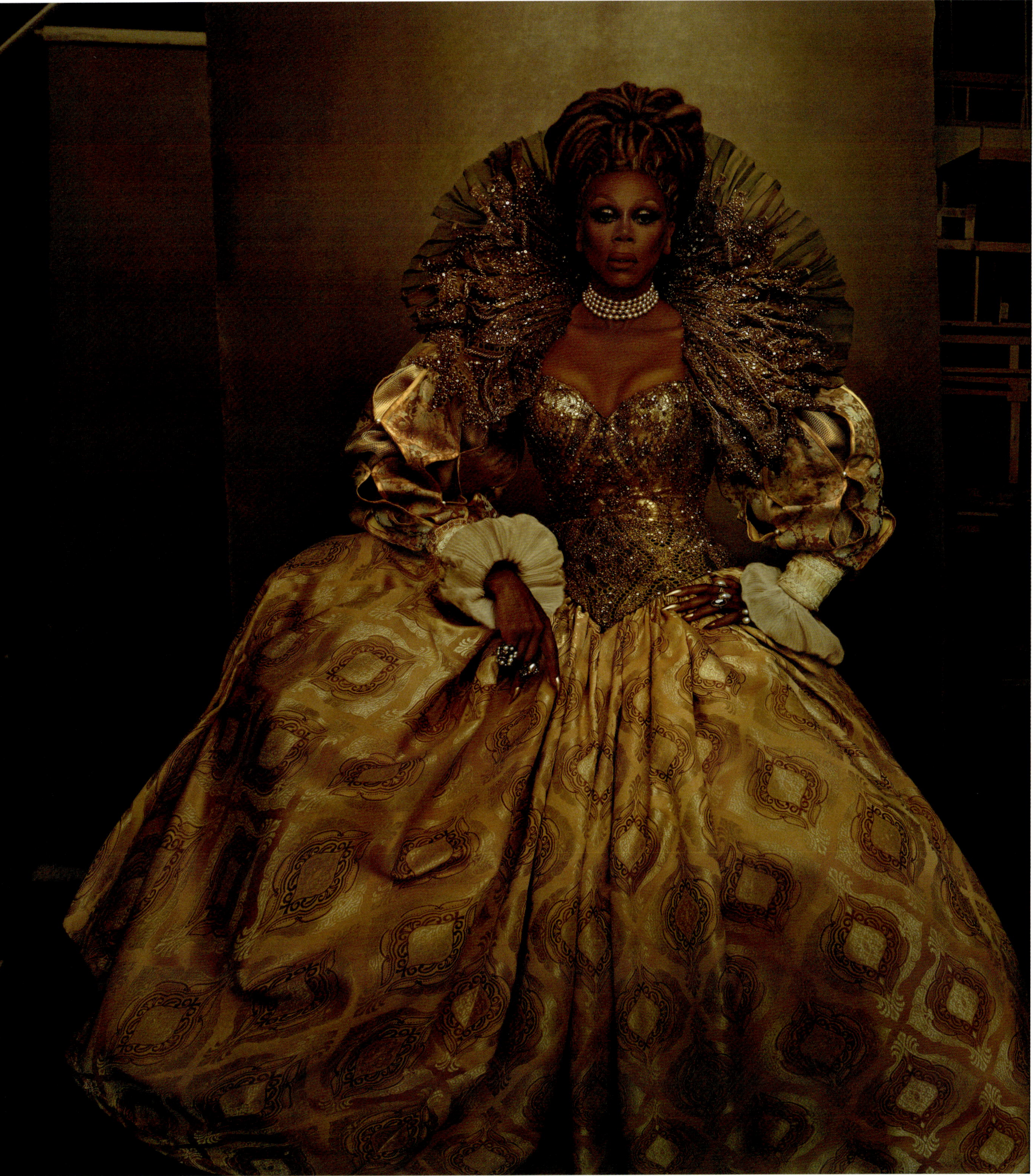

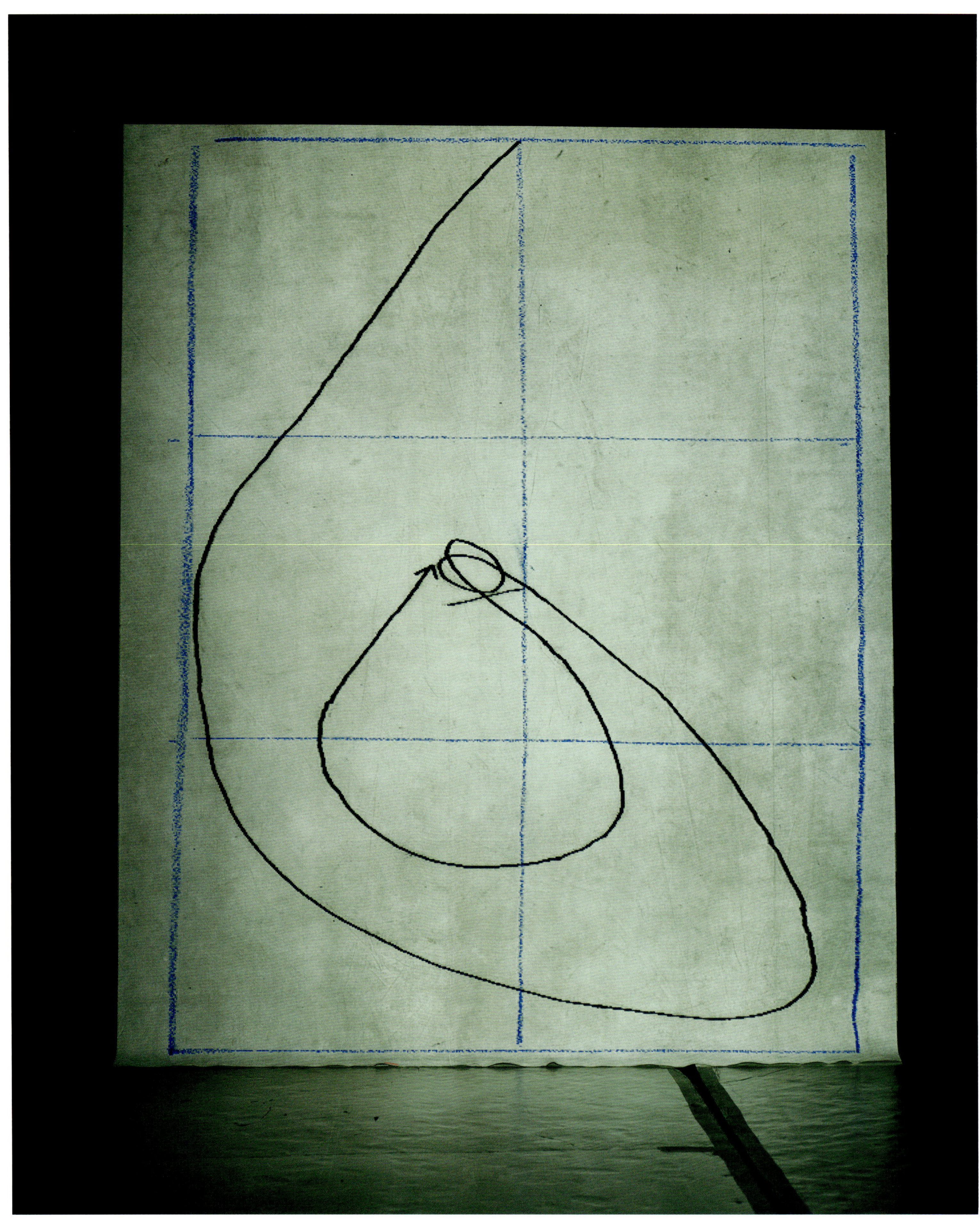

Twyla Tharp's dance notes, New York City, 2018
Opposite: Twyla Tharp

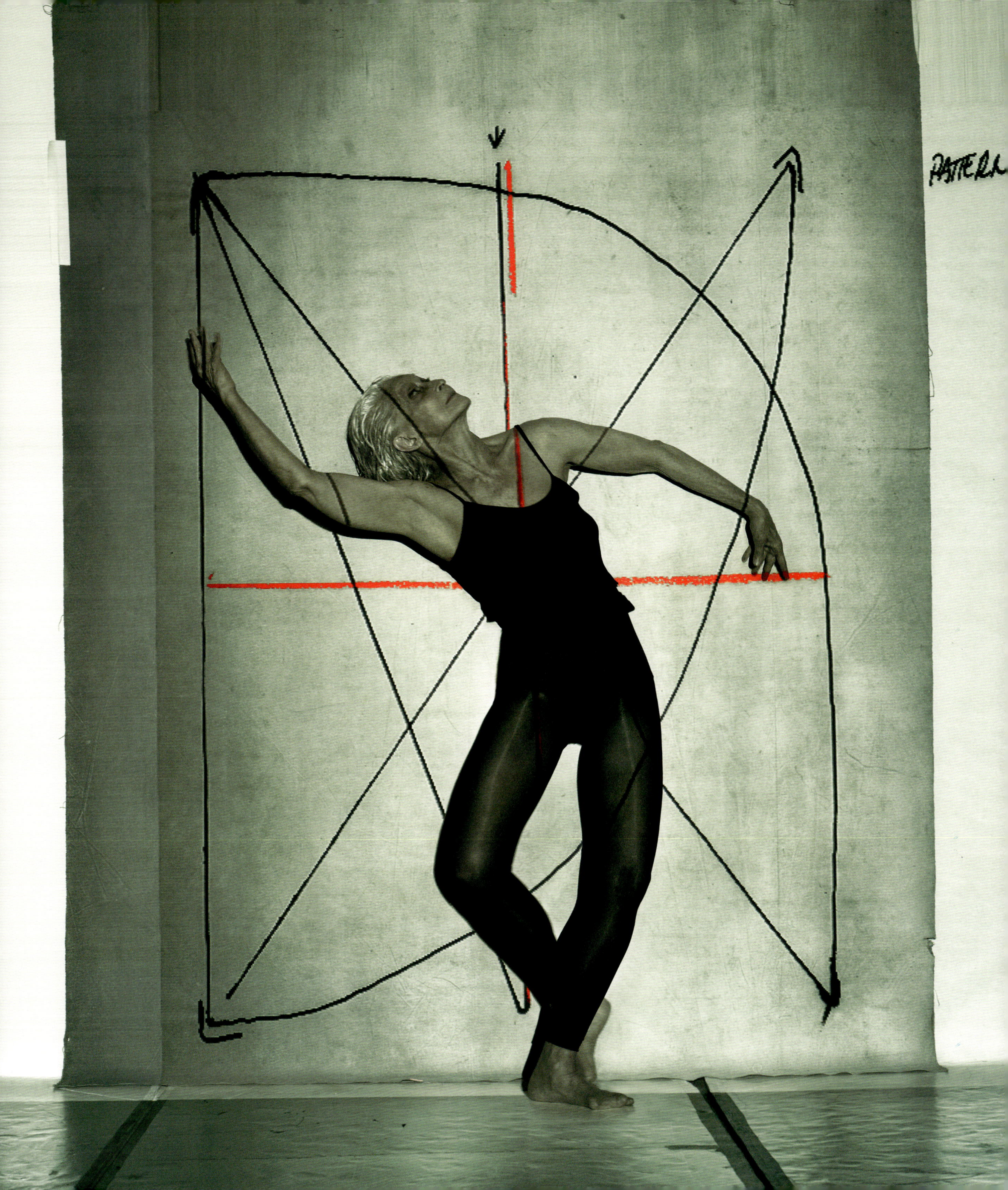
PATTERN

“Karl Lagerfeld collected beautiful things: houses, furniture, books, paintings, music. And he collected information about them. He was an insatiable accumulator. He said that he needed everything for his work.

Toward the end of his life, he did much of the work in a futuristic apartment on two floors of a house overlooking the Louvre on the Quai Voltaire in Paris. When a shoot was being arranged with me for a series on designers, a location was chosen nearby—a photo studio Karl had set up in the back room of a bookshop specializing in elegant illustrated books. He was a publisher, a writer, an editor, and a sometime photographer.

The photo studio was striking. There were walls with thousands of books in them and then in the middle of the room some backdrops and lights. I wanted to do a simple portrait of Karl and I spent a lot of time setting this up, but an hour before the shoot, we got word that he didn’t want us there.

It was frustrating, but I agreed to meet him at an apartment he used as an office and for storage, a few blocks away. There was no sense of intimacy there, just files everywhere and posters of Karl. When he finally came in, he was in his armor: the glasses, the powdered wig, the gloves, the black suit. I started to take some pictures and then I stopped.

When I was doing research for the assignment, I read an interview with him where he said that he worked at home, either in bed or wandering around in the morning in a white nightshirt, drawing. The nightshirt would have smears of charcoal and pastels all over it. I told him that’s the way I wanted to photograph him. Working.

He thought about this, and then he said that I could come to his apartment if I came alone. No one else could be there.”

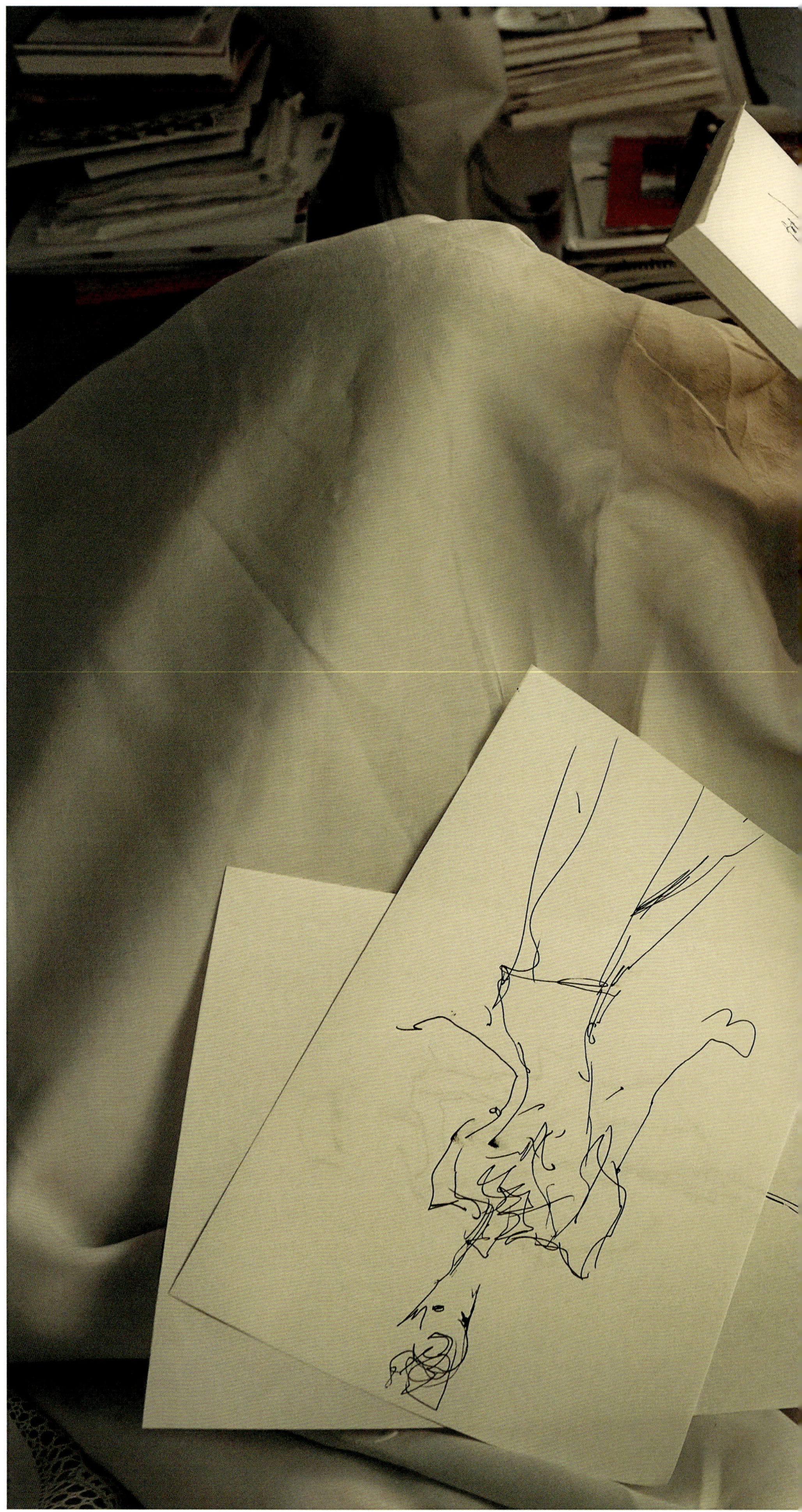

Karl Lagerfeld, Paris, 2018

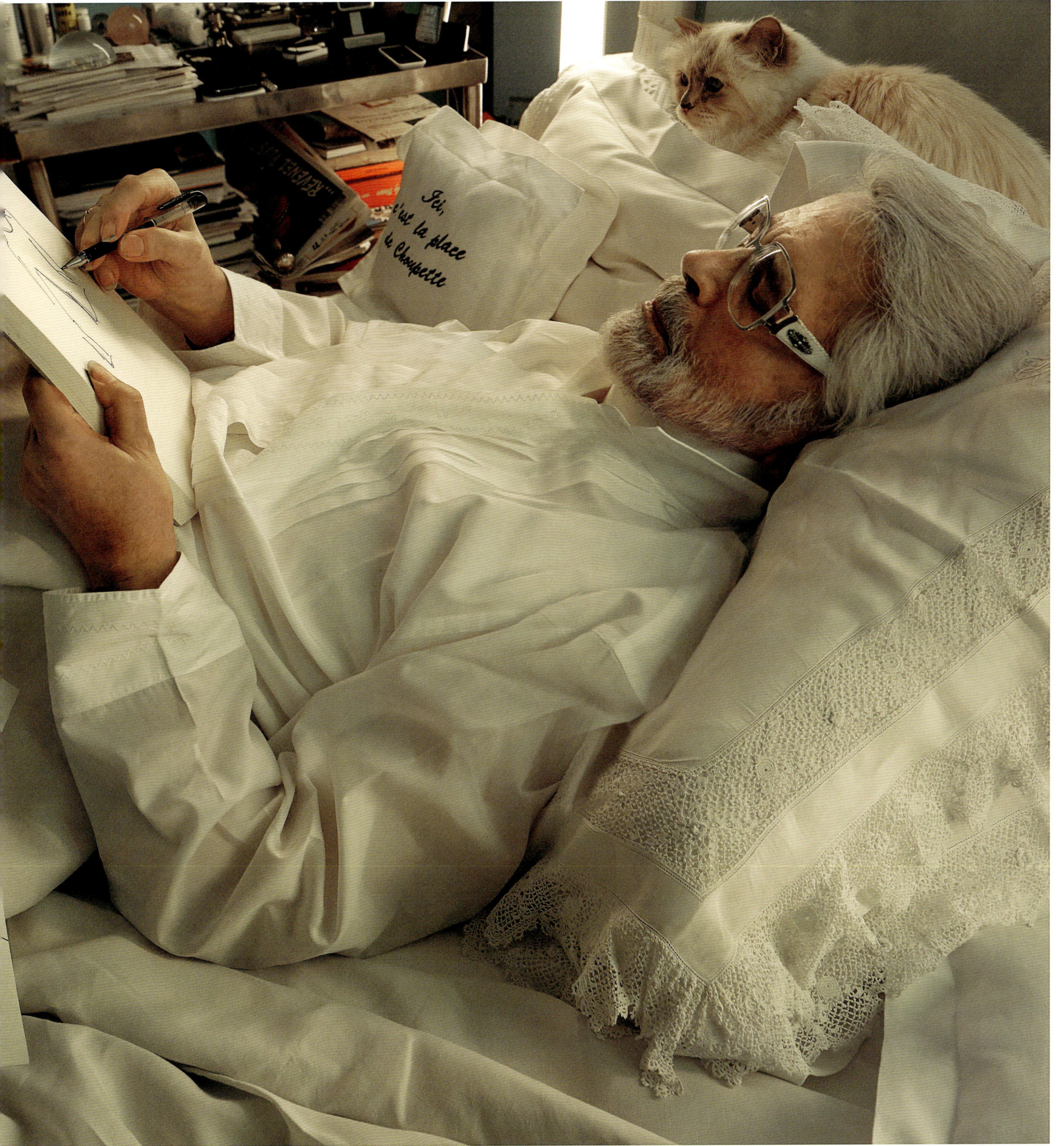
Ici,
'est la place
e Choupette

"I was very impressed that he wanted to try. Six months later, after several appointments had been made and postponed, I went to see him on the Quai Voltaire. I was nervous, and I couldn't believe the condition of the apartment. It didn't look anything like the pictures in the architectural design magazines. It was covered in mountains of books and papers. You couldn't see the furniture.

Karl took me in back where there was a tiny bedroom and a dressing room. Rows of flat files were filled with white nightshirts, all different, all folded up, beautifully pressed. He asked me to pick one. I asked him where he drew but we couldn't find the desk. I had to clear out some books and papers to make a space for him. I photographed him there for a while, and then he got into bed with his famous cat, Choupette, and continued to draw."

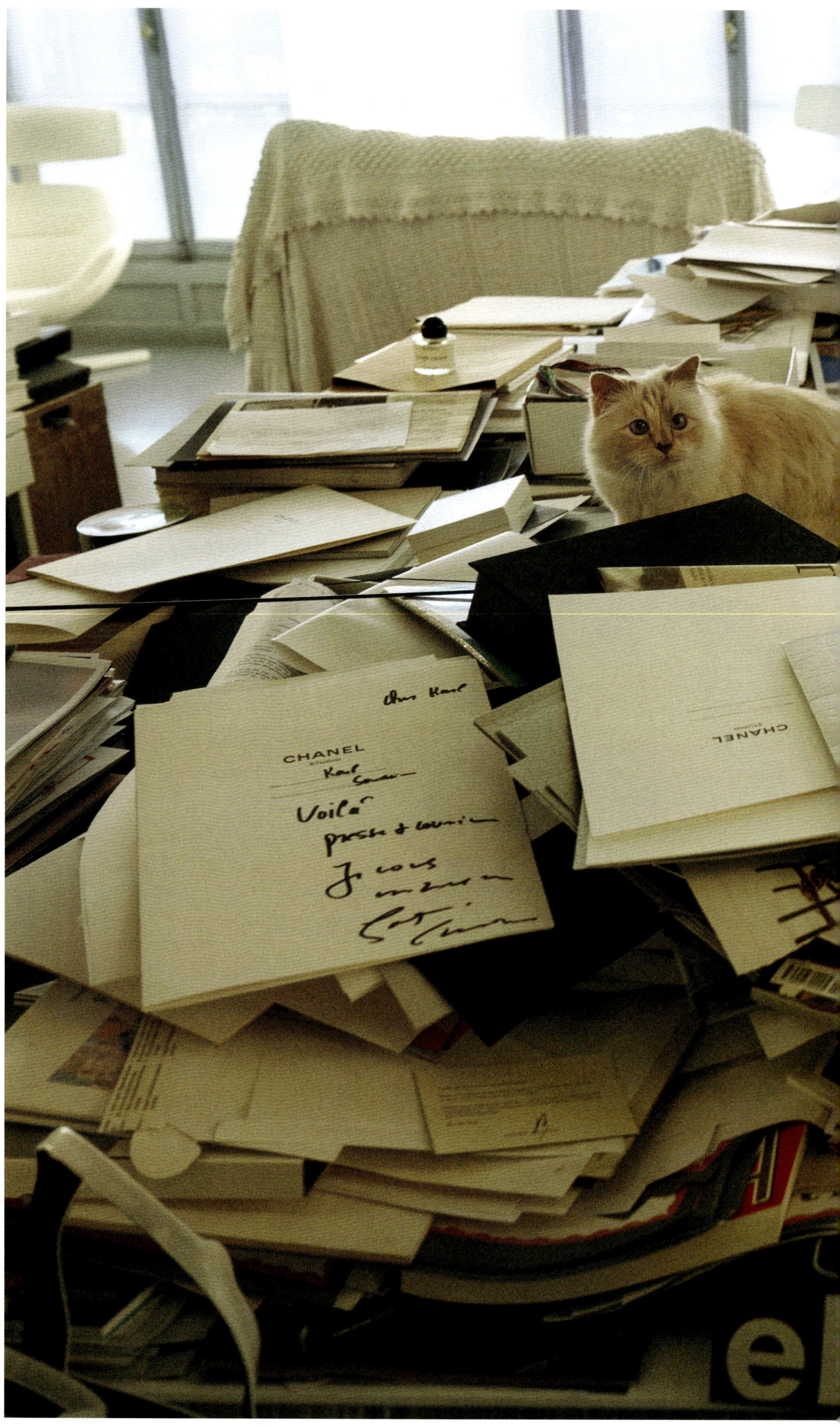

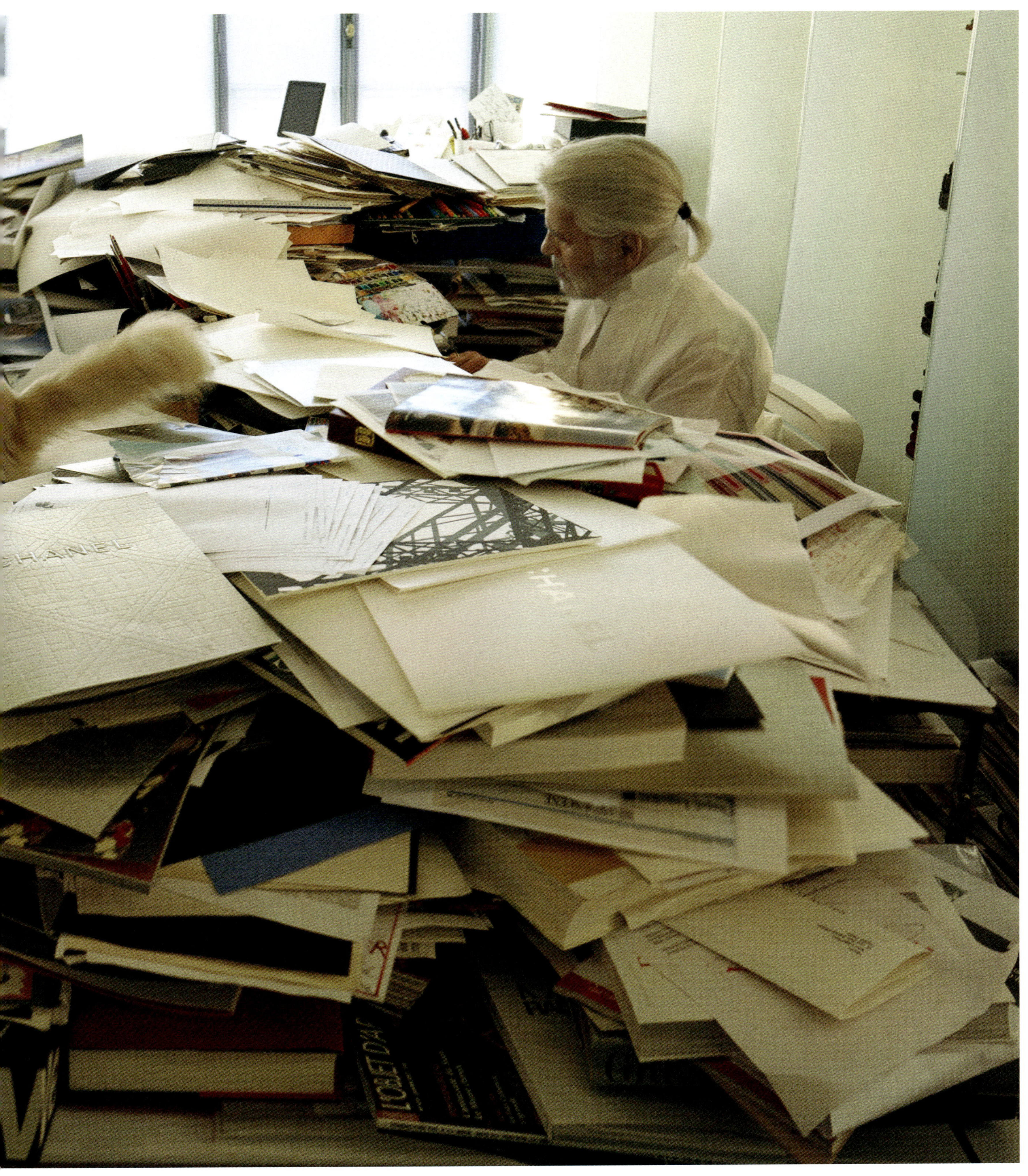
CHANEL

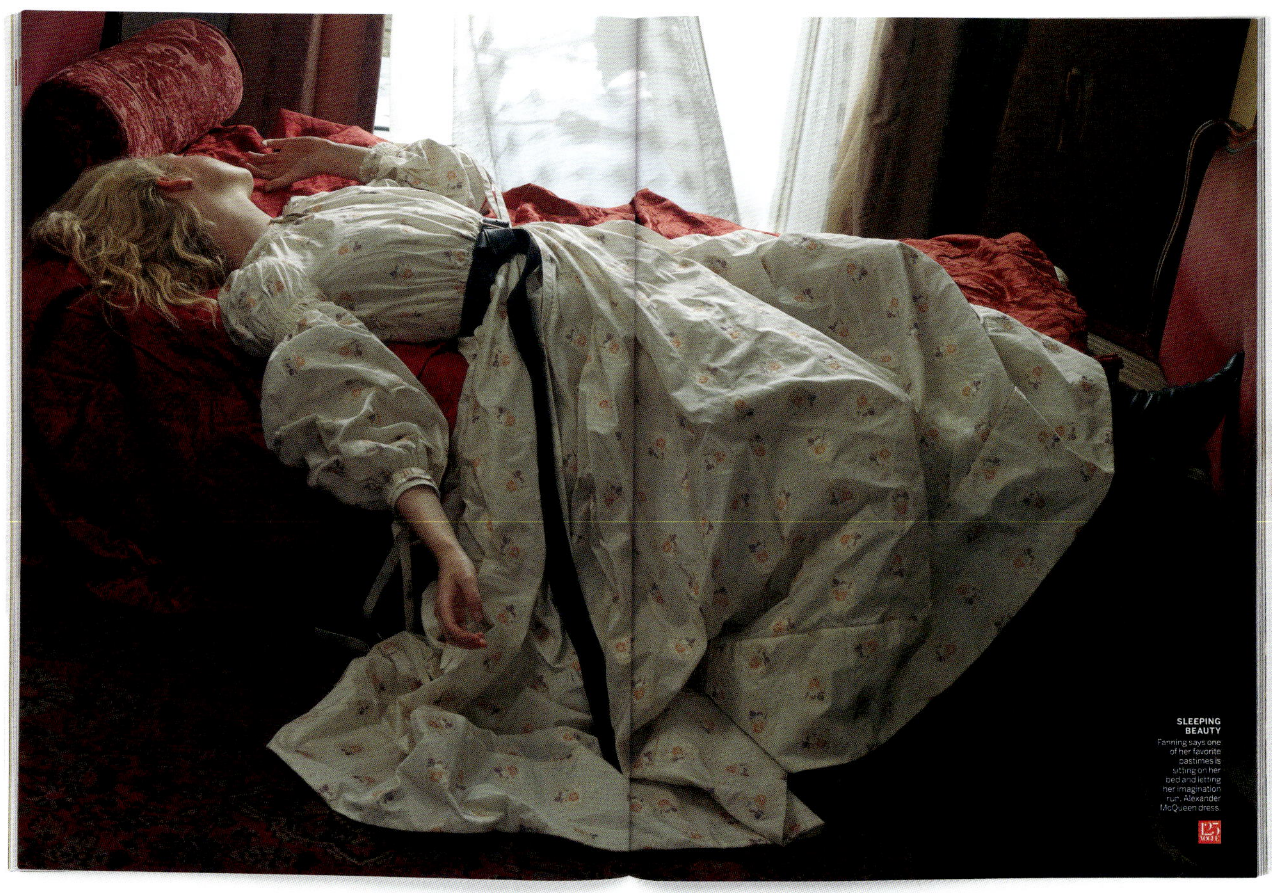

"Sofia Coppola has an impeccable sense of where to inhabit her stories. I was very aware of this when we were exploring places to shoot at Versailles after Sofia had shot *Marie Antoinette* there. And it is crucial to films like *Lost in Translation*, which is critically dependent on Tokyo. We photographed Elle Fanning after she worked in New Orleans with Sofia on a remake of *The Beguiled*. I wanted to know exactly where Sofia filmed, and I used many of her locations in our story. She goes to places that are visually arresting and rich in history."

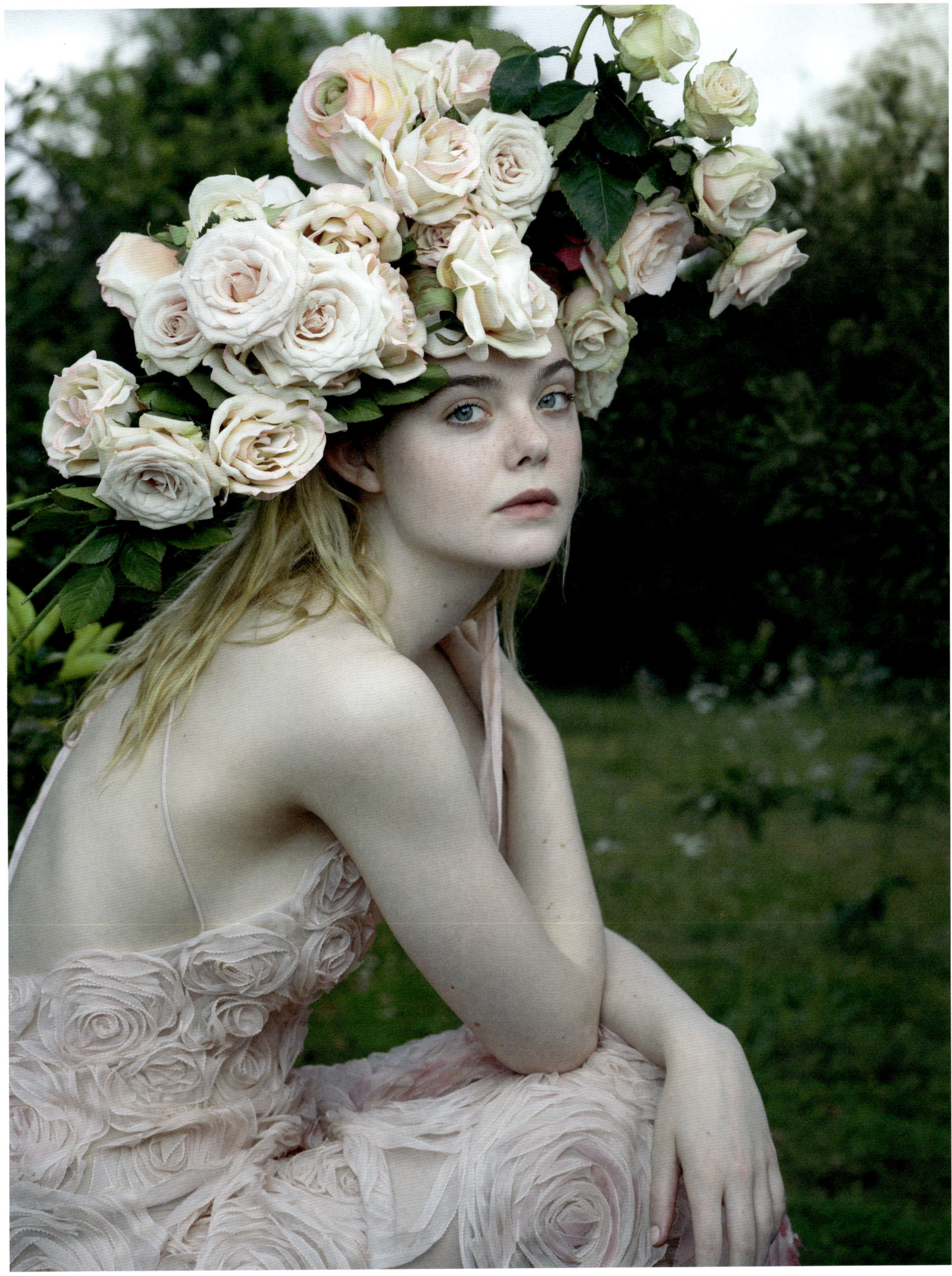

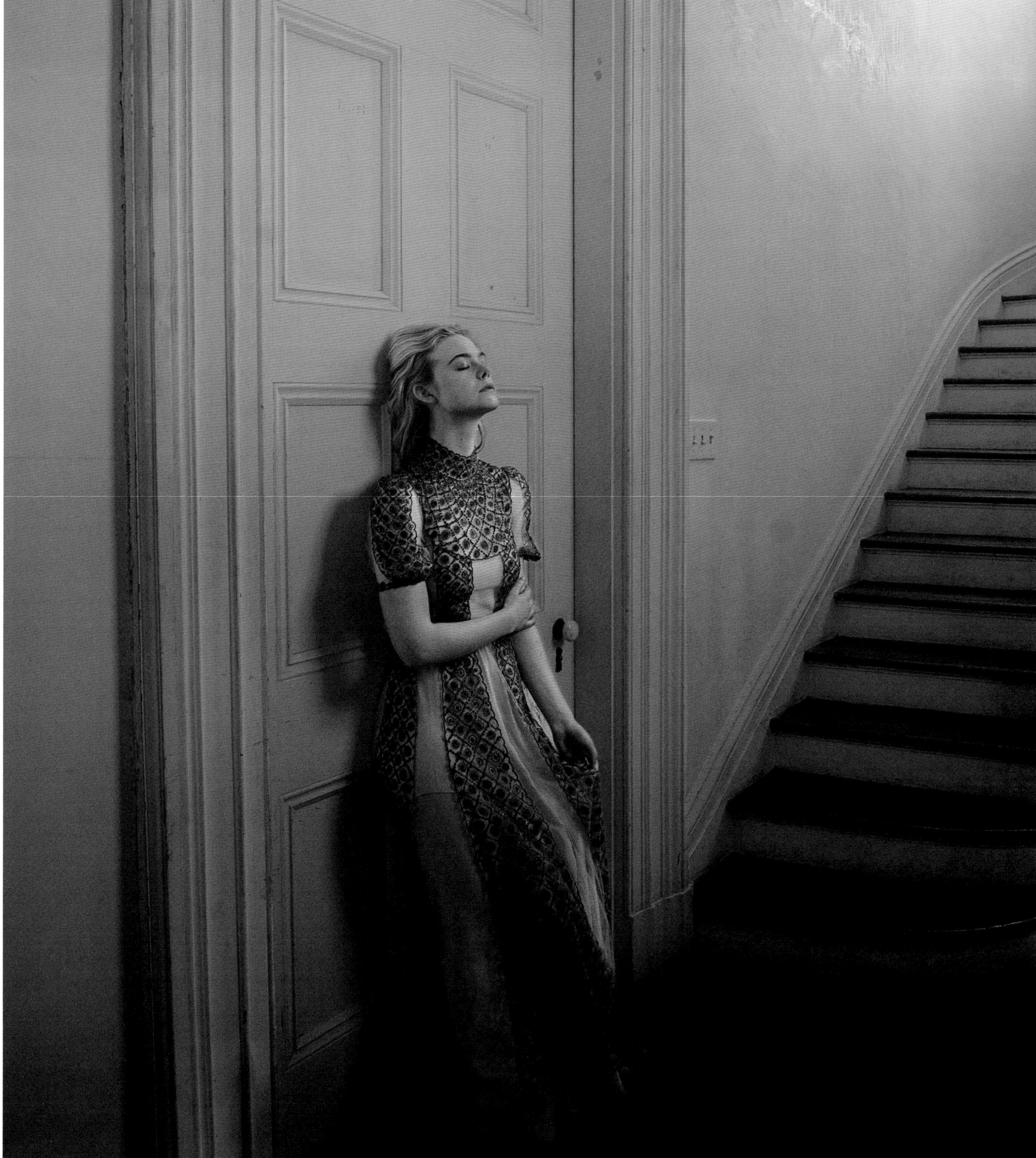

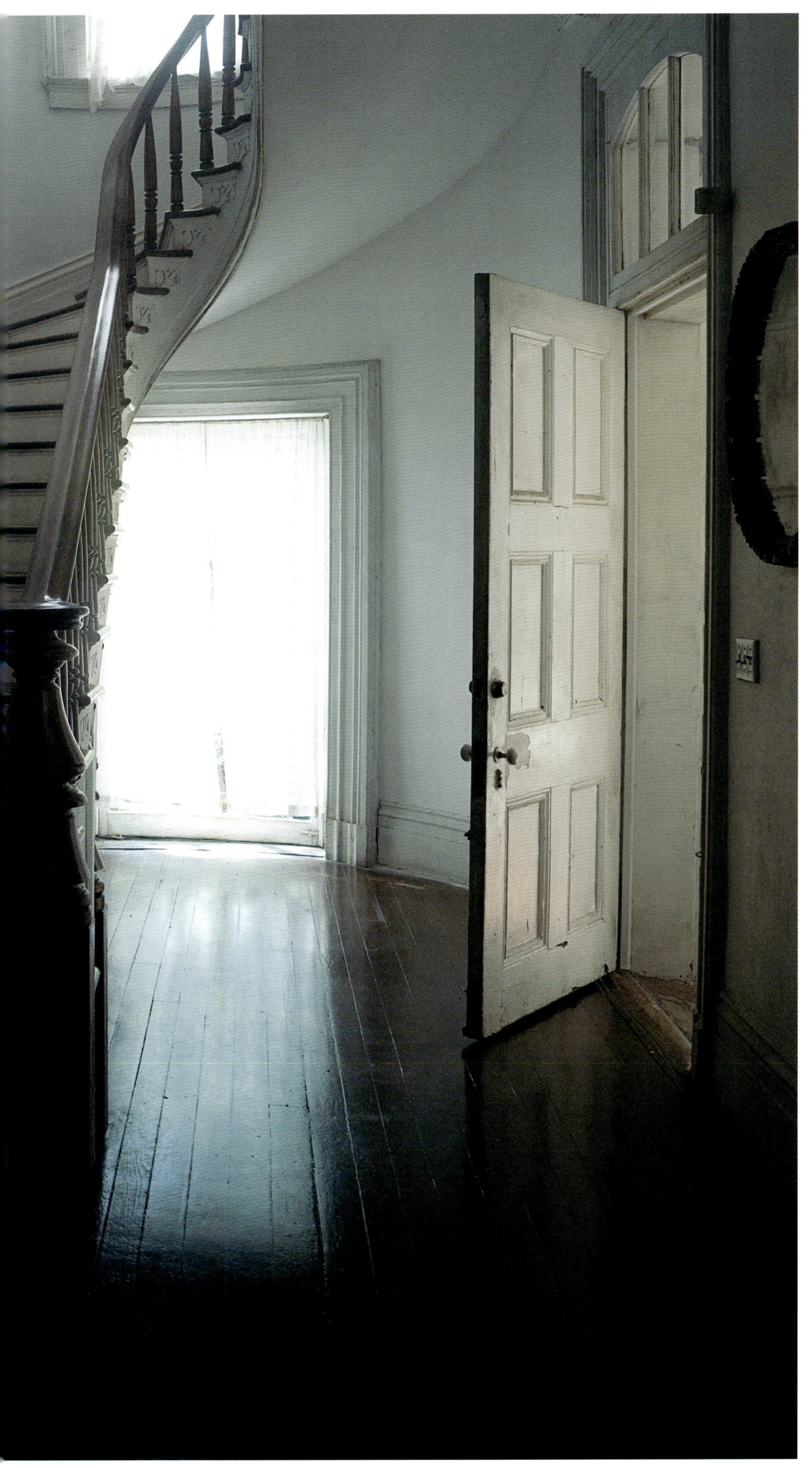

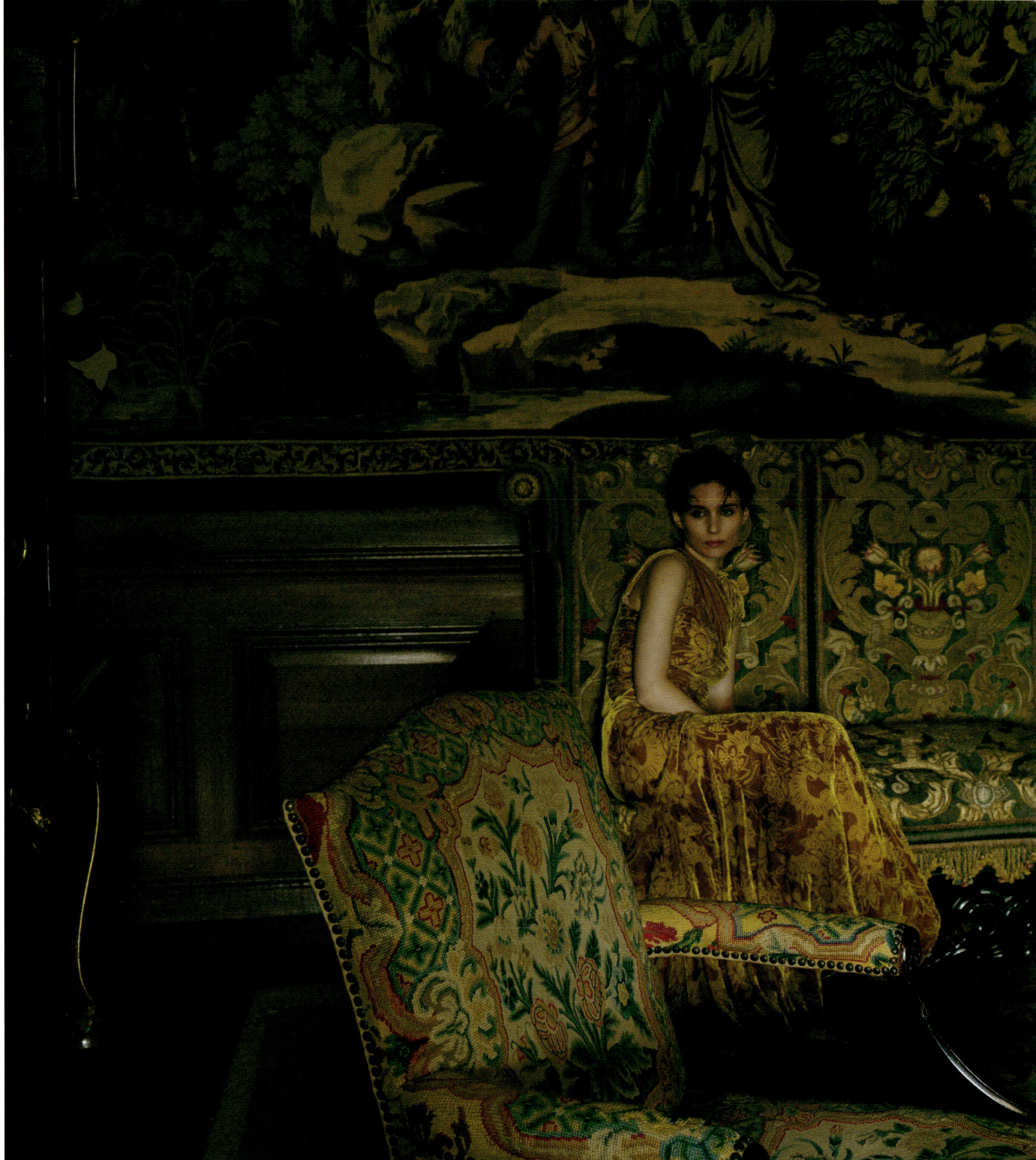

Rooney Mara has an enigmatic, brooding quality. She somehow manages to stay quietly under the radar. It is a temperament compatible with the isolated, luminously wild landscape of Cornwall, on England's extreme southwestern coast. Annie has worked in Cornwall several times, including for a shoot with Kate Winslet on a rocky, stormy beach and for a portrait of John le Carré at his farm overlooking the ocean.

Antony House, where the Mara photographs are set, was built in the early eighteenth century on an estate that has been home to one family for six hundred years. The house has been spared extensive modernization, and many of the oak-paneled rooms have the original furniture and tapestries.

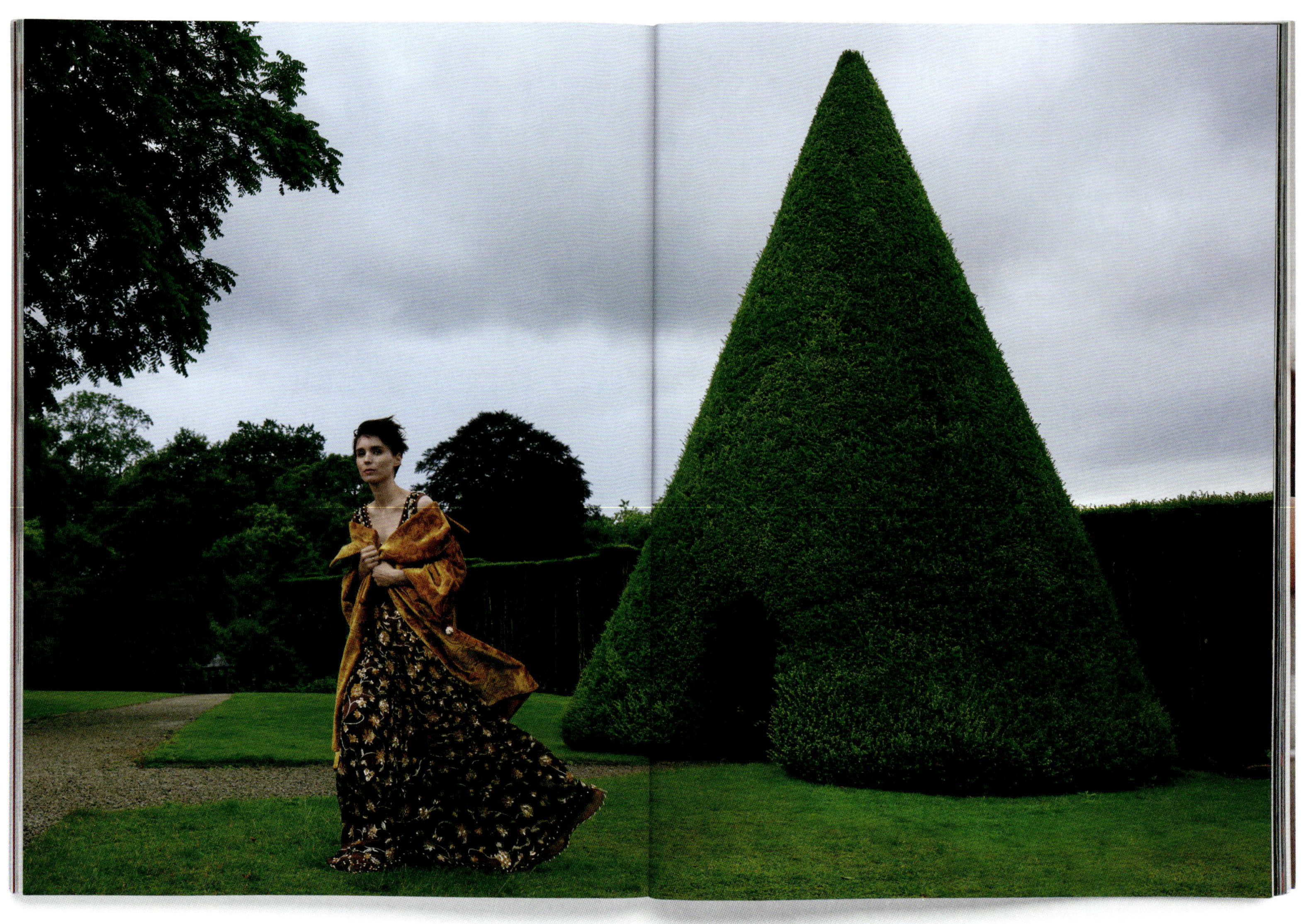

The gardens of Antony House,
Cornwall, England, 2017

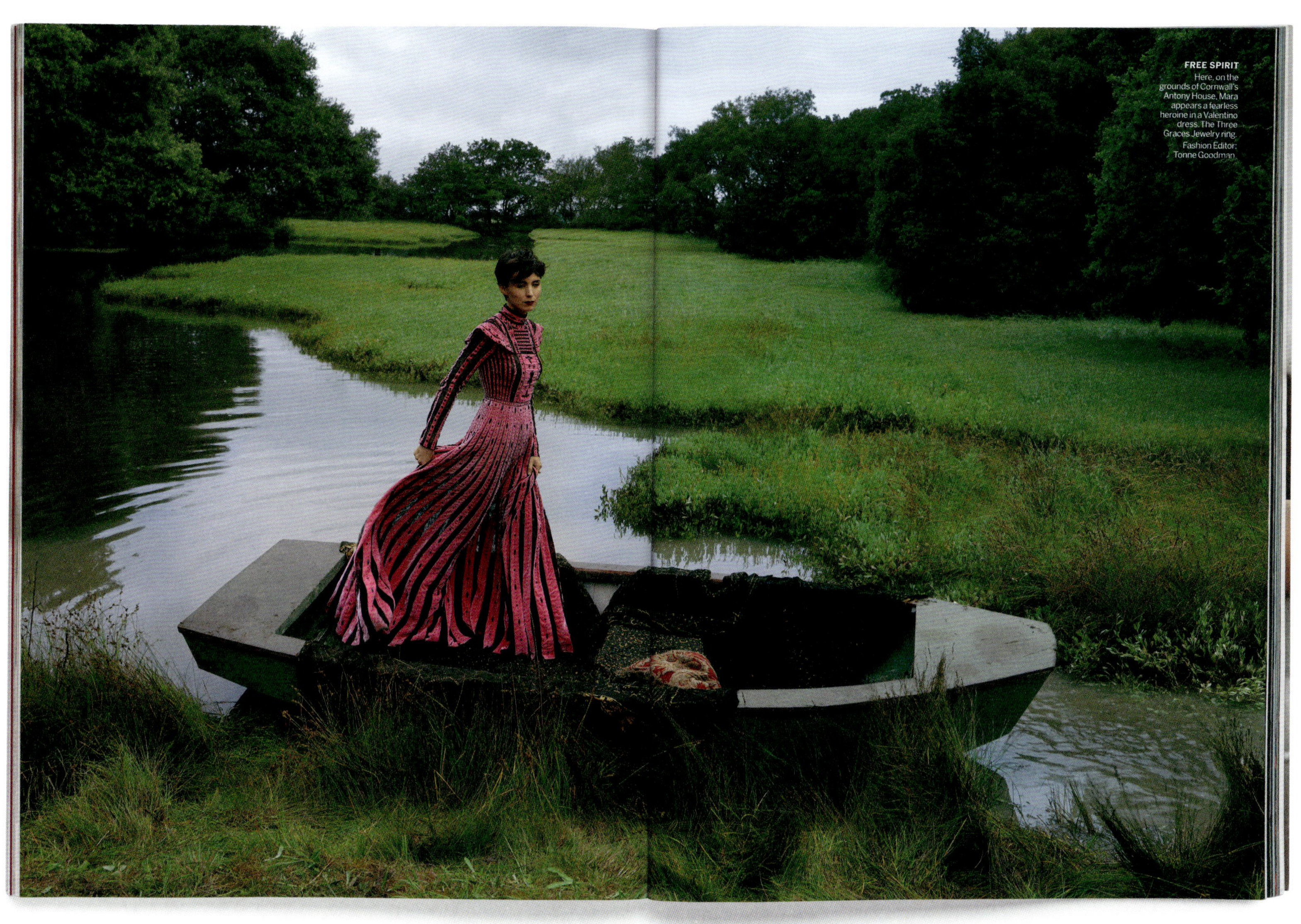
FREE SPIRIT
Here, on the grounds of Cornwall's Antony House, Mara appears a fearless heroine in a Valentino dress. The Three Graces Jewelry ring.
Fashion Editor: Tonne Goodman.

Misty Copeland,
New York City, 2015

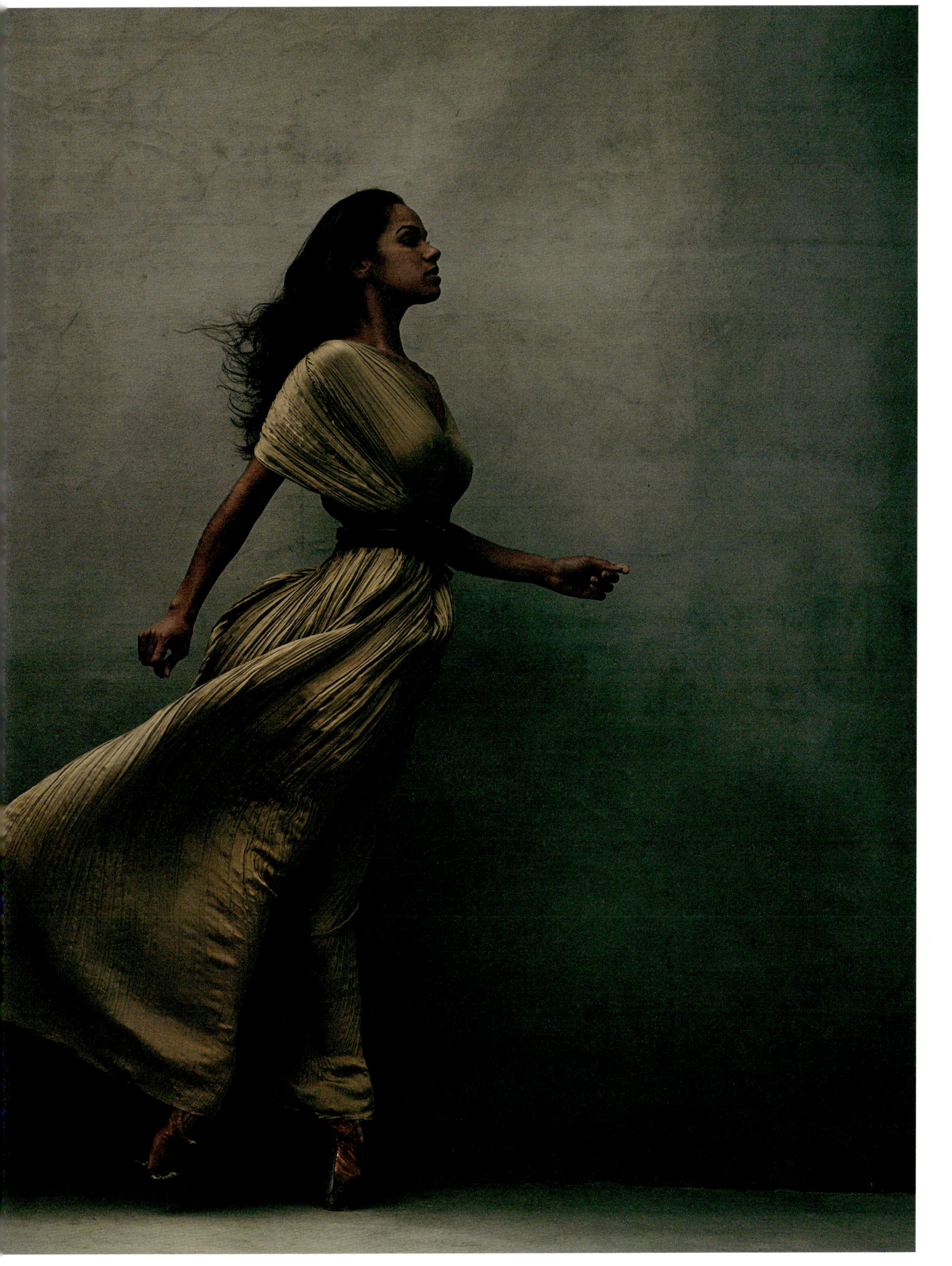

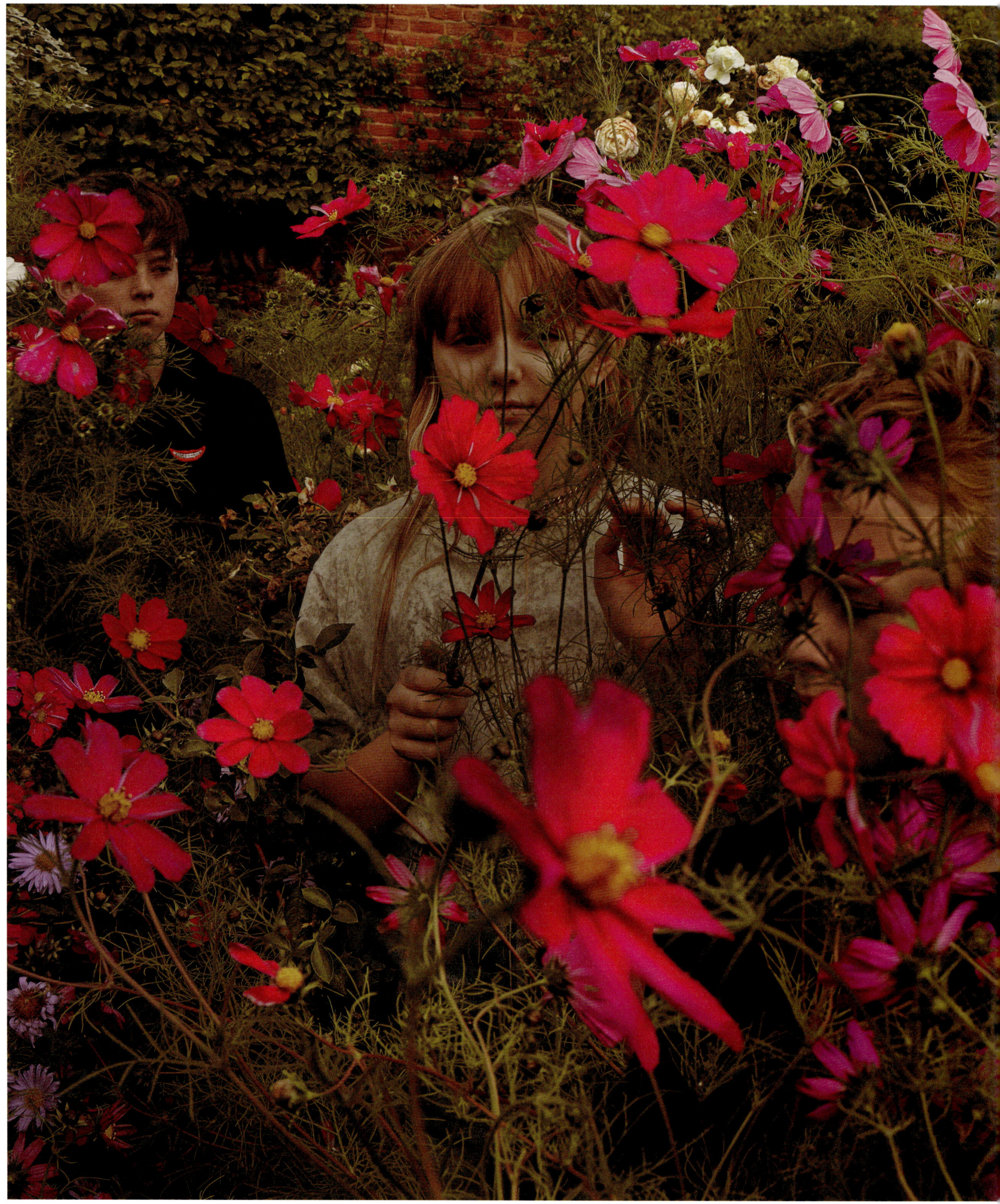

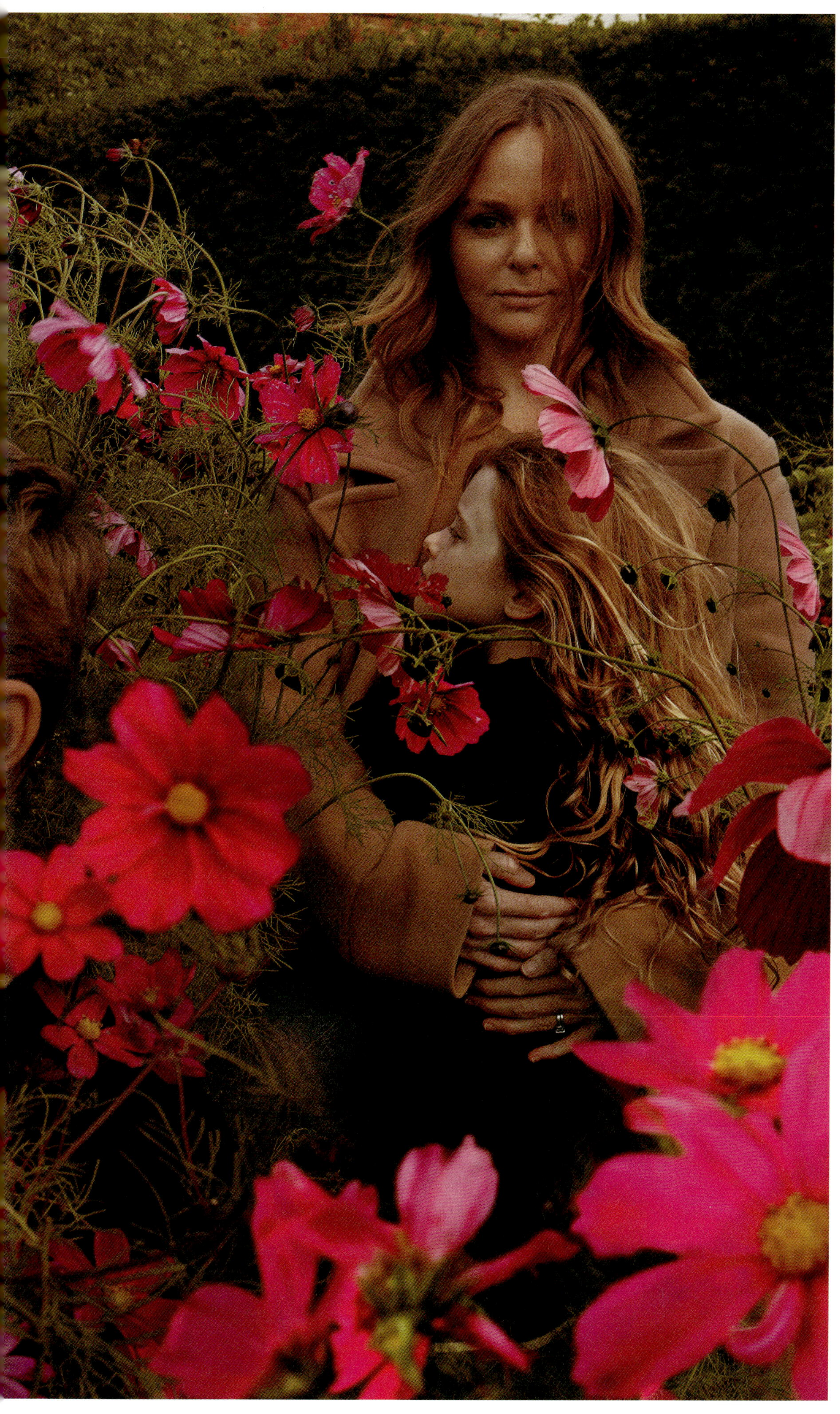

Stella McCartney with her children, Miller, Bailey, Beckett, and Reiley, Gloucestershire, England, 2019

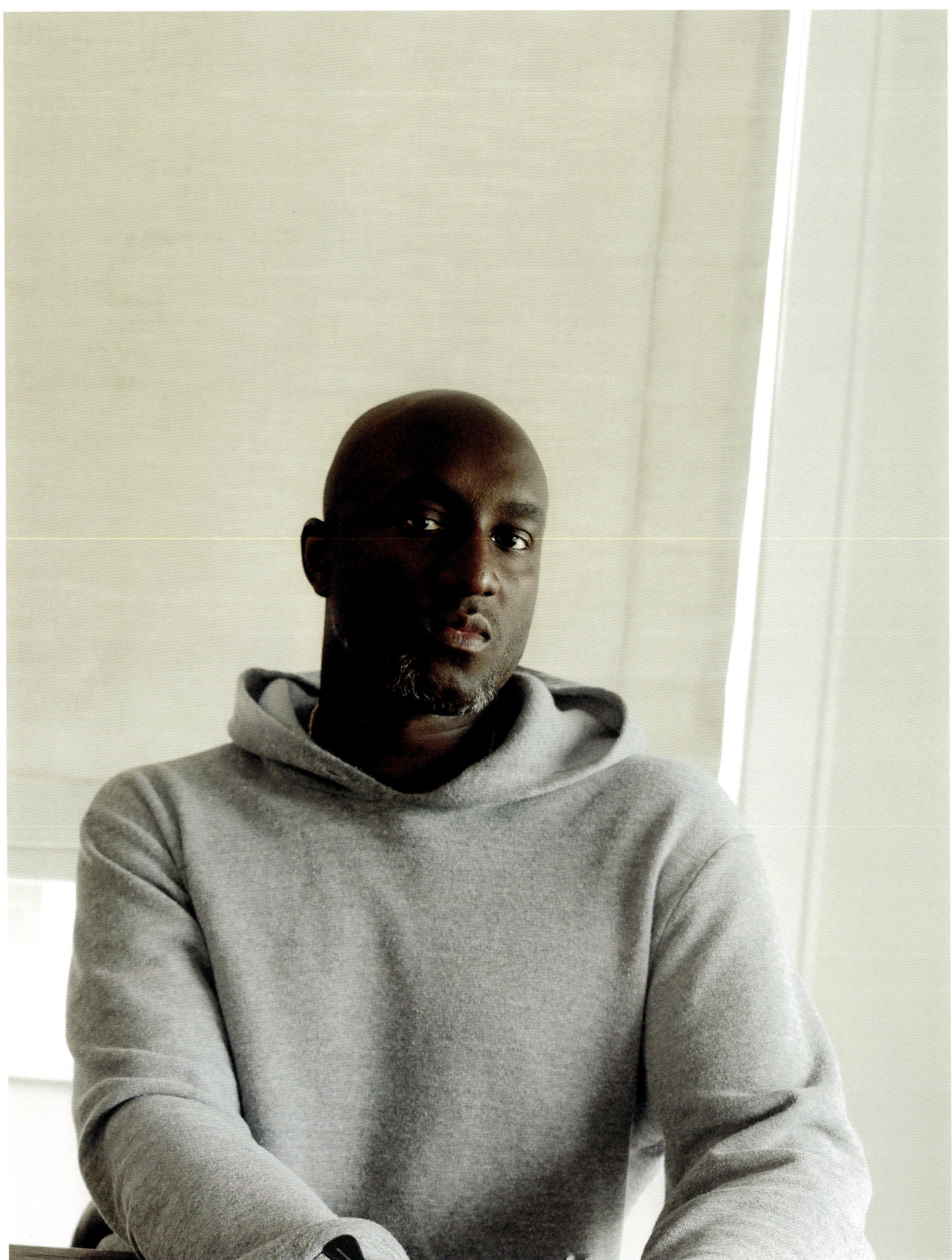

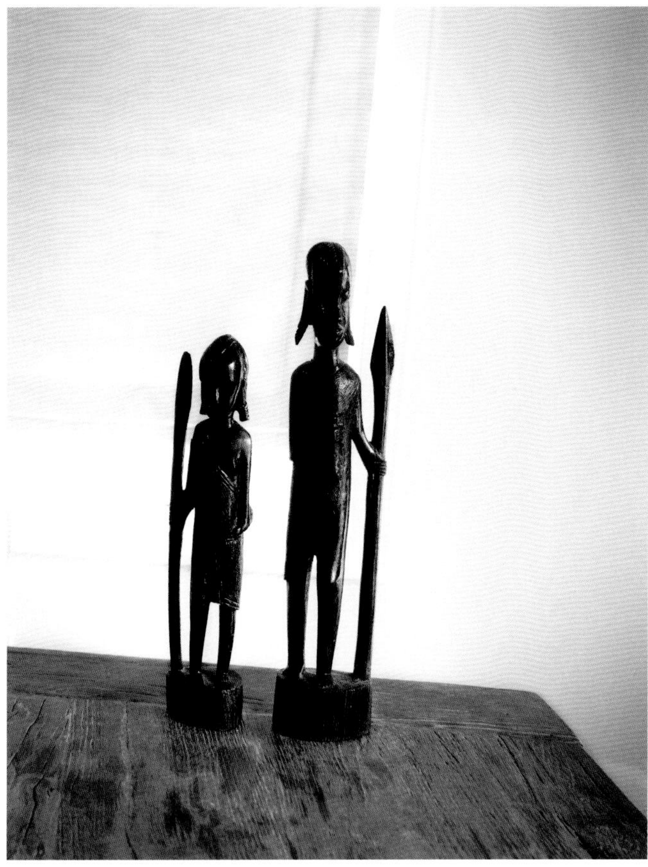

"Virgil Abloh's portrait was made in a virtual photo session during the first months of the COVID-19 pandemic. We used Zoom, but Virgil had been sent a laptop and a conventional camera with lenses and tripods. The camera was tethered to the laptop, which I controlled remotely. Since I had no ability to set up lights, we looked for the place with the best natural light. Virgil had to actually move the camera around himself. That was frustrating. So much of photography depends on peripheral vision—what you are not seeing through the camera.

The day of the shoot, Virgil brought out two ebony statues that looked very old. He said they belonged to his parents and that he kept them in his bedroom. His parents are from Ghana.

He also has a photograph of his maternal grandmother in his bedroom. She is wrapped in a kente cloth, the colorful textile with geometric patterns that is traditionally woven by the Ashanti people of Ghana. It was his inspiration for the wrap worn by Amanda Gorman on the May 2021 cover of *Vogue*."

Virgil Abloh at his home outside of Chicago, 2020

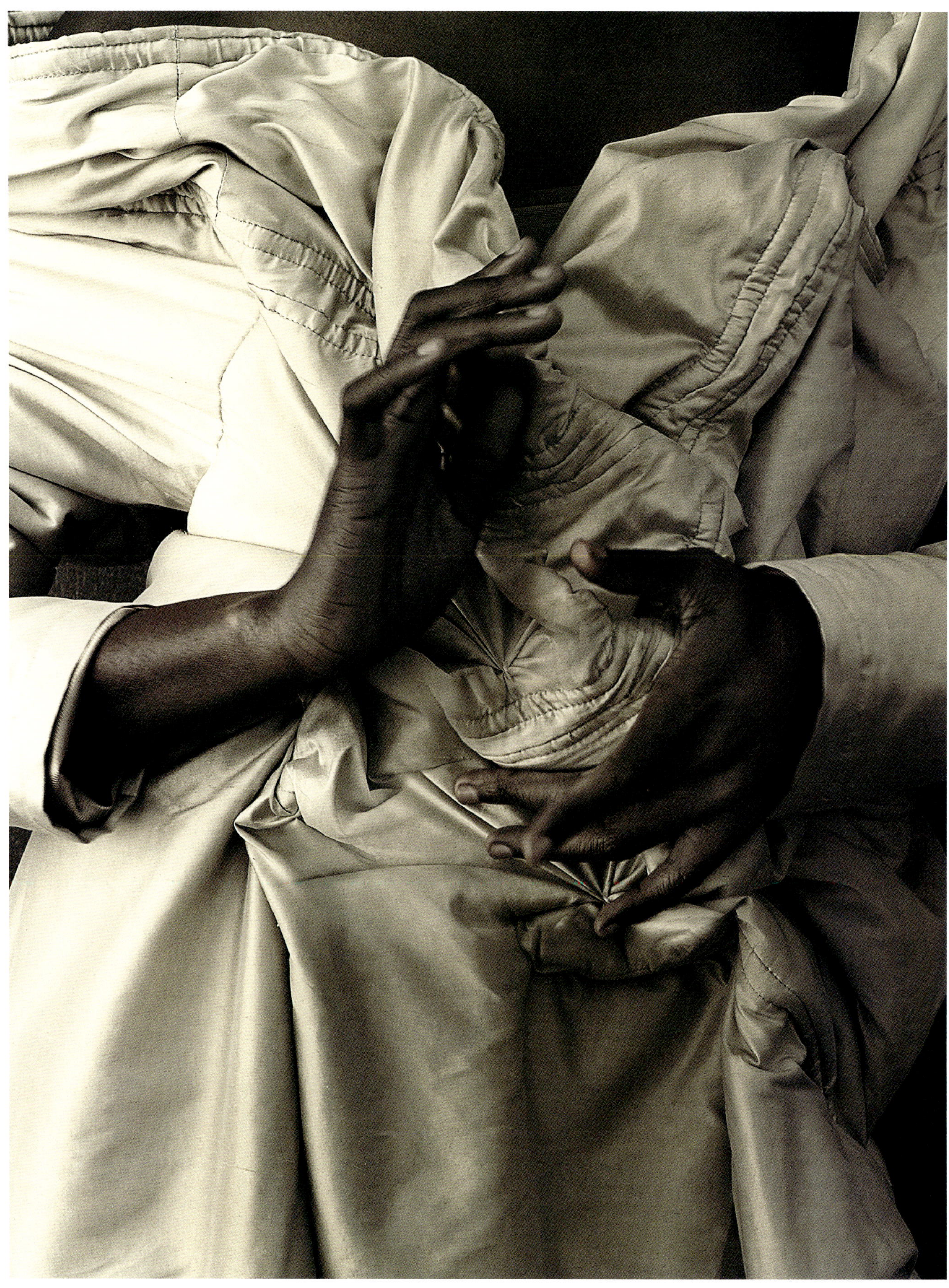

Amanda Gorman, the San Fernando
Valley, California, 2021

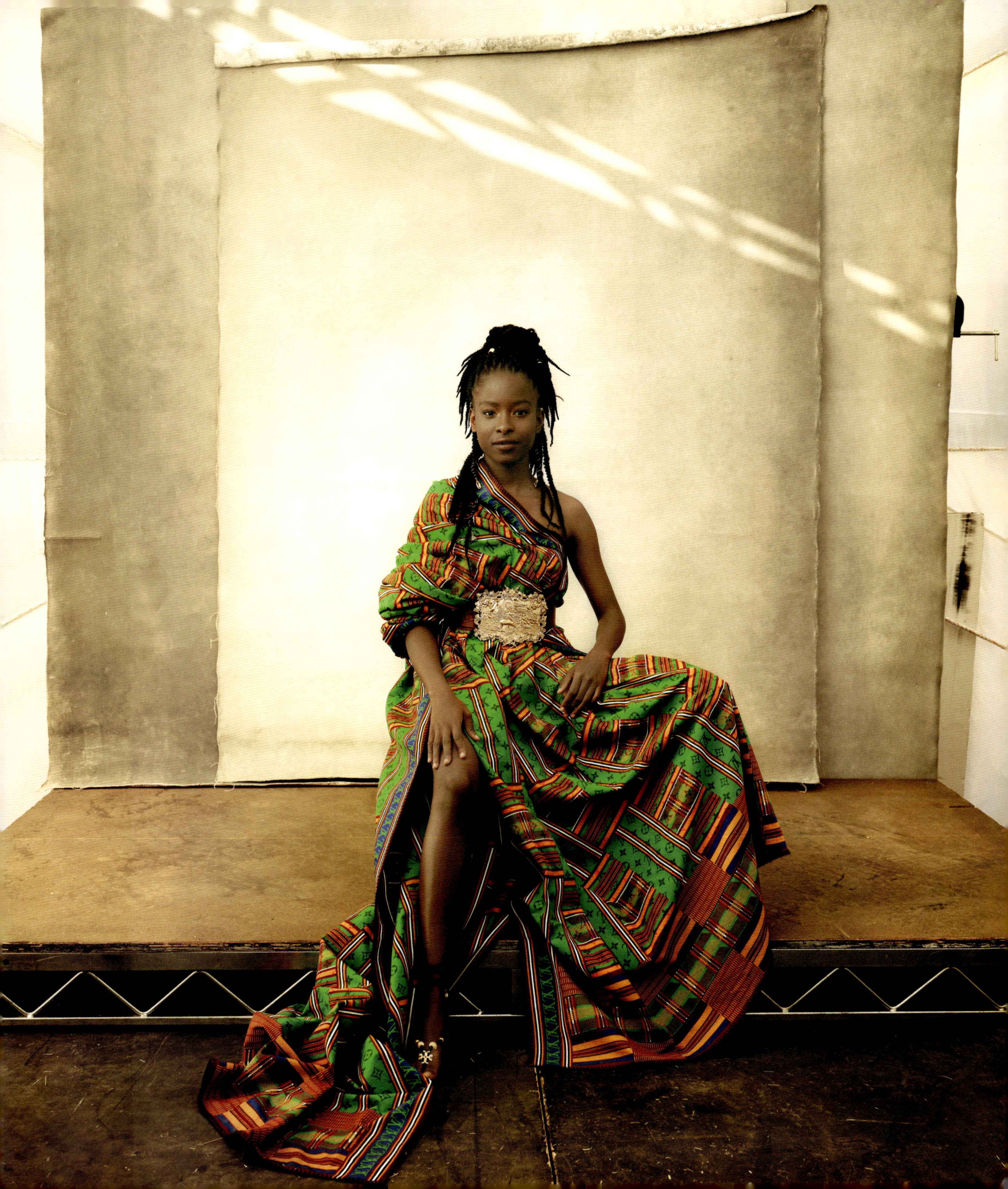

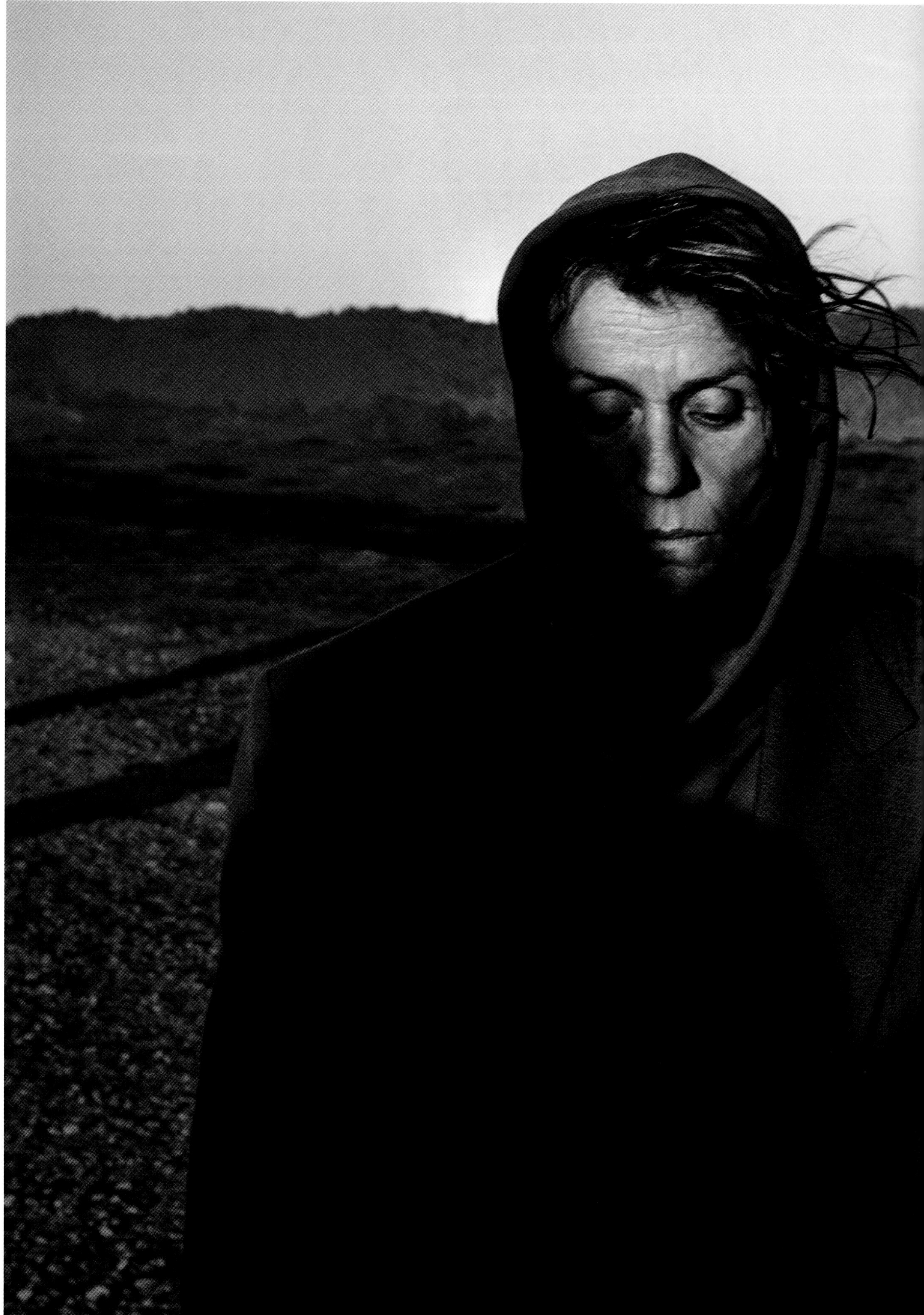

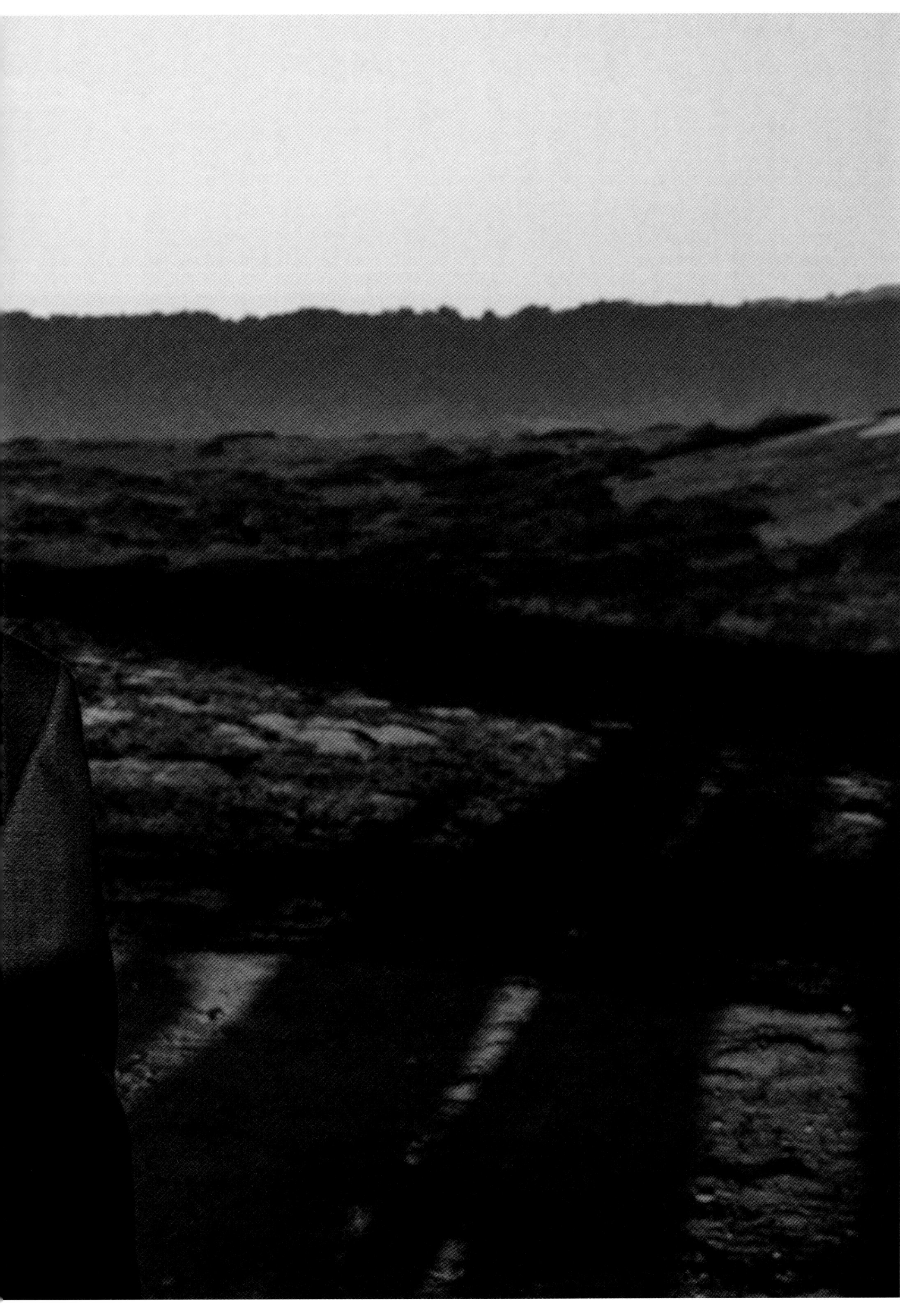

Frances McDormand,
Northern California, 2020

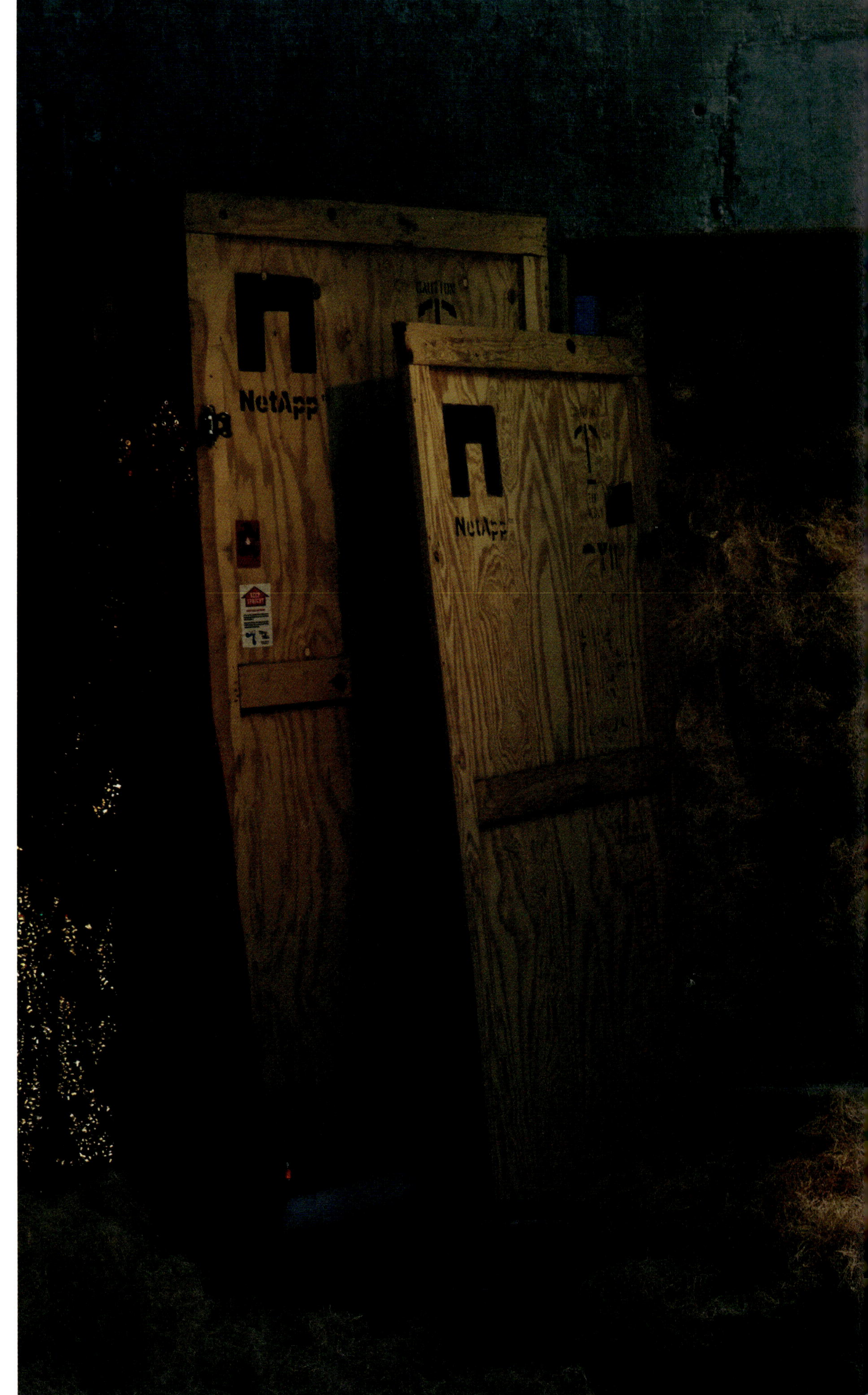

"Grace Coddington and I worked together on the shoot for Alexander McQueen's last collection. We hardly said a thing to each other when we were with the clothes, which had been shipped to New York in their original packing crates for us to photograph before they were formally presented in Paris to a small group of editors. There was an understanding that we were paying homage to a great artist."

New York, April 2010

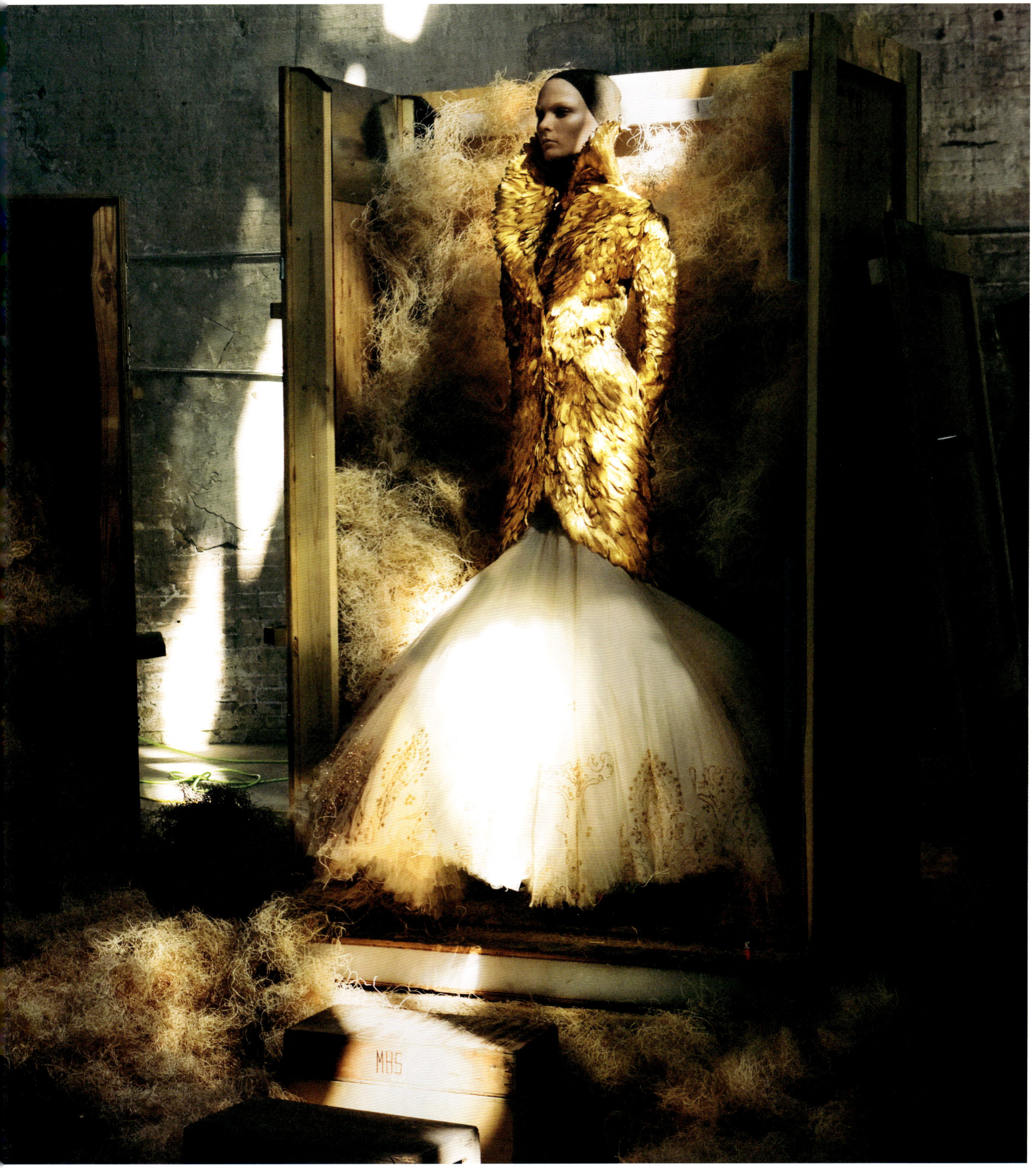
MHS

FASHION STORY CREDITS

"That Girl," *Vogue*, February 2014
Fashion Editor: Tonne Goodman.
Hair: Jimmy Paul. Makeup: Stéphane Marais.
Set Design: Mary Howard.
6–7: Lena Dunham in Zac Posen dress.

"The Big Stare," *Vanity Fair*, October 1986
Set Design: Susan Beeson.
23: David Byrne in a costume designed by Adelle Lutz for *True Stories*.

"Art of Fashion" campaign for Neiman Marcus, spring 1995
Stylist: Lori Goldstein.
Hair: Richard Keo. Makeup: Diane Kendal.
24: Jennifer Jason Leigh in Bill Blass dress.
25: Valentino Boutique suit.

"Puffy Takes Paris," *Vogue*, October 1999
Fall 1999 Couture
Fashion Editor: Grace Coddington.
Hair: Julien d'Ys. Makeup: Diane Kendal.
Styling for Sean Combs: Andrea Lieberman.
Hair: Mike Daddy.
Set Design: Jean-Hugues de Chatillon.
Prop Stylist: Ricky Floyd.
Locations: Frédéric Jagueneau.
Sittings Editor: Alexandra Kotur.
58–59: Kate Moss in Gaultier Paris coat and pants. Sean Combs in Versace coat, jacket, and pants. 60–61: Kate Moss in Atelier Versace dress. Sean Combs in Gucci pants and boots. 62–63: *Top left*, Kate Moss in Emanuel Ungaro Haute Couture leopard-print coat. Sean Combs in coat by Nija Furs. *Top center*, dress by Karl Lagerfeld for Chanel Haute Couture. *Top right*, Yves Saint Laurent Haute Couture top and skirt; Gaultier Paris dress. *Bottom left*, Christian Dior Haute Couture jacket and skirt; Givenchy Haute Couture dress and hat. *Bottom center*, Christian Dior Haute Couture dresses; Atelier Versace catsuit, T-shirt, and pants; Valentino Couture evening dress. *Bottom right*, Amanda Harlech in Chanel Haute Couture dress. Sean Combs in Sean Jean tank top, Jean Paul Gaultier, Karl Lagerfeld, Kate Moss in Gaultier Paris turtle-neck and pants, Oscar de la Renta, Alek Wek in Christian Dior Haute Couture dress, John Galliano. 64–65: Christian Dior Haute Couture jacket, headdress, and earrings. 66–67: Pierre Balmain Haute Couture dress and coat.

"Funny Face," *Vogue*, October 2001
Fall 2001 Couture
Fashion Editor: Grace Coddington.
Hair: Julien d'Ys. Makeup: Stéphane Marais.
Set Design: Jean-Hugues de Chatillon.
Locations: Frédéric Jagueneau.
Prop Stylist: Ricky Floyd.
80–81: Jacquetta Wheeler in Atelier Versace coat, Ai Tominaga in Givenchy Haute Couture dress, Karolina Kurkova in Emanuel Ungaro Haute Couture coat and dress, Oluchi Onweagba in Valentino Couture Collection dress, Stella Tennant in Yves Saint Laurent Haute Couture dress, Ben Stiller in Prada. 82: *Top*, Stella Tennant in Christian Lacroix Haute Couture dress, Ben Stiller in Prada. *Bottom*, Chez Castel on rue Princesse: Oluchi Onweagba, Stella Tennant, and Jacquetta Wheeler in Christian Dior Haute Couture coats, jacket, pants, and skirt; Ben Stiller in Christian Dior. 83: *Top*, Stella Tennant in Pierre Balmain Haute Couture by Oscar de la Renta, Jacquetta Wheeler in Spanish wedding dress, Ben Stiller in Tom Ford for Gucci. *Bottom*, Lapérouse restaurant on the Quai des Grands Augustins: Stella Tennant and Jacquetta Wheeler in Gaultier Paris coat, pants, and dress; Ben Stiller in Prada. 84: *Top*, Ai Tominaga, Jacquetta Wheeler, Stella Tennant, and Oluchi Onweagba in Gaultier Paris dresses, pants, jumpsuit, and coat. *Bottom*, Stella Tennant in Chanel Haute Couture tunic and overall, Ben Stiller in Prada. 85: *Top*, Stella Tennant and Jacquetta Wheeler in Valentino Couture Collection dresses, Ben Stiller in Hermès swimming trunks. *Bottom*, Stella Tennant and Jacquetta Wheeler in Christian Dior Haute Couture coat, pants, top, jacket, and skirt; Ben Stiller in Christian Dior Haute Couture hat. 86: Karl Lagerfeld, Ben Stiller in Christian Dior, Hedi Slimane. 87: Stella Tennant, Oluchi Onweagba, Ai Tominaga, and Jacquetta Wheeler in Chanel Haute Couture dresses, cape, tunic, and pants.

"Alice in Wonderland," *Vogue*, December 2003
Fashion Editor: Grace Coddington.
Hair: Julien d'Ys. Makeup: Gucci Westman.
Set Design: Mary Howard.
Set Design (Paris): Jean-Hugues de Chatillon.
Locations and Production: Frédéric Jagueneau.
Prop Stylist: Ricky Floyd.
Sittings Editor: Alexandra Kotur.
88: Natalia Vodianova in Chanel Haute Couture jacket, skirt, and pants. 88–89: Tom Ford for Yves Saint Laurent Rive Gauche dress. 90–91: Helmut Lang dress. 92: *Top*, Marc Jacobs minidress. *Bottom*, Gaultier Paris dress. 93: *Top*, Natalia Vodianova in Viktor and Rolf dress, Rolf Snoeren and Viktor Horsting in Viktor and Rolf. *Bottom*, Natalia Vodianova in Atelier Versace dress, Donatella Versace and Rupert Everett in Versace. 94–95: Natalia Vodianova in Christian Lacroix Haute Couture dress, Stephen Jones in his custom-made hat and vintage Emilio Pucci tie. 96–97: Natalia Vodianova in Dior Haute Couture dress by John Galliano, Galliano in Dior Haute Couture coat. 98–99: Balenciaga by Nicolas Ghesquière dress and boots.

"A Hollywood Elusive," *Vanity Fair*, February 2009
Fashion Editor: Michael Roberts.
Hair: Odile Gilbert. Makeup: Mary Greenwell.
102–3: Cate Blanchett in Ralph Lauren Collection gown.

"Truth or Dare," *Vogue*, December 2009
Fashion Editor: Tonne Goodman.
Hair: Sam McKnight. Makeup: Mary Greenwell.
Set Design: Mary Howard.
104–5: Cate Blanchett in Oscar de la Renta gown.

"French Twists," *Vogue*, May 2004
Fashion Editor: Grace Coddington.
Hair: Julien d'Ys. Makeup: Gucci Westman.
Set Design: Jean-Hugues de Chatillon.
Sittings Editor: Alexandra Kotur.
116–17: Gisele Bündchen in Christian Lacroix Haute Couture dress, Gérard Depardieu in a shirt from the private collection of Claudine Lachaud for Atelier Caraco. 118: *Top*, Karen Elson, Gisele Bündchen, and Gemma Ward in Gaultier Paris dresses; Gérard Depardieu in a Gucci trench coat. *Bottom*, unpublished photograph. 119: *Top*, Karen Elson, Gemma Ward, and Gisele Bündchen in Chanel Haute Couture dresses and coat; Louis Garrel in Alexander McQueen; Gérard Depardieu in a shirt from the private collection of Claudine Lachaud for Atelier Caraco. *Bottom*, Lily Cole, Gemma Ward, Gisele Bündchen, Daria Werbowy, and Karen Elson in Christian Dior Haute Couture dresses by John Galliano; Men's clothes by John Galliano.

"The Wizard of Oz," *Vogue*, December 2005
Fashion Editor: Grace Coddington.
Hair: Julien d'Ys. Makeup: Gucci Westman.
Set Design: Mary Howard.
Costumer: Wendy Schecter.
Sittings Editor: Alexandra Kotur.
120–21: Keira Knightley in Vera Wang dress. 122: *Top*, Balenciaga Edition dress by Nicolas Ghesquière. *Bottom*, Rochas dress and shoes. 123: *Top*, Oscar de la Renta dress. *Bottom*, Comme des Garçon dress. 124–25: Kara Walker in Dior Haute Couture ball dress by John Galliano, Keira Knightley in Marc Jacobs dress and sandals. 126–27: Donna Karan dress. 128–29: Keira Knightley in Yves Saint Laurent dress and loafers, Kiki Smith in Chanel Haute Couture cape.

"Straight from the Heart," *Vogue*, November 2005
Fashion Editor: Camilla Nickerson.
Hair: Recine. Makeup: Molly R. Stern.
Set Design: Mary Howard.
130–31: Reese Witherspoon in Rochas jacket and dress. 132: *Top*, Chloé dress. *Bottom*, Balenciaga top and skirt by Nicolas Ghesquière. 133: *Top*, Reese Witherspoon in Prada shirtdress, Joaquin Phoenix in Marc Jacobs sports jacket and Levi's jeans. *Bottom*, Oscar de la Renta dress.

"The Bold and the Beautiful," *Vogue*, January 2007
Fashion Editor: Phyllis Posnick.
Hair: Garren. Makeup: Toni G.
Set Design: Mary Howard.
Sittings Editor: Alexandra Kotur.
134–35: Angelina Jolie in Ralph Lauren Collection dress.

"Rebel with a Cause," *Vogue*, November 2015
Fashion Editor: Tonne Goodman.
Hair: Adam Campbell. Makeup: Toni G.
Set Design: Theresa Rivera for Mary Howard Studio.
136: *Top*, Angelina Jolie in an Oscar de la Renta dress. *Bottom*, Calvin Klein Collection dress. 137: *Top*, Wolford bodysuit and Bottega Veneta skirt. *Bottom*, Lanvin tank top and skirt.

"Teen Queen," *Vogue*, September 2006
Fashion Editor: Grace Coddington.
Hair: Odile Gilbert. Makeup: Stéphane Marais.
Set Design: Jean-Hughes de Chatillon.
Prop Stylist: Ricky Floyd.
Sittings Editor: Alexandra Kotur.
146–47: Kirsten Dunst and Jason Schwartzman in costumes created by Milena Canonero; Wigs by Rocchetti. 148–49: John-Paul Scarpitta, Alexandre Cornillon, Aurore Clément, Jamie Dornan, Victoire de Castellane, Matilde Agostinelli, Rose Byrne, Jason Schwartzman, Kirsten Dunst, Clementine Poidatz, and Mary Nighy in costumes created by Milena Canonero; Wigs by Rocchetti. 150: Kirsten Dunst in a costume created by Milena Canonero (unpublished alternate cover). 151: Alexander McQueen ball gown (unpublished alternate). 152–53: Oscar de la Renta gown. 154–55: Balenciaga by Nicolas Ghesquière dress. 156–57: Rochas by Olivier Theyskens gown. 158–59: Dior Couture by John Galliano dress.

"Made in Spain," *Vogue*, December 2007
Fashion Editor: Tonne Goodman.
Hair: Didier Malige. Makeup: Gucci Westman.
Set Design: Mary Howard.
Sittings Editor: Alexandra Kotur.
160–61: Unpublished photograph. 162–63: Penélope Cruz in Marchesa ball dress. 164–65: Donna Karan Collection dress. 166: *Top*, Dior Haute Couture by John Galliano coatdress. *Bottom*, Penélope Cruz in L'Wren Scott dress; Men in Armani Collezioni shirt and suit, Emporio Armani shirts, Dior Homme vest, Giorgio Armani shirt and shoes. 167: *Top*, Dior Haute Couture by John Galliano dress. *Bottom*, Armani Privé dress.

"Pillow Talk," *Vogue*, September 2005
Fashion Editor: Camilla Nickerson
Hair: Serge Normant. Makeup: Tom Pecheux.
Set Design: Mary Howard.
Sittings Editor: Alexandra Kotur.
172–73: Sarah Jessica Parker in Carolina Herrera blouse and skirt. 174–75: Oscar de la Renta dress. 176–77: Yves Saint Laurent tuxedo.

"Rebel Romance," *Vogue*, June 2008
Fashion Editor: Phyllis Posnick.
Hair: Serge Normant. Makeup: Stéphane Marais.
Set Design: Mary Howard.
Men's Stylist: Wendy Schecter.
Sittings Editor: Alexandra Kotur.
178: *Top*, Sarah Jessica Parker in Chanel suit; Chris Noth in Valentino suit and shirt, Tom Ford coat. *Bottom*, Sarah Jessica Parker in Alexander McQueen dress, Chris Noth in Valentino suit. 179: *Top*, Sarah Jessica Parker in Lanvin evening dress; Chris Noth in Tom Ford coat, Hugo Boss Shirt, Valentino pants. *Bottom*, Sarah Jessica Parker in Nina Ricci dress; Chris Noth in Tom Ford vest, Valentino shirt and trousers. 180–81: Sarah Jessica Parker in Narciso Rodriguez dress, Chris Noth in Valentino suit and Tom Ford vest. 182–83: Sarah Jessica Parker in Versace dress, Chris Noth in Tom Ford tuxedo and Brooks Brothers shirt. 184–85: Sarah Jessica Parker in Dolce & Gabbana evening dress, Chris Noth in Valentino suit.

"La Dolce Diva," *Vogue*, October 2008
Fashion Editor: Phyllis Posnick.
Hair: Odile Gilbert. Makeup: Stéphane Marais.
Set Design: Mary Howard.
Sittings Editor: Alexandra Kotur.
186–87: Renée Fleming in Christian Lacroix gown.

"Love of a Lifetime," *Vogue*, December 2008
Fashion Editor: Grace Coddington.
Hair: Julien d'Ys. Makeup: Gucci Westman.
Set Design: Mary Howard.
Costumer: Hannah Teare.
Sittings Editor: Alexandra Kotur.
188–89: Coco Rocha in Nina Ricci dress. 190–91: Proenza Schouler dress. 192–93: Coco Rocha in Christian Lacroix Couture, guests in dresses from the Christian Lacroix Couture archive. 196: Dolce & Gabbana dress. 197: Alexander McQueen dress and body stocking.

"The Other Man," *Vogue*, October 2013
Fashion Editor: Grace Coddington.
Menswear Editor: Michael Philouze.
Hair: Didier Malige.
Set Design: Mary Howard.
198–99: Karen Elson in Nina Ricci jacket and skirt. 200–201: Dior coat. 202: *Top*, Karen Elson in Rochas coat, sweater, and skirt; Hugh Dancy in Ralph Lauren suit and Turnbull & Asser sweater; Michael Shannon in Calvin Klein suit and Dior Homme turtleneck. *Bottom*, Karen Elson in Carolina Herrera ball dress, Hugh Dancy in Brooks Brothers suit and Salvatore Ferragamo shirt. 203: *Top*, Karen Elson in Dolce & Gabbana skirt and jacket, Michael Shannon in Turnbull & Asser shirt and Calvin Klein Collection pants. *Bottom*, Karen Elson in Bottega Veneta sweater and Jil Sander skirt, Hugh Dancy in Polo Ralph Lauren suit, Michael Shannon in Calvin Klein Collection suit.

"Frock and Roll," *Vogue*, June 2010
Fashion Editor: Grace Coddington.
Hair: Julien d'Ys. Makeup: Gucci Westman.
Set Design: Mary Howard.
204–5: Karen Elson in Nina Ricci sweater and skirt. 206–7: Alberta Ferretti jacket and skirt. 208: Marc Jacobs dress. 209: Rochas sweater and skirt, Moschino blouse. 210–11: Karen Elson in Nina Ricci coat and dress.

"Little Girl & Boy Lost," *Vogue*, December 2009
Fashion Editor: Grace Coddington.
Hair: Julien d'Ys. Makeup: Gucci Westman.
Set Design: Mary Howard.
Metropolitan Opera costumes: John Macfarlane.
Sittings Editor: Alexandra Kotur.
218: *Top*, Lily Cole in Dolce & Gabbana dress, Andrew Garfield in Martin Margiela shirt and Ann Demeulemeester pants. *Bottom*, Balenciaga by Nicolas Ghesquière jacket and skirt. 219: *Top*, Dior dress (unpublished alternate). *Bottom*, unpublished alternate. 220–21: Lady Gaga in Marc Jacobs bra, blouse, and shorts; Lily Cole in Yves Saint Laurent dress.

"Breaking Away," *Vogue*, December 2011
Fashion Editor: Camilla Nickerson.
Hair: Enzo Angileri. Makeup: Shane Paish.
Set Design: Mary Howard.
Locations: Ernie Liberati.
224–25: Charlize Theron in Marchesa dress.
226–27: Salvatore Ferragamo halter dress.

"Katy Perry's Grand Tour," *Vanity Fair*, June 2011
Fashion Editor: Jessica Diehl.
Hair: Julien d'Ys. Makeup: Stéphane Marais.
Set Design: Mary Howard.
Vanity Fair Production: Kathryn MacLeod.
Locations and Production: Frédéric Jagueneau.
228: Katy Perry in a Christian Dior Haute Couture corset. 229: Christian Dior Haute Couture. 230: *Top*, Christian Dior Haute Couture (unpublished alternate). *Bottom*, Jean Paul Gaultier Haute Couture. 231: *Top*, Christian Dior Haute Couture. *Bottom*, Jean Paul Gaultier Haute Couture (unpublished).

"In Lady Gaga's Wake," *Vanity Fair*, January 2012
Fashion Editor: Jessica Diehl.
Hair: Orlando Pita. Makeup: James Kaliardos.
Set Design: Mary Howard.
Stylist for Lady Gaga: Nicola Formichetti.
Vanity Fair Production: Kathryn MacLeod.
Locations: Ernie Liberati.
232: *Top*, Lady Gaga in Valentino Haute Couture. *Bottom*, Versace bra and skirt. 233: *Top*, Alexander McQueen coat. *Bottom*, Atelier Versace. 234–35: Chanel sunglasses.

"The Fall Classic," *Vogue*, October 2014
Fashion Editor: Camilla Nickerson.
Hair: Recine. Makeup: Diane Kendal.
Set Design: Mary Howard.
238–39: Natalia Vodianova in Balmain jacket, Céline sweater and skirt, Zadig & Voltaire fur collar.

"Grand Entrance," *Vogue*, November 2014
Fashion Editor: Tonne Goodman.
Hair: Oribe. Makeup: Stéphane Marais.
240–41: Natalia Vodianova in Donna Karan New York silk halter dress.

"Brief Encounter," *Vogue*, February 2010
Fashion Editor: Grace Coddington.
Hair: Julien d'Ys. Makeup: Gucci Westman.
Styling for Sean Combs: Sean Spellman.
Men's Hair: Curtis Smith. Men's Grooming: AJ Crimson.
Set Design: Mary Howard.
242–43: Natalia Vodianova in Nina Ricci trench coat. 244–45: Natalia Vodianova in Chanel suit dress, Sean Combs in Tom Ford coat and suit. 246: *Top*, Giambattista Valli jacket and skirt. *Bottom*, Natalia Vodianova in Nina Ricci dress, Sean Combs in Salvatore Ferragamo shirt and Louis Vuitton trousers. 247: *Top*, Natalia Vodianova in Christian Dior jacket and shorts, Sean Combs in Calvin Klein T-shirt. *Bottom*, Christian Dior jacket and skirt.

"The Custom of the Country," *Vogue*, September 2012
Fashion Editor: Grace Coddington.
Hair: Julien d'Ys. Makeup: Stéphane Marais.
Set Design: Mary Howard.
Men's Styling: Hannah Teare.
248–49: Natalia Vodianova in Nina Ricci dress.
250–51: Natalia Vodianova in Donna Karan coat, Jeffrey Eugenides in Paul Stuart coat, Elijah Wood in Angels the Costumiers coat, Jack Huston in Polo Ralph Lauren suit. 252–53: Natalia Vodianova in Rochas blouse and skirt.
254–55: Natalia Vodianova in Balenciaga by Nicolas Ghesquière jacket and skirt, James Corden and Jeffrey Eugenides in Polo Ralph Lauren suits. 256: *Top*, Natalia Vodianova in Alberta Ferretti dress, Juno Temple in Ralph Lauren Collection jacket and skirt. *Bottom*, Natalia Vodianova in Chanel dress, Nate Lowman in Budd Shirtmakers shirt, Jeffrey Eugenides in Polo Ralph Lauren suit. 257: *Top*, Natalia Vodianova in Louis Vuitton jacket and dress, Mamie Gummer in vintage Ralph Lauren Collection blouse and Lanvin skirt, Jeffrey Eugenides in Burberry London suit, Junot Díaz and Jack Huston in suits from Angels the Costumiers, Jonathan Safran Foer in a waistcoat from Angels the Costumiers and a Prada shirt, Max Minghella in Giorgio Armani shirt and Burberry London pants. *Bottom*, Natalia Vodianova in Oscar de la Renta blouse and skirt, Jack Huston in Angels the Costumiers suit, Jeffrey Eugenides in Angels the Costumiers vest and jacket and Prada pants.

"That Girl," *Vogue*, February 2014
Fashion Editor: Tonne Goodman.
Hair: Jimmy Paul. Makeup: Stéphane Marais.
Set Design: Mary Howard.
Locations: Ernie Liberati.
310: Lena Dunham in Rochas top and skirt, Adam Driver in J. Crew sweater and Levi's jeans.
311: Alexander McQueen dress and capelet.

"The Flip Side," *Vogue*, July 2009
Fashion Editor: Phyllis Posnick.
Hair: Julien d'Ys. Makeup: Stéphane Marais.
Set design: Mary Howard.
312–13: Karlie Kloss in Zac Posen dress.

"Country Strong," *Vogue*, June 2012
Fashion Editor: Tonne Goodman.
Hair: Oribe. Makeup: Fulvia Farolfi.
Set Design: Mary Howard.
314–15: Karlie Kloss in Stella McCartney gold lamé dress. 316: *Top*, Karlie Kloss in Victoria Beckham dress, Jonathan Horton in Adidas pants. *Bottom*, Vera Wang dress. 317: *Top*, Karlie Kloss in Oscar de la Renta dress, Dwyane Wade in Jordan shorts and Jordan Nike Fly Wade 2 sneakers. *Bottom*, Alexander McQueen dress.

"Wild Irish Rose," *Vogue*, September 2013
Fashion Editor: Grace Coddington.
Hair: Julien d'Ys.
Set Design: Mary Howard.
322–23: Daria Werbowy in Céline coat, Rochas sweater, and Jil Sander skirt; Adam Driver in Doyle+Mueser jacket and pants. 324: *Top*, Rochas jacket, Ralph Lauren Collection skirt.
325: *Top*, Daria Werbowy in Belstaff cable-knit sweater, Rochas skirt, and Michael Kors coat; Adam Driver in Hollander & Lexer shirt. *Bottom*, Donna Karan New York sweater and Chanel skirt.

"Without a Net," *Vogue*, September 2017
Fashion Editor: Tonne Goodman
Hair: Shay Ashual. Makeup: Hannah Murray.
326–27: Jennifer Lawrence in Dior (unpublished). 328–29: Ralph Lauren Collection dress.

"How Many People Does It Take to Design a Dress?" *Vogue*, September 2000
Fashion Editor: Camilla Nickerson.
Makeup: James Kaliardos.
Sittings Editor: Alexandra Kotur.
334–35: Pina Bausch in vintage Yohji Yamamoto (unpublished alternate).

"Wonder Women," *Vanity Fair*, Hollywood 2017
Fashion Editor: Jessica Diehl
Hair: Ben Skervin. Makeup: Mark Carrasquillo.
Vanity Fair Production: Kathryn MacLeod.
336–37: Greta Gerwig in The Row coat and Rag & Bone dress.

"Sisters at Court," *Vogue*, May 1998
Fashion Editor: Camilla Nickerson.
Makeup: Julie Harris.
340: Venus Williams in tank top by Liza Bruce.

"Queen of the Court," *Vogue*, April 2015
Fashion Editor: Sara Moonves.
Hair: Holli Smith. Makeup: Francelle Daly.
343: Serena Williams in Donna Karan New York dress.

"Serena's Love Match," *Vanity Fair*, August 2017
Fashion Editor: Jessica Diehl.
Hair: Vernon François. Makeup: Tyron Machhausen.
Set Design: Mary Howard.
Vanity Fair Production: Kathryn MacLeod.
344–45: Serena Williams in Issey Miyake Pleats Please dress.

"Princess Bride," *Vogue*, October 2014
Fashion Editor: Phyllis Posnick.
Hair: Orlando Pita. Makeup: Alice Lane.
Set Design: Mary Howard.
346–47 Amal Clooney in Oscar de la Renta dress.

"All Eyes on Claire," *Vogue*, August 2013
Fashion Editor: Tonne Goodman.
Menswear Editor: Michael Philouze.
Hair: Oribe. Makeup: Val Garland.
Set Design: Mary Howard.
358–59: Claire Danes in Victoria Beckham dress. 360: Claire Danes in Hermès jacket and skirt, Damian Lewis in Polo Ralph Lauren jacket and Tom Ford sweater. 361: Claire Danes in Donna Karan New York dress, Damian Lewis in Prada shirt.

"Brand-New Day," *Vogue*, May 2014
Fashion Editor: Phyllis Posnick.
Hair: Julien d'Ys. Victoria Beckham's makeup: Sally Branka.
Location Support: Mary Howard.
362–63: Liya Kebede in Lemlem for Born Free dress and Joie jacket (unpublished alternate).
366: *Top*, Liya Kebede in Marni for Born Free dress. 367: *Top*, Liya Kebede in Isabel Marant for Born Free blouse, Vera Wang for Born Free top, Nili Lotan pants. *Bottom*, Victoria Beckham in her own clothes.

"Keeping Up with Kimye," *Vogue*, April 2014
Fashion Editor: Grace Coddington.
Hair: Anthony Turner. Makeup: Aaron de Mey.
Set Design: Mary Howard.
Styling for Kanye West: Renelou Padora.
Grooming: Ibn Jasper.
368–69: Kim Kardashian in Schiaparelli Haute Couture top and skirt, Kanye West in Fear of God T-shirt and Prada pants.
370: *Top*, Kim Kardashian in Lanvin Blanche Collection by Alber Elbaz dress, Kanye West in Louis Vuitton coat and Alternative Apparel hoodie. 371: *Top*, Kim Kardashian in Dolce & Gabbana Alta Moda dress and skirt, North West in Dolce & Gabbana Childrenswear dress. *Bottom*, Nina Ricci dress.
372–73: Kim Kardashian in Givenchy by Riccardo Tisci fox stole and skirt, Kanye West in Balmain T-shirt.

"He Says Goodbye, She Says Hello," *Vanity Fair*, July 2015
Fashion Editor: Jessica Diehl.
Hair: Oribe. Makeup: Mark Carrasquillo.
Set Design: Mary Howard.
Vanity Fair Production: Kathryn MacLeod.
374–75: Caitlyn Jenner in Halston Heritage gown and Helen Yarmak stole. 376–77: Zac Posen gown. 378–79: Trashy Lingerie.

"Rihanna's Solo Scene," *Vanity Fair*, November 2015
Fashion Editor: Jessica Diehl.
Hair: Yusef Jamal.
Set Design: Mary Howard.
Vanity Fair Production: Kathryn MacLeod.
384–85: Rihanna in Carine Gilson top and pants. 386: *Top*, Manolo Blahnik shoes. *Bottom*, Dior coat and briefs. 387: *Top*, Valentino jumpsuit. *Bottom*, Ralph Lauren Collection gown.
388–89: Zuhair Murad dress (unpublished photograph).

"A Secret Passion," *Vogue*, January 2014
Fashion Editor: Grace Coddington.
Hair: Julian d'Ys. Makeup: Stéphane Marais.
Set Design: Mary Howard.
Men's Stylist: Hannah Teare.
392–93: Felicity Jones in Oscar de la Renta blouse and skirt (unpublished). 394–95: Alexander McQueen jacket and skirt.

"The Voice," *Vogue*, March 2016
Fashion Editor: Tonne Goodman.
Hair: Shay Ashual. Makeup: Mark Carrasquillo.
Set Design: Mary Howard.
Locations: Charlie Borradaile.
400–401: Adele in Alexander McQueen dress.
402: *Top*, Giambattista Valli dress. *Bottom*, Salvatore Ferragamo dress. 403: *Top*, Burberry dress. *Bottom*, Gucci dress.

"All Hail," *Vogue*, May 2019
Fashion Stylist: Madeline Weeks.
Hair: Curtis William Foreman. Makeup: David Petruschin.
405: RuPaul in costume tailored by Shana Albery.

"Swept Away," *Vogue*, June 2017
Fashion Editor: Grace Coddington.
Hair: Julien d'Ys. Makeup: Lauren Parsons.
Set Design: Mary Howard.
412: Elle Fanning in Alexander McQueen dress. 413: Valentino Haute Couture dress.
414–15: Dior dress.

"Rooney on the Move," *Vogue*, October 2017
Fashion Editor: Tonne Goodman.
Hair: Odile Gilbert. Makeup: Lauren Parsons.
Set Design: Mary Howard.
Locations: Charlie Borradaile.
416–17: Rooney Mara in Erdem dress.
418: Altuzarra dress and Erdem coat.
419: Valentino dress.

"Supernova," *Vogue*, May 2021
Fashion Editor: Gabriella Karefa-Johnson.
Hair: Lacy Redway. Makeup: Raisa Flowers.
Set Design: Mary Howard.
426: Y/Project dress.
427: Wrap by Virgil Abloh for Louis Vuitton.

"The Real World," *Vogue*, January 2021
Sittings Editor: Jorden Bickham.
Hair and Makeup: Cydney Cornell.
Set Design: Mary Howard.
428-429: Fear of God Suit and hoodie.

1997 PLAN-A-MONTH® Brand

SEPTEMBER

SUN	MON	TUE	WED	THUR	FRI	SAT
NOTES	1 244/121 LABOR DAY HOLIDAY	2 245/120 STUDIO BACK	3 246/119 VF to DC Katharine graham #2081	4 247/118 VF Katharine graham #2081 Wash DC	5 248/117 10 book meeting 12 Alexandra Kotur 1 Dancer MIN #2086	6 249/116
7 250/115	8 251/114 Amy grant MILK/LA #2087	9 252/113 3pm/LA #2088 NYPD Prep. Will & Jada #2082 VF-LA	10 253/112 Ambassador Will + Jada VF #2082 LA	11 254/111 Studio Day	12 255/110 MISS AMERICA #2079 NEW YORKER Atlantic City, NJ	13 256/109
14 257/108 Miss America AC → NYC	15 258/107 Prep Claire Danes #2072 VF/cover	16 259/106 Claire Danes #2072 VF/Cover	17 260/105 Claire Danes #2072 VF/Cover	18 261/104 MILK MOMS #2089	19 262/103 Vanity Fair Evander Holyfield #2080 Atlanta, GA	20 263/102
21 264/101	22 265/100 MARS Scientists #2091 Pasadena	23 266/99 Studio Day Ruth@1pm	24 267/98	25 268/97 Sandra Day O'Connor Justice Ginsburg #2083	26 269/96	27 270/95
28 271/94	29 272/93 Ralph Lauren #2092 VF/Montauk	30 273/92 Women's Book- Ruth 10- Mark 12-2p	NOTES			

JANUARY S M T W T F S
1 2 3 4 / 5 6 7 8 9 10 11 / 12 13 14 15 16 17 18 / 19 20 21 22 23 24 25 / 26 27 28 29 30 31

FEBRUARY S M T W T F S
1 / 2 3 4 5 6 7 8 / 9 10 11 12 13 14 15 / 16 17 18 19 20 21 22 / 23 24 25 26 27 28

MARCH S M T W T F S
1 / 2 3 4 5 6 7 8 / 9 10 11 12 13 14 15 / 16 17 18 19 20 21 22 / 23 24 25 26 27 28 29 / 30 31

APRIL S M T W T F S
1 2 3 4 5 / 6 7 8 9 10 11 12 / 13 14 15 16 17 18 19 / 20 21 22 23 24 25 26 / 27 28 29 30

MAY S M T W T F S
1 2 3 / 4 5 6 7 8 9 10 / 11 12 13 14 15 16 17 / 18 19 20 21 22 23 24 / 25 26 27 28 29 30 31

JUNE S M T W T F S
1 2 3 4 5 6 7 / 8 9 10 11 12 13 14 / 15 16 17 18 19 20 21 / 22 23 24 25 26 27 28 / 29 30

JULY S M T W T F S
1 2 3 4 5 / 6 7 8 9 10 11 12 / 13 14 15 16 17 18 19 / 20 21 22 23 24 25 26 / 27 28 29 30 31

AUGUST S M T W T F S
1 2 / 3 4 5 6 7 8 9 / 10 11 12 13 14 15 16 / 17 18 19 20 21 22 23 / 24 25 26 27 28 29 30 / 31

SEPTEMBER S M T W T F S
1 2 3 4 5 6 / 7 8 9 10 11 12 13 / 14 15 16 17 18 19 20 / 21 22 23 24 25 26 27 / 28 29 30

OCTOBER S M T W T F S
1 2 3 4 / 5 6 7 8 9 10 11 / 12 13 14 15 16 17 18 / 19 20 21 22 23 24 25 / 26 27 28 29 30 31

NOVEMBER S M T W T F S
1 / 2 3 4 5 6 7 8 / 9 10 11 12 13 14 15 / 16 17 18 19 20 21 22 / 23 24 25 26 27 28 29 / 30

DECEMBER S M T W T F S
1 2 3 4 5 6 / 7 8 9 10 11 12 13 / 14 15 16 17 18 19 20 / 21 22 23 24 25 26 27 / 28 29 30 31

A CONVERSATION WITH ANNIE LEIBOVITZ AND KAREN MULLIGAN

Karen Mulligan: When I started working for you over twenty years ago, you were probably doing between eighty and ninety shoots per year . . . There were trips to make portraits for books, and assignments for *Vanity Fair* and *Vogue*. And advertising work. In one of those early years, I think you did over a hundred shoots. There were some weeks when you were in five different cities in five days.

Annie Leibovitz: It was hard to turn down assignments. They were big, interesting jobs, so we were traveling constantly. Things were pretty crazy.

KM: I was dropping out of graduate school at NYU, and Kara Glynn, who was a friend through a friend from college, was starting to work as your studio manager. She said that you were looking for someone to do research for a book about women. I said that I could do that. It sounded interesting.

I met Leslie Simitch, your producer at the time, who worked with Jimmy Moffat, your photo agent, and she said, "I love you; you're hired." And I said, "Maybe I should meet Annie." She said that first I would meet Jimmy, so I went to his office. He was wearing sneakers and his feet were on his desk and he said, "Can you start this week?"

And I said, "Shouldn't I meet Annie?"

Jimmy said, "Well, she's in South Africa with Hillary Clinton. When she comes back, we will call you and you can come in."

This was 1997. People didn't really use cell phones. But I happened to be home when Leslie called and said, "Can you come and meet Annie right now?" I wasn't dressed for an interview, but I got in a cab and went to the studio on Vandam Street and buzzed to go upstairs. Someone on the intercom kept saying, "Who are you here to see?"

And I would say, "I have an appointment with Annie Leibovitz." And he would say, "But what is this about? I don't know about this." I asked him if he could check with you. I was so worried about my outfit.

When I finally got in, Jimmy was sitting there with you and Leslie. You said, "What are you wearing? Are you wearing a skirt? Do you wear skirts?" I said that I usually wore skirts. Or dresses. And you said, "Well, OK. Do you want to start this afternoon?"

Basically, I started a couple of days after I met you. Kara put the fear of God into me. She said, "Don't touch the phone if line four rings. Do not answer it. And don't look at Annie."

You would come off the elevator, and I would say cheerily, "Good morning, Annie." Kara said, "You've got to take it down a notch. Annie thinks there's something wrong with you. When she comes in, don't say anything." The next time you came in, I turned around and tried to look busy.

About a month later you called me into your office and said that you would like me to come on a shoot. You were photographing the Harlem Girls Choir for the *Women* book. I said OK and that I wanted you to know that I wouldn't be cheerful. But could I say, "Good morning"? You said that was fine.

I was really excited to be on my way to my first shoot. I was sitting in the back of the van, and I saw that you wanted to say something to me but didn't remember my name. You were calling me "the new girl." So I said, "Annie, my name is Karen," which freaked the photo assistants out.

That was the beginning.

You kept giving me more and more responsibility. It was never formal. Three or four years after I started, Kara decided to leave, and you asked me if I wanted to take her place as studio manager. I said I would give it a try.

A page from Karen Mulligan's calendar

AL: The bottom line is that people like you, and you care about them. I've always been driven and focused, and you allowed me to work while you handled the rest. At this point, we are a team. I get to be a photographer, and you handle everything else.

KM: It all started at that studio on Vandam Street. A few months after I began working for you, there was a big fashion shoot. Hair and makeup was done at the studio, and everyone drove to the locations—Harlem, the Meatpacking District, Westbury Gardens out on Long Island, and Chinatown. It was your first shoot with Grace Coddington. Her assistant was Samira Nasr, who became the executive fashion director for *Vanity Fair* and has moved on to become the editor in chief at *Harper's Bazaar*. It's so interesting how many people started out as Grace's assistants and went on.

The story was about designers' visions: Yohji Yamamoto, Rei Kawakubo, Jean Paul Gaultier, Galliano . . .

AL: Anna [Wintour] loved that shoot. I could never understand why she liked it. It was the beginning of us doing fashion for *Vogue*.

KM: We were working on the *Women* book at the same time. I was putting together lists of women to photograph with Sharon DeLano, the editor. Then I was setting up shoots, not knowing what I was doing. I would call friends and ask them things like how to get a van.

I first met Susan Sontag when she came to the studio to discuss the *Women* book. I worked with Susan and Sharon on the biographies for the book. I remember Susan sitting and smoking at the kitchen table in front of the window at the Vandam Street studio.

We did everything by fax. I would work with Sharon during the day and then fax to Susan overnight and wake up to faxes back from Susan.

A while after that you called me into your office and said that Susan wanted me to work with her one day a week. She had an apartment in London Terrace that was so overheated that her assistant worked in his underwear. I would help her organize her books and go through the mail, and she would ask me what movies I was seeing, which restaurants I was dining at, and which clubs I was going to.

Susan was interested in fashion. She would talk to me about clothes. One day she called me up and said she had something for me that only I would appreciate. It was her Claude Montana black leather trench coat. The one that Avedon photographed her in. Susan gave me the coat for Christmas. She brought it to me the night of one of our infamous holiday parties. One year the studio was converted into a snow-covered forest with twelve-foot pine trees scattered throughout. And we had Hank Williams Jr. fly up from Nashville to play.

AL: Another person who started around the time you did and who became essential to the whole operation is Mary Howard. It's hard to give her a title. Officially, she is the set designer, but she does everything. If I go on a shoot and I can bring only one person plus my assistants, it would be Mary Howard. Fashion is important, but creating the framework to put the fashion in is crucial to a photograph.

I have my personal favorites of Mary Howard shoots. One of them is Natalia Vodianova playing Edith Wharton at The Mount [Wharton's home in the Berkshires in Massachusetts]. The shoot was so smooth and so beautiful. I could turn to Mary and say, "Edith Wharton liked driving around in the countryside. Can we get a car?" And she would find the car that Edith Wharton might have driven.

Or the wings on Jeff Koons as the Flying Monkey in the *Wizard of Oz* shoot. You can imagine what those wings looked like, and then Mary Howard has an idea and draws them and meets with the fabricators. And after they were created, we said, "How are we going to get them up in the air?" And there was a crane.

Mary is incredibly resourceful. If we travel, say, to South Africa, she won't have an assistant. She packs a small kit of things she thinks she might need and then sources everything else on-site. She will figure things out. If a wall is in the wrong place, she will knock it down and rebuild it.

KM: Mary wasn't traveling with us much yet in 1999, when we did the first couture shoot in Paris. I hadn't been working very long myself, and I was nervous. Fortunately, someone had given me Fred Jagueneau's name. He worked with us finding locations.

We were looking for a factory or something like it. A friend who was scouting for a film at the time had seen the factory, and he gave Fred the number of the person who had the keys. The person with the keys said he didn't want anything to do with it but that we could come and go as we pleased. There wasn't really an owner. The place was sort of condemned. After we shot there, it closed down forever.

AL: Fred was really unbelievable. We felt that we owned Paris when we worked with him. He could get us on top of the Eiffel Tower and into the Louvre. I guess the most ambitious time was the Ben Stiller shoot, where we had a plexiglass bubble suspended from a crane over the Seine. The sitting with Ben was based on great fashion photography. Our bubble was made by the same fabricator who made Melvin Sokolsky's bubble in 1963. Sokolsky had a model in the bubble and suspended it in several places in Paris. Our bubble had Ben in it.

KM: Fred said, "I have permission. But we have to do it at three a.m." I remember telling Ben. He said, "You mean three p.m." And I said, "No, three a.m."

We were testing the bubble when Ben arrived. He was looking up at it, and you know he is thinking, "This is insane."

And then his publicist shows up. And she says, "Karen, what if that falls into the river?" I explain that there is a barge ready to pick it up and scuba divers on standby.

And then she said, "Are there holes in it? Can he breathe?" And we showed her the seam.

AL: We hadn't really figured it out. I didn't even know what he was going to do in the bubble. France couldn't have been a more difficult place to get permits, although everything is more difficult now than it used to be.

KM: The logistics of working in another country are always difficult. Something inevitably gets lost in translation. Which is not to say that we don't have crazy shoots in the US. For instance, the Charlize Theron shoot that was based somewhat loosely on the theme of water.

AL: The principal location was a waterfall in the Poconos. Ernie Liberati, who has been scouting locations for us for twenty-five years, knew about it because it's where he takes his family. It seemed great, and I asked Ernie about the access. He said, "No problem. You just walk right down."

KM: So we go to the place, Bushkill Falls, and we're looking out the car window and thinking it doesn't look easy to get to.

Ernie says, totally typically, "Well, you just walk down the steps."

Almost a mile.

AL: It was a slippery, wet path. The guys were carrying the equipment like Sherpas. Then when we got to the falls, Charlize had to walk around this precarious rock base. There are shots where she is literally in the falls. And it was freezing. Mary Howard had built scaffolding where I could stand and where the guys held the lights.

KM: Ernie also found a place in Rhode Island for that shoot. There was a rocky ledge by the ocean that we wanted. It was a four-and-a-half-hour drive to get there. On the way back, we stopped at the aquarium in Mystic, Connecticut, to do what we thought would be the most complicated shot. Charlize would be swimming in a tank.

The people at the aquarium told me and Ernie that Charlize could jump right in.

So I go into the room and I say, "Why are the seals still in there?"

And they say, "They're fine. Don't worry about it." They would herd the seals to the side. Someone could be in there feeding them when Charlize was in.

I say, "Well, I don't think Charlize is going to want to get in with the seals." And they say, "OK. We'll take them out."

By now Charlize has walked into the room, and they are trying to get the seals out, and there is all this screaming. And a disgusting smell.

Charlize said, very politely, "I don't think I can go into that tank. I just had my hair colored and I'm worried about that."

She didn't say, "Are you completely nuts?"

At one point, you may recall, you said, "Karen, maybe you should go in to make her feel more comfortable."

We ended up doing the picture in a tank in LA that is used for shoots.

AL: That was a *Vogue* shoot. For the *Vanity Fair* shoots, Kathryn MacLeod was always with us. Kathryn went on every shoot I did for *Vanity Fair*, starting in 1997. Then when *Vanity Fair* changed editors and reorganized their staff in 2018, she came on board to work with us in the studio. Kathryn has been involved in almost every one of our shoots since then.

Kathryn wears many hats. She started on the fashion side of things, working with Grace Mirabella and Michael Roberts. But her great area of expertise is photography itself. She is passionate about photographs and has an encyclopedic knowledge of the history of photography.

Kathryn takes into consideration the time we have—and Kathryn has a very acute understanding of who the subject is—and what might be possible.

KM: And then there is Jeff Streeper, who was working with you several years before I came.

AL: Like many people I've worked with over the years, it's hard to say what it is that Jeff really does. First and foremost, he is my art director. He has held my hand through it all. Jeff and I have worked together since my first book in the late eighties to create the stories that make up my work. Jeff has great patience, a quiet demeanor. He knows when something is good.

KM: There have been many photo assistants.

AL: There has been a steady, small flow of extraordinary people who have worked as my first assistant, side by side over the years. One can imagine how hard that position is—actually, I'm not sure one can imagine it. My current first assistant, Matthias Gaggl, is a rock. Strong, steadfast, and true.

KM: They usually stay for four or five years and move on. Except for Nick Rogers. He was with us in Paris for the first couture shoot.

AL: We found Nick in England. He had been one of a raft of assistants on a Bruce Weber shoot that Jo Matthews worked on. She was producing a shoot for me and she recommended Nick. We hired him right away and he never went home. He was in his early twenties then, and after he had worked for me for about twenty years, he said that he had bought some land in Costa Rica and wanted to spend more time there to build a house, start a farm, and surf. Nick had developed a gift for handling a movable light; he was really good at it. It's an art. The nuances are not obvious. After all that time, Nick and I had a system for working. Like all relationships, Nick and I had our ups and downs, but I admired Nick and respected him and loved him.

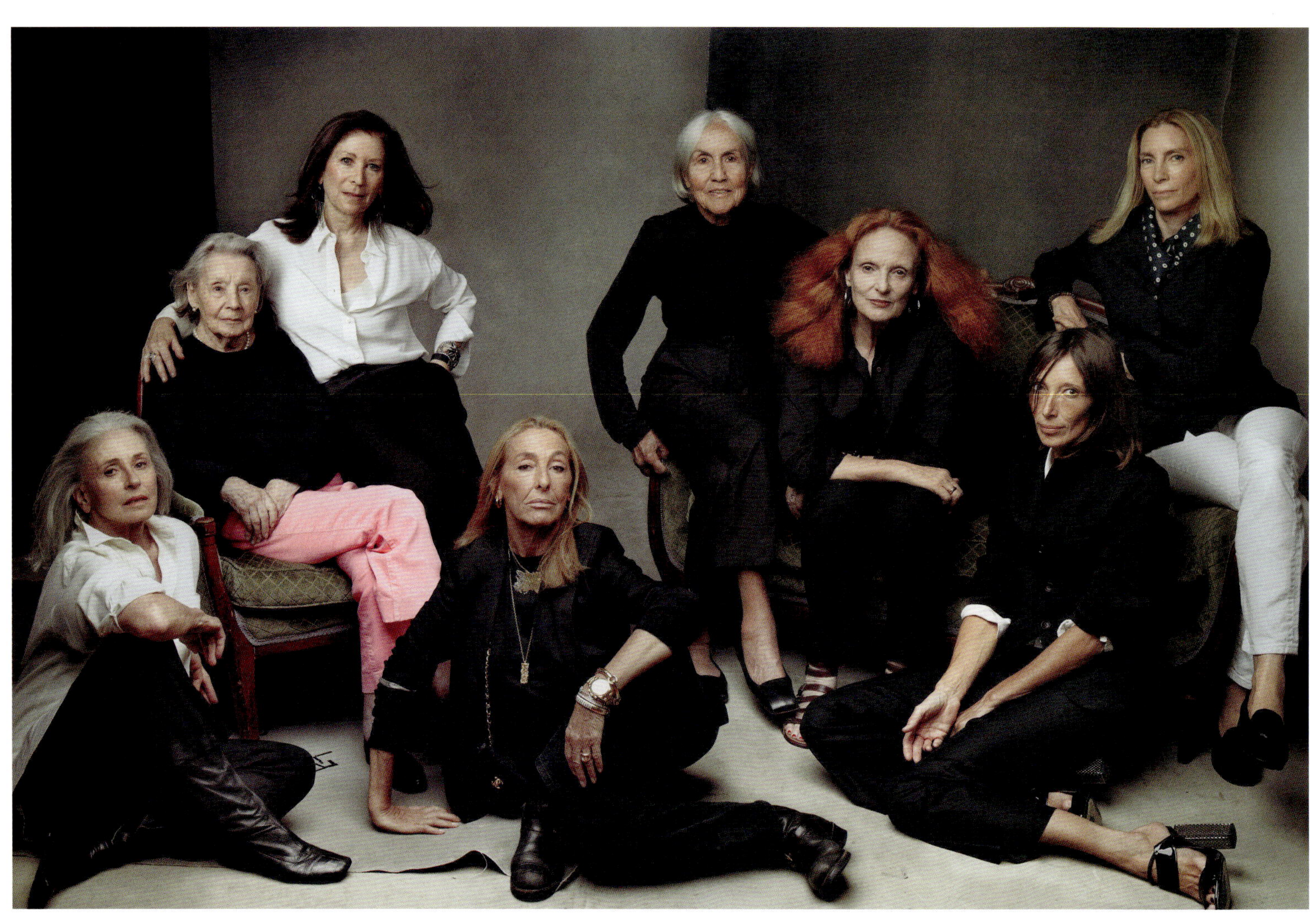

The editors: Jade Hobson, Babs Simpson, Phyllis Posnick, Carlyne Cerf de Dudzeele, Polly Allen Mellen, Grace Coddington, Camilla Nickerson, Tonne Goodman, Rye, New York, 2012

ACKNOWLEDGMENTS

LEIBOVITZ STUDIO Karen Mulligan
Anna Sabatini, Chelsea Sillars, Frankie Alduino, Laura Viteri
Laura Cali, Matthew Currie
Matthias Gaggl, David Jaffe
Marco Giannavola, Jonathan Ragle
Will Kennedy, Stanislav Ginzburg
Janine Cramner, Jo Jude
Baha and Hasan Gluhic, Julia Dickens, Craig St. John

Mary Howard, Kathryn MacLeod
Ernie Liberati

CONDE NAST S.I. Newhouse • Jonathan Newhouse

VOGUE Anna Wintour
Raul Martinez, Jill Demling
Grace Coddington, Tonne Goodman, Phyllis Posnick, Camilla Nickerson
Gabriella Karefa-Johnson

VANITY FAIR Graydon Carter • Radhika Jones
Kira Pollack
Chris Garrett, Jane Sarkin, Jessica Diehl, Susan White

WYLIE, ATKEN & STONE Andrew Wylie
Jeffrey Posternak

PHAIDON Keith Fox
Deborah Aaronson
Lynne Ciccaglione, Julia Hasting, Nerissa Vales
Elaine Ward, Adela Cory
Siobhan Bent, Amy Hordes, Imogen Blackwell, Ellen Bashford, Alex Coumbis

Phaidon Press Limited
2 Cooperage Yard
London E15 2QR

Phaidon Press Inc.
65 Bleecker Street
New York, NY 10012

phaidon.com

First published 2021

ISBN 978 1 83866 152 6 (Trade edition)
ISBN 978 1 83866 233 2 (Signed edition)
ISBN 978 1 83866 408 4 (Luxury edition)

A CIP catalogue record for this book is available from the British Library and the Library of Congress.

GLOSS STUDIO
Raja Sethuraman
Magnus Andersson, Laxman Sethuraman
Kaitlyn Buzzetti, Aqeela Reddy Khan, Satoe Onizuka
B.J. DeLorenzo, Sean Ross

Text is a collaboration with Sharon Delano

EDITOR: Sharon Delano

ART DIRECTOR: Jeff Streeper

Printed in China